Houghton
Mifflin
Harcourt

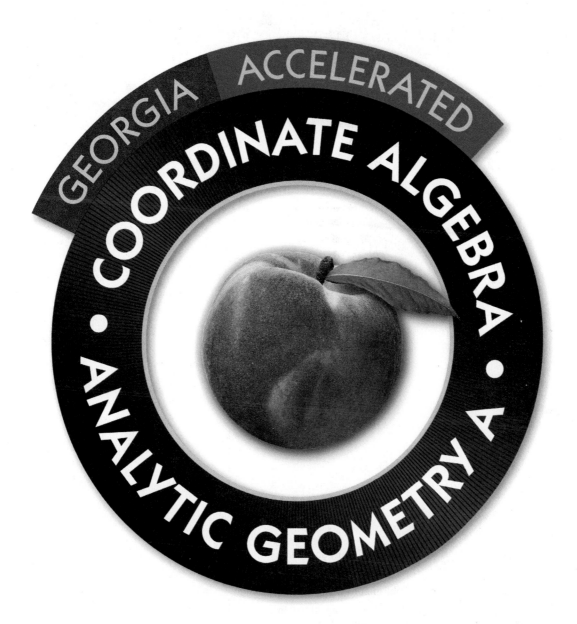

GEORGIA ACCELERATED

COORDINATE ALGEBRA · ANALYTIC GEOMETRY A

Edward B. Burger
David J. Chard
Paul A. Kennedy
Steven J. Leinwand
Freddie L. Renfro
Tom W. Roby
Dale G. Seymour
Bert K. Waits

10000002782051

Printed in the U.S.A.

ISBN   978-0-544-23663-9

1 2 3 4 5 6 7 8 9 10   0868   22 21 20 19 18 17 16 15 14 13

4500429205   A B C D E F G

Authors

Edward B. Burger, Ph.D., is Professor of Mathematics at Williams College and is the author of numerous articles, books, and videos. He has won several of the most prestigious writing and teaching awards offered by the Mathematical Association of America. Dr. Burger has made numerous television and radio appearances and has given countless mathematical presentations around the world.

Freddie L. Renfro, MA, has 35 years of experience in Texas education as a classroom teacher and director/coordinator of Mathematics PreK-12 for school districts in the Houston area. She has served as a reviewer and TXTEAM trainer for Texas Math Institutes and has presented at numerous math workshops.

David J. Chard, Ph.D., is the Leon Simmons Dean of the School of Education and Human Development at Southern Methodist University. He is a past president of the Divison of Research at the Council for Exceptional Children, a member of the International Academy for Research on Learning Disabilities, and has been the Principal Investigator on numerous research projects for the U.S. Department of Education.

Tom W. Roby, Ph.D., is Associate Professor of Mathematics and Director of the Quantitative Learning Center at the University of Connecticut. He founded and directed the Bay Area-based ACCLAIM professional development program. He also chaired the advisory board of the California Mathematics Project and reviewed content for the California Standards Tests.

Paul A. Kennedy, Ph.D., is a professor and Distinguished University Teaching Scholar in the Department of Mathematics at Colorado State University. Dr. Kennedy is a leader in mathematics education. His research focuses on developing algebraic thinking by using multiple representations and technology. He is the author of numerous publications.

Dale G. Seymour is a retired mathematics teacher, author, speaker and publisher. Dale founded Creative Publications in 1968, and went on to found two other mathematics publishing companies. Creating mathematical sculptures is one of his many hobbies.

Steven J. Leinwand is a Principal Research Analyst at the American Institutes for Research in Washington, D.C. He was previously, for 22 years, the Mathematics Supervisor with the Connecticut Department of Education.

Bert K. Waits, Ph.D., is a Professor Emeritus of Mathematics at The Ohio State University and cofounder of T^3 (Teachers Teaching with Technology), a national professional development program. Dr. Waits is also a former board member of the NCTM and an author of the original NCTM Standards.

Georgia Reviewers

Michelle Genovese
Sandy Creek High School
Tyrone, GA

C. Mark Henderson
Starr's Mill High School
Fayette County Board of
    Education
Fayetteville, GA

Steve Martin
Carrollton High School
Carrollton, GA

Ashley McAfee
McIntosh High School
Peachtree City, GA

Judy Riddell
Math Department Chair
Northgate High School
Newnan, GA

Susan S. Roach Ed.S.
Instructional Coach,
    Mathematics
Newnan High School
Newnan, GA

Kimberly Snell, Ed.S
Mathematics Teacher
Campbell High School
Smyrna, GA

Melanie Tomlinson
East Coweta High School
Coweta County, GA

Contributing Authors

Linda Antinone
Fort Worth, TX

Carmen Whitman
Pflugerville, TX

Contributing Writer

Karen Droga Campe
Instructor
Yale University
New Haven, CT

Field Test Participants

John Bakelaar
Peebles Middle School
Jackson, MS

Carey Carter
Alvarado High School
Alvarado, TX

Jill Morris
Navasota High School
Navasota, TX

Vicky Petty
Central Middle School
Murfreesboro, TN

Ruth Stutzman
Jefferson Forest High School
Forest, VA

Len Zigment
Mesa Ridge High School
Colorado Springs, CO

Reviewers

John Bakelaar
Assistant Principal
Whitten Middle School
Jackson, MS

Jennifer Bauer
Mathematics Instructional Leader
East Haven High School
East Haven, CT

Doug Becker
Mathematics Teacher
Gaylord High School
Gaylord, MI

Joe Brady
Mathematics Department Chair
Ensworth High School
Nashville, TN

Sharon Butler
Adjunct Faculty
Montgomery College of The
Woodlands
Spring, TX

Kathy Dean Davis
Mathematics Department Chair,
retired
Bowling Green Junior High
Bowling Green, KY

Maureen "Willie" DiLaura
Middle School Math Specialist,
retired
Lockerman Middle School
Denton, MD

Arlane Frederick
Curriculum & Learning Specialist
in Mathematics, retired
Kenmore-Town of Tonawanda
UFSD
Buffalo, NY

Marieta W. Harris
Mathematics Specialist
Memphis, TN

Connie Johnsen
Mathematics Teacher
Harker Heights High School
Harker Heights, TX

Mary Jones
Mathematics Supervisor/Teacher
Grand Rapids Public Schools
Grand Rapids, MI

Lendy Jones
Algebra Teacher
Liberty Hill Middle School
Killeen, TX

Mary Joy
Algebra Teacher
Mayfield High School
Las Cruces, NM

Vilma Martinez
Algebra Teacher
Nikki Rowe High School
McAllen, TX

Mende Mays
Algebra Teacher
Crockett Junior High
Odessa, TX

Rebecca Newburn
Lead Math Teacher
Davidson Middle School
San Rafael, CA

Vicki Petty
Mathematics Teacher
Central Middle School
Murfreesboro, TN

Susan Pippen
Mathematics Department Chair
Hinsdale South High School
Darien, IL

Elaine Rafferty
Mathematics Learning Specialist
Charleston County SD
Charleston, SC

Susan Rash
Manager of Secondary
Curriculum
Red Clay CSD
Wilmington, DE

John Remensky
Mathematics Department Chair
South Park High School
South Park, PA

Raymond Seymour
Mathematics Department Head,
retired
Kirby Middle School
San Antonio, TX

Jennifer J. Southers
Mathematics Teacher
Hillcrest High School
Simpsonville, SC

Jill Springer
Mathematics Teacher
Henderson County High School
Henderson, KY

Dr. Katherine Staltare
Mathematics Consultant &
Graduate Level
   Course Developer
NYSUT, Effective Teaching
Program
New York State

Pam Walker
Curriculum Teacher Specialist
Nacogdoches ISD
Nacogdoches, TX

Larry Ward
Mathematics Supervisor, retired
Carrollton-Farmers Branch ISD
Carrollton, TX

Carmen Whitman
Director, Mathematics for All
Consulting
Pflugerville, TX

Mastering the Standards

for Mathematical Practice

The topics described in the Standards for Mathematical Content will vary from year to year. However, the *way* in which you learn, study, and think about mathematics will not. The Standards for Mathematical Practice describe skills that you will use in all of your math courses.

Mathematical Practices

1. *Make sense of problems and persevere in solving them.*
2. *Reason abstractly and quantitatively.*
3. *Construct viable arguments and critique the reasoning of others.*
4. *Model with mathematics.*
5. *Use appropriate tools strategically.*
6. *Attend to precision.*
7. *Look for and make use of structure.*
8. *Look for and express regularity in repeated reasoning.*

❶ Make sense of problems and persevere in solving them.

Mathematically proficient students start by explaining to themselves the meaning of a problem... They analyze givens, constraints, relationships, and goals. They make conjectures about the form... of the solution and plan a solution pathway...

In your book

Focus on Problem Solving describes a four-step plan for problem solving. The plan is introduced at the beginning of your book, and practice with the plan appears throughout the book.

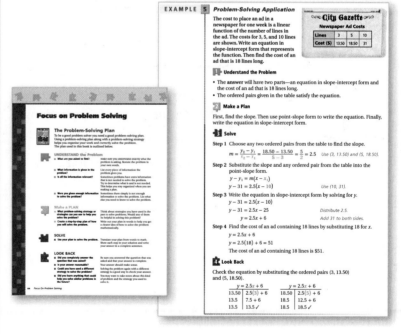

Relationships Between Quantities

Reasoning with Equations and Inequalities

UNIT **2**

UNIT 2 CONTINUED

Linear and Exponential Functions

UNIT 3 CONTINUED

Describing Data

UNIT 4

COMMON CORE GPS

UNIT

5 Transformations in the Coordinate Plane

Connecting Algebra and Geometry Through Coordinates

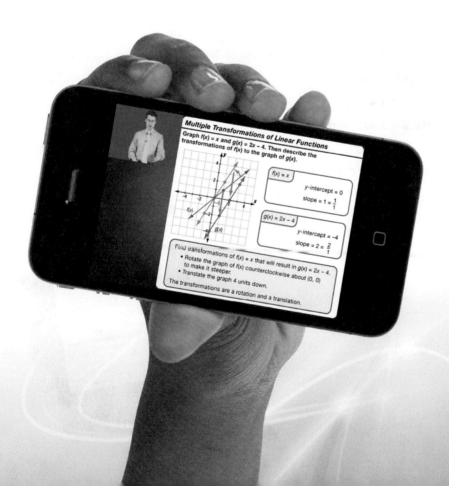

UNIT 7

Similarity, Congruence, and Proofs

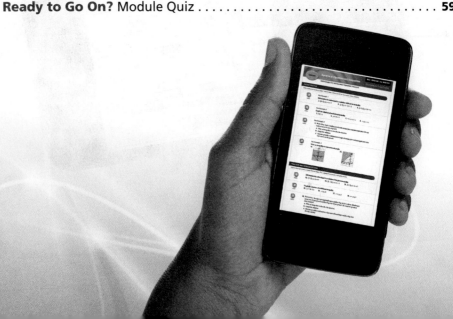

UNIT 7 CONTINUED

Right Triangle Trigonometry

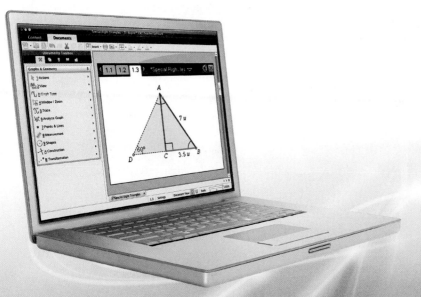

UNIT
9
Circles and Volume

Appendix of Additional Lessons

Correlation for Georgia Accelerated Coordinate Algebra/Analytic Geometry A

Standard	Descriptor	Page Citation
Number and Quantity: Quantities*		
Reason quantitatively and use units to solve problems		
MCC9-12.N.Q.1	Use units as a way to understand problems and to guide the solution of multi-step problems; choose and interpret units consistently in formulas; choose and interpret the scale and the origin in graphs and data displays.*	**SE:** 6–11, 32–38, 39–44, 45–51, 92–97
MCC9-12.N.Q.2	Define appropriate quantities for the purpose of descriptive modeling.*	**SE:** 13–18, 20–26, 39–44
MCC9-12.N.Q.3	Choose a level of accuracy appropriate to limitations on measurement when reporting quantities.*	**SE:** 45–51
Algebra: Seeing Structure in Expressions		
Interpret the structure of expressions		
MCC9-12.A.SSE.1	Interpret expressions that represent a quantity in terms of its context.*	**SE:** 6–11
MCC9-12.A.SSE.1a	a. Interpret parts of an expression, such as terms, factors, and coefficients.*	**SE:** 6–11
MCC9-12.A.SSE.1b	b. Interpret complicated expressions by viewing one or more of their parts as a single entity. For example, interpret $P(1 + r)^n$ as the product of P and a factor not depending on P.*	**SE:** 19

SE = Student Edition
+ = Advanced
* = Also a Modeling Standard

Standard	Descriptor	Page Citation
Algebra: Creating Equations*		
Create equations that describe numbers or relationships		
MCC9-12.A.CED.1	Create equations and inequalities in one variable and use them to solve problems. Include equations arising from linear and quadratic functions, and simple rational and exponential functions.*	**SE:** 6–11, 13–18, 20–26, 32–38, 39–44, 62–68, 70–76, 92–97, 98–103, 108–113, 114–120, 121–127, 531–537, 538–545, 641–648, 649–655, 662–669, 687–693, 733–739, 740–747, 748–755, 797–803, 878–883, 914–922, 924–931
MCC9-12.A.CED.2	Create equations in two or more variables to represent relationships between quantities; graph equations on coordinate axes with labels and scales.*	**SE:** 20–26, 133–138, 140–146, 147–153, 158–163, 203–209, 274–279, 280–286, 287–294, 516–521
MCC9-12.A.CED.3	Represent constraints by equations or inequalities, and by systems of equations and/or inequalities, and interpret solutions as viable or non-viable options in a modeling context. *For example, represent inequalities describing nutritional and cost constraints on combinations of different foods.**	**SE:** 13–18, 20–26, 86–91
MCC9-12.A.CED.4	Rearrange formulas to highlight a quantity of interest, using the same reasoning as in solving equations. *For example, rearrange Ohm's law V = IR to highlight resistance R.**	**SE:** 77–81

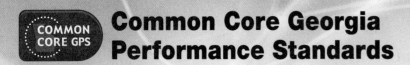

Correlation for Georgia Accelerated Coordinate Algebra/Analytic Geometry A

Standard	Descriptor	Page Citation
Algebra: Reasoning with Equations and Inequalities		
Understand solving equations as a process of reasoning and explain the reasoning		
MCC9-12.A.REI.1	Explain each step in solving a simple equation as following from the equality of numbers asserted at the previous step, starting from the assumption that the original equation has a solution. Construct a viable argument to justify a solution method.	**SE:** 12, 13–18, 20–26, 62–68, 69, 70–76, 77–81
Solve equations and inequalities in one variable		
MCC9-12.A.REI.3	Solve linear equations and inequalities in one variable, including equations with coefficients represented by letters.	**SE:** 13–18, 20–26, 27, 62–68, 69, 70–76, 77–81, 86–91, 92–97, 98–103, 108–113, 114–120, 121–127
MCC9-12.A.REI.4b	b. Solve quadratic equations by inspection (e.g., for $x^2 = 49$), taking square roots, completing the square, the quadratic formula and factoring, as appropriate to the initial form of the equation. Recognize when the quadratic formula gives complex solutions and write them as $a \pm bi$ for real numbers a and b.	**SE:** 820–827
Solve systems of equations		
MCC9-12.A.REI.5	Prove that, given a system of two equations in two variables, replacing one equation by the sum of that equation and a multiple of the other produces a system with the same solutions.	**SE:** 147–153
MCC9-12.A.REI.6	Solve systems of linear equations exactly and approximately (e.g., with graphs), focusing on pairs of linear equations in two variables.	**SE:** 132, 139, 133–138, 140–146, 147–153, 158–163

SE = Student Edition
+ = Advanced
* = Also a Modeling Standard

Standard	Descriptor	Page Citation
Represent and solve equations and inequalities graphically		
MCC9-12.A.REI.10	Understand that the graph of an equation in two variables is the set of all its solutions plotted in the coordinate plane, often forming a curve (which could be a line).	**SE:** 188–193, 214–220, 314–320
MCC9-12.A.REI.11	Explain why the x-coordinates of the points where the graphs of the equations $y = f(x)$ and $y = g(x)$ intersect are the solutions of the equation $f(x) = g(x)$; find the solutions approximately, e.g., using technology to graph the functions, make tables of values, or find successive approximations. Include cases where $f(x)$ and/or $g(x)$ are linear, polynomial, rational, absolute value, exponential, and logarithmic functions.*	**SE:** 27, 133–138
MCC9-12.A.REI.12	Graph the solutions to a linear inequality in two variables as a half-plane (excluding the boundary in the case of a strict inequality), and graph the solution set to a system of linear inequalities in two variables as the intersection of the corresponding half-planes.	**SE:** 164–170, 171–176, 177

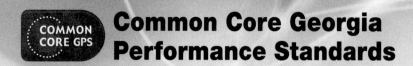
Correlation for Georgia Accelerated Coordinate Algebra/Analytic Geometry A

Standard	Descriptor	Page Citation
Functions: Interpreting Functions		
Understand the concept of a function and use function notation		
MCC9-12.F.IF.1	Understand that a function from one set (called the domain) to another set (called the range) assigns to each element of the domain exactly one element of the range. If f is a function and x is an element of its domain, then f(x) denotes the output of f corresponding to the input x. The graph of f is the graph of the equation y = f(x).	**SE:** 203–209, 280–286, 287–294
MCC9-12.F.IF.2	Use function notation, evaluate functions for inputs in their domains, and interpret statements that use function notation in terms of a context.	**SE:** 202, 203–209
MCC9-12.F.IF.3	Recognize that sequences are functions, sometimes defined recursively, whose domain is a subset of the integers. *For example, the Fibonacci sequence is defined recursively by f(0) = f(1) = 1, f(n+1) = f(n) + f(n−1) for n ≥ 1 (n is greater than or equal to 1).*	**SE:** 230–235, 308–313, 332–335
Interpret functions that arise in applications in terms of the context		
MCC9-12.F.IF.4	For a function that models a relationship between two quantities, interpret key features of graphs and tables in terms of the quantities, and sketch graphs showing key features given a verbal description of the relationship. Key features include: intercepts; intervals where the function is increasing, decreasing, positive, or negative; relative maximums and minimums; symmetries; end behavior; and periodicity.*	**SE:** 188–193, 247–252, 254–261, 264–269
MCC9-12.F.IF.5	Relate the domain of a function to its graph and, where applicable, to the quantitative relationship it describes. *For example, if the function h(n) gives the number of person-hours it takes to assemble n engines in a factory, then the positive integers would be an appropriate domain for the function.*†	**SE:** 188–193, 214–220, 240–246, 247–252, 254–261, 280–286, 314–320
MCC9-12.F.IF.6	Calculate and interpret the average rate of change of a function (presented symbolically or as a table) over a specified interval. Estimate the rate of change from a graph.*	**SE:** 254–261, 262–263, 264–269, 348–351

SE = Student Edition
+ = Advanced
* = Also a Modeling Standard

Standard	Descriptor	Page Citation
Analyze functions using different representations		
MCC9-12.F.IF.7	Graph functions expressed symbolically and show key features of the graph, by hand in simple cases and using technology for more complicated cases.*	**SE:** 214–220, 280–286, 295, 314–320
MCC9-12.F.IF.7a	a. Graph linear and quadratic functions and show intercepts, maxima, and minima.*	**SE:** 214–220, 280–286
MCC9-12.F.IF.7e	e. Graph exponential and logarithmic functions, showing intercepts and end behavior, and trigonometric functions, showing period, midline, and amplitude.*	**SE:** 314–320
MCC9-12.F.IF.9	Compare properties of two functions each represented in a different way (algebraically, graphically, numerically in tables, or by verbal descriptions). *For example, given a graph of one quadratic function and an algebraic expression for another, say which has the larger maximum.*	**SE:** 352–357
Functions: Building Functions		
Build a function that models a relationship between two quantities		
MCC9-12.F.BF.1	Write a function that describes a relationship between two quantities.*	**SE:** 203–209, 280–286, 287–294
MCC9-12.F.BF.1a	a. Determine an explicit expression, a recursive process, or steps for calculation from a context.	**SE:** 203–209, 280–286, 287–294
MCC9-12.F.BF.1b	b. Combine standard function types using arithmetic operations. *For example, build a function that models the temperature of a cooling body by adding a constant function to a decaying exponential, and relate these functions to the model.*	**SE:** 279, 347
MCC9-12.F.BF.2	Write arithmetic and geometric sequences both recursively and with an explicit formula, use them to model situations, and translate between the two forms.*	**SE:** 230–235, 308–313, 321
Build new functions from existing functions		
MCC9-12.F.BF.3	Identify the effect on the graph of replacing f(x) by f(x) + k, k f(x), f(kx), and f(x + k) for specific values of k (both positive and negative); find the value of k given the graphs. Experiment with cases and illustrate an explanation of the effects on the graph using technology. *Include recognizing even and odd functions from their graphs and algebraic expressions for them.*	**SE:** 222–229, 296, 297–303, 358–359, 466

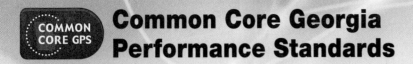

Common Core Georgia Performance Standards

Correlation for Georgia Accelerated Coordinate Algebra/Analytic Geometry A

Standard	Descriptor	Page Citation
Functions: Linear, Quadratic, and Exponential Models*		
Construct and compare linear, quadratic, and exponential models and solve problems		
MCC9-12.F.LE.1	Distinguish between situations that can be modeled with linear functions and with exponential functions.*	**SE:** 430–433
MCC9-12.F.LE.1a	a. Prove that linear functions grow by equal differences over equal intervals, and that exponential functions grow by equal factors over equal intervals.*	**SE:** 240–246, 357
MCC9-12.F.LE.1b	b. Recognize situations in which one quantity changes at a constant rate per unit interval relative to another.*	**SE:** 240–246, 274–279, 314–320, 341–347
MCC9-12.F.LE.1c	c. Recognize situations in which a quantity grows or decays by a constant percent rate per unit interval relative to another.*	**SE:** 314–320, 323–330
MCC9-12.F.LE.2	Construct linear and exponential functions, including arithmetic and geometric sequences, given a graph, a description of a relationship, or two input-output pairs (include reading these from a table).*	**SE:** 230–235, 322, 323–330, 341–347
MCC9-12.F.LE.3	Observe using graphs and tables that a quantity increasing exponentially eventually exceeds a quantity increasing linearly, quadratically, or (more generally) as a polynomial function.*	**SE:** 341–347
Interpret expressions for functions in terms of the situation they model		
MCC9-12.F.LE.5	interpret the parameters in a linear or exponential function in terms of a context.*	**SE:** 214–220, 243, 254–261, 264–269, 280–286, 314–320, 323–330

SE = Student Edition
+ = Advanced
* = Also a Modeling Standard

Standard	Descriptor	Page Citation
Geometry: Congruence		
Experiment with transformations in the plane		
MCC9-12.G.CO.1	Know precise definitions of angle, circle, perpendicular line, parallel line, and line segment, based on the undefined notions of point, line, distance along a line, and distance around a circular arc.	SE: 444–449, 452–458, 459–465
MCC9-12.G.CO.2	Represent transformations in the plane using, e.g., transparencies and geometry software; describe transformations as functions that take points in the plane as inputs and give other points as outputs. Compare transformations that preserve distance and angle to those that do not (e.g., translation versus horizontal stretch).	SE: 444–449, 450–451, 452–458, 459–465, 467–473
MCC9-12.G.CO.3	Given a rectangle, parallelogram, trapezoid, or regular polygon, describe the rotations and reflections that carry it onto itself.	SE: 484–490
MCC9-12.G.CO.4	Develop definitions of rotations, reflections, and translations in terms of angles, circles, perpendicular lines, parallel lines, and line segments.	SE: 444–449, 452–458, 459–465, 467–473
MCC9-12.G.CO.5	Given a geometric figure and a rotation, reflection, or translation, draw the transformed figure using, e.g., graph paper, tracing paper, or geometry software. Specify a sequence of transformations that will carry a given figure onto another.	SE: 452–458, 459–465, 467–473, 478–483, 491–497
Understand congruence in terms of rigid motions		
MCC9-12.G.CO.6	Use geometric descriptions of rigid motions to transform figures and to predict the effect of a given rigid motion on a given figure; given two figures, use the definition of congruence in terms of rigid motions to decide if they are congruent.	SE: 632–639
MCC9-12.G.CO.7	Use the definition of congruence in terms of rigid motions to show that two triangles are congruent if and only if corresponding pairs of sides and corresponding pairs of angles are congruent.	SE: 649–655, 678–683
MCC9-12.G.CO.8	Explain how the criteria for triangle congruence (ASA, SAS, and SSS) follow from the definition of congruence in terms of rigid motions.	SE: 660–661

Common Core Georgia Performance Standards

Correlation for Georgia Accelerated Coordinate Algebra/Analytic Geometry A

Standard	Descriptor	Page Citation
Prove geometric theorems		
MCC9-12.G.CO.9	Prove theorems about lines and angles. Theorems include: vertical angles are congruent; when a transversal crosses parallel lines, alternate interior angles are congruent and corresponding angles are congruent; points on a perpendicular bisector of a line segment are exactly those equidistant from the segment's endpoints.	**SE:** 570–575, 576–581, 582–588, 589, 590–597, 602, 603–609, 610–617, 620–626, 700–706, 707–713, 797–803
MCC9-12.G.CO.10	Prove theorems about triangles. Theorems include: measures of interior angles of a triangle sum to 180°; base angles of isosceles triangles are congruent; the segment joining midpoints of two sides of a triangle is parallel to the third side and half the length; the medians of a triangle meet at a point.	**SE:** 640, 641–648, 649–655, 678–683, 687–693, 714–720, 722–727
MCC9-12.G.CO.11	Prove theorems about parallelograms. Theorems include: opposite sides are congruent, opposite angles are congruent, the diagonals of a parallelogram bisect each other, and conversely, rectangles are parallelograms with congruent diagonals.	**SE:** 732, 733–739, 740–747, 748–755, 756–757, 758–765
Make geometric constructions		
MCC9-12.G.CO.12	Make formal geometric constructions with a variety of tools and methods (compass and straightedge, string, reflective devices, paper folding, dynamic geometric software, etc.). Copying a segment; copying an angle; bisecting a segment; bisecting an angle; constructing perpendicular lines, including the perpendicular bisector of a line segment; and constructing a line parallel to a given line through a point not on the line.	**SE:** 530, 531–537, 538–545, 618–619, 627, 721, 796, 835
MCC9-12.G.CO.13	Construct an equilateral triangle, a square, and a regular hexagon inscribed in a circle.	**SE:** 694–695

SE = Student Edition
+ = Advanced
* = Also a Modeling Standard

Standard	Descriptor	Page Citation
Geometry: Similarity, Right Triangles, and Trigonometry		
Understand similarity in terms of similarity transformations		
MCC9-12.G.SRT.1	Verify experimentally the properties of dilations given by a center and a scale factor:	**SE:** 776–783, 804–809
MCC9-12.G.SRT.1a	a. A dilation takes a line not passing through the center of the dilation to a parallel line, and leaves a line passing through the center unchanged.	**SE:** 776–783, 804–809
MCC9-12.G.SRT.1b	b. The dilation of a line segment is longer or shorter in the ratio given by the scale factor.	**SE:** 776–783, 804–809
MCC9-12.G.SRT.2	Given two figures, use the definition of similarity in terms of similarity transformations to decide if they are similar; explain using similarity transformations the meaning of similarity for triangles as the equality of all corresponding pairs of angles and the proportionality of all corresponding pairs of sides.	**SE:** 770–775, 804–809
MCC9-12.G.SRT.3	Use the properties of similarity transformations to establish the AA criterion for two triangles to be similar.	**SE:** 784–785, 786–793

Common Core Georgia Performance Standards

Correlation for Georgia Accelerated Coordinate Algebra/Analytic Geometry A

Standard	Descriptor	Page Citation
Prove theorems involving similarity		
MCC9-12.G.SRT.4	Prove theorems about triangles. Theorems include: a line parallel to one side of a triangle divides the other two proportionally, and conversely; the Pythagorean Theorem proved using triangle similarity.	**SE:** 786–793, 794–795, 797–803
MCC9-12.G.SRT.5	Use congruence and similarity criteria for triangles to solve problems and to prove relationships in geometric figures.	**SE:** 662–669, 670–677, 678–683, 684–685, 786–793, 797–803, 804–809
Define trigonometric ratios and solve problems involving right triangles		
MCC9-12.G.SRT.6	Understand that by similarity, side ratios in right triangles are properties of the angles in the triangle, leading to definitions of trigonometric ratios for acute angles.	**SE:** 828–834, 840, 841–848
MCC9-12.G.SRT.7	Explain and use the relationship between the sine and cosine of complementary angles.	**SE:** 849–850
MCC9-12.G.SRT.8	Use trigonometric ratios and the Pythagorean Theorem to solve right triangles in applied problems.	**SE:** 794–795, 820–827, 828–834, 841–848, 852–859, 860–865, 878–883, 885–892, 914–922, 924–931, 932–937

SE = Student Edition
 + = Advanced
 * = Also a Modeling Standard

Standard	Descriptor	Page Citation
Geometry: Circles		
Understand and apply theorems about circles		
MCC9-12.G.C.1	Prove that all circles are similar.	**SE:** 776–783
MCC9-12.G.C.2	Identify and describe relationships among inscribed angles, radii, and chords. Include the relationship between central, inscribed, and circumscribed angles; inscribed angles on a diameter are right angles; the radius of a circle is perpendicular to the tangent where the radius intersects the circle.	**SE:** 914–922, 924–931, 940–947
MCC9-12.G.C.3	Construct the inscribed and circumscribed circles of a triangle, and prove properties of angles for a quadrilateral inscribed in a circle.	**SE:** 707–713, 940–947
MCC9-12.G.C.4(+)	Construct a tangent line from a point outside a given circle to the circle.	**SE:** 940–947
Find arc lengths and areas of sectors of circles		
MCC9-12.G.C.5	Derive using similarity the fact that the length of the arc intercepted by an angle is proportional to the radius, and define the radian measure of the angle as the constant of proportionality; derive the formula for the area of a sector.	**SE:** 932–937, 938–939

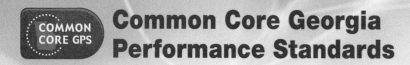

Common Core Georgia Performance Standards

Correlation for Georgia Accelerated Coordinate Algebra/Analytic Geometry A

Standard	Descriptor	Page Citation
Geometry: Expressing Geometric Properties with Equations		
Use coordinates to prove simple geometric theorems algebraically		
MCC9-12.G.GPE.4	Use coordinates to prove simple geometric theorems algebraically. For example, prove or disprove that a figure defined by four given points in the coordinate plane is a rectangle; prove or disprove that the point $(1, \sqrt{3})$ lies on the circle centered at the origin and containing the point $(0, 2)$.	**SE:** 509–515, 678–683, 714–720, 722–727, 733–739, 740–747, 748–755, 804–809
MCC9-12.G.GPE.5	Prove the slope criteria for parallel and perpendicular lines and use them to solve geometric problems (e.g., find the equation of a line parallel or perpendicular to a given line that passes through a given point).	**SE:** 509–515
MCC9-12.G.GPE.6	Find the point on a directed line segment between two given points that partitions the segment in a given ratio.	**SE:** 516–521
MCC9-12.G.GPE.7	Use coordinates to compute perimeters of polygons and areas of triangles and rectangles, e.g., using the distance formula.*	**SE:** 508, 516–521

SE = Student Edition
+ = Advanced
* = Also a Modeling Standard

Standard	Descriptor	Page Citation
Geometry: Geometric Measurement and Dimension		
Explain volume formulas and use them to solve problems		
MCC9-12.G.GMD.1	Give an informal argument for the formulas for the circumference of a circle, area of a circle, volume of a cylinder, pyramid, and cone. Use dissection arguments, Cavalieri's principle, and informal limit arguments.	**SE:** 878–877, 878–883, 885–892, 893–900
MCC9-12.G.GMD.2(+)	Give an informal argument using Cavalieri's principle for the formulas for the volume of a sphere and other solid figures.	**SE:** 885–892, 902–909
MCC9-12.G.GMD.3	Use volume formulas for cylinders, pyramids, cones, and spheres to solve problems.*	**SE:** 885–892, 893–900, 902–909

Common Core Georgia Performance Standards

Correlation for Georgia Accelerated Coordinate Algebra/Analytic Geometry A

Standard	Descriptor	Page Citation
Statistics and Probability: Interpreting Categorical and Quantitative Data*		
Summarize, represent, and interpret data on a single count or measurable variable		
MCC9-12.S.ID.1	Represent data with plots on the real number line (dot plots, histograms, and box plots).*	**SE:** 370–378, 379–385, 394–401, 402–405, 406–407
MCC9-12.S.ID.2	Use statistics appropriate to the shape of the data distribution to compare center (median, mean) and spread (interquartile range, standard deviation) of two or more different data sets.*	**SE:** 394–401, 402–405
MCC9-12.S.ID.3	Interpret differences in shape, center, and spread in the context of the data sets, accounting for possible effects of extreme data points (outliers).*	**SE:** 394–401, 402–405

SE = Student Edition
+ = Advanced
* = Also a Modeling Standard

Standard	Descriptor	Page Citation
Summarize, represent, and interpret data on two categorical and quantitative variables		
MCC9-12.S.ID.5	Summarize categorical data for two categories in two-way frequency tables. Interpret relative frequencies in the context of the data (including joint, marginal, and conditional relative frequencies). Recognize possible associations and trends in the data.*	**SE:** 379–385, 386–393
MCC9-12.S.ID.6	Represent data on two quantitative variables on a scatter plot, and describe how the variables are related.*	**SE:** 412–419
MCC9-12.S.ID.6a	a. Fit a function to the data; use functions fitted to data to solve problems in the context of the data. Use given functions or choose a function suggested by the context. Emphasize linear and exponential models.*	**SE:** 412–419, 420, 421–428
MCC9-12.S.ID.6b	b. Informally assess the fit of a function by plotting and analyzing residuals.*	**SE:** 412–419, 421–428
MCC9-12.S.ID.6c	c. Fit a linear function for a scatter plot that suggests a linear association.*	**SE:** 412–419, 420, 421–428
Interpret linear models		
MCC9-12.S.ID.7	Interpret the slope (rate of change) and the intercept (constant term) of a linear model in the context of the data.*	**SE:** 429, 412–419, 421–428
MCC9-12.S.ID.8	Compute (using technology) and interpret the correlation coefficient of a linear fit.*	**SE:** 420, 421–428
MCC9-12.S.ID.9	Distinguish between correlation and causation.*	**SE:** 412–419, 421–428

Mastering the Standards
for Mathematical Practice

The topics described in the Standards for Mathematical Content will vary from year to year. However, the way in which you learn, study, and think about mathematics will not. The Standards for Mathematical Practice describe skills that you will use in all of your math courses. These pages show some features of your book and the *Explorations in Core Math* workbook that will help you gain these skills and use them to master this year's topics.

1 Make sense of problems and persevere in solving them.

Mathematically proficient students start by explaining to themselves the meaning of a problem… They analyze givens, constraints, relationships, and goals. They make conjectures about the form… of the solution and plan a solution pathway…

In your book

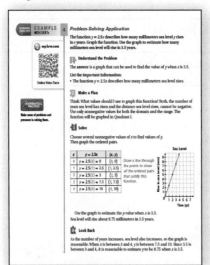

Problem Solving Applications in your book describe and illustrate a four-step plan for problem solving.

In *Explorations*

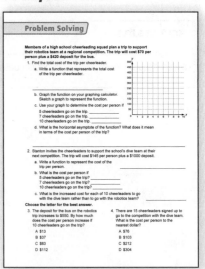

Problem Solving in *Explorations* provides an opportunity to practice and refine your problem-solving skills.

2 Reason abstractly and quantitatively.

Mathematically proficient students... bring two complementary abilities to bear on problems...: the ability to decontextualize—to abstract a given situation and represent it symbolically...and the ability to contextualize, to pause... in order to probe into the referents for the symbols involved.

In your book

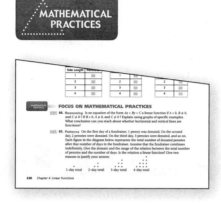

In *Explorations*

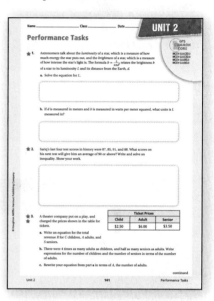

Focus on Mathematical Practices exercises in your book and **Performance Tasks** in *Explorations* require you to use logical reasoning, represent situations symbolically, use mathematical models to solve problems, and state your answers in terms of a problem context.

3 Construct viable arguments and critique the reasoning of others.

Mathematically proficient students... justify their conclusions, [and]... distinguish correct... reasoning from that which is flawed.

In your book

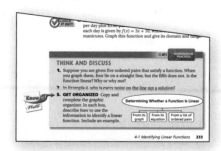

In *Explorations*

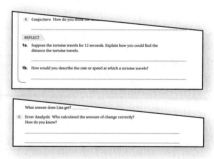

Think and Discuss in your book and **Reflect and Error Analysis** in *Explorations* ask you to evaluate statements, explain relationships, apply mathematical principles, make conjectures, construct arguments, and justify your reasoning.

4 Model with mathematics.

Mathematically proficient students can apply… mathematics… to problems… in everyday life, society, and the workplace…

In your book

In *Explorations*

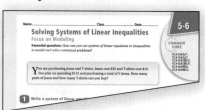

Real-World Connections in your book and **Focus on Modeling** in *Explorations* apply mathematics to other disciplines and real-world contexts such as science and business.

5 Use appropriate tools strategically.

Mathematically proficient students consider the available tools when solving a problem… [and] are… able to use technological tools to explore and deepen their understanding…

In your book

In *Explorations*

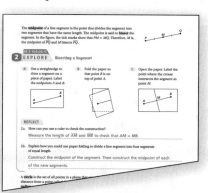

Hands-On Tasks and **Technology Tasks** in your book and **Explore** in *Explorations* use concrete and technological tools, such as manipulatives or graphing calculators, to explore mathematical concepts.

6 Attend to precision.

Mathematically proficient students… communicate precisely… with others and in their own reasoning… [They] give carefully formulated explanations…

In your book

83. **Write About It** Explain why the FC binomials at a time.

In *Explorations*

Key Vocabulary

Precision refers not only to the correctness of calculations but also to the proper use of mathematical language and symbols. **Write About It** in your book and **Key Vocabulary** in *Explorations* help you learn and use the language of math to communicate mathematics precisely.

Getty Images/PhotoDisc

7 Look for and make use of structure.

Mathematically proficient students… look closely to discern a pattern or structure… They can also step back for an overview and shift perspective.

In your book

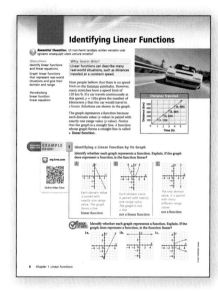

In *Explorations*

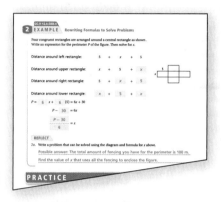

In both your book and *Explorations*, you will study regularity in mathematical structures, such as expressions, equations, operations, geometric figures, tables, graphs, and diagrams. Understanding the underlying structures of mathematics allows you to generalize beyond a specific case and to make connections between related problems.

8 Look for and express regularity in repeated reasoning.

Mathematically proficient students… look both for general methods and for shortcuts… [and] maintain oversight of the process, while attending to the details…

In your book

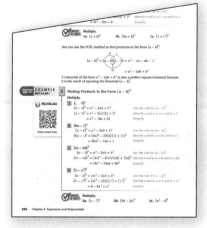

In *Explorations*

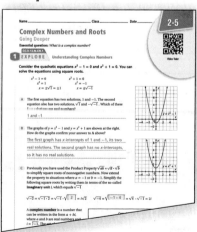

In both your book and *Explorations*, examples group similar types of problems together, and the solutions are carefully stepped out. This allows you to look for patterns or regularity and make generalizations while noticing variations in the details.

Are You Ready?

my.hrw.com
Assessment and Intervention

✔ Vocabulary

Match each term on the left with a definition on the right.

1. constant

2. expression

3. order of operations

4. variable

A. a mathematical phrase that contains operations, numbers, and/or variables

B. a mathematical statement that two expressions are equivalent

C. a process for evaluating expressions

D. a symbol used to represent a quantity that can change

E. a value that does not change

✔ Order of Operations

Simplify each expression.

5. $(7 - 3) \div 2$

6. $4 \cdot 6 \div 3$

7. $12 - 3 + 1$

8. $2 \cdot 10 \div 5$

9. $125 \div 5^2$

10. $7 \cdot 6 + 5 \cdot 4$

✔ Add and Subtract Integers

Add or subtract.

11. $-15 + 19$

12. $-6 - (-18)$

13. $6 + (-8)$

14. $-12 + (-3)$

✔ Add and Subtract Fractions

Perform each indicated operation. Give your answer in the simplest form.

15. $\frac{1}{4} + \frac{2}{3}$

16. $1\frac{1}{2} - \frac{3}{4}$

17. $\frac{3}{8} + \frac{2}{3}$

18. $\frac{3}{2} - \frac{2}{3}$

✔ Evaluate Expressions

Evaluate each expression for the given value of the variable.

19. $2x + 3$ for $x = 7$

20. $3n - 5$ for $n = 7$

21. $13 - 4a$ for $a = 2$

22. $3y + 5$ for $y = 5$

Career Readiness Biologists

Biologists study living things and their relationship to the environment. Most biologists specialize in one area, such as botany (the study of plants) or zoology (the study of animals). They use many different kinds of math, including algebra, probability, and statistics. For example, a biologist may use equations, graphs, and proportions to study populations. Biologists usually have at least a bachelor's degree. Many biologists work in scientific research, in medicine, or in colleges.

Relationships Between Quantities

Online Edition

my.hrw.com

Access the complete online textbook, interactive features, and additional resources.

Multilingual Glossary

Enhance your math vocabulary with this illustrated online glossary in 13 languages.

Homework Help

Get instant help with tutorial videos, practice problems, and step-by-step solutions.

Portable Devices

On the Spot

Watch video tutorials anywhere, anytime with this app for iPhone® and iPad®.

eTextbook

Access your full textbook on your tablet or e-reader.

Chapter Resources

Scan with your smart phone to jump directly to the online edition.

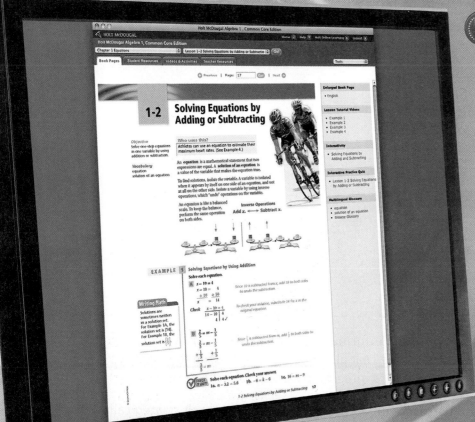

COMMON CORE GPS

Unit Contents

Module 1 Creating Expressions and Equations

MCC9-12.A.CED.1, MCC9-12.A.REI.1, MCC9-12.A.SSE.1, MCC9-12.N.Q.2

Module 2 Choosing Appropriate Units

MCC9-12.A.CED.1, MCC9-12.N.Q.1, MCC9-12.N.Q.2, MCC9-12.N.Q.3

The online edition of your textbook is enhanced with videos and interactive features for every lesson.

1 Creating Expressions and Equations

COMMON
CORE GPS

Contents

MATHEMATICAL PRACTICES   The Common Core Georgia Performance Standards for Mathematical Practice describe varieties of expertise that all students should seek to develop. Opportunities to develop these practices are integrated throughout this program.

1 Make sense of problems and persevere in solving them.

2 Reason abstractly and quantitatively.

3 Construct viable arguments and critique the reasoning of others.

4 Model with mathematics.

5 Use appropriate tools strategically.

6 Attend to precision.

7 Look for and make use of structure.

8 Look for and express regularity in repeated reasoning.

Unpacking the Standards

Understanding the standards and the vocábulary terms in the standards will help you know exactly what you are expected to learn in this chapter.

 MCC9-12.A.SSE.1

Interpret expressions that represent a quantity in terms of its context.

Key Vocabulary

expression (expresión)
A mathematical phrase that contains operations, numbers, and/or variables.

What It Means For You

Variables in formulas and other math expressions are used to represent specific quantities.

EXAMPLE

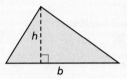

$$A = \frac{1}{2}bh$$

A = area of the triangle

b = length of the base

h = height

 MCC9-12.A.CED.1

Create equations … in one variable and use them to solve problems.

Key Vocabulary

equation (ecuación)
A mathematical statement that two expressions are equivalent.
variable (variable)
A symbol used to represent a quantity that can change.

What It Means For You

You can write an equation to represent a real-world problem and then use algebra to solve the equation and find the answer.

EXAMPLE

Michael is saving money to buy a trumpet. The trumpet costs $670. He has $350 saved, and each week he adds $20 to his savings. How long will it take him to save enough money to buy the trumpet?

Let w represent the number of weeks.

cost of trumpet	=	current savings	+	additional savings
670	=	350	+	$20w$
320	=	$20w$		
16	=	w		

It will take Michael 16 weeks to save enough money.

1-1 Variables and Expressions

Essential Question: How can you use variables to write an expression that represents a quantity in terms of its context?

Objectives
Translate between words and algebra.

Evaluate algebraic expressions.

Vocabulary
variable
constant
numerical expression
algebraic expression
evaluate

Why learn this?

Variables and expressions can be used to determine how many plastic drink bottles must be recycled to make enough carpet for a house.

Container City, in East London, UK, is a development of buildings made from recycled shipping containers.

A home that is "green built" uses many recycled products, including carpet made from recycled plastic drink bottles. You can determine how many square feet of carpet can be made from a certain number of plastic drink bottles by using *variables, constants,* and *expressions*.

A **variable** is a letter or symbol used to represent a value that can change.

A **constant** is a value that does not change.

A **numerical expression** may contain only constants and/or operations.

An **algebraic expression** may contain variables, constants, and/or operations.

You will need to translate between algebraic expressions and words to be successful in math. The diagram below shows some of the ways to write mathematical operations with words.

Plus, sum, increased by | Minus, difference, less than | Times, product, equal groups of | Divided by, quotient

COMMON CORE GPS
MCC9-12.A.SSE.1

EXAMPLE 1 Translating from Algebraic Symbols to Words

 my.hrw.com

Online Video Tutor

Give two ways to write each algebraic expression in words.

A $x + 3$
the sum of x and 3
x increased by 3

B $m - 7$
the difference of m and 7
7 less than m

C $2 \cdot y$
2 times y
the product of 2 and y

D $k \div 5$
k divided by 5
the quotient of k and 5

 CHECK IT OUT! Give two ways to write each algebraic expression in words.

1a. $4 - n$ **1b.** $\dfrac{t}{5}$ **1c.** $9 + q$ **1d.** $3(h)$

To translate words into algebraic expressions, look for words that indicate the action that is taking place.

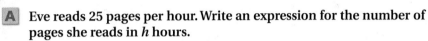

Add	**Subtract**	**Multiply**	**Divide**
↑	↑	↑	↑
Put together, combine	Find how much more or less	Put together equal groups	Separate into equal groups

my.hrw.com

Online Video Tutor

EXAMPLE **2**
MCC9-12.N.Q.1
COMMON CORE GPS

Translating from Words to Algebraic Symbols

A Eve reads 25 pages per hour. Write an expression for the number of pages she reads in h hours.

h represents the number of hours that Eve reads.

$25 \cdot h$ or $25h$ *Think: h groups of 25 pages.*

B Sam is 2 years younger than Sue, who is y years old. Write an expression for Sam's age.

y represents Sue's age.

$y - 2$ *Think: "younger than" means "less than."*

C William runs a mile in 12 minutes. Write an expression for the number of miles that William runs in m minutes.

m represents the total time William runs.

$\dfrac{m}{12}$ *Think: How many groups of 12 are in m?*

 CHECK IT OUT!

2a. Lou drives at 65 mi/h. Write an expression for the number of miles that Lou drives in t hours.

2b. Miriam is 5 cm taller than her sister, who is m cm tall. Write an expression for Miriam's height in centimeters.

2c. Elaine earns \$32 per day. Write an expression for the amount that she earns in d days.

To **evaluate** an expression is to find its value. To evaluate an algebraic expression, substitute numbers for the variables in the expression and then simplify the expression.

my.hrw.com

Online Video Tutor

EXAMPLE **3**
MCC9-12.A.SSE.1a
COMMON CORE GPS

Evaluating Algebraic Expressions

Evaluate each expression for $x = 8$, $y = 5$, and $z = 4$.

A $x + y$
$x + y = 8 + 5$ *Substitute 8 for x and 5 for y.*
$= 13$ *Simplify.*

B $\dfrac{x}{z}$
$\dfrac{x}{z} = \dfrac{8}{4}$ *Substitute 8 for x and 4 for z.*
$= 2$ *Simplify.*

 CHECK IT OUT!

Evaluate each expression for $m = 3$, $n = 2$, and $p = 9$.

3a. mn **3b.** $p - n$ **3c.** $p \div m$

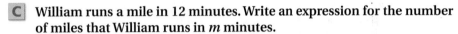

COMMON CORE GPS

EXAMPLE **4**
Prep. for MCC9-12.A.CED.1

my.hrw.com

Online Video Tutor

Helpful Hint

A *replacement set* is a set of numbers that can be substituted for a variable. The replacement set in Example 4 is {40, 120, 224}.

Recycling Application

Approximately fourteen 20-ounce plastic drink bottles must be recycled to produce 1 square foot of carpet.

a. Write an expression for the number of bottles needed to make c square feet of carpet.

The expression $14c$ models the number of bottles needed to make c square feet of carpet.

b. Find the number of bottles needed to make 40, 120, and 224 square feet of carpet.

Evaluate $14c$ for $c = 40$, 120, and 224.

c	$14c$
40	$14(40) = 560$
120	$14(120) = 1680$
224	$14(224) = 3136$

To make 40 ft^2 of carpet, 560 bottles are needed.
To make 120 ft^2 of carpet, 1680 bottles are needed.
To make 224 ft^2 of carpet, 3136 bottles are needed.

CHECK IT OUT!

4. To make one sweater, sixty-three 20-ounce plastic drink bottles must be recycled.

  a. Write an expression for the number of bottles needed to make s sweaters.

  b. Find the number of bottles needed to make 12, 25, and 50 sweaters.

MCC.MP.6

MATHEMATICAL PRACTICES

THINK AND DISCUSS

1. Write two ways to suggest each of the following, using words or phrases: addition, subtraction, multiplication, division.

2. Explain the difference between a numerical expression and an algebraic expression.

Know it!
Note

3. GET ORGANIZED Copy and complete the graphic organizer. Next to each operation, write a word phrase in the left box and its corresponding algebraic expression in the right box.

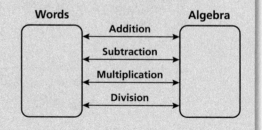

Words

Addition
Subtraction
Multiplication
Division

Algebra

GUIDED PRACTICE

1. **Vocabulary** A(n) _____?_____ is a value that can change. (*algebraic expression, constant,* or *variable*)

SEE EXAMPLE 1 Give two ways to write each algebraic expression in words.

2. $n - 5$
3. $\frac{f}{3}$
4. $c + 15$
5. $9 - y$

6. $\frac{x}{12}$
7. $t + 12$
8. $8x$
9. $x - 3$

SEE EXAMPLE 2 10. George drives at 45 mi/h. Write an expression for the number of miles George travels in h hours.

11. The length of a rectangle is 4 units greater than its width w. Write an expression for the length of the rectangle.

SEE EXAMPLE 3 Evaluate each expression for $a = 3$, $b = 4$, and $c = 2$.

12. $a - c$
13. ab
14. $b \div c$
15. ac

SEE EXAMPLE 4 16. Brianna practices the piano 30 minutes each day.

a. Write an expression for the number of hours she practices in d days.

b. Find the number of hours Brianna practices in 2, 4, and 10 days.

PRACTICE AND PROBLEM SOLVING

Independent Practice

For Exercises	See Example
17–24	1
25–26	2
27–30	3
31	4

my.hrw.com

Online Extra Practice

Give two ways to write each algebraic expression in words.

17. $5p$
18. $4 - y$
19. $3 + x$
20. $3y$

21. $-3s$
22. $r \div 5$
23. $14 - t$
24. $x + 0.5$

25. Friday's temperature was 20° warmer than Monday's temperature t. Write an expression for Friday's temperature.

26. Ann sleeps 8 hours per night. Write an expression for the number of hours Ann sleeps in n nights.

Evaluate each expression for $r = 6$, $s = 5$, and $t = 3$.

27. $r - s$
28. $s + t$
29. $r \div t$
30. sr

31. Jim is paid for overtime when he works more than 40 hours per week.

a. Write an expression for the number of hours he works overtime when he works h hours.

b. Find the number of hours Jim works overtime when he works 40, 44, 48, and 52 hours.

H.O.T. 32. **Write About It** Write a paragraph that explains to another student how to evaluate an expression.

Write an algebraic expression for each verbal expression. Then write a real-world situation that could be modeled by the expression.

33. the product of 2 and x
34. b less than 17
35. 10 more than y

36. The air around you puts pressure on your body equal to 14.7 pounds per square inch (psi). When you are underwater, the water exerts additional pressure on your body. For each foot you are below the surface of the water, the pressure increases by 0.445 psi.

   a. What does 14.7 represent in the expression $14.7 + 0.445d$?

   b. What does d represent in the expression?

   c. What is the total pressure exerted on a person's body when $d = 8$ ft?

37. **Geometry** The length of a rectangle is 9 inches. Write an expression for the area of the rectangle if the width is w inches. Find the area of the rectangle when the width is 1, 8, 9, and 11 inches.

38. **Geometry** The perimeter of any rectangle is the sum of its lengths and widths. The area of any rectangle is the length ℓ times the width w.

   a. Write an expression for the perimeter of a rectangle.

   b. Find the perimeter of the rectangle shown.

   c. Write an expression for the area of a rectangle.

   d. Find the area of the rectangle shown.

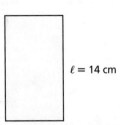

$\ell = 14$ cm

$w = 8$ cm

Complete each table. Evaluate the expression for each value of x.

39.

x	$x + 12$
1	
2	
3	
4	

40.

x	$10x$
1	
5	
10	
15	

41.

x	$x \div 2$
12	
20	
26	
30	

Astronomy

A crater on Canada's Devon Island is geologically similar to the surface of Mars. However, the temperature on Devon Island is about 37 °F in summer, and the average summer temperature on Mars is −85 °F.

42. **Astronomy** An object's weight on Mars can be found by multiplying 0.38 by the object's weight on Earth.

   a. An object weighs p pounds on Earth. Write an expression for its weight on Mars.

   b. Dana weighs 120 pounds, and her bicycle weighs 44 pounds. How much would Dana and her bicycle together weigh on Mars?

43. **Meteorology** Use the bar graph to write an expression for the average annual precipitation in New York, New York.

   a. The average annual precipitation in New York is m inches more than the average annual precipitation in Houston, Texas.

   b. The average annual precipitation in New York is s inches less than the average annual precipitation in Miami, Florida.

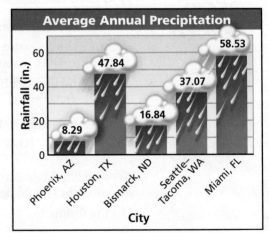

Average Annual Precipitation

Rainfall (in.)

Phoenix, AZ — 8.29
Houston, TX — 47.84
Bismarck, ND — 16.84
Seattle–Tacoma, WA — 37.07
Miami, FL — 58.53

City

44. **Critical Thinking** Compare algebraic expressions and numerical expressions. Give examples of each.

Write an algebraic expression for each verbal expression. Then evaluate the algebraic expression for the given values of x.

	Verbal	Algebraic	x = 12	x = 14
	x reduced by 5	x − 5	12 − 5 = 7	14 − 5 = 9
45.	7 more than x	�	▪	▪
46.	The quotient of x and 2	▪	▪	▪
47.	The sum of x and 3	▪	▪	▪

TEST PREP

48. Claire has had her driver's license for 3 years. Bill has had his license for *b* fewer years than Claire. Which expression can be used to show the number of years Bill has had his driver's license?

   Ⓐ 3 + b   Ⓑ b + 3   Ⓒ 3 − b   Ⓓ b − 3

49. Which expression represents *x*?

   Ⓕ 12 − 5   Ⓗ 12(5)

   Ⓖ 12 + 5   Ⓙ 12 ÷ 5

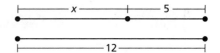

50. Which situation is best modeled by the expression 25 − x?

   Ⓐ George places *x* more video games on a shelf with 25 games.

   Ⓑ Sarah has driven *x* miles of a 25-mile trip.

   Ⓒ Amelia paid 25 dollars of an *x* dollar lunch that she shared with Ariel.

   Ⓓ Jorge has 25 boxes full of *x* baseball cards each.

CHALLENGE AND EXTEND

Evaluate each expression for the given values of the variables.

51. $2ab$; $a = 6$, $b = 3$ **52.** $2x + y$; $x = 4$, $y = 5$ **53.** $3x \div 6y$; $x = 6$, $y = 3$

54. **Multi-Step** An Internet service provider charges \$9.95/month for the first 20 hours and \$0.50 for each additional hour. Write an expression representing the charges for *h* hours of use in one month when *h* is more than 20 hours. What is the charge for 35 hours?

FOCUS ON MATHEMATICAL PRACTICES

H.O.T. 55. **Reasoning** Are there any values of *x* and *y* for which $x + y$ is equal to $x - y$? If so, give an example.

H.O.T. 56. **Patterns** $x + 2$ is an odd number. Write an expression for each of the next 4 odd numbers. Is $x + 75$ even or odd? Explain.

H.O.T. 57. **Error Analysis** One insect crawled for 5 minutes at a rate of 2.5 inches per minute while another insect crawled the same amount of time at a rate of 2.5 inches per second. Kevin used the variable *t* for the time (in minutes) each insect crawled, wrote the expression $2.5t$ for each insect's distance, and found that each insect crawled the same distance. Explain Kevin's error.

Model One-Step Equations

You can use algebra tiles and an equation mat to model and solve equations. To find the value of the variable, place or remove tiles to get the x-tile by itself on one side of the mat. You must place or remove the same number of yellow tiles or the same number of red tiles on both sides.

  Use appropriate tools strategically.

Use with Solving Equations by Adding or Subtracting

MCC9-12.A.REI.1 Explain each step in solving a simple equation as following from the equality of numbers asserted at the previous step, starting from the assumption that the original equation has a solution. Construct a viable argument to justify a solution method. *Also* **MCC9-12.A.REI.3**

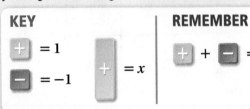

KEY	REMEMBER
$+$ = 1	$+$ + $-$ = 0
$-$ = −1 $+$ = x	

Activity

Use algebra tiles to model and solve $x + 6 = 2$.

MODEL		ALGEBRA
	Model $x + 6$ on the left side of the mat and 2 on the right side of the mat.	$x + 6 = 2$
	Place 6 red tiles on both sides of the mat. This represents adding −6 to both sides of the equation.	$x + 6 + (-6) = 2 + (-6)$
	Remove zero pairs from both sides of the mat.	$x + 0 = 0 + (-4)$
	One x-tile is equivalent to 4 red tiles.	$x = -4$

Try This

Use algebra tiles to model and solve each equation.

1. $x + 2 = 5$ **2.** $x - 7 = 8$ **3.** $x - 5 = 9$ **4.** $x + 4 = 7$

1-2 Solving Equations by Adding or Subtracting

Essential Question: How can you use addition or subtraction to solve equations?

Objective
Solve one-step equations in one variable by using addition or subtraction.

Vocabulary
equation
solution of an equation

Animated Math

Who uses this?

Athletes can use an equation to estimate their maximum heart rates. (See Example 4.)

An **equation** is a mathematical statement that two expressions are equal. A **solution of an equation** is a value of the variable that makes the equation true.

To find solutions, *isolate the variable.* A variable is isolated when it appears by itself on one side of an equation, and not at all on the other side. Isolate a variable by using inverse operations, which "undo" operations on the variable.

An equation is like a balanced scale. To keep the balance, perform the same operation on both sides.

Inverse Operations

Add *x.* ⟷ Subtract *x.*

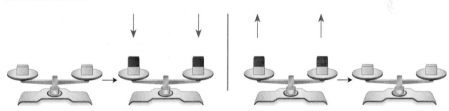

COMMON CORE GPS
EXAMPLE 1
MCC9-12.A.REI.3

my.hrw.com

Online Video Tutor

Solving Equations by Using Addition

Solve each equation.

A $x - 10 = 4$

$$x - 10 = 4$$
$$\underline{+ 10 \quad + 10}$$
$$x = 14$$

Since 10 is subtracted from x, add 10 to both sides to undo the subtraction.

Check
$$\frac{x - 10 = 4}{14 - 10 \mid 4}$$
$$4 \mid 4 \checkmark$$

To check your solution, substitute 14 for x in the original equation.

B $\frac{2}{5} = m - \frac{1}{5}$

$$\frac{2}{5} = m - \frac{1}{5}$$
$$\underline{+ \frac{1}{5} \qquad + \frac{1}{5}}$$
$$\frac{3}{5} = m$$

Since $\frac{1}{5}$ is subtracted from m, add $\frac{1}{5}$ to both sides to undo the subtraction.

Writing Math

Solutions are sometimes written in a *solution set.* For Example 1A, the solution set is {14}. For Example 1B, the solution set is $\left\{\frac{3}{5}\right\}$.

CHECK IT OUT!

Solve each equation. Check your answer.

1a. $n - 3.2 = 5.6$ **1b.** $-6 = k - 6$ **1c.** $16 = m - 9$

© Duomo/CORBIS

1-2 Solving Equations by Adding or Subtracting   **13**

COMMON CORE GPS
EXAMPLE **2**
MCC9-12.A.REI.3

Solving Equations by Using Subtraction

Solve each equation. Check your answer.

my.hrw.com

Online Video Tutor

A $x + 7 = 9$

$$x + 7 = \quad 9$$
$$\underline{\quad -7 \quad \quad -7}$$
$$x = \quad 2$$

Since 7 is added to x, subtract 7 from both sides to undo the addition.

Check
$$\begin{array}{c|c} x + 7 = 9 \\ \hline 2 + 7 & 9 \\ 9 & 9 \checkmark \end{array}$$

To check your solution, substitute 2 for x in the original equation.

B $0.7 = r + 0.4$

$$0.7 = r + 0.4$$
$$\underline{-0.4 \quad \quad -0.4}$$
$$0.3 = r$$

Since 0.4 is added to r, subtract 0.4 from both sides to undo the addition.

Check
$$\begin{array}{c|c} 0.7 = r + 0.4 \\ \hline 0.7 & 0.3 + 0.4 \\ 0.7 & 0.7 \checkmark \end{array}$$

To check your solution, substitute 0.3 for r in the original equation.

Solve each equation. Check your answer.

2a. $d + \dfrac{1}{2} = 1$ **2b.** $-5 = k + 5$ **2c.** $6 + t = 14$

Remember that subtracting is the same as adding the opposite. When solving equations, you will sometimes find it easier to add an opposite to both sides instead of subtracting. For example, this method may be useful when the equation contains negative numbers.

COMMON CORE GPS
EXAMPLE **3**
MCC9-12.A.REI.3

Solving Equations by Adding the Opposite

Solve $-8 + b = 2$.

$$-8 + b = \quad 2$$
$$\underline{+8 \quad \quad +8}$$
$$b = \quad 10$$

Since −8 is added to b, add 8 to both sides.

my.hrw.com

Online Video Tutor

Solve each equation. Check your answer.

3a. $-2.3 + m = 7$ **3b.** $-\dfrac{3}{4} + z = \dfrac{5}{4}$ **3c.** $-11 + x = 33$

Student to Student

Ama Walker
Carson High School

Zero As a Solution

I used to get confused when I got a solution of 0. But my teacher reminded me that 0 is a number just like any other number, so it can be a solution of an equation. Just check your answer and see if it works.

$$x + 6 = \quad 6$$
$$\underline{-6 \quad -6}$$
$$x = \quad 0$$

Check
$$\begin{array}{c|c} x + 6 = 6 \\ \hline 0 + 6 & 6 \\ 6 & 6 \checkmark \end{array}$$

EXAMPLE 4
MCC9-12.A.CED.1

Fitness Application

A person's maximum heart rate is the highest rate, in beats per minute, that the person's heart should reach. One method to estimate maximum heart rate states that your age added to your maximum heart rate is 220. Using this method, write and solve an equation to find the maximum heart rate of a 15-year-old.

Age	added to	maximum heart rate	is	220.
a	$+$	r	$=$	220

$$a + r = 220$$ *Write an equation to represent the relationship.*

$$15 + r = 220$$

$$\underline{-15 \qquad -15}$$ *Substitute 15 for a. Since 15 is added to r, subtract 15 from both sides to undo the addition.*

$$r = 205$$

The maximum heart rate for a 15-year-old is 205 beats per minute. Since age added to maximum heart rate is 220, the answer should be less than 220. So 205 is a reasonable answer.

CHECK IT OUT!

4. **What if...?** Use the method above to find a person's age if the person's maximum heart rate is 185 beats per minute.

The properties of equality allow you to perform inverse operations, as in the previous examples. These properties say that you can perform the same operation on both sides of an equation.

Properties of Equality

WORDS	NUMBERS	ALGEBRA
Addition Property of Equality You can add the same number to both sides of an equation, and the statement will still be true.	$3 = 3$ $3 + 2 = 3 + 2$ $5 = 5$	$a = b$ $a + c = b + c$
Subtraction Property of Equality You can subtract the same number from both sides of an equation, and the statement will still be true.	$7 = 7$ $7 - 5 = 7 - 5$ $2 = 2$	$a = b$ $a - c = b - c$

MCC.MP.3   MATHEMATICAL PRACTICES

THINK AND DISCUSS

1. Describe how the Addition and Subtraction Properties of Equality are like a balanced scale.

2. **GET ORGANIZED** Copy and complete the graphic organizer. In each box, write an example of an equation that can be solved by using the given property, and solve it.

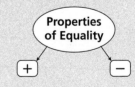

Properties of Equality

$+$ $-$

1-2 Exercises

my.hrw.com
Homework Help

GUIDED PRACTICE

1. **Vocabulary** Will the *solution of an equation* such as $x - 3 = 9$ be a variable or a number? Explain.

Solve each equation. Check your answer.

SEE EXAMPLE 1

2. $s - 5 = 3$
3. $17 = w - 4$
4. $k - 8 = -7$
5. $x - 3.9 = 12.4$
6. $8.4 = y - 4.6$
7. $\frac{3}{8} = t - \frac{1}{8}$

SEE EXAMPLE 2

8. $t + 5 = -25$
9. $9 = s + 9$
10. $42 = m + 36$
11. $2.8 = z + 0.5$
12. $b + \frac{2}{3} = 2$
13. $n + 1.8 = 3$

SEE EXAMPLE 3

14. $-10 + d = 7$
15. $20 = -12 + v$
16. $-46 + q = 5$
17. $2.8 = -0.9 + y$
18. $-\frac{2}{3} + c = \frac{2}{3}$
19. $-\frac{5}{6} + p = 2$

SEE EXAMPLE 4

20. **Geology** In 1673, the Hope diamond was reduced from its original weight by about 45 carats, resulting in a diamond weighing about 67 carats. Write and solve an equation to find how many carats the original diamond weighed. Show that your answer is reasonable.

PRACTICE AND PROBLEM SOLVING

Independent Practice

For Exercises	See Example
21–30	1
31–40	2
41–48	3
49	4

my.hrw.com

Online Extra Practice

Solve each equation. Check your answer.

21. $1 = k - 8$
22. $u - 15 = -8$
23. $x - 7 = 10$
24. $-9 = p - 2$
25. $\frac{3}{7} = p - \frac{1}{7}$
26. $q - 0.5 = 1.5$
27. $6 = t - 4.5$
28. $4\frac{2}{3} = r - \frac{1}{3}$
29. $6 = x - 3$
30. $1.75 = k - 0.75$
31. $19 + a = 19$
32. $4 = 3.1 + y$
33. $m + 20 = 3$
34. $-12 = c + 3$
35. $v + 2300 = -800$
36. $b + 42 = 300$
37. $3.5 = n + 4$
38. $b + \frac{1}{2} = \frac{1}{2}$
39. $x + 5.34 = 5.39$
40. $2 = d + \frac{1}{4}$
41. $-12 + f = 3$
42. $-9 = -4 + g$
43. $-1200 + j = 345$
44. $90 = -22 + a$
45. $26 = -4 + y$
46. $1\frac{3}{4} = -\frac{1}{4} + w$
47. $-\frac{1}{6} + h = \frac{1}{6}$
48. $-5.2 + a = -8$

49. **Finance** Luis deposited $500 into his bank account. He now has $4732. Write and solve an equation to find how much was in his account before the deposit. Show that your answer is reasonable.

50. **///ERROR ANALYSIS///** Below are two possible solutions to $x + 12.5 = 21.6$. Which is incorrect? Explain the error.

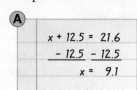

A

$$x + 12.5 = 21.6$$
$$\underline{- 12.5 \quad - 12.5}$$
$$x = 9.1$$

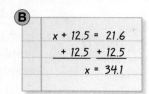

B

$$x + 12.5 = 21.6$$
$$\underline{+ 12.5 \quad + 12.5}$$
$$x = 34.1$$

Write an equation to represent each relationship. Then solve the equation.

51. Ten less than a number is equal to 12.

52. A number decreased by 13 is equal to 7.

53. Eight more than a number is 16.

54. A number minus 3 is –8.

55. The sum of 5 and a number is 6.

56. Two less than a number is –5.

57. The difference of a number and 4 is 9.

58. Geology The sum of the Atlantic Ocean's average depth (in feet) and its greatest depth is 43,126. Use the information in the graph to write and solve an equation to find the average depth of the Atlantic Ocean. Show that your answer is reasonable.

59. School Helene's marching band needs money to travel to a competition. Band members have raised $560. They need to raise a total of $1680. Write and solve an equation to find how much more they need. Show that your answer is reasonable.

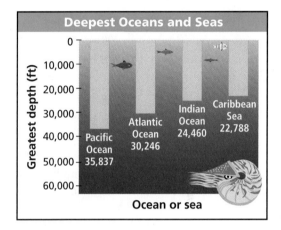

60. Economics When you receive a loan to make a purchase, you often must make a down payment in cash. The amount of the loan is the purchase cost minus the down payment. Riva made a down payment of $1500 on a used car. She received a loan of $2600. Write and solve an equation to find the cost of the car. Show that your answer is reasonable.

Geometry The angles in each pair are complementary. Write and solve an equation to find each value of x. (*Hint:* The measures of complementary angles add to 90°.)

61.

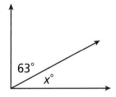

62.

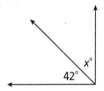

63.

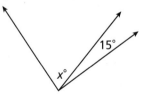

64. *Rates* are often used to describe how quickly something is moving or changing.

  a. A wildfire spreads at a rate of 1000 acres per day. How many acres will the fire cover in 2 days? Show that your answer is reasonable.

  b. How many acres will the fire cover in 5 days? Explain how you found your answer.

  c. Another wildfire spread for 7 days and covered a total of 780 square miles. How can you estimate the number of square miles the fire covered per day?

65. Statistics The range of a set of scores is 28, and the lowest score is 47. Write and solve an equation to find the highest score. (*Hint:* In a data set, the range is the difference between the highest and the lowest values.) Show that your answer is reasonable.

H.O.T. 66. Write About It Describe a real-world situation that can be modeled by $x + 5 = 25$. Tell what the variable represents in your situation. Then solve the equation and tell what the solution means in the context of your problem.

H.O.T. 67. Critical Thinking Without solving, tell whether the solution of $-3 + z = 10$ will be greater than 10 or less than 10. Explain.

TEST PREP

68. Which situation is best represented by $x - 32 = 8$?

Ⓐ Logan withdrew $32 from her bank account. After her withdrawal, her balance was $8. How much was originally in her account?

Ⓑ Daniel has 32 baseball cards. Joseph has 8 fewer baseball cards than Daniel. How many baseball cards does Joseph have?

Ⓒ Room A contains 32 desks. Room B has 8 fewer desks. How many desks are in Room B?

Ⓓ Janelle bought a bag of 32 craft sticks for a project. She used 8 craft sticks. How many craft sticks does she have left?

69. For which equation is $a = 8$ a solution?

Ⓕ $15 - a = 10$ Ⓖ $10 + a = 23$ Ⓗ $a - 18 = 26$ Ⓙ $a + 8 = 16$

70. Short Response Julianna used a gift card to pay for an $18 haircut. The remaining balance on the card was $22.

a. Write an equation that can be used to determine the original value of the card.

b. Solve your equation to find the original value of the card.

CHALLENGE AND EXTEND

Solve each equation. Check your answer.

71. $3\frac{1}{5} + b = \frac{4}{5}$ **72.** $x - \frac{7}{4} = \frac{2}{3}$ **73.** $x + \frac{7}{4} = \frac{2}{3}$ **74.** $x - \frac{4}{9} = \frac{4}{9}$

75. If $p - 4 = 2$, find the value of $5p - 20$.   **76.** If $t + 6 = 21$, find the value of $-2t$.

77. If $x + 3 = 15$, find the value of $18 + 6x$.   **78.** If $2 + n = -11$, find the value of $6n$.

FOCUS ON MATHEMATICAL PRACTICES

H.O.T. 79. Reasoning Compare the equations $w + 3 = 65$ and $3 = w + 65$. How are the solutions related?

H.O.T. 80. Make a Conjecture Consider the equation $8 = 8$.

a. How can you obtain the equation $3 = 3$ by using the Subtraction Property of Equality? How can you obtain the equation $3 = 3$ by using the Addition Property of Equality?

b. Is the Subtraction Property of Equality ever *needed* to solve an equation? Explain.

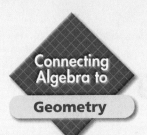

Area of Composite Figures

Review the area formulas for squares, rectangles, and triangles in the table below.

Squares	Rectangles	Triangles
![square with side s]	![rectangle with width w and length ℓ]	![triangle with height h and base b]
$A = s^2$	$A = \ell w$	$A = \frac{1}{2}bh$

A *composite figure* is a figure that is composed of basic shapes. You can divide composite figures into combinations of squares, rectangles, and triangles to find their areas.

Example

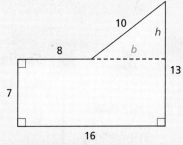

Find the area of the figure shown.

Divide the figure into a rectangle and a right triangle. Notice that you do not know the base or the height of the triangle. Use b and h to represent these lengths.

The bottom of the rectangle is 16 units long; the top of the rectangle is 8 units long plus the base of the triangle. Use this information to write and solve an equation.

$$\begin{array}{r} b + 8 = 16 \\ \underline{-8 -8} \\ b = 8 \end{array}$$

The right side of the figure is 13 units long: 7 units from the rectangle plus the height of the triangle. Use this information to write and solve an equation.

$$\begin{array}{r} h + 7 = 13 \\ \underline{-7 -7} \\ h = 6 \end{array}$$

The area of the figure is the sum of the areas of the rectangle and the triangle.

Area of rectangle → ← Area of triangle

$$A = \ell w + \frac{1}{2}bh$$
$$A = 16(7) + \frac{1}{2}(8)(6)$$
$$A = 112 + 24$$
$$A = 136 \text{ square units}$$

Try This

Find the area of each composite figure.

1.

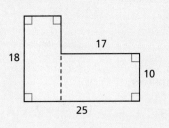

2.

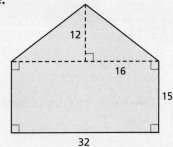

3.

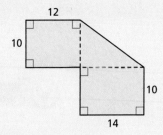

Solving Equations by Multiplying or Dividing

  Essential Question: How can you use multiplication or division to solve equations?

Objective
Solve one-step equations in one variable by using multiplication or division.

Who uses this?
Pilots can make quick calculations by solving one-step equations. (See Example 4.)

Solving an equation that contains multiplication or division is similar to solving an equation that contains addition or subtraction. Use inverse operations to undo the operations on the variable.

Remember that an equation is like a balanced scale. To keep the balance, whatever you do on one side of the equation, you must also do on the other side.

Inverse Operations
Multiply by x. ⟷ Divide by x.

EXAMPLE
MCC9-12.A.REI.3

1

 my.hrw.com

Online Video Tutor

Solving Equations by Using Multiplication

Solve each equation. Check your answer.

A $-4 = \dfrac{k}{-5}$

$(-5)(-4) = (-5)\left(\dfrac{k}{-5}\right)$ *Since k is divided by −5, multiply both sides by −5 to undo the division.*

$20 = k$

Check $-4 = \dfrac{k}{-5}$ *To check your solution, substitute 20 for k in the original equation.*

$$
\begin{array}{c|c}
-4 & \dfrac{20}{-5} \\
\hline
-4 & -4 \checkmark
\end{array}
$$

B $\dfrac{m}{3} = 1.5$

$(3)\left(\dfrac{m}{3}\right) = (3)(1.5)$ *Since m is divided by 3, multiply both sides by 3 to undo the division.*

$m = 4.5$

Check $\dfrac{m}{3} = 1.5$ *To check your solution, substitute 1.5 for m in the original equation.*

$$
\begin{array}{c|c}
\dfrac{4.5}{3} & 1.5 \\
\hline
1.5 & 1.5 \checkmark
\end{array}
$$

 CHECK IT OUT!   Solve each equation. Check your answer.

1a. $\dfrac{p}{5} = 10$ **1b.** $-13 = \dfrac{y}{3}$ **1c.** $\dfrac{c}{8} = 7$

EXAMPLE 2 Solving Equations by Using Division

Solve each equation. Check your answers.

A $7x = 56$

$$\frac{7x}{7} = \frac{56}{7}$$

$$x = 8$$

Since x is multiplied by 7, divide both sides by 7 to undo the multiplication.

Check

$$7x = 56$$
$$\overline{7(8) \mid 56}$$
$$56 \mid 56 \checkmark$$

To check your solution, substitute 8 for x in the original equation.

B $13 = -2w$

$$\frac{13}{-2} = \frac{-2w}{-2}$$

$$-6.5 = w$$

Since w is multiplied by −2, divide both sides by −2 to undo the multiplication.

Check

$$13 = -2w$$
$$\overline{13 \mid -2(-6.5)}$$
$$13 \mid 13 \checkmark$$

To check your solution, substitute −6.5 for w in the original equation.

CHECK IT OUT!

Solve each equation. Check your answer.

2a. $16 = 4c$ **2b.** $0.5y = -10$ **2c.** $15k = 75$

Remember that dividing is the same as multiplying by the reciprocal. When solving equations, you will sometimes find it easier to multiply by a reciprocal instead of dividing. This is often true when an equation contains fractions.

EXAMPLE 3 Solving Equations That Contain Fractions

Solve each equation.

A $\frac{5}{9}v = 35$

$$\left(\frac{9}{5}\right)\frac{5}{9}v = \left(\frac{9}{5}\right)35$$

$$v = 63$$

The reciprocal of $\frac{5}{9}$ is $\frac{9}{5}$. Since v is multiplied by $\frac{5}{9}$, multiply both sides by $\frac{9}{5}$.

B $\frac{5}{2} = \frac{4y}{3}$

$$\frac{5}{2} = \frac{4y}{3}$$

$$\frac{5}{2} = \frac{4}{3}y$$

$\frac{4y}{3}$ is the same as $\frac{4}{3}y$.

$$\left(\frac{3}{4}\right)\frac{5}{2} = \left(\frac{3}{4}\right)\frac{4}{3}y$$

$$\frac{15}{8} = y$$

The reciprocal of $\frac{4}{3}$ is $\frac{3}{4}$. Since y is multiplied by $\frac{4}{3}$, multiply both sides by $\frac{3}{4}$.

CHECK IT OUT!

Solve each equation. Check your answer.

3a. $-\frac{1}{4} = \frac{1}{5}b$ **3b.** $\frac{4j}{6} = \frac{2}{3}$ **3c.** $\frac{1}{6}w = 102$

EXAMPLE **4** *Aviation Application*

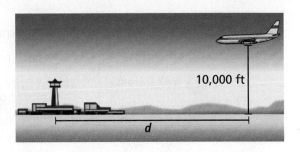

10,000 ft

The distance in miles from the airport that a plane should begin descending, divided by 3, equals the plane's height above the ground in thousands of feet. If a plane is 10,000 feet above the ground, write and solve an equation to find the distance at which the pilot should begin descending.

my.hrw.com

Online Video Tutor

| Distance | divided by 3 | equals | height in thousands of feet. |

$$\frac{d}{3} = h \qquad \text{Write an equation to represent the relationship.}$$

$$\frac{d}{3} = 10 \qquad \text{Substitute 10 for } h. \text{ Since } d \text{ is divided by 3, multiply both sides by 3 to undo the division.}$$

$$(3)\frac{d}{3} = (3)10$$

$$d = 30$$

The pilot should begin descending 30 miles from the airport.

Caution! ////

The equation uses the plane's height above the ground in *thousands* of feet. So substitute 10 for *h*, not 10,000.

4. **What if...?** A plane began descending 45 miles from the airport. Use the equation above to find how high the plane was flying when the descent began.

You have now used four properties of equality to solve equations. These properties are summarized in the box below.

Properties of Equality

WORDS	NUMBERS	ALGEBRA
Addition Property of Equality You can add the same number to both sides of an equation, and the statement will still be true.	$3 = 3$ $3 + 2 = 3 + 2$ $5 = 5$	$a = b$ $a + c = b + c$
Subtraction Property of Equality You can subtract the same number from both sides of an equation, and the statement will still be true.	$7 = 7$ $7 - 5 = 7 - 5$ $2 = 2$	$a = b$ $a - c = b - c$
Multiplication Property of Equality You can multiply both sides of an equation by the same number, and the statement will still be true.	$6 = 6$ $6(3) = 6(3)$ $18 = 18$	$a = b$ $ac = bc$
Division Property of Equality You can divide both sides of an equation by the same nonzero number, and the statement will still be true.	$8 = 8$ $\frac{8}{4} = \frac{8}{4}$ $2 = 2$	$a = b$ $(c \neq 0)$ $\frac{a}{c} = \frac{b}{c}$

THINK AND DISCUSS

1. Tell how the Multiplication and Division Properties of Equality are similar to the Addition and Subtraction Properties of Equality.

2. **GET ORGANIZED** Copy and complete the graphic organizer. In each box, write an example of an equation that can be solved by using the given property, and solve it.

Properties of Equality

$\times$ $\div$

1-3 Exercises

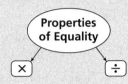

my.hrw.com
Homework Help

GUIDED PRACTICE

Solve each equation. Check your answer.

SEE EXAMPLE 1

1. $\dfrac{k}{4} = 8$

2. $\dfrac{z}{3} = -9$

3. $-2 = \dfrac{w}{-7}$

4. $6 = \dfrac{t}{-5}$

5. $\dfrac{g}{1.9} = 10$

6. $2.4 = \dfrac{b}{5}$

SEE EXAMPLE 2

7. $4x = 28$

8. $-64 = 8c$

9. $-9j = -45$

10. $84 = -12a$

11. $4m = 10$

12. $2.8 = -2h$

SEE EXAMPLE 3

13. $\dfrac{1}{2}d = 7$

14. $15 = \dfrac{5}{6}f$

15. $\dfrac{2}{3}s = -6$

16. $9 = -\dfrac{3}{8}r$

17. $\dfrac{1}{10} = \dfrac{4}{5}y$

18. $\dfrac{1}{4}v = -\dfrac{3}{4}$

SEE EXAMPLE 4

19. **Recreation** The Baseball Birthday Batter Package at a minor league ballpark costs $192. The package includes tickets, drinks, and cake for a group of 16 children. Write and solve an equation to find the cost per child.

20. **Nutrition** An orange contains about 80 milligrams of vitamin C, which is 10 times as much as an apple contains. Write and solve an equation to find the amount of vitamin C in an apple.

PRACTICE AND PROBLEM SOLVING

Solve each equation. Check your answer.

21. $\dfrac{x}{2} = 12$

22. $-40 = \dfrac{b}{5}$

23. $-\dfrac{j}{6} = 6$

24. $-\dfrac{n}{3} = -4$

25. $-\dfrac{q}{5} = 30$

26. $1.6 = \dfrac{d}{3}$

27. $\dfrac{v}{10} = 5.5$

28. $\dfrac{h}{8.1} = -4$

29. $5t = -15$

30. $49 = 7c$

31. $-12 = -12u$

32. $-7m = 63$

33. $-52 = -4c$

34. $11 = -2z$

35. $5f = 1.5$

36. $-8.4 = -4n$

Independent Practice

For Exercises	See Example
21–28	1
29–36	2
37–44	3
45	4

my.hrw.com

Online Extra Practice

Solve each equation. Check your answer.

37. $\frac{5}{2}k = 5$

38. $-9 = \frac{3}{4}d$

39. $-\frac{5}{8}b = 10$

40. $-\frac{4}{5}g = -12$

41. $\frac{4}{7}t = -2$

42. $-\frac{4}{5}p = \frac{2}{3}$

43. $\frac{2}{3} = -\frac{1}{3}q$

44. $-\frac{5}{8} = -\frac{3}{4}a$

45. Finance After taxes, Alexandra's take-home pay is $\frac{7}{10}$ of her salary before taxes. Write and solve an equation to find Alexandra's salary before taxes for the pay period that resulted in $392 of take-home pay.

46. Earth Science Your weight on the Moon is about $\frac{1}{6}$ of your weight on Earth. Write and solve an equation to show how much a person weighs on Earth if he weighs 16 pounds on the Moon. How could you check that your answer is reasonable?

47. ///ERROR ANALYSIS/// For the equation $\frac{x}{3} = 15$, a student found the value of x to be 5. Explain the error. What is the correct answer?

Geometry The perimeter of a square is given. Write and solve an equation to find the length of each side of the square.

48. $P = 36$ in.

49. $P = 84$ in.

50. $P = 100$ yd

51. $P = 16.4$ cm

Write an equation to represent each relationship. Then solve the equation.

52. Five times a number is 45.

53. A number multiplied by negative 3 is 12.

54. A number divided by 4 is equal to 10.

55. The quotient of a number and 3 is negative 8.

56. Statistics The mean height of the students in Marta's class is 60 in. There are 18 students in her class. Write and solve an equation to find the total measure of all students' heights. (*Hint:* The mean is found by dividing the sum of all data values by the number of data values.)

57. Finance Lisa earned $6.25 per hour at her after-school job. Each week she earned $50. Write and solve an equation to show how many hours she worked each week.

58. Critical Thinking Will the solution of $\frac{x}{2.1} = 4$ be greater than 4 or less than 4? Explain.

59. Consumer Economics Dion's long-distance phone bill was $13.80. His long-distance calls cost $0.05 per minute. Write and solve an equation to find the number of minutes he was charged for. Show that your answer is reasonable.

60. Nutrition An 8 oz cup of coffee has about 184 mg of caffeine. This is 5 times as much caffeine as in a 12 oz soft drink. Write and solve an equation to find about how much caffeine is in a 12 oz caffeinated soft drink. Round your answer to the nearest whole number. Show that your answer is reasonable.

Statistics

American Robert P. Wadlow (1918–1940) holds the record for world's tallest man— 8 ft 11.1 in. He also holds world records for the largest feet and hands.

Source: Guinness World Records 2005

Use the equation $8y = 4x$ to find y for each value of x.

	x	$4x$	$8y = 4x$	y
61.	−4	$4(-4) = -16$	$8y = -16$	▪
62.	−2	▪	▪	▪
63.	0	▪	▪	▪
64.	2	▪	▪	▪

© Bettmann/CORBIS

65. **a.** The formula for the mean of a data set is mean = $\frac{\text{sum of data values}}{\text{number of data values}}$. One summer, there were 1926 wildfires in Arizona. Which value does this number represent in the formula?

   b. The mean number of acres burned by each wildfire was 96.21. Which value does this number represent in the formula?

   c. Use the formula and information given to find how many acres were burned by wildfires in Arizona that summer. Round your answer to the nearest acre. Show that your answer is reasonable.

Solve each equation. Check your answer.

66. $\frac{m}{6} = 1$ 67. $4x = 28$ 68. $1.2h = 14.4$ 69. $\frac{1}{5}x = 121$

70. $2w = 26$ 71. $4b = \frac{3}{4}$ 72. $5y = 11$ 73. $\frac{n}{1.9} = 3$

Biology Use the table for Exercises 74 and 75.

Average Weight			
Animal	At Birth (g)	Adult Female (g)	Adult Male (g)
Hamster	2	130	110
Guinea pig	85	800	1050
Rat	5	275	480

74. The mean weight of an adult male rat is 16 times the mean weight of an adult male mouse. Write and solve an equation to find the mean weight of an adult male mouse. Show that your answer is reasonable.

75. On average, a hamster at birth weighs $\frac{2}{3}$ the weight of a gerbil at birth. Write and solve an equation to find the average weight of a gerbil at birth. Show that your answer is reasonable.

H.O.T. 76. **Write About It** Describe a real-world situation that can be modeled by $3x = 42$. Solve the equation and tell what the solution means in the context of your problem.

TEST PREP

77. Which situation does NOT represent the equation $\frac{d}{2} = 10$?

   Ⓐ Leo bought a box of pencils. He gave half of them to his brother. They each got 10 pencils. How many pencils were in the box Leo bought?
   Ⓑ Kasey evenly divided her money from baby-sitting into two bank accounts. She put $10 in each account. How much did Kasey earn?
   Ⓒ Gilbert cut a piece of ribbon into 2-inch strips. When he was done, he had ten 2-inch strips. How long was the ribbon to start?
   Ⓓ Mattie had 2 more CDs than her sister Leona. If Leona had 10 CDs, how many CDs did Mattie have?

78. Which equation below shows a correct first step for solving $3x = -12$?

   Ⓕ $3x + 3 = -12 + 3$ Ⓗ $3(3x) = 3(-12)$
   Ⓖ $3x - 3 = -12 - 3$ Ⓙ $\frac{3x}{3} = \frac{-12}{3}$

79. In a regular pentagon, all of the angles are equal in measure. The sum of the angle measures is 540°. Which of the following equations could be used to find the measure of each angle?

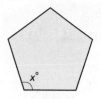

Ⓐ $\dfrac{x}{540} = 5$ Ⓒ $540x = 5$

Ⓑ $5x = 540$ Ⓓ $\dfrac{x}{5} = 540$

80. For which equation is $m = 10$ a solution?

Ⓕ $5 = 2m$ Ⓖ $5m = 2$ Ⓗ $\dfrac{m}{2} = 5$ Ⓘ $\dfrac{m}{10} = 2$

81. **Short Response** Luisa bought 6 cans of cat food that each cost the same amount. She spent a total of $4.80.

   a. Write an equation to determine the cost of one can of cat food. Tell what each part of your equation represents.

   b. Solve your equation to find the cost of one can of cat food. Show each step.

CHALLENGE AND EXTEND

Solve each equation. Check your answer.

82. $\left(3\dfrac{1}{5}\right)b = \dfrac{4}{5}$ 83. $\left(1\dfrac{1}{3}\right)x = 2\dfrac{2}{3}$ 84. $\left(5\dfrac{4}{5}\right)x = -52\dfrac{1}{5}$

85. $\left(-2\dfrac{9}{10}\right)k = -26\dfrac{1}{10}$ 86. $\left(1\dfrac{2}{3}\right)w = 15\dfrac{1}{3}$ 87. $\left(2\dfrac{1}{4}\right)d = 4\dfrac{1}{2}$

Find each indicated value.

88. If $2p = 4$, find the value of $6p + 10$.   89. If $6t = 24$, find the value of $-5t$.

90. If $3x = 15$, find the value of $12 - 4x$.   91. If $\dfrac{n}{2} = -11$, find the value of $6n$.

92. To isolate x in $ax = b$, what should you divide both sides by?

93. To isolate x in $\frac{x}{a} = b$, what operation should you perform on both sides of the equation?

H.O.T. 94. **Travel** The formula $d = rt$ gives the distance d that is traveled at a rate r in time t.

   a. If $d = 400$ and $r = 25$, what is the value of t?

   b. If $d = 400$ and $r = 50$, what is the value of t?

   c. What if...? How did t change when r increased from 25 to 50?

   d. What if...? If r is doubled while d remains the same, what is the effect on t?

FOCUS ON MATHEMATICAL PRACTICES

H.O.T. 95. **Problem Solving** Teo did not know how many ounces of liquid his rice cooker cup would hold. He used the cup to put an entire 32-oz container of broth into the cooker, filling the cup $5\dfrac{1}{3}$ times. How much liquid does the cup hold?

H.O.T. 96. **Communication** Suppose a and b are any nonzero numbers. Solve the equations $\dfrac{1}{a}x = b$ and $\dfrac{1}{b}x = a$ for x. Are the solutions the same? Provide an example that supports your answer.

H.O.T. 97. **Number Sense** Write four equations that each have a solution of 0 and that are solved by using a different property of equality.

1-3
Technology
TASK
Solve Equations by Graphing

You can use graphs to solve equations. As you complete this activity, you will learn some of the connections between graphs and equations.

Use with Solving Equations by Multiplying or Dividing

Use appropriate tools strategically.

MCC9-12.A.REI.11 Explain why the x-coordinates of the points where the graphs of the equations $y = f(x)$ and $y = g(x)$ intersect are the solutions of the equation $f(x) = g(x)$; find the solutions approximately, e.g., using technology to graph the functions, make tables of values, ...* *Also* **MCC9-12.A.REI.3**

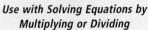

Solve $3x - 4 = 5$.

1. Press [Y=]. In Y_1, enter the left side of the equation, $3x - 4$.

   [Y=] 3 [X,T,θ,n] [−] 4 [ENTER]

   In Y_2, enter the right side of the equation, 5.

   [Y=] 5 [ENTER]

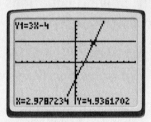

2. Press [GRAPH]. Press [TRACE]. The display will show the x- and y-values of a point on the first line. Press the right arrow key several times. Notice that the x- and y-values change.

3. Continue to trace as close as possible to the intersection of the two lines. The x-value of this point 2.9787…, is an approximation of the solution. The solution is about 3.

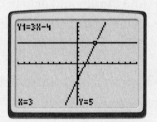

4. While still in trace mode, to check, press 3 [ENTER]. The display will show the y-value when $x = 3$. When $x = 3$, $y = 5$. So 3 is the solution. You can also check this solution by substituting 3 for x in the equation:

$$\begin{array}{c|c} \textbf{Check} & 3x - 4 = 5 \\ \hline 3(3) - 4 & 5 \\ 9 - 4 & 5 \\ 5 & 5 \checkmark \end{array}$$

1. Solve $3x - 4 = 2$, $3x - 4 = 17$, and $3x - 4 = -7$ by graphing.

2. What does each line represent?

3. Describe a procedure for finding the solution of $3x - 4 = y$ for any value of y.

4. Solve $\frac{1}{2}x - 7 = -4$, $\frac{1}{2}x - 7 = 0$, and $\frac{1}{2}x - 7 = 2$ by graphing.

Ready to Go On?

my.hrw.com
Assessment and Intervention

1-1 Variables and Expressions

Give two ways to write each algebraic expression in words.

1. $4 + n$

2. $m - 9$

3. $\dfrac{g}{2}$

4. $4z$

5. Grapes cost \$1.99 per pound. Write an expression for the cost of g pounds of grapes.

6. Today's temperature is 3 degrees warmer than yesterday's temperature t. Write an expression for today's temperature.

Evaluate each expression for $p = 5$ and $q = 1$.

7. qp

8. $p \div q$

9. $q + p$

10. Each member of the art club will make the same number of posters to advertise their club. They will make 150 posters total. Write an expression for how many posters each member will make if there are m members. Find how many posters each member will make if there are 5, 6, and 10 members.

1-2 Solving Equations by Adding or Subtracting

Solve each equation.

11. $x - 32 = -18$

12. $1.1 = m - 0.9$

13. $j + 4 = -17$

14. $\dfrac{9}{8} = g + \dfrac{1}{2}$

Solve each equation. Check your answer.

15. $b - 16 = 20$

16. $4 + x = 2$

17. $9 + a = -12$

18. $z - \dfrac{1}{4} = \dfrac{7}{8}$

19. When she first purchased it, Soledad's computer had 400 GB of hard drive space. After six months, there were only 313 GB available. Write and solve an equation to find the amount of hard drive space that Soledad used in the first six months.

20. Robin needs 108 signatures for her petition. So far, she has 27. Write and solve an equation to determine how many more signatures she needs.

1-3 Solving Equations by Multiplying or Dividing

Solve each equation.

21. $\dfrac{h}{3} = -12$

22. $-2.8 = \dfrac{w}{-3}$

23. $42 = 3c$

24. $-0.1b = 3.7$

Solve each equation. Check your answer.

25. $35 = 5x$

26. $-30 = \dfrac{n}{3}$

27. $5y = 0$

28. $-4.6r = 9.2$

29. A fund-raiser raised \$2400, which was $\dfrac{3}{5}$ of the goal. Write and solve an equation to find the amount of the goal.

PARCC Assessment Readiness

Selected Response

1. Give two ways to write the algebraic expression $p \div 10$ in words.

   Ⓐ the product of p and 10; p times 10

   Ⓑ the quotient of p and 10; p divided by 10

   Ⓒ the quotient of 10 and p; 10 divided by p

   Ⓓ p subtracted from 10; p less than 10

2. Julia wrote 14 letters to friends each month for y months in a row. Write an expression to show how many total letters Julia wrote.

   Ⓕ $14y$ Ⓗ $14 - y$

   Ⓖ $14 + y$ Ⓙ $\frac{14}{y}$

3. Solve $p - 6 = 16$. Check your answer.

   Ⓐ $p = 22$ Ⓒ $p = 10$

   Ⓑ $p = -22$ Ⓓ $p = -10$

4. Solve $\frac{q}{5} = 41$. Check your answer.

   Ⓕ $q = 8\frac{1}{5}$ Ⓗ $q = 205$

   Ⓖ $q = 36$ Ⓙ $q = 46$

5. Salvador's class has collected 88 cans in a food drive. They plan to sort the cans into x bags, with an equal number of cans in each bag. Write an expression to show how many cans there will be in each bag.

   Ⓐ $88 - x$ Ⓒ $88 + x$

   Ⓑ $88x$ Ⓓ $\frac{88}{x}$

6. Evaluate the expression xy for $x = 6$ and $y = 3$.

   Ⓕ 9   Ⓗ 18

   Ⓖ 24   Ⓙ 21

7. Evaluate the expression $a \div b$ for $a = 24$ and $b = 8$.

   Ⓐ 3   Ⓒ 16

   Ⓑ 4   Ⓓ 192

8. Evaluate the expression $2m + n$ for $m = 7$ and $n = 9$.

   Ⓕ 25   Ⓗ 23

   Ⓖ 18   Ⓙ 32

9. The range of a set of scores is 23, and the lowest score is 33. Write and solve an equation to find the highest score. (*Hint*: In a data set, the range is the difference between the highest and the lowest values.)

   Ⓐ $h - 33 = 2 \cdot 23$ The highest score is 79.

   Ⓑ $h + 23 = 33$ The highest score is 10.

   Ⓒ $h + 33 = 23$ The highest score is -10.

   Ⓓ $h - 33 = 23$ The highest score is 56.

10. The time between a flash of lightning and the sound of its thunder can be used to estimate the distance from a lightning strike. The distance from the strike is the number of seconds between seeing the flash and hearing the thunder divided by 5. Suppose you are 17 miles from a lightning strike. Write and solve an equation to find how many seconds there would be between the flash and thunder.

   Ⓕ $\frac{5}{t} = d$, so t is about 0.3 seconds.

   Ⓖ $t = \frac{d}{5}$, so t is about 3.4 seconds.

   Ⓗ $t - 5 = d$, so t is about 22 seconds.

   Ⓙ $\frac{t}{5} = d$, so t is about 85 seconds.

11. If $4x = 32$, find the value of $35 - 5x$.

   Ⓐ -5 Ⓒ -3

   Ⓑ 3   Ⓓ 5

Mini-Task

12. Fatima enrolled in a traveler rewards program. She begins with 10,000 bonus points. For every trip she takes, she collects 3000 bonus points.

   a. Write a rule for the number of bonus points Fatima has after x trips.

   b. Make a table showing the number of bonus points Fatima has after 0, 1, 2, 3, 4, and 5 trips.

   c. When Fatima has collected 20,000 bonus points, she gets a free vacation. How many trips does Fatima need to take to get a free vacation?

UNIT 1

Module

2 Choosing Appropriate Units

MCC9-12.N.Q.1

MCC9-12.A.CED.1, MCC9-12.N.Q.2

MCC9-12.N.Q.3

Contents

MATHEMATICAL PRACTICES The Common Core Georgia Performance Standards for Mathematical Practice describe varieties of expertise that all students should seek to develop. Opportunities to develop these practices are integrated throughout this program.

1 Make sense of problems and persevere in solving them.

2 Reason abstractly and quantitatively.

3 Construct viable arguments and critique the reasoning of others.

4 Model with mathematics.

5 Use appropriate tools strategically.

6 Attend to precision.

7 Look for and make use of structure.

8 Look for and express regularity in repeated reasoning.

Unpacking the Standards

Understanding the standards and the vocabulary terms in the standards will help you know exactly what you are expected to learn in this chapter.

 MCC9-12.N.Q.1

Use units as a way to understand problems and to guide the solution of multi-step problems; …

Key Vocabulary

unit analysis/dimensional analysis
(análisis dimensional) A process that uses rates to convert measurements from one unit to another.

What It Means For You

Keeping track of units in problem solving will help you identify a solution method and interpret the results.

EXAMPLE

Li's car gets 40 miles per gallon of gas. At this rate, she can go 620 miles on a full tank. She has driven 245 miles on the current tank. How many gallons of gas g are left in the tank?

$$\underbrace{620 \text{ mi}}_{\text{Distance}} = \underbrace{245 \text{ mi}}_{\text{Distance}} + \underbrace{\frac{40 \text{ mi}}{1 \text{ gal}} \cdot g \text{ gal}}_{\text{Distance}}$$

 MCC9-12.A.CED.1

Create equations … in one variable and use them to solve problems.

Key Vocabulary

equation (ecuación)
A mathematical statement that two expressions are equivalent.
variable (variable)
A symbol used to represent a quantity that can change.

What It Means For You

You can write an equation to represent a real-world problem and then use algebra to solve the equation and find the answer.

EXAMPLE

Michael is saving money to buy a trumpet. The trumpet costs $670. He has $350 saved, and each week he adds $20 to his savings. How long will it take him to save enough money to buy the trumpet?

Let w represent the number of weeks.

cost of trumpet	=	current savings	+	additional savings
670	=	350	+	$20w$
320	=	$20w$		
16	=	w		

It will take Michael 16 weeks to save enough money.

2-1 Rates, Ratios, and Proportions

Essential Question: How can you use units to understand problems and guide the solution of proportions?

Objectives
Write and use ratios, rates, and unit rates.

Write and solve proportions.

Vocabulary
ratio proportion
rate cross products
scale scale drawing
unit rate scale model
conversion dimensional
factor analysis

Why learn this?
Ratios and proportions are used to draw accurate maps. (See Example 5.)

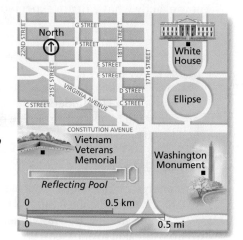

A **ratio** is a comparison of two quantities by division. The ratio of a to b can be written $a:b$ or $\frac{a}{b}$, where $b \neq 0$. Ratios that name the same comparison are said to be *equivalent*.

A statement that two ratios are equivalent, such as $\frac{1}{12} = \frac{2}{24}$, is called a **proportion**.

COMMON CORE GPS MCC9-12.N.Q.1

 **EXAMPLE 1 Using Ratios**

my.hrw.com

Online Video Tutor

The ratio of faculty members to students at a college is 1:15. There are 675 students. How many faculty members are there?

$$\frac{\text{faculty}}{\text{students}} \rightarrow \frac{1}{15}$$ *Write a ratio comparing faculty to students.*

$$\frac{1}{15} = \frac{x}{675}$$ *Write a proportion. Let x be the number of faculty members.*

$$675\left(\frac{x}{675}\right) = 675\left(\frac{1}{15}\right)$$ *Since x is divided by 675, multiply both sides of the equation by 675.*

$$x = 45$$

There are 45 faculty members.

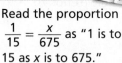 **CHECK IT OUT!**   **1.** The ratio of games won to games lost for a baseball team is $3:2$. The team won 18 games. How many games did the team lose?

 Reading Math

Read the proportion $\frac{1}{15} = \frac{x}{675}$ as "1 is to 15 as x is to 675."

A **rate** is a ratio of two quantities with different units, such as $\frac{34 \text{ mi}}{2 \text{ gal}}$. Rates are usually written as *unit rates*. A **unit rate** is a rate with a second quantity of 1 unit, such as $\frac{17 \text{ mi}}{1 \text{ gal}}$, or 17 mi/gal. You can convert any rate to a unit rate.

COMMON CORE GPS MCC9-12.N.Q.1

 EXAMPLE 2 Finding Unit Rates

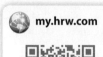
my.hrw.com

Online Video Tutor

Takeru Kobayashi of Japan ate 53.5 hot dogs in 12 minutes to win a contest. Find the unit rate in hot dogs per minute. Round to the nearest hundredth.

$$\frac{53.5}{12} = \frac{x}{1}$$ *Write a proportion to find an equivalent ratio with a second quantity of 1.*

$$4.46 \approx x$$ *Divide on the left side to find x.*

The unit rate is approximately 4.46 hot dogs per minute.

 CHECK IT OUT!   **2.** Cory earns $52.50 in 7 hours. Find the unit rate in dollars per hour.

Dimensional analysis is a process that uses rates to convert measurements from one unit to another. A rate such as $\frac{12 \text{ in.}}{1 \text{ ft}}$, in which the two quantities are equal but use different units, is called a **conversion factor**. To convert from one set of units to another, multiply by a conversion factor.

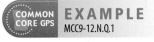
EXAMPLE 3
MCC9-12.N.Q.1

Using Dimensional Analysis

my.hrw.com

Online Video Tutor

A **A large adult male human has about 12 pints of blood. Use dimensional analysis to convert this quantity to gallons.**

Step 1 Convert pints to quarts.

$12 \text{ pt} \cdot \dfrac{1 \text{ qt}}{2 \text{ pt}}$ *Multiply by a conversion factor whose first quantity is quarts and whose second quantity is pints.*

6 qt

12 pints is 6 quarts.

Step 2 Convert quarts to gallons.

$6 \text{ qt} \cdot \dfrac{1 \text{ gal}}{4 \text{ qt}}$ *Multiply by a conversion factor whose first quantity is gallons and whose second quantity is quarts.*

$\dfrac{6}{4} \text{ gal} = 1\frac{1}{2} \text{ gal}$

A large adult male human has about $1\frac{1}{2}$ gallons of blood.

B **The dwarf sea horse *Hippocampus zosterae* swims at a rate of 52.68 feet per hour. Use dimensional analysis to convert this speed to inches per minute.**

Use the conversion factor $\frac{12 \text{ in.}}{1 \text{ ft}}$ to convert feet to inches, and use the conversion factor $\frac{1 \text{ h}}{60 \text{ min}}$ to convert hours to minutes.

$\dfrac{52.68 \text{ ft}}{1 \text{ h}} \cdot \dfrac{12 \text{ in.}}{1 \text{ ft}} \cdot \dfrac{1 \text{ h}}{60 \text{ min}} = \dfrac{10.536 \text{ in.}}{1 \text{ min}}$

The speed is 10.536 inches per minute.

> Check that the answer is reasonable. The answer is about 10 in./min.
> - There are 60 min in 1 h, so 10 in./min is $60(10) = 600$ in./h.
> - There are 12 in. in 1 ft, so 600 in./h is $\frac{600}{12} = 50$ ft/h. This is close to the rate given in the problem, 52.68 ft/h.

Hippocampus zosterae

CHECK
IT OUT!

3. A cyclist travels 56 miles in 4 hours. Use dimensional analysis to convert the cyclist's speed to feet per second. Round your answer to the nearest tenth, and show that your answer is reasonable.

In the proportion $\frac{a}{b} = \frac{c}{d}$, the products $a \cdot d$ and $b \cdot c$ are called **cross products**. You can solve a proportion for a missing value by using the Cross Products Property.

Know it!
Note

Cross Products Property

WORDS	NUMBERS	ALGEBRA
In a proportion, cross products are equal.	$\dfrac{2}{3} \diagup\!\!\!\!\times \dfrac{4}{6}$ $2 \cdot 6 = 3 \cdot 4$	If $\dfrac{a}{b} \diagup\!\!\!\!\times \dfrac{c}{d}$ and $b \neq 0$ and $d \neq 0$, then $ad = bc$.

EXAMPLE **4** **Solving Proportions**
MCC9-12.A.REI.2

Solve each proportion.

A $\dfrac{5}{9} = \dfrac{3}{w}$

$\dfrac{5}{9} \diagdown \dfrac{3}{w}$

$5(w) = 9(3)$ *Use cross*
products.

$5w = 27$

$\dfrac{5w}{5} = \dfrac{27}{5}$ *Divide both sides*
by 5.

$w = \dfrac{27}{5}$

B $\dfrac{8}{x + 10} = \dfrac{1}{12}$

$\dfrac{8}{x + 10} \diagdown \dfrac{1}{12}$

$8(12) = 1(x + 10)$ *Use cross*
products.

$96 = x + 10$

$\underline{-10 \qquad -10}$ *Subtract 10 from*
both sides.

$86 = x$

 Solve each proportion.

4a. $\dfrac{-5}{2} = \dfrac{y}{8}$ **4b.** $\dfrac{g + 3}{5} = \dfrac{7}{4}$

A **scale** is a ratio between two sets of measurements, such as 1 in : 5 mi. A **scale drawing** or **scale model** uses a scale to represent an object as smaller or larger than the actual object. A map is an example of a scale drawing.

EXAMPLE **5** **Scale Drawings and Scale Models**
MCC9-12.A.CED.1

A On the map, the distance from Chicago to Evanston is 0.625 in. What is the actual distance?

1 in : 18 mi

$\dfrac{\text{map}}{\text{actual}} \rightarrow \dfrac{1 \text{ in.}}{18 \text{ mi}}$ *Write the scale as*
a fraction.

$\dfrac{1}{18} \diagdown \dfrac{0.625}{x}$ *Let x be the*
actual distance.

$x \cdot 1 = 18(0.625)$ *Use cross products*
to solve.

$x = 11.25$

The actual distance is 11.25 mi.

B The actual distance between North Chicago and Waukegan is 4 mi. What is this distance on the map? Round to the nearest tenth.

$\dfrac{\text{map}}{\text{actual}} \rightarrow \dfrac{1 \text{ in.}}{18 \text{ mi}}$ *Write the scale as a fraction.*

$\dfrac{1}{18} \diagdown \dfrac{x}{4}$ *Let x be the distance on the map.*

$4 = 18x$ *Use cross products to solve the proportion.*

$\dfrac{4}{18} = \dfrac{18x}{18}$ *Since x is multiplied by 18, divide both sides by 18 to undo the multiplication.*

$0.2 \approx x$ *Round to the nearest tenth.*

The distance on the map is about 0.2 in.

Reading Math

A scale written without units, such as 32 : 1, means that 32 units of any measure correspond to 1 unit of that same measure.

 5. A scale model of a human heart is 16 ft long. The scale is 32 : 1. How many inches long is the actual heart it represents?

THINK AND DISCUSS

1. Explain two ways to solve the proportion $\frac{t}{4} = \frac{3}{5}$.

2. How could you show that the answer to Example 5A is reasonable?

3. GET ORGANIZED Copy and complete the graphic organizer. In each box, write an example of each use of ratios.

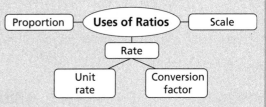

2-1 Exercises

my.hrw.com
Homework Help

GUIDED PRACTICE

1. Vocabulary What does it mean when two ratios form a *proportion*?

SEE EXAMPLE 1

2. The ratio of the sale price of a jacket to the original price is $3:4$. The original price is $64. What is the sale price?

3. Chemistry The ratio of hydrogen atoms to oxygen atoms in water is $2:1$. If an amount of water contains 341 trillion atoms of oxygen, how many hydrogen atoms are there?

SEE EXAMPLE 2

4. A computer's fan rotates 2000 times in 40 seconds. Find the unit rate in rotations per second.

5. Twelve cows produce 224,988 pounds of milk. Find the unit rate in pounds per cow.

6. A yellow jacket can fly 4.5 meters in 9 seconds. Find the unit rate in meters per second.

SEE EXAMPLE 3

7. Lydia wrote $4\frac{1}{2}$ pages of her science report in one hour. What was her writing rate in pages per minute?

8. A model airplane flies 18 feet in 2 seconds. What is the airplane's speed in miles per hour? Round your answer to the nearest hundredth.

9. A vehicle uses 1 tablespoon of gasoline to drive 125 yards. How many miles can the vehicle travel per gallon? Round your answer to the nearest mile. (*Hint:* There are 256 tablespoons in a gallon.)

SEE EXAMPLE 4

Solve each proportion.

10. $\frac{3}{z} = \frac{1}{8}$

11. $\frac{x}{3} = \frac{1}{5}$

12. $\frac{b}{4} = \frac{3}{2}$

13. $\frac{f+3}{12} = \frac{7}{2}$

14. $\frac{-1}{5} = \frac{3}{2d}$

15. $\frac{3}{14} = \frac{s-2}{21}$

16. $\frac{-4}{9} = \frac{7}{x}$

17. $\frac{3}{s-2} = \frac{1}{7}$

18. $\frac{10}{h} = \frac{52}{13}$

Alfred Sheppard, one of the builders of Stonehenge II.

SEE EXAMPLE 5

19. **Archaeology** Stonehenge II in Hunt, Texas, is a scale model of the ancient construction in Wiltshire, England. The scale of the model to the original is $3:5$. The Altar Stone of the original construction is 4.9 meters tall. Write and solve a proportion to find the height of the model of the Altar Stone.

PRACTICE AND PROBLEM SOLVING

Independent Practice	
For Exercises	See Example
20–21	1
22–23	2
24–25	3
26–37	4
38	5

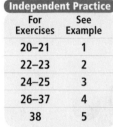

my.hrw.com

Online Extra Practice

20. **Gardening** The ratio of the height of a bonsai ficus tree to the height of a full-size ficus tree is $1:9$. The bonsai ficus is 6 inches tall. What is the height of a full-size ficus?

21. **Manufacturing** At one factory, the ratio of defective light bulbs produced to total light bulbs produced is about $3:500$. How many light bulbs are expected to be defective when 12,000 are produced?

22. Four gallons of gasoline weigh 25 pounds. Find the unit rate in pounds per gallon.

23. Fifteen ounces of gold cost $6058.50. Find the unit rate in dollars per ounce.

24. **Biology** The tropical giant bamboo can grow 11.9 feet in 3 days. What is this rate of growth in inches per hour? Round your answer to the nearest hundredth, and show that your answer is reasonable.

25. **Transportation** The maximum speed of the Tupolev Tu-144 airliner is 694 m/s. What is this speed in kilometers per hour?

Solve each proportion.

26. $\dfrac{v}{6} = \dfrac{1}{2}$ 27. $\dfrac{2}{5} = \dfrac{4}{y}$ 28. $\dfrac{2}{h} = \dfrac{-5}{6}$ 29. $\dfrac{3}{10} = \dfrac{b+7}{20}$

30. $\dfrac{5t}{9} = \dfrac{1}{2}$ 31. $\dfrac{2}{3} = \dfrac{6}{q-4}$ 32. $\dfrac{x}{8} = \dfrac{7.5}{20}$ 33. $\dfrac{3}{k} = \dfrac{45}{18}$

34. $\dfrac{6}{a} = \dfrac{15}{17}$ 35. $\dfrac{9}{2} = \dfrac{5}{x+1}$ 36. $\dfrac{3}{5} = \dfrac{x}{100}$ 37. $\dfrac{38}{19} = \dfrac{n-5}{20}$

38. **Science** The image shows a dust mite as seen under a microscope. The scale of the drawing to the dust mite is 100:1. Use a ruler to measure the length of the dust mite in the image in millimeters. What is the actual length of the dust mite?

39. **Finance** On a certain day, the exchange rate was 60 U.S. dollars for 50 euro. How many U.S. dollars were 70 euro worth that day? Show that your answer is reasonable.

40. **Environmental Science** An environmental scientist wants to estimate the number of carp in a pond. He captures 100 carp, tags all of them, and releases them. A week later, he captures 85 carp and records how many have tags. His results are shown in the table. Write and solve a proportion to estimate the number of carp in the pond.

Status	Number Captured
Tagged	20
Not tagged	65

© Linda Owen

41. **/// ERROR ANALYSIS ///** Below is a bonus question that appeared on an algebra test and a student's response.

> The ratio of junior varsity members to varsity members on the track team is 3:5. There are 24 members on the team. Write a proportion to find the number of junior varsity members.
>
> $\dfrac{3}{5} = \dfrac{x}{24}$

The student did not receive the bonus points. Why is this proportion incorrect?

42. **Sports** The table shows world record times for women's races of different distances.

a. Find the speed in meters per second for each race. Round your answers to the nearest hundredth.

b. Which race has the fastest speed? the slowest?

c. **Critical Thinking** Give a possible reason why the speeds are different.

World Records (Women)	
Distance (m)	Time (s)
100	10.5
200	21.3
800	113.3
5000	864.7

43. **Entertainment** Lynn, Faith, and Jeremy are film animators. In one 8-hour day, Lynn rendered 203 frames, Faith rendered 216 frames, and Jeremy rendered 227 frames. How many more frames per hour did Faith render than Lynn did?

Solve each proportion.

44. $\dfrac{x-1}{3} = \dfrac{x+1}{5}$

45. $\dfrac{m}{3} = \dfrac{m+4}{7}$

46. $\dfrac{1}{x-3} = \dfrac{3}{x-5}$

47. $\dfrac{a}{2} = \dfrac{a-4}{30}$

48. $\dfrac{3}{2y} = \dfrac{16}{y+2}$

49. $\dfrac{n+3}{5} = \dfrac{n-1}{2}$

50. $\dfrac{1}{y} = \dfrac{1}{6y-1}$

51. $\dfrac{2}{n} = \dfrac{4}{n+3}$

52. $\dfrac{5t-3}{-2} = \dfrac{t+3}{2}$

53. $\dfrac{3}{d+3} = \dfrac{4}{d+12}$

54. $\dfrac{3x+5}{14} = \dfrac{x}{3}$

55. $\dfrac{5}{2n} = \dfrac{8}{3n-24}$

56. **Decorating** A particular shade of paint is made by mixing 5 parts red paint with 7 parts blue paint. To make this shade, Shannon mixed 12 quarts of blue paint with 8 quarts of red paint. Did Shannon mix the correct shade? Explain.

H.O.T. **57.** **Write About It** Give three examples of proportions. How do you know they are proportions? Then give three nonexamples of proportions. How do you know they are not proportions?

Real-World Connections

58. a. Marcus is shopping for a new jacket. He finds one with a price tag of $120. Above the rack is a sign that says that he can take off $\frac{1}{5}$. Find out how much Marcus can deduct from the price of the jacket.

b. What price will Marcus pay for the jacket?

c. Copy the model below. Complete it by placing numerical values on top and the corresponding fractional parts below.

d. Explain how this model shows proportional relationships.

59. One day the U.S. dollar was worth approximately 100 yen. An exchange of 2500 yen was made that day. What was the value of the exchange in dollars?

 Ⓐ $25   Ⓑ $400   Ⓒ$2500   Ⓓ $40,000

60. Brett walks at a speed of 4 miles per hour. He walks for 20 minutes in a straight line at this rate. Approximately what distance does Brett walk?

 Ⓕ 0.06 miles Ⓖ 1.3 miles Ⓗ 5 miles Ⓙ 80 miles

61. A shampoo company conducted a survey and found that 3 out of 8 people use their brand of shampoo. Which proportion could be used to find the expected number of users n in a city of 75,000 people?

 Ⓐ $\dfrac{3}{8} = \dfrac{75,000}{n}$ Ⓑ $\dfrac{3}{75,000} = \dfrac{n}{8}$ Ⓒ $\dfrac{8}{3} = \dfrac{n}{75,000}$ Ⓓ $\dfrac{3}{8} = \dfrac{n}{75,000}$

62. A statue is 3 feet tall. The display case for a model of the statue can fit a model that is no more than 9 inches tall. Which of the scales below allows for the tallest model of the statue that will fit in the display case?

 Ⓕ 2:1   Ⓖ 1:1   Ⓗ 1:3   Ⓙ 1:4

CHALLENGE AND EXTEND

63. Geometry Complementary angles are two angles whose measures add up to 90°. The ratio of the measures of two complementary angles is 4:5. What are the measures of the angles?

64. A customer wanted 24 feet of rope. The clerk at the hardware store used what she thought was a yardstick to measure the rope, but the yardstick was actually 2 inches too short. How many inches were missing from the customer's piece of rope?

65. Population The population density of Jackson, Mississippi, is 672.2 people per square kilometer. What is the population density in people per square meter? Show that your answer is reasonable. (*Hint:* There are 1000 meters in 1 kilometer. How many square meters are in 1 square kilometer?)

FOCUS ON MATHEMATICAL PRACTICES

H.O.T 66. Error Analysis Sofia says that any real number is a solution to the equation $\frac{4}{2x-4} = \frac{2}{x-2}$. What mistake did she make?

H.O.T 67. Make a Conjecture Examine the graph.

 a. Do the two points on Line 1 satisfy the proportion $\frac{y_1}{x_1} = \frac{y_2}{x_2}$? Explain.

 b. Do the two points on Line 2 satisfy the proportion $\frac{y_1}{x_1} = \frac{y_2}{x_2}$? Explain.

 c. Another point on Line 1 is (1, 3). Replace one of the points from part a with this point. Do these two points satisfy the proportion?

 d. Another point on Line 1 is (6, 4). Replace one of the points from part b with this point. Do these two points satisfy the proportion?

 e. Make a conjecture about whether the coordinates of any two points on each line will form a proportion.

H.O.T 68. Problem Solving Find a solution of $\frac{12}{x} = \frac{x}{3}$. Explain how you found it.

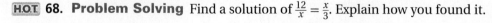

2-2 Applications of Proportions

Essential Question: How can you create proportions and use them to solve problems?

Objectives
Use proportions to solve problems involving geometric figures.

Use proportions and similar figures to measure objects indirectly.

Vocabulary
similar
corresponding sides
corresponding angles
indirect measurement
scale factor

Animated Math

Reading Math

- $\overline{AB}$ means segment AB. AB means the length of $\overline{AB}$.
- $\angle A$ means angle A. $m\angle A$ means the measure of angle A.

Why learn this?
Proportions can be used to find the heights of tall objects, such as totem poles, that would otherwise be difficult to measure. (See Example 2.)

Similar figures have exactly the same shape but not necessarily the same size.

Corresponding sides of two figures are in the same relative position, and **corresponding angles** are in the same relative position. Two figures are similar if and only if the lengths of corresponding sides are proportional and all pairs of corresponding angles have equal measures.

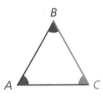

$$\frac{AB}{DE} = \frac{BC}{EF} = \frac{AC}{DF}$$

$m\angle A = m\angle D$
$m\angle B = m\angle E$
$m\angle C = m\angle F$

When stating that two figures are similar, use the symbol ~. For the triangles above, you can write $\triangle ABC \sim \triangle DEF$. Make sure corresponding vertices are in the same order. It would be incorrect to write $\triangle ABC \sim \triangle EFD$.

You can use proportions to find missing lengths in similar figures.

COMMON CORE GPS
MCC9-12.A.CED.1

EXAMPLE **1** **Finding Missing Measures in Similar Figures**

Find the value of x in each diagram.

my.hrw.com

Online Video Tutor

A $\triangle RST \sim \triangle BCD$

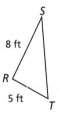
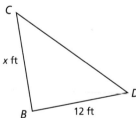

R corresponds to B, S corresponds to C, and T corresponds to D.

$$\frac{5}{12} = \frac{8}{x}$$

$$5x = 96$$

$$\frac{5x}{5} = \frac{96}{5}$$

$$x = 19.2$$

$\frac{RT}{BD} = \frac{RS}{BC}$

Use cross products.

Since x is multiplied by 5, divide both sides by 5 to undo the multiplication.

The length of $\overline{BC}$ is 19.2 ft.

Find the value of *x* in each diagram.

B *FGHJKL* ~ *MNPQRS*

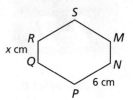

$$\frac{6}{4} = \frac{x}{2}$$ $$\frac{NP}{GH} = \frac{RQ}{KJ}$$

$4x = 12$ *Use cross products.*

$$\frac{4x}{4} = \frac{12}{4}$$ *Since x is multiplied by 4, divide both sides by 4 to undo the multiplication.*

$x = 3$

The length of $\overline{QR}$ is 3 cm.

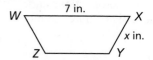

CHECK IT OUT!

1. Find the value of *x* in the diagram if *ABCD* ~ *WXYZ*.

You can solve a proportion involving similar triangles to find a length that is not easily measured. This method of measurement is called **indirect measurement**. If two objects form right angles with the ground, you can apply indirect measurement using their shadows.

COMMON CORE GPS MCC9-12.A.CED.1

EXAMPLE 2

Measurement Application

my.hrw.com

Online Video Tutor

A totem pole casts a shadow 45 feet long at the same time that a 6-foot-tall man casts a shadow that is 3 feet long. Write and solve a proportion to find the height of the totem pole.

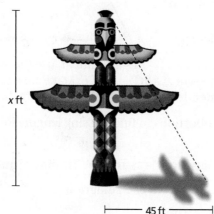

x ft

— 45 ft —

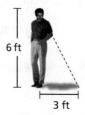

Both the man and the totem pole form right angles with the ground, and their shadows are cast at the same angle. You can form two similar right triangles.

6 ft

3 ft

Helpful Hint

A height of 90 ft seems reasonable for a totem pole. If you got 900 or 9000 ft, that would not be reasonable, and you should check your work.

$$\frac{6}{x} = \frac{3}{45}$$

$3x = 270$

$$\frac{3x}{3} = \frac{270}{3}$$

$x = 90$

The totem pole is 90 feet tall.

$$\frac{man's\ height}{pole's\ height} = \frac{man's\ shadow}{pole's\ shadow}$$

Use cross products. Since x is multiplied by 3, divide both sides by 3 to undo the multiplication.

CHECK IT OUT!

2a. A forest ranger who is 150 cm tall casts a shadow 45 cm long. At the same time, a nearby tree casts a shadow 195 cm long. Write and solve a proportion to find the height of the tree.

2b. A woman who is 5.5 feet tall casts a shadow 3.5 feet long. At the same time, a building casts a shadow 28 feet long. Write and solve a proportion to find the height of the building.

If every dimension of a figure is multiplied by the same number, the result is a similar figure. The multiplier is called a **scale factor**.

my.hrw.com

Online Video Tutor

Changing Dimensions

A Every dimension of a 2-by-4-inch rectangle is multiplied by 1.5 to form a similar rectangle. How is the ratio of the perimeters related to the ratio of corresponding sides? How is the ratio of the areas related to the ratio of corresponding sides?

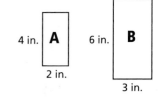

4 in. A 6 in. B
2 in. 3 in.

	Rectangle A	Rectangle B
$P = 2\ell + 2w$	$2(2) + 2(4) = 12$	$2(6) + 2(3) = 18$
$A = \ell w$	$4(2) = 8$	$6(3) = 18$

Sides: $\dfrac{4}{6} = \dfrac{2}{3}$ Perimeters: $\dfrac{12}{18} = \dfrac{2}{3}$ Areas: $\dfrac{8}{18} = \dfrac{4}{9} = \left(\dfrac{2}{3}\right)^2$

The ratio of the perimeters is equal to the ratio of corresponding sides. The ratio of the areas is the square of the ratio of corresponding sides.

Helpful Hint

A scale factor between 0 and 1 reduces a figure. A scale factor greater than 1 enlarges it.

B Every dimension of a cylinder with radius 4 cm and height 6 cm is multiplied by $\frac{1}{2}$ to form a similar cylinder. How is the ratio of the volumes related to the ratio of corresponding dimensions?

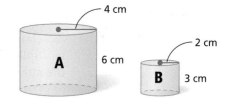

4 cm
2 cm
A 6 cm B 3 cm

	Cylinder A	Cylinder B
$V = \pi r^2 h$	$\pi(4)^2(6) = 96\pi$	$\pi(2)^2(3) = 12\pi$

Radii: $\dfrac{4}{2} = \dfrac{2}{1} = 2$ Heights: $\dfrac{6}{3} = \dfrac{2}{1} = 2$ Volumes: $\dfrac{96\pi}{12\pi} = \dfrac{8}{1} = 8 = 2^3$

The ratio of the volumes is the cube of the ratio of corresponding dimensions.

CHECK IT OUT!

3. A rectangle has width 12 inches and length 3 inches. Every dimension of the rectangle is multiplied by $\frac{1}{3}$ to form a similar rectangle. How is the ratio of the perimeters related to the ratio of the corresponding sides?

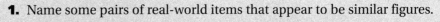

MCC.MP.4 **MATHEMATICAL PRACTICES**

THINK AND DISCUSS

1. Name some pairs of real-world items that appear to be similar figures.

Know it! Note

2. GET ORGANIZED Copy and complete the graphic organizer. In the top box, sketch and label two similar triangles. Then list the corresponding sides and angles in the bottom boxes.

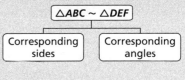

$\triangle ABC \sim \triangle DEF$
Corresponding sides Corresponding angles

GUIDED PRACTICE

1. **Vocabulary** What does it mean for two figures to be *similar*?

SEE EXAMPLE 1 **Find the value of *x* in each diagram.**

2. $\triangle ABC \sim \triangle DEF$

3. $RSTV \sim WXYZ$

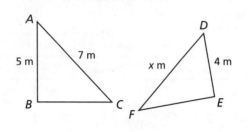

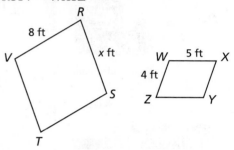

SEE EXAMPLE 2
4. Roger is 5 feet tall and casts a shadow 3.5 feet long. At the same time, the flagpole outside his school casts a shadow 14 feet long. Write and solve a proportion to find the height of the flagpole.

SEE EXAMPLE 3
5. A rectangle has length 12 feet and width 8 feet. Every dimension of the rectangle is multiplied by $\frac{3}{4}$ to form a similar rectangle. How is the ratio of the areas related to the ratio of corresponding sides?

PRACTICE AND PROBLEM SOLVING

Independent Practice	
For Exercises	See Example
6–7	1
8	2
9	3

my.hrw.com

Online Extra Practice

Find the value of *x* in each diagram.

6. $\triangle LMN \sim \triangle RST$

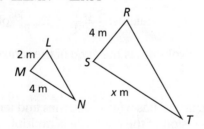

7. prism $A \sim$ prism B

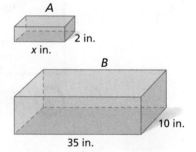

8. Write and solve a proportion to find the height of the taller tree in the diagram at right.

9. A triangle has side lengths of 5 inches, 12 inches, and 15 inches. Every dimension is multiplied by $\frac{1}{5}$ to form a new triangle. How is the ratio of the perimeters related to the ratio of corresponding sides?

10. **Hobbies** For a baby shower gift, Heather crocheted a baby blanket whose length was $2\frac{1}{2}$ feet and whose width was 2 feet. She plans to crochet a proportionally larger similar blanket for the baby's mother. If she wants the length of the mother's blanket to be $6\frac{1}{4}$ feet, what should the width be? Show that your answer is reasonable.

11. **Real Estate** Refer to the home builder's advertisement. The family rooms in both models are rectangular. How much carpeting is needed to carpet the family room in the Weston model?

12. A rectangle has an area of 16 ft². Every dimension is multiplied by a scale factor, and the new rectangle has an area of 64 ft². What was the scale factor?

Our Homes Are Made for Families!

Our Easton model includes a 120-square-foot family room. In the new Weston model, we've doubled the dimensions of the family room!

120 ft² Family room

13. A cone has a volume of 98π cm³. Every dimension is multiplied by a scale factor, and the new cone has a volume of 6272π cm³. What was the scale factor?

Find the value of x in each diagram.

14. $FGHJK \sim MNPQR$

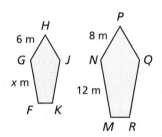

15. cylinder $A \sim$ cylinder B

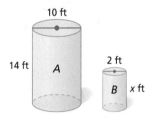

16. $\triangle BCD \sim \triangle FGD$

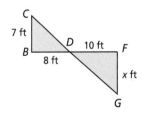

17. $\triangle RST \sim \triangle QSV$

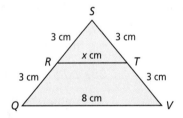

18. A tower casts a 450 ft shadow at the same time that a 4 ft child casts a 6 ft shadow. Write and solve a proportion to find the height of the tower.

H.O.T. 19. **Write About It** At Pizza Palace, a pizza with a diameter of 8 inches costs $6.00. The restaurant manager says that a 16-inch pizza should be priced at $12.00 because it is twice as large. Do you agree? Explain why or why not.

Real-World Connections

20. Another common application of proportion is *percents*. A percent is a ratio of a number to 100. For example, $80\% = \frac{80}{100}$.

   a. Write 12%, 18%, 25%, 67%, and 98% as ratios.

   b. Percents can also be written as decimals. Write each of your ratios from part **a** as a decimal.

   c. What do you notice about a percent and its decimal equivalent?

21. A lighthouse casts a shadow that is 36 meters long. At the same time, a person who is 1.5 meters tall casts a shadow that is 4.5 meters long. Write and solve a proportion to find the height of the lighthouse.

22. In the diagram, $\triangle ABC \sim \triangle DEC$. What is the distance across the river from A to B?

H.O.T. 23. Critical Thinking If every dimension of a two-dimensional figure is multiplied by k, by what quantity is the area multiplied?

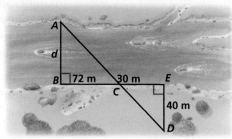

TEST PREP

24. A beach ball holds 800 cubic inches of air. Another beach ball has a radius that is half that of the larger ball. How much air does the smaller ball hold?

   Ⓐ 400 cubic inches   Ⓒ 100 cubic inches

   Ⓑ 200 cubic inches   Ⓓ 80 cubic inches

25. For two similar triangles, $\dfrac{SG}{MW} = \dfrac{GT}{WR} = \dfrac{TS}{RM}$. Which statement below is NOT correct?

   Ⓕ $\triangle SGT \sim \triangle MWR$ Ⓗ $\triangle TGS \sim \triangle RWM$

   Ⓖ $\triangle GST \sim \triangle MRW$ Ⓙ $\triangle GTS \sim \triangle WRM$

26. Gridded Response A rectangle has length 5 centimeters and width 3 centimeters. A similar rectangle has length 7.25 centimeters. What is the width in centimeters of this rectangle?

CHALLENGE AND EXTEND

27. Find the values of w, x, and y given that $\triangle ABC \sim \triangle DEF \sim \triangle GHJ$.

28. $\triangle RST \sim \triangle VWX$ and $\dfrac{RT}{VX} = b$.

  What is $\dfrac{\text{area of } \triangle RST}{\text{area of } \triangle VWX}$?

29. Multi-Step Rectangles A and B are similar. The area of A is 30.195 cm². The length of B is 6.1 cm. Each dimension of B is $\frac{2}{3}$ the corresponding dimension of A. What is the perimeter of B?

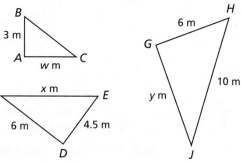

FOCUS ON MATHEMATICAL PRACTICES

H.O.T. 30. Modeling It takes Padma 6 minutes to cut a length of timber into 3 pieces. How long would it take her to cut a length into 9 pieces? (*Hint:* Think about how many *cuts* it takes to cut the timber into 3 pieces or 9 pieces.)

H.O.T. 31. Problem Solving You have a stack of $8\frac{1}{2}$ in. wide by 11 in. long sheets of paper, and start laying the sheets out as shown. The shape is the same number of sheets wide as it is long.

   a. When the shape is 68 in. wide, how long is it?

   b. When the area of the shape is 3366 in.², how many sheets are in it?

2-3 Precision and Accuracy

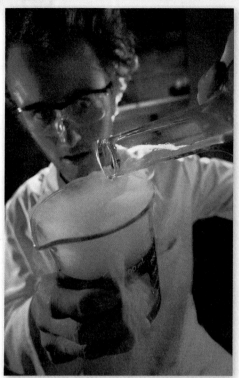

? Essential Question: How can you choose appropriate levels of precision and accuracy when solving problems?

Objectives
Analyze and compare measurements for precision and accuracy.

Choose an appropriate level of accuracy when reporting measurements.

Vocabulary
precision
accuracy
tolerance

Who uses this?
Chemists must understand precision and accuracy when weighing or mixing specific amounts of chemicals. (See Example 2.)

When you measure an object, you must use an instrument that will give an appropriate measurement. A scale to measure the mass of a person may show mass to the nearest kilogram. A scale to measure chemicals in a lab may show mass to the nearest milligram.

Precision is the level of detail in a measurement and is determined by the smallest unit or fraction of a unit that you can reasonably measure. Sometimes, the instrument determines the precision of a measurement. At other times, measurements are rounded to a specified precision.

A scale that shows the mass of an object to the nearest milligram is more precise than a scale that shows the mass of an object to the nearest kilogram, because a milligram is a smaller unit of measure than a kilogram. Likewise, a scale that shows the mass of an object as 24.23 grams is more precise than a scale that shows the mass of the same object as 24.2 grams.

EXAMPLE 1 MCC9-12.N.Q.3

my.hrw.com

Online Video Tutor

Comparing Precision of Measurements

Choose the more precise measurement in each pair.

A 3.4 kg; 3421 g

3.4 kg — *Nearest tenth of a kilogram*
3421 g — *Nearest gram*

A gram is smaller than a tenth of a kilogram, so 3421 g is more precise.

B 3.4 cm; 3.43 cm

3.4 cm — *Nearest tenth of a centimeter*
3.43 cm — *Nearest hundredth of a centimeter*

A hundredth of a centimeter is smaller than a tenth of a centimeter, so 3.43 cm is more precise.

C 3 ft; 36 in.

3 ft — *Nearest foot*
36 in. — *Nearest inch*

An inch is smaller than a foot, so 36 in. is more precise.

Choose the more precise measurement in each pair.

1a. 2 lb; 17 oz   **1b.** 7.85 m; 7.8 m   **1c.** 6 kg; 6000 g

A precise measurement is only useful if the measurement is also *accurate*. The **accuracy** of a measurement is the closeness of a measured value to the actual or true value. Two measurement tools may measure to the same precision, but not have the same accuracy. Similarly, using a more precise measuring instrument will not necessarily give a more accurate measurement.

my.hrw.com

Online Video Tutor

Comparing Precision and Accuracy

Sam is a technician in a pharmaceutical lab. Each week, she must test the scales in the lab to make sure they are accurate. She uses a standard mass that is *exactly* 5.000 grams and gets the following results:

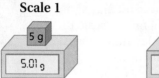
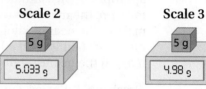

a. Which scale is the most precise?

Scales 1 and 3 measure to the nearest hundredth of a gram.

Scale 2 measures to the nearest thousandth of a gram.

Because a thousandth of a gram is smaller than a hundredth of a gram, Scale 2 is the most precise.

b. Which scale is the most accurate?

For each scale, find the absolute value of the difference of the standard mass and the scale reading.

Scale 1: $|5.000 - 5.01| = 0.01$
Scale 2: $|5.000 - 5.033| = 0.033$
Scale 3: $|5.000 - 4.98| = 0.02$

Because $0.01 < 0.02 < 0.033$, Scale 1 is the most accurate.

 2. A standard mass of 16 ounces is used to test three postal scales. The results are shown below.

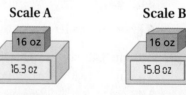

a. Which scale is the most precise?
b. Which scale is the most accurate?

When you measure a group of objects that are expected to be similar, you may find that there are variations from the expected value. **Tolerance** describes the amount by which a measurement is permitted to vary from a specified value. Tolerance is often expressed as a range of values, such as 5 mm ± 0.3 mm, which is equivalent to 4.7 mm–5.3 mm.

EXAMPLE 3
MCC9-12.N.Q.1

my.hrw.com

Online Video Tutor

Using a Specified Tolerance

Acme Nuts & Bolts is manufacturing a bolt to use in an airplane. The length of the bolt should be 50 mm, with a tolerance of 0.5 mm (50 mm ± 0.5 mm). A batch of bolts had the lengths shown in the table. Do all of the bolts measure within the specified tolerance? If not, which bolt(s) are not within the specified tolerance?

Bolt	Length (mm)
A	49.8
B	50.4
C	49.5
D	50.1
E	49.4
F	50.0

$50 - 0.5 = 49.5$ *50 mm ± 0.5 mm means that the*
$50 + 0.5 = 50.5$ *bolts must be between 49.5 and 50.5 mm.*

Bolt E measures 49.4 mm, so it is not within the specified tolerance.

Writing Math

The final zero in a decimal measurement such as 50.0 mm should not be dropped. 50.0 mm indicates a precision of one-tenth of a millimeter. 50 mm indicates a precision of one millimeter, and is less precise than 50.0 mm.

CHECK IT OUT!

3. A lacrosse ball must weigh 5.25 oz ± 0.25 oz. The weights of the lacrosse balls in one box are given in the table. Do all of the lacrosse balls weigh within the specified tolerance? If not, which lacrosse ball(s) are not within the specified tolerance?

Ball	Weight (oz)
A	5.41
B	5.23
C	5.54
D	5.33
E	5.21

Tolerance can also be expressed as a percent. A measurement written as 5 mm ± 5% means that the measurement can be greater or less than 5 mm by an amount equal to 5% of 5 mm, or 0.25 mm. Therefore, the measurement can have a range of 4.75 mm–5.25 mm.

EXAMPLE 4
MCC9-12.N.Q.2

my.hrw.com

Online Video Tutor

Using Tolerance Expressed as a Percent

Write the possible range of each measurement. Round to the nearest hundredth if necessary.

A 50 kg ± 2%
$50(0.02) = 1$ *Find 2% of 50.*
$50 \text{ kg} \pm 1 \text{ kg}$ *Write the measurement and tolerance.*
49 kg–51 kg   *Write the measurement as a range.*

B 125 lb ± 1.5%
$125(0.015) = 1.875$ *Find 1.5% of 125.*
$125 \text{ lb} \pm 1.88 \text{ lb}$ *Write the measurement and tolerance. Round to the nearest hundredth.*
123.12 lb–126.88 lb   *Write the measurement as a range.*

C 45 mm ± 0.3%
$45(0.003) = 0.135$ *Find 0.3% of 45.*
$45 \text{ mm} \pm 0.14 \text{ mm}$ *Write the measurement and tolerance. Round to the nearest hundredth.*
44.86 mm–45.14 mm   *Write the measurement as a range.*

CHECK IT OUT! Write the possible range of each measurement. Round to the nearest hundredth if necessary.

4a. 4.1 in. ± 5%   **4b.** 475 m ± 2.5%   **4c.** 85 mg ± 0.5%

THINK AND DISCUSS

1. Explain the difference between precision and accuracy.

2. Describe a situation where the expected size of an object might be specified as 10 in. ± 0.5 in.

3. **GET ORGANIZED** Copy and complete the graphic organizer. In each box, write an example of when that characteristic of measurement would be important.

Measurement
Precision Accuracy Tolerance

2-3 Exercises

my.hrw.com
Homework Help

GUIDED PRACTICE

Vocabulary Apply the vocabulary from this lesson to answer each question.

1. A ruler that can measure length to a smaller unit than another ruler is said to be more _____?_____. (*precise* or *acurate*)

2. A scale that gives a mass closer to the true mass of an object than another scale of the exact same type is said to be more _____?_____. (*precise* or *accurate*)

SEE EXAMPLE 1 Choose the more precise measurement in each pair.

3. 4 mL; 4.3 mL   4. 7 m; 6.8 m   5. 2.4 mg; 2.37 mg

6. 7 lb; 6.5 lb   7. 47 ft; 47.3 ft   8. 14 oz; 13.9 oz

SEE EXAMPLE 2

9. Sarah is comparing five different scales using a standard mass that is exactly 10 grams. Her results are shown below.

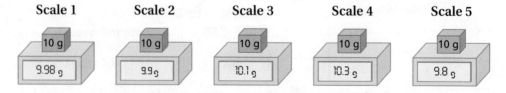

Scale 1   Scale 2   Scale 3   Scale 4   Scale 5
10 g   10 g   10 g   10 g   10 g
9.98 g   9.9 g   10.1 g   10.3 g   9.8 g

a. Which scale is the most precise?

b. Which scale is the most accurate?

10. A group of students compare the odometer readings on their bicycle computers after riding their bikes on a one-mile track. Their odometer readings are shown in the table. Whose odometer is the most precise? Whose is the most accurate?

Student	Distance (mi)
Jen	1.01
Bill	0.97
Rasheed	0.989
Sasha	1.02

SEE EXAMPLE 3

11. **Sports** A basketball for men's college games must have a mass of 595.5 ± 28.5 grams. Several basketballs are tested. Their masses are shown in the table. Do all of the basketballs fall within the specified tolerance? If not, which basketball(s) do not fall within the specified tolerance?

Basketball	1	2	3	4	5
Mass (g)	617.5	567.5	608	624.5	593.5

12. **Sports** A basketball for men's college games must bounce 51.5 ± 2.5 in. when dropped from a height of 6 feet. The bounce heights of several basketballs when dropped from a height of 6 feet are shown in the graph. Do all of the basketballs fall within the specified tolerance? If not, which basketball(s) do not have a bounce height within the specified tolerance?

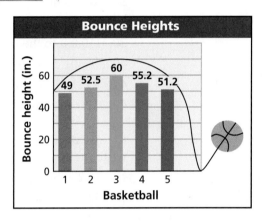

SEE EXAMPLE 4

Write the possible range of each measurement. Round to the nearest hundredth if necessary.

13. 50 lb ± 2%
14. 100 yd ± 0.5%
15. 25 cm ± 4%
16. 400 L ± 6%
17. 250 mm ± 4%
18. 70 kg ± 3%

PRACTICE AND PROBLEM SOLVING

Independent Practice

For Exercises	See Example
19–26	1
27	2
28	3
29–36	4

my.hrw.com

Online Extra Practice

Choose the more precise measurement in each pair.

19. 4.33 g; 4337 mg
20. 11 ft; 122 in.
21. 6 tons; 11,000 lb
22. 3 c; 2 pt
23. 67 mm; 6.83 cm
24. 4.5 km; 3 mi
25. 12 cm; 0.0127 m
26. 7.23 lb; 115 oz

27. Maria is trying to beat the school record for the 400-meter dash. Her friends timed her using the stopwatch functions in their cell phones. The official track timer, which is highly accurate, reported that she ran the race in 51.12 seconds. Her friends recorded the times shown in the table.

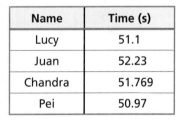

Name	Time (s)
Lucy	51.1
Juan	52.23
Chandra	51.769
Pei	50.97

   a. Who recorded the most precise time?

   b. Who recorded the most accurate time?

28. Anael cut several boards to build a deck. The boards must be 100 in. ± 0.25 in. Her measurements of the boards after cutting them are shown in the graph. Which boards, if any, can she not use?

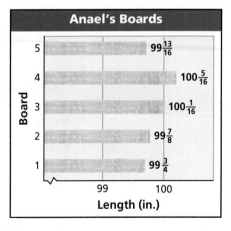

Write the possible range of each measurement. Round to the nearest hundredth if necessary.

29. 45 lb ± 2%   **30.** 3 m ± 5%   **31.** 37 °C ± 1.5%   **32.** 750 kg ± 3%

33. 30 ft ± 4%   **34.** 550 mL ± 8%   **35.** 0.2 cm ± 5%   **36.** 0.25 kg ± 10%

Round each measurement to the specified precision.

37. 5456.3 mi to the nearest mile

38. 3.627 m to the nearest hundredth of a meter

39. 119.8 ft to the nearest ten feet

40. 62.301 cg to the nearest tenth of a centigram

41. 5,721 mg to the nearest kilogram

42. 0.4586 km to the nearest meter

Choose the more precise measurement in each pair. If they are equally precise, write "neither."

43. 16.270 liters; 16,453.2 mL   **44.** 437 cm; 437 mm   **45.** 0.265 cm; 260 mm

46. 5.20 kg; 5200.0 mg   **47.** 55 yd; 165 ft   **48.** 67 min; 1.1 h

49. 33 mg; 0.033 g   **50.** 42.7 cm; 427.0 mm   **51.** 475.0 mL; 0.475 L

Technology

Rewrite each specified tolerance as a percent.

52. 100 m ± 2 m   **53.** 50 g ± 2 g   **54.** 240 ft ± 12 ft   **55.** 750 kg ± 15 kg

56. 25 in. ± 0.25 in.   **57.** 425 lb ± 8.5 lb   **58.** 60 oz ± 1.5 oz   **59.** 175 km ± 5.25 km

 60. Technology Postcards that do not fit in the U.S. Postal Service's automatic sorting machines require additional postage for mailing. The machine will accept postcards whose length is between 5 and 6 inches and whose width is between $3\frac{1}{2}$ and $4\frac{1}{4}$ inches. Write these requirements as tolerances.

61. Sports For women's collegiate competition, a basketball's circumference, mass, and bounce height must fall within given tolerance levels of regulation measurements. The table shows these tolerance levels as well as measurements taken on five different basketballs. Which basketball meets all of the specified tolerances?

	Circumference (mm)	Mass (g)	Bounce Height (mm)
Tolerance	730.56 ± 6.5	538.5 ± 28.5	1358.5 ± 63.5
Basketball #1	729.8	509.3	1343.4
Basketball #2	723.5	529.8	1299.8
Basketball #3	734.2	542.6	1293.5
Basketball #4	725.5	528.0	1364.5
Basketball #5	740.0	555.9	1407.4

H.O.T. 62. Write About It Linda wants to purchase a new sofa. Before buying the sofa, Linda must measure her doorway to make sure that the sofa will fit through the door. The sofa manufacturer says that the sofa measures 39 inches from front to back. What level of precision would you recommend Linda measure to? Explain.

H.O.T. 63. Critical Thinking Yusuf measured a board and determined that it was 125.5 centimeters long. He then cut the board into eight equal pieces. His calculator shows that 125.5 ÷ 8 = 15.6875. Is it reasonable for Yusuf to record the length of the 8 smaller boards as 15.6875 centimeters? Explain why or why not.

Automated equipment plays a large role in processing the approximately 584 million pieces of mail that the U.S. Postal Service delivers each day. Machines sort mail, cancel stamps, scan barcodes, and even "read" handwritten addresses.

Source: Postal Facts 2010, USPS

TEST PREP

64. The mass of a crystal is 0.9728 grams. What is the mass of the crystal to the nearest milligram?

    (A) 1 milligram   (C) 973 milligrams

    (B) 9.73 milligrams   (D) 972.8 milligrams

65. A piece used to assemble a computer must be 1.4 millimeters ± 0.02 millimeters in diameter. Which of the following measurements does NOT meet the specified tolerance?

    (F) 1.420 millimeters   (H) 1.382 millimeters

    (G) 1.402 millimeters   (J) 1.378 millimeters

66. Which measurement is most precise?

    (A) 475.3 milliliters   (C) 0.475 liter

    (B) 475 milliliters   (D) 0.5 liter

CHALLENGE AND EXTEND

Percent accuracy or *percent error* indicates how far a measurement is from the true value. An instrument that has 1.5% accuracy means that the measured value is within 1.5% of the true value.

67. A scale shows that a standard mass of exactly 5.000 grams has a mass of 5.002 grams. What is the percent accuracy of the scale?

68. A car odometer is accurate to within 0.5%. The odometer records the distance from Charlotte, North Carolina, to Orlando, Florida, as 525.3 miles. What is the range of possible values for the actual mileage?

69. Astronomy A scientist measures the distance to the moon using a method that has a percent error of 0.02%. He finds that the distance at a particular time is 384,403 kilometers. What is the range of possible values for the actual distance?

FOCUS ON MATHEMATICAL PRACTICES

H.O.T. 70. Problem Solving An Internet sports site polled its readers with the question "Which team will win the division?" and posted the results. What is the smallest number of readers that could have picked Atlanta? Explain your answer.

Atlanta	33%
Tampa	29%
New Orleans	24%
Carolina	14%

3651 Responses

H.O.T. 71. Communication Would you prefer to have an accurate room thermometer that is not very precise or a precise thermometer that is not very accurate? Explain.

H.O.T. 72. Error Analysis Caleb uses the ruler shown to measure the length of a card. He says that the length is 3.1875 inches, so the measurement is precise to one ten-thousandth of an inch. Is he correct? Explain.

Ready to Go On?

my.hrw.com
Assessment and Intervention

✓ 2-1 Rates, Ratios, and Proportions

1. Last week, the ratio of laptops to desktops sold at a computer store was $2:3$. Eighteen desktop models were sold. How many laptop models were sold?

2. Anita read 150 pages in 5 hours. What is her reading rate in pages per minute?

3. Twenty-six crackers contain 156 Calories. Find the unit rate in Calories per cracker.

4. A store developed 1024 photographs in 8 hours. Find the unit rate in photographs per hour.

Solve each proportion.

5. $\dfrac{-18}{n} = \dfrac{9}{2}$

6. $\dfrac{d}{5} = \dfrac{2}{4}$

7. $\dfrac{4}{12} = \dfrac{r+2}{16}$

8. $\dfrac{-3}{7} = \dfrac{6}{x+6}$

✓ 2-2 Applications of Proportions

Find the value of n in each diagram.

9. $\triangle RST \sim \triangle XYZ$

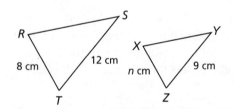

10. $ABCD \sim FGHJ$

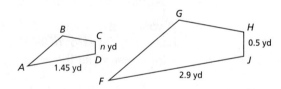

✓ 2-3 Precision and Accuracy

Choose the more precise measurement in each pair.

11. 2.5 ft; 2 ft

12. 1 yd; 3 ft

13. 5910 g; 5.9 kg

14. 16 oz; 16.0 oz

Write the possible range of each measurement. Round to the nearest hundredth if necessary.

15. $300 \text{ m} \pm 1\%$

16. $150 \text{ lb} \pm 6\%$

17. $60 \text{ L} \pm 0.5\%$

18. $220 \text{ kg} \pm 1.5\%$

PARCC Assessment Readiness

Selected Response

1. The fuel for a chain saw is a mix of oil and gasoline. The ratio of ounces of oil to gallons of gasoline is 7:19. There are 38 gallons of gasoline. How many ounces of oil are there?

- (A) 14 ounces
- (B) 20 ounces
- (C) 103.1 ounces
- (D) 3.5 ounces

2. A pipe is leaking at the rate of 8 fluid ounces per minute. Use dimensional analysis to find out how many gallons the pipe is leaking per hour.

- (F) 3,840 gal/h
- (G) 0.02 gal/h
- (H) 3.75 gal/h
- (J) 17.07 gal/h

3. Solve the proportion $\frac{5}{6} = \frac{x}{30}$.

- (A) $x = 0.03$
- (B) $x = 36$
- (C) $x = 26$
- (D) $x = 25$

4. Find the value of MN if $AB = 21$ cm, $BC = 16.8$ cm, and $LM = 28$ cm. $ABCD \sim LMNO$

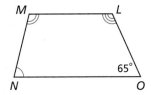 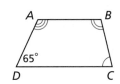

- (F) 23.8 cm
- (H) 12.6 cm
- (G) 22.4 cm
- (J) 22.8 cm

5. Complementary angles are two angles whose measures add to 90°. The ratio of the measures of two complementary angles is 4:11. What are the measures of the angles?

- (A) 24°, 66°
- (C) 51.4°, 38.6°
- (B) 26°, 64°
- (D) 24°, 114°

6. A weight that measures *exactly* 3.000 ounces is placed on three different balance scales. Scale 1 shows a weight of 3.03 ounces, scale 2 shows a weight of 2.99 ounces, and scale 3 shows a weight of 3.014 ounces. Which scale is the most precise? Which is the most accurate?

- (F) Scale 1 is the most precise.
  Scale 3 is the most accurate.
- (G) Scale 3 is the most precise.
  Scale 2 is the most accurate.
- (H) Scale 1 is the most precise.
  Scale 2 is the most accurate.
- (J) Scale 3 is the most precise.
  Scale 3 is the most accurate.

7. Round the measurement and underline the last significant digit.
254.8 liters to the nearest liter.

- (A) 25<u>4</u> liters
- (B) 2<u>6</u>0 liters
- (C) 25<u>5</u> liters
- (D) 2<u>5</u>0 liters

8. Write the possible range of the measurement to the nearest hundredth.
40 km ± 1%

- (F) 39.8 km—40.2 km
- (G) 39.99 km—40.01 km
- (H) 39 km—41 km
- (J) 39.6 km—40.4 km

Mini-Task

9. A recipe for a casserole calls for 2 cups of rice. The recipe makes 6 servings of casserole.

- **a.** How many cups of rice will you need to make 10 servings of casserole?
- **b.** If you have 5 cups of rice, how many servings can you make?

PARCC Assessment Readiness

Selected Response

1. A clock loses 5 minutes every day. How much time will it lose in 2 hours?

- Ⓐ 0.417 second
- Ⓑ 25 seconds
- Ⓒ 240 seconds
- Ⓓ 600 seconds

2. A statue is 8 feet tall. The display case for a model of the statue is 18 inches tall. Which scale allows for the tallest model of the statue that will fit in the display case?

- Ⓕ 1 inch : 2 inches
- Ⓖ 1 inch : 7 inches
- Ⓗ 1 inch : 5 inches
- Ⓙ 1 inch : 10 inches

3. Mr. Phillips wants to install hardwood flooring in his den. The flooring costs $25.86 per square yard. The blueprint below shows his house. What other information do you need in order to find the total cost of the flooring?

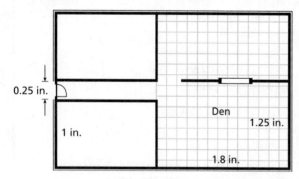

- Ⓐ The lengths and widths of the adjoining rooms in the blueprint
- Ⓑ The total area of the blueprint
- Ⓒ The scale of inches in the blueprint to yards in the house
- Ⓓ The width of the den

4. Which two phrases are equivalent to the expression $7t$?

- Ⓕ the product of 7 and t; 7 multiplied by t
- Ⓖ t subtracted from 7; t less than 7
- Ⓗ t more than 7; t added to 7
- Ⓙ the quotient of 7 and t; 7 divided by t

5. What is the solution of the equation $f - 10 = 10$?

- Ⓐ $f = 20$
- Ⓑ $f = -101$
- Ⓒ $f = -20$
- Ⓓ $f = 0$

6. On her math test, Suki was asked to round the measurement 718.4 meters to the nearest ten meters and underline the last significant digit. What should Suki write?

- Ⓕ 72<u>9</u> meters
- Ⓖ 7<u>2</u>0 meters
- Ⓗ 71<u>0</u> meters
- Ⓙ 72<u>8</u> meters

7. An architect built a scale model of a shopping mall. On the model, a circular fountain is 20 inches tall and 22.5 inches in diameter. The actual fountain is to be 8 feet tall. What will be the diameter of the fountain?

- Ⓐ 7.1 feet
- Ⓑ 9 feet
- Ⓒ 7 feet
- Ⓓ 10.5 feet

8. What is the solution of the equation $17a = 17$?

- Ⓕ $a = 1$
- Ⓖ $a = 17$
- Ⓗ $a = -17$
- Ⓙ $a = -1$

9. Ramon drives his car 150 miles in 3 hours. What is the unit rate?

Ⓐ 1 mile per 50 hours

Ⓑ 50 miles per hour

Ⓒ 30 miles per hour

Ⓓ 150 miles per 3 hours

10. Which is the most precise measurement?

Ⓕ $14\frac{3}{4}$ ft

Ⓖ 23 in.

Ⓗ 4 ft

Ⓙ $2\frac{11}{16}$ in.

11. What is the solution of $3n = 42$?

Ⓐ $n = 45$

Ⓑ $n = 39$

Ⓒ $n = 14$

Ⓓ $n = 15$

12. Which range of measurements is equivalent to 25 km ± 5%?

Ⓕ 24.95 km − 25.05 km

Ⓖ 23.75 km − 26.25 km

Ⓗ 24.38 km − 25.63 km

Ⓙ 20 km − 30 km

13. Isabel reads 15 books from the library each month for y months in a row. Which expression shows how many books Isabel read in all?

Ⓐ $15 + y$

Ⓑ $15 - y$

Ⓒ $15y$

Ⓓ $\frac{15}{y}$

14. If $8y = 32$, what is the value of $2y$?

Ⓕ 2

Ⓖ 8

Ⓗ 11

Ⓙ 24

15. What is the value of the expression $m + o$ when $m = 9$ and $o = 7$?

Ⓐ 15

Ⓑ 63

Ⓒ 2

Ⓓ 16

If you are stuck on a problem, skip it and come back later. Another problem might remind you of something that will help. If you feel yourself become tense, take a few deep breaths to relax.

16. Melissa invested her savings in a retirement account that pays simple interest. A portion of her account record is shown below. What is the interest rate on Melissa's account?

Date	Transaction	Amount	Balance
8/1	Beginning deposit	$6000.00	$6000.00
8/31	Interest payment	$192.00	$6192.00
9/1	Withdrawal	$1000.00	$5192.00
9/30	Interest payment	$166.14	$5358.14

Ⓕ 0.31%   Ⓗ 3.1%

Ⓖ 0.32%   Ⓙ 3.2%

17. At 2:45 P.M. you are 112 miles from Dallas. You want to be in Dallas at 4:30 P.M. What is the average speed you must travel to be on time?

Ⓐ 49.8 mi/h

Ⓑ 51 mi/h

Ⓒ 64 mi/h

Ⓓ 89.6 mi/h

18. A cyclist travels 45 miles in 4 hours. What is her speed in feet per second?

Ⓕ 16.5 ft/s

Ⓖ 31 ft/s

Ⓗ 66 ft/s

Ⓙ 59,400 ft/s

19. Julie's total cell phone bill consists of a monthly fee plus a charge per minute used. The expression that describes the total of Julie's cell phone bill is $0.07x + 29.99$. What does the variable x represent?

    (A) The number of months billed

    (B) The total amount of the bill

    (C) The number of minutes used

    (D) The monthly fee

20. In a test, a hybrid car drove 619 yards on 1 ounce of gasoline. To the nearest tenth, what is this rate in miles per gallon?

    (F) 7.5 miles/gallon

    (G) 15.0 miles/gallon

    (H) 22.5 miles/gallon

    (J) 45.0 miles/gallon

21. Which equation has the solution $x = -3$?

    (A) $2x = 6$

    (B) $-9 = -3x$

    (C) $-6 = 2x$

    (D) $-18x = 6$

22. In a scale model, a monument is 4.5 inches tall and 2.5 inches wide. The actual monument is 60 feet wide. How tall is the actual monument?

    (F) $33\frac{1}{3}$ feet

    (G) 90 feet

    (H) 108 feet

    (J) $112\frac{1}{2}$ feet

23. A consultant charges for her services based on the number of hours worked. The expression that gives the total cost for h hours is $125h + 150$. Which is the best interpretation of this expression?

    (A) The consultant charges $150 per hour plus a fee of $125.

    (B) The consultant charges $125 per hour plus a fee of $150.

    (C) The consultant charges $275 per hour.

    (D) The consultant's hourly charge varies from $125 to $150.

24. A rectangle has a length of 8 meters and a width of 3 meters. A larger, similar rectangle has a length of 22 meters. What is the width of the larger rectangle?

    (F) 58.67 meters   (H) 8.25 meters

    (G) 17 meters   (J) 9 meters

Mini-Tasks

25. Triangles C and D are similar. The area of triangle C is 47.6 in². The base of triangle D is 6.72 in. Each dimension of D is $\frac{6}{5}$ the corresponding dimension of C. What is the height of D?

26. A company sells furniture for home assembly. Their largest bookcase has shelves that should be 115 cm, with a tolerance of 0.6 cm. A set of six shelves had lengths of 115.2 cm, 114.9 cm, 115.0 cm, 114.3 cm, 114.7 cm, and 115.7 cm. Which, if any, of the shelves are not within the specified tolerance?

27. A toy company's total payment for salaries for the first two months of 2011 was $21,894.

    a. The total salaries for the first month of 2011 were $10,205. Write an equation to find the total salaries for the second month.

    b. What were the total salaries for the second month?

28. A plane is cruising at an altitude of 24,000 feet. It begins to descend at a constant rate of 20 feet per second.

    a. Write an expression for the altitude of the plane after t seconds.

    b. What is the altitude of the plane after 5 min?

29. Juan scored 26 points in the first half of the basketball game, and he scored n points in the second half of the game.

    a. Write an expression to determine the number of points he scored in all.

    b. Juan scored 44 points in all. Find the number of points he scored in the second half of the game.

30. On a sunny day, a 5-foot red kangaroo casts a shadow that is 7 feet long. The shadow of a nearby eucalyptus tree is 35 feet long.

    a. Write a proportion to determine the height of the tree.

    b. What is the height of the tree?

31. A right triangle has legs 15 inches and 12 inches. Every dimension is multiplied by $\frac{1}{3}$ to form a new right triangle with legs 5 inches and 4 inches. How is the ratio of the areas of the two triangles related to the ratio of corresponding sides?

32. Let p represent the price of a pair of jeans. Miles has a coupon for $10 off each pair of jeans that he buys.

    a. Use the variable p to write an expression for Miles's cost of a pair of a jeans with his coupon.

    b. Miles decides to buy 4 identical pairs of jeans. Write an expression for the total cost.

    c. Miles also buys a pair of socks for $5. Write an expression for Miles's total cost.

33. One day, the exchange rate was 60 U.S. dollars for 50 euro. At this rate, about how many U.S. dollars would be equivalent to 70 euro?

34. A map has the scale 1 inch:10 miles. On this map, the area of a national park is about 12.5 square inches. What is the approximate area of the park in acres? (1 square mile = 640 acres)

35. The table shows the typing rates of four applicants for a typing job.

Applicant	Words	Minute
Ann	112	6
Theo	206	8
June	195	7
Andy	120	5

    a. Based on typing rates, which applicant is the best choice to hire?

    b. What other information besides typing rate might you want to consider when choosing an applicant?

36. A polygon has an area of 3 square feet. What is the area of the polygon in square inches?

37. In the 2004 Olympics, the ratio of gold medals to silver medals won by the team from Hungary was 4:3. The ratio of silver medals to bronze medals won by the team was 2:1. The team won 3 bronze medals. How many gold medals did they win?

Performance Tasks

38. Luke is buying food for a neighborhood block party. He has $139 to spend, and he has already spent $121. He wants to buy some bags of hamburger buns that cost $4 each.

    a. How much money does Luke have left to spend?

    b. Define a variable or variables needed to model this situation.

    c. Using the number you found in part **a** and the variable(s) defined in part **b**, write an equation to find the number of bags of hamburger buns Luke can buy.

    d. Luke wants to buy 6 bags of hamburger buns. Does he have enough money? Explain how you found your answer.

39. Suppose a report indicates that the surveyed distance between two points is 1200 feet.

    a. If this is all of the information given about the surveyed distance, what might a reader think the measurement error is? Why?

    b. The error in the measurement is actually ± 0.1 feet. Explain how the distance might have been reported in a way that better indicates the true accuracy of the measurement.

40. To build an accurate scale model of the solar system, choose a diameter for the model of the Sun. Then other distances and sizes can be calculated proportionally.

	Sun	Mars	Pluto
Diameter (mi)	865,000	4,200	1,500
Distance from Sun (million mi)	—	141	3,670

    a. Sara wants to draw a scale model of the solar system in which the diameter of the Sun is 1 inch. What should the diameter of Pluto be?

    b. Do you think it is reasonable for Sara to draw this model? Why or why not?

my.hrw.com
Online Assessment
Go online for updated, PARCC-aligned assessment readiness.

Are You Ready?

my.hrw.com
Assessment and Intervention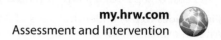

✓ Vocabulary

Match each term on the left with a definition on the right.

1. equation

2. evaluate

3. inverse operations

4. like terms

5. solution of an equation

A. mathematical phrase that contains operations, numbers, and/or variables

B. mathematical statement that two expressions are equivalent

C. value of a variable that makes a statement true

D. terms that contain the same variables raised to the same powers

E. to find the value of an expression

F. operations that undo each other

✓ Evaluate Expressions

Evaluate each expression for $a = 2$ and $b = 6$.

6. $b - a$

7. ab

8. $b \div a$

9. $a + b$

✓ Compare and Order Real Numbers

Compare. Write <, >, or =.

10. $10 \ \blacksquare\ 21$

11. $5.27 \ \blacksquare\ 5.23$

12. $20\% \ \blacksquare\ 0.2$

13. $\dfrac{1}{3} \ \blacksquare\ \dfrac{2}{5}$

✓ Combine Like Terms

Simplify each expression by combining like terms.

14. $6x + x$

15. $-8a + 3a$

16. $9x^2 - 15x^2$

17. $2.1x + 4.3x$

✓ Distributive Property

Simplify each expression.

18. $2(x + 3)$

19. $(3 - d)5$

20. $4(r - 1)$

21. $3(4 + m)$

Career Readiness Small Business Owners

Owners of small businesses need to have knowledge of many aspects of business, including expenses, income, taxes, licenses, and fees. They must be able to predict how their business will perform. Small business owners can use systems of equations to predict sales necessary to break even or make a profit. Preparation for starting a small business should include a business math class and a study of laws governing hiring, record keeping, and accounting.

Reasoning with Equations and Inequalities

Online Edition

my.hrw.com

Access the complete online textbook, interactive features, and additional resources.

Online Video Tutor

Watch full explanations of every example in the textbook with these online videos.

Animated Math

Interactively explore key concepts with these online tutorials.

Portable Devices

eTextbook

Access your full textbook on your tablet or e-reader.

HMH Fuse

Make your learning experience completely portable and interactive with this app for iPad®.

Chapter Resources

Scan with your smart phone to jump directly to the online edition.

COMMON CORE GPS Unit Contents

Module 3 Solving Equations in One Variable
MCC9-12.A.CED.1, MCC9-12.A.CED.4, MCC9-12.A.REI.1, MCC9-12.A.REI.3

Module 4 Solving Inequalities in One Variable
MCC9-12.A.CED.1, MCC9-12.A.CED.3, MCC9-12.A.REI.3

Module 5 Solving Multi-Step Inequalities
MCC9-12.A.CED.1, MCC9-12.A.CED.3, MCC9-12.A.REI.3

Module 6 Solving Systems of Equations
MCC9-12.A.CED.1, MCC9-12.A.REI.5, MCC9-12.A.REI.6, MCC9-12.A.REI.11

Module 7 Special Systems and Systems of Inequalities
MCC9-12.A.CED.1, MCC9-12.A.CED.3, MCC9-12.A.REI.6, MCC9-12.A.REI.12

Homework Help provides video tutorials, step-by-step solutions, and additional practice for lesson exercises.

3

Solving Equations in One Variable

COMMON CORE GPS

Contents

MATHEMATICAL PRACTICES
The Common Core Georgia Performance Standards for Mathematical Practice describe varieties of expertise that all students should seek to develop. Opportunities to develop these practices are integrated throughout this program.

1 Make sense of problems and persevere in solving them.

2 Reason abstractly and quantitatively.

3 Construct viable arguments and critique the reasoning of others.

4 Model with mathematics.

5 Use appropriate tools strategically.

6 Attend to precision.

7 Look for and make use of structure.

8 Look for and express regularity in repeated reasoning.

Unpacking the Standards

Understanding the standards and the vocabulary terms in the standards will help you know exactly what you are expected to learn in this chapter.

 MCC9-12.A.CED.1

Create equations ... in one variable and use them to solve problems.

Key Vocabulary

equation (ecuación)
A mathematical statement that two expressions are equivalent.

variable (variable)
A symbol used to represent a quantity that can change.

What It Means For You

You can write an equation to represent a real-world problem and then use algebra to solve the equation and find the answer.

EXAMPLE

Michael is saving money to buy a trumpet. The trumpet costs $670. He has $350 saved, and each week he adds $20 to his savings. How long will it take him to save enough money to buy the trumpet?

Let w represent the number of weeks.

cost of trumpet	=	current savings	+	additional savings
670	=	350	+	$20w$
320	=	$20w$		
16	=	w		

It will take Michael 16 weeks to save enough money.

 MCC9-12.A.REI.3

Solve linear equations ... in one variable, including equations with coefficients represented by letters.

Key Vocabulary

linear equation in one variable
(ecuación lineal en una variable)
An equation that can be written in the form $ax = b$ where a and b are constants and $a \neq 0$.

coefficient (coeficiente) A number that is multiplied by a variable.

solution of an equation in one variable (solución de una ecuación en una variable) A value or values that make the equation true.

What It Means For You

You solve equations by finding the value of the variable that makes both sides equal.

EXAMPLE

The Fahrenheit temperature that corresponds to 35°C is the solution of the equation $35 = \frac{5}{9}(F - 32)$.

F	70	75	80	85	90	95
$\frac{5}{9}(F - 32)$	21.1	23.9	26.7	29.4	32.2	35

When it is 35°C, it is 95°F.

Equation is true.

3-1 Solving Two-Step and Multi-Step Equations

? Essential Question: How can you solve equations that involve more than one operation?

Objective
Solve equations in one variable that contain more than one operation.

Why learn this?
Equations containing more than one operation can model real-world situations, such as the cost of a music club membership.

Alex belongs to a music club. In this club, students can buy a student discount card for $19.95. This card allows them to buy CDs for $3.95 each. After one year, Alex has spent $63.40.

To find the number of CDs c that Alex bought, you can solve an equation.

Cost of discount card
↓
Cost per CD → $3.95c + 19.95 = 63.40$ ← Total cost

Notice that this equation contains multiplication and addition. Equations that contain more than one operation require more than one step to solve. Identify the operations in the equation and the order in which they are applied to the variable. Then use inverse operations and work backward to undo them one at a time.

$$3.95c + 19.95 = 63.40$$

Operations in the Equation
❶ First c is multiplied by 3.95.

❷ Then 19.95 is added.

Work Backward →

To Solve
❶ Subtract 19.95 from both sides of the equation.

❷ Then divide both sides by 3.95.

EXAMPLE 1
MCC9-12.A.REI.3

my.hrw.com

Online Video Tutor

Solving Two-Step Equations

Solve $10 = 6 - 2x$. Check your answer.

$$
\begin{aligned}
10 &= 6 - 2x & &\text{First } x \text{ is multiplied by } -2. \text{ Then 6 is added.}\\
\underline{-6} & \underline{-6} & &\text{Work backward: Subtract 6 from both sides.}\\
4 &= -2x & &\text{Since } x \text{ is multiplied by } -2, \text{ divide both sides}\\
\frac{4}{-2} &= \frac{-2x}{-2} & &\text{by } -2 \text{ to undo the multiplication.}\\
-2 &= 1x\\
-2 &= x
\end{aligned}
$$

Check

$10 = 6 - 2x$	
10	$6 - 2(-2)$
10	$6 - (-4)$
10	$10 \checkmark$

CHECK IT OUT! Solve each equation. Check your answer.

1a. $-4 + 7x = 3$ **1b.** $1.5 = 1.2y - 5.7$ **1c.** $\frac{n}{7} + 2 = 2$

© Tom Stewart/CORBIS

62 *Module 3 Solving Equations in One Variable*

Online Video Tutor

EXAMPLE 2
MCC9-12.A.REI.3

Solving Two-Step Equations That Contain Fractions

Solve $\dfrac{q}{15} - \dfrac{1}{5} = \dfrac{3}{5}$.

Method 1 Use fraction operations.

$$\dfrac{q}{15} - \dfrac{1}{5} = \dfrac{3}{5}$$

$$\underline{+\dfrac{1}{5}+\dfrac{1}{5}}$$

Since $\dfrac{1}{5}$ is subtracted from $\dfrac{q}{15}$, add $\dfrac{1}{5}$ to both sides to undo the subtraction.

$$\dfrac{q}{15} = \dfrac{4}{5}$$

Since q is divided by 15, multiply both sides by 15 to undo the division.

$$15\left(\dfrac{q}{15}\right) = 15\left(\dfrac{4}{5}\right)$$

$$q = \dfrac{15 \cdot 4}{5}$$

Simplify.

$$q = \dfrac{60}{5}$$

$$q = 12$$

Method 2 Multiply by the least common denominator (LCD) to clear the fractions.

$$\dfrac{q}{15} - \dfrac{1}{5} = \dfrac{3}{5}$$

$$15\left(\dfrac{q}{15} - \dfrac{1}{5}\right) = 15\left(\dfrac{3}{5}\right)$$

Multiply both sides by 15, the LCD of the fractions.

$$15\left(\dfrac{q}{15}\right) - 15\left(\dfrac{1}{5}\right) = 15\left(\dfrac{3}{5}\right)$$

Distribute 15 on the left side.

$$q - 3 = 9$$

Simplify.

$$\underline{+3+3}$$

$$q = 12$$

Since 3 is subtracted from q, add 3 to both sides to undo the subtraction.

CHECK IT OUT! Solve each equation. Check your answer.

2a. $\dfrac{2x}{5} - \dfrac{1}{2} = 5$ **2b.** $\dfrac{3}{4}u + \dfrac{1}{2} = \dfrac{7}{8}$ **2c.** $\dfrac{1}{5}n - \dfrac{1}{3} = \dfrac{8}{3}$

Equations that are more complicated may have to be simplified before they can be solved. You may have to use the Distributive Property or combine like terms before you begin using inverse operations.

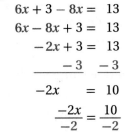

Online Video Tutor

EXAMPLE 3
MCC9-12.A.REI.3

Simplifying Before Solving Equations

Solve each equation.

A $6x + 3 - 8x = 13$

$$6x + 3 - 8x = 13$$

$$6x - 8x + 3 = 13$$

Use the Commutative Property of Addition.

$$-2x + 3 = 13$$

Combine like terms.

$$\underline{-3-3}$$

Since 3 is added to $-2x$, subtract 3 from both sides to undo the addition.

$$-2x = 10$$

$$\dfrac{-2x}{-2} = \dfrac{10}{-2}$$

Since x is multiplied by -2, divide both sides by -2 to undo the multiplication.

$$x = -5$$

Solve each equation.

B $9 = 6 - (x + 2)$

$9 = 6 + (-1)(x + 2)$ *Write subtraction as addition of the opposite.*

$9 = 6 + (-1)(x) + (-1)(2)$ *Distribute −1 on the right side.*
Simplify.

$9 = 6 - x - 2$ *Use the Commutative Property of Addition.*

$9 = 6 - 2 - x$ *Combine like terms.*

$9 = \quad 4 - x$

$\underline{-4 \quad -4}$ *Since 4 is added to −x, subtract 4 from both*
sides to undo the addition.

$5 = \quad\quad -x$

$\dfrac{5}{-1} = \dfrac{-x}{-1}$ *Since x is multiplied by −1, divide both sides*
by −1 to undo the multiplication.

$-5 = x$

 Solve each equation. Check your answer.

3a. $2a + 3 - 8a = 8$

3b. $-2(3 - d) = 4$

3c. $4(x - 2) + 2x = 40$

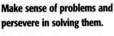
Problem-Solving Application

Alex belongs to a music club. In this club, students can buy a student discount card for $19.95. This card allows them to buy CDs for $3.95 each. After one year, Alex has spent $63.40. Write and solve an equation to find how many CDs Alex bought during the year.

1 **Understand the Problem**

The **answer** will be the number of CDs that Alex bought during the year.

List the important information:

• Alex paid $19.95 for a student discount card.

• Alex pays $3.95 for each CD purchased.

• After one year, Alex has spent $63.40.

2 **Make a Plan**

Let c represent the number of CDs that Alex purchased. That means Alex has spent $3.95c$. However, Alex must also add the amount spent on the card. Write an equation to represent this situation.

total cost	=	cost of compact discs	+	cost of discount card
63.40	=	3.95c	+	19.95

Solve

$$63.40 = 3.95c + 19.95$$
$$\underline{-19.95 \qquad\quad -19.95}$$
$$43.45 = 3.95c$$
$$\frac{43.45}{3.95} = \frac{3.95c}{3.95}$$
$$11 = c$$

Since 19.95 is added to 3.95c, subtract 19.95 from both sides to undo the addition.

Since c is multiplied by 3.95, divide both sides by 3.95 to undo the multiplication.

Alex bought 11 CDs during the year.

 Look Back

Check that the answer is reasonable. The cost per CD is about \$4, so if Alex bought 11 CDs, this amount is about $11(4) = \$44$.

Add the cost of the discount card, which is about \$20: $44 + 20 = 64$. So the total cost was about \$64, which is close to the amount given in the problem, \$63.40.

CHECK IT OUT! **4.** Sara paid \$15.95 to become a member at a gym. She then paid a monthly membership fee. Her total cost for 12 months was \$735.95. How much was the monthly fee?

 **EXAMPLE 5**
MCC9-12.A.REI.3

 my.hrw.com

Online Video Tutor

Solving Equations to Find an Indicated Value

If $3a + 12 = 30$, find the value of $a + 4$.

Step 1 Find the value of a.

$$3a + 12 = 30$$
$$\underline{\quad -12 \quad -12}$$
$$3a \quad\;\; = 18$$
$$\frac{3a}{3} = \frac{18}{3}$$
$$a = 6$$

Since 12 is added to 3a, subtract 12 from both sides to undo the addition.

Since a is multiplied by 3, divide both sides by 3 to undo the multiplication.

Step 2 Find the value of $a + 4$.

$$a + 4$$
$$6 + 4$$
$$10$$

To find the value of a + 4, substitute 6 for a.

Simplify.

CHECK IT OUT! **5.** If $2x + 4 = -24$, find the value of $3x$.

 MCC.MP.3

MATHEMATICAL PRACTICES

THINK AND DISCUSS

1. Explain the steps you would follow to solve $2x + 1 = 7$. How is this procedure different from the one you would follow to solve $2x - 1 = 7$?

 2. GET ORGANIZED Copy and complete the graphic organizer. In each box, write and solve a multi-step equation. Use addition, subtraction, multiplication, and division at least one time each.

Solving Multi-Step Equations	

GUIDED PRACTICE

Solve each equation. Check your answer.

SEE EXAMPLE **1**

1. $4a + 3 = 11$

2. $8 = 3r - 1$

3. $42 = -2d + 6$

4. $x + 0.3 = 3.3$

5. $15y + 31 = 61$

6. $9 - c = -13$

SEE EXAMPLE **2**

7. $\frac{x}{6} + 4 = 15$

8. $\frac{1}{3}y + \frac{1}{4} = \frac{5}{12}$

9. $\frac{2}{7}j - \frac{1}{7} = \frac{3}{14}$

10. $15 = \frac{a}{3} - 2$

11. $4 - \frac{m}{2} = 10$

12. $\frac{x}{8} - \frac{1}{2} = 6$

SEE EXAMPLE **3**

13. $28 = 8x + 12 - 7x$

14. $2y - 7 + 5y = 0$

15. $2.4 = 3(m + 4)$

16. $3(x - 4) = 48$

17. $4t + 7 - t = 19$

18. $5(1 - 2w) + 8w = 15$

SEE EXAMPLE **4**

19. Transportation Paul bought a student discount card for the bus. The card cost $7 and allows him to buy daily bus passes for $1.50. After one month, Paul spent $29.50. How many daily bus passes did Paul buy?

SEE EXAMPLE **5**

20. If $3x - 13 = 8$, find the value of $x - 4$.

21. If $3(x + 1) = 7$, find the value of $3x$.

22. If $-3(y - 1) = 9$, find the value of $\frac{1}{2}y$.

23. If $4 - 7x = 39$, find the value of $x + 1$.

PRACTICE AND PROBLEM SOLVING

For Exercises	See Example
24–29	1
30–35	2
36–41	3
42	4
43–46	5

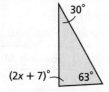

my.hrw.com

Online Extra Practice

Solve each equation. Check your answer.

24. $5 = 2g + 1$

25. $6h - 7 = 17$

26. $0.6v + 2.1 = 4.5$

27. $3x + 3 = 18$

28. $0.6g + 11 = 5$

29. $32 = 5 - 3t$

30. $2d + \frac{1}{5} = \frac{3}{5}$

31. $1 = 2x + \frac{1}{2}$

32. $\frac{z}{2} + 1 = \frac{3}{2}$

33. $\frac{2}{3} = \frac{4j}{6}$

34. $\frac{3}{4} = \frac{3}{8}x - \frac{3}{2}$

35. $\frac{1}{5} - \frac{x}{5} = -\frac{2}{5}$

36. $6 = -2(7 - c)$

37. $5(h - 4) = 8$

38. $-3x - 8 + 4x = 17$

39. $4x + 6x = 30$

40. $2(x + 3) = 10$

41. $17 = 3(p - 5) + 8$

42. Consumer Economics Jennifer is saving money to buy a bike. The bike costs $245. She has $125 saved, and each week she adds $15 to her savings. How long will it take her to save enough money to buy the bike?

43. If $2x + 13 = 17$, find the value of $3x + 1$.

44. If $-(x - 1) = 5$, find the value of $-4x$.

45. If $5(y + 10) = 40$, find the value of $\frac{1}{4}y$.

46. If $9 - 6x = 45$, find the value of $x - 4$.

Geometry Write and solve an equation to find the value of x for each triangle. (*Hint:* The sum of the angle measures in any triangle is 180°.)

47.

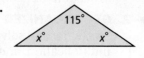

30°
$(2x + 7)°$ 63°

48.

115°
$x°$ $x°$

49.

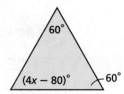

60°
$(4x - 80)°$ 60°

Write an equation to represent each relationship. Solve each equation.

50. Seven less than twice a number equals 19.

51. Eight decreased by 3 times a number equals 2.

52. The sum of two times a number and 5 is 11.

History

Martin Luther King Jr. entered college at age 15. During his life he earned 3 degrees and was awarded 20 honorary degrees.
Source: lib.lsu.edu

53. **History** In 1963, Dr. Martin Luther King Jr. began his famous "I have a dream" speech with the words "Five score years ago, a great American, in whose symbolic shadow we stand, signed the Emancipation Proclamation." The proclamation was signed by President Abraham Lincoln in 1863.

    a. Using the dates given, write and solve an equation that can be used to find the number of years in a score.

    b. How many score would represent 60?

Solve each equation. Check your answer.

54. $3t + 44 = 50$ **55.** $3(x - 2) = 18$ **56.** $15 = \dfrac{c}{3} - 2$ **57.** $2x + 6.5 = 15.5$

58. $3.9w - 17.9 = -2.3$ **59.** $17 = x - 3(x + 1)$ **60.** $5x + 9 = 39$ **61.** $15 + 5.5m = 70$

Biology Use the graph for Exercises 62 and 63.

62. The height of an ostrich is 20 inches more than 4 times the height of a kiwi. Write and solve an equation to find the height of a kiwi. Show that your answer is reasonable.

63. Five times the height of a kakapo minus 70 equals the height of an emu. Write and solve an equation to find the height of a kakapo. Show that your answer is reasonable.

64. The sum of two consecutive whole numbers is 57. What are the two numbers? (*Hint:* Let n represent the first number. Then $n + 1$ is the next consecutive whole number.)

65. Stan's, Mark's, and Wayne's ages are consecutive whole numbers. Stan is the youngest, and Wayne is the oldest. The sum of their ages is 111. Find their ages.

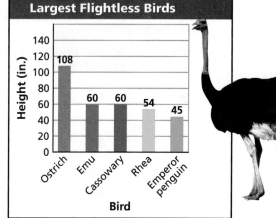

Source: The Top Ten of Everything

66. The sum of two consecutive even whole numbers is 206. What are the two numbers? (*Hint:* Let n represent the first number. What expression can you use to represent the second number?)

Real-World Connections

67. **a.** The cost of fighting a certain forest fire is $225 per acre. Complete the table.

    b. Write an equation for the relationship between the cost c of fighting the fire and the number of acres n.

Cost of Fighting Fire	
Acres	Cost ($)
100	22,500
200	▮
500	▮
1000	▮
1500	▮
n	▮

68. **Critical Thinking** The equation $2(m - 8) + 3 = 17$ has more than one solution method. Give at least two different "first steps" to solve this equation.

69. **Write About It** Write a series of steps that you can use to solve any multi-step equation.

TEST PREP

70. Lin sold 4 more shirts than Greg. Fran sold 3 times as many shirts as Lin. In total, the three sold 51 shirts. Which represents the number of shirts Greg sold?

    (A) $3g = 51$ (B) $3 + g = 51$ (C) $8 + 5g = 51$ (D) $16 + 5g = 51$

71. If $\frac{4m - 3}{7} = 3$, what is the value of $7m - 5$?

    (F) 6   (G) 10.5   (H) 37   (J) 68.5

72. The equation $c = 48 + 0.06m$ represents the cost c of renting a car and driving m miles. Which statement best describes this cost?

    (A) The cost is a flat rate of \$0.06 per mile.

    (B) The cost is \$0.48 for the first mile and \$0.06 for each additional mile.

    (C) The cost is a \$48 fee plus \$0.06 per mile.

    (D) The cost is a \$6 fee plus \$0.48 per mile.

73. **Gridded Response** A telemarketer earns \$150 a week plus \$2 for each call that results in a sale. Last week she earned a total of \$204. How many of her calls resulted in sales?

CHALLENGE AND EXTEND

Solve each equation. Check your answer.

74. $\frac{9}{2}x + 18 + 3x = \frac{11}{2}$

75. $\frac{15}{4}x - 15 = \frac{33}{4}$

76. $(x + 6) - (2x + 7) - 3x = -9$

77. $(4x + 2) - (12x + 8) + 2(5x - 3) = 6 + 11$

78. Find a value for b so that the solution of $4x + 3b = -1$ is $x = 2$.

79. Find a value for b so that the solution of $2x - 3b = 0$ is $x = -9$.

H.O.T. 80. **Business** The formula $p = nc - e$ gives the profit p when a number of items n are each sold at a cost c and expenses e are subtracted.

   a. If $p = 2500$, $n = 2000$, and $e = 800$, what is the value of c?

   b. If $p = 2500$, $n = 1000$, and $e = 800$, what is the value of c?

   c. **What if...?** If n is divided in half while p and e remain the same, what is the effect on c?

FOCUS ON MATHEMATICAL PRACTICES

H.O.T. 81. **Problem Solving** The temperature inside Earth increases as you get closer to its molten core. The temperature increases by about 25 °C for every kilometer you go below the surface. If the surface temperature is 19 °C and the temperature inside a mine is 64 °C, what is the depth of the mine?

H.O.T. 82. **Analysis** Solve $2x + b = c$ and $2(x + b) = c$ for x. Explain why the solution to the first equation will be greater than the solution to the second equation when $b > 0$.

3-2 Algebra TASK

Model Equations with Variables on Both Sides

Algebra tile models can help you understand how to solve equations with variables on both sides.

Use with Solving Equations with Variables on Both Sides

 Use appropriate tools strategically.

MCC9-12.A.REI.1 Explain each step in solving a simple equation as following from the equality of numbers asserted at the previous step, starting from the assumption that the original equation has a solution. Construct a viable argument to justify a solution method. *Also* **MCC9-12.A.REI.3**

KEY

 $= 1$

 $= -1$

 $= x$ $= -x$

REMEMBER

 $+$ $= 0$

Activity

Use algebra tiles to model and solve $5x - 2 = 2x + 10$.

MODEL		ALGEBRA
	Model $5x - 2$ on the left side of the mat and $2x + 10$ on the right side. Remember that $5x - 2$ is the same as $5x + (-2)$.	$5x - 2 = 2x + 10$
	Remove 2 x-tiles from both sides. This represents subtracting $2x$ from both sides of the equation.	$5x - 2 - 2x = 2x - 2x + 10$ $3x - 2 = 10$
	Place 2 yellow tiles on both sides. This represents adding 2 to both sides of the equation. Remove zero pairs.	$3x - 2 + 2 = 10 + 2$ $3x = 12$
	Separate each side into 3 equal groups. Each group is $\frac{1}{3}$ of the side. One x-tile is equivalent to 4 yellow tiles.	$\frac{1}{3}(3x) = \frac{1}{3}(12)$ $x = 4$

Try This

Use algebra tiles to model and solve each equation.

1. $3x + 2 = 2x + 5$ **2.** $5x + 12 = 2x + 3$ **3.** $9x - 5 = 6x + 13$ **4.** $x = -2x + 9$

3-2 Solving Equations with Variables on Both Sides

Essential Question: How can you solve equations that have the variable on both sides?

Objective
Solve equations in one variable that contain variable terms on both sides.

Vocabulary
identity

Why learn this?
You can compare prices and find the best value.

Many phone companies offer low rates for long-distance calls without requiring customers to sign up for their services. To compare rates, solve an equation with variables on both sides.

To solve an equation like this, use inverse operations to "collect" variable terms on one side of the equation.

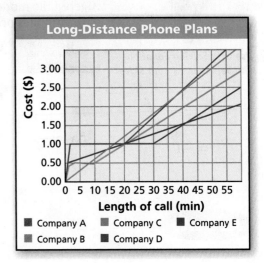

Long-Distance Phone Plans

■ Company A   ■ Company C   ■ Company E
■ Company B   ■ Company D

EXAMPLE 1
MCC9-12.A.REI.3

Solving Equations with Variables on Both Sides

Solve each equation.

my.hrw.com

Online Video Tutor

A $7k = 4k + 15$

$$7k = 4k + 15$$
$$\underline{-4k \quad -4k}$$
$$3k = \quad 15$$
$$\frac{3k}{3} = \frac{15}{3}$$
$$k = 5$$

To collect the variable terms on one side, subtract 4k from both sides.

Since k is multiplied by 3, divide both sides by 3 to undo the multiplication.

B $5x - 2 = 3x + 4$

$$5x - 2 = 3x + 4$$
$$\underline{-3x \qquad -3x}$$
$$2x - 2 = \qquad 4$$
$$\underline{+2 \qquad +2}$$
$$2x = \qquad 6$$
$$\frac{2x}{2} = \frac{6}{2}$$
$$x = 3$$

To collect the variable terms on one side, subtract 3x from both sides.

Since 2 is subtracted from 2x, add 2 to both sides to undo the subtraction.

Since x is multiplied by 2, divide both sides by 2 to undo the multiplication.

Helpful Hint

Equations are often easier to solve when the variable has a positive coefficient. Keep this in mind when deciding on which side to "collect" variable terms.

Check

$5x - 2 = 3x + 4$	
$5(3) - 2$	$3(3) + 4$
$15 - 2$	$9 + 4$
13	13 ✓

To check your solution, substitute 3 for x in the original equation.

Solve each equation. Check your answer.

1a. $4b + 2 = 3b$

1b. $0.5 + 0.3y = 0.7y - 0.3$

To solve more complicated equations, you may need to first simplify by using the Distributive Property or combining like terms.

EXAMPLE 2 Simplifying Each Side Before Solving Equations

my.hrw.com

Online Video Tutor

Solve each equation.

A $2(y + 6) = 3y$

$$2(y + 6) = 3y$$
$$2(y) + 2(6) = 3y$$ Distribute 2 to the expression in parentheses.
$$2y + 12 = 3y$$
$$\underline{-2y \qquad\quad -2y}$$ To collect the variable terms on one side, subtract 2y from both sides.
$$12 = y$$

Check $2(y + 6) = 3y$ To check your solution, substitute 12 for y in the original equation.

$2(12 + 6)$	$3(12)$
$2(18)$	36
36	36 ✓

B $2k - 5 = 3(1 - 2k)$

$$2k - 5 = 3(1 - 2k)$$
$$2k - 5 = 3(1) - 3(2k)$$ Distribute 3 to the expression in parentheses.
$$2k - 5 = 3 - 6k$$
$$\underline{+6k \qquad\qquad +6k}$$ To collect the variable terms on one side, add 6k to both sides.
$$8k - 5 = 3$$
$$\underline{+5 \qquad +5}$$ Since 5 is subtracted from 8k, add 5 to both sides.
$$8k = 8$$
$$\frac{8k}{8} = \frac{8}{8}$$ Since k is multiplied by 8, divide both sides by 8.
$$k = 1$$

C $3 - 5b + 2b = -2 - 2(1 - b)$

$$3 - 5b + 2b = -2 - 2(1 - b)$$
$$3 - 5b + 2b = -2 - 2(1) - 2(-b)$$ Distribute −2 to the expression in parentheses.
$$3 - 5b + 2b = -2 - 2 + 2b$$
$$3 - 3b = -4 + 2b$$ Combine like terms.
$$\underline{+3b \qquad\quad +3b}$$ Add 3b to both sides.
$$3 = -4 + 5b$$
$$\underline{+4 \qquad +4}$$ Since −4 is added to 5b, add 4 to both sides.
$$7 = 5b$$
$$\frac{7}{5} = \frac{5b}{5}$$ Since b is multiplied by 5, divide both sides by 5.
$$1.4 = b$$

 Solve each equation. Check your answer.

2a. $\dfrac{1}{2}(b + 6) = \dfrac{3}{2}b - 1$ **2b.** $3x + 15 - 9 = 2(x + 2)$

An **identity** is an equation that is always true, no matter what value is substituted for the variable. The solutions of an identity are all real numbers. Some equations are always false. These equations have no solutions.

Online Video Tutor

EXAMPLE 3 MCC9-12.A.REI.3

Infinitely Many Solutions or No Solutions

Solve each equation.

A $x + 4 - 6x = 6 - 5x - 2$

$x + 4 - 6x = 6 - 5x - 2$ *Identify like terms.*

$4 - 5x = 4 - 5x$ *Combine like terms on the left and the right.*

$\underline{+ 5x \qquad + 5x}$ *Add 5x to both sides.*

$4 \quad = 4 \checkmark$ *True statement*

The equation $x + 4 - 6x = 6 - 5x - 2$ is an identity. All values of x will make the equation true. All real numbers are solutions.

B $-8x + 6 + 9x = -17 + x$

$-8x + 6 + 9x = -17 + x$ *Identify like terms.*

$x + 6 = -17 + x$ *Combine like terms.*

$\underline{- x \qquad\qquad - x}$ *Subtract x from both sides.*

$6 = -17$ ✗   *False statement*

The equation $-8x + 6 + 9x = -17 + x$ is always false. There is no value of x that will make the equation true. There are no solutions.

Solve each equation.

3a. $4y + 7 - y = 10 + 3y$ **3b.** $2c + 7 + c = -14 + 3c + 21$

Writing Math

The solution set for Example 3B is an empty set—it contains no elements. The empty set can be written as $\varnothing$ or {}.

Online Video Tutor

EXAMPLE 4 MCC9-12.A.CED.1

Consumer Application

The long-distance rates of two phone companies are shown in the table. How long is a call that costs the same amount no matter which company is used? What is the cost of that call?

Phone Company	Charges
Company A	36¢ plus 3¢ per minute
Company B	6¢ per minute

Let m represent minutes, and write expressions for each company's cost.

When is	36¢	plus	3¢ per minute	times number of minutes	the same as	6¢ per minute	times number of minutes	?
	36	+	3	(m)	=	6	(m)	

$36 + 3m = 6m$

$\underline{- 3m \quad\; - 3m}$ *To collect the variable terms on one side,*

$36 \quad = 3m$ *subtract 3m from both sides.*

$\dfrac{36}{3} = \dfrac{3m}{3}$ *Since m is multiplied by 3, divide both sides by 3 to undo the multiplication.*

$12 = m$

The charges will be the same for a 12-minute call using either phone service. To find the cost of this call, evaluate either expression for $m = 12$:

$$36 + 3m = 36 + 3(12) = 36 + 36 = 72 \qquad 6m = 6(12) = 72$$

The cost of a 12-minute call through either company is 72¢.

4. Four times Greg's age, decreased by 3 is equal to 3 times Greg's age, increased by 7. How old is Greg?

THINK AND DISCUSS

1. Tell which of the following is an identity. Explain your answer.

    a. $4(a + 3) - 6 = 3(a + 3) - 6$ **b.** $8.3x - 9 + 0.7x = 2 + 9x - 11$

2. GET ORGANIZED Copy and complete the graphic organizer. In each box, write an example of an equation that has the indicated number of solutions.

An equation with variables on both sides can have...

| one solution: | many solutions: | no solution: |

3-2 Exercises

GUIDED PRACTICE

1. Vocabulary How can you recognize an identity?

Solve each equation. Check your answer.

SEE EXAMPLE **1**
2. $2c - 5 = c + 4$
3. $8r + 4 = 10 + 2r$
4. $2x - 1 = x + 11$
5. $28 - 0.3y = 0.7y - 12$

SEE EXAMPLE **2**
6. $-2(x + 3) = 4x - 3$
7. $3c - 4c + 1 = 5c + 2 + 3$
8. $5 + 3(q - 4) = 2(q + 1)$
9. $5 - (t + 3) = -1 + 2(t - 3)$

SEE EXAMPLE **3**
10. $7x - 4 = -2x + 1 + 9x - 5$
11. $8x + 6 - 9x = 2 - x - 15$
12. $6y = 8 - 9 + 6y$
13. $6 - 2x - 1 = 4x + 8 - 6x - 3$

SEE EXAMPLE **4**
14. Consumer Economics A house-painting company charges $376 plus $12 per hour. Another painting company charges $280 plus $15 per hour.

    a. How long is a job for which both companies will charge the same amount?

    b. What will that cost be?

PRACTICE AND PROBLEM SOLVING

Solve each equation. Check your answer.

15. $7a - 17 = 4a + 1$
16. $2b - 5 = 8b + 1$
17. $4x - 2 = 3x + 4$

18. $2x - 5 = 4x - 1$
19. $8x - 2 = 3x + 12.25$
20. $5x + 2 = 3x$

21. $3c - 5 = 2c + 5$
22. $-17 - 2x = 6 - x$
23. $3(t - 1) = 9 + t$

24. $5 - x - 2 = 3 + 4x + 5$
25. $2(x + 4) = 3(x - 2)$
26. $3m - 10 = 2(4m - 5)$

27. $5 - (n - 4) = 3(n + 2)$
28. $6(x + 7) - 20 = 6x$
29. $8(x + 1) = 4x - 8$

30. $x - 4 - 3x = -2x - 3 - 1$
31. $-2(x + 2) = -2x + 1$
32. $2(x + 4) - 5 = 2x + 3$

Independent Practice

For Exercises	See Example
15–22	1
23–29	2
30–32	3
33	4

my.hrw.com

Online Extra Practice

33. **Sports** Justin and Tyson are beginning an exercise program to train for football season. Justin weighs 150 lb and hopes to gain 2 lb per week. Tyson weighs 195 lb and hopes to lose 1 lb per week.

   a. If the plan works, in how many weeks will the boys weigh the same amount?

   b. What will that weight be?

Write an equation to represent each relationship. Then solve the equation.

34. Three times the sum of a number and 4 is the same as 18 more than the number.

35. A number decreased by 30 is the same as 14 minus 3 times the number.

36. Two less than 2 times a number is the same as the number plus 64.

Solve each equation. Check your answer.

37. $2x - 2 = 4x + 6$

38. $3x + 5 = 2x + 2$

39. $4x + 3 = 5x - 4$

40. $-\frac{2}{5}p + 2 = \frac{1}{5}p + 11$

41. $5x + 24 = 2x + 15$

42. $5x - 10 = 14 - 3x$

43. $12 - 6x = 10 - 5x$

44. $5x - 7 = -6x - 29$

45. $1.8x + 2.8 = 2.5x + 2.1$

46. $2.6x + 18 = 2.4x + 22$

47. $1 - 3x = 2x + 8$

48. $\frac{1}{2}(8 - 6h) = h$

49. $3(x + 1) = 2x + 7$

50. $9x - 8 + 4x = 7x + 16$

51. $3(2x - 1) + 5 = 6(x + 1)$

52. **Travel** Rapid Rental Car company charges a $40 rental fee, $15 for gas, and $0.25 per mile driven. For the same car, Capital Cars charges $45 for rental and gas and $0.35 per mile.

   a. Find the number of miles for which the companies' charges will be the same. Then find that charge. Show that your answers are reasonable.

   b. The Barre family estimates that they will drive about 95 miles during their vacation to Hershey, Pennsylvania. Which company should they rent their car from? Explain.

   c. **What if...?** The Barres have extended their vacation and now estimate that they will drive about 120 miles. Should they still rent from the same company as in part **b**? Why or why not?

   d. Give a general rule for deciding which company to rent from.

53. **Geometry** The triangles shown have the same perimeter. What is the value of x?

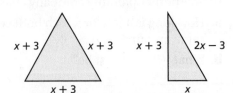

Real-World Connections

54. a. A fire currently covers 420 acres and continues to spread at a rate of 60 acres per day. How many total acres will be covered in the next 2 days? Show that your answer is reasonable.

   b. Write an expression for the total area covered by the fire in d days.

   c. The firefighters estimate that they can put out the fire at a rate of 80 acres per day. Write an expression for the total area that the firefighters can put out in d days.

   d. Set the expressions in parts **b** and **c** equal. Solve for d. What does d represent?

Biology

A cheetah's body is well designed for fast running. Its tail acts like a boat's rudder to help it make sharp turns. Its spine acts like a spring to propel it forward.

Source:
www.cheetahspot.com

55. Critical Thinking Write an equation with variables on both sides that has no solution.

56. Biology The graph shows the maximum recorded speeds of the four fastest mammals.

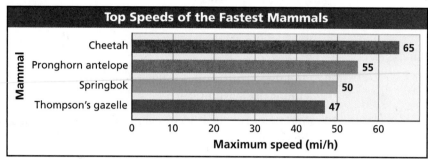

Source: The Top 10 of Everything

a. Write an expression for the distance in miles that a Thompson's gazelle can run at top speed in *x* hours.

b. Write an expression for the distance in miles that a cheetah can run at top speed in *x* hours.

c. A cheetah and a Thompson's gazelle are running at their top speeds. The cheetah is one mile behind the gazelle. Write an expression for the distance the cheetah must run to catch up with the gazelle.

d. Write and solve an equation that represents how long the cheetah will have to run at top speed to catch up with the gazelle.

e. A cheetah can maintain its top speed for only 300 yards. Will the cheetah be able to catch the gazelle? Explain.

H.O.T. 57. Write About It Write a series of steps that you can use to solve any equation with variables on both sides.

TEST PREP

58. Lindsey's monthly magazine subscription costs $1.25 per issue. Kenzie's monthly subscription costs $1.50 per issue, but she received her first 2 issues free. Which equation can be used to find the number of months after which the girls will have paid the same amount?

(A) $1.25m = 1.50m - 2$

(C) $1.25m = 1.50(m - 2)$

(B) $1.25m = 1.50m - 2m$

(D) $1.25m = 3m - 1.50$

59. What is the numerical solution of the equation *7 times a number equals 3 less than 5 times that number*?

(F) -1.5 (G) 0.25 (H) $\frac{2}{3}$ (J) 4

60. Three packs of markers cost $9.00 less than 5 packs of markers. Which equation best represents this situation?

(A) $5x + 9 = 3x$ (B) $3x + 9 = 5x$ (C) $3x - 9 = 5x$ (D) $9 - 3x = 5x$

61. Nicole has $120. If she saves $20 per week, in how many days will she have $500?

(F) 19 (G) 25 (H) 133 (J) 175

62. Gridded Response Solve $-2(x - 1) + 5x = 2(2x - 1)$.

Solve each equation.

63. $4x + 2[4 - 2(x + 2)] = 2x - 4$

64. $\dfrac{x + 5}{2} + \dfrac{x - 1}{2} = \dfrac{x - 1}{3}$

65. $\dfrac{2}{3}w - \dfrac{1}{4} = \dfrac{2}{3}\left(w - \dfrac{1}{4}\right)$

66. $-5 - 7 - 3f = -f - 2(f + 6)$

67. $\dfrac{2}{3}x + \dfrac{1}{2} = \dfrac{3}{5}x - \dfrac{5}{6}$

68. $x - \dfrac{1}{4} = \dfrac{x}{3} + 7\dfrac{3}{4}$

69. Find three consecutive integers such that twice the greatest integer is 2 less than 3 times the least integer.

70. Find three consecutive integers such that twice the least integer is 12 more than the greatest integer.

71. Rob had twice as much money as Sam. Then Sam gave Rob 1 quarter, 2 nickels, and 3 pennies. Rob then gave Sam 8 dimes. If they now have the same amount of money, how much money did Rob originally have? Check your answer.

FOCUS ON MATHEMATICAL PRACTICES

H.O.T. 72. Comparison One store charges $1.30 an ounce for a spice. Another store charges $1.20 an ounce but includes a half-ounce container when weighing. For what number of ounces is the cost at each store the same?

H.O.T. 73. Justify Name the property that justifies each numbered step.

$$2x + 5 = 3(x - 3)$$
(1) $\qquad 2x + 5 = 3x - 9$
(2) $\qquad 2x + 5 + 9 = 3x - 9 + 9$
(3) $\quad 2x + 14 - 2x = 3x - 2x$
$$14 = x$$

H.O.T. 74. Modeling Create an equation with variables on both sides of the equation and integer coefficients that has a solution of $n = -\dfrac{7}{12}$. Explain how you created the equation.

Career Path

Beth Simmons
Biology major

Q: What math classes did you take in high school?
A: Algebra 1 and 2, Geometry, and Precalculus

Q: What math classes have you taken in college?
A: Two calculus classes and a calculus-based physics class

Q: How do you use math?
A: I use math a lot in physics. Sometimes I would think a calculus topic was totally useless, and then we would use it in physics class! In biology, I use math to understand populations.

Q: What career options are you considering?
A: When I graduate, I could teach, or I could go to graduate school and do more research. I have a lot of options.

3-3 Solving for a Variable

 Essential Question: How can you solve for a given variable in formulas or equations with more than one variable?

Objectives
Solve a formula for a given variable.

Solve an equation in two or more variables for one of the variables.

Vocabulary
formula
literal equation

Who uses this?
Athletes can "rearrange" the distance formula to calculate their average speed.

Many wheelchair athletes compete in marathons, which cover about 26.2 miles. Using the time t it took to complete the race, the distance d, and the *formula* $d = rt$, racers can find their average speed r.

A **formula** is an equation that states a rule for a relationship among quantities.

In the formula $d = rt$, d is isolated. You can "rearrange" a formula to isolate any variable by using inverse operations. This is called *solving for a variable*.

Solving for a Variable
Step 1 Locate the variable you are asked to solve for in the equation.
Step 2 Identify the operations on this variable and the order in which they are applied.
Step 3 Use inverse operations to undo operations and isolate the variable.

COMMON CORE GPS
EXAMPLE **1**
MCC9-12.A.CED.4

my.hrw.com

Online Video Tutor

Helpful Hint

A number divided by itself equals 1. For $t \neq 0$, $\frac{t}{t} = 1$.

Sports Application

In 2004, Ernst Van Dyk won the wheelchair race of the Boston Marathon with a time of about 1.3 hours. The race was about 26.2 miles. What was his average speed? Use the formula $d = rt$ and round your answer to the nearest tenth.

The question asks for speed, so first solve the formula $d = rt$ for r.

$d = \mathbf{r}t$ *Locate r in the equation.*

$\dfrac{d}{t} = \dfrac{rt}{t}$ *Since r is multiplied by t, divide both sides by t to undo the multiplication.*

$\dfrac{d}{t} = r$, or $r = \dfrac{d}{t}$

Now use this formula and the information given in the problem.

$r = \dfrac{d}{t} \approx \dfrac{26.2}{1.3}$

≈ 20.2

Van Dyk's average speed was about 20.2 miles per hour.

CHECK IT OUT!

1. Solve the formula $d = rt$ for t. Find the time in hours that it would take Van Dyk to travel 26.2 miles if his average speed was 18 miles per hour. Round to the nearest hundredth.

© Ezra Shaw/Getty Images

EXAMPLE **2** Solving Formulas for a Variable

MCC9-12.A.CED.4

A The formula for a Fahrenheit temperature in terms of degrees Celsius is $F = \frac{9}{5}C + 32$. Solve for C.

$$F = \frac{9}{5}\mathbf{C} + 32 \qquad \textit{Locate C in the equation.}$$

$$\underline{-32 \qquad\qquad -32} \qquad \textit{Since 32 is added to } \frac{9}{5}\textit{C, subtract 32 from both}$$
$$F - 32 = \frac{9}{5}C \qquad\qquad \textit{sides to undo the addition.}$$

$$\left(\frac{5}{9}\right)(F - 32) = \left(\frac{5}{9}\right)\frac{9}{5}C \qquad \textit{Since C is multiplied by } \frac{9}{5}\textit{, divide both}$$
$$\frac{5}{9}(F - 32) = C \qquad\qquad \textit{sides by } \frac{9}{5} \left(\textit{multiply by } \frac{5}{9}\right) \textit{ to undo the}$$
$$\textit{multiplication.}$$

Remember!

Dividing by a fraction is the same as multiplying by the reciprocal.

B The formula for a person's typing speed is $s = \frac{w - 10e}{m}$, where s is speed in words per minute, w is number of words typed, e is number of errors, and m is number of minutes typing. Solve for w.

$$s = \frac{w - 10e}{m} \qquad \textit{Locate w in the equation.}$$

$$m(s) = m\left(\frac{w - 10e}{m}\right) \qquad \textit{Since w − 10e is divided by m, multiply both}$$
$$\textit{sides by m to undo the division.}$$

$$ms = w - 10e$$

$$\underline{+ 10e \qquad\quad + 10e} \qquad \textit{Since 10e is subtracted from w, add 10e to}$$
$$ms + 10e = w \qquad\qquad \textit{both sides to undo the subtraction.}$$

2. The formula for an object's final velocity f is $f = i - gt$, where i is the object's initial velocity, g is acceleration due to gravity, and t is time. Solve for i.

A formula is a type of *literal equation*. A **literal equation** is an equation with two or more variables. To solve for one of the variables, use inverse operations.

EXAMPLE **3** Solving Literal Equations for a Variable

MCC9-12.A.REI.3

A Solve $m - n = 5$ for m.

$$m - n = \quad 5 \qquad \textit{Locate m in the equation.}$$
$$\underline{+ n \quad + n} \qquad \textit{Since n is subtracted from m, add n to both sides to}$$
$$m = 5 + n \qquad\qquad \textit{undo the subtraction.}$$

B Solve $\frac{m}{k} = x$ for k.

$$\frac{m}{k} = x \qquad \textit{Locate k in the equation.}$$

$$k\left(\frac{m}{k}\right) = kx \qquad \textit{Since k appears in the denominator, multiply both}$$
$$\textit{sides by k.}$$
$$m = kx$$

$$\frac{m}{x} = \frac{kx}{x} \qquad \textit{Since k is multiplied by x, divide both sides by x to}$$
$$\textit{undo the multiplication.}$$
$$\frac{m}{x} = k$$

3a. Solve $5 - b = 2t$ for t.   **3b.** Solve $D = \frac{m}{V}$ for V.

THINK AND DISCUSS

1. Describe a situation in which a formula could be used more easily if it were "rearranged." Include the formula in your description.

2. Explain how to solve $P = 2\ell + 2w$ for w.

3. **GET ORGANIZED** Copy and complete the graphic organizer. Write a formula that is used in each subject. Then solve the formula for each of its variables.

Common Formulas	
Subject	**Formula**
Geometry	
Physical science	
Earth science	

3-3 Exercises

my.hrw.com
Homework Help

GUIDED PRACTICE

1. **Vocabulary** Explain why a *formula* is a type of *literal equation*.

SEE EXAMPLE 1
2. **Construction** The formula $a = 46c$ gives the floor area a in square meters that can be wired using c circuits.
   a. Solve $a = 46c$ for c.
   b. If a room is 322 square meters, how many circuits are required to wire this room?

SEE EXAMPLE 2
3. The formula for the volume of a rectangular prism with length ℓ, width w, and height h is $V = \ell wh$. Solve this formula for w.

SEE EXAMPLE 3
4. Solve $st + 3t = 6$ for s.
5. Solve $m - 4n = 8$ for m.
6. Solve $\frac{f+4}{g} = 6$ for f.
7. Solve $b + c = \frac{10}{a}$ for a.

PRACTICE AND PROBLEM SOLVING

my.hrw.com
Online Extra Practice

8. **Geometry** The formula $C = 2\pi r$ relates the circumference C of a circle to its radius r. (Recall that π is the constant ratio of circumference to diameter.)
   a. Solve $C = 2\pi r$ for r.
   b. If a circle's circumference is 15 inches, what is its radius? Leave the symbol π in your answer.

C is the distance around the circle.

r is the distance from the center of the circle to any point on the circle.

9. **Finance** The formula $A = P + I$ shows that the total amount of money A received from an investment equals the principal P (the original amount of money invested) plus the interest I. Solve this formula for I.

10. Solve $-2 = 4r + s$ for s.
11. Solve $xy - 5 = k$ for x.
12. Solve $\frac{m}{n} = p - 6$ for n.
13. Solve $\frac{x-2}{y} = z$ for y.

Solve for the indicated variable.

14. $S = 180n - 360$ for n
15. $\frac{x}{5} - g = a$ for x
16. $A = \frac{1}{2}bh$ for b

17. $y = mx + b$ for x
18. $a = 3n + 1$ for n
19. $PV = nRT$ for T

20. $T + M = R$ for T
21. $M = T - R$ for T
22. $PV = nRT$ for R

23. $2a + 2b = c$ for b
24. $5p + 9c = p$ for c
25. $ax + r = 7$ for r

26. $3x + 7y = 2$ for y
27. $4y + 3x = 5$ for x
28. $y = 3x + 3b$ for b

29. Estimation The table shows the flying time and distance traveled for five flights on a certain airplane.

   a. Use the data in the table to write a rule that *estimates* the relationship between flying time t and distance traveled d.

   b. Use your rule from part **a** to estimate the time that it takes the airplane to fly 1300 miles.

   c. Solve your rule for d.

   d. Use your rule from part **c** to estimate the distance the airplane can fly in 8 hours.

Flying Times		
Flight	**Time (h)**	**Distance (mi)**
A	2	1018
B	3	1485
C	4	2103
D	5	2516
E	6	2886

30. Sports To find a baseball pitcher's earned run average (ERA), you can use the formula $Ei = 9r$, where E represents ERA, i represents number of innings pitched, and r represents number of earned runs allowed. Solve the equation for E. What is a pitcher's ERA if he allows 5 earned runs in 18 innings pitched?

31. Meteorology For altitudes up to 36,000 feet, the relationship between temperature and altitude can be described by the formula $t = -0.0035a + g$, where t is the temperature in degrees Fahrenheit, a is the altitude in feet, and g is the ground temperature in degrees Fahrenheit. Solve this formula for a.

H.O.T. **32. Write About It** In your own words, explain how to solve a literal equation for one of the variables.

33. Critical Thinking How is solving $a - ab = c$ for a different from the problems in this lesson? How might you solve this equation for a?

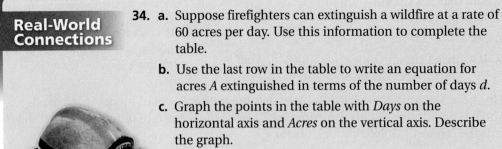

Real-World Connections

34. a. Suppose firefighters can extinguish a wildfire at a rate of 60 acres per day. Use this information to complete the table.

   b. Use the last row in the table to write an equation for acres A extinguished in terms of the number of days d.

   c. Graph the points in the table with *Days* on the horizontal axis and *Acres* on the vertical axis. Describe the graph.

Days	Acres
1	60
2	▨
3	180
4	▨
5	▨
d	▨

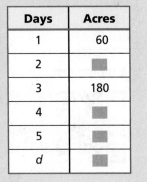

TEST PREP

35. Which equation is the result of solving $9 + 3x = 2y$ for x?

    Ⓐ $\dfrac{9 + 3y}{2} = x$ Ⓑ $\dfrac{2}{3}y - 9 = x$ Ⓒ $x = \dfrac{2}{3}y - 3$ Ⓓ $x = 2y - 3$

36. Which of the following is a correct method for solving $2a - 5b = 10$ for b?

    Ⓕ Add $5b$ to both sides, then divide both sides by 2.

    Ⓖ Subtract $5b$ from both sides, then divide both sides by 2.

    Ⓗ Divide both sides by 5, then add $2a$ to both sides.

    Ⓙ Subtract $2a$ from both sides, then divide both sides by -5.

37. The formula for the volume of a rectangular prism is $V = \ell wh$. Anna wants to make a cardboard box with a length of 7 inches, a width of 5 inches, and a volume of 210 cubic inches. Which variable does Anna need to solve for in order to build her box?

    Ⓐ V Ⓑ ℓ Ⓒ w Ⓓ h

CHALLENGE AND EXTEND

Solve for the indicated variable.

38. $3.3x + r = 23.1$ for x **39.** $\dfrac{2}{5}a - \dfrac{3}{4}b = c$ for a **40.** $\dfrac{3}{5}x + 1.4y = \dfrac{2}{5}$ for y

41. $t = \dfrac{d}{500} + \dfrac{1}{2}$ for d **42.** $s = \dfrac{1}{2}gt^2$ for g **43.** $v^2 = u^2 + 2as$ for s

44. Solve $y = mx + 6$ for m. What can you say about y if $m = 0$?

45. Entertainment The formula $S = \dfrac{h \cdot w \cdot f \cdot t}{35{,}000}$ gives the approximate size in kilobytes (Kb) of a compressed video. The variables h and w represent the height and width of the frame measured in pixels, f is the number of frames per second (fps) the video plays, and t is the time the video plays in seconds. Estimate the time a movie trailer will play if it has a frame height of 320 pixels, has a frame width of 144 pixels, plays at 15 fps, and has a size of 2370 Kb.

FOCUS ON MATHEMATICAL PRACTICES

H.O.T. 46. Analysis Solve the equation $2x + 5y = 12 - y$ for y. Use the resulting equation to solve for x. Then, solve the original equation for x. Are both results for x the same? Why?

H.O.T. 47. Problem Solving In ice hockey, the Goals Against Average (GAA) is calculated by multiplying the number of goals allowed by 60 and dividing by minutes played.

    a. How can you use the calculation to find the number of goals allowed by a goalie if the GAA and minutes played are known?

    b. Use the result of part a to find the number of goals allowed by a goalie who has a 2.80 GAA and has played 1050 minutes.

Ready to Go On?

3-1 Solving Two-Step and Multi-Step Equations

Solve each equation.

1. $2r + 20 = 200$ **2.** $\frac{3}{5}k + 5 = 7$ **3.** $5n + 6 - 3n = -12$ **4.** $4(x - 7) = 2$

5. A taxicab company charges $2.10 plus $0.80 per mile. Carmen paid a fare of $11.70. Write and solve an equation to find the number of miles she traveled.

6. $4t - 13 = 57$ **7.** $5 - 2y = 15$ **8.** $\frac{k}{5} - 6 = 2$

9. $\frac{5}{6}f - \frac{3}{4}f + \frac{3}{4} = \frac{1}{2}$ **10.** $7x - 19x = 6$ **11.** $4 + 3a - 6 = 43$

12. If $8n + 22 = 70$, find the value of $3n$.

13. If $0 = 6n - 36$, find the value of $n - 5$.

14. The sum of the measures of two angles is 180°. One angle measures $3a$ and the other angle measures $2a - 25$ Find a. Then find the measure of each angle.

3-2 Solving Equations with Variables on Both Sides

Solve each equation.

15. $4x - 3 = 2x + 5$ **16.** $3(2x - 5) = 2(3x - 2)$ **17.** $2(2t - 3) = 6(t + 2)$

18. $7(x + 5) = -7(x + 5)$ **19.** $4x + 2 = 3x$ **20.** $-3r - 8 = -5r - 12$

21. $-a - 3 + 7 = 3a$ **22.** $-(x - 4) = 2x + 6$ **23.** $\frac{2}{3}n = 4n - \frac{10}{3}n - \frac{1}{2}$

24. $0.2(7 + 2t) = 0.4t + 1.4$

25. One photo shop charges $0.36 per print. Another photo shop charges $2.52 plus $0.08 per print. Juan finds that the cost of printing his photos is the same at either shop. How many photos does Juan have to print?

3-3 Solving for a Variable

26. Solve $2x + 3y = 12$ for x. **27.** Solve $\frac{x}{r} = v$ for x.

28. Solve $5j + s = t - 2$ for t. **29.** Solve $h + p = 3(k - 8)$ for k.

Solve for the indicated variable.

30. $C = \frac{360}{n}$ for n **31.** $S = \frac{n}{2}(a + \ell)$ for a

32. The formula $a = \frac{d}{g}$ gives the average gas mileage a of a vehicle that uses g gallons of gas to travel d miles. Use the formula to find how many gallons of gas a vehicle with an average gas mileage of 20.2 miles per gallon will use to travel 75 miles. Round your answer to the nearest tenth.

PARCC Assessment Readiness

Selected Response

1. Solve $\frac{h}{50} - \frac{1}{10} = \frac{1}{10}$.

  (A) $h = -250$ (C) $h = -10$

  (B) $h = 10$ (D) $h = 250$

2. Solve $30a + 23 - 25a = 28$.

  (F) $a = 5$ (H) $a = 1$

  (G) $a = -1$ (J) $a = -5$

3. Devon pays $49.95 for her roller skates. After that she pays $5.95 for each visit to the roller rink. What is the greatest number of visits she can afford if the total amount she spends cannot be more than $115.40?

  (A) 2   (C) 65

  (B) 11   (D) 19

4. If $3x - 8 = 31$, find the value of $4x$.

  (F) 8   (H) 36

  (G) 18   (J) 52

5. The formula $p = nc - e$ gives the profit p when a number of items n are each sold at a cost c and expenses e are subtracted. If $p = 4150$, $n = 3000$, and $e = 500$, what is the value of c?

  (A) $1.38   (C) $0.72

  (B) $1.55   (D) $1.22

6. Solve $50s - 13 = 55s - 93$.

  (F) $s = 16$ (H) $s = 80$

  (G) $s = -80$ (J) $s = -16$

7. Solve $4x - 3 - 2x = 9 + 2x - 12$. Tell whether the equation has infinitely many solutions or no solutions.

  (A) Infinitely many solutions

  (B) Only one solution

  (C) Two solutions

  (D) No solutions

8. An online video service charges a monthly membership fee of $7.50 and a charge of $1.00 per movie watched. Another service has no membership fee but charges $2.50 for each movie. How many movies need to be rented each month for the total fees to be the same from either company?

  (F) 9 movies   (H) 3 movies

  (G) 5 movies   (J) 7 movies

9. The formula for the resistance of a conductor with voltage V and current I is $r = \frac{V}{I}$. Solve for V.

  (A) $I = Vr$ (C) $V = \frac{I}{r}$

  (B) $V = \frac{r}{I}$ (D) $V = Ir$

10. A professional cyclist is training for the Tour de France. What was his average speed in kilometers per hour if he rode the 194 kilometers from Laval to Blois in 4.5 hours? Use the formula $d = rt$, and round your answer to the nearest tenth.

  (F) 43.1 kph   (H) 189.5 kph

  (G) 873.0 kph   (J) 116.3 kph

Mini-Task

11. Find three consecutive integers such that twice the greatest integer is 6 less than 3 times the least integer.

UNIT 2

Module

4

Solving Inequalities in One Variable

COMMON CORE GPS

MCC9-12.A.CED.3

MCC9-12.A.REI.3

MCC9-12.A.REI.3

Contents

The Common Core Georgia Performance Standards for Mathematical Practice describe varieties of expertise that all students should seek to develop. Opportunities to develop these practices are integrated throughout this program.

1 Make sense of problems and persevere in solving them.

2 Reason abstractly and quantitatively.

3 Construct viable arguments and critique the reasoning of others.

4 Model with mathematics.

5 Use appropriate tools strategically.

6 Attend to precision.

7 Look for and make use of structure.

8 Look for and express regularity in repeated reasoning.

Unpacking the Standards

Understanding the standards and the vocabulary terms in the standards will help you know exactly what you are expected to learn in this chapter.

 MCC9-12.A.CED.3

Represent constraints by ... inequalities ... and interpret solutions as viable or nonviable options in a modeling context.

Key Vocabulary

inequality (desigualdad) A statement that compares two expressions by using one of the following signs: $<$, $>$, $\leq$, $\geq$, or $\neq$.

solution of an inequality in one variable (solución de una desigualdad en una variable) A value or values that make the inequality true.

What It Means For You

You can use inequalities to represent limits on the values in a situation so that the solutions make sense in a real-world context.

EXAMPLE

Anyone riding the large water slide at a park must be at least 40 inches tall.

Let h represent the heights that are allowed.

Height is at least 40 inches.

| h | $\geq$ | 40 |

 MCC9-12.A.REI.3

Solve linear ... inequalities in one variable, ...

Key Vocabulary

linear inequality in one variable (desigualdad lineal en una variable) An inequality that can be written in one of the following forms: $ax < b$, $ax > b$, $ax \leq b$, $ax \geq b$, or $ax \neq b$, where a and b are constants and $a \neq 0$.

What It Means For You

Solving inequalities lets you answer questions where a range of solutions is possible.

EXAMPLE

Solve the inequality for t to find what grades on the final exam will give Cleo a course grade of "A".

$705 + 2t \geq 895$	*Cleo has 705 points and needs at least 895.*
$2t \geq 190$	*Subtract 705 from both sides.*
$t \geq 95$	*Divide both sides by 2.*

Cleo needs to earn a 95 or above on the final exam.

Graphing and Writing Inequalities

Essential Question: How can you graph and write inequalities?

Objectives
Identify solutions of inequalities in one variable.

Write and graph inequalities in one variable.

Vocabulary
inequality
solution of an inequality

Who uses this?
Members of a crew team can use inequalities to be sure they fall within a range of weights. (See Example 4.)

The athletes on a lightweight crew team must weigh 165 pounds or less. The acceptable weights for these athletes can be described using an *inequality*.

An **inequality** is a statement that two quantities are not equal. The quantities are compared by using one of the following signs:

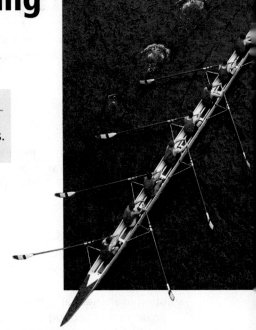

 Animated Math

$<$	$>$	$\leq$	$\geq$	$\neq$
$A < B$	$A > B$	$A \leq B$	$A \geq B$	$A \neq B$
A is less than B.	A is greater than B.	A is less than or equal to B.	A is greater than or equal to B.	A is not equal to B.

A **solution of an inequality** is any value of the variable that makes the inequality true.

 COMMON CORE GPS
MCC9-12.A.REI.3

EXAMPLE **1** **Identifying Solutions of Inequalities**

Describe the solutions of $3 + x < 9$ in words.

 my.hrw.com

Online Video Tutor

Test values of x that are positive, negative, and 0.

x	-2.75	0	5.99	6	6.01	6.1
$3 + x$	0.25	3	8.99	9	9.01	9.1
$3 + x \overset{?}{<} 9$	$0.25 \overset{?}{<} 9$	$3 \overset{?}{<} 9$	$8.99 \overset{?}{<} 9$	$9 \overset{?}{<} 9$	$9.01 \overset{?}{<} 9$	$9.1 \overset{?}{<} 9$
Solution?	Yes	Yes	Yes	No	No	No

When the value of x is a number less than 6, the value of $3 + x$ is less than 9.
When the value of x is 6, the value of $3 + x$ is equal to 9.
When the value of x is a number greater than 6, the value of $3 + x$ is greater than 9.

The solutions of $3 + x < 9$ are numbers less than 6.

Writing Math

The solutions in Example 1 can be written in *set-builder notation* as $\{x \mid x < 6\}$, read as "x such that x is less than 6."

 CHECK IT OUT!

1. Describe the solutions of $2p > 8$ in words.

© Charles Crust

An inequality like $3 + x < 9$ has too many solutions to list. You can use a graph on a number line to show all the solutions.

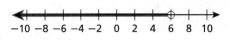

The solutions are shaded and an arrow shows that the solutions continue past those shown on the graph. To show that an endpoint is a solution, draw a solid circle at the number. To show that an endpoint is not a solution, draw an empty circle.

Graphing Inequalities

WORDS	ALGEBRA	GRAPH
All real numbers less than 5	$x < 5$	
All real numbers greater than -1	$x > -1$	
All real numbers less than or equal to $\frac{1}{2}$	$x \le \frac{1}{2}$	
All real numbers greater than or equal to 0	$x \ge 0$	

COMMON CORE GPS
EXAMPLE Prep. for MCC9-12.A.REI.12

2 **Graphing Inequalities**

Graph each inequality.

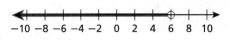
my.hrw.com

Online Video Tutor

A $b < -1.5$

> Draw an empty circle at -1.5.
> Shade all the numbers less than -1.5 and draw an arrow pointing to the left.

B $r \ge 2$

> Draw a solid circle at 2.
> Shade all the numbers greater than 2 and draw an arrow pointing to the right.

CHECK IT OUT! Graph each inequality.

2a. $c > 2.5$ **2b.** $2^2 - 4 \ge w$ **2c.** $m \le -3$

Student to Student

Graphing Inequalities

Victor Solomos
Palmer High School

To know which direction to shade a graph, I write inequalities with the variable on the left side of the inequality symbol. I know that the symbol has to point to the same number after I rewrite the inequality.

For example, I write $4 < y$ as $y > 4$.

Now the inequality symbol points in the direction that I should draw the shaded arrow on my graph.

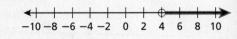

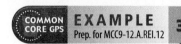

EXAMPLE 3
Prep. for MCC9-12.A.REI.12

my.hrw.com

Online Video Tutor

Writing an Inequality from a Graph

Write the inequality shown by each graph.

A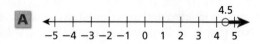

Use any variable. The arrow points to the right, so use either > or ≥.
The empty circle at 4.5 means that 4.5 is not a solution, so use >.

$h > 4.5$

B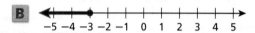

Use any variable. The arrow points to the left, so use either < or ≤.
The solid circle at −3 means that −3 is a solution, so use ≤.

$m \leq -3$

CHECK IT OUT! **3.** Write the inequality shown by the graph.

EXAMPLE 4
MCC9-12.A.CED.3

my.hrw.com

Online Video Tutor

Sports Application

The members of a lightweight crew team can weigh no more than 165 pounds each. Define a variable and write an inequality for the acceptable weights of the team members. Graph the solutions.

Let w represent the weights that are allowed.

Athletes may weigh	no more than	165 pounds.
w	$\leq$	165

$w \leq 165$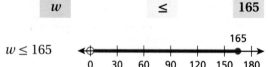

Stop the graph at 0 because a person's weight must be a positive number.

"No more than" means "less than or equal to."

"At least" means "greater than or equal to."

CHECK IT OUT! **4.** A store's employees earn at least $8.25 per hour. Define a variable and write an inequality for the amount the employees may earn per hour. Graph the solutions.

MCC.MP.6

MATHEMATICAL PRACTICES

THINK AND DISCUSS

Know it! Note

1. Compare the solutions of $x > 2$ and $x \geq 2$.

2. GET ORGANIZED Copy and complete the graphic organizer. Draw a graph in the first row and write the correct inequality in the second row.

Inequality	Graph
$x > 1$	
	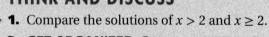

GUIDED PRACTICE

1. **Vocabulary** How is a *solution of an inequality* like a solution of an equation?

SEE EXAMPLE **1**   Describe the solutions of each inequality in words.

     2. $g - 5 \geq 6$ **3.** $-2 < h + 1$ **4.** $20 > 5t$ **5.** $5 - x \leq 2$

SEE EXAMPLE **2**   Graph each inequality.

     6. $x < -5$ **7.** $c \geq 3\frac{1}{2}$ **8.** $(4 - 2)^3 > m$ **9.** $p \geq \sqrt{17 + 8}$

SEE EXAMPLE **3**   Write the inequality shown by each graph.

10.
```
←—+——+——+——+——●——+——+——+——+——+——+——→
  -6  -5  -4  -3  -2  -1   0   1   2   3   4
```

11. $-8\frac{1}{2}$
```
←—+——○——+——+——+——+——+——+——+——+——+——→
  -9  -8  -7  -6  -5  -4  -3  -2  -1   0   1
```

12.
```
←————+——+——+——+——+——+——+——+——+——○——+——→
     -4  -3  -2  -1   0   1   2   3   4  5.5 6
```

13. -7
```
←—————————+——+——○——+——+——+——+——→
         -12 -10  -8   -6  -4  -2   0
```

14.
```
←—+——+——+——+——+——+——●——+——+——+——+——→
  -4  -3  -2  -1   0   1   2   3   4   5   6
```

15.
```
←——————————————————————————●——+——+——→
  -2   0   2   4   6   8  10  12  14  16  18
```

SEE EXAMPLE **4**   Define a variable and write an inequality for each situation. Graph the solutions.

   16. There must be at least 20 club members present in order to hold a meeting.

   17. A trainer advises an athlete to keep his heart rate under 140 beats per minute.

PRACTICE AND PROBLEM SOLVING

Independent Practice	
For Exercises	See Example
18–21	1
22–25	2
26–31	3
32–33	4

my.hrw.com

Online Extra Practice

Describe the solutions of each inequality in words.

18. $-2t > -8$ **19.** $0 > w - 2$ **20.** $3k > 9$ **21.** $\frac{1}{2}b \leq 6$

Graph each inequality.

22. $7 < x$ **23.** $t \leq -\frac{1}{2}$ **24.** $d > 4(5 - 8)$ **25.** $t \leq 3^2 - 2^2$

Write the inequality shown by each graph.

26.
```
←—+——+——+——+——+——+——+——+——●——+——+——→
  -4  -3  -2  -1   0   1   2   3   4   5   6
```

27. -11
```
←———————————+——○——+——+——+——+——+——→
        -16 -14 -12 -10  -8   -6  -4
```

28. -3.5
```
←—+——○——+——+——+——+——+——+——+——+——+——→
  -6  -5  -4  -3  -2  -1   0   1   2   3   4
```

29. -3.3
```
←—+——○——+——+——+——+——+——+——+——+——+——→
  -5  -4  -3  -2  -1   0   1   2   3   4   5
```

30.
```
←—+——+——+——+——+——+——+——+——+——○——+——→
  -5  -4  -3  -2  -1   0   1   2   3   4   5
```

31. 9
```
←—+——+——+——+——+——●——+——+——+——+——+——→
  -2   0   2   4   6   8  10  12  14  16  18
```

Define a variable and write an inequality for each situation. Graph the solutions.

32. The maximum speed allowed on Main Street is 25 miles per hour.

33. Applicants must have at least 5 years of experience.

Write each inequality in words.

34. $x > 7$ **35.** $h < -5$ **36.** $d \leq 23$ **37.** $r \geq -2$

Write each inequality with the variable on the left. Graph the solutions.

38. $19 < g$ **39.** $17 \geq p$ **40.** $10 < e$ **41.** $0 < f$

Define a variable and write an inequality for each situation. Graph the solutions.

42. The highest temperature ever recorded on Earth was 135.9 °F at Al Aziziyah, Libya, on September 13, 1922.

43. Businesses with profits less than $10,000 per year will be shut down.

44. You must be at least 46 inches tall to ride a roller coaster at an amusement park.

45. Due to a medical condition, a hiker can hike only in areas with an elevation no more than 5000 feet above sea level.

Write a real-world situation that could be described by each inequality.

46. $x \geq 0$ **47.** $x < 10$ **48.** $x \leq 12$ **49.** $x > 8.5$

Match each inequality with its graph.

50. $x \geq 5$

A.

51. $x < 5$

B.

52. $x > 5$

C.

53. $x \leq 5$

D.

H.O.T. 54. ///**ERROR ANALYSIS**/// Two students graphed the inequality $4 > b$. Which graph is incorrect? Explain the error.

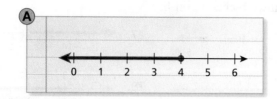

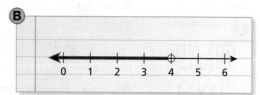

Real-World Connections

55. a. Mirna earned $125 baby-sitting during the spring break. She needs to save $90 for the German Club trip. She wants to spend the remainder of the money shopping. Write an inequality to show how much she can spend.

b. Graph the inequality you wrote in part **a.**

c. Mirna spends $15 on a bracelet. Write an inequality to show how much money she has left to spend.

56. Critical Thinking Graph all positive integer solutions of the inequality $x < 5$.

H.O.T. 57. Write About It Explain how to write an inequality that is modeled by a graph. What characteristics do you look for in the graph?

58. Write About It You were told in the lesson that the phrase "no more than" means "less than or equal to" and the phrase "at least" means "greater than or equal to."

   a. What does the phrase "at most" mean?

   b. What does the phrase "no less than" mean?

TEST PREP

59. Which is NOT a solution of the inequality $5 - 2x \geq -3$?

   (A) 0   (B) 2   (C) 4   (D) 5

60. Which is NOT a solution of the inequality $3 - x < 2$?

   (F) 1   (G) 2   (H) 3   (J) 4

61. Which graph represents the solutions of $-2 \leq 1 - t$?

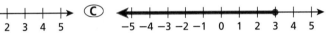

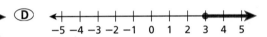

CHALLENGE AND EXTEND

Describe the values for x and y that make each inequality true.

62. $x + y \leq |x + y|$ **63.** $x^2 < xy$ **64.** $x - y \geq y - x$

Complete each statement. Write < or >.

65. If $a > b$, then $b \blacksquare a$.   **66.** If $x > y$ and $y > z$, then $x \blacksquare z$.

67. Name a value of x that makes the statement $0.35 < x < 1.27$ true.

68. Is $\frac{5}{6}$ a solution of $x < 1$? How many solutions of $x < 1$ are between 0 and 1?

69. Write About It Explain how to graph all the solutions of $x \neq 5$.

FOCUS ON MATHEMATICAL PRACTICES

H.O.T. 70. Modeling In order for Ramon to remain in his current weight class for a wrestling match on Saturday morning, he must weigh in at 152 pounds or more, but less than 160 pounds. Write a pair of inequalities that expresses the set of acceptable weights for Ramon. Define your variable.

H.O.T. 71. Problem Solving Cary is making brownies using a recipe that calls for "at least 5 cups of flour but no more than 6 cups of flour." The only measuring cup he could find holds one quarter of a cup. Write a pair of inequalities to express how many *quarter cups* of flour Cary can use.

H.O.T. 72. Analysis Imani and Trey are planning the seating at their wedding reception. They have 168 guests and each table can hold up to 16 guests, so they calculate that they need at least 10.5 tables to seat all of their guests. Graph their solution. In this context, how is the graph inaccurate? Make another graph that takes the context into account.

4-2 Solving Inequalities by Adding or Subtracting

Essential Question: How can you use addition or subtraction to solve inequalities?

Objectives
Solve one-step inequalities by using addition.

Solve one-step inequalities by using subtraction.

Who uses this?
You can use inequalities to determine how many more photos you can take. (See Example 2.)

Tenea has a cell phone that also takes pictures. After taking some photos, Tenea can use a one-step inequality to determine how many more photos she can take.

Solving one-step inequalities is much like solving one-step equations. To solve an inequality, you need to isolate the variable using the properties of inequality and inverse operations.

Properties of Inequality

Addition and Subtraction

WORDS	NUMBERS	ALGEBRA
Addition You can add the same number to both sides of an inequality, and the statement will still be true.	$3 < 8$ $3 + 2 < 8 + 2$ $5 < 10$	$a < b$ $a + c < b + c$
Subtraction You can subtract the same number from both sides of an inequality, and the statement will still be true.	$9 < 12$ $9 - 5 < 12 - 5$ $4 < 7$	$a < b$ $a - c < b - c$

These properties are also true for inequalities that use the symbols $>$, $\geq$, and $\leq$.

COMMON CORE GPS
MCC9-12.A.REI.3

EXAMPLE 1 Using Addition and Subtraction to Solve Inequalities

Solve each inequality and graph the solutions.

my.hrw.com

Online Video Tutor

A $x + 9 < 15$

$$x + 9 < 15$$
$$\underline{-9 \quad -9}$$
$$x \quad < 6$$

Since 9 is added to x, subtract 9 from both sides to undo the addition.

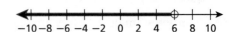

B $d - 3 > -6$

$$d - 3 > -6$$
$$\underline{+3 \quad +3}$$
$$d \quad > -3$$

Since 3 is subtracted from d, add 3 to both sides to undo the subtraction.

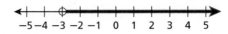

© Mingasson/Getty/HMH

Solve each inequality and graph the solutions.

C $0.7 \geq n - 0.4$

$$0.7 \geq n - 0.4$$
$$\underline{+\,0.4 \qquad +\,0.4}$$
$$1.1 \geq n$$
$$n \leq 1.1$$

Since 0.4 is subtracted from n, add 0.4 to both sides to undo the subtraction.

A number line with a point at 1.1, with arrow pointing left, marked from −5 to 5.

 **Solve each inequality and graph the solutions.**

1a. $s + 1 \leq 10$ **1b.** $2\frac{1}{2} > -3 + t$ **1c.** $q - 3.5 < 7.5$

Since there can be an infinite number of solutions to an inequality, it is not possible to check all the solutions. You can check the endpoint and the direction of the inequality symbol.

The solutions of $x + 9 < 15$ are given by $x < 6$.

Step 1 Check the endpoint.

Substitute 6 for x in the related equation $x + 9 = 15$. The endpoint should be a solution of the equation.

$x + 9 = 15$	
$6 + 9$	15
15	15 ✓

Step 2 Check the inequality symbol.

Substitute a number less than 6 for x in the original inequality. The number you choose should be a solution of the inequality.

$x + 9 < 15$		
$4 + 9$	$<$	15
13	$<$	15 ✓

COMMON CORE GPS
EXAMPLE **2**
MCC9-12.N.Q.1

my.hrw.com

Online Video Tutor

MATHEMATICAL PRACTICES

Make sence of problems and persevere in solving them.

Problem Solving Application

The memory in Tenea's camera phone allows her to take up to 20 pictures. Tenea has already taken 16 pictures. Write, solve, and graph an inequality to show how many more pictures Tenea could take.

1 **Understand the Problem**

The **answer** will be an inequality and a graph that show all the possible numbers of pictures that Tenea can take.

> **List the important information:**
> • Tenea can take up to, or *at most*, 20 pictures.
> • Tenea has taken 16 pictures already.

2 **Make a Plan**

Write an inequality.

Let p represent the remaining number of pictures Tenea can take.

Number taken	plus	number remaining	is at most	20 pictures.
16	+	p	$\leq$	20

Solve

$$16 + p \le 20$$
$$\underline{-16 \qquad -16}$$
$$p \le \quad 4$$

Since 16 is added to p, subtract 16 from both sides to undo the addition.

It is not reasonable for Tenea to take a negative or fractional number of pictures, so graph the nonnegative integers less than or equal to 4.

Tenea could take 0, 1, 2, 3, or 4 more pictures.

 Look Back

Check   Check the endpoint, 4.

$$16 + p = 20$$

$16 + 4$	20
20	20 ✓

Check a number less than 4.

$$16 + p \le 20$$

$16 + 2$	$\le$	20
18	$\le$	20 ✓

Adding 0, 1, 2, 3, or 4 more pictures will not exceed 20.

 **2.** The Recommended Dietary Allowance (RDA) of iron for a female in Sarah's age group (14–18 years) is 15 mg per day. Sarah has consumed 11 mg of iron today. Write and solve an inequality to show how many more milligrams of iron Sarah can consume without exceeding the RDA.

COMMON CORE GPS
EXAMPLE 3
MCC9-12.A.CED.1

Sports Application

my.hrw.com

Online Video Tutor

Josh can bench press 220 pounds. He wants to bench press at least 250 pounds. Write and solve an inequality to determine how many more pounds Josh must lift to reach his goal. Check your answer.

Let *p* represent the number of additional pounds Josh must lift.

220 pounds	plus	additional pounds	is at least	250 pounds.
220	+	*p*	≥	250

$$220 + p \ge 250$$
$$\underline{-220 \qquad -220}$$
$$p \ge \quad 30$$

Since 220 is added to p, subtract 220 from both sides to undo the addition.

Check   Check the endpoint, 30.

$$220 + p = 250$$

$220 + 30$	250
250	250 ✓

Check a number greater than 30.

$$220 + p \ge 250$$

$220 + 40$	$\ge$	250
260	$\ge$	250 ✓

Josh must lift at least 30 additional pounds to reach his goal.

 3. What if...? Josh has reached his goal of 250 pounds and now wants to try to break the school record of 282 pounds. Write and solve an inequality to determine how many more pounds Josh needs to break the school record. Check your answer.

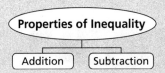
MATHEMATICAL PRACTICES

THINK AND DISCUSS

1. Show how to check your solution to Example 1B.

2. Explain how the Addition and Subtraction Properties of Inequality are like the Addition and Subtraction Properties of Equality.

3. **GET ORGANIZED** Copy and complete the graphic organizer. In each box, write an inequality that you must use the specified property to solve. Then solve and graph the inequality.

Properties of Inequality

Addition | Subtraction

4-2 Exercises

my.hrw.com
Homework Help

GUIDED PRACTICE

SEE EXAMPLE **1**

Solve each inequality and graph the solutions.

1. $12 < p + 6$ **2.** $w + 3 \geq 4$ **3.** $-5 + x \leq -20$ **4.** $z - 2 > -11$

SEE EXAMPLE **2**

5. **Health** For adults, the maximum safe water temperature in a spa is 104 °F. The water temperature in Bill's spa is 102 °F. The temperature is increased by t °F. Write, solve, and graph an inequality to show the values of t for which the water temperature is still safe.

SEE EXAMPLE **3**

6. **Consumer Economics** A local restaurant will deliver food to your house if the purchase amount of your order is at least $25.00. The total for part of your order is $17.95. Write and solve an inequality to determine how much more you must spend for the restaurant to deliver your order.

PRACTICE AND PROBLEM SOLVING

Independent Practice	
For Exercises	See Example
7–10	1
11	2
12	3

my.hrw.com

Online Extra Practice

Solve each inequality and graph the solutions.

7. $a - 3 \geq 2$ **8.** $2.5 > q - 0.8$ **9.** $-45 + x < -30$ **10.** $r + \frac{1}{4} \leq \frac{3}{4}$

11. **Engineering** The maximum load for a certain elevator is 2000 pounds. The total weight of the passengers on the elevator is 1400 pounds. A delivery man who weighs 243 pounds enters the elevator with a crate of weight w. Write, solve, and graph an inequality to show the values of w that will not exceed the weight limit of the elevator.

12. **Transportation** The gas tank in Mindy's car holds at most 15 gallons. She has already filled the tank with 7 gallons of gas. She will continue to fill the tank with g gallons more. Write and solve an inequality that shows all values of g that Mindy can add to the car's tank.

Write an inequality to represent each statement. Solve the inequality and graph the solutions.

13. Ten less than a number x is greater than 32.

14. A number n increased by 6 is less than or equal to 4.

15. A number r decreased by 13 is at most 15.

Solve each inequality and graph the solutions.

16. $x + 4 \leq 2$ **17.** $-12 + q > 39$ **18.** $x + \frac{3}{5} < 7$ **19.** $4.8 \geq p + 4$

20. $-12 \leq x - 12$ **21.** $4 < 206 + c$ **22.** $y - \frac{1}{3} > \frac{2}{3}$ **23.** $x + 1.4 \geq 1.4$

24. Use the inequality $s + 12 \geq 20$ to fill in the missing numbers.

    a. $s \geq$ ▇   **b.** $s +$ ▇ ≥ 30 **c.** $s - 8 \geq$ ▇

25. **Health** A particular type of contact lens can be worn up to 30 days in a row. Alex has been wearing these contact lenses for 21 days. Write, solve, and graph an inequality to show how many more days Alex could wear his contact lenses.

Solve each inequality and match the solutions to the correct graph.

26. $1 \leq x - 2$

A. ⟵ + + + + + + + ⊕ + + ⟶
    −5 −4 −3 −2 −1 0 1 2 3 4 5

27. $8 > x - (-5)$

B. ⟵ + + + + + + + ⊕ + + ⟶
    −5 −4 −3 −2 −1 0 1 2 3 4 5

28. $x + 6 > 9$

C. ⟵ + + + + + + + ● + + ⟶
    −5 −4 −3 −2 −1 0 1 2 3 4 5

29. $-4 \geq x - 7$

D. ⟵ + + + + + + + ● + + ⟶
    −5 −4 −3 −2 −1 0 1 2 3 4 5

H.O.T. **30.** **Estimation** Is $x < 10$ a reasonable estimate for the solutions to the inequality $11.879 + x < 21.709$? Explain your answer.

31. **Sports** At the Seattle Mariners baseball team's home games, there are 45,611 seats in the four areas listed in the table. Suppose all the suite level and club level seats during a game are filled. Write and solve an inequality to determine how many people p could be sitting in the other types of seats.

Mariners Home Game Seating	
Type of Seat	**Number of Seats**
Main bowl	24,399
Upper bowl	16,022
Club level	4,254
Suite level	936

32. **Critical Thinking** Recall that a balance scale was used to model solving equations. Describe how a balance scale could model solving inequalities.

33. **Critical Thinking** Explain why $x + 4 \geq 6$ and $x - 4 \geq -2$ have the same solutions.

H.O.T. **34.** **Write About It** How do the solutions of $x + 2 \geq 3$ differ from the solutions of $x + 2 > 3$? How do the graphs of the solutions differ?

35. **a.** Daryl finds that the distance from Columbus, Ohio, to Washington, D.C., is 411 miles. What is the round-trip distance?

    b. Daryl can afford to drive a total of 1000 miles. Write an inequality to show the number of miles m he can drive while in Washington, D.C.

    c. Solve the inequality and graph the solutions on a number line. Show that your answer is reasonable.

Health

Special-effects contact lenses are sometimes part of costumes for movies. All contact lenses should be worn under an eye doctor's supervision.

Real-World Connections

(tl), Buzz Orr/The Gazette/AP/Wide World Photos; (cr), PhotoDisc/gettyimages; (bl), © Creatas

36. Which is a reasonable solution of $4.7367 + p < 20.1784$?

    Ⓐ 15   Ⓑ 16   Ⓒ 24   Ⓓ 25

37. Which statement can be modeled by $x + 3 \leq 12$?

    Ⓕ Sam has 3 bottles of water. Together, Sam and Dave have at most 12 bottles of water.

    Ⓖ Jennie sold 3 cookbooks. To earn a prize, Jennie must sell at least 12 cookbooks.

    Ⓗ Peter has 3 baseball hats. Peter and his brothers have fewer than 12 baseball hats.

    Ⓙ Kathy swam 3 laps in the pool this week. She must swim more than 12 laps.

38. Which graph represents the solutions of $p + 3 < 1$?

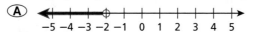
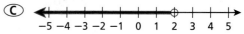
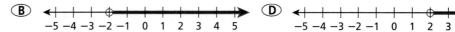

39. Which inequality does NOT have the same solutions as $n + 12 \leq 26$?

    Ⓕ $n \leq 14$ Ⓖ $n + 6 \leq 20$ Ⓗ $10 \geq n - 4$ Ⓙ $n - 12 \leq 14$

CHALLENGE AND EXTEND

Solve each inequality and graph the solutions.

40. $6\frac{9}{10} \geq 4\frac{4}{5} + x$ **41.** $r - 1\frac{2}{5} \leq 3\frac{7}{10}$ **42.** $6\frac{2}{3} + m > 7\frac{1}{6}$

Determine whether each statement is sometimes, always, or never true. Explain.

43. $a + b > a - b$

44. If $a > c$, then $a + b > c + b$.

45. If $a > b$ and $c > d$, then $a + c > b + d$.

46. If $x + b > c$ and $x > 0$ have the same solutions, what is the relationship between b and c?

FOCUS ON MATHEMATICAL PRACTICES

H.O.T. **47. Estimation** In 10 weeks, Yuri wants to have enough money to buy a racing bicycle that costs $1487.95. He currently has $292.50 in his savings account.

    a. Write an inequality that expresses how much Yuri still needs to save.

    b. Rewrite this inequality in a simpler form by rounding all numerical values to the nearest $100, and then solve it.

    c. Use the solution you just found to estimate how much money Yuri needs to save each week in order to purchase the bicycle.

H.O.T. **48. Modeling** A psychotherapist needs to complete a minimum number of internship hours before he or she can receive certification. Candace wrote the inequality $1840 + h \geq 3000$ to represent the hours she needs complete her certification. In total, how many hours does Candace need to serve as an intern? How many hours has Candace completed? How many hours does Candace still need to perform?

Solving Inequalities by Multiplying or Dividing

Essential Question: How can you use multiplication or division to solve inequalities?

Objectives

Solve one-step inequalities by using multiplication.

Solve one-step inequalities by using division.

Who uses this?

You can solve an inequality to determine how much you can buy with a certain amount of money. (See Example 3.)

Remember, solving inequalities is similar to solving equations. To solve an inequality that contains multiplication or division, undo the operation by dividing or multiplying both sides of the inequality by the same number.

The rules below show the properties of inequality for multiplying or dividing by a positive number. The rules for multiplying or dividing by a negative number appear later in this lesson.

"This is all I have, so I'll take 3 pencils, 3 notebooks, a binder, and 0.9 calculators."

Properties of Inequality

Multiplication and Division by Positive Numbers

WORDS	NUMBERS	ALGEBRA
Multiplication You can multiply both sides of an inequality by the same *positive* number, and the statement will still be true.	$7 < 12$ $7(3) < 12(3)$ $21 < 36$	If $a < b$ and $c > 0$, then $ac < bc$.
Division You can divide both sides of an inequality by the same *positive* number, and the statement will still be true.	$15 < 35$ $\dfrac{15}{5} < \dfrac{35}{5}$ $3 < 7$	If $a < b$ and $c > 0$, then $\dfrac{a}{c} < \dfrac{b}{c}$.

These properties are also true for inequalities that use the symbols $>$, $\geq$, and $\leq$.

 EXAMPLE 1
MCC9-12.A.REI.3

Multiplying or Dividing by a Positive Number

Solve each inequality and graph the solutions.

A $3x > -27$

$3x > -27$ *Since x is multiplied by 3, divide both sides by 3 to*

$\dfrac{3x}{3} > \dfrac{-27}{3}$ *undo the multiplication.*

$x > -9$

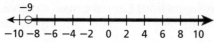

 my.hrw.com

Online Video Tutor

Solve each inequality and graph the solutions.

B $\quad \dfrac{2}{3}r < 6$

$\qquad \dfrac{2}{3}r < 6 \qquad$ *Since r is multiplied by $\frac{2}{3}$, multiply both sides by*

$\qquad \dfrac{3}{2}\left(\dfrac{2}{3}r\right) < \dfrac{3}{2}(6) \qquad$ *the reciprocal of $\frac{2}{3}$.*

$\qquad\qquad r < 9$

 Solve each inequality and graph the solutions.

1a. $4k > 24$ $\qquad$ **1b.** $-50 \geq 5q$ $\qquad$ **1c.** $\dfrac{3}{4}g > 27$

What happens when you multiply or divide both sides of an inequality by a negative number?

Look at the number line below.

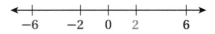

$2 < 6$		$6 > -2$	
$-2 \;\blacksquare\; -6$	*Multiply both sides by -1.*	$-6 \;\blacksquare\; 2$	*Multiply both sides by -1.*
$-2 > -6$	*Use the number line to determine the direction of the inequality.*	$-6 < 2$	*Use the number line to determine the direction of the inequality.*

Notice that when you multiply (or divide) both sides of an inequality by a negative number, you must reverse the inequality symbol. This means there is another set of properties of inequality for multiplying or dividing by a negative number.

Properties of Inequality

Multiplication and Division by Negative Numbers

WORDS	NUMBERS	ALGEBRA
Multiplication If you multiply both sides of an inequality by the same *negative* number, you must reverse the inequality symbol for the statement to still be true.	$8 > 4$ $8(-2) < 4(-2)$ $-16 < -8$	If $a > b$ and $c < 0$, then $ac < bc$.
Division If you divide both sides of an inequality by the same *negative* number, you must reverse the inequality symbol for the statement to still be true.	$12 > 4$ $\dfrac{12}{-4} < \dfrac{4}{-4}$ $-3 < -1$	If $a > b$ and $c < 0$, then $\dfrac{a}{c} < \dfrac{b}{c}$.

These properties are also true for inequalities that use the symbols $<$, $\geq$, and $\leq$.

 **EXAMPLE** **2** MCC9-12.A.REI.3

Multiplying or Dividing by a Negative Number

Solve each inequality and graph the solutions.

 my.hrw.com

Online Video Tutor

A $-8x > 72$

$$\frac{-8x}{-8} < \frac{72}{-8}$$

$$x < -9$$

Since x is multiplied by −8, divide both sides by −8. Change > to <.

B $-3 \le \dfrac{x}{-5}$

$$-5(-3) \ge -5\left(\frac{x}{-5}\right)$$

$$15 \ge x \ (\text{or } x \le 15)$$

Since x is divided by −5, multiply both sides by −5. Change ≤ to ≥.

CHECK IT OUT! Solve each inequality and graph the solutions.

2a. $10 \ge -x$ **2b.** $4.25 > -0.25h$

 **EXAMPLE** **3** MCC9-12.A.CED.1

Consumer Application

 **my.hrw.com**

Online Video Tutor

Ryan has a $16 gift card for a health store where a smoothie costs $2.50 with tax. What are the possible numbers of smoothies that Ryan can buy?

Let *s* represent the number of smoothies Ryan can buy.

$2.50	times	number of smoothies	is at most	$16.00.
2.50	•	s	≤	16.00

$$2.50s \le 16.00$$

$$\frac{2.50s}{2.50} \le \frac{16.00}{2.50}$$

Since s is multiplied by 2.50, divide both sides by 2.50. The symbol does not change.

$$s \le 6.4$$

Ryan can buy only a whole number of smoothies.

Ryan can buy 0, 1, 2, 3, 4, 5, or 6 smoothies.

CHECK IT OUT! **3.** A pitcher holds 128 ounces of juice. What are the possible numbers of 10-ounce servings that one pitcher can fill?

MCC.MP.8 **MATHEMATICAL PRACTICES**

THINK AND DISCUSS

1. Compare the Multiplication and Division Properties of Inequality and the Multiplication and Division Properties of Equality.

 2. GET ORGANIZED Copy and complete the graphic organizer. In each cell, write and solve an inequality.

Solving Inequalities by Using Multiplication and Division		
	By a Positive Number	**By a Negative Number**
Divide		
Multiply		

100 *Module 4 Solving Inequalities in One Variable*

GUIDED PRACTICE

Solve each inequality and graph the solutions.

SEE EXAMPLE 1

1. $3b > 27$ **2.** $-40 \geq 8b$ **3.** $\dfrac{d}{3} > 6$ **4.** $24d \leq 6$

5. $1.1m \leq 1.21$ **6.** $\dfrac{2}{3}k > 6$ **7.** $9s > -18$ **8.** $\dfrac{4}{5} \geq \dfrac{r}{2}$

SEE EXAMPLE 2

9. $-2x < -10$ **10.** $\dfrac{b}{-2} \geq 8$ **11.** $-3.5n < 1.4$ **12.** $4 > -8g$

13. $\dfrac{d}{-6} < \dfrac{1}{2}$ **14.** $-10h \geq -6$ **15.** $12 > \dfrac{t}{-6}$ **16.** $-\dfrac{1}{2}m \geq -7$

SEE EXAMPLE 3

17. Travel Tom saved $550 to go on a school trip. The cost for a hotel room, including tax, is $80 per night. What are the possible numbers of nights Tom can stay at the hotel?

PRACTICE AND PROBLEM SOLVING

Independent Practice

For Exercises	See Example
18–29	1
30–41	2
42	3

my.hrw.com

Online Extra Practice

Solve each inequality and graph the solutions.

18. $10 < 2t$ **19.** $\dfrac{1}{3}j \leq 4$ **20.** $-80 < 8c$ **21.** $21 > 3d$

22. $\dfrac{w}{4} \geq -2$ **23.** $\dfrac{h}{4} \leq \dfrac{2}{7}$ **24.** $6y < 4.2$ **25.** $12c \leq -144$

26. $\dfrac{4}{5}x \geq \dfrac{2}{5}$ **27.** $6b \geq \dfrac{3}{5}$ **28.** $-25 > 10p$ **29.** $\dfrac{b}{8} \leq -2$

30. $-9a > 81$ **31.** $\dfrac{1}{2} < \dfrac{r}{-3}$ **32.** $-6p > 0.6$ **33.** $\dfrac{y}{-4} > -\dfrac{1}{2}$

34. $-\dfrac{1}{6}f < 5$ **35.** $-2.25t < -9$ **36.** $24 \leq -10w$ **37.** $-11z > 121$

38. $\dfrac{3}{5} < \dfrac{f}{-5}$ **39.** $-k \geq 7$ **40.** $-2.2b < -7.7$ **41.** $16 \geq -\dfrac{4}{3}p$

42. Camping The rope Roz brought with her camping gear is 54 inches long. Roz needs to cut shorter pieces of rope that are each 18 inches long. What are the possible number of pieces Roz can cut?

Solve each inequality and graph the solutions.

43. $-8x < 24$ **44.** $3t \leq 24$ **45.** $\dfrac{1}{4}x < 5$ **46.** $\dfrac{4}{5}p \geq -24$

47. $54 \leq -9p$ **48.** $3t > -\dfrac{1}{2}$ **49.** $-\dfrac{3}{4}b > -\dfrac{3}{2}$ **50.** $216 > 3.6r$

Write an inequality for each statement. Solve the inequality and graph the solutions.

51. The product of a number and 7 is not less than 21.

52. The quotient of h and -6 is at least 5.

53. The product of $-\dfrac{4}{5}$ and b is at most -16.

54. Ten is no more than the quotient of t and 4.

H.O.T. **55. Write About It** Explain how you know whether to reverse the inequality symbol when solving an inequality.

56. Geometry The area of a rectangle is at most 21 square inches. The width of the rectangle is 3.5 inches. What are the possible measurements for the length of the rectangle?

Solve each inequality and match the solution to the correct graph.

57. $-0.5t \geq 1.5$

A.

$$\text{—|—|—|—|—|—|—|—|—•—|—|—→}$$
$$-5\ -4\ -3\ -2\ -1\quad 0\quad 1\quad 2\quad 3\quad 4\quad 5$$

58. $\dfrac{1}{9}t \leq -3$

B.

$$\text{←|—|—|—|—|—|—|—|—•—|—|—}$$
$$-5\ -4\ -3\ -2\ -1\quad 0\quad 1\quad 2\quad 3\quad 4\quad 5$$

59. $-13.5 \leq -4.5t$

C.

$$\text{←|—|—•—|—|—|—|—|—|—|—|—→}$$
$$-5\ -4\ -3\ -2\ -1\quad 0\quad 1\quad 2\quad 3\quad 4\quad 5$$

60. $\dfrac{t}{-6} \leq -\dfrac{1}{2}$

D.

$$\text{←|—|—|—•—|—|—|—|—→}$$
$$-45\ -36\ -27\ -18\ -9\quad 0\quad 9$$

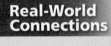
61. **Animals** A wildlife shelter is home to birds, mammals, and reptiles. If cat chow is sold in 20 lb bags, what is the least number of bags of cat chow needed for one year at this shelter?

Food Consumed at a Wildlife Shelter per Week	
Type of Food	**Amount of Food (lb)**
Grapes	4
Mixed seed	10
Peanuts	5
Cat chow	10
Kitten chow	5

62. **Education** In order to earn an A in a college math class, a student must score no less than 90% of all possible points. One semester, a student with 567 points earned an A in the class. Write an inequality to show the numbers of points possible.

H.O.T. **63.** **Critical Thinking** Explain why you cannot solve an inequality by multiplying both sides by zero.

H.O.T. **64.** **///ERROR ANALYSIS///** Two students have different answers for a homework problem. Which answer is incorrect? Explain the error.

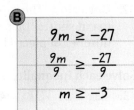

A

$$9m \geq -27$$
$$\dfrac{9m}{9} \geq \dfrac{-27}{9}$$
$$m \leq -3$$

B

$$9m \geq -27$$
$$\dfrac{9m}{9} \geq \dfrac{-27}{9}$$
$$m \geq -3$$

65. Jan has a budget of $800 for catering. The catering company charges $12.50 per guest. Write and solve an inequality to show the numbers of guests Jan can invite.

Real-World Connections

66. a. The Swimming Club can spend a total of $250 for hotel rooms for its spring trip. One hotel costs $75 per night. Write an inequality to find the number of rooms the club can reserve at this hotel. Let n be the number of rooms.

b. Solve the inequality you wrote in part **a.** Graph the solutions on a number line. Make sure your answer is reasonable.

c. Another hotel offers a rate of $65 per night. Does this allow the club to reserve more rooms? Explain your reasoning.

TEST PREP

67. Which inequality does NOT have the same solutions as $-\frac{2}{3}y > 4$?

Ⓐ $12 < -2y$

Ⓒ $-\frac{3}{4}y > \frac{9}{2}$

Ⓑ $\frac{y}{2} < -12$

Ⓓ $-3y > 18$

68. The solutions of which inequality are NOT represented by the following graph?

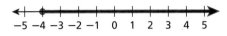

Ⓕ $\frac{x}{2} \geq -2$

Ⓗ $3x \geq -12$

Ⓖ $-5x \geq 20$

Ⓙ $-7x \leq 28$

69. Which inequality can be used to find the number of 39-cent stamps you can purchase for $4.00?

Ⓐ $0.39s \geq 4.00$

Ⓒ $\frac{s}{0.39} \leq 4.00$

Ⓑ $0.39s \leq 4.00$

Ⓓ $\frac{4.00}{0.39} \leq s$

70. Short Response Write three different inequalities that have the same solutions as $x > 4$. Show your work and explain each step.

CHALLENGE AND EXTEND

Solve each inequality.

71. $2\frac{1}{3} \leq -\frac{5}{6}g$

72. $\frac{2x}{3} < 8.25$

73. $2\frac{5}{8}m > \frac{7}{10}$

74. $3\frac{3}{5}f \geq 14\frac{2}{5}$

75. Estimation What is the greatest possible integer solution of the inequality $3.806x < 19.902$?

76. Critical Thinking The Transitive Property of Equality states that if $a = b$ and $b = c$, then $a = c$. Is there a Transitive Property of Inequality using the symbol <? Give an example to support your answer.

77. Critical Thinking The Symmetric Property of Equality states that if $a = b$, then $b = a$. Is there a Symmetric Property of Inequality? Give an example to support your answer.

FOCUS ON MATHEMATICAL PRACTICES

H.O.T. **78. Error Analysis** Marigold solves an inequality as shown.

$$\frac{4}{5}x \geq -20$$
$$\frac{5}{4}\left(\frac{4}{5}x\right) \geq \frac{5}{4}(-20)$$
$$x \leq -\frac{100}{4}$$
$$x \leq -25$$

What mistake did Marigold make? What is the correct answer?

H.O.T. **79. Make a Conjecture** The solution to the inequality $kx < 6$ is $x > -2$.

a. What can you say about the value of k just by looking at the inequality and its solution, without actually solving the problem?

b. Find another solution for x by dividing both sides of $kx < 6$ by k.

c. Use $x > -2$ and your solution from part b to make an equation, then solve for k. Does the solution support your conjecture from part a?

Ready to Go On?

my.hrw.com
Assessment and Intervention

☑ **4-1** **Graphing and Writing Inequalities**

Describe the solutions of each inequality in words.

1. $-2 < r$ **2.** $t - 1 \le 7$ **3.** $2s \ge 6$ **4.** $4 > 5 - x$

Graph each inequality.

5. $x > -2$ **6.** $m \le 1\frac{1}{2}$ **7.** $g < \sqrt{8 + 1}$ **8.** $h \ge 2^3$

Write the inequality shown by each graph.

9.
```
←|——+——●——+——+——+——+——+——+——+——→
 -5 -4 -3 -2 -1  0  1  2  3  4  5
```

10.
```
←+——+——+——+——+——+——+——+——○——+——→
 -4 -3 -2 -1  0  1  2  3  4  5  6
```

11.
```
           -1.5
←+——+——+——+●——+——+——+——+——+——→
 -6 -5 -4 -3 -2 -1  0  1  2  3  4
```

Write an inequality for each situation and graph the solutions.

12. You must purchase at least 5 tickets to receive a discount.

13. Children under 13 are not admitted to certain movies without an adult.

14. A cell phone plan allows up to 250 free minutes per month.

☑ **4-2** **Solving Inequalities by Adding or Subtracting**

Solve each inequality and graph the solutions.

15. $k + 5 \le 7$ **16.** $4 > p - 3$ **17.** $r - 8 \ge -12$ **18.** $-3 + p < -6$

19. Allie must sell at least 50 gift baskets for the band fund-raiser. She already sold 36 baskets. Write and solve an inequality to determine how many more baskets Allie must sell for the fund-raiser.

20. Dante has at most $12 to spend on entertainment each week. So far this week, he spent $7.50. Write and solve an inequality to determine how much money Dante can spend on entertainment the rest of the week.

☑ **4-3** **Solving Inequalities by Multiplying or Dividing**

Solve each inequality and graph the solutions.

21. $-4x < 8$ **22.** $\frac{d}{3} \ge -3$ **23.** $\frac{3}{4}t \le 12$ **24.** $8 > -16c$

25. A spool of ribbon is 80 inches long. Riley needs to cut strips of ribbon that are 14 inches long. What are the possible numbers of strips that Riley can cut?

PARCC Assessment Readiness

Selected Response

1. Graph the inequality $m < -3.4$.

Ⓐ
```
←+—●—+—+—+—+—+—+—+—+—+→
 −5 −4 −3 −2 −1  0  1  2  3  4  5
```

Ⓑ
```
←+—●—+—+—+—+—+—+—+—+—+→
 −5 −4 −3 −2 −1  0  1  2  3  4  5
```

Ⓒ
```
←+—○—+—+—+—+—+—+—+—+—+→
 −5 −4 −3 −2 −1  0  1  2  3  4  5
```

Ⓓ
```
←+—+○—+—+—+—+—+—+—+—+→
 −5 −4 −3 −2 −1  0  1  2  3  4  5
```

2. Describe the solutions of $6 + y < 10$ in words.

Ⓕ The value of y is a number less than or equal to 3.

Ⓖ The value of y is a number less than 4.

Ⓗ The value of y is a number equal to 3.

Ⓙ The value of y is a number greater than 4.

3. To join the school swim team, swimmers must be able to swim at least 800 yards without stopping. Let n represent the number of yards a swimmer can swim without stopping. Write an inequality describing which values of n will result in a swimmer making the team.

Ⓐ $n \leq 800$ 　　Ⓒ $n > 800$

Ⓑ $n \geq 800$ 　　Ⓓ $n < 800$

4. Solve the inequality $n + 6 < -1.5$ and graph the solutions.

Ⓕ $n < 4.5$
```
←+—+—+—+—+—+—○—+—+—+→
−10 −8 −6 −4 −2  0  2  4  6  8  10
```

Ⓖ $n < -7.5$
```
←+—○—+—+—+—+—+—+—+—+→
−10 −8 −6 −4 −2  0  2  4  6  8  10
```

Ⓗ $n < -7.5$
```
←+—●—+—+—+—+—+—+—+—+→
−10 −8 −6 −4 −2  0  2  4  6  8  10
```

Ⓙ $n < 4.5$
```
←+—+—+—+—+—+—○—+—+—+→
−10 −8 −6 −4 −2  0  2  4  6  8  10
```

5. Solve the inequality $\frac{z}{-4} \leq 2$.

Ⓐ $z \geq -8$ 　　Ⓒ $z \leq 8$

Ⓑ $z \leq -8$ 　　Ⓓ $z \geq 8$

6. Carlotta subscribes to the HotBurn music service. She can download no more than 11 song files per week. Carlotta has already downloaded 8 song files this week. Write, solve, and graph an inequality to show how many more songs Carlotta can download.

Ⓕ $s \leq 3$
```
←●—●—●—●—+—+—+—+—+—+—+→
 0  1  2  3  4  5  6  7  8  9  10
```

Ⓖ $s > 3$
```
←+—+—+—+—●—●—●—●—●—●—●→
 0  1  2  3  4  5  6  7  8  9 10 11
```

Ⓗ $s \geq 3$
```
←+—+—+—●———————————————→
 0  1  2  3  4  5  6  7  8  9  10
```

Ⓙ $s < 3$
```
←————————○—+—+—+—+—+—+→
 0  1  2  3  4  5  6  7  8  9  10
```

7. Marco's Drama class is performing a play. He wants to buy as many tickets as he can afford. If tickets cost $2.50 each and he has $14.75 to spend, how many tickets can he buy?

Ⓐ 4 tickets 　　Ⓒ 6 tickets

Ⓑ 0 tickets 　　Ⓓ 5 tickets

Mini-Task

8. Glen raised $275 for his softball team's fundraiser. He wants to raise at least $715.

　a. Write and solve an inequality to determine how much more money Glen must raise to reach his goal. Let d represent the amount of money in dollars Glen must raise to reach his goal.

　b. If Glen raises $50 per week, what is the minimum number of weeks it will take him to reach his goal?

5 Solving Multi-Step Inequalities

COMMON
CORE GPS

Contents

MATHEMATICAL PRACTICES   The Common Core Georgia Performance Standards for Mathematical Practice describe varieties of expertise that all students should seek to develop. Opportunities to develop these practices are integrated throughout this program.

1 Make sense of problems and persevere in solving them.

2 Reason abstractly and quantitatively.

3 Construct viable arguments and critique the reasoning of others.

4 Model with mathematics.

5 Use appropriate tools strategically.

6 Attend to precision.

7 Look for and make use of structure.

8 Look for and express regularity in repeated reasoning.

Unpacking the Standards

Understanding the standards and the vocabulary terms in the standards will help you know exactly what you are expected to learn in this chapter.

 MCC9-12.A.CED.1

Create … inequalities … in one variable and use them to solve problems.

What It Means For You

You can write an inequality to represent a real-world problem and then solve the inequality to find the possible answers.

EXAMPLE

Amy uses $\frac{3}{4}$ cup of vanilla yogurt to make a smoothie. What are the possible whole numbers of smoothies that Amy can make using 1 quart of vanilla yogurt?

Let s represent the number of smoothies Amy can make.

cups per smoothie	•	number of smoothies	≤	cups per quart
$\frac{3}{4}$	•	s	≤	4
		$\frac{3}{4}s$	≤	4
		s	≤	$\frac{16}{3}$

Amy can make 0, 1, 2, 3, 4, or 5 smoothies.

 MCC9-12.A.REI.3

Solve linear … inequalities in one variable, …

Key Vocabulary

linear inequality in one variable
(desigualdad lineal en una variable)
An inequality that can be written in one of the following forms: $ax < b$, $ax > b$, $ax \le b$, $ax \ge b$, or $ax \ne b$, where a and b are constants and $a \ne 0$.

What It Means For You

Solving inequalities lets you answer questions where a range of solutions is possible.

EXAMPLE

Solve the inequality for t to find what grades on the final exam will give Cleo a course grade of "A".

$705 + 2t \ge 895$ *Cleo has 705 points and needs at least 895.*

$2t \ge 190$ *Subtract 705 from both sides.*

$t \ge 95$ *Divide both sides by 2.*

Cleo needs to earn a 95 or above on the final exam.

5-1 Solving Two-Step and Multi-Step Inequalities

Essential Question: How can you solve inequalities that involve more than one operation?

Objective
Solve inequalities that contain more than one operation.

Who uses this?
Contestants at a county fair can solve an inequality to find how many pounds a prize-winning pumpkin must weigh. (See Example 3.)

At the county fair, contestants can enter contests that judge animals, recipes, crops, art projects, and more. Sometimes an average score or average weight is used to determine the winner of the blue ribbon. A contestant can use a multi-step inequality to determine what score or weight is needed in order to win.

Inequalities that contain more than one operation require more than one step to solve. Use inverse operations to undo the operations in the inequality one at a time.

COMMON CORE GPS
EXAMPLE **1**
MCC9-12.A.REI.3

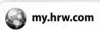

Online Video Tutor

Solving Multi-Step Inequalities

Solve each inequality and graph the solutions.

A $160 + 4f \le 500$

$$160 + 4f \le 500$$
$$\underline{-160 \qquad\quad -160}$$
$$4f \le 340$$
$$\frac{4f}{4} \le \frac{340}{4}$$
$$f \le 85$$

Since 160 is added to 4f, subtract 160 from both sides to undo the addition.

Since f is multiplied by 4, divide both sides by 4 to undo the multiplication.

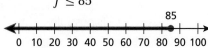

0 10 20 30 40 50 60 70 80 90 100

B $7 - 2t \le 21$

$$7 - 2t \le 21$$
$$\underline{-7 \qquad\quad -7}$$
$$-2t \le 14$$
$$\frac{-2t}{-2} \ge \frac{14}{-2}$$
$$t \ge -7$$

Since 7 is added to −2t, subtract 7 from both sides to undo the addition.

Since t is multiplied by −2, divide both sides by −2 to undo the multiplication. Change ≤ to ≥.

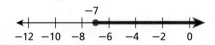

−12 −10 −8 −6 −4 −2 0

CHECK IT OUT! **Solve each inequality and graph the solutions.**

1a. $-12 \ge 3x + 6$ **1b.** $\dfrac{x+5}{-2} > 3$ **1c.** $\dfrac{1-2n}{3} \ge 7$

To solve more complicated inequalities, you may first need to simplify the expressions on one or both sides by using the order of operations, combining like terms, or using the Distributive Property.

COMMON CORE GPS   **EXAMPLE**   2   MCC9-12.A.REI.3

Simplifying Before Solving Inequalities

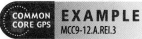 my.hrw.com

Online Video Tutor

Solve each inequality and graph the solutions.

A $-4 + (-8) < -5c - 2$

$-12 < -5c - 2$ *Combine like terms. Since 2 is subtracted from $-5c$,*

$\underline{+2 \qquad\quad +2}$ *add 2 to both sides to undo the subtraction.*

$-10 < -5c$

$\dfrac{-10}{-5} > \dfrac{-5c}{-5}$ *Since c is multiplied by -5, divide both sides by -5*

$2 > c \,(\text{or } c < 2)$ *to undo the multiplication. Change $<$ to $>$.*

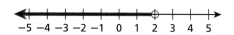

B $-3(3 - x) < 4^2$

$-3(3 - x) < 4^2$ *Distribute -3 on the left side.*

$-3(3) - (-3)x < 4^2$

$-9 + 3x < 4^2$

$-9 + 3x < 16$ *Simplify the right side.*

$-9 + 3x < 16$ *Since -9 is added to $3x$, add 9 to both sides*

$\underline{+9 \qquad\quad +9}$ *to undo the addition.*

$3x < 25$ *Since x is multiplied by 3, divide both sides by*

$\dfrac{3x}{3} < \dfrac{25}{3}$ *3 to undo the multiplication.*

$x < 8\dfrac{1}{3}$

C $\dfrac{4}{5}x + \dfrac{1}{2} > \dfrac{3}{5}$

$10\left(\dfrac{4}{5}x + \dfrac{1}{2}\right) > 10\left(\dfrac{3}{5}\right)$ *Multiply both sides by 10, the LCD of the fractions.*

$10\left(\dfrac{4}{5}x\right) + 10\left(\dfrac{1}{2}\right) > 10\left(\dfrac{3}{5}\right)$ *Distribute 10 on the left side.*

$8x + 5 > 6$ *Since 5 is added to $8x$, subtract 5 from*

$\underline{\quad -5 \quad -5}$ *both sides to undo the addition.*

$8x > 1$

$\dfrac{8x}{8} > \dfrac{1}{8}$ *Since x is multiplied by 8, divide both sides by 8 to undo the multiplication.*

$x > \dfrac{1}{8}$

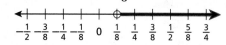

 Solve each inequality and graph the solutions.

2a. $2m + 5 > 5^2$ **2b.** $3 + 2(x + 4) > 3$ **2c.** $\dfrac{5}{8} < \dfrac{3}{8}x - \dfrac{1}{4}$

Gardening Application

my.hrw.com

Online Video Tutor

To win the blue ribbon for the Heaviest Pumpkin Crop at the county fair, the average weight of John's two pumpkins must be greater than 819 lb. One of his pumpkins weighs 887 lb. What is the least number of pounds the second pumpkin could weigh in order for John to win the blue ribbon?

Let p represent the weight of the second pumpkin. The average weight of the pumpkins is the sum of each weight divided by 2.

(887	plus	p)	divided by	2	must be greater than	819.
(887	+	p)	÷	2	>	819

$$\frac{887 + p}{2} > 819$$

Since 887 + p is divided by 2, multiply both sides by 2 to undo the division.

$$2\left(\frac{887 + p}{2}\right) > 2(819)$$

$$887 + p > 1638$$

Since 887 is added to p, subtract 887 from both sides to undo the addition.

$$\underline{-887 \qquad -887}$$
$$p > 751$$

The second pumpkin must weigh more than 751 pounds.

Check   Check the endpoint, 751.   Check a number greater than 751.

$\frac{887 + p}{2} = 819$			$\frac{887 + p}{2} > 819$		
$\frac{887 + 751}{2}$	819		$\frac{887 + 755}{2}$	>	819
$\frac{1638}{2}$	819		$\frac{1642}{2}$	>	819
819	819 ✓		821	>	819 ✓

3. The average of Jim's two test scores must be at least 90 to make an A in the class. Jim got a 95 on his first test. What scores can Jim get on his second test to make an A in the class?

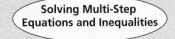

MCC.MP.1, MCC.MP.7   MATHEMATICAL PRACTICES

THINK AND DISCUSS

1. The inequality $v \geq 25$ states that 25 is the ___?___. (*value of v, minimum value of v,* or *maximum value of v*)

2. Describe two sets of steps for solving the inequality $\frac{x+5}{3} > 7$.

3. GET ORGANIZED Copy and complete the graphic organizer.

Solving Multi-Step Equations and Inequalities

How are they alike?   How are they different?

GUIDED PRACTICE

Solve each inequality and graph the solutions.

SEE EXAMPLE 1

1. $2m + 1 > 13$ **2.** $2d + 21 \leq 11$ **3.** $6 \leq -2x + 2$ **4.** $4c - 7 > 5$

5. $\dfrac{4 + x}{3} > -4$ **6.** $1 < 0.2x - 0.7$ **7.** $\dfrac{3 - 2x}{3} \leq 7$ **8.** $2x + 5 \geq 2$

SEE EXAMPLE 2

9. $4(x + 2) > 6$ **10.** $\dfrac{1}{4}x + \dfrac{2}{3} < \dfrac{3}{4}$ **11.** $4 - x + 6^2 \geq 21$

12. $4 - x > 3(4 - 2)$ **13.** $0.2(x - 10) > -1.8$ **14.** $3(j + 41) \leq 35$

SEE EXAMPLE 3

15. Business A sales representative is given a choice of two paycheck plans. One choice includes a monthly base pay of $300 plus 10% commission on his sales. The second choice is a monthly salary of $1200. For what amount of sales would the representative make more money with the first plan?

PRACTICE AND PROBLEM SOLVING

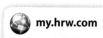

For Exercises	See Example
16–27	1
28–36	2
37	3

my.hrw.com

Online Extra Practice

Solve each inequality and graph the solutions.

16. $4r - 9 > 7$ **17.** $3 \leq 5 - 2x$ **18.** $\dfrac{w + 3}{2} > 6$ **19.** $11w + 99 < 77$

20. $9 \geq \dfrac{1}{2}v + 3$ **21.** $-4x - 8 > 16$ **22.** $8 - \dfrac{2}{3}z \leq 2$ **23.** $f + 2\dfrac{1}{2} < -2$

24. $\dfrac{3n - 8}{5} \geq 2$ **25.** $-5 > -5 - 3w$ **26.** $10 > \dfrac{5 - 3p}{2}$ **27.** $2v + 1 > 2\dfrac{1}{3}$

28. $4(x + 3) > -24$ **29.** $4 > x - 3(x + 2)$ **30.** $-18 \geq 33 - 3h$

31. $-2 > 7x - 2(x - 4)$ **32.** $9 - (9)^2 > 10x - x$ **33.** $2a - (-3)^2 \geq 13$

34. $6 - \dfrac{x}{3} + 1 > \dfrac{2}{3}$ **35.** $12(x - 3) + 2x > 6$ **36.** $15 \geq 19 + 2(q - 18)$

37. Communications One cell phone company offers a plan that costs $29.99 and includes unlimited night and weekend minutes. Another company offers a plan that costs $19.99 and charges $0.35 per minute during nights and weekends. For what numbers of night and weekend minutes does the second company's plan cost more than the first company's plan?

Solve each inequality and graph the solutions.

38. $-12 > -4x - 8$ **39.** $5x + 4 \leq 14$ **40.** $\dfrac{2}{3}x - 5 > 7$

41. $x - 3x > 2 - 10$ **42.** $5 - x - 2 > 3$ **43.** $3 < 2x - 5(x + 3)$

44. $\dfrac{1}{6} - \dfrac{2}{3}m \geq \dfrac{1}{4}$ **45.** $4 - (r - 2) > 3 - 5$ **46.** $0.3 - 0.5n + 1 \geq 0.4$

47. $6^2 > 4(x + 2)$ **48.** $-4 - 2n + 4n > 7 - 2^2$ **49.** $\dfrac{1}{4}(p - 10) \geq 6 - 4$

50. Use the inequality $-4t - 8 \leq 12$ to fill in the missing numbers.

    a. $t \geq \blacksquare$ **b.** $t + 4 \geq \blacksquare$ **c.** $t - \blacksquare \geq 0$

    d. $t + 10 \geq \blacksquare$ **e.** $3t \geq \blacksquare$ **f.** $\dfrac{t}{\blacksquare} \geq -5$

Write an inequality for each statement. Solve the inequality and graph the solutions.

51. One-half of a number, increased by 9, is less than 33.

52. Six is less than or equal to the sum of 4 and $-2x$.

53. The product of 4 and the sum of a number and 12 is at most 16.

54. The sum of half a number and two-thirds of the number is less than 14.

Solve each inequality and match the solution to the correct graph.

55. $4x - 9 \geq 7$

A.

56. $-6 \geq 3(x - 2)$

B.

57. $-2x - 6 \geq -4 + 2$

C.

58. $\frac{1}{2} - \frac{1}{3}x \leq \left(\frac{2}{3} + \frac{1}{3}\right)^2$

D.

59. Entertainment A digital video recorder (DVR) records television shows on an internal hard drive. To use a DVR, you need a subscription with a DVR service company. Two companies advertise their charges for a DVR machine and subscription service.

For what numbers of months will a consumer pay less for the machine and subscription at Easy Electronics than at Cable Solutions?

60. Geometry The area of the triangle shown is less than 55 square inches.

a. Write an inequality that can be used to find x.

b. Solve the inequality you wrote in part **a.**

c. What is the maximum height of the triangle?

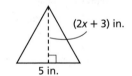

Real-World Connections

61. a. A band wants to create a CD of their last concert. They received a donation of $500 to cover the cost. The total cost is $350 plus $3 per CD. Complete the table to find a relationship between the number of CDs and the total cost.

Number	Process	Cost
1	350 + 3	353
2	■	■
3	■	■
10	■	■
n	■	

b. Write an equation for the cost c of the CDs based on the number of CDs n.

c. Write an inequality that can be used to determine how many CDs can be made with the $500 donation. Solve the inequality and determine how many CDs the band can have made from the $500 donation.

H.O.T. 62. Critical Thinking What is the least whole number that is a solution of $4r - 4.9 > 14.95$?

H.O.T. 63. Write About It Describe two sets of steps to solve $2(x + 3) > 10$.

64. What are the solutions of $3y > 2x + 4$ when $y = 6$?

   Ⓐ $7 > x$ Ⓑ $x > 7$ Ⓒ $x > 11$ Ⓓ $11 > x$

65. Cecilia has $30 to spend at a carnival. Admission costs $5.00, lunch will cost $6.00, and each ride ticket costs $1.25. Which inequality represents the number of ride tickets x that Cecilia can buy?

   Ⓕ $30 - (5 - 6) + 1.25x \le 30$ Ⓗ $30 - (5 + 6) \le 1.25x$

   Ⓖ $5 + 6 + 1.25x \le 30$ Ⓙ $30 + 1.25x \le 5 + 6$

66. Which statement is modeled by $2p + 5 < 11$?

   Ⓐ The sum of 5 and 2 times p is at least 11.

   Ⓑ Five added to the product of 2 and p is less than 11.

   Ⓒ Two times p plus 5 is at most 11.

   Ⓓ The product of 2 and p added to 5 is 11.

67. Gridded Response A basketball team scored 8 points more in its second game than in its first. In its third game, the team scored 42 points. The total number of points scored in the three games was more than 150. What is the least number of points the team might have scored in its *second* game?

Solve each inequality and graph the solutions.

68. $3(x + 2) - 6x + 6 \le 0$ **69.** $-18 > -(2x + 9) - 4 + x$ **70.** $\dfrac{2 + x}{2} - (x - 1) > 1$

Write an inequality for each statement. Graph the solutions.

71. x is a positive number.   **72.** x is a negative number.

73. x is a nonnegative number.   **74.** x is not a positive number.

75. x times negative 3 is positive.   **76.** The opposite of x is greater than 2.

FOCUS ON MATHEMATICAL PRACTICES

H.O.T. 77. Modeling Mario wants to spend no more than $85 per month for texting. He is considering a plan that provides him with 200 free text messages for $40 per month, plus $0.10 for each additional text sent or received.

   a. Complete the table to show how much Mario would pay for each number of text messages sent or received.

Number of messages	200	400	600	800	1000
Cost in dollars	▪	▪	▪	▪	▪

   b. Based on the table, write and solve an inequality that represents the maximum number of texts that Mario can send or receive under this plan.

5-2 Solving Inequalities with Variables on Both Sides

? Essential Question: How can you solve inequalities that have the variable on both sides?

Objective
Solve inequalities that contain variable terms on both sides.

Who uses this?
Business owners can use inequalities to find the most cost-efficient services. (See Example 2.)

Some inequalities have variable terms on both sides of the inequality symbol. You can solve these inequalities like you solved equations with variables on both sides.

Use the properties of inequality to "collect" all the variable terms on one side and all the constant terms on the other side.

COMMON CORE GPS
EXAMPLE **1**
MCC9-12.A.REI.3

my.hrw.com

Online Video Tutor

Solving Inequalities with Variables on Both Sides

Solve each inequality and graph the solutions.

A $x < 3x + 8$

$$
\begin{array}{rl}
x < & 3x + 8 \\
\underline{-x \quad -x} & \\
0 < & 2x + 8 \\
\underline{-8 \quad\quad -8} & \\
-8 < & 2x
\end{array}
$$

To collect the variable terms on one side, subtract x from both sides.

Since 8 is added to 2x, subtract 8 from both sides to undo the addition.

$$\dfrac{-8}{2} < \dfrac{2x}{2}$$

Since x is multiplied by 2, divide both sides by 2 to undo the multiplication.

$-4 < x$ (or $x > -4$)

-5 -4 -3 -2 -1 0 1 2 3 4 5

B $6x - 1 \le 3.5x + 4$

$$
\begin{array}{rl}
6x - 1 \le & 3.5x + 4 \\
\underline{-6x \quad\quad -6x} & \\
-1 \le & -2.5x + 4 \\
\underline{-4 \quad\quad\quad -4} & \\
-5 \le & -2.5x
\end{array}
$$

Subtract 6x from both sides.

Since 4 is added to −2.5x, subtract 4 from both sides to undo the addition.

$$\dfrac{-5}{-2.5} \ge \dfrac{-2.5x}{-2.5}$$

$2 \ge x$

Since x is multiplied by −2.5, divide both sides by −2.5 to undo the multiplication. Reverse the inequality symbol.

Helpful Hint

When you divide by a negative number, remember to reverse the inequality symbol.

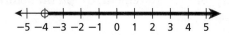

-5 -4 -3 -2 -1 0 1 2 3 4 5

CHECK IT OUT!

Solve each inequality and graph the solutions.

1a. $4x \ge 7x + 6$

1b. $5t + 1 < -2t - 6$

© Ariel Skelley/CORBIS

Business Application

The *Daily Info* charges a fee of $650 plus $80 per week to run an ad. The *People's Paper* charges $145 per week. For how many weeks will the total cost at *Daily Info* be less expensive than the cost at *People's Paper*?

Let w be the number of weeks the ad runs in the paper.

Daily Info fee	plus	$80 per week	times	number of weeks	is less expensive than	*People's Paper* charge per week	times	number of weeks.
$650	+	$80	·	w	<	$145	·	w

$$650 + 80w < 145w$$

$$\underline{\quad -80w \qquad -80w \quad}$$ *Subtract 80w from both sides.*

$$650 \quad < \quad 65w$$ *Since w is multiplied by 65, divide both sides by 65 to undo the multiplication.*

$$\frac{650}{65} < \frac{65w}{65}$$

$$10 < w$$

The total cost at *Daily Info* is less than the cost at *People's Paper* if the ad runs for more than 10 weeks.

 CHECK IT OUT!

2. A-Plus Advertising charges a fee of $24 plus $0.10 per flyer to print and deliver flyers. Print and More charges $0.25 per flyer. For how many flyers is the cost at A-Plus Advertising less than the cost at Print and More?

You may need to simplify one or both sides of an inequality before solving it. Look for like terms to combine and places to use Distributive Property.

Simplifying Each Side Before Solving

Solve each inequality and graph the solutions.

A $6(1 - x) < 3x$

$$6(1 - x) < 3x$$ *Distribute 6 on the left side of the inequality.*

$$6(1) - 6(x) < 3x$$

$$6 - 6x < 3x$$ *Add 6x to both sides so that the coefficient of x is positive.*

$$\underline{\quad +6x \qquad +6x \quad}$$

$$6 \quad < \quad 9x$$

$$\frac{6}{9} < \frac{9x}{9}$$ *Since x is multiplied by 9, divide both sides by 9 to undo the multiplication.*

$$\frac{2}{3} < x$$

```
 ←——+——+——⊕——+——+——+——+——+——+——→
   -⅓   0   ⅓   ⅔   1  1⅓  1⅔   2  2⅓  2⅔   3
```

Solve each inequality and graph the solutions.

B $1.6x \leq -0.2x + 0.9$

$$
\begin{array}{ll}
1.6x \leq -0.2x + 0.9 & \\
\underline{+\ 0.2x \qquad +\ 0.2x} & \text{Since } -0.2x \text{ is added to 0.9, subtract } -0.2x \text{ from} \\
1.8x \leq \qquad\quad 0.9 & \text{both sides. Subtracting } -0.2x \text{ is the same as} \\
& \text{adding } 0.2x. \\
\dfrac{1.8x}{1.8} \leq \dfrac{0.9}{1.8} & \text{Since } x \text{ is multiplied by 1.8, divide both sides by 1.8} \\
& \text{to undo the multiplication.} \\
x \leq \dfrac{1}{2} &
\end{array}
$$

 **Solve each inequality and graph the solutions. Check your answer.**

3a. $5(2 - r) \geq 3(r - 2)$ **3b.** $0.5x - 0.3 + 1.9x < 0.3x + 6$

Some inequalities are true no matter what value is substituted for the variable. For these inequalities, all real numbers are solutions.

Some inequalities are false no matter what value is substituted for the variable. These inequalities have no solutions.

If both sides of an inequality are fully simplified and the same variable term appears on both sides, then the inequality has all real numbers as solutions or it has no solutions. Look at the other terms in the inequality to decide which is the case.

EXAMPLE **4**

All Real Numbers as Solutions or No Solutions

Solve each inequality.

A $x + 5 \geq x + 3$

$x + 5 \geq x + 3$

The same variable term (x) appears on both sides. Look at the other terms.

For any number x, adding 5 will always result in a greater number than adding 3.

All values of x make the inequality true.
All real numbers are solutions.

B $2(x + 3) < 5 + 2x$

$2x + 6 < 5 + 2x$ *Distribute 2 on the left side.*

The same variable term ($2x$) appears on both sides. Look at the other terms.

For any number $2x$, adding 6 will never result in a lesser number than adding 5.

No values of x make the inequality true.
There are no solutions.

 Solve each inequality.

4a. $4(y - 1) \geq 4y + 2$ **4b.** $x - 2 < x + 1$

MATHEMATICAL PRACTICES

THINK AND DISCUSS

1. Explain how you would collect the variable terms to solve the inequality $5c - 4 > 8c + 2$.

Know it!
Note

2. GET ORGANIZED Copy and complete the graphic organizer. In each box, give an example of an inequality of the indicated type.

Solutions of Inequalities with Variables on Both Sides

| All real numbers | No solutions |

5-2 Exercises

my.hrw.com
Homework Help

GUIDED PRACTICE

SEE EXAMPLE 1 Solve each inequality and graph the solutions.

1. $2x > 4x - 6$

2. $7y + 1 \le y - 5$

3. $27x + 33 > 58x - 29$

4. $-3r < 10 - r$

5. $5c - 4 > 8c + 2$

6. $4.5x - 3.8 \ge 1.5x - 2.3$

SEE EXAMPLE 2 **7. School** The school band will sell pizzas to raise money for new uniforms. The supplier charges $100 plus $4 per pizza. If the band members sell the pizzas for $7 each, how many pizzas will they have to sell to make a profit?

SEE EXAMPLE 3 Solve each inequality and graph the solutions.

8. $5(4 + x) \le 3(2 + x)$

9. $-4(3 - p) > 5(p + 1)$

10. $2(6 - x) < 4x$

11. $4x > 3(7 - x)$

12. $\frac{1}{2}f + \frac{3}{4} \ge \frac{1}{4}f$

13. $-36.72 + 5.65t < 0.25t$

SEE EXAMPLE 4 Solve each inequality.

14. $2(x - 2) \le -2(1 - x)$

15. $4(y + 1) < 4y + 2$

16. $4v + 1 < 4v - 7$

17. $b - 4 \ge b - 6$

18. $3(x - 5) > 3x$

19. $2k + 7 \ge 2(k + 14)$

PRACTICE AND PROBLEM SOLVING

Solve each inequality and graph the solutions.

20. $3x \le 5x + 8$

21. $9y + 3 > 4y - 7$

22. $1.5x - 1.2 < 3.1x - 2.8$

23. $7 + 4b \ge 3b$

24. $7 - 5t < 4t - 2$

25. $2.8m - 5.2 > 0.8m + 4.8$

26. Geometry For what values of x is the area of the rectangle greater than the area of the triangle?

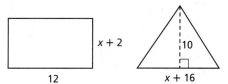

Solve each inequality and graph the solutions.

27. $4(2 - x) \leq 5(x - 2)$ **28.** $-3(n + 4) < 6(1 - n)$ **29.** $9(w + 2) \leq 12w$

30. $4.5 + 1.3t > 3.8t - 3$ **31.** $\frac{1}{2}r + \frac{2}{3} \geq \frac{1}{3}r$ **32.** $2(4 - n) < 3n - 7$

Solve each inequality.

33. $3(2 - x) < -3(x - 1)$ **34.** $7 - y > 5 - y$ **35.** $3(10 + z) \leq 3z + 36$

36. $-5(k - 1) \geq 5(2 - k)$ **37.** $4(x - 1) \leq 4x$ **38.** $3(v - 9) \geq 15 + 3v$

my.hrw.com

Online Extra Practice

Solve each inequality and graph the solutions.

39. $3t - 12 > 5t + 2$ **40.** $-5(y + 3) - 6 < y + 3$

41. $3x + 9 - 5x < x$ **42.** $18 + 9p > 12p - 31$

43. $2(x - 5) < -3x$ **44.** $-\frac{2}{5}x \leq \frac{4}{5} - \frac{3}{5}x$

45. $-2(x - 7) - 4 - x < 8x + 32$ **46.** $-3(2r - 4) \geq 2(5 - 3r)$

47. $-7x - 10 + 5x \geq 3(x + 4) + 8$ **48.** $-\frac{1}{3}(n + 8) + \frac{1}{3}n \leq 1 - n$

Recreation

The American Kitefliers Association has over 4000 members in 35 countries. Kitefliers participate in festivals, competitions, and kite-making workshops.

49. Recreation A red kite is 100 feet off the ground and is rising at 8 feet per second. A blue kite is 180 feet off the ground and is rising at 5 feet per second. How long will it take for the red kite to be higher than the blue kite? Round your answer to the nearest second.

50. Education The table shows the enrollment in Howard High School and Phillips High School for three school years.

School Enrollment			
	Year 1	Year 2	Year 3
Howard High School	1192	1188	1184
Phillips High School	921	941	961

 a. How much did the enrollment change each year at Howard?

 b. Use the enrollment in year 1 and your answer from part **a** to write an expression for the enrollment at Howard in any year x.

 c. How much did the enrollment change each year at Phillips?

 d. Use the enrollment in year 1 and your answer from part **c** to write an expression for the enrollment at Phillips in any year x.

 e. Assume that the pattern in the table continues. Use your expressions from parts **b** and **d** to write an inequality that can be solved to find the year in which the enrollment at Phillips High School will be greater than the enrollment at Howard High School. Solve your inequality and graph the solutions.

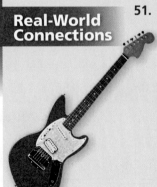

Real-World Connections

51. a. The school orchestra is creating a CD of their last concert. The total cost is $400 + 4.50 per CD. Write an expression for the cost of creating the CDs based on the number of CDs n.

 b. The orchestra plans to sell the CDs for $12. Write an expression for the amount the orchestra earns from the sale of n CDs.

 c. In order for the orchestra to make a profit, the amount they make selling the CDs must be greater than the cost of creating the CDs. Write an inequality that can be solved to find the number of CDs the orchestra must sell in order to make a profit. Solve your inequality.

(b), © Brand X Pictures; (cl), HMH

Write an inequality to represent each relationship. Solve your inequality.

52. Four more than twice a number is greater than two-thirds of the number.

53. Ten less than five times a number is less than six times the number decreased by eight.

54. The sum of a number and twenty is less than four times the number decreased by one.

55. Three-fourths of a number is greater than or equal to five less than the number.

56. Entertainment Use the table to determine how many movies you would have to rent for Video View to be less expensive than Movie Place.

	Membership Fee ($)	Cost per Rental ($)
Movie Place	None	2.99
Video View	19.99	1.99

57. Geometry In an acute triangle, all angles measure less than 90°. Also, the sum of the measures of any two angles is greater than the measure of the third angle. Can the measures of an acute triangle be x, $x - 1$, and $2x$? Explain.

H.O.T. 58. Write About It Compare the steps you would follow to solve an inequality to the steps you would follow to solve an equation.

H.O.T. 59. Critical Thinking How can you tell just by looking at the inequality $x > x + 1$ that it has no solutions?

H.O.T. 60. ///ERROR ANALYSIS/// Two students solved the inequality $5x < 3 - 4x$. Which is incorrect? Explain the error.

Ⓐ
$$5x < 3 - 4x$$
$$+ 4x \quad\quad + 4x$$
$$9x < 3$$
$$x < \frac{1}{3}$$

Ⓑ
$$5x < 3 - 4x$$
$$- 4x \quad\quad - 4x$$
$$x < 3$$

TEST PREP

61. If $a - b > a + b$, which statement is true?

Ⓐ The value of a is positive.   Ⓒ The value of a is negative.

Ⓑ The value of b is positive.   Ⓓ The value of b is negative.

62. If $-a < b$, which statement is always true?

Ⓕ $a < b$ Ⓖ $a > b$ Ⓗ $a < -b$ Ⓙ $a > -b$

63. Which is a solution of the inequality $7(2 - x) > 4(x - 2)$?

Ⓐ -2 Ⓑ 2 Ⓒ 4 Ⓓ 7

64. Which is the graph of $-5x < -2x - 6$?

Ⓕ ◄─┼─┼─┼─┼─┼─┼─⊕─┼─┼─┼─►
    −5 −4 −3 −2 −1 0 1 2 3 4 5

Ⓗ ◄─┼─┼─┼─┼─⊕─┼─┼─┼─┼─┼─┼─►
    −5 −4 −3 −2 −1 0 1 2 3 4 5

Ⓖ ◄─┼─┼─┼─⊕━━━━━━━━━►
    −5 −4 −3 −2 −1 0 1 2 3 4 5

Ⓙ ◄━━━━━━━━━⊕─┼─┼─►
    −5 −4 −3 −2 −1 0 1 2 3 4 5

65. Short Response Write a real-world situation that could be modeled by the inequality $7x + 4 > 4x + 13$. Explain how the inequality relates to your situation.

CHALLENGE AND EXTEND

Solve each inequality.

66. $2\frac{1}{2} + 2x \geq 5\frac{1}{2} + 2\frac{1}{2}x$

67. $1.6x - 20.7 > 6.3x - (-2.2x)$

68. $1.3x - 7.5x < 8.5x - 29.4$

69. $-4w + \dfrac{-8 - 37}{9} \leq \dfrac{75 - 3}{9} + 3w$

70. Replace the square and circle with numbers so that the inequality has all real numbers as solutions. $\square - 2x < \bigcirc - 2x$

71. Replace the square and circle with numbers so that the inequality has no solutions. $\square - 2x < \bigcirc - 2x$

H.O.T. 72. Critical Thinking Explain whether there are any numbers that can replace the square and circle so that the inequality has all real numbers as solutions. $\square + 2x < \bigcirc + x$

FOCUS ON MATHEMATICAL PRACTICES

H.O.T. 73. Analysis The table below shows a step-by-step solution to the inequality $2x + 5 > 7x - 35$. Fill in the remaining inequality symbols and steps.

Left Side	Symbol	Right Side	Step
$2x + 5$	$>$	$7x - 35$	None
$2x$		$7x - 40$	Subtract 5
$-5x$		-40	
x		8	

Career Path

Katie Flannigan
Culinary Arts program

Q: What math classes did you take in high school?

A: Algebra 1, Geometry, and Algebra 2

Q: What math classes have you taken since high school?

A: I have taken a basic accounting class and a business math class.

Q: How do you use math?

A: I use math to estimate how much food I need to buy. I also use math when adjusting recipe amounts to feed large groups of people.

Q: What are your future plans?

A: I plan to start my own catering business. The math classes I took will help me manage the financial aspects of my business.

Solving Compound Inequalities

Essential Question: How can you solve compound inequalities and graph their solutions?

Objectives
Solve compound inequalities in one variable.

Graph solution sets of compound inequalities in one variable.

Vocabulary
compound inequality
intersection
union

Who uses this?
A lifeguard can use compound inequalities to describe the safe pH levels in a swimming pool. (See Example 1.)

The inequalities you have seen so far are simple inequalities. When two simple inequalities are combined into one statement by the words AND or OR, the result is called a **compound inequality**.

Compound Inequalities

WORDS	ALGEBRA	GRAPH
All real numbers greater than 2 AND less than 6	$x > 2$ AND $x < 6$ $2 < x < 6$	0 2 4 6 8
All real numbers greater than or equal to 2 AND less than or equal to 6	$x \geq 2$ AND $x \leq 6$ $2 \leq x \leq 6$	0 2 4 6 8
All real numbers less than 2 OR greater than 6	$x < 2$ OR $x > 6$	0 2 4 6 8
All real numbers less than or equal to 2 OR greater than or equal to 6	$x \leq 2$ OR $x \geq 6$	0 2 4 6 8

COMMON CORE GPS
MCC9-12.A.CED.1

EXAMPLE 1

my.hrw.com

Online Video Tutor

Helpful Hint

The phrase "between 7.2 and 7.6 *inclusive*" means 7.2 and 7.6 are solutions. Use a solid circle for endpoints that are solutions.

Chemistry Application

A water analyst recommends that the pH level of swimming pool water be between 7.2 and 7.6 inclusive. Write a compound inequality to show the pH levels that are within the recommended range. Graph the solutions.

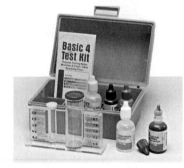

Let p be the pH level of swimming pool water.

7.2	is less than or equal to	pH level	is less than or equal to	7.6
7.2	$\leq$	p	$\leq$	7.6

$7.2 \leq p \leq 7.6$

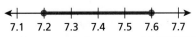
7.1 7.2 7.3 7.4 7.5 7.6 7.7

1. The free chlorine level in a pool should be between 1.0 and 3.0 parts per million inclusive. Write a compound inequality to show the levels that are within this range. Graph the solutions.

In this diagram, oval *A* represents some integer solutions of $x < 10$, and oval *B* represents some integer solutions of $x > 0$. The overlapping region represents numbers that belong in both ovals. Those numbers are solutions of *both $x < 10$ and $x > 0$.*

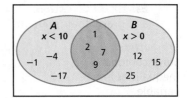

You can graph the solutions of a compound inequality involving AND by using the idea of an overlapping region. The overlapping region is called the **intersection** and shows the numbers that are solutions of both inequalities.

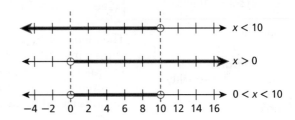

EXAMPLE 2

Solving Compound Inequalities Involving AND

Solve each compound inequality and graph the solutions.

A $4 \le x + 2 \le 8$

$4 \le x + 2$	AND	$x + 2 \le 8$	*Write the compound inequality using AND.*
$\underline{-2 \quad -2}$		$\underline{-2 \quad -2}$	*Solve each simple inequality.*
$2 \le x$	AND	$x \quad \le 6$	

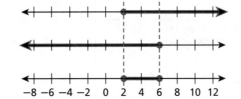

Graph $2 \le x$.

Graph $x \le 6$.

Graph the intersection by finding where the two graphs overlap.

Remember!

The statement $-5 \le 2x + 3 \le 9$ consists of two inequalities connected by AND. Example 2B shows a "shorthand" method for solving this type of inequality.

B $-5 \le 2x + 3 < 9$

$$-5 \le 2x + 3 < 9$$ *Since 3 is added to 2x, subtract 3 from each part of the inequality.*
$$\underline{-3 \qquad -3 \quad -3}$$
$$-8 \le 2x \qquad < 6$$

$$\frac{-8}{2} \le \frac{2x}{2} < \frac{6}{2}$$ *Since x is multiplied by 2, divide each part of the inequality by 2.*
$$-4 \le x < 3$$

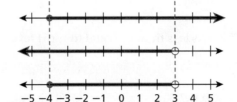

Graph $-4 \le x$.

Graph $x < 3$.

Graph the intersection by finding where the two graphs overlap.

Solve each compound inequality and graph the solutions.

2a. $-9 < x - 10 < -5$ **2b.** $-4 \le 3n + 5 < 11$

In this diagram, circle *A* represents some integer solutions of $x < 0$, and circle *B* represents some integer solutions of $x > 10$. The combined shaded regions represent numbers that are solutions of *either* $x < 0$ *or* $x > 10$.

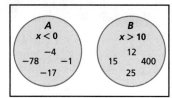

You can graph the solutions of a compound inequality involving OR by using the idea of combining regions. The combined regions are called the **union** and show the numbers that are solutions of either inequality.

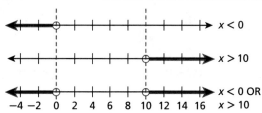

COMMON CORE GPS | **EXAMPLE** | **3**
MCC9-12.A.REI.3

my.hrw.com

Online Video Tutor

Solving Compound Inequalities Involving OR

Solve each compound inequality and graph the solutions.

A $-4 + a > 1$ OR $-4 + a < -3$

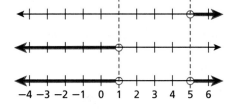

$$-4 + a > 1 \text{ OR } -4 + a < -3$$
$$\underline{+4 \qquad +4 \qquad +4 \qquad +4}$$
$$a > 5 \text{ OR } \qquad a < 1$$

Solve each simple inequality.

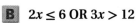

Graph $a > 5$.

Graph $a < 1$.

Graph the union by combining the regions.

B $2x \leq 6$ OR $3x > 12$

$$2x \leq 6 \text{ OR } 3x > 12$$
$$\frac{2x}{2} \leq \frac{6}{2} \qquad \frac{3x}{3} > \frac{12}{3}$$
$$x \leq 3 \text{ OR } \quad x > 4$$

Solve each simple inequality.

Graph $x \leq 3$.

Graph $x > 4$.

Graph the union by combining the regions.

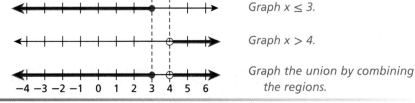

CHECK IT OUT! Solve each compound inequality and graph the solutions.

3a. $2 + r < 12$ OR $r + 5 > 19$

3b. $7x \geq 21$ OR $2x < -2$

Every solution of a compound inequality involving AND must be a solution of both parts of the compound inequality. If no numbers are solutions of *both* simple inequalities, then the compound inequality has no solutions.

The solutions of a compound inequality involving OR are not always two separate sets of numbers. There may be numbers that are solutions of both parts of the compound inequality.

5-3 Solving Compound Inequalities **123**

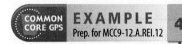

COMMON CORE GPS **EXAMPLE 4** Prep. for MCC9-12.A.REI.12

Writing a Compound Inequality from a Graph

my.hrw.com

Online Video Tutor

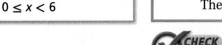

Write the compound inequality shown by each graph.

A

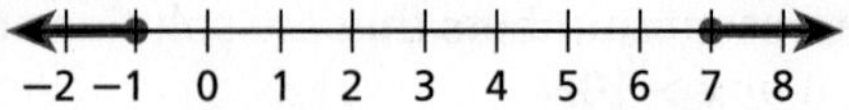

The shaded portion of the graph is not between two values, so the compound inequality involves OR.

On the left, the graph shows an arrow pointing left, so use either < or ≤.
The solid circle at −1 means −1 is a solution, so use ≤.

$x \leq -1$

On the right, the graph shows an arrow pointing right, so use either > or ≥.
The solid circle at 7 means 7 is a solution, so use ≥.

$x \geq 7$

The compound inequality is $x \leq -1$ OR $x \geq 7$.

B

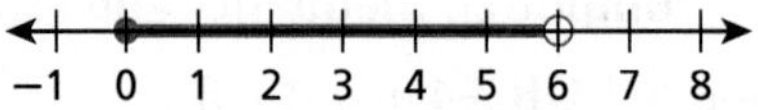

The shaded portion of the graph is between the values 0 and 6, so the compound inequality involves AND.

The shaded values are to the right of 0, so use > or ≥.
The solid circle at 0 means 0 is a solution, so use ≥.

$x \geq 0$

The shaded values are to the left of 6, so use < or ≤.
The empty circle at 6 means 6 is not a solution, so use <.

$x < 6$

The compound inequality is $x \geq 0$ AND $x < 6$.

Writing Math

The compound inequality in Example 4B can also be written with the variable between the two endpoints.
$0 \leq x < 6$

CHECK IT OUT! **Write the compound inequality shown by the graph.**

4a.

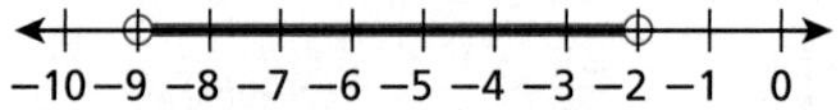

4b.

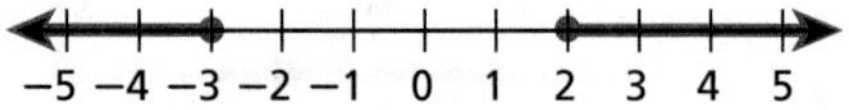

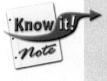

MCC.MP.2 MATHEMATICAL PRACTICES

THINK AND DISCUSS

1. Describe how to write the compound inequality $y > 4$ AND $y \leq 12$ without using the joining word AND.

Know it! Note

2. GET ORGANIZED Copy and complete the graphic organizers. Write three solutions in each of the three sections of the diagram. Then write each of your nine solutions in the appropriate column or columns of the table.

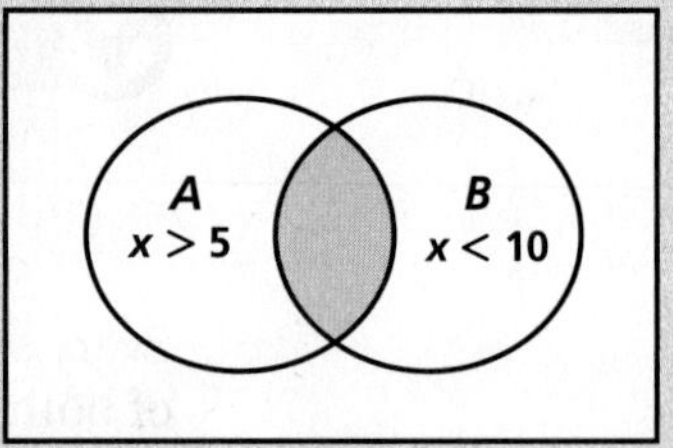

$x > 5$ AND $x < 10$	$x > 5$ OR $x < 10$

GUIDED PRACTICE

1. **Vocabulary** The graph of a(n) ___?___ shows all values that are solutions to both simple inequalities that make a compound inequality. (*union* or *intersection*)

SEE EXAMPLE **1**

2. **Biology** An iguana needs to live in a warm environment. The temperature in a pet iguana's cage should be between 70 °F and 95 °F inclusive. Write a compound inequality to show the temperatures that are within the recommended range. Graph the solutions.

Solve each compound inequality and graph the solutions.

SEE EXAMPLE **2**

3. $-3 < x + 2 < 7$

4. $5 \le 4x + 1 \le 13$

5. $2 < x + 2 < 5$

6. $11 < 2x + 3 < 21$

SEE EXAMPLE **3**

7. $x + 2 < -6 \text{ OR } x + 2 > 6$

8. $r - 1 < 0 \text{ OR } r - 1 > 4$

9. $n + 2 < 3 \text{ OR } n + 3 > 7$

10. $x - 1 < -1 \text{ OR } x - 5 > -1$

SEE EXAMPLE **4**

Write the compound inequality shown by each graph.

11.

12.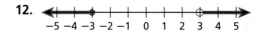

13.
−6 −5 −4 −3 −2 −1 0 1 2 3 4

14.
−10 −8 −6 −4 −2 0 2 4 6 8 10

PRACTICE AND PROBLEM SOLVING

Independent Practice

For Exercises	See Example
15	1
16–19	2
20–23	3
24–27	4

my.hrw.com

Online Extra Practice

15. **Meteorology** One layer of Earth's atmosphere is called the stratosphere. At one point above Earth's surface the stratosphere extends from an altitude of 16 km to an altitude of 50 km. Write a compound inequality to show the altitudes that are within the range of the stratosphere. Graph the solutions.

Solve each compound inequality and graph the solutions.

16. $-1 < x + 1 < 1$

17. $1 \le 2n - 5 \le 7$

18. $-2 < x - 2 < 2$

19. $5 < 3x - 1 < 17$

20. $x - 4 < -7 \text{ OR } x + 3 > 4$

21. $2x + 1 < 1 \text{ OR } x + 5 > 8$

22. $x + 1 < 2 \text{ OR } x + 5 > 8$

23. $x + 3 < 0 \text{ OR } x - 2 > 0$

Write the compound inequality shown by each graph.

24.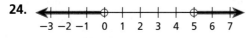

25.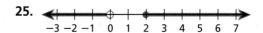

26.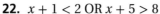
−10 −8 −6 −4 −2 0 2 4 6 8 10

27.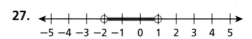

28. **Music** A typical acoustic guitar has a range of three octaves. When the guitar is tuned to "concert pitch," the range of frequencies for those three octaves is between 82.4 Hz and 659.2 Hz inclusive. Write a compound inequality to show the frequencies that are within the range of a typical acoustic guitar. Graph the solutions.

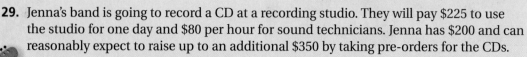

29. Jenna's band is going to record a CD at a recording studio. They will pay $225 to use the studio for one day and $80 per hour for sound technicians. Jenna has $200 and can reasonably expect to raise up to an additional $350 by taking pre-orders for the CDs.

   a. Explain how the inequality $200 \leq 225 + 80n \leq 550$ can be used to find the number of hours Jenna and her band can afford to use the studio and sound technicians.

   b. Solve the inequality. Are there any numbers in the solution set that are not reasonable in this situation?

   c. Suppose Jenna raises $350 in pre-orders. How much more money would she need to raise if she wanted to use the studio and sound technicians for 6 hours?

Write and graph a compound inequality for the numbers described.

30. all real numbers between -6 and 6

31. all real numbers less than or equal to 2 and greater than or equal to 1

32. all real numbers greater than 0 and less than 15

33. all real numbers between -10 and 10 inclusive

Chemistry

34. Transportation The cruise-control function on Georgina's car should keep the speed of the car within 3 mi/h of the set speed. Write a compound inequality to show the acceptable speeds s if the set speed is 55 mi/h. Graph the solutions.

35. Chemistry Water is not a liquid if its temperature is above 100 °C or below 0 °C. Write a compound inequality for the temperatures t when water is not a liquid.

The element gallium is in a solid state at room temperature but becomes a liquid at about 30 °C. Gallium stays in a liquid state until it reaches a temperature of about 2204 °C.

Solve each compound inequality and graph the solutions.

36. $5 \leq 4b - 3 \leq 9$

37. $-3 < x - 1 < 4$

38. $r + 2 < -2$ OR $r - 2 > 2$

39. $2a - 5 < -5$ OR $3a - 2 > 1$

40. $x - 4 \geq 5$ AND $x - 4 \leq 5$

41. $n - 4 < -2$ OR $n + 1 > 6$

42. Sports The ball used in a soccer game may not weigh more than 16 ounces or less than 14 ounces at the start of the match. After $1\frac{1}{2}$ ounces of air was added to a ball, the ball was approved for use in a game. Write and solve a compound inequality to show how much the ball might have weighed before the air was added.

43. Meteorology Tornado damage is rated using the Fujita scale shown in the table. A tornado has a wind speed of 200 miles per hour. Write and solve a compound inequality to show how many miles per hour the wind speed would need to increase for the tornado to be rated "devastating" but not "incredible."

Fujita Tornado Scale		
Category	Type	Wind Speed (mi/h)
F0	Weak	40 to 72
F1	Moderate	73 to 112
F2	Significant	113 to 157
F3	Severe	158 to 206
F4	Devastating	207 to 260
F5	Incredible	261 to 318

44. Give a real-world situation that can be described by a compound inequality. Write the inequality that describes your situation.

H.O.T. **45. Write About It** How are the graphs of the compound inequality $x < 3$ AND $x < 7$ and the compound inequality $x < 3$ OR $x < 7$ different? How are the graphs alike? Explain.

H.O.T. 46. Critical Thinking If there is no solution to a compound inequality, does the compound inequality involve OR or AND? Explain.

TEST PREP

47. Which of the following describes the solutions of $-x + 1 > 2$ OR $x - 1 > 2$?

    Ⓐ all real numbers greater than 1 or less than 3

    Ⓑ all real numbers greater than 3 or less than 1

    Ⓒ all real numbers greater than −1 or less than 3

    Ⓓ all real numbers greater than 3 or less than −1

48. Which of the following is a graph of the solutions of $x - 3 < 2$ AND $x + 3 > 2$?

    Ⓕ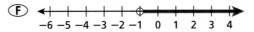
    Ⓗ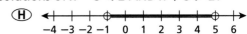

    Ⓖ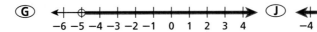
    Ⓙ

49. Which compound inequality is shown by the graph?

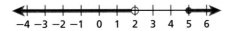

    Ⓐ $x \le 2$ OR $x > 5$
        Ⓒ $x \le 2$ OR $x \ge 5$

    Ⓑ $x < 2$ OR $x \ge 5$
        Ⓓ $x \ge 2$ OR $x > 5$

50. Which of the following is a solution of $x + 1 \ge 3$ AND $x + 1 \le 3$?

    Ⓕ 0   Ⓖ 1   Ⓗ 2   Ⓙ 3

CHALLENGE AND EXTEND

Solve and graph each compound inequality.

51. $2c - 10 < 5 - 3c < 7c$
         52. $5p - 10 < p + 6 < 3p$

53. $2s \le 18 - s$ OR $5s \ge s + 36$
     54. $9 - x \ge 5x$ OR $20 - 3x \le 17$

55. Write a compound inequality that represents all values of x that are NOT solutions to $x < -1$ OR $x > 3$.

56. For the compound inequality $x + 2 \ge a$ AND $x - 7 \le b$, find values of a and b for which the only solution is $x = 1$.

FOCUS ON MATHEMATICAL PRACTICES

H.O.T. 57. Modeling Ronaldo purchased a gym membership at a special rate that allows him at most 15 workouts per month. He has a trainer who requires him to work out at least 9 days per month. In the first half of April, Ronaldo completed d_1, workouts, with $d_1 \le 9$. Using the variable d_2, write a compound inequality to describe how many times Ronaldo should work out in the second half of April.

H.O.T. 58. Counterexample While working on a problem involving inequalities, Loretta noticed $12 \le x \le 16$ has 4 integer solutions, 12, 13, 14, and 15, but $12 < x < 16$ has only 2 integer solutions, 13 and 14. She proposed that $a \le x \le b$ always has 2 more integer solutions than $a < x < b$ whenever $a < b$. Can you think of a counterexample to disprove Loretta's conjecture?

Ready to Go On?

my.hrw.com
Assessment and Intervention

5-1 Solving Two-Step and Multi-Step Inequalities

Solve each inequality and graph the solutions.

1. $2x + 3 < 9$

2. $3t - 2 > 10$

3. $7 \geq 1 - 6r$

Solve each inequality.

4. $2(x - 3) > -1$

5. $\frac{1}{3}a + \frac{1}{2} > \frac{2}{3}$

6. $15 < 5(m - 7)$

7. $2 + (-6) > 0.8p$

8. The average of Mindy's two test scores must be at least 92 to make an A in the class. Mindy got an 88 on her first test. What scores can she get on her second test to make an A in the class?

9. Carl's Cable Company charges $55 for monthly service plus $4 for each pay-per-view movie. Teleview Cable Company charges $110 per month with no fee for movies. For what number of movies is the cost of Carl's Cable Company less than the cost of Teleview?

5-2 Solving Inequalities with Variables on Both Sides

Solve each inequality and graph the solutions.

10. $5x < 3x + 8$

11. $6p - 3 > 9p$

12. $r - 8 \geq 3r - 12$

Solve each inequality.

13. $3(y + 6) > 2(y + 4)$

14. $4(5 - g) \geq g$

15. $4x < 4(x - 1)$

16. $3(1 - x) \geq -3(x + 2)$

17. Phillip has $100 in the bank and deposits $18 per month. Gil has $145 in the bank and deposits $15 per month. For how many months will Gil have a larger bank balance than Phillip?

18. Hanna has a savings account with a balance of $210 and deposits $16 per month. Faith has a savings account with a balance of $175 and deposits $20 per month. Write and solve an inequality to determine the number of months Hanna's account balance will be greater than Faith's account balance.

5-3 Solving Compound Inequalities

Solve each compound inequality and graph the solutions.

19. $-2 \leq x + 3 < 9$

20. $m + 2 < -1 \text{ OR } m - 2 > 6$

21. $-3 \geq x - 1 > 2$

22. $-2 > r + 2 \text{ OR } r + 4 < 5$

23. It is recommended that a certain medicine be stored in temperatures above 32 °F and below 70 °F. Write a compound inequality to show the acceptable storage temperatures for this medicine.

PARCC Assessment Readiness

Selected Response

1. Solve the inequality $3n - 6 - n \leq 4$ and graph the solutions.

(A) $n \leq -1$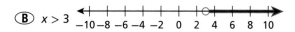

(B) $n \geq -1$

(C) $n \geq 5$

(D) $n \leq 5$

2. A family travels to Bryce Canyon for three days. On the first day, they drove 150 miles. On the second day, they drove 190 miles. What is the least number of miles they drove on the third day if their average number of miles per day was at least 185?

(F) 200 mi   (H) 555 mi

(G) 175 mi   (J) 215 mi

3. Solve the inequality $6x < 3x + 15$ and graph the solutions.

(A) $x < 5$

(B) $x > 3$

(C) $x < -5$

(D) $x > 5$

4. Mrs. Williams is deciding between two field trips for her class. The Science Center charges $360 plus $5 per student. The Dino Discovery Museum simply charges $11 per student. For how many students will the Science Center charge less than the Dino Discovery Museum?

(F) Fewer than 60 students

(G) 354 or more students

(H) More than 60 students

(J) 354 or fewer students

5. Solve the inequality $3(y - 3) \leq 3y + 2$.

(A) $y \leq -1\frac{1}{6}$ (C) $y \leq 1\frac{5}{6}$

(B) no solutions   (D) All real numbers are solutions.

6. Fly with Us owns an airplane that has seats for 240 people. The company flies this airplane only if there are at least 100 people on the plane. Write a compound inequality to show the possible number of people in a flight on this airplane. Let n represent the possible number of people in the flight.

(F) $100 \geq n \geq 240$

(G) $100 \leq n \leq 240$

(H) $n \leq 240$

(J) $100 < n < 240$

7. Solve the compound inequality $1 < 3x - 2 \leq 10$ and graph the solutions.

(A) $1 < x$ AND $x \leq 4$ (C) $1 \leq x$ AND $x \leq 4$

(B) $1 < x$ AND $x < 4$ (D) $1 > x$ AND $x \geq 4$

8. Write the compound inequality shown by the graph.

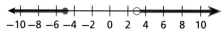

(F) $x < -5$ OR $x > 3$ (H) $x \leq -5$ OR $x > 3$

(G) $x \leq 3$ AND $x > -5$ (J) $x \leq -5$ AND $x > 3$

9. Which of the following is a solution of $x - 9 < 5$ AND $x + 5 \geq -1$?

(A) 13   (C) 14

(B) 16   (D) −7

Mini-Tasks

10. A volleyball team scored 6 more points in its first game than in its third game. In the second game, the team scored 23 points. The total number of points scored was less than 55.

   a. Write and solve an inequality to find the number of points the team could have scored in its first game.

   b. Janie scored 8 points in the first game. Is it possible that she scored exactly half the team's points in that game? Explain.

6 Solving Systems of Equations

Contents

The Common Core Georgia Performance Standards for Mathematical Practice describe varieties of expertise that all students should seek to develop. Opportunities to develop these practices are integrated throughout this program.

1 Make sense of problems and persevere in solving them.

2 Reason abstractly and quantitatively.

3 Construct viable arguments and critique the reasoning of others.

4 Model with mathematics.

5 Use appropriate tools strategically.

6 Attend to precision.

7 Look for and make use of structure.

8 Look for and express regularity in repeated reasoning.

Unpacking the Standards

Understanding the standards and the vocabulary terms in the standards will help you know exactly what you are expected to learn in this chapter.

 MCC9-12.A.CED.2

Create equations in two or more variables to represent relationships between quantities; graph equations on coordinate axes with labels and scales.

Key Vocabulary

equation (ecuación)
A mathematical statement that two expressions are equivalent.

What It Means For You

Creating equations in two variables to describe relationships gives you access to the tools of graphing and algebra to solve the equations.

EXAMPLE

A customer spent $29 on a bouquet of roses and daisies.

r = number of roses in bouquet
d = number of daises in bouquet

$2.5r + 1.75d = 29$

ROSES $2.50 each   DAISIES $1.75 each

 MCC9-12.A.REI.6

Solve systems of linear equations exactly and approximately (e.g., with graphs), focusing on pairs of linear equations in two variables.

Key Vocabulary

system of linear equations (sistema de ecuaciones lineales) A system of equations in which all of the equations are linear.

What It Means For You

You can solve systems of equations to find out when two relationships involving the same variables are true at the same time.

EXAMPLE

The cost of bowling at bowling alley **A** or **B** is a function of the number of games g.

$$\text{Cost } \mathbf{A} = 2.5g + 2$$
$$\text{Cost } \mathbf{B} = 2g + 4$$

When are the costs the same?

$$\text{Cost } \mathbf{A} = \text{Cost } \mathbf{B}$$
$$2.5g + 2 = 2g + 4$$

The cost is $12 at both bowling alleys when g is 4.

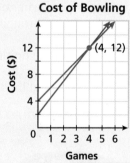

Cost of Bowling

(4, 12)

Cost ($)

Games

6-1 Technology TASK

Solve Linear Equations by Using a Spreadsheet

You can use a spreadsheet to answer "What if...?" questions. By changing one or more values, you can quickly model different scenarios.

Use with Solving Systems by Graphing

Use appropriate tools strategically.

MCC9-12.A.REI.3 Solve linear equations and inequalities in one variable, including equations with coefficients represented by letters.

Activity

Company Z makes DVD players. The company's costs are $400 per week plus $20 per DVD player. Each DVD player sells for $45. How many DVD players must company Z sell in one week to make a profit?

Let *n* represent the number of DVD players company Z sells in one week.

$c = 400 + 20n$ *The total cost is $400 plus $20 times the number of DVD players made.*

$s = 45n$ *The total sales income is $45 times the number of DVD players sold.*

$p = s - c$ *The total profit is the sales income minus the total cost.*

1 Set up your spreadsheet with columns for number of DVD players, total cost, total income, and profit.

2 Under Number of DVD Players, enter 1 in cell A2.

3 Use the equations above to enter the formulas for total cost, total sales, and total profit in row 2.

  • In cell B2, enter the formula for total cost.

  • In cell C2, enter the formula for total sales income.

  • In cell D2, enter the formula for total profit.

4 Fill columns A, B, C, and D by selecting cells A1 through D1, clicking the small box at the bottom right corner of cell D2, and dragging the box down through several rows.

5 Find the point where the profit is $0. This is known as the breakeven point, where total cost and total income are the same.

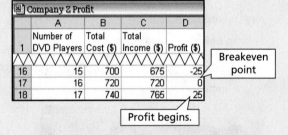

Company Z must sell 17 DVD players to make a profit. The profit is $25.

Try This

For Exercises 1 and 2, use the spreadsheet from the activity.

1. If company Z sells 10 DVD players, will they make a profit? Explain. What if they sell 16?

2. Company Z makes a profit of $225 dollars. How many DVD players did they sell?

For Exercise 3, make a spreadsheet.

3. Company Y's costs are $400 per week plus $20 per DVD player. They want the breakeven point to occur with sales of 8 DVD players. What should the sales price be?

6-1 Solving Systems by Graphing

Essential Question: How can you solve systems of linear equations by using graphs?

Objectives
Identify solutions of systems of linear equations in two variables.

Solve systems of linear equations in two variables by graphing.

Vocabulary
system of linear equations
solution of a system of linear equations

Why learn this?

You can compare costs by graphing a system of linear equations. (See Example 3.)

Sometimes there are different charges for the same service or product at different places. For example, Bowl-o-Rama charges $2.50 per game plus $2 for shoe rental while Bowling Pinz charges $2 per game plus $4 for shoe rental. A *system of linear equations* can be used to compare these charges.

A **system of linear equations** is a set of two or more linear equations containing two or more variables. A **solution of a system of linear equations** with two variables is an ordered pair that satisfies each equation in the system. So, if an ordered pair is a solution, it will make both equations true.

 EXAMPLE MCC9-12.A.REI.6 **1** **Identifying Solutions of Systems**

Tell whether the ordered pair is a solution of the given system.

 my.hrw.com

Online Video Tutor

A $(4, 1); \begin{cases} x + 2y = 6 \\ x - y = 3 \end{cases}$

$x + 2y = 6$	
$4 + 2(1)$	6
$4 + 2$	6
6	6 ✓

$x - y = 3$	
$4 - 1$	3
3	3 ✓

Substitute 4 for x and 1 for y in each equation in the system.

The ordered pair $(4, 1)$ makes both equations true.

$(4, 1)$ is a solution of the system.

 Animated Math

B $(-1, 2); \begin{cases} 2x + 5y = 8 \\ 3x - 2y = 5 \end{cases}$

$2x + 5y = 8$	
$2(-1) + 5(2)$	8
$-2 + 10$	8
8	8 ✓

$3x - 2y = 5$	
$3(-1) - 2(2)$	5
$-3 - 4$	5
-7	5 ✗

Substitute −1 for x and 2 for y in each equation in the system.

The ordered pair $(-1, 2)$ makes one equation true, but not the other.

$(-1, 2)$ is not a solution of the system.

Helpful Hint

If an ordered pair does not satisfy the first equation in the system, there is no need to check the other equations.

 CHECK IT OUT! **Tell whether the ordered pair is a solution of the given system.**

1a. $(1, 3); \begin{cases} 2x + y = 5 \\ -2x + y = 1 \end{cases}$

1b. $(2, -1); \begin{cases} x - 2y = 4 \\ 3x + y = 6 \end{cases}$

© Kwame Zikomo/SuperStock

All solutions of a linear equation are on its graph. To find a solution of a system of linear equations, you need a point that each line has in common. In other words, you need their point of intersection.

$$\begin{cases} y = 2x - 1 \\ y = -x + 5 \end{cases}$$

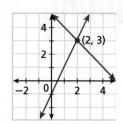

The point $(2, 3)$ is where the two lines intersect and is a solution of both equations, so $(2, 3)$ is the solution of the system.

COMMON CORE GPS **EXAMPLE** **2** MCC9-12.A.REI.6

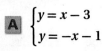

Solving a System of Linear Equations by Graphing

Solve each system by graphing. Check your answer.

A $$\begin{cases} y = x - 3 \\ y = -x - 1 \end{cases}$$

Graph the system.

The solution appears to be at $(1, -2)$.

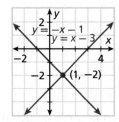

Check

Substitute $(1, -2)$ into the system.

$y = x - 3$	
-2	$1 - 3$
-2	-2 ✓

$y = -x - 1$	
-2	$-1 - 1$
-2	-2 ✓

The solution is $(1, -2)$.

B $$\begin{cases} x + y = 0 \\ y = -\dfrac{1}{2}x + 1 \end{cases}$$

$$\begin{array}{r} x + y = 0 \\ \underline{-x \qquad -x} \\ y = -x \end{array}$$ *Rewrite the first equation in slope-intercept form.*

Graph using a calculator and then use the intersection command.

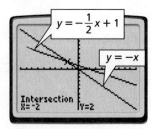

Check   Substitute $(-2, 2)$ into the system.

$x + y = 0$	
$-2 + 2$	0
0	0 ✓

$y = -\dfrac{1}{2}x + 1$	
2	$-\dfrac{1}{2}(-2) + 1$
2	$1 + 1$
2	2 ✓

The solution is $(-2, 2)$.

Helpful Hint

Sometimes it is difficult to tell exactly where the lines cross when you solve by graphing. It is good to confirm your answer by substituting it into both equations.

Solve each system by graphing. Check your answer.

2a. $$\begin{cases} y = -2x - 1 \\ y = x + 5 \end{cases}$$ **2b.** $$\begin{cases} y = \dfrac{1}{3}x - 3 \\ 2x + y = 4 \end{cases}$$

Problem-Solving Application

Bowl-o-Rama charges $2.50 per game plus $2 for shoe rental, and Bowling Pinz charges $2 per game plus $4 for shoe rental. For how many games will the cost to bowl be the same at both places? What is that cost?

my.hrw.com

Online Video Tutor

1 Understand the Problem

The **answer** will be the number of games played for which the total cost is the same at both bowling alleys. **List the important information:**

• Game price: Bowl-o-Rama $2.50   Bowling Pinz: $2
• Shoe-rental fee: Bowl-o-Rama $2   Bowling Pinz: $4

2 Make a Plan

Write a system of equations, one equation to represent the price at each company. Let x be the number of games played and y be the total cost.

	Total cost	is	price per game	times	games	plus	shoe rental.
Bowl-o-Rama	y	=	2.5	•	x	+	2
Bowling Pinz	y	=	2	•	x	+	4

3 Solve

Graph $y = 2.5x + 2$ and $y = 2x + 4$. The lines appear to intersect at $(4, 12)$. So, the cost at both places will be the same for 4 games bowled and that cost will be $12.

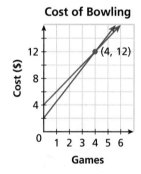

Cost of Bowling

4 Look Back

Check $(4, 12)$ using both equations.

Cost of bowling 4 games at Bowl-o-Rama:
$\$2.5(4) + \$2 = 10 + 2 = 12$ ✓

Cost of bowling 4 games at Bowling Pinz:
$\$2(4) + \$4 = 8 + 4 = 12$ ✓

CHECK IT OUT! 3. Video club A charges $10 for membership and $3 per movie rental. Video club B charges $15 for membership and $2 per movie rental. For how many movie rentals will the cost be the same at both video clubs? What is that cost?

MCC.MP.6   MATHEMATICAL PRACTICES

THINK AND DISCUSS

1. Explain how to use a graph to solve a system of linear equations.

2. Explain how to check a solution of a system of linear equations.

3. **GET ORGANIZED** Copy and complete the graphic organizer. In each box, write a step for solving a linear system by graphing. More boxes may be added.

Know it! Note

Solving a Linear System by Graphing

1. → 2. → 3.

GUIDED PRACTICE

1. **Vocabulary** Describe a *solution of a system of linear equations*.

SEE EXAMPLE 1 Tell whether the ordered pair is a solution of the given system.

2. $(2, -2);$ $\begin{cases} 3x + y = 4 \\ x - 3y = -4 \end{cases}$

3. $(3, -1);$ $\begin{cases} x - 2y = 5 \\ 2x - y = 7 \end{cases}$

4. $(-1, 5);$ $\begin{cases} -x + y = 6 \\ 2x + 3y = 13 \end{cases}$

SEE EXAMPLE 2 Solve each system by graphing. Check your answer.

5. $\begin{cases} y = \dfrac{1}{2}x \\ y = -x + 3 \end{cases}$

6. $\begin{cases} y = x - 2 \\ 2x + y = 1 \end{cases}$

7. $\begin{cases} -2x - 1 = y \\ x + y = 3 \end{cases}$

SEE EXAMPLE 3 8. To deliver mulch, Lawn and Garden charges $30 per cubic yard of mulch plus a $30 delivery fee. Yard Depot charges $25 per cubic yard of mulch plus a $55 delivery fee. For how many cubic yards will the cost be the same? What will that cost be?

PRACTICE AND PROBLEM SOLVING

Independent Practice

For Exercises	See Example
9–11	1
12–15	2
16	3

my.hrw.com

Online Extra Practice

Tell whether the ordered pair is a solution of the given system.

9. $(1, -4);$ $\begin{cases} x - 2y = 8 \\ 4x - y = 8 \end{cases}$

10. $(-2, 1);$ $\begin{cases} 2x - 3y = -7 \\ 3x + y = -5 \end{cases}$

11. $(5, 2);$ $\begin{cases} 2x + y = 12 \\ -3y - x = -11 \end{cases}$

Solve each system by graphing. Check your answer.

12. $\begin{cases} y = \dfrac{1}{2}x + 2 \\ y = -x - 1 \end{cases}$

13. $\begin{cases} y = x \\ y = -x + 6 \end{cases}$

14. $\begin{cases} -2x - 1 = y \\ x = -y + 3 \end{cases}$

15. $\begin{cases} x + y = 2 \\ y = x - 4 \end{cases}$

16. **Multi-Step** Angelo runs 7 miles per week and increases his distance by 1 mile each week. Marc runs 4 miles per week and increases his distance by 2 miles each week. In how many weeks will Angelo and Marc be running the same distance? What will that distance be?

17. **School** The school band sells carnations on Valentine's Day for $2 each. They buy the carnations from a florist for $0.50 each, plus a $16 delivery charge.

   a. Write a system of equations to describe the situation.

   b. Graph the system. What does the solution represent?

   c. Explain whether the solution shown on the graph makes sense in this situation. If not, give a reasonable solution.

Real-World Connections

18. a. The Warrior baseball team is selling hats as a fund-raiser. They contacted two companies. Hats Off charges a $50 design fee and $5 per hat. Top Stuff charges a $25 design fee and $6 per hat. Write an equation for each company's pricing.

   b. Graph the system of equations from part **a**. For how many hats will the cost be the same? What is that cost?

   c. Explain when it is cheaper for the baseball team to use Top Stuff and when it is cheaper to use Hats Off.

Graphing Calculator Use a graphing calculator to graph and solve the systems of equations in Exercises 19–22. Round your answer to the nearest tenth.

19. $\begin{cases} y = 4.7x + 2.1 \\ y = 1.6x - 5.4 \end{cases}$

20. $\begin{cases} 4.8x + 0.6y = 4 \\ y = -3.2x + 2.7 \end{cases}$

21. $\begin{cases} y = \dfrac{5}{4}x - \dfrac{2}{3} \\ \dfrac{8}{3}x + y = \dfrac{5}{9} \end{cases}$

22. $\begin{cases} y = 6.9x + 12.4 \\ y = -4.1x - 5.3 \end{cases}$

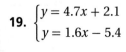

Middleton Place Gardens, South Carolina, are the United States' oldest landscaped gardens. The gardens were established in 1741 and opened to the public in the 1920s.

23. **Landscaping** The gardeners at Middleton Place Gardens want to plant a total of 45 white and pink hydrangeas in one flower bed. In another flower bed, they want to plant 120 hydrangeas. In this bed, they want 2 times the number of white hydrangeas and 3 times the number of pink hydrangeas as in the first bed. Use a system of equations to find how many white and how many pink hydrangeas the gardeners should buy altogether.

24. **Fitness** Rusty burns 5 Calories per minute swimming and 11 Calories per minute jogging. In the morning, Rusty burns 200 Calories walking and swims for x minutes. In the afternoon, Rusty will jog for x minutes. How many minutes must he jog to burn at least as many Calories y in the afternoon as he did in the morning? Round your answer up to the next whole number of minutes.

25. A tree that is 2 feet tall is growing at a rate of 1 foot per year. A 6-foot tall tree is growing at a rate of 0.5 foot per year. In how many years will the trees be the same height?

26. **Critical Thinking** Write a real-world situation that could be represented by the system $\begin{cases} y = 3x + 10 \\ y = 5x + 20 \end{cases}$.

27. **Write About It** When you graph a system of linear equations, why does the intersection of the two lines represent the solution of the system?

TEST PREP

28. Taxi company A charges $4 plus $0.50 per mile. Taxi company B charges $5 plus $0.25 per mile. Which system best represents this problem?

Ⓐ $\begin{cases} y = 4x + 0.5 \\ y = 5x + 0.25 \end{cases}$

Ⓒ $\begin{cases} y = -4x + 0.5 \\ y = -5x + 0.25 \end{cases}$

Ⓑ $\begin{cases} y = 0.5x + 4 \\ y = 0.25x + 5 \end{cases}$

Ⓓ $\begin{cases} y = -0.5x + 4 \\ y = -0.25x + 5 \end{cases}$

29. Which system of equations represents the given graph?

Ⓕ $\begin{cases} y = 2x - 1 \\ y = \dfrac{1}{3}x + 3 \end{cases}$

Ⓗ $\begin{cases} y = 2x + 1 \\ y = \dfrac{1}{3}x - 3 \end{cases}$

Ⓖ $\begin{cases} y = -2x + 1 \\ y = 2x - 3 \end{cases}$

Ⓙ $\begin{cases} y = -2x - 1 \\ y = 3x - 3 \end{cases}$

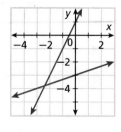

30. **Gridded Response** Which value of b will make the system $y = 2x + 2$ and $y = 2.5x + b$ intersect at the point $(2, 6)$?

CHALLENGE AND EXTEND

31. **Entertainment** If the pattern in the table continues, in what month will the number of sales of VCRs and DVD players be the same? What will that number be?

Total Number Sold				
Month	1	2	3	4
VCRs	500	490	480	470
DVD Players	250	265	280	295

32. Long Distance Inc. charges a $1.45 connection charge and $0.03 per minute. Far Away Calls charges a $1.52 connection charge and $0.02 per minute.

   a. For how many minutes will a call cost the same from both companies? What is that cost?

   b. When is it better to call using Long Distance Inc.? Far Away Calls? Explain.

   c. What if...? Long Distance Inc. raised its connection charge to $1.50 and Far Away Calls decreased its connection charge by 2 cents. How will this affect the graphs? Now which company is better to use for calling long distance? Why?

FOCUS ON MATHEMATICAL PRACTICES

H.O.T. 33. **Error Analysis** Mario says $(-1, 5)$ is a solution of the system of equations shown. Do you agree? Explain.

$$\begin{cases} x + y = 4 \\ x - y = 6 \end{cases}$$

H.O.T. 34. **Problem Solving** Amanda cut an 8-foot length of ribbon into two pieces. One piece is three times as long as the other.

   a. Write and graph a system of equations for the length of each piece of ribbon. Use x for the length of the shorter piece, and y for the longer.

   b. What does the point where the lines intersect represent?

   c. What is the system of equations if you define y as the length of the shorter piece and x as the longer piece? What is the solution?

Career Path

Ethan Reynolds
Applied Sciences major

Q: What math classes did you take in high school?

A: Career Math, Algebra, and Geometry

Q: What are you studying and what math classes have you taken?

A: I am really interested in aviation. I am taking Statistics and Trigonometry. Next year I will take Calculus.

Q: How is math used in aviation?

A: I use math to interpret aeronautical charts. I also perform calculations involving wind movements, aircraft weight and balance, and fuel consumption. These skills are necessary for planning and executing safe air flights.

Q: What are your future plans?

A: I could work as a commercial or corporate pilot or even as a flight instructor. I could also work toward a bachelor's degree in aviation management, air traffic control, aviation electronics, aviation maintenance, or aviation computer science.

6-2
Algebra TASK
Model Systems of Linear Equations

You can use algebra tiles to model and solve some systems of linear equations.

Use with Solving Systems by Substitution

Use appropriate tools strategically.

MCC9-12.A.REI.6 Solve systems of linear equations exactly ... , focusing on pairs of linear equations in two variables.

KEY

$\boxed{+} = 1$

$\boxed{-} = -1$

$\boxed{+} = x$ $\boxed{-} = -x$

REMEMBER

When two expressions are equal, you can substitute one for the other in any expression or equation.

Activity

Use algebra tiles to model and solve $\begin{cases} y = 2x - 3 \\ x + y = 9 \end{cases}$.

MODEL		ALGEBRA
The first equation is solved for y. Model the second equation, x + y = 9, by substituting 2x − 3 for y.		$x + y = 9$ $x + (2x - 3) = 9$ $3x - 3 = 9$
Add 3 yellow tiles on both sides of the mat. This represents adding 3 to both sides of the equation. *Remove zero pairs.*		$3x - 3 = \quad 9$ $\underline{+3 \quad +3}$ $3x \quad = \quad 12$
Divide each side into 3 equal groups. Align one x-tile with each group on the right side. One x-tile is equivalent to 4 yellow tiles. x = 4		$\dfrac{3x}{3} = \dfrac{12}{3}$ $x = 4$

To solve for y, substitute 4 for x in one of the equations:
$$y = 2x - 3$$
$$= 2(4) - 3$$
$$= 5$$

The solution is (4, 5).

Try This

Model and solve each system of equations.

1. $\begin{cases} y = x + 3 \\ 2x + y = 6 \end{cases}$

2. $\begin{cases} 2x + 3 = y \\ x + y = 6 \end{cases}$

3. $\begin{cases} 2x + 3y = 1 \\ x = -1 - y \end{cases}$

4. $\begin{cases} y = x + 1 \\ 2x - y = -5 \end{cases}$

6-2 Solving Systems by Substitution

CAMPING OUT FOR THE BEST TICKETS ISN'T WHAT IT USED TO BE...

Off the Mark by Mark Parisi. Cartoon copyrighted by Mark Parisi, printed with permission.

? *Essential Question:* How can you solve systems of linear equations by using substitution?

Objective
Solve systems of linear equations in two variables by substitution.

Why learn this?

You can solve systems of equations to help select the best value among high-speed Internet providers. (See Example 3.)

Sometimes it is difficult to identify the exact solution to a system by graphing. In this case, you can use a method called *substitution*.

The goal when using substitution is to reduce the system to one equation that has only one variable. Then you can solve this equation, and substitute into an original equation to find the value of the other variable.

Solving Systems of Equations by Substitution
Step 1 Solve for one variable in at least one equation, if necessary.
Step 2 Substitute the resulting expression into the other equation.
Step 3 Solve that equation to get the value of the first variable.
Step 4 Substitute that value into one of the original equations and solve.
Step 5 Write the values from Steps 3 and 4 as an ordered pair, (x, y), and check.

COMMON CORE GPS **EXAMPLE 1** MCC9-12.A.REI.6

my.hrw.com

Online Video Tutor

Helpful Hint

You can substitute the value of one variable into *either* of the original equations to find the value of the other variable.

Solving a System of Linear Equations by Substitution

Solve each system by substitution.

A $\begin{cases} y = 2x \\ y = x + 5 \end{cases}$

Step 1 $y = 2x$ *Both equations are solved for y.*
        $y = x + 5$

Step 2 $y = \quad x + 5$ *Substitute 2x for y in the second equation.*
        $2x = \quad x + 5$

Step 3 $\dfrac{-x \quad -x}{x = \quad 5}$ *Solve for x.*

Step 4 $y = 2x$ *Write one of the original equations.*
        $y = 2(5)$ *Substitute 5 for x.*
        $y = 10$

Step 5 $(5, 10)$ *Write the solution as an ordered pair.*

Check Substitute $(5, 10)$ into both equations in the system.

$y = 2x$	
10	$2(5)$
10	10 ✓

$y = x + 5$	
10	$5 + 5$
10	10 ✓

Solve each system by substitution.

 $\begin{cases} 2x + y = 5 \\ y = x - 4 \end{cases}$

Step 1 $y = x - 4$ *The second equation is solved for y.*

Step 2 $2x + y = 5$

$2x + (x - 4) = 5$ *Substitute x − 4 for y in the first equation.*

Step 3 $3x - 4 = 5$ *Simplify. Then solve for x.*

$\underline{\quad +4 \quad +4}$ *Add 4 to both sides.*

$3x \quad = 9$

$\dfrac{3x}{3} = \dfrac{9}{3}$ *Divide both sides by 3.*

$x = 3$

Step 4 $y = x - 4$ *Write one of the original equations.*

$y = 3 - 4$ *Substitute 3 for x.*

$y = -1$

Step 5 $(3, -1)$ *Write the solution as an ordered pair.*

C $\begin{cases} x + 4y = 6 \\ x + y = 3 \end{cases}$

Step 1 $x + 4y = 6$ *Solve the first equation for x by subtracting*

$\underline{\quad -4y \quad -4y}$ *4y from both sides.*

$x = 6 - 4y$

Step 2 $x + y = 3$

$(6 - 4y) + y = 3$ *Substitute 6 − 4y for x in the second equation.*

Step 3 $6 - 3y = 3$ *Simplify. Then solve for y.*

$\underline{\quad -6 \qquad -6}$ *Subtract 6 from both sides.*

$-3y = -3$

$\dfrac{-3y}{-3} = \dfrac{-3}{-3}$ *Divide both sides by −3.*

$y = 1$

Step 4 $x + y = 3$ *Write one of the original equations.*

$x + 1 = 3$ *Substitute 1 for y.*

$\underline{\quad -1 \quad -1}$ *Subtract 1 from both sides.*

$x = 2$

Step 5 $(2, 1)$ *Write the solution as an ordered pair.*

Helpful Hint

Sometimes neither equation is solved for a variable. You can begin by solving either equation for either *x* or *y*.

 Solve each system by substitution.

1a. $\begin{cases} y = x + 3 \\ y = 2x + 5 \end{cases}$ **1b.** $\begin{cases} x = 2y - 4 \\ x + 8y = 16 \end{cases}$ **1c.** $\begin{cases} 2x + y = -4 \\ x + y = -7 \end{cases}$

Sometimes you substitute an expression for a variable that has a coefficient. When solving for the second variable in this situation, you can use the Distributive Property.

EXAMPLE 2 **Using the Distributive Property**

MCC9-12.A.REI.6

my.hrw.com

Online Video Tutor

Solve $\begin{cases} 4y - 5x = 9 \\ x - 4y = 11 \end{cases}$ by substitution.

Step 1
$$x - 4y = 11$$
$$+ 4y \quad + 4y$$
$$x = 4y + 11$$

Solve the second equation for x by adding 4y to each side.

Step 2
$$4y - 5x = 9$$
$$4y - 5(4y + 11) = 9$$

Substitute 4y + 11 for x in the first equation.

Step 3
$$4y - 5(4y) - 5(11) = 9$$
$$4y - 20y - 55 = 9$$
$$-16y - 55 = 9$$
$$ + 55 \quad + 55$$
$$-16y = 64$$
$$\frac{-16y}{-16} = \frac{64}{-16}$$
$$y = -4$$

Distribute −5 to the expression in parentheses. Simplify. Solve for y.

Add 55 to both sides.

Divide both sides by −16.

Step 4
$$x - 4y = 11$$
$$x - 4(-4) = 11$$
$$x + 16 = 11$$
$$ - 16 \quad - 16$$
$$x = -5$$

Write one of the original equations.

Substitute −4 for y.

Simplify.

Subtract 16 from both sides.

Step 5 $(-5, -4)$

Write the solution as an ordered pair.

> **Caution!**
>
> When you solve one equation for a variable, you must substitute the value or expression into the *other* original equation, not the one that has just been solved.

 CHECK IT OUT!

2. Solve $\begin{cases} -2x + y = 8 \\ 3x + 2y = 9 \end{cases}$ by substitution.

Student to Student

Solving Systems by Substitution

Erika Chu
Terrell High School

I always look for a variable with a coefficient of 1 or −1 when deciding which equation to solve for x or y.

For the system

$$\begin{cases} 2x + y = 14 \\ -3x + 4y = -10 \end{cases}$$

I would solve the first equation for y because it has a coefficient of 1.

$$2x + y = 14$$
$$y = -2x + 14$$

Then I use substitution to find the values of x and y.

$$-3x + 4y = -10$$
$$-3x + 4(-2x + 14) = -10$$
$$-3x + (-8x) + 56 = -10$$
$$-11x + 56 = -10$$
$$-11x = -66$$
$$x = 6$$

$$y = -2x + 14$$
$$y = -2(6) + 14 = 2$$

The solution is (6, 2).

Consumer Economics Application

One high-speed Internet provider has a $50 setup fee and costs $30 per month. Another provider has no setup fee and costs $40 per month.

a. In how many months will both providers cost the same? What will that cost be?

Write an equation for each option. Let t represent the total amount paid and m represent the number of months.

	Total paid	is	setup fee	plus	cost per month	times	months.
Option 1	t	$=$	50	$+$	30	$\cdot$	m
Option 2	t	$=$	0	$+$	40	$\cdot$	m

Step 1 $t = 50 + 30m$ *Both equations are solved for t.*
$\qquad\quad t = 40m$

Step 2 $50 + 30m = \quad 40m$ *Substitute 50 + 30m for t in the second equation.*

Step 3 $\dfrac{-30m \qquad\; -30m}{\;50 \qquad = \quad 10m}$ *Solve for m. Subtract 30m from both sides.*

$\qquad\qquad \dfrac{50}{10} = \dfrac{10m}{10}$ *Divide both sides by 10.*

$\qquad\qquad\quad 5 = m$

Step 4 $\quad t = 40m$ *Write one of the original equations.*
$\qquad\qquad = 40(5)$ *Substitute 5 for m.*
$\qquad\qquad = 200$

Step 5 $(5, 200)$ *Write the solution as an ordered pair.*

In 5 months, the total cost for each option will be the same—$200.

b. If you plan to cancel in 1 year, which is the cheaper provider? Explain.

Option 1: $t = 50 + 30(12) = 410$ Option 2: $t = 40(12) = 480$
Option 1 is cheaper.

CHECK IT OUT!

3. One cable television provider has a $60 setup fee and charges $80 per month, and another provider has a $160 equipment fee and charges $70 per month.

   a. In how many months will the cost be the same? What will that cost be?

   b. If you plan to move in 6 months, which is the cheaper option? Explain.

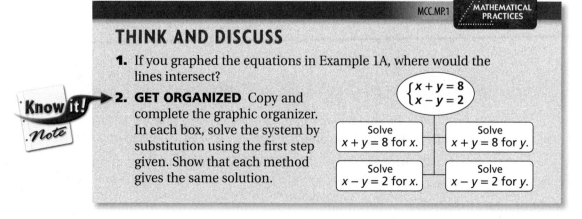

MCC.MP.1

MATHEMATICAL PRACTICES

THINK AND DISCUSS

1. If you graphed the equations in Example 1A, where would the lines intersect?

2. GET ORGANIZED Copy and complete the graphic organizer. In each box, solve the system by substitution using the first step given. Show that each method gives the same solution.

Know it! Note

$$\begin{cases} x + y = 8 \\ x - y = 2 \end{cases}$$

| Solve $x + y = 8$ for x. | Solve $x + y = 8$ for y. |
| Solve $x - y = 2$ for x. | Solve $x - y = 2$ for y. |

GUIDED PRACTICE

Solve each system by substitution.

SEE EXAMPLE 1

1. $\begin{cases} y = 5x - 10 \\ y = 3x + 8 \end{cases}$

2. $\begin{cases} 3x + y = 2 \\ 4x + y = 20 \end{cases}$

3. $\begin{cases} y = x + 5 \\ 4x + y = 20 \end{cases}$

SEE EXAMPLE 2

4. $\begin{cases} x - 2y = 10 \\ \frac{1}{2}x - 2y = 4 \end{cases}$

5. $\begin{cases} y - 4x = 3 \\ 2x - 3y = 21 \end{cases}$

6. $\begin{cases} x = y - 8 \\ -x - y = 0 \end{cases}$

SEE EXAMPLE 3

7. **Consumer Economics** The Strauss family is deciding between two lawn-care services. Green Lawn charges a $49 startup fee, plus $29 per month. Grass Team charges a $25 startup fee, plus $37 per month.

   a. In how many months will both lawn-care services cost the same? What will that cost be?

   b. If the family will use the service for only 6 months, which is the better option? Explain.

PRACTICE AND PROBLEM SOLVING

Independent Practice

For Exercises	See Example
8–10	1
11–16	2
17	3

Solve each system by substitution.

8. $\begin{cases} y = x + 3 \\ y = 2x + 4 \end{cases}$

9. $\begin{cases} y = 2x + 10 \\ y = -2x - 6 \end{cases}$

10. $\begin{cases} x + 2y = 8 \\ x + 3y = 12 \end{cases}$

11. $\begin{cases} 2x + 2y = 2 \\ -4x + 4y = 12 \end{cases}$

12. $\begin{cases} y = 0.5x + 2 \\ -y = -2x + 4 \end{cases}$

13. $\begin{cases} -x + y = 4 \\ 3x - 2y = -7 \end{cases}$

14. $\begin{cases} 3x + y = -8 \\ -2x - y = 6 \end{cases}$

15. $\begin{cases} x + 2y = -1 \\ 4x - 4y = 20 \end{cases}$

16. $\begin{cases} 4x = y - 1 \\ 6x - 2y = -3 \end{cases}$

17. **Recreation** Casey wants to buy a gym membership. One gym has a $150 joining fee and costs $35 per month. Another gym has no joining fee and costs $60 per month.

    a. In how many months will both gym memberships cost the same? What will that cost be?

    b. If Casey plans to cancel in 5 months, which is the better option for him? Explain.

Solve each system by substitution. Check your answer.

18. $\begin{cases} x = 5 \\ x + y = 8 \end{cases}$

19. $\begin{cases} y = -3x + 4 \\ x = 2y + 6 \end{cases}$

20. $\begin{cases} 3x - y = 11 \\ 5y - 7x = 1 \end{cases}$

21. $\begin{cases} \frac{1}{2}x + \frac{1}{3}y = 6 \\ x - y = 2 \end{cases}$

22. $\begin{cases} x = 7 - 2y \\ 2x + y = 5 \end{cases}$

23. $\begin{cases} y = 1.2x - 4 \\ 2.2x + 5 = y \end{cases}$

24. The sum of two numbers is 50. The first number is 43 less than twice the second number. Write and solve a system of equations to find the two numbers.

25. **Money** A jar contains n nickels and d dimes. There are 20 coins in the jar, and the total value of the coins is $1.40. How many nickels and how many dimes are in the jar? (*Hint:* Nickels are worth $0.05 and dimes are worth $0.10.)

26. Multi-Step Use the receipts below to write and solve a system of equations to find the cost of a large popcorn and the cost of a small drink.

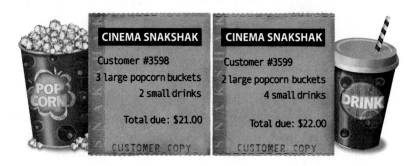

CINEMA SNAKSHAK

Customer #3598

3 large popcorn buckets

2 small drinks

Total due: $21.00

CUSTOMER COPY

CINEMA SNAKSHAK

Customer #3599

2 large popcorn buckets

4 small drinks

Total due: $22.00

CUSTOMER COPY

27. Finance Helene invested a total of $1000 in two simple-interest bank accounts. One account paid 5% annual interest; the other paid 6% annual interest. The total amount of interest she earned after one year was $58. Write and solve a system of equations to find the amount invested in each account. (*Hint:* Change the interest rates into decimals first.)

Geometry Two angles whose measures have a sum of 90° are called complementary angles. For Exercises 28–30, *x* and *y* represent the measures of complementary angles. Use this information and the equation given in each exercise to find the measure of each angle.

28. $y = 4x - 10$ **29.** $x = 2y$ **30.** $y = 2(x - 15)$

31. Aviation With a headwind, a small plane can fly 240 miles in 3 hours. With a tailwind, the plane can fly the same distance in 2 hours. Follow the steps below to find the rates of the plane and wind.

   a. Copy and complete the table. Let *p* be the rate of the plane and *w* be the rate of the wind.

	Rate	•	Time	=	Distance
With Headwind	$p - w$	•	▓	=	240
With Tailwind	▓	•	2	=	▓

   b. Use the information in each row to write a system of equations.

   c. Solve the system of equations to find the rates of the plane and wind.

H.O.T. 32. Write About It Explain how to solve a system of equations by substitution.

H.O.T. 33. Critical Thinking Explain the connection between the solution of a system solved by graphing and the solution of the same system solved by substitution.

Real-World Connections

34. At the school store, Juanita bought 2 books and a backpack for a total of $26 before tax. Each book cost $8 less than the backpack.

   a. Write a system of equations that can be used to find the price of each book and the price of the backpack.

   b. Solve this system by substitution.

   c. Solve this system by graphing. Discuss advantages and disadvantages of solving by substitution and solving by graphing.

Victoria Smith/HMH

35. Estimation Use the graph to estimate the solution to

$$\begin{cases} 2x - y = 6 \\ x + y = -0.6 \end{cases}$$. Round your answer to the nearest tenth.

Then solve the system by substitution.

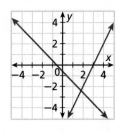

TEST PREP

36. Elizabeth met 24 of her cousins at a family reunion. The number of male cousins m was 6 less than twice the number of female cousins f. Which system can be used to find the number of male cousins and female cousins?

(A) $\begin{cases} m + f = 24 \\ f = 2m - 6 \end{cases}$ (B) $\begin{cases} m + f = 24 \\ f = 2m \end{cases}$ (C) $\begin{cases} m = 24 + f \\ m = f - 6 \end{cases}$ (D) $\begin{cases} f = 24 - m \\ m = 2f - 6 \end{cases}$

37. Which problem is best represented by the system $\begin{cases} d = n + 5 \\ d + n = 12 \end{cases}$?

(F) Roger has 12 coins in dimes and nickels. There are 5 more dimes than nickels.

(G) Roger has 5 coins in dimes and nickels. There are 12 more dimes than nickels.

(H) Roger has 12 coins in dimes and nickels. There are 5 more nickels than dimes.

(J) Roger has 5 coins in dimes and nickels. There are 12 more nickels than dimes.

CHALLENGE AND EXTEND

38. A car dealership has 378 cars on its lot. The ratio of new cars to used cars is 5:4. Write and solve a system of equations to find the number of new and used cars on the lot.

Solve each system by substitution.

39. $\begin{cases} 2r - 3s - t = 12 \\ s + 3t = 10 \\ t = 4 \end{cases}$ **40.** $\begin{cases} x + y + z = 7 \\ y + z = 5 \\ 2y - 4z = -14 \end{cases}$ **41.** $\begin{cases} a + 2b + c = 19 \\ -b + c = -5 \\ 3b + 2c = 15 \end{cases}$

FOCUS ON MATHEMATICAL PRACTICES

H.O.T. 42. Reasoning Examine the system. $\begin{cases} 2m + 3n = 31 \\ n - m = 7 \end{cases}$

a. Solve the system by substitution.

b. Would you get the same answer whether you solved for m or n first? Explain.

c. Why does it make sense to solve for n in the second equation first?

H.O.T. 43. Error Analysis Marjorie attempted to solve the system of equations shown, but ran into trouble. What mistake did she make? $\begin{cases} 3x + y = 3 \\ 14x + 4y = 2 \end{cases}$

Step 1: $3x + y = 3 \rightarrow y = 3 - 3x$

Step 2: $3x + y = 3 \rightarrow 3x + (3 - 3x) = 3$

Step 3: $3x + (3 - 3x) = 3$

$3 = 3$

H.O.T. 44. Precision Explain why it is not always possible to solve a system of linear equations by graphing, but it is always possible to solve a system using substitution.

6-3 Solving Systems by Elimination

Essential Question: How can you solve systems of linear equations by using elimination?

Objectives
Solve systems of linear equations in two variables by elimination.

Compare and choose an appropriate method for solving systems of linear equations.

Why learn this?
You can solve a system of linear equations to determine how many flowers of each type you can buy to make a bouquet. (See Example 4.)

Another method for solving systems of equations is *elimination*. Like substitution, the goal of elimination is to get one equation that has only one variable.

Remember that an equation stays balanced if you add equal amounts to both sides. Consider the system $\begin{cases} x - 2y = -19 \\ 5x + 2y = 1 \end{cases}$. Since $5x + 2y = 1$, you can add $5x + 2y$ to one side of the first equation and 1 to the other side and the balance is maintained.

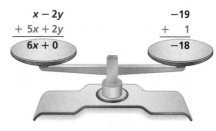

Since $-2y$ and $2y$ have **opposite coefficients**, you can eliminate the y by adding the two equations. The result is one equation that has only one variable: $6x = -18$.

When you use the elimination method to solve a system of linear equations, align all like terms in the equations. Then determine whether any like terms can be eliminated because they have opposite coefficients.

Solving Systems of Equations by Elimination
Step 1 Write the system so that like terms are aligned.
Step 2 Eliminate one of the variables and solve for the other variable.
Step 3 Substitute the value of the variable into one of the original equations and solve for the other variable.
Step 4 Write the answers from Steps 2 and 3 as an ordered pair, (x, y), and check.

Later in this lesson you will learn how to multiply one or more equations by a number in order to produce opposites that can be eliminated.

EXAMPLE **1**
MCC9-12.A.REI.6

Elimination Using Addition

Solve $\begin{cases} x - 2y = -19 \\ 5x + 2y = 1 \end{cases}$ by elimination.

my.hrw.com

Online Video Tutor

Step 1	$x - 2y = -19$	*Write the system so that like terms are aligned.*
	$+ \; 5x + 2y = \quad 1$	*Notice that −2y and 2y are opposites.*
Step 2	$6x \; + 0 = -18$	*Add the equations to eliminate y.*
	$6x = -18$	*Simplify and solve for x.*
	$\dfrac{6x}{6} = \dfrac{-18}{6}$	*Divide both sides by 6.*
	$x = -3$	

Step 3	$x - 2y = -19$	*Write one of the original equations.*
	$-3 - 2y = -19$	*Substitute −3 for x.*
	$\underline{+ 3 \qquad\quad + 3}$	*Add 3 to both sides.*
	$-2y = -16$	
	$\dfrac{-2y}{-2} = \dfrac{-16}{-2}$	*Divide both sides by −2.*
	$y = 8$	

Step 4 $(-3, 8)$ — *Write the solution as an ordered pair.*

Helpful Hint

Check your answer.

$x - 2y = -19$	
$-3 - 2(8)$	-19
$-3 - 16$	-19
-19	$-19 ✓$

$5x + 2y = 1$	
$5(-3) + 2(8)$	1
$-15 + 16$	1
1	$1 ✓$

1. Solve $\begin{cases} y + 3x = -2 \\ 2y - 3x = 14 \end{cases}$ by elimination. Check your answer.

When two equations each contain the same term, you can subtract one equation from the other to solve the system. To subtract an equation, add the opposite of *each* term.

EXAMPLE **2**
MCC9-12.A.REI.6

Elimination Using Subtraction

Solve $\begin{cases} 3x + 4y = 18 \\ -2x + 4y = 8 \end{cases}$ by elimination.

my.hrw.com

Online Video Tutor

Step 1	$3x + 4y = 18$	
	$-(-2x + 4y = \; 8)$	*Notice that both equations contain 4y.*
	$3x + 4y = \; 18$	*Add the opposite of each term*
	$\underline{+ 2x - 4y = -8}$	*in the second equation.*
Step 2	$5x + \; 0 = 10$	*Eliminate y.*
	$5x = 10$	*Simplify and solve for x.*
	$x = 2$	

Step 3	$-2x + 4y = \; 8$	*Write one of the original equations.*
	$-2(2) + 4y = \; 8$	*Substitute 2 for x.*
	$-4 + 4y = \; 8$	
	$\underline{+ 4 \qquad\quad + 4}$	*Add 4 to both sides.*
	$4y = 12$	*Simplify and solve for y.*
	$y = 3$	

Step 4 $(2, 3)$ — *Write the solution as an ordered pair.*

Remember!

Remember to check by substituting your answer into both original equations.

148 *Module 6 Solving Systems of Equations*

2. Solve $\begin{cases} 3x + 3y = 15 \\ -2x + 3y = -5 \end{cases}$ by elimination. Check your answer.

In some cases, you will first need to multiply one or both of the equations by a number so that one variable has opposite coefficients.

 my.hrw.com

Online Video Tutor

Helpful Hint

In Example 3A, you could have also multiplied the first equation by −3 to eliminate y.

Elimination Using Multiplication First

Solve each system by elimination.

A $\begin{cases} 2x + y = 3 \\ -x + 3y = -12 \end{cases}$

Step 1 $\qquad$ $2x + y = 3$
$+ 2(-x + 3y = -12)$
$2x + y = 3$
$+ (-2x + 6y = -24)$

Multiply each term in the second equation by 2 to get opposite x-coefficients.

Add the new equation to the first equation to eliminate x.

Step 2 $\qquad 7y = -21$
$y = -3$ $\qquad$ *Solve for y.*

Step 3 $\quad 2x + y = 3$ $\qquad$ *Write one of the original equations.*
$2x + (-3) = 3$ $\qquad$ *Substitute −3 for y.*
$\underline{+ 3 \quad + 3}$ $\qquad$ *Add 3 to both sides.*
$2x = 6$ $\qquad$ *Solve for x.*
$x = 3$

Step 4 $(3, -3)$ $\qquad$ *Write the solution as an ordered pair.*

B $\begin{cases} 7x - 12y = -22 \\ 5x - 8y = -14 \end{cases}$

Step 1 $\qquad 2(7x - 12y = -22)$
$+ (-3)(5x - 8y = -14)$
$14x - 24y = -44$
$+ (-15x + 24y = 42)$

Multiply the first equation by 2 and the second equation by −3 to get opposite y-coefficients.

Add the new equations to eliminate y.

Step 2 $\quad -x = -2$
$x = 2$ $\qquad$ *Solve for x.*

Step 3 $\quad 7x - 12y = -22$ $\qquad$ *Write one of the original equations.*
$7(2) - 12y = -22$ $\qquad$ *Substitute 2 for x.*
$14 - 12y = -22$
$\underline{-14 \qquad -14}$ $\qquad$ *Subtract 14 from both sides.*
$-12y = -36$ $\qquad$ *Solve for y.*
$y = 3$

Step 4 $\quad (2, 3)$ $\qquad$ *Write the solution as an ordered pair.*

 Solve each system by elimination. Check your answer.

3a. $\begin{cases} 3x + 2y = 6 \\ -x + y = -2 \end{cases}$ $\qquad$ **3b.** $\begin{cases} 2x + 5y = 26 \\ -3x - 4y = -25 \end{cases}$

Consumer Economics Application

my.hrw.com

Online Video Tutor

Sam spent $24.75 to buy 12 flowers for his mother. The bouquet contained roses and daisies. How many of each type of flower did Sam buy?

Write a system. Use r for the number of roses and d for the number of daisies.

$$2.50r + 1.75d = 24.75 \qquad \textit{The cost of roses and daisies totals \$24.75.}$$

$$r + d = 12 \qquad \textit{The total number of roses and daisies is 12.}$$

Step 1

$$2.50r + 1.75d = 24.75$$
$$+ (-2.50)(r + d = 12)$$
$$\rightarrow \quad 2.50r + 1.75d = \quad 24.75$$

Multiply the second equation by −2.50 to get opposite r-coefficients.

$$+ (-2.50r - 2.50d = -30.00)$$

Add this equation to the first equation to eliminate r.

Step 2

$$-0.75d = -5.25$$

$$d = 7 \qquad \textit{Solve for d.}$$

Step 3

$$r + d = 12 \qquad \textit{Write one of the original equations.}$$
$$r + 7 = 12 \qquad \textit{Substitute 7 for d.}$$
$$\underline{\quad -7 \quad -7} \qquad \textit{Subtract 7 from both sides.}$$
$$r = 5$$

Step 4

$$(5, 7) \qquad \textit{Write the solution as an ordered pair.}$$

Sam can buy 5 roses and 7 daisies.

ROSES
$2.50 each

DAISIES
$1.75 each

CHECK IT OUT!

4. What if...? Sally spent $14.85 to buy 13 flowers. She bought lilies, which cost $1.25 each, and tulips, which cost $0.90 each. How many of each flower did Sally buy?

All systems can be solved in more than one way. For some systems, some methods may be better than others.

Know it! Note

Systems of Linear Equations

METHOD	USE WHEN...	EXAMPLE
Graphing	• Both equations are solved for *y*. • You want to estimate a solution.	$\begin{cases} y = 3x + 2 \\ y = -2x + 6 \end{cases}$
Substitution	• A variable in either equation has a coefficient of 1 or −1. • Both equations are solved for the same variable. • Either equation is solved for a variable.	$\begin{cases} x + 2y = 7 \\ x = 10 - 5y \end{cases}$ or $\begin{cases} x = 2y + 10 \\ x = 3y + 5 \end{cases}$
Elimination	• Both equations have the same variable with the same or opposite coefficients. • A variable term in one equation is a multiple of the corresponding variable term in the other equation.	$\begin{cases} 3x + 2y = 8 \\ 5x + 2y = 12 \end{cases}$ or $\begin{cases} 6x + 5y = 10 \\ 3x + 2y = 15 \end{cases}$

THINK AND DISCUSS

1. Explain how multiplying the second equation in a system by -1 and eliminating by adding is the same as elimination by subtraction. Give an example of a system for which this applies.

2. Explain why it does not matter which variable you solve for first when solving a system by elimination.

3. GET ORGANIZED Copy and complete the graphic organizer. In each box, write an example of a system of equations that you could solve using the given method.

Solving Systems of Linear Equations

- Substitution
- Elimination using addition or subtraction
- Elimination using multiplication

6-3 Exercises

my.hrw.com
Homework Help

GUIDED PRACTICE

Solve each system by elimination. Check your answer.

SEE EXAMPLE 1

1. $\begin{cases} -x + y = 5 \\ x - 5y = -9 \end{cases}$

2. $\begin{cases} x + y = 12 \\ x - y = 2 \end{cases}$

3. $\begin{cases} 2x + 5y = -24 \\ 3x - 5y = 14 \end{cases}$

SEE EXAMPLE 2

4. $\begin{cases} x - 10y = 60 \\ x + 14y = 12 \end{cases}$

5. $\begin{cases} 5x + y = 0 \\ 5x + 2y = 30 \end{cases}$

6. $\begin{cases} -5x + 7y = 11 \\ -5x + 3y = 19 \end{cases}$

SEE EXAMPLE 3

7. $\begin{cases} 2x + 3y = 12 \\ 5x - y = 13 \end{cases}$

8. $\begin{cases} -3x + 4y = 12 \\ 2x + y = -8 \end{cases}$

9. $\begin{cases} 2x + 4y = -4 \\ 3x + 5y = -3 \end{cases}$

SEE EXAMPLE 4

10. Consumer Economics Each family in a neighborhood is contributing $20 worth of food to the neighborhood picnic. The Harlin family is bringing 12 packages of buns. The hamburger buns cost $2.00 per package. The hot-dog buns cost $1.50 per package. How many packages of each type of bun did they buy?

PRACTICE AND PROBLEM SOLVING

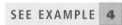

Independent Practice	
For Exercises	See Example
11–13	1
14–16	2
17–19	3
20	4

Solve each system by elimination. Check your answer.

11. $\begin{cases} -x + y = -1 \\ 2x - y = 0 \end{cases}$

12. $\begin{cases} -2x + y = -20 \\ 2x + y = 48 \end{cases}$

13. $\begin{cases} 3x - y = -2 \\ -2x + y = 3 \end{cases}$

14. $\begin{cases} x - y = 4 \\ x - 2y = 10 \end{cases}$

15. $\begin{cases} x + 2y = 5 \\ 3x + 2y = 17 \end{cases}$

16. $\begin{cases} 3x - 2y = -1 \\ 3x - 4y = 9 \end{cases}$

17. $\begin{cases} x - y = -3 \\ 5x + 3y = 1 \end{cases}$

18. $\begin{cases} 9x - 3y = 3 \\ 3x + 8y = -17 \end{cases}$

19. $\begin{cases} 5x + 2y = -1 \\ 3x + 7y = 11 \end{cases}$

20. Multi-Step Mrs. Gonzalez bought centerpieces to put on each table at a graduation party. She spent $31.50. There are 8 tables each requiring either a candle or vase. Candles cost $3 and vases cost $4.25. How many of each type did she buy?

my.hrw.com

Online Extra Practice

21. **Geometry** The difference between the length and width of a rectangle is 2 units. The perimeter is 40 units. Write and solve a system of equations to determine the length and width of the rectangle. (*Hint:* The perimeter of a rectangle is $2\ell + 2w$.)

22. ///**ERROR ANALYSIS**/// Which is incorrect? Explain the error.

Ⓐ
$$\begin{cases} x + y = -3 \qquad x + y = -3 \\ 3x + y = 3 \quad -(3x + y = 3) \end{cases}$$
$$\underline{\qquad\qquad\qquad -2x = 0}$$
$$x = 0$$

Ⓑ
$$\begin{cases} x + y = -3 \qquad x + y = -3 \\ 3x + y = 3 \quad -(3x + y = 3) \end{cases}$$
$$\underline{\qquad\qquad\qquad -2x = -6}$$
$$x = 3$$

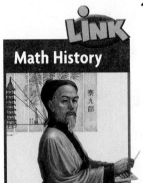

Math History

In 1247, Qin Jiushao wrote *Mathematical Treatise in Nine Sections.* Its contents included solving systems of equations and the Chinese Remainder Theorem.

23. **Chemistry** A chemist has a bottle of a 1% acid solution and a bottle of a 5% acid solution. She wants to mix the two solutions to get 100 mL of a 4% acid solution. Follow the steps below to find how much of each solution she should use.

	1% Solution	+	5% Solution	=	4% Solution
Amount of Solution (mL)	x	+	y	=	▨
Amount of Acid (mL)	$0.01x$	+	▨	=	$0.04(100)$

a. Copy and complete the table.

b. Use the information in the table to write a system of equations.

c. Solve the system of equations to find how much she will use from each bottle to get 100 mL of a 4% acid solution.

Critical Thinking Which method would you use to solve each system? Explain.

24. $\begin{cases} \dfrac{1}{2}x - 5y = 30 \\ \dfrac{1}{2}x + 7y = 6 \end{cases}$

25. $\begin{cases} -x + 2y = 3 \\ 4x - 5y = -3 \end{cases}$

26. $\begin{cases} 3x - y = 10 \\ 2x - y = 7 \end{cases}$

27. $\begin{cases} 3y + x = 10 \\ x = 4y + 2 \end{cases}$

28. $\begin{cases} y = -4x \\ y = 2x + 3 \end{cases}$

29. $\begin{cases} 2x + 6y = 12 \\ 4x + 5y = 15 \end{cases}$

30. **Business** A local boys club sold 176 bags of mulch and made a total of $520. They did not sell any of the expensive cocoa mulch. Use the table to determine how many bags of each type of mulch they sold.

Mulch Prices ($)	
Cocoa	4.75
Hardwood	3.50
Pine Bark	2.75

Real-World Connections

31. a. The school store is running a promotion on school supplies. Different supplies are placed on two shelves. You can purchase 3 items from shelf A and 2 from shelf B for $16. Or you can purchase 2 items from shelf A and 3 from shelf B for $14. Write a system of equations that can be used to find the individual prices for the supplies on shelf A and on shelf B.

b. Solve the system of equations by elimination.

c. If the supplies on shelf A are normally $6 each and the supplies on shelf B are normally $3 each, how much will you save on each package plan from part **a**?

H.O.T. 32. Write About It Solve the system $\begin{cases} 3x + y = 1 \\ 2x + 4y = -6 \end{cases}$. Explain how you can check your solution algebraically and graphically.

TEST PREP

33. A math test has 25 problems. Some are worth 2 points, and some are worth 3 points. The test is worth 60 points total. Which system can be used to determine the number of 2-point problems and the number of 3-point problems on the test?

Ⓐ $\begin{cases} x + y = 25 \\ 2x + 3y = 60 \end{cases}$ Ⓑ $\begin{cases} x + y = 60 \\ 2x + 3y = 25 \end{cases}$ Ⓒ $\begin{cases} x - y = 25 \\ 2x + 3y = 60 \end{cases}$ Ⓓ $\begin{cases} x - y = 60 \\ 2x - 3y = 25 \end{cases}$

34. An electrician charges $15 plus $11 per hour. Another electrician charges $10 plus $15 per hour. For what amount of time will the cost be the same? What is that cost?

    Ⓕ 1 hour; $25   Ⓗ $1\frac{1}{2}$ hours; $30

    Ⓖ $1\frac{1}{4}$ hours; $28.75   Ⓙ $1\frac{3}{4}$ hours; $32.50

35. Short Response Three hundred fifty-eight tickets to the school basketball game on Friday were sold. Student tickets were $1.50, and nonstudent tickets were $3.25. The school made $752.25.

    a. Write a system of linear equations that could be used to determine how many student and how many nonstudent tickets were sold. Define the variables you use.

    b. Solve the system you wrote in part **a.** How many student and how many nonstudent tickets were sold?

CHALLENGE AND EXTEND

H.O.T. 36. If two equations in a system are represented by $Ax + By = C$ and $Dx + Ey = F$, where A, B, C, D, E, and F are constants, you can write a third equation by doing the following:

Multiply the second equation by a nonzero constant k to get $kDx + kEy = kF$.

Add this new equation to the first equation $Ax + By = C$ to get $(A + kD)x + (B + kE)y = C + kF$.

Prove that if (x_1, y_1) is a solution of the original system, then it is a solution of the system represented by $Ax + By = C$ and $(A + kD)x + (B + kE)y = C + kF$.

FOCUS ON MATHEMATICAL PRACTICES

H.O.T. 37. Reasoning To solve the system of linear equations shown by elimination, which variable would you eliminate first? Explain your thinking, then find the solution of the system. $\begin{cases} 3x - 2y = 1 \\ 2x + 2y = 4 \end{cases}$

H.O.T. 38. Comparison To solve the system of linear equations shown by elimination, Mateo began by multiplying the first equation by 3. Mariana began by multiplying the second equation by -2. What will each student find as the sum of the equations? Which sum will be easier to solve? $\begin{cases} \frac{2}{3}x + 12y = 14 \\ -2x + 6y = 0 \end{cases}$

Ready to Go On?

my.hrw.com
Assessment and Intervention

✅ 6-1 Solving Systems by Graphing

Tell whether the ordered pair is a solution of the given system.

1. $(-2, 1)$; $\begin{cases} y = -2x - 3 \\ y = x + 3 \end{cases}$

2. $(9, 2)$; $\begin{cases} x - 4y = 1 \\ 2x - 3y = 3 \end{cases}$

3. $(3, -1)$; $\begin{cases} y = -\frac{1}{3}x \\ y + 2x = 5 \end{cases}$

Solve each system by graphing.

4. $\begin{cases} y = x + 5 \\ y = \frac{1}{2}x + 4 \end{cases}$

5. $\begin{cases} y = -x - 2 \\ 2x - y = 2 \end{cases}$

6. $\begin{cases} \frac{2}{3}x + y = -3 \\ 4x + y = 7 \end{cases}$

7. **Banking** Christiana and Marlena opened their first savings accounts on the same day. Christiana opened her account with $50 and plans to deposit $10 every month. Marlena opened her account with $30 and plans to deposit $15 every month. After how many months will their two accounts have the same amount of money? What will that amount be?

✅ 6-2 Solving Systems by Substitution

Solve each system by substitution.

8. $\begin{cases} y = -x + 5 \\ 2x + y = 11 \end{cases}$

9. $\begin{cases} 4x - 3y = -1 \\ 3x - y = -2 \end{cases}$

10. $\begin{cases} y = -x \\ y = -2x - 5 \end{cases}$

11. $\begin{cases} x + y = -1 \\ y = -2x + 3 \end{cases}$

12. $\begin{cases} x = y - 7 \\ -y - 2x = 8 \end{cases}$

13. $\begin{cases} \frac{1}{2}x + y = 9 \\ 3x - 4y = -6 \end{cases}$

14. The Nash family's car needs repairs. Estimates for parts and labor from two garages are shown.

Garage	Parts ($)	Labor ($ per hour)
Motor Works	650	70
Jim's Car Care	800	55

For how many hours of labor will the total cost of fixing the car be the same at both garages? What will that cost be? Which garage will be cheaper if the repairs require 8 hours of labor? Explain.

✅ 6-3 Solving Systems by Elimination

Solve each system by elimination.

15. $\begin{cases} x + 3y = 15 \\ 2x - 3y = -6 \end{cases}$

16. $\begin{cases} x + y = 2 \\ 2x + y = -1 \end{cases}$

17. $\begin{cases} -2x + 5y = -1 \\ 3x + 2y = 11 \end{cases}$

18. It takes Akira 10 minutes to make a black and white drawing and 25 minutes for a color drawing. On Saturday he made a total of 9 drawings in 2 hours. Write and solve a system of equations to determine how many drawings of each type Akira made.

1. The Fun Guys game rental store charges an annual fee of $5 plus $5.50 per game rented. The Game Bank charges an annual fee of $17 plus $2.50 per game. For how many game rentals will the cost be the same at both stores? What is that cost?

   (A) 4 games; $27   (C) 3 games; $22

   (B) 6 games; $38   (D) 2 games; $16

2. If the pattern in the table continues, in what month will the number of sales of CDs and movie tickets be the same? What number will that be?

Total Number Sold				
Month	1	2	3	4
CDs	700	685	670	655
Movie tickets	100	145	190	235

   (F) Month 10; 550   (H) Month 8; 580

   (G) Month 9; 580   (J) Month 11; 550

3. Solve $\begin{cases} 4x - 4y = -16 \\ x - 2y = -12 \end{cases}$ by substitution. Express your answer as an ordered pair.

   (A) (8, −4)   (C) (−2, 4)

   (B) (4, 8)   (D) (4, −8)

4. Solve $\begin{cases} 2x - 5y = -7 \\ 5x - 3y = 11 \end{cases}$ by elimination.

   Express your answer as an ordered pair.

   (F) (3, 4)   (H) $\left(\frac{4}{7}, \frac{8}{5}\right)$

   (G) (3, 2)   (J) (4, 3)

5. At the local pet store, zebra fish cost $2.10 each and neon tetras cost $1.85 each. If Marsha bought 13 fish for a total cost of $25.80, not including tax, how many of each type of fish did she buy?

   (A) 5 zebra fish, 8 neon tetras

   (B) 7 zebra fish, 6 neon tetras

   (C) 8 zebra fish, 5 neon tetras

   (D) 6 zebra fish, 7 neon tetras

6. Which system of equations is shown on the graph?

   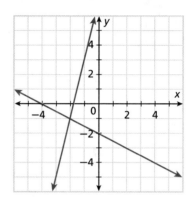

   (F) $\begin{cases} x + 2y = -4 \\ y = 4x + 7 \end{cases}$ (H) $\begin{cases} x = \frac{1}{2}x - 2 \\ y = 4x + 7 \end{cases}$

   (G) $\begin{cases} y = -\frac{1}{2}x - 2 \\ y = -4x + 7 \end{cases}$ (J) $\begin{cases} x + 2y = 4 \\ 4x - y = -7 \end{cases}$

7. The sum of the digits of a two-digit number is 8. If the number is multiplied by 4, the result is 104. Write and solve a system of equations. Find the number.

   (A) $\begin{cases} x + y = 8 \\ 4(x + y) = 104 \end{cases}$ (C) $\begin{cases} x + y = 8 \\ 4(2x + y) = 104 \end{cases}$

   The number is 35.   The number is 18.

   (B) $\begin{cases} x + y = 8 \\ 4(10x + y) = 104 \end{cases}$ (D) $\begin{cases} x + y = 8 \\ 4(10x + y) = 104 \end{cases}$

   The number is 17.   The number is 26.

Mini-Task

8. Gracey's little sister Eliza was born when Gracey was 7 years old. Now, Eliza is half as old as Gracey. Write and solve an equation to find the age of each sister.

Special Systems and Systems of Inequalities

COMMON CORE GPS

Contents

MATHEMATICAL PRACTICES The Common Core Georgia Performance Standards for Mathematical Practice describe varieties of expertise that all students should seek to develop. Opportunities to develop these practices are integrated throughout this program.

1 Make sense of problems and persevere in solving them.

2 Reason abstractly and quantitatively.

3 Construct viable arguments and critique the reasoning of others.

4 Model with mathematics.

5 Use appropriate tools strategically.

6 Attend to precision.

7 Look for and make use of structure.

8 Look for and express regularity in repeated reasoning.

Unpacking the Standards

my.hrw.com
Multilingual Glossary

Understanding the standards and the vocabulary terms in the standards will help you know exactly what you are expected to learn in this chapter.

COMMON CORE GPS MCC9-12.A.REI.12

Graph the solutions to a linear inequality in two variables as a half-plane (excluding the boundary in the case of a strict inequality), and graph the solution set to a system of linear inequalities in two variables as the intersection of the corresponding half-planes.

Key Vocabulary

half-plane (semiplano) The part of the coordinate plane on one side of a line, which may include the line.

solution of a linear inequality in two variables (solución de una desigualdad lineal en dos variables) An ordered pair or ordered pairs that make the inequality true.

system of linear inequalities (sistema de desigualdades lineales) A system of inequalities in which all of the inequalities are linear.

What It Means For You

Systems of linear inequalities model many real-life situations where you want to know when one or more conditions are met, but where there are many possible solutions.

EXAMPLE **Linear Inequality**

$y > \frac{2}{3}x - 1$

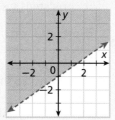

EXAMPLE **System of Two Linear Inequalities**

$$\begin{cases} y > \frac{2}{3}x - 1 \\ y \leq -2x - 2 \end{cases}$$

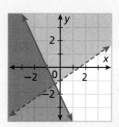

EXAMPLE **System of Three Linear Inequalities**

Tracy works at least 5 hours per week as a cashier: $c \geq 5$

Tracy works at least 10 hours per week at a library: $p \geq 10$

Tracy works at most 24 hours per week: $c + p \leq 24$

How can Tracy divide her time between the two jobs?

Sample Solutions	
Cashier (hours)	Page (hours)
5	10
5	16
8	12
8	16
10	12
12	12

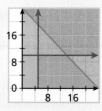

© SW Productions/PhotoDisc/Getty Image

Unpacking the Standards **157**

7-1 Solving Special Systems

Essential Question: How can you solve consistent and inconsistent systems of linear equations?

Objectives
Solve special systems of linear equations in two variables.

Classify systems of linear equations and determine the number of solutions.

Vocabulary
consistent system
inconsistent system
independent system
dependent system

Why learn this?
Linear systems can be used to analyze business growth, such as comic book sales. (See Example 4.)

When two lines intersect at a point, there is exactly one solution to the system. A system with at least one solution is a **consistent system**.

When the two lines in a system do not intersect, they are parallel lines. There are no ordered pairs that satisfy both equations, so there is no solution. A system that has no solution is an **inconsistent system**.

  EXAMPLE MCC9-12.A.REI.6 **1**

my.hrw.com

Online Video Tutor

Systems with No Solution

Show that $\begin{cases} y = x - 1 \\ -x + y = 2 \end{cases}$ has no solution.

Method 1 Compare slopes and y-intercepts.

$y = x - 1 \rightarrow y = 1x - 1$ *Write both equations in slope-intercept form.*
$-x + y = 2 \rightarrow y = 1x + 2$ *The lines are parallel because they have the same slope and different y-intercepts.*

This system has no solution.

Method 2 Graph the system.
The lines are parallel.

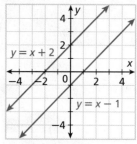

This system has no solution.

Method 3 Solve the system algebraically. Use the substitution method.

$-x + (x - 1) = 2$ *Substitute x − 1 for y in the second equation, and solve.*
$-1 = 2$ ✗   *False*

This system has no solution.

 1. Show that $\begin{cases} y = -2x + 5 \\ 2x + y = 1 \end{cases}$ has no solution.

If two linear equations in a system have the same graph, the graphs are coincident lines, or the same line. There are infinitely many solutions of the system because every point on the line represents a solution of both equations.

EXAMPLE 2 Systems with Infinitely Many Solutions

Show that $\begin{cases} y = 2x + 1 \\ 2x - y + 1 = 0 \end{cases}$ has infinitely many solutions.

Method 1 Compare slopes and y-intercepts.

$$y = 2x + 1 \rightarrow y = 2x + 1$$
$$2x - y + 1 = 0 \rightarrow y = 2x + 1$$

Write both equations in slope-intercept form. The lines have the same slope and the same y-intercept.

If this system were graphed, the graphs would be the same line. There are infinitely many solutions.

Method 2 Solve the system algebraically. Use the elimination method.

$$y = 2x + 1 \rightarrow -2x + y = 1 \quad \text{Write equations to line up like terms.}$$
$$2x - y + 1 = 0 \rightarrow \underline{+2x - y = -1} \quad \text{Add the equations.}$$
$$0 = 0 \checkmark \quad \text{True. The equation is an identity.}$$

There are infinitely many solutions.

Caution!

$0 = 0$ is a true statement. It does not mean the system has zero solutions or no solution.

 2. Show that $\begin{cases} y = x - 3 \\ x - y - 3 = 0 \end{cases}$ has infinitely many solutions.

Consistent systems can either be independent or dependent.

- An **independent system** has exactly one solution. The graph of an independent system consists of two intersecting lines.

- A **dependent system** has infinitely many solutions. The graph of a dependent system consists of two coincident lines.

Classification of Systems of Linear Equations

CLASSIFICATION	CONSISTENT AND INDEPENDENT	CONSISTENT AND DEPENDENT	INCONSISTENT
Number of Solutions	Exactly one	Infinitely many	None
Description	Different slopes	Same slope, same y-intercept	Same slope, different y-intercepts
Graph	Intersecting lines	Coincident lines	Parallel lines

EXAMPLE **3** MCC9-12.A.REI.6

Online Video Tutor

Classifying Systems of Linear Equations

Classify each system. Give the number of solutions.

A $\begin{cases} 2y = x + 2 \\ -\dfrac{1}{2}x + y = 1 \end{cases}$

$2y = x + 2 \rightarrow y = \dfrac{1}{2}x + 1$ *Write both equations in slope-intercept form.*

$-\dfrac{1}{2}x + y = 1 \rightarrow y = \dfrac{1}{2}x + 1$ *The lines have the same slope and the same y-intercepts. They are the same.*

The system is consistent and dependent. It has infinitely many solutions.

B $\begin{cases} y = 2(x - 1) \\ y = x + 1 \end{cases}$

$y = 2(x - 1) \rightarrow y = 2x - 2$ *Write both equations in slope-intercept form.*

$y = x + 1 \rightarrow y = 1x + 1$ *The lines have different slopes. They intersect.*

The system is consistent and independent. It has one solution.

CHECK IT OUT! Classify each system. Give the number of solutions.

3a. $\begin{cases} x + 2y = -4 \\ -2(y + 2) = x \end{cases}$ **3b.** $\begin{cases} y = -2(x - 1) \\ y = -x + 3 \end{cases}$ **3c.** $\begin{cases} 2x - 3y = 6 \\ y = \dfrac{2}{3}x \end{cases}$

EXAMPLE **4** MCC9-12.A.CED.2

Online Video Tutor

Business Application

The sales manager at Comics Now is comparing its sales with the sales of its competitor, Dynamo Comics. If the sales patterns continue, will the sales for Comics Now ever equal the sales for Dynamo Comics? Explain.

Comic Books Sold per Year (thousands)	2005	2006	2007	2008
Comics Now	130	170	210	250
Dynamo Comics	180	220	260	300

Use the table to write a system of linear equations. Let *y* represent the sales total and *x* represent the number of years since 2005.

	Sales total	equals	increase in sales per year	times	years	plus	beginning sales.
Comics Now	y	$=$	40	$\cdot$	x	$+$	130
Dynamo Comics	y	$=$	40	$\cdot$	x	$+$	180

$\begin{cases} y = 40x + 130 \\ y = 40x + 180 \end{cases}$

$y = 40x + 130$ *Both equations are in slope-intercept form.*

$y = 40x + 180$ *The lines have the same slope, but different y-intercepts.*

The graphs of the two equations are parallel lines, so there is no solution. If the patterns continue, sales for the two companies will never be equal.

Helpful Hint

The increase in sales is the difference between sales each year.

CHECK IT OUT!

4. Matt has $100 in a checking account and deposits $20 per month. Ben has $80 in a checking account and deposits $30 per month. Will the accounts ever have the same balance? Explain.

THINK AND DISCUSS

1. What methods can be used to determine the number of solutions of a system of linear equations?

2. GET ORGANIZED Copy and complete the graphic organizer. In each box, write the word or words that describes a system with that number of solutions and sketch a graph.

Linear System of Equations

No solution

Exactly one | Infinitely many

7-1 Exercises

my.hrw.com
Homework Help

GUIDED PRACTICE

1. Vocabulary A _____?_____ system can be independent or dependent. (*consistent* or *inconsistent*)

SEE EXAMPLE 1 Show that each system has no solution.

2. $\begin{cases} y = x + 1 \\ -x + y = 3 \end{cases}$

3. $\begin{cases} 3x + y = 6 \\ y = -3x + 2 \end{cases}$

4. $\begin{cases} -y = 4x + 1 \\ 4x + y = 2 \end{cases}$

SEE EXAMPLE 2 Show that each system has infinitely many solutions.

5. $\begin{cases} y = -x + 3 \\ x + y - 3 = 0 \end{cases}$

6. $\begin{cases} y = 2x - 4 \\ 2x - y - 4 = 0 \end{cases}$

7. $\begin{cases} -7x + y = -2 \\ 7x - y = 2 \end{cases}$

SEE EXAMPLE 3 Classify each system. Give the number of solutions.

8. $\begin{cases} y = 2x + 3 \\ -2y = 2x + 6 \end{cases}$

9. $\begin{cases} y = -3x - 1 \\ 3x + y = 1 \end{cases}$

10. $\begin{cases} 9y = 3x + 18 \\ \frac{1}{3}x - y = -2 \end{cases}$

SEE EXAMPLE 4 **11. Athletics** Micah walks on a treadmill at 4 miles per hour. He has walked 2 miles when Luke starts running at 6 miles per hour on the treadmill next to him. If their rates continue, will Luke's distance ever equal Micah's distance? Explain.

PRACTICE AND PROBLEM SOLVING

Show that each system has no solution.

12. $\begin{cases} y = 2x - 2 \\ -2x + y = 1 \end{cases}$

13. $\begin{cases} x + y = 3 \\ y = -x - 1 \end{cases}$

14. $\begin{cases} x + 2y = -4 \\ y = -\frac{1}{2}x - 4 \end{cases}$

15. $\begin{cases} -6 + y = 2x \\ y = 2x - 36 \end{cases}$

Show that each system has infinitely many solutions.

16. $\begin{cases} y = -2x + 3 \\ 2x + y - 3 = 0 \end{cases}$

17. $\begin{cases} y = x - 2 \\ x - y - 2 = 0 \end{cases}$

18. $\begin{cases} x + y = -4 \\ y = -x - 4 \end{cases}$

19. $\begin{cases} -9x - 3y = -18 \\ 3x + y = 6 \end{cases}$

Independent Practice

For Exercises	See Example
12–15	1
16–19	2
20–22	3
23	4

my.hrw.com

Online Extra Practice

Classify each system. Give the number of solutions.

20. $\begin{cases} y = -x + 5 \\ x + y = 5 \end{cases}$
21. $\begin{cases} y = -3x + 2 \\ y = 3x \end{cases}$
22. $\begin{cases} y - 1 = 2x \\ y = 2x - 1 \end{cases}$

23. Sports Mandy is skating at 5 miles per hour. Nikki is skating at 6 miles per hour and started 1 mile behind Mandy. If their rates stay the same, will Mandy catch up with Nikki? Explain.

24. Multi-Step Photocopier A can print 35 copies per minute. Photocopier B can print 35 copies per minute. Copier B is started and makes 10 copies. Copier A is then started. If the copiers continue, will the number of copies from machine A ever equal the number of copies from machine B? Explain.

25. Entertainment One week Trey rented 4 DVDs and 2 video games for $18. The next week he rented 2 DVDs and 1 video game for $9. Find the rental costs for each video game and DVD. Explain your answer.

26. Rosa bought 1 pound of cashews and 2 pounds of peanuts for $10. At the same store, Sabrina bought 2 pounds of cashews and 1 pound of peanuts for $11. Find the cost per pound for cashews and peanuts.

Geology

27. Geology Pam and Tommy collect geodes. Pam's parents gave her 2 geodes to start her collection, and she buys 4 every year. Tommy has 2 geodes that were given to him for his birthday. He buys 4 every year. If Pam and Tommy continue to buy the same amount of geodes per year, when will Tommy have as many geodes as Pam? Explain your answer.

28. Use the data given in the tables.

x	3	4	5	6
y	6	8	10	12

x	12	13	14	15
y	24	26	28	30

Geodes are rounded, hollow rock formations. Most are partially or completely filled with layers of colored quartz crystals. The world's largest geode was discovered in Spain in 2000. It is 26 feet long and 5.6 feet high.

a. Write an equation to describe the data in each table.

b. Graph the system of equations from part **a**. Describe the graph.

c. How could you have predicted the graph by looking at the equations?

d. What if...? Each y-value in the second table increases by 1. How does this affect the graphs of the two equations? How can you tell how the graphs would be affected without actually graphing?

29. Critical Thinking Describe the graphs of two equations if the result of solving the system by substitution or elimination is the statement $1 = 3$.

Real-World Connections

30. The Crusader pep club is selling team buttons that support the sports teams. They contacted Buttons, Etc. which charges $50 plus $1.10 per button, and Logos, which charges $40 plus $1.10 per button.

a. Write an equation for each company's cost.

b. Use the system from part **a** to find when the price for both companies is the same. Explain.

c. What part of the equation should the pep club negotiate to change so that the cost of Buttons, Etc. is the same as Logos? What part of the equation should change in order to get a better price?

H.O.T. 31. **///ERROR ANALYSIS///** Student A says there is no solution to the graphed system of equations. Student B says there is one solution. Which student is incorrect? Explain the error.

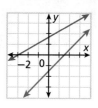

H.O.T. 32. **Write About It** Compare the graph of a system that is consistent and independent with the graph of a system that is consistent and dependent.

TEST PREP

33. Which of the following classifications fit the following system?

$$\begin{cases} 2x - y = 3 \\ 6x - 3y = 9 \end{cases}$$

   (A) Inconsistent and independent
   (B) Consistent and independent
   (C) Inconsistent and dependent
   (D) Consistent and dependent

34. Which of the following would be enough information to classify a system of two linear equations?
   (F) The graphs have the same slope.
   (G) The y-intercepts are the same.
   (H) The graphs have different slopes.
   (J) The y-intercepts are different.

CHALLENGE AND EXTEND

H.O.T. 35. What conditions are necessary for the system $\begin{cases} y = 2x + p \\ y = 2x + q \end{cases}$ to have infinitely many solutions? no solution?

H.O.T. 36. Solve the systems in parts **a** and **b**. Use this information to make a conjecture about all solutions that exist for the system in part **c**.

a. $\begin{cases} 3x + 4y = 0 \\ 4x + 3y = 0 \end{cases}$ b. $\begin{cases} 2x + 5y = 0 \\ 5x + 2y = 0 \end{cases}$ c. $\begin{cases} ax + by = 0 \\ bx + ay = 0 \end{cases}$, for $a > 0, b > 0, a \neq b$

FOCUS ON MATHEMATICAL PRACTICES

H.O.T. 37. **Reasoning** In the graph of a linear system of equations, the lines have different slopes and the same y-intercept.
   a. Write and solve a system of equations whose graph fits this description.
   b. In general, what is the solution to a system like this? Explain.

H.O.T. 38. **Analysis** Chris manages a video rental store and an online video rental service. He found equations for how the number of rentals for each service changed over time and graphed them as shown. Explain what the graph means in this context.

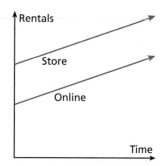

Solving Linear Inequalities

? Essential Question: How can you solve linear inequalities by using graphs?

Objective
Graph and solve linear inequalities in two variables.

Vocabulary
linear inequality
solution of a linear inequality

Animated Math

Who uses this?
Consumers can use linear inequalities to determine how much food they can buy for an event. (See Example 3.)

A **linear inequality** is similar to a linear equation, but the equal sign is replaced with an inequality symbol. A **solution of a linear inequality** is any ordered pair that makes the inequality true.

 COMMON CORE GPS **EXAMPLE** **1**
Prep. for MCC9-12.A.REI.12

my.hrw.com

Online Video Tutor

Identifying Solutions of Inequalities

Tell whether the ordered pair is a solution of the inequality.

A $(7, 3); y < x - 1$

$$
\begin{array}{c|c}
y & < x - 1 \\
\hline
3 & 7 - 1 \\
3 & < 6 \checkmark
\end{array}
$$

Substitute (7, 3) for (x, y).

$(7, 3)$ is a solution.

B $(4, 5); y > 3x + 2$

$$
\begin{array}{c|c}
y & > 3x + 2 \\
\hline
5 & 3(4) + 2 \\
5 & 12 + 2 \\
5 & > 14 \; \text{✗}
\end{array}
$$

Substitute (4, 5) for (x, y).

$(4, 5)$ is not a solution.

 CHECK IT OUT! Tell whether the ordered pair is a solution of the inequality.

1a. $(4, 5); y < x + 1$ **1b.** $(1, 1); y > x - 7$

A linear inequality describes a region of a coordinate plane called a *half-plane*. All points in the region are solutions of the linear inequality. The boundary line of the region is the graph of the related equation.

When the inequality is written as $y \le$ or $y \ge$, the points on the boundary line are solutions of the inequality, and the line is **solid**.

When the inequality is written as $y <$ or $y >$, the points on the boundary line are not solutions of the inequality, and the line is **dashed**.

When the inequality is written as $y >$ or $y \ge$, the points **above** the boundary line are solutions of the inequality.

When the inequality is written as $y <$ or $y \le$, the points **below** the boundary line are solutions of the inequality.

Graphing Linear Inequalities	
Step 1	Solve the inequality for *y*.
Step 2	Graph the boundary line. Use a solid line for ≤ or ≥. Use a dashed line for < or >.
Step 3	Shade the half-plane above the line for *y* > or *y* ≥. Shade the half-plane below the line for *y* < or *y* ≤. Check your answer.

EXAMPLE **2** MCC9-12.A.REI.12

Graphing Linear Inequalities in Two Variables

Graph the solutions of each linear inequality.

A $y < 3x + 4$

my.hrw.com

Online Video Tutor

Step 1 The inequality is already solved for *y*.

Step 2 Graph the boundary line $y = 3x + 4$. Use a dashed line for <.

Step 3 The inequality is <, so shade below the line.

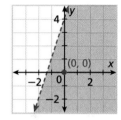

Helpful Hint

The point (0, 0) is a good test point to use if it does not lie on the boundary line.

Check

y	<	$3x + 4$
0		$3(0) + 4$
0		$0 + 4$
0	<	4 ✓

Substitute (0, 0) for (x, y) because it is not on the boundary line.

The point (0, 0) satisfies the inequality, so the graph is shaded correctly.

B $3x + 2y \geq 6$

Step 1 Solve the inequality for *y*.

$$3x + 2y \geq 6$$
$$\underline{-3x \qquad -3x}$$
$$2y \geq -3x + 6$$
$$y \geq -\frac{3}{2}x + 3$$

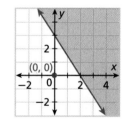

Step 2 Graph the boundary line $y = -\frac{3}{2}x + 3$. Use a solid line for ≥.

Step 3 The inequality is ≥, so shade above the line.

Check

y	≥	$\frac{3}{2}x + 3$
0		$\frac{3}{2}(0) + 3$
0		$0 + 3$
0	≥	3 ✗

A false statement means that the half-plane containing (0, 0) should NOT be shaded. (0, 0) is not one of the solutions, so the graph is shaded correctly.

Graph the solutions of each linear inequality.

2a. $4x - 3y > 12$ **2b.** $2x - y - 4 > 0$ **2c.** $y \geq -\frac{2}{3}x + 1$

EXAMPLE 3 **Consumer Economics Application**

Sarah can spend at most $7.50 on vegetables for a party. Broccoli costs $1.25 per bunch and carrots cost $0.75 per package.

a. Write a linear inequality to describe the situation.

Let x represent the number of bunches of broccoli and let y represent the number of packages of carrots.

Write an inequality. Use $\leq$ for "at most."

Cost of broccoli	plus	cost of carrots	is at most	$7.50.
1.25x	+	0.75y	$\leq$	7.50

Solve the inequality for y.

$$1.25x + 0.75y \leq 7.50$$

$$100(1.25x + 0.75y) \leq 100(7.50)$$ *You can multiply both sides of the inequality by 100 to eliminate the decimals.*

$$125x + 75y \leq 750$$
$$\underline{-125x \qquad\quad -125x}$$ *Subtraction Property of Inequality*

$$75y \leq 750 - 125x$$

$$\frac{75y}{75} \leq \frac{750 - 125x}{75}$$ *Division Property of Inequality*

$$y \leq 10 - \frac{5}{3}x$$

b. Graph the solutions.

Step 1 Since Sarah cannot buy a negative amount of vegetables, the system is graphed only in Quadrant I. Graph the boundary line $y = -\frac{5}{3}x + 10$. Use a solid line for $\leq$.

Step 2 Shade below the line. Sarah must buy whole numbers of bunches or packages. All points on or below the line with whole-number coordinates represent combinations of broccoli and carrots that Sarah can buy.

Vegetable Combinations

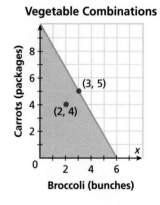

c. Give two combinations of vegetables that Sarah can buy.

Two different combinations that Sarah could buy for $7.50 or less are 2 bunches of broccoli and 4 packages of carrots, or 3 bunches of broccoli and 5 packages of carrots.

3. Dirk is going to bring two types of olives to the Honor Society induction and can spend no more than $6. Green olives cost $2 per pound and black olives cost $2.50 per pound.

   a. Write a linear inequality to describe the situation.

   b. Graph the solutions.

   c. Give two combinations of olives that Dirk could buy.

EXAMPLE **4**
Ext. of MCC9-12.A.REI.12

Online Video Tutor

Writing an Inequality from a Graph

Write an inequality to represent each graph.

A

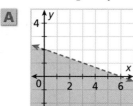

y-intercept: **2**; slope: $-\frac{1}{3}$

Write an equation in slope-intercept form.

$$y = mx + b \longrightarrow y = -\frac{1}{3}x + 2$$

The graph is shaded *below* a *dashed* boundary line.

Replace = with < to write the inequality $y < -\frac{1}{3}x + 2$.

B

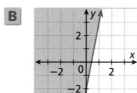

y-intercept: **−2**; slope: **5**

Write an equation in slope-intercept form.

$$y = mx + b \longrightarrow y = 5x + (-2)$$

The graph is shaded *above* a *solid* boundary line.

Replace = with ≥ to write the inequality $y \geq 5x - 2$.

C

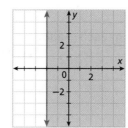

y-intercept: **none**; slope: **undefined**

The graph is a vertical line at $x = -2$.

The graph is shaded on the *right* side of a *solid* boundary line.

Replace = with ≥ to write the inequality $x \geq -2$.

Write an inequality to represent each graph.

4a.

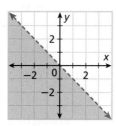

4b.

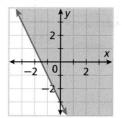

MCC.MP.6 **MATHEMATICAL PRACTICES**

THINK AND DISCUSS

1. Tell how graphing a linear inequality is the same as graphing a linear equation. Tell how it is different.

2. Explain how you would write a linear inequality from a graph.

3. GET ORGANIZED Copy and complete the graphic organizer.

Inequality	$y < 5x + 2$	$y > 7x - 3$	$y \leq 9x + 1$	$y \geq -3x - 2$
Symbol	<			
Boundary Line	Dashed			
Shading	Below			

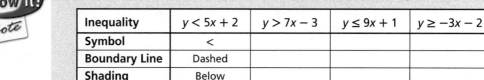

GUIDED PRACTICE

1. **Vocabulary** Can a *solution of a linear inequality* lie on a dashed boundary line? Explain.

SEE EXAMPLE 1   **Tell whether the ordered pair is a solution of the given inequality.**

2. $(0, 3); y \leq -x + 3$ 3. $(2, 0); y > -2x - 2$ 4. $(-2, 1); y < 2x + 4$

SEE EXAMPLE 2   **Graph the solutions of each linear inequality.**

5. $y \leq -x$ 6. $y > 3x + 1$ 7. $-y < -x + 4$ 8. $-y \geq x + 1$

SEE EXAMPLE 3   9. **Multi-Step** Jack is making punch with orange juice and pineapple juice. He can make at most 16 cups of punch.

   a. Write an inequality to describe the situation.

   b. Graph the solutions.

   c. Give two combinations of cups of orange juice and pineapple juice that Jack can use in his punch.

SEE EXAMPLE 4   **Write an inequality to represent each graph.**

10.
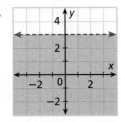

11.
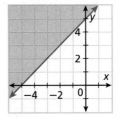

PRACTICE AND PROBLEM SOLVING

my.hrw.com

Online Extra Practice

Tell whether the ordered pair is a solution of the given inequality.

12. $(2, 3); y \geq 2x + 3$ 13. $(1, -1); y < 3x - 3$ 14. $(0, 7); y > 4x + 7$

Graph the solutions of each linear inequality.

15. $y > -2x + 6$ 16. $-y \geq 2x$ 17. $x + y \leq 2$ 18. $x - y \geq 0$

19. **Multi-Step** Beverly is serving hamburgers and hot dogs at her cookout. Hamburger meat costs $3 per pound, and hot dogs cost $2 per pound. She wants to spend no more than $30.

   a. Write an inequality to describe the situation.

   b. Graph the solutions.

   c. Give two combinations of pounds of hamburger and hot dogs that Beverly can buy.

Write an inequality to represent each graph.

20.
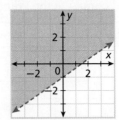

21.
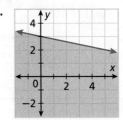

22. **Business** An electronics store makes $125 profit on every DVD player it sells and $100 on every CD player it sells. The store owner wants to make a profit of at least $500 a day selling DVD players and CD players.

    a. Write a linear inequality to determine the number of DVD players x and the number of CD players y that the owner needs to sell to meet his goal.

    b. Graph the linear inequality.

    c. Describe the possible values of x. Describe the possible values of y.

    d. List three combinations of DVD players and CD players that the owner could sell to meet his goal.

Graph the solutions of each linear inequality.

23. $y \leq 2 - 3x$ **24.** $-y < 7 + x$ **25.** $2x - y \leq 4$ **26.** $3x - 2y > 6$

27. **Geometry** Marvin has 18 yards of fencing that he can use to put around a rectangular garden.

    a. Write an inequality to describe the possible lengths and widths of the garden.

    b. Graph the inequality and list three possible solutions to the problem.

    c. What are the dimensions of the largest *square* garden that can be fenced in with whole-number dimensions?

28. **Hobbies** Stephen wants to buy yellow tangs and clown fish for his saltwater aquarium. He wants to spend no more than $77 on fish. At the store, yellow tangs cost $15 each and clown fish cost $11 each. Write and graph a linear inequality to find the number of yellow tangs x and the number of clown fish y that Stephen could purchase. Name a solution of your inequality that is not reasonable for the situation. Explain.

Graph each inequality on a coordinate plane.

29. $y > 1$ **30.** $-2 < x$ **31.** $x \geq -3$ **32.** $y \leq 0$

33. $0 \geq x$ **34.** $-12 + y > 0$ **35.** $x + 7 < 7$ **36.** $-4 \geq x - y$

37. **School** At a high school football game, tickets at the gate cost $7 per adult and $4 per student. Write a linear inequality to determine the number of adult and student tickets that need to be sold so that the amount of money taken in at the gate is at least $280. Graph the inequality and list three possible solutions.

H.O.T. **38. Critical Thinking** Why must a region of a coordinate plane be shaded to show all solutions of a linear inequality?

39. Write About It Give a real-world situation that can be described by a linear inequality. Then graph the inequality and give two solutions.

Real-World Connections

40. Gloria is making teddy bears. She is making boy and girl bears. She has enough stuffing to create 50 bears. Let x represent the number of girl bears and y represent the number of boy bears.

    a. Write an inequality that shows the possible number of boy and girl bears Gloria can make.

    b. Graph the inequality.

    c. Give three possible solutions for the numbers of boy and girl bears that can be made.

H.O.T. 41. ///ERROR ANALYSIS/// Student A wrote $y < 2x - 1$ as the inequality represented by the graph. Student B wrote $y \leq 2x - 1$ as the inequality represented by the graph. Which student is incorrect? Explain the error.

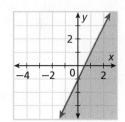

H.O.T. 42. Write About It How do you decide to shade above or below a boundary line? What does this shading represent?

TEST PREP

43. Which point is a solution of the inequality $y > -x + 3$?

    (A) $(0, 3)$ (B) $(1, 4)$ (C) $(-1, 4)$ (D) $(0, -3)$

44. Which inequality is represented by the graph at right?

    (F) $2x + y \geq 3$ (H) $2x + y \leq 3$

    (G) $2x + y > 3$ (J) $2x + y < 3$

45. Which of the following describes the graph of $3 \leq x$?

    (A) The boundary line is dashed, and the shading is to the right.

    (B) The boundary line is dashed, and the shading is to the left.

    (C) The boundary line is solid, and the shading is to the right.

    (D) The boundary line is solid, and the shading is to the left.

CHALLENGE AND EXTEND

Graph each inequality.

46. $0 \geq -6 - 2x - 5y$ **47.** $y > |x|$ **48.** $y \geq |x - 3|$

49. A linear inequality has the points $(0, 3)$ and $(-3, 1.5)$ as solutions on the boundary line. Also, the point $(1, 1)$ is not a solution. Write the linear inequality.

50. Two linear inequalities are graphed on the same coordinate plane. The point $(0, 0)$ is a solution of both inequalities. The entire coordinate plane is shaded except for Quadrant I. What are the two inequalities?

FOCUS ON MATHEMATICAL PRACTICES

H.O.T. 51. Analysis Equivalent inequalities have the same boundaries and contain the same points in their solutions. Is the inequality $x - y < 12$ equivalent to $y < x - 12$? Explain why or why not.

H.O.T. 52. Modeling Angie volunteers at the local animal sanctuary. They are fencing a space that will house no more than 10 dogs. They want to house some adult dogs x and some puppies y.

    a. Write an inequality that describes the situation.

    b. Graph the inequality. How is your graphed inequality different than the actual situation?

H.O.T. 53. Make a Conjecture The solutions to an inequality of the form $y > ax + b$ are always found above the boundary line. Where do you think the solutions to an inequality of the form $x > ay + b$ can be found? Explain your reasoning.

7-3 Solving Systems of Linear Inequalities

Essential Question: How can you solve systems of linear inequalities by using graphs?

Objective
Graph and solve systems of linear inequalities in two variables.

Vocabulary
system of linear inequalities
solutions of a system of linear inequalities

Who uses this?
The owner of a surf shop can use systems of linear inequalities to determine how many surfboards and wakeboards need to be sold to make a certain profit. (See Example 4.)

A **system of linear inequalities** is a set of two or more linear inequalities containing two or more variables. The **solutions of a system of linear inequalities** are all of the ordered pairs that satisfy all the linear inequalities in the system.

COMMON CORE GPS
Prep. for MCC9-12.A.REI.12

EXAMPLE 1

my.hrw.com

Online Video Tutor

Remember!
An ordered pair must be a solution of all inequalities to be a solution of the system.

Identifying Solutions of Systems of Linear Inequalities

Tell whether the ordered pair is a solution of the given system.

A $(2, 1)$; $\begin{cases} y < -x + 4 \\ y \le x + 1 \end{cases}$

$$(2, 1)$$
$$\begin{array}{c|c} y < -x + 4 \\ \hline 1 & -2 + 4 \\ 1 < 2 \checkmark \end{array}$$

$$(2, 1)$$
$$\begin{array}{c|c} y \le x + 1 \\ \hline 1 & 2 + 1 \\ 1 \le 3 \checkmark \end{array}$$

$(2, 1)$ is a solution to the system because it satisfies both inequalities.

B $(2, 0)$; $\begin{cases} y \ge 2x \\ y < x + 1 \end{cases}$

$$(2, 0)$$
$$\begin{array}{c|c} y \ge 2x \\ \hline 0 & 2(2) \\ 0 \ge 4 \ X \end{array}$$

$$(2, 0)$$
$$\begin{array}{c|c} y < x + 1 \\ \hline 0 & 2 + 1 \\ 0 < 3 \checkmark \end{array}$$

$(2, 0)$ is not a solution to the system because it does not satisfy both inequalities.

CHECK IT OUT!

Tell whether the ordered pair is a solution of the given system.

1a. $(0, 1)$; $\begin{cases} y < -3x + 2 \\ y \ge x - 1 \end{cases}$

1b. $(0, 0)$; $\begin{cases} y > -x + 1 \\ y > x - 1 \end{cases}$

To show all the solutions of a system of linear inequalities, graph the solutions of each inequality. The solutions of the system are represented by the overlapping shaded regions. Below are graphs of Examples 1A and 1B.

Example 1A

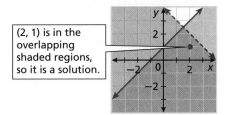

(2, 1) is in the overlapping shaded regions, so it is a solution.

Example 1B

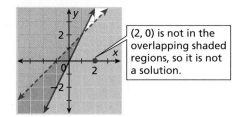

(2, 0) is not in the overlapping shaded regions, so it is not a solution.

EXAMPLE 2
MCC9-12.A.REI.12

Solving a System of Linear Inequalities by Graphing

Graph the system of linear inequalities. Give two ordered pairs that are solutions and two that are not solutions.

$$\begin{cases} 8x + 4y \le 12 \\ y > \dfrac{1}{2}x - 2 \end{cases}$$

$$8x + 4y \le 12$$ *Solve the first inequality for y.*
$$4y \le -8x + 12$$
$$y \le -2x + 3$$

Graph the system.

$$\begin{cases} y \le -2x + 3 \\ y > \dfrac{1}{2}x - 2 \end{cases}$$

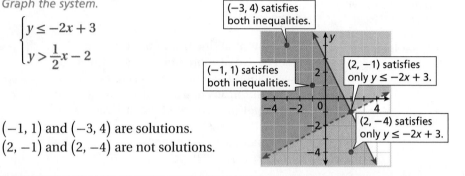

(−3, 4) satisfies both inequalities.

(−1, 1) satisfies both inequalities.

(2, −1) satisfies only $y \le -2x + 3$.

(2, −4) satisfies only $y \le -2x + 3$.

$(-1, 1)$ and $(-3, 4)$ are solutions.
$(2, -1)$ and $(2, -4)$ are not solutions.

CHECK IT OUT!

Graph each system of linear inequalities. Give two ordered pairs that are solutions and two that are not solutions.

2a. $\begin{cases} y \le x + 1 \\ y > 2 \end{cases}$

2b. $\begin{cases} y > x - 7 \\ 3x + 6y \le 12 \end{cases}$

Previously, you saw that in systems of linear equations, if the lines are parallel, there are no solutions. With systems of linear inequalities, that is not always true.

EXAMPLE 3
MCC9-12.A.REI.12

Graphing Systems with Parallel Boundary Lines

Graph each system of linear inequalities. Describe the solutions.

A $\begin{cases} y < 2x - 3 \\ y > 2x + 2 \end{cases}$

B $\begin{cases} y > x - 3 \\ y \le x + 1 \end{cases}$

C $\begin{cases} y \le -3x - 2 \\ y \le -3x + 4 \end{cases}$

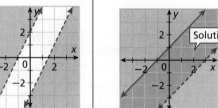   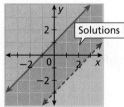 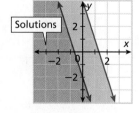

This system has no solution.

The solutions are all points between the parallel lines and on the solid line.

The solutions are the same as the solutions of $y \le -3x - 2$.

Graph each system of linear inequalities. Describe the solutions.

3a. $\begin{cases} y > x + 1 \\ y \le x - 3 \end{cases}$ **3b.** $\begin{cases} y \ge 4x - 2 \\ y \le 4x + 2 \end{cases}$ **3c.** $\begin{cases} y > -2x + 3 \\ y > -2x \end{cases}$

 EXAMPLE 4
COMMON CORE GPS
MCC9-12.A.CED.3

Business Application

my.hrw.com

Online Video Tutor

A surf shop makes the profits given in the table. The shop owner sells at least 10 surfboards and at least 20 wakeboards per month. He wants to earn at least $2000 a month. Show and describe all possible combinations of surfboards and wakeboards that the store owner needs to sell to meet his goals. List two possible combinations.

Profit per Board Sold ($)	
Surfboard	150
Wakeboard	100

Step 1 Write a system of inequalities.
Let x represent the number of surfboards and y represent the number of wakeboards.

$x \ge 10$ *He sells at least 10 surfboards.*

$y \ge 20$ *He sells at least 20 wakeboards.*

$150x + 100y \ge 2000$ *He wants to earn a total of at least $2000.*

Step 2 Graph the system.
The graph should be in only the first quadrant because sales are not negative.

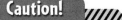 Caution!

An ordered pair solution of the system need not have whole numbers, but answers to many application problems may be restricted to whole numbers.

Step 3 Describe all possible combinations.
To meet the sales goals, the shop could sell any combination represented by an ordered pair of whole numbers in the solution region. Answers must be whole numbers because the shop cannot sell part of a surfboard or wakeboard.

Step 4 List two possible combinations.
Two possible combinations are:
15 surfboards and 25 wakeboards
25 surfboards and 20 wakeboards

Sales Goals

Solutions

(15, 25)

(25, 20)

 4. At her party, Alice is serving pepper jack cheese and cheddar cheese. She wants to have at least 2 pounds of each. Alice wants to spend at most $20 on cheese. Show and describe all possible combinations of the two cheeses Alice could buy. List two possible combinations.

Price per Pound ($)	
Pepper Jack	4
Cheddar	2

 MCC.MP.1   MATHEMATICAL PRACTICES

THINK AND DISCUSS

1. How would you write a system of linear inequalities from a graph?

 Know it! Note

2. GET ORGANIZED Copy and complete each part of the graphic organizer. In each box, draw a graph and list one solution.

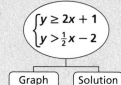 $\begin{cases} y \ge 2x + 1 \\ y > \frac{1}{2}x - 2 \end{cases}$

Graph   Solution

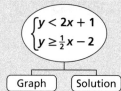 $\begin{cases} y < 2x + 1 \\ y \ge \frac{1}{2}x - 2 \end{cases}$

Graph   Solution

GUIDED PRACTICE

1. **Vocabulary** A solution of a system of inequalities is a solution of _____?_____ of the inequalities in the system. (*at least one* or *all*)

SEE EXAMPLE 1 Tell whether the ordered pair is a solution of the given system.

2. $(0, 0); \begin{cases} y < -x + 3 \\ y < x + 2 \end{cases}$

3. $(0, 0); \begin{cases} y < 3 \\ y > x - 2 \end{cases}$

4. $(1, 0); \begin{cases} y > 3x \\ y \le x + 1 \end{cases}$

SEE EXAMPLE 2 Graph each system of linear inequalities. Give two ordered pairs that are solutions and two that are not solutions.

5. $\begin{cases} y < 2x - 1 \\ y > 2 \end{cases}$

6. $\begin{cases} x < 3 \\ y > x - 2 \end{cases}$

7. $\begin{cases} y \ge 3x \\ 3x + y \ge 3 \end{cases}$

8. $\begin{cases} 2x - 4y \le 8 \\ y > x - 2 \end{cases}$

SEE EXAMPLE 3 Graph each system of linear inequalities. Describe the solutions.

9. $\begin{cases} y > 2x + 3 \\ y < 2x \end{cases}$

10. $\begin{cases} y \le -3x - 1 \\ y \ge -3x + 1 \end{cases}$

11. $\begin{cases} y > 4x - 1 \\ y \le 4x + 1 \end{cases}$

12. $\begin{cases} y < -x + 3 \\ y > -x + 2 \end{cases}$

13. $\begin{cases} y > 2x - 1 \\ y > 2x - 4 \end{cases}$

14. $\begin{cases} y \le -3x + 4 \\ y \le -3x - 3 \end{cases}$

SEE EXAMPLE 4 15. **Business** Sandy makes $2 profit on every cup of lemonade that she sells and $1 on every cupcake that she sells. Sandy wants to sell at least 5 cups of lemonade and at least 5 cupcakes per day. She wants to earn at least $25 per day. Show and describe all the possible combinations of lemonade and cupcakes that Sandy needs to sell to meet her goals. List two possible combinations.

PRACTICE AND PROBLEM SOLVING

Tell whether the ordered pair is a solution of the given system.

16. $(0, 0); \begin{cases} y > -x - 1 \\ y < 2x + 4 \end{cases}$

17. $(0, 0); \begin{cases} x + y < 3 \\ y > 3x - 4 \end{cases}$

18. $(1, 0); \begin{cases} y > 3x \\ y > 3x + 1 \end{cases}$

my.hrw.com

Online Extra Practice

Graph each system of linear inequalities. Give two ordered pairs that are solutions and two that are not solutions.

19. $\begin{cases} y < -3x - 3 \\ y \ge 0 \end{cases}$

20. $\begin{cases} y < -1 \\ y > 2x - 1 \end{cases}$

21. $\begin{cases} y > 2x + 4 \\ 6x + 2y \ge -2 \end{cases}$

22. $\begin{cases} 9x + 3y \le 6 \\ y > x \end{cases}$

Graph each system of linear inequalities. Describe the solutions.

23. $\begin{cases} y < 3 \\ y > 5 \end{cases}$

24. $\begin{cases} y < x - 1 \\ y > x - 2 \end{cases}$

25. $\begin{cases} x \ge 2 \\ x \le 2 \end{cases}$

26. $\begin{cases} y > -4x - 3 \\ y < -4x + 2 \end{cases}$

27. $\begin{cases} y > -1 \\ y > 2 \end{cases}$

28. $\begin{cases} y \le 2x + 1 \\ y \le 2x - 4 \end{cases}$

29. **Multi-Step** Linda works at a pharmacy for $15 an hour. She also baby-sits for $10 an hour. Linda needs to earn at least $90 per week, but she does not want to work more than 20 hours per week. Show and describe the number of hours Linda could work at each job to meet her goals. List two possible solutions.

30. **Farming** Tony wants to plant at least 40 acres of corn and at least 50 acres of soybeans. He wants no more than 200 acres of corn and soybeans. Show and describe all the possible combinations of the number of acres of corn and of soybeans Tony could plant. List two possible combinations.

Graph each system of linear inequalities.

31. $\begin{cases} y \geq -3 \\ y \geq 2 \end{cases}$
32. $\begin{cases} y > -2x - 1 \\ y > -2x - 3 \end{cases}$
33. $\begin{cases} x \leq -3 \\ x \geq 1 \end{cases}$
34. $\begin{cases} y < 4 \\ y > 0 \end{cases}$

Write a system of linear inequalities to represent each graph.

35.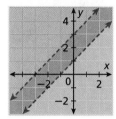

36.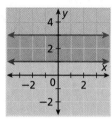

37.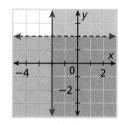

38. **Military** For males to enter the United States Air Force Academy, located in Colorado Springs, CO, they must be at least 17 but less than 23 years of age. Their standing height must be not less than 60 inches and not greater than 80 inches. Graph all possible heights and ages for eligible male candidates. Give three possible combinations.

39. **///ERROR ANALYSIS///** Two students wrote a system of linear inequalities to describe the graph. Which student is incorrect? Explain the error.

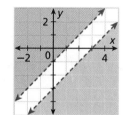

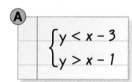 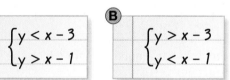

40. **Recreation** Vance wants to fence in a rectangular area for his dog. He wants the length of the rectangle to be at least 30 feet and the perimeter to be no more than 150 feet. Graph all possible dimensions of the rectangle.

H.O.T. 41. **Critical Thinking** Can the solutions of a system of linear inequalities be the points on a line? Explain.

Real-World Connections

42. Gloria is starting her own company making teddy bears. She has enough bear bodies to create 40 bears. She will make girl bears and boy bears.
   a. Write an inequality to show this situation.
   b. Gloria will charge $15 for girl bears and $12 for boy bears. She wants to earn at least $540 a week. Write an inequality to describe this situation.
   c. Graph this situation and locate the solution region.

H.O.T. **43. Write About It** What must be true of the boundary lines in a system of two linear inequalities if there is no solution of the system? Explain.

TEST PREP

44. Which point is a solution of $\begin{cases} 2x + y \geq 3 \\ y \geq -2x + 1 \end{cases}$?

    Ⓐ $(0, 0)$ Ⓑ $(0, 1)$ Ⓒ $(1, 0)$ Ⓓ $(1, 1)$

45. Which system of inequalities best describes the graph?

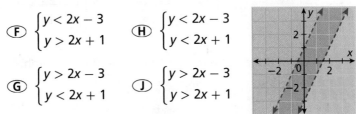

   Ⓕ $\begin{cases} y < 2x - 3 \\ y > 2x + 1 \end{cases}$ Ⓗ $\begin{cases} y < 2x - 3 \\ y < 2x + 1 \end{cases}$

   Ⓖ $\begin{cases} y > 2x - 3 \\ y < 2x + 1 \end{cases}$ Ⓙ $\begin{cases} y > 2x - 3 \\ y > 2x + 1 \end{cases}$

46. Short Response Graph and describe $\begin{cases} y + x > 2 \\ y \leq -3x + 4 \end{cases}$. Give two possible solutions of the system.

CHALLENGE AND EXTEND

47. Estimation Graph the given system of inequalities. Estimate the area of the overlapping solution regions.

$$\begin{cases} y \geq 0 \\ y \leq x + 3.5 \\ y \leq -x + 3.5 \end{cases}$$

48. Write a system of linear inequalities for which $(-1, 1)$ and $(1, 4)$ are solutions and $(0, 0)$ and $(2, -1)$ are not solutions.

49. Graph $|y| < 1$.

50. Write a system of linear inequalities for which the solutions are all the points in the third quadrant.

FOCUS ON MATHEMATICAL PRACTICES

H.O.T. **51. Problem Solving** Without graphing, describe the solution or solutions to the system of inequalities shown. How did you find your answer?

       $\begin{cases} x - y < 3 \\ x - y > 3 \end{cases}$

H.O.T. **52. Analysis** Is it possible for a system of two linear inequalities to have a single point as a solution? What about a system of more than two inequalities? If either case is possible, write such a system and name the solution.

H.O.T. **53. Reasoning** Use a graph to find three solutions to the system of inequalities shown. What approach did you use to graph the system?

       $\begin{cases} y < x^2 + 5 \\ y > x^2 \end{cases}$

7-3 Technology TASK

Solve Systems of Linear Inequalities

A graphing calculator gives a visual solution to a system of linear inequalities.

Use with Solving Systems of Linear Inequalities

MATHEMATICAL PRACTICES

Use appropriate tools strategically.

MCC9-12.A.REI.12 Graph the … solution set to a system of linear inequalities in two variables as the intersection of the corresponding half-planes.

Activity

Graph the system $\begin{cases} y > 2x - 4 \\ 2.75y - x < 6 \end{cases}$. Give two ordered pairs that are solutions.

1 The first inequality is solved for y.

2 Graph the first inequality. First graph the boundary line $y = 2x - 4$. Press and enter $2x - 4$ for **Y1.**

The inequality contains the symbol >. The solution region is above the boundary line. Press ◄ to move the cursor to the left of **Y1.** Press ENTER until the icon that looks like a region above a line appears. Press GRAPH.

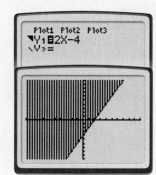

3 Solve the second inequality for y.

$2.75y - x < 6$

$\qquad 2.75y < x + 6$

$\qquad\quad y < \dfrac{x + 6}{2.75}$

4 Graph the second inequality. First graph the boundary line $y = \dfrac{x + 6}{2.75}$. Press Y= and enter $(x + 6)/2.75$ for **Y2.**
The inequality contains the symbol <. The solution region is below the boundary line. Press ◄ to move the cursor to the left of **Y2.** Press ENTER until the icon that looks like a region below a line appears. Press GRAPH.

5 The solutions of the system are represented by the overlapping shaded regions. The points $(0, 0)$ and $(-1, 0)$ are in the shaded region.

Check Test $(0, 0)$ in both inequalities.

$y > 2x - 4$		$2.75y - x < 6$	
0	$2(0) - 4$	$2.75(0) - 0$	6
0	$>$ -4 ✓	0	$<$ 6 ✓

Test $(-1, 0)$ in both inequalities.

$y > 2x - 4$		$2.75y - x < 6$	
0	$2(-1) - 4$	$2.75(0) - (-1)$	6
0	$>$ -6 ✓	1	$<$ 6 ✓

Try This

Graph each system. Give two ordered pairs that are solutions.

1. $\begin{cases} x + 5y > -10 \\ x - y < 4 \end{cases}$
2. $\begin{cases} y > x - 2 \\ y \le x + 2 \end{cases}$
3. $\begin{cases} y > x - 2 \\ y \le 3 \end{cases}$
4. $\begin{cases} y < x - 3 \\ y - 3 > x \end{cases}$

Ready to Go On?

my.hrw.com
Assessment and Intervention

7-1 Solving Special Systems

Solve each system of linear equations.

1. $\begin{cases} y = -2x - 6 \\ 2x + y = 5 \end{cases}$

2. $\begin{cases} x + y = 2 \\ 2x + 2y = -6 \end{cases}$

3. $\begin{cases} y = -2x + 4 \\ 2x + y = 4 \end{cases}$

Classify each system. Give the number of solutions.

4. $\begin{cases} 3x = -6y + 3 \\ 2y = -x + 1 \end{cases}$

5. $\begin{cases} y = -4x + 2 \\ 4x + y = -2 \end{cases}$

6. $\begin{cases} 4x - 3y = 8 \\ y = 4(x + 2) \end{cases}$

7-2 Solving Linear Inequalities

Tell whether the ordered pair is a solution of the inequality.

7. $(3, -2); y < -2x + 1$

8. $(2, 1); y \geq 3x - 5$

9. $(1, -6); y \leq 4x - 10$

Graph the solutions of each linear inequality.

10. $y \geq 4x - 3$

11. $3x - y < 5$

12. $2x + 3y < 9$

13. $y \leq -\frac{1}{2}x$

14. Theo's mother has given him at most $150 to buy clothes for school. The pants cost $30 each and the shirts cost $15 each. Write a linear inequality to describe the situation. Graph the solutions and give three combinations of pants and shirts that Theo could buy.

Write an inequality to represent each graph.

15.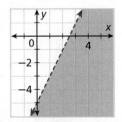

16.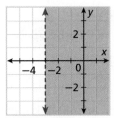

17.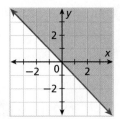

7-3 Solving Systems of Linear Inequalities

Tell whether the ordered pair is a solution of the given system.

18. $(-3, -1); \begin{cases} y > -2 \\ y < x + 4 \end{cases}$

19. $(-3, 0); \begin{cases} y \leq x + 4 \\ y \geq -2x - 6 \end{cases}$

20. $(0, 0); \begin{cases} y \geq 3x \\ 2x + y < -1 \end{cases}$

Graph each system of linear inequalities. Give two ordered pairs that are solutions and two that are not solutions.

21. $\begin{cases} y > -2 \\ y < x + 3 \end{cases}$

22. $\begin{cases} x + y \leq 2 \\ 2x + y \geq -1 \end{cases}$

23. $\begin{cases} 2x - 5y \leq -5 \\ 3x + 2y < 10 \end{cases}$

Graph each system of linear inequalities. Describe the solutions.

24. $\begin{cases} y \geq x + 1 \\ y \geq x - 4 \end{cases}$

25. $\begin{cases} y \geq 2x - 1 \\ y < 2x - 3 \end{cases}$

26. $\begin{cases} y < -3x + 5 \\ y > -3x - 2 \end{cases}$

27. A grocer sells mangos for \$4/lb and apples for \$3/lb. The grocer starts with 45 lb of mangos and 50 lb of apples each day. The grocer's goal is to make at least \$300 by selling mangos and apples each day. Show and describe all possible combinations of mangos and apples that could be sold to meet the goal. List two possible combinations.

PARCC Assessment Readiness

Selected Response

1. Elena and her husband Marc both drive to work. Elena's car has a current mileage (total distance driven) of 5,000 and she drives 15,000 miles more each year. Marc's car has a current mileage of 32,000 and he drives 15,000 miles more each year. Will the mileages for the two cars ever be equal? Explain.

   Ⓐ No; The equations have different slopes, so the lines do not intersect.

   Ⓑ Yes; The equations have different y-intercepts, so the lines intersect.

   Ⓒ No; the equations have equal slopes but different y-intercepts, so the lines do not intersect.

   Ⓓ Yes; The equations have different slopes, so the lines intersect.

2. Classify $\begin{cases} x - 8y = 6 \\ 2x - 16y = 12 \end{cases}$. Give the number of solutions.

   Ⓕ This system is consistent. It has infinitely many solutions.

   Ⓖ This system is inconsistent. It has infinitely many solutions.

   Ⓗ This system is inconsistent. It has no solutions.

   Ⓙ This system is consistent. It has one solution.

3. Solve $\begin{cases} y = -x + 8 \\ x + y = 7 \end{cases}$

   Ⓐ This system has infinitely many solutions.

   Ⓑ This system has no solutions.

   Ⓒ $\left(\dfrac{1}{2}, \dfrac{15}{2}\right)$

   Ⓓ $\left(-\dfrac{1}{2}, \dfrac{17}{2}\right)$

4. Write an inequality to represent the graph.

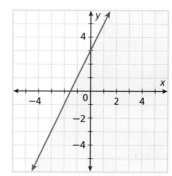

   Ⓕ $y > 2x + 3$ Ⓗ $y < 3x + 2$

   Ⓖ $y \leq 2x + 3$ Ⓙ $y < 2x + 3$

Mini-Task

5. Graph the system of linear inequalities $\begin{cases} y < -3x + 2 \\ y \geq 4x - 1 \end{cases}$.

   Give two ordered pairs that are solutions and two that are not solutions.

PARCC Assessment Readiness

Selected Response

1. What value of *n* makes the equation below have no solution?

$$2x + 2 = nx - 3$$

Ⓐ −2

Ⓑ 0

Ⓒ 2

Ⓓ 3

2. Which of the equations below represents the second step of the solution process?

Step 1: $3(5x - 2) + 27 = -24$
Step 2:
Step 3: $15x + 21 = -24$
Step 4: $15x = -45$
Step 5: $x = -3$

Ⓕ $3(5x + 27) - 2 = -24$

Ⓖ $3(5x + 25) = -24$

Ⓗ $15x - 2 + 27 = -24$

Ⓙ $15x - 6 + 27 = -24$

3. Cass drove 3 miles to school, and then she drove *m* miles to a friend's house. The total mileage for these two trips was 8 miles. Which equation CANNOT be used to determine the number of miles Cass drove?

Ⓐ $3 + m = 8$

Ⓑ $3 - m = 8$

Ⓒ $8 - 3 = m$

Ⓓ $8 - m = 3$

4. If $\dfrac{20}{x} = \dfrac{4}{x - 5}$, which of the following is a true statement?

Ⓕ $x(x - 5) = 80$

Ⓖ $20x = 4(x - 5)$

Ⓗ $20(x - 5) = 4x$

Ⓙ $24 = 2x - 5$

5. A bike rental shop charges a one-time charge of $8 plus an hourly fee to rent a bike. Dan paid $24.50 to rent a bike for $5\frac{1}{2}$ hours. What is the bike shop's hourly fee in dollars?

Ⓐ $3.00   Ⓒ $5.50

Ⓑ $4.45   Ⓓ $8

6. Which algebraic expression means "5 less than *y*"?

Ⓕ $5 - y$

Ⓖ $y - 5$

Ⓗ $5 < y$

Ⓙ $5 \div y$

7. If $t + 8 = 2$, find the value of $2t$.

Ⓐ −12

Ⓑ −6

Ⓒ 12

Ⓓ 20

8. The length of the rectangle is $2(x + 1)$ meters and the perimeter is 60 meters. What is the length of the rectangle?

Ⓕ 12 meters

Ⓖ 26 meters

Ⓗ 28 meters

Ⓙ 56 meters

9. Samantha opened a bank account in June and deposited some money. She deposited twice that amount in August. At the end of August, Samantha had less than $600 in her account. If she made no other withdrawals or deposits, which inequality could be used to determine the maximum amount Samantha could have deposited in June?

Ⓐ $2x < 600$

Ⓑ $2x > 600$

Ⓒ $3x < 600$

Ⓓ $3x > 600$

10. For which inequality is −2 a solution?

Ⓕ $2x < -4$

Ⓖ $-2x < 4$

Ⓗ $-2x > -4$

Ⓙ $-2x < -4$

11. Which graph shows the solutions of
$-2(1 - x) < 3(x - 2)$?

Ⓐ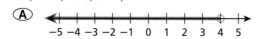
−5 −4 −3 −2 −1 0 1 2 3 4 5

Ⓑ
−5 −4 −3 −2 −1 0 1 2 3 4 5

Ⓒ
−5 −4 −3 −2 −1 0 1 2 3 4 5

Ⓓ
−5 −4 −3 −2 −1 0 1 2 3 4 5

12. Which compound inequality has no solution?

Ⓕ $x > 1$ OR $x < -2$

Ⓖ $x < 1$ AND $x > -2$

Ⓗ $x < 1$ OR $x < -2$

Ⓙ $x > 1$ AND $x < -2$

13. Which inequality has the same solutions
as $p < -2$?

Ⓐ $p + 1 < -2$

Ⓑ $p + 4 < 2$

Ⓒ $2p + 1 < -4$

Ⓓ $3p < -12$

14. What is the greatest integer solution of
$5 - 3m > 11$?

Ⓕ 0

Ⓖ −1

Ⓗ −2

Ⓙ −3

15. The sum of the measures of any two sides of a
triangle must be greater than the measure of the
third side. What is the greatest possible integer
value for x?

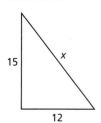

Ⓐ 27

Ⓑ 3

Ⓒ 26

Ⓓ 180

16. For which inequality is 3 a solution?

Ⓕ $x - 5 > -2$ Ⓗ $2x + 1 \leq 4$

Ⓖ $x + 4 \leq 7$ Ⓙ $2x - 1 \geq 7$

17. Which of the problems below could be solved by
finding the solution of this system?

$$\begin{cases} 2x + 2y = 56 \\ y = \dfrac{1}{3}x \end{cases}$$

Ⓐ The area of a rectangle is 56 square units.
The width is one-third the length. Find the
length of the rectangle.

Ⓑ The area of a rectangle is 56 square units.
The length is one-third the perimeter. Find
the length of the rectangle.

Ⓒ The perimeter of a rectangle is 56 units. The
length is one-third more than the width. Find
the length of the rectangle.

Ⓓ The perimeter of a rectangle is 56 units. The
width is one-third the length. Find the length
of the rectangle.

18. What is the slope of a line perpendicular to a line
that passes through $(3, 8)$ and $(1, -4)$?

Ⓕ $-\dfrac{1}{6}$ Ⓗ 2

Ⓖ $-\dfrac{1}{2}$ Ⓙ 6

19. Which inequality is graphed below?

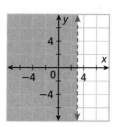

Ⓐ $-x > -3$ Ⓒ $2x < -6$

Ⓑ $-y > -3$ Ⓓ $3y < 9$

20. A chemist has a bottle of a 10% acid solution
and a bottle of a 30% acid solution. He mixes the
solutions together to get 500 mL of a 25% acid
solution. How much of the 30% solution did
he use?

Ⓕ 125 mL   Ⓗ 375 mL

Ⓖ 150 mL   Ⓙ 450 mL

21. Which ordered pair is NOT a solution of the system graphed below?

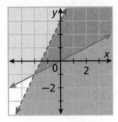

Ⓐ (0, 0)

Ⓑ (0, 3)

Ⓒ (1, 1)

Ⓓ (2, 1)

22. The fare for a cab is $3.50 per trip plus $1.25 per mile. Which describes the cab fare in dollars as a function of miles traveled?

Ⓕ $f(x) = 3.5x + 1.25$

Ⓖ $f(x) = 3.5x + 0.125$

Ⓗ $f(x) = 1.25x + 3.5$

Ⓙ $f(x) = 1.25x + 0.35$

23. Hillary needs markers and poster board for a project. The markers are $0.79 each and the poster board is $1.89 per sheet. She needs at least 4 sheets of poster board. Hillary has $15 to spend on project materials. Which system models this information?

Ⓐ $\begin{cases} p \geq 4 \\ 0.79m + 1.89p \leq 15 \end{cases}$

Ⓑ $\begin{cases} 0.79m \geq 1.89p \\ 4p \leq 15 \end{cases}$

Ⓒ $\begin{cases} 4p \geq 1.89 \\ m + 4p \leq 15 \end{cases}$

Ⓓ $\begin{cases} p + m \leq 15 \\ 0.79m + 1.89p \geq 4 \end{cases}$

Mini-Tasks

24. Alex buys 5 calendars to give as gifts. Each calendar has the same price. When the cashier rings up Alex's calendars, the total cost before tax is $58.75.

a. Write and solve an equation to find the cost of each calendar.

b. The total cost of Alex's calendars after tax is $63.45. Find the percent sales tax. Show your work and explain in words how you found your answer.

25. Write 2 different inequalities that have the same solution as $n > 3$ such that

a. the first inequality uses the symbol > and requires addition or subtraction to solve.

b. the second inequality uses the symbol < and requires multiplication or division to solve.

26. Alison has twice as many video games as Kyle. Maurice has 5 more video games than Alison. The total number of video games is less than 40.

a. Write an inequality to represent this situation.

b. Solve the inequality to determine the greatest number of video games Maurice could have. Justify each step in your solution.

27. Donna's Deli delivers lunches for $7 per person plus a $35 delivery fee. Larry's Lunches delivers lunches for $11 per person.

a. Write an expression to represent the cost of x lunches from Donna's Deli. Write an expression to represent the cost of ordering x lunches from Larry's Lunches.

b. Write an inequality to determine the number of lunches for which the cost of Larry's Lunches is less than the cost of Donna's Deli.

c. Solve the inequality and explain what the answer means. Which restaurant charges less for an order of 10 lunches?

28. Graph $y > \dfrac{-x}{3} - 1$ on a coordinate plane. Name one point that is a solution of the inequality.

29. Marc and his brother Ty start saving money at the same time. Marc has $145 and will add $10 to his savings every week. Ty has $20 and will add $15 to his savings every week. After how many weeks will Marc and Ty have the same amount saved? What is that amount? Show your work.

30. A movie producer is looking for extras to act as office employees in his next movie. The producer needs extras that are at least 40 years old but less than 70 years old. They should be at least 60 inches tall but less than 75 inches tall. Graph all the possible combinations of ages and heights for extras that match the producer's needs. Let x represent age and y represent height. Show your work.

Performance Tasks

31. Korena is laying out a flower garden in her front yard. The garden will be 6 feet wide, and one side will be flush against her house. She wants to add a decorative border around the other three sides, and she has 22 feet of decorative border. She also needs the garden to have an area of at least 50 square feet to fit all of her plants.

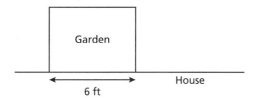

a. Write formulas for the area of the garden and for the length of the decorative border. Write both formulas in terms of length ℓ and width w.

b. Solve both formulas from part **a** for ℓ.

c. Use your formulas to find out if there is a length ℓ that satisfies Korena's requirement for the area and fits the amount of border she has. Explain your reasoning.

d. Describe one way Korena could change her plans so that she has the materials she needs to make her garden. Explain your reasoning and detail your changes.

32. Serena wants to use the interest earned for one year from her college savings to update the software on her computer. She can invest up to $10,000, and she needs at least $300 for the software. She wants to put part of this amount into a money market account that earns 2.5% simple interest per year. She puts the other part in a certificate of deposit (CD), which earns 4% simple interest per year.

a. Use x to represent the money invested in the CD and y to represent the money invested in the money market account. Write an inequality to represent the amount of money she can invest.

b. Using the same variables as in part **a**, write an inequality to represent the amount of interest she needs to earn in one year.

c. Graph the system of inequalities. Identify a solution that meets Serena's requirements, and calculate how much money she will earn on interest with that solution.

d. Serena wants to put as little money in the CD as possible, because unlike the money market account, she can't withdraw any money from the CD until the end of the year. What is the least amount of money Serena can put in the CD and still earn enough interest? Round to the nearest whole dollar, and explain how you found your answer.

Are You Ready?

my.hrw.com
Assessment and Intervention

✓ Vocabulary

Match each term on the left with a definition on the right.

1. absolute value
2. algebraic expression
3. input
4. output
5. x-axis

A. a letter used to represent a value that can change

B. the value generated for y

C. a group of numbers, symbols, and variables with one or more operations

D. the distance of a number from zero on the number line

E. the horizontal number line in the coordinate plane

F. a value substituted for x

✓ Ordered Pairs

Graph each point on the same coordinate plane.

6. $(-2, 4)$
7. $(0, -5)$
8. $(1, -3)$
9. $(4, 2)$
10. $(3, -2)$
11. $(-1, -2)$
12. $(-1, 3)$
13. $(-4, 0)$

✓ Function Tables

Generate ordered pairs for each function for $x = -2, -1, 0, 1, 2$.

14. $y = -2x - 1$
15. $y = x + 1$
16. $y = -x^2$
17. $y = \frac{1}{2}x + 2$
18. $y = (x + 1)^2$
19. $y = (x - 1)^2$

✓ Solve Multi-Step Equations

Solve each equation. Check your answer.

20. $17x - 15 = 12$
21. $-7 + 2t = 7$
22. $-6 = \frac{p}{3} + 9$
23. $5n - 10 = 35$
24. $3r - 14 = 7$
25. $9 = \frac{x}{2} + 1$
26. $-2.4 + 1.6g = 5.6$
27. $34 - 2x = 12$
28. $2(x + 5) = -8$

Career Readiness Market Researchers

Market researchers gather information and statistical data. They use graphs, including trend lines, to analyze the data. They determine what kinds of products people want to buy, and how much they are willing to pay. Market researchers advise companies about the types of people who are likely to buy their products. They usually need a college degree, with a strong background in math, especially statistics. They work in all areas of industry and as self-employed consultants.

Linear and Exponential Functions

UNIT

3

Online Edition

my.hrw.com

Access the complete online textbook, interactive features, and additional resources.

Animated Math

Interactively explore key concepts with these online tutorials.

Multilingual Glossary

Enhance your math vocabulary with this illustrated online glossary in 13 languages.

Portable Devices

On the Spot

Watch video tutorials anywhere, anytime with this app for iPhone® and iPad®.

HMH Fuse

Make your learning experience completely portable and interactive with this app for iPad®.

Chapter Resources

Scan with your smart phone to jump directly to the online edition.

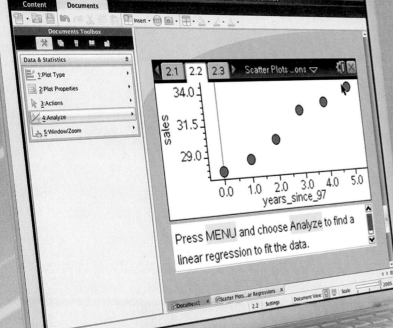

Press MENU and choose Analyze to find a linear regression to fit the data.

Use a computer or handheld to explore scatter plots with TI-Nspire™ activities.

8 Functional Relationships

COMMON
CORE GPS

MATHEMATICAL
PRACTICES
The Common Core Georgia Performance Standards for Mathematical Practice
describe varieties of expertise that all students should seek to develop.
Opportunities to develop these practices are integrated throughout this program.

1 Make sense of problems and persevere in solving them.

2 Reason abstractly and quantitatively.

3 Construct viable arguments and critique the reasoning of others.

4 Model with mathematics.

5 Use appropriate tools strategically.

6 Attend to precision.

7 Look for and make use of structure.

8 Look for and express regularity in repeated reasoning.

Unpacking the Standards

Understanding the standards and the vocabulary terms in the standards will help you know exactly what you are expected to learn in this chapter.

 MCC9-12.F.IF.1

Understand that a function from one set (called the domain) to another set (called the range) assigns to each element of the domain exactly one element of the range. ...

Key Vocabulary

function (función)
A relation in which every domain value is paired with exactly one range value.

domain (dominio)
The set of all first coordinates (or *x*-values) of a relation or function.

range of a function or relation (rango de una función o relación)
The set of all second coordinates (or *y*-values) of a function or relation.

element (elemento)
Each member in a set.

What It Means For You

A function model guarantees you that for any input value, you will get a unique output value.

EXAMPLE   **Relationship is a function**

$y = x^2$

One output for every input: When −2 is input, the output is always 4.

NON-EXAMPLE   **Relationship is NOT a function**

$y^2 = x$

Two outputs for every input but 0: When 4 is input, the output can be −2 or 2.

 MCC9-12.F.IF.4

For a function that models a relationship between two quantities, interpret key features of graphs and tables in terms of the quantities, and sketch graphs showing key features given a verbal description of the relationship.

What It Means For You

Learning to interpret a graph enables a deep visual understanding of all sorts of relationships.

EXAMPLE

A group of friends walked to the town market, did some shopping there, then returned home.

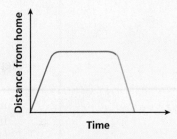

8-1 Graphing Relationships

? *Essential Question:* How can you use key features to sketch a graph of a real-world situation?

Objectives
Match simple graphs with situations.

Graph a relationship.

Vocabulary
continuous graph
discrete graph

Who uses this?
Cardiologists can use graphs to analyze their patients' heartbeats. (See Example 2.)

Graphs can be used to illustrate many different situations. For example, trends shown on a cardiograph can help a doctor see how the patient's heart is functioning.

To relate a graph to a given situation, use key words in the description.

 EXAMPLE MCC9-12.F.IF.4 **1** **Relating Graphs to Situations**

my.hrw.com

Online Video Tutor

The air temperature was constant for several hours at the beginning of the day and then rose steadily for several hours. It stayed the same temperature for most of the day before dropping sharply at sundown. Choose the graph that best represents this situation.

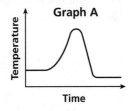 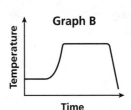 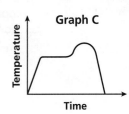

Step 1 Read the graphs from left to right to show time passing.

Step 2 List key words in order and decide which graph shows them.

Key Words	Segment Description	Graphs
Was constant	Horizontal	Graphs A and B
Rose steadily	Slanting upward	Graphs A and B
Stayed the same	Horizontal	Graph B
Dropped sharply	Slanting downward	Graph B

Step 3 Pick the graph that shows all the key phrases in order.

horizontal, slanting upward, horizontal, slanting downward

The correct graph is B.

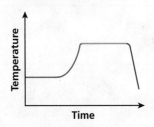

 1. The air temperature increased steadily for several hours and then remained constant. At the end of the day, the temperature increased slightly again before dropping sharply. Choose the graph above that best represents this situation.

As seen in Example 1, some graphs are connected lines or curves called **continuous graphs** . Some graphs are only distinct points. These are called **discrete graphs** .

The graph on theme-park attendance is an example of a discrete graph. It consists of distinct points because each year is distinct and people are counted in whole numbers only. The values between the whole numbers are not included, since they have no meaning for the situation.

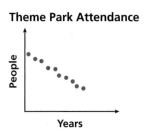

Theme Park Attendance

COMMON CORE GPS

EXAMPLE 2

MCC9-12.F.IF.4

my.hrw.com

Online Video Tutor

Sketching Graphs for Situations

Sketch a graph for each situation. Tell whether the graph is continuous or discrete.

A Simon is selling candles to raise money for the school dance. For each candle he sells, the school will get $2.50. He has 10 candles that he can sell.

Simon's Earnings

The amount earned (y-axis) increases by $2.50 for each candle Simon sells (x-axis).

Since Simon can only sell whole numbers of candles, the graph is 11 distinct points.

The graph is discrete.

B Angelique's heart rate is being monitored while she exercises on a treadmill. While walking, her heart rate remains the same. As she increases her pace, her heart rate rises at a steady rate. When she begins to run, her heart rate increases more rapidly and then remains high while she runs. As she decreases her pace, her heart rate slows down and returns to her normal rate.

As time passes during her workout (moving left to right along the *x*-axis), her heart rate (*y*-axis) does the following:

- remains the same,
- rises at a steady rate,
- increases more rapidly (steeper than previous segment),
- remains high,
- slows down,
- and then returns to her normal rate.

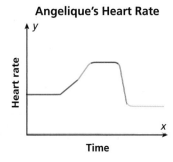

Angelique's Heart Rate

The graph is continuous.

CHECK IT OUT!

Sketch a graph for each situation. Tell whether the graph is continuous or discrete.

2a. Jamie is taking an 8-week keyboarding class. At the end of each week, she takes a test to find the number of words she can type per minute. She improves each week.

2b. Henry begins to drain a water tank by opening a valve. Then he opens another valve. Then he closes the first valve. He leaves the second valve open until the tank is empty.

When sketching or interpreting a graph, pay close attention to the labels on each axis. Both graphs below show a relationship about a child going down a slide. **Graph A** represents the child's *distance from the ground* over time. **Graph B** represents the child's *speed* over time.

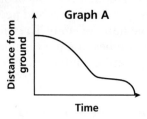

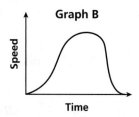

COMMON CORE GPS

EXAMPLE 3
Ext. of MCC9-12.F.IF.4

my.hrw.com

Online Video Tutor

Writing Situations for Graphs

Write a possible situation for the given graph.

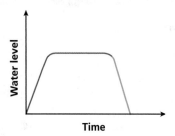

Step 1 Identify labels.
x-axis: time y-axis: water level

Step 2 Analyze sections.
Over time, the water level
- **increases steadily,**
- **remains unchanged,**
- and then decreases steadily.

Possible Situation: A watering can is filled with water. It sits for a while until some flowers are planted. The water is then emptied on top of the planted flowers.

CHECK IT OUT!

3. Write a possible situation for the given graph.

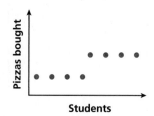

MCC.MP.2, MCC.MP.4

MATHEMATICAL PRACTICES

THINK AND DISCUSS

1. Should a graph of age related to height be a continuous graph or a discrete graph? Explain.

2. Give an example of a situation that, when graphed, would include a horizontal segment.

Know it! Note

3. GET ORGANIZED Copy and complete the graphic organizer. Write an example of key words that suggest the given segments on a graph. One example for each segment is given for you.

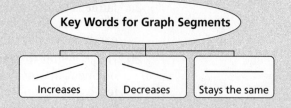

Key Words for Graph Segments

Increases   Decreases   Stays the same

GUIDED PRACTICE

Vocabulary Apply the vocabulary from this lesson to answer each question.

1. A ____?____ graph is made of connected lines or curves. (*continuous* or *discrete*)

2. A ____?____ graph is made of only distinct points. (*continuous* or *discrete*)

SEE EXAMPLE **1** **Choose the graph that best represents each situation.**

3. A person alternates between running and walking.

4. A person gradually speeds up to a constant running pace.

5. A person walks, gradually speeds up to a run, and then slows back down to a walk.

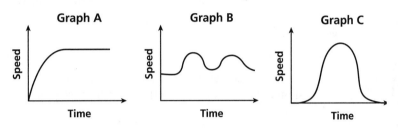

SEE EXAMPLE **2** **6.** Maxine is buying extra pages for her photo album. Each page holds exactly 8 photos. Sketch a graph to show the maximum number of photos she can add to her album if she buys 1, 2, 3, or 4 extra pages. Tell whether the graph is continuous or discrete.

SEE EXAMPLE **3** **Write a possible situation for each graph.**

7. 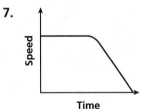 **8.** 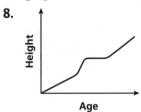 **9.**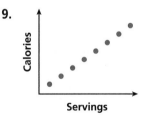

PRACTICE AND PROBLEM SOLVING

Choose the graph that best represents each situation.

10. A flag is raised up a flagpole quickly at the beginning and then more slowly near the top.

11. A flag is raised up a flagpole in a jerky motion, using a hand-over-hand method.

12. A flag is raised up a flagpole at a constant rate of speed.

Independent Practice

For Exercises	See Example
10–12	1
13	2
14–16	3

my.hrw.com

Online Extra Practice

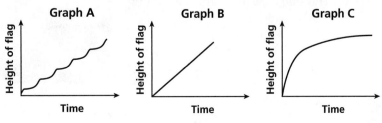

13. For six months, a puppy gained weight at a steady rate. Sketch a graph to illustrate the weight of the puppy during that time period. Tell whether the graph is continuous or discrete.

Write a possible situation for each graph.

14.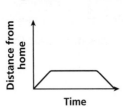

15.

16.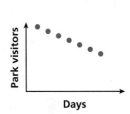

17. Data Collection Use a graphing calculator and motion detector for the following.

    a. On a coordinate plane, draw a graph relating distance from a starting point walking at various speeds and time.

    b. Using the motion detector as the starting point, walk away from the motion detector to make a graph on the graphing calculator that matches the one you drew.

    c. Compare your walking speeds to each change in steepness on the graph.

18. Sports The graph shows the speed of a horse during and after a race. Use it to describe the changing pace of the horse during the race.

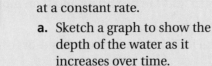

19. Recreation You hike up a mountain path starting at 10 A.M. You camp overnight and then walk back down the same path at the same pace at 10 A.M. the next morning. On the same set of axes, graph the relationship between distance from the top of the mountain and the time of day for both the hike up and the hike down. What does the point of intersection of the graphs represent?

20. Critical Thinking Suppose that you sketched a graph of speed related to time for a brick that fell from the top of a building. Then you sketched a graph for speed related to time for a ball that was rolled down a hill and then came to rest. How would the graphs be the same? How would they be different?

H.O.T. 21. Write About It Describe a real-life situation that could be represented by a distinct graph. Then describe a real-life situation that could be represented by a continuous graph.

Real-World Connections

22. A rectangular pool that is 4 feet deep at all places is being filled at a constant rate.

    a. Sketch a graph to show the depth of the water as it increases over time.

    b. The side view of another swimming pool is shown. If the pool is being filled at a constant rate, sketch a graph to show the depth of the water as it increases over time.

(cl),© Bettmann/CORBIS; (b), Sam Dudgeon/HMH

23. Which situation would NOT be represented by a discrete graph?

    Ⓐ Amount of money earned based on the number of cereal bars sold

    Ⓑ Number of visitors to a grocery store per day for one week

    Ⓒ The amount of iced tea in a pitcher at a restaurant during the lunch hour

    Ⓓ The total cost of buying 1, 2, or 3 CDs at the music store

24. Which situation is best represented by the graph?

    Ⓕ A snowboarder starts at the bottom of the hill and takes a ski lift to the top.

    Ⓖ A cruise boat travels at a steady pace from the port to its destination.

    Ⓗ An object falls from the top of a building and gains speed at a rapid pace before hitting the ground.

    Ⓙ A marathon runner starts at a steady pace and then runs faster at the end of the race before stopping at the finish line.

H.O.T. 25. Short Response Marla participates in a triathlon consisting of swimming, biking, and running. Would a graph of Marla's speed during the triathlon be a continuous graph or a distinct graph? Explain.

CHALLENGE AND EXTEND

Pictured are three vases and graphs representing the height of water as it is poured into each of the vases at a constant rate. Match each vase with the correct graph.

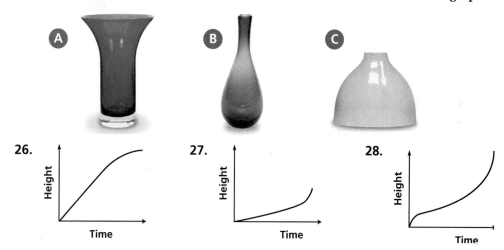

A   B   C

26.   **27.**   **28.**

FOCUS ON MATHEMATICAL PRACTICES

H.O.T. 29. Modeling As Kayla burns a candle, she records the amount of time that passes and the height of the burning candle. Which graph could reasonably represent her data? Explain your choice.

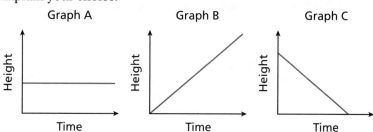

Graph A   Graph B   Graph C

8-2 Relations and Functions

Essential Question: How can you identify the domain and range of a relation and tell whether a relation is a function?

Objectives
Identify functions.

Find the domain and range of relations and functions.

Vocabulary
relation
domain
range
function

Why learn this?
You can use a relation to show finishing positions and scores in a track meet.

Previously, you saw relationships represented by graphs. Relationships can also be represented by a set of ordered pairs, called a **relation**.

In the scoring system of some track meets, **first place** is worth 5 points, **second place** is worth 3 points, **third place** is worth 2 points, and **fourth place** is worth 1 point. This scoring system is a relation, so it can be shown as ordered pairs, $\{(1, 5), (2, 3), (3, 2), (4, 1)\}$. You can also show relations in other ways, such as tables, graphs, or *mapping diagrams*.

COMMON CORE GPS
Prep. for MCC9-12.F.IF.1

EXAMPLE 1

Showing Multiple Representations of Relations

Express the relation for the track meet scoring system, $\{(1, 5), (2, 3), (3, 2), (4, 1)\}$, as a table, as a graph, and as a mapping diagram.

my.hrw.com

Online Video Tutor

Table

Track Scoring	
Place	Points
1	5
2	3
3	2
4	1

Write all x-values under "Place" and all y-values under "Points."

Graph

Use the x- and y-values to plot the ordered pairs.

Mapping Diagram

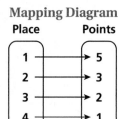

Write all x-values under "Place" and all y-values under "Points." Draw an arrow from each x-value to its corresponding y-value.

1. Express the relation $\{(1, 3)\ (2, 4),\ (3, 5)\}$ as a table, as a graph, and as a mapping diagram.

The **domain** of a relation is the set of first coordinates (or *x*-values) of the ordered pairs. The **range** of a relation is the set of second coordinates (or *y*-values) of the ordered pairs. The domain of the track meet scoring system is {1, 2, 3, 4}. The range is {5, 3, 2, 1}.

Aflo Foto Agency

EXAMPLE **2**
MCC9-12.F.IF.5

Finding the Domain and Range of a Relation

Give the domain and range of the relation.

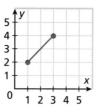

The domain is all *x*-values from 1 through 3, inclusive.

The range is all *y*-values from 2 through 4, inclusive.

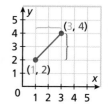

D: $1 \le x \le 3$ R: $2 \le y \le 4$

 Give the domain and range of each relation.

2a.

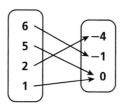

2b.

x	y
1	1
4	4
8	1

A **function** is a special type of relation that pairs each domain value with exactly one range value.

 EXAMPLE **3**
MCC.9-12.F.IF.1

Identifying Functions

Give the domain and range of each relation. Tell whether the relation is a function. Explain.

A

Field Trip	
Students x	**Buses y**
75	2
68	2
125	3

D: $\{75, 68, 125\}$
R: $\{2, 3\}$

Even though 2 appears twice in the table, it is written only once when writing the range.

This relation is a function. Each domain value is paired with exactly one range value.

Writing Math

When there is a finite number of values in a domain or range, list the values inside braces.

B

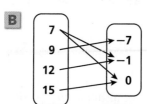

Use the arrows to determine which domain values correspond to each range value.

D: $\{7, 9, 12, 15\}$

R: $\{-7, -1, 0\}$

This relation is not a function. Each domain value does not have exactly one range value. The domain value 7 is paired with the range values −1 and 0.

Give the domain and range of each relation. Tell whether the relation is a function. Explain.

To find the domain and range of a graph, it may help to draw lines to see the *x*- and *y*-values.

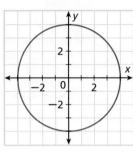

C

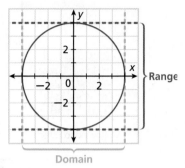

Draw lines to see the domain and range values.

Range

Domain

D: $-4 \leq x \leq 4$ R: $-4 \leq y \leq 4$

x	4	0	0	−4
y	0	4	−4	0

To compare domain and range values, make a table using points from the graph.

This relation is not a function because there are several domain values that have more than one range value. For example, the domain value 0 is paired with both 4 and −4.

CHECK IT OUT! **Give the domain and range of each relation. Tell whether the relation is a function. Explain.**

3a. $\{(8, 2), (-4, 1), (-6, 2), (1, 9)\}$ **3b.**

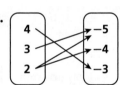

Student to Student   *Functions*

I decide whether a list of ordered pairs is a function by looking at the x-values. If they're all different, then it's a function.

(1, 6), (2, 5), (6, 5), (0, 8)
All different x-values
Function

(5, 6), (7, 2), (5, 8), (6, 3)
Same x-value (with different *y*-values)
Not a function

Eric Dawson
Boone High School

MCC.MP.3   MATHEMATICAL PRACTICES

THINK AND DISCUSS

1. Describe how to tell whether a set of ordered pairs is a function.

2. Can the graph of a vertical line segment represent a function? Explain.

3. GET ORGANIZED Copy and complete the graphic organizer by explaining when a relation is a function and when it is not a function.

A relation is...	
A function if...	Not a function if...

my.hrw.com
Homework Help

GUIDED PRACTICE

Vocabulary Apply the vocabulary from this lesson to answer each question.

1. Use a mapping diagram to show a relation that is not a *function*.

2. The set of *x*-values for a relation is also called the __?__. (*domain* or *range*)

SEE EXAMPLE 1 Express each relation as a table, as a graph, and as a mapping diagram.

3. $\{(1, 1), (1, 2)\}$

4. $\left\{(-1, 1), \left(-2, \frac{1}{2}\right), \left(-3, \frac{1}{3}\right), \left(-4, \frac{1}{4}\right)\right\}$

5. $\{(-1, 1), (-3, 3), (5, -5), (-7, 7)\}$

6. $\{(0, 0), (2, -4), (2, -2)\}$

SEE EXAMPLE 2 Give the domain and range of each relation.

7. $\{(-5, 7), (0, 0), (2, -8), (5, -20)\}$

8. $\{(1, 2), (2, 4), (3, 6), (4, 8), (5, 10)\}$

9.
x	3	5	2	8	6
y	9	25	4	81	36

10.
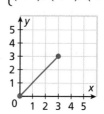

SEE EXAMPLE 3 **Multi-Step** Give the domain and range of each relation. Tell whether the relation is a function. Explain.

11. $\{(1, 3), (1, 0), (1, -2), (1, 8)\}$

12. $\{(-2, 1), (-1, 2), (0, 3), (1, 4)\}$

13.
x	−2	−1	0	1	2
y	1	1	1	1	1

14.

PRACTICE AND PROBLEM SOLVING

For Exercises	See Example
15–16	1
17–18	2
19–20	3

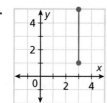

my.hrw.com

Online Extra Practice

Express each relation as a table, as a graph, and as a mapping diagram.

15. $\{(-2, -4), (-1, -1), (0, 0), (1, -1), (2, -4)\}$

16. $\left\{(2, 1), \left(2, \frac{1}{2}\right), (2, 2), \left(2, 2\frac{1}{2}\right)\right\}$

Give the domain and range of each relation.

17.

18.
x	y
4	4
5	5
6	6
7	7
8	8

Multi-Step Give the domain and range of each relation. Tell whether the relation is a function. Explain.

19.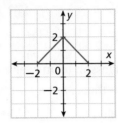

20.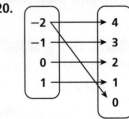

21. **Consumer Application** An electrician charges a base fee of $75 plus $50 for each hour of work. Create a table that shows the amount the electrician charges for 1, 2, 3, and 4 hours of work. Let *x* represent the number of hours and *y* represent the amount charged for *x* hours. Is this relation a function? Explain.

22. **Geometry** Write a relation as a set of ordered pairs in which the *x*-value represents the side length of a square and the *y*-value represents the area of that square. Use a domain of 2, 4, 6, 9, and 11.

23. **Multi-Step** Create a mapping diagram to display the numbers of days in 1, 2, 3, and 4 weeks. Is this relation a function? Explain.

24. **Nutrition** The illustrations list the number of grams of fat and the number of Calories from fat for selected foods.

 a. Create a graph for the relation between grams of fat and Calories from fat.

 b. Is this relation a function? Explain.

Hamburger
Fat (g):   14
Fat (Cal): 126

Cheeseburger
Fat (g):   18
Fat (Cal): 162

Grilled chicken filet
Fat (g):   3.5
Fat (Cal): 31.5

Breaded chicken filet
Fat (g):   11
Fat (Cal): 99

Taco salad
Fat (g):   19
Fat (Cal): 171

25. **Recreation** A shop rents canoes for a $7 equipment fee plus $2 per hour, with a maximum cost of $15 per day. Express the number of hours *x* and the cost *y* as a relation in table form, and find the cost to rent a canoe for 1, 2, 3, 4, and 5 hours. Is this relation a function? Explain.

26. **Health** You can burn about 6 Calories per minute bicycling. Let *x* represent the number of minutes bicycled, and let *y* represent the number of Calories burned.

 a. Write ordered pairs to show the number of Calories burned by bicycling for 60, 120, 180, 240, or 300 minutes. Graph the ordered pairs.

 b. Find the domain and range of the relation.

 c. Does this graph represent a function? Explain.

27. **Critical Thinking** For a function, can the number of elements in the range be greater than the number of elements in the domain? Explain.

28. **Critical Thinking** Tell whether each statement is true or false. If false, explain why.

 a. All relations are functions.   b. All functions are relations.

29. **a.** The graph shows the amount of water being pumped into a pool over a 5-hour time period. Find the domain and range.

   b. Does the graph represent a function? Explain.

   c. Give the time and volume as ordered pairs at 2 hours and at 3 hours 30 minutes.

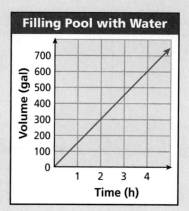

Filling Pool with Water

HO.T. 30. **///ERROR ANALYSIS///** When asked whether the relation $\{(-4, 16), (-2, 4),$ $(0, 0), (2, 4)\}$ is a function, a student stated that the relation is not a function because 4 appears twice. What error did the student make? How would you explain to the student why this relation is a function?

HO.T. 31. **Write About It** Describe a real-world situation for a relation that is NOT a function. Create a mapping diagram to show why the relation is not a function.

TEST PREP

32. Which of the following relations is NOT a function?

   Ⓐ $\{(6, 2), (-1, 2), (-3, 2), (-5, 2)\}$ Ⓒ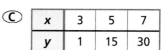

   Ⓑ 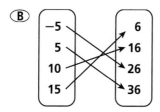   Ⓓ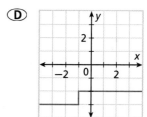

33. Which is NOT a correct way to describe the function $\{(-3, 2), (1, 8),$ $(-1, 5), (3, 11)\}$?

   Ⓕ 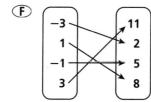   Ⓗ Domain: $\{-3, 1, -1, 3\}$

                                                  Range: $\{2, 8, 5, 11\}$

   Ⓖ 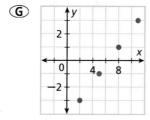   Ⓙ

x	y
−3	2
−1	5
1	8
3	11

34. Which graph represents a function?

 A   B   C 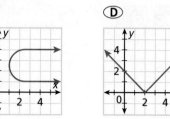 D

35. Extended Response Use the table for the following.

x	−3	−1	0	1	3
y	5	7	9	11	13

    a. Express the relation as ordered pairs.

    b. Give the domain and range of the relation.

    c. Does the relation represent a function? Explain your answer.

CHALLENGE AND EXTEND

36. What values of a make the relation $\{(a, 1), (2, 3), (4, 5)\}$ a function? Explain.

37. What values of b make the relation $\{(5, 6), (7, 8), (9, b)\}$ a function? Explain.

38. The *inverse* of a relation is created by interchanging the x- and y- coordinates of each ordered pair in the relation.

    a. Find the inverse of the following relation: $\{(-2, 5), (0, 4), (3, -8), (7, 5)\}$.

    b. Is the original relation a function? Why or why not? Is the inverse of the relation a function? Why or why not?

    c. The statement "If a relation is a function, then the inverse of the relation is also a function" is sometimes true. Give an example of a relation and its inverse that are both functions. Then give an example of a relation and its inverse that are both not functions.

FOCUS ON MATHEMATICAL PRACTICES

H.O.T. 39. Analysis Gina surveys 15 high school students, asking them what grade they're in and how much they spent that day on lunch. She makes a table of the data, and then draws a graph. She labels her x-axis *Grade Level* and her y-axis *Cost of Lunch*.

    a. What is the domain of her graph?

    b. Can you find the range of the graph from the information given? If not, describe the range in general terms.

    c. What is the maximum possible number of elements in the range? What is the minimum?

    d. Is it likely that the graph is a function? Explain your answer.

H.O.T. 40. Error Analysis Nick matches each day of the week to anyone in his class of 20 students that was born on that day. He says this is a function. Oscar says this relation is not a function.

    a. Who do you think is correct? Explain why.

    b. How could Nick relate the same two sets in a way that creates a function?

8-2 Algebra TASK

Use with Relations and Functions

The Vertical-Line Test

The *vertical-line test* can be used to visually determine whether a graphed relation is a function.

MATHEMATICAL PRACTICES

Look for and express regularity in repeated reasoning.

MCC9-12.F.IF.1 Understand that a function from one set (called the domain) to another set (called the range) assigns to each element of the domain exactly one element of the range. . . .

Activity

1 Look at the values in Table 1. Is every *x*-value paired with exactly one *y*-value? If not, what *x*-value(s) are paired with more than one *y*-value?

2 Is the relation a function? Explain.

3 Graph the points from the Table 1. Draw a vertical line through each point of the graph. Does any vertical line touch more than one point?

Table 1	
x	**y**
−2	−5
−1	−3
0	−1
1	1
2	3
3	5

4 Look at the values in Table 2. Is every *x*-value paired with exactly one *y*-value? If not, what *x*-value(s) are paired with more than one *y*-value?

5 Is the relation a function? Explain.

6 Graph the points from the Table 2. Draw a vertical line through each point of the graph. Does any vertical line touch more than one point?

7 What is the *x*-value of the two points that are on the same vertical line? Is that *x*-value paired with more than one *y*-value?

Table 2	
x	**y**
−2	−3
1	4
0	5
1	2
2	3
3	5

8 Write a statement describing how to use a vertical line to tell if a relation is a function. This is called the vertical-line test.

9 Why does the vertical-line test work?

Try This

Use the vertical-line test to determine whether each relation is a function. If a relation is not a function, list two ordered pairs that show the same *x*-value with two different *y*-values.

1.

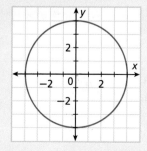

2.

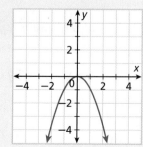

3.

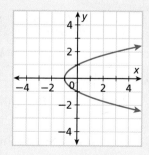

8-3
Algebra
TASK

Model Variable Relationships

You can use models to represent an algebraic relationship. Using these models, you can write an algebraic expression to help describe and extend patterns.

Use with Writing Functions

Look for and express regularity in repeated reasoning.

The diagrams below represent the side views of tables. Each has a tabletop and a base. Copy and complete the chart using the pattern shown in the diagrams.

Tabletop →
Base →

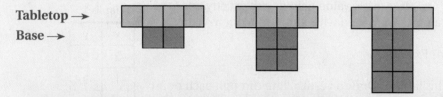

TERM NUMBER	FIGURE	DESCRIPTION OF FIGURE	EXPRESSION FOR NUMBER OF BLOCKS	VALUE OF TERM (NUMBER OF BLOCKS)	ORDERED PAIR
1		length of tabletop = 4 height of base = 1	4 + (2)1	6	(1, 6)
2		length of tabletop = 4 height of base = 2	▪	8	▪
3		length of tabletop = 4 height of base = 3	▪	10	▪
4	▪	▪	▪	▪	▪
5	▪	▪	▪	▪	▪
n	✕	▪	▪	✕	▪

Try This

1. Explain why you must multiply the height of the base by 2.

2. What does the ordered pair (1, 6) mean?

3. Does the ordered pair (10, 24) belong in this pattern? Why or why not?

4. Which expression from the table describes how you would find the total number of blocks for any term number n?

5. Use your rule to find the 25th term in this pattern.

8-3 # Writing Functions

? ***Essential Question:*** How can you use function notation to write and evaluate functions?

Objectives
Identify independent and dependent variables.

Write an equation in function notation and evaluate a function for given input values.

Vocabulary
independent variable
dependent variable
function rule
function notation

Why learn this?

You can use a function rule to calculate how much money you will earn for working specific amounts of time.

Suppose Tasha baby-sits and charges $5 per hour.

Time Worked (h) *x*	1	2	3	4
Amount Earned ($) *y*	5	10	15	20

The amount of money Tasha earns is $5 times the number of hours she works. Write an equation using two different variables to show this relationship.

Amount earned is $5 times the number of hours worked.

$$y \quad = 5 \cdot \quad x$$

Tasha can use this equation to find how much money she will earn for any number of hours she works.

  EXAMPLE 1 MCC9-12.A.CED.2

 my.hrw.com

Online Video Tutor

Using a Table to Write an Equation

Determine a relationship between the *x*- and *y*-values. Write an equation.

x	1	2	3	4
y	−2	−1	0	1

Step 1 List possible relationships between the first *x*- and *y*-values.

$1 - 3 = -2$ or $1(-2) = -2$

Step 2 Determine if one relationship works for the remaining values.

$2 - 3 = -1$ ✓ $\quad 2(-2) \neq -1$ ✗

$3 - 3 = 0$ ✓ $\quad 3(-2) \neq 0$ ✗

$4 - 3 = 1$ ✓ $\quad 4(-2) \neq 1$ ✗

The first relationship works. The value of *y* is 3 less than *x*.

Step 3 Write an equation.

$y = x - 3$ *The value of y is 3 less than x.*

 CHECK IT OUT! 1. Determine a relationship between the *x*- and *y*-values in the relation $\{(1, 3), (2, 6), (3, 9), (4, 12)\}$. Write an equation.

The equation in Example 1 describes a function because for each *x*-value (input), there is only one *y*-value (output).

RubberBall/Alamy

The input of a function is the **independent variable**. The output of a function is the **dependent variable**. The value of the dependent variable *depends* on, or is a function of, the value of the independent variable. For Tasha, the amount she earns depends on, or is a function of, the amount of time she works.

Online Video Tutor

EXAMPLE 2
MCC9-12.F.IF.1

Identifying Independent and Dependent Variables

Identify the independent and dependent variables in each situation.

A In the winter, more electricity is used when the temperature goes down, and less is used when the temperature rises.

The amount of electricity used *depends on* the temperature.

Dependent: **amount of electricity**   Independent: temperature

B The cost of shipping a package is based on its weight.

The cost of shipping a package *depends on* its weight.

Dependent: **cost**   Independent: weight

C The faster Ron walks, the quicker he gets home.

The time it takes Ron to get home *depends on* the speed he walks.

Dependent: **time**   Independent: speed

CHECK IT OUT! Identify the independent and dependent variables in each situation.

2a. A company charges $10 per hour to rent a jackhammer.

2b. Apples cost $0.99 per pound.

An algebraic expression that defines a function is a **function rule**. 5 · x in the equation about Tasha's earnings is a function rule.

If x is the independent variable and y is the dependent variable, then **function notation** for y is $f(x)$, read "f of x," where f names the function. When an equation in two variables describes a function, you can use function notation to write it.

Helpful Hint

There are several different ways to describe the variables of a function.

Independent Variable	Dependent Variable
x-values	y-values
Domain	Range
Input	Output
x	f(x)

The dependent variable   is   a function of   the independent variable.

y	is a function of	x.
y	=	f (x)

Since $y = f(x)$, Tasha's earnings, $y = 5x$, can be rewritten in function notation by substituting $f(x)$ for y: $f(x) = 5x$. Sometimes functions are written using y, and sometimes functions are written using $f(x)$.

Online Video Tutor

EXAMPLE 3
MCC9-12.F.IF.2

Writing Functions

Identify the independent and dependent variables. Write an equation in function notation for each situation.

A A lawyer's fee is $200 per hour for her services.

The fee for the lawyer depends on how many hours she works.

Dependent: **fee**   Independent: hours

Let *h* represent the number of hours the lawyer works.

The function for the lawyer's fee is $f(h) = 200h$.

Identify the independent and dependent variables. Write an equation in function notation for each situation.

B The admission fee to a local carnival is $8. Each ride costs $1.50.

The **total cost** depends on *the number of rides* ridden, plus $8.

Dependent: **total cost**　　Independent: *number of rides*

Let *r* represent the number of rides ridden.

The function for the total cost of the carnival is $f(r) = 1.50r + 8$.

 CHECK IT OUT! Identify the independent and dependent variables. Write an equation in function notation for each situation.

3a. Steven buys lettuce that costs $1.69/lb.

3b. An amusement park charges a $6.00 parking fee plus $29.99 per person.

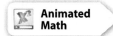
Animated Math

You can think of a function as an **input-output** machine. For Tasha's earnings, $f(x) = 5x$, if you input a value *x*, the output is $5x$.

If Tasha wanted to know how much money she would earn by working 6 hours, she could input 6 for *x* and find the output. This is called *evaluating the function*.

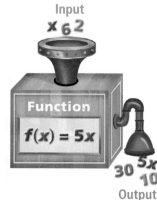

Input

x 6 2

Function

$f(x) = 5x$

30 5x
10

Output

COMMON CORE GPS
MCC9-12.F.IF.2

EXAMPLE 4 **Evaluating Functions**

my.hrw.com

Online Video Tutor

Evaluate each function for the given input values.

A For $f(x) = 5x$, find $f(x)$ when $x = 6$ and when $x = 7.5$.

$$f(x) = 5x \qquad\qquad\qquad f(x) = 5x$$
$$f(6) = 5(6) \quad \text{Substitute 6 for x.} \qquad f(7.5) = 5(7.5) \quad \text{Substitute 7.5 for x.}$$
$$= 30 \quad \text{Simplify.} \qquad\qquad\qquad = 37.5 \quad \text{Simplify.}$$

B For $g(t) = 2.30t + 10$, find $g(t)$ when $t = 2$ and when $t = -5$.

$$g(t) = 2.30t + 10 \qquad\qquad g(t) = 2.30t + 10$$
$$g(2) = 2.30(2) + 10 \qquad\qquad g(-5) = 2.30(-5) + 10$$
$$= 4.6 + 10 \qquad\qquad\qquad = -11.5 + 10$$
$$= 14.6 \qquad\qquad\qquad\qquad = -1.5$$

 **Reading Math**

Functions can be named with any letter; *f*, *g*, and *h* are the most common. You read $f(6)$ as "*f* of 6," and $g(2)$ as "*g* of 2."

C For $h(x) = \frac{1}{2}x - 3$, find $h(x)$ when $x = 12$ and when $x = -8$.

$$h(x) = \frac{1}{2}x - 3 \qquad\qquad h(x) = \frac{1}{2}x - 3$$
$$h(12) = \frac{1}{2}(12) - 3 \qquad\qquad h(-8) = \frac{1}{2}(-8) - 3$$
$$= 6 - 3 \qquad\qquad\qquad = -4 - 3$$
$$= 3 \qquad\qquad\qquad\qquad = -7$$

 CHECK IT OUT! Evaluate each function for the given input values.

4a. For $h(c) = 2c - 1$, find $h(c)$ when $c = 1$ and $c = -3$.

4b. For $g(t) = \frac{1}{4}t + 1$, find $g(t)$ when $t = -24$ and $t = 400$.

When a function describes a real-world situation, every real number is not always reasonable for the domain and range. For example, a number representing the length of an object cannot be negative, and only whole numbers can represent a number of people.

EXAMPLE **5**
MCC9-12.F.IF.5

my.hrw.com

Online Video Tutor

Finding the Reasonable Domain and Range of a Function

Manuel has already sold $20 worth of tickets to the school play. He has 4 tickets left to sell at $2.50 per ticket. Write a function to describe how much money Manuel can collect from selling tickets. Find the reasonable domain and range for the function.

Money collected from ticket sales	is	$2.50	per	ticket	plus	the $20 already sold.
$f(x)$	=	$2.50	·	x	+	20

If he sells x more tickets, he will have collected $f(x) = 2.50x + 20$ dollars.

Manuel has only 4 tickets left to sell, so he could sell 0, 1, 2, 3, or 4 tickets. A reasonable domain is {0, 1, 2, 3, 4}.

Substitute these values into the function rule to find the range values.

x	0	1	2	3	4
$f(x)$	2.50(0) + 20 = 20	2.50(1) + 20 = 22.50	2.50(2) + 20 = 25	2.50(3) + 20 = 27.50	2.50(4) + 20 = 30

The reasonable range for this situation is {$20, $22.50, $25, $27.50, $30}.

 5. The settings on a space heater are the whole numbers from 0 to 3. The total number of watts used for each setting is 500 times the setting number. Write a function to describe the number of watts used for each setting. Find the reasonable domain and range for the function.

MCC.MP.4, MCC.MP.6   MATHEMATICAL PRACTICES

THINK AND DISCUSS

1. When you input water into an ice machine, the output is ice cubes. Name another real-world object that has an input and an output.

2. How do you identify the independent and dependent variables in a situation?

3. Explain how to find reasonable domain values for a function.

 4. GET ORGANIZED Copy and complete the graphic organizer. Use the function $y = x + 3$ and the domain {−2, −1, 0, 1, 2}.

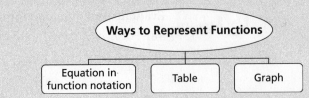

Ways to Represent Functions
Equation in function notation — Table — Graph

GUIDED PRACTICE

Vocabulary Apply the vocabulary from this lesson to answer each question.

1. The output of a function is the ___?___ variable. (*independent* or *dependent*)

2. An algebraic expression that defines a function is a ___?___. (*function rule* or *function notation*)

SEE EXAMPLE 1 Determine a relationship between the *x*- and *y*-values. Write an equation.

3.

x	1	2	3	4
y	−1	0	1	2

4. $\{(1, 4), (2, 7), (3, 10), (4, 13)\}$

SEE EXAMPLE 2 Identify the independent and dependent variables in each situation.

5. A small-size bottle of water costs $1.99 and a large-size bottle of water costs $3.49.

6. An employee receives 2 vacation days for every month worked.

SEE EXAMPLE 3 Identify the independent and dependent variables. Write an equation in function notation for each situation.

7. An air-conditioning technician charges customers $75 per hour.

8. An ice rink charges $3.50 for skates and $1.25 per hour.

SEE EXAMPLE 4 Evaluate each function for the given input values.

9. For $f(x) = 7x + 2$, find $f(x)$ when $x = 0$ and when $x = 1$.

10. For $g(x) = 4x - 9$, find $g(x)$ when $x = 3$ and when $x = 5$.

11. For $h(t) = \frac{1}{3}t - 10$, find $h(t)$ when $t = 27$ and when $t = -15$.

SEE EXAMPLE 5 12. A construction company uses beams that are 2, 3, or 4 meters long. The measure of each beam must be converted to centimeters. Write a function to describe the situation. Find the reasonable domain and range for the function. (*Hint*: 1 m = 100 cm)

PRACTICE AND PROBLEM SOLVING

Independent Practice

For Exercises	See Example
13–14	1
15–16	2
17–19	3
20–22	4
23	5

my.hrw.com

Online Extra Practice

Determine a relationship between the *x*- and *y*-values. Write an equation.

13.

x	1	2	3	4
y	−2	−4	−6	−8

14. $\{(1, -1), (2, -2), (3, -3), (4, -4)\}$

Identify the independent and dependent variables in each situation.

15. Gardeners buy fertilizer according to the size of a lawn.

16. The cost to gift wrap an order is $3 plus $1 per item wrapped.

Identify the independent and dependent variables. Write an equation in function notation for each situation.

17. To rent a DVD, a customer must pay $3.99 plus $0.99 for every day that it is late.

18. Stephen charges $25 for each lawn he mows.

19. A car can travel 28 miles per gallon of gas.

Evaluate each function for the given input values.

20. For $f(x) = x^2 - 5$, find $f(x)$ when $x = 0$ and when $x = 3$.

21. For $g(x) = x^2 + 6$, find $g(x)$ when $x = 1$ and when $x = 2$.

22. For $f(x) = \frac{2}{3}x + 3$, find $f(x)$ when $x = 9$ and when $x = -3$.

23. A mail-order company charges $5 per order plus $2 per item in the order, up to a maximum of 4 items. Write a function to describe the situation. Find the reasonable domain and range for the function.

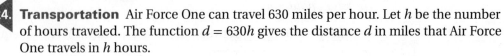

Transportation

Air Force One refers to two specially configured Boeing 747-200B airplanes. The radio call sign when the president is aboard either aircraft or any Air Force aircraft is "Air Force One."

24. Transportation Air Force One can travel 630 miles per hour. Let h be the number of hours traveled. The function $d = 630h$ gives the distance d in miles that Air Force One travels in h hours.

    a. Identify the independent and dependent variables. Write $d = 630h$ using function notation.

    b. What are reasonable values for the domain and range in the situation described?

    c. How far can Air Force One travel in 12 hours?

25. Complete the table for $g(z) = 2z - 5$.

z	1	2	3	4
g(z)				

26. Complete the table for $h(x) = x^2 + x$.

x	0	1	2	3
h(x)				

27. Estimation For $f(x) = 3x + 5$, estimate the output when $x = -6.89$, $x = 1.01$, and $x = 4.67$.

28. Transportation A car can travel 30 miles on a gallon of gas and has a 20-gallon gas tank. Let g be the number of gallons of gas the car has in its tank. The function $d = 30g$ gives the distance d in miles that the car travels on g gallons.

    a. What are reasonable values for the domain and range in the situation described?

    b. How far can the car travel on 12 gallons of gas?

H.O.T. 29. Critical Thinking Give an example of a real-life situation for which the reasonable domain consists of 1, 2, 3, and 4 and the reasonable range consists of 2, 4, 6, and 8.

H.O.T. 30. ///ERROR ANALYSIS/// Rashid saves $150 each month. He wants to know how much he will have saved in 2 years. He writes the rule $s = m + 150$ to help him figure out how much he will save, where s is the amount saved and m is the number of months he saves. Explain why his rule is incorrect.

31. Write About It Give a real-life situation that can be described by a function. Identify the independent variable and the dependent variable.

Real-World Connections

32. The table shows the volume v of water pumped into a pool after t hours.

    a. Determine a relationship between the time and the volume of water and write an equation.

    b. Identify the independent and dependent variables.

    c. If the pool holds 10,000 gallons, how long will it take to fill?

Amount of Water in Pool

Time (h)	Volume (gal)
0	0
1	1250
2	2500
3	3750
4	5000

TEST PREP

33. Marsha buys x pens at \$0.70 per pen and one pencil for \$0.10. Which function gives the total amount Marsha spends?

    (A) $c(x) = 0.70x + 0.10x$ (C) $c(x) = (0.70 + 0.10)x$

    (B) $c(x) = 0.70x + 1$ (D) $c(x) = 0.70x + 0.10$

34. Belle is buying pizzas for her daughter's birthday party, using the prices in the table. Which equation best describes the relationship between the total cost c and the number of pizzas p?

Pizzas	Total Cost ($)
5	26.25
10	52.50
15	78.75

    (F) $c = 26.25p$ (H) $c = p + 26.25$

    (G) $c = 5.25p$ (J) $c = 6p - 3.75$

35. Gridded Response What is the value of $f(x) = 5 - \frac{1}{2}x$ when $x = 3$?

CHALLENGE AND EXTEND

36. The formula to convert a temperature that is in degrees Celsius x to degrees Fahrenheit $f(x)$ is $f(x) = \frac{9}{5}x + 32$. What are reasonable values for the domain and range when you convert to Fahrenheit the temperature of water as it rises from 0° to 100° Celsius?

37. Math History In his studies of the motion of free-falling objects, Galileo Galilei found that regardless of its mass, an object will fall a distance d that is related to the square of its travel time t in seconds. The modern formula that describes free-fall motion is $d = \frac{1}{2}gt^2$, where g is the acceleration due to gravity and t is the length of time in seconds the object falls. Find the distance an object falls in 3 seconds. (*Hint*: Research to find acceleration due to gravity in meters per second squared.)

FOCUS ON MATHEMATICAL PRACTICES

H.O.T. **38. Problem Solving** Alejandro's grandmother gives him \$25 dollars to start his savings account. For every dollar d he adds to this account, his grandmother puts in an additional \$5.

    a. Write an equation that describes t, the total in his savings account, after he has added d dollars.

    b. What is the independent variable for this equation? What is the dependent variable? Explain how you know.

    c. Write the equation from part a in function notation.

H.O.T. **39. Modeling** Jasmine's monthly cell phone bill varies according to the number of minutes she uses. The table shows the relationship.

Minutes	0	100	200	300	400
Monthly Cost	\$15	\$25	\$35	\$45	\$55

Write a function in the form $f(x) = mx + b$ that relates the number of minutes Jasmine uses to her monthly cost. What does the value of m mean in the context of Jasmine's bill? What about the value of b?

H.O.T. **40. Analysis** You can perform basic operations, such as addition, subtraction, multiplication, and division, with functions. For example, when $f(x) = 4x$ and $g(x) = 2x - 1$, $f(x) + g(x) = 4x + (2x - 1) = 6x - 1$. Find $f(x) - g(x)$.

Ready to Go On?

my.hrw.com
Assessment and Intervention

✓ 8-1 Graphing Relationships

Choose the graph that best represents each situation.

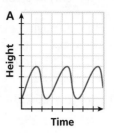
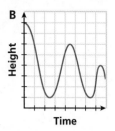

1. A person bungee jumps from a high platform.

2. A person jumps on a trampoline in a steady motion.

3. Xander takes a quiz worth 100 points. Each question is worth 20 points. Sketch a graph to show his score if he misses 1, 2, 3, 4, or 5 questions.

✓ 8-2 Relations and Functions

Give the domain and range of each relation. Tell whether the relation is a function. Explain.

4.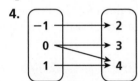

5.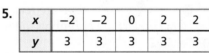

x	−2	−2	0	2	2
y	3	3	3	3	3

6.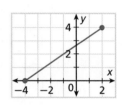

7. A local parking garage charges $5.00 for the first hour plus $1.50 for each additional hour or part of an hour. Write a relation as a set of ordered pairs in which the x-value represents the number of hours and the y-value represents the cost for x hours. Use a domain of 1, 2, 3, 4, 5. Is this relation a function? Explain.

8. A baseball coach is taking the team for ice cream. Four students can ride in each car. Create a mapping diagram to show the number of cars needed to transport 8, 10, 14, and 16 students. Is this relation a function? Explain.

✓ 8-3 Writing Functions

Determine a relationship between the x- and y-values. Write an equation.

9.

x	1	2	3	4
y	−6	−5	−4	−3

10.

x	1	2	3	4
y	−3	−6	−9	−12

11. A printer can print 8 pages per minute. Identify the dependent and independent variables for the situation. Write an equation in function notation.

Evaluate each function for the given input values.

12. For $f(x) = 3x - 1$, find $f(x)$ when $x = 2$.

13. For $g(x) = x^2 - x$, find $g(x)$ when $x = -2$.

14. A photographer charges a sitting fee of $15 plus $3 for each pose. Write a function to describe the situation. Find a reasonable domain and range for up to 5 poses.

PARCC Assessment Readiness

Selected Response

1. Give the domain and range of the relation.

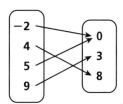

- Ⓐ D: {−2, 4, 5, 9}; R: {0, 3, 8}
- Ⓑ D: {0, 3, 8}; R: {−2, 4, 5, 9}
- Ⓒ D: −2 < x < 9; R: 0 < x < 8
- Ⓓ D: −2 ≤ x ≤ 9; R: 0 ≤ x ≤ 8

2. Which graph represents a function?

Ⓕ
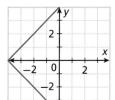

Ⓖ
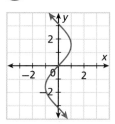

Ⓗ
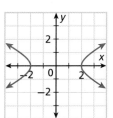

Ⓙ
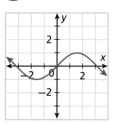

3. Write a possible situation for the graph.

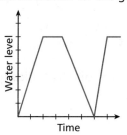

Ⓐ A pool is filled with water, and people are having fun swimming and jumping in and out of the pool.

Ⓑ A pool is filled with water using one valve. Shortly after it is full, the pool needs to be emptied. Then it is refilled immediately, using two valves this time.

Ⓒ A pool is filled with water using one valve. Immediately after it is full, the pool needs to be emptied. It is refilled immediately after it is completely empty, using two valves this time.

Ⓓ A pool is filled with water. Shortly after it is full, the pool needs to be emptied. It is refilled immediately after it is completely empty, using one valve.

4. Determine a relationship between the x- and y-values. Write an equation.

x	1	2	3	4
y	4	5	6	7

- Ⓕ y = −x + 3
- Ⓖ y = x + 4
- Ⓗ y = x + 3
- Ⓙ y = 3x + 1

Mini-Task

5. A function is graphed below.

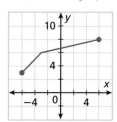

What are the domain and range of the function?

Graphs and Transformations

The Common Core Georgia Performance Standards for Mathematical Practice describe varieties of expertise that all students should seek to develop. Opportunities to develop these practices are integrated throughout this program.

1 Make sense of problems and persevere in solving them.

2 Reason abstractly and quantitatively.

3 Construct viable arguments and critique the reasoning of others.

4 Model with mathematics.

5 Use appropriate tools strategically.

6 Attend to precision.

7 Look for and make use of structure.

8 Look for and express regularity in repeated reasoning.

Unpacking the Standards

Understanding the standards and the vocabulary terms in the standards will help you know exactly what you are expected to learn in this chapter.

 MCC9-12.F.IF.1

Understand that a function from one set (called the domain) to another set (called the range) assigns to each element of the domain exactly one element of the range. …

Key Vocabulary

function (función)
A relation in which every domain value is paired with exactly one range value.

domain (dominio)
The set of all first coordinates (or x-values) of a relation or function.

range of a function or relation (rango de una función o relación)
The set of all second coordinates (or y-values) of a function or relation.

element (elemento)
Each member in a set.

What It Means For You

A function model guarantees you that for any input value, you will get a unique output value.

EXAMPLE   **Relationship is a function**

$$y = x^2$$

One output for every input: When -2 is input, the output is always 4.

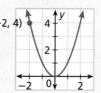

NON-EXAMPLE   **Relationship is NOT a function**

$$y^2 = x$$

Two outputs for every input but 0: When 4 is input, the output can be -2 or 2.

9-1 Graphing Functions

Essential Question: How can you graph functions over a given domain?

Objectives
Graph functions given a limited domain.

Graph functions given a domain of all real numbers.

Who uses this?
Scientists can use a function to make conclusions about rising sea level.

Sea level is rising at an approximate rate of 2.5 millimeters per year. If this rate continues, the function $y = 2.5x$ can describe how many millimeters y sea level will rise in the next x years.

One way to understand functions such as the one above is to graph them. You can graph a function by finding ordered pairs that satisfy the function.

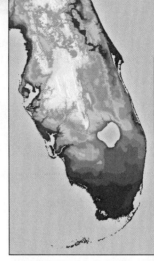
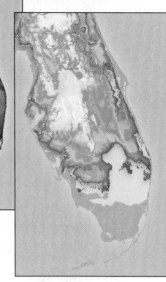

Current Florida coastline.

Possible Florida coastline in 2400 years.

EXAMPLE 1
MCC9-12.F.IF.5

 my.hrw.com

Online Video Tutor

Graphing Solutions Given a Domain

Graph each function for the given domain.

A $-x + 2y = 6$; D: $\{-4, -2, 0, 2\}$

Step 1 Solve for y since you are given values of the domain, or x.

$$-x + 2y = 6$$

$$\underline{+x \qquad\qquad +x}$$ *Add x to both sides.*

$$2y = x + 6$$

$$\frac{2y}{2} = \frac{x + 6}{2}$$ *Since y is multiplied by 2, divide both sides by 2.*

$$y = \frac{x}{2} + \frac{6}{2}$$ *Rewrite $\frac{x+6}{2}$ as two separate fractions.*

$$y = \frac{1}{2}x + 3$$ *Simplify.*

Sometimes solving for y first makes it easier to substitute values of x and find an ordered pair.

Step 2 Substitute the given values of the domain for x and find values of y.

x	$y = \frac{1}{2}x + 3$	(x, y)
-4	$y = \frac{1}{2}(-4) + 3 = 1$	$(-4, 1)$
-2	$y = \frac{1}{2}(-2) + 3 = 2$	$(-2, 2)$
0	$y = \frac{1}{2}(0) + 3 = 3$	$(0, 3)$
2	$y = \frac{1}{2}(2) + 3 = 4$	$(2, 4)$

Step 3 Graph the ordered pairs.

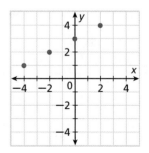

Graph each function for the given domain.

B $f(x) = |x|$; D: $\{-2, -1, 0, 1, 2\}$

Step 1 Use the given values of the domain to find values of $f(x)$.

x	$f(x) = |x|$	$(x, f(x))$
-2	$f(x) = |-2| = 2$	$(-2, 2)$
-1	$f(x) = |-1| = 1$	$(-1, 1)$
0	$f(x) = |0| = 0$	$(0, 0)$
1	$f(x) = |1| = 1$	$(1, 1)$
2	$f(x) = |2| = 2$	$(2, 2)$

Step 2 Graph the ordered pairs.

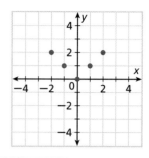

 Graph each function for the given domain.

1a. $-2x + y = 3$; D: $\{-5, -3, 1, 4\}$

1b. $f(x) = x^2 + 2$; D: $\{-3, -1, 0, 1, 3\}$

If the domain of a function is all real numbers, any number can be used as an input value. This process will produce an infinite number of ordered pairs that satisfy the function. Therefore, arrowheads are drawn at both "ends" of a smooth line or curve to represent the infinite number of ordered pairs. If a domain is not given, assume that the domain is all real numbers.

Graphing Functions Using a Domain of All Real Numbers	
Step 1	Use the function to generate ordered pairs by choosing several values for x.
Step 2	Plot enough points to see a pattern for the graph.
Step 3	Connect the points with a line or smooth curve.

COMMON CORE GPS
EXAMPLE **2** **Graphing Functions**
MCC9-12.F.IF.7a

Graph each function.

A $2x + 1 = y$

Step 1 Choose several values of x and generate ordered pairs.

x	$2x + 1 = y$	(x, y)
-3	$2(-3) + 1 = -5$	$(-3, -5)$
-2	$2(-2) + 1 = -3$	$(-2, -3)$
-1	$2(-1) + 1 = -1$	$(-1, -1)$
0	$2(0) + 1 = 1$	$(0, 1)$
1	$2(1) + 1 = 3$	$(1, 3)$
2	$2(2) + 1 = 5$	$(2, 5)$
3	$2(3) + 1 = 7$	$(3, 7)$

Step 2 Plot enough points to see a pattern.

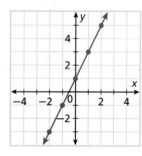

Step 3 The ordered pairs appear to form a line. **Draw a line** through all the points to show all the ordered pairs that satisfy the function. Draw arrowheads on both "ends" of the line.

my.hrw.com

Online Video Tutor

Helpful Hint

When choosing values of x, be sure to choose both positive and negative values. You may not need to graph all the points to see the pattern.

9-1 Graphing Functions **215**

Graph each function.

B $y = x^2$

Step 1 Choose several values of x and generate ordered pairs.

Step 2 Plot enough points to see a pattern.

x	$y = x^2$	(x, y)
-3	$y = (-3)^2 = 9$	$(-3, 9)$
-2	$y = (-2)^2 = 4$	$(-2, 4)$
-1	$y = (-1)^2 = 1$	$(-1, 1)$
0	$y = (0)^2 = 0$	$(0, 0)$
1	$y = (1)^2 = 1$	$(1, 1)$
2	$y = (2)^2 = 4$	$(2, 4)$

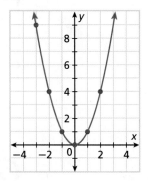

Step 3 The ordered pairs appear to form an almost U-shaped graph. **Draw a smooth curve** through the points to show all the ordered pairs that satisfy the function. Draw arrowheads on the "ends" of the curve.

Check If the graph is correct, any point on it will satisfy the function. Choose an ordered pair on the graph that was not in your table, such as $(3, 9)$. Check whether it satisfies $y = x^2$.

$$\frac{y = x^2}{9 \mid 3^2}$$
$$9 \mid 9 \checkmark$$

Substitute the values for x and y into the function. Simplify.

The ordered pair (3, 9) satisfies the function.

 Graph each function.

2a. $f(x) = 3x - 2$ **2b.** $y = |x - 1|$

EXAMPLE **3**
MCC9-12.F.IF.2

 my.hrw.com

Online Video Tutor

Finding Values Using Graphs

Use a graph of the function $f(x) = \frac{1}{3}x + 2$ to find the value of $f(x)$ when $x = 6$. Check your answer.

Locate 6 on the x-axis. Move up to the graph of the function. Then move left to the y-axis to find the corresponding value of y.

$f(x) = 4$

Check Use substitution.

$$\frac{f(x) = \frac{1}{3}x + 2}{}$$
$$4 \mid \frac{1}{3}(6) + 2$$
$$4 \mid 2 + 2$$
$$4 \mid 4 \checkmark$$

Substitute the values for x and y into the function.

Simplify.

The ordered pair (4, 6) satisfies the function.

Writing Math

"The value of y is 4 when $x = 6$" can also be written as $f(6) = 4$.

 3. Use the graph above to find the value of x when $f(x) = 3$. Check your answer.

Recall that in real-world situations you may have to limit the domain to make answers reasonable. For example, quantities such as time, distance, and number of people can be represented using only nonnegative values. When both the domain and the range are limited to nonnegative values, the function is graphed only in Quadrant I.

Online Video Tutor

EXAMPLE 4
MCC9-12.F.IF.7a

Make sense of problems and persevere in solving them.

Problem-Solving Application

The function $y = 2.5x$ describes how many millimeters sea level y rises in x years. Graph the function. Use the graph to estimate how many millimeters sea level will rise in 3.5 years.

 Understand the Problem

The **answer** is a graph that can be used to find the value of y when x is 3.5.

List the important information:
• The function $y = 2.5x$ describes how many millimeters sea level rises.

2 Make a Plan

Think: What values should I use to graph this function? Both, the number of years sea level has risen and the distance sea level rises, cannot be negative. Use only nonnegative values for both the domain and the range. The function will be graphed in Quadrant I.

3 Solve

Choose several nonnegative values of x to find values of y. Then graph the ordered pairs.

x	$y = 2.5x$	(x, y)
0	$y = 2.5(0) = 0$	$(0, 0)$
1	$y = 2.5(1) = 2.5$	$(1, 2.5)$
2	$y = 2.5(2) = 5$	$(2, 5)$
3	$y = 2.5(3) = 7.5$	$(3, 7.5)$
4	$y = 2.5(4) = 10$	$(4, 10)$

Draw a line through the points to show all the ordered pairs that satisfy this function.

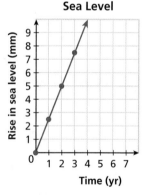

Sea Level

Use the graph to estimate the y-value when x is 3.5.
Sea level will rise about 8.75 millimeters in 3.5 years.

 Look Back

As the number of years increases, sea level also increases, so the graph is reasonable. When x is between 3 and 4, y is between 7.5 and 10. Since 3.5 is between 3 and 4, it is reasonable to estimate y to be 8.75 when x is 3.5.

4. The fastest recorded Hawaiian lava flow moved at an average speed of 6 miles per hour. The function $y = 6x$ describes the distance y the lava moved on average in x hours. Graph the function. Use the graph to estimate how many miles the lava moved after 5.5 hours.

THINK AND DISCUSS

1. How do you find the range of a function if the domain is all real numbers?

2. Explain how to use a graph to find the value of a function for a given value of x.

3. **GET ORGANIZED** Copy and complete the graphic organizer. Explain how to graph a function for each situation.

Graphing a Function
- Not a real-world situation
- Real-world situation

9-1 Exercises

my.hrw.com
Homework Help

GUIDED PRACTICE

SEE EXAMPLE 1

Graph each function for the given domain.

1. $3x - y = 1$; D: $\{-3, -1, 0, 4\}$

2. $f(x) = -|x|$; D: $\{-5, -3, 0, 3, 5\}$

3. $f(x) = x + 4$; D: $\{-5, -3, 0, 4\}$

4. $y = x^2 - 1$; D: $\{-3, -1, 0, 1, 3\}$

SEE EXAMPLE 2

Graph each function.

5. $f(x) = 6x + 4$

6. $y = \frac{1}{2}x + 4$

7. $x + y = 0$

8. $y = |x| - 4$

9. $f(x) = 2x^2 - 7$

10. $y = -x^2 + 5$

SEE EXAMPLE 3

11. Use a graph of the function $f(x) = \frac{1}{2}x - 2$ to find the value of y when $x = 2$. Check your answer.

SEE EXAMPLE 4

12. **Oceanography** The floor of the Atlantic Ocean is spreading at an average rate of 1 inch per year. The function $y = x$ describes the number of inches y the ocean floor spreads in x years. Graph the function. Use the graph to estimate the number of inches the ocean floor will spread in $10\frac{1}{2}$ years.

PRACTICE AND PROBLEM SOLVING

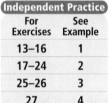

For Exercises	See Example
13–16	1
17–24	2
25–26	3
27	4

my.hrw.com

Online Extra Practice

Graph each function for the given domain.

13. $2x + y = 4$; D: $\{-3, -1, 4, 7\}$

14. $y = |x| - 1$; D: $\{-4, -2, 0, 2, 4\}$

15. $f(x) = -7x$; D: $\{-2, -1, 0, 1\}$

16. $y = (x + 1)^2$; D: $\{-2, -1, 0, 1, 2\}$

Graph each function.

17. $y = -3x + 5$

18. $f(x) = 3x$

19. $x + y = 8$

20. $f(x) = 2x + 2$

21. $y = -|x| + 10$

22. $f(x) = -5 + x^2$

23. $y = |x + 1| + 1$

24. $y = (x - 2)^2 - 1$

25. Use a graph of the function $f(x) = -2x - 3$ to find the value of y when $x = -4$. Check your answer.

26. Use a graph of the function $f(x) = \frac{1}{3}x + 1$ to find the value of y when $x = 6$. Check your answer.

27. **Transportation** An electric motor scooter can travel at 0.25 miles per minute. The function $y = 0.25x$ describes the number of miles y the scooter can travel in x minutes. Graph the function. Use the graph to estimate the number of miles an electric motor scooter travels in 15 minutes.

Graph each function.

28. $f(x) = x - 1$ 29. $12 - x - 2y = 0$ 30. $3x - y = 13$

31. $y = x^2 - 2$ 32. $x^2 - y = -4$ 33. $2x^2 = f(x)$

34. $f(x) = |2x| - 2$ 35. $y = |-x|$ 36. $-|2x + 1| = y$

37. Find the value of x so that $(x, 12)$ satisfies $y = 4x + 8$.

38. Find the value of x so that $(x, 6)$ satisfies $y = -x - 4$.

39. Find the value of y so that $(-2, y)$ satisfies $y = -2x^2$.

For each function, determine whether the given points are on the graph.

40. $y = 7x - 2$; $(1, 5)$ and $(2, 10)$ 41. $y = |x| + 2$; $(3, 5)$ and $(-1, 3)$

42. $y = x^2$; $(1, 1)$ and $(-3, -9)$ 43. $y = \frac{1}{4}x - 2$; $\left(1, -\frac{3}{4}\right)$ and $(4, -1)$

H.O.T. 44. **///ERROR ANALYSIS///** Student A says that $(3, 2)$ is on the graph of $y = 4x - 5$, but student B says that it is not. Who is incorrect? Explain the error.

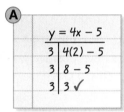 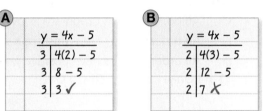

A	
y = 4x − 5	
3	4(2) − 5
3	8 − 5
3	3 ✓

B	
y = 4x − 5	
2	4(3) − 5
2	12 − 5
2	7 ✗

Determine whether $(0, -7)$, $\left(-6, -\frac{5}{3}\right)$, **and** $(-2, -3)$ **lie on the graph of each function.**

45. $x + 3y = -11$ 46. $y + |x| = -1$ 47. $x^2 - y = 7$

For each function, find three ordered pairs that lie on the graph of the function.

48. $-6 = 3x + 2y$ 49. $y = 1.1x + 2$

50. $y = \frac{4}{5}x$ 51. $y = 3x - 1$

52. $y = |x| + 6$ 53. $y = x^2 - 5$

54. **Critical Thinking** Graph the functions $y = |x|$ and $y = -|x|$. Describe how they are alike. How are they different?

 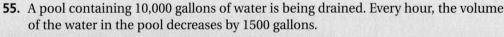 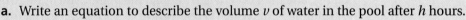

Real-World Connections

55. A pool containing 10,000 gallons of water is being drained. Every hour, the volume of the water in the pool decreases by 1500 gallons.

a. Write an equation to describe the volume v of water in the pool after h hours.

b. How much water is in the pool after 1 hour?

c. Create a table of values showing the volume of the water in gallons in the pool as a function of the time in hours and graph the function.

56. Estimation Use the graph to estimate the value of y when $x = 2.117$.

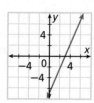

H.O.T. 57. Write About It Why is a graph a convenient way to show the ordered pairs that satisfy a function?

TEST PREP

58. Which function is graphed?

    Ⓐ $2y - 3x = 2$ Ⓒ $y = 2x - 1$

    Ⓑ $5x + y = 1$ Ⓓ $y = 5x + 8$

59. Which ordered pair is NOT on the graph of $y = 4 - |x|$?

    Ⓕ $(0, 4)$ Ⓗ $(-1, 3)$

    Ⓖ $(4, 0)$ Ⓙ $(3, -1)$

60. Which function has $(3, 2)$ on its graph?

    Ⓐ $2x - 3y = 12$ Ⓒ $y = -\dfrac{2}{3}x + 4$

    Ⓑ $-2x - 3y = 12$ Ⓓ $y = -\dfrac{3}{2}x + 4$

61. Which statement(s) is true about the function $y = x^2 + 1$?

    I.   All points on the graph are above the origin.

    II.   All ordered pairs have positive x-values.

    III. All ordered pairs have positive y-values.

    Ⓕ I Only   Ⓖ II Only   Ⓗ I and II   Ⓙ I and III

CHALLENGE AND EXTEND

62. Graph the function $y = x^3$. Make sure you have enough ordered pairs to see the shape of the graph.

63. The temperature of a liquid that started at 64 °F is increasing by 4 °F per hour. Write a function that describes the temperature of the liquid over time. Graph the function to show the temperatures over the first 10 hours.

FOCUS ON MATHEMATICAL PRACTICES

H.O.T. 64. Modeling Does the ordered pair $\left(\dfrac{1}{2}, 1\right)$ name a point on the graph of $f(x) = 2x$?

Can you find an ordered pair on the graph where *both* coordinates are non-integers? If the function is graphed on a coordinate plane where every integer has a grid line, where can you find points with two non-integer coordinates?

H.O.T. 65. Analysis When you graph a function by making a table of values and plotting the points, and then draw a line through the points, you draw arrowheads on both ends of the graphed line. What do these arrowheads tell you about the line? Is it possible to draw a coordinate plane large enough that the arrowheads are no longer necessary? Explain.

9-1
Technology TASK

Connect Function Rules, Tables, and Graphs

You can use a graphing calculator to understand the connections among function rules, tables, and graphs.

Use with Graphing Functions

MATHEMATICAL PRACTICES

Use appropriate tools strategically.

MCC9-12.F.IF.1 Understand that a function . . . assigns to each element of the domain exactly one element of the range. . . . The graph of *f* is the graph of the equation $y = f(x)$.

Activity

Make a table of values for the function $f(x) = 4x + 3$.
Then graph the function.

1 Press **Y=** and enter the function rule **4x + 3**.

2 Press **2nd** **WINDOW** (TBLSET). Make sure **Indpnt: Auto** and **Depend: Auto** are selected.

3 To view the table, press **2nd** **GRAPH** (TABLE). The *x*-values and the corresponding *y*-values appear in table form. Use the up and down arrow keys to scroll through the table.

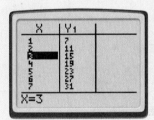

4 To view the table with the graph, press **MODE** and select **G-T** view. Press **ENTER**. Be sure to use the standard window.

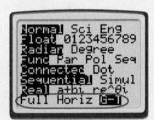

5 Press **TRACE** to see both the graph and a table of values.

6 Press the left arrow key several times to move the cursor. Notice that the point on the graph and the values in the table correspond.

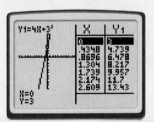

Try This

Make a table of values for each function. Then graph the function.

1. $f(x) = 2x - 1$

2. $f(x) = 1.5x$

3. $f(x) = \frac{1}{2}x + 2$

4. Explain the relationship between a function, its table of values, and the graph of the function.

Exploring Transformations

? **Essential Question:** How can you identify the effect of a given transformation on a graph?

Objectives
Apply transformations to points and sets of points.

Interpret transformations of real-world data.

Vocabulary
transformation
translation
reflection
stretch
compression

Why learn this?
Changes in recording studio fees can be modeled by transformations. (See Example 4.)

A **transformation** is a change in the position, size, or shape of a figure. A **translation**, or slide, is a transformation that moves each point in a figure the same distance in the same direction.

 EXAMPLE **1** **Translating Points**
Prep. for MCC9-12.F.BF.3

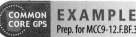

Online Video Tutor

Perform the given translation on the point $(2, -1)$. Give the coordinates of the translated point.

A **4 units left**

Translating $(2, -1)$ 4 units left results in the point $(-2, -1)$.

B **2 units right and 3 units up**

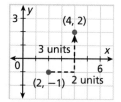

Translating $(2, -1)$ 2 units right and 3 units up results in the point $(4, 2)$.

CHECK IT OUT! Perform the given translation on the point $(-1, 3)$. Give the coordinates of the translated point.

1a. 4 units right

1b. 1 unit left and 2 units down

Notice that when you translate **left or right**, the x-coordinate changes, and when you translate **up or down**, the y-coordinate changes.

Translations	
Horizontal Translation	**Vertical Translation**
Each point shifts *right* or *left* by a number of units.	Each point shifts *up* or *down* by a number of units.
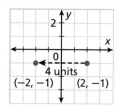 The x-coordinate changes. $(1, 2) \to (1 + 3, 2)$ $(x, y) \to (x + h, y)$	The y-coordinate changes. $(1, 2) \to (1, 2 + 2)$ $(x, y) \to (x, y + k)$
left if $h < 0$ right if $h > 0$	down if $k < 0$ up if $k > 0$

A **reflection** is a transformation that flips a figure across a line called the line of reflection. Each reflected point is the same distance from the line of reflection, but on the opposite side of the line.

Reflections	
Reflection Across y-axis	**Reflection Across x-axis**
Each point flips across the y-axis.	Each point flips across the x-axis.

Reflection Across y-axis: The x-coordinate changes.
$$(1, 2) \rightarrow (-1, 2)$$
$$(x, y) \rightarrow (-x, y)$$

Reflection Across x-axis: The y-coordinate changes.
$$(1, 2) \rightarrow (1, -2)$$
$$(x, y) \rightarrow (x, -y)$$

You can transform a function by transforming its ordered pairs. When a function is translated or reflected, the original graph and the graph of the transformation are *congruent* because the size and shape of the graphs are the same.

COMMON CORE GPS MCC9-12.F.BF.3

EXAMPLE 2

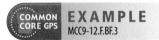

Online Video Tutor

Translating and Reflecting Functions

Use a table to perform each transformation of $y = f(x)$. Use the same coordinate plane as the original function.

A translation 2 units down

Identify important points from the graph and make a table.

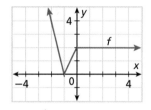

x	y	y − 2
−2	4	4 − 2 = 2
−1	0	0 − 2 = −2
0	2	2 − 2 = 0
2	2	2 − 2 = 0

The entire graph shifts 2 units down. Subtract 2 from each y-coordinate.

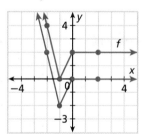

Helpful Hint

Transform x by adding a table column on the left side; transform y by adding a column on the right side.

B reflection across y-axis

Identify important points from the graph and make a table.

−x	x	y
−1(−2) = 2	−2	4
−1(−1) = 1	−1	0
−1(0) = 0	0	2
−1(2) = −2	2	2

Multiply each x-coordinate by −1. The entire graph flips across the y-axis.

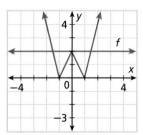

CHECK IT OUT! For the function from Example 2, use a table to perform each transformation of $y = f(x)$. Use the same coordinate plane as the original function.

2a. translation 3 units right   **2b.** reflection across x-axis

Imagine grasping two points on the graph of a function that lie on opposite sides of the *y*-axis. If you pull the points away from the *y*-axis, you would create a horizontal **stretch** of the graph. If you push the points towards the *y*-axis, you would create a horizontal **compression** .

Stretches and compressions are not congruent to the original graph.

Stretches and Compressions		
	Horizontal	**Vertical**
Stretch	Each point is *pulled away* from the *y*-axis. The *x*-coordinate changes. $(4, 0) \rightarrow (2(4), 0)$ $(x, y) \rightarrow (bx, y)$ $\lvert b \rvert > 1$	Each point is *pulled away* from the *x*-axis. The *y*-coordinate changes. $(0, 4) \rightarrow (0, 2(4))$ $(x, y) \rightarrow (x, ay)$ $\lvert a \rvert > 1$
Compression	Each point is *pushed toward* the *y*-axis. The *x*-coordinate changes. $(4, 0) \rightarrow \left(\frac{1}{2}(4), 0\right)$ $(x, y) \rightarrow (bx, y)$ $0 < \lvert b \rvert < 1$	Each point is *pushed toward* the *x*-axis. The *y*-coordinate changes. $(0, 4) \rightarrow \left(0, \frac{1}{2}(4)\right)$ $(x, y) \rightarrow (x, ay)$ $0 < \lvert a \rvert < 1$

COMMON CORE GPS **EXAMPLE** MCC9-12.F.BF.3 **3**

Stretching and Compressing Functions

my.hrw.com

Online Video Tutor

Use a table to perform a horizontal compression of $y = f(x)$ by a factor of $\frac{1}{2}$. Use the same coordinate plane as the original function.

Identify important points from the graph and make a table.

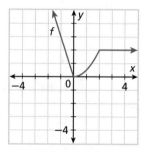

$\frac{1}{2}x$	*x*	*y*
$\frac{1}{2}(-1) = -\frac{1}{2}$	−1	3
$\frac{1}{2}(0) = 0$	0	0
$\frac{1}{2}(2) = 1$	2	2
$\frac{1}{2}(4) = 2$	4	2

Multiply each x-coordinate by $\frac{1}{2}$.

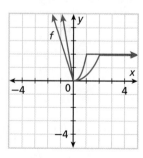

 3. For the function from Example 3, use a table to perform a vertical stretch of $y = f(x)$ by a factor of 2. Graph the transformed function on the same coordinate plane as the original function.

MCC9-12.F.BF.3

my.hrw.com

Online Video Tutor

Business Application

Recording studio fees are usually based on an hourly rate, but the rate can be modified due to various options. The graph shows a basic hourly studio rate. Sketch a graph to represent each situation below and identify the transformation of the original graph that it represents.

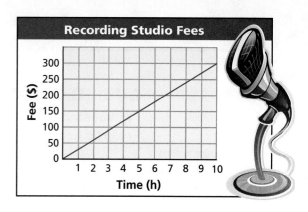

A The engineer's time is needed, so the hourly rate is 1.5 times the original rate.

If the fees are 1.5 times the basic hourly rate, the value of each *y*-coordinate would be multiplied by 1.5. This represents a vertical stretch by a factor of 1.5.

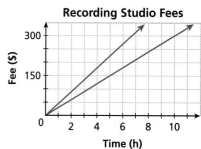

B A $20 setup fee is added to the basic hourly rate.

If the prices are $20 more than the original estimate, the value of each *y*-coordinate would increase by 20. This represents a vertical translation up 20 units.

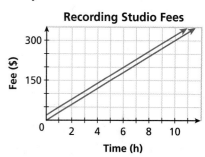

4. What if...? Suppose that a discounted rate is $\frac{3}{4}$ of the original rate. Sketch a graph to represent the situation and identify the transformation of the original graph that it represents.

MCC.MP.1, MCC.MP.7   MATHEMATICAL PRACTICES

THINK AND DISCUSS

1. Describe two ways to transform $(4, 2)$ to $(2, 2)$.

2. Compare a vertical stretch with a horizontal compression.

3. GET ORGANIZED Copy and complete the graphic organizer. In each box, describe the transformations indicated by the given rule.

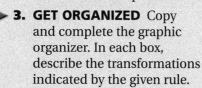

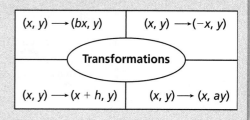

| $(x, y) \longrightarrow (bx, y)$ | $(x, y) \longrightarrow (-x, y)$ |

Transformations

| $(x, y) \longrightarrow (x + h, y)$ | $(x, y) \longrightarrow (x, ay)$ |

9-2 Exploring Transformations **225**

GUIDED PRACTICE

1. **Vocabulary** A transformation that pushes a graph toward the *x*-axis is a ___?___ .
   (*reflection* or *compression*)

SEE EXAMPLE **1** Perform the given translation on the point $(4, 2)$ and give the coordinates of the translated point.

    2. 5 units left   **3.** 3 units down   **4.** 1 unit right, 6 units up

SEE EXAMPLE **2** Use a table to perform each transformation of $y = f(x)$. Use the same coordinate plane as the original function.

    5. translation 2 units up

    6. reflection across the *y*-axis

    7. reflection across the *x*-axis

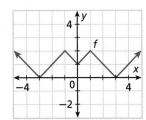

SEE EXAMPLE **3** Use a table to perform each transformation of $y = f(x)$. Use the same coordinate plane as the original function.

    8. horizontal stretch by a factor of 3

    9. vertical stretch by a factor of 3

    10. vertical compression by a factor of $\frac{1}{3}$

SEE EXAMPLE **4** **Recreation** The graph shows the price for admission by age at a local zoo. Sketch a graph to represent each situation and identify the transformation of the original graph that it represents.

    11. Admission is half price on Wednesdays.

    12. To raise funds for endangered species, the zoo charges $1.50 extra per ticket.

    13. The maximum age for each ticket price is increased by 5 years.

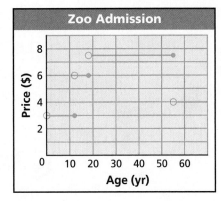

Zoo Admission

PRACTICE AND PROBLEM SOLVING

Independent Practice	
For Exercises	See Example
14–16	1
17–20	2
21–24	3
25–27	4

Perform the given translation on $(3, 1)$. Give the coordinates of the translated point.

    14. 2 units right   **15.** 4 units up   **16.** 5 units left, 4 units down

Use a table to perform each transformation of $y = f(x)$. Use the same coordinate plane as the original function.

    17. translation 2 units down   **18.** reflection across the *x*-axis

    19. translation 3 units right   **20.** reflection across the *y*-axis

    21. vertical compression by a factor of $\frac{2}{3}$ **22.** horizontal compression by a factor of $\frac{1}{2}$

    23. horizontal stretch by a factor of $\frac{3}{2}$ **24.** vertical stretch by a factor of 2

Technology The graph shows the cost of Web page hosting depending on the Web space used. Sketch a graph to represent each situation and identify the transformation of the original graph that it represents.

Web Page Hosting

25. The prices are reduced by $5.

26. The prices are discounted by 25%.

27. A special is offered for double the amount of Web space for the same price.

Estimation The table gives the coordinates for the vertices of a triangle. Estimate the area of each transformed triangle by graphing it and counting the number of squares it covers on the coordinate plane. How does the area of each transformed triangle compare with the area of the original triangle?

x	y
−2	2
2	−4
4	−2

28. reflection across the y-axis

29. 5 units left, 3 units up

30. horizontal stretch by a factor of 2

31. horizontal compression by a factor of $\frac{2}{3}$

32. vertical compression by a factor of $\frac{2}{3}$

33. reflection across the x-axis

34. 1 unit left, 6 units down

35. vertical stretch by a factor of 3

Entertainment

The amusement park industry in the United States includes about 700 parks and accounted for over $8.5 billion in revenues in 2001.
Source: Statistical Abstract of the United States

36. **Entertainment** The revenue from an amusement park ride is given by the admission price of $3 times the number of riders. As part of a promotion, the first 10 riders ride for free.

  a. What kind of transformation describes the change in the revenue based on the promotion?

  b. Write a function rule for this transformation.

37. **Business** An automotive mechanic charges $50 to diagnose the problem in a vehicle and $65 per hour for labor to fix it.

  a. If the mechanic increases his diagnostic fee to $60, what kind of transformation is this to the graph of the total repair bill?

  b. If the mechanic increases his labor rate to $75 per hour, what kind of transformation is this to the graph of the total repair bill?

  c. If it took 3 hours to repair your car, which of the two rate increases would have a greater effect on your total bill?

38. The student council wants to buy vases for the flowers for the school prom. A florist charges a $20 delivery fee plus $1.25 per vase. A home-decorating store charges a $10 delivery fee plus $1.25 per vase.

  a. The function $f(x) = 20 + 1.25x$ models the cost of ordering x vases from the florist, and the function $g(x) = 10 + 1.25x$ models the cost of ordering x vases from the home-decorating store. What do the graphs of these functions look like?

  b. How are the graphs related to each other?

  c. How could you modify these functions so that their graphs are identical?

  d. If the florist decided to waive the $20 delivery fee as long as the number of vases ordered was more than 150, how would the graph of f change? How would it compare with the graph of the other function?

Transportation Use the graph and the following information for Exercises 39–43.

Roberta left her house at 10:00 A.M. and drove to the library. She was at the library studying until 11:30 A.M. Then she drove to the grocery store. At 12:15 P.M. Roberta left the grocery store and drove home. The graph shows Roberta's position with respect to time.

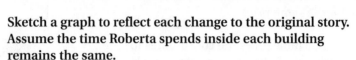

Sketch a graph to reflect each change to the original story. Assume the time Roberta spends inside each building remains the same.

39. Roberta drove at half the speed from her house to the library.

40. The grocery store she went to is twice as far from the library.

41. The grocery store is 2.5 miles closer to the house than the library is.

Change the original story about Roberta to match each graph.

42.

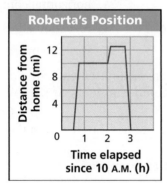

43.

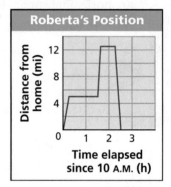

H.O.T. **44. Critical Thinking** Suppose two transformations are performed on a single point: a translation and a reflection. Does the order in which the transformations are performed make a difference? Does the type of translation or reflection matter? Explain your reasoning.

H.O.T. **45. Write About It** Describe how transformations might make graphing easier.

TEST PREP

46. The function $c(p) = 0.99p$ represents the cost in dollars of p pounds of peaches. If the cost per pound increases by 10%, how will the graph of the function change?

Ⓐ Translation 0.1 unit up
Ⓒ Horizontal stretch by a factor of 1.1
Ⓑ Translation 0.1 unit right
Ⓓ Vertical stretch by a factor of 1.1

47. Which transformation would change the point $(5, 3)$ into $(-5, 3)$?

Ⓕ Reflection across the x-axis
Ⓗ Reflection across the y-axis
Ⓖ Translation 5 units down
Ⓙ Translation 5 units left

48. The graph of the function f is a line that intersects the y-axis at the point $(0, 3)$ and the x-axis at the point $(3, 0)$. Which transformation of f does NOT intersect the y-axis at the point $(0, 6)$?

Ⓐ Translation 3 units up
Ⓒ Vertical stretch by a factor of 2
Ⓑ Translation 3 units right
Ⓓ Horizontal compression by a factor of $\frac{1}{2}$

49. Which transformation is displayed in the graph?

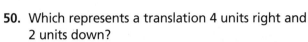

  ⒡ Reflection across the *x*-axis

  ⒢ Translation 5 units down

  ⒣ Reflection across the *y*-axis

  ⒥ Translation 5 units left

50. Which represents a translation 4 units right and 2 units down?

  ⒜ From $(4, 2)$ to $(0, 0)$ ⒞ From $(-4, -2)$ to $(0, 0)$

  ⒝ From $(4, -2)$ to $(0, 0)$ ⒟ From $(-4, 2)$ to $(0, 0)$

51. Short Response Graph the points $(-1, 3)$ and $(-1, -3)$. Describe two different transformations that would transform $(-1, 3)$ to $(-1, -3)$.

CHALLENGE AND EXTEND

52. Suppose the rule $(x, y) \rightarrow (2x, y - 3)$ is used to translate a point. If the coordinates of the translated point are $(22, 7)$, what was the original point?

53. History From 1999 to 2001 the cost for mailing *n* first class letters through the United States Postal Service was $c(n) = 0.33n$. In 2001 the rate was increased by $0.01 per letter. In 2002 the rate was increased an additional $0.03 per letter.

  a. Write an equation that represents the cost of mailing *n* first class letters in 2002.

  b. What transformation describes the total change in price?

  c. Graph both functions and estimate the maximum number of first class letters you could mail for $5.00 in both 1999 and 2002.

  d. Explain the effect of the reasonable domain and range for these functions on your answer for part **c**.

54. Name a point that when reflected across the *x*-axis has the same coordinates as if it were reflected across the *y*-axis. How many points are there that satisfy this condition?

FOCUS ON MATHEMATICAL PRACTICES

H.O.T. **55. Communication** Germaine says, "I'm a little confused by the difference between translations and transformations. Is a translation a transformation or is a transformation a translation?" Answer her question and explain.

H.O.T. **56. Properties** Rudy reflects a rectangle across the *y*-axis and then translates it 3 units right and 4 units down. Is the new rectangle congruent to the old? Justify your answer.

H.O.T. **57. Analysis** The function $y = x$ is transformed into a new function $y = 3x$. How does this transformation affect the graph of the function?

H.O.T. **58. Make a Conjecture** A point undergoes a reflection across the *x*-axis, but stays in the same location.

  a. Find two different sets of coordinates that the point might have.

  b. Make a conjecture about which points stay in the same place when reflected across the *x*-axis.

  c. Use the coordinate definition of a reflection across the *x*-axis to justify your conjecture in part b.

9-3 Arithmetic Sequences

? Essential Question: How can you recognize and extend an arithmetic sequence and find a given term of the sequence?

Objectives
Recognize and extend an arithmetic sequence.

Find a given term of an arithmetic sequence.

Vocabulary
sequence
term
arithmetic sequence
common difference

Why learn this?
The distance between you and a lightning strike can be approximated by using an arithmetic sequence.

During a thunderstorm, you can estimate your distance from a lightning strike by counting the number of seconds from the time you see the lightning until the time you hear the thunder.

Time (s)	Distance (mi)
1	0.2
2	0.4
3	0.6
4	0.8
5	1.0
6	1.2
7	1.4
8	1.6

+ 0.2
+ 0.2
+ 0.2
+ 0.2
+ 0.2
+ 0.2
+ 0.2

When you list the times and distances in order, each list forms a *sequence*. A **sequence** is a list of numbers that may form a pattern. Each number in a sequence is a **term**.

In the distance sequence, each distance is 0.2 mi greater than the previous distance. When the terms of a sequence differ by the same nonzero number d, the sequence is an **arithmetic sequence** and d is the **common difference**. The distances in the table form an arithmetic sequence with $d = 0.2$.

The variable a is often used to represent terms in a sequence. The variable a_9, read "a sub 9," is the ninth term in a sequence. To designate any term, or the nth term, in a sequence, you write a_n, where n can be any number.

To find a term in an arithmetic sequence, add d to the previous term.

Finding a Term of an Arithmetic Sequence

The nth term of an arithmetic sequence with **common difference** d is

$$a_n = a_{n-1} + d.$$

EXAMPLE 1
MCC9-12.F.BF.2

Online Video Tutor

Identifying Arithmetic Sequences

Determine whether each sequence appears to be an arithmetic sequence. If so, find the common difference and the next three terms in the sequence.

A 12, 8, 4, 0, ...

Step 1 Find the difference between successive terms.

12, 8, 4, 0, ...
 − 4 − 4 − 4

Add −4 to each term to find the next term. The common difference is −4.

Step 2 Use the common difference to find the next 3 terms.

12, 8, 4, 0, −4, −8, −12
 − 4 − 4 − 4

$a_n = a_{n-1} + d$

The sequence appears to be an arithmetic sequence with a common difference of −4. The next 3 terms are −4, −8, −12.

B 1, 4, 9, 16, …

Find the difference between successive terms.

1, 4, 9, 16, …
+ 3 + 5 + 7

The difference between successive terms is not the same.

This sequence is not an arithmetic sequence.

CHECK IT OUT! Determine whether each sequence appears to be an arithmetic sequence. If so, find the common difference and the next three terms.

1a. $-\dfrac{3}{4}, -\dfrac{1}{4}, \dfrac{1}{4}, \dfrac{3}{4}, \dots$

1b. $-4, -2, 1, 5, \dots$

To find the *n*th term of an arithmetic sequence when *n* is a large number, you need an equation or rule. Look for a pattern to find a rule for the sequence below.

$$
\begin{array}{ccccc}
1 & 2 & 3 & 4\dots & n \leftarrow \text{Position}\\
\downarrow & \downarrow & \downarrow & \downarrow & \\
3, & 5, & 7, & 9\dots & \leftarrow \text{Term}\\
a_1 & a_2 & a_3 & a_4 & a_n
\end{array}
$$

The sequence starts with 3. The common difference *d* is 2. You can use the first term and the common difference to write a rule for finding a_n.

Words	Numbers	Algebra
1st term	3	a_1
2nd term = 1st term plus common difference	$3 + (1)2 = 5$	$a_1 + 1d$
3nd term = 1st term plus 2 common differences	$3 + (2)2 = 7$	$a_1 + 2d$
4th term = 1st term plus 3 common differences	$3 + (3)2 = 9$	$a_1 + 3d$
$\vdots$	$\vdots$	$\vdots$
*n*th term = 1st term plus $(n - 1)$ common differences	$3 + (n - 1)2$	$a_1 + (n - 1)d$

The pattern in the table shows that to find the *n*th term, add the first term to the product of $(n - 1)$ and the common difference.

Finding the *n*th Term of an Arithmetic Sequence

The *n*th term of an arithmetic sequence with common difference *d* and first term a_1 is

$$a_n = a_1 + (n - 1)d.$$

EXAMPLE 2 Finding the *n*th Term of an Arithmetic Sequence

Find the indicated term of each arithmetic sequence.

A 22nd term: 5, 2, −1, −4, …

Step 1 Find the common difference.

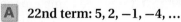
5, 2, −1, −4, …   *The common difference is −3.*
−3 −3 −3

my.hrw.com

Online Video Tutor

Step 2 Find the 22nd term.

$$a_n = a_1 + (n-1)d$$ *Write the rule to find the nth term.*

$$a_{22} = 5 + (22-1)(-3)$$ *Substitute 5 for a_1, 22 for n, and −3 for d.*

$$= 5 + (21)(-3)$$ *Simplify the expression in parentheses.*

$$= 5 - 63$$ *Multiply.*

$$= -58$$ *Subtract.*

B   15th term: $a_1 = 7$; $d = 3$

$$a_n = a_1 + (n-1)d$$ *Write the rule to find the nth term.*

$$a_{15} = 7 + (15-1)3$$ *Substitute 7 for a_1, 15 for n, and 3 for d.*

$$= 7 + (14)3$$ *Simplify the expression in parentheses.*

$$= 7 + 42$$ *Multiply.*

$$= 49$$ *Add.*

 Find the indicated term of each arithmetic sequence.

2a. 60th term: 11, 5, −1, −7, …   **2b.** 12th term: $a_1 = 4.2$; $d = 1.4$

Online Video Tutor

EXAMPLE 3   *Travel Application*

The odometer on a car reads 60,473 on day 1. Every day, the car is driven 54 miles. If this pattern continues, what is the odometer reading on day 20?

Notice that the sequence for the situation is arithmetic with $d = 54$ because the odometer reading will increase by **54** miles per day.

Since the odometer reading on day 1 is 60,473 miles, $a_1 = 60{,}473$.

Since you want to find the odometer reading on day 20, you will need to find the **20th term** of the sequence, so $n = 20$.

$$a_n = a_1 + (n-1)d$$ *Write the rule to find the nth term.*

$$a_{20} = 60{,}473 + (20-1)54$$ *Substitute 60,473 for a_1, 54 for d, and 21 for n.*

$$= 60{,}473 + (19)54$$ *Simplify the expression in parentheses.*

$$= 60{,}473 + 1026$$ *Multiply.*

$$= 61{,}499$$ *Add.*

The odometer will read 61,499 miles on day 20.

 3. Each time a truck stops, it drops off 250 pounds of cargo. After stop 1, its cargo weighed 2000 pounds. How much does the load weigh after stop 6?

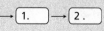 MCC.MP.3   **MATHEMATICAL PRACTICES**

THINK AND DISCUSS

1. Explain how to determine if a sequence appears to be arithmetic.

2. GET ORGANIZED Copy and complete the graphic organizer with steps for finding the *n*th term of an arithmetic sequence.

Finding the *n*th Term of an Arithmetic Sequence → 1. → 2.

GUIDED PRACTICE

1. **Vocabulary** When trying to find the *n*th term of an arithmetic sequence you must first know the _____?_____. (*common difference* or *sequence*)

SEE EXAMPLE **1** **Multi-Step** Determine whether each sequence appears to be an arithmetic sequence. If so, find the common difference and the next three terms.

2. 2, 8, 14, 20, …

3. 2.1, 1.4, 0.7, 0, …

4. 1, 1, 2, 3, …

5. 0.1, 0.3, 0.9, 2.7, …

SEE EXAMPLE **2** Find the indicated term of each arithmetic sequence.

6. 21st term: 3, 8, 13, 18, …

7. 18th term: $a_1 = -2$; $d = -3$

SEE EXAMPLE **3** 8. **Shipping** To package and ship an item, it costs $5.75 for the first pound and $0.75 for each additional pound. What is the cost of shipping a 12-pound package?

PRACTICE AND PROBLEM SOLVING

Independent Practice	
For Exercises	See Example
9–12	1
13–14	2
15	3

my.hrw.com

Online Extra Practice

Multi-Step Determine whether each sequence appears to be an arithmetic sequence. If so, find the common difference and the next three terms.

9. −1, 10, −100, 1,100, …

10. 0, −2, −4, −6, …

11. −22, −31, −40, −49, …

12. 0.2, 0.5, 0.9, 1.1, …

Find the indicated term of each arithmetic sequence.

13. 31st term: 1.40, 1.55, 1.70, …

14. 50th term: $a_1 = 2.2$; $d = 1.1$

15. **Travel** Rachel signed up for a frequent-flier program. She receives 4300 frequent-flier miles for her first round trip and 1300 frequent-flier miles for each additional round-trip. How many frequent-flier miles will she have after 5 round-trips?

Find the common difference for each arithmetic sequence.

16. 0, 6, 12, 18, …

17. $\frac{1}{2}, \frac{3}{4}, 1, \frac{5}{4}, …$

18. 107, 105, 103, 101, …

19. 7.9, 5.7, 3.5, 1.3, …

20. $\frac{1}{5}, \frac{2}{5}, \frac{3}{5}, \frac{4}{5}, …$

21. 4.25, 4.32, 4.39, 4.46, …

Find the next four terms in each arithmetic sequence.

22. −4, −7, −10, −13, …

23. $\frac{1}{8}, 0, -\frac{1}{8}, -\frac{1}{4}, …$

24. 505, 512, 519, 526, …

25. 1.8, 1.3, 0.8, 0.3, …

26. $\frac{2}{3}, \frac{4}{3}, 2, \frac{8}{3}, …$

27. −1.1, −0.9, −0.7, −0.5

Find the given term of each arithmetic sequence.

28. 5, 10, 15, 20, …; 17th term

29. 121, 110, 99, 88, …; 10th term

30. −2, −5, −8, −11, …; 41st term

31. −30, −22, −14, −6, …; 20th term

H.O.T. 32. **Critical Thinking** Is the sequence $5a - 1, 3a - 1, a - 1, -a - 1, …$ arithmetic? If not, explain why not. If so, find the common difference and the next three terms.

33. Recreation The rates for a go-cart course are shown.

   a. Explain why the relationship described on the flyer could be represented by an arithmetic sequence.

   b. Find the cost for 1, 2, 3, and 4 laps. Write a rule to find the *n*th term of the sequence.

   c. How much would 15 laps cost?

   d. **What if...?** After 9 laps, you get the 10th one free. Will the sequence still be arithmetic? Explain.

JESSIKA'S SPEEDWAY
License: $7
Per Lap: $2

Find the given term of each arithmetic sequence.

34. 2.5, 8.5, 14.5, 20.5, …; 30th term

35. 189.6, 172.3, 155, 137.7, …; 18th term

36. $\frac{1}{4}, \frac{3}{4}, \frac{5}{4}, \frac{7}{4}$, …; 15th term

37. $\frac{2}{3}, \frac{11}{12}, \frac{7}{6}, \frac{17}{12}$, …; 25th term

38. Number Theory The sequence 1, 1, 2, 3, 5, 8, 13, … is a famous sequence called the Fibonacci sequence. After the first two terms, each term is the sum of the previous two terms.

   a. Write the first 10 terms of the Fibonacci sequence. Is the Fibonacci sequence arithmetic? Explain.

   b. Notice that the third term is divisible by 2. Are the 6th and 9th terms also divisible by 2? What conclusion can you draw about every third term? Why is this true?

   c. Can you find any other patterns? (*Hint:* Look at every 4th and 5th term.)

39. Entertainment Seats in a concert hall are arranged in the pattern shown.

   a. The numbers of seats in the rows form an arithmetic sequence. Write a rule for the arithmetic sequence.

   b. How many seats are in the 15th row?

   c. A ticket costs $40. Suppose every seat in the first 10 rows is filled. What is the total revenue from those seats?

   d. **What if...?** An extra chair is added to each row. Write the new rule for the arithmetic sequence and find the new total revenue from the first 10 rows.

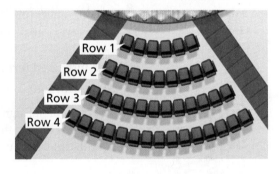

Row 1
Row 2
Row 3
Row 4

H.O.T. **40. Write About It** Explain how to find the common difference of an arithmetic sequence. How can you determine whether the arithmetic sequence has a positive common difference or a negative common difference?

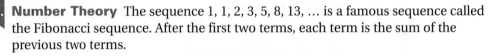

Number Theory

Fibonacci numbers occur frequently throughout nature. The number of petals on many flowers are numbers of the Fibonacci sequence. Two petals on a flower are rare but 3, 5, and even 34 petals are common.

Real-World Connections

STATE

41. Juan is traveling to visit universities. He notices mile markers along the road. He records the mile marker every 10 minutes. His father is driving at a constant speed.

   a. Copy and complete the table.

   b. Write the rule for the sequence.

   c. What does the common difference represent?

   d. If this sequence continues, find the mile marker for time interval 10.

Time Interval	Mile Marker
1	520
2	509
3	498
4	▮
5	▮
6	▮

(t),Digital Vision/gettyimages; (bl),comstock/Getty Photos

TEST PREP

42. What are the next three terms in the arithmetic sequence −21, −12, −3, 6, … ?

Ⓐ 9, 12, 15   Ⓑ 15, 24, 33   Ⓒ 12, 21, 27   Ⓓ 13, 20, 27

43. What is the common difference for the data listed in the second column?

Ⓕ −1.8   Ⓗ 2.8

Ⓖ 1.8   Ⓙ −3.6

Altitude (ft)	Boiling Point of Water (°F)
1000	210.2
2000	208.4
3000	206.6

44. Which of the following sequences is NOT arithmetic?

Ⓐ −4, 2, 8, 14, …   Ⓑ 9, 4, −1, −6, …   Ⓒ 2, 4, 8, 16, …   Ⓓ $\frac{1}{3}$, $1\frac{1}{3}$, $2\frac{1}{3}$, $3\frac{1}{3}$, …

CHALLENGE AND EXTEND

45. The first term of an arithmetic sequence is 2, and the common difference is 9. Find two consecutive terms of the sequence that have a sum of 355. What positions in the sequence are the terms?

46. The 60th term of an arithmetic sequence is 106.5, and the common difference is 1.5. What is the first term of the sequence?

47. **Athletics** Verona is training for a marathon. The first part of her training schedule is shown below.

Session	1	2	3	4	5	6
Distance Run (mi)	3.5	5	6.5	8	9.5	11

    a. If Verona continues this pattern, during which training session will she run 26 miles? Is her training schedule an arithmetic sequence? Explain.

    b. If Verona's training schedule starts on a Monday and she runs every third day, on which day will she run 26 miles?

FOCUS ON MATHEMATICAL PRACTICES

H.O.T. **48. Communication** As part of a game, Darryl says "I wrote an arithmetic sequence that has a common difference of +5. What is my sequence?" Pat says, "I can't tell. You haven't given me enough information." Is Pat correct? If so, what other information does Darryl have to provide? If not, what is Darryl's sequence?

H.O.T. **49. Problem Solving** Gena starts an exercise program by running half a mile on Saturday morning. Each week, she increases the distance she runs by a quarter mile. Is this pattern an arithmetic sequence? Explain. If it is, find the common difference and write the first 6 terms of the sequence.

H.O.T. **50. Patterns** Many sequences are not arithmetic but still form a clear pattern. Predict the next three terms of each sequence. Are any of them arithmetic sequences?
a. 1, 2, 4, 8, 16, …   b. 9, 6, 3, 0, …   c. 2, −2, 3, −3, 4, −4, …

H.O.T. **51. Modeling** Arithmetic sequences can be written as functions, in which the input is the position of the term and the output is the value of the term. Write a function that models the sequence 4, 7, 10, 13,…. (*Hint:* Remember that the position of the first term of a sequence is 1, not 0.)

Ready to Go On?

my.hrw.com
Assessment and Intervention

9-1 Graphing Functions

Graph each function for the given domain.

1. $2x - y = 3$; D: $\{-2, 0, 1, 3\}$ **2.** $y = 4 - x^2$; D: $\{-1, 0, 1, 2\}$ **3.** $y = 3 - 2x$; D: $\{-1, 0, 1, 3\}$

Graph each function.

4. $x + y = 6$ **5.** $y = |x| - 3$ **6.** $y = x^2 + 1$

7. The function $y = 8x$ represents how many miles y a certain storm travels in x hours. Graph the function and estimate the number of miles the storm travels in 10.5 h.

9-2 Exploring Transformations

The graph shows some credit card fees for cash advances. Sketch a graph to represent each situation and identify the transformation of the original graph that it represents.

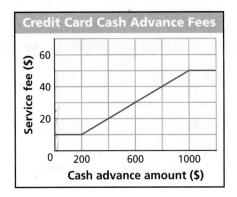

8. Each fee is increased by $15.

9. Each fee is decreased by 40%.

9-3 Arithmetic Sequences

Determine whether each sequence appears to be an arithmetic sequence. If so, find the common difference and the next three terms.

10. $7, 3, -1, -5, \ldots$ **11.** $3, 6, 12, 24, \ldots$ **12.** $-3.5, -2, -0.5, 1, \ldots$

Find the indicated term of the arithmetic sequence.

13. 31st term: $12, 7, 2, -3, \ldots$ **14.** 22nd term: $a_1 = 6$; $d = 4$

15. With no air resistance, an object would fall 16 feet during the first second, 48 feet during the second second, 80 feet during the third second, 112 feet during the fourth second, and so on. How many feet will the object fall during the ninth second?

PARCC Assessment Readiness

Selected Response

1. Find the 20th term in the arithmetic sequence
−4, 1, 6, 11, 16,…

- Ⓐ 96
- Ⓑ 72
- Ⓒ 95
- Ⓓ 91

2. Which situation is best represented by the graph?

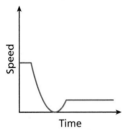

- Ⓕ An airplane starts slowly on the runway, and then quickly takes off before finding a nice cruising speed.

- Ⓖ A swimmer starts at a steady pace, slows down to a stop, and then starts swimming again, but at a slower pace than when she first started.

- Ⓗ After a ball is thrown into the air, it falls back to the ground and bounces.

- Ⓙ The driver of a car starts on flat ground and drives quickly up a hill, then keeps driving.

3. Use the graph of the function $f(x) = 2x + 2$ to find the value of y when $x = 2$.

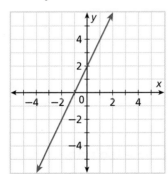

- Ⓐ −2
- Ⓑ 7
- Ⓒ 6
- Ⓓ 0

4. Determine whether the sequence appears to be an arithmetic sequence. If so, find the common difference and the next three terms in the sequence. −5, −11, −17, −23, −29, . . .

- Ⓕ Not an arithmetic sequence

- Ⓖ Yes; common difference −7; next three terms are −36, −43, −50

- Ⓗ Yes; common difference −6; next 3 terms are −35, −41, −47

- Ⓙ Yes; common difference 6; next three terms are −23, −17, −11

5. Sylvie is going on vacation. She has already driven 60 miles in one hour. Her average speed for the rest of the trip is 57 miles per hour. How far will Sylvie have driven 7 hours later?

- Ⓐ 399 miles
- Ⓑ 402 miles
- Ⓒ 459 miles
- Ⓓ 420 miles

6. Graph the function $y = -x^2 - 2$.

Ⓕ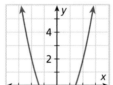

Ⓖ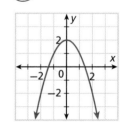

Ⓗ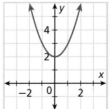

Ⓙ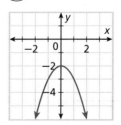

Mini-Task

7. A motorist is driving across the country at a steady speed at 54.5 miles per hour. At the end of the 17th hour, the odometer reads 62,416. What was the odometer reading when she started her trip?

10 Linear Functions and Slope

Contents

The Common Core Georgia Performance Standards for Mathematical Practice describe varieties of expertise that all students should seek to develop. Opportunities to develop these practices are integrated throughout this program.

1 Make sense of problems and persevere in solving them.

2 Reason abstractly and quantitatively.

3 Construct viable arguments and critique the reasoning of others.

4 Model with mathematics.

5 Use appropriate tools strategically.

6 Attend to precision.

7 Look for and make use of structure.

8 Look for and express regularity in repeated reasoning.

Unpacking the Standards

my.hrw.com
Multilingual Glossary

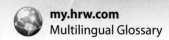

Understanding the standards and the vocabulary terms in the standards will help you know exactly what you are expected to learn in this chapter.

COMMON CORE GPS **MCC9-12.F.IF.6**

Calculate and interpret the average rate of change of a function (presented symbolically or as a table) over a specified interval. Estimate the rate of change from a graph.

Key Vocabulary

rate of change (tasa de cambio)
A ratio that compares the amount of change in a dependent variable to the amount of change in an independent variable.

What It Means For You

Average rate of change measures the change in the dependent variable against the change in the independent variable over a specific interval. This helps you understand how quickly the values in a function change.

EXAMPLE

Time (hours)	1	2	3	4
Distance (miles)	60	120	180	240

$$\text{Average rate of change} = \frac{180 - 60}{3 - 1} = 60 \text{ mi/h}$$

10-1 Identifying Linear Functions

Essential Question: How can you identify and graph linear functions?

Objectives
Identify linear functions and linear equations.

Graph linear functions that represent real-world situations and give their domain and range.

Vocabulary
linear function
linear equation

Why learn this?
Linear functions can describe many real-world situations, such as distances traveled at a constant speed.

Most people believe that there is no speed limit on the German autobahn. However, many stretches have a speed limit of 120 km/h. If a car travels continuously at this speed, $y = 120x$ gives the number of kilometers y that the car would travel in x hours. Solutions are shown in the graph.

The graph represents a function because each domain value (x-value) is paired with exactly one range value (y-value). Notice that the graph is a straight line. A function whose graph forms a straight line is called a **linear function**.

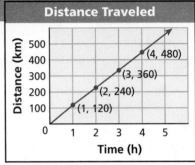

Distance Traveled

COMMON CORE GPS
MCC9-12.F.LE.1b

EXAMPLE 1

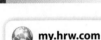

Online Video Tutor

Identifying a Linear Function by Its Graph

Identify whether each graph represents a function. Explain. If the graph does represent a function, is the function linear?

A

Each domain value is paired with exactly one range value. The graph forms a line.

linear function

B

Each domain value is paired with exactly one range value. The graph is not a line.

not a linear function

C

The only domain value, 3, is paired with many different range values.

not a function

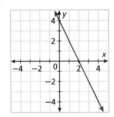

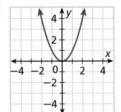

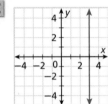

Identify whether each graph represents a function. Explain. If the graph does represent a function, is the function linear?

1a.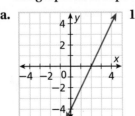

1b.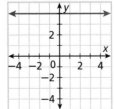

1c.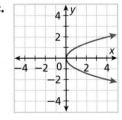

You can sometimes identify a linear function by looking at a table or a list of ordered pairs. In a linear function, a constant change in x corresponds to a constant change in y.

x	y
−2	7
−1	4
0	1
1	−2
2	−5

+1 ⟶ −3
+1 ⟶ −3
+1 ⟶ −3
+1 ⟶ −3

x	y
−2	6
−1	3
0	2
1	3
2	6

+1 ⟶ −3
+1 ⟶ −1
+1 ⟶ +1
+1 ⟶ +3

In this table, a constant change of +1 in x corresponds to a constant change of −3 in y. These points satisfy a linear function.

The points from this table lie on a line.

In this table, a constant change of +1 in x does *not* correspond to a constant change in y. These points do *not* satisfy a linear function.

The points from this table do not lie on a line.

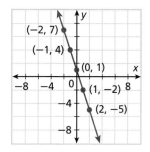

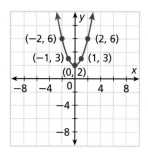

Caution!

If you find a constant change in the y-values, check for a constant change in the x-values. Both need to be constant for the function to be linear.

COMMON CORE GPS
EXAMPLE 2
MCC9-12.F.LE.1b

my.hrw.com

Online Video Tutor

Identifying a Linear Function by Using Ordered Pairs

Tell whether each set of ordered pairs satisfies a linear function. Explain.

A $\{(2, 4), (5, 3), (8, 2), (11, 1)\}$

x	y
2	4
5	3
8	2
11	1

+3 ⟶ −1
+3 ⟶ −1
+3 ⟶ −1

Write the ordered pairs in a table. Look for a pattern.

A constant change of +3 in x corresponds to a constant change of −1 in y.

These points satisfy a linear function.

B $\{(-10, 10), (-5, 4), (0, 2), (5, 0)\}$

x	y
−10	10
−5	4
0	2
5	0

+5 ⟶ −6
+5 ⟶ −2
+5 ⟶ −2

Write the ordered pairs in a table. Look for a pattern.

A constant change of +5 in x corresponds to different changes in y.

These points do not satisfy a linear function.

2. Tell whether the set of ordered pairs $\{(3, 5), (5, 4), (7, 3), (9, 2), (11, 1)\}$ satisfies a linear function. Explain.

Another way to determine whether a function is linear is to look at its equation. A function is linear if it is described by a *linear equation*. A **linear equation** is any equation that can be written in the *standard form* shown below.

Standard Form of a Linear Equation

$Ax + By = C$ where A, B, and C are real numbers and A and B are not both 0

Notice that when a linear equation is written in standard form
- x and y both have exponents of 1.
- x and y are not multiplied together.
- x and y do not appear in denominators, exponents, or radical signs.

Linear		Not Linear	
$3x + 2y = 10$	Standard form	$3xy + x = 1$	x and y are multiplied.
$y - 2 = 3x$	Can be written as $3x - y = -2$	$x^3 + y = -1$	x has an exponent other than 1.
$-y = 5x$	Can be written as $5x + y = 0$	$x + \dfrac{6}{y} = 12$	y is in a denominator.

For any two points, there is exactly one line that contains them both. This means you need only two ordered pairs to graph a line.

EXAMPLE 3
MCC9-12.F.IF.7a

my.hrw.com

Online Video Tutor

Graphing Linear Functions

Tell whether each function is linear. If so, graph the function.

A $y = x + 3$

$$y = \quad x + 3 \qquad \textit{Write the equation in standard form.}$$
$$\underline{-x \quad -x} \qquad \textit{Subtraction Property of Equality}$$
$$y - x = \qquad 3$$
$$-x + y = \qquad 3 \qquad \textit{The equation is in standard form } (A = -1, B = 1, C = 3).$$

The equation can be written in standard form, so the function is linear.

To graph, choose three values of x, and use them to generate ordered pairs. (You only need two, but graphing three points is a good check.)

Plot the points and connect them with a straight line.

x	$y = x + 3$	(x, y)
0	$y = 0 + 3 = 3$	$(0, 3)$
1	$y = 1 + 3 = 4$	$(1, 4)$
2	$y = 2 + 3 = 5$	$(2, 5)$

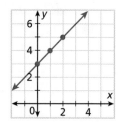

Remember!

- $y - x = y + (-x)$
- $y + (-x) = -x + y$
- $-x = -1x$
- $y = 1y$

B $y = x^2$

This is not linear, because x has an exponent other than 1.

CHECK IT OUT! Tell whether each function is linear. If so, graph the function.

3a. $y = 5x - 9$ **3b.** $y = 12$ **3c.** $y = 2^x$

For linear functions whose graphs are not horizontal, the domain and range are all real numbers. However, in many real-world situations, the domain and range must be restricted. For example, some quantities cannot be negative, such as time.

Sometimes domain and range are restricted even further to a set of points. For example, a quantity such as number of people can only be whole numbers. When this happens, the graph is not actually connected because every point on the line is not a solution. However, you may see these graphs shown connected to indicate that the linear pattern, or trend, continues.

EXAMPLE 4
MCC9-12.F.IF.7a

Career Application

my.hrw.com

Online Video Tutor

Remember!

$f(x) = y$, so in Example 4, graph the function values (dependent variable) on the *y*-axis.

Sue rents a manicure station in a salon and pays the salon owner $5.50 for each manicure she gives. The amount Sue pays each day is given by $f(x) = 5.50x$, where *x* is the number of manicures. Graph this function and give its domain and range.

Choose several values of x and make a table of ordered pairs.

Graph the ordered pairs.

x	f(x) = 5.50x
0	$f(0) = 5.50(0) = 0$
1	$f(1) = 5.50(1) = 5.50$
2	$f(2) = 5.50(2) = 11.00$
3	$f(3) = 5.50(3) = 16.50$
4	$f(4) = 5.50(4) = 22.00$
5	$f(5) = 5.50(5) = 27.50$

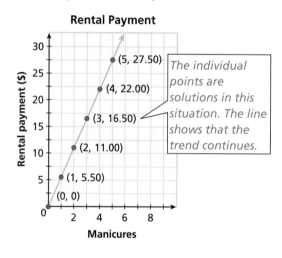

The individual points are solutions in this situation. The line shows that the trend continues.

The number of manicures must be a whole number, so the domain is $\{0, 1, 2, 3, \ldots\}$. The range is $\{0, 5.50, 11.00, 16.50, \ldots\}$.

4. What if...? At another salon, Sue can rent a station for $10.00 per day plus $3.00 per manicure. The amount she would pay each day is given by $f(x) = 3x + 10$, where *x* is the number of manicures. Graph this function and give its domain and range.

MCC.MP.3 | MATHEMATICAL PRACTICES

THINK AND DISCUSS

1. Suppose you are given five ordered pairs that satisfy a function. When you graph them, four lie on a straight line, but the fifth does not. Is the function linear? Why or why not?

2. In Example 4, why is every point on the line not a solution?

3. GET ORGANIZED Copy and complete the graphic organizer. In each box, describe how to use the information to identify a linear function. Include an example.

Determining Whether a Function Is Linear

| From its graph | From its equation | From a list of ordered pairs |

GUIDED PRACTICE

1. **Vocabulary** Is the *linear equation* $3x - 2 = y$ in standard form? Explain.

SEE EXAMPLE 1   Identify whether each graph represents a function. Explain. If the graph does represent a function, is the function linear?

2.
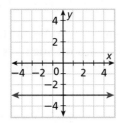

3.
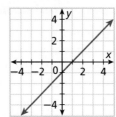

4.
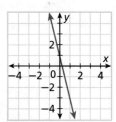

SEE EXAMPLE 2   Tell whether the given ordered pairs satisfy a linear function. Explain.

5.

x	5	4	3	2	1
y	0	2	4	6	8

6.

x	1	4	9	16	25
y	1	2	3	4	5

7. $\{(0, 5), (-2, 3), (-4, 1), (-6, -1), (-8, -3)\}$

8. $\{(2, -2), (-1, 0), (-4, 1), (-7, 3), (-10, 6)\}$

SEE EXAMPLE 3   Tell whether each function is linear. If so, graph the function.

9. $2x + 3y = 5$ 10. $2y = 8$ 11. $\dfrac{x^2 + 3}{5} = y$ 12. $\dfrac{x}{5} = \dfrac{y}{3}$

SEE EXAMPLE 4

13. **Transportation** A train travels at a constant speed of 75 mi/h. The function $f(x) = 75x$ gives the distance that the train travels in x hours. Graph this function and give its domain and range.

14. **Entertainment** A movie rental store charges a $6.00 membership fee plus $2.50 for each movie rented. The function $f(x) = 2.50x + 6$ gives the cost of renting x movies. Graph this function and give its domain and range.

PRACTICE AND PROBLEM SOLVING

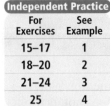

For Exercises	See Example
15–17	1
18–20	2
21–24	3
25	4

Online Extra Practice

Identify whether each graph represents a function. Explain. If the graph does represent a function, is the function linear?

15.
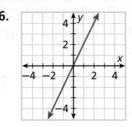

16.

17.

Tell whether the given ordered pairs satisfy a linear function. Explain.

18.

x	−3	0	3	6	9
y	−2	−1	0	2	4

19.

x	−1	0	1	2	3
y	−3	−2	−1	0	1

20. $\{(3, 4), (0, 2), (-3, 0), (-6, -2), (-9, -4)\}$

Tell whether each function is linear. If so, graph the function.

21. $y = 5$ **22.** $4y - 2x = 0$ **23.** $\dfrac{3}{x} + 4y = 10$ **24.** $5 + 3y = 8$

25. Transportation The gas tank in Tony's car holds 15 gallons, and the car can travel 25 miles for each gallon of gas. When Tony begins with a full tank of gas, the function $f(x) = -\dfrac{1}{25}x + 15$ gives the amount of gas $f(x)$ that will be left in the tank after traveling x miles (if he does not buy more gas). Graph this function and give its domain and range.

Tell whether the given ordered pairs satisfy a function. If so, is it a linear function?

26. $\{(2, 5), (2, 4), (2, 3), (2, 2), (2, 1)\}$ **27.** $\{(-8, 2), (-6, 0), (-4, -2), (-2, -4), (0, -6)\}$

28.

x	−10	−6	−2	2	4
y	0	0.25	0.50	0.75	1

29.

x	−5	−1	3	7	11
y	1	1	1	1	1

Tell whether each equation is linear. If so, write the equation in standard form and give the values of A, B, and C.

30. $2x - 8y = 16$ **31.** $y = 4x + 2$ **32.** $2x = \dfrac{y}{3} - 4$ **33.** $\dfrac{4}{x} = y$

34. $\dfrac{x+4}{2} = \dfrac{y-4}{3}$ **35.** $x = 7$ **36.** $xy = 6$ **37.** $3x - 5 + y = 2y - 4$

38. $y = -x + 2$ **39.** $5x = 2y - 3$ **40.** $2y = -6$ **41.** $y = \sqrt{x}$

Graph each linear function.

42. $y = 3x + 7$ **43.** $y = x + 25$ **44.** $y = 8 - x$ **45.** $y = 2x$

46. $-2y = -3x + 6$ **47.** $y - x = 4$ **48.** $y - 2x = -3$ **49.** $x = 5 + y$

50. Measurement One inch is equal to approximately 2.5 centimeters. Let x represent inches and y represent centimeters. Write an equation in standard form relating x and y. Give the values of A, B, and C.

51. Wages Molly earns $8.00 an hour at her job.
   a. Let x represent the number of hours that Molly works. Write a function using x and $f(x)$ that describes Molly's pay for working x hours.
   b. Graph this function and give its domain and range.

H.O.T. 52. Write About It For $y = 2x - 1$, make a table of ordered pairs and a graph. Describe the relationships between the equation, the table, and the graph.

H.O.T. 53. Critical Thinking Describe a real-world situation that can be represented by a linear function whose domain and range must be limited. Give your function and its domain and range.

Real-World Connections

54. a. Juan is running on a treadmill. The table shows the number of Calories Juan burns as a function of time. Explain how you can tell that this relationship is linear by using the table.
   b. Create a graph of the data.
   c. How can you tell from the graph that the relationship is linear?

Time (min)	Calories
3	27
6	54
9	81
12	108
15	135
18	162
21	189

55. Physical Science A ball was dropped from a height of 100 meters. Its height above the ground in meters at different times after its release is given in the table. Do these ordered pairs satisfy a linear function? Explain.

Time (s)	0	1	2	3
Height (m)	100	90.2	60.8	11.8

H.O.T. **56. Critical Thinking** Is the equation $x = 9$ a linear equation? Does it describe a linear function? Explain.

TEST PREP

57. Which is NOT a linear function?

Ⓐ $y = 8x$ Ⓑ $y = x + 8$ Ⓒ $y = \frac{8}{x}$ Ⓓ $y = 8 - x$

58. The speed of sound in 0 °C air is about 331 feet per second. Which function could be used to describe the distance in feet d that sound will travel in air in s seconds?

Ⓕ $d = s + 331$ Ⓖ $d = 331s$ Ⓗ $s = 331d$ Ⓙ $s = 331 - d$

H.O.T. **59. Extended Response** Write your own linear function. Show that it is a linear function in at least three different ways. Explain any connections you see between your three methods.

CHALLENGE AND EXTEND

60. What equation describes the x-axis? the y-axis? Do these equations represent linear functions?

Geometry Copy and complete each table below. Then tell whether the table shows a linear relationship.

61.

Perimeter of a Square	
Side Length	Perimeter
1	▨
2	▨
3	▨
4	▨

62.

Area of a Square	
Side Length	Area
1	▨
2	▨
3	▨
4	▨

63.

Volume of a Cube	
Side Length	Volume
1	▨
2	▨
3	▨
4	▨

FOCUS ON MATHEMATICAL PRACTICES

H.O.T. **64. Reasoning** A function crosses the x-axis at the points (0,0) and (4,0) and nowhere else. Could the function be a linear function? Explain your answer.

H.O.T. **65. Analysis** Fill each of the three areas of the Venn diagram with two different equations.

H.O.T. **66. Modeling** Describe a problem situation that can be modeled by a linear function with a domain of D: $0 < x \le 10$, where 0 is not part of the range. Give the function and its range.

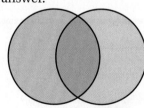

Linear   Function

10-2 Using Intercepts

Essential Question: How can you find *x*- and *y*-intercepts and use them to graph linear functions?

Objectives
Find *x*- and *y*-intercepts and interpret their meanings in real-world situations.

Use *x*- and *y*-intercepts to graph lines.

Vocabulary
y-intercept
x-intercept

Who uses this?
Divers can use intercepts to determine the time a safe ascent will take.

A diver explored the ocean floor 120 feet below the surface and then ascended at a rate of 30 feet per minute. The graph shows the diver's elevation below sea level during the ascent.

The **y-intercept** is the *y*-coordinate of the point where the graph intersects the *y*-axis. The *x*-coordinate of this point is always 0.

The **x-intercept** is the *x*-coordinate of the point where the graph intersects the *x*-axis. The *y*-coordinate of this point is always 0.

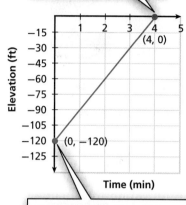

The x-intercept is 4. It represents the time that the diver reaches the surface, or when depth = 0.

The y-intercept is −120. It represents the diver's elevation at the start of the ascent, when time = 0.

EXAMPLE 1 Finding Intercepts

Find the *x*- and *y*-intercepts.

A

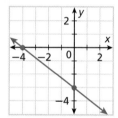

The graph intersects the x-axis at (−4, 0).
The *x*-intercept is −4.

The graph intersects the y-axis at (0, −3).
The *y*-intercept is −3.

B $3x - 2y = 12$

To find the *x*-intercept, replace *y* with 0 and solve for *x*.

$$3x - 2y = 12$$
$$3x - 2(0) = 12$$
$$3x - 0 = 12$$
$$3x = 12$$
$$\frac{3x}{3} = \frac{12}{3}$$
$$x = 4$$

The *x*-intercept is 4.

To find the *y*-intercept, replace *x* with 0 and solve for *y*.

$$3x - 2y = 12$$
$$3(0) - 2y = 12$$
$$0 - 2y = 12$$
$$-2y = 12$$
$$\frac{-2y}{-2} = \frac{12}{-2}$$
$$y = -6$$

The *y*-intercept is −6.

CHECK IT OUT! Find the *x*- and *y*-intercepts.

1a.

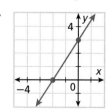

1b. $-3x + 5y = 30$

1c. $4x + 2y = 16$

I use the "cover-up" method to find intercepts. To use this method, make sure the equation is in standard form first.

If I have 4x − 3y = 12:

First, I cover 4x with my finger and solve the equation I can still see.

$$\text{✋} - 3y = 12$$
$$y = -4$$

The y-intercept is −4.

Then I cover −3y with my finger and do the same thing.

$$4x \; \text{✋} = 12$$
$$x = 3$$

The x-intercept is 3.

Madison Stewart
Jefferson High School

COMMON CORE GPS

EXAMPLE **2**
MCC9-12.F.IF.7a

my.hrw.com

Online Video Tutor

Travel Application

The Sandia Peak Tramway in Albuquerque, New Mexico, travels a distance of about 4500 meters to the top of Sandia Peak. Its speed is 300 meters per minute. The function $f(x) = 4500 - 300x$ gives the tram's distance in meters from the top of the peak after x minutes. Graph this function and find the intercepts. What does each intercept represent?

Neither time nor distance can be negative, so choose several nonnegative values for x. Use the function to generate ordered pairs.

x	0	2	5	10	15
f(x) = 4500 − 300x	4500	3900	3000	1500	0

Graph the ordered pairs. Connect the points with a line.

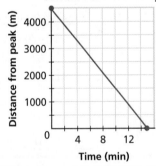

Sandia Peak Tramway

• *y*-intercept: 4500. This is the starting distance from the top (time = 0).

• *x*-intercept: 15. This the time when the tram reaches the peak (distance = 0).

Caution!

The graph is not the path of the tram. Even though the line is descending, the graph describes the distance from the peak as the tram goes *up* the mountain.

CHECK IT OUT!

2. The school store sells pens for $2.00 and notebooks for $3.00. The equation $2x + 3y = 60$ describes the number of pens x and notebooks y that you can buy for $60.

a. Graph the function and find its intercepts.

b. What does each intercept represent?

Remember, to graph a linear function, you need to plot only two ordered pairs. It is often simplest to find the ordered pairs that contain the intercepts.

EXAMPLE 3 MCC9-12.F.IF.7a

Graphing Linear Equations by Using Intercepts

Use intercepts to graph the line described by each equation.

A $2x - 4y = 8$

Step 1 Find the intercepts.

x-intercept:	y-intercept:
$2x - 4y = 8$	$2x - 4y = 8$
$2x - 4(0) = 8$	$2(0) - 4y = 8$
$2x = 8$	$-4y = 8$
$\dfrac{2x}{2} = \dfrac{8}{2}$	$\dfrac{-4y}{-4} = \dfrac{8}{-4}$
$x = 4$	$y = -2$

Step 2 Graph the line.

Plot (4, 0) and (0, −2).
Connect with a straight line.

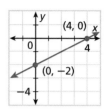

B $\dfrac{2}{3}y = 4 - \dfrac{1}{2}x$

Step 1 Write the equation in standard form.

$$6\left(\dfrac{2}{3}y\right) = 6\left(4 - \dfrac{1}{2}x\right)$$

Multiply both sides by 6, the LCD of the fractions, to clear the fractions.

$$4y = 24 - 3x$$
$$3x + 4y = 24$$

Write the equation in standard form.

Step 2 Find the intercepts.

x-intercept:	y-intercept:
$3x + 4y = 24$	$3x + 4y = 24$
$3x + 4(0) = 24$	$3(0) + 4y = 24$
$3x = 24$	$4y = 24$
$\dfrac{3x}{3} = \dfrac{24}{3}$	$\dfrac{4y}{4} = \dfrac{24}{4}$
$x = 8$	$y = 6$

Step 3 Graph the line.

Plot (8, 0) and (0, 6).
Connect with a straight line.

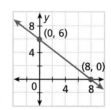

my.hrw.com

Online Video Tutor

Helpful Hint

You can use a third point to check your line. Either choose a point from your graph and check it in the equation, or use the equation to generate a point and check that it is on your graph.

Use intercepts to graph the line described by each equation.

3a. $-3x + 4y = -12$ **3b.** $y = \dfrac{1}{3}x - 2$

THINK AND DISCUSS

1. A function has x-intercept 4 and y-intercept 2. Name two points on the graph of this function.

2. What is the y-intercept of $2.304x + y = 4.318$? What is the x-intercept of $x - 92.4920y = -21.5489$?

3. GET ORGANIZED Copy and complete the graphic organizer.

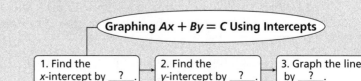

Graphing $Ax + By = C$ Using Intercepts

| 1. Find the x-intercept by ___?___. | 2. Find the y-intercept by ___?___. | 3. Graph the line by ___?___. |

my.hrw.com
Homework Help

GUIDED PRACTICE

1. **Vocabulary** The ___?___ is the *y*-coordinate of the point where a graph crosses the *y*-axis. (*x-intercept* or *y-intercept*)

SEE EXAMPLE 1 | Find the *x*- and *y*-intercepts.

2.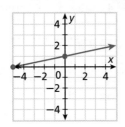

3.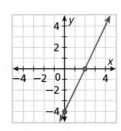

4.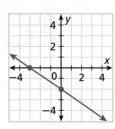

5. $2x - 4y = 4$ 6. $-2y = 3x - 6$ 7. $4y + 5x = 2y - 3x + 16$

SEE EXAMPLE 2 | 8. **Biology** To thaw a specimen stored at -25 °C, the temperature of a refrigeration tank is raised 5 °C every hour. The temperature in the tank after *x* hours can be described by the function $f(x) = -25 + 5x$.

   a. Graph the function and find its intercepts.

   b. What does each intercept represent?

SEE EXAMPLE 3 | Use intercepts to graph the line described by each equation.

9. $4x - 5y = 20$ 10. $y = 2x + 4$ 11. $\frac{1}{3}x - \frac{1}{4}y = 2$ 12. $-5y + 2x = -10$

PRACTICE AND PROBLEM SOLVING

my.hrw.com

Online Extra Practice

Find the *x*- and *y*-intercepts.

13.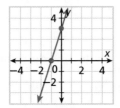

14.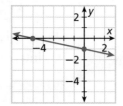

15.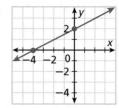

16. $6x + 3y = 12$ 17. $4y - 8 = 2x$ 18. $-2y + x = 2y - 8$

19. $4x + y = 8$ 20. $y - 3x = -15$ 21. $2x + y = 10x - 1$

22. **Environmental Science** A fishing lake was stocked with 300 bass. Each year, the population decreases by 25. The population of bass in the lake after *x* years is represented by the function $f(x) = 300 - 25x$.

   a. Graph the function and find its intercepts.

   b. What does each intercept represent?

23. **Sports** Julie is running a 5-kilometer race. She runs 1 kilometer every 5 minutes. Julie's distance from the finish line after *x* minutes is represented by the function $f(x) = 5 - \frac{1}{5}x$.

   a. Graph the function and find its intercepts.

   b. What does each intercept represent?

Use intercepts to graph the line described by each equation.

24. $4x - 6y = 12$ **25.** $2x + 3y = 18$ **26.** $\frac{1}{2}x - 4y = 4$

27. $y - x = -1$ **28.** $5x + 3y = 15$ **29.** $x - 3y = -1$

30. Biology A bamboo plant is growing 1 foot per day. When you first measure it, it is 4 feet tall.

   a. Write an equation to describe the height y, in feet, of the bamboo plant x days after you measure it.

   b. What is the y-intercept?

   c. What is the meaning of the y-intercept in this problem?

31. Estimation Look at the scatter plot and trend line.

   a. Estimate the x- and y-intercepts.

   b. What is the real-world meaning of each intercept?

32. Personal Finance A bank employee notices an abandoned checking account with a balance of $412. If the bank charges a $4 monthly fee for the account, the function $b = 412 - 4m$ shows the balance b in the account after m months.

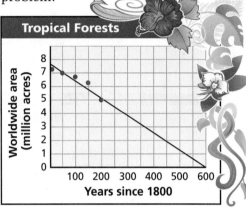

   a. Graph the function and give its domain and range. (*Hint:* The bank will keep charging the monthly fee even after the account is empty.)

   b. Find the intercepts. What does each intercept represent?

   c. When will the bank account balance be 0?

H.O.T. 33. Critical Thinking Complete the following to learn about intercepts and horizontal and vertical lines.

   a. Graph $x = -6$, $x = 1$, and $x = 5$. Find the intercepts.

   b. Graph $y = -3$, $y = 2$, and $y = 7$. Find the intercepts.

   c. Write a rule describing the intercepts of linear equations whose graphs are horizontal and vertical lines.

Match each equation with a graph.

34. $-2x - y = 4$ **35.** $y = 4 - 2x$ **36.** $2y + 4x = 8$ **37.** $4x - 2y = 8$

A.

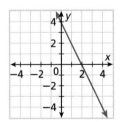

B.

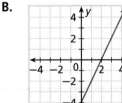

C.

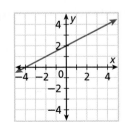

D.

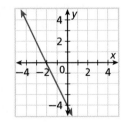

38. Kristyn rode a stationary bike at the gym. She programmed the timer for 20 minutes. The display counted backward to show how much time remained in her workout. It also showed her mileage.

a. What are the intercepts?

b. What do the intercepts represent?

Time Remaining (min)	Distance Covered (mi)
20	0
16	0.35
12	0.70
8	1.05
4	1.40
0	1.75

H.O.T. 39. Write About It Write a real-world problem that could be modeled by a linear function whose *x*-intercept is 5 and whose *y*-intercept is 60.

TEST PREP

40. Which is the *x*-intercept of $-2x = 9y - 18$?

Ⓐ −9 Ⓑ −2 Ⓒ 2 Ⓓ 9

41. Which of the following situations could be represented by the graph?

Ⓕ Jamie owed her uncle $200. Each week for 40 weeks she paid him $5.

Ⓖ Jamie owed her uncle $200. Each week for 5 weeks she paid him $40.

Ⓗ Jamie owed her uncle $40. Each week for 5 weeks she paid him $200.

Ⓙ Jamie owed her uncle $40. Each week for 200 weeks she paid him $5.

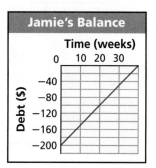

42. Gridded Response What is the *y*-intercept of $60x + 55y = 660$?

CHALLENGE AND EXTEND

Use intercepts to graph the line described by each equation.

43. $\frac{1}{2}x + \frac{1}{5}y = 1$ **44.** $0.5x - 0.2y = 0.75$ **45.** $y = \frac{3}{8}x + 6$

46. For any linear equation $Ax + By = C$, what are the intercepts?

47. Find the intercepts of $22x - 380y = 20,900$. Explain how to use the intercepts to determine appropriate scales for the graph.

FOCUS ON MATHEMATICAL PRACTICES

H.O.T. 48. Reasonableness Teresa wants to graph the equation $\frac{x}{4.8} - \frac{y}{8.8} = 5$. What is a reasonable scale for each axis that would show both intercepts near the edge of the graph?

H.O.T. 49. Analysis Consider the equation $\frac{x}{a} + \frac{y}{b} = 1$.

a. What are the intercepts?

b. Write a linear equation in this form with an *x*-intercept of 15 and a *y*-intercept of 60.

c. Rewrite your answer to part b using integer coefficients.

Victoria Smith/HMH

Mastering *the* Standards

for Mathematical Practice

The topics described in the Standards for Mathematical Content will vary from year to year. However, the *way* in which you learn, study, and think about mathematics will not. The Standards for Mathematical Practice describe skills that you will use in all of your math courses.

Mathematical Practices

1. Make sense of problems and persevere in solving them.
2. Reason abstractly and quantitatively.
3. Construct viable arguments and critique the reasoning of others.
4. Model with mathematics.
5. Use appropriate tools strategically.
6. Attend to precision.
7. Look for and make use of structure.
8. Look for and express regularity in repeated reasoning.

---

① Make sense of problems and persevere in solving them.

Mathematically proficient students start by explaining to themselves the meaning of a problem... They analyze givens, constraints, relationships, and goals. They make conjectures about the form... of the solution and plan a solution pathway...

In your book

Focus on Problem Solving describes a four-step plan for problem solving. The plan is introduced at the beginning of your book, and practice with the plan appears throughout the book.

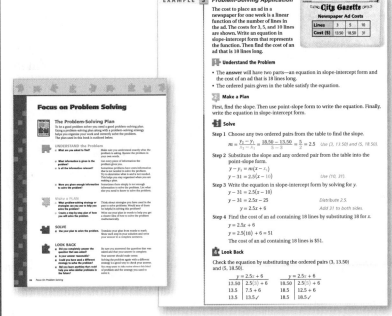

10-3 Rate of Change and Slope

Essential Question: How can you calculate and interpret the rate of change of a linear function?

Objectives
Find rates of change and slopes.

Relate a constant rate of change to the slope of a line.

Vocabulary
rate of change
rise
run
slope

Animated Math

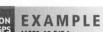

Why learn this?

Rates of change can be used to find how quickly costs have increased.

In 1985, the cost of sending a 1-ounce letter was 22 cents. In 1988, the cost was 25 cents. How fast did the cost change from 1985 to 1988? In other words, at what *rate* did the cost change?

A **rate of change** is a ratio that compares the amount of change in a dependent variable to the amount of change in an independent variable.

$$\text{rate of change} = \frac{\text{change in dependent variable}}{\text{change in independent variable}}$$

COMMON CORE GPS MCC9-12.F.IF.6

EXAMPLE 1 Consumer Application

The table shows the cost of mailing a 1-ounce letter in different years. Find the rate of change in cost for each time interval. During which time interval did the cost increase at the greatest rate?

Year	1988	1990	1991	2004	2008
Cost (¢)	25	25	29	37	42

Step 1 Identify the dependent and independent variables.

dependent: cost   independent: year

Step 2 Find the rates of change.

1988 to 1990 $\dfrac{\text{change in cost}}{\text{change in years}} = \dfrac{25 - 25}{1990 - 1988} = \dfrac{0}{2} = 0$ *0 cents / year*

1990 to 1991 $\dfrac{\text{change in cost}}{\text{change in years}} = \dfrac{29 - 25}{1991 - 1990} = \dfrac{4}{1} = 4$ *4 cents / year*

1991 to 2004 $\dfrac{\text{change in cost}}{\text{change in years}} = \dfrac{37 - 29}{2004 - 1991} = \dfrac{8}{13} \approx 0.62 \approx$ *0.62 cents / year*

2004 to 2008 $\dfrac{\text{change in cost}}{\text{change in years}} = \dfrac{42 - 37}{2008 - 2004} = \dfrac{5}{4} = 1.25$ *1.25 cents / year*

The cost increased at the greatest rate from 1990 to 1991.

Caution!

A rate of change of 1.25 cents per year for a 4-year period means that the *average* change was 1.25 cents per year. The *actual* change in each year may have been different.

CHECK IT OUT!

1. The table shows the balance of a bank account on different days of the month. Find the rate of change for each time interval. During which time interval did the balance decrease at the greatest rate?

Day	1	6	16	22	30
Balance ($)	550	285	210	210	175

EXAMPLE MCC9-12.F.IF.6

2

Finding Rates of Change from a Graph

Graph the data from Example 1 and show the rates of change.

my.hrw.com

Online Video Tutor

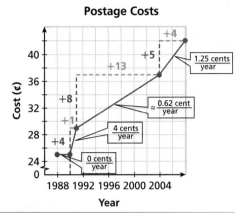

Graph the ordered pairs. The vertical blue segments show the changes in the dependent variable, and the horizontal green segments show the changes in the independent variable.

Notice that the greatest rate of change is represented by the steepest of the red line segments.

Also notice that between 1988 and 1990, when the cost did not change, the red line segment is horizontal.

2. Graph the data from Check It Out Problem 1 and show the rates of change.

If all of the connected segments have the same rate of change, then they all have the same steepness and together form a straight line. The constant rate of change of a nonvertical line is called the *slope* of the line.

Slope of a Line

The **rise** is the difference in the *y*-values of two points on a line.

The **run** is the difference in the *x*-values of two points on a line.

The **slope** of a line is the ratio of rise to run for any two points on the line.

$$\text{slope} = \frac{\text{rise}}{\text{run}} = \frac{\text{change in } y}{\text{change in } x}$$

(Remember that *y* is the **dependent** variable and *x* is the **independent** variable.)

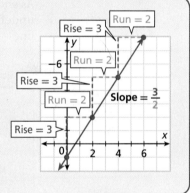

EXAMPLE MCC9-12.F.IF.6

3

Finding Slope

Find the slope of the line.

my.hrw.com

Online Video Tutor

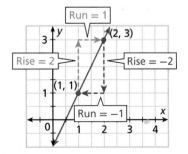

Begin at one point and count vertically to find the rise.

Then count horizontally to the second point to find the run.

It does not matter which point you start with. The slope is the same.

$$\text{slope} = \frac{2}{1} = 2$$

$$\text{slope} = \frac{-2}{-1} = 2$$

3. Find the slope of the line that contains $(0, -3)$ and $(5, -5)$.

EXAMPLE 4
MCC9-12.F.IF.6

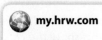

Online Video Tutor

Finding Slopes of Horizontal and Vertical Lines

Find the slope of each line.

A

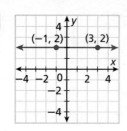

$$\frac{\text{rise}}{\text{run}} = \frac{0}{4} = 0$$

The slope is 0.

B

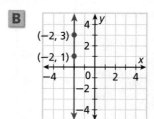

$$\frac{\text{rise}}{\text{run}} = \frac{2}{0}$$ *You cannot divide by 0.*

The slope is undefined.

Find the slope of each line.

4a.

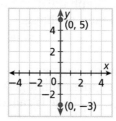

4b.

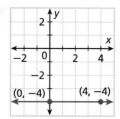

As shown in the previous examples, slope can be positive, negative, zero, or undefined. You can tell which of these is the case by looking at the graph of a line—you do not need to calculate the slope.

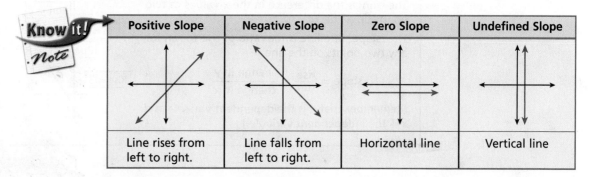

Positive Slope	Negative Slope	Zero Slope	Undefined Slope
Line rises from left to right.	Line falls from left to right.	Horizontal line	Vertical line

Describing Slope

EXAMPLE 5
MCC9-12.F.IF.4

my.hrw.com

Online Video Tutor

Tell whether the slope of each line is positive, negative, zero, or undefined.

A

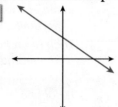

The line falls from left to right.

The slope is negative.

B

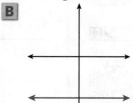

The line is horizontal.

The slope is 0.

Tell whether the slope of each line is positive, negative, zero, or undefined.

5a.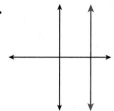

5b.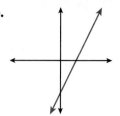

A line's slope is a measure of its steepness. Some lines are steeper than others. As the absolute value of the slope increases, the line becomes steeper.
As the absolute value of the slope decreases, the line becomes less steep.

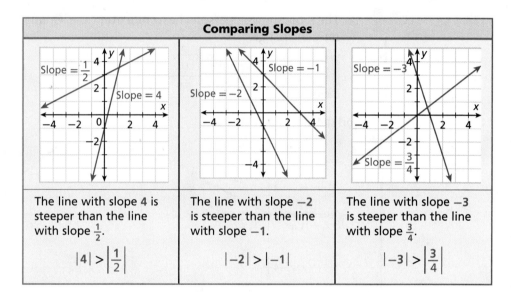

Comparing Slopes		
The line with slope 4 is steeper than the line with slope $\frac{1}{2}$. $$\left|4\right| > \left|\frac{1}{2}\right|$$	The line with slope −2 is steeper than the line with slope −1. $$\left|-2\right| > \left|-1\right|$$	The line with slope −3 is steeper than the line with slope $\frac{3}{4}$. $$\left|-3\right| > \left|\frac{3}{4}\right|$$

MCC.MP.1, MCC.MP.4 MATHEMATICAL PRACTICES

THINK AND DISCUSS

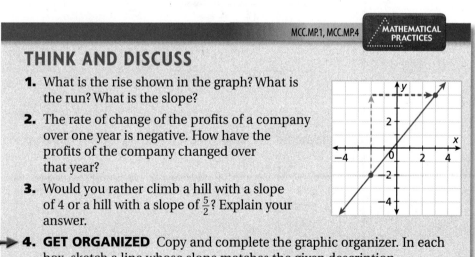

1. What is the rise shown in the graph? What is the run? What is the slope?

2. The rate of change of the profits of a company over one year is negative. How have the profits of the company changed over that year?

3. Would you rather climb a hill with a slope of 4 or a hill with a slope of $\frac{5}{2}$? Explain your answer.

4. GET ORGANIZED Copy and complete the graphic organizer. In each box, sketch a line whose slope matches the given description.

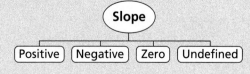

Slope
Positive | Negative | Zero | Undefined

my.hrw.com
Homework Help

GUIDED PRACTICE

1. **Vocabulary** The *slope* of any nonvertical line is ___?___. (*positive* or *constant*)

SEE EXAMPLE 1

2. The table shows the volume of gasoline in a gas tank at different times. Find the rate of change for each time interval. During which time interval did the volume decrease at the greatest rate?

Time (h)	0	1	3	6	7
Volume (gal)	12	9	5	1	1

SEE EXAMPLE 2

3. The table shows a person's heart rate over time. Graph the data and show the rates of change.

Time (min)	0	2	5	7	10
Heart Rate (beats/min)	64	92	146	84	64

Find the slope of each line.

SEE EXAMPLE 3

4.

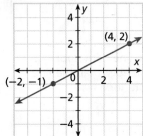

5.

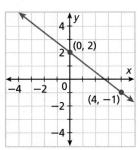

SEE EXAMPLE 4

6.

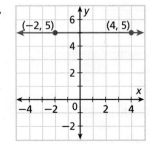

7.

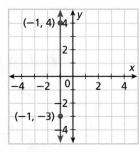

SEE EXAMPLE 5

Tell whether the slope of each line is positive, negative, zero, or undefined.

8.

9.

10.

11.

PRACTICE AND PROBLEM SOLVING

Independent Practice

For Exercises	See Example
12	1
13	2
14–15	3
16–17	4
18–19	5

my.hrw.com

Online Extra Practice

12. The table shows the length of a baby at different ages. Find the rate of change for each time interval. Round your answers to the nearest tenth. During which time interval did the baby have the greatest growth rate?

Age (mo)	3	9	18	26	33
Length (in.)	23.5	27.5	31.6	34.5	36.7

13. The table shows the distance of an elevator from the ground floor at different times. Graph the data and show the rates of change.

Time (s)	0	15	23	30	35
Distance (m)	30	70	0	45	60

Find the slope of each line.

14.

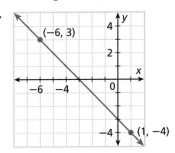

15.

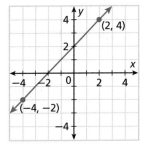

16.

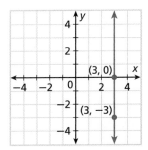

17.

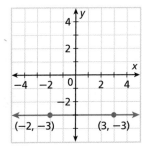

Tell whether the slope of each line is positive, negative, zero, or undefined.

18.

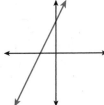

19.

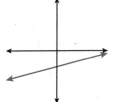

20. Travel The Lookout Mountain Incline Railway in Chattanooga, Tennessee, is the steepest passenger railway in the world. A section of the railway has a slope of about 0.73. In this section, a vertical change of 1 unit corresponds to a horizontal change of what length? Round your answer to the nearest hundredth.

21. Critical Thinking Previously you learned that in a linear function, a constant change in x corresponds to a constant change in y. How is this related to slope?

Travel

The Incline Railway's climb up Lookout Mountain has been called "America's Most Amazing Mile." A round-trip on the railway lasts about 1.5 hours.

© Dave G. Houser/CORBIS

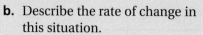

Real-World Connections

22. **a.** The graph shows a relationship between a person's age and his or her estimated maximum heart rate in beats per minute. Find the slope.

    b. Describe the rate of change in this situation.

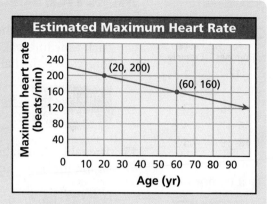

Estimated Maximum Heart Rate

(graph with y-axis "Maximum heart rate (beats/min)" marked 40, 80, 120, 160, 200, 240 and x-axis "Age (yr)" marked 10 20 30 40 50 60 70 80 90, showing points (20, 200) and (60, 160))

23. **Construction** Most staircases in use today have 9-inch treads and $8\frac{1}{2}$-inch risers. What is the slope of a staircase with these measurements?

24. A ladder is leaned against a building. The bottom of the ladder is 9 feet from the building. The top of the ladder is 16 feet above the ground.

    a. Draw a diagram to represent this situation.

    b. What is the slope of the ladder?

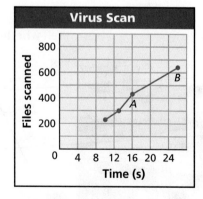

Tread

Riser

H.O.T. 25. **Write About It** Why will the slope of any horizontal line be 0? Why will the slope of any vertical line be undefined?

26. The table shows the distance traveled by a car during a five-hour road trip.

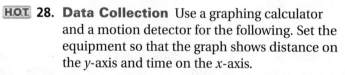

Time (h)	0	1	2	3	4	5
Distance (mi)	0	40	80	80	110	160

    a. Graph the data and show the rates of change.

    b. The rate of change represents the average speed. During which hour was the car's average speed the greatest?

27. **Estimation** The graph shows the number of files scanned by a computer virus detection program over time.

    a. Estimate the coordinates of point *A*.

    b. Estimate the coordinates of point *B*.

    c. Use your answers from parts **a** and **b** to estimate the rate of change (in files per second) between points *A* and *B*.

Virus Scan

(graph with y-axis "Files scanned" marked 200, 400, 600, 800 and x-axis "Time (s)" marked 4 8 12 16 20 24, showing points A and B)

H.O.T. 28. **Data Collection** Use a graphing calculator and a motion detector for the following. Set the equipment so that the graph shows distance on the *y*-axis and time on the *x*-axis.

    a. Experiment with walking in front of the motion detector. How must you walk to graph a straight line? Explain.

    b. Describe what you must do differently to graph a line with a positive slope vs. a line with a negative slope.

    c. How can you graph a line with slope 0? Explain.

29. The slope of which line has the greatest absolute value?

Ⓐ line A   Ⓒ line C

Ⓑ line B   Ⓓ line D

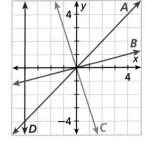

30. For which line is the run equal to 0?

Ⓐ line A   Ⓒ line C

Ⓑ line B   Ⓓ line D

31. Which line has a slope of 4?

Ⓕ

Ⓗ

Ⓖ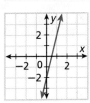

Ⓙ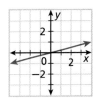

32. Recreation Tara and Jade are hiking up a hill. Each has a different stride. The run for Tara's stride is 32 inches, and the rise is 8 inches. The run for Jade's stride is 36 inches. What is the rise of Jade's stride?

H.O.T. 33. Economics The table shows cost in dollars charged by an electric company for various amounts of energy in kilowatt-hours.

Energy (kWh)	0	200	400	600	1000	2000
Cost ($)	3	3	31	59	115	150

a. Graph the data and show the rates of change.

b. Compare the rates of change for each interval. Are they all the same? Explain.

c. What do the rates of change represent?

d. Describe in words the electric company's billing plan.

H.O.T. 34. Estimation Estimate each slope, then order them from least to greatest.

A   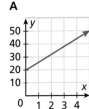

B

C   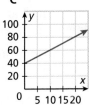

D   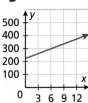

10-3

Algebra TASK

Explore Constant Changes

There are many real-life situations in which the amount of change is constant. In these activities, you will explore what happens when

- a quantity increases by a constant amount.

- a quantity decreases by a constant amount.

Use with Rate of Change and Slope

MATHEMATICAL PRACTICES | **Reason abstractly and quantitatively.**

MCC9-12.F.IF.6 Calculate and interpret the average rate of change of a function (presented symbolically or as a table) over a specified interval. Estimate the rate of change from a graph.

Activity 1

Janice has read 7 books for her summer reading club. She plans to read 2 books each week for the rest of the summer. The table shows the total number of books that Janice will have read after different numbers of weeks have passed.

1 What number is added to the number of books in each row to get the number of books in the next row?

2 What does your answer to Problem 1 represent in Janice's situation? Describe the meaning of the constant change.

3 Graph the ordered pairs from the table. Describe how the points are related.

4 Look again at your answer to Problem 1. Explain how this number affects your graph.

Janice's Summer Reading	
Week	Total Books Read
0	7
1	9
2	11
3	13
4	15
5	17

Try This

At a particular college, a full-time student must take at least 12 credit hours per semester and may take up to 18 credit hours per semester. Tuition costs $200 per credit hour.

1. Copy and complete the table by using the information above.

2. What number is added to the cost in each row to get the cost in the next row?

3. What does your answer to Problem 2 above represent in the situation? Describe the meaning of the constant change.

4. Graph the ordered pairs from the table. Describe how the points are related.

5. Look again at your answer to Problem 2. Explain how this number affects your graph.

6. Compare your graphs from Activity 1 and Problem 4. How are they alike? How are they different?

7. Make a Conjecture Describe the graph of any situation that involves repeated addition of a positive number. Why do you think your description is correct?

Tuition Costs	
Credit Hours	Cost ($)
12	
13	
14	
15	
16	
17	
18	

Activity 2

An airplane is 3000 miles from its destination. The plane is traveling at a rate of 540 miles per hour. The table shows how far the plane is from its destination after various amounts of time have passed.

1 What number is subtracted from the distance in each row to get the distance in the next row?

2 What does your answer to Problem 1 represent in the situation? Describe the meaning of the constant change.

3 Graph the ordered pairs from the table. Describe how the points are related.

4 Look again at your answer to Problem 1. Explain how this number affects your graph.

Airplane's Distance	
Time (h)	Distance to Destination (mi)
0	3000
1	2460
2	1920
3	1380
4	840

Try This

A television game show begins with 20 contestants. Each week, the players vote 2 contestants off the show.

8. Copy and complete the table by using the information above.

9. What number is subtracted from the number of contestants in each row to get the number of contestants in the next row?

10. What does your answer to Problem 9 represent in the situation? Describe the meaning of the constant change.

11. Graph the ordered pairs from the table. Describe how the points are related.

12. Look again at your answer to Problem 9. Explain how this number affects your graph.

13. Compare your graphs from Activity 2 and Problem 11. How are they alike? How are they different?

14. **Make a Conjecture** Describe the graph of any situation that involves repeated subtraction of a positive number. Why do you think your description is correct?

15. Compare your two graphs from Activity 1 with your two graphs from Activity 2. How are they alike? How are they different?

16. **Make a Conjecture** How are graphs of situations involving repeated subtraction different from graphs of situations involving repeated addition? Explain your answer.

Game Show	
Week	Contestants Remaining
0	20
1	▨
2	▨
3	▨
4	▨
5	▨
6	▨

10-4 The Slope Formula

? ***Essential Question:*** How can you calculate and interpret the slope of a linear function?

Objective
Find slope by using the slope formula.

Why learn this?

You can use the slope formula to find how quickly a quantity, such as the amount of water in a reservoir, is changing. (See Example 3.)

In a previous lesson, slope was described as the constant rate of change of a line. You saw how to find the slope of a line by using its graph.

There is also a formula you can use to find the slope of a line, which is usually represented by the letter *m*. To use this formula, you need the coordinates of two different points on the line.

	Slope Formula	
WORDS	**FORMULA**	**EXAMPLE**
The slope of a line is the ratio of the difference in *y*-values to the difference in *x*-values between any two different points on the line.	If (x_1, y_1) and (x_2, y_2) are any two different points on a line, the slope of the line is $m = \dfrac{y_2 - y_1}{x_2 - x_1}$.	If $(2, -3)$ and $(1, 4)$ are two points on a line, the slope of the line is $m = \dfrac{4 - (-3)}{1 - 2} = \dfrac{7}{-1} = -7$.

EXAMPLE 1 MCC9-12.F.IF.6

Finding Slope by Using the Slope Formula

Find the slope of the line that contains $(4, -2)$ and $(-1, 2)$.

my.hrw.com

Online Video Tutor

$m = \dfrac{y_2 - y_1}{x_2 - x_1}$ *Use the slope formula.*

$= \dfrac{2 - (-2)}{-1 - 4}$ *Substitute $(4, -2)$ for (x_1, y_1) and $(-1, 2)$ for (x_2, y_2).*

$= \dfrac{4}{-5}$ *Simplify.*

$= -\dfrac{4}{5}$

The slope of the line that contains $(4, -2)$ and $(-1, 2)$ is $-\dfrac{4}{5}$.

1a. Find the slope of the line that contains $(-2, -2)$ and $(7, -2)$.

1b. Find the slope of the line that contains $(5, -7)$ and $(6, -4)$.

1c. Find the slope of the line that contains $\left(\dfrac{3}{4}, \dfrac{7}{5}\right)$ and $\left(\dfrac{1}{4}, \dfrac{2}{5}\right)$.

Sometimes you are not given two points to use in the formula. You might have to choose two points from a graph or a table.

Online Video Tutor

EXAMPLE 2   Finding Slope from Graphs and Tables

Each graph or table shows a linear relationship. Find the slope.

A

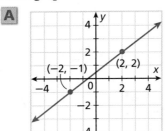

Let $(2, 2)$ be (x_1, y_1) and $(-2, -1)$ be (x_2, y_2).

$$m = \frac{y_2 - y_1}{x_2 - x_1}$$ *Use the slope formula.*

$$= \frac{-1 - 2}{-2 - 2}$$ *Substitute $(2, 2)$ for (x_1, y_1) and $(-2, -1)$ for (x_2, y_2).*

$$= \frac{-3}{-4}$$ *Simplify.*

$$= \frac{3}{4}$$

B

x	2	2	2	2
y	0	1	3	5

Step 1 Choose any two points from the table. Let $(2, 0)$ be (x_1, y_1) and $(2, 3)$ be (x_2, y_2).

Step 2 Use the slope formula.

$$m = \frac{y_2 - y_1}{x_2 - x_1}$$ *Use the slope formula.*

$$= \frac{3 - 0}{2 - 2}$$ *Substitute $(2, 0)$ for (x_1, y_1) and $(2, 3)$ for (x_2, y_2).*

$$= \frac{3}{0}$$ *Simplify.*

The slope is undefined.

Each graph or table shows a linear relationship. Find the slope.

2a.

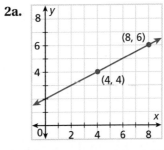

2b.

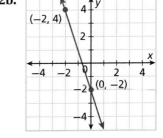

2c.

x	0	2	5	6
y	1	5	11	13

2d.

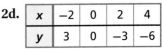

Remember that slope is a rate of change. In real-world problems, finding the slope can give you information about how a quantity is changing.

10-4 The Slope Formula   **265**

EXAMPLE **3**

MCC9-12.F.IF.4

Environmental Science Application

The graph shows how much water is in a reservoir at different times. Find the slope of the line. Then tell what the slope represents.

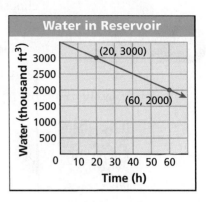

Water in Reservoir

Step 1 Use the slope formula.

$$m = \frac{y_2 - y_1}{x_2 - x_1}$$

$$= \frac{2000 - 3000}{60 - 20}$$

$$= \frac{-1000}{40} = -25$$

Step 2 Tell what the slope represents.

In this situation, y represents **volume of water** and x represents **time**. So slope represents $\frac{\text{change in volume}}{\text{change in time}}$ in units of $\frac{\text{thousands of cubic feet}}{\text{hours}}$.

A slope of -25 means the amount of water in the reservoir is decreasing (negative change) at a rate of 25 thousand cubic feet each hour.

3. The graph shows the height of a plant over a period of days. Find the slope of the line. Then tell what the slope represents.

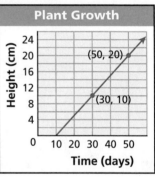

Plant Growth

If you know the equation that describes a line, you can find its slope by using any two ordered-pair solutions. It is often easiest to use the ordered pairs that contain the intercepts.

EXAMPLE **4**

MCC9-12.F.IF.6

Finding Slope from an Equation

Find the slope of the line described by $6x - 5y = 30$.

Step 1 Find the x-intercept.

$6x - 5y = 30$

$6x - 5(0) = 30$ *Let y = 0.*

$6x = 30$

$\dfrac{6x}{6} = \dfrac{30}{6}$

$x = 5$

Step 2 Find the y-intercept.

$6x - 5y = 30$

$6(0) - 5y = 30$ *Let x = 0.*

$-5y = 30$

$\dfrac{-5y}{-5} = \dfrac{30}{-5}$

$y = -6$

Step 3 The line contains $(5, 0)$ and $(0, -6)$. Use the slope formula.

$$m = \frac{y_2 - y_1}{x_2 - x_1} = \frac{-6 - 0}{0 - 5} = \frac{-6}{-5} = \frac{6}{5}$$

4. Find the slope of the line described by $2x + 3y = 12$.

THINK AND DISCUSS

1. The slope of a line is the difference of the ___?___ divided by the difference of the ___?___ for any two points on the line.

2. Two points lie on a line. When you substitute their coordinates into the slope formula, the value of the denominator is 0. Describe this line.

3. **GET ORGANIZED** Copy and complete the graphic organizer. In each box, describe how to find slope using the given method.

Finding Slope — From a graph | From a table | From an equation

10-4 Exercises

my.hrw.com
Homework Help

GUIDED PRACTICE

SEE EXAMPLE 1 Find the slope of the line that contains each pair of points.

1. $(3, 6)$ and $(6, 9)$
2. $(2, 7)$ and $(4, 4)$
3. $(-1, -5)$ and $(-9, -1)$

SEE EXAMPLE 2 Each graph or table shows a linear relationship. Find the slope.

4.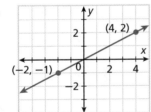

5.

x	y
0	25
2	45
4	65
6	85

SEE EXAMPLE 3 Find the slope of each line. Then tell what the slope represents.

6.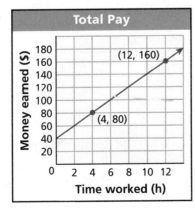

7.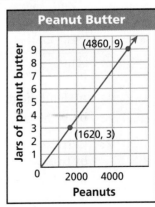

SEE EXAMPLE 4 Find the slope of the line described by each equation.

8. $8x + 2y = 96$
9. $5x = 90 - 9y$
10. $5y = 160 + 9x$

PRACTICE AND PROBLEM SOLVING

Independent Practice

For Exercises	See Example
11–13	1
14–15	2
16–17	3
18–20	4

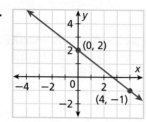

my.hrw.com

Online Extra Practice

Find the slope of the line that contains each pair of points.

11. $(2, 5)$ and $(3, 1)$ **12.** $(-9, -5)$ and $(6, -5)$ **13.** $(3, 4)$ and $(3, -1)$

Each graph or table shows a linear relationship. Find the slope.

14.

x	y
1	18.5
2	22
3	25.5
4	29

15.

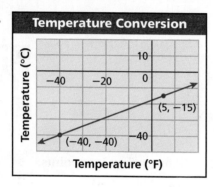

Find the slope of each line. Then tell what the slope represents.

16.

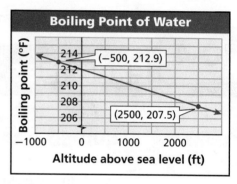

17.

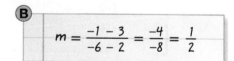

Find the slope of the line described by each equation.

18. $7x + 13y = 91$ **19.** $5y = 130 - 13x$ **20.** $7 - 3y = 9x$

H.O.T. 21. /// **ERROR ANALYSIS** /// Two students found the slope of the line that contains $(-6, 3)$ and $(2, -1)$. Who is incorrect? Explain the error.

Ⓐ
$$m = \frac{-1 - 3}{2 - (-6)} = \frac{-4}{8} = -\frac{1}{2}$$

Ⓑ
$$m = \frac{-1 - 3}{-6 - 2} = \frac{-4}{-8} = \frac{1}{2}$$

H.O.T. 22. Environmental Science The table shows how the number of cricket chirps per minute changes with the air temperature.

Temperature (°F)	40	50	60	70	80	90
Chirps per minute	0	40	80	120	160	200

   a. Find the rates of change.

   b. Is the graph of the data a line? If so, what is the slope? If not, explain why not.

23. Critical Thinking The graph shows the distance traveled by two cars.

   a. Which car is going faster? How much faster?

   b. How are the speeds related to slope?

   c. At what rate is the distance between the cars changing?

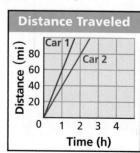

H.O.T. 24. Write About It You are given the coordinates of two points on a line. Describe two different ways to find the slope of that line.

Real-World Connections

25. **a.** One way to estimate your maximum heart rate is to subtract your age from 220. Write a function to describe the relationship between maximum heart rate y and age x.

b. The graph of this function is a line. Find its slope. Then tell what the slope represents.

TEST PREP

26. The equation $2y + 3x = -6$ describes a line with what slope?

(A) $\dfrac{3}{2}$ (B) 0 (C) $\dfrac{1}{2}$ (D) $-\dfrac{3}{2}$

27. A line with slope $-\dfrac{1}{3}$ could pass through which of the following pairs of points?

(F) $\left(0, -\dfrac{1}{3}\right)$ and $(1, 1)$ (H) $(0, 0)$ and $\left(-\dfrac{1}{3}, -\dfrac{1}{3}\right)$

(G) $(-6, 5)$ and $(-3, 4)$ (J) $(5, -6)$ and $(4, 3)$

28. **Gridded Response** Find the slope of the line that contains $(-1, 2)$ and $(5, 5)$.

CHALLENGE AND EXTEND

Find the slope of the line that contains each pair of points.

29. $(a, 0)$ and $(0, b)$ 30. $(2x, y)$ and $(x, 3y)$ 31. (x, y) and $(x + 2, 3 - y)$

Find the value of x so that the points lie on a line with the given slope.

32. $(x, 2)$ and $(-5, 8)$, $m = -1$ 33. $(4, x)$ and $(6, 3x)$, $m = \dfrac{1}{2}$

34. $(1, -3)$ and $(3, x)$, $m = -1$ 35. $(-10, -4)$ and (x, x), $m = \dfrac{1}{7}$

36. A line contains the point $(1, 2)$ and has a slope of $\dfrac{1}{2}$. Use the slope formula to find another point on this line.

37. The points $(-2, 4)$, $(0, 2)$, and $(3, x - 1)$ all lie on the same line. What is the value of x? (*Hint:* Remember that the slope of a line is constant for any two points on the line.)

FOCUS ON MATHEMATICAL PRACTICES

H.O.T. 38. **Error Analysis** Kayla incorrectly estimated that the slope of a line segment connecting the points $(3, 21)$ and $(45, 61)$ is slightly greater than 1. Name one way that she could have made this mistake.

H.O.T. 39. **Problem Solving** A bicyclist starts traveling back to town at a speed of 16 miles per hour from a rest stop 56 miles away. Write ordered pairs that relate her hours traveled to her distance from town after 1 hour of biking and after 3 hours of biking. Then, find the slope between the two points. What does the sign of the slope mean in this context?

Ready to Go On?

my.hrw.com
Assessment and Intervention

✅ 10-1 Identifying Linear Functions

Tell whether the given ordered pairs satisfy a linear function. Explain.

1.

x	−2	−1	0	1	2
y	1	0	1	4	9

2. $\{(-3, 8), (-2, 6), (-1, 4), (0, 2), (1, 0)\}$

✅ 10-2 Using Intercepts

Use intercepts to graph the line described by each equation.

3. $2x - 4y = 16$

4. $-3y + 6x = -18$

5. $y = -3x + 3$

✅ 10-3 Rate of Change and Slope

6. The chart gives the amount of water in a rain gauge in inches at various times. Graph the data and show the rates of change.

Time (h)	1	2	3	4	5
Rain (in.)	0.2	0.4	0.7	0.8	1.0

7. Find the slope of the line graphed below.

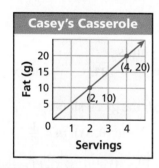

✅ 10-4 The Slope Formula

Find the slope of each line. Then tell what the slope represents.

8.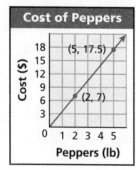

9.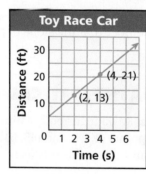

10.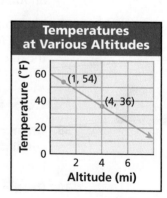

PARCC Assessment Readiness

Selected Response

1. Tell whether the set of ordered pairs $\{(1, 1),(3, 5), (5, 9), (7, 13)\}$ is a linear function. Explain.

  (A) No; there is a constant change in x that corresponds to a constant change in y.

  (B) Yes; there is no constant change in x that corresponds to a constant change in y.

  (C) No; there is no constant change in x that corresponds to a constant change in y.

  (D) Yes; there is a constant change in x that corresponds to a constant change in y.

2. This table shows the number of swimmers in the ocean at a given time. Find the rate of change for each time period. During which period did the number of swimmers increase at the fastest rate?

Time	10:30 am	12:30 pm	1:30 pm	3:30 pm	5:30 pm
Number of swimmers	41	55	64	70	80

  (F) Between 10:30 and 12:30: 7 $\frac{\text{swimmers}}{\text{hour}}$

  (G) Between 3:30 and 5:30: 5 $\frac{\text{swimmers}}{\text{hour}}$

  (H) Between 12:30 and 1:30: 9 $\frac{\text{swimmers}}{\text{hour}}$

  (J) Between 1:30 and 3:30: 3 $\frac{\text{swimmers}}{\text{hour}}$

3. Identify whether each graph represents a function. If the graph does represent a function, is the function linear?

Graph A

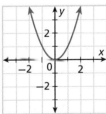

Graph B

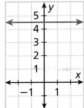

Graph C

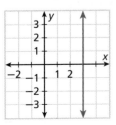

  (A) Graph A: not a linear function
      Graph B: not a function
      Graph C: not a function

  (B) Graph A: not a function
      Graph B: not a function
      Graph C: linear function

  (C) Graph A: not a linear function
      Graph B: linear function
      Graph C: linear function

  (D) Graph A: not a linear function
      Graph B: linear function
      Graph C: not a function

4. Find the x- and y-intercepts of $-x + 2y = 8$.

  (F) x-intercept: -8, y-intercept: 4

  (G) x-intercept: -8, y-intercept: 3

  (H) x-intercept: -11, y-intercept: 4

  (J) x-intercept: -11, y-intercept: 3

5. Find the slope of the line that contains $(1, 6)$ and $(10, -9)$.

  (A) $-\frac{3}{11}$ (C) $-\frac{5}{3}$

  (B) $-\frac{3}{5}$ (D) $-\frac{11}{3}$

6. Find the x- and y-intercepts.

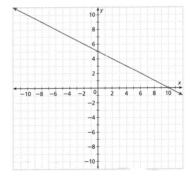

  (F) x-intercept: 10, y-intercept: 5

  (G) x-intercept: 5, y-intercept: 10

  (H) x-intercept: -10, y-intercept: 5

  (J) x-intercept: 10, y-intercept: -5

Mini-Task

7. Find the value of a such that the points $(4, a)$ and $(8, 3a)$ lie on a line with slope $m = \frac{1}{3}$.

11 Graphs and Equations of Linear Functions

COMMON CORE GPS

Contents

MATHEMATICAL PRACTICES

The Common Core Georgia Performance Standards for Mathematical Practice describe varieties of expertise that all students should seek to develop. Opportunities to develop these practices are integrated throughout this program.

1 Make sense of problems and persevere in solving them.

2 Reason abstractly and quantitatively.

3 Construct viable arguments and critique the reasoning of others.

4 Model with mathematics.

5 Use appropriate tools strategically.

6 Attend to precision.

7 Look for and make use of structure.

8 Look for and express regularity in repeated reasoning.

Unpacking the Standards

Understanding the standards and the vocabulary terms in the standards will help you know exactly what you are expected to learn in this chapter.

 MCC9-12.A.CED.2

Create equations in two ... variables to represent relationships between quantities; graph equations on coordinate axes with labels and scales.

Key Vocabulary

equation (ecuación)
A mathematical statement that two expressions are equivalent.

What It Means For You

You can represent mathematical relationships with words, equations, tables, and graphs.

EXAMPLE

Membership costs $150 plus $75 per month.

$$y = 75x + 150$$

Months	0	1	2	3	4
Cost ($)	150	225	300	375	450

Gym Membership

 MCC9-12.F.BF.3

Identify the effect on the graph of replacing $f(x)$ by $f(x) + k$, $k\,f(x)$, $f(kx)$, and $f(x + k)$ for specific values of k (both positive and negative); ...

Key Vocabulary

function notation (notación de función)
If x is the independent variable and y is the dependent variable, then the function notation for y is $f(x)$, read "f of x," where f names the function.

What It Means For You

You can change a function by adding or multiplying by a constant. The result will be a new function that is a transformation of the original function.

EXAMPLE **Vertical translations of the function $f(x) = x$**

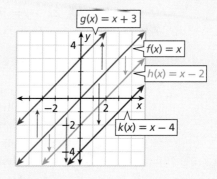

Direct Variation

Essential Question: How can you identify, write, and graph direct variation equations?

Objective
Identify, write, and graph direct variation.

Vocabulary
direct variation
constant of variation

Who uses this?
Chefs can use direct variation to determine ingredients needed for a certain number of servings.

A recipe for paella calls for 1 cup of rice to make 5 servings. In other words, a chef needs 1 cup of rice for every 5 servings.

Rice (c) x	1	2	3	4
Servings y	5	10	15	20

Paella is a rice dish that originated in Valencia, Spain.

The equation $y = 5x$ describes this relationship. In this relationship, the number of servings *varies directly* with the number of cups of rice.

A **direct variation** is a special type of linear relationship that can be written in the form $y = kx$, where k is a nonzero constant called the **constant of variation**.

 **COMMON CORE GPS**
 EXAMPLE
MCC9-12.F.LE.1b

1

 my.hrw.com

Online Video Tutor

Identifying Direct Variations from Equations

Tell whether each equation represents a direct variation. If so, identify the constant of variation.

A $y = 4x$

This equation represents a direct variation because it is in the form $y = kx$. The constant of variation is 4.

B $-3x + 5y = 0$

$$
\begin{array}{ll}
-3x + 5y = 0 & \textit{Solve the equation for y.} \\
\underline{+3x \qquad +3x} & \textit{Since −3x is added to 5y, add 3x to both sides.} \\
5y = 3x & \\
\dfrac{5y}{5} = \dfrac{3x}{5} & \textit{Since y is multiplied by 5, divide both sides by 5.} \\
y = \dfrac{3}{5}x &
\end{array}
$$

This equation represents a direct variation because it can be written in the form $y = kx$. The constant of variation is $\frac{3}{5}$.

C $2x + y = 10$

$$
\begin{array}{ll}
2x + y = 10 & \textit{Solve the equation for y.} \\
\underline{-2x \qquad -2x} & \textit{Since 2x is added to y, subtract 2x from both sides.} \\
y = -2x + 10 &
\end{array}
$$

This equation does not represent a direct variation because it cannot be written in the form $y = kx$.

 CHECK IT OUT! Tell whether each equation represents a direct variation. If so, identify the constant of variation.

1a. $3y = 4x + 1$ **1b.** $3x = -4y$ **1c.** $y + 3x = 0$

What happens if you solve $y = kx$ for k?

$$y = kx$$

$$\frac{y}{x} = \frac{kx}{x}$$ *Divide both sides by x (x ≠ 0).*

$$\frac{y}{x} = k$$

So, in a direct variation, the ratio $\frac{y}{x}$ is equal to the constant of variation. Another way to identify a direct variation is to check whether $\frac{y}{x}$ is the same for each ordered pair (except where $x = 0$).

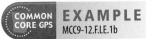

COMMON CORE GPS
MCC9-12.F.LE.1b

my.hrw.com

Online Video Tutor

EXAMPLE 2   Identifying Direct Variations from Ordered Pairs

Tell whether each relationship is a direct variation. Explain.

A

x	1	3	5
y	6	18	30

Method 1 Write an equation.

$y = 6x$ *Each y-value is 6 times the corresponding x-value.*

This is a direct variation because it can be written as $y = kx$, where $k = 6$.

Method 2 Find $\frac{y}{x}$ for each ordered pair.

$$\frac{6}{1} = 6 \qquad \frac{18}{3} = 6 \qquad \frac{30}{5} = 6$$

This is a direct variation because $\frac{y}{x}$ is the same for each ordered pair.

B

x	2	4	8
y	−2	0	4

Method 1 Write an equation.

$y = x - 4$ *Each y-value is 4 less than the corresponding x-value.*

This is not a direct variation because it cannot be written as $y = kx$.

Method 2 Find $\frac{y}{x}$ for each ordered pair.

$$\frac{-2}{2} = -1 \qquad \frac{0}{4} = 0 \qquad \frac{4}{8} = \frac{1}{2}$$

This is not a direct variation because $\frac{y}{x}$ is not the same for all ordered pairs.

 CHECK IT OUT!   **Tell whether each relationship is a direct variation. Explain.**

2a.

x	y
−3	0
1	3
3	6

2b.

x	y
2.5	−10
5	−20
7.5	−30

2c.

x	y
−2	5
1	3
4	1

If you know one ordered pair that satisfies a direct variation, you can write the equation. You can also find other ordered pairs that satisfy the direct variation.

EXAMPLE **3**
MCC9-12.A.CED.2

Writing and Solving Direct Variation Equations

The value of y varies directly with x, and $y = 6$ when $x = 12$. Find y when $x = 27$.

Method 1 Find the value of k and then write the equation.

$y = kx$	*Write the equation for a direct variation.*
$6 = k(12)$	*Substitute 6 for y and 12 for x. Solve for k.*
$\dfrac{1}{2} = k$	*Since k is multiplied by 12, divide both sides by 12.*

The equation is $y = \dfrac{1}{2}x$. When $x = 27$, $y = \dfrac{1}{2}(27) = 13.5$.

Method 2 Use a proportion.

$\dfrac{6}{12} \times \dfrac{y}{27}$	*In a direct variation, $\dfrac{y}{x}$ is the same for all values of x and y.*
$12y = 162$	*Use cross products.*
$y = 13.5$	*Since y is multiplied by 12, divide both sides by 12.*

 3. The value of y varies directly with x, and $y = 4.5$ when $x = 0.5$. Find y when $x = 10$.

EXAMPLE **4**
MCC9-12.A.CED.2

Graphing Direct Variations

The three-toed sloth is an extremely slow animal. On the ground, it travels at a speed of about 6 feet per minute. Write a direct variation equation for the distance y a sloth will travel in x minutes. Then graph.

Step 1 Write a direct variation equation.

distance	=	6 feet per minute	times	number of minutes
y	=	6	•	x

Step 2 Choose values of x and generate ordered pairs.

x	$y = 6x$	(x, y)
0	$y = 6(0) = 0$	$(0, 0)$
1	$y = 6(1) = 6$	$(1, 6)$
2	$y = 6(2) = 12$	$(2, 12)$

Step 3 Graph the points and connect.

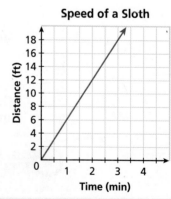

Speed of a Sloth

 4. The perimeter y of a square varies directly with its side length x. Write a direct variation equation for this relationship. Then graph.

Look at the graph in Example 4. It passes through $(0, 0)$ and has a slope of 6. The graph of any direct variation $y = kx$

- is a line through $(0, 0)$.   • has a slope of k.

MATHEMATICAL PRACTICES

THINK AND DISCUSS

1. How do you know that a direct variation is linear?

2. How does the graph of a direct variation differ from the graphs of other types of linear relationships?

3. **GET ORGANIZED** Copy and complete the graphic organizer. In each box, describe how you can use the given information to identify a direct variation.

Know it!
Note

Recognizing a Direct Variation		
From an Equation	From Ordered Pairs	From a Graph

11-1 Exercises

my.hrw.com
Homework Help

GUIDED PRACTICE

1. **Vocabulary** If x varies directly with y, then the relationship between the two variables is said to be a _____?_____. (*direct variation* or *constant of variation*)

SEE EXAMPLE 1 Tell whether each equation represents a direct variation. If so, identify the constant of variation.

2. $y = 4x + 9$ 3. $2y = -8x$ 4. $x + y = 0$

SEE EXAMPLE 2 Tell whether each relationship is a direct variation. Explain.

5.

x	10	5	2
y	12	7	4

6.

x	3	−1	−4
y	−6	2	8

SEE EXAMPLE 3

7. The value of y varies directly with x, and $y = -3$ when $x = 1$. Find y when $x = -6$.

8. The value of y varies directly with x, and $y = 6$ when $x = 18$. Find y when $x = 12$.

SEE EXAMPLE 4

9. **Wages** Cameron earns $7 per hour at her after-school job. The total amount of her paycheck varies directly with the amount of time she works. Write a direct variation equation for the amount of money y that she earns for working x hours. Then graph.

PRACTICE AND PROBLEM SOLVING

Tell whether each equation represents a direct variation. If so, identify the constant of variation.

10. $y = \frac{1}{6}x$ 11. $4y = x$ 12. $x = 2y - 12$

Tell whether each relationship is a direct variation. Explain.

13.

x	6	9	17
y	13.2	19.8	37.4

14.

x	−6	3	12
y	4	−2	−8

Independent Practice	
For Exercises	**See Example**
10–12	1
13–14	2
15–16	3
17	4

my.hrw.com

Online Extra Practice

15. The value of y varies directly with x, and $y = 8$ when $x = -32$. Find y when $x = 64$.

16. The value of y varies directly with x, and $y = \frac{1}{2}$ when $x = 3$. Find y when $x = 1$.

17. While on his way to school, Norman saw that the cost of gasoline was $2.50 per gallon. Write a direct variation equation to describe the cost y of x gallons of gas. Then graph.

Tell whether each relationship is a direct variation. Explain your answer.

18. The equation $-15x + 4y = 0$ relates the length of a videotape in inches x to its approximate playing time in seconds y.

19. The equation $y - 2.00x = 2.50$ relates the cost y of a taxicab ride to distance x of the cab ride in miles.

Each ordered pair is a solution of a direct variation. Write the equation of direct variation. Then graph your equation and show that the slope of the line is equal to the constant of variation.

20. $(2, 10)$ **21.** $(-3, 9)$ **22.** $(8, 2)$ **23.** $(1.5, 6)$

24. $(7, 21)$ **25.** $(1, 2)$ **26.** $(2, -16)$ **27.** $\left(\frac{1}{7}, 1\right)$

28. $(-2, 9)$ **29.** $(9, -2)$ **30.** $(4, 6)$ **31.** $(3, 4)$

32. $(5, 1)$ **33.** $(1, -6)$ **34.** $\left(-1, \frac{1}{2}\right)$ **35.** $(7, 2)$

Astronomy

36. **Astronomy** Weight varies directly with gravity. A Mars lander weighed 767 pounds on Earth but only 291 pounds on Mars. Its accompanying Mars rover weighed 155 pounds on Mars. How much did it weigh on Earth? Round your answer to the nearest pound.

The Mars rover *Spirit* landed on Mars in January 2004 and immediately began sending photos of the planet's surface back to Earth.

37. **Environment** Mischa bought an energy-efficient washing machine. She will save about 15 gallons of water per wash load.

    a. Write an equation of direct variation to describe how many gallons of water y Mischa saves for x loads of laundry she washes.

    b. Graph your direct variation from part **a.** Is every point on the graph a solution in this situation? Why or why not?

    c. If Mischa does 2 loads of laundry per week, how many gallons of water will she have saved at the end of a year?

H.O.T. **38.** **Critical Thinking** If you double an x-value in a direct variation, will the corresponding y-value double? Explain.

H.O.T. **39.** **Write About It** In a direct variation $y = kx$, k is sometimes called the "constant of proportionality." How are proportions related to direct variations?

Real-World Connections

40. Rhea exercised on a treadmill at the gym. When she was finished, the display showed that she had walked at an average speed of 3 miles per hour.

    a. Write an equation that gives the number of miles y that Rhea would cover in x hours if she walked at this speed.

    b. Explain why this is a direct variation and find the value of k. What does this value represent in Rhea's situation?

TEST PREP

41. Which equation does NOT represent a direct variation?

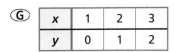

Ⓐ $y = \frac{1}{3}x$ Ⓑ $y = -2x$ Ⓒ $y = 4x + 1$ Ⓓ $6x - y = 0$

42. Identify which set of data represents a direct variation.

Ⓕ
x	1	2	3
y	1	2	3

Ⓗ
x	1	2	3
y	3	5	7

Ⓖ
x	1	2	3
y	0	1	2

Ⓙ
x	1	2	3
y	3	4	5

43. Two yards of fabric cost $13, and 5 yards of fabric cost $32.50. Which equation relates the cost of the fabric c to its length ℓ?

Ⓐ $c = 2.6\ell$ Ⓑ $c = 6.5\ell$ Ⓒ $c = 13\ell$ Ⓓ $c = 32.5\ell$

44. Gridded Response A car is traveling at a constant speed. After 3 hours, the car has traveled 180 miles. If the car continues to travel at the same constant speed, how many hours will it take to travel a total of 270 miles?

CHALLENGE AND EXTEND

45. Transportation The function $y = 20x$ gives the number of miles y that a sport-utility vehicle (SUV) can travel on x gallons of gas. The function $y = 60x$ gives the number of miles y that a hybrid car can travel on x gallons of gas.

   a. If you drive 120 miles, how much gas will you save by driving the hybrid instead of the SUV?

   b. Graph both functions on the same coordinate plane. Will the lines ever meet other than at the origin? Explain.

   c. What if...? Shannon drives 15,000 miles in one year. How many gallons of gas will she use if she drives the SUV? the hybrid?

46. Suppose the equation $ax + by = c$, where a, b, and c are real numbers, describes a direct variation. What do you know about the value of c?

FOCUS ON MATHEMATICAL PRACTICES

H.O.T. **47. Error Analysis** Jon is on the 30th floor of a building where each floor is 10 feet high. The building next door has floors that are 12 feet high. Jon sets up the direct variation equation $30 = 10k$, solves for k, and calculates that the floor across from him in the other building is the 36th floor. What error did Jon make? What is the correct answer?

H.O.T. **48. Communication** Write three different direct variation equations that have 0.75 as the constant of variation. Use different coefficients and variables in each equation and identify each independent variable.

H.O.T. **49. Problem Solving** The function $p = 10 + 12t$ gives the cost of renting a kayak at Boatwerks for t hours, and $p = 10 + 7t$ gives the cost of renting a paddleboard. Subtract $10 + 7t$ from $10 + 12t$ to create a new function.

   a. What does the new function represent?

   b. Which, if any, of the three functions represents direct variation?

11-2 # Slope-Intercept Form

Essential Question: How can you write a linear equation in slope-intercept form and use that form to draw its graph?

Objectives
Write a linear equation in slope-intercept form.

Graph a line using slope-intercept form.

Who uses this?
Consumers can use slope-intercept form to model and calculate costs, such as the cost of renting a moving van. (See Example 4.)

You have seen that you can graph a line if you know two points on the line. Another way is to use the slope of the line and the point that contains the y-intercept.

COMMON CORE GPS **EXAMPLE** MCC9-12.F.IF.7a

1

 my.hrw.com

Online Video Tutor

Graphing by Using Slope and y-intercept

Graph the line with slope -2 and y-intercept 4.

Step 1 The y-intercept is 4, so the line contains $(0, 4)$. Plot $(0, 4)$.

Step 2 Slope $= \dfrac{\text{change in } y}{\text{change in } x} = \dfrac{-2}{1}$

Count **2 units down** and **1 unit right** from $(0, 4)$ and plot another point.

Step 3 Draw the line through the two points.

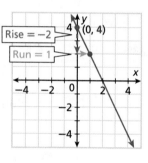

Writing Math

Any integer can be written as a fraction with 1 in the denominator.

$$-2 = \frac{-2}{1}$$

CHECK IT OUT! **Graph each line given the slope and y-intercept.**

1a. slope $= 2$, y-intercept $= -3$ **1b.** slope $= -\dfrac{2}{3}$, y-intercept $= 1$

If you know the slope of a line and the y-intercept, you can write an equation that describes the line.

Step 1 If a line has slope 2 and the y-intercept is 3, then $m = 2$ and $(0, 3)$ is on the line. Substitute these values into the slope formula.

Slope formula $\rightarrow$ $m = \dfrac{y_2 - y_1}{x_2 - x_1}$ $2 = \dfrac{y - 3}{x - 0}$ $\leftarrow$ Since you don't know (x_2, y_2), use (x, y).

Step 2 Solve for y: $2 = \dfrac{y - 3}{x - 0}$

$2 = \dfrac{y - 3}{x}$ *Simplify the denominator.*

$2 \cdot x = \left(\dfrac{y - 3}{x}\right) \cdot x$ *Multiply both sides by x.*

$2x = y - 3$

$\underline{+3 \qquad +3}$ *Add 3 to both sides.*

$2x + 3 = y$, or $y = 2x + 3$

Slope-Intercept Form of a Linear Equation

If a line has **slope** m and the **y-intercept** is b, then the line is described by the equation $y = mx + b$.

Any linear equation can be written in slope-intercept form by solving for y and simplifying. In this form, you can immediately see the slope and y-intercept. Also, you can quickly graph a line when the equation is written in slope-intercept form.

EXAMPLE **2**
MCC9-12.A.CED.2

my.hrw.com

Online Video Tutor

Animated Math

Writing Linear Equations in Slope-Intercept Form

Write the equation that describes each line in slope-intercept form.

A slope $= \dfrac{1}{3}$, y-intercept $= 6$

$y = mx + b$ *Substitute the given*
values for m and b.
$y = \dfrac{1}{3}x + 6$ *Simplify if necessary.*

B slope $= 0$, y-intercept $= -5$

$y = mx + b$

$y = 0x + (-5)$

$y = -5$

C

Step 1 Find the y-intercept. The graph crosses the y-axis at $(0, 1)$, so $b = 1$.

Step 2 Find the slope. The line contains the points $(0, 1)$ and $(1, 3)$.

$m = \dfrac{y_2 - y_1}{x_2 - x_1}$ *Use the slope formula.*

$m = \dfrac{3 - 1}{1 - 0} = \dfrac{2}{1} = 2$ *Substitute (0, 1) for (x_1, y_1)*
and (1, 3) for (x_2, y_2).

Step 3 Write the equation.

$y = mx + b$ *Write the slope-intercept form.*

$y = 2x + 1$ *Substitute 2 for m and 1 for b.*

D slope $= 4$, $(2, 5)$ is on the line

Step 1 Find the y-intercept.

$y = mx + b$ *Write the slope-intercept form.*

$5 = 4(2) + b$ *Substitute 4 for m, 2 for x, and 5 for y.*

$5 = 8 + b$ *Solve for b. Since 8 is added to b, subtract 8 from both*
sides to undo the addition.

$\underline{-8 -8}$

$-3 = b$

Step 2 Write the equation.

$y = mx + b$ *Write the slope-intercept form.*

$y = 4x + (-3)$ *Substitute 4 for m and −3 for b.*

$y = 4x - 3$

Write the equation that describes each line in slope-intercept form.

2a. slope $= -12$, y-intercept $= -\dfrac{1}{2}$

2b. slope $= 1$, y-intercept $= 0$

2c. slope $= 8$, $(-3, 1)$ is on the line.

EXAMPLE 3
MCC9-12.F.IF.7a

Using Slope-Intercept Form to Graph

Write each equation in slope-intercept form. Then graph the line described by the equation.

A $y = 4x - 3$

$y = 4x - 3$ is in the form $y = mx + b$.

slope: $m = 4 = \dfrac{4}{1}$

y-intercept: $b = -3$

Step 1 Plot $(0, -3)$.

Step 2 Count 4 units up and 1 unit right and plot another point.

Step 3 Draw the line connecting the two points.

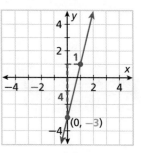

B $y = -\dfrac{2}{3}x + 2$

$y = -\dfrac{2}{3}x + 2$ is in the form $y = mx + b$.

slope: $m = -\dfrac{2}{3} = \dfrac{-2}{3}$

y-intercept: $b = 2$

Step 1 Plot $(0, 2)$

Step 2 Count 2 units down and 3 units right and plot another point.

Step 3 Draw the line connecting the two points.

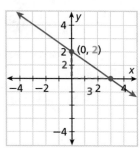

C $3x + 2y = 8$

Step 1 Write the equation in slope-intercept form by solving for y.

$$3x + 2y = 8$$
$$\underline{-3x \qquad\qquad -3x}$$
Subtract 3x from both sides.
$$2y = 8 - 3x$$
$$\dfrac{2y}{2} = \dfrac{8 - 3x}{2}$$
Since y is multiplied by 2, divide both sides by 2.
$$y = 4 - \dfrac{3}{2}x \qquad \dfrac{3x}{2} = \dfrac{3}{2}x$$
$$y = -\dfrac{3}{2}x + 4$$
Write the equation in the form y = mx + b.

Step 2 Graph the line.

$y = -\dfrac{3}{2}x + 4$ is in the form $y = mx + b$.

slope: $m = -\dfrac{3}{2} = \dfrac{-3}{2}$

y-intercept: $b = 4$

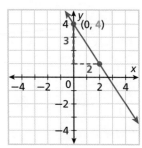

• Plot $(0, 4)$.

• Then count 3 units down and 2 units right and plot another point.

• Draw the line connecting the two points.

Helpful Hint

To divide $(8 - 3x)$ by 2, you can multiply by $\dfrac{1}{2}$ and use the Distributive Property.

$\dfrac{8 - 3x}{2} = \dfrac{1}{2}(8 - 3x)$

$= \dfrac{1}{2}(8) + \dfrac{1}{2}(-3x)$

$= 4 - \dfrac{3}{2}x$

Write each equation in slope-intercept form. Then graph the line described by the equation.

3a. $y = \dfrac{2}{3}x$ **3b.** $6x + 2y = 10$ **3c.** $y = -4$

EXAMPLE **4**
MCC9-12.F.BF.1

Consumer Application

To rent a van, a moving company charges $30.00 plus $0.50 per mile. The cost as a function of the number of miles driven is shown in the graph.

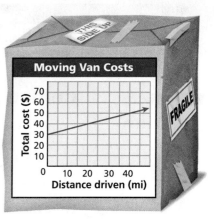

a. Write an equation that represents the cost as a function of the number of miles.

Cost	is	$0.50 per mile	times	miles	plus	$30.00
y	=	0.5	•	x	+	30

An equation is $y = 0.5x + 30$.

b. Identify the slope and y-intercept and describe their meanings.

The y-intercept is 30. This is the cost for 0 miles, or the initial fee of $30.00.

The slope is 0.5. This is the rate of change of the cost: $0.50 per mile.

c. Find the cost of the van for 150 miles.

$y = 0.5x + 30$

$\quad = 0.5(150) + 30 = 105$ *Substitute 150 for x in the equation.*

The cost of the van for 150 miles is $105.

4. A caterer charges a $200 fee plus $18 per person served. The cost as a function of the number of guests is shown in the graph.

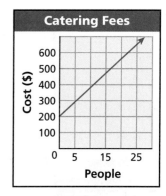

   a. Write an equation that represents the cost as a function of the number of guests.

   b. Identify the slope and y-intercept and describe their meanings.

   c. Find the cost of catering an event for 200 guests.

THINK AND DISCUSS

1. If a linear function has a y-intercept of b, at what point does its graph cross the y-axis?

2. Where does the line described by $y = 4.395x - 23.75$ cross the y-axis?

3. GET ORGANIZED Copy and complete the graphic organizer.

> **Graphing the Line Described by $y = mx + b$**
>
> | 1. Plot the point __?__ . | → | 2. Find a second point on the line by __?__ . | → | 3. Draw __?__ . |

GUIDED PRACTICE

SEE EXAMPLE 1 Graph each line given the slope and *y*-intercept.

1. slope = $\frac{1}{3}$, *y*-intercept = −3

2. slope = 0.5, *y*-intercept = 3.5

3. slope = 5, *y*-intercept = −1

4. slope = −2, *y*-intercept = 2

SEE EXAMPLE 2 Write the equation that describes each line in slope-intercept form.

5.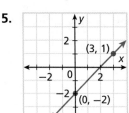

6. slope = 8, *y*-intercept = 2

7. slope = 0, *y*-intercept = −3

8. slope = 5, (2, 7) is on the line.

9. slope = −2, (1, −3) is on the line.

SEE EXAMPLE 3 Write each equation in slope-intercept form. Then graph the line described by the equation.

10. $y = \frac{2}{5}x - 6$

11. $3x - y = 1$

12. $2x + y = 4$

SEE EXAMPLE 4

13. Helen is in a bicycle race. She has already biked 10 miles and is now biking at a rate of 18 miles per hour. Her distance as a function of time is shown in the graph.

   a. Write an equation that represents the distance Helen has biked as a function of time.

   b. Identify the slope and *y*-intercept and describe their meanings.

   c. How far will Helen have biked after 2 hours?

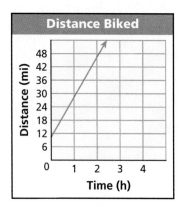

Distance Biked

PRACTICE AND PROBLEM SOLVING

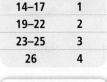

Independent Practice

For Exercises	See Example
14–17	1
19–22	2
23–25	3
26	4

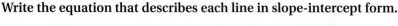

Graph each line given the slope and *y*-intercept.

14. slope = $\frac{1}{4}$, *y*-intercept = 7

15. slope = −6, *y*-intercept = −3

16. slope = 1, *y*-intercept = −4

17. slope = $-\frac{4}{5}$, *y*-intercept = 6

Write the equation that describes each line in slope-intercept form.

18.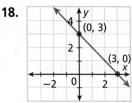

19. slope = 5, *y*-intercept = −9

20. slope = $-\frac{2}{3}$, *y*-intercept = 2

21. slope = $-\frac{1}{2}$, $(6, 4)$ is on the line.

22. slope = 0, $(6, -8)$ is on the line.

my.hrw.com

Online Extra Practice

Write each equation in slope-intercept form. Then graph the line described by the equation.

23. $-\frac{1}{2}x + y = 4$

24. $\frac{2}{3}x + y = 2$

25. $2x + y = 8$

26. Fitness Pauline's health club has an enrollment fee of $175 and costs $35 per month. Total cost as a function of number of membership months is shown in the graph.

    a. Write an equation that represents the total cost as a function of months.

    b. Identify the slope and y-intercept and describe their meanings.

    c. Find the cost of one year of membership.

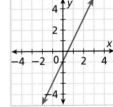

Health Club Membership Costs

27. A company rents video games. The table shows the linear relationship between the number of games a customer can rent at one time and the monthly cost of the service.

    a. Graph the relationship.

    b. Write an equation that represents the monthly cost as a function of games rented at one time.

Games Rented at One Time	1	2	3
Monthly Cost ($)	14	18	22

H.O.T. Critical Thinking Tell whether each situation is possible or impossible. If possible, draw a sketch of the graphs. If impossible, explain.

28. Two different lines have the same slope.

29. Two different linear functions have the same y-intercept.

30. Two intersecting lines have the same slope.

31. A linear function does not have a y-intercept.

Match each equation with its corresponding graph.

32.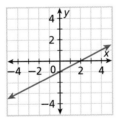

33.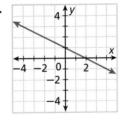

34.

A. $y = 2x - 1$

B. $y = \frac{1}{2}x - 1$

C. $y = -\frac{1}{2}x + 1$

H.O.T. 35. Write About It Write an equation that describes a vertical line. Can you write this equation in slope-intercept form? Why or why not?

Real-World Connections

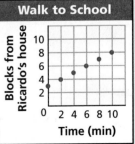

36. a. Ricardo and Sam walk from Sam's house to school. Sam lives 3 blocks from Ricardo's house. The graph shows their distance from Ricardo's house as they walk to school. Create a table of these values.

    b. Find an equation for the distance as a function of time.

    c. What are the slope and y-intercept? What do they represent in this situation?

Walk to School

TEST PREP

37. Which function has the same y-intercept as $y = \frac{1}{2}x - 2$?

Ⓐ $2x + 3y = 6$ Ⓑ $x + 4y = -8$ Ⓒ $-\frac{1}{2}x + y = 4$ Ⓓ $\frac{1}{2}x - 2y = -2$

38. What is the slope-intercept form of $x - y = -8$?

Ⓕ $y = -x - 8$ Ⓖ $y = x - 8$ Ⓗ $y = -x + 8$ Ⓘ $y = x + 8$

39. Which function has a y-intercept of 3?

Ⓐ $2x - y = 3$ Ⓑ $2x + y = 3$ Ⓒ $2x + y = 6$ Ⓓ $y = 3x$

40. **Gridded Response** What is the slope of the line described by $-6x = -2y + 5$?

41. **Short Response** Write a function whose graph has the same slope as the line described by $3x - 9y = 9$ and the same y-intercept as $8x - 2y = 6$. Show your work.

CHALLENGE AND EXTEND

42. The standard form of a linear equation is $Ax + By = C$. Rewrite this equation in slope-intercept form. What is the slope? What is the y-intercept?

43. What value of n in the equation $nx + 5 = 3y$ would give a line with slope -2?

44. If b is the y-intercept of a linear function whose graph has slope m, then $y = mx + b$ describes the line. Below is an incomplete justification of this statement. Fill in the missing information.

Statements	Reasons
1. $m = \dfrac{y_2 - y_1}{x_2 - x_1}$	1. Slope formula
2. $m = \dfrac{y - b}{x - 0}$	2. By definition, if b is the y-intercept, then $\left(\blacksquare, b\right)$ is a point on the line. (x, y) is any other point on the line.
3. $m = \dfrac{y - b}{x}$	3. _____ ?
4. $m\blacksquare = y - b$	4. Multiplication Property of Equality (Multiply both sides of the equation by x.)
5. $mx + b = y$, or $y = mx + b$	5. _____ ?

FOCUS ON MATHEMATICAL PRACTICES

H.O.T. **45.** **Modeling** Create a real-world situation that could be modeled by a linear function with a slope of 2 and a y-intercept of -30. Explain the meaning of the slope and the y-intercept in your context.

H.O.T. **46.** **Proof** The graph of $y = 2x + 1$ is shown. Suppose n is any value of x. Prove that, as n increases by any positive number k, the linear function $y = 2x + 1$ grows by an amount related only to k and not to n. (*Hint:* Evaluate y for the two values of x shown on the graph and subtract.)

11-3 Point-Slope Form

© Pixtal/SuperStock

Essential Question: How can you write a linear equation in point-slope form and use two points to draw its graph?

Objectives
Graph a line and write a linear equation using point-slope form.

Write a linear equation given two points.

Why learn this?
You can use point-slope form to represent a cost function, such as the cost of placing a newspaper ad. (See Example 5.)

If you know the slope and any point on the line, you can write an equation of the line by using the slope formula. For example, suppose a line has a slope of 3 and contains $(2, 1)$. Let (x, y) be any other point on the line.

$$m = \frac{y_2 - y_1}{x_2 - x_1} \longrightarrow 3 = \frac{y - 1}{x - 2}$$ *Substitute into the slope formula.*

$$3(x - 2) = \left(\frac{y - 1}{x - 2}\right)(x - 2)$$ *Multiplication Property of Equality*

$$3(x - 2) = y - 1$$ *Simplify.*

$$y - 1 = 3(x - 2)$$

Slope formula

Point-Slope Form of a Linear Equation

The line with slope m that contains the point (x_1, y_1) can be described by the equation $y - y_1 = m(x - x_1)$.

COMMON CORE GPS
MCC9-12.A.CED.2

EXAMPLE 1

my.hrw.com

Online Video Tutor

Writing Linear Equations in Point-Slope Form

Write an equation in point-slope form for the line with the given slope that contains the given point.

A slope $= \frac{5}{2}$; $(-3, 0)$

$y - y_1 = m(x - x_1)$ *Write the point-slope form.*

$y - 0 = \frac{5}{2}[x - (-3)]$ *Substitute $\frac{5}{2}$ for m, -3 for x_1, and 0 for y_1.*

$y - 0 = \frac{5}{2}(x + 3)$ *Rewrite subtraction of negative numbers as addition.*

B slope $= -7$; $(4, 2)$

$y - y_1 = m(x - x_1)$

$y - 2 = -7(x - 4)$

C slope $= 0$; $(-2, -3)$

$y - y_1 = m(x - x_1)$

$y - (-3) = 0[x - (-2)]$

$y + 3 = 0(x + 2)$

CHECK IT OUT!

Write an equation in point-slope form for the line with the given slope that contains the given point.

1a. slope $= 2$; $\left(\frac{1}{2}, 1\right)$

1b. slope $= 0$; $(3, -4)$

Previously, you graphed a line given its equation in slope-intercept form. You can also graph a line when given its equation in point-slope form. Start by using the equation to identify a point on the line. Then use the slope of the line to identify a second point.

EXAMPLE 2
MCC9-12.A.CED.2

my.hrw.com

Online Video Tutor

Using Point-Slope Form to Graph

Graph the line described by each equation.

A $y - 1 = 3(x - 1)$

$y - 1 = 3(x - 1)$ is in the form $y - y_1 = m(x - x_1)$.

The line contains the point $(1, 1)$.

slope: $m = 3 = \dfrac{3}{1}$

Step 1 Plot $(1, 1)$.

Step 2 Count **3 units up** and **1 unit right** and plot another point.

Step 3 Draw the line connecting the two points.

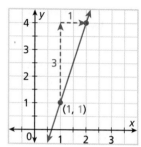

B $y + 2 = -\dfrac{1}{2}(x - 3)$

Step 1 Write the equation in point-slope form: $y - y_1 = m(x - x_1)$.

$y - (-2) = -\dfrac{1}{2}(x - 3)$ *Rewrite addition of 2 as subtraction of −2.*

Step 2 Graph the line.

The line contains the point $(3, -2)$.

slope: $m = -\dfrac{1}{2} = \dfrac{1}{-2}$

• Plot $(3, -2)$.

• Count **1 unit up** and **2 units left** and plot another point.

• Draw the line connecting the two points.

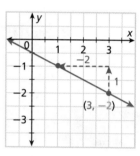

Helpful Hint

For a negative fraction, you can write the negative sign in one of three places.

$-\dfrac{1}{2} = \dfrac{-1}{2} = \dfrac{1}{-2}$

CHECK IT OUT!

Graph the line described by each equation.

2a. $y + 2 = -(x - 2)$ **2b.** $y + 3 = -2(x - 1)$

EXAMPLE 3
MCC9-12.A.CED.2

my.hrw.com

Online Video Tutor

Writing Linear Equations in Slope-Intercept Form

Write the equation that describes each line in slope-intercept form.

A slope $= -4$, $(-1, -2)$ is on the line.

Step 1 Write the equation in point-slope form: $y - y_1 = m(x - x_1)$.

$y - (-2) = -4[x - (-1)]$

Step 2 Write the equation in slope-intercept form by solving for y.

$y - (-2) = -4[x - (-1)]$

$y + 2 = -4(x + 1)$ *Rewrite subtraction of negative numbers as*
addition. Distribute −4 on the right side.

$y + 2 = -4x - 4$

$\underline{\ -2 \qquad\qquad -2}$ *Subtract 2 from both sides.*

$y \quad\ = -4x - 6$

B **(1, −4) and (3, 2) are on the line.**

Step 1 Find the slope.

$$m = \frac{y_2 - y_1}{x_2 - x_1} = \frac{2 - (-4)}{3 - 1} = \frac{6}{2} = 3$$

Step 2 Substitute the slope and one of the points into the point-slope form. Then write the equation in slope-intercept form.

$$y - y_1 = m(x - x_1)$$
$$y - 2 = 3(x - 3) \qquad \textit{Use (3, 2).}$$
$$y - 2 = 3x - 9 \qquad \textit{Distribute 3 on the right side.}$$
$$y = 3x - 7 \qquad \textit{Add 2 to both sides.}$$

C **x-intercept = −2, y-intercept = 4**

Step 1 Use the intercepts to find two points: (−2, 0) and (0, 4).

Step 2 Find the slope.

$$m = \frac{y_2 - y_1}{x_2 - x_1} = \frac{4 - 0}{0 - (-2)} = \frac{4}{2} = 2$$

Step 3 Write the equation in slope-intercept form.

$$y = mx + b \qquad \textit{Write the slope-intercept form.}$$
$$y = 2x + 4 \qquad \textit{Substitute 2 for m and 4 for b.}$$

 Write the equation that describes each line in slope-intercept form.

3a. slope $= \frac{1}{3}$, (−3, 1) is on the line.

3b. (1, −2) and (3, 10) are on the line.

EXAMPLE 4 **Using Two Points to Find Intercepts**
MCC9-12.F.IF.8

The points (4, 8) and (−1, −12) are on a line. Find the intercepts.

Step 1 Find the slope.
$$m = \frac{y_2 - y_1}{x_2 - x_1} = \frac{-12 - 8}{-1 - 4} = \frac{-20}{-5} = 4$$

my.hrw.com

Online Video Tutor

Step 2 Write the equation in slope-intercept form.
$$y - y_1 = m(x - x_1) \qquad \textit{Write the point-slope form.}$$
$$y - 8 = 4(x - 4) \qquad \textit{Substitute (4, 8) for } (x_1, y_1) \textit{ and 4 for m.}$$
$$y - 8 = 4x - 16 \qquad \textit{Distribute 4 on the right side.}$$
$$y = 4x - 8 \qquad \textit{Add 8 to both sides.}$$

Step 3 Find the intercepts.

x-intercept:
$$y = 4x - 8 \qquad \textit{Replace y with}$$
$$0 = 4x - 8 \qquad \textit{0 and solve}$$
$$8 = 4x \qquad \textit{for x.}$$
$$2 = x$$

y-intercept:
$$y = 4x - 8 \qquad \textit{Use the slope-}$$
$$b = -8 \qquad \textit{intercept form to identify the y-intercept.}$$

The x-intercept is 2, and the y-intercept is −8.

 4. The points (2, 15) and (−4, −3) are on a line. Find the intercepts.

EXAMPLE **5**

MCC9-12.F.BF.1a

my.hrw.com

Online Video Tutor

MATHEMATICAL PRACTICES

Make sense of problems and persevere in solving them.

Problem-Solving Application

The cost to place an ad in a newspaper for one week is a linear function of the number of lines in the ad. The costs for 3, 5, and 10 lines are shown. Write an equation in slope-intercept form that represents the function. Then find the cost of an ad that is 18 lines long.

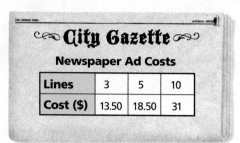

City Gazette

Newspaper Ad Costs

Lines	3	5	10
Cost ($)	13.50	18.50	31

1. Understand the Problem

- The **answer** will have two parts—an equation in slope-intercept form and the cost of an ad that is 18 lines long.
- The ordered pairs given in the table satisfy the equation.

2. Make a Plan

First, find the slope. Then use point-slope form to write the equation. Finally, write the equation in slope-intercept form.

3. Solve

Step 1 Choose any two ordered pairs from the table to find the slope.

$$m = \frac{y_2 - y_1}{x_2 - x_1} = \frac{18.50 - 13.50}{5 - 3} = \frac{5}{2} = 2.5 \quad \textit{Use (3, 13.50) and (5, 18.50).}$$

Step 2 Substitute the slope and any ordered pair from the table into the point-slope form.

$$y - y_1 = m(x - x_1)$$
$$y - 31 = 2.5(x - 10) \qquad \textit{Use (10, 31).}$$

Step 3 Write the equation in slope-intercept form by solving for y.

$$y - 31 = 2.5(x - 10)$$
$$y - 31 = 2.5x - 25 \qquad \textit{Distribute 2.5.}$$
$$y = 2.5x + 6 \qquad \textit{Add 31 to both sides.}$$

Step 4 Find the cost of an ad containing 18 lines by substituting 18 for x.

$$y = 2.5x + 6$$
$$y = 2.5(18) + 6 = 51$$

The cost of an ad containing 18 lines is $51.

4. Look Back

Check the equation by substituting the ordered pairs (3, 13.50) and (5, 18.50).

$y = 2.5x + 6$	
13.50	2.5(3) + 6
13.5	7.5 + 6
13.5	13.5 ✓

$y = 2.5x + 6$	
18.50	2.5(5) + 6
18.5	12.5 + 6
18.5	18.5 ✓

5. What if...? At a different newspaper, the costs to place an ad for one week are shown. Write an equation in slope-intercept form that represents this linear function. Then find the cost of an ad that is 21 lines long.

Lines	Cost ($)
3	12.75
5	17.25
10	28.50

THINK AND DISCUSS

1. How are point-slope form and slope-intercept form alike? different?

2. When is point-slope form useful? When is slope-intercept form useful?

3. GET ORGANIZED Copy and complete the graphic organizer. In each box, describe how to find the equation of a line by using the given method.

Writing the Equation of a Line

| If you know two points on the line | If you know the slope and *y*-intercept | If you know the slope and a point on the line |

11-3 Exercises

my.hrw.com
Homework Help

GUIDED PRACTICE

SEE EXAMPLE 1 Write an equation in point-slope form for the line with the given slope that contains the given point.

1. slope $= \frac{1}{5}$; $(2, -6)$ **2.** slope $= -4$; $(1, 5)$ **3.** slope $= 0$; $(3, -7)$

SEE EXAMPLE 2 Graph the line described by each equation.

4. $y - 1 = -(x - 3)$ **5.** $y + 2 = -2(x + 4)$ **6.** $y + 1 = -\frac{1}{2}(x + 4)$

SEE EXAMPLE 3 Write the equation that describes each line in slope-intercept form.

7. slope $= -\frac{1}{3}$, $(-3, 8)$ is on the line. **8.** slope $= 2$; $(1, 1)$ is on the line.

9. $(-2, 2)$ and $(2, -2)$ are on the line. **10.** $(1, 1)$ and $(-5, 3)$ are on the line.

11. *x*-intercept $= 8$, *y*-intercept $= 4$ **12.** *x*-intercept $= -2$, *y*-intercept $= 3$

SEE EXAMPLE 4 Each pair of points is on a line. Find the intercepts.

13. $(5, 2)$ and $(7, 4)$ **14.** $(-1, 5)$ and $(-3, -5)$ **15.** $(2, 9)$ and $(-4, -9)$

SEE EXAMPLE 5 **16. Measurement** An oil tank is being filled at a constant rate. The depth of the oil is a function of the number of minutes the tank has been filling, as shown in the table. Write an equation in slope-intercept form that represents this linear function. Then find the depth of the oil after one-half hour.

Time (min)	Depth (ft)
0	3
10	5
15	6

PRACTICE AND PROBLEM SOLVING

Write an equation in point-slope form for the line with the given slope that contains the given point.

17. slope $= \frac{2}{9}$; $(-1, 5)$ **18.** slope $= 0$; $(4, -2)$ **19.** slope $= 8$; $(1, 8)$

Independent Practice

For Exercises	See Example
17–19	1
20–22	2
23–30	3
31–33	4
34	5

my.hrw.com

Online Extra Practice

Graph the line described by each equation.

20. $y - 4 = -\dfrac{1}{2}(x + 3)$ **21.** $y + 2 = \dfrac{3}{5}(x - 1)$ **22.** $y - 0 = 4(x - 1)$

Write the equation that describes each line in slope-intercept form.

23. slope $= -\dfrac{2}{7}$, $(14, -3)$ is on the line. **24.** slope $= \dfrac{4}{5}$, $(-15, 1)$ is on the line.

25. slope $= -6$, $(9, 3)$ is on the line. **26.** $(7, 8)$ and $(-7, 6)$ are on the line.

27. $(2, 7)$ and $(4, -4)$ are on the line. **28.** $(-1, 2)$ and $(4, -23)$ are on the line.

29. x-intercept $= 3$, y-intercept $= -6$ **30.** x-intercept $= 4$, y-intercept $= -1$

Each pair of points is on a line. Find the intercepts.

31. $(-1, -4)$ and $(6, 10)$ **32.** $(3, 4)$ and $(-6, 16)$ **33.** $(4, 15)$ and $(-2, 6)$

34. History The amount of fresh water left in the tanks of a 19th-century clipper ship is a linear function of the time since the ship left port, as shown in the table. Write an equation in slope-intercept form that represents the function. Then find the amount of water that will be left in the ship's tanks 50 days after leaving port.

Fresh Water Aboard Ship	
Time (days)	Amount (gal)
1	3555
8	3240
15	2925

Science

As altitude increases, the amount of breathable oxygen decreases. At elevations above 8000 feet, this can cause altitude sickness. To prevent this, mountain climbers often use tanks containing a mixture of air and pure oxygen.

35. Science At higher altitudes, water boils at lower temperatures. This relationship between altitude and boiling point is linear. At an altitude of 1000 feet, water boils at 210 °F. At an altitude of 3000 feet, water boils at 206 °F. Write an equation in slope-intercept form that represents this linear function. Then find the boiling point at 6000 feet.

36. Consumer Economics Lora has a gift card from an online music store where all downloads cost the same amount. After downloading 2 songs, the balance on her card was $18.10. After downloading a total of 5 songs, the balance was $15.25.

a. Write an equation in slope-intercept form that represents the amount in dollars remaining on the card as a function of songs downloaded.

b. Identify the slope of the line and tell what the slope represents.

c. Identify the y-intercept of the line and tell what it represents.

d. How many additional songs can Lora download when there is $15.25 left on the card?

Graph the line with the given slope that contains the given point.

37. slope $= -3$; $(2, 4)$ **38.** slope $= -\dfrac{1}{4}$; $(0, 0)$ **39.** slope $= \dfrac{1}{2}$; $(-2, -1)$

Tell whether each statement is sometimes, always, or never true.

40. A line described by the equation $y = mx + b$ contains the point $(0, b)$.

41. The slope of the line that contains the points $(0, 0)$ and (c, d) is negative if both c and d are negative.

42. The y-intercept of the graph of $y - y_1 = m(x - x_1)$ is negative if y_1 is negative.

43. Meteorology Snowfall accumulates at an average rate of 2.5 inches per hour during a snowstorm. Two hours after the snowstorm begins, the average depth of snow on the ground is 11 inches.

a. Write an equation in point-slope form that represents the depth of the snow in inches as a function of hours since the snowstorm began.

b. How much snow is on the ground when the snowstorm starts?

c. The snowstorm begins at 2:15 P.M. and continues until 6:30 P.M. How much snow is on the ground at the end of the storm?

© Royal Geographical Society/Alamy

Write an equation in point-slope form that describes each graph.

44.

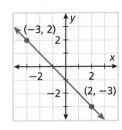

45.

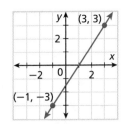

46.

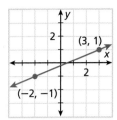

The tables show linear relationships between x and y. Copy and complete the tables.

47.

x	−2	0	▨	7
y	−18	▨	12	27

48.

x	−4	1	0	▨
y	14	4	▨	−6

H.O.T. 49. ▮▮**ERROR ANALYSIS**▮▮▮ Two students used point-slope form to find an equation that describes the line with slope -3 through $(-5, 2)$. Who is incorrect? Explain the error.

Ⓐ
$$y - y_1 = m(x - x_1)$$
$$y - 2 = -3(x - 5)$$

Ⓑ
$$y - y_1 = m(x - x_1)$$
$$y - 2 = -3[x - (-5)]$$
$$y - 2 = -3(x + 5)$$

50. Critical Thinking Compare the methods for finding the equation that describes a line when you know

- a point on the line and the slope of the line.
- two points on the line.

How are the methods alike? How are they different?

H.O.T. 51. Write About It Explain why the first statement is false but the second is true.

- All linear equations can be written in point-slope form.
- All linear equations that describe functions can be written in point-slope form.

52. Multi-Step The table shows the mean scores on a standardized test for several different years.

Years Since 1985	0	5	10	17	21
Mean Combined Score	994	1009	1001	1016	1020

a. Make a scatter plot of the data and add a trend line to your graph.

b. Use your trend line to estimate the slope and y-intercept, and write an equation in slope-intercept form.

c. What do the slope and y-intercept represent in this situation?

53. a. Stephen is walking from his house to his friend Sharon's house. When he is 12 blocks away, he looks at his watch. He looks again when he is 8 blocks away and finds that 6 minutes have passed. Write two ordered pairs for these data in the form (time, blocks).

b. Write a linear equation for these two points.

c. What is the total amount of time it takes Stephen to reach Sharon's house? Explain how you found your answer.

TEST PREP

54. Which equation describes the line through $(-5, 1)$ with slope of 1?

   Ⓐ $y + 1 = x - 5$ Ⓒ $y - 1 = -5(x - 1)$

   Ⓑ $y + 5 = x - 1$ Ⓓ $y - 1 = x + 5$

55. A line contains $(4, 4)$ and $(5, 2)$. What are the slope and y-intercept?

   Ⓕ slope = -2; y-intercept = 2   Ⓗ slope = -2; y-intercept = 12

   Ⓖ slope = 1.2; y-intercept = -2 Ⓙ slope = 12; y-intercept = 1.2

CHALLENGE AND EXTEND

56. A linear function has the same y-intercept as $x + 4y = 8$ and its graph contains the point $(2, 7)$. Find the slope and y-intercept.

57. Write the equation of a line in slope-intercept form that contains $\left(\frac{3}{4}, \frac{1}{2}\right)$ and has the same slope as the line described by $y + 3x = 6$.

58. Write the equation of a line in slope-intercept form that contains $\left(-\frac{1}{2}, -\frac{1}{3}\right)$ and $\left(1\frac{1}{2}, 1\right)$.

FOCUS ON MATHEMATICAL PRACTICES

H.O.T. **59. Analysis** A line contains $(8, 16)$ and has a negative y-intercept. Write a possible point-slope equation of the line.

H.O.T. **60. Comparison** The slope-intercept and point-slope forms are related.

   a. A line has a slope of 3 and y-intercept of -4. Write equations of the line in slope-intercept form and point-slope form. What do you notice?

   b. For any slope m and y-intercept $(0, b)$, show that the point-slope and slope-intercept form of the line are equivalent.

Career Path

Michael Raynor
Data mining major

Q: What math classes did you take in high school?

A: Algebra 1 and 2, Geometry, and Statistics

Q: What math classes have you taken in college?

A: Applied Statistics, Data Mining Methods, Web Mining, and Artificial Intelligence

Q: How do you use math?

A: Once for a class, I used software to analyze basketball statistics. What I learned helped me develop strategies for our school team.

Q: What are your future plans?

A: There are many options for people with data mining skills. I could work in banking, pharmaceuticals, or even the military. But my dream job is to develop game strategies for an NBA team.

© Ocean/Corbis

11-3 Technology TASK

Use with Point-Slope Form

Graph Linear Functions

You can use a graphing calculator to quickly graph lines whose equations are in point-slope form. To enter an equation into your calculator, it must be solved for y, but it does not necessarily have to be in slope-intercept form.

 MATHEMATICAL PRACTICES **Use appropriate tools strategically.**

MCC9-12.F.IF.7 Graph functions expressed symbolically and show key features of the graph, by hand in simple cases and using technology for more complicated cases.

Activity

Graph the line with slope 2 that contains the point $(2, 6.09)$.

1 Use point-slope form.
$$y - y_1 = m(x - x_1)$$
$$y - 6.09 = 2(x - 2)$$

2 Solve for y by adding 6.09 to both sides of the equation.
$$y - 6.09 = 2(x - 2)$$
$$\underline{+ 6.09 \qquad + 6.09}$$
$$y \qquad = 2(x - 2) + 6.09$$

3 Enter this equation into your calculator.

 Y= 2 (X,T,θ,n − 2) + 6.09 ENTER

4 Graph in the *standard viewing window* by pressing ZOOM and selecting **6:ZStandard**. In this window, both the x- and y-axes go from -10 to 10.

5 Notice that the scale on the y-axis is smaller than the scale on the x-axis. This is because the width of the calculator screen is about 50% greater than its height. To see a more accurate graph of this line, use the *square viewing window*. Press ZOOM and select **5:ZSquare**.

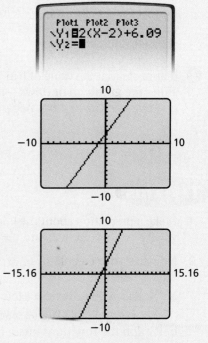

Try This

1. Graph the function represented by the line with slope -1.5 that contains the point $(2.25, -3)$. View the graph in the standard viewing window.

2. Now view the graph in the square viewing window. Press WINDOW and write down the minimum and maximum values on the x- and y-axes.

3. In which graph does the line appear steeper? Why?

4. Explain why it might sometimes be useful to look at a graph in a square window.

Technology TASK

Use with Transforming
Linear Functions

The Family of Linear Functions

A *family of functions* is a set of functions whose graphs have basic characteristics in common. For example, all linear functions form a family. You can use a graphing calculator to explore families of functions.

Use appropriate tools strategically.

MCC9-12.F.BF.3 Identify the effect on the graph of replacing $f(x)$ by $f(x) + k$, $kf(x)$, $f(kx)$, and $f(x + k)$ for specific values of k (both positive and negative); ... . Experiment with cases and illustrate an explanation of the effects on the graph using technology.

Activity

Graph the lines described by $y = x - 2$, $y = x - 1$, $y = x$, $y = x + 1$, $y = x + 2$, $y = x + 3$, and $y = x + 4$. How does the value of b affect the graph described by $y = x + b$?

1 All of the functions are in the form $y = x + b$. Enter them into the **Y=** editor.

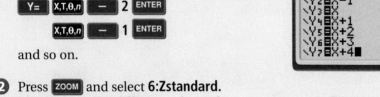

and so on.

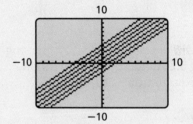

2 Press ZOOM and select **6:Zstandard.** Think about the different values of b as you watch the graphs being drawn. Notice that the lines are all parallel.

3 It appears that the value of b in $y = x + b$ shifts the graph up or down—up if b is positive and down if b is negative.

Try This

1. Make a prediction about the lines described by $y = 2x - 3$, $y = 2x - 2$, $y = 2x - 1$, $y = 2x$, $y = 2x + 1$, $y = 2x + 2$, and $y = 2x + 3$. Then graph. Was your prediction correct?

2. Now use your calculator to explore what happens to the graph of $y = mx$ when you change the value of m.

   a. **Make a Prediction** How do you think the lines described by $y = -2x$, $y = -x$, $y = x$, and $y = 2x$ will be related? How will they be alike? How will they be different?

   b. Graph the functions given in part **a**. Was your prediction correct?

   c. How is the effect of m different when m is positive from when m is negative?

11-4 Transforming Linear Functions

? **Essential Question:** How can you identify the effect of a given transformation on the graph of a linear function?

Objectives
Transform linear functions.

Solve problems involving linear transformations.

Why learn this?
Transformations allow you to visualize and compare many different functions at once.

You have learned to transform functions by transforming each point. Transformations can also be expressed by using function notation.

Helpful Hint

To remember the difference between vertical and horizontal translations, think: "Add to *y*, go high." "Add to *x*, go left."

Translations and Reflections	
Translations	
Horizontal Shift of $|h|$ Units	**Vertical Shift of $|k|$ Units**
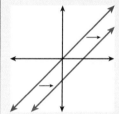 Input value changes. $f(x) \to f(x - h)$ $h > 0$ moves right $h < 0$ moves left	Output value changes. $f(x) \to f(x) + k$ $k > 0$ moves up $k < 0$ moves down
Reflections	
Reflection Across *y*-axis	**Reflection Across *x*-axis**
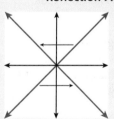 Input value changes. $f(x) \to f(-x)$ The lines are symmetric about the *y*-axis.	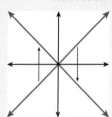 Output value changes. $f(x) \to -f(x)$ The lines are symmetric about the *x*-axis.

COMMON CORE GPS
MCC9-12.F.BF.3

EXAMPLE 1

my.hrw.com

Online Video Tutor

Translating and Reflecting Linear Functions

Let $g(x)$ be the indicated transformation of $f(x)$. Write the rule for $g(x)$.

A $f(x) = 2x + 3$; vertical translation 4 units up

Translating $f(x)$ 4 units up adds 4 to each output value.

$g(x) = f(x) + 4$ *Add 4 to $f(x)$.*

$g(x) = (2x + 3) + 4$ *Substitute $2x + 3$ for $f(x)$.*

$g(x) = 2x + 7$ *Simplify.*

Check Graph $f(x)$ and $g(x)$ on a graphing calculator. The slopes are the same, but the *y*-intercept has moved 4 units up from 3 to 7. ✔

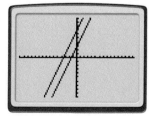

Let $g(x)$ be the indicated transformation of $f(x)$. Write the rule for $g(x)$.

B linear function defined in the table; reflection across y-axis

x	f(x)
−1	0
0	2
1	4

Step 1 Write the rule for $f(x)$ in slope-intercept form.

The y-intercept is 2.   *The table contains (0, 2).*

Find the slope:

$$m = \frac{2 - 0}{0 - (-1)} = \frac{2}{1} = 2 \quad \textit{Use } (-1, 0) \textit{ and } (0, 2).$$

$y = mx + b$ *Slope-intercept form*

$y = 2x + 2$ *Substitute 2 for m and 2 for b.*

$f(x) = 2x + 2$ *Replace y with f (x).*

Step 2 Write the rule for $g(x)$. Reflecting $f(x)$ across the y-axis replaces each x with $-x$.

$g(x) = 2(-x) + 2$ $g(x) = f(-x)$

$g(x) = -2x + 2$

Check Graph $f(x)$ and $g(x)$ on a graphing calculator. The graphs are symmetric about the y-axis. ✔

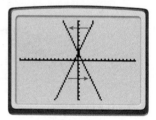

CHECK IT OUT! Let $g(x)$ be the indicated transformation of $f(x)$. Write the rule for $g(x)$.

1a. $f(x) = 3x + 1$; translation 2 units right

1b. linear function defined in the table; a reflection across the x-axis

x	−1	0	1
y	1	2	3

Stretches and compressions change the slope of a linear function. If the line becomes steeper, the function has been stretched vertically or compressed horizontally. If the line becomes flatter, the function has been compressed vertically or stretched horizontally.

Know it! Note

Stretches and Compressions	
Horizontal	**Vertical**
Horizontal Stretch/Compression by a Factor of b	**Vertical Stretch/Compression by a Factor of a**
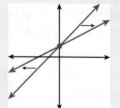 Input value changes. $f(x) \to f\left(\frac{1}{b}x\right)$	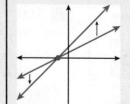 Output value changes. $f(x) \to a \cdot f(x)$
$b > 1$ stretches away from the y-axis. $0 < \lvert b \rvert < 1$ compresses toward the y-axis.	$a > 1$ stretches away from the x-axis. $0 < \lvert a \rvert < 1$ compresses toward the x-axis.

COMMON CORE GPS MCC9-12.F.BF.3

EXAMPLE **2**

Stretching and Compressing Linear Functions

Let $g(x)$ be a horizontal compression of $f(x) = 2x - 1$ by a factor of $\frac{1}{3}$. Write the rule for $g(x)$, and graph the function.

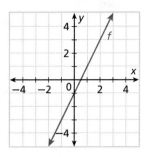

Horizontally compressing $f(x)$ by a factor of $\frac{1}{3}$ replaces each x with $\frac{1}{b}x$ where $b = \frac{1}{3}$.

$g(x) = 2\left(\dfrac{1}{b}\right)x - 1$ *For horizontal compression, use $\frac{1}{b}$.*

$\quad\quad = 2\left(\dfrac{1}{\frac{1}{3}}\right)x - 1$ *Substitute $\frac{1}{3}$ for b.*

$\quad\quad = 2(3x) - 1$ *Replace x with 3x.*

$g(x) = 6x - 1$ *Simplify.*

Check Graph both functions on the same coordinate plane. The graph of $g(x)$ is steeper than $f(x)$, which indicates that $g(x)$ has been horizontally compressed from $f(x)$, or pushed toward the y-axis.

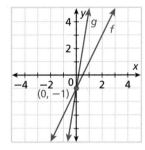

Helpful Hint

These don't change!
• y-intercepts in a horizontal stretch or compression
• x-intercepts in a vertical stretch or compression

2. Let $g(x)$ be a vertical compression of $f(x) = 3x + 2$ by a factor of $\frac{1}{4}$. Write the rule for $g(x)$.

Some linear functions involve more than one transformation. Combine transformations by applying individual transformations one at a time in the order in which they are given.

For multiple transformations, create a temporary function—such as $h(x)$ in Example 3 below—to represent the first transformation, and then transform it to find the combined transformation.

COMMON CORE GPS MCC9-12.F.BF.3

EXAMPLE **3**

Combining Transformations of Linear Functions

Let $g(x)$ be a vertical shift of $f(x) = x$ down 2 units followed by a vertical stretch by a factor of 5. Write the rule for $g(x)$.

Step 1 First perform the translation.

Translating $f(x) = x$ down 2 units subtracts 2 from the function. You can use $h(x)$ to represent the translated function.

$h(x) = f(x) - 2$ *Subtract 2 from the function.*

$h(x) = x - 2$ *Substitute x for f(x).*

Step 2 Then perform the stretch.

Stretching $h(x)$ vertically by a factor of 5 multiplies the function by 5.

$g(x) = 5 \cdot h(x)$ *Multiply the function by 5.*

$g(x) = 5(x - 2)$ *Because h(x) = x − 2, substitute x − 2 for h(x).*

$g(x) = 5x - 10$ *Simplify.*

3. Let $g(x)$ be a vertical compression of $f(x) = x$ by a factor of $\frac{1}{2}$ followed by a horizontal shift 8 units left. Write the rule for $g(x)$.

COMMON CORE GPS **EXAMPLE** **4**
MCC9-12.F.BF.1

my.hrw.com

Online Video Tutor

Fund-raising Application

The Dance Club is selling beaded purses as a fund-raiser. The function $R(n) = 12.5n$ represents the club's revenue in dollars where n is the number of purses sold.

a. The club paid \$75 for the materials needed to make the purses. Write a new function $P(n)$ for the club's profit.

The initial costs must be subtracted from the revenue.

$R(n) = 12.5n$ *Original function*

$P(n) = 12.5n - 75$ *Subtract the expenses.*

b. Graph $P(n)$ and $R(n)$ on the same coordinate plane.

Graph both functions. The lines have the same slope but different y-intercepts.

Note that the profit can be negative but the number of purses sold cannot be less than 0.

c. Describe the transformation(s) that have been applied.

The graphs indicate that $P(n)$ is a translation of $R(n)$. Because 75 was subtracted, $P(n) = R(n) - 75$. This indicates a vertical shift 75 units down.

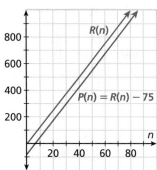

4. What if...? The club members decided to double the price of each purse.

a. Write a new profit function $S(n)$ for the club.

b. Graph $S(n)$ and $P(n)$ on the same coordinate plane.

c. Describe the transformation(s) that have been applied.

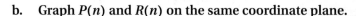

MCC.MP.1, MCC.MP.6   MATHEMATICAL PRACTICES

THINK AND DISCUSS

1. Identify the horizontal translation that would have the same effect on the graph of $f(x) = x$ as a vertical translation of 6 units.

2. Give an example of two different transformations of $f(x) = 2x$ that would result in $g(x) = 2x - 6$.

3. Describe the transformation that would cause all of the function values to double.

4. GET ORGANIZED Copy and complete the graphic organizer. In each box, give an example of the indicated transformation of the parent function $f(x) = x$. Include an equation and a graph.

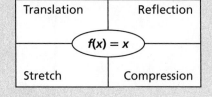

Translation	Reflection
$f(x) = x$	
Stretch	Compression

GUIDED PRACTICE

SEE EXAMPLE 1

Let $g(x)$ be the indicated transformation of $f(x)$.
Write the rule for $g(x)$.

1. linear function defined by the table; vertical translation 1.5 units up

x	−2	−1	0
f(x)	3.5	2	0.5

SEE EXAMPLE 2

2. $f(x) = -x + 5$; horizontal translation 2 units left

3. $f(x) = \frac{1}{3}x - 2$; vertical stretch by a factor of 3

4. $f(x) = -2x + 0.5$; horizontal stretch by a factor of $\frac{4}{3}$.

SEE EXAMPLE 3

Let $g(x)$ be the indicated combined transformation of $f(x) = x$. Write the rule for $g(x)$.

5. vertical compression by a factor of $\frac{2}{3}$ followed by a vertical shift 6 units down

6. horizontal shift right 4 units followed by a horizontal stretch by a factor of $\frac{3}{2}$

SEE EXAMPLE 4

7. **Advertising** An electronics company is changing its Internet ad from a banner ad to a pop-up ad. The cost of the banner ad in dollars is represented by $C(n) = 0.30n + 5.00$ where n is the average number of hits per hour. The cost of the pop-up ad will double the cost per hit.

a. Write a new cost function $D(n)$ for the ads.

b. Graph $C(n)$ and $D(n)$ on the same coordinate plane.

c. Describe the transformation(s) that have been applied.

PRACTICE AND PROBLEM SOLVING

Independent Practice

For Exercises	See Example
8–9	1
10–12	2
13–14	3
15	4

my.hrw.com

Online Extra Practice

Let $g(x)$ be the indicated transformation of $f(x)$. Write the rule for $g(x)$.

8.

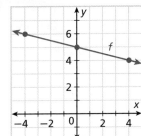

Reflection across the x-axis

9.

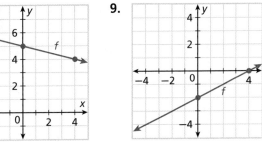

Vertical translation 2 units down

10.

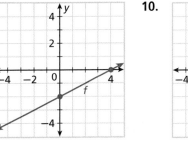

Horizontal compression by a factor of 0.5

11. linear function defined by the table; vertical stretch by a factor of 1.2 units

x	1	5	9
f(x)	0	−2	−4

12. $f(x) = -3x + 7$; vertical compression by a factor of $\frac{3}{4}$

Let $g(x)$ be the indicated combined transformation of $f(x) = x$. Write the rule for $g(x)$.

13. horizontal stretch by a factor of 2.75 followed by a horizontal shift 1 unit left

14. vertical shift 6 units down followed by a vertical compression by a factor of $\frac{2}{3}$

15. Consumer Economics In 1997, Southwestern Bell increased the price for local pay-phone calls. Before then, the price of a call could be determined by $f(x) = 0.15x + 0.25$, where x was the number of minutes after the *first* minute. The company increased the cost of the first minute by 10 cents.

    a. Write a new price function $g(x)$ for a phone call.

    b. Graph $f(x)$ and $g(x)$ on the same coordinate plane.

    c. Describe the transformation(s) that have been applied.

Write the rule for the transformed function $g(x)$ and graph.

16.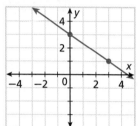

Reflection across
the y-axis

17.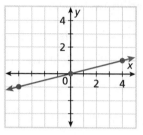

Vertical stretch
by a factor of 8

18.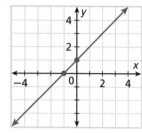

Horizontal stretch
by a factor of 3

History Historic tolls for traveling on the Cumberland Road in Pennsylvania are shown on the sign. Toll was paid every 15 miles.

19. Write a function to represent the cost for 1 horse and rider to travel n miles with a score of sheep. What transformation describes the change in cost if the sheep were replaced by cattle?

20. Write a function to represent the cost for a carriage with 2 horses and 4 wheels to travel n miles. Name two different transformations that would represent a 6¢ increase in the toll rate.

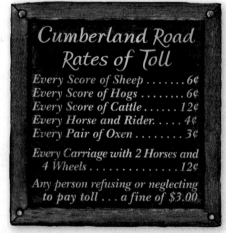

H.O.T. 21. Critical Thinking Consider the linear function $f(x) = x$.

    a. Shift $f(x)$ 2 units up and then reflect it over the x-axis.

    b. Perform the same transformations on $f(x)$ again but in reverse order.

    c. Make a conjecture about the order in which transformations are performed.

H.O.T. 22. Write About It Which transformations affect the slope of a linear function, and which transformations affect the y-intercept? Support your answers.

23. Use the data set $\{1, 5, 10, 17, 23, 23, 38, 60\}$.

    a. Find the mean, median, mode, and range.

    b. How does adding 7 to each number affect the mean, median, mode, and range?

    c. How does multiplying each number by 4 affect the mean, median, mode, and range?

    d. How does multiplying each number by 2 and then adding 5 affect the mean, median, mode, and range?

24. The cost function C of rent at an apartment complex increased $50 last year and another $60 this year. Which function accurately reflects these changes?

Ⓐ $60(C + 50)$ Ⓑ $60(50C)$ Ⓒ $(C + 50) + 60$ Ⓓ $50C + 60$

25. Given $f(x) = 28.5x + 45.6$, which function decreases the y-intercept by 20.3?

Ⓕ $g(x) = 8.2x + 45.6$ Ⓗ $g(x) = 28.5x + 25.3$

Ⓖ $g(x) = 8.2x + 66.1$ Ⓙ $g(x) = 28.5x + 66.1$

26. Which transformation describes a line that is parallel to $f(x)$?

Ⓐ $f(3x)$ Ⓑ $f\left(\dfrac{x}{2}\right)$ Ⓒ $f(x - 4)$ Ⓓ $f(-2x)$

27. Which transformation of $f(x) = \dfrac{1}{2}x - 1$ could result in the graph shown?

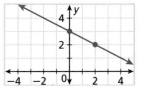

Ⓕ vertical shift 2 units down and reflection across x-axis

Ⓖ horizontal shift 2 units left and reflection across x-axis

Ⓗ vertical shift 2 units up and reflection across x-axis

Ⓙ horizontal shift 2 units right and reflection across x-axis

CHALLENGE AND EXTEND

28. Give two different combinations of transformations that would transform $f(x) = 3x + 4$ into $g(x) = 15x - 10$.

29. Give an example of two transformations of $f(x) = x$ that can be performed in any order and result in the same transformed function.

30. Education The graph shows the tuition at a university based on the number of credit hours taken. The rate per credit hour varies according to the number of hours taken: less than 12 hours, 12 to 18 hours, and greater than 18 hours.

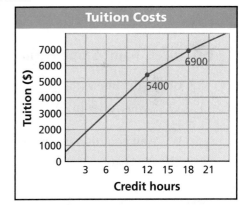

   a. Write the linear function that represents each segment of the graph.

   b. Write the linear functions that would reflect a 12% increase in all tuition costs.

FOCUS ON MATHEMATICAL PRACTICES

MATHEMATICAL PRACTICES

H.O.T. **31. Modeling** What transformation would you use to triple the slope of a line while leaving its x-intercept constant?

H.O.T. **32. Reasoning** Explain why reflecting the function $f(x) = 0$ across either axis does not change the graph.

H.O.T. **33. Analysis** Let $f(x) = 2x + 1$.

   a. $f(x)$ is reflected across the x-axis to obtain $g(x)$. Write the equation of $g(x)$.

   b. $g(x)$ is reflected across the y-axis to obtain $h(x)$. Write the equation of $h(x)$. How is the slope of $h(x)$ related to the slope of $f(x)$?

   c. What single transformation of $f(x)$ could you use to get $h(x)$?

Ready to Go On?

my.hrw.com
Assessment and Intervention

11-1 Direct Variation

Tell whether each relationship is a direct variation. If so, identify the constant of variation.

1.

x	1	4	8	12
y	3	6	10	14

2.

x	−6	−2	0	3
y	−3	−1	0	1.5

11-2 Slope-Intercept Form

Write each equation in slope-intercept form. Then graph the line described by the equation.

3. $2x + y = 5$

4. $2x - 6y = 6$

5. $3x + y = 3x - 4$

6. Entertainment At a chili cook-off, people pay a $3.00 entrance fee and $0.50 for each bowl of chili they taste. The graph shows the total cost per person as a function of the number of bowls of chili tasted.

a. Write an equation that represents the total cost per person as a function of the number of bowls of chili tasted.

b. Identify the slope and y-intercept and describe their meanings.

11-3 Point-Slope Form

Graph the line with the given slope that contains the given point.

7. slope $= -3$; $(0, 3)$

8. slope $= -\frac{2}{3}$; $(-3, 5)$

9. slope $= 2$; $(-3, -1)$

Write an equation in slope-intercept form for the line through the two points.

10. $(3, 1)$ and $(4, 3)$

11. $(-1, -1)$ and $(1, 7)$

12. $(1, -4)$ and $(-2, 5)$

11-4 Transforming Linear Functions

Graph $f(x)$ and $g(x)$. Then describe the transformation(s) from the graph of $f(x)$ to the graph of $g(x)$.

13. $f(x) = 5x$, $g(x) = -5x$

14. $f(x) = \frac{1}{2}x - 1$, $g(x) = \frac{1}{2}x + 4$

PARCC Assessment Readiness

Selected Response

1. Write a function to describe the following:

The graph of $f(x) = |x|$ is made narrower, reflected across the x-axis, and translated 8 units up.

(A) $g(x) = -\left|\frac{1}{5}x + 8\right|$

(B) $g(x) = \left|-\frac{1}{5}x + 8\right|$

(C) $g(x) = -|5x| + 8$

(D) $g(x) = |-5x + 8|$

2. The points $(-4, -3)$ and $(-1, -8)$ are on a line. Find the intercepts to the nearest tenth.

(F) $x = 5.8$; $y = -9.7$

(G) $x = 3$; $y = -5$

(H) $x = -5.8$; $y = -9.7$

(J) $x = -5$; $y = -11$

3. The cost $f(x)$ in dollars to fill a car's tank with gas and get a car wash is a linear function of the capacity in gallons x of gas of the tank. The costs of a fill-up and a car wash for three different customers are shown in the table. Write an equation for the function in slope-intercept form. Then, find the cost of a fill-up and a car wash for a customer with a truck whose tank size is 22 gallons.

Tank size (gal) (x)	Total cost ($) $f(x)$
11	21.45
15	28.25
17	31.65

(A) $f(x) = 1.50x + 3.00$; Cost for truck = $36.00

(B) $f(x) = 1.70x + 2.75$; Cost for truck = $40.15

(C) $f(x) = 0.59x + 1.62$; Cost for truck = $14.60

(D) $f(x) = 1.60x + 2.25$; Cost for truck = $37.45

4. The value of y varies directly with x, and $y = 27$ when $x = 18$. Find y when $x = 36$.

(F) $y = 36$

(G) $y = 24$

(H) $y = 1.5$

(J) $y = 54$

5. Identify the vertex and give the minimum or maximum value of the function. Explain.
$y = |x - 3| + 1$

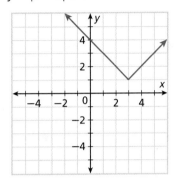

(A) The vertex is $(3, 1)$. The graph opens upward, so the function has a minimum. The minimum is 1.

(B) The vertex is $(3, 1)$. The graph does not intersect the x-axis, so the function has no minimum.

(C) The vertex is $(3, 1)$. The graph opens upward, so the function has a maximum. The maximum is 6.

(D) The vertex is $(1, 3)$. The graph opens upward, so the function has a minimum. The minimum is 1.

6. Write the equation that describes the line in slope-intercept form.
slope = 4, point $(3, -2)$ is on the line

(F) $y = 4x + 14$ (H) $y = 4x + 10$

(G) $y = 4x - 14$ (J) $y = 4x - 2$

Mini-Task

7. The water level of a river is 34 feet and it is receding at a rate of 0.5 foot per day.

a. Write an equation that represents the water level, w, after d days.

b. Identify the slope and y-intercept and describe their meanings.

c. In how many days will the water level be 26 feet?

Exponential Functions

COMMON CORE GPS

Contents

MATHEMATICAL PRACTICES The Common Core Georgia Performance Standards for Mathematical Practice describe varieties of expertise that all students should seek to develop. Opportunities to develop these practices are integrated throughout this program.

1 Make sense of problems and persevere in solving them.

2 Reason abstractly and quantitatively.

3 Construct viable arguments and critique the reasoning of others.

4 Model with mathematics.

5 Use appropriate tools strategically.

6 Attend to precision.

7 Look for and make use of structure.

8 Look for and express regularity in repeated reasoning.

Unpacking the Standards

Understanding the standards and the vocabulary terms in the standards will help you know exactly what you are expected to learn in this chapter.

 MCC9-12.F.BF.2

Write arithmetic and geometric sequences both recursively and with an explicit formula, use them to model situations, and translate between the two forms.

Key Vocabulary

arithmetic sequence (sucesión aritmética) A sequence whose successive terms differ by the same nonzero number d, called the *common difference*.

geometric sequence (sucesión geométrica) A sequence in which the ratio of successive terms is a constant r, called the *common ratio*, where $r \neq 0$ and $r \neq 1$.

recursive formula (fórmula recurrente) A formula for a sequence in which one or more previous terms are used to generate the next term.

What It Means For You

You can write rules for arithmetic and geometric sequences as a function of the term number or with respect to the previous term. You can use the form that is more useful for a particular situation.

EXAMPLE   **Explicit and Recursive Formulas**

In the geometric sequence below, each term is twice the previous term. So, the common ratio is $r = 2$.

$$
\begin{array}{cccc}
1 & 2 & 3 & 4 \quad \longleftarrow \text{Position, } n \\
\downarrow & \downarrow & \downarrow & \downarrow \\
3 & 6 & 12 & 24 \quad \longleftarrow \text{Term, } a_n \\
a_1 & a_2 & a_3 & a_4
\end{array}
$$

Explicit formula: $a_n = a_1 r^{n-1}$, so $a_n = 3 \cdot 2^{n-1}$

Recursive formula: The recursive formula gives the first term and for finding successive terms:
$a_n = a_{n-1} r$, so $a_1 = 3$, $a_n = 2a_{n-1}$

 MCC9-12.F.IF.7e

Graph exponential … functions, showing intercepts and end behavior, …

Key Vocabulary

exponential function (función exponencial) A function of the form $f(x) = ab^x$, where a and b are real numbers with $a \neq 0$, $b > 0$, and $b \neq 1$.

What It Means For You

The graph of an exponential function $f(x) = ab^x$ has y-intercept a. If $a > 0$, the function may model growth or decay.

EXAMPLE

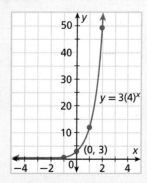

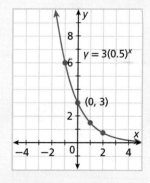

The graph nears the x-axis as x decreases and rises faster and faster as x increases.

The graph nears the x-axis as x increases and rises faster and faster as x decreases.

12-1 Geometric Sequences

? ***Essential Question:*** How can you recognize, extend, and find a given term of a geometric sequence?

Objectives
Recognize and extend geometric sequences.

Find the *n*th term of a geometric sequence.

Vocabulary
geometric sequence
common ratio

Who uses this?
Bungee jumpers can use geometric sequences to calculate how high they will bounce.

The table shows the heights of a bungee jumper's bounces.

The height of the bounces shown in the table form a *geometric sequence*. In a **geometric sequence**, the ratio of successive terms is the same number *r*, called the **common ratio**.

Bounce	1	2	3
Height (ft)	200	80	32

 Writing Math

The variable *a* is often used to represent terms in a sequence. The variable a_4 (read "*a* sub 4") is the fourth term in a sequence.

Geometric sequences can be thought of as functions. The term number, or position in the sequence, is the input, and the term itself is the output.

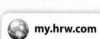

1	2	3	4	⟵ Position

| 3 | 6 | 12 | 24 | ⟵ Term |
| a_1 | a_2 | a_3 | a_4 | |

To find a term in a geometric sequence, multiply the previous term by *r*.

Finding a Term of a Geometric Sequence

The *n*th term of a geometric sequence with **common ratio** *r* is

$$a_n = a_{n-1} r$$

 EXAMPLE 1
MCC9-12.F.BF.2

 my.hrw.com

Online Video Tutor

Extending Geometric Sequences

Find the next three terms in each geometric sequence.

A 1, 3, 9, 27, …

Step 1 Find the value of *r* by dividing each term by the one before it.

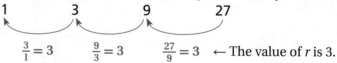

$\frac{3}{1} = 3$ $\frac{9}{3} = 3$ $\frac{27}{9} = 3$ ⟵ The value of *r* is 3.

Step 2 Multiply each term by 3 to find the next three terms.

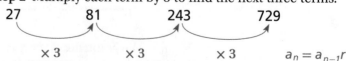

× 3   × 3   × 3 $a_n = a_{n-1} r$

The next three terms are 81, 243, and 729.

Mark A. Johnson/photolibrary

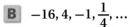

Helpful Hint

When the terms in a geometric sequence alternate between positive and negative, the value of r is negative.

B $-16, 4, -1, \frac{1}{4}, \dots$

Step 1 Find the value of r by dividing each term by the one before it.

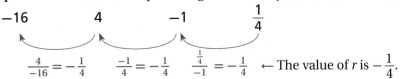

$$-16 \qquad 4 \qquad -1 \qquad \frac{1}{4}$$

$$\frac{4}{-16} = -\frac{1}{4} \qquad \frac{-1}{4} = -\frac{1}{4} \qquad \frac{\frac{1}{4}}{-1} = -\frac{1}{4} \qquad \leftarrow \text{The value of } r \text{ is } -\frac{1}{4}.$$

Step 2 Multiply each term by $-\frac{1}{4}$ to find the next three terms.

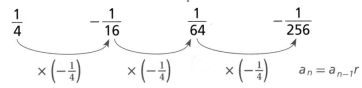

$$\frac{1}{4} \qquad -\frac{1}{16} \qquad \frac{1}{64} \qquad -\frac{1}{256}$$

$$\times \left(-\frac{1}{4}\right) \qquad \times \left(-\frac{1}{4}\right) \qquad \times \left(-\frac{1}{4}\right) \qquad a_n = a_{n-1}r$$

The next three terms are $-\frac{1}{16}, \frac{1}{64},$ and $-\frac{1}{256}$.

CHECK IT OUT! **Find the next three terms in each geometric sequence.**
1a. $5, -10, 20, -40, \dots$ **1b.** $512, 384, 288, \dots$

To find the output a_n of a geometric sequence when n is a large number, you need an equation, or function rule.

The pattern in the table shows that to get the nth term, multiply the first term by the common ratio raised to the power $n - 1$.

Words	Numbers	Algebra
1st term	3	a_1
2nd term	$3 \cdot 2^1 = 6$	$a_1 \cdot r^1$
3rd term	$3 \cdot 2^2 = 12$	$a_1 \cdot r^2$
4th term	$3 \cdot 2^3 = 24$	$a_1 \cdot r^3$
nth term	$3 \cdot 2^{n-1}$	$a_1 \cdot r^{n-1}$

If the first term of a geometric sequence is a_1, the nth term is a_n, and the common ratio is r, then

$$a_n = a_1 r^{n-1}$$

nth term   1st term   Common ratio

EXAMPLE 2
MCC9-12.F.BF.2

my.hrw.com

Online Video Tutor

Finding the nth Term of a Geometric Sequence

A The first term of a geometric sequence is 128, and the common ratio is 0.5. What is the 10th term of the sequence?

$a_n = a_1 r^{n-1}$ *Write the formula.*

$a_{10} = 128(0.5)^{10-1}$ *Substitute 128 for a_1, 10 for n, and 0.5 for r.*

$= 128(0.5)^9$ *Simplify the exponent.*

$= 0.25$ *Use a calculator.*

B For a geometric sequence, $a_1 = 8$ and $r = 3$. Find the 5th term of this sequence.

$a_n = a_1 r^{n-1}$ *Write the formula.*

$a_5 = 8(3)^{5-1}$ *Substitute 8 for a_1, 5 for n, and 3 for r.*

$= 8(3)^4$ *Simplify the exponent.*

$= 648$ *Use a calculator.*

C What is the 13th term of the geometric sequence 8, −16, 32, −64, … ?

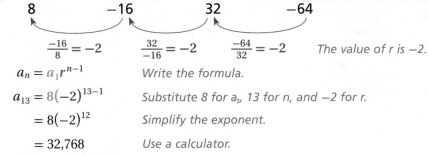

$$\frac{-16}{8} = -2 \qquad \frac{32}{-16} = -2 \qquad \frac{-64}{32} = -2 \qquad \text{The value of } r \text{ is } -2.$$

$a_n = a_1 r^{n-1}$	Write the formula.
$a_{13} = 8(-2)^{13-1}$	Substitute 8 for a_1, 13 for n, and −2 for r.
$= 8(-2)^{12}$	Simplify the exponent.
$= 32{,}768$	Use a calculator.

CHECK IT OUT! **2.** What is the 8th term of the sequence 1000, 500, 250, 125, … ?

 **EXAMPLE** **3**
MCC9-12.F.BF.2

my.hrw.com

Online Video Tutor

Sports Application

A bungee jumper jumps from a bridge. The diagram shows the bungee jumper's height above the ground at the top of each bounce. The heights form a geometric sequence. What is the bungee jumper's height at the top of the 5th bounce?

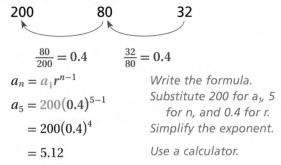

$$\frac{80}{200} = 0.4 \qquad \frac{32}{80} = 0.4$$

$a_n = a_1 r^{n-1}$	Write the formula.
$a_5 = 200(0.4)^{5-1}$	Substitute 200 for a_1, 5 for n, and 0.4 for r.
$= 200(0.4)^4$	Simplify the exponent.
$= 5.12$	Use a calculator.

The height of the 5th bounce is 5.12 feet.

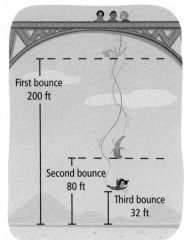

First bounce
200 ft

Second bounce
80 ft

Third bounce
32 ft

CHECK IT OUT! **3.** The table shows a car's value for 3 years after it is purchased. The values form a geometric sequence. How much will the car be worth in the 10th year?

Year	Value ($)
1	10,000
2	8,000
3	6,400

MCC.MP.3  MATHEMATICAL PRACTICES

THINK AND DISCUSS

1. How do you determine whether a sequence is geometric?

2. GET ORGANIZED Copy and complete the graphic organizer. In each box, write a way to represent the geometric sequence.

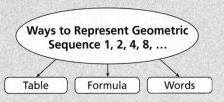

Ways to Represent Geometric Sequence 1, 2, 4, 8, …

Table Formula Words

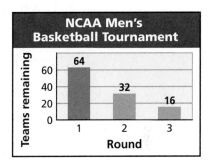
GUIDED PRACTICE

1. **Vocabulary** What is the *common ratio* of a geometric sequence?

SEE EXAMPLE **1** — **Find the next three terms in each geometric sequence.**

2. 2, 4, 8, 16, …   3. 400, 200, 100, 50, …   4. 4, −12, 36, −108, …

SEE EXAMPLE **2**

5. The first term of a geometric sequence is 1, and the common ratio is 10. What is the 10th term of the sequence?

6. What is the 11th term of the geometric sequence 3, 6, 12, 24, … ?

SEE EXAMPLE **3**

7. **Sports** In the NCAA men's basketball tournament, 64 teams compete in round 1. Fewer teams remain in each following round, as shown in the graph, until all but one team have been eliminated. The numbers of teams in each round form a geometric sequence. How many teams compete in round 5?

PRACTICE AND PROBLEM SOLVING

Independent Practice	
For Exercises	See Example
8–13	1
14–15	2
16	3

my.hrw.com

Online Extra Practice

Find the next three terms in each geometric sequence.

8. −2, 10, −50, 250, …   9. 32, 48, 72, 108, …   10. 625, 500, 400, 320, …

11. 6, 42, 294, …   12. 6, −12, 24, −48, …   13. 40, 10, $\frac{5}{2}$, $\frac{5}{8}$, …

14. The first term of a geometric sequence is 18 and the common ratio is 3.5. What is the 5th term of the sequence?

15. What is the 14th term of the geometric sequence 1000, 100, 10, 1, … ?

16. **Physical Science** A ball is dropped from a height of 500 meters. The table shows the height of each bounce, and the heights form a geometric sequence. How high does the ball bounce on the 8th bounce? Round your answer to the nearest tenth of a meter.

Bounce	Height (m)
1	400
2	320
3	256

Find the missing term(s) in each geometric sequence.

17. 20, 40, ▬, ▬, …   18. ▬, 6, 18, ▬, …   19. 9, 3, 1, ▬, …

20. 3, 12, ▬, 192, ▬, …   21. 7, 1, ▬, ▬, $\frac{1}{343}$, …   22. ▬, 100, 25, ▬, $\frac{25}{16}$, …

23. −3, ▬, −12, 24, ▬, …   24. ▬, ▬, 1, −3, 9, …   25. 1, 17, 289, ▬, …

Determine whether each sequence could be geometric. If so, give the common ratio.

26. 2, 10, 50, 250, …   27. 15, 5, $\frac{5}{3}$, $\frac{5}{9}$, …   28. 6, 18, 24, 38, …

29. 9, 3, −1, −5, …   30. 7, 21, 63, 189, …   31. 4, 1, −2, −4, …

H.O.T. 32. Multi-Step Billy earns money by mowing lawns for the summer. He offers two payment plans, as shown at right.

a. Do the payments for plan 2 form a geometric sequence? Explain.

b. If you were one of Billy's customers, which plan would you choose? (Assume that the summer is 10 weeks long.) Explain your choice.

33. Measurement When you fold a piece of paper in half, the thickness of the folded piece is twice the thickness of the original piece. A piece of copy paper is about 0.1 mm thick.

a. How thick is a piece of copy paper that has been folded in half 7 times?

b. Suppose that you could fold a piece of copy paper in half 12 times. How thick would it be? Write your answer in centimeters.

List the first four terms of each geometric sequence.

34. $a_1 = 3, a_n = 3(2)^{n-1}$ **35.** $a_1 = -2, a_n = -2(4)^{n-1}$ **36.** $a_1 = 5, a_n = 5(-2)^{n-1}$

37. $a_1 = 2, a_n = 2(2)^{n-1}$ **38.** $a_1 = 2, a_n = 2(5)^{n-1}$ **39.** $a_1 = 12, a_n = 12\left(\dfrac{1}{4}\right)^{n-1}$

H.O.T. 40. Critical Thinking What happens to the terms of a geometric sequence when r is doubled? Use an example to support your answer.

41. Geometry The steps below describe how to make a geometric figure by repeating the same process over and over on a smaller and smaller scale.

Step 1 (stage 0) Draw a large square.

Step 2 (stage 1) Divide the square into four equal squares.

Step 3 (stage 2) Divide each small square into four equal squares.

Step 4 Repeat Step 3 indefinitely.

a. Draw stages 0, 1, 2, and 3.

b. How many small squares are in each stage? Organize your data relating stage and number of small squares in a table.

c. Does the data in part **b** form a geometric sequence? Explain.

d. Write a rule to find the number of small squares in stage n.

H.O.T. 42. Write About It Write a series of steps for finding the nth term of a geometric sequence when you are given the first several terms.

Real-World Connections

43.
a. Three years ago, the annual tuition at a university was $3000. The following year, the tuition was $3300, and last year, the tuition was $3630. If the tuition has continued to grow in the same manner, what is the tuition this year? What do you expect it to be next year?

b. What is the common ratio?

c. What would you predict the tuition was 4 years ago? How did you find that value?

44. Which of the following is a geometric sequence?

    (A) $\frac{1}{2}$, 1, $\frac{3}{2}$, 2, ...   (C) 3, 8, 13, 18, ...

    (B) −2, −6, −10, −14, ...   (D) 5, 10, 20, 40, ...

45. Which equation represents the nth term in the geometric sequence
2, −8, 32, −128, ...?

    (F) $a_n = (-4)^n$ (G) $a_n = (-4)^{n-1}$ (H) $a_n = 2(-4)^n$ (J) $a_n = 2(-4)^{n-1}$

46. The frequency of a musical note, measured in hertz (Hz), is called its pitch. The pitches of the A keys on a piano form a geometric sequence, as shown.

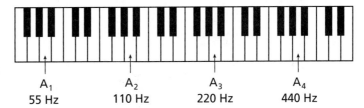

    A_1 A_2 A_3 A_4
    55 Hz   110 Hz   220 Hz   440 Hz

What is the frequency of A_7?

    (A) 880 Hz   (B) 1760 Hz   (C) 3520 Hz   (D) 7040 Hz

CHALLENGE AND EXTEND

Find the next three terms in each geometric sequence.

47. $x, x^2, x^3, \ldots$ **48.** $2x^2, 6x^3, 18x^4, \ldots$ **49.** $\frac{1}{y^3}, \frac{1}{y^2}, \frac{1}{y}, \ldots$ **50.** $\frac{1}{(x+1)^2}, \frac{1}{x+1}, 1, \ldots$

51. The 10th term of a geometric sequence is 0.78125. The common ratio is −0.5. Find the first term of the sequence.

52. The first term of a geometric sequence is 12 and the common ratio is $\frac{1}{2}$. Is 0 a term in this sequence? Explain.

53. A geometric sequence starts with 14 and has a common ration of 0.4. Colin finds that another number in the sequence is 0.057344. Which term in the sequence did Colin find?

H.O.T. 54. The first three terms of a sequence are 1, 2, and 4. Susanna said the 8th term of this sequence is 128. Paul said the 8th term is 29. Explain how the students found their answers. Why could these both be considered correct answers?

FOCUS ON MATHEMATICAL PRACTICES

H.O.T. 55. Reasoning A geometric sequence can be written as a function, in which the input p is the position of the term and the output is the term's value. Write the first 4 terms of each sequence.

    a. $f(p) = 2(1.5)^{p-1}$ **b.** $f(p) = 256\left(\frac{1}{4}\right)^{p-1}$ **c.** $f(p) = 3(-3)^p$

H.O.T. 56. Reasonableness A company promises that its Superbounce Ball will reach at least 50% of its drop height after the third bounce. The heights of successive bounces form a geometric sequence. Jay drops the ball and measures its first bounce at 80% of the drop height. Is the company's claim reasonable? Explain.

Exponential Functions

Essential Question: How can you identify, evaluate, and graph exponential functions?

Objectives
Evaluate exponential functions.

Identify and graph exponential functions.

Vocabulary
exponential function

Who uses this?
Scientists model populations with exponential functions.

The table and the graph show an insect population that increases over time.

Time (days)	Population
0	2
1	6
2	18
3	54

$\times 3$
$\times 3$
$\times 3$

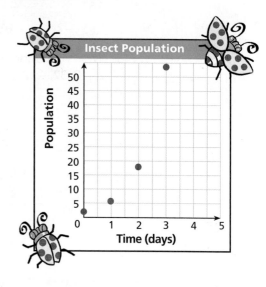

A function rule that describes the pattern above is $f(x) = 2(3)^x$. This type of function, in which the independent variable appears in an exponent, is an **exponential function**. Notice that 2 is the starting population and 3 is the amount by which the population is multiplied each day.

Exponential Functions

An exponential function has the form $f(x) = ab^x$, where $a \neq 0$, $b \neq 1$, and $b > 0$.

COMMON CORE GPS
MCC9-12.F.BF.1a

EXAMPLE **1** **Evaluating an Exponential Function**

 my.hrw.com

Online Video Tutor

A The function $f(x) = 2(3)^x$ models an insect population after x days. What will the population be on the 5th day?

$f(x) = 2(3)^x$ *Write the function.*

$f(5) = 2(3)^5$ *Substitute 5 for x.*

$\quad = 2(243)$ *Evaluate 3^5.*

$\quad = 486$ *Multiply.*

There will be 486 insects on the 5th day.

B The function $f(x) = 1500(0.995)^x$, where x is the time in years, models a prairie dog population. How many prairie dogs will there be in 8 years?

$f(x) = 1500(0.995)^x$

$f(8) = 1500(0.995)^8$ *Substitute 8 for x.*

$\quad \approx 1441$ *Use a calculator. Round to the nearest whole number.*

There will be about 1441 prairie dogs in 8 years.

Helpful Hint

In Example 1B, round your answer to the nearest whole number because there can only be a whole number of prairie dogs.

 CHECK IT OUT!

1. The function $f(x) = 8(0.75)^x$ models the width of a photograph in inches after it has been reduced by 25% x times. What is the width of the photograph after it has been reduced 3 times?

Remember that linear functions have constant first differences and quadratic functions have constant second differences. Exponential functions do not have constant differences, but they do have *constant ratios*.

As the *x*-values increase by a constant amount, the *y*-values are multiplied by a constant amount. This amount is the constant ratio and is the value of *b* in $f(x) = ab^x$.

x	$f(x) = 2(3)^x$
1	6
2	18
3	54
4	162

+ 1 | × 3 (between rows)

COMMON CORE GPS
MCC9-12.F.LE.1c

🌐 **my.hrw.com**

Online Video Tutor

EXAMPLE 2

Identifying an Exponential Function

Tell whether each set of ordered pairs satisfies an exponential function. Explain your answer.

A $\{(-1, 1.5), (0, 3), (1, 6), (2, 12)\}$

x	y
−1	1.5
0	3
1	6
2	12

+1 | × 2 (between each row)

This is an exponential function. As the *x*-values increase by a constant amount, the *y*-values are multiplied by a constant amount.

B $\{(-1, -9), (1, 9), (3, 27), (5, 45)\}$

x	y
−1	−9
1	9
3	27
5	45

+2 | × (−1); +2 | × 3; +2 | × $\frac{5}{3}$

This is *not* an exponential function. As the *x*-values increase by a constant amount, the *y*-values are *not* multiplied by a constant amount.

 CHECK IT OUT! Tell whether each set of ordered pairs satisfies an exponential function. Explain your answer.

2a. $\{(-1, 1), (0, 0), (1, 1), (2, 4)\}$ **2b.** $\{(-2, 4), (-1, 2), (0, 1), (1, 0.5)\}$

To graph an exponential function, choose several values of *x* (positive, negative, and 0) and generate ordered pairs. Plot the points and connect them with a smooth curve.

COMMON CORE GPS
MCC9-12.F.IF.7e

🌐 **my.hrw.com**

Online Video Tutor

EXAMPLE 3

Graphing $y = ab^x$ with $a > 0$ and $b > 1$

Graph $y = 3(4)^x$.

Choose several values of x and generate ordered pairs.

x	$y = 3(4)^x$
−1	0.75
0	3
1	12
2	48

Graph the ordered pairs and connect with a smooth curve.

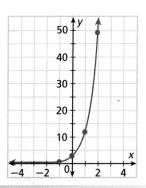

 CHECK IT OUT!   **3a.** Graph $y = 2^x$.   **3b.** Graph $y = 0.2(5)^x$.

COMMON CORE GPS MCC9-12.F.IF.7e **EXAMPLE 4**

Graphing $y = ab^x$ with $a < 0$ and $b > 1$

Graph $y = -5(2)^x$.

Choose several values of x and generate ordered pairs.

x	$y = -5(2)^x$
-1	-2.5
0	-5
1	-10
2	-20

Graph the ordered pairs and connect with a smooth curve.

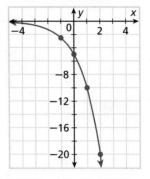

CHECK IT OUT!   **4a.** Graph $y = -6^x$.   **4b.** Graph $y = -3(3)^x$.

COMMON CORE GPS MCC9-12.F.IF.7e **EXAMPLE 5**

Graphing $y = ab^x$ with $0 < b < 1$

Graph each exponential function.

 my.hrw.com

Online Video Tutor

A $y = 3\left(\dfrac{1}{2}\right)^x$

Choose several values of x and generate ordered pairs.

x	$y = 3\left(\dfrac{1}{2}\right)^x$
-1	6
0	3
1	1.5
2	0.75

Graph the ordered pairs and connect with a smooth curve.

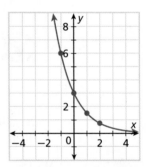

B $y = -2(0.4)^x$

Choose several values of x and generate ordered pairs.

x	$y = -2(0.4)^x$
-2	-12.5
-1	-5
0	-2
1	-0.8

Graph the ordered pairs and connect with a smooth curve.

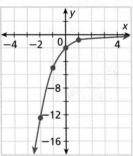

CHECK IT OUT!   Graph each exponential function.

5a. $y = 4\left(\dfrac{1}{4}\right)^x$ **5b.** $y = -2(0.1)^x$

The box summarizes the general shapes of exponential function graphs.

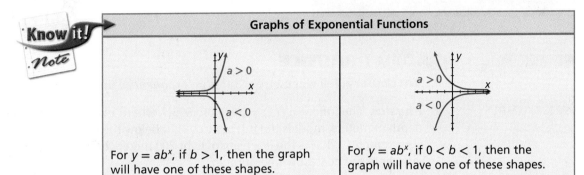

Graphs of Exponential Functions	
For $y = ab^x$, if $b > 1$, then the graph will have one of these shapes.	For $y = ab^x$, if $0 < b < 1$, then the graph will have one of these shapes.

COMMON CORE GPS
MCC9-12.F.BF.1a

EXAMPLE 6

Statistics Application

my.hrw.com

Online Video Tutor

In the year 2000, the world population was about 6 billion, and it was growing by 1.21% each year. At this growth rate, the function $f(x) = 6(1.0121)^x$ gives the population, in billions, x years after 2000. Using this model, in about what year does the population reach 7 billion?

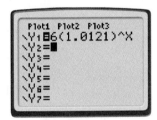

Enter the function into the Y= editor of a graphing calculator.

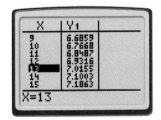

TABLE
Press **2nd** **GRAPH**. *Use the arrow keys to find a y-value as close to 7 as possible. The corresponding x-value is 13.*

Caution!

The function values give the population *in billions*, so a *y*-value of 7 means 7 billion.

The world population reaches 7 billion in about 2013.

CHECK IT OUT!

6. An accountant uses $f(x) = 12{,}330(0.869)^x$, where x is the time in years since the purchase, to model the value of a car. When will the car be worth $2000?

MCC.MP.7 **MATHEMATICAL PRACTICES**

THINK AND DISCUSS

1. How can you find the constant ratio of a set of exponential data?

2. GET ORGANIZED Copy and complete the graphic organizer. In each box, give an example of an appropriate exponential function and sketch its graph.

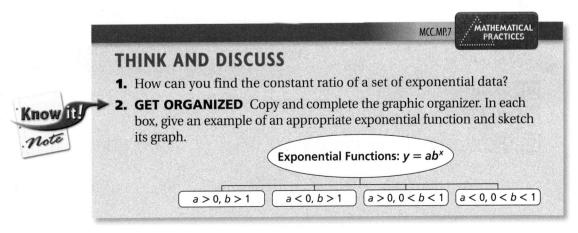

Exponential Functions: $y = ab^x$

| $a > 0, b > 1$ | $a < 0, b > 1$ | $a > 0, 0 < b < 1$ | $a < 0, 0 < b < 1$ |

GUIDED PRACTICE

1. **Vocabulary** Tell whether $y = 3x^4$ is an *exponential function*. Explain your answer.

SEE EXAMPLE 1

2. **Physics** The function $f(x) = 50{,}000(0.975)^x$, where x represents the underwater depth in meters, models the intensity of light below the water's surface in lumens per square meter. What is the intensity of light 200 meters below the surface? Round your answer to the nearest whole number.

SEE EXAMPLE 2

Tell whether each set of ordered pairs satisfies an exponential function. Explain your answer.

3. $\{(-1, -1), (0, 0), (1, -1), (2, -4)\}$ 4. $\{(0, 1), (1, 4), (2, 16), (3, 64)\}$

Graph each exponential function.

SEE EXAMPLE 3

5. $y = 3^x$ 6. $y = 5^x$

7. $y = 10(3)^x$ 8. $y = 5(2)^x$

SEE EXAMPLE 4

9. $y = -2(3)^x$ 10. $y = -4(2)^x$

11. $y = -3(2)^x$ 12. $y = 2(3)^x$

SEE EXAMPLE 5

13. $y = -\left(\frac{1}{4}\right)^x$ 14. $y = \left(\frac{1}{3}\right)^x$

15. $y = 2\left(\frac{1}{4}\right)^x$ 16. $y = -2(0.25)^x$

SEE EXAMPLE 6

17. The function $f(x) = 57.8(1.02)^x$ gives the number of passenger cars, in millions, in the United States x years after 1960. Using this model, in about what year does the number of passenger cars reach 200 million?

PRACTICE AND PROBLEM SOLVING

Independent Practice	
For Exercises	See Example
18–20	1
21–24	2
25–27	3
28–30	4
31–33	5
34	6

my.hrw.com

Online Extra Practice

18. **Sports** If a golf ball is dropped from a height of 27 feet, the function $f(x) = 27\left(\frac{2}{3}\right)^x$ gives the height in feet of each bounce, where x is the bounce number. What will be the height of the 4th bounce?

19. Suppose the depth of a lake can be described by the function $y = 334(0.976)^x$, where x represents the number of weeks from today. Today, the depth of the lake is 334 ft. What will the depth be in 6 weeks? Round your answer to the nearest whole number.

20. **Physics** A ball rolling down a slope travels continuously faster. Suppose the function $y = 1.3(1.41)^x$ describes the speed of the ball in inches per minute. How fast will the ball be rolling in 15 minutes? Round your answer to the nearest hundredth.

Tell whether each set of ordered pairs satisfies an exponential function. Explain your answer.

21. $\left\{(-2, 9), (-1, 3), (0, 1), \left(1, \frac{1}{3}\right)\right\}$ 22. $\{(-1, 0), (0, 1), (1, 4), (2, 9)\}$

23. $\{(-1, -5), (0, -3), (1, -1), (2, 1)\}$ 24. $\{(-3, 6.25), (-2, 12.5), (-1, 25), (0, 50)\}$

Graph each exponential function.

25. $y = 1.5^x$

26. $y = \frac{1}{3}(3)^x$

27. $y = 100(0.7)^x$

28. $y = -2(4)^x$

29. $y = -1(5)^x$

30. $y = -\frac{1}{2}(4)^x$

31. $y = 4\left(\frac{1}{2}\right)^x$

32. $y = -2\left(\frac{1}{3}\right)^x$

33. $y = 0.5(0.25)^x$

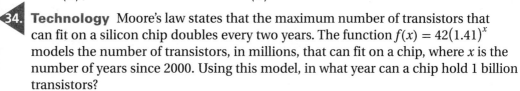

Technology

34. Technology Moore's law states that the maximum number of transistors that can fit on a silicon chip doubles every two years. The function $f(x) = 42(1.41)^x$ models the number of transistors, in millions, that can fit on a chip, where x is the number of years since 2000. Using this model, in what year can a chip hold 1 billion transistors?

35. Multi-Step A computer randomly creates three different functions. The functions are $y = (3.1x + 7)^2$, $y = 4.8(2)^x$, and $y = \frac{1}{5}(6)^x$. The computer then generates the y value 38.4. Given the three different functions, determine which one is exponential *and* produces the generated number.

Early silicon chips were about the size of your pinky finger and held one transistor. Today, chips the size of a baby's fingernail hold over 100 million transistors.

36. Contests As a promotion, a clothing store draws the name of one of its customers each week. The prize is a coupon for the store. If the winner is not present at the drawing, he or she cannot claim the prize, and the amount of the coupon increases for the following week's drawing. The function $f(x) = 20(1.2)^x$ gives the amount of the coupon in dollars after x weeks of the prize going unclaimed.

a. What is the amount of the coupon after 2 weeks of the prize going unclaimed?

b. After how many weeks of the prize going unclaimed will the amount of the coupon be greater than $100?

c. What is the original amount of the coupon?

d. Find the percent increase each week.

H.O.T. 37. Critical Thinking In the definition of exponential function, the value of b cannot be 1, and the value of a cannot be 0. Why?

Graphing Calculator Graph each group of functions on the same screen. How are their graphs alike? How are they different?

38. $y = 2^x, y = 3^x, y = 4^x$

39. $y = \left(\frac{1}{2}\right)^x, y = \left(\frac{1}{3}\right)^x, y = \left(\frac{1}{4}\right)^x$

Evaluate each of the following for the given value of x.

40. $f(x) = 4^x; x = 3$

41. $f(x) = -(0.25)^x; x = 1.5$

42. $f(x) = 0.4(10)^x; x = -3$

Real-World Connections

43. a. The annual tuition at a community college since 2001 is modeled by the equation $C = 2000(1.08)^n$, where C is the tuition cost and n is the number of years since 2001. What was the tuition cost in 2001?

b. What is the annual percentage of tuition increase?

c. Find the tuition cost in 2006.

Lucidio Studio, Inc./Alamy

H.O.T. **44. Write About It** Your employer offers two salary plans. With plan A, your salary is $f(x) = 10,000(2x)$, where x is the number of years you have worked for the company. With plan B, your salary is $g(x) = 10,000(2)^x$. Which plan would you choose? Why?

TEST PREP

45. Which graph shows an exponential function?

(A)

(C)

(B)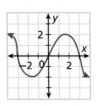

(D)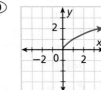

46. The function $f(x) = 15(1.4)^x$ represents the area in square inches of a photograph after it has been enlarged x times by a factor of 140%. What is the area of the photograph after it has been enlarged 4 times?

(F) 5.6 square inches   (H) 41.16 square inches

(G) 57.624 square inches   (J) 560 square inches

47. Look at the pattern. How many squares will there be in the nth stage?

Stage 0   Stage 1   Stage 2

(A) $5n$ (B) $2.5 \cdot 2^n$ (C) 25^{n-1} (D) 5^n

CHALLENGE AND EXTEND

Solve each equation.

48. $4^x = 64$ **49.** $\left(\frac{1}{3}\right)^x = \frac{1}{27}$ **50.** $2^x = \frac{1}{16}$

H.O.T. **51.** Graph the following functions: $y = 2(2)^x$, $y = 3(2)^x$, $y = -2(2)^x$. Then make a conjecture about the relationship between the value of a and the y-intercept of $y = ab^x$.

FOCUS ON MATHEMATICAL PRACTICES

H.O.T. **52. Problem Solving** $p = 0.915^d$ approximates the probability that a professional golfer will sink a putt from a distance of d feet. At what whole number of feet does the probability first drop below 0.5?

H.O.T. **53. Communication** The population of a bacteria colony after t hours can be modeled by the function $f(x) = 32(1.25)^t$. What do the numbers 32 and 1.25 represent in the context of the situation?

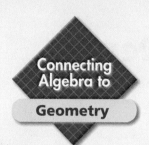

Changing Dimensions

Connecting Algebra to

Geometry

What happens to the volume of a three-dimensional figure when you repeatedly double the dimensions?

Recall these formulas for the volumes of common three-dimensional figures.

Cube $V = s^3$

Rectangular Prism $V = \ell wh$

Pyramid $V = \frac{1}{3}(\text{area of base}) \cdot h$

Base

Changing the dimensions of three-dimensional figures results in geometric sequences.

Example

Find the volume of a cube with a side length of 3 cm. Double the side length and find the new volume. Repeat two more times. Show the patterns for the side lengths and volumes as geometric sequences. Identify the common ratios.

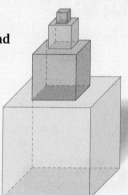

Cube	Side Length (cm)	Volume (cm³)
1	3	27
2	6	216
3	12	1,728
4	24	13,824

×2, ×2, ×2 (side lengths); ×8, ×8, ×8 (volumes)

The side lengths and the volumes form geometric sequences. The sequence of the side lengths has a common ratio of 2. The sequence of the volumes has a common ratio of 2^3, or 8.

The patterns in the example above are a specific instance of a general rule.

> When the dimensions of a solid figure are multiplied by x, the volume of the figure is multiplied by x^3.

Try This

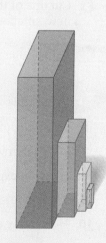

1. The large rectangular prism at right is 8 in. wide, 16 in. long, and 32 in. tall. The dimensions are multiplied by $\frac{1}{2}$ to create each next smaller prism. Show the patterns for the dimensions and the volumes as geometric sequences. Identify the common ratios.

2. A pyramid has a height of 8 cm and a square base of 3 cm on each edge. Triple the dimensions two times. Show the patterns for the dimensions and the volumes as geometric sequences. Identify the common ratios.

12-3

Model Growth and Decay

You can fold and cut paper to model quantities that increase
or decrease exponentially.

Use with Exponential
Growth and Decay

Look for and express
regularity in repeated
reasoning.

MCC.9-12.F.IE.2 Construct ... exponential functions ... given ...
a description of a relationship .... Also MCC.9-12.F.IE.1

Activity 1

1. Copy the table at right.

2. Fold a piece of notebook paper in half. Then open it back up. Count the
number of regions created by the fold. Record your answer in the table.

3. Now fold the paper in half twice. Record the number of regions created
by the folds in the table.

4. Repeat this process for 3, 4, and 5 folds.

Folds	Regions
0	1
1	
2	
3	
4	
5	

Try This

1. When the number of folds increases by 1, the number of regions ___?___ .

2. For each row of the table, write the number of regions as a power of 2.

3. Write an exponential expression for the number of regions formed by n folds.

4. If you could fold the paper 8 times, how many regions would be formed?

5. How many times would you have to fold the paper to make 512 regions?

Activity 2

1. Copy the table at right.

2. Begin with a square piece of paper. The area of the paper is 1 square
unit. Cut the paper in half. Each piece has an area of $\frac{1}{2}$ square unit.
Record the result in the table.

3. Cut one of those pieces in half again, and record the area of one of the
new, smaller pieces in the table.

4. Repeat this process for 3, 4, and 5 cuts.

Cuts	Area
0	1
1	
2	
3	
4	
5	

Try This

6. When the number of cuts increases by 1, the area ___?___ .

7. For each row of the table, write the area as a power of 2.

8. Write an exponential expression for the area after n cuts.

9. What would be the area after 7 cuts?

10. How many cuts would you have to make to get an area of $\frac{1}{256}$ square unit?

Exponential Growth and Decay

 Essential Question: How can you use exponential growth and decay functions to solve problems?

Objective
Solve problems involving exponential growth and decay.

Vocabulary
exponential growth
compound interest
exponential decay
half-life

 Animated Math

Why learn this?
Exponential growth and decay describe many real-world situations, such as the value of artwork. (See Example 1.)

Exponential growth occurs when a quantity increases by the same rate *r* in each time period *t*. When this happens, the value of the quantity at any given time can be calculated as a function of the rate and the original amount.

 **Exponential Growth**

An exponential growth function has the form $y = a(1 + r)^t$, where $a > 0$.

y represents the final amount.

a represents the original amount.

r represents the rate of growth expressed as a decimal.

t represents time.

COMMON CORE GPS
EXAMPLE 1
MCC9-12.F.LE.2

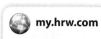 **my.hrw.com**

Online Video Tutor

Exponential Growth

The original value of a painting is $1400, and the value increases by 9% each year. Write an exponential growth function to model this situation. Then find the value of the painting in 25 years.

Step 1 Write the exponential growth function for this situation.

$$y = a(1 + r)^t \qquad \text{\textit{Write the formula.}}$$
$$= 1400(1 + 0.09)^t \qquad \text{\textit{Substitute 1400 for a and 0.09 for r.}}$$
$$= 1400(1.09)^t \qquad \text{\textit{Simplify.}}$$

Step 2 Find the value in 25 years.

$$y = 1400(1.09)^t$$
$$= 1400(1.09)^{25} \qquad \text{\textit{Substitute 25 for t.}}$$
$$\approx 12{,}072.31 \qquad \text{\textit{Use a calculator and round to the nearest hundredth.}}$$

The value of the painting in 25 years is $12,072.31.

Helpful Hint

In Example 1, round to the nearest hundredth because the problem deals with money. This means you are rounding to the nearest cent.

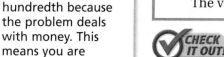 **1.** A sculpture is increasing in value at a rate of 8% per year, and its value in 2000 was $1200. Write an exponential growth function to model this situation. Then find the sculpture's value in 2006.

A common application of exponential growth is *compound interest*. Recall that simple interest is earned or paid only on the principal. **Compound interest** is interest earned or paid on *both* the principal and previously earned interest.

Compound Interest

$$A = P\left(1 + \frac{r}{n}\right)^{nt}$$

A represents the balance after *t* years.

P represents the principal, or original amount.

r represents the annual interest rate expressed as a decimal.

n represents the number of times interest is compounded per year.

t represents time in years.

COMMON CORE GPS MCC9-12.F.LE.2

EXAMPLE 2

Finance Application

Write a compound interest function to model each situation. Then find the balance after the given number of years.

Online Video Tutor

A $1000 invested at a rate of 3% compounded quarterly; 5 years

Step 1 Write the compound interest function for this situation.

$$A = P\left(1 + \frac{r}{n}\right)^{nt} \qquad \text{Write the formula.}$$

$$= 1000\left(1 + \frac{0.03}{4}\right)^{4t} \qquad \text{Substitute 1000 for P, 0.03 for r, and 4 for n.}$$

$$= 1000(1.0075)^{4t} \qquad \text{Simplify.}$$

Step 2 Find the balance after 5 years.

$$A = 1000(1.0075)^{4(5)} \qquad \text{Substitute 5 for t.}$$

$$= 1000(1.0075)^{20}$$

$$\approx 1161.18 \qquad \text{Use a calculator and round to the nearest hundredth.}$$

The balance after 5 years is $1161.18.

B $18,000 invested at a rate of 4.5% compounded annually; 6 years

Step 1 Write the compound interest function for this situation.

$$A = P\left(1 + \frac{r}{n}\right)^{nt} \qquad \text{Write the formula.}$$

$$= 18,000\left(1 + \frac{0.045}{1}\right)^{t} \qquad \text{Substitute 18,000 for P, 0.045 for r, and 1 for n.}$$

$$= 18,000(1.045)^{t} \qquad \text{Simplify.}$$

Step 2 Find the balance after 6 years.

$$A = 18,000(1.045)^{6} \qquad \text{Substitute 6 for t.}$$

$$\approx 23,440.68 \qquad \text{Use a calculator and round to the nearest hundredth.}$$

The balance after 6 years is $23,440.68.

For compound interest,
- *annually* means "once per year" ($n = 1$).
- *quarterly* means "4 times per year" ($n = 4$).
- *monthly* means "12 times per year" ($n = 12$).

Write a compound interest function to model each situation. Then find the balance after the given number of years.

2a. $1200 invested at a rate of 3.5% compounded quarterly; 4 years

2b. $4000 invested at a rate of 3% compounded monthly; 8 years

Exponential decay occurs when a quantity decreases by the same rate *r* in each time period *t*. Just like exponential growth, the value of the quantity at any given time can be calculated by using the rate and the original amount.

Exponential Decay

An exponential decay function has the form $y = a(1 - r)^t$, where $a > 0$.

y represents the final amount.

a represents the original amount.

r represents the rate of decay as a decimal.

t represents time.

Notice an important difference between exponential growth functions and exponential decay functions. For exponential growth, the value inside the parentheses will be greater than 1 because *r* is added to 1. For exponential decay, the value inside the parentheses will be less than 1 because *r* is subtracted from 1.

EXAMPLE MCC9-12.F.LE.2

3

Exponential Decay

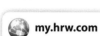

my.hrw.com

Online Video Tutor

The population of a town is decreasing at a rate of 1% per year. In 2000 there were 1300 people. Write an exponential decay function to model this situation. Then find the population in 2008.

Step 1 Write the exponential decay function for this situation.

$$y = a(1 - r)^t \qquad \text{\textit{Write the formula.}}$$

$$= 1300(1 - 0.01)^t \qquad \text{\textit{Substitute 1300 for a and 0.01 for r.}}$$

$$= 1300(0.99)^t \qquad \text{\textit{Simplify.}}$$

Step 2 Find the population in 2008.

$$y = 1300(0.99)^8 \qquad \text{\textit{Substitute 8 for t.}}$$

$$\approx 1200 \qquad \text{\textit{Use a calculator and round to the nearest whole number.}}$$

The population in 2008 is approximately 1200 people.

Helpful Hint

In Example 3, round your answer to the nearest whole number because there can only be a whole number of people.

3. The fish population in a local stream is decreasing at a rate of 3% per year. The original population was 48,000. Write an exponential decay function to model this situation. Then find the population after 7 years.

A common application of exponential decay is *half-life*. The **half-life** of a substance is the time it takes for one-half of the substance to decay into another substance.

Half-life

$A = P(0.5)^t$

A represents the final amount.

P represents the original amount.

t represents the number of half-lives in a given time period.

EXAMPLE **4**
MCC9-12.F.LE.2

Science Application

Fluorine-20 has a half-life of 11 seconds.

A Find the amount of fluorine-20 left from a 40-gram sample after 44 seconds.

Step 1 Find t, the number of half-lives in the given time period.

$$\frac{44\text{ s}}{11\text{ s}} = 4$$ *Divide the time period by the half-life. The value of t is 4.*

Step 2 $A = P(0.5)^t$ *Write the formula.*

$= 40(0.5)^4$ *Substitute 40 for P and 4 for t.*

$= 2.5$ *Use a calculator.*

There are 2.5 grams of fluorine-20 remaining after 44 seconds.

B Find the amount of fluorine-20 left from a 40-gram sample after 2.2 minutes. Round your answer to the nearest hundredth.

Step 1 Find t, the number of half-lives in the given time period.

$$2.2(60) = 132$$ *Find the number of seconds in 2.2 minutes.*

$$\frac{132\text{ s}}{11\text{ s}} = 12$$ *Divide the time period by the half-life. The value of t is $\frac{132}{11} = 12$.*

Step 2 $A = P(0.5)^t$ *Write the formula.*

$= 40(0.5)^{12}$ *Substitute 40 for P and 12 for t.*

≈ 0.01 *Use a calculator. Round to the nearest hundredth.*

There is about 0.01 gram of fluorine-20 remaining after 2.2 minutes.

4a. Cesium-137 has a half-life of 30 years. Find the amount of cesium-137 left from a 100-milligram sample after 180 years.

4b. Bismuth-210 has a half-life of 5 days. Find the amount of bismuth-210 left from a 100-gram sample after 5 weeks. (*Hint:* Change 5 weeks to days.)

MCC.MP.6   **MATHEMATICAL PRACTICES**

THINK AND DISCUSS

1. Describe three real-world situations that can be described by exponential growth or exponential decay functions.

2. The population of a town after t years can be modeled by $P = 1000(1.02)^t$. Is the population increasing or decreasing? By what percentage rate?

3. An exponential function is a function of the form $y = ab^x$. Explain why both exponential growth functions and exponential decay functions are exponential functions.

4. GET ORGANIZED Copy and complete the graphic organizer.

> **Exponential Growth vs. Exponential Decay**
>
> How are they alike? ↔ How are they different?

GUIDED PRACTICE

1. **Vocabulary** The function $y = 0.68(2)^x$ is an example of _____?_____.
   (*exponential growth* or *exponential decay*)

SEE EXAMPLE 1 Write an exponential growth function to model each situation. Then find the value of the function after the given amount of time.

2. The cost of tuition at a college is $12,000 and is increasing at a rate of 6% per year; 4 years.

3. The number of student-athletes at a local high school is 300 and is increasing at a rate of 8% per year; 5 years.

SEE EXAMPLE 2 Write a compound interest function to model each situation. Then find the balance after the given number of years.

4. $1500 invested at a rate of 3.5% compounded annually; 4 years

5. $4200 invested at a rate of 2.8% compounded quarterly; 6 years

SEE EXAMPLE 3 Write an exponential decay function to model each situation. Then find the value of the function after the given amount of time.

6. The value of a car is $18,000 and is depreciating at a rate of 12% per year; 10 years.

7. The amount (to the nearest hundredth) of a 10-mg dose of a certain antibiotic decreases in your bloodstream at a rate of 16% per hour; 4 hours.

SEE EXAMPLE 4 8. Bismuth-214 has a half-life of approximately 20 minutes. Find the amount of bismuth-214 left from a 30-gram sample after 1 hour.

9. Mendelevium-258 has a half-life of approximately 52 days. Find the amount of mendelevium-258 left from a 44-gram sample after 156 days.

PRACTICE AND PROBLEM SOLVING

Independent Practice	
For Exercises	See Example
10–13	1
14–17	2
18–19	3
20	4

my.hrw.com

Online Extra Practice

Write an exponential growth function to model each situation. Then find the value of the function after the given amount of time.

10. Annual sales for a company are $149,000 and are increasing at a rate of 6% per year; 7 years.

11. The population of a small town is 1600 and is increasing at a rate of 3% per year; 10 years.

12. A new savings account starts at $700 and increases at 1.2% yearly; 8 years.

13. Membership of a local club grows at a rate of 7.8% yearly and currently has 30 members; 6 years.

Write a compound interest function to model each situation. Then find the balance after the given number of years.

14. $28,000 invested at a rate of 4% compounded annually; 5 years

15. $7000 invested at a rate of 3% compounded quarterly; 10 years

16. $3500 invested at a rate of 1.8% compounded monthly; 4 years

17. $12,000 invested at a rate of 2.6% compounded annually; 15 years

Write an exponential decay function to model each situation. Then find the value of the function after the given amount of time.

18. The population of a town is 18,000 and is decreasing at a rate of 2% per year; 6 years.

19. The value of a book is $58 and decreases at a rate of 10% per year; 8 years.

20. The half-life of bromine-82 is approximately 36 hours. Find the amount of bromine-82 left from an 80-gram sample after 6 days.

Identify each of the following functions as exponential growth or decay. Then give the rate of growth or decay as a percent.

21. $y = 3(1.61)^t$

22. $y = 39(0.098)^t$

23. $y = a\left(\dfrac{2}{3}\right)^t$

24. $y = a\left(\dfrac{3}{2}\right)^t$

25. $y = a(1.1)^t$

26. $y = a(0.8)^t$

27. $y = a\left(\dfrac{5}{4}\right)^t$

28. $y = a\left(\dfrac{1}{2}\right)^t$

Write an exponential growth or decay function to model each situation. Then find the value of the function after the given amount of time.

29. The population of a country is 58,000,000 and grows by 0.1% per year; 3 years.

30. An antique car is worth $32,000, and its value grows by 7% per year; 5 years.

31. An investment of $8200 loses value at a rate of 2% per year; 7 years.

32. A new car is worth $25,000, and its value decreases by 15% each year; 6 years.

33. The student enrollment in a local high school is 970 students and increases by 1.2% per year; 5 years.

Atlantic Ocean

North Sea

England

Testwood●

34. **Archaeology** Carbon-14 dating is a way to determine the age of very old organic objects. Carbon-14 has a half-life of about 5700 years. An organic object with $\frac{1}{2}$ as much carbon-14 as its living counterpart died 5700 years ago. In 1999, archaeologists discovered the oldest bridge in England near Testwood, Hampshire. Carbon dating of the wood revealed that the bridge was 3500 years old. Suppose that when the bridge was built, the wood contained 15 grams of carbon-14. How much carbon-14 would it have contained when it was found by the archaeologists? Round to the nearest hundredth.

A computer-generated image of what the bridge at Testwood might have looked like

H.O.T. 35. **/// ERROR ANALYSIS ///** Two students were asked to find the value of a $1000-item after 3 years. The item was depreciating (losing value) at a rate of 40% per year. Which is incorrect? Explain the error.

Ⓐ
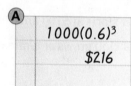
$1000(0.6)^3$
$216

Ⓑ
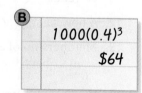
$1000(0.4)^3$
$64

H.O.T. 36. **Critical Thinking** The value of a certain car can be modeled by the function $y = 20,000(0.84)^t$, where t is time in years. Will the value ever be zero? Explain.

37. The value of a rare baseball card increases every year at a rate of 4%. Today, the card is worth $300. The owner expects to sell the card as soon as the value is over $600. How many years will the owner wait before selling the card? Round your answer to the nearest whole number.

Real-World Connections

38. **a.** The annual tuition at a prestigious university was $20,000 in 2002. It generally increases at a rate of 9% each year. Write a function to describe the cost as a function of the number of years since 2002. Use 2002 as year zero when writing the function rule.

   b. What do you predict the cost of tuition will be in 2008?

   c. Use a table of values to find the first year that the cost of the tuition is more than twice the cost in 2002.

39. **Multi-Step** At bank A, $600 is invested with an interest rate of 5% compounded annually. At bank B, $500 is invested with an interest rate of 6% compounded quarterly. Which account will have a larger balance after 10 years? 20 years?

40. **Estimation** The graph shows the decay of 100 grams of sodium-24. Use the graph to estimate the number of hours it will take the sample to decay to 10 grams. Then estimate the half-life of sodium-24.

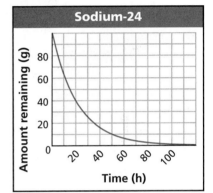

Sodium-24

41. **Graphing Calculator** Use a graphing calculator to graph $y = 10(1 + r)^x$ for $r = 10\%$ and $r = 20\%$. Compare the two graphs. How does the value of r affect the graphs?

42. **Write About It** Write a real-world situation that could be modeled by $y = 400(1.08)^t$.

43. **Write About It** Write a real-world situation that could be modeled by $y = 800(0.96)^t$.

44. **Critical Thinking** The amount of water in a container doubles every minute. After 6 minutes, the container is full. Your friend says it was half full after 3 minutes. Do you agree? Why or why not?

TEST PREP

45. A population of 500 is decreasing by 1% per year. Which function models this situation?

   (A) $y = 500(0.01)^t$ (B) $y = 500(0.1)^t$ (C) $y = 500(0.9)^t$ (D) $y = 500(0.99)^t$

46. Which function is NOT an exponential decay model?

   (F) $y = 5\left(\frac{1}{3}\right)^x$ (G) $y = -5\left(\frac{1}{3}\right)^x$ (H) $y = 5(3)^{-x}$ (J) $y = 5(3^{-1})^x$

47. Stephanie wants to save $1000 for a down payment on a car that she wants to buy in 3 years. She opens a savings account that pays 5% interest compounded annually. About how much should Stephanie deposit now to have enough money for the down payment in 3 years?

   (A) $295   (B) $333   (C) $500   (D) $865

48. **Short Response** In 2000, the population of a town was 1000 and was growing at a rate of 5% per year.

   a. Write an exponential growth function to model this situation.

   b. In what year is the population 1300? Show how you found your answer.

CHALLENGE AND EXTEND

49. You invest $700 at a rate of 6% compounded quarterly. Use a graph to estimate the number of years it will take for your investment to increase to $2300.

50. Omar invested $500 at a rate of 4% compounded annually. How long will it take for Omar's money to double? How long would it take if the interest were 8% compounded annually?

51. An 80-gram sample of a radioactive substance decayed to 10 grams after 300 minutes. Find the half-life of the substance.

52. Praseodymium-143 has a half-life of 2 weeks. The original measurement for the mass of a sample was lost. After 6 weeks, 15 grams of praseodymium-143 remain. How many grams was the original sample?

53. Phillip invested some money in a business 8 years ago. Since then, his investment has grown at an average rate of 1.3% compounded quarterly. Phillip's investment is now worth $250,000. How much was his original investment? Round your answer to the nearest dollar.

54. Personal Finance Anna has a balance of $200 that she owes on her credit card. She plans to make a $30 payment each month. There is also a 1.5% finance charge (interest) on the remaining balance each month. Copy and complete the table to answer the questions below. You may add more rows to the table as necessary.

Month	Balance ($)	Monthly Payment ($)	Remaining Balance ($)	1.5% Finance Charge ($)	New Balance ($)
1	200	30	170	2.55	172.55
2	172.55	30	▨	▨	▨
3	▨	30	▨	▨	▨
4	▨	30	▨	▨	▨

a. How many months will it take Anna to pay the entire balance?

b. By the time Anna pays the entire balance, how much total interest will she have paid?

FOCUS ON MATHEMATICAL PRACTICES

H.O.T. 55. Counterexamples Show that $y = (1 + 0.2)^x$ and $y = 1^x + 0.2^x$ are not equivalent.

H.O.T. 56. Modeling Ricardo is researching a groundhog population.

   a. Ricardo finds that the population increases by 4% every 6 months. Write an exponential function with t in *years* that models the size of the population in terms of percent of the original population.

   b. Ricardo wonders when the population will reach 180% of its initial value. He finds that $(1.04)^{15} \approx 1.8$. Use this and your function from part **a** to find the number of years needed. Show your work.

H.O.T. 57. Estimation Phosphorus-32 has a half-life of 14.29 days. Consider what percent of a sample remains after each of the first three periods of 14.29 days. Then estimate how long it would take for 11.5% of a sample of phosphorus-32 to remain. Explain your reasoning.

Mastering *the* Standards

for Mathematical Practice

The topics described in the Standards for Mathematical Content will vary from year to year. However, the *way* in which you learn, study, and think about mathematics will not. The Standards for Mathematical Practice describe skills that you will use in all of your math courses.

Mathematical Practices

1. *Make sense of problems and persevere in solving them.*
2. *Reason abstractly and quantitatively.*
3. *Construct viable arguments and critique the reasoning of others.*
4. *Model with mathematics.*
5. *Use appropriate tools strategically.*
6. *Attend to precision.*
7. *Look for and make use of structure.*
8. *Look for and express regularity in repeated reasoning.*

④ Model with mathematics.

Mathematically proficient students can apply... mathematics... to... problems... in everyday life, society, and the workplace...

In your book

Real-World Connections and **Focus on Mathematical Practices** exercises apply mathematics to other disciplines and in real-world scenarios.

Real-World Connections

61. **a.** A band wants to create a CD of their last concert. They received a donation of $500 to cover the cost. The total cost is $350 plus $3 per CD. Complete the table to find a relationship between the number of CDs and the total cost.
b. Write an equation for the cost *c* of the CDs based on the number of CDs *n*.
c. Write an inequality that can be used to determine how many CDs can be made with the $500 donation. Solve the inequality and determine how many CDs the band can have made from the $500 donation.

Number	Process	Cost
1	350 + 3	353
2		
3		
10		
n		

124 Chapter 2 Inequalities

FOCUS ON MATHEMATICAL PRACTICES

HOT 70. **Modeling** In order for Ramon to remain in his current weight class for a wrestling match on Saturday morning, he must weigh in at 152 pounds or more, but less than 160 pounds. Write a pair of inequalities that expresses the set of acceptable weights for Ramon. Define your variable.

HOT 71. **Problem Solving** Cary is making brownies using a recipe that calls for "at least 5 cups of flour but no more than 6 cups of flour." The only measuring cup he could find holds one quarter of a cup. Write a pair of inequalities to express how many *quarter cups* of flour Cary can use.

HOT 72. **Analysis** Imani and Trey are planning the seating at their wedding reception. They have 168 guests and each table can hold up to 16 guests, so they calculate that they need at least 10.5 tables to seat all of their guests. Graph their solution. In this context, how is the graph inaccurate? Make another graph that takes the context into account.

2-1 Graphing and Writing Inequalities **105**

EXTENSION # Patterns and Recursion

? *Essential Question:* How can you use recursion to identify and extend a sequence or function?

Objective
Identify and extend patterns using recursion.

Vocabulary
recursive pattern

In a **recursive pattern** or *recursive sequence*, each term is defined using one or more previous terms. For example, the sequence 1, 4, 7, 10, 13, ... can be defined recursively as follows: The first term is 1 and each term after the first is equal to the preceding term plus 3.

You can use recursive techniques to identify patterns. The table summarizes the characteristics of four types of patterns.

Using Recursive Techniques to Identify Patterns	
Type of Pattern	**Characteristics**
Linear	First differences are constant.
Quadratic	Second differences are constant.
Cubic	Third differences are constant.
Exponential	Ratios between successive terms are constant.

COMMON CORE GPS **EXAMPLE** **1** Prep. for MCC9-12.F.IF.3

Identifying and Extending a Pattern

Identify the type of pattern. Then find the next three numbers in the pattern.

Helpful Hint

You may need to use trial and error when identifying a pattern. If first, second, and third differences are not constant, check for constant ratios.

A **4, 6, 10, 16, 24, ...**

Find first, second, and, if necessary, third differences.

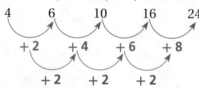

Second differences are constant, so the pattern is quadratic.

Extend the pattern by continuing the sequence of first and second differences.

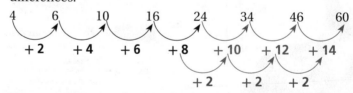

The next three numbers in the pattern are 34, 46, and 60.

B $\frac{1}{8}, \frac{1}{2}, 2, 8, 32$

Find the ratio between successive terms.

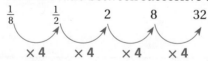

Ratios between terms are constant, so the pattern is exponential.

Extend the pattern by continuing the sequence of ratios.

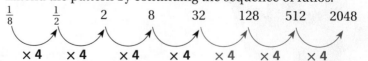

The next three numbers in the pattern are 128, 512, and 2048.

Identify the type of pattern. Then find the next three numbers in the pattern.

1a. 56, 47, 38, 29, 20, ...　　　　**1b.** 1, 8, 27, 64, 125, ...

You can use a similar process to determine whether a function is linear, quadratic, cubic, or exponential. Note that before comparing y-values, you must first make sure there is a constant change in the corresponding x-values.

Using Recursive Techniques to Identify Functions	
Type of Function	Characteristics (Given a Constant Change in x-values)
Linear	First differences of y-values are constant.
Quadratic	Second differences of y-values are constant.
Cubic	Third differences of y-values are constant.
Exponential	Ratios between successive y-values are constant.

COMMON CORE GPS Prep. for MCC9-12.F.IF.3 **EXAMPLE 2**

Identifying a Function

The ordered pairs {(−4, −4), (0, 0), (4, 4), (8, 32), (12, 108)} satisfy a function. Determine whether the function is linear, quadratic, cubic, or exponential. Then find three additional ordered pairs that satisfy the function.

Make a table. Check for a constant change in the x-values. Then find first, second, and third differences of y-values.

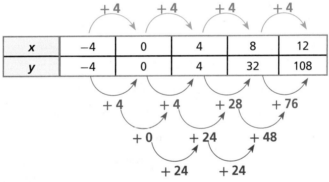

There is a constant change in the x-values. Third differences are constant. The function is a cubic function.

To find additional ordered pairs, extend the pattern by working backward from the constant third differences.

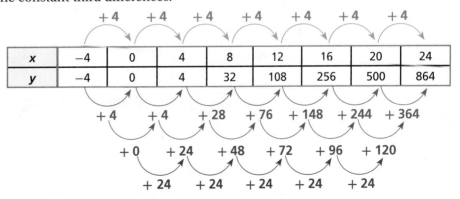

Helpful Hint

In Example 2, the constant third differences are 24. To extend the pattern, first find each second difference by adding 24 to the previous second difference. Then find each first difference by adding the second difference below to the previous first difference.

Three additional ordered pairs that satisfy this function are (16, 256), (20, 500), and (24, 864).

CHECK IT OUT! Several ordered pairs that satisfy a function are given. Determine whether the function is linear, quadratic, cubic, or exponential. Then find three additional ordered pairs that satisfy the function.

2a. {(0, 1), (1, 3), (2, 9), (3, 19), (4, 33)}

2b. $\left\{\left(1, \frac{1}{2}\right), \left(3, \frac{1}{6}\right), \left(5, \frac{1}{18}\right), \left(7, \frac{1}{54}\right), \left(9, \frac{1}{162}\right)\right\}$

EXTENSION

Exercises

my.hrw.com
Homework Help

Identify the type of pattern. Then find the next three numbers in the pattern.

1. 25, 28, 31, 34, 37, ...

2. 20, 45, 80, 125, 180, ...

3. 128, 64, 32, 16, 8, ...

4. 4, 32, 108, 256, 500, ...

5. $\frac{1}{2}, \frac{3}{4}, 1, 1\frac{1}{4}, 1\frac{1}{2}, ...$

6. 0.3, 0.03, 0.003, 0.0003, 0.00003, ...

7. 127, 66, 29, 10, 3, ...

8. 2, 8, 18, 32, 50, ...

Several ordered pairs that satisfy a function are given. Determine whether the function is linear, quadratic, cubic, or exponential. Then find three additional ordered pairs that satisfy the function.

9. {(3, 1), (5, –3), (7, –7), (9, –11), (11, –15)}

10. {(–1, –2), (2, 7), (5, 124), (8, 511), (11, 1330)}

11. $\left\{\left(2, \frac{1}{4}\right), \left(3, \frac{1}{8}\right), \left(4, \frac{1}{16}\right), \left(5, \frac{1}{32}\right), \left(6, \frac{1}{64}\right)\right\}$

12. {(–3, –7), (0, 2), (3, –7), (6, –34), (9, –79)}

13. {(0, 600), (10, 480), (20, 384), (30, 307.2), (40, 245.76)}

14. {(–8, 2), (–5, 7), (–2, 12), (1, 17), (4, 22)}

15. Entertainment The table shows the cost of using an online DVD rental service for different numbers of months.

Online DVD Rentals	
Months	**Cost ($)**
3	50
6	92
9	134
12	176
15	218

  a. Determine whether the function that models the data is linear, quadratic, cubic, or exponential. Explain.

  b. Graph the data in the table.

  c. What do you notice about your graph? Why does this make sense?

  d. Predict the cost of the service for 18 months.

16. A student claimed that the function shown in the table is a quadratic function. Do you agree or disagree? Explain.

x	3	7	10	14	17
y	2	6	12	20	30

      + 4   + 6   + 8   + 10

           + 2   + 2   + 2

17. **Business** The table shows the annual sales for a small company.

Annual Sales	
Year	Sales ($)
2006	513,000
2007	516,000
2008	521,000
2009	528,000
2010	537,000

   a. Determine whether the function that models the data is linear, quadratic, cubic, or exponential. Explain.

   b. Suppose sales continue to grow according to the pattern in the table. Predict the annual sales for 2011, 2012, and 2013.

   c. If the pattern continues, in what year will annual sales be $17,000 greater than the previous year's sales?

18. **Critical Thinking** Use the table for the following problems.

x	0	1	2	3	4
y	3	6			

   a. Copy and complete the table so that the function is a linear function.

   b. Copy and complete the table so that the function is a quadratic function.

   c. Copy and complete the table so that the function is an exponential function.

   d. For which of these three types of functions is there more than one correct way to complete the table? Explain.

Use the description to write the first five terms in each numerical pattern.

19. The first term is 8. Each following term is 11 less than the term before it.

20. The first term is 1000. Each following term is 40% of the term before it.

21. The first two terms are 1 and 2. Each following term is the sum of the two terms before it.

Make a table for a function that has the given characteristics. Include at least five ordered pairs.

22. The function is linear. The first differences are -3.

23. The function is quadratic. The second differences are 6.

24. The function is cubic. The third differences are 1.

A *recursive formula* for a sequence shows how to find the value of a term from one or more terms that come before it. For example, the recursive formula $a_n = a_{n-1} + 3$ tells you that each term is equal to the preceding term plus 3. Given that $a_1 = 5$, you can use the formula to generate the sequence 5, 8, 11, 14, ...

Write the first four terms of each sequence.

25. $a_n = a_{n-1} + 2; a_1 = 12$

26. $a_n = a_{n-1} - 7; a_1 = 16$

27. $a_n = 2a_{n-1}; a_1 = 4$

28. $a_n = 0.6a_{n-1}; a_1 = 100$

29. $a_n = 5a_{n-1} - 2; a_1 = 0$

30. $a_n = (a_{n-1})^2; a_1 = -2$

31. A *recursive function* defines a function for whole numbers by referring to the value of the function at previous whole numbers. Consider the recursive function $f(n) = f(n-1) + 5$ with $f(0) = 1$.

   a. According to the formula, $f(1) = f(0) + 5$. What is the value of $f(1)$?

   b. Use the formula to find $f(2), f(3), f(4)$, and $f(5)$.

   c. Graph $f(n)$ by plotting points at $x = 0, x = 1, x = 2, x = 3, x = 4$, and $x = 5$.

   d. What do you notice about your graph? What does this tell you about $f(n)$?

Ready to Go On?

my.hrw.com
Assessment and Intervention

12-1 Geometric Sequences

Find the next three terms in each geometric sequence.

1. 3, 6, 12, 24, …

2. −1, 2, −4, 8, …

3. −2400, −1200, −600, −300, …

4. The first term of a geometric sequence is 2 and the common ratio is 3. What is the 8th term of the sequence?

5. What is the 15th term of the geometric sequence 4, 12, 36, 108, …?

12-2 Exponential Functions

6. The function $f(x) = 3(1.1)^x$ gives the length (in inches) of an image after being enlarged by 10% x times. What is the length of the image after it has been enlarged 4 times? Round your answer to the nearest hundredth.

Graph each exponential function.

7. $y = 3^x$

8. $y = 2(2)^x$

9. $y = -2(4)^x$

10. $y = -(0.5)^x$

11. The function $f(x) = 40(0.8)^x$ gives the amount of a medication in milligrams present in a patient's system x hours after taking a 40-mg dose. In how many hours will there be less than 2 mg of the drug in a patient's system?

Tell whether each set of ordered pairs satisfies an exponential function. Explain.

12. $\{(0, 1), (2, 9), (4, 81), (6, 729)\}$

13. $\{(-2, -8), (-1, -4), (0, 0), (1, 4)\}$

12-3 Exponential Growth and Decay

Write a function to model each situation. Then find the value of the function after the given amount of time.

14. Fiona's salary is $30,000, and she expects to receive a 3% raise each year; 10 years.

15. $2000 is invested at a rate of 4.5% compounded monthly; 3 years.

16. A $1200 computer is losing value at a rate of 20% per year; 4 years.

17. Strontium-90 has a half-life of 29 years. About how much strontium-90 will be left from a 100-mg sample after 290 years? Round your answer to the nearest thousandth.

PARCC Assessment Readiness

Selected Response

1. The function $f(x) = 5{,}000(0.972)^x$, where x is the time in years, models a declining lemming population. How many lemmings will there be in 6 years?

Ⓐ About 30,006 lemmings

Ⓑ About 29,160 lemmings

Ⓒ About 5,001 lemmings

Ⓓ About 4,217 lemmings

2. Find the next three terms in the geometric sequence $-36, 6, -1, \frac{1}{6}, \ldots$

Ⓕ $-\frac{1}{1296}, \frac{1}{216}, -\frac{1}{36}$

Ⓖ $\frac{1}{36}, -\frac{1}{216}, \frac{1}{1296}$

Ⓗ $-1, 6, -36$

Ⓙ $-\frac{1}{36}, \frac{1}{216}, -\frac{1}{1296}$

3. The value of a gold coin picturing the head of the Roman Emperor Vespasian is $105. This value is increasing at a rate of 10% per year. Write an exponential growth function to model this situation. Then find the value of the coin in 11 years.

Ⓐ $f(t) = 1.1(105)^t$; about $1270.

Ⓑ $f(t) = 105(1.1)^t$; about $300.

Ⓒ $f(t) = 105 + 1.1t$; about $117.

Ⓓ $f(t) = 105(1.1t)$; about $1271.

4. Write a compound interest function to model the following situation. Then, find the balance after the given number of years.

$17,400 invested at a rate of 2.5% compounded annually; 8 years

Ⓕ $17{,}400 \, (1.025)^{8t}$; $84,504

Ⓖ $17{,}400 \, (0.025)^t$; $26,550,293

Ⓗ $17{,}400 \, (1.025)^t$; $21,200

Ⓙ $17{,}400 \, (3.5)^t$; $391,826,318

5. Graph $y = 3(2)^x$.

Ⓐ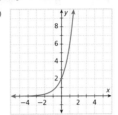

Ⓑ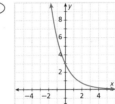

Ⓒ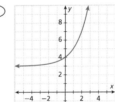

Ⓓ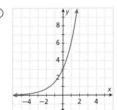

6. The first term of a geometric sequence is 512, and the common ratio is 0.5. What is the 8th term of the sequence?.

Ⓕ 4   Ⓗ 22.63

Ⓖ 8   Ⓙ 2

Mini-Task

7. Tell whether the set of ordered pairs satisfies an exponential function. Explain your answer.
$\{(1, -6), (2, -18), (3, -54), (4, -162)\}$

13 Comparing and Modeling with Functions

COMMON CORE GPS

Contents

MATHEMATICAL PRACTICES   The Common Core Georgia Performance Standards for Mathematical Practice describe varieties of expertise that all students should seek to develop. Opportunities to develop these practices are integrated throughout this program.

1 Make sense of problems and persevere in solving them.

2 Reason abstractly and quantitatively.

3 Construct viable arguments and critique the reasoning of others.

4 Model with mathematics.

5 Use appropriate tools strategically.

6 Attend to precision.

7 Look for and make use of structure.

8 Look for and express regularity in repeated reasoning.

Unpacking the Standards

Understanding the standards and the vocabulary terms in the standards will help you know exactly what you are expected to learn in this chapter.

MCC9-12.F.LE.2

Construct linear and exponential functions, including arithmetic and geometric sequences, given a graph, a description of a relationship, or two input-output pairs (include reading these from a table).

What It Means For You

You can construct a model of a linear or exponential function from different descriptions or displays of the same situation.

EXAMPLE   Geometric Sequence

A ball is dropped 81 inches onto a hard surface. The table shows the ball's height on successive bounces. Write a model for the height reached as a function of the number of bounces.

Bounce	1	2	3	4
Height (in.)	54	36	24	16

Consecutive terms have a common ratio of $\frac{2}{3}$. You can write a model as an exponential function or as a geometric sequence:

Exponential function: $f(x) = 81\left(\frac{2}{3}\right)^x$, where x is the bounce number

Geometric sequence: $a_1 = 54$, $a_n = \frac{2}{3} a_{n-1}$, where n is the bounce number

Mastering *the* Standards

for Mathematical Practice

The topics described in the Standards for Mathematical Content will vary from year to year. However, the *way* in which you learn, study, and think about mathematics will not. The Standards for Mathematical Practice describe skills that you will use in all of your math courses.

Mathematical Practices

1. Make sense of problems and persevere in solving them.
2. Reason abstractly and quantitatively.
3. Construct viable arguments and critique the reasoning of others.
4. Model with mathematics.
5. Use appropriate tools strategically.
6. Attend to precision.
7. Look for and make use of structure.
8. Look for and express regularity in repeated reasoning.

⑤ Use appropriate tools strategically.

Mathematically proficient students consider the available tools when solving a... problem... [and] are... able to use technological tools to explore and deepen their understanding...

In your book

Algebra Tasks and **Technology Tasks** use concrete and technological tools to explore mathematical concepts.

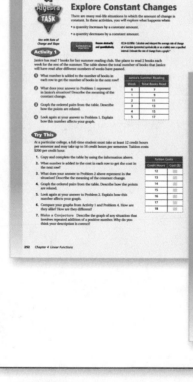

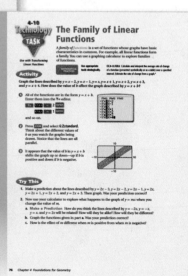

13-1 Linear, Quadratic, and Exponential Models

Essential Question: How can you distinguish between situations that can be modeled by linear and exponential functions?

Objectives
Compare linear, quadratic, and exponential models.

Given a set of data, decide which type of function models the data and write an equation to describe the function.

Why learn this?
Different situations in sports can be described by linear, quadratic, or exponential models.

Look at the tables and graphs below. The data show three ways you have learned that variable quantities can be related. The relationships shown are linear, quadratic, and exponential.

Remember!

A linear function is a function whose rule is a first-degree polynomial and whose graph is a line. A quadratic function is a function whose rule is a second-degree polynomial and whose graph is a U-shaped curve called a parabola.

Linear

Training Heart Rate

Age (yr)	Beats/min
20	170
30	161.5
40	153
50	144.5

Quadratic

Volleyball Height

Time (s)	Height (ft)
0.4	10.44
0.8	12.76
1	12
1.2	9.96

Exponential

Volleyball Tournament

Round	Teams Left
1	16
2	8
3	4
4	2

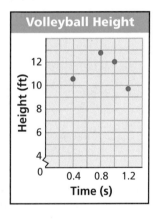

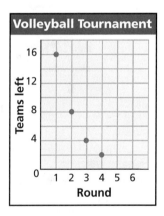

In the real world, people often gather data and then must decide what kind of relationship (if any) they think best describes their data.

COMMON CORE GPS
MCC9-12.F.LE.1

EXAMPLE 1 Graphing Data to Choose a Model

my.hrw.com

Online Video Tutor

Graph each data set. Which kind of model best describes the data?

A

Time (h)	0	1	2	3
Bacteria	10	20	40	80

Plot the data points and connect them.
The data appear to be exponential.

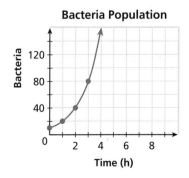

Bacteria Population

© Stan Liu/Icon SMI/ZUMA Press

13-1 Linear, Quadratic, and Exponential Models **341**

Graph each data set. Which kind of model best describes the data?

°C	0	5	10	15	20
°F	32	41	50	59	68

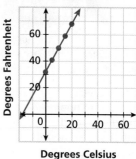

Celsius to Fahrenheit

Plot the data points and connect them.

The data appear to be linear.

CHECK IT OUT!

Graph each data set. Which kind of model best describes the data?

1a. $\{(-3, 0.30), (-2, 0.44), (0, 1), (1, 1.5), (2, 2.25), (3, 3.38)\}$

1b. $\{(-3, -14), (-2, -9), (-1, -6), (0, -5), (1, -6), (2, -9), (3, -14)\}$

Another way to decide which kind of relationship (if any) best describes a data set is to use patterns.

COMMON CORE GPS
MCC9-12.F.LE.1

EXAMPLE 2

Using Patterns to Choose a Model

Look for a pattern in each data set to determine which kind of model best describes the data.

my.hrw.com

Online Video Tutor

A

Height of Bridge Suspension Cables

Cable's Distance from Tower (ft)	Cable's Height (ft)
0	400
100	256
200	144
300	64

+ 100 for distance; − 144, − 112, − 80 with + 32 second difference

For every constant change in distance of +100 feet, there is a constant second difference of +32.

The data appear to be quadratic.

B

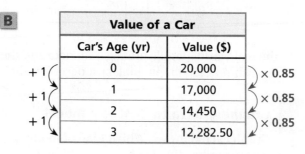

Value of a Car

Car's Age (yr)	Value ($)
0	20,000
1	17,000
2	14,450
3	12,282.50

+ 1 for age; × 0.85 ratio

For every constant change in age of +1 year, there is a constant ratio of 0.85.

The data appear to be exponential.

Remember!

When the independent variable changes by a constant amount,
• linear functions have constant first differences.
• quadratic functions have constant second differences.
• exponential functions have a constant ratio.

CHECK IT OUT!

2. Look for a pattern in the data set $\{(-2, 10), (-1, 1), (0, -2), (1, 1), (2, 10)\}$ to determine which kind of model best describes the data.

After deciding which model best fits the data, you can write a function. The general forms of linear, quadratic, and exponential functions are shown below.

General Forms of Functions

LINEAR	QUADRATIC	EXPONENTIAL
$y = mx + b$	$y = ax^2 + bx + c$	$y = ab^x$

COMMON CORE GPS **EXAMPLE** **3** MCC9-12.F.LE.2

Problem-Solving Application

Use the data in the table to describe how the ladybug population is changing. Then write a function that models the data. Use your function to predict the ladybug population after one year.

Ladybug Population

Time (mo)	Ladybugs
0	10
1	30
2	90
3	270

my.hrw.com

Online Video Tutor

1 **Understand the Problem**

The **answer** will have three parts—a description, a function, and a prediction.

2 **Make a Plan**

Determine whether the data is linear, quadratic, or exponential. Use the general form to write a function. Then use the function to find the population after one year.

MATHEMATICAL PRACTICES

Make sense of problems and persevere in solving them.

3 **Solve**

Step 1 Describe the situation in words.

Ladybug Population

	Time (mo)	Ladybugs	
+1	0	10	×3
+1	1	30	×3
+1	2	90	×3
	3	270	

Each month, the ladybug population is multiplied by 3. In other words, the population triples each month.

Step 2 Write the function.

There is a constant ratio of 3. The data appear to be exponential.

$y = ab^x$	*Write the general form of an exponential function.*
$y = a(3)^x$	*Substitute the constant ratio, 3, for b.*
$10 = a(3)^0$	*Choose an ordered pair from the table, such as (0, 10). Substitute for x and y.*
$10 = a(1)$	*Simplify. $3^0 = 1$*
$10 = a$	*The value of a is 10.*
$y = 10(3)^x$	*Substitute 10 for a in $y = a(3)^x$.*

Helpful Hint

You can choose any given ordered pair to substitute for *x* and *y*. However, it is often easiest to choose an ordered pair that contains 0.

Christine Lee Zilka/Getty Images

Step 3 Predict the ladybug population after one year.

$y = 10(3)^x$ *Write the function.*

$\quad = 10(3)^{12}$ *Substitute 12 for x (1 year = 12 mo).*

$\quad = 5{,}314{,}410$ *Use a calculator.*

There will be 5,314,410 ladybugs after one year.

4 Look Back

You chose the ordered pair $(0, 10)$ to write the function. Check that every other ordered pair in the table satisfies your function.

$y = 10(3)^x$	
30	$10(3)^1$
30	$10(3)$
30	$30 \checkmark$

$y = 10(3)^x$	
90	$10(3)^2$
90	$10(9)$
90	$90 \checkmark$

$y = 10(3)^x$	
270	$10(3)^3$
270	$10(27)$
270	$270 \checkmark$

3. Use the data in the table to describe how the oven temperature is changing. Then write a function that models the data. Use your function to predict the temperature after 1 hour.

Oven Temperature

Time (min)	0	10	20	30
Temperature (°F)	375	325	275	225

MCC.MP.3

MATHEMATICAL PRACTICES

THINK AND DISCUSS

1. Do you think that every data set will be able to be modeled by a linear, quadratic, or exponential function? Why or why not?

2. In Example 3, is it certain that there will be 5,314,410 ladybugs after one year? Explain.

3. GET ORGANIZED Copy and complete the graphic organizer. In each box, list some characteristics and sketch a graph of each type of model.

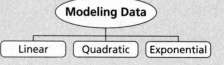

Modeling Data

Linear   Quadratic   Exponential

age fotostock

13-1 Exercises

my.hrw.com
Homework Help

GUIDED PRACTICE

SEE EXAMPLE **1** — Graph each data set. Which kind of model best describes the data?

1. $\{(-1, 4), (-2, 0.8), (0, 20), (1, 100), (-3, 0.16)\}$
2. $\{(0, 3), (1, 9), (2, 11), (3, 9), (4, 3)\}$
3. $\{(2, -7), (-2, -9), (0, -8), (4, -6), (6, -5)\}$

SEE EXAMPLE **2** — Look for a pattern in each data set to determine which kind of model best describes the data.

4. $\{(-2, 1), (-1, 2.5), (0, 3), (1, 2.5), (2, 1)\}$
5. $\{(-2, 0.75), (-1, 1.5), (0, 3), (1, 6), (2, 12)\}$
6. $\{(-2, 2), (-1, 4), (0, 6), (1, 8), (2, 10)\}$

SEE EXAMPLE **3** —

7. **Consumer Economics** Use the data in the table to describe the cost of grapes. Then write a function that models the data. Use your function to predict the cost of 6 pounds of grapes.

Total Cost of Grapes				
Amount (lb)	1	2	3	4
Cost ($)	1.79	3.58	5.37	7.16

PRACTICE AND PROBLEM SOLVING

Independent Practice	
For Exercises	See Example
8–10	1
11–13	2
14	3

my.hrw.com

Online Extra Practice

Graph each data set. Which kind of model best describes the data?

8. $\{(-3, -5), (-2, -8), (-1, -9), (0, -8), (1, -5), (2, 0), (3, 7)\}$
9. $\{(-3, -1), (-2, 0), (-1, 1), (0, 2), (1, 3), (2, 4), (3, 5)\}$
10. $\{(0, 0.1), (2, 0.9), (3, 2.7), (4, 8.1)\}$

Look for a pattern in each data set to determine which kind of model best describes the data.

11. $\{(-2, 5), (-1, 4), (0, 3), (1, 2), (2, 1)\}$
12. $\{(-2, 12), (-1, 15), (0, 16), (1, 15), (2, 12)\}$
13. $\{(-2, 8), (-1, 4), (0, 2), (1, 1), (2, 0.5)\}$

14. **Business** Use the data in the table to describe how the company's sales are changing. Then write a function that models the data. Use your function to predict the amount of sales after 10 years.

Company Sales				
Year	0	1	2	3
Sales ($)	25,000	30,000	36,000	43,200

15. **Multi-Step** Jay's hair grows about 6 inches each year. Write a function that describes the length ℓ in inches that Jay's hair will grow for each year k. Which kind of model best describes the function?

13-1 Linear, Quadratic, and Exponential Models **345**

Tell which kind of model best describes each situation.

16. The height of a plant at weekly intervals over the last 6 weeks was 1 inches, 1.5 inches, 2 inches, 2.5 inches, 3 inches., and 3.5 inches.

17. The number of games a baseball player played in the last four years was 162, 162, 162, and 162.

18. The height of a ball in a certain time interval was recorded as 30.64 feet, 30.96 feet, 31 feet, 30.96 feet, and 30.64 feet.

Write a function to model each set of data.

19.

x	−1	0	1	2	4
y	0.05	0.2	0.8	3.2	51.2

20.

x	−2	0	2	4	8
y	5	4	3	2	0

Tell which kind of model best describes each graph.

21.

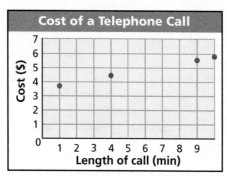

22.

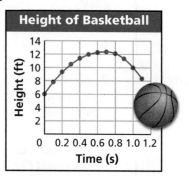

H.O.T. 23. **Write About It** Write a set of data that you could model with an exponential function. Explain why the exponential model would work.

24. **///ERROR ANALYSIS///** A student concluded that the data set would best be modeled by a quadratic function. Explain the student's error.

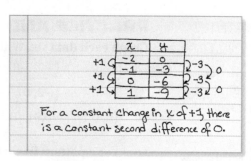

H.O.T. 25. **Critical Thinking** Sometimes the graphs of quadratic data and exponential data can look very similar. Describe how you can tell them apart.

Real-World Connections

26. **a.** Examine the two models that represent annual tuition for two colleges. Describe each model as linear, quadratic, or exponential.

   b. Write a function rule for each model.

   c. Both models have the same values for 2004. What does this mean?

   d. Why do both models have the same value for year 1?

Years After 2004	Tuition at College 1 ($)	Tuition at College 2 ($)
0	2000.00	2000.00
1	2200.00	2200.00
2	2400.00	2420.00
3	2600.00	2662.00
4	2800.00	2928.20

27. Which function best models the data: $\{(-4, -2), (-2, -1), (0, 0), (2, 1), (4, 2)\}$?

(A) $y = \left(\frac{1}{2}\right)^x$ (B) $y = \frac{1}{2}x^2$ (C) $y = \frac{1}{2}x$ (D) $y = \left(\frac{1}{2}x\right)^2$

28. A city's population is increasing at a rate of 2% per year. Which type of model describes this situation?

(F) Exponential (G) Quadratic (H) Linear (J) None of these

29. Which data set is best modeled by a linear function?

(A) $\{(-2, 0), (-1, 2), (0, -4), (1, -1), (2, 2)\}$
(B) $\{(-2, 2), (-1, 4), (0, 6), (1, 16), (2, 32)\}$
(C) $\{(-2, 2), (-1, 4), (0, 6), (1, 8), (2, 10)\}$
(D) $\{(-2, 0), (-1, 5), (0, 7), (1, 5), (2, 0)\}$

CHALLENGE AND EXTEND

30. **Finance** An accountant estimates that a certain new automobile worth $18,000 will lose value at a rate of 16% per year.

   a. Make a table that shows the worth of the car for years 0, 1, 2, 3, and 4. What is the real-world meaning of year 0?

   b. Which type of model best represents the data in your table? Explain.

   c. Write a function for your data.

   d. What is the value of the car after $5\frac{1}{2}$ years?

   e. What is the value of the car after 8 years?

31. **Pet Care** The table shows general guidelines for the weight of a Great Dane at various ages.

   a. None of the three models in this lesson—linear, quadratic, or exponential—fits this data exactly. Which of these is the *best* model for the data? Explain your choice.

   b. What would you predict for the weight of a Great Dane who is 1 year old?

   c. Do you think you could use your model to find the weight of a Great Dane at any age? Why or why not?

Great Dane	
Age (mo)	Weight (kg)
2	12
4	23
6	33
8	40
10	45

FOCUS ON MATHEMATICAL PRACTICES

H.O.T. **32.** **Reasoning** For $f(x) = 5^x$ and $g(x) = 2^x$, $h(x) = f(x) - g(x)$. Evaluate $h(x)$ for $x = 3, 4, 5, 6, 7$. Which type of function best models $h(x)$? Explain.

H.O.T. **33.** **Properties** You know that a function is linear, quadratic, or exponential. You find that the average rate of change between two values of x is positive, but between two other values of x, the rate of change is negative. What type of function is it? How do you know?

H.O.T. **34.** **Modeling** Yvonne knows that a home was valued at $150,000 initially and $180,000 one year later. Find a linear function that describes the data, and then find an exponential function. Finally, find the value of the house after 5 years using each function.

Linear and Nonlinear Rates of Change

? **Essential Question:** How can you identify linear and nonlinear rates of change and the functions they are associated with?

Objectives

Identify linear and nonlinear rates of change.

Compare rates of change.

Recall that a *rate of change* is a ratio that compares the amount of change in a dependent variable to the amount of change in an independent variable.

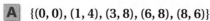

$$\text{rate of change} = \frac{\text{change in dependent variable}}{\text{change in independent variable}}$$

The table shows the price of one ounce of gold in 2005 and 2008. The year is the independent variable and the price is the dependent variable. The rate of change is $\frac{870-513}{2008-2005} = \frac{357}{3} = 119$, or \$119 per year.

Price of Gold	
Year	Price ($/oz)
2005	513
2008	870

COMMON CORE GPS
MCC9-12.F.IF.6

EXAMPLE 1

Identifying Constant and Variable Rates of Change

Determine whether each function has a constant or variable rate of change.

A {(0, 0), (1, 4), (3, 8), (6, 8), (8, 6)}

Find the ratio of the amount of change in the dependent variable *y* to the corresponding amount of change in the independent variable *x*.

x	y
0	0
1	4
3	8
6	8
8	6

+1) +4
+2) +4
+3) +0
+2) −2

The rates of change are

$\frac{4}{1} = 4$, $\frac{4}{2} = 2$, $\frac{0}{3} = 0$, and $\frac{-2}{2} = -1$.

The function has a variable rate of change.

B {(0, 1), (1, 2), (4, 5), (6, 7), (7, 8)}

Find the ratio of the amount of change in the dependent variable *y* to the corresponding amount of change in the independent variable *x*.

x	y
0	1
1	2
4	5
6	7
7	8

+1) +1
+3) +3
+2) +2
+1) +1

The rates of change are

$\frac{1}{1} = 1$, $\frac{3}{3} = 1$, $\frac{2}{2} = 1$, and $\frac{1}{1} = 1$.

The function has a constant rate of change.

 CHECK IT OUT! **Determine whether each function has a constant or variable rate of change.**

1a. {(−3, 10), (0, 7), (1, 6), (4, 3), (7, 0)}

1b. {(−2, −3), (2, 5), (3, 7), (5, 9), (8, 12)}

The functions in Examples 1A and 1B are graphed below.

Example 1A (variable rate of change)

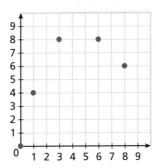

Example 1B (constant rate of change)

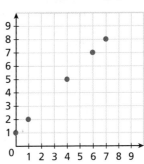

A function is a *linear function* if and only if the function has a constant rate of change. The graph of such a function is a straight line and the rate of change is the slope of the line, as in Example 1B.

A function with a variable rate of change, as in Example 1A, is a *nonlinear function*. Examples of nonlinear functions include quadratic functions and exponential functions.

EXAMPLE 2
MCC9-12.F.LE.1

Identifying Linear and Nonlinear Functions

Use rates of change to determine whether each function is linear or nonlinear.

A

	x	y	
+2	−2	0	+1
+1	0	1	+0.5
+3	1	1.5	+1.5
+6	4	3	+3
	10	6	

Find the rates of change.

$\frac{1}{2}$ $\frac{0.5}{1}=\frac{1}{2}$ $\frac{1.5}{3}=\frac{1}{2}$ $\frac{3}{6}=\frac{1}{2}$

There is a constant rate of change, $\frac{1}{2}$, so this function is linear.

B

	x	y	
+4	−6	18	−16
+4	−2	2	+0
−2	2	2	−2
+4	0	0	+8
	4	8	

Find the rates of change.

$\frac{-16}{4}=-4$ $\frac{0}{4}=0$ $\frac{-2}{-2}=1$ $\frac{8}{4}=\frac{1}{2}$

The rates of change are not constant, so this function is nonlinear.

CHECK IT OUT! Use rates of change to determine whether each function is linear or nonlinear.

2a.

x	y
−2	$\frac{1}{4}$
−1	$\frac{1}{2}$
0	1
3	8
4	16

2b.

x	y
−5	3
−1	3
1	3
3	3
7	3

When you are given a verbal description of a function, you can determine whether the function is linear or nonlinear by making a table of values and examining the rates of change. You can compare two functions by comparing their rates of change.

EXAMPLE **3** *Physical Science Application*

Two water tanks contain 512 gallons of water each. Tank A begins to drain, losing half of its volume of water every hour. Tank B begins to drain at the same time and loses 40 gallons of water every hour. Identify the function that gives the volume of water in each tank as linear or nonlinear. Which tank loses water more quickly between hour 4 and hour 5?

Use the verbal descriptions to make a table for the volume of water in each tank.

Time (h)	0	1	2	3	4	5
Water in Tank A (gal)	512	256	128	64	32	16

Time (h)	0	1	2	3	4	5
Water in Tank B (gal)	512	472	432	392	352	312

For tank A, the rates of change are –256, –128, –64, –32, and –16, so the rate of change is variable and the function is nonlinear.

For tank B, the rates of change are all –40, so the rate of change is constant and the function is linear.

Between hours 4 and 5, the volume of water in tank A decreases at a rate of 16 gallons per hour. The volume of water in tank B decreases at a rate of 40 gallons per hour. Tank B loses water more quickly.

CHECK IT OUT!

3. Reka and Charlotte each invest $500. Each month, Charlotte's investment grows by $25, while Reka's investment grows by 5% of the previous month's amount. Identify the function that gives the value of each investment as linear or nonlinear. Who is earning money more quickly between month 3 and month 4?

EXTENSION

Exercises

my.hrw.com
Homework Help

Use rates of change to determine whether each function is linear or nonlinear.

1.

x	4	5	7	10	12
y	–2	–1	1	4	6

2.

x	–2	3	4	6	8
y	–4	6	8	14	20

3.

x	0	3	9	12	18
y	14	12	8	6	2

4.

x	–8	–6	–4	–2	0
y	–3	1	3	5	9

5. Hobbies Caitlin and Greg collect stamps. Each starts with a collection of 50 stamps. Caitlin adds 15 stamps to her collection each week. Greg adds 1 stamp to his collection the first week, 3 stamps the second week, 5 stamps the third week, and so on. Identify the function that gives the number of stamps in each collection as linear or nonlinear. Which collection is growing more quickly between week 5 and week 6?

Determine whether each function has a constant or variable rate of change.

6.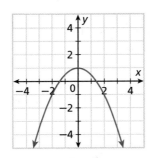

7.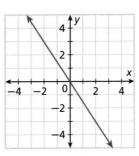

8.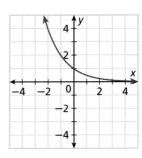

9. $y = 2x^2$

10. $y + 1 = 3x$

11. $y = -7$

12. $y = \frac{1}{5}x$

13. $y = 5^x$

14. $y = x^2 + 1$

15. $y = 3\sqrt{x}$

16. $y = \frac{x - 3}{2x}$

17. $x + y = 6.25$

Determine whether each statement is sometimes, always, or never true.

18. A function whose graph is a straight line has a variable rate of change.

19. A quadratic function has a constant rate of change.

20. The rate of change of a linear function is negative.

21. The rate of change between two points on the graph of a nonlinear function is 0.

22. Critical Thinking The figure shows the graph of the exponential function $y = \left(\frac{1}{2}\right)^x$.

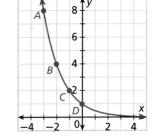

    a. Find the rates of change between points A and B, between points B and C, and between points A and D.

    b. What do you notice about the rates of change you found in part **a**? Do you think this would be true for the rate of change between any two points on the graph?

    c. How do your findings about the rates of change relate to the shape of the graph?

23. A model rocket is launched from the ground. The graph shows the height of the rocket at various times.

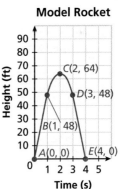

Model Rocket

    a. Find the rates of change between points A and B and between points B and C.

    b. Which rate of change is greater? What does this tell you about the motion of the rocket?

    c. Find the rates of change between points C and D and between points D and E.

    d. What does the sign of the rates of change you found in part **c** tell you about the motion of the rocket? Explain.

13-2 Comparing Functions

? *Essential Question:* How can you compare properties of two functions each represented in a different way?

Objectives
Compare functions in different representations.

Estimate and compare rates of change.

Vocabulary
average rate of change

Who uses this?
Investment analysts can use different function representations to compare investments. (See Example 2.)

You have studied how linear, quadratic, and exponential functions can be used to model various kinds of situations. The table below shows the three types of functions and some of their key properties.

	Linear	Quadratic	Exponential
Equation	$y = mx + b$ Example: $y = 2x + 1$	$y = ax^2 + bx + c,$ $a \neq 0$ Example: $y = x^2 - 2x + 3$	$y = ab^x, a \neq 0, b \neq 1,$ $b > 0$ Example: $y = 0.5(2)^x$
Graph			
Table	x : 0,1,2,3,4 / y : 1,3,5,7,9 with +2, +2, +2, +2 Constant first differences	x : 0,1,2,3,4 / y : 3,2,3,6,11 with −1,+1,+3,+5 and +2,+2,+2 Constant second differences	x : 0,1,2,3,4 / y : 0.5,1,2,4,8 with ×2,×2,×2,×2 Constant ratios

COMMON CORE GPS
MCC9-12.F.IF.9

EXAMPLE 1

Comparing Linear Functions

Deirdre and Beth each deposit money into their checking accounts weekly. Their account information for the past several weeks is shown below.

my.hrw.com

Online Video Tutor

Deirdre's Account

Weeks	Account Balance ($)
0	60
1	75
2	90
3	105
4	120

Beth's Account

Compare the accounts by finding slopes and *y*-intercepts and interpreting those values in the context of the situation.

Deirdre	Beth	Interpret and Compare.
Slope	**Slope**	The slope is the rate of change. Beth is saving at a higher rate.
Use (1, 75) and (2, 90). $\frac{90-75}{2-1} = 15$	Use (1, 60) and (2, 80). $\frac{80-60}{2-1} = 20$	
***y*-intercept** (0, 60) *y*-intercept = 60	***y*-intercept** (0, 40) *y*-intercept = 40	The *y*-intercept is the beginning account balance. Deirdre started with more money.

 1. Dave and Arturo each deposit money into their checking accounts weekly. Their account information for the past several weeks is shown. Compare the accounts by finding and interpreting slopes and *y*-intercepts.

Arturo's Account

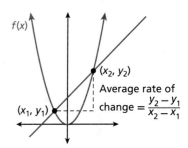

Dave's Account

Weeks	0	1	2	3
Account Balance ($)	30	42	54	66

Remember that nonlinear functions do not have a constant rate of change. One way to compare two nonlinear functions is to calculate their *average rates of change* over a certain interval. For a function $f(x)$ whose graph contains the points (x_1, y_1) and (x_2, y_2), the **average rate of change** over the interval $[x_1, x_2]$ is the slope of the line through (x_1, y_1) and (x_2, y_2).

The notation [0, 20] means all *x*-values from 0 to 20, including 0 and 20.

MCC9-12.F.IF.9

EXAMPLE 2

my.hrw.com

Online Video Tutor

Comparing Exponential Functions

An investment analyst offers two different investment options for her customers. Compare the investments by finding and interpreting the average rates of change from year 0 to year 20.

Investment A

Years	Value ($)
0	10.00
5	13.38
10	17.91
15	23.97
20	32.07
25	42.92

Investment B

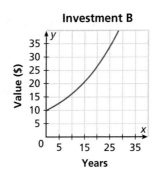

Calculate the average rates of change over [0, 20] by using the points whose x-coordinates are 0 and 20.

Investment A

$$\frac{32.07 - 10.00}{20-0} = \frac{22.07}{20} \approx 1.10$$ *Use (0, 10.00) and (20, 32.07).*

Investment B

$$\frac{27 - 10}{20-0} = \frac{17}{20} = 0.85$$ *Use the graph to estimate. When x = 20, y ≈ 27. Use (0, 10) and (20, 27).*

From year 0 to year 20, investment A increased at an average rate of $1.10 per year, while investment B increased at an average rate of $0.85 per year.

 2. Compare the same investments' average rates of change from year 10 to year 25.

EXAMPLE 3
MCC9-12.F.LE.3

my.hrw.com

Online Video Tutor

Comparing Different Types of Functions

A town has approximately 1000 homes. The town council is considering plans for future development. Plan A calls for an increase of 200 homes per year. Plan B calls for a 10% increase each year. Compare the plans.

Let *x* be the number of years. Let *y* be the number of homes. Write functions to model each plan.

Plan A: $y = 200x + 1000$

Plan B: $y = 1000(1.10)^x$

Use your calculator to graph both functions.

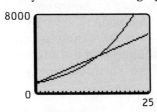

The graphs show that under plan A, there will be more homes built than under plan B in early years.

But by the end of the 15th year, the number of homes built under plan B exceeds the number of homes built under plan A. From that point on, plan B results in more homes than plan A by ever-increasing amounts every year.

 3. Two neighboring schools use different models for anticipated growth in enrollment: School A has 850 students and predicts an increase of 100 students per year. School B also has 850 students, but predicts an increase of 8% per year. Compare the models.

THINK AND DISCUSS

1. Explain why you need to use the word *average* when comparing rates of change for quadratic or exponential functions, but not for linear functions.

2. A function can be represented by an equation or a graph. Describe a possible advantage of each representation.

3. GET ORGANIZED Copy and complete the graphic organizer. Complete the sentence in each column by writing important values to compare.

Comparing Functions			
Linear to Linear	**Exponential to Exponential**	**Quadratic to Quadratic**	**Linear to Quadratic**
Compare…	Compare…	Compare…	Compare…

13-2 Exercises

my.hrw.com
Homework Help

GUIDED PRACTICE

SEE EXAMPLE 1

1. Personal Finance Fay and Kara each withdraw money from their savings accounts weekly, as shown. Compare the accounts by finding and interpreting slopes and *y*-intercepts.

Fay's Account

Weeks	0	1	2	3
Account Balance ($)	425	375	325	255

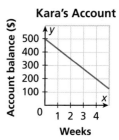

Kara's Account

SEE EXAMPLE 2

2. Biology A biologist tracked the hourly growth of two different strains of bacteria in the lab. Her data are shown below. Compare the number of bacteria by finding and interpreting the average rates of change from hour 0 to hour 4.

Bacteria A

Hours	Number of Bacteria
0	5
1	15
2	45
3	135
4	405

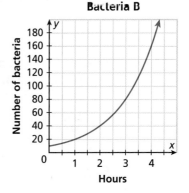

Bacteria B

SEE EXAMPLE **3**

3. **Business** A bicycle store has approximately 200 bicycles in stock. The store owner is considering plans for expanding his inventory. Plan A calls for an increase of 30 bicycles per year. Plan B calls for a 10% increase each year. Compare the plans.

PRACTICE AND PROBLEM SOLVING

H.O.T. 4. **Recreation** Kevin and Darius each hiked a mountain trail at different rates, as shown below. Compare the hikes by finding and interpreting slopes and y-intercepts.

Kevin's Hike

Time (h)	0	1	2	3
Distance from Camp (mi)	1.5	3.5	5.5	7.5

Darius's Hike

$y = 2.2x + 1$

5. **Anthropology** An archeologist used these functions to model the changing populations of two ancient cities as they grew in size. Compare the populations by finding and interpreting the average rates of change over the interval [0, 40].

City A

Area (mi²)	Population
0	0
10	31
20	89
30	164
40	252
50	353

City B

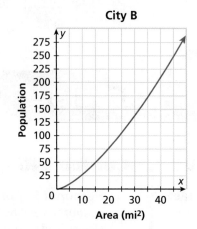

H.O.T. 6. **Recreation** A summer boating camp has 75 boats. The camp director is considering two proposals for increasing the number of boats to match the increase in the number of campers. Proposal A recommends increasing the number of boats by 5 boats per year. Proposal B recommends a 5% increase each year. Compare the proposals.

7. **Business** The revenue of a company based on the price of its product is modeled by the function below.

   a. Estimate the average rate of change over [0, 4].

   b. What price that will yield the maximum revenue?

Product Price and Revenue

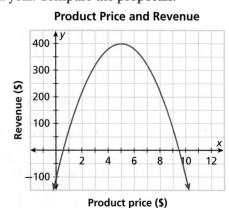

8. **Critical Thinking** A karate center has 120 students. The director wants to set a goal to motivate her instructors to increase student enrollment. Under plan A, the goal is to increase the number of students by 12% each year. Under plan B, the goal is to increase the number of students by 20 each year.

   a. Compare the plans.

   b. Which plan should the director choose to double the enrollment in the shortest amount of time? Explain.

   c. Which plan should she use to triple the enrollment in the shortest amount of time? Explain.

9. **Write About It** Compare the characteristics of linear, quadratic, and exponential functions. Explain how to decide which type of function is being shown on a graph and in a table.

TEST PREP

10. Tanya has $2000 in savings. She wants to save more money. She is considering two plans. Under plan A, she will increase her balance by $1000 per year. Under plan B, she will increase her balance by 20% each year. How much more will she save with plan B after 10 years? Round your answer to the nearest dollar.

    (A) $383   (B) $9,562   (C) $12,000   (D) $12,383

CHALLENGE AND EXTEND

H.O.T. 11. Prove that linear functions grow by equal differences over equal intervals.

Given: $x_2 - x_1 = x_4 - x_3$;

f is a linear function of the form $f(x) = mx + b$.

Prove: $f(x_2) - f(x_1) = f(x_4) - f(x_3)$

H.O.T. 12. Prove that exponential functions grow by equal factors over equal intervals.

Given: $x_2 - x_1 = x_4 - x_3$;

g is an exponential function of the form $g(x) = ab^x$.

Prove: $\dfrac{g(x_2)}{g(x_1)} = \dfrac{g(x_4)}{g(x_3)}$

FOCUS ON MATHEMATICAL PRACTICES

H.O.T. 13. **Comparison** For a math project, two groups of students wrote functions to describe a six-month repayment plan for a loan. Group A set up the function $f(t) = 100 + 100(1.2)^t$, where $t = 0$ for the first month, $t = 1$ for the second, and so on. Group B described their function using a table. The first three months' payments are shown.

Month	1	2	3
Payment	$150	$187.50	$234.38

Compare the total amounts repaid in 6 months using the two plans.

H.O.T. 14. **Analysis** For each function pair, use your knowledge of transformations to explain how the graph of $g(x)$ differs from the graph of $f(x)$.

   a. $f(x) = 500(1.45)^x$; $g(x) = 500(1.45)^x + 50$

   b. $f(x) = 5(0.85)^x$; $g(x) = 5(0.85)^{x-3}$

   c. $f(x) = 2(5)^x$; $g(x) = 6(5)^x$

EXTENSION

Transforming Exponential Functions

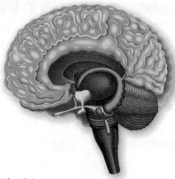

? Essential Question: How can you identify the effect of a given transformation on the graph of an exponential function?

Objectives

Transform exponential functions by changing parameters.

Describe the effects of changes in the coefficients of exponential functions.

You can perform the same transformations on exponential functions that you performed on polynomial, quadratic, and linear functions.

The hippocampus, in orange, directs the storage of memory in the brain.

 Know it! Note

 Helpful Hint

It may help you remember the direction of the shift if you think of "*h* is for horizontal."

Transformations of Exponential Functions		
Transformation	**$f(x)$ Notation**	**Examples**
Vertical translation	$f(x) + k$	$y = 2^x + 3$ — 3 units up $y = 2^x - 6$ — 6 units down
Horizontal translation	$f(x - h)$	$y = 2^{x-2}$ — 2 units right $y = 2^{x+1}$ — 1 unit left
Vertical stretch or compression	$af(x)$	$y = 6(2^x)$ — stretch by 6 $y = \frac{1}{2}(2^x)$ — compression by $\frac{1}{2}$
Horizontal stretch or compression	$f\left(\frac{1}{b}x\right)$	$y = 2^{\left(\frac{1}{5}x\right)}$ — stretch by 5 $y = 2^{3x}$ — compression by $\frac{1}{3}$
Reflection	$-f(x)$ $f(-x)$	$y = -2^x$ — across x-axis $y = 2^{-x}$ — across y-axis

COMMON CORE GPS **EXAMPLE 1**
MCC9-12.F.BF.3

Translating Exponential Functions

Make a table of values, and graph the function $g(x) = 2^x - 4$. Describe the asymptote. Tell how the graph is transformed from the graph of $f(x) = 2^x$.

x	-2	-1	0	1	2	3
$g(x)$	-3.75	-3.5	-3	-2	0	4

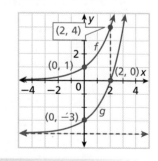

The asymptote is $y = -4$, and the graph approaches this line as the value of x decreases. The transformation moves the graph of $f(x) = 2^x$ down 4 units. The range changes to $\left\{y \mid y > -4\right\}$.

 CHECK IT OUT!

1. Make a table of values, and graph $j(x) = 2^{x-2}$. Describe the asymptote. Tell how the graph is transformed from the graph of $f(x) = 2^x$.

358 Module 13 Comparing and Modeling with Functions

EXAMPLE **2** **Stretching, Compressing, and Reflecting Exponential Functions**

Graph the exponential function. Find the *y*-intercept and the asymptote. Describe how the graph is transformed from the graph of its parent function.

A $g(x) = 2(3^x)$

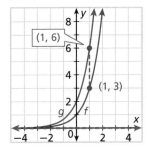

parent function: $f(x) = 3^x$

y-intercept: 2, asymptote: $y = 0$

The graph of $g(x)$ is a vertical stretch of the parent function $f(x) = 3^x$ by a factor of 2.

B $h(x) = -\frac{1}{4}(2^x)$

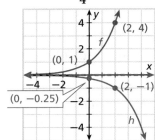

parent function: $f(x) = 2^x$

y-intercept: $-\frac{1}{4}$, asymptote: $y = 0$

The graph of $h(x)$ is a reflection of the parent function $f(x) = 2^x$ across the *x*-axis and a vertical compression by a factor of $\frac{1}{4}$. The range is $\{y \mid y < 0\}$.

 CHECK IT OUT! Graph the exponential function. Find the *y*-intercept and the asymptote. Describe how the graph is transformed from the graph of its parent function.

2a. $h(x) = \frac{1}{3}(5^x)$ **2b.** $g(x) = 2(2^{-x})$

EXTENSION
Exercises

my.hrw.com
Homework Help

Make a table of values, and graph each function. Describe the asymptote. Tell how the graph is transformed from the graph of $f(x) = 3^x$.

1. $g(x) = 3^x + 2$ **2.** $h(x) = 3^x - 2$ **3.** $j(x) = 3^{x+1}$

Graph each exponential function. Find the *y*-intercept and the asymptote. Describe how the graph is transformed from the graph of its parent function.

4. $g(x) = 3(4^x)$ **5.** $h(x) = \frac{1}{3}(4^x)$ **6.** $j(x) = -\frac{1}{3}(4^x)$

7. $k(x) = -2(4^x)$ **8.** $m(x) = -(4^{-x})$ **9.** $n(x) = e^{2x}$

Make a table of values, and graph each function. Describe the asymptote. Tell how the graph is transformed from the graph of $f(x) = 5^x$.

10. $g(x) = 5^x - 1$ **11.** $h(x) = 5^{x+2}$ **12.** $j(x) = 5^{x-1} - 1$

Graph each exponential function. Find the *y*-intercept and the asymptote. Describe how the graph is transformed from the graph of its parent function.

13. $g(x) = 4\left(\frac{1}{2}\right)^x$ **14.** $h(x) = 0.25\left(\frac{1}{2}\right)^x$ **15.** $j(x) = -0.25\left(\frac{1}{2}\right)^x$

16. $k(x) = -\left(\frac{1}{2}\right)^{\frac{x}{2}}$ **17.** $m(x) = 4\left(\frac{1}{2}\right)^{-x}$ **18.** $n(x) = -4\left(\frac{1}{2}\right)^{-x}$

Ready to Go On?

my.hrw.com
Assessment and Intervention

 13-1 **Linear, Quadratic, and Exponential Models**

Graph each data set. Which kind of model best describes the data?

1. $\{(-2, 5), (3, 10), (0, 1), (1, 2), (0.5, 1.25)\}$ **2.** $\{(0, 3), (2, 12), (-1, 1.5), (-3, 0.375), (4, 48)\}$

Look for a pattern in each data set to determine which kind of model best describes the data.

3. $\{(-2, -6), (-1, -5), (0, -4), (1, -3), (2, -2)\}$ **4.** $\{(-2, -24), (-1, -12), (0, -6), (1, -3)\}$

5. Write a function that models the data. Then use your function to predict how long the humidifier will produce steam with 10 quarts of water.

Input and Output of a Humidifier	
Water Volume (qt)	Steam Time (h)
3	4.5
4	6
5	7.5
6	9

 13-2 **Comparing Functions**

6. Sam has $5000 in a savings account. He is considering two plans to save more money. Under plan A, Sam will increase his account balance by $500 per year. Under plan B, he will increase his account balance by 10% per year. How much money will Sam have in his account with each plan after 5 years? Which is the better plan to save more money? Explain.

7. Decide which linear function is increasing at a greater rate.

- Function 1 has x-intercept −7 and y-intercept 4.

- Function 2 includes the points in the table.

x	0	2	4	6
y	−8	−3	2	7

8. Michael is studying population changes in two types of birds living on an island. Compare the populations by finding and interpreting the average rates of change over the interval [0, 18]

Bird A

Time (months)	0	6	12	18
Population (thousands)	8.3	8.6	8.8	9.1

Bird B

$y = 3.6(1.06)^x$

PARCC Assessment Readiness

Selected Response

1. Look for a pattern in the data set. Which kind of model best describes the data?

Population Growth of Bacteria	
Time (hours)	Number of Bacteria
0	2,000
1	5,000
2	12,500
3	31,250
4	78,125

(A) cubic   (C) quadratic

(B) exponential   (D) linear

2. Two insect colonies start out with the same populations but have different growth rates. Compare the colonies by finding and interpreting the average rates of change from week 0 to week 15.

Colony A

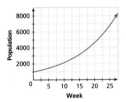

Colony B

Week	0	5	10	15	20	25
Population	1000	1539	2367	3642	5604	8623

(F) Colony A: about 150 per week, Colony B: about 176 per week.

(G) Colony A: about 150 per week, Colony B: about 243 per week.

(H) Colony A: about 2200 per week, Colony B: about 2642 per week.

(J) Colony A: about 2200 per week, Colony B: about 176 per week.

3. Use the information in the table to predict the number of termites in the termite colony after one year.

Termite Colony Population	
Time (months)	Number of Termites
0	20
1	80
2	320
3	1,280

(A) 16,777,216 termites

(B) 9,920 termites

(C) 5,120 termites

(D) 335,544,320 termites

Mini-Tasks

4. Suppose you have $10,000 to invest and a choice between two investment plans. In each plan, the interest you earn each year is added to the value of the investment.
In Plan A, you earn $500 in interest every year.
In Plan B, you earn 4% of your current investment value every year.

a. Write a function for each of the plans.

b. Which plan has a greater value in year 10?

c. Which plan has a greater value in year 20?

5. A realtor estimates that a certain new house worth $500,000 will gain value at a rate of 6% per year.

a. Make a table that shows the worth of the house for years 0, 1, 2, 3, and 4.

b. What is the real-world meaning of year 0?

c. Which type of model best represents the data in your table? Explain.

d. Write a function for the data.

PARCC Assessment Readiness

Selected Response

1. Benito has x apples. He cuts each apple in half and gives each half to a different horse. Which expression represents the number of horses Benito feeds?

   (A) $x \cdot \frac{1}{2}$

   (B) $x \div \frac{1}{2}$

   (C) $x \cdot 1\frac{1}{2}$

   (D) $x \div 1\frac{1}{2}$

2. What is the value of $\frac{2a}{a^3}$ if $4 - a = -6$?

   (F) $\frac{1}{50}$

   (G) 8

   (H) $\frac{1}{2}$

   (J) 10

3. Which equation describes the relationship between x and y in the table below?

x	−8	−4	0	4	8
y	2	1	0	−1	−2

   (A) $y = -4x$

   (B) $y = -\frac{1}{4}x$

   (C) $y = 4x$

   (D) $y = \frac{1}{4}x$

4. Which graph is described by $x - 3y = -3$?

   (F)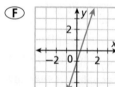

   (G)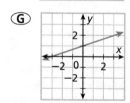

   (H)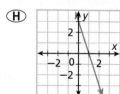

   (J)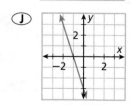

5. Which steps could you use to graph the line that has slope 2 and contains the point $(-1, 3)$?

   (A) Plot $(-1, 3)$. Move 1 unit up and 2 units right and plot another point.

   (B) Plot $(-1, 3)$. Move 2 units up and 1 unit right and plot another point.

   (C) Plot $(-1, 3)$. Move 1 unit up and 2 units left and plot another point.

   (D) Plot $(-1, 3)$. Move 2 units up and 1 unit left and plot another point.

6. Which relation is NOT a function?

   (F) $\{(1, -5), (3, 1), (-5, 4), (4, -2)\}$

   (G) $\{(2, 7), (3, 7), (4, 7), (5, 8)\}$

   (H) $\{(1, -5), (-1, 6), (1, 5), (6, -3)\}$

   (J) $\{(3, -2), (5, -6), (7, 7), (8, 8)\}$

7. A bird flies from the ground to the top of a tree, sits there and sings for a while, flies down to the top of a picnic table to eat crumbs, and then flies back to the top of the tree to sing some more. Which graph best represents this situation?

   (A)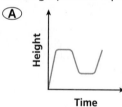

   (B)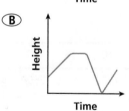

   (C)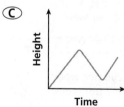

   (D)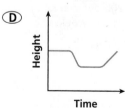

HOT TIP! If possible, use the same calculator you usually use in math class. A timed test is not the right place to figure out where buttons are and how they work. Also, replace your batteries the night before the test. If your batteries run out, you may be given a replacement calculator you are not familiar with.

8. The graph below shows a function.

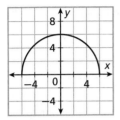

What is the domain of the function?

Ⓕ $x \geq 0$

Ⓖ $x \geq -6$

Ⓗ $0 \leq x \leq 6$

Ⓙ $-6 \leq x \leq 6$

9. Frank borrowed $5000 with an annual simple interest rate. The amount of interest he owed after 6 months was $300. What is the interest rate of the loan?

Ⓐ 1%

Ⓑ 6%

Ⓒ 10%

Ⓓ 12%

10. What is the value of $f(x) = -3 - x$ when $x = -7$?

Ⓕ −10

Ⓖ −4

Ⓗ 4

Ⓙ 10

11. Which relationship is a direct variation?

Ⓐ

x	1	2	3	4
y	−1	0	1	2

Ⓑ

x	1	2	3	4
y	0	−1	−2	−3

Ⓒ

x	1	2	3	4
y	3	5	7	9

Ⓓ

x	1	2	3	4
y	3	6	9	12

12. Which shows the slope-intercept form of $2x + 3y = 6$?

Ⓕ $y = \frac{2}{3}x + 2$

Ⓖ $y = \frac{2}{3}x + 6$

Ⓗ $y = -\frac{2}{3}x + 2$

Ⓙ $y = -\frac{2}{3}x + 6$

13. Company A charges $30 plus $0.40 per mile for a car rental. The total charge for *m* miles is given by $f(m) = 30 + 0.4m$. For a similar car, company B charges $30 plus $0.30 per mile. The total charge for *m* miles is given by $g(m) = 30 + 0.3m$. Which best describes the transformation from the graph of $f(m)$ to the graph of $g(m)$?

Ⓐ Translation up

Ⓑ Translation down

Ⓒ Rotation

Ⓓ Reflection

14. For $h(x) = x^3 + 2x$, what is $h(4)$?

Ⓕ 20

Ⓖ 24

Ⓗ 48

Ⓙ 72

15. A sequence is defined by the rule $a_n = -3(2)^{n-1}$. What is the 5th term of the sequence?

Ⓐ 5

Ⓑ −30

Ⓒ −48

Ⓓ −216

16. Which could be the graph of $y = -2^x$?

Ⓕ

Ⓖ

Ⓗ

Ⓙ

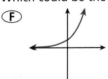

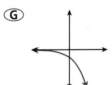

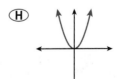

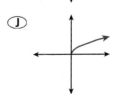

17. Which equation models exponential decay?

   Ⓐ $y = -0.12(1.05)^t$

   Ⓑ $y = 0.12(1.05)^t$

   Ⓒ $y = 1.05(0.12)^t$

   Ⓓ $y = 0.12(1 + 0.5)^t$

18. Which ordered pair lies on the graph of $y = 3(2)^{x+1}$?

   Ⓕ $(-1, 0)$

   Ⓖ $(0, 9)$

   Ⓗ $(1, 12)$

   Ⓙ $(3, 24)$

19. Which rule defines the sequence –3, 15, –75, 375...?

   Ⓐ $a_n = -5(3)^{n-1}$

   Ⓑ $a_n = -3(-5)^{n-1}$

   Ⓒ $a_n = 3(-5)^{n-1}$

   Ⓓ $a_n = 5(-3)^{n-1}$

20. The function $f(t) = 30,000(0.8)^t$ gives the value of a vehicle where t is the number of years after purchase. According to the function, what will be the value of the car 8 years after purchase, rounded to the nearest dollar?

   Ⓕ $5,033

   Ⓖ $19,200

   Ⓗ $24,000

   Ⓙ $192,000

21. Brian calculates the charge for each lawn that he mows using the function $y = 4x + 5.5$, where x is the number of hours spent mowing the lawn. Brian never takes more than 2 hours to mow a lawn. Which best represents the reasonable range for the function?

   Ⓐ $0 < y \leq 2$

   Ⓑ $0 < y \leq 13.5$

   Ⓒ $5.5 < y \leq 13.5$

   Ⓓ $y > 13.5$

22. A line passes through the point $(5, -1)$. The slope of the line is $-\frac{1}{2}$. Which of these is the equation of the line?

   Ⓕ $2x - y = 11$

   Ⓖ $x - 2y = 3$

   Ⓗ $2x + y = 9$

   Ⓙ $x + 2y = 3$

23. A gym membership costs $25 a month plus $3 per visit. This is modeled by the function $c = 3v + 25$, where c is the cost per month and v is the number of visits. If the slope of this function's graph were to increase, what does that mean about the prices that the gym charges?

   Ⓐ The gym raised its monthly fee.

   Ⓑ The gym lowered the cost per visit.

   Ⓒ The gym raised the cost per visit.

   Ⓓ The gym lowered its monthly fee.

24. A video club costs $25 to join and it costs $2.50 to rent a video. Which gives the independent and dependent variables and a function that describes this situation?

   Ⓕ Independent: number of videos rented; dependent: total cost; $f(x) = 2.5x - 25$

   Ⓖ Independent: number of videos rented; dependent: total cost; $f(x) = 2.5x + 25$

   Ⓗ Independent: number of videos rented; dependent: total cost; $f(x) = 25x + 2.5$

   Ⓙ Independent: total cost; dependent: number of videos rented; $f(x) = 25x - 2.5$

Mini-Tasks

25. A video store charges a $10 membership fee plus $2 for each movie rental. The total cost for x movie rentals is given by $f(x) = 2x + 10$.

   a. Graph this function.

   b. Give a reasonable domain and range.

26. The table below shows the federal minimum wage in different years.

Year	1960	1970	1980	1990	2000
Minimum Wage ($)	1.00	1.60	3.10	3.80	5.15

   a. Find the rate of change for each ten-year time period. Show your work.

   b. During which time period did the minimum wage increase the fastest? Explain what the rate of change for this time period means.

27. **a.** Find the slope of the line below. Explain how you found your answer.

   b. Write an equation in slope-intercept form for the line. Explain how you found your answer.

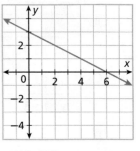

28. The table shows the number of people newly infected by a certain virus with one person as the original source.

Week	1	2	3	4	5	6	7
Newly Infected People	1	3	9	27	81	243	729

    a. Is the data set best described by a linear function or an exponential function? Write a function to model the data.

    b. Use the function to predict the number of people that will become infected in the 10th week. Show your work.

29. Ella and Mia went on a camping trip. The total cost for their trip was $124, which the girls divided evenly. Ella paid for 4 nights at the campsite and $30 for supplies. Mia paid for 2 nights at the campsite and $46 for supplies.

    a. Write an equation that could be used to find the cost of one night's stay at the campsite. Explain what the variable in your equation represents.

    b. Solve your equation from part **a** to find the cost of one night's stay at the campsite. Show your work.

30. Study the sequence below.

    18, 24.5, 31, 37.5, 44,…

    a. Could this sequence be arithmetic? Explain.

    b. Find the 100th term of the sequence. Show your work.

31. The fare for a taxi ride depends on the distance traveled. It costs $9.50 to go 3 miles and $17 to go 6 miles.

    a. Assume that taxi fare is a linear function of distance. Write an equation that gives the fare y for a trip of x miles.

    b. How much do you pay for each additional mile that you ride in the taxi?

Performance Tasks

32. Connie is interested in yoga classes. Yoga Studio charges a one-time fee of $75 for a medical examination and $20 for each class. Stretch Classic charges $25 for each class. Both companies only allow full-hour sessions.

    a. Sketch a graph of the cost associated with each facility on the same coordinate grid. Tell whether each graph is continuous or discrete.

    b. Write functions for the cost associated with each facility.

    c. Connie wants to do yoga at home, but she read an article that recommended at least 28 sessions with a trainer before starting a home yoga practice. Assuming the quality of the classes is the same, which company should Connie choose? Explain your reasoning.

33. A loan's interest rate for an entire year is called its annual percentage rate, or APR, but APR can have two meanings. When the compounding of the interest is not taken into account, it is called the *nominal* APR, and when the compounding is taken into account, it is called the *effective* APR. To convert from nominal APR to effective APR, you can use the formula

$$\text{effective APR} = \left(1 + \frac{\text{nominal APR}}{n}\right)^n - 1,$$

where n is the number of times the interest is compounded per year. You can use this formula to compare the loans offered by two used car dealerships for different compounding periods.

    a. Secondhand Cars is offering a loan with a nominal APR of 13.2%, compounded monthly. Convert this nominal APR to an effective APR, and round to the nearest tenth of a percent.

    b. Gently Used Motors is offering a loan with a nominal APR of 13.4%, compounded semi-annually. Convert this nominal APR to an effective APR and round to the nearest tenth of a percent. Which dealership offers the better interest rate? Explain.

    c. Suppose both Secondhand Cars and Gently Used Motors are offering you a loan of $5000. For both, your first payment is not due for one year, but you have to pay interest for that year. What is the difference in the amounts owed after one year?

    d. Why would a used car dealership offering a loan be more likely to advertise the nominal APR instead of the effective APR?

my.hrw.com
Online Assessment
Go online for updated, PARCC-aligned assessment readiness.

Are You Ready?

my.hrw.com
Assessment and Intervention

✓ Vocabulary

Match each term on the left with a definition on the right.

1. difference
2. factor
3. natural numbers
4. ratio
5. sum

   A. the result of an addition

   B. a whole number that is multiplied by another whole number to get a product

   C. numbers that can be expressed in the form $\frac{a}{b}$, where a and b are both integers and $b \neq 0$

   D. the result of a subtraction

   E. a comparison of two quantities by division

   F. the counting numbers: 1, 2, 3, …

✓ Solve Proportions

Solve each proportion.

6. $\frac{3}{4} = \frac{x}{12}$

7. $\frac{15}{9} = \frac{3}{x}$

8. $\frac{10}{20} = \frac{x}{100}$

9. $\frac{250}{1500} = \frac{x}{100}$

✓ Compare and Order Real Numbers

Compare. Write <, >, or =.

10. 20 ▨ 13

11. $\frac{2}{3}$ ▨ $\frac{1}{2}$

12. $\frac{3}{4}$ ▨ $\frac{7}{9}$

13. 0.75 ▨ $\frac{9}{12}$

Order the numbers from least to greatest.

14. $\frac{1}{2}, \frac{4}{5}, \frac{1}{8}, \frac{3}{4}, \frac{2}{3}$

15. $0.12, \frac{2}{5}, \frac{3}{4}, 0.3, \frac{1}{3}$

✓ Multiply Decimals

Multiply.

16. 0.25×300

17. 0.5×4000

18. 0.05×200

19. 0.125×9600

✓ Divide Decimals

Divide.

20. $435 \div 10$

21. $32 \div 100$

22. $777 \div 1000$

23. $295 \div 10{,}000$

Career Readiness Statisticians

Statisticians apply mathematical principles to collect, analyze, and present numerical data. They design surveys and experiments, and interpret the results. Statisticians work in many different fields, such as government, economics, scientific research, software engineering, education, and sports. Most statisticians have a college degree in statistics or mathematics. However, sports statisticians require less academic training.

Describing Data

Online Edition

my.hrw.com

Access the complete online textbook, interactive features, and additional resources.

Online Video Tutor

Watch full explanations of every example in the textbook with these online videos.

TI-Nspire™ Activities

Enhance your learning with cutting edge technology from Texas Instruments.

Portable Devices

eTextbook

Access your full textbook on your tablet or e-reader.

On the Spot

Watch video tutorials anywhere, anytime with this app for iPhone® and iPad®.

Chapter Resources

Scan with your smart phone to jump directly to the online edition.

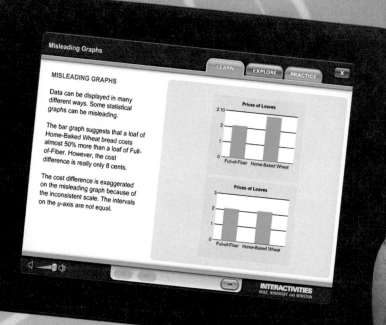

Unit Contents

Module 14 Data Distributions
MCC9-12.S.ID.1, MCC9-12.S.ID.2, MCC9-12.S.ID.3, MCC9-12.S.ID.5

Module 15 Linear and Exponential Models
MCC9-12.F.LE.1, MCC9-12.S.ID.6, MCC9-12.S.ID.7, MCC9-12.S.ID.9

 Use this **Animated Math** activity to explore misleading graphs.

14 Data Distributions

COMMON
CORE GPS

Contents

MATHEMATICAL
PRACTICES   The Common Core Georgia Performance Standards for Mathematical Practice describe varieties of expertise that all students should seek to develop. Opportunities to develop these practices are integrated throughout this program.

1 Make sense of problems and persevere in solving them.

2 Reason abstractly and quantitatively.

3 Construct viable arguments and critique the reasoning of others.

4 Model with mathematics.

5 Use appropriate tools strategically.

6 Attend to precision.

7 Look for and make use of structure.

8 Look for and express regularity in repeated reasoning.

Unpacking the Standards

my.hrw.com
Multilingual Glossary

Understanding the standards and the vocabulary terms in the standards will help you know exactly what you are expected to learn in this chapter.

 MCC9-12.S.ID.1

Represent data with plots on the real number line (dot plots, histograms, and box plots).

Key Vocabulary

histogram (histograma) A bar graph used to display data grouped in intervals

box-and-whisker plot (gráfica de mediana y rango) A method of showing how data are distributed by using the median, quartiles, and minimum and maximum values; also called a box plot.

What It Means For You

Displaying numerical data on the real number line gives you an instant visual image of how the data are distributed, and helps you draw conclusions about the center and spread of the data.

EXAMPLE **Histogram**

A histogram gives you an overall picture of how data are distributed, but does not indicate any particular values or statistics.

EXAMPLE **Box-and-whisker plot**

A box-and-whisker plot includes five statistical values.

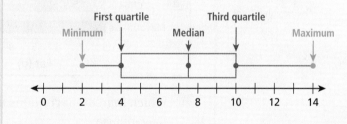

 MCC9-12.S.ID.3

Interpret differences in shape, center, and spread in the context of the data sets, accounting for possible effects of extreme data points (outliers).

Key Vocabulary

outlier (valor extremo) A data value that is far removed from the rest of the data.

What It Means For You

Always examine the displays and statistics for a data set in its own particular context so that you can draw valid conclusions.

EXAMPLE **Outliers**

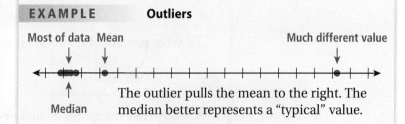

The outlier pulls the mean to the right. The median better represents a "typical" value.

14-1 Organizing and Displaying Data

 Essential Question: How can you use various types of graphs to organize and display data?

Objectives
Organize data in tables and graphs.

Choose a table or graph to display data.

Vocabulary
bar graph
line graph
circle graph

Who uses this?
Nutritionists can display health information about food in bar graphs.

Bar graphs, line graphs, and *circle graphs* can be used to present data in a visual way.

A **bar graph** displays data with vertical or horizontal bars. Bar graphs are a good way to display data that can be organized into categories. Using a bar graph, you can quickly compare the categories.

COMMON CORE GPS
EXAMPLE **1**
MCC9-12.S.ID.1

my.hrw.com
Online Video Tutor

Reading and Interpreting Bar Graphs

Use the graph to answer each question.

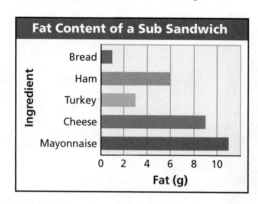

A Which ingredient contains the most fat?
mayonnaise   *The bar for mayonnaise is the longest.*

B How many more grams of fat are in ham than in turkey?
$6 - 3 = 3$ *There are 6 grams of fat in ham and 3 grams of fat in turkey.*

C How many total fat grams are in this sandwich?
$1 + 6 + 3 + 9 + 11 = 30$ *Add the number of fat grams for each ingredient.*

D What percent of the total fat grams in this sandwich are from turkey?
$\dfrac{3}{30} = \dfrac{1}{10} = 10\%$ *Out of 30 total fat grams, 3 fat grams are from turkey.*

 CHECK IT OUT! Use the graph to answer each question.
1a. Which ingredient contains the least amount of fat?
1b. Which ingredients contain at least 8 grams of fat?

Victoria Smith/HMH

A double-bar graph can be used to compare two data sets. A double-bar graph has a key to distinguish between the two sets of data.

EXAMPLE 2   MCC9-12.S.ID.1

Reading and Interpreting Double Bar Graphs

Use the graph to answer each question.

my.hrw.com

Online Video Tutor

A In which year did State College have the greatest average attendance for basketball?

2003

Find the tallest orange bar.

B On average, how many more people attended a football game than a basketball game in 2001?

$20,000 - 13,000 = 7000$

Find the height of each bar for 2001 and subtract.

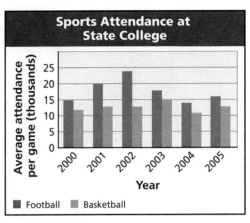

Sports Attendance at State College

■ Football ■ Basketball

CHECK IT OUT! **2.** Use the graph to determine which years had the same average basketball attendance. What was the average attendance for those years?

A **line graph** displays data using line segments. Line graphs are a good way to display data that changes over a period of time.

EXAMPLE 3   MCC9-12.S.ID.1

Reading and Interpreting Line Graphs

Use the graph to answer each question.

my.hrw.com

Online Video Tutor

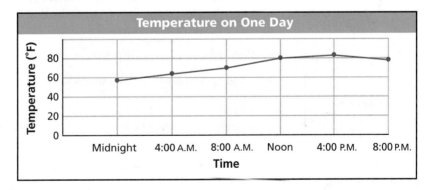

Temperature on One Day

A At what time was the temperature the warmest?

4:00 P.M.   *Identify the highest point.*

B During which 4-hour time period did the temperature increase the most?

From 8:00 A.M. to noon   *Look for the segment with the greatest positive slope.*

CHECK IT OUT! **3.** Use the graph to estimate the difference in temperature between 4:00 A.M. and noon.

A double-line graph can be used to compare how two related data sets change over time. A double-line graph has a key to distinguish between the two sets of data.

EXAMPLE 4 MCC9-12.S.ID.1

Reading and Interpreting Double-Line Graphs

Use the graph to answer each question.

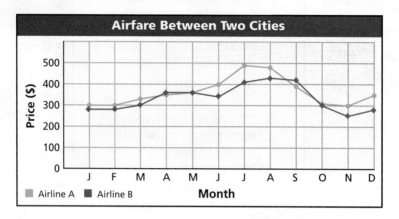

A In which month(s) did airline B charge more than airline A?

April and September   *Identify the points when the purple line is higher than the blue line.*

B During which month(s) did the airlines charge the same airfare?

May   *Look for the point where the data points overlap.*

 4. Use the graph to describe the general trend of the data.

A **circle graph** shows parts of a whole. The entire circle represents 100% of the data and each sector represents a percent of the total. Circle graphs are good for comparing each category of data to the whole set.

EXAMPLE 5 MCC9-12.S.ID.1

Reading and Interpreting Circle Graphs

Use the graph to answer each question.

A Which two fruits together make up half of the fruit salad?

bananas and strawberries

Look for two fruits that together make up half of the circle.

B Which fruit is used more than any other?

cantaloupe

Look for the largest sector of the graph.

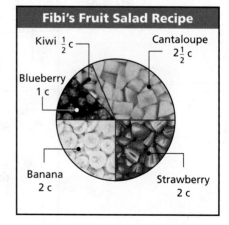

Reading Math

The sections of a circle graph are called *sectors*.

 5. Use the graph to determine what percent of the fruit salad is cantaloupe.

EXAMPLE **6**
MCC9-12.S.ID.1

Choosing and Creating an Appropriate Display

Use the given data to make a graph. Explain why you chose that type of graph.

A

Livestock Show Entries	
Animal	**Number**
Chicken	38
Goat	10
Horse	32
Pig	12
Sheep	25

A bar graph is appropriate for this data because it will be a good way to compare categories.

Step 1 Determine an appropriate scale and interval. The scale must include all of the data values. The scale is separated into equal parts, called intervals.

Step 2 Use the data to determine the lengths of the bars. Draw bars of equal width. The bars should not touch.

Step 3 Title the graph and label the horizontal and vertical scales.

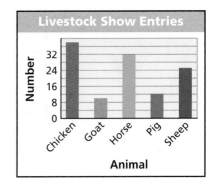

B

Division of Crops	
Crop	**Area (acres)**
Corn	70
Fallow	50
Mixed vegetables	10
Soybeans	40
Wheat	30

A circle graph is appropriate for this data because it shows categories as parts of a whole.

Step 1 Calculate the percent of the total represented by each category.

Corn: $\frac{70}{200} = 0.35 = 35\%$

Soybeans: $\frac{40}{200} = 0.2 = 20\%$

Fallow: $\frac{50}{200} = 0.25 = 25\%$

Wheat: $\frac{30}{200} = 0.15 = 15\%$

Mixed vegetables: $\frac{10}{200} = 0.05 = 5\%$

Step 2 Find the angle measure for each sector of the graph. Since there are 360° in a circle, multiply each percent by 360°.
Corn: $0.35 \times 360° = 126°$
Fallow: $0.25 \times 360° = 90°$
Mixed vegetables: $0.05 \times 360° = 18°$
Soybeans: $0.2 \times 360° = 72°$
Wheat: $0.15 \times 360° = 54°$

Step 3 Use a compass to draw a circle. Mark the center and use a straightedge to draw one radius. Then use a protractor to draw each central angle.

Step 4 Title the graph and label each sector.

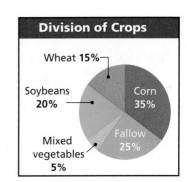

Use the given data to make a graph. Explain why you chose that type of graph.

Chinnick College Enrollment	
Year	Students
1930	586
1955	2,361
1980	15,897
2005	21,650

A line graph is appropriate for this data because it will show the change in enrollment over a period of time.

Step 1 Determine the scale and interval for each set of data. Time should be plotted on the horizontal axis because it is independent.

Step 2 Plot a point for each pair of values. Connect the points using line segments.

Step 3 Title the graph and label the horizontal and vertical scales.

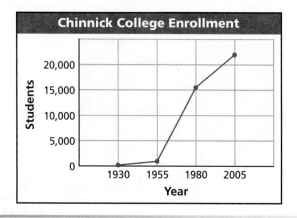

---

6. Use the given data to make a graph. Explain why you chose that type of graph.

The data below shows how Vera spends her time during a typical 5-day week during the school year.

Vera's Schedule						
Activity	Sleeping	Eating	School	Sports	Homework	Other
Time (h)	45	8	30	10	10	17

MCC.MP.7 | MATHEMATICAL PRACTICES

THINK AND DISCUSS

1. What are some comparisons you can make by looking at a bar graph?

2. Name some key components of a good line graph.

3. GET ORGANIZED Copy and complete the graphic organizer. In each box, tell which kind of graph is described.

```
                    Graph Type
        ┌───────────────┼───────────────┐
   Compares         Shows change    Shows how a whole
   categories       over time       is divided in parts
```

GUIDED PRACTICE

Vocabulary Use the vocabulary from this lesson to answer the following questions.

1. In a *circle graph*, what does each sector represent?

2. In a *line graph*, how does the slope of a line segment relate to the rate of change?

SEE EXAMPLE **1** Use the bar graph for Exercises 3 and 4.

3. Estimate the total number of animals at the shelter.

4. There are 3 times as many ___?___ as ___?___ at the animal shelter.

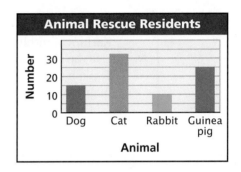

SEE EXAMPLE **2** Use the double-bar graph for Exercises 5–7.

5. About how much more is a club level seat at stadium A than at stadium B?

6. Which type of seat is the closest in price at the two stadiums?

7. Describe one relationship between the ticket prices at stadium A and stadium B.

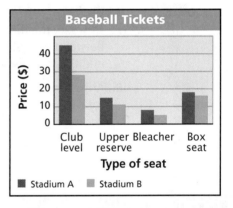

SEE EXAMPLE **3** Use the line graph for Exercises 8 and 9.

8. Estimate the number of tickets sold during the week of the greatest sales.

9. Which one-week period of time saw the greatest change in sales?

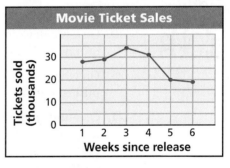

SEE EXAMPLE **4** Use the double-line graph for Exercises 10–12.

10. When was the support for the two candidates closest?

11. Estimate the difference in voter support for the two candidates five weeks before the election.

12. Describe the general trend(s) of voter support for the two candidates.

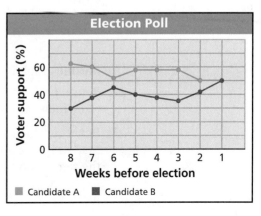

Use the circle graph for Exercises 13–15.

13. Which color is least represented in the ball playpen?

14. There are 500 balls in the playpen. How many are yellow?

15. Which two colors are approximately equally represented in the ball playpen?

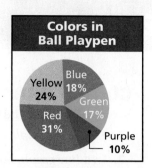

Colors in Ball Playpen

Yellow 24%
Blue 18%
Green 17%
Red 31%
Purple 10%

16. The table shows the breakdown of Karim's monthly budget of $100. Use the given data to make a graph. Explain why you chose that type of graph.

Item/Activity	Spending ($)
Clothing	35
Food	25
Entertainment	25
Other	15

PRACTICE AND PROBLEM SOLVING

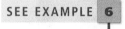

Independent Practice

For Exercises	See Example
17–18	1
19–21	2
22–23	3
24–26	4
27–28	5
29	6

my.hrw.com

Online Extra Practice

Use the bar graph for Exercises 17 and 18.

17. Estimate the difference in population between the tribes with the largest and the smallest population.

18. Approximately what percent of the total population shown in the table is Cherokee?

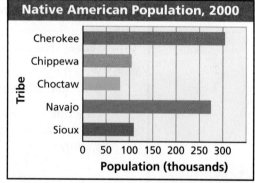

Native American Population, 2000

Tribe: Cherokee, Chippewa, Choctaw, Navajo, Sioux

Population (thousands): 0 50 100 150 200 250 300

Source: U.S. Census Bureau

Use the double bar graph for Exercises 19–21.

19. On what day did Ray do the most overall business?

20. On what day did Ray have the busiest lunch?

21. On Sunday, about how many times as great was the number of dinner customers as the number of lunch customers?

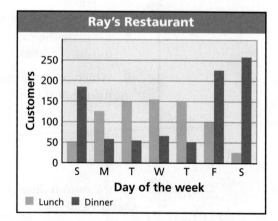

Ray's Restaurant

Customers: 0 50 100 150 200 250

Day of the week: S M T W T F S

■ Lunch ■ Dinner

Use the line graph for Exercises 22 and 23.

22. Between which two games did Marlon's score increase the most?

23. Between which three games did Marlon's score increase by about the same amount?

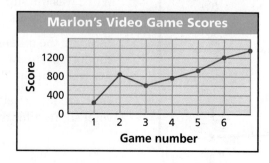

Marlon's Video Game Scores

Score: 0 400 800 1200

Game number: 1 2 3 4 5 6

Use the double-line graph for Exercises 24–26.

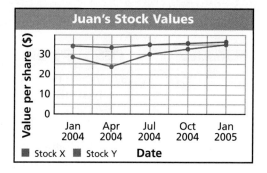

Juan's Stock Values

24. What was the average value per share of Juan's two stocks in July 2004?

25. Which stock's value changed the most over any time period?

26. Describe the trend of the values of both stocks.

Use the circle graph for Exercises 27 and 28.

27. About what percent of the total number of cars are hopper cars?

28. About what percent of the total number of cars are gondola or tank cars?

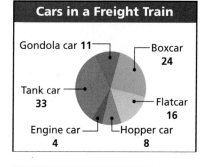

Cars in a Freight Train

29. The table shows the weight of twin babies at various times from birth to four weeks old. Use the given data to make a graph. Explain why you chose that type of graph.

Age (days)	Boy's Weight (lb)	Girl's Weight (lb)
1	5.3	5.7
3	5.0	5.2
7	5.5	5.9
14	6.2	6.8
28	7.9	7.5

Write *bar*, *double-bar*, *line*, *double-line*, or *circle* to indicate the type of graph that would best display the data described.

30. attendance at a carnival each year over a ten-year period

31. attendance at two different carnivals each year over a ten-year period

32. attendance at five different carnivals during the same year

33. attendance at a carnival by age group as it relates to total attendance

34. **Critical Thinking** Give an example of real-world data that would best be displayed by each type of graph: line graph, circle graph, double-bar graph.

Real-World Connections

35. The first modern Olympic Games took place in 1896 in Athens, Greece. The circle graph shows the total number of medals won by several countries at the Olympic Games of 1896.

a. Which country won the most medals? Estimate the percent of the medals won by this country.

b. Which country won the second most medals? Estimate the percent of the medals won by this country.

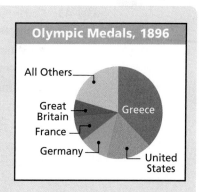

Olympic Medals, 1896

36. Write About It Explain how you could use a line graph to make predictions.

TEST PREP

37. Which type of graph would best display the contribution of each high school basketball player to the team, in terms of points scored?

    Ⓐ Bar graph   Ⓑ Line graph   Ⓒ Double-line graph   Ⓓ Circle graph

38. At what age did Marianna have 75% more magazine subscriptions than she did at age 40?

    Ⓕ 25

    Ⓖ 30

    Ⓗ 35

    Ⓙ 45

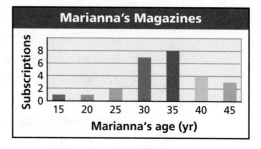

39. Short Response The table shows the number of students in each algebra class. Make a graph to display the data. Explain why you chose that type of graph.

Teacher	Students
Mr. Abrams	34
Ms. Belle	29
Mr. Marvin	25
Ms. Swanson	27

CHALLENGE AND EXTEND

Students and teachers at Lauren's school went on one of three field trips.

40. On which trip were there more boys than girls?

41. A total of 60 people went to the museum. Estimate the number of girls who went to the museum.

42. Explain why it is not possible to determine whether fewer teachers went to the museum than to the zoo or the opera.

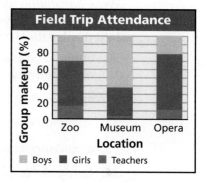

FOCUS ON MATHEMATICAL PRACTICES

43. Communication A double–line graph displays the high temperatures and the low temperatures for each day of a week.

    a. What does a temperature that lies between the high temperature line and the low temperature line represent?

    b. Armin says a double-bar graph would better represent the data than a double-line graph. How might Armin support his choice?

44. Error Analysis Darnell says the best graphical display for the data in the table is a circle graph. Do you agree? If not, what display would you chose?

Favorite Lunch	Male	Female
Pizza	23	17
Turkey Burger	14	9
Veggie Lasagna	3	21

Frequency and Histograms

Essential Question: How can you organize and display data using stem-and-leaf plots and histograms?

Objectives
Create stem-and-leaf plots.

Create frequency tables and histograms.

Vocabulary
stem-and-leaf plot
frequency
frequency table
histogram
cumulative frequency

Why learn this?

Stem-and-leaf plots can be used to organize data, like the number of students in elective classes. (See Example 1.)

A **stem-and-leaf plot** arranges data by dividing each data value into two parts. This allows you to see each data value.

The digits other than the last digit of each value are called a stem. ⟶ 2|3 ⟵ The last digit of a value is called a leaf.

Key: 2|3 means 23 ⟵ The key tells you how to read each value.

EXAMPLE MCC9-12.S.ID.1 **1** Making a Stem-and-Leaf Plot

my.hrw.com

Online Video Tutor

A The numbers of students in each of the elective classes at a school are given below. Use the data to make a stem-and-leaf plot.

24, 14, 12, 25, 32, 18, 23, 24, 9, 18, 34, 28, 24, 27

Number of Students in Elective Classes

Stem	Leaves
0	9
1	2 4 8 8
2	3 4 4 4 5 7 8
3	2 4

Key: 2|3 means 23

The tens digits are the stems.

The ones digits are the leaves. List the leaves from least to greatest within each row.

Title the graph and add a key.

Writing Math

Stems are always consecutive numbers. In Example 1B, neither player has scores that start with 15, so there are no leaves in that row.

B Marty's and Bill's scores for ten games of bowling are given below. Use the data to make a back-to-back stem-and-leaf plot.

Marty: 137, 149, 167, 134, 121, 127, 143, 123, 168, 162
Bill: 129, 138, 141, 124, 139, 160, 149, 145, 128, 130

Bowling Scores

Marty		Bill
7 3 1	12	4 8 9
7 4	13	0 8 9
9 3	14	1 5 9
	15	
8 7 2	16	0

Key: |14|1 means 141
3|14| means 143

The first two digits are the stems.

The ones digits are the leaves.

Put Marty's scores on the left side and Bill's scores on the right.

Title the graph and add a key.

The graph shows that three of Marty's scores were higher than Bill's highest score.

 1. The temperatures in degrees Celsius for two weeks are given below. Use the data to make a stem-and-leaf plot.

7, 32, 34, 31, 26, 27, 23, 19, 22, 29, 30, 36, 35, 31

Tom Stewart/CORBIS

The **frequency** of a data value is the number of times it occurs. A **frequency table** shows the frequency of each data value. If the data is divided into intervals, the table shows the frequency of each interval.

Making a Frequency Table

The final scores for each golfer in a tournament are given below. Use the data to make a frequency table with intervals.

77, 71, 70, 82, 75, 76, 72, 70, 77, 74, 71, 75, 68, 72, 75, 74

Step 1 Identify the least and greatest values.

The least value is 68. The greatest value is 82.

Step 2 Divide the data into equal intervals.

For this data set, use an interval of 3.

Step 3 List the intervals in the first column of the table. Count the number of data values in each interval and list the count in the last column. Give the table a title.

Golf Tournament Scores	
Scores	Frequency
68–70	3
71–73	4
74–76	6
77–79	2
80–82	1

2. The numbers of days of Maria's last 15 vacations are listed below. Use the data to make a frequency table with intervals.

4, 8, 6, 7, 5, 4, 10, 6, 7, 14, 12, 8, 10, 15, 12

A **histogram** is a bar graph used to display the frequency of data divided into equal intervals. The bars must be of equal width and should touch, but not overlap.

Making a Histogram

Use the frequency table in Example 2 to make a histogram.

Step 1 Use the scale and interval from the frequency table.

Step 2 Draw a bar for the number of scores in each interval.

All bars should be the same width. The bars should touch, but not overlap.

Step 3 Title the graph and label the horizontal and vertical scales.

Helpful Hint

The intervals in a histogram must be of equal size.

3. Make a histogram for the number of days of Maria's last 15 vacations.

4, 8, 6, 7, 5, 4, 10, 6, 7, 14, 12, 8, 10, 15, 12

Cumulative frequency shows the frequency of all data values less than or equal to a given value. You could just count the number of values, but if the data set has many values, you might lose track. Recording the data in a cumulative frequency table can help you keep track of the data values as you count.

Making a Cumulative Frequency Table

The heights in inches of the players on a school basketball team are given below.

72, 68, 71, 70, 73, 69, 79, 76, 72, 75, 72, 74, 68, 70, 69, 75, 72, 71, 73, 76

a. Use the data to make a cumulative frequency table.

Step 1 Choose intervals for the first column of the table.

Step 2 Record the frequency of values in each interval for the second column.

Step 3 Add the frequency of each interval to the frequencies of all the intervals before it. Put that number in the third column of the table.

Step 4 Title the table.

Basketball Players' Heights

Height (in.)	Frequency	Cumulative Frequency
68–70	6	6
71–73	8	14
74–76	5	19
77–79	1	20

b. How many players have heights under 74 in?

All heights under 74 in. are displayed in the first two rows of the table, so look at the cumulative frequency shown in the second row.

There are 14 players with heights under 74 in.

CHECK IT OUT!

4. The numbers of vowels in each sentence of a short essay are listed below.

33, 36, 39, 37, 34, 35, 43, 35, 28, 32, 36, 35, 29, 40, 33, 41, 37

a. Use the data to make a cumulative frequency table.

b. How many sentences contain 35 vowels or fewer?

MCC.MP.6   MATHEMATICAL PRACTICES

THINK AND DISCUSS

1. In a stem-and-leaf plot, the number of _____?_____ is always the same as the number of data values. (*stems* or *leaves*)

2. Explain how to make a histogram from a stem-and-leaf plot.

3. GET ORGANIZED Copy and complete the graphic organizer.

Bar Graphs vs Histograms

How are they alike?   How are they different?

GUIDED PRACTICE

1. **Vocabulary** A(n) _____?_____ is a data display that shows individual data values. (*stem-and-leaf plot* or *histogram*)

SEE EXAMPLE 1

2. **Sports** The ages of professional basketball players at the time the players were recruited are given. Use the data to make a stem-and-leaf plot.

Ages When Recruited
21 23 21 18 22 19 24 22 21 22 20 21

3. **Weather** The average monthly rainfall for two cities (in inches) is given below. Use the data to make a back-to-back stem-and-leaf plot.

Average Monthly Rainfall (in.)											
Austin, TX	1.9	2.4	1.9	3.0	3.6	3.3	1.9	2.1	3.2	3.5	2.2	2.3
New York, NY	3.3	3.1	3.9	3.7	4.2	3.3	4.1	4.1	3.6	3.3	4.2	3.6

SEE EXAMPLE 2

4. **Sports** The finishing times of runners in a 5K race, to the nearest minute, are given. Use the data to make a frequency table with intervals.

Finishing Times in 5K Race (to the nearest minute)
19 25 23 29 32 30 21 22 24
19 28 26 31 34 30 28 25 24

SEE EXAMPLE 3

5. **Biology** The breathing intervals of gray whales are given. Use the frequency table to make a histogram for the data.

Breathing Intervals (min)	
Interval	**Frequency**
5–7	4
8–10	7
11–13	7
14–16	8

SEE EXAMPLE 4

6. The scores made by a group of eleventh-grade students on the mathematics portion of the SAT are given.

Scores on Mathematics Portion of SAT
520 560 720 690 540 630 790 540
600 580 710 500 540 660 630

   a. Use the data to make a cumulative frequency table.

   b. How many students scored 650 or higher on the mathematics portion of the SAT?

PRACTICE AND PROBLEM SOLVING

7. The numbers of people who visited a park each day over two weeks during different seasons are given below. Use the data to make a back-to-back stem-and-leaf plot.

Visitors to a Park													
Summer	25	25	26	27	27	57	59	22	23	29	22	23	54	53
Winter	11	12	13	9	30	27	4	19	14	19	21	33	35	9

my.hrw.com

Online Extra Practice

8. **Weather** The daily high temperatures in degrees Fahrenheit in a town during one month are given. Use the data to make a stem-and-leaf plot.

Daily High Temperatures (°F)									
68	72	79	77	70	72	75	71	64	64
68	62	70	71	78	83	83	87	91	89
87	75	73	70	69	69	62	58	71	76

9. The overall GPAs of several high school seniors are given. Use the data to make a frequency table with intervals.

Overall GPAs							
3.6	2.9	3.1	3.0	2.5	2.6	3.8	2.9
2.2	2.9	3.1	3.3	3.6	3.0	2.3	2.8	2.9

10. **Chemistry** The atomic masses of the nonmetal elements are given in the table. Use the frequency table to make a histogram for the data.

Atomic Masses of Nonmetal Elements					
Interval	0–49.9	50–99.9	100–149.9	150–199.9	200–249.9
Frequency	11	3	2	0	2

11. The numbers of pretzels found in several samples of snack mix are given in the table.
   a. Use the data to make a cumulative frequency table.
   b. How many samples of snack mix had fewer than 42 pretzels?

Numbers of Pretzels				
42	39	39	38	40
41	44	42	38	44
47	36	40	40	43	38

12. **Automobiles** The table shows gas mileage for the most economical cars in July 2004, including three hybrids.

Gas Mileage of Economical Cars									
Mileage in City (mi/gal)	32	60	48	38	36	60	35	38	32
Mileage on Highway (mi/gal)	38	51	47	46	47	66	43	46	40

Make a back-to-back stem-and-leaf plot for the data.

LINK

Automobiles

Solar cars usually weigh between 330 and 880 pounds. A conventional car weighs over 4000 pounds.

13. Damien's math test scores are given in the table:
   a. Make a stem-and-leaf plot of Damien's test scores.
   b. Make a histogram of the test scores using intervals of 5.
   c. Make a histogram of the test scores using intervals of 10.
   d. Make a histogram of the test scores using intervals of 20.
   e. How does the size of the interval affect the appearance of the histogram?
   f. **Write About It** Which histogram makes Damien's grades look highest? Explain.

Damien's Math Test Scores		
75	84	68
72	59	88
72	77	81
84	60	70

H.O.T. 14. **///ERROR ANALYSIS///** Two students made stem-and-leaf plots for the following data: 530, 545, 550, 555, 570. Which is incorrect? Explain the error.

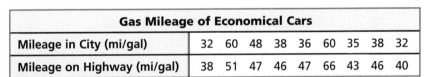

A

Stem	Leaves
53	0
54	5
55	0 5
57	0

Key: 52|5 means 525

B

Stem	Leaves
53	0
54	5
55	0 5
56	
57	0

Key: 52|5 means 525

15. The 2004 Olympic results for women's weightlifting in the 48 kg weight class are 210, 205, 200, 190, 187.5, 182.5, 180, 177.5, 175, 172.5, 170, 167.5, and 165, measured in kilograms. Medals are awarded to the athletes who can lift the most weight.

   a. Create a frequency table beginning at 160 and using intervals of 10 kg.

   b. Create a histogram of the data.

   c. Tara Cunningham from the United States lifted 172.5 kg. Did she win a medal? How do you know?

16. **Entertainment** The top ten movies in United States theaters for the weekend of June 25–27, 2004, grossed the following amounts (in millions of dollars). Create a histogram for the data. Make the first interval 5–9.9.

Ticket Sales (million $)				
23.9	19.7	18.8	13.5	13.1
11.2	10.2	7.5	6.1	5.1

H.O.T. 17. **Critical Thinking** Margo's homework assignment is to make a data display of some data she finds in a newspaper. She found a frequency table with the given intervals.

Explain why Margo must be careful when drawing the bars of the histogram.

Age
Under 18
18–30
31–54
55 and older

TEST PREP

18. What data value occurs most often in the stem-and-leaf plot?

   Ⓐ 7

   Ⓑ 4.7

   Ⓒ 47

   Ⓓ 777

Stem	Leaves
3	2 3 4 4 7 9
4	0 1 5 7 7 7 8
5	1 2 2 3

Key: 3|2 means 3.2

19. The table shows the results of a survey about time spent on the Internet each month. Which statement is NOT supported by the data in the table?

Time Spent on the Internet per Month		
Time (h)	Frequency	Cumulative Frequency
0–4	4	4
5–9	6	10
10–14	3	13
15–19	16	29
20–24	12	41
25–29	7	48
30–34	2	50

   Ⓕ The interval of 30 to 34 h/mo has the lowest frequency.

   Ⓖ More than half of those who responded spend more than 20 h/mo on the Internet.

   Ⓗ Only four people responded that they spend less than 5 h/mo on the Internet.

   Ⓙ Sixteen people responded that they spend less than 20 h/mo on the Internet.

20. The frequencies of starting salary ranges for college graduates are noted in the table. Which histogram best reflects the data?

Starting Salaries	
Salary Range ($)	Frequency
20,000–29,000	ЖЖ ЖЖ ЖЖ ЖЖ II
30,000–39,000	ЖЖ ЖЖ ЖЖ ЖЖ ЖЖ ЖЖ
40,000–49,000	ЖЖ ЖЖ ЖЖ I
50,000–59,000	I

Ⓐ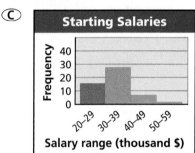

Ⓒ

Ⓑ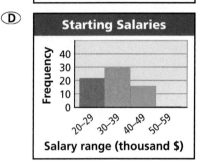

Ⓓ

CHALLENGE AND EXTEND

21. The cumulative frequencies of each interval have been given. Use this information to complete the frequency column.

Interval	Frequency	Cumulative Frequency
13–16		8
17–20		16
21–24		57
25–28		123

FOCUS ON MATHEMATICAL PRACTICES

H.O.T. 22. Error Analysis Rajiv says that a stem-and-leaf plot with 12 stems definitely represents a data set of 12 values. Do you agree? Explain.

H.O.T. 23. Reasoning The table shows the lengths of students' right feet.

a. Find the cumulative frequencies for the intervals in the table.

b. How many students have a right foot length greater than 19 cm but less than 26 cm?

c. How many students have a right foot length of 21 cm? Explain.

d. Which type of graphical display would you use for the data in the table? Justify your choice.

Students' Right Foot Lengths	
Length (cm)	Frequency
14–16	2
17–19	19
20–22	13
23–25	6
26–28	1

14-3 Two-Way Tables

Essential Question: How can you construct and interpret two-way frequency tables?

Objectives
Construct and interpret two-way frequency tables of data when two categories are associated with each object being classified.

Vocabulary
joint relative frequency
marginal relative frequency
conditional relative frequency

Who uses this?
Commuters can use two-way tables to determine the best route to work. (See Example 3.)

A *two-way table* is a useful way to organize data that can be categorized by two variables. Suppose you asked 20 children and adults whether they liked broccoli. The table shows one way to arrange the data.

The **joint relative frequencies** are the values in each category divided by the total number of values, shown by the shaded cells in the table. Each value is divided by 20, the total number of individuals.

The **marginal relative frequencies** are found by adding the joint relative frequencies in each row and column.

	Yes	No
Children	3	8
Adults	7	2

	Yes	No	Total
Children	0.15	0.4	0.55
Adults	0.35	0.1	0.45
Total	0.5	0.5	1

EXAMPLE 1
MCC9-12.S.ID.5

Online Video Tutor

Finding Joint and Marginal Relative Frequencies

The table shows the results of a poll of 80 randomly selected high school students who were asked if they prefer math or English. Make a table of the joint and marginal relative frequencies.

	9th grade	10th grade	11th grade	12th grade
Math	10	12	11	8
English	12	11	8	8

Divide each value by the total of 80 to find the joint relative frequencies, and add each row and column to find the marginal relative frequencies.

	9th grade	10th grade	11th grade	12th grade	Total
Math	0.125	0.15	0.1375	0.1	0.5125
English	0.15	0.1375	0.1	0.1	0.4875
Total	0.275	0.2875	0.2375	0.2	1

1. The table shows the number of books sold at a library sale. Make a table of the joint and marginal relative frequencies.

	Fiction	Nonfiction
Hardcover	28	52
Paperback	94	36

To find a **conditional relative frequency**, divide the joint relative frequency by the marginal relative frequency. Conditional relative frequencies can be used to find conditional probabilities.

EXAMPLE 2 Using Conditional Relative Frequency to Find Probability

A sociologist collected data on the types of pets in 100 randomly selected households, and summarized the results in a table.

		Owns a cat	
		Yes	No
Owns a dog	Yes	15	24
	No	18	43

A Make a table of the joint and marginal relative frequencies.

		Owns a cat		
		Yes	No	Total
Owns a dog	Yes	0.15	0.24	0.39
	No	0.18	0.43	0.61
	Total	0.33	0.67	1

B If you are given that a household has a dog, what is the probability that the household also has a cat?

Use the conditional relative frequency for the row with the condition "Owns a dog." The total for households with dogs is 0.39, or 39%. Out of these, 0.15, or 15%, also have cats. The conditional relative frequency is $\frac{0.15}{0.39} \approx 0.38$.

Given that a household has a dog, there is a probability of about 0.38 that the household also has a cat.

CHECK IT OUT! The classes at a dance academy include ballet and tap dancing. Enrollment in these classes is shown in the table.

		Ballet	
		Yes	No
Tap	Yes	38	52
	No	86	24

2a. Copy and complete the table of the joint relative frequencies and marginal relative frequencies.

		Ballet		
		Yes	No	Total
Tap	Yes			
	No			
	Total			1

2b. If you are given that a student is taking ballet, what is the probability that the student is not taking tap?

Notice that in Example 2, the conditional relative frequency could have been found from the original data:

$$\frac{0.15}{0.39} = \frac{15}{39} \approx 0.38$$

EXAMPLE 3
MCC9-12.S.CP.4

Comparing Conditional Probabilities

my.hrw.com

Online Video Tutor

Tomas is trying to decide on the best possible route to drive to work. He has a choice of three possible routes. On each day, he randomly selects a route and keeps track of whether he is late. After a 40-day trial, his notes look like this.

	Late	Not Late
Route A	IIII	HHT HHT
Route B	II	HHT II
Route C	IIII	HHT HHT II

Use conditional probabilities to determine the best route for Tomas to take to work.

Create a table of joint and marginal relative frequencies. There are 40 data values, so divide each frequency by 40.

	Late	Not late	Total
Route A	0.1	0.25	0.35
Route B	0.075	0.175	0.25
Route C	0.1	0.3	0.4
Total	0.275	0.725	1

To find the conditional probabilities, divide the joint relative frequency of being late by the marginal relative frequency in each row.

$P(\text{being late if driving Route A}) = \dfrac{0.1}{0.35} \approx 0.29$

$P(\text{being late if driving Route B}) = \dfrac{0.075}{0.25} = 0.3$

$P(\text{being late if driving Route C}) = \dfrac{0.1}{0.4} = 0.25$

The probability of being late is least for Route C. Based on the sample, Tomas is least likely to be late if he takes Route C.

CHECK IT OUT!

3. Francine is evaluating three driving schools. She asked 50 people who attended the schools whether they passed their driving tests on the first try.

Use conditional probabilities to determine which is the best school.

	Pass	Fail
Al's Driving	HHT HHT IIII	HHT III
Drive Time	HHT HHT I	HHT II
Crash Course	HHT	HHT

MCC.MP.6

MATHEMATICAL PRACTICES

THINK AND DISCUSS

1. Describe the relationship between joint relative frequencies and marginal relative frequencies.

2. Explain how to find the conditional relative frequencies from a two-way table showing joint and marginal relative frequencies.

Know it!
.note

3. GET ORGANIZED Copy and complete the graphic organizer at right. In each column, explain how to find the relative frequency from a two-way table.

Relative Frequencies		
Joint	Marginal	Conditional

Exercises

my.hrw.com
Homework Help

GUIDED PRACTICE

Vocabulary Apply the vocabulary from this lesson to answer each question.

1. The ___?___ relative frequencies are the sums of each row and column in a two-way table. (*joint, marginal,* or *conditional*)

2. You can compare ___?___ probabilities to evaluate the best one out of a number of options. (*joint, marginal,* or *conditional*)

SEE EXAMPLE 1

3. The table shows the results of a poll of randomly selected high school students who were asked if they prefer to hear all-school announcements in the morning or afternoon.

	Underclassmen	Upperclassmen
Morning	8	14
Afternoon	18	10

Make a table of the joint and marginal relative frequencies.

4. **Customer Service** The table shows the results of a customer satisfaction survey for a cellular service provider, by location of the customer. In the survey, customers were asked whether they would recommend a plan with the provider to a friend.

	Arlington	Towson	Parkville
Yes	40	35	41
No	18	10	6

Make a table of the joint and marginal relative frequencies. Round to the nearest hundredth where appropriate.

SEE EXAMPLE 2

5. **School** Pamela has collected data on the number of students in the sophomore class who play a sport or play a musical instrument.

		Plays a sport	
		Yes	No
Plays an instrument	**Yes**	47	38
	No	51	67

a. Copy and complete the table of the joint and marginal relative frequencies. Round to the nearest hundredth where appropriate.

		Play Sport		
		Yes	No	Total
Play instrument	**Yes**			
	No			
	Total			

b. If you are given that a student plays an instrument, what is the probability that the student also plays a sport? Round your answer to the nearest hundredth.

c. If you are given that a student plays a sport, what is the probability that the student also plays an instrument? Round your answer to the nearest hundredth.

Artville/Getty Images

6. **Business** Roberto is the owner of a car dealership. He is assessing the success rates of his top three salespeople in order to offer one of them a promotion. Over two months, for each attempted sale, he records whether the salesperson made a successful sale or not. The results are shown in the chart below.

	Successful	Unsuccessful
Becky	6	6
Raul	4	5
Darrell	6	9

    a. Make a table of the joint relative frequencies and marginal relative frequencies. Round to the nearest hundredth where appropriate.

    b. Find the probability that each salesperson will make a successful sale. Round to the nearest hundredth where appropriate.

    c. Determine which salesperson has the highest success rate.

PRACTICE AND PROBLEM SOLVING

Independent Practice

For Exercises	See Example
7–8	1
9–12	2
13	3

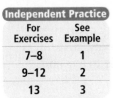

my.hrw.com

Online Extra Practice

7. **Fundraising** The table shows the number of T-shirts and sweatshirts sold at a fundraiser during parent visitation night at Preston High School.

	Students	Adults
T-Shirts	16	23
Sweatshirts	7	14

Make a table of the joint relative frequencies and marginal relative frequencies.

8. **Write About It** Describe in your own words the process you use to write marginal relative frequencies for data given in a two-way table.

9. **Customer Service** The claims handlers at a car insurance company help customers with insurance issues when there has been an accident, so their customer service skills are very important.

The claims handlers at the Trust Auto Insurance Company are divided into three teams. For one month, a customer satisfaction survey was given for each team. The results of the surveys are shown below.

	Satisfied	Dissatisfied
Team 1	20	8
Team 2	34	12
Team 3	34	10

    a. Make a table of the joint relative frequencies and marginal relative frequencies. Round to the nearest hundredth where appropriate.

    b. Find the probability that a customer will be satisfied after working with each team. Round to the nearest hundredth where appropriate.

    c. Determine which team has the highest rate of customer satisfaction.

10. **Critical Thinking** What do you notice about the value that always falls in the cell to the lower right of a two-way table when marginal relative frequencies have been written in? What does this value represent?

H.O.T. 11. ///ERROR ANALYSIS/// One hundred adults and children were randomly selected and asked whether they spoke more than one language fluently. The data were recorded in a two-way table. Maria and Brennan each used the data to make the tables of joint relative frequencies shown below, but their results are slightly different. The difference is shaded. Can you tell by looking at the tables which of them made an error? Explain.

Maria's table

	Yes	No
Children	0.15	0.25
Adults	0.1	0.6

Brennan's table

	Yes	No
Children	0.15	0.25
Adults	0.1	0.5

H.O.T. 12. Estimation A total of 107 brownies and muffins was sold at a school bake sale. The joint relative frequency representing muffins sold to seniors was 0.48. Use mental math to find approximately how many muffins were sold to seniors.

13. Public Transit A town planning committee is considering a new system for public transit. Residents of the town were randomly selected to answer two questions: "Do you work within 5 miles of your home?" and "Would you use the new system to get to work, if it were available?"
The results are shown below.

Work less than 5 miles from home?

Use new system?		Yes	No
	Yes	24	32
	No	44	20

a. Make a table of the joint relative frequencies and marginal relative frequencies. Round to the nearest hundredth where appropriate.

b. If residents work less than 5 miles from home, what is the probability that they would use the new system? Round to the nearest hundredth.

c. If residents are willing to use the new system, what is the probability that they don't work less than 5 miles from home? Round to the nearest hundredth.

TEST PREP

14. Students and teachers at a school were polled to see if they were in favor of extending the parking lot into part of the athletic fields. The results of the poll are shown in the two-way table.

	In Favor	Not in Favor
Students	16	23
Teachers	9	14

Which of the following statements is false?

Ⓐ Thirty-nine students were polled in all.

Ⓑ Fourteen teachers were polled in all.

Ⓒ Twenty-three students are not in favor of extending the parking lot.

Ⓓ Nine teachers are in favor of extending the parking lot.

15. A group of students were polled to find out how many were planning to major in a scientific field of study in college. The results of the poll are shown in the two-way table.

		Majoring in a science field	
		Yes	No
Class	Junior	150	210
	Senior	112	200

Which of the following statements is true?

Ⓐ Three hundred sixty students were polled in all.

Ⓑ A student in the senior class is more likely to be planning on a scientific major than a nonscientific major.

Ⓒ A student planning on a scientific major is more likely to be a junior than a senior.

Ⓓ More seniors than juniors plan to enter a scientific field of study.

16. Gridded Response A group of children and adults were polled about whether they watch a particular TV show. The survey results, showing the joint relative frequencies and marginal relative frequencies, are shown in the two-way table.

	Yes	No	Total
Children	0.3	0.4	0.7
Adults	0.25	x	0.3
Total	0.55	0.45	1

What is the value of x?

CHALLENGE AND EXTEND

The table shows the joint relative frequencies for data on how many children and teenagers attended a fair in one evening, and whether each bought a booklet of tickets for rides at the entrance gate.

	Yes	No
Children	0.125	0.1
Teenagers	0.725	0.05

Use the table to answer questions 17–20. Round answers to the nearest hundredth where appropriate.

17. Find the marginal relative frequencies for the data.

18. Based on this data, use a percentage to express how likely it is that tomorrow evening a teenager at the fair will buy a ticket booklet at the entrance. Round your answer to the nearest whole percent, if necessary.

19. If the data represent 80 teenagers and children altogether, how many children will have bought a ticket booklet at the entrance?

20. If 12 children did not buy ticket booklets at the entrance, then how many children and teenagers altogether does the data represent?

21. A poll with the options of 'yes' and 'no' was given. If the marginal relative frequency of 'yes' is 1.0, what was the marginal relative frequency of 'no'?

	Yes	No	Total
Group 1	0.24	?	?
Group 2	0.76	?	?
Total	1.0	?	?

22. Short Response What is the maximum a marginal relative frequency can be, and why?

FOCUS ON MATHEMATICAL PRACTICES

H.O.T. **23. Problem Solving** A survey of a sheep farm reveals that 27% of the sheep have long white wool, 8% have short black wool, and 3% have short white wool.

    a. Draw a two-way relative frequency table to show this information. Include marginal relative frequencies in your table.

    b. What percent of the sheep have black wool?

    c. If the farm has a total of 300 sheep, how many of them have short black wool or long white wool?

H.O.T. **24. Reasoning** The table shows the relative frequencies of the results of a survey of whether children and adults have recently used crayons. If 2 of the adults surveyed have recently used crayons, how many children were surveyed in all?

	Child	Adult	Total
Yes	0.55	0.05	0.6
No	0.1	0.30	0.4
Total	0.65	0.35	1

H.O.T. **25. Analysis** The partial frequency table compares the class year of students in a high school to where they like to eat lunch. Is enough information given to complete the table? If so, complete it. If not, complete as much as possible and explain what further information is needed.

	Freshman	Sophomore	Junior	Senior	Total
Cafeteria	75				
Library	20			10	65
Outside		30	50	55	
Total	125	110	140	100	475

Data Distributions

Essential Question: How can you describe data using measures of central tendency and spread, including displaying data on box-and-whisker plots?

Objectives

Describe the central tendency of a data set.

Create and interpret box-and-whisker plots.

Vocabulary

mean
median
mode
range
outlier
first quartile
third quartile
interquartile range (IQR)
box-and-whisker plot

Who uses this?

Sports analysts examine data distributions to make predictions. (See Example 4.)

A *measure of central tendency* describes the center of a set of data. Measures of central tendency include the *mean*, *median*, and *mode*.

- The **mean** is the average of the data values, or the sum of the values in the set divided by the number of values in the set.

- The **median** is the middle value when the values are in numerical order, or the mean of the two middle numbers if there are an even number of values.

- The **mode** is the value or values that occur most often. A data set may have one mode or more than one mode. If no value occurs more often than another, the data set has no mode.

The **range** of a set of data is the difference between the greatest and least values in the set. The range is one measure of the spread of a data set.

COMMON CORE GPS
EXAMPLE 1
Prep. for MCC9-12.S.ID.2

my.hrw.com

Online Video Tutor

Finding Mean, Median, Mode, and Range of a Data Set

The numbers of hours Isaac did homework on six days are 3, 8, 4, 6, 5, and 4. Find the mean, median, mode, and range of the data set.

3, 4, 4, 5, 6, 8   *Write the data in numerical order.*

mean: $\dfrac{3+4+4+5+6+8}{6} = \dfrac{30}{6} = 5$ *Add all the values and divide by the number of values.*

median: 3, 4, ④, ⑤, 6, 8   *There is an even number of values. Find the*
The median is 4.5.   *mean of the two middle values.*

mode: 4   *4 occurs more than any other value.*

range: $8 - 3 = 5$ *Subtract the least value from the greatest value.*

---

1. The weights in pounds of five cats are 12, 14, 12, 16, and 16. Find the mean, median, mode, and range of the data set.

A value that is very different from the other values in a data set is called an **outlier**. In the data set below, one value is much greater than the other values.

Most of data   Mean   Much different value

AP Photo/Dave Martin

EXAMPLE 2 MCC9-12.S.ID.3

Determining the Effects of Outliers

Identify the outlier in the data set $\{7, 10, 54, 9, 12, 8, 5\}$, and determine how the outlier affects the mean, median, mode, and range of the data.

5, 7, 8, 9, 10, 12, 54   *Write the data in numerical order.*

The outlier is 54.   *Look for a value much greater or less than the rest.*

With the Outlier:

mean: $\dfrac{5 + 7 + 8 + 9 + 10 + 12 + 54}{7}$
$= 15$

median: 5, 7, 8, ⑨ 10, 12, 54
The median is 9.

mode: Each value occurs once.
There is no mode.

range: $54 - 5 = 49$

Without the Outlier:

mean: $\dfrac{5 + 7 + 8 + 9 + 10 + 12}{6}$
$= 8.5$

median: 5, 7, ⑧⑨ 10, 12
The median is 8.5.

mode: Each value occurs once.
There is no mode.

range: $12 - 5 = 7$

The outlier increases the mean by 6.5, the median by 0.5, and the range by 42. It has no effect on the mode.

2. Identify the outlier in the data set $\{21, 24, 3, 27, 30, 24\}$, and determine how the outlier affects the mean, median, mode, and range of the data.

As you can see in Example 2, an outlier can strongly affect the mean of a data set, while having little or no impact on the median and mode. Therefore, the mean may not be the best measure to describe a data set that contains an outlier. In such cases, the median or mode may better describe the center of the data set.

EXAMPLE 3 MCC9-12.S.ID.3

Choosing a Measure of Central Tendency

Niles scored 70, 74, 72, 71, 73, and 96 on his six geography tests. For each question, choose the mean, median, or mode, and give its value.

A Which measure gives Niles's test average?
The average of Niles's scores is the mean.

mean: $\dfrac{70 + 74 + 72 + 71 + 73 + 96}{6} = 76$

B Which measure best describes Niles's typical score? Explain.
The outlier of 96 causes the mean to be greater than all but one of the test scores, so it is not the best measure in this situation.

The data set has no mode.

The median best describes the typical score.

median: 70, 71, ⑦②│⑦③ 74, 96   *Find the mean of the two middle values.*
The median is 72.5.

Josh scored 75, 75, 81, 84, and 85 on five tests. For each question, choose the mean, median, or mode, and give its value.

3a. Which measure describes the score Josh received most often?

3b. Which measure should Josh use to convince his parents that he is doing well in school? Explain.

Measures of central tendency describe how data cluster around one value. Another way to describe a data set is by its spread—how the data values are spread out from the center.

Quartiles divide a data set into four equal parts. Each quartile contains one-fourth of the values in the set. The **first quartile** is the median of the lower half of the data set. The second quartile is the median of the data set, and the **third quartile** is the median of the upper half of the data set.

The **interquartile range (IQR)** of a data set is the difference between the third and first quartiles. It represents the range of the middle half of the data.

Reading Math

The first quartile is sometimes called the lower quartile, and the third quartile is sometimes called the upper quartile.

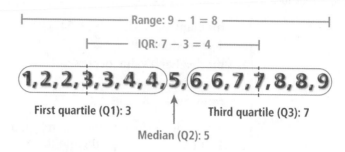

A **box-and-whisker plot** can be used to show how the values in a data set are distributed. You need five values to make a box-and-whisker plot: the minimum (or least value), first quartile, median, third quartile, and maximum (or greatest value).

COMMON CORE GPS **EXAMPLE** **4**
MCC9-12.S.ID.1

my.hrw.com

Online Video Tutor

Sports Application

The numbers of runs scored by a softball team in 20 games are given. Use the data to make a box-and-whisker plot.

3, 4, 8, 12, 7, 5, 4, 12, 3, 9, 11, 4, 14, 8, 2, 10, 3, 10, 9, 7

Step 1 Order the data from least to greatest.

2, 3, 3, 3, 4, 4, 4, 5, 7, 7, 8, 8, 9, 9, 10, 10, 11, 12, 12, 14

Step 2 Identify the five needed values.

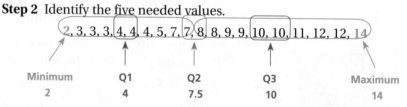

Step 3 Draw a number line and plot a point above each of the five needed values. Draw a box through the first and third quartiles and a vertical line through the median. Draw lines from the box to the minimum and maximum.

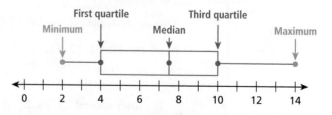

4. Use the data to make a box-and-whisker plot.

13, 14, 18, 13, 12, 17, 15, 12, 13, 19, 11, 14, 14, 18, 22, 23

EXAMPLE **5** Reading and Interpreting Box-and-Whisker Plots

The box-and-whisker plots show the ticket sales, in millions of dollars, of the top 25 movies in 2000 and 2007 (for the United States only).

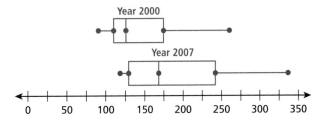

A **Which data set has a greater median? Explain.**

The vertical line in the box for 2007 is farther to the right than the vertical line in the box for 2000.

The data set for 2007 has a greater median.

B **Which data set has a greater interquartile range? Explain.**

The length of the box for 2007 is greater than the length of the box for 2000.

The data set for 2007 has a greater interquartile range.

C **About how much more were the ticket sales for the top movie in 2007 than for the top movie in 2000?**

2007 maximum: **about \$335 million**   *Read the maximum values from*
2000 maximum: **about \$260 million**   *the box-and-whisker plots.*
$335 - 260 = 75$ *Subtract the maximum values.*

The ticket sales for the top movie in 2007 were about \$75 million more than for the top movie in 2000.

 Use the box-and-whisker plots above to answer each question.

5a. Which data set has a smaller range? Explain.

5b. About how much more was the median ticket sales for the top 25 movies in 2007 than in 2000?

 MCC.MP.1, MCC.MP.6   **MATHEMATICAL PRACTICES**

THINK AND DISCUSS

1. Explain when the median is a value in the data set.

2. Give an example of a data set for which the mean is twice the median. Explain how you determined your answer.

3. Suppose the minimum in a data set is the same as the first quartile. How would this affect a box-and-whisker plot of the data?

4. GET ORGANIZED Copy and complete the graphic organizer. Tell which measure of central tendency answers each question.

Measures of Central Tendency	
Measure	**Used to Answer**
	What is the average?
	What is the halfway point of the data?
	What is the most common value?

my.hrw.com
Homework Help

GUIDED PRACTICE

1. **Vocabulary** What is the difference between the *range* and the *interquartile range* of a data set?

SEE EXAMPLE 1 Find the mean, median, mode, and range of each data set.

2. 85, 83, 85, 82

3. 12, 22, 33, 34, 44, 44

4. 10, 26, 25, 10, 20, 22, 25, 20

5. 71, 73, 75, 78, 78, 80, 85, 86

SEE EXAMPLE 2 Identify the outlier in each data set, and determine how the outlier affects the mean, median, mode, and range of the data.

6. 10, 96, 12, 17, 15

7. 64, 75, 72, 13, 64

SEE EXAMPLE 3 Adrienne scored 82, 54, 85, 91, and 83 on her last five science tests. For each question, choose the mean, median, or mode, and give its value.

8. Which measure best describes Adrienne's typical score? Explain.

9. Which measure should Adrienne use to convince her soccer coach she is doing well in science? Explain.

SEE EXAMPLE 4 Use the data to make a box-and-whisker plot.

10. 21, 31, 26, 24, 28, 26

11. 12, 13, 42, 62, 62, 82

SEE EXAMPLE 5 The box-and-whisker plots show the scores, in thousands of points, of two players on a video game. Use the box-and-whisker plots to answer each question.

12. Which player has a higher median score? Explain.

13. Which player had the lowest score? Estimate this score.

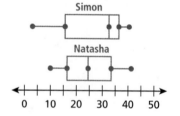

PRACTICE AND PROBLEM SOLVING

Find the mean, median, mode, and range of each data set.

14. 75, 63, 89, 91

15. 1, 2, 2, 2, 3, 3, 3, 4

16. 19, 25, 31, 19, 34, 22, 31, 34

17. 58, 58, 60, 60, 60, 61, 63

Identify the outlier in each data set, and determine how the outlier affects the mean, median, mode, and range of the data.

18. 42, 8, 54, 37, 29

19. 3, 8, 3, 3, 23, 8

Lamont bowled 153, 145, 148, and 166 in four games. For each question, choose the mean, median, or mode, and give its value.

20. Which measure gives Lamont's average score?

21. Which measure should Lamont use to convince his parents to let him join a bowling league? Explain.

Use the data to make a box-and-whisker plot.

22. 62, 63, 62, 64, 68, 62, 62

23. 85, 90, 81, 100, 92, 85

Independent Practice	
For Exercises	See Example
14–17	1
18–19	2
20–21	3
22–23	4
24-26	5

my.hrw.com

Online Extra Practice

The box-and-whisker plots show the prices, in dollars, of athletic shoes at two sports apparel stores. Use the box-and-whisker plots to answer each question.

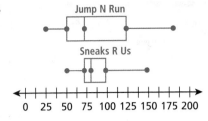

24. Which store has the greater median price? About how much greater?

25. Which store has the smaller interquartile range? What does this tell you about the data sets?

26. Estimate the difference in price between the most expensive shoe type at Jump N Run and the most expensive shoe at Sneaks R Us.

Find the mean, median, mode, and range of each data set.

27. 1, 2, 3, 4, 5, 6, 7, 8, 9, 10

28. 5, 6, 6, 5, 5

29. 2.1, 4.3, 6.5, 1.2, 3.4

30. $0, \frac{1}{4}, \frac{1}{2}, \frac{3}{4}, 1$

31. 23, 25, 26, 25, 23

32. −3, −3, −3, −2, −2, −1

33. 1, 4, 9, 16, 25, 36

34. 1, 0, 0, 1, 1, 4

35. **Estimation** Estimate the mean of $16\frac{7}{8}$, $12\frac{1}{4}$, $22\frac{1}{10}$, $18\frac{5}{7}$, $19\frac{1}{3}$, $13\frac{8}{11}$, and $13\frac{8}{11}$.

Tell whether each statement is sometimes, always, or never true.

36. The mean is a value in the data set.

37. The median is a value in the data set.

38. If a data set has one mode, the mode is a value in the data set.

39. The mean is affected by including an outlier.

40. The mode is affected by including an outlier.

H.O.T. 41. **Sports** The table shows the attendance at six football games at Jefferson High School. Which measure of central tendency best indicates the typical attendance at a football game? Why?

Attendance at Football Games	
Eagles vs. Bulldogs	743
Eagles vs. Panthers	768
Eagles vs. Coyotes	835
Eagles vs. Bears*	1218
Eagles vs. Colts	797
Eagles vs. Mustangs	854

*Homecoming Game

42. **Weather** The high temperatures in degrees Fahrenheit on 11 consecutive days were 68, 71, 75, 74, 75, 71, 73, 71, 72, 74, and 79. Find the mean, median, mode, and range of the temperatures. Describe the effect on the mean, median, mode, and range if the next day's temperature was 70 °F.

H.O.T. 43. **Advertising** A home-decorating store sells five types of candles, which are priced at $3, $2, $2, $2, and $15. If the store puts an ad in the paper titled "Best Local Candle Prices," which measure of central tendency should it advertise? Justify your answer.

Use the data to make a box-and-whisker plot.

44. 25, 28, 26, 16, 18, 15, 25, 28, 26, 16

45. 2, 3, 5, 7, 11, 13, 17, 19, 23, 29, 31

46. 1, 1, 1, 1, 2, 2, 2, 2, 3, 3, 4, 4, 4, 4, 4

47. 50, 52, 45, 62, 36, 55, 40, 50, 65, 33

Real-World Connections

48. The results in Olympic pole-vaulting are given as heights in meters. In the 2008 Olympic Games in Beijing, the following results occurred for the men's pole-vault finals: 5.96, 5.85, 5.70, 5.70, 5.70, 5.70, 5.60, 5.60, 5.60, 5.45, 5.45.

   a. Find the mean, median, mode, and range of this data set. Round to the nearest hundredth if needed.

   b. The gold medal was won by Steve Hooker of Australia. What was his height in the pole-vault finals?

49. **Business** The salaries for the eight employees at a small company are shown in the stem-and-leaf plot. Find the mean and median of the salaries. Which measure better describes the typical salary of an employee at this company? Explain.

Salaries ($1000)

Stem	Leaves
2	0 0 3 5 5
3	0 5
4	
5	
6	
7	8

Key: 2|0 means $20,000

50. **Critical Thinking** Use the data set {1, 2, 3, 5, 8, 13, 21, 34} to complete the following.

   a. Find the mean of the data set.

   b. What happens to the mean of the data set if every number is increased by 2?

   c. What happens to the mean of the data set if every number is multiplied by 2?

51. Allison has taken 5 tests worth 100 points each. Her scores are shown in the grade book below. What score does she need on her next test to have a mean of 90%?

Student	Test 1	Test 2	Test 3	Test 4	Test 5	Test 6	Average
Allison	88	85	89	92	90		

52. **Astronomy** The table shows the number of moons of the planets in our solar system. What is the mean number of moons per planet? Is Earth's value of one moon typical for the solar system? Explain.

Planet	Mercury	Venus	Earth	Mars	Jupiter	Saturn	Uranus	Neptune
Moons	0	0	1	2	63	60	27	13

H.O.T. 53. **Write About It** Explain how an outlier with a large value will affect the mean. Explain how an outlier with a small value will affect the mean.

TEST PREP

54. Which value is always represented on a box-and-whisker plot?

   (A) Mean   (B) Median   (C) Mode   (D) Range

55. The lengths in feet of the alligators at a zoo are 9, 7, 12, 6, and 10. The lengths in feet of the crocodiles at the zoo are 13, 10, 8, 19, 18, and 16. What is the difference between the mean length of the crocodiles and the mean length of the alligators?

   (F) 0.5 foot   (G) 5.2 feet   (H) 8 feet   (J) 11.4 feet

56. The mean score on a test is 50. Which CANNOT be true?

 Ⓐ Half the scores are 0, and half the scores are 100.

 Ⓑ The range is 50.

 Ⓒ Half the scores are 25, and half the scores are 50.

 Ⓓ Every score is 50.

57. Short Response The table shows the weights in pounds of six dogs. How does the mean weight of the dogs change if Rex's weight is not included in the data set?

Weights of Dogs (lb)			
Duffy	23	Rex	62
Rocky	15	Skipper	34
Pepper	21	Sunny	19

CHALLENGE AND EXTEND

58. List a set of data values with the following measures of central tendency:

mean: 8   median: 7   mode: 6

59. Collect a set of data about your classmates or your school. For example, you might collect data about the number of points per game scored by your school's basketball team. Use the data you collect to make a box-and-whisker plot.

60. A *weighted average* is an average in which each data value has an importance, or weight, assigned to it. A teacher uses the following weights when determining course grades: homework 25%, tests 30%, and final exam 45%. The table shows Nathalie's scores in the class.

Homework	78, 83, 95, 82, 79, 93
Tests	88, 92, 81
Final exam	90

 a. Find the mean of Nathalie's homework scores and the mean of her test scores.

 b. Find Nathalie's weighted average for the class. To do so, multiply the homework mean, the test mean, and the final exam score by their corresponding weights. Then add the products.

 c. What if...? What would Nathalie's mean score for the class be if her teacher did not use a weighted average?

FOCUS ON MATHEMATICAL PRACTICES

H.O.T. **61. Precision** A data set has an even number of values. What do you know about the median?

H.O.T. **62. Problem Solving** The table shows the teams with the most World Series appearances as of 2011. It is missing the number of Yankee appearances.

MLB Team	World Series Appearances
Yankees	
Cardinals	18
Giants	18
Dodgers	18
Athletics	14

 a. The article with the table states that the mean of the data is 21.6. Find the missing data value. Show your work.

 b. What is the range of the data?

 c. Do you think the number of Yankee appearances is an outlier for this data set? Explain.

H.O.T. **63. Communication** Can a data set have two outliers? Can removing the two outliers not have an effect on the mean? Justify your responses.

EXTENSION # Dot Plots and Distributions

 Essential Question: How can you use dot plots to describe the shape of a data distribution?

A **dot plot** is a data representation that uses a number line and x's, dots, or other symbols to show frequency. Dot plots are sometimes called line plots.

COMMON CORE GPS **EXAMPLE** MCC9-12.S.ID.1

1 ### Making a Dot Plot

Objectives
Create dot plots.

Use a dot plot to describe the shape of a data distribution.

Vocabulary
dot plot
uniform distribution
symmetric distribution
skewed distribution

Mrs. Montoya asked her junior and senior students how many minutes each of them spent studying math in one day, rounded to the nearest five minutes. The results are shown below. Make a dot plot showing the data for juniors and a dot plot showing the data for seniors.

Time Spent Studying Math (min)	Frequency (Juniors)	Frequency (Seniors)
5	2	0
10	1	1
15	3	2
20	4	3
25	5	4
30	5	4
35	4	6
40	3	5
45	2	4

Find the least and greatest values in each data set. Then use these values to draw a number line for each graph. For each student, place a dot above the number line for the number of minutes he or she spent studying.

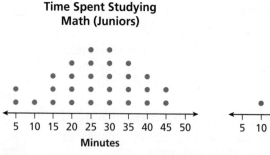

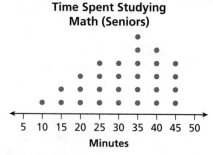

 1. The cafeteria offers items at six different prices. John counted how many items were sold at each price for one week. Make a dot plot of the data.

Price ($)	1.50	2.00	2.50	3.00	3.50	4.00	4.50
Items	3	3	5	8	6	5	3

A dot plot gives a visual representation of the distribution, or "shape", of the data. The dot plots in Example 1 have different shapes because the data sets are distributed differently.

Types of Distributions

UNIFORM DISTRIBUTION	SYMMETRIC DISTRIBUTION	SKEWED DISTRIBUTION
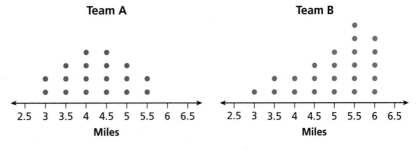		
In a **uniform distribution**, all data points have an approximately equal frequency.	In a **symmetric distribution**, a vertical line can be drawn and the result is a graph divided in two parts that are approximate mirror images of each other.	In a **skewed distribution**, the data is not uniform or symmetric. The data may be skewed to the right or skewed to the left.

COMMON CORE GPS **EXAMPLE** **2** **Shapes of Data Distributions**
MCC9-12.S.ID.3

The data table shows the number of miles run by members of two track teams during one day. Make a dot plot and determine the type of distribution for each team. Explain what the distribution means for each.

Miles	3	3.5	4	4.5	5	5.5	6
Team A	2	3	4	4	3	2	0
Team B	1	2	2	3	4	6	5

Make dot plots of the data.

Team A

Team B

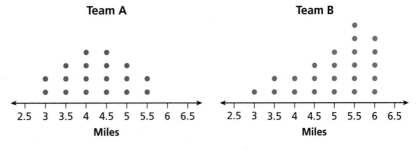

The data for team A show a symmetric distribution. The distances run are evenly distributed about the mean.

The data for team B show a skewed left distribution. Most team members ran a distance greater than the mean.

 CHECK IT OUT! **2.** Data for team C members are shown below. Make a dot plot and determine the type of distribution. Explain what the distribution means.

Miles	3	3.5	4	4.5	5	5.5	6
Team C	3	2	2	2	3	2	2

Exercises

1. **Biology** Michael is collecting data for the growth of plants after one week. He planted nine seeds for each of three different types of plants and recorded his data in the table below.

Growth of Plants (in.)		
Type A	Type B	Type C
0.9	2.1	1.9
0.9	2.2	2.0
1.0	2.2	2.0
1.0	2.2	2.1
1.1	2.3	2.1
1.2	2.3	2.1
1.2	2.4	2.2
1.3	2.5	2.2
1.4	2.6	2.3

   a. Create a dot plot for each type of plant.

   b. Describe the distributions.

   c. Which data value(s) occur(s) the most often in each dot plot? the least often?

   d. For each dot plot, list the heights in order from least frequent to most frequent.

2. **Nutrition** Julia researched grape juice brands to determine how many grams of sugar each brand contained per serving (8 fluid ounces = 1 serving). The data she collected is shown in the table.

Grams of Sugar in Grape Juice (per serving)					
15	0	36	18	30	10
30	15	35	30	36	30
36	30	38	16	35	16

   a. Identify any outlier(s) in the data set.

   b. Make a dot plot for the data with the outlier(s) and a dot plot for the data without the outlier(s).

   c. Describe the distribution of the data with and without the outlier(s).

   d. How does excluding the outlier(s) affect the mean, median, and mode of the data set?

3. The frequency table shows the number of siblings of each student in a class. Use the table to make a dot plot of the data, and describe the distribution.

Number of Siblings	Frequency
0	7
1	9
2	5
3	1
4	1

4. **School** The list below shows which grade each member of a high school marching band belongs to.

$$9, 12, 9, 10, 9, 12, 9, 9, 11, 12, 12, 10, 10, 9, 9, 11, 9, 10,$$
$$10, 12, 9, 12, 11, 9, 12, 11, 10, 9, 12, 12, 9, 9, 11, 12$$

a. Make a dot plot of the data.

b. Explain how you can use the dot plot to find the mean, median, and mode of the data set. Then find each of these values.

Use the dot plot for Exercises 5 and 6.

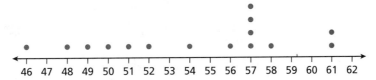

5. **Write About It** Compare stem-and-leaf plots and dot plots.

a. How are they similar and how are they different?

b. What information can you get from each graph?

c. Can you make a dot plot given a stem-and-leaf plot? Explain.

d. Can you make a stem-and-leaf plot given a dot plot? If so, make a stem-and-leaf plot of the data in the dot plot at right. If not, explain why not.

6. **Write About It** Compare histograms and dot plots.

a. How are they similar and how are they different?

b. What information can you get from each graph?

c. Can you make a dot plot given a histogram? Explain.

d. Can you make a histogram given a dot plot? If so, make a histogram of the data in the dot plot at right. If not, explain why not.

Biology

Even though identical twins share the same DNA, they are often of different heights. According to one study, the average height difference between identical twins is 1.7 cm.

7. **Multi-Step** Gather data on the heights of people in your classroom. Separate the data for males from the data for females. Make two dot plots representing the data collected for each group. Compare the dot plots and the distributions of the data.

8. The dot plot at right shows an example of a *bimodal distribution*. Why is this an appropriate name for this type of distribution?

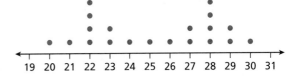

9. **Critical Thinking** Magdalene and Peter conducted the same experiment. Both of their data sets had the same mean. Both made dot plots of their data that showed symmetric distributions, but Peter's dot plot shows a greater range than Magdalene's dot plot. Identify which plot below belongs to Peter and which belongs to Magdalene.

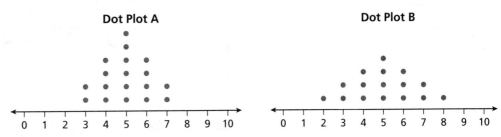

Dot Plot A   Dot Plot B

14-4 Technology TASK

Use Technology to Make Graphs

You can use a spreadsheet program to create bar graphs, line graphs, and circle graphs. You can also use a graphing calculator to make a box-and-whisker plot.

Use with Data Distributions

 MATHEMATICAL PRACTICES Use appropriate tools strategically.

MCC9-12.S.ID.1 Represent data with plots on the real number line (... box plots).

Activity 1

Many colors are used on the flags of the 50 United States. The table shows the number of flags that use each color. Use a spreadsheet program to make a bar graph to display the data.

Color	Black	Blue	Brown	Gold	Green	Purple	Red	White
Number	27	46	20	36	24	4	34	42

1. Enter the data from the table in the first two columns of the spreadsheet.

2. Select the cells containing the titles and the data.

   Then click the Chart Wizard icon, 📊. Click Column from the list on the left, and then choose the small picture of a vertical bar graph. Click Next.

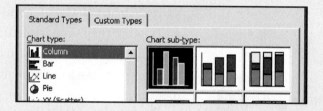

3. The next screen shows the range of cells used to make the graph. Click Next.

4. Give the chart a title and enter titles for the *x*-axis and *y*-axis. Click the Legend tab, and then click the box next to Show Legend to turn off the key. (A key is needed when making a double-bar graph.) Click Next.

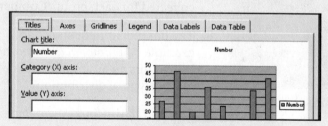

5. Click Finish to place the chart in the spreadsheet.

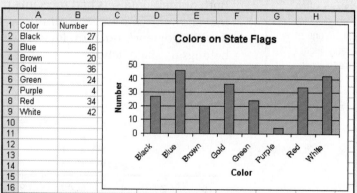

1. The table shows the average number of hours of sleep people at different ages get each night. Use a spreadsheet program to make a bar graph to display the data.

Age (yr)	3–9	10–13	14–18	19–30	31–45	46–50	51+
Sleep (h)	11	10	9	8	7.5	6	5.5

Activity 2

Adrianne is a waitress at a restaurant. The amounts Adrianne made in tips during her last 15 shifts are listed below. Use a graphing calculator to make a box-and-whisker plot to display the data. Give the minimum, first quartile, median, third quartile, and maximum values.

$58, $63, $40, $44, $57, $59, $61, $53, $54, $58, $57, $57, $58, $58, $56

1 To make a list of the data, press STAT , select **Edit**, and enter the values in List 1 **(L1)**. Press ENTER after each value.

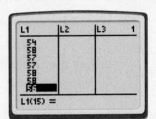

2 To use the **STAT PLOT** editor to set up the box-and-whisker

plot, press 2nd   **STAT PLOT** **Y=** , and then ENTER .

Press ENTER to select **Plot 1**.

3 Select **On**. Then use the arrow keys to choose the fifth type of graph, a box-and-whisker plot.

Xlist should be **L1** and **Freq:** should be 1.

4 Press ZOOM and select **9: ZoomStat** to see the graph in the statistics window.

5 Use TRACE and the arrow keys to move the cursor along the graph to the five important values: minimum **(MinX)**, first quartile **(Q1)**, median **(MED)**, third quartile **(Q3)**, and maximum **(MaxX)**.

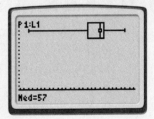

minimum: 40

first quartile: 54

median: 57

third quartile: 58

maximum: 63

Try This

2. The average length in inches of the ten longest bones in the human body are listed. Use a graphing calculator to make a box-and-whisker plot to display the data. What are the minimum, first quartile, median, third quartile, and maximum values of the data set?

19.88, 16.94, 15.94, 14.35, 11.10, 10.40, 9.45, 9.06, 7.28, 6.69

Ready to Go On?

my.hrw.com
Assessment and Intervention

14-1 Organizing and Displaying Data

1. The table shows the total proceeds for a fund-raiser at various times during the day. Choose a type of graph to display the given data. Make the graph, and explain why you chose that type of graph.

Time	Total Proceeds (thousand $)	Time	Total Proceeds (thousand $)
3:00 P.M.	1.5	6:00 P.M.	6.5
4:00 P.M.	2	7:00 P.M.	8
5:00 P.M.	4	8:00 P.M.	9.5

14-2 Frequency and Histograms

2. The number of people at a caterer's last 12 parties are given below.

    16, 18, 17, 19, 15, 25, 18, 17, 18, 16, 17, 19

   a. Use the data to make a frequency table with intervals.
   b. Use your frequency table from part **a** to make a histogram.

14-3 Two-Way Tables

A bookshop surveys its customers about their magazine-buying habits, summarized in the table.

3. Make a table of the joint relative frequencies and the marginal relative frequencies.

4. Given that a customer reads *Super News,* what is the probability that he or she also reads *Look Around?*

		Reads *Look Around*	
		Yes	No
Reads *Super News*	Yes	62	15
	No	21	136

14-4 Data Distributions

5. The daily high temperatures on 14 consecutive days in one city were 59 °F, 49 °F, 48 °F, 46 °F, 47 °F, 51 °F, 49 °F, 43 °F, 45 °F, 52 °F, 51 °F, 51 °F, 51 °F, and 38 °F.

   a. Find the mean, median, and mode of the temperatures.
   b. Which value describes the average high temperature for the 14 days?
   c. Which value best describes the high temperatures? Explain.

6. Use the temperature data above to make a box-and-whisker plot.

Selected Response

1. How many more victories did the 8th grade basketball team have than the 10th grade team? Use the graph to answer the question.

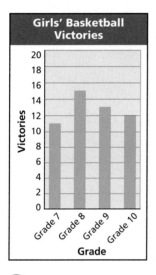

Girls' Basketball Victories

- Ⓐ 2
- Ⓑ 3
- Ⓒ 1
- Ⓓ 27

2. The cumulative frequencies of each interval have been given. Use this information to complete the frequency column.

Interval	Frequency	Cumulative Frequency
45–52	?	6
53–60	?	23
61–68	?	32
69–76	?	41
77–84	?	75
85–92	?	134

- Ⓕ 7, 16, 16, 25, 50, 84
- Ⓖ 6, 17, 6, 26, 15, 60, 74
- Ⓗ 7, 30, 39, 48, 82, 141
- Ⓙ 6, 17, 9, 9, 34, 59

Mini-Tasks

3. Identify the sample space and the outcome shown for spinning the game spinner.

4. The table shows the numbers of points scored by the top three scorer's in a basketball tournament that were made as 1-point (free throws), 2-point, and 3-point shots.

	1-point	2-point	3-point
Tina	11	38	21
Stella	7	24	42
Misha	17	46	6

a. What is the joint relative frequency that represents points scored by Misha as 2-point shots?

b. What is the marginal relative frequency of the points that were made as 3-point shots?

UNIT 4

Module

15 Linear and Exponential Models

COMMON
CORE GPS

Contents

MATHEMATICAL
PRACTICES
The Common Core Georgia Performance Standards for Mathematical Practice
describe varieties of expertise that all students should seek to develop.
Opportunities to develop these practices are integrated throughout this program.

1 Make sense of problems and persevere in solving them.

2 Reason abstractly and quantitatively.

3 Construct viable arguments and critique the reasoning of others.

4 Model with mathematics.

5 Use appropriate tools strategically.

6 Attend to precision.

7 Look for and make use of structure.

8 Look for and express regularity in repeated reasoning.

Unpacking the Standards

Understanding the standards and the vocabulary terms in the standards will help you know exactly what you are expected to learn in this chapter.

 MCC9-12.F.LE.1

Distinguish between situations that can be modeled with linear functions and with exponential functions.

Key Vocabulary

linear function (función lineal)
A function that can be written in the form $y = mx + b$, where x is the independent variable and m and b are real numbers. Its graph is a line.

What It Means For You

A linear function models a *constant amount* of change for equal intervals. An exponential function models a *constant factor*, or *constant ratio* of change for equal intervals.

EXAMPLE **Exponential model**

Value of a car	
Car's Age (yr)	Value ($)
0	20,000
1	17,000
2	14,450
3	12,282.50

+1 → ×0.85
+1 → ×0.85
+1 → ×0.85

Ratio is constant.

NON-EXAMPLE **Nonlinear, non-exponential model**

Height of Bridge Suspension Cables	
Cable's Distance from Tower (ft)	Cable's Height (ft)
0	400
100	256
200	144
300	64

+100 → − 144, × 0.64
+100 → − 112, × 0.56
+100 → − 80, × 0.44

Neither difference nor ratio is constant.

15-1 Scatter Plots and Trend Lines

Essential Question: How can you represent data on a scatter plot and use trend lines to make predictions?

Objectives
Create and interpret scatter plots.

Use trend lines to make predictions.

Vocabulary
scatter plot
correlation
positive correlation
negative correlation
no correlation
trend line

Who uses this?
Ecologists can use scatter plots to help them analyze data about endangered species, such as ocelots. (See Example 1.)

In this chapter, you have examined relationships between sets of ordered pairs, or data. Displaying data visually can help you see relationships.

A **scatter plot** is a graph with points plotted to show a possible relationship between two sets of data. A scatter plot is an effective way to display some types of data.

EXAMPLE 1
MCC9-12.S.ID.6

Graphing a Scatter Plot from Given Data

The table shows the number of species added to the list of endangered and threatened species in the United States during the given years. Graph a scatter plot using the given data.

Increase in List							
Calendar Year	1996	1997	1998	1999	2000	2001	2002
Species	91	79	62	11	39	10	9

Source: U.S. Fish and Wildlife Service

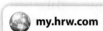
my.hrw.com

Online Video Tutor

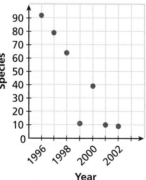

Species Added to List

Use the table to make ordered pairs for the scatter plot.

The x-value represents the calendar year and the y-value represents the number of species added.

Plot the ordered pairs.

Animated Math

Helpful Hint

The point (2000, 39) tells you that in the year 2000, the list increased by 39 species.

CHECK IT OUT!

1. The table shows the number of points scored by a high school football team in the first four games of a season. Graph a scatter plot using the given data.

Game	1	2	3	4
Score	6	21	46	34

A **correlation** describes a relationship between two data sets. A graph may show the correlation between data. The correlation can help you analyze trends and make predictions. There are three types of correlations between data.

Correlations

Positive Correlation	Negative Correlation	No Correlation
Both sets of data values increase.	One set of data values increases as the other set decreases.	There is no relationship between the data sets.
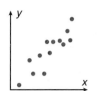		

In the endangered species graph, as time increases, the number of new species added decreases. So the correlation between the data is negative.

COMMON CORE GPS
MCC9-12.S.ID.6

EXAMPLE 2 Describing Correlations from Scatter Plots

my.hrw.com

Online Video Tutor

Describe the correlation illustrated by the scatter plot.

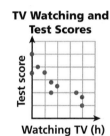

As the number of hours spent watching TV increased, test scores decreased.

There is a negative correlation between the two data sets.

 2. Describe the correlation illustrated by the scatter plot.

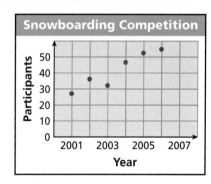

COMMON CORE GPS
MCC9-12.S.IC.6

EXAMPLE 3 Identifying Correlations

my.hrw.com

Online Video Tutor

Identify the correlation you would expect to see between each pair of data sets. Explain.

A the number of empty seats in a classroom and the number of students seated in the class

You would expect to see a negative correlation. As the number of students increases, the number of empty seats decreases.

B the number of pets a person owns and the number of books that person read last year

You would expect to see no correlation. The number of pets a person owns has nothing to do with how many books the person has read.

Identify the correlation you would expect to see between each pair of data sets. Explain.

 C the monthly rainfall and the depth of water in a reservoir

You would expect to see a positive correlation. As more rain falls, there is more water in the reservoir.

 Identify the correlation you would expect to see between each pair of data sets. Explain.

3a. the temperature in Houston and the number of cars sold in Boston

3b. the number of members in a family and the size of the family's grocery bill

3c. the number of times you sharpen your pencil and the length of your pencil

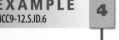

COMMON CORE GPS

EXAMPLE **4**
MCC9-12.S.ID.6

Matching Scatter Plots to Situations

Choose the scatter plot that best represents the relationship between the number of days since a sunflower seed was planted and the height of the plant. Explain.

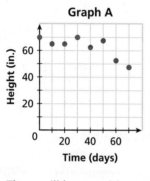

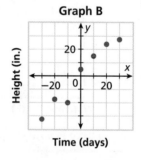

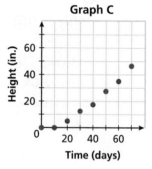

There will be a positive correlation between the number of days and the height because the plant will grow each day.

Neither the number of days nor the plant heights can be negative.

This graph shows all positive coordinates and a positive correlation, so it could represent the data sets.

Graph A has a negative correlation, so it is incorrect.

Graph B shows negative values, so it is incorrect.

Graph C is the correct scatter plot.

 4. Choose the scatter plot that best represents the relationship between the number of minutes since a pie has been taken out of the oven and the temperature of the pie. Explain.

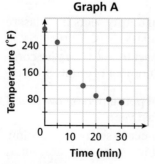

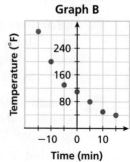

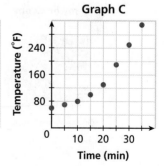

You can graph a line on a scatter plot to help show a relationship in the data. This line, called a **trend line,** helps show the correlation between data sets more clearly. It can also be helpful when making predictions based on the data.

EXAMPLE 5
MCC9-12.S.ID.6c

my.hrw.com

Online Video Tutor

Fund-raising Application

The scatter plot shows a relationship between the total amount of money collected and the total number of rolls of wrapping paper sold as a school fund-raiser. Based on this relationship, predict how much money will be collected when 175 rolls have been sold.

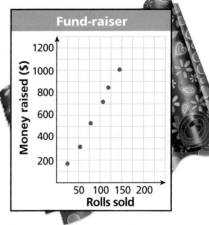

Draw a trend line and use it to make a prediction.

Draw a line that has about the same number of points above and below it. Your line may or may not go through data points.

Find the point on the line whose x-value is 175. The corresponding y-value is 1200.

Based on the data, $1200 is a reasonable prediction of how much money will be collected when 175 rolls have been sold.

CHECK IT OUT!
5. Based on the trend line above, predict how many wrapping paper rolls need to be sold to raise $500.

MCC.MP.3, MCC.MP.4   MATHEMATICAL PRACTICES

THINK AND DISCUSS

1. Is it possible to make a prediction based on a scatter plot with no correlation? Explain your answer.

2. GET ORGANIZED Copy and complete the graphic organizer with either a scatter plot, a real-world example, or both.

	Graph	Example
Positive Correlation		
Negative Correlation		The amount of water in a watering can and the number of flowers watered
No Correlation		

GUIDED PRACTICE

Vocabulary Apply the vocabulary from this lesson to answer each question.

1. Give an example of a graph that is not a *scatter plot*.

2. How is a scatter plot that shows *no correlation* different from a scatter plot that shows a *negative correlation*?

3. Does a *trend line* always pass through every point on a scatter plot? Explain.

SEE EXAMPLE **1** **4.** Graph a scatter plot using the given data.

Garden Statue	Cupid	Gnome	Lion	Flamingo	Wishing well
Height (in.)	32	18	35	28	40
Price ($)	50	25	80	15	75

SEE EXAMPLE **2** Describe the correlation illustrated by each scatter plot.

5.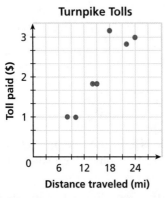

6.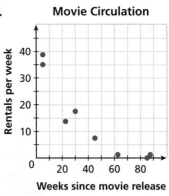

SEE EXAMPLE **3** Identify the correlation you would expect to see between each pair of data sets. Explain.

7. the volume of water poured into a container and the amount of empty space left in the container

8. a person's shoe size and the length of the person's hair

9. the outside temperature and the number of people at the beach

SEE EXAMPLE **4** Choose the scatter plot that best represents the described relationship. Explain.

10. age of car and number of miles traveled

11. age of car and sales price of car

12. age of car and number of states traveled to

Graph A	Graph B	Graph C

SEE EXAMPLE 5

13. **Transportation** The scatter plot shows the total number of miles passengers flew on U.S. domestic flights in the month of April for the years 1997–2004. Based on this relationship, predict how many miles passengers flew in April 2008.

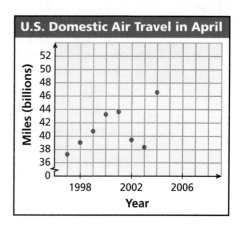

PRACTICE AND PROBLEM SOLVING

Independent Practice

For Exercises	See Example
14	1
15–16	2
17–18	3
19–20	4
21	5

14. Graph a scatter plot using the given data.

Train Arrival Time	6:45 A.M.	7:30 A.M.	8:15 A.M.	9:45 A.M.	10:30 A.M.
Passengers	160	148	194	152	64

Describe the correlation illustrated by each scatter plot.

15.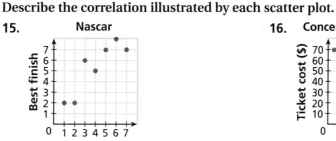

16.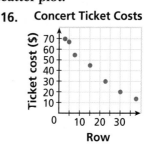

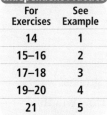

my.hrw.com

Online Extra Practice

Identify the correlation you would expect to see between each pair of data sets. Explain.

17. the speed of a runner and the distance she can cover in 10 minutes

18. the year a car was made and the total mileage

Choose the scatter plot that best represents the described relationship. Explain.

19. the number of college classes taken and the number of roommates

20. the number of college classes taken and the hours of free time.

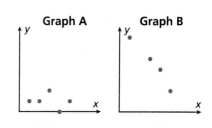

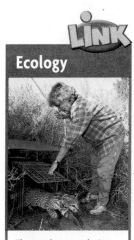

Ecology

The ocelot population in Texas is dwindling due in part to their habitat being destroyed. The ocelot population at Laguna Atascosa National Wildlife Refuge is monitored by following 5–10 ocelots yearly by radio telemetry.

Roy Toft

21. **Ecology** The scatter plot shows a projection of the average ocelot population living in Laguna Atascosa National Wildlife Refuge near Brownsville, Texas. Based on this relationship, predict the number of ocelots living at the wildlife refuge in 2014 if nothing is done to help manage the ocelot population.

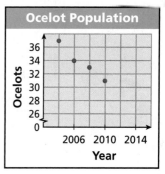

22. Estimation Angie enjoys putting jigsaw puzzles together. The scatter plot shows the number of puzzle pieces and the time in minutes it took her to complete each of her last six puzzles. Use the trend line to estimate the time in minutes it will take Angie to complete a 1200-piece puzzle.

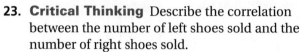

23. Critical Thinking Describe the correlation between the number of left shoes sold and the number of right shoes sold.

24. Roma had guests for dinner at her house eight times and has recorded the number of guests and the total cost for each meal in the table.

Guests	3	4	4	6	6	7	8	8
Cost ($)	30	65	88	90	115	160	150	162

    a. Graph a scatter plot of the data.

    b. Describe the correlation.

    c. Draw a trend line.

    d. Based on the trend line you drew, predict the cost of dinner for 11 guests.

    e. What if...? Suppose that each cost in the table increased by $5. How will this affect the cost of dinner for 11 guests?

25. ///ERROR ANALYSIS/// Students graphed a scatter plot for the temperature of hot bath water and time if no new water is added. Which graph is incorrect? Explain the error.

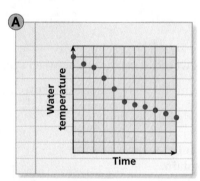

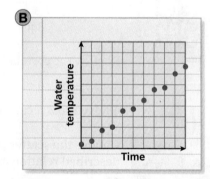

H.O.T. 26. Critical Thinking Will more people or fewer people buy an item if the price goes up? Explain the relationship and describe the correlation.

Real-World Connections

27. Juan and his parents are visiting a university 205 miles from their home. As they travel, Juan uses the car odometer and his watch to keep track of the distance.

    a. Make a scatter plot for this data set.

    b. Describe the correlation. Explain.

    c. Draw a trend line for the data and predict the distance Juan would have traveled going to a university 4 hours away.

Time (min)	Distance (mi)
0	0
30	28
60	58
90	87
120	117
150	148
180	178
210	205

28. **Write About It** Conduct a survey of your classmates to find the number of siblings they have and the number of pets they have. Predict whether there will be a positive, negative, or no correlation. Then graph the data in a scatter plot. What is the relationship between the two data sets? Was your prediction correct?

TEST PREP

29. Which graph is the best example of a negative correlation?

Ⓐ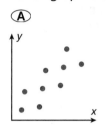

Ⓑ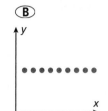

Ⓒ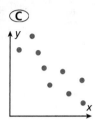

Ⓓ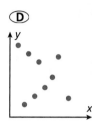

30. Which situation best describes a positive correlation?

Ⓕ The amount of rainfall on Fridays

Ⓖ The height of a candle and the amount of time it stays lit

Ⓗ The price of a pizza and the number of toppings added

Ⓙ The temperature of a cup of hot chocolate and the length of time it sits

31. **Short Response** Write a real-world situation for the graph. Explain your answer.

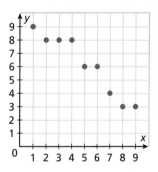

CHALLENGE AND EXTEND

32. Describe a situation that involves a positive correlation. Gather data on the situation. Make a scatter plot showing the correlation. Use the scatter plot to make a prediction. Repeat for a negative correlation and for no correlation.

33. Research an endangered or threatened species in your state. Gather information on its population for several years. Make a scatter plot using the data you gather. Is there a positive or negative correlation? Explain. Draw a trend line and make a prediction about the species population over the next 5 years.

FOCUS ON MATHEMATICAL PRACTICES

H.O.T. 34. **Patterns** Gigi draws a scatter plot for a table that compares the weight of a bird to its wingspan. Would you expect this plot to show a positive correlation, no correlation, or a negative correlation? Why?

H.O.T. 35. **Analysis** When you graph the function $y = x + 3$, you make a table with pairs of values, graph those ordered pairs, and then draw a line with arrows that joins the points. Contrast this to the way you draw the trend line for a scatter plot. How do the two lines differ?

15-1 Technology TASK

Interpret Scatter Plots and Trend Lines

You can use a graphing calculator to graph a trend line on a scatter plot.

Use with Scatter Plots and Trend Lines

MATHEMATICAL PRACTICES

Use appropriate tools strategically.

MCC9-12.S.ID.6 Represent data on two quantitative variables on a scatter plot, ... *Also* **MCC9-12.S.ID.6a, MCC9-12.S.ID.6c**

Activity

The table shows the recommended dosage of a particular medicine as related to a person's weight. Graph a scatter plot of the given data. Draw the trend line. Then predict the dosage for a person weighing 240 pounds.

Weight (lb)	90	100	110	125	140	155	170	180	200
Dosage (mg)	20	25	30	35	40	53	60	66	75

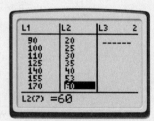

1 First enter the data. Press **STAT** and select **1: Edit**. In **L1**, enter the first weight. Press **ENTER**. Continue entering all weights. Use ▶ to move to **L2**. Enter the first dosage. Press **ENTER**. Continue entering all dosages.

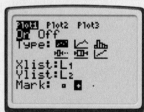

2 To view the scatter plot, press **2nd** **Y=**. Select **Plot 1**. Select **On**, the first plot type, and the plot mark **+**. Press **ZOOM**. Select **9: ZoomStat**. You should see a scatter plot of the data.

3 To find the trend line, press **STAT** and select the **CALC** menu. Select **LinReg (ax+b)**. Press **ENTER**. This gives you the values of *a* and *b* in the trend line.

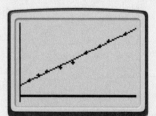

4 To enter the equation for the trend line, press **Y=**, and then input **.5079441502x − 26.78767453**. Press **GRAPH**.

5 Now predict the dosage for a weight of 240 pounds. Press **VARS**. Select **Y-VARS** menu and select **1:Function**. Select **1:Y1**. Enter **(240)**. Press **ENTER**. The dosage is about 95 milligrams.

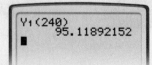

Try This

1. The table shows the price of a stock over an 8-month period. Graph a scatter plot of the given data. Draw the trend line. Then predict what the price of one share of stock will be in the twelfth month.

Month	1	2	3	4	5	6	7	8
Price ($)	32	35	37	41	46	50	54	59

15-2 Line of Best Fit

Essential Question: How can you use residuals and linear regression to determine the line of best fit?

Objectives
Determine a line of best fit for a set of linear data.

Determine and interpret the correlation coefficient.

Vocabulary
residual
least-squares line
line of best fit
linear regression
correlation coefficient

Who uses this?
Climate scientists can use a least-squares line to study temperature-latitude relationships. (See Example 2.)

Recall that a scatter plot shows two data sets as one set of ordered pairs. A trend line, or line of fit, is a model for the data.

Some trend lines will fit a data set better than others. One way to evaluate how well a line fits a data set is to use *residuals*. A **residual** is the signed vertical distance between a data point and a line of fit. The closer the sum of the squared residuals is to 0, the better the line fits the data.

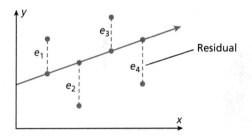

COMMON CORE GPS MCC9-12.S.ID.6b

EXAMPLE 1 Calculating Residuals

my.hrw.com

Online Video Tutor

The data in the table are graphed along with two lines of fit. For each line, find the sum of the squares of the residuals. Which line is a better fit?

x	2	4	6	8
y	6	3	7	5

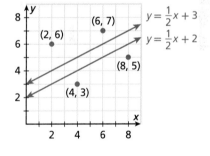
$y = \frac{1}{2}x + 3$
$y = \frac{1}{2}x + 2$

Find the residuals.

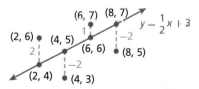

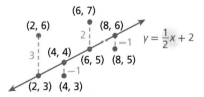

Sum of squared residuals:

$(2)^2 + (-2)^2 + (1)^2 + (-2)^2$
$4 + 4 + 1 + 4 = 13$

Sum of squared residuals:

$(3)^2 + (-1)^2 + (2)^2 + (-1)^2$
$9 + 1 + 4 + 1 = 15$

The line $y = \frac{1}{2}x + 3$ is a better fit for the data.

Helpful Hint

By using *squares* of residuals, positive and negative residuals do not "cancel out," and residuals with squares greater than 1 have a magnified effect on the sum.

©Gordon Wiltsie/National Geographic/Getty Images

1. Two lines of fit for this data are $y = -\frac{1}{2}x + 6$ and $y = -x + 8$. For each line, find the sum of the squares of the residuals. Which line is a better fit?

x	2	4	6	8
y	3	6	1	4

The **least-squares line** for a data set is the line of fit for which the sum of the squares of the residuals is as small as possible. So, the least-squares line is a *line of best fit*. A **line of best fit** is the line that comes closest to all of the points in the data set, using a given process. **Linear regression** is a process of finding the least-squares line.

COMMON CORE GPS **EXAMPLE** **2**
MCC9-12.S.ID.6a

Finding the Least-Squares Line

The table shows the latitudes and average temperatures of several cities.

my.hrw.com

Online Video Tutor

City	Latitude	Average Temperature (°C)
Barrow, Alaska, USA	71.2° N	−12.7
Yakutsk, Russia	62.1° N	−10.1
London, England	51.3° N	10.4
Chicago, Illinois, USA	41.9° N	10.3
San Francisco, California, USA	37.5° N	13.8
Yuma, Arizona, USA	32.7° N	22.8
Tindouf, Algeria	27.7° N	22.8
Dakar, Senegal	14.0° N	24.5
Mangalore, India	12.5° N	27.1

A **Find an equation for a line of best fit.**

Use your calculator. To enter the data, press **STAT** and select **1:Edit**. Enter the latitudes in the **L1** column and the average temperatures in the **L2** column.

Then press **STAT** and choose **CALC**. Choose **4:LinReg(ax+b)** and press **ENTER**. An equation for a line of best fit is $y \approx -0.69x + 39.11$.

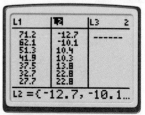

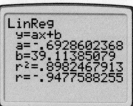

B **Interpret the meaning of the slope and *y*-intercept.**

The slope, −0.69, means that for each 1-degree increase in latitude, the average temperature decreases 0.69 °C. The *y*-intercept, 39.11, means that the average temperature is 39.11 °C at 0° N latitude.

C **The approximate latitude of Vancouver, Canada, is 49.1° N. Use your equation to predict Vancouver's average temperature.**

$y \approx -0.69x + 39.11$

$y \approx -0.69(49.1) + 39.11 \approx 5.23$

The average temperature of Vancouver should be close to 5 °C.

2. The table shows the prices and the lengths in yards of several balls of yarn at Knit Mart.

Length (yd)	1680	100	153	99	109	109	176	100	1440	61
Price ($)	65.85	7.85	9.80	10.85	8.35	7.85	19.85	5.35	65.85	14.85

a. Find an equation for a line of best fit.

b. Interpret the meaning of the slope and y-intercept.

c. Knit Mart also sells yarn in a 1000-yard ball. Use your equation to predict the cost of this yarn.

In Example 2, you may have noticed the last value the calculator gave you, r. This is the *correlation coefficient*. The **correlation coefficient** is a number r, where $-1 \le r \le 1$, that describes how closely the points in a scatter plot cluster around a line of best fit.

Properties of the Correlation Coefficient r

r is a value in the range $-1 \le r \le 1$.

If $r = 1$, the data set forms a straight line with a positive slope.

If $r = 0$, the data set has no correlation.

If $r = -1$, the data set forms a straight line with a negative slope.

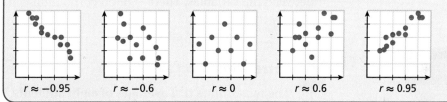

$r \approx -0.95$ $r \approx -0.6$ $r \approx 0$ $r \approx 0.6$ $r \approx 0.95$

Helpful Hint

r-values close to 1 or −1 indicate a very strong correlation. The closer r is to 0, the weaker the correlation.

COMMON CORE GPS MCC9-12.S.ID.8

EXAMPLE 3

my.hrw.com

Online Video Tutor

Correlation Coefficient

The table shows a relationship between a city's population and the average time the city's citizens spend commuting to work each day.

City	Population (thousands)	Average Commute Time (min)
Albuquerque, NM	505	21.5
Atlanta, GA	486	31.1
Austin, TX	710	23.2
Charlotte, NC	630	25.1
Chicago, IL	2833	30.6
Eugene, OR	146	17.9
Houston, TX	2144	27.7
Las Vegas, NV	553	25.2
New York, NY	8496	34.0
New Orleans, LA	223	24.2

Find an equation for a line of best fit. How well does the line represent the data?

Use your calculator.

Enter the data into the lists **L1** and **L2**.

Then press and choose **CALC**. Choose

4:LinReg(ax+b) and press ENTER . An equation for a line of best fit is $y \approx 0.001x + 23.8$. The value of r is about 0.71, which indicates a moderate positive correlation.

```
LinReg
 y=ax+b
 a=.0013555626
 b=23.78268592
 r²=.5068914082
 r=.7119630666
```

3. Kylie and Marcus designed a quiz to measure how much information adults retain after leaving school. The table below shows the quiz scores of several adults, matched with the number of years each person had been out of school. Find an equation for a line of best fit. How well does the line represent the data?

Time Out of School (yr)	1	1	1	2	2	3	5	7	10	10	14	25
Quiz Score	85	94	98	75	80	77	63	56	45	50	34	33

Causation refers to cause-and-effect. If a change in one variable directly causes a change in the other variable, then there is a cause-and-effect relationship between the variables. There is often correlation without causation.

COMMON CORE GPS
MCC9-12.S.ID.9

EXAMPLE 4

Correlation and Causation

The table shows test averages of eight students. The equation of the least-squares line for the data is $y \approx 0.77x + 18.12$ and $r \approx 0.87$. Discuss correlation and causation for the data set.

U.S. History Test Average	90	70	75	100	90	85	80	90
Science Test Average	80	75	72	95	92	82	80	92

There is a strong positive correlation between the U.S. history test average and the science test average for these students. There is *not* a likely cause-and-effect relationship because there is no apparent reason why test scores in one subject would directly affect test scores in the other subject.

my.hrw.com

Online Video Tutor

Caution!

Notice in Example 4, there is a strong correlation, but no causation. Two variables can be strongly correlated without having a direct cause-and-effect relationship.

4. Eight adults were surveyed about their education and earnings. The table shows the survey results. The equation of the least-squares line for the data is $y \approx 5.59x - 30.28$ and $r \approx 0.86$. Discuss correlation and causation for the data set.

Years of Education	12	16	20	14	18	16	16	18
Earnings Last Year (thousand $)	40	65	75	44	70	50	54	86

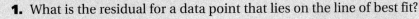

THINK AND DISCUSS

1. What is the residual for a data point that lies on the line of best fit?
2. **GET ORGANIZED** Copy and complete the graphic organizer. For each *r*-value, sketch a possible scatter plot and describe the correlation, choosing from the following: strong positive, weak positive, none, strong negative, weak negative.

r-value	−0.9	−0.4	0	0.4	0.9
Scatter Plot					
Description of Correlation					

15-2 Exercises

my.hrw.com
Homework Help

GUIDED PRACTICE

Vocabulary Apply the vocabulary from this lesson to answer each question.

1. A signed vertical distance between a data point and its corresponding model point is called a _____?_____ (*residual* or *correlation coefficient*)

2. A _____?_____ (*least squares line* or *correlation coefficient*) is a measure of how well a line of best fit models a data set.

SEE EXAMPLE 1

3. The data in the table are graphed along with two lines of fit. For each line, find the sum of the squares of the residuals. Which line is a better fit for the data?

x	2	3	4	5
y	2	5	6	2

SEE EXAMPLE 2

4. The table shows numbers of books read by students in an English class over a summer and the students' grades for the following semester.

Books	0	0	0	0	1	1	1	2	3	5	6	8	10	12	20
Grade	65	69	70	73	70	75	78	77	86	85	89	90	95	99	98

a. Find an equation for a line of best fit.
b. Interpret the meaning of the slope and *y*-intercept.
c. Use your equation to predict the grade of a student who reads 15 books.

SEE EXAMPLE 3

5. A negative correlation exists between the time Shawnda spends on homework during an evening and the amount of sleep she gets that night. The table shows data for several nights. Find an equation for a line of best fit. How well does the line represent the data?

Homework (h)	0.5	0.5	1	1	1.5	2	2	2.5	3	3	3	4	4.5	5
Sleep (h)	8	9	8	8.5	8	7.5	8	7.5	7	7	8	6.5	6.5	6

SEE EXAMPLE 4

6. Some students were surveyed about how much time they spent playing video games last week and their overall test average. The equation of the least-squares line for the data is $y \approx -2.93x + 89.70$ and $r \approx -0.92$. Discuss correlation and causation for the data set.

Hours Playing Video Games	1	3	3	6	2	1	9	10
Test Average for all Subjects	80	85	78	70	86	92	60	64

PRACTICE AND PROBLEM SOLVING

Independent Practice

For Exercise	See Example
7	1
8	2
9	3
10	4

my.hrw.com

Online Extra Practice

7. The data in the table are graphed along with two lines of fit. For each line, find the sum of the squares of the residuals. Which line is a better fit for the data?

x	2	4	6	8
y	5	6	1	1

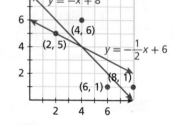

8. The table shows the mean outside temperature for each of six months and the amount of heating oil used by a family for each of those months.

Mean Outside Temperature (°F)	30	28	44	56	62	76
Heating Oil Used (gal)	112	115	94	60	35	12

a. Find an equation for a line of best fit.

b. Interpret the meaning of the slope and y-intercept.

c. Use your equation to predict the amount of heating oil used in a month in which the mean outside temperature is 20 °F.

9. The table shows the number of customers at a coffee shop and the number of cookies sold for several days. Find an equation for a line of best fit. How well does the line represent the data?

Customers	10	12	25	27	40	55	67	109
Cookies Sold	2	6	5	9	10	11	20	22

10. Some students were surveyed about how much time they spent watching television one week and how much time they spent playing video games the next week. The equation of the least-squares line for the data is $y \approx 0.76x + 1.63$ and $r \approx 0.77$. Discuss correlation and causation for the data set.

Week 1: Hours Watching Television	4	2	0	1	3	1	8	10
Week 2: Hours Playing Video Games	1	3	3	6	2	1	9	10

11. H.O.T. **Write About It** Tell which correlation coefficient, $r = 0.65$ or $r = -0.78$, indicates a stronger linear relationship between two variables. Explain your answer.

12. Critical Thinking What can you conclude if the sum of the squared residuals is 0? Explain why the same conclusion might not apply when the sum of the residuals is 0.

Sports

13. Sports The table shows hits and runs scored by eight New York Yankees in the 2009 baseball season.

a. Find the equation of the least-squares line.

b. Interpret the meaning of the slope.

c. Interpret the meaning of the y-intercept mathematically.

d. Describe any possible correlation for the data set. Use the correlation coefficient to support your answer.

e. Use the equation of the least-squares line from part **a** to predict how many runs a player will score if he gets 100 hits.

Player	Hits	Runs
Jorge Posada	109	55
Mark Teixeira	178	103
Robinson Cano	204	103
Derek Jeter	212	107
Johnny Damon	155	107
Melky Cabrera	133	66
Nick Swisher	124	84
Hideki Matsui	125	62

The New York Yankees opened a new stadium in 2009. Although the new stadium seats fewer fans than the old stadium (50,287 versus 56,886), the seats in the new stadium are wider, and there is more legroom between rows.

14. Community The table shows data about temperature and how much bottled water was sold at an annual summer festival in past years. The high temperature for the day of this year's festival is predicted to be 89 °F. The festival organizer must order bottled water in cases of 100. Find the equation of the least-squares line. Use the equation to decide how many cases the organizer should order.

Midtown Summer Fest						
Year	1	2	3	4	5	6
Daily High Temperature (°F)	75	82	95	92	80	84
Bottled Waters Sold	465	517	1052	940	611	625

Use the table for Exercises 15 and 16.

Regional Historical Museum						
Year	0	2	4	6	8	10
Visitors	980	1,251	1,667	1,785	2,110	2,056
Gift Shop Sales ($)	8,890	12,365	15,100	18,060	20,650	22,600

15. Complete parts **a–d** for the relationship between the year and the number of visitors.

a. Find the equation of the least-squares line and the correlation coefficient.

b. Interpret the meaning of the slope and the y-intercept.

c. Is it reasonable to use your equation to make predictions? Explain.

d. Is it reasonable to say there is a cause-and-effect relationship? Explain.

16. Complete parts **a–d** above for the relationship between the number of visitors and the gift shop sales.

©Sandra Baker/Getty Images

17. Which could be the correlation coefficient of this graph?

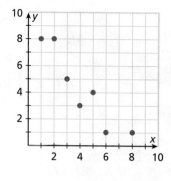

Ⓐ −1.00

Ⓑ −0.93

Ⓒ 0.93

Ⓓ 1.00

18. The table shows how much time five students studied for a test and their test scores. The equation of a line of fit for the data is $y = 5x + 60$. What is the sum of the squares of the residuals for the line of fit?

Hours Studying	0	2	4	6	8
Test Score	60	70	90	80	100

Ⓕ 0   Ⓖ 20   Ⓗ 40   Ⓙ 200

CHALLENGE AND EXTEND

H.O.T. 19. The heights and weights of eight basketball players are graphed along with a line of fit.

    a. Find the sum of the squares of the residuals.

    b. Find the *mean absolute deviation.* (The mean absolute deviation is the mean of the absolute values of the residuals.) Explain why the mean absolute deviation might be more useful than the sum of the squares of the residuals in some cases.

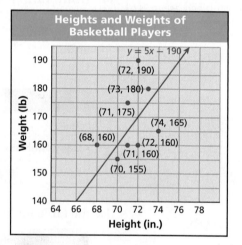

20. Use these facts to complete the data table:
The equation of a line of fit is $y = 2x - 3$.
The sum of the residuals is 0.
The sum of the squares of the residuals is 14.

x	1	3	4	5
y	1	▇	▇	8

FOCUS ON MATHEMATICAL PRACTICES

MATHEMATICAL PRACTICES

H.O.T. 21. Error Analysis Lainey calculated the correlation coefficient between the prices of items at two stores as −0.97, and found the line of best fit to be $y = 1.02x - 0.15$. Explain why Lainey must have made a mistake in her calculations.

H.O.T. 22. Analysis Examine the data in the table.

x	2	5	6	8	11
y	9	7	4	3	4

    a. Find the line of best fit and the correlation coefficient.

    b. Suppose each value of y is increased by 5. Find the new line of best fit and correlation coefficient. How did they change?

Interpreting Trend Lines

Connecting
Algebra to

Data Analysis

Previously, you learned how to draw trend lines on scatter plots. Now you will learn how to find the equations of trend lines and write them in slope-intercept form.

Example

Write an equation for the trend line on the scatter plot.

Two points on the trend line are (30, 75) and (60, 90).

To find the slope of the line that contains (30, 75) and (60, 90), use the slope formula.

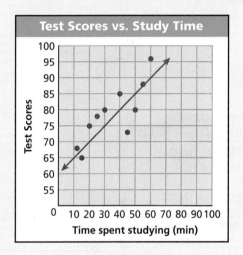

Test Scores vs. Study Time

$m = \dfrac{y_2 - y_1}{x_2 - x_1}$ *Use the slope formula.*

$m = \dfrac{90 - 75}{60 - 30}$ *Substitute (30, 75) for (x_1, y_1) and (60, 90) for (x_2, y_2).*

$m = \dfrac{15}{30}$ *Simplify.*

$m = \dfrac{1}{2}$

Use the slope and the point (30, 75) to find the *y*-intercept of the line.

$y = mx + b$ *Slope-intercept form*

$75 = \dfrac{1}{2}(30) + b$ *Substitute $\frac{1}{2}$ for m, 30 for x, and 75 for y.*

$75 = 15 + b$ *Solve for b.*

$60 = b$

Write the equation.

$y = \dfrac{1}{2}x + 60$ *Substitute $\frac{1}{2}$ for m and 60 for b.*

Try This

1. In the example above, what is the meaning of the slope?

2. What does the *y*-intercept represent?

3. Use the equation to predict the test score of a student who spent 25 minutes studying.

4. Use the table to create a scatter plot. Draw a trend line and find the equation of your trend line. Tell the meaning of the slope and *y*-intercept. Then use your equation to predict the race time of a runner who ran 40 miles in training.

Distance Run in Training (mi)	12	15	16	18	21	23	24	25	33
Race Time (min)	65	64	55	58	55	50	50	47	36

EXTENSION

Curve Fitting with Exponential Models

Essential Question: How can you use exponential regression to fit a curve to data?

Objectives
Model data by using exponential functions.

Use exponential models to analyze and predict.

Vocabulary
exponential regression

Analyzing data values can identify a pattern, or repeated relationship, between two quantities.

Look at this table of values for the exponential function $f(x) = 2(3^x)$.

Remember!

For linear functions (first degree), first differences are constant. For quadratic functions, second differences are constant, and so on.

x	−1	0	1	2	3
f(x)	$\frac{2}{3}$	2	6	18	54

$\times 3 \quad \times 3 \quad \times 3 \quad \times 3$

Notice that the *ratio* of each *y*-value and the previous one is constant. Each value is three times the one before it, so the ratio of function values is constant for equally spaced *x*-values. This data can be fit by an exponential function of the form $f(x) = ab^x$.

COMMON CORE GPS
MCC9-12.F.LE.1

EXAMPLE 1 Identifying Exponential Data

Determine whether *f* is an exponential function of *x* of the form $f(x) = ab^x$. If so, find the constant ratio.

A

x	−1	0	1	2	3
f(x)	−3	−1	1	3	5

$+2 \quad +2 +2 +2$ *First differences*

y is a linear function of *x*.

B

x	−1	0	1	2	3
f(x)	$\frac{1}{2}$	1	2	4	8

$+\frac{1}{2} \quad +1 +2 \quad +4$

Ratios $\frac{1}{\frac{1}{2}} = \frac{2}{1} = \frac{4}{2} = \frac{8}{4} = 2$

This data set is exponential, with a constant ratio of 2.

Determine whether *y* is an exponential function of *x* of the form $f(x) = ab^x$. If so, find the constant ratio.

1a.

x	−1	0	1	2	3
f(x)	$2.\overline{6}$	4	6	9	13.5

1b.

x	−1	0	1	2	3
f(x)	−3	2	7	12	17

Steve Taylor/Getty Images

You have used a graphing calculator to perform *linear regressions* and *quadratic regressions* to make predictions. You can also use an *exponential model,* which is an exponential function that represents a real data set.

Once you know that data are exponential, you can use **ExpReg** (exponential regression) on your calculator to find a function that fits. This method of using data to find an exponential model is called an **exponential regression** . The calculator fits exponential functions to ab^x, so translations cannot be modeled.

EXAMPLE MCC9-12.F.LE.2

2 | ***Gemology Application***

The table gives the approximate values of diamonds of the same quality. Find an exponential model for the data. Use the model to estimate the weight of a diamond worth $2325.

Diamond Values	
Weight (carats)	Value ($)
0.5	920
1.0	1160
2.0	1580
3.0	2150
4.0	2900

Step 1 Enter the data into two lists in a graphing calculator. Use the exponential regression feature.

An exponential model is $V(w) \approx 814.96(1.38)^w$, where V is the diamond value and w is the weight in carats.

Step 2 Graph the data and the function model to verify that it fits the data.

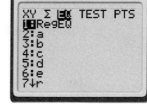

To enter the regression equation as **Y1** from the [Y=] screen, press [VARS], choose **5:Statistics**, press [ENTER], scroll to the **EQ** menu and select **1:RegEQ.**

Enter 2325 as **Y2**. Use the intersection feature. You may need to adjust the window dimensions to find the intersection.

A diamond weighing about 3.26 carats will have a value of $2325.

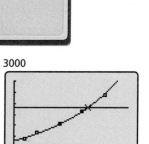

> **Remember!**
>
> If you do not see r^2 and r when you calculate regression, use
> CATALOG
> [2nd] [0] and
> turn these features on by selecting **DiagnosticOn**.

2. Use exponential regression to find a function that models this data. When will the number of bacteria reach 2000?

Time (min)	0	1	2	3	4	5
Bacteria	200	248	312	390	489	610

Determine whether f is an exponential function of x of the form $f(x) = ab^x$. If so, find the constant ratio.

1.

x	−1	0	1	2	3
$f(x)$	$-2\frac{5}{7}$	−1	11	95	683

2.

x	−1	0	1	2	3
$f(x)$	27	18	12	8	$5\frac{1}{3}$

3.

x	−1	0	1	2	3
$f(x)$	5	1	−3	−7	−11

4.

x	−1	0	1	2	3
$f(x)$	$2\frac{1}{4}$	3	4	$5\frac{1}{3}$	$7\frac{1}{9}$

5. Physics The table gives the approximate number of degrees Fahrenheit above room temperature of a cup of tea as it cools. Find an exponential model for the data. Use the model to estimate how long it will take the tea to reach a temperature that is less than 40 degrees above room temperature.

Cooling Tea					
Time (min)	0	1	2	3	4
Degrees above room temperature (°F)	132	120	110	101	93

Determine whether f is an exponential function of x of the form $f(x) = ab^x$. If so, find the constant ratio.

6.

x	−1	0	1	2	3
$f(x)$	1.25	1	0.75	0.5	0.25

7.

x	−5	−3	1	3	5
$f(x)$	20	6	2	12	30

8.

x	−1	0	1	2	3
$f(x)$	0.667	1	1.5	2.25	3.375

9.

x	−1	0	1	2	3
$f(x)$	−16	−8	−4	−2	−1

10. Social Studies The table gives the United States Hispanic population from 1980 to 2000. Find an exponential model for the data. Use the model to predict when the Hispanic population will exceed 120 million.

United States Hispanic Population			
Years After 1970	10	20	30
Population (millions)	14.6	22.5	35.3

Source: Census 2000

11. Telecommunication The table gives the number of telecommuters in the United States from 1990 to 2000. Find an exponential model for the data. Use the model to estimate when the number of telecommuters will exceed 100 million.

U.S. Telecommuters											
Years After 1990	0	1	2	3	4	5	6	7	8	9	10
Telecommuters (millions)	4.4	5.5	6.6	7.3	9.1	8.5	8.7	11.1	15.7	19.6	23.6

Source: Federal Highway Administration

Decide whether the data set is exponential, and if it is, use exponential regression to find a function that models the data.

12.

x	1	2	3	4
f(x)	11	95	683	4799

13.

x	−1	0	2	3
f(x)	4	2	0.5	0.25

American alligator, Everglades National Park

14. Critical Thinking According to one source, the population of nesting wading birds in the wetlands of the Florida Everglades Park System has decreased from more than a half-million in the 1930s to less than 15,000 today. What do you need to know to determine whether this decrease in numbers is exponential? Explain.

15. Ecology One research study showed that the rate of calf survival in Yellowstone elk herds depends on spring snow depths. At snow depths of about 5000 mm, the rate of survival is about 0.9 per hundred cows; at 6700 mm it is about 0.3; and at 8250 mm, it is about 0.17. Find an exponential function to model the data. Use the model to predict the calf survival rate per hundred cows at snow depths of 4000 mm.

16. Technology Holiday season sales of a portable digital music player are shown in the graph. Assume that growth rate continues in the same way. Write an exponential function to model the data. Use the model to predict sales in three years.

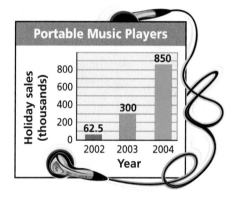

17. Make a Conjecture Make a table of values for an exponential function with $x = 1, 2, 3, \ldots 8$. Find the first differences, second differences, and third differences. Make a conjecture about the nth differences, assuming that the domain of the function is all natural numbers.

18. The table shows the total amount of farmland in Vermont since 1970.

   a. Use exponential regression to find a function that models the data.

   b. According to the model, by what percent does the amount of farmland decrease each year?

   c. Predict the amount of farmland in 2010.

Farmland in Vermont	
Year	Farmland (thousands of acres)
1970	2010
1980	1740
1990	1440
2000	1270

Ready to Go On?

my.hrw.com
Assessment and Intervention

✓ **15-1 Scatter Plots and Trend Lines**

The table shows the time it takes different people to read a given number of pages.

Pages Read	2	6	6	8	8	10	10
Time (min)	10	15	20	15	30	25	30

1. Graph a scatter plot using the given data.

2. Describe the correlation illustrated by the scatter plot.

3. The scatter plot shows the estimated annual sales for an electronics and appliance chain of stores for the years 2004–2009. Based on this relationship, predict the annual sales in 2012.

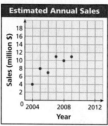

4. The table shows the value of a car for the given years. Graph a scatter plot using the given data. Describe the correlation illustrated by the scatter plot.

Year	2000	2001	2002	2003
Value (thousand $)	28	25	23	20

5. The graph shows the results of a 2003–2004 survey on class size at the given grade levels. Based on this relationship, predict the class size for the 9th grade.

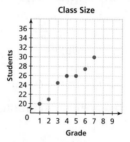

✓ **15-2 Line of Best Fit**

6. A street vendor noted the daily high temperature and the number of ice cream cones she sold each day for one week. Find an equation for a line of best fit. How well does the line represent the data?

Temperature (°F)	80	73	65	90	96	100	82
Ice Cream Cones Sold	32	27	22	38	45	48	35

7. Two lines of fit for the data in the table are $y = 0.5x$ and $y = x - 1$. For each line, find the sum of the squares of the residuals. Which line is a better fit?

x	1	2	4	5
y	2	0	1	3

8. The lengths and weights of 6 koi in a pond are shown in the table. Find an equation of a line of best fit. How well does the line fit the data?

Length (in.)	9	12	11	15	8	10
Weight (oz)	5	11	9	20	4	7

9. Four friends recorded the numbers of CDs and video games their families purchased in the last month, as shown in the table. Find an equation of a line of best fit. How well does the line fit the data?

CDs	2	3	5	6
Games	2	5	4	6

PARCC Assessment Readiness

Selected Response

1. Make a scatter plot using the given data.

x	3	6	5	2	7	4	8	1
y	4.5	6.5	6.5	3.5	6.5	4.5	8	4

Ⓐ
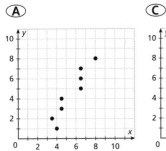

Ⓒ
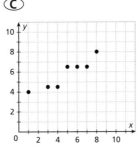

Ⓑ
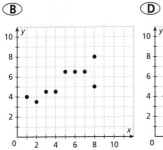

Ⓓ
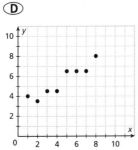

2. The table and accompanying scatter plot show forearm lengths *f* and heights *h* from a randomly selected sample of people. Find an equation of the line of best fit. Then use your equation to predict how tall a person is if the forearm length is 27.5 centimeters.

Forearm length (cm)	24	27	24	26	32	30	29	28
Body height (cm)	157	177	164	175	195	178	180	172

Ⓕ $h = 3.64f + 74.57$

about 175 centimeters tall

Ⓖ $h = -1.16f + 203.24$

about 171 centimeters tall

Ⓗ $h = 2.34f + 116.23$

about 181 centimeters tall

Ⓙ $h = 0.23f + 152.49$

about 159 centimeters tall

3. Describe the correlation illustrated by the scatter plot.

Ⓐ positive correlation

Ⓑ negative correlation

Ⓒ no correlation

Ⓓ cannot determine

Mini-Task

4. The table shows the relationship between typical weight and typical lifespan for several dog breeds. Find an equation of the line of best fit, and the correlation coefficient. How well does the line represent the data?

Breed	Weight (pounds)	Lifespan (years)
Yorkshire Terrier	5.5	15
Shih Tzu	12.5	13
Pug	16	13.5
Boston Terrier	20	13
Welsh Corgi (Pembroke)	26	13
Bulldog	45	7
Siberian Husky	47.5	12
Golden Retriever	65	12
German Shepherd	72.5	11
Rottweiler	107.5	10
Great Dane	135	8.5

PARCC Assessment Readiness

Selected Response

1. How many total victories did the four teams have?

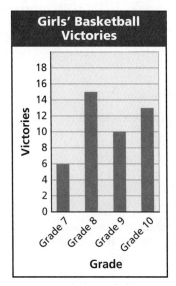

Girls' Basketball Victories

Victories / Grade

(A) 42   (C) 31

(B) 41   (D) 44

2. The graph shows the profit made at a family yard sale that lasted 8 hours. Between which hours did the profit increase at the slowest rate?

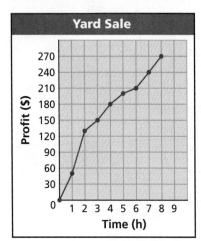

Yard Sale

Profit ($) / Time (h)

(F) 0–1   (H) 5–6

(G) 1–2   (J) 7–8

3. Which of the following is one of the five values needed to make a box-and-whisker plot?

(A) Mean   (C) Mode

(B) Median   (D) Average

4. What is the median of the data presented in this stem-and-leaf plot?

Stem	Leaves
6	0 2 2 2 5 8
7	3 4 4 6 7
8	2 5 8 9

Key: 8 | 2 means 0.82

(F) 0.62

(G) 0.74

(H) 6.2

(J) 7.4

5. The numbers of students in different classes at a community college are given below. Which is a correct histogram of these data?

25, 15, 28, 52, 22, 38, 42, 44, 24, 32, 19, 28, 29, 20, 31

(A)

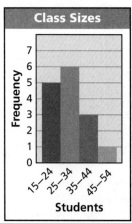

Class Sizes

Frequency / Students

(B)

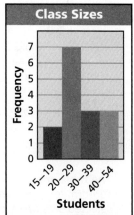

Class Sizes

Frequency / Students

(C)

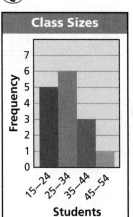

Class Sizes

Frequency / Students

(D)

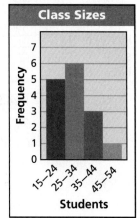

Class Sizes

Frequency / Students

If you are allowed to write in your test booklet, you may want to add additional information to a given diagram. Be sure to mark your answer on the answer sheet since your marks on the test booklet will not be graded.

6. The cumulative frequencies of each interval have been given. What numbers should be placed in the frequency column?

Interval	Frequency	Cumulative Frequency
6–15	?	1
16–25	?	11
26–35	?	64
36–45	?	112
46–55	?	127
56–65	?	131

F   10, 53, 48, 15, 4, 0

G   0, 1, 12, 76, 188, 315

H   1, 10, 53, 48, 15, 4

J   1, 12, 76, 188, 315, 446

7. The table shows the number of stars that make up various constellations. What are the mean, median, mode, and range of the data set?

Constellation Number	Number of Stars in Constellation
Constellation 1	17
Constellation 2	35
Constellation 3	49
Constellation 4	17
Constellation 5	24

A   mean = 42.5; median = 24; mode = 23; range = 32

B   mean − 28.4; median = 24; mode = 17; range = 32

C   mean = 28.4; median = 49; mode = 17; range = 49

D   mean = 42.5; median = 49; mode = 17; range = 32

8. Which set of data values can be represented by the box-and-whisker plot shown?

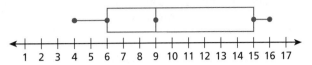

F   4, 5, 6, 9, 11, 15, 16

G   4, 5, 6, 7, 8, 9, 11, 13, 14, 15, 16

H   4, 6, 8, 11, 15, 16

J   4, 6, 7, 11, 15, 16

9. What is the outlier in the data set {42, 13, 23, 24, 5, 5, 13, 8}, and how does it affect the mean, median, mode(s), and range of the data?

A   The outlier is 42. The outlier increases the mean by 3.6 and the range by 18. The outlier has no effect on the median or the modes.

B   The outlier is 42. The outlier increases the mean by 3.6, the median by 5, and the range by 18. The outlier has no effect on the modes.

C   The outlier is 42. The outlier increases the mean by 5.2 and the range by 18. The outlier has no effect on the median and the modes.

D   The outlier is 42. The outlier increases the median by 3.6 and the range by 18. The outlier has no effect on the mean and the modes.

10. Between which of the following variables would you expect there to be a negative correlation?

F   A person's height and weight

G   The amount of time spent studying and a test grade

H   The outside temperature and the number of layers of clothing a person wears

J   The number of years spent in school and salary

11. Which of the following data sets has the greatest interquartile range?

A   3, 4, 6, 5, 7, 5, 7

B   8, 8, 8, 8, 8, 8, 8

C   10, 3, 11, 11, 12, 11, 11

D   2, 1, 2, 6, 4, 5, 6

12. The table shows the relationship between the typical weight and typical lifespan for several mammals. Which gives an equation of the line of best fit and the correlation coefficient? What does the correlation indicate about the data?

Mammal	Weight (pounds)	Lifespan (years)
African Elephant	9500	70
Hippopotamus	6500	40
Grizzly bear	800	25
Water buffalo	2075	25
Red panda	16	8
Kangaroo	120	10
Cottontail rabbit	3	3
Spotted hyena	200	25
Wolf	110	8
Skunk	1	3
Leopard seal	840	11.5

Ⓕ $y \approx 0.006x + 10$
The value of r is about 0.93, which indicates a strong positive correlation.

Ⓖ $y \approx -0.006x + 10$
The value of r is about -0.93, which indicates a strong negative correlation.

Ⓗ $y \approx 0.006x + 10$
The value of r is about -0.07, which indicates a weak negative correlation.

Ⓙ $y \approx -0.006x + 10$
The value of r is about 0.934, which indicates that weight and lifespan are not correlated.

13. Will has the following quiz scores in his Geography class.

86, 90, 80, 75, 80, 95, 97, 80

Will takes a ninth quiz, and his median score increases by 1. What score did he get on the ninth quiz?

Ⓐ 82

Ⓑ 83

Ⓒ 84

Ⓓ 85

14. Lionel observes that traffic is getting worse and it's taking him longer to get to work. He records the following data for several weeks. Which scatter plot shows Lionel's data?

Week	1	2	3	4	5	6	7	8
Time (min)	8.2	8.9	8.6	8.3	9	9.7	8.4	10.1

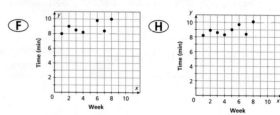

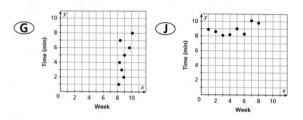

Mini-Tasks

15. The numbers of people who attended two different plays are shown in the table below. Make a back-to-back stem-and-leaf plot.

Play Attendance	
Comedy Camp	Days and Days
104 62 83 102 104 120 81 126 122	103 105 80 135 109 128 82 132 139

16. The capacities of the gas tanks on several new vehicles are shown below. Use the data to make a frequency table with intervals.

Gas Tank Capacity (gal)
15 12 12 15 18 26 25 12 15 18 11 10 12 16 15 16 18 25 21 18 20 21

A teacher collected data on the activities the class performed on their summer break and summarized the data in a table.

Went to Beach

		Yes	No
Joined a sports team	Yes	10	9
	No	11	6

17. Make a table of the joint and marginal relative frequencies.

18. Given that a student went to the beach, what is the probability he or she joined a sports team?

19. Given that a student did not go to the beach, what is the probability he or she did not join a sports team?

20. The table shows the number of Atlantic hurricanes for the years 1997–2004.

Atlantic Hurricanes			
Year	Number	Year	Number
1997	3	2001	9
1998	10	2002	4
1999	8	2003	7
2000	8	2004	9

  a. Make a box-and-whisker plot of the hurricane data.

  b. What is the mean number of hurricanes per year for the time period shown in the table?

21. On four math tests, Clark scored 90, 94, 97, and 93. Give an example of a score Clark could receive on his next test that would raise his mean test score but have no effect on the range or mode of his scores. Justify your answer.

Performance Tasks

22. Gustavo is comparing his basketball statistics for the current year with those from the previous year when he won the conference scoring championship. The points he has scored through the first ten games this year are given in this table.

22	17	10	23	31
3	18	26	18	18

The points Gustavo scored last year in all 12 games are given in this table.

23	35	19	11	28	21
25	17	18	15	24	28

  a. Make a double box-and-whisker plot for the two sets of data.

  b. Find the ranges and interquartile ranges of the two data sets.

  c. Identify any outliers in each set of data.

  d. The school newspaper reported that Gustavo's performance this year has been less consistent than and not as good as last year. Is this accurate? Use your results from parts **a–c** to explain why or why not.

23. The table shows the number of sales of a popular hybrid car in the U.S. for the first four years it was on sale.

Year	1	2	3	4
Number of cars sold	21,386	17,173	14,787	11,182

  a. Graph the data in a scatter plot with year number on the x-axis and number of cars on the y-axis.

  b. Graph a trend line for the data and write an equation for your trend line.

  c. If the trend continues into year 5, how many cars should the manufacturer expect to sell? Include this point on your graph.

  d. The manufacturer expects that rising gas prices and some upgrades to the car will help increase sales. They predict that after year 5, their sales will increase by 1,000 cars per year. Graph the data for years 6 through 8 based on their prediction, and write the equation of a trend line that models the data from year 5 on.

my.hrw.com
Online Assessment

Go online for updated, PARCC-aligned assessment readiness.

Are You Ready?

my.hrw.com
Assessment and Intervention

✅ Vocabulary

Match each term on the left with a definition on the right.

1. image
2. preimage
3. transformation
4. *y*-coordinate

A. a mapping of a figure from its original position to a new position

B. the first number in an ordered pair

C. a shape that undergoes a transformation

D. the second number in an ordered pair

E. the shape that results from a transformation of a figure

✅ Ordered Pairs

Graph each ordered pair.

5. $(0, 4)$
6. $(-3, 2)$
7. $(4, 3)$
8. $(3, -1)$
9. $(-1, -3)$
10. $(-2, 0)$

✅ Identify Similar Figures

Can you conclude that the given figures are similar? If so, explain why.

11. $\triangle JKL$ and $\triangle JMN$

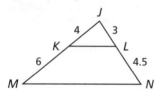

12. rectangle *PQRS* and rectangle *UVWX*

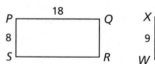

✅ Find Missing Measures in Similar Figures

13. $\triangle PQR \sim \triangle XYZ$. $m\angle PQR = 48°$ and $m\angle PRQ = 52°$. What is $m\angle XZY$?

14. $\square ABCD \sim \square JKLM$. $AD = 16$, $DC = 12$, and $JM = 24$. What is ML?

15. $\square WXYZ \sim \square CDEF$. $XY = 84$, $ZY = 54$, and $DE = 14$. What is FE?

Career Readiness Fabric Designers

Fabric designers create designs for all sorts of fabrics. Fabric designers may use the latest computer design methods or traditional hand-printing techniques. Both may involve using transformations and tessellations to produce designs. Fabric designers must be artistic and have good design skills. They may have a college degree in fine art or design. Some fabric designers work with clothing or furniture manufacturers or with fashion designers. Others work as artists, creating fabrics as art.

Transformations in the Coordinate Plane

UNIT 5

Online Edition

my.hrw.com

Access the complete online textbook, interactive features, and additional resources.

Animated Math

Interactively explore key concepts with these online tutorials.

Homework Help

Get instant help with tutorial videos, practice problems, and step-by-step solutions.

Portable Devices

On the Spot

Watch video tutorials anywhere, anytime with this app for iPhone® and iPad®.

HMH Fuse

Make your learning experience completely portable and interactive with this app for iPad®.

Chapter Resources

Scan with your smart phone to jump directly to the online edition.

COMMON CORE GPS — Unit Contents

Module 16 Transformations
MCC9-12.G.CO.1, MCC9-12.G.CO.2, MCC9-12.G.CO.4, MCC9-12.G.CO.5

Module 17 Combined Transformations and Symmetry
MCC9-12.G.CO.3, MCC9-12.G.CO.5

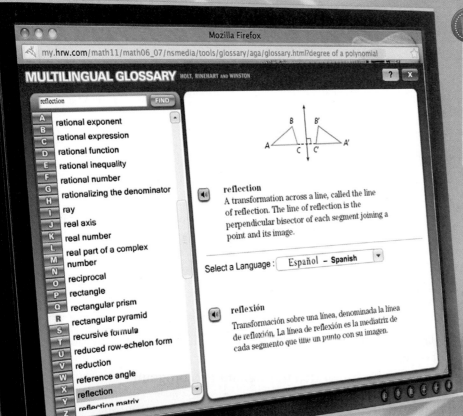

The **Multilingual Glossary** contains illustrated definitions and translations of chapter vocabulary words.

16 Transformations

MATHEMATICAL PRACTICES The Common Core Georgia Performance Standards for Mathematical Practice describe varieties of expertise that all students should seek to develop. Opportunities to develop these practices are integrated throughout this program.

1 Make sense of problems and persevere in solving them.

2 Reason abstractly and quantitatively.

3 Construct viable arguments and critique the reasoning of others.

4 Model with mathematics.

5 Use appropriate tools strategically.

6 Attend to precision.

7 Look for and make use of structure.

8 Look for and express regularity in repeated reasoning.

Unpacking the Standards

my.hrw.com
Multilingual Glossary

Understanding the standards and the vocabulary terms in the standards will help you know exactly what you are expected to learn in this chapter.

 MCC9-12.G.CO.2

Represent transformations in the plane using, e.g., transparencies and geometry software; describe transformations as functions that take points in the plane as inputs and give other points as outputs. Compare transformations that preserve distance and angle to those that do not (e.g., translation versus horizontal stretch).

Key Vocabulary

transformation (transformación) A change in the position, size, or shape of a figure or graph.

function (función) A relation in which every input is paired with exactly one output.

What It Means For You

Representing transformations as functions of points in the plane lets you use algebra tools such as the distance formula to investigate the results of transformations.

EXAMPLE   **Translation and Rotation**

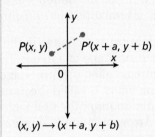

$(x, y) \rightarrow (x + a, y + b)$

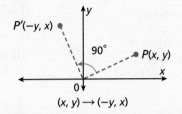

$(x, y) \rightarrow (-y, x)$

The function $P(x, y)$ slides the point (x, y) by a units horizontally and b units vertically to the point $(x + a, y + b)$.

The function $P(x, y)$ rotates the point (x, y) by 90° in a counterclockwise direction about the origin to the point $(-y, x)$.

 MCC9-12.G.CO.5

Given a geometric figure and a rotation, reflection, or translation, draw the transformed figure using, e.g., graph paper, tracing paper, or geometry software. Specify a sequence of transformations that will carry a given figure onto another.

Key Vocabulary

rotation (rotación) A transformation that rotates or turns a figure about a point called the center of rotation.

reflection (reflexión) A transformation that reflects, or "flips," a graph or figure across a line, called the line of reflection, such that each reflected point is the same distance from the line of reflection but is on the opposite side of the line.

translation (traslación) A transformation that shifts or slides every point of a figure or graph the same distance in the same direction.

What It Means For You

Rotations, reflections, and translations do not change the shape or size of a figure. You can move a figure onto another of the same size by one or more of these transformations.

EXAMPLE

The diagram represents the whirling pockets of air that form behind a fast-moving truck.

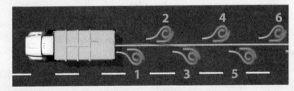

To carry whirl **1** onto whirl **2**: translate right and reflect up.

To carry whirl **2** onto whirl **3**: translate right and reflect down.

In the same way, you can carry each whirl onto the next.

16-1 Transformations in the Coordinate Plane

Essential Question: How can you define rotations, reflections, and translations of geometric figures?

Objectives
Identify reflections, rotations, and translations.

Graph transformations in the coordinate plane.

Vocabulary
transformation
preimage
image
reflection
rotation
translation

Who uses this?

Artists use transformations to create decorative patterns. (See Example 4.)

The Alhambra, a 13th-century palace in Granada, Spain, is famous for the geometric patterns that cover its walls and floors. To create a variety of designs, the builders based the patterns on several different *transformations*.

A **transformation** is a change in the position, size, or shape of a figure. The original figure is called the **preimage**. The resulting figure is called the **image**. A transformation *maps* the preimage to the image. Arrow notation (→) is used to describe a transformation, and primes (′) are used to label the image.

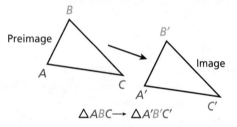

$\triangle ABC \rightarrow \triangle A'B'C'$

Know it! .Note

Transformations

REFLECTION	ROTATION	TRANSLATION
	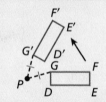	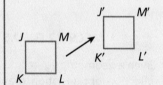
A **reflection** (or *flip*) is a transformation across a line, called the line of reflection. Each point and its image are the same distance from the line of reflection.	A **rotation** (or *turn*) is a transformation about a point *P*, called the center of rotation. Each point and its image are the same distance from *P*.	A **translation** (or *slide*) is a transformation in which all the points of a figure move the same distance in the same direction.

COMMON CORE GPS
MCC9-12.G.CO.4

EXAMPLE **Identifying Transformations**

Identify the transformation. Then use arrow notation to describe the transformation.

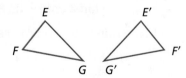

The transformation cannot be a translation because each point and its image are not in the same position.

The transformation is a reflection. $\triangle EFG \rightarrow \triangle E'F'G'$

my.hrw.com

Online Video Tutor

Identify the transformation. Then use arrow notation to describe the transformation.

B

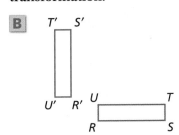

The transformation cannot be a reflection because each point and its image are not the same distance from a line of reflection.

The transformation is a 90° rotation. $RSTU \rightarrow R'S'T'U'$

Identify each transformation. Then use arrow notation to describe the transformation.

1a.

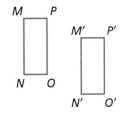

1b.

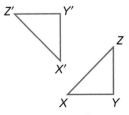

COMMON CORE GPS
MCC9-12.G.CO.5

EXAMPLE 2

my.hrw.com

Online Video Tutor

Drawing and Identifying Transformations

A figure has vertices at $A(-1, 4)$, $B(-1, 1)$, and $C(3, 1)$. After a transformation, the image of the figure has vertices at $A'(-1, -4)$, $B'(-1, -1)$, and $C'(3, -1)$. Draw the preimage and image. Then identify the transformation.

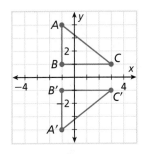

Plot the points. Then use a ruler to connect the vertices.

The transformation is a reflection across the *x*-axis because each point and its image are the same distance from the *x*-axis.

2. A figure has vertices at $E(2, 0)$, $F(2, -1)$, $G(5, -1)$, and $H(5, 0)$. After a transformation, the image of the figure has vertices at $E'(0, 2)$, $F'(1, 2)$, $G'(1, 5)$, and $H'(0, 5)$. Draw the preimage and image. Then identify the transformation.

To find coordinates for the image of a figure in a translation, add *a* to the *x*-coordinates of the preimage and add *b* to the *y*-coordinates of the preimage. Translations can also be described by a rule such as $(x, y) \rightarrow (x + a, y + b)$.

COMMON CORE GPS
MCC9-12.G.CO.5

EXAMPLE 3

Translations in the Coordinate Plane

Find the coordinates for the image of $\triangle ABC$ after the translation $(x, y) \rightarrow (x + 3, y - 4)$. Draw the image.

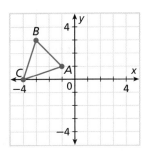

Step 1 Find the coordinates of $\triangle ABC$.

The vertices of $\triangle ABC$ are $A(-1, 1)$, $B(-3, 3)$, and $C(-4, 0)$.

Online Video Tutor

Step 2 Apply the rule to find the vertices of the image.

$$A'(-1 + 3, 1 - 4) = A'(2, -3)$$
$$B'(-3 + 3, 3 - 4) = B'(0, -1)$$
$$C'(-4 + 3, 0 - 4) = C'(-1, -4)$$

Step 3 Plot the points. Then finish drawing the image by using a ruler to connect the vertices.

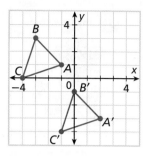

CHECK IT OUT!

3. Find the coordinates for the image of *JKLM* after the translation $(x, y) \rightarrow (x - 2, y + 4)$. Draw the image.

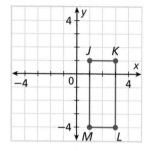

Art History Application

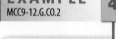

Online Video Tutor

The pattern shown is similar to a pattern on a wall of the Alhambra. Write a rule for the translation of square 1 to square 2.

Step 1 Choose 2 points

Choose a point *A* on the preimage and a corresponding point *A'* on the image. *A* has coordinates $(3, 1)$, and *A'* has coordinates $(1, 3)$.

Step 2 Translate

To translate *A* to *A'*, 2 units are subtracted from the *x*-coordinate and 2 units are added to the *y*-coordinate. Therefore, the translation rule is $(x, y) \rightarrow (x - 2, y + 2)$.

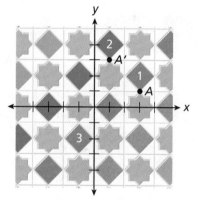

CHECK IT OUT!

4. Use the diagram to write a rule for the translation of square 1 to square 3.

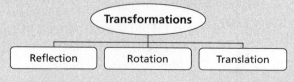

MCC.MP.6   MATHEMATICAL PRACTICES

THINK AND DISCUSS

1. Explain how to recognize a reflection when given a figure and its image.

2. GET ORGANIZED Copy and complete the graphic organizer. In each box, sketch an example of each transformation.

```
              Transformations
      ┌────────────┬────────────┐
  Reflection    Rotation    Translation
```

GUIDED PRACTICE

Vocabulary Apply the vocabulary from this lesson to answer each question.

1. Given the transformation $\triangle XYZ \rightarrow \triangle X'Y'Z'$, name the preimage and image of the transformation.

2. The types of transformations of geometric figures in the coordinate plane can be described as a slide, a flip, or a turn. What are the other names used to identify these transformations?

SEE EXAMPLE 1 | Identify each transformation. Then use arrow notation to describe the transformation.

3.

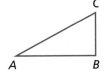

4.

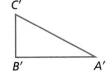

SEE EXAMPLE 2

5. A figure has vertices at $A(-3, 2)$, $B(-1, -1)$, and $C(-4, -2)$. After a transformation, the image of the figure has vertices at $A'(3, 2)$, $B'(1, -1)$, and $C'(4, -2)$. Draw the preimage and image. Then identify the transformation.

SEE EXAMPLE 3

6. **Multi-Step** The coordinates of the vertices of $\triangle DEF$ are $D(2, 3)$, $E(1, 1)$, and $F(4, 0)$. Find the coordinates for the image of $\triangle DEF$ after the translation $(x, y) \rightarrow (x - 3, y - 2)$. Draw the preimage and image.

SEE EXAMPLE 4

7. **Animation** In an animated film, a simple scene can be created by translating a figure against a still background. Write a rule for the translation that maps the rocket from position 1 to position 2.

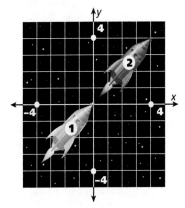

PRACTICE AND PROBLEM SOLVING

Identify each transformation. Then use arrow notation to describe the transformation.

For Exercises	See Example
8–9	1
10	2
11	3
12	4

Independent Practice

my.hrw.com

Online Extra Practice

8.

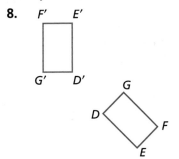

9.

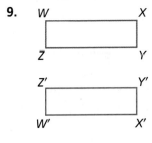

10. A figure has vertices at $J(-2, 3)$, $K(0, 3)$, $L(0, 1)$, and $M(-2, 1)$. After a transformation, the image of the figure has vertices at $J'(2, 1)$, $K'(4, 1)$, $L'(4, -1)$, and $M'(2, -1)$. Draw the preimage and image. Then identify the transformation.

11. **Multi-Step** The coordinates of the vertices of rectangle *ABCD* are $A(-4, 1)$, $B(1, 1)$, $C(1, -2)$, and $D(-4, -2)$. Find the coordinates for the image of rectangle *ABCD* after the translation $(x, y) \rightarrow (x + 3, y - 2)$. Draw the preimage and the image.

12. **Travel** Write a rule for the translation that maps the descent of the hot air balloon.

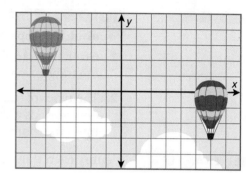

Which transformation is suggested by each of the following?

13. mountain range and its image on a lake

14. straight line path of a band marching down a street

15. wings of a butterfly

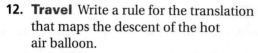

Given points $F(3, 5)$, $G(-1, 4)$, and $H(5, 0)$, draw $\triangle FGH$ and its reflection across each of the following lines.

16. the *x*-axis　　　　　　17. the *y*-axis

18. Find the vertices of one of the triangles on the graph. Then use arrow notation to write a rule for translating the other three triangles.

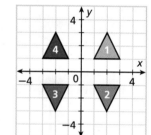

A transformation maps *A* onto *B* and *C* onto *D*.

19. Name the image of *A*.　　20. Name the preimage of *B*.

21. Name the image of *C*.　　22. Name the preimage of *D*.

23. Find the coordinates for the image of $\triangle RST$ with vertices $R(1, -4)$, $S(-1, -1)$, and $T(-5, 1)$ after the translation $(x, y) \rightarrow (x - 2, y - 8)$.

24. **Critical Thinking** Consider the translations $(x, y) \rightarrow (x + 5, y + 3)$ and $(x, y) \rightarrow (x + 10, y + 5)$. Compare the two translations.

Graph each figure and its image after the given translation.

25. $\overline{MN}$ with endpoints $M(2, 8)$ and $N(-3, 4)$ after the translation $(x, y) \rightarrow (x + 2, y - 5)$

26. $\overline{KL}$ with endpoints $K(-1, 1)$ and $L(3, -4)$ after the translation $(x, y) \rightarrow (x - 4, y + 3)$

27. **Write About It** Given a triangle in the coordinate plane, explain how to draw its image after the translation $(x, y) \rightarrow (x + 1, y + 1)$.

28. Greg wants to rearrange a triangular pattern of colored stones on his patio. What combination of transformations could he use to transform $\triangle CAE$ to the image on the coordinate plane?

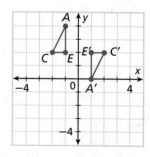

29. Which type of transformation maps △XYZ to △X′Y′Z′?

ⒶReflection ⒸTranslation

ⒷRotation ⒹNot here

30. △DEF has vertices at $D(-4, 2)$, $E(-3, -3)$, and $F(1, 4)$. Which of these points is a vertex of the image of △DEF after the translation $(x, y) \rightarrow (x - 2, y + 1)$?

Ⓕ $(-2, 1)$ Ⓗ $(-5, -2)$

Ⓖ $(3, 3)$ Ⓙ $(-6, -1)$

31. Consider the translation $(1, 4) \rightarrow (-2, 3)$. What number was added to the x-coordinate?

Ⓐ -3 Ⓑ -1 Ⓒ 1 Ⓓ 7

32. Consider the translation $(-5, -7) \rightarrow (-2, -1)$. What number was added to the y-coordinate?

Ⓕ -3 Ⓖ 3 Ⓗ 6 Ⓙ 8

CHALLENGE AND EXTEND

33. △RST with vertices $R(-2, -2)$, $S(-3, 1)$, and $T(1, 1)$ is translated by $(x, y) \rightarrow (x - 1, y + 3)$. Then the image, △R′S′T′, is translated by $(x, y) \rightarrow (x + 4, y - 1)$, resulting in △R″S″T″.

a. Find the coordinates for the vertices of △R″S″T″.

b. Write a rule for a single translation that maps △RST to △R″S″T″.

34. Find the angle through which the minute hand of a clock rotates over a period of 12 minutes. (*Hint:* There are 360° in a circle.)

35. A triangle has vertices $A(1, 0)$, $B(5, 0)$, and $C(2, 3)$. The triangle is rotated 90° counterclockwise about the origin. Draw and label the image of the triangle.

Determine the coordinates for the reflection image of any point $A(x, y)$ across the given line.

36. x-axis **37.** y-axis

FOCUS ON MATHEMATICAL PRACTICES

H.O.T. 38. Reasoning A figure has vertices at $(1, 3)$, $(1, 5)$, $(3, 5)$, and $(3, 3)$. After a transformation, the image has vertices at $(1, -5)$, $(1, -3)$, $(3, -3)$, and $(3, -5)$. Sylvia says this transformation is a translation that is described by $(x, y) \rightarrow (x, y - 8)$. Helene says it is a reflection across the x-axis. Who is correct? Why?

H.O.T. 39. Problem Solving A circle with its center at $(-3, -4)$ is reflected across the x-axis. What is the center of the image?

H.O.T. 40. Analysis A point (x, y) undergoes the translation $(x + 6, y)$. This image is then translated again by $(x - 2, y)$. Write a rule for a single translation that has the same effect as these two translations.

H.O.T. 41. Problem Solving The graph of triangle ABC is within the first quadrant. Describe a transformation that would result in an image $A′B′C′$ that is within the second quadrant.

H.O.T. 42. Communication Under what circumstances is the image of a preimage also a preimage?

16-2
Technology TASK

Use with Transformations in the Coordinate Plane

Explore Transformations

A transformation is a movement of a figure from its original position (preimage) to a new position (image). In this lab, you will use geometry software to perform transformations and explore their properties.

Use appropriate tools strategically.

MCC9-12.G.CO.2 Represent transformations in the plane using… geometry software… *Also* **MCC9-12.G.CO.5**

Activity 1

1. Construct a triangle using the segment tool. Use the text tool to label the vertices *A*, *B*, and *C*.

2. Select points *A* and *B* in that order. Choose Mark Vector from the Transform menu.

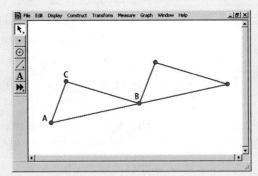

3. Select △*ABC* by clicking on all three segments of the triangle.

4. Choose Translate from the Transform menu, using *Marked* as the translation vector. What do you notice about the relationship between your preimage and its image?

5. What happens when you drag a vertex or a side of △*ABC*?

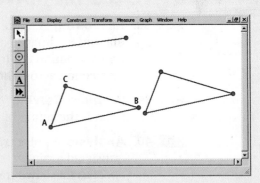

Try This

For Problems 1 and 2 choose New Sketch from the File menu.

1. Construct a triangle and a segment outside the triangle. Mark this segment as a translation vector as you did in Step 2 of Activity 1. Use Step 4 of Activity 1 to translate the triangle. What happens when you drag an endpoint of the new segment?

2. Instead of translating by a marked vector, use *Rectangular* as the translation vector and translate by a horizontal distance of 1 cm and a vertical distance of 2 cm. Compare this method with the marked vector method. What happens when you drag a side or vertex of the triangle?

3. Select the angles and sides of the preimage and image triangles. Use the tools in the Measure menu to measure length, angle measure, perimeter, and area. What do you think is true about these two figures?

Activity 2

1 Construct a triangle. Label the vertices *G*, *H*, and *I*.

2 Select point *H* and choose Mark Center from the Transform menu.

3 Select ∠*GHI* by selecting points *G*, *H*, and *I* in that order. Choose Mark Angle from the Transform menu.

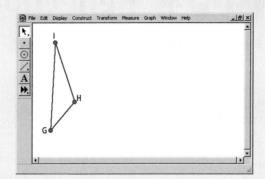

4 Select the entire triangle △*GHI* by dragging a selection box around the figure.

5 Choose Rotate from the Transform menu, using *Marked Angle* as the angle of rotation.

6 What happens when you drag a vertex or a side of △*GHI*?

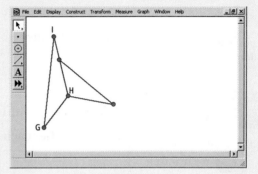

Try This

For Problems 4–6 choose New Sketch from the File menu.

4. Instead of selecting an angle of the triangle as the rotation angle, draw a new angle outside of the triangle. Mark this angle. Mark ∠*GHI* as Center and rotate the triangle. What happens when you drag one of the points that form the rotation angle?

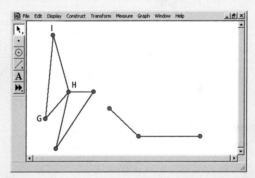

5. Construct △*QRS*, a new rotation angle, and a point *P* not on the triangle. Mark *P* as the center and mark the angle. Rotate the triangle. What happens when you drag *P* outside, inside, or on the preimage triangle?

6. Instead of rotating by a marked angle, use *Fixed Angle* as the rotation method and rotate by a fixed angle measure of 30°. Compare this method with the marked angle method.

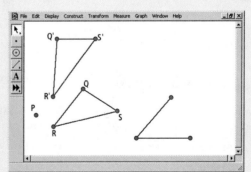

7. Using the fixed angle method of rotation, can you find an angle measure that will result in an image figure that exactly covers the preimage figure?

16-2 Reflections

Essential Question: How can you identify the effect of a reflection on a geometric figure?

Objective
Identify and draw reflections.

Vocabulary
isometry

Who uses this?
Trail designers use reflections to find shortest paths. (See Example 3.)

An **isometry** is a transformation that does not change the shape or size of a figure. Reflections, translations, and rotations are all isometries. Isometries are also called *congruence transformations* or *rigid motions*.

 Animated Math

Recall that a reflection is a transformation that moves a figure (the preimage) by flipping it across a line. The reflected figure is called the image. A reflection is an isometry, so the image is always congruent to the preimage.

 COMMON CORE GPS
EXAMPLE MCC9-12.G.CO.4

1 **Identifying Reflections**

Tell whether each transformation appears to be a reflection. Explain.

 my.hrw.com

Online Video Tutor

A

Yes; the image appears to be flipped across a line.

B

No; the figure does not appear to be flipped.

✓ **CHECK IT OUT!** Tell whether each transformation appears to be a reflection.

1a.

1b.

Reflect a Figure Using Patty Paper

1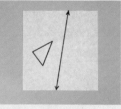

Draw a triangle and a line of reflection on a piece of patty paper.

2

Fold the patty paper back along the line of reflection.

3

Trace the triangle. Then unfold the paper.

Remember!

A perpendicular bisector is a line perpendicular to a segment that passes through its midpoint.

Draw a segment from each vertex of the preimage to the corresponding vertex of the image. Your drawing should show that the line of reflection is the perpendicular bisector of every segment connecting a point and its image.

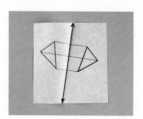

(tl), ©Ocean/CORBIS; (b), Sam Dudgeon/HMH

A reflection is a transformation across a line, called the line of reflection, so that the line of reflection is the perpendicular bisector of each segment joining each point and its image.

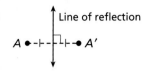

EXAMPLE 2
MCC9-12.G.CO.5

my.hrw.com

Online Video Tutor

Drawing Reflections

Copy the quadrilateral and the line of reflection. Draw the reflection of the quadrilateral across the line.

Step 1 Through each vertex draw a line perpendicular to the line of reflection.

Step 2 Measure the distance from each vertex to the line of reflection. Locate the image of each vertex on the opposite side of the line of reflection and the same distance from it.

Step 3 Connect the images of the vertices.

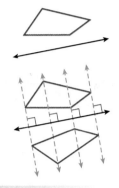

2. Copy the quadrilateral and the line of reflection. Draw the reflection of the quadrilateral across the line.

EXAMPLE 3
MCC9-12.G.CO.5

my.hrw.com

Online Video Tutor

Problem-Solving Application

A trail designer is planning two trails that connect campsites *A* and *B* to a point on the river. He wants the total length of the trails to be as short as possible. Where should the trail meet the river?

1 Understand the Problem

The problem asks you to locate point *X* on the river so that $AX + XB$ has the least value possible.

2 Make a Plan

Let B' be the reflection of point *B* across the river. For any point *X* on the river, $\overline{XB'} \cong \overline{XB}$, so $AX + XB = AX + XB'$. $AX + XB'$ is least when *A*, *X*, and B' are collinear.

MATHEMATICAL PRACTICES

Make sense of problems and persevere in solving them.

3 Solve

Reflect *B* across the river to locate B'. Draw $\overline{AB'}$ and locate *X* at the intersection of $\overline{AB'}$ and the river.

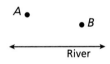

4 Look Back

To verify your answer, choose several possible locations for *X* and measure the total length of the trails for each location.

Remember!

The symbol $\cong$ is read as "is congruent to".

3. What if...? If *A* and *B* were the same distance from the river, what would be true about $\overline{AX}$ and $\overline{BX}$?

Reflections in the Coordinate Plane

ACROSS THE x-AXIS	ACROSS THE y-AXIS	ACROSS THE LINE y = x
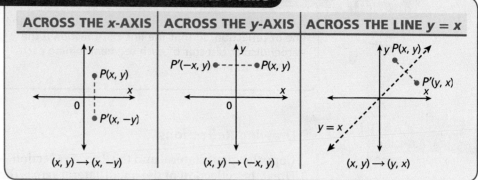		
$(x, y) \rightarrow (x, -y)$	$(x, y) \rightarrow (-x, y)$	$(x, y) \rightarrow (y, x)$

 EXAMPLE **4**
MCC9-12.G.CO.5

Drawing Reflections in the Coordinate Plane

Reflect the figure with the given vertices across the given line.

 my.hrw.com

Online Video Tutor

A $M(1, 2), N(1, 4), P(3, 3)$; y-axis
The reflection of (x, y) is $(-x, y)$.
$$M(1, 2) \rightarrow M'(-1, 2)$$
$$N(1, 4) \rightarrow N'(-1, 4)$$
$$P(3, 3) \rightarrow P'(-3, 3)$$
Graph the preimage and image.

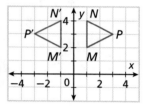

B $D(2, 0), E(2, 2), F(5, 2), G(5, 1)$; $y = x$
The reflection of (x, y) is (y, x).
$$D(2, 0) \rightarrow D'(0, 2)$$
$$E(2, 2) \rightarrow E'(2, 2)$$
$$F(5, 2) \rightarrow F'(2, 5)$$
$$G(5, 1) \rightarrow G'(1, 5)$$
Graph the preimage and image.

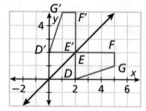

 4. Reflect the rectangle with vertices $S(3, 4)$, $T(3, 1)$, $U(-2, 1)$, and $V(-2, 4)$ across the x-axis.

 MCC.MP.6 **MATHEMATICAL PRACTICES**

THINK AND DISCUSS

1. Acute scalene $\triangle ABC$ is reflected across $\overline{BC}$. Classify quadrilateral $ABA'C$. Explain your reasoning.

2. Point A' is a *reflection* of point A across line ℓ. What is the relationship of ℓ to $\overline{AA'}$?

 3. GET ORGANIZED Copy and complete the graphic organizer.

Line of Reflection	Image of (a, b)	Example
x-axis		
y-axis		
y = x		

GUIDED PRACTICE

1. **Vocabulary** If a transformation is an *isometry*, how would you describe the relationship between the preimage and the image?

SEE EXAMPLE 1 Tell whether each transformation appears to be a reflection.

2.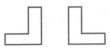

3.

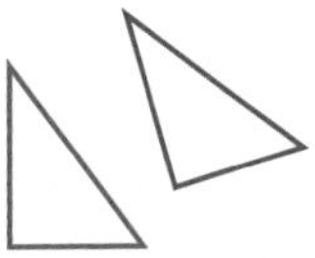

4.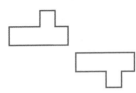

5.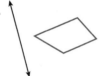

SEE EXAMPLE 2 **Multi-Step** Copy each figure and the line of reflection. Draw the reflection of the figure across the line.

6.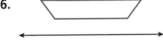

7.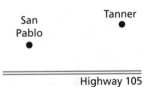

SEE EXAMPLE 3 8. **City Planning** The towns of San Pablo and Tanner are located on the same side of Highway 105. Two access roads are planned that connect the towns to a point P on the highway. Draw a diagram that shows where point P should be located in order to make the total length of the access roads as short as possible.

San Pablo   Tanner

Highway 105

SEE EXAMPLE 4 Reflect the figure with the given vertices across the given line.

9. $A(-2, 1)$, $B(2, 3)$, $C(5, 2)$; x-axis

10. $R(0, -1)$, $S(2, 2)$, $T(3, 0)$; y-axis

11. $M(2, 1)$, $N(3, 1)$, $P(2, -1)$, $Q(1, -1)$; $y = x$

12. $A(-2, 2)$, $B(-1, 3)$, $C(1, 2)$, $D(-2, -2)$; $y = x$

PRACTICE AND PROBLEM SOLVING

Tell whether each transformation appears to be a reflection.

Independent Practice	
For Exercises	See Example
13–16	1
17–18	2
19	3
20–23	4

13.

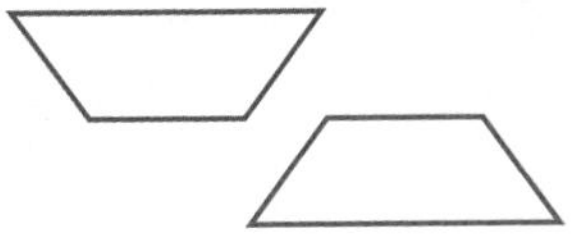

14.

15.

16.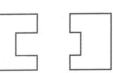

my.hrw.com

Online Extra Practice

Multi-Step Copy each figure and the line of reflection. Draw the reflection of the figure across the line.

17.

18.

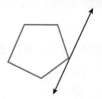

19. Recreation Cara is playing pool. She wants to hit the ball at point *A* without hitting the ball at point *B*. She has to bounce the cue ball, located at point *C*, off the side rail and into her ball. Draw a diagram that shows the exact point along the rail that Cara should aim for.

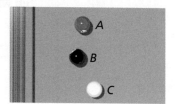

Reflect the figure with the given vertices across the given line.

20. $A(-3, 2)$, $B(0, 2)$, $C(-2, 0)$; *y*-axis

21. $M(-4, -1)$, $N(-1, -1)$, $P(-2, -2)$; $y = x$

22. $J(1, 2)$, $K(-2, -1)$, $L(3, -1)$; *x*-axis

23. $S(-1, 1)$, $T(1, 4)$, $U(3, 2)$, $V(1, -3)$; $y = x$

Copy each figure. Then complete the figure by drawing the reflection image across the line.

24.

25.

26.

Chemistry

Louis Pasteur (1822–1895) is best known for the pasteurization process, which kills germs in milk. He discovered chemical chirality when he observed that two salt crystals were mirror images of each other.

27. Chemistry In chemistry, *chiral* molecules are mirror images of each other. Although they have similar structures, chiral molecules can have very different properties. For example, the compound R-(+)-limonene smells like oranges, while its mirror image, S-(−)-limonene, smells like lemons. Use the figure and the given line of reflection to draw S-(−)-limonene.

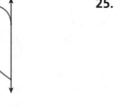

R-(+)-limonene

Each figure shows a preimage and image under a reflection. Copy the figure and draw the line of reflection.

28.

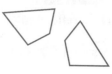

29.

30.

Use arrow notation to describe the mapping of each point when it is reflected across the given line.

31. $(5, 2)$; *x*-axis

32. $(-3, -7)$; *y*-axis

33. $(0, 12)$; *x*-axis

34. $(-3, -6)$; $y = x$

35. $(0, -5)$; $y = x$

36. $(4, 4)$; $y = x$

Real-World Connections

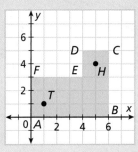

37. The figure shows one hole of a miniature golf course.

    a. Is it possible to hit the ball in a straight line from the tee T to the hole H?

    b. Find the coordinates of H', the reflection of H across $\overline{BC}$.

    c. The point at which a player should aim in order to make a hole in one is the intersection of $\overline{TH'}$ and $\overline{BC}$. What are the coordinates of this point?

H.O.T. **38. Critical Thinking** Sketch the next figure in the sequence below.

Ⱶ Ɒ ꝏ ꜧ ꜵ ꜷ ▽

H.O.T. **39. Critical Thinking** Under a reflection in the coordinate plane, the point $(3, 5)$ is mapped to the point $(5, 3)$. What is the line of reflection? Is this the only possible line of reflection? Explain.

Draw the reflection of the graph of each function across the given line.

40. x-axis

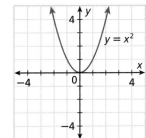

$y = x^2$

41. y-axis

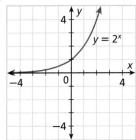

$y = 2^x$

H.O.T. **42. Write About It** Imagine reflecting all the points in a plane across line ℓ. Which points remain fixed under this transformation? That is, for which points is the image the same as the preimage? Explain.

TEST PREP

43. Daryl is using a coordinate plane to plan a garden. He draws a flower bed with vertices $(3, 1)$, $(3, 4)$, $(-2, 4)$, and $(-2, 1)$. Then he creates a second flower bed by reflecting the first one across the x-axis. Which of these is a vertex of the second flower bed?

    Ⓐ $(-2, -4)$

    Ⓑ $(-3, 1)$

    Ⓒ $(2, 1)$

    Ⓓ $(-3, -4)$

©Brian Hagiwara/Brand X Pictures/Getty Images

44. In the reflection shown, the shaded figure is the preimage. Which of these represents the mapping?

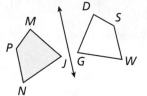

　　Ⓕ *MJNP → DSWG*　　　　Ⓗ *JMPN → GWSD*

　　Ⓖ *DGWS → MJNP*　　　　Ⓙ *PMJN → SDGW*

45. What is the image of the point $(-3, 4)$ when it is reflected across the *y*-axis?

　　Ⓐ $(4, -3)$　　　　　　　Ⓒ $(3, 4)$

　　Ⓑ $(-3, -4)$　　　　　　Ⓓ $(-4, -3)$

CHALLENGE AND EXTEND

Find the coordinates of the image when each point is reflected across the given line.

46. $(4, 2); y = 3$　　　　**47.** $(-3, 2); x = 1$　　　　**48.** $(3, 1); y = x + 2$

FOCUS ON MATHEMATICAL PRACTICES

H.O.T. **49. Analysis** Selina draws a pattern for the quilt she is going to make. As part of the pattern, she reflects a triangle with vertices at (3, 1), (6, 1), and (6, 4) across the line $x = y$ and then reflects this image across the *y*-axis. What are the coordinates of the final image?

H.O.T. **50. Draw Conclusions** Henri takes an original 4 inch by 6 inch photo and enlarges it to be a new photo that is 8 inches by 10 inches.

　　a. Is this a transformation? Explain.

　　b. Is this an example of an isometry? Explain.

H.O.T. **51. Properties** Triangle *JKL* is reflected across the line $y = x$ to form the image *J'K'L'*. Is the distance from *J* to the line $y = x$ the same as the distance from the line $y = x$ to *J'*? Explain how you know.

H.O.T. **52. Communication** Is the transformation shown a reflection? Explain.

H.O.T. **53. Make a Conjecture** An isosceles trapezoid is reflected across a line.

　　a. What type of quadrilateral is the image? Classify it without drawing the figure.

　　b. How can you be sure without drawing the image?

H.O.T. **54. Draw Conclusions** A figure in Quadrant II is reflected across the *x*-axis.

　　a. In what quadrant is the image?

　　b. What conclusion can you draw about the signs of the coordinates of the vertices of the image?

16-3 Translations

Essential Question: How can you identify the effect of a translation on a geometric figure?

Objective
Identify and draw translations.

Vocabulary
translation vector

Who uses this?
Marching band directors use translations to plan their bands' field shows. (See Example 4.)

A translation is a transformation where all the points of a figure are moved the same distance in the same direction. The distance and direction are indicated by a ray called the **translation vector**. A vector is a quantity that has both length and direction, and can be thought of as a line segment with a starting point and an endpoint. A translation is an isometry, so the image of a translated figure is congruent to the preimage.

EXAMPLE 1
MCC9-12.G.CO.4

my.hrw.com

Online Video Tutor

Identifying Translations

Tell whether each transformation appears to be a translation. Explain.

A

No; not all of the points have moved the same distance.

B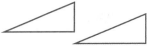

Yes; all of the points have moved the same distance in the same direction.

 CHECK IT OUT!

Tell whether each transformation appears to be a translation.

1a.

1b.

Translate a Figure Using Patty Paper

1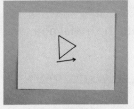

Draw a triangle and a translation vector on a sheet of paper.

2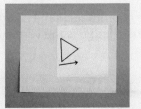

Place a sheet of patty paper on top of the diagram. Trace the triangle and vector.

3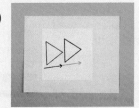

Slide the bottom paper in the direction of the vector until the head of the top vector aligns with the tail of the bottom vector. Trace the triangle.

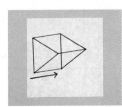

Draw a segment from each vertex of the preimage to the corresponding vertex of the image. Your drawing should show that every segment connecting a point and its image is the same length as the translation vector. These segments are also parallel to the translation vector.

(tr), ©Steve Boyle/NewSport/CORBIS; (cl),(c),(cr),(br), Sam Dudgeon/HMH

Translations

A translation is a transformation along a vector such that each segment joining a point and its image has the same length as the vector and is parallel to the vector.

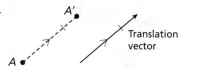

EXAMPLE **2**
MCC9-12.G.CO.5

my.hrw.com

Online Video Tutor

Drawing Translations

Copy the triangle and the translation vector. Draw the translation of the triangle along $\vec{v}$.

Step 1 Draw a line parallel to the vector through each vertex of the triangle.

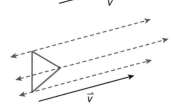

Step 2 Measure the length of the vector. Then, from each vertex mark off this distance in the same direction as the vector, on each of the parallel lines.

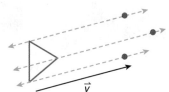

Reading Math

A vector *v* can be represented by the symbol $\vec{v}$.

Step 3 Connect the images of the vertices.

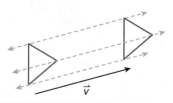

 CHECK IT OUT!

2. Copy the quadrilateral and the translation vector. Draw the translation of the quadrilateral along $\vec{w}$.

Reading Math

The vector form $\langle a, b \rangle$ is called component form.

A vector in the coordinate plane can be written as $\langle a, b \rangle$, where *a* is the horizontal change and *b* is the vertical change from the initial point to the terminal point.

Translations in the Coordinate Plane

HORIZONTAL TRANSLATION ALONG VECTOR $\langle a, 0 \rangle$	VERTICAL TRANSLATION ALONG VECTOR $\langle 0, b \rangle$	GENERAL TRANSLATION ALONG VECTOR $\langle a, b \rangle$
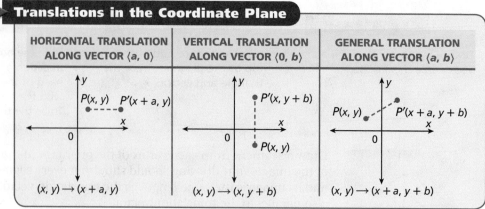		
$(x, y) \rightarrow (x + a, y)$	$(x, y) \rightarrow (x, y + b)$	$(x, y) \rightarrow (x + a, y + b)$

EXAMPLE 3 — Drawing Translations in the Coordinate Plane

MCC9-12.G.CO.2

Translate the triangle with vertices $A(-2, -4)$, $B(-1, -2)$, and $C(-3, 0)$ along the vector $\langle 2, 4 \rangle$.

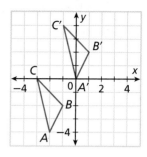

The image of (x, y) is $(x + 2, y + 4)$.

$A(-2, -4) \rightarrow A'(-2 + 2, -4 + 4) = A'(0, 0)$

$B(-1, -2) \rightarrow B'(-1 + 2, -2 + 4) = B'(1, 2)$

$C(-3, 0) \rightarrow C'(-3 + 2, 0 + 4) = C'(-1, 4)$

Graph the preimage and image.

CHECK IT OUT!
3. Translate the quadrilateral with vertices $R(2, 5)$, $S(0, 2)$, $T(1, -1)$, and $U(3, 1)$ along the vector $\langle -3, -3 \rangle$.

EXAMPLE 4 — Entertainment Application

MCC9-12.G.CO.5

In a marching drill, it takes 8 steps to march 5 yards. A drummer starts 8 steps to the left and 8 steps up from the center of the field. She marches 16 steps to the right to her second position. Then she marches 24 steps down the field to her final position. What is the drummer's final position? What single translation vector moves her from the starting position to her final position?

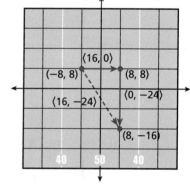

The drummer's starting coordinates are $(-8, 8)$.

Her second position is $(-8 + 16, 8) = (8, 8)$.

Her final position is $(8, 8 - 24) = (8, -16)$.

The vector that moves her directly from her starting position to her final position is $\langle 16, 0 \rangle + \langle 0, -24 \rangle = \langle 16, -24 \rangle$.

CHECK IT OUT!
4. What if...? Suppose another drummer started at the center of the field and marched along the same vectors as above. What would this drummer's final position be?

MCC.MP.1, MCC.MP.6 — MATHEMATICAL PRACTICES

THINK AND DISCUSS

1. Point A' is a *translation* of point A along $\vec{v}$. What is the relationship of $\vec{v}$ to $\overline{AA'}$?

2. $\overline{AB}$ is translated to form $\overline{A'B'}$. Classify quadrilateral $AA'B'B$. Explain your reasoning.

3. GET ORGANIZED Copy and complete the graphic organizer.

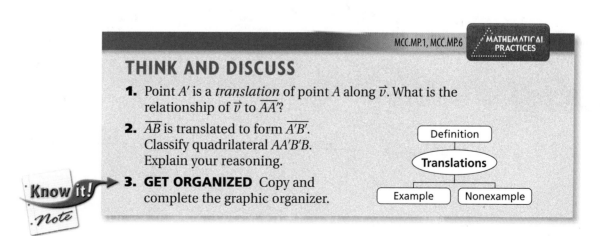

Know it!
.Note

GUIDED PRACTICE

SEE EXAMPLE 1   Tell whether each transformation appears to be a translation.

1.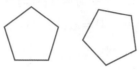

2.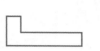

3.

4.

SEE EXAMPLE 2   **Multi-Step** Copy each figure and the translation vector. Draw the translation of the figure along the given vector.

5.

6.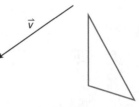

SEE EXAMPLE 3   Translate the figure with the given vertices along the given vector.

7. $A(-4, -4)$, $B(-2, -3)$, $C(-1, 3)$; $\langle 5, 0 \rangle$

8. $R(-3, 1)$, $S(-2, 3)$, $T(2, 3)$, $U(3, 1)$; $\langle 0, -4 \rangle$

9. $J(-2, 2)$, $K(-1, 2)$, $L(-1, -2)$, $M(-3, -1)$; $\langle 3, 2 \rangle$

SEE EXAMPLE 4   10. **Art** The Zulu people of southern Africa are known for their beadwork. To create a typical Zulu pattern, translate the polygon with vertices $(1, 5)$, $(2, 3)$, $(1, 1)$, and $(0, 3)$ along the vector $\langle 0, -4 \rangle$. Translate the image along the same vector. Repeat to generate a pattern. What are the vertices of the fourth polygon in the pattern?

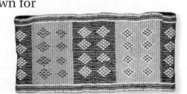

PRACTICE AND PROBLEM SOLVING

Tell whether each transformation appears to be a translation.

Independent Practice

For Exercises	See Example
11–14	1
15–16	2
17–19	3
20	4

11.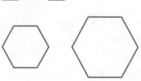

12.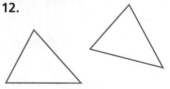

13.

14.

Multi-Step Copy each figure and the translation vector. Draw the translation of the figure along the given vector.

15.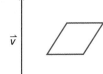

16.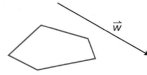

Animation

Each frame of a computer-animated feature represents $\frac{1}{24}$ of a second of film.

Source: www.pixar.com

Translate the figure with the given vertices along the given vector.

17. $P(-1, 2)$, $Q(1, -1)$, $R(3, 1)$, $S(2, 3)$; $\langle -3, 0 \rangle$

18. $A(1, 3)$, $B(-1, 2)$, $C(2, 1)$, $D(4, 2)$; $\langle -3, -3 \rangle$

19. $D(0, 15)$, $E(-10, 5)$, $F(10, -5)$; $\langle 5, -20 \rangle$

20. Animation An animator draws the ladybug shown and then translates it along the vector $\langle 1, 1 \rangle$, followed by a translation of the new image along the vector $\langle 2, 2 \rangle$, followed by a translation of the second image along the vector $\langle 3, 3 \rangle$.

    a. Sketch the ladybug's final position.

    b. What single vector moves the ladybug from its starting position to its final position?

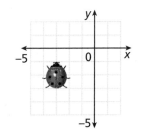

Draw the translation of the graph of each function along the given vector.

21. $\langle 3, 0 \rangle$

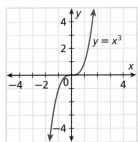

22. $\langle -1, -1 \rangle$

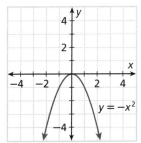

23. Probability The point $P(3, 2)$ is translated along one of the following four vectors chosen at random: $\langle -3, 0 \rangle$, $\langle -1, -4 \rangle$, $\langle 3, -2 \rangle$, and $\langle 2, 3 \rangle$. Find the probability of each of the following.

    a. The image of P is in the fourth quadrant.

    b. The image of P is on an axis.

    c. The image of P is at the origin.

Real-World Connections

24. The figure shows one hole of a miniature golf course and the path of a ball from the tee T to the hole H.

    a. What translation vector represents the path of the ball from T to $\overline{DC}$?

    b. What translation vector represents the path of the ball from $\overline{DC}$ to H?

    c. Show that the sum of these vectors is equal to the vector that represents the straight path from T to H.

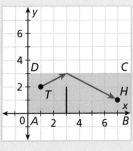

Each figure shows a preimage (blue) and its image (red) under a translation. Copy the figure and draw the vector along which the polygon is translated.

25.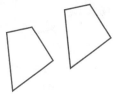

26.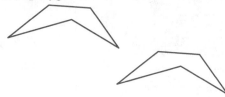

H.O.T. 27. Critical Thinking The points of a plane are translated along the given vector $\overrightarrow{AB}$. Do any points remain fixed under this transformation? That is, are there any points for which the image coincides with the preimage? Explain.

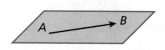

28. **Carpentry** Carpenters use a tool called *adjustable parallels* to set up level work areas and to draw parallel lines. Describe how a carpenter could use this tool to translate a given point along a given vector. What additional tools, if any, would be needed?

Find the vector associated with each translation. Then use arrow notation to describe the mapping of the preimage to the image.

29. the translation that maps point A to point B

30. the translation that maps point B to point A

31. the translation that maps point C to point D

32. the translation that maps point E to point B

33. the translation that maps point C to the origin

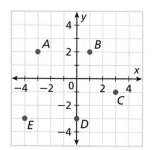

34. **Multi-Step** The rectangle shown is translated two-thirds of the way along one of its diagonals. Find the area of the region where the rectangle and its image overlap.

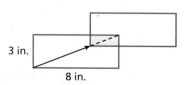

3 in.

8 in.

H.O.T. 35. Write About It Point P is translated along the vector $\langle a, b \rangle$. Explain how to find the distance between point P and its image.

TEST PREP

36. What is the image of $P(1, 3)$ when it is translated along the vector $\langle -3, 5 \rangle$?

   Ⓐ $(-2, 8)$ Ⓑ $(0, 6)$ Ⓒ $(1, 3)$ Ⓓ $(0, 4)$

37. After a translation, the image of $A(-6, -2)$ is $B(-4, -4)$. What is the image of the point $(3, -1)$ after this translation?

   Ⓕ $(-5, 1)$ Ⓖ $(5, -3)$ Ⓗ $(5, 1)$ Ⓙ $(-5, -3)$

38. Which vector translates point Q to point P?

    Ⓐ $\langle -2, -4 \rangle$ Ⓒ $\langle -2, 4 \rangle$

    Ⓑ $\langle 4, -2 \rangle$ Ⓓ $\langle 2, -4 \rangle$

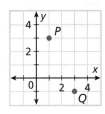

CHALLENGE AND EXTEND

39. The point $M(1, 2)$ is translated along a vector that is parallel to the line $y = 2x + 4$. The translation vector has magnitude $\sqrt{5}$. What are the possible images of point M?

40. A cube has edges of length 2 cm. Point P is translated along $\vec{u}$, $\vec{v}$, and $\vec{w}$ as shown.

    a. Describe a single translation vector that maps point P to point Q.

    b. Find the magnitude of this vector to the nearest hundredth.

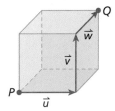

FOCUS ON MATHEMATICAL PRACTICES

H.O.T. 41. Analysis Does this transformation appear to be a translation? Explain why or why not.

H.O.T. 42. Problem Solving Shelly graphs the line $y = x$ and then translates it along the vector $\langle 0, 3 \rangle$.

    a. What are the slopes of the preimage and the image?

    b. What are the y-intercepts of the preimage and the image?

    c. Is this an isometry? How do you know?

H.O.T. 43. Justify Harold draws a translation of triangle ABC where the measure of angle B is 56°. He says that the measure of angle B' is also 56°. Justify his conclusion.

H.O.T. 44. Draw Conclusions The red parabola is the image of the blue parabola.

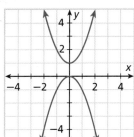

    a. If the image was created by a translation followed by a reflection, describe the transformations that could have taken place.

    b. If the image was created by a reflection followed by a translation, describe the transformations that could have taken place.

H.O.T. 45. Error Analysis The graph of the equation $y = |x|$ is translated so that the V-shape of the graph is moved up 3 units. Deb says the equation of the image is $y = |x| + 3$. Sara says it is $y = |x + 3|$. Who is correct? Use a point on the graph to justify your answer.

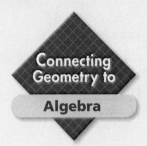

Transformations of Functions

Transformations can be used to graph complicated functions by using the graphs of simpler functions called *parent functions*. The following are examples of parent functions and their graphs.

$y = |x|$ $y = \sqrt{x}$ $y = x^2$

Transformation of Parent Function $y = f(x)$		
Reflection	**Vertical Translation**	**Horizontal Translation**
Across x-axis: $y = -f(x)$	$y = f(x) + k$	$y = f(x - h)$
Across y-axis: $y = f(-x)$	Up k units if $k > 0$	Right h units if $h > 0$
	Down k units if $k < 0$	Left h units if $h < 0$

Example

For the parent function $y = x^2$, write a function rule for the given transformation and graph the preimage and image.

A a reflection across the x-axis
function rule: $y = -x^2$
graph:

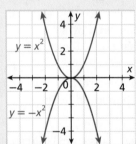

B a translation up 2 units and right 3 units
function rule: $y = (x - 3)^2 + 2$
graph:

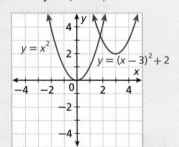

Try This

For each parent function, write a function rule for the given transformation and graph the preimage and image.

1. parent function: $y = x^2$
   transformation: a translation down 1 unit and right 4 units

2. parent function: $y = \sqrt{x}$
   transformation: a reflection across the x-axis

3. parent function: $y = |x|$
   transformation: a translation up 2 units and left 1 unit

16-4 Rotations

 Essential Question: How can you identify the effect of a rotation on a geometric figure?

Objective
Identify and draw rotations.

Who uses this?
Astronomers can use properties of rotations to analyze photos of star trails. (See Exercise 35.)

Remember that a rotation is a transformation that turns a figure around a fixed point, called the center of rotation. A rotation is an isometry, so the image of a rotated figure is congruent to the preimage.

COMMON CORE GPS **EXAMPLE** MCC9-12.G.CO.4

1 **Identifying Rotations**

my.hrw.com

Online Video Tutor

Tell whether each transformation appears to be a rotation. Explain.

A

Yes; the figure appears to be turned around a point.

B

No; the figure appears to be flipped, not turned.

CHECK IT OUT! Tell whether each transformation appears to be a rotation.

1a.   **1b.**

Rotate a Figure Using Patty Paper

1
On a sheet of paper, draw a triangle and a point. The point will be the center of rotation.

2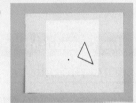
Place a sheet of patty paper on top of the diagram. Trace the triangle and the point.

3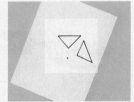
Hold your pencil down on the point and rotate the bottom paper counterclockwise. Trace the triangle.

Remember!
An angle is a figure formed by two rays with a common endpoint.

Draw a segment from each vertex to the center of rotation. Your drawing should show that a point's distance to the center of rotation is equal to its image's distance to the center of rotation. The angle formed by a point, the center of rotation, and the point's image is the angle by which the figure was rotated.

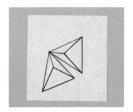

Rotations

A rotation is a transformation about a point P, called the center of rotation, such that each point and its image are the same distance from P, and such that all angles with vertex P formed by a point and its image are congruent. In the figure, $\angle APA'$ is the angle of rotation.

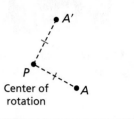

Center of rotation

 EXAMPLE **2**
MCC9-12.G.CO.5

Drawing Rotations

Copy the figure and the angle of rotation. Draw the rotation of the triangle about point P by m$\angle A$.

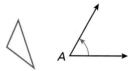

my.hrw.com

Online Video Tutor

Step 1 Draw a segment from each vertex to point P.

Step 2 Draw an angle congruent to $\angle A$ onto each segment. Measure the distance from each vertex to point P and mark off this distance on the corresponding ray to locate the image of each vertex.

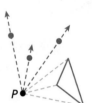

Helpful Hint

Unless otherwise stated, all rotations in this book are counterclockwise.

Step 3 Connect the images of the vertices.

 2. Copy the figure and the angle of rotation. Draw the rotation of the segment about point Q by m$\angle X$.

Rotations in the Coordinate Plane

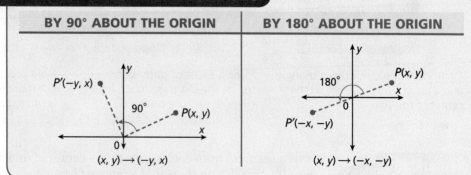

BY 90° ABOUT THE ORIGIN	BY 180° ABOUT THE ORIGIN
$(x, y) \rightarrow (-y, x)$	$(x, y) \rightarrow (-x, -y)$

EXAMPLE 3
MCC9-12.G.CO.2

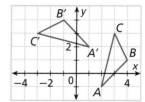

my.hrw.com

Online Video Tutor

Drawing Rotations in the Coordinate Plane

A Rotate △*ABC* with vertices $A(2, -1)$, $B(4, 1)$, and $C(3, 3)$ by 90° about the origin.

The rotation of (x, y) is $(-y, x)$.

$A(2, -1) \rightarrow A'(1, 2)$

$B(4, 1) \rightarrow B'(-1, 4)$

$C(3, 3) \rightarrow C'(-3, 3)$

Graph the preimage and image.

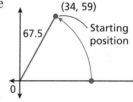

B The London Eye observation wheel has a radius of 67.5 m and takes 30 minutes to make a complete rotation. A car starts at position (34, 59). What are the coordinates of the car's location after 15 minutes?

Step 1 Find the angle of rotation. Fifteen minutes is $\frac{15}{30} = \frac{1}{2}$ of a complete rotation, or $\frac{1}{2}(360°) = 180°$.

Step 2 Draw a diagram to represent the car's starting location at (34, 59).

Step 3 Use the formula for the 180° rotation in the coordinate plane about the origin to find the new coordinates of the car's location.

The rotation of (x, y) is $(-x, -y)$.

$(34, 59) \rightarrow (-34, -59)$

The car's location after 15 minutes is $(-34, -59)$.

3a. Rotate △*ABC* by 180° about the origin.

3b. Find the coordinates of the location of the observation car after 7.5 minutes.

MCC.MP.1 **MATHEMATICAL PRACTICES**

THINK AND DISCUSS

1. Describe the image of a rotation of a figure by an angle of 360°.

2. Point A' is a rotation of point A about point P. What is the relationship of $\overline{AP}$ to $\overline{A'P}$?

3. GET ORGANIZED Copy and complete the graphic organizer.

	Reflection	Translation	Rotation
Definition			
Example			

©Robert Harding Picture Library Ltd/Alamy Photos

Know it! Note

CHECK IT OUT!

GUIDED PRACTICE

SEE EXAMPLE 1

Tell whether each transformation appears to be a rotation.

1.

2.

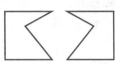

3.

4.

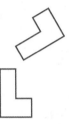

SEE EXAMPLE 2

Copy each figure and the angle of rotation. Draw the rotation of the figure about point P by m∠A.

5.

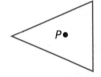

6.

SEE EXAMPLE 3

Rotate the figure with the given vertices about the origin using the given angle of rotation.

7. $A(1, 0)$, $B(3, 2)$, $C(5, 0)$; 90°

8. $J(2, 1)$, $K(4, 3)$, $L(2, 4)$, $M(-1, 2)$; 90°

9. $D(2, 3)$, $E(-1, 2)$, $F(2, 1)$; 180°

10. $P(-1, -1)$, $Q(-4, -2)$, $R(0, -2)$; 180°

PRACTICE AND PROBLEM SOLVING

Independent Practice	
For Exercises	See Example
11–14	1
15–16	2
11–21	3

Tell whether each transformation appears to be a rotation.

11.

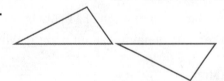

12.

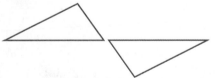

13.

14.

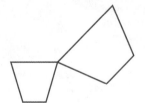

Copy each figure and the angle of rotation. Draw the rotation of the figure about point *P* by m∠*A*.

15.
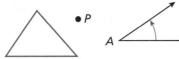

16.
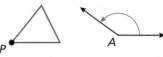

Rotate the figure with the given vertices about the origin using the given angle of rotation.

17. *E*(−1, 2), *F*(3, 1), *G*(2, 3); 90°

18. *A*(−1, 0), *B*(−1, −3), *C*(1, −3), *D*(1, 0); 90°

19. *P*(0, −2), *Q*(2, 0), *R*(3, −3); 180°

20. *L*(2, 0), *M*(−1, −2), *N*(2, −2); 180°

21. Architecture The CN Tower in Toronto, Canada, features a revolving restaurant that takes 72 minutes to complete a full rotation. A table that is 50 feet from the center of the restaurant starts at position (50, 10). What are the coordinates of the table after 18 minutes?

Copy each figure. Then draw the rotation of the figure about the red point using the given angle measure.

22. 90°

23. 180°

24. 180°

25. Point *Q* has coordinates (2, 3). After a rotation about the origin, the image of point *Q* lies on (−2, −3).

    a. Find the angle of rotation.

    b. Find the coordinates of the image of point *Q* after a 90º rotation about the origin.

Rectangle *RSTU* is the image of rectangle *LMNP* under a 180° rotation about point *A*. Name each of the following.

26. the image of point *N*

27. the preimage of point *S*

28. the image of $\overline{MN}$

29. the preimage of $\overline{TU}$

Real-World Connections

30. A miniature golf course includes a hole with a windmill. Players must hit the ball through the opening at the base of the windmill while the blades rotate.

    a. The blades take 20 seconds to make a complete rotation. Through what angle do the blades rotate in 5 seconds?

    b. Find the coordinates of point *A* after 5 seconds. (*Hint:* (4, 3) is the center of rotation.)

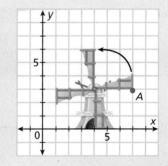

Each figure shows a preimage and its image under a rotation. Copy the figure and locate the center of rotation.

31.

32.

33.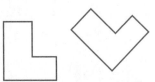

H.O.T. **34. Astronomy** The photograph was made by placing a camera on a tripod and keeping the camera's shutter open for a long time. Because of Earth's rotation, the stars appear to rotate around Polaris, also known as the North Star.

    a. Estimation Estimate the angle of rotation of the stars in the photo.

    b. Estimation Use your result from part **a** to estimate the length of time that the camera's shutter was open. (*Hint:* If the shutter was open for 24 hours, the stars would appear to make one complete rotation around Polaris.)

H.O.T. **35. Estimation** In the diagram, $\triangle ABC \rightarrow \triangle A'B'C'$ under a rotation about point P.

    a. Estimate the angle of rotation.

    b. Explain how you can draw two segments and can then use a protractor to measure the angle of rotation.

    c. Copy the figure. Use the method from part **b** to find the angle of rotation. How does your result compare to your estimate?

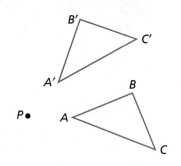

H.O.T. **36. Critical Thinking** A student wrote the following in his math journal. "Under a rotation, every point moves around the center of rotation by the same angle measure. This means that every point moves the same distance." Do you agree? Explain.

Use the figure for Exercises 37–39.

37. Sketch the image of pentagon *ABCDE* under a rotation of 90° about the origin. Give the vertices of the image.

38. Sketch the image of pentagon *ABCDE* under a rotation of 180° about the origin. Give the vertices of the image.

H.O.T. **39. Write About It** Is the image of *ABCDE* under a rotation of 180° about the origin the same as its image under a reflection across the *x*-axis? Explain your reasoning.

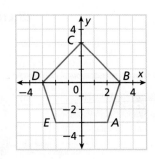

TEST PREP

40. What is the image of the point $(-2, 5)$ when it is rotated about the origin by 90°?

　Ⓐ $(-5, 2)$　　　Ⓑ $(5, -2)$　　　Ⓒ $(-5, -2)$　　　Ⓓ $(2, -5)$

41. The six cars of a Ferris wheel are located at the vertices of a regular hexagon. Which rotation about point *P* maps car *A* to car *C*?

　Ⓕ 60°　　Ⓖ 90°　　Ⓗ 120°　　Ⓙ 135°

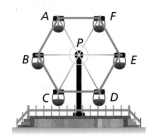

42. **Gridded Response** Under a rotation about the origin, the point $(-3, 4)$ is mapped to the point $(3, -4)$. What is the measure of the angle of rotation?

CHALLENGE AND EXTEND

H.O.T. **43.** **Engineering** Gears are used to change the speed and direction of rotating parts in pieces of machinery. In the diagram, suppose gear B makes one complete rotation in the counterclockwise direction. Give the angle of rotation and direction for the rotation of gear A. Explain how you got your answer.

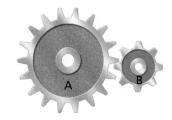

FOCUS ON MATHEMATICAL PRACTICES

H.O.T. **44.** **Reasoning** Cole rotates the point $(3, 4)$ about the origin by 270°. What is the image of this point? Explain how you found your answer.

H.O.T. **45.** **Make a Conjecture** Tell whether each figure appears to be a rotation. Explain. If it is not, name the translation it appears to be.

　a.

　b.

H.O.T. **46.** **Problem Solving** Rotate the figure with vertices $(1, 1), (5, 1), (4, 3)$ 90° about the origin. What are the coordinates of the image?

H.O.T. **47.** **Communication** What are the formal mathematical terms for flips, turns, and slides?

H.O.T. **48.** **Error Analysis** Landon says this figure has been rotated about the origin 90°. Garrett says that it has been rotated 270°. Who is correct? Explain.

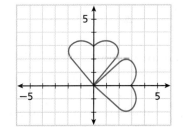

H.O.T. **49.** **Number Sense** The figure *ABCD* is rotated about point *P* to form the image *A'B'C'D'*. Which distance is equal to *PA*?

H.O.T. **50.** **Modeling** To make the design for a tile border, Alexie rotates this figure 180° about the red point. Copy the figure and then draw the image.

Ready to Go On?

✓ **16-1** **Transformations in the Coordinate Plane**

1. A graphic designer used the translation $(x, y) \rightarrow (x - 3, y + 2)$ to transform square *HJKL*. Find the coordinates and graph the image *H'J'K'L'* of square *HJKL*.

2. A figure has vertices at $X(1, 1)$, $Y(3, 1)$, and $Z(3, 4)$. After a transformation, the image of the figure has vertices at $X'(-1, -1)$, $Y'(-3, -1)$, and $Z'(-3, -4)$. Graph the preimage and image. Then identify the transformation.

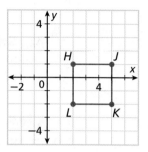

✓ **16-2** **Reflections**

Copy each figure and the line of reflection. Draw the reflection of the figure across the line.

3.

4.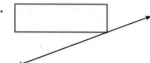

Reflect the figure with the given vertices across the given line.

5. $E(-3, 2)$, $F(0, 2)$, $G(-2, 5)$; *x*-axis

6. $J(2, -1)$, $K(4, -2)$, $L(4, -3)$, $M(2, -3)$; *y*-axis

✓ **16-3** **Translations**

7. A landscape architect represents a flower bed by a polygon with vertices $(1, 0)$, $(4, 0)$, $(4, 2)$, and $(1, 2)$. She decides to move the flower bed to a new location by translating it along the vector $\langle -4, -3 \rangle$. Draw the flower bed in its final position.

Translate the figure with the given vertices along the given vector.

8. $R(1, -1)$, $S(1, -3)$, $T(4, -3)$, $U(4, -1)$; $\langle -5, 2 \rangle$

9. $A(-4, -1)$, $B(-3, 2)$, $C(-1, -2)$; $\langle 6, 0 \rangle$

✓ **16-4** **Rotations**

Rotate the figure with the given vertices about the origin using the given angle of rotation.

10. $A(1, 0)$, $B(4, 1)$, $C(3, 2)$; 180°

11. $R(-2, 0)$, $S(-2, 4)$, $T(-3, 4)$, $U(-3, 0)$; 90°

Rotate the figure with the given vertices about the origin using the given angle of rotation.

12. $A(1, 3)$, $B(4, 1)$, $C(4, 4)$; 90°

13. $A(1, 3)$, $B(4, 1)$, $C(4, 4)$; 180°

PARCC Assessment Readiness

Selected Response

1. A designer used the translation $(x, y) \rightarrow (x + 3, y - 3)$ to transform a triangular-shaped pin *ABC*. Find the coordinates and draw the image of △*ABC*. Which point is a vertex of the image?

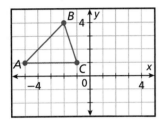

- Ⓐ (−4, 4)
- Ⓑ (−5, 1)
- Ⓒ (1, 1)
- Ⓓ (1, −1)

2. △*QRS* has vertices at *Q*(3, 5), *R*(3, 9), and *S*(7, 5). Which of these points is a vertex of the image of △*QRS* after the translation $(x, y) \rightarrow (x - 7, y - 6)$?

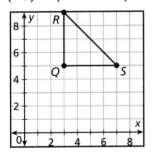

- Ⓕ (−4, 3)
- Ⓖ (0, 0)
- Ⓗ (4, 1)
- Ⓙ (4, −3)

3. △*ABC* is reflected across the *x*-axis. Then its image is rotated 180° about the origin. What are the coordinates of the image of point *B* after the reflection?

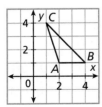

- Ⓐ (−4, −1)
- Ⓑ (−1, 4)
- Ⓒ (1, −4)
- Ⓓ (4, −1)

4. What is the image of the following figure after rotating it clockwise by 90°?

- Ⓕ
- Ⓖ
- Ⓗ
- Ⓙ

Mini-Task

5. The picture below shows half of a stenciled design. The full design should resemble a sun. Name two transformations that can be performed on the image so that the image and its preimage form a complete picture. Be as specific as possible, referring to *L* and *P*.

17 Combined Transformations and Symmetry

Contents

The Common Core Georgia Performance Standards for Mathematical Practice describe varieties of expertise that all students should seek to develop. Opportunities to develop these practices are integrated throughout this program.

1 Make sense of problems and persevere in solving them.

2 Reason abstractly and quantitatively.

3 Construct viable arguments and critique the reasoning of others.

4 Model with mathematics.

5 Use appropriate tools strategically.

6 Attend to precision.

7 Look for and make use of structure.

8 Look for and express regularity in repeated reasoning.

Unpacking the Standards

Understanding the standards and the vocabulary terms in the standards will help you know exactly what you are expected to learn in this chapter.

 MCC9-12.G.CO.3

Given a rectangle, parallelogram, trapezoid, or regular polygon, describe the rotations and reflections that carry it onto itself.

Key Vocabulary

rectangle (rectángulo)
A quadrilateral with four right angles.

parallelogram (paralelogramo)
A quadrilateral with two pairs of parallel sides.

trapezoid (trapecio)
A quadrilateral with exactly one pair of parallel sides.

regular polygon (polígono regular)
A polygon that is both equilateral and equiangular.

What It Means For You

The rotations and reflections that carry a figure onto itself determine what kind of symmetry, if any, that the figure has. Reflections determine line symmetry, and rotations determine rotational symmetry.

EXAMPLE　　Line symmetry and rotational symmetry

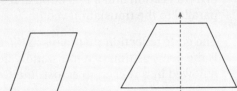 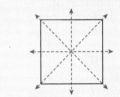

Parallelogram:

no line symmetry

180° rotational symmetry

Isosceles Trapezoid:

1 line of symmetry

no rotational symmetry

Square:

4 lines of symmetry

90° rotational symmetry

17-1 Compositions of Transformations

? **Essential Question:** How can you identify the effect of a composition of transformations on a geometric figure?

Objectives
Apply theorems about isometries.

Identify and draw compositions of transformations, such as glide reflections.

Vocabulary
composition of transformations
glide reflection

Why learn this?
Compositions of transformations can be used to describe chess moves. (See Exercise 11.)

A **composition of transformations** is one transformation followed by another. For example, a **glide reflection** is the composition of a translation and a reflection across a line parallel to the translation vector.

The glide reflection that maps △*JKL* to △*J'K'L'* is the composition of a translation along $\vec{v}$ followed by a reflection across line ℓ.

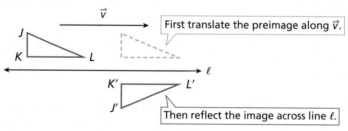

First translate the preimage along $\vec{v}$.

Then reflect the image across line ℓ.

The image after each transformation is congruent to the previous image. By the Transitive Property of Congruence, the final image is congruent to the preimage. This leads to the following theorem.

Know it! *Note*

Theorem 17-1-1

A composition of two isometries is an isometry.

COMMON CORE GPS MCC9-12.G.CO.5 **EXAMPLE 1** **Drawing Compositions of Isometries**

my.hrw.com

Online Video Tutor

Draw the result of the composition of isometries.

A Reflect △*ABC* across line ℓ and then translate it along $\vec{v}$.

Step 1 Draw △*A'B'C'*, the reflection image of △*ABC*.

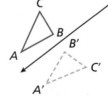

Step 2 Translate △*A'B'C'* along $\vec{v}$ to find the final image, △*A"B"C"*.

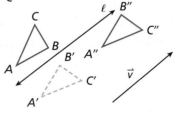

©George B. Diebold/CORBIS

B △RST has vertices R(1, 2), S(1, 4), and T(-3, 4). Rotate △RST 90° about the origin and then reflect it across the y-axis.

Step 1 The rotation image of (x, y) is (-y, x).
R(1, 2) → R'(-2, 1), S(1, 4) → S'(-4, 1), and T(-3, 4) → T'(-4, -3).

Step 2 The reflection image of (x, y) is (-x, y).
R'(-2, 1) → R"(2, 1), S'(-4, 1) → S"(4, 1), and T'(-4, -3) → T"(4, -3).

Step 3 Graph the preimage and images.

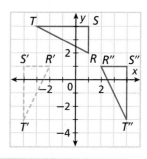

 1. △JKL has vertices J(1, -2), K(4, -2), and L(3, 0). Reflect △JKL across the x-axis and then rotate it 180° about the origin.

Theorem 17-1-2

The composition of two reflections across two parallel lines is equivalent to a translation.

- The translation vector is perpendicular to the lines.
- The length of the translation vector is twice the distance between the lines.

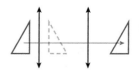

The composition of two reflections across two intersecting lines is equivalent to a rotation.

- The center of rotation is the intersection of the lines.
- The angle of rotation is twice the measure of the angle formed by the lines.

COMMON CORE GPS
MCC9-12.G.CO.5

EXAMPLE 2

my.hrw.com

Online Video Tutor

Art Application

Tabitha is creating a design for an art project. She reflects a figure across line ℓ and then reflects the image across line m. Describe a single transformation that moves the figure from its starting position to its final position.

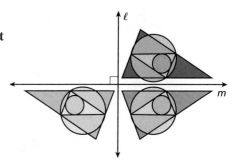

By Theorem 17-1-2, the composition of two reflections across intersecting lines is equivalent to a rotation about the point of intersection. Since the lines are perpendicular, they form a 90° angle. By Theorem 17-1-2, the angle of rotation is 2 · 90° = 180°.

 2. What if...? Suppose Tabitha reflects the figure across line n and then the image across line p. Describe a single transformation that is equivalent to the two reflections.

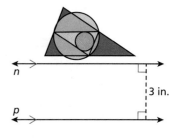

3 in.

Theorem 17-1-3

Any translation or rotation is equivalent to a composition of two reflections.

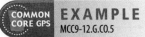
Describing Transformations in Terms of Reflections

Copy each figure and draw two lines of reflection that produce an equivalent transformation.

A translation: $\triangle ABC \rightarrow \triangle A'B'C'$

> **Step 1** Draw $\overline{AA'}$ and locate the midpoint M of $\overline{AA'}$.
>
> **Step 2** Draw the perpendicular bisectors of $\overline{AM}$ and $\overline{A'M}$.

Remember!

To draw the perpendicular bisector of a segment, use a ruler to locate the midpoint, and then use a right angle to draw a perpendicular line. To draw the angle bisector of an angle, use a protractor to find the measure of the angle and then use a ruler to draw a ray from the vertex through the point that represents half the measure.

B rotation with center P: $\triangle DEF \rightarrow \triangle D'E'F'$

> **Step 1** Draw $\angle DPD'$. Draw the angle bisector $\overrightarrow{PX}$.
>
> **Step 2** Draw the bisectors of $\angle DPX$ and $\angle D'PX$.

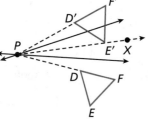

CHECK IT OUT!

3. Copy the figure showing the translation that maps $LMNP \rightarrow L'M'N'P'$. Draw the lines of reflection that produce an equivalent transformation.

MCC.MP.1, MCC.MP.6 — **MATHEMATICAL PRACTICES**

THINK AND DISCUSS

1. Which theorem explains why the image of a rectangle that is translated and then rotated is congruent to the preimage?

2. Point A' is a glide reflection of point A along $\vec{v}$ and across line ℓ. What is the relationship between $\vec{v}$ and ℓ? Explain the steps you would use to draw a glide reflection.

3. GET ORGANIZED Copy and complete the graphic organizer. In each box, describe an equivalent transformation and sketch an example.

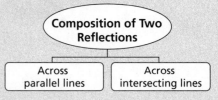

Composition of Two Reflections
- Across parallel lines
- Across intersecting lines

GUIDED PRACTICE

1. **Vocabulary** Explain the steps you would use to draw a *glide reflection*.

SEE EXAMPLE 1   **Draw the result of each composition of isometries.**

2. Translate △*DEF* along $\vec{u}$ and then reflect it across line ℓ.

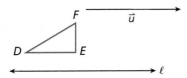

3. Reflect rectangle *PQRS* across line *m* and then translate it along $\vec{v}$.

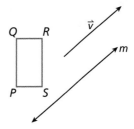

4. △*ABC* has vertices $A(1, -1)$, $B(4, -1)$, and $C(3, 2)$. Reflect △*ABC* across the *y*-axis and then translate it along the vector $\langle 0, -2 \rangle$.

SEE EXAMPLE 2

5. **Sports** To create the opening graphics for a televised football game, an animator reflects a picture of a football helmet across line ℓ. She then reflects its image across line *m*, which intersects line ℓ at a 50° angle. Describe a single transformation that moves the helmet from its starting position to its final position.

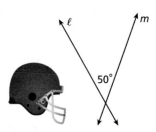

SEE EXAMPLE 3   **Copy each figure and draw two lines of reflection that produce an equivalent transformation.**

6. translation:
△*EFG* → △*E'F'G'*

7. rotation with center *P*:
△*ABC* → △*A'B'C'*

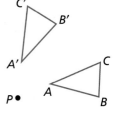

PRACTICE AND PROBLEM SOLVING

Draw the result of each composition of isometries.

8. Translate △*RST* along $\vec{u}$ and then translate it along $\vec{v}$.

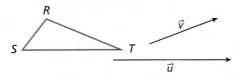

9. Rotate △*ABC* 90° about point *P* and then reflect it across line ℓ.

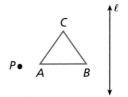

10. △*GHJ* has vertices $G(1, -1)$, $H(3, 1)$, and $J(3, -2)$. Reflect △*GHJ* across the line $y = x$ and then reflect it across the *x*-axis.

11. Games In chess, a knight moves in the shape of the letter L. The piece moves two spaces horizontally or vertically. Then it turns 90° in either direction and moves one more space.

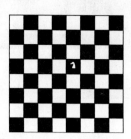

   a. Describe a knight's move as a composition of transformations.

   b. Copy the chessboard with the knight. Label all the positions the knight can reach in one move.

   c. Label all the positions the knight can reach in two moves.

Copy each figure and draw two lines of reflection that produce an equivalent transformation.

12. translation:
   $ABCD \rightarrow A'B'C'D'$

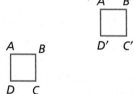

13. rotation with center Q:
   $\triangle JKL \rightarrow \triangle J'K'L'$

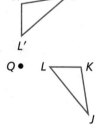

H.O.T. 14. /// **ERROR ANALYSIS** /// The segment with endpoints $A(4, 2)$ and $B(2, 1)$ is reflected across the y-axis. The image is reflected across the x-axis. What transformation is equivalent to the composition of these two reflections? Which solution is incorrect? Explain the error.

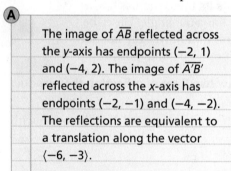

Ⓐ The image of $\overline{AB}$ reflected across the y-axis has endpoints $(-2, 1)$ and $(-4, 2)$. The image of $\overline{A'B'}$ reflected across the x-axis has endpoints $(-2, -1)$ and $(-4, -2)$. The reflections are equivalent to a translation along the vector $\langle -6, -3 \rangle$.

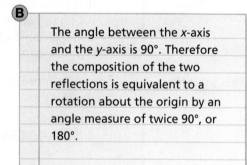

Ⓑ The angle between the x-axis and the y-axis is 90°. Therefore the composition of the two reflections is equivalent to a rotation about the origin by an angle measure of twice 90°, or 180°.

15. Equilateral $\triangle ABC$ is reflected across $\overline{AB}$. Then its image is translated along $\overrightarrow{BC}$. Copy $\triangle ABC$ and draw its final image.

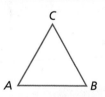

Tell whether each statement is sometimes, always, or never true.

16. The composition of two reflections is equivalent to a rotation.

17. An isometry changes the size of a figure.

18. The composition of two isometries is an isometry.

19. A rotation is equivalent to a composition of two reflections.

H.O.T. 20. Critical Thinking Given a composition of reflections across two parallel lines, does the order of the reflections matter? For example, does reflecting $\triangle ABC$ across m and then its image across n give the same result as reflecting $\triangle ABC$ across n and then its image across m? Explain.

21. Write About It Under a glide reflection, $\triangle RST \rightarrow \triangle R'S'T'$. The vertices of $\triangle RST$ are $R(-3, -2)$, $S(-1, -2)$, and $T(-1, 0)$. The vertices of $\triangle R'S'T'$ are $R'(2, 2)$, $S'(4, 2)$, and $T'(4, 0)$. Describe the reflection and translation that make up the glide reflection.

Real-World Connections

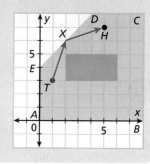

22. The figure shows one hole of a miniature golf course where T is the tee and H is the hole.

a. Yuriko makes a hole in one as shown by the red arrows. Write the ball's path as a composition of translations.

b. Find a different way to make a hole in one, and write the ball's path as a composition of translations.

TEST PREP

23. $\triangle ABC$ is reflected across the y-axis. Then its image is rotated 90° about the origin. What are the coordinates of the final image of point A under this composition of transformations?

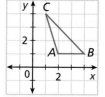

    (A) $(-1, -2)$ (B) $(-2, 1)$ (C) $(1, 2)$ (D) $(-2, -1)$

24. Which composition of transformations maps $\triangle ABC$ into the fourth quadrant?

    (F) Reflect across the x-axis and then reflect across the y-axis.

    (G) Rotate about the origin by 180° and then reflect across the y-axis.

    (H) Translate along the vector $\langle -5, 0 \rangle$ and then rotate about the origin by 90°.

    (J) Rotate about the origin by 90° and then translate along the vector $\langle 1, -2 \rangle$.

25. Which is equivalent to the composition of two translations?

    (A) Reflection   (B) Rotation   (C) Translation   (D) Glide reflection

CHALLENGE AND EXTEND

26. The point $A(3, 1)$ is rotated 90° about the point $P(-1, 2)$ and then reflected across the line $y = 5$. Find the coordinates of the image A'.

27. For any two congruent figures in a plane, one can be transformed to the other by a composition of no more than three reflections. Copy the figure. Show how to find a composition of three reflections that maps $\triangle MNP$ to $\triangle M'N'P'$.

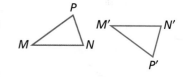

28. A figure in the coordinate plane is reflected across the line $y = x + 1$ and then across the line $y = x + 3$. Find a translation vector that is equivalent to the composition of the reflections. Write the vector in component form.

FOCUS ON MATHEMATICAL PRACTICES

H.O.T. 29. Communication Describe the two transformations that make up a glide reflection.

H.O.T. 30. Problem Solving A figure is reflected across the x-axis and the resulting image is then reflected across the y-axis. Describe a single transformation that is equivalent to the composition of these two reflections. Explain.

H.O.T. 31. Draw Conclusions A figure is reflected across the line $x = 2$ and the resulting image is then reflected across the line $x = 5$. Where is the image in comparison to the preimage? How do you know?

17-2 Symmetry

? Essential Question: How can you identify and describe symmetry in a geometric figure?

Objective
Identify and describe symmetry in geometric figures.

Vocabulary
symmetry
line symmetry
line of symmetry
rotational symmetry

Who uses this?
Marine biologists use symmetry to classify diatoms.

Diatoms are microscopic algae that are found in aquatic environments. Scientists use a system that was developed in the 1970s to classify diatoms based on their *symmetry*.

A figure has **symmetry** if there is a transformation of the figure such that the image coincides with the preimage.

Line Symmetry

A figure has **line symmetry** (or reflection symmetry) if it can be reflected across a line so that the image coincides with the preimage. The **line of symmetry** (also called the axis of symmetry) divides the figure into two congruent halves.

COMMON CORE GPS
MCC9-12.G.CO.3

EXAMPLE 1

Identifying Line Symmetry

Tell whether each figure has line symmetry. If so, copy the shape and draw all lines of symmetry.

A   yes; one line of symmetry

my.hrw.com

Online Video Tutor

B 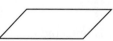   no line symmetry

C   yes; five lines of symmetry

✓ CHECK IT OUT!   Tell whether each figure has line symmetry. If so, copy the shape and draw all lines of symmetry.

1a.   **1b.** **B**   **1c.**

(tr), Jan Hinsch/Photo Researchers, Inc.; (br), ©One Mile Up, Inc

Rotational Symmetry

A figure has **rotational symmetry** (or *radial symmetry*) if it can be rotated about a point by an angle greater than 0° and less than 360° so that the image coincides with the preimage.

The *angle of rotational symmetry* is the smallest angle through which a figure can be rotated to coincide with itself. The number of times the figure coincides with itself as it rotates through 360° is called the *order* of the rotational symmetry.

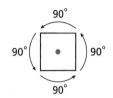

Angle of rotational symmetry: 90°
Order: 4

COMMON CORE GPS
MCC9-12.G.CO.3

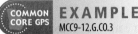

EXAMPLE 2

 my.hrw.com

Online Video Tutor

Identifying Rotational Symmetry

Tell whether each figure has rotational symmetry. If so, give the angle of rotational symmetry and the order of the symmetry.

A

yes; 180°;
order: 2

B

no rotational
symmetry

C

yes; 60°;
order: 6

 CHECK IT OUT! Tell whether each figure has rotational symmetry. If so, give the angle of rotational symmetry and the order of the symmetry.

2a.

2b.
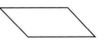

2c.

COMMON CORE GPS
MCC9-12.G.CO.3

EXAMPLE 3

 my.hrw.com

Online Video Tutor

Biology Application

Describe the symmetry of each diatom. Copy the shape and draw any lines of symmetry. If there is rotational symmetry, give the angle and order.

A

line symmetry and rotational symmetry; angle of rotational symmetry: 180°; order: 2

B
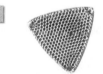

line symmetry and rotational symmetry; angle of rotational symmetry: 120°; order: 3

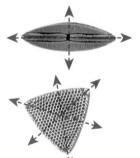

 CHECK IT OUT! Describe the symmetry of each diatom. Copy the shape and draw any lines of symmetry. If there is rotational symmetry, give the angle and order.

3a.

3b.

A three-dimensional figure has *plane symmetry* if a plane can divide the figure into two congruent reflected halves.

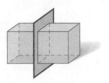
Plane symmetry

A three-dimensional figure has *symmetry about an axis* if there is a line about which the figure can be rotated (by an angle greater than 0° and less than 360°) so that the image coincides with the preimage.

Symmetry about an axis

Identifying Symmetry in Three Dimensions

Tell whether each figure has plane symmetry, symmetry about an axis, or neither.

A trapezoidal prism

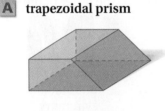

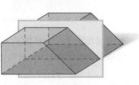

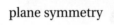

plane symmetry

B equilateral triangular prism

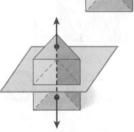

plane symmetry and symmetry about an axis

CHECK IT OUT!

Tell whether each figure has plane symmetry, symmetry about an axis, or no symmetry.

4a. cone

4b. pyramid

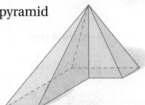

MCC.MP.6

MATHEMATICAL PRACTICES

THINK AND DISCUSS

1. Explain how you could use scissors and paper to cut out a shape that has line symmetry.

2. Describe how you can find the angle of rotational symmetry for a regular polygon with *n* sides.

3. **GET ORGANIZED** Copy and complete the graphic organizer. In each region, draw a figure with the given type of symmetry.

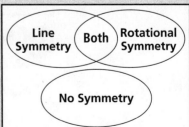

Line Symmetry | Both | Rotational Symmetry

No Symmetry

Know it! Note

my.hrw.com
Homework Help

GUIDED PRACTICE

Vocabulary Apply the vocabulary from this lesson to answer each question.

1. Describe the *line of symmetry* of an isosceles triangle.

2. The capital letter T has ___?___ . (*line symmetry* or *rotational symmetry*)

SEE EXAMPLE **1** Tell whether each figure has line symmetry. If so, copy the shape and draw all lines of symmetry.

3.

4.

5.

SEE EXAMPLE **2** Tell whether each figure has rotational symmetry. If so, give the angle of rotational symmetry and the order of the symmetry.

6. S

7.

8.

SEE EXAMPLE **3**

9. **Architecture** The Pentagon in Alexandria, Virginia, is the world's largest office building. Copy the shape of the building and draw all lines of symmetry. Give the angle and order of rotational symmetry.

SEE EXAMPLE **4** Tell whether each figure has plane symmetry, symmetry about an axis, or neither.

10. prism

11. cylinder

12. rectangular prism

PRACTICE AND PROBLEM SOLVING

| Independent Practice | |
For Exercises	See Example
13–15	1
16–18	2
19	3
20–22	4

Tell whether each figure has line symmetry. If so, copy the shape and draw all lines of symmetry.

13.

14.

15.

Tell whether each figure has rotational symmetry. If so, give the angle of rotational symmetry and the order of the symmetry.

16.

17.

18.

19. **Art** *Op art* is a style of art that uses optical effects to create an impression of movement in a painting or sculpture. The painting at right, *Vega-Tek*, by Victor Vasarely, is an example of op art. Sketch the shape in the painting and draw any lines of symmetry. If there is rotational symmetry, give the angle and order.

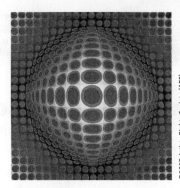

©2007 Artists Rights Society (ARS), New York/ADAGP, Paris

Tell whether each figure has plane symmetry, symmetry about an axis, or neither.

20. sphere

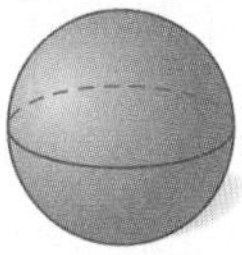

21. triangular pyramid

22. torus

Draw a triangle with the following number of lines of symmetry. Then classify the triangle.

23. exactly one line of symmetry

24. three lines of symmetry

25. no lines of symmetry

Data Analysis The graph shown, called the *standard normal curve*, is used in statistical analysis. The area under the curve is 1 square unit. There is a vertical line of symmetry at $x = 0$. The areas of the shaded regions are indicated on the graph.

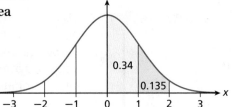

26. Find the area under the curve for $x > 0$.

27. Find the area under the curve for $x > 2$.

28. If a point under the curve is selected at random, what is the probability that the x-value of the point will be between -1 and 1?

Tell whether the figure with the given vertices has line symmetry and/or rotational symmetry. Give the angle and order if there is rotational symmetry. Draw the figure and any lines of symmetry.

29. $A(-2, 2), B(2, 2), C(1, -2), D(-1, -2)$

30. $R(-3, 3), S(3, 3), T(3, -3), U(-3, -3)$

31. $J(4, 4), K(-2, 2), L(2, -2)$

32. $A(3, 1), B(0, 2), C(-3, 1), D(-3, -1), E(0, -2), F(3, -1)$

33. **Art** The Chokwe people of Angola are known for their traditional sand designs. These complex drawings are traced out to illustrate stories that are told at evening gatherings. Classify the symmetry of the Chokwe design shown.

Graph each function. Tell whether the graph has line symmetry and/or rotational symmetry. If there is rotational symmetry, give the angle and order. Write the equations of any lines of symmetry.

34. $y = x^2$

35. $y = (x - 2)^2$

36. $y = x^3$

(tr), (c) ARS, NY/Art Resource, NY

37. This woodcut, entitled *Circle Limit III*, was made by Dutch artist M. C. Escher.

  a. Does the woodcut have line symmetry? If so, describe the lines of symmetry. If not, explain why not.

  b. Does the woodcut have rotational symmetry? If so, give the angle and order of the symmetry. If not, explain why not.

  c. Does your answer to part **b** change if color is not taken into account? Explain.

Classify the quadrilateral that meets the given conditions. First make a conjecture and then verify your conjecture by drawing a figure.

38. two lines of symmetry perpendicular to the sides and order-2 rotational symmetry

39. no line symmetry and order-2 rotational symmetry

40. two lines of symmetry through opposite vertices and order-2 rotational symmetry

41. four lines of symmetry and order-4 rotational symmetry

42. one line of symmetry through a pair of opposite vertices and no rotational symmetry

43. Physics High-speed photography makes it possible to analyze the physics behind a water splash. When a drop lands in a bowl of liquid, the splash forms a crown of evenly spaced points. What is the angle of rotational symmetry for a crown with 24 points?

H.O.T. **44. Critical Thinking** What can you conclude about a rectangle that has four lines of symmetry? Explain.

45. Geography The Isle of Man is an island in the Irish Sea. The island's symbol is a *triskelion* that consists of three running legs radiating from the center. Describe the symmetry of the triskelion.

46. Critical Thinking Draw several examples of figures that have two perpendicular lines of symmetry. What other type of symmetry do these figures have? Make a conjecture based on your observation.

Each figure shows part of a shape with a center of rotation and a given rotational symmetry. Copy and complete each figure.

47. order 4

48. order 6

49. order 2

H.O.T. **50. Write About It** Explain the connection between the angle of rotational symmetry and the order of the rotational symmetry. That is, if you know one of these, explain how you can find the other.

51. What is the order of rotational symmetry for the hexagon shown?

     Ⓐ 2   Ⓑ 3   Ⓒ 4   Ⓓ 6

52. Which of these figures has exactly four lines of symmetry?

     Ⓕ Regular octagon   Ⓗ Isosceles triangle

     Ⓖ Equilateral triangle   Ⓙ Square

53. Consider the graphs of the following equations. Which graph has the *y*-axis as a line of symmetry?

     Ⓐ $y = (x - 3)^2$ Ⓑ $y = x^3$ Ⓒ $y = x^2 - 3$ Ⓓ $y = |x + 3|$

54. Donnell designed a garden plot that has rotational symmetry, but not line symmetry. Which of these could be the shape of the plot?

     Ⓕ   Ⓖ   Ⓗ   Ⓙ

CHALLENGE AND EXTEND

55. A regular polygon has an angle of rotational symmetry of 5°. How many sides does the polygon have?

 56. A polygon with *n* sides is called an *n*-gon. How many lines of symmetry does a regular *n*-gon have if *n* is even? if *n* is odd? Explain your reasoning.

Give the number of axes of symmetry for each regular solid. Describe all axes of symmetry.

57. cube   **58.** tetrahedron   **59.** octahedron

FOCUS ON MATHEMATICAL PRACTICES

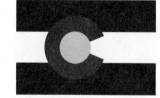

 60. Make a Conjecture Describe any lines of symmetry in this design for the state flag of Colorado. What changes could be made to this design in order for it to have more types of symmetry?

 61. Analysis Give the angle of rotational symmetry and the order of the symmetry for this letter. How many lines of symmetry does the letter have?

 62. Analysis Tell whether the figure with vertices at $(-1, -1)$, $(-4, -1)$, $(-4, -4)$, $(-1, -4)$ has line symmetry, rotational symmetry, or both, and describe any symmetry.

 63. Modeling Describe any symmetry of the graph of $y = |x|$.

 64. Make a Conjecture A certain figure has an order of rotational symmetry of 9. What would you predict for the angle of rotational symmetry? Explain.

 65. Properties A bass drum has a cylindrical shape, as shown. Does it have plane symmetry, symmetry about an axis, both, or neither?

17-3 Tessellations

Essential Question: How can you use transformations to draw tessellations?

Objectives

Use transformations to draw tessellations.

Identify regular and semiregular tessellations and figures that will tessellate.

Vocabulary

translation symmetry
frieze pattern
glide reflection symmetry
tessellation
regular tessellation
semiregular tessellation

Who uses this?

Repeating patterns play an important role in traditional Native American art.

A pattern has **translation symmetry** if it can be translated along a vector so that the image coincides with the preimage. A **frieze pattern** is a pattern that has translation symmetry along a line.

Both of the frieze patterns shown below have translation symmetry. The pattern on the right also has *glide reflection symmetry*. A pattern with **glide reflection symmetry** coincides with its image after a glide reflection.

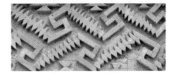

COMMON CORE GPS
MCC9-12.G.CO.5

EXAMPLE 1

Art Application

my.hrw.com

Online Video Tutor

Identify the symmetry in each frieze pattern.

A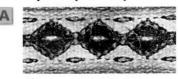

translation symmetry and glide reflection symmetry

B

translation symmetry

CHECK IT OUT!

Identify the symmetry in each frieze pattern.

1a.

1b.

A **tessellation**, or *tiling*, is a repeating pattern that completely covers a plane with no gaps or overlaps. The measures of the angles that meet at each vertex must add up to 360°.

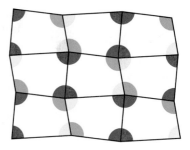

In the tessellation shown, each angle of the quadrilateral occurs once at each vertex. Because the angle measures of any quadrilateral add to 360°, any quadrilateral can be used to tessellate the plane. Four copies of the quadrilateral meet at each vertex.

The angle measures of any triangle add up to 180°. This means that any triangle can be used to tessellate a plane. Six copies of the triangle meet at each vertex, as shown.

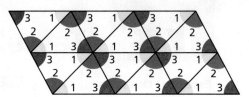

$$m\angle 1 + m\angle 2 + m\angle 3 = 180°$$
$$m\angle 1 + m\angle 2 + m\angle 3 + m\angle 1 + m\angle 2 + m\angle 3 = 360°$$

COMMON CORE GPS
EXAMPLE 2
MCC9-12.G.CO.5

my.hrw.com

Online Video Tutor

Using Transformations to Create Tessellations

Copy the given figure and use it to create a tessellation.

A

Step 1 Rotate the triangle 180° about the midpoint of one side.

Step 2 Translate the resulting pair of triangles to make a row of triangles.

Step 3 Translate the row of triangles to make a tessellation.

B

Step 1 Rotate the quadrilateral 180° about the midpoint of one side.

Step 2 Translate the resulting pair of quadrilaterals to make a row of quadrilaterals.

Step 3 Translate the row of quadrilaterals to make a tessellation.

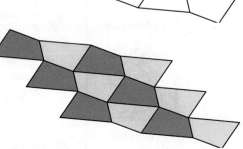

✓ CHECK IT OUT!

2. Copy the given figure and use it to create a tessellation.

A **regular tessellation** is formed by congruent regular polygons. A **semiregular tessellation** is formed by two or more different regular polygons, with the same number of each polygon occurring in the same order at every vertex.

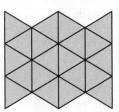

Regular tessellation

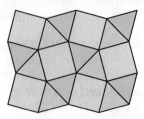

Semiregular tessellation

Every vertex has two squares and three triangles in this order: square, triangle, square, triangle, triangle.

Student to Student

Tessellations

Ryan Gray
Sunset High School

When I need to decide if given figures can be used to tessellate a plane, I look at angle measures. To form a regular tessellation, the angle measures of a regular polygon must be a divisor of 360°. To form a semiregular tessellation, the angle measures around a vertex must add up to 360°.

For example, regular octagons and equilateral triangles cannot be used to make a semiregular tessellation because no combination of 135° and 60° adds up to exactly 360°.

COMMON CORE GPS CC.MP.7

EXAMPLE 3

my.hrw.com

Online Video Tutor

Classifying Tessellations

Classify each tessellation as regular, semiregular, or neither.

A

Two regular octagons and one square meet at each vertex. The tessellation is semiregular.

B

Only squares are used. The tessellation is regular.

C

Irregular hexagons are used in the tessellation. It is neither regular nor semiregular.

CHECK IT OUT! Classify each tessellation as regular, semiregular, or neither.

3a.   **3b.**   **3c.**

COMMON CORE GPS CC.MP.7

EXAMPLE 4

my.hrw.com

Online Video Tutor

Determining Whether Polygons Will Tessellate

Determine whether the given regular polygon(s) can be used to form a tessellation. If so, draw the tessellation.

A

No; each angle of the pentagon measures 108°, and 108 is not a divisor of 360.

B

Yes; two octagons and one square meet at each vertex.
$135° + 135° + 90° = 360°$

CHECK IT OUT! Determine whether the given regular polygon(s) can be used to form a tessellation. If so, draw the tessellation.

4a.   **4b.**

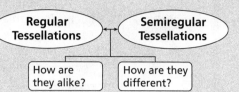
THINK AND DISCUSS

1. Explain how you can identify a frieze pattern that has glide reflection symmetry.

2. Is it possible to tessellate a plane using circles? Why or why not?

3. **GET ORGANIZED** Copy and complete the graphic organizer.

Know it!
Note

17-3 Exercises

my.hrw.com
Homework Help

GUIDED PRACTICE

Vocabulary Apply the vocabulary from this lesson to answer each question.

1. Sketch a pattern that has *glide reflection symmetry*.

2. Describe a real-world example of a *regular tessellation*.

SEE EXAMPLE 1

Transportation The tread of a tire is the part that makes contact with the ground. Various tread patterns help improve traction and increase durability. Identify the symmetry in each tread pattern.

3.

4.

5.

SEE EXAMPLE 2

Copy the given figure and use it to create a tessellation.

6.

7.

8.

SEE EXAMPLE 3

Classify each tessellation as regular, semiregular, or neither.

9.

10.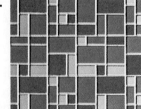

11.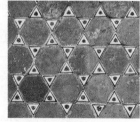

SEE EXAMPLE 4

Determine whether the given regular polygon(s) can be used to form a tessellation. If so, draw the tessellation.

12.

13.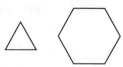

14.

PRACTICE AND PROBLEM SOLVING

Interior Decorating Identify the symmetry in each wallpaper border.

15.

16.

17.

Copy the given figure and use it to create a tessellation.

18.

19.

20.

Classify each tessellation as regular, semiregular, or neither.

21.

22.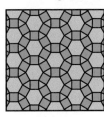

23.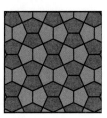

Determine whether the given regular polygon(s) can be used to form a tessellation. If so, draw the tessellation.

24.

25.

26.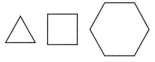

27. **Physics** A truck moving down a road creates whirling pockets of air called a *vortex train*. Use the figure to classify the symmetry of a vortex train.

Identify all of the types of symmetry (translation, glide reflection, and/or rotation) in each tessellation.

28.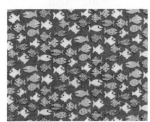

29.

30.

Tell whether each statement is sometimes, always, or never true.

31. A triangle can be used to tessellate a plane.

32. A frieze pattern has glide reflection symmetry.

33. The angles at a vertex of a tessellation add up to 360°.

34. It is possible to use a regular pentagon to make a regular tessellation.

35. A semiregular tessellation includes scalene triangles.

Real-World Connections

36. Many of the patterns in M. C. Escher's works are based on simple tessellations. For example, the pattern at right is based on a tessellation of equilateral triangles. Identify the figure upon which each pattern is based.

a.
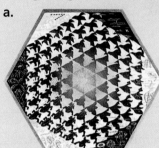

b.

Use the given figure to draw a frieze pattern with the given symmetry.

37. translation symmetry

38. glide reflection symmetry

39. translation symmetry

40. glide reflection symmetry

41. Optics A kaleidoscope is formed by three mirrors joined to form the lateral surface of a triangular prism. Copy the triangular faces and reflect it over each side. Repeat to form a tessellation. Describe the symmetry of the tessellation.

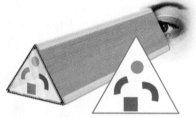

H.O.T. 42. Critical Thinking The pattern on a soccer ball is a tessellation of a sphere using regular hexagons and regular pentagons. Can these two shapes be used to tessellate a plane? Explain your reasoning.

43. Chemistry A *polymer* is a substance made of repeating chemical units or molecules. The *repeat unit* is the smallest structure that can be repeated to create the chain. Draw the repeat unit for polypropylene, the polymer shown below.

$$- CH_2 - CH - CH_2 - CH - CH_2 - CH - CH_2 - CH -$$
$$\qquad\quad | \qquad\qquad\quad | \qquad\qquad\quad | \qquad\qquad\quad |$$
$$\qquad\quad CH_3 \qquad\qquad CH_3 \qquad\qquad CH_3 \qquad\qquad CH_3$$

44. The *dual* of a tessellation is formed by connecting the centers of adjacent polygons with segments. Copy or trace the semiregular tessellation shown and draw its dual. What type of polygon makes up the dual tessellation?

H.O.T. 45. Write About It You can make a regular tessellation from an equilateral triangle, a square, or a regular hexagon. Explain why these are the only three regular tessellations that are possible.

TEST PREP

46. Which frieze pattern has glide reflection symmetry?

Ⓐ 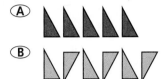   Ⓒ

Ⓑ   Ⓓ

47. Which shape CANNOT be used to make a regular tessellation?

Ⓕ Equilateral triangle   Ⓗ Regular pentagon

Ⓖ Square   Ⓙ Regular hexagon

48. Which pair of regular polygons can be used to make a semiregular tessellation?

Ⓐ 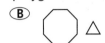   Ⓑ   Ⓒ   Ⓓ

CHALLENGE AND EXTEND

49. Some shapes can be used to tessellate a plane in more than one way. Three tessellations that use the same rectangle are shown. Draw a parallelogram and draw at least three tessellations using that parallelogram.

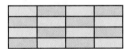   

Determine whether each figure can be used to tessellate three-dimensional space.

50.   **51.**   **52.**

FOCUS ON MATHEMATICAL PRACTICES

H.O.T. **53. Reasoning** Explain why the measures of the angles that meet at each vertex of a tessellation must add to 360°.

H.O.T. **54. Error Analysis** Fred says this tiling is a tessellation. Hari says it is not. Who is correct? Explain.

H.O.T. **55. Problem Solving** Can a non-isosceles trapezoid be used to tessellate a plane? Explain.

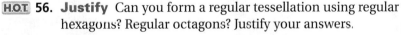

H.O.T. **56. Justify** Can you form a regular tessellation using regular hexagons? Regular octagons? Justify your answers.

H.O.T. **57. Draw Conclusions** Is this tiling a regular tessellation, a semiregular tessellation, or neither? Explain.

H.O.T. **58. Problem Solving** Can a triangle with three different side lengths be used to tessellate a plane? If so, give a method. If not, explain why not.

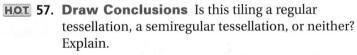
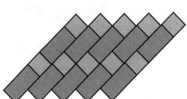

Ready to Go On?

my.hrw.com
Assessment and Intervention

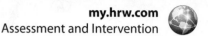

17-1 Compositions of Transformations

1. Draw the result of the following composition of transformations. Translate *GHJK* along $\vec{v}$, and then reflect it across line *m*.

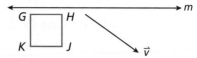

2. $\triangle ABC$ with vertices $A(1, 0)$, $B(1, 3)$, and $C(2, 3)$ is reflected across the *y*-axis, and then its image is reflected across the *x*-axis. Describe a single transformation that moves the triangle from its starting position to its final position.

17-2 Symmetry

Explain whether each figure has line symmetry. If so, copy the figure and draw all lines of symmetry.

3.     4.    5.

Explain whether each figure has rotational symmetry. If so, give the angle of rotational symmetry and the order of the symmetry.

6.   7.    8.

17-3 Tessellations

Copy the given figure and use it to create a tessellation.

9. 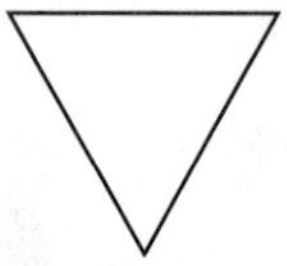 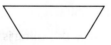   10.    11.

Classify each tessellation as regular, semiregular, or neither.

12. 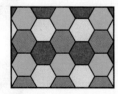   13.    14.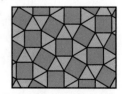

15. Determine whether it is possible to tessellate a plane with regular octagons. If so, draw the tessellation. If not, explain why.

Selected Response

1. Ann wants to create a design to decorate her Geometry binder. She draws a figure on a coordinate grid and reflects the figure across the y-axis. She then reflects the image across the x-axis. Describe a single transformation that moves the part of the design from its starting position to its final position.

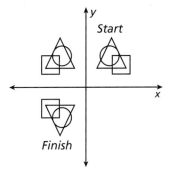

(A) rotation of 180° about the origin

(B) rotation of 90° about the origin

(C) translation along the line y = x

(D) reflection across the line y = x

2. Tell whether the figure has rotational symmetry. If so, give the angle of rotational symmetry and the order of the symmetry.

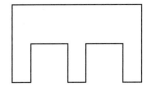

(F) The figure has no rotational symmetry.

(G) Yes, the figure has rotational symmetry. The angle of rotational symmetry is 180°, and the order of the symmetry is 2.

(H) Yes, the figure has rotational symmetry. The angle of rotational symmetry is 90°, and the order of the symmetry is 4.

(J) Yes, the figure has rotational symmetry. The angle of rotational symmetry is 45°, and the order of the symmetry is 8.

3. Identify the symmetry in the pattern. Assume that the pattern continues forever in both directions.

(A) Both translation symmetry and glide reflection symmetry

(B) Only translation symmetry

(C) Only glide reflection symmetry

(D) No symmetry

4. After a composition of transformations, the line segment from $A(1, 4)$ to $B(4, 2)$ maps to the line segment from $C(-1, -2)$ to $D(-4, -4)$. Which of the following describes the composition that is applied to $\overline{AB}$ to obtain $\overline{CD}$?

(F) Translate 5 units to the left and then reflect across the y-axis.

(G) Reflect across the y-axis and then reflect across the x-axis.

(H) Reflect across the y-axis and then translate 6 units down.

(J) Translate 6 units down and then reflect across the x-axis.

Mini-Task

5. Copy the given figure and use it to create a tessellation.

PARCC Assessment Readiness

COMMON CORE GPS

Selected Response

1. The change in position from the solid figure to the dashed figure is best described as a _____.

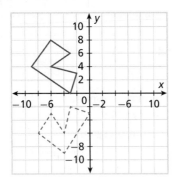

   (A) transmission
   (B) translation
   (C) rotation
   (D) reflection

2. The image of point A under a 90° rotation about the origin is A'(10, −4). What are the coordinates of point A?

   (F) (−10, −4)
   (G) (−10, 4)
   (H) (−4, −10)
   (J) (4, 10)

3. Which are the angle of rotation and the order of rotational symmetry for the figure?

   (A) 90°; 2
   (B) 180°; 2
   (C) 90°; 4
   (D) 180°; 4

Use the graph for items 4–6.

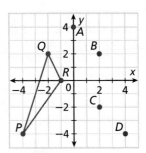

4. What are the coordinates of the image of point C under the same translation that maps point D to point B?

   (F) (4, 4)
   (G) (0, 4)
   (H) (0, 8)
   (J) (4, −8)

5. $\triangle PQR$ is rotated 180° about the origin. Which point is the image of point Q?

   (A) A   (C) C
   (B) B   (D) D

6. For which of the following combinations of transformations of $\triangle PQR$ would point A NOT be the image of point P?

   (F) Reflection across the x-axis, followed by a horizontal translation of 4 units
   (G) Reflection across the y-axis, followed by a horizontal translation of 4 units
   (H) 180° rotation followed by a horizontal translation of −4 units
   (J) Reflection across the line x = −2 followed by a vertical translation of 8 units

7. Which mapping represents three successive rotations of 90° about the origin?

   (A) $(x, y) \rightarrow (-x, -y)$
   (B) $(x, y) \rightarrow (x, -y)$
   (C) $(x, y) \rightarrow (-y, -x)$
   (D) $(x, y) \rightarrow (y, -x)$

8. Which regular polygon can be used with an equilateral triangle to tessellate a plane?

　Ⓕ Heptagon

　Ⓖ Octagon

　Ⓗ Nonagon

　Ⓙ Dodecagon

When problems involve geometric figures in the coordinate plane, it may be useful to describe properties of the figures algebraically. For example, you can use slope to verify that sides of a figure are parallel or perpendicular, or you can use the Distance Formula to find side lengths of the figure.

9. Which shows the image of △EFG after the translation $(x, y) \rightarrow (x - 6, y + 2)$?

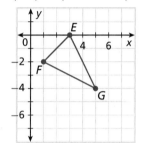

Ⓐ
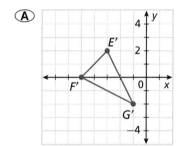

Ⓑ
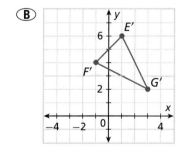

Ⓒ
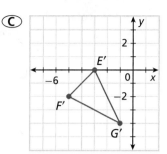

Ⓓ
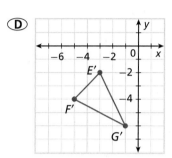

10. What are the coordinates of the image of the point (5, 5) when it is reflected across the line $y = 8$?

　Ⓕ (5, 13)

　Ⓖ (5, −3)

　Ⓗ (5, 11)

　Ⓙ (5, −5)

11. The point $G(6, 7)$ is rotated 90° about point $M(-9, -3)$ and then reflected across the line $y = 9$. What are the coordinates of the image G′?

　Ⓐ (37, 6)

　Ⓑ (−24, 11)

　Ⓒ (−7, 12)

　Ⓓ (−19, 6)

12. How many lines of symmetry does a regular hexagon have?

　Ⓕ 1

　Ⓖ 3

　Ⓗ 6

　Ⓙ 12

13. What is the x-coordinate of the image of the point $A(12, -7)$ after A is reflected across the x-axis?

　Ⓐ −12

　Ⓑ −7

　Ⓒ 7

　Ⓓ 12

14. Quadrilateral *LMNO* has vertices *L*(0, 4), *M*(3, 6), *N*(5, 4), and *O*(3, 0). If *LMNO* is reflected across the *x*-axis, which point(s) will not change location?

(F) *L* and *O*

(G) *L*

(H) *O*

(J) *L* and *N*

15. A triangle has vertices (0, 3), (0, 5), and (4, 5). The triangle is translated 2 units to the right and 2 units down. Which is one of the vertices of the translated triangle?

(A) (2, 3)

(B) (0, 1)

(C) (4, 2)

(D) (−2, 1)

16. Which of the following represents a reflection across the line $y = 0$?

(F) $(x, y) \rightarrow (-x, y)$

(G) $(x, y) \rightarrow (x, -y)$

(H) $(x, y) \rightarrow (-x, -y)$

(J) $(x, y) \rightarrow (y, x)$

17. What would be the coordinates of *M*(4, 3) after a rotation of 90° about the origin?

(A) (0, 5)

(B) (−2, 6)

(C) (−3, 4)

(D) (−1, 0)

18. A triangle has vertices *A*(1, 1), *B*(4, 1), and *C*(4, 3). After a transformation, the image has vertices *A'*(−1, 1), *B'*(−4, 1), and *C'*(−4, 3). Which of the following describes the transformation?

(F) A rotation of 180° about the origin

(G) A reflection across the *x*-axis

(H) A reflection across the *y*-axis

(J) A translation 2 units to the left

19. The vertices of triangle *JKL* are *J*(−3, −1), *K*(−1, −3), and *L*(−4, −4). Triangle *JKL* is reflected across the *x*-axis. What are the coordinates of *K'*?

(A) (1, −3)

(B) (−1, 3)

(C) (−1, −3)

(D) (1, 3)

20. Triangle *PQR* has vertices at *P*(2, 3), *Q*(3, 5), and *R*(5, 1). The triangle will be translated 4 units up. What will be the coordinates of point *R'*?

(F) (2, 7)

(G) (7, 5)

(H) (9, 5)

(J) (5, 5)

Mini-Tasks

21. △*ABC* is reflected across line *m*. What observations can be made about △*ABC* and its reflected image △*A'B'C'* regarding the following properties: collinearity, betweenness, angle measure, triangle congruence, and orientation? Explain.

For items 22 and 23, identify the transformation. Then use arrow notation to describe the transformation.

22.

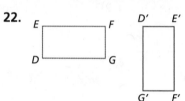

23.

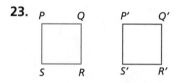

24. The coordinates for the vertices of △*XYZ* are *X*(−5, −4), *Y*(−3, −1), and *Z*(−2, −2). Find the coordinates for the image of △*XYZ* after the translation $(x, y) \rightarrow (x + 4, y + 5)$.

For items 25 and 26, tell whether the figure has line symmetry. If so, copy the figure and draw all lines of symmetry.

25.

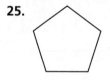

26.

For items 27 and 28, tell whether the figure has rotational symmetry. If so, give the angle of rotational symmetry and the order of symmetry.

27.

28.

For items 29 and 30, copy the given figure and use it to create a tessellation.

29.

30.

31. The coordinates of the vertices of rectangle *HJKL* are *H*(2, −1), *J*(5, −1), *K*(5, −3), and *L*(2, −3).

   a. Graph *HJKL* in the coordinate plane.

   b. Graph *H′J′K′L′* by applying the translation $(x, y) \rightarrow (x − 4, y + 1)$ to *HJKL*.

32. A triangle has vertices at (−1, 1), (1, 3), and (4, −2). After a reflection and a translation, the coordinates of the image are (5, 3), (3, 5), and (0, 0). Describe the reflection and the translation.

For items 33–36, reflect the figure with the given vertices across the given line.

33. *E*(−3, 2), *F*(0, 2), *G*(−2, 5); *x*-axis

34. *J*(2, −1), *K*(4, −2), *L*(4, −3), *M*(2, −3); *y*-axis

35. *P*(2, −2), *Q*(4, −2), *R*(3, −4); *y* = *x*

36. *A*(2, 2), *B*(−2, 2), *C*(−1, 4); *y* = *x*

37. Many of the capital letters in our alphabet have horizontal or vertical lines of symmetry.

   a. Make a list of the capital letters that have horizontal lines of symmetry.

   b. Make a list of the capital letters that have vertical lines of symmetry.

   c. Which capital letters have both horizontal and vertical lines of symmetry?

Performance Tasks

38. Archeologists examine digital images of their excavations on a computer screen. They have the ability to move the image left, right, up, or down. They can also rotate the image. Suppose a computer screen has a coordinate grid transposed over it, and a bone fragment is in the shape of a rectangle that has the vertices *A*(4, −6), *B*(4, −8), *C*(8, −6) and *D*(8, −8). Determine the effects that an archeologist's actions will have on the bone fragment's position on the screen.

   a. First, the archeologist moves the bone fragment up 5 units on the screen. Find its new vertices.

   b. Next, the archeologist moves the bone fragment left 4 units on the screen. What are its vertices now?

39. Square *ABCD* was transformed using the rule $(x, y \rightarrow x + 5, y − 5)$ to produce the image *A′B′C′D′*.

   a. Is the transformation a reflection, a rotation, or a translation? How do you know?

   b. The vertices of square *ABCD* are *A*(−3 −7), *B*(−1, −5), *C*(1, −7), and *D*(−1, −9). What are the coordinates of *A′B′C′D′*?

   c. Right triangle *QRS* is transformed using the rule to produce the image *Q′R′S′*. Will △*Q′R′S′* be a right triangle? Explain.

my.hrw.com
Online Assessment

Go online for updated, PARCC-aligned assessment readiness.

Are You Ready?

my.hrw.com
Assessment and Intervention

Vocabulary
Match each term on the left with a definition on the right.

1. coefficient

2. coordinate plane

3. transformation

4. perpendicular

A. a change in the size or position of a figure

B. forming right angles

C. a two-dimensional system formed by the intersection of a horizontal number line and a vertical number line

D. an ordered pair of numbers that gives the location of a point

E. a number that is multiplied by a variable

Solve for a Variable
Solve each equation for the indicated variable.

5. $2x + y = 8$; y

6. $5y = 5x - 10$; y

7. $2y = 6x - 8$; y

8. $10x + 25 = 5y$; y

Evaluate Expressions
Evaluate each expression for the given value of the variable.

9. $4g - 3$; $g = -2$

10. $8p - 12$; $p = 4$

11. $4x + 8$; $x = -2$

12. $-5t - 15$; $t = 1$

Connect Words and Algebra

13. The value of a stock begins at \$0.05 and increases by \$0.01 each month. Write an equation representing the value of the stock v in any month m.

14. Write a situation that could be modeled by the equation $b = 100 - s$.

Career Readiness Personal Trainers

Personal trainers are fitness professionals who motivate and provide feedback to their clients. They use fitness assessments that may involve formulas for the following:
• Body Mass Index, or BMI
• Basal Metabolic Rate, or BMR
• Maximum Heart Rate, or MHR
• Training Zone Heart Rate
Personal trainers must be certified. Most trainers have college degrees and many of them are employed by gyms or health clubs.

Connecting Algebra and Geometry Through Coordinates

UNIT 6

Online Edition

my.hrw.com

Access the complete online textbook, interactive features, and additional resources.

Homework Help

Get instant help with tutorial videos, practice problems, and step-by-step solutions.

TI-Nspire™ Activities

Enhance your learning with cutting edge technology from Texas Instruments.

Portable Devices

eTextbook

Access your full textbook on your tablet or e-reader.

On the Spot

Watch video tutorials anywhere, anytime with this app for iPhone® and iPad®.

Chapter Resources

Scan with your smart phone to jump directly to the online edition.

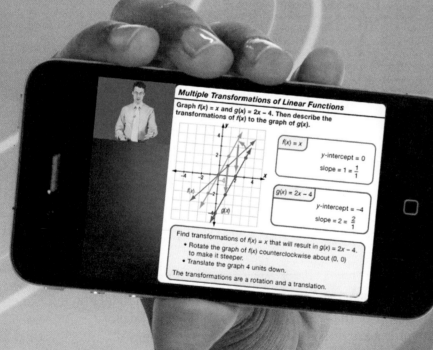

Multiple Transformations of Linear Functions

Graph $f(x) = x$ and $g(x) = 2x - 4$. Then describe the transformations of $f(x)$ to the graph of $g(x)$.

$f(x) = x$

y-intercept = 0

slope = $1 = \frac{1}{1}$

$g(x) = 2x - 4$

y-intercept = -4

slope = $2 = \frac{2}{1}$

Find transformations of $f(x) = x$ that will result in $g(x) = 2x - 4$.
- Rotate the graph of $f(x)$ counterclockwise about (0, 0) to make it steeper.
- Translate the graph 4 units down.

The transformations are a rotation and a translation.

Use **On the Spot** videos to see linear functions and transformations in action.

18 Coordinate Geometry

MCC9-12.G.GPE.7

MCC9-12.G.GPE.4, MCC9-12.G.GPE.5

MCC9-12.G.GPE.6, MCC9-12.G.GPE.7

Contents

MATHEMATICAL PRACTICES   The Common Core Georgia Performance Standards for Mathematical Practice describe varieties of expertise that all students should seek to develop. Opportunities to develop these practices are integrated throughout this program.

1 Make sense of problems and persevere in solving them.

2 Reason abstractly and quantitatively.

3 Construct viable arguments and critique the reasoning of others.

4 Model with mathematics.

5 Use appropriate tools strategically.

6 Attend to precision.

7 Look for and make use of structure.

8 Look for and express regularity in repeated reasoning.

Unpacking the Standards

Understanding the standards and the vocabulary terms in the standards will help you know exactly what you are expected to learn in this chapter.

 MCC9-12.G.GPE.4

Use coordinates to prove simple geometric theorems algebraically.

Key Vocabulary

coordinate (coordenada) A number used to identify the location of a point. On a number line, one coordinate is used. On a coordinate plane, two coordinates are used, called the x-coordinate and the y-coordinate. In space, three coordinates are used, called the x-coordinate, the y-coordinate, and the z-coordinate.

What It Means For You

You can prove some properties of geometric figures by using coordinates and algebra. These proofs sometimes involve the distance formula or the midpoint formula.

EXAMPLE

The midpoint of $\overline{AB}$, point M, has coordinates $M\left(\frac{0+x}{2}, \frac{0+y}{2}\right)$.

Area $\triangle AMC = \frac{1}{2}(x)\left(\frac{y}{2}\right) = \frac{xy}{4}$.

Area $\triangle ABC = \frac{1}{2}(x)(y) = \frac{xy}{2}$.

The area of triangle AMC is half the area of triangle ABC.

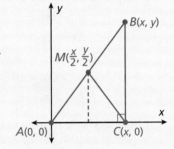

 MCC9-12.G.GPE.5

Prove the slope criteria for parallel and perpendicular lines and use them to solve geometric problems (e.g., find the equation of a line parallel or perpendicular to a given line that passes through a given point).

Key Vocabulary

slope (pendiente) A measure of the steepness of a line. If (x_1, y_1) and (x_2, y_2) are any two points on the line, the slope of the line, known as m, is represented by the equation $m = \frac{y_2 - y_1}{x_2 - x_1}$.

What It Means For You

Parallel lines have the same slope. Perpendicular lines have slopes whose product is −1. You can use these facts to conclude that lines are parallel or perpendicular, or to identify slopes of lines.

EXAMPLE

The slope of $\overleftrightarrow{AB}$ is −4.

The slope of $\overleftrightarrow{CD}$ is −4.

The slopes are the same.

So, $\overleftrightarrow{AB} \parallel \overleftrightarrow{CD}$.

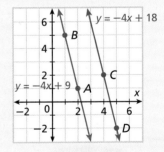

The slope of $\overleftrightarrow{FG}$ is 1.

The slope of $\overleftrightarrow{JH}$ is −1.

The product of the slopes is −1.

So, $\overleftrightarrow{FG} \perp \overleftrightarrow{JH}$.

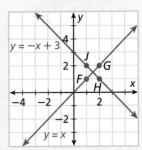

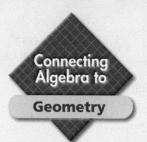

Area in the Coordinate Plane

Lines in the coordinate plane can form the sides of polygons. You can use points on these lines to help you find the areas of these polygons.

Example

Find the area of the triangle formed by the x-axis, the y-axis, and the line described by $3x + 2y = 18$.

Step 1 Find the intercepts of $3x + 2y = 18$.

x-intercept:	*y*-intercept:
$3x + 2y = 18$	$3x + 2y = 18$
$3x + 2(0) = 18$	$3(0) + 2y = 18$
$3x = 18$	$2y = 18$
$x = 6$	$y = 9$

Step 2 Use the intercepts to graph the line. The *x*-intercept is 6, so plot $(6, 0)$. The *y*-intercept is 9, so plot $(0, 9)$. Connect with a straight line. Then shade the triangle formed by the line and the axes, as described.

Step 3 Recall that the area of a triangle is given by $A = \frac{1}{2}bh$.

• The length of the base is 6.

• The height is 9.

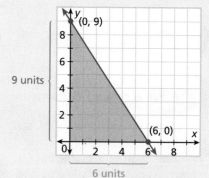

Step 4 Substitute these values into the formula.

$$A = \frac{1}{2}bh$$

$$A = \frac{1}{2}(6)(9) \qquad \textit{Substitute into the area formula.}$$

$$= \frac{1}{2}(54) \qquad \textit{Simplify.}$$

$$= 27$$

The area of the triangle is 27 square units.

Try This

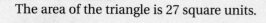

1. Find the area of the triangle formed by the x-axis, the y-axis, and the line described by $3x + 2y = 12$.

2. Find the area of the triangle formed by the x-axis, the y-axis, and the line described by $y = 6 - x$.

3. Find the area of the polygon formed by the x-axis, the y-axis, the line described by $y = 6$, and the line described by $x = 4$.

18-1 Slopes of Parallel and Perpendicular Lines

Essential Question: How can you use the relationships between the slopes of parallel and perpendicular lines to solve problems?

Objectives
Identify and graph parallel and perpendicular lines.

Write equations to describe lines parallel or perpendicular to a given line.

Vocabulary
parallel lines
perpendicular lines

Animated Math

Why learn this?
Parallel lines and their equations can be used to model costs, such as the cost of a booth at a farmers' market.

To sell at a particular farmers' market for a year, there is a $100 membership fee. Then you pay $3 for each hour that you sell at the market. However, if you were a member the previous year, the membership fee is reduced to $50.

- The **red** line shows the total cost if you are a new member.

- The **blue** line shows the total cost if you are a returning member.

These two lines are *parallel*. **Parallel lines** are lines in the same plane that have no points in common. In other words, they do not intersect.

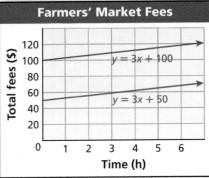

Farmers' Market Fees

Parallel Lines

WORDS	Two different nonvertical lines are parallel if and only if they have the same slope.	All different vertical lines are parallel.
GRAPH	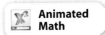	

COMMON CORE GPS
MCC9-12.G.GPE.5

EXAMPLE 1

my.hrw.com

Online Video Tutor

Identifying Parallel Lines

Identify which lines are parallel.

A $y = \frac{4}{3}x + 3$; $y = 2$; $y = \frac{4}{3}x - 5$; $y = -3$

The lines described by $y = \frac{4}{3}x + 3$ and $y = \frac{4}{3}x - 5$ both have slope $\frac{4}{3}$. These lines are parallel. The lines described by $y = 2$ and $y = -3$ both have slope 0. These lines are parallel.

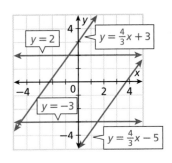

Identify which lines are parallel.

B $y = 3x + 2; \ y = -\dfrac{1}{2}x + 4; \ x + 2y = -4; \ y - 5 = 3(x - 1)$

Write all equations in slope-intercept form to determine the slopes.

$y = 3x + 2$	$y = -\dfrac{1}{2}x + 4$
slope-intercept form ✓	slope-intercept form ✓

$$x + 2y = -4$$
$$\underline{-x \qquad\qquad -x}$$
$$2y = -x - 4$$
$$\dfrac{2y}{2} = \dfrac{-x - 4}{2}$$
$$y = -\dfrac{1}{2}x - 2$$

$$y - 5 = 3(x - 1)$$
$$y - 5 = 3x - 3$$
$$\underline{+5 \qquad\qquad +5}$$
$$y = 3x + 2$$

The lines described by $y = 3x + 2$ and $y - 5 = 3(x - 1)$ have the same slope, but they are not parallel lines. They are the same line.

The lines described by $y = -\dfrac{1}{2}x + 4$ and $x + 2y = -4$ represent parallel lines. They each have slope $-\dfrac{1}{2}$.

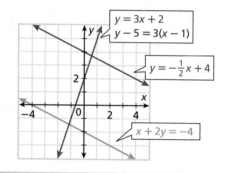

CHECK IT OUT! Identify which lines are parallel.

1a. $y = 2x + 2; \ y = 2x + 1; \ y = -4; \ x = 1$

1b. $y = \dfrac{3}{4}x + 8; \ -3x + 4y = 32; \ y = 3x; \ y - 1 = 3(x + 2)$

COMMON CORE GPS
MCC9-12.G.GPE.5

EXAMPLE 2

Geometry Application

my.hrw.com

Online Video Tutor

Show that *ABCD* is a parallelogram.

Use the ordered pairs and the slope formula to find the slopes of $\overline{AB}$ and $\overline{CD}$.

$$\text{slope of } \overline{AB} = \dfrac{7 - 5}{4 - (-1)} = \dfrac{2}{5}$$

$$\text{slope of } \overline{CD} = \dfrac{3 - 1}{4 - (-1)} = \dfrac{2}{5}$$

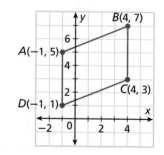

$\overline{AB}$ is parallel to $\overline{CD}$ because they have the same slope.

$\overline{AD}$ is parallel to $\overline{BC}$ because they are both vertical.

Therefore, *ABCD* is a parallelogram because both pairs of opposite sides are parallel.

Remember!

In a parallelogram, opposite sides are parallel.

CHECK IT OUT! **2.** Show that the points $A(0, 2)$, $B(4, 2)$, $C(1, -3)$, and $D(-3, -3)$ are the vertices of a parallelogram.

Perpendicular lines are lines that intersect to form right angles (90°).

Perpendicular Lines

WORDS	Two nonvertical lines are perpendicular if and only if the product of their slopes is −1.	Vertical lines are perpendicular to horizontal lines.
GRAPH	$y = -\frac{2}{3}x + 3$ $y = \frac{3}{2}x - 2$	$y = 3$ $x = 2$

COMMON CORE GPS MCC9-12.G.GPE.5

EXAMPLE 3 **Identifying Perpendicular Lines**

my.hrw.com

Online Video Tutor

Identify which lines are perpendicular: $x = -2$; $y = 1$; $y = -4x$; $y + 2 = \frac{1}{4}(x + 1)$.

The graph described by $x = -2$ is a vertical line, and the graph described by $y = 1$ is a horizontal line. These lines are perpendicular.

The slope of the line described by $y = -4x$ is −4. The slope of the line described by $y + 2 = \frac{1}{4}(x - 1)$ is $\frac{1}{4}$.

$$(-4)\left(\frac{1}{4}\right) = -1$$

These lines are perpendicular because the product of their slopes is −1.

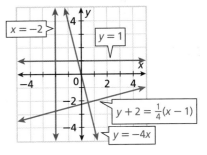

CHECK IT OUT! 3. Identify which lines are perpendicular: $y = -4$; $y - 6 = 5(x + 4)$; $x = 3$; $y = -\frac{1}{5}x + 2$.

COMMON CORE GPS MCC9-12.G.GPE.4

EXAMPLE 4 *Geometry Application*

my.hrw.com

Online Video Tutor

Show that *PQR* is a right triangle.

If *PQR* is a right triangle, $\overline{PQ}$ will be perpendicular to $\overline{QR}$.

$$\text{slope of } \overline{PQ} = \frac{3 - 1}{3 - 0} = \frac{2}{3}$$

$$\text{slope of } \overline{QR} = \frac{3 - 0}{3 - 5} = \frac{3}{-2} = -\frac{3}{2}$$

$\overline{PQ}$ is perpendicular to $\overline{QR}$ because $\frac{2}{3}\left(-\frac{3}{2}\right) = -1$.

Therefore, *PQR* is a right triangle because it contains a right angle.

CHECK IT OUT! 4. Show that $P(1, 4)$, $Q(2, 6)$, and $R(7, 1)$ are the vertices of a right triangle.

Writing Equations of Parallel and Perpendicular Lines

 my.hrw.com

Online Video Tutor

A Write an equation in slope-intercept form for the line that passes through $(4, 5)$ and is parallel to the line described by $y = 5x + 10$.

Step 1 Find the slope of the line.

$y = 5x + 10$ *The slope is 5.*

The parallel line also has a slope of 5.

Step 2 Write the equation in point-slope form.

$y - y_1 = m(x - x_1)$ *Use point-slope form.*

$y - 5 = 5(x - 4)$ *Substitute 5 for m, 4 for x_1, and 5 for y_1.*

Step 3 Write the equation in slope-intercept form.

$y - 5 = 5(x - 4)$

$y - 5 = 5x - 20$ *Distributive Property*

$y = 5x - 15$ *Addition Property of Equality*

B Write an equation in slope-intercept form for the line that passes through $(3, 2)$ and is perpendicular to the line described by $y = 3x - 1$.

Step 1 Find the slope of the line.

$y = 3x - 1$ *The slope is 3.*

The perpendicular line has a slope of $-\frac{1}{3}$, because $3\left(-\frac{1}{3}\right) = -1$.

Step 2 Write the equation in point-slope form.

$y - y_1 = m(x - x_1)$ *Use point-slope form.*

$y - 2 = -\frac{1}{3}(x - 3)$ *Substitute $-\frac{1}{3}$ for m, 3 for x_1, and 2 for y_1.*

Step 3 Write the equation in slope-intercept form.

$y - 2 = -\frac{1}{3}(x - 3)$

$y - 2 = -\frac{1}{3}x + 1$ *Distributive Property*

$y = -\frac{1}{3}x + 3$ *Addition Property of Equality*

Helpful Hint

If you know the slope of a line, the slope of a perpendicular line will be the "opposite reciprocal."

$\frac{2}{3} \rightarrow -\frac{3}{2}$

$\frac{1}{5} \rightarrow -5$

$-7 \rightarrow \frac{1}{7}$

 CHECK IT OUT!

5a. Write an equation in slope-intercept form for the line that passes through $(5, 7)$ and is parallel to the line described by $y = \frac{4}{5}x - 6$.

5b. Write an equation in slope-intercept form for the line that passes through $(-5, 3)$ and is perpendicular to the line described by $y = 5x$.

MCC.MP.6, MCC.MP.7   MATHEMATICAL PRACTICES

THINK AND DISCUSS

1. Are the lines described by $y = \frac{1}{2}x$ and $y = 2x$ perpendicular? Explain.

2. Describe the slopes and y-intercepts when two nonvertical lines are parallel.

 Know it! Note

3. GET ORGANIZED Copy and complete the graphic organizer. In each box, sketch an example and describe the slopes.

Parallel lines	Perpendicular lines

GUIDED PRACTICE

1. **Vocabulary** ____?____ lines have the same slope. (*Parallel* or *Perpendicular*)

SEE EXAMPLE 1 | **Identify which lines are parallel.**

2. $y = 6$; $y = 6x + 5$; $y = 6x - 7$; $y = -8$

3. $y = \frac{3}{4}x - 1$; $y = -2x$; $y - 3 = \frac{3}{4}(x - 5)$; $y - 4 = -2(x + 2)$

SEE EXAMPLE 2 | 4. **Geometry** Show that *ABCD* is a trapezoid. (*Hint:* In a trapezoid, exactly one pair of opposite sides is parallel.)

SEE EXAMPLE 3 | **Identify which lines are perpendicular.**

5. $y = \frac{2}{3}x - 4$; $y = -\frac{3}{2}x + 2$; $y = -1$; $x = 3$

6. $y = -\frac{3}{7}x - 4$; $y - 4 = -7(x + 2)$;

$y - 1 = \frac{1}{7}(x - 4)$; $y - 7 = \frac{7}{3}(x - 3)$

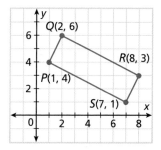

SEE EXAMPLE 4 | 7. **Geometry** Show that *PQRS* is a rectangle. (*Hint:* In a rectangle, all four angles are right angles.)

SEE EXAMPLE 5 | 8. Write an equation in slope-intercept form for the line that passes through (5, 0) and is perpendicular to the line described by $y = -\frac{5}{2}x + 6$.

PRACTICE AND PROBLEM SOLVING

Identify which lines are parallel.

Independent Practice	
For Exercises	See Example
9–11	1
12	2
13–15	3
16	4
17	5

9. $x = 7$; $y = -\frac{5}{6}x + 8$; $y = -\frac{5}{6}x - 4$; $x = -9$

10. $y = -x$; $y - 3 = -1(x + 9)$; $y - 6 = \frac{1}{2}(x - 14)$; $y + 1 = \frac{1}{2}x$

11. $y = -3x + 2$; $y = \frac{1}{2}x - 1$; $-x + 2y = 17$; $3x + y = 27$

12. **Geometry** Show that *LMNP* is a parallelogram.

Identify which lines are perpendicular.

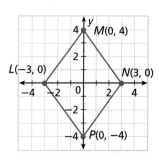

my.hrw.com

Online Extra Practice

13. $y = 6x$; $y = \frac{1}{6}x$; $y = -\frac{1}{6}x$; $y = -6x$

14. $y - 9 = 3(x + 1)$; $y = -\frac{1}{3}x + 5$; $y = 0$; $x = 6$

15. $x - 6y = 15$; $y = 3x - 2$; $y = -3x - 3$; $y = -6x - 8$; $3y = -x - 11$

16. Geometry Show that ABC is a right triangle.

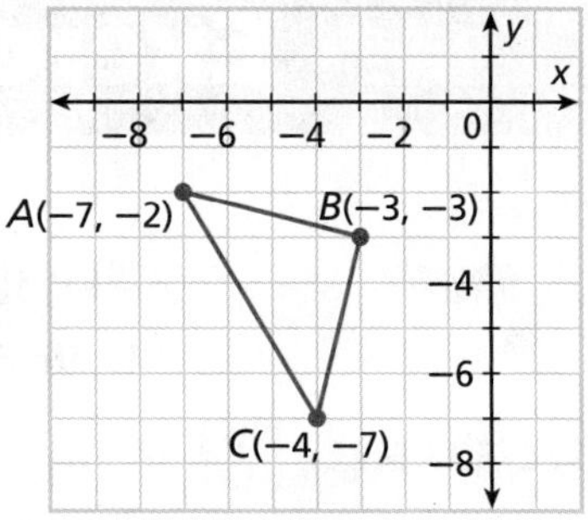

17. Write an equation in slope-intercept form for the line that passes through $(0, 0)$ and is parallel to the line described by $y = -\frac{6}{7}x + 1$.

The graph shows a coordinate plane with points $A(-7, -2)$, $B(-3, -3)$, and $C(-4, -7)$ connected to form a triangle. The axes are labeled with values -8, -6, -4, -2, 0 on the x-axis and -4, -6, -8 on the y-axis.

Without graphing, tell whether each pair of lines is parallel, perpendicular, or neither.

18. $x = 2$ and $y = -5$

19. $y = 7x$ and $y - 28 = 7(x - 4)$

20. $y = 2x - 1$ and $y = \frac{1}{2}x + 2$

21. $y - 3 = \frac{1}{4}(x - 3)$ and $y + 13 = \frac{1}{4}(x + 1)$

Write an equation in slope-intercept form for the line that is parallel to the given line and that passes through the given point.

22. $y = 3x - 7; (0, 4)$

23. $y = \frac{1}{2}x + 5; (4, -3)$

24. $4y = x; (4, 0)$

25. $y = 2x + 3; (1, 7)$

26. $5x - 2y = 10; (3, -5)$

27. $y = 3x - 4; (-2, 7)$

28. $y = 7; (2, 4)$

29. $x + y = 1; (2, 3)$

30. $2x + 3y = 7; (4, 5)$

31. $y = 4x + 2; (5, -3)$

32. $y = \frac{1}{2}x - 1; (0, -4)$

33. $3x + 4y = 8; (4, -3)$

Write an equation in slope-intercept form for the line that is perpendicular to the given line and that passes through the given point.

34. $y = -3x + 4; (6, -2)$

35. $y = x - 6; (-1, 2)$

36. $3x - 4y = 8; (-6, 5)$

37. $5x + 2y = 10; (3, -5)$

38. $y = 5 - 3x; (2, -4)$

39. $-10x + 2y = 8; (4, -3)$

40. $2x + 3y = 7; (4, 5)$

41. $4x - 2y = -6; (3, -2)$

42. $-2x - 8y = 16; (4, 5)$

43. $y = -2x + 4; (-2, 5)$

44. $y = x - 5; (0, 5)$

45. $x + y = 2; (8, 5)$

46. Write an equation describing the line that is parallel to the y-axis and that is 6 units to the right of the y-axis.

47. Write an equation describing the line that is perpendicular to the y-axis and that is 4 units below the x-axis.

48. Critical Thinking Is it possible for two linear functions whose graphs are parallel lines to have the same y-intercept? Explain.

49. Estimation Estimate the slope of a line that is perpendicular to the line through $(2.07, 8.95)$ and $(-1.9, 25.07)$.

H.O.T. **50. Write About It** Explain in words how to write an equation in slope-intercept form that describes a line parallel to $y - 3 = -6(x - 3)$.

 **Real-World Connections**

51. a. Flora walks from her home to the bus stop at a rate of 50 steps per minute. Write a rule that gives her distance from home (in steps) as a function of time.

b. Flora's neighbor Dan lives 30 steps closer to the bus stop. He begins walking at the same time and at the same pace as Flora. Write a rule that gives Dan's distance from *Flora's* house as a function of time.

c. Will Flora meet Dan along the walk? Use a graph to help explain your answer.

TEST PREP

52. Which describes a line parallel to the line described by $y = -3x + 2$?

    Ⓐ $y = -3x$ Ⓑ $y = \frac{1}{3}x$ Ⓒ $y = 2 - 3x$ Ⓓ $y = \frac{1}{3}x + 2$

53. Which describes a line passing through $(3, 3)$ that is perpendicular to the line described by $y = \frac{3}{5}x + 2$?

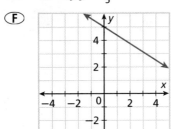

    Ⓖ $y = \frac{5}{3}x - 2$ Ⓙ $y = \frac{3}{5}x + \frac{6}{5}$

54. Gridded Response The graph of a linear function $f(x)$ is parallel to the line described by $2x + y = 5$ and contains the point $(6, -2)$. What is the y-intercept of $f(x)$?

CHALLENGE AND EXTEND

H.O.T. 55. Three or more points that lie on the same line are called *collinear points*. Explain why the points A, B, and C must be collinear if the line containing A and B has the same slope as the line containing B and C.

56. The lines described by $y = (a + 12)x + 3$ and $y = 4ax$ are parallel. What is the value of a?

57. The lines described by $y = (5a + 3)x$ and $y = -\frac{1}{2}x$ are perpendicular. What is the value of a?

58. Geometry The diagram shows a square in the coordinate plane. Use the diagram to show that the diagonals of a square are perpendicular.

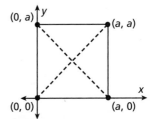

FOCUS ON MATHEMATICAL PRACTICES

H.O.T. 59. Error Analysis Trent found that both the lines shown had the same slope and concluded that the equations represent parallel lines. Is Trent correct? Explain.

$$5x + 2y = 12$$
$$4(y - 6) = -10x$$

H.O.T. 60. Problem Solving Three points are shown.

    a. Write an equation of a line that contains two of the points.

    b. Write an equation of a line through the third point that is parallel to your line.

    c. Write an equation of the line through the third point that is perpendicular to your line.

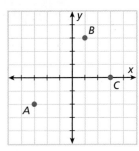

18-2 The Midpoint and Distance Formulas

Essential Question: How can you apply the Midpoint and Distance Formulas?

Objectives
Apply the formula for midpoint.

Use the Distance Formula to find the distance between two points.

Vocabulary
midpoint

Why learn this?

You can use the coordinate plane to model and solve problems involving distances, such as the distance across a lake. (See Example 4.)

You have used the coordinates of points to determine the slope of lines. You can also use coordinates to determine the *midpoint* of a line segment on the coordinate plane.

The **midpoint** of a line segment is the point that divides the segment into two congruent segments. *Congruent segments* are segments that have the same length.

You can find the midpoint of a segment by using the coordinates of its endpoints. Calculate the average of the *x*-coordinates and the average of the *y*-coordinates of the endpoints.

Midpoint Formula

The midpoint M of $\overline{AB}$ with endpoints $A(x_1, y_1)$ and $B(x_2, y_2)$ is

$$M\left(\frac{x_1 + x_2}{2}, \frac{y_1 + y_2}{2}\right).$$

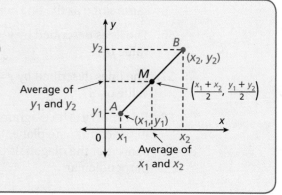

Average of y_1 and y_2

$\left(\frac{x_1 + x_2}{2}, \frac{y_1 + y_2}{2}\right)$

Average of x_1 and x_2

EXAMPLE MCC9-12.G.GPE.6

1 **Finding the Coordinates of a Midpoint**

Find the coordinates of the midpoint of $\overline{CD}$ with endpoints $C(-2, -1)$ and $D(4, 2)$.

$M\left(\dfrac{x_1 + x_2}{2}, \dfrac{y_1 + y_2}{2}\right)$ *Write the formula.*

$M\left(\dfrac{-2 + 4}{2}, \dfrac{-1 + 2}{2}\right)$ *Substitute.*

$M\left(\dfrac{2}{2}, \dfrac{1}{2}\right) = M\left(1, \dfrac{1}{2}\right)$ *Simplify.*

my.hrw.com

Online Video Tutor

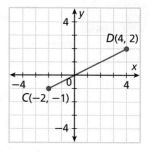

 CHECK IT OUT!

1. Find the coordinates of the midpoint of $\overline{EF}$ with endpoints $E(-2, 3)$ and $F(5, -3)$.

Ilene MacDonald/Alamy

EXAMPLE **2**
Ext. of MCC9-12.G.GPE.6

Finding the Coordinates of an Endpoint

M is the midpoint of $\overline{AB}$. *A* has coordinates $(2, 2)$, and *M* has coordinates $(4, -3)$. **Find the coordinates of *B*.**

Step 1 Let the coordinates of *B* equal (x, y).

Step 2 Use the Midpoint Formula.

$$(4, -3) = \left(\frac{2 + x}{2}, \frac{2 + y}{2} \right)$$

Step 3 Find the *x*-coordinate.   Find the *y*-coordinate.

$4 = \dfrac{2 + x}{2}$	*Set the coordinates equal.*	$-3 = \dfrac{2 + y}{2}$
$2(4) = 2\left(\dfrac{2 + x}{2}\right)$	*Multiply both sides by 2.*	$2(-3) = 2\left(\dfrac{2 + y}{2}\right)$
$8 = \;\; 2 + x$	*Simplify.*	$-6 = \;\; 2 + y$
$\dfrac{-2 \quad -2}{6 = \qquad x}$	*Subtract 2 from both sides.* *Simplify.*	$\dfrac{-2 \quad -2}{-8 = \qquad y}$

The coordinates of *B* are $(6, -8)$.

Check Graph points *A* and *B* and midpoint *M*.

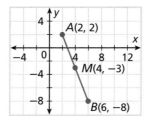

Point M appears to be the midpoint of $\overline{AB}$.

2. *S* is the midpoint of $\overline{RT}$. *R* has coordinates $(-6, -1)$, and *S* has coordinates $(-1, 1)$. Find the coordinates of *T*.

You can also use coordinates to find the distance between two points or the length of a line segment. To find the length of segment *PQ*, draw a horizontal segment from *P* and a vertical segment from *Q* to form a right triangle.

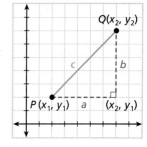

Remember!

The *Pythagorean Theorem* states that if a right triangle has legs of lengths *a* and *b* and a hypotenuse of length *c*, then $a^2 + b^2 = c^2$.

$c^2 = a^2 + b^2$	*Pythagorean Theorem*
$c = \sqrt{a^2 + b^2}$	*Solve for c. Use the positive square root to represent distance.*

$$PQ = \sqrt{\underbrace{(x_2 - x_1)^2}_{} + \underbrace{(y_2 - y_1)^2}_{}}$$

Length of   Length of
horizontal segment   vertical segment

This equation represents the Distance Formula.

Distance Formula

In a coordinate plane, the distance *d* between two points (x_1, y_1) and (x_2, y_2) is

$$d = \sqrt{(x_2 - x_1)^2 + (y_2 - y_1)^2}.$$

EXAMPLE 3
Prep. for MCC9-12.G.GPE.7

Finding Distance in the Coordinate Plane

Use the Distance Formula to find the distance, to the nearest hundredth, from $A(-2, 3)$ to $B(2, -2)$.

my.hrw.com

Online Video Tutor

$d = \sqrt{(x_2 - x_1)^2 + (y_2 - y_1)^2}$ *Distance Formula*

$d = \sqrt{[2 - (-2)]^2 + (-2 - 3)^2}$ *Substitute (−2, 3) for (x₁, y₁) and (2, −2) for (x₂, y₂).*

$d = \sqrt{4^2 + (-5)^2}$ *Subtract.*

$d = \sqrt{16 + 25}$ *Simplify powers.*

$d = \sqrt{41}$ *Add.*

$d \approx 6.40$ *Find the square root to the nearest hundredth.*

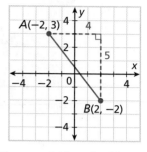

CHECK IT OUT!   **3.** Use the Distance Formula to find the distance, to the nearest hundredth, from $R(3, 2)$ to $S(-3, -1)$.

EXAMPLE 4
MCC9-12.A.CED.2

Geography Application

my.hrw.com

Online Video Tutor

Each unit on the map of Lake Okeechobee represents 1 mile. Delia and her father plan to travel from point A near the town of Okeechobee to point B at Pahokee. To the nearest tenth of a mile, how far do Delia and her father plan to travel?

$d = \sqrt{(x_2 - x_1)^2 + (y_2 - y_1)^2}$

$d = \sqrt{(33 - 22)^2 + (13 - 39)^2}$ *Substitute.*

$d = \sqrt{11^2 + (-26)^2}$ *Subtract.*

$d = \sqrt{121 + 676}$ *Simplify powers.*

$d = \sqrt{797}$ *Add.*

$d \approx 28.2$ *Find the square root to the nearest tenth.*

Delia and her father plan to travel about 28.2 miles.

CHECK IT OUT!   **4.** Jacob takes a boat from Pahokee to Clewiston. To the nearest tenth of a mile, how far does he travel?

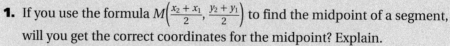
MCC.MP.3   MATHEMATICAL PRACTICES

THINK AND DISCUSS

1. If you use the formula $M\left(\frac{x_2 + x_1}{2}, \frac{y_2 + y_1}{2}\right)$ to find the midpoint of a segment, will you get the correct coordinates for the midpoint? Explain.

Know it! Note

2. GET ORGANIZED Copy and complete the graphic organizer. In each box, write a formula. Then make a sketch that will illustrate the formula.

Formulas
— Midpoint Formula
— Distance Formula

GUIDED PRACTICE

1. **Vocabulary** In your own words, describe the *midpoint* of a line segment.

SEE EXAMPLE 1 **Find the coordinates of the midpoint of each segment.**

2. $\overline{AB}$ with endpoints $A(4, -6)$ and $B(-4, 2)$

3. $\overline{CD}$ with endpoints $C(0, -8)$ and $D(3, 0)$

4. $\overline{EF}$ with endpoints $E(-8, 17)$ and $F(-12, -16)$

SEE EXAMPLE 2 5. M is the midpoint of $\overline{LN}$. L has coordinates $(-3, -1)$, and M has coordinates $(0, 1)$. Find the coordinates of N.

6. B is the midpoint of $\overline{AC}$. A has coordinates $(-3, 4)$, and B has coordinates $\left(-1\frac{1}{2}, 1\right)$. Find the coordinates of C.

SEE EXAMPLE 3 **Use the Distance Formula to find the distance, to the nearest hundredth, between each pair of points.**

7. $A(1, -2)$ and $B(-4, -4)$

8. $X(-2, 7)$ and $Y(-2, -8)$

9. $V(2, -1)$ and $W(-4, 8)$

SEE EXAMPLE 4 10. **Recreation** Each unit on the map of a public park represents 1 kilometer. To the nearest tenth of a kilometer, what is the distance from the campground to the waterfall?

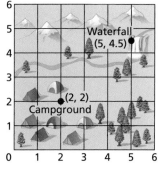

PRACTICE AND PROBLEM SOLVING

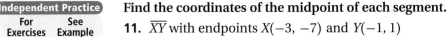

my.hrw.com

Online Extra Practice

Find the coordinates of the midpoint of each segment.

11. $\overline{XY}$ with endpoints $X(-3, -7)$ and $Y(-1, 1)$

12. $\overline{MN}$ with endpoints $M(12, -7)$ and $N(-5, -2)$

13. M is the midpoint of $\overline{QR}$. Q has coordinates $(-3, 5)$, and M has coordinates $(7, -9)$. Find the coordinates of R.

14. D is the midpoint of $\overline{CE}$. E has coordinates $(-3, -2)$, and D has coordinates $\left(2\frac{1}{2}, 1\right)$. Find the coordinates of C.

15. Y is the midpoint of $\overline{XZ}$. X has coordinates $(0, -1)$, and Y has coordinates $\left(1, -4\frac{1}{2}\right)$. Find the coordinates of Z.

Use the Distance Formula to find the distance, to the nearest hundredth, between each pair of points.

16. $U(0, 1)$ and $V(-3, -9)$

17. $M(10, -1)$ and $N(2, -5)$

18. $P(-10, 1)$ and $Q(5, 5)$

19. $F(6, 15)$ and $G(4, 24)$

20. **Astronomy** Each unit on the map of a section of a moon represents 1 kilometer. To the nearest tenth of a kilometer, what is the distance between the two craters?

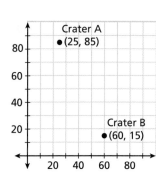

For Exercises 21 and 22, use the map, and round your answers to the nearest tenth of a mile. Each unit on the map represents 1 mile.

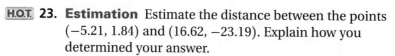

21. How far is it from Cedar City to Milltown along Highway 201?

22. A car breaks down on Route 1 halfway between Jefferson and Milltown. A tow truck is sent out from Jefferson. How far does the truck travel to reach the car?

H.O.T 23. **Estimation** Estimate the distance between the points $(-5.21, 1.84)$ and $(16.62, -23.19)$. Explain how you determined your answer.

24. **Geometry** The coordinates of the vertices of $\triangle ABC$ are $A(1, 4)$, $B(-2, -1)$, and $C(3, -2)$. Find the perimeter of $\triangle ABC$ to the nearest whole number.

Find the distance, to the nearest hundredth, between each pair of points.

25. $J(0, 3)$ and $K(-6, -9)$ 26. $L(-5, 2)$ and $M(-8, 10)$ 27. $N(4, -6)$ and $P(-2, 7)$

28. **Aviation** A Coast Guard helicopter receives a distress signal from a boat. The units on the map represent miles. To the nearest minute, how long will it take the helicopter to reach the boat if the helicopter travels at an average speed of 75 miles per hour?

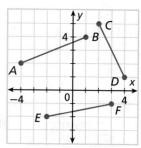

29. **Geometry** A diameter of a circle has endpoints $(-2, -5)$ and $(2, 1)$.

   a. Find the length of the diameter to the nearest tenth.

   b. Find the coordinates of the center of the circle.

   c. Find the circumference of the circle to the nearest whole number.

30. **Travel** A group of tourists is traveling by camel in the desert. They are following a straight path from point $(2, 4)$ to point $(8, 12)$ on a map. Each unit on the map represents 1 mile. An oasis lies at the midpoint of the path. The group has already traveled 3.2 miles. How much farther do they need to go to reach the oasis?

31. **Multi-Step** Use the Distance Formula to order $\overline{AB}$, $\overline{CD}$, and $\overline{EF}$ from shortest to longest.

H.O.T 32. **Critical Thinking** Rebecca found the x-coordinate of the midpoint of $\overline{AB}$ with endpoints $A(x_1, y_1)$ and $B(x_2, y_2)$ by dividing the difference between x_2 and x_1 by 2 and then adding the quotient to x_1. Did this method give the correct x-coordinate for the midpoint? Explain.

H.O.T 33. **Write About It** Explain why the Distance Formula is not needed to find the distance between two points that lie on a horizontal or vertical line.

34. On a map of a city park, the ordered pairs $(3, 5)$ and $(8, 17)$ mark the starting and ending points of a straight jogging trail. Each unit on the map represents 0.1 mile.

   a. What is the length of the trail in miles?

   b. How many back-and-forth trips would Marisol need to make on the trail in order to run at least 7 miles?

TEST PREP

35. Which segment has a length closest to 4 units?

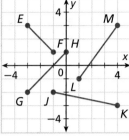

(A) $\overline{EF}$ (C) $\overline{JK}$

(B) $\overline{GH}$ (D) $\overline{LM}$

36. What is the distance between the points $(7, -3)$ and $(-5, 6)$?

(F) 4   (H) 15

(G) 9   (J) 21

37. A coordinate plane is placed over the map of a town. A library is located at $(-5, 1)$, and a museum is located at $(3, 5)$. What is the distance, to the nearest tenth, from the library to the museum?

(A) 4.5 units   (B) 5.7 units   (C) 6.3 units   (D) 8.9 units

H.O.T. 38. Short Response Brian is driving along a straight highway. His truck can travel 22 miles per gallon of gasoline, and it has 2 gallons of gas remaining. On a map, the truck's current location is $(7, 12)$, and the nearest gas station on the highway is located at $(16, 52)$. Each unit on the map represents 1 mile. Will the truck reach the gas station before running out of gas? Support your answer.

CHALLENGE AND EXTEND

39. Geometry Find the area of a trapezoid with vertices $A(-4, 2)$, $B(0, 4)$, $C(3, 3)$, and $D(-3, 0)$. (*Hint:* The formula for the area of a trapezoid is $A = \frac{1}{2}h(b_1 + b_2)$.)

40. X has coordinates $(a, 3a)$, and Y has coordinates $(-5a, 0)$. Find the coordinates of the midpoint of $\overline{XY}$.

41. The coordinates of P are $(a - 5, 0)$. The coordinates of Q are $(a + 1, a)$. The distance between P and Q is 10 units. Find the value of a.

42. Find two points on the y-axis that are a distance of 5 units from $(4, 2)$.

43. The coordinates of S are $(4, 5)$. The coordinates of the midpoint of $\overline{ST}$ are $(-1, -7)$. Find the length of $\overline{ST}$.

FOCUS ON MATHEMATICAL PRACTICES

H.O.T. 44. Reasoning Two line segments on a graph are parallel and congruent.

  a. Will they have the same midpoint? Explain.

  b. Are the distances between the endpoints of each segment the same? Explain.

H.O.T. 45. Analysis On a graph, $\overline{DF}$ is a line segment and point E is equidistant from D and F. Is E the midpoint of $\overline{DF}$? Justify your answer.

H.O.T. 46. Reasoning Carmen says she can find the distance between two points on a graph by using this formula: $d = \sqrt{(x_1 - x_2)^2 + (y_2 - y_1)^2}$. Is she correct? Explain your answer.

H.O.T. 47. Draw Conclusions Alex graphs the line segment from $(0, 0)$ to $(5, 5)$ and labels it $\overline{AB}$. He graphs segment $\overline{AC}$ from $(0, 0)$ to $(-5, -5)$. Without calculating, determine whether $\overline{AB}$ or $\overline{AC}$ is longer, or if they are the same length. Explain.

Ready to Go On?

my.hrw.com
Assessment and Intervention

18-1 Slopes of Parallel and Perpendicular Lines

Identify which lines are parallel.

1. $y = -\frac{1}{3}x$; $y = 3x + 2$; $y = -\frac{1}{3}x - 6$; $y = 3$

2. $y - 2 = -4(x - 1)$; $y = 4x - 4$; $y = \frac{1}{4}x$; $y = -4x - 2$

3. $y = -2x$; $y = 2x + 1$; $y = 2x$; $y = 2(x + 5)$

4. $-3y = x$; $y = -\frac{1}{3}x + 1$; $y = -3x$; $y + 2 = x + 4$

Identify which lines are perpendicular.

5. $y = -4x - 1$; $y = \frac{1}{4}x$; $y = 4x - 6$; $x = -4$

6. $y = -\frac{3}{4}x$; $y = \frac{3}{4}x - 3$; $y = \frac{4}{3}x$; $y = 4$; $x = 3$

7. $y - 1 = -5(x - 6)$; $y = \frac{1}{5}x + 2$; $y = 5$; $y = 5x + 8$

8. $y = 2x$; $y - 2 = 3(x + 1)$; $y = \frac{2}{3}x - 4$; $y = -\frac{1}{3}x$

9. Write an equation in slope-intercept form for the line that passes through $(1, -1)$ and is parallel to the line described by $y = 2x - 4$.

18-2 The Midpoint and Distance Formulas

Find the coordinates of the midpoint of each segment.

10. $\overline{EF}$ with endpoints $E(9, 12)$ and $F(21, 18)$

11. $\overline{GH}$ with endpoints $G(-5, -7)$ and $H(4, -11)$

12. Find the coordinates of the midpoint of $\overline{XY}$ with endpoints $X(-4, 6)$ and $Y(3, 8)$.

Use the Distance Formula to find the distance, to the nearest hundredth, between each pair of points.

13. $J(3, 10)$ and $K(-2, 4)$

14. $L(-6, 0)$ and $M(8, -7)$

15. Each unit on a map of a forest represents 1 mile. To the nearest tenth of a mile, what is the distance from a ranger station at $(1, 2)$ on the map to a river crossing at $(2, 4)$?

16. On a treasure map, the coordinates of a crooked palm tree are $(3, 6)$, and the coordinates of a buried treasure chest are $(12, 18)$. Each unit on the map represents 10 feet. What is the distance in feet between the palm tree and the treasure chest?

PARCC Assessment Readiness

Selected Response

1. The equations of four lines are given. Identify which lines are parallel.

Line 1: $y = 8x - 3$

Line 2: $y - 6 = \dfrac{1}{8}(x - 4)$

Line 3: $y = 3x + 4$

Line 4: $x - \dfrac{1}{3}y = -4$

(A) Lines 2 and 3 are parallel.

(B) Lines 3 and 4 are parallel.

(C) All four lines are parallel.

(D) None of the lines are parallel.

2. Identify the lines that are perpendicular:
$y = 4;\ y = \dfrac{1}{5}x - 5;\ x = 8;\ y + 5 = -5(x + 1)$

(F) Only $y = \dfrac{1}{5}x - 5$ and $y + 5 = -5(x + 1)$ are perpendicular.

(G) Only $y = 4$ and $x = 8$ are perpendicular.

(H) $y = 4$ and $x = 8$ are perpendicular; $y = \dfrac{1}{5}x - 5$ and $y + 5 = -5(x + 1)$ are perpendicular.

(J) None of the lines are perpendicular.

3. M is the midpoint of $\overline{AN}$, A has coordinates $(-2, 6)$, and M has coordinates $(1, 2)$. Find the coordinates of N.

(A) $(4, -2)$ (C) $(-1, 8)$

(B) $\left(4\dfrac{1}{2}, -\dfrac{1}{2}\right)$ (D) $\left(-\dfrac{1}{2}, 4\right)$

4. What is the area of the square?

(F) 16

(G) 25

(H) 32

(J) 36

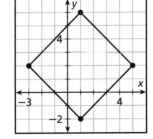

5. The line segment between the points $(4, 0)$ and $(2, -2)$ forms one side of a rectangle. Which of the following coordinates could determine another vertex of that rectangle?

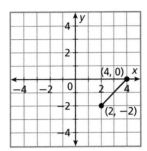

(A) $(-2, 6)$

(B) $(-2, -2)$

(C) $(0, 6)$

(D) $(1, 2)$

6. Find CD and EF. Then determine if $\overline{CD} \cong \overline{EF}$.

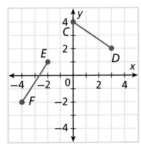

(F) $CD = \sqrt{13}$, $EF = \sqrt{13}$, $\overline{CD} \cong \overline{EF}$

(G) $CD = \sqrt{5}$, $EF = \sqrt{13}$, $\overline{CD} \not\cong \overline{EF}$

(H) $CD = \sqrt{13}$, $EF = 3\sqrt{5}$, $\overline{CD} \not\cong \overline{EF}$

(J) $CD = \sqrt{5}$, $EF = \sqrt{5}$, $\overline{CD} \cong \overline{EF}$

Mini-Task

7. Sketch the polygon with vertices $D(-1, 3)$, $E(2, 3)$, and $F(2, -5)$. Then find the area.

PARCC Assessment Readiness

COMMON
CORE GPS

Selected Response

1. A line passes through point *A* at (2, 3) and point *B* at (4, 7). Which is the equation of $\overleftrightarrow{BC}$ if $\overleftrightarrow{AB} \perp \overleftrightarrow{BC}$?

Ⓐ $y = -2x + 5$

Ⓑ $y = -\frac{1}{2}x + 5$

Ⓒ $y = -\frac{1}{2}x + 9$

Ⓓ $y = \frac{1}{2}x + 5$

2. Which line is parallel to the line described by $2x + 3y = 6$?

Ⓕ $3x + 2y = 6$

Ⓖ $3x - 2y = -6$

Ⓗ $2x + 3y = -6$

Ⓙ $2x - 3y = 6$

3. Which function's graph is NOT perpendicular to the line described by $4x - y = -2$?

Ⓐ $y + \frac{1}{4}x = 0$

Ⓑ $\frac{1}{2}x = 10 - 2y$

Ⓒ $3y = \frac{3}{4}x + 3$

Ⓓ $y = -\frac{1}{4}x + \frac{3}{2}$

4. Which equation describes a line perpendicular to $y = 8x - 9$ that passes through the point (9, −9)?

Ⓕ $y = 8x - 81$

Ⓖ $y = -\frac{1}{8}x - \frac{63}{8}$

Ⓗ $y = 8x - 9$

Ⓙ $y = -\frac{1}{8}x + \frac{585}{8}$

5. Point *P* is on the line segment from point *A*(−11, 4) to point *B*(−1, −6) and divides the segment in the ratio 1 to 3. Which could be the coordinates of *P*?

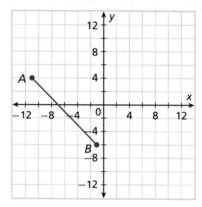

Ⓐ $P(-6, -1)$

Ⓑ $P(-3, -4)$

Ⓒ $P\left(-\frac{7}{2}, -\frac{7}{2}\right)$

Ⓓ $P\left(-\frac{9}{5}, \frac{2}{5}\right)$

6. What is the area of the polygon?

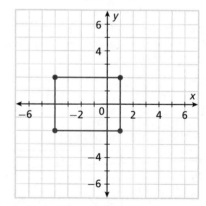

Ⓕ 18 units²

Ⓖ 18 units

Ⓗ 20 units²

Ⓙ 20 units

When answering multiple-choice test items, check that the test item number matches the number on your answer sheet, especially if you skip test items that you plan to come back to.

7. Which are the vertices of a polygon with a perimeter of $10\sqrt{5}$ units?

   (A) $A(5, -1)$, $B(-1, -4)$, $C(-3, 1)$

   (B) $K(-4, 1)$, $L(0, 4)$, $M(4, 0)$, $N(-2, -3)$

   (C) $P(-4, 1)$, $Q(2, 4)$, $R(4, 0)$, $S(-2, -3)$

   (D) $T(5, -1)$, $U(-1, -4)$, $V(0, 3)$

8. What are the coordinates of the midpoint of $\overline{BL}$ with endpoints $B(-7, -4)$ and $L(2, 3)$?

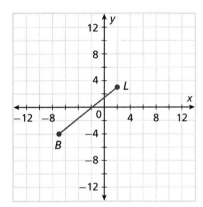

   (F) $\left(-3\frac{1}{2}, -1\frac{1}{2}\right)$ (H) $\left(-1\frac{1}{2}, 0\right)$

   (G) $\left(-2\frac{1}{2}, -\frac{1}{2}\right)$ (J) $(-5, -1)$

9. Jocelyn writes the equation of a line that passes through the point $(4, 0)$ and is perpendicular to the line $y = 2x + 1$. Jocelyn writes her equation in the form $y = mx + b$. What are the values of m and b?

   (A) $m = 2$, $b = 1$ (C) $m = -\frac{1}{2}$, $b = 2$

   (B) $m = 2$, $b = 2$ (D) $m = -\frac{1}{2}$, $b = 4$

10. Nadine graphs a line using the tables of values shown. Mei graphs a line that is parallel to Nadine's line. Which of these could be the equation of Mei's line?

x	y
−2	6
−1	4
2	−2
4	6

   (F) $-x + 2y = 8$ (H) $2x + y = 8$

   (G) $x + 2y = 8$ (J) $-2x + y = -8$

11. Ricardo plots the points $(0, 0)$, $(6, 0)$, and $(0, 8)$. Then he connects the points to form a right triangle. What is the length of the triangle's hypotenuse?

   (A) 5 units   (C) 14 units

   (B) 10 units   (D) 100 units

Mini-Tasks

12. Find the coordinates of the midpoint of each side of the parallelogram.

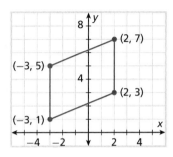

13. Each unit on a coordinate map of a bay represents 1 kilometer. Two buoys are located at $(1, 5)$ and $(3, 6)$. To the nearest tenth of a kilometer, what is the distance between the two buoys?

Performance Task

14. Show that LMN is a right triangle.

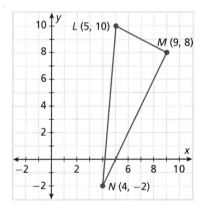

my.hrw.com
Online Assessment

Go online for updated, PARCC-aligned assessment readiness.

Are You Ready?

my.hrw.com
Assessment and Intervention

☑ Vocabulary

Match each term on the left with a definition on the right.

1. coordinate

2. metric system of measurement

3. expression

4. order of operations

A. a mathematical phrase that contains operations, numbers, and/or variables

B. the measurement system often used in the United States

C. one of the numbers of an ordered pair that locates a point on a coordinate graph

D. a list of rules for evaluating expressions

E. a decimal system of weights and measures that is used universally in science and commonly throughout the world

☑ Measure with Customary and Metric Units

For each object tell which is the better measurement.

5. length of an unsharpened pencil
$7\frac{1}{2}$ in. or $9\frac{3}{4}$ in.

6. the diameter of a quarter
1 m or $2\frac{1}{2}$ cm

7. length of a soccer field
100 yd or 40 yd

8. height of a classroom
5 ft or 10 ft

9. height of a student's desk
30 in. or 4 ft

10. length of a dollar bill
15.6 cm or 35.5 cm

☑ Combine Like Terms

Simplify each expression.

11. $-y + 3y - 6y + 12y$

12. $63 + 2x - 7 - 4x$

13. $-5 - 9 - 7x + 6x$

14. $24 - 3y + y + 7$

☑ Evaluate Expressions

Evaluate each expression for the given value of the variable.

15. $x + 3x + 7x$ for $x = -5$

16. $5p + 10$ for $p = 78$

Career Readiness Lawyers

Lawyers represent clients in civil or criminal trials, and advise people and businesses on what they can and can't do under the law. In a trial, a lawyer must convince a judge or a jury by presenting chains of logical reasoning, much as you would prove a theorem. A lawyer must have a college degree plus three years of law school. Finally, a lawyer must pass a bar exam. Lawyers may work in government, in law offices or law schools, in for-profit or non-profit organizations, or be self-employed.

COMMON CORE GPS

UNIT 7

Similarity, Congruence, and Proofs

Online Edition

my.hrw.com
Access the complete online textbook, interactive features, and additional resources.

Animated Math
Interactively explore key concepts with these online tutorials.

Multilingual Glossary
Enhance your math vocabulary with this illustrated online glossary in 13 languages.

Portable Devices

On the Spot
Watch video tutorials anywhere, anytime with this app for iPhone® and iPad®.

HMH Fuse
Make your learning experience completely portable and interactive with this app for iPad®.

Chapter Resources
Scan with your smart phone to jump directly to the online edition.

Homework Help provides video tutorials, step-by-step solutions, and additional practice for lesson exercises.

COMMON CORE GPS
Unit Contents

Module 19 Tools of Geometry
MCC9-12.G.CO.12

Module 20 Algebraic and Geometric Proofs
MCC9-12.A.REI.1, MCC9-12.G.CO.9

Module 21 Proving Theorems about Lines and Angles
MCC9-12.G.CO.9, MCC9-12.G.CO.12

Module 22 Congruence and Triangles
MCC9-12.G.CO.5, MCC9-12.G.CO.6, MCC9-12.G.CO.7, MCC9-12.G.CO.10

Module 23 Proving Triangles Congruent
MCC9-12.G.CO.7, MCC9-12.G.CO.8, MCC9-12.G.CO.10, MCC9-12.G.CO.13

Module 24 Special Points and Segments in Triangles
MCC9-12.G.C.3, MCC9-12.G.CO.9, MCC9-12.G.CO.10, MCC9-12.G.CO.12

Module 25 Proving Theorems about Parallelograms
MCC9-12.G.CO.11

Module 26 Similarity
MCC9-12.G.C.1, MCC9-12.G.CO.12, MCC9-12.G.SRT.2, MCC9-12.G.SRT.4

19

Tools of Geometry

COMMON CORE GPS

Contents

The Common Core Georgia Performance Standards for Mathematical Practice describe varieties of expertise that all students should seek to develop. Opportunities to develop these practices are integrated throughout this program.

1 Make sense of problems and persevere in solving them.

2 Reason abstractly and quantitatively.

3 Construct viable arguments and critique the reasoning of others.

4 Model with mathematics.

5 Use appropriate tools strategically.

6 Attend to precision.

7 Look for and make use of structure.

8 Look for and express regularity in repeated reasoning.

Unpacking the Standards

Understanding the standards and the vocabulary terms in the standards will help you know exactly what you are expected to learn in this chapter.

 MCC9-12.G.CO.12

Make formal geometric constructions with a variety of tools and methods (compass and straightedge, string, reflective devices, paper folding, dynamic geometric software, etc.).

Key Vocabulary

construction (construcción) A method of creating a figure that is considered to be mathematically precise. Figures may be constructed by using a compass and straightedge, geometry software, or paper folding.

What It Means For You

Construction methods give you precise ways to create or copy geometric figures without having to measure and/or estimate.

EXAMPLE

How can you divide $\overline{XY}$ in half without measuring?

Fold the paper in half so that the points X and Y line up exactly.

Unfold the paper and mark the point M where the fold meets the segment. You have found the midpoint of $\overline{XY}$!

19-1
Technology TASK

Use with Measuring and Constructing Segments

Explore Properties Associated with Points

The two endpoints of a segment determine its length. Other points on the segment are *between* the endpoints. Only one of these points is the *midpoint* of the segment. In this task, you will use geometry software to measure lengths of segments and explore properties of points on segments.

Use appropriate tools strategically.

MCC9-12.G.CO.1 Know precise definitions ... based on the undefined notions of point, line, distance along a line ...

Activity

1 Construct a segment and label its endpoints *A* and *C*.

2 Create point *B* on $\overline{AC}$.

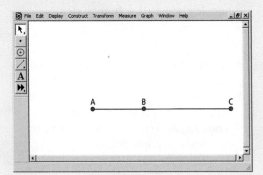

3 Measure the distances from *A* to *B* and from *B* to *C*. Use the Calculate tool to calculate the sum of *AB* and *BC*.

4 Measure the length of $\overline{AC}$. What do you notice about this length compared with the measurements found in Step 3?

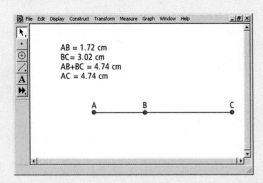

5 Drag point *B* along $\overline{AC}$. Drag one of the endpoints of $\overline{AC}$. What relationships do you think are true about the three measurements?

6 Construct the midpoint of $\overline{AC}$ and label it *M*.

7 Measure $\overline{AM}$ and $\overline{MC}$. What relationships do you think are true about the lengths of $\overline{AC}$, $\overline{AM}$, and $\overline{MC}$? Use the Calculate tool to confirm your findings.

8 How many midpoints of $\overline{AC}$ exist?

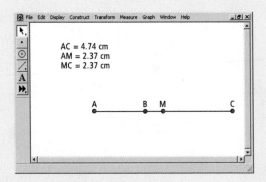

Try This

1. Repeat the activity with a new segment. Drag each of the points in your figure (the endpoints, the point on the segment, and the midpoint). Write down any relationships you observe about the measurements.

2. Create a point *D* not on $\overline{AC}$. Measure $\overline{AD}$, $\overline{DC}$, and $\overline{AC}$. Does *AD* + *DC* = *AC*? What do you think has to be true about *D* for the relationship to always be true?

19-1 Measuring and Constructing Segments

Essential Question: How can you measure, construct, and describe segments?

Objectives
Use length and midpoint of a segment.

Construct midpoints and congruent segments.

Vocabulary
coordinate
distance
length
congruent segments
construction
between
midpoint
bisect
segment bisector

Why learn this?
You can measure a segment to calculate the distance between two locations. Maps of a race are used to show the distance between stations on the course. (See Example 4.)

A ruler can be used to measure the distance between two points. A point corresponds to one and only one number on the ruler. This number is called a **coordinate** . The following postulate summarizes this concept.

Postulate 19-1-1 | **Ruler Postulate**

The points on a line can be put into a one-to-one correspondence with the real numbers.

The **distance** between any two points is the absolute value of the difference of the coordinates. If the coordinates of points A and B are a and b, then the distance between A and B is $|a - b|$ or $|b - a|$. The distance between A and B is also called the **length** of $\overline{AB}$, or AB.

$$AB = |a - b| = |b - a|$$

EXAMPLE 1
MCC9-12.G.CO.1

Finding the Length of a Segment

Find each length.

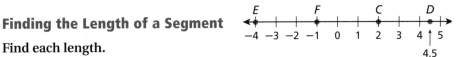

A DC
$$DC = |4.5 - 2|$$
$$= |2.5|$$
$$= 2.5$$

B EF
$$EF = |-4 - (-1)|$$
$$= |-4 + 1|$$
$$= |-3|$$
$$= 3$$

my.hrw.com

Online Video Tutor

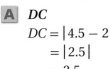

CHECK IT OUT!

Find each length.
1a. XY
1b. XZ

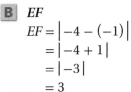

Caution!

PQ represents a number, while $\overline{PQ}$ represents a geometric figure. Be sure to use equality for numbers ($PQ = RS$) and congruence for figures ($\overline{PQ} \cong \overline{RS}$).

Congruent segments are segments that have the same length. In the diagram, $PQ = RS$, so you can write $\overline{PQ} \cong \overline{RS}$. This is read as "segment PQ is congruent to segment RS." *Tick marks* are used in a figure to show congruent segments.

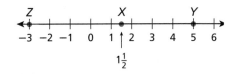

Tick marks

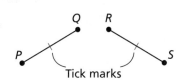

You can make a sketch or measure and draw a segment. These may not be exact. A **construction** is a way of creating a figure that is more precise. One way to make a geometric construction is to use a compass and straightedge.

Construction   Congruent Segment

Construct a segment congruent to $\overline{AB}$.

❶

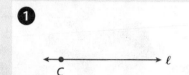

Draw ℓ. Choose a point on ℓ and label it C.

❷

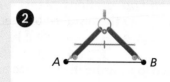

Open the compass to distance AB.

❸

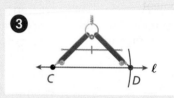

Place the point of the compass at C and make an arc through ℓ. Find the point where the arc and ℓ intersect and label it D.

$$\overline{CD} \cong \overline{AB}$$

COMMON CORE GPS
MCC9-12.G.CO.12

EXAMPLE 2   Copying a Segment

Sketch, draw, and construct a segment congruent to $\overline{MN}$.

my.hrw.com

Online Video Tutor

Step 1 Estimate and sketch.
Estimate the length of $\overline{MN}$ and sketch $\overline{PQ}$ approximately the same length.

Step 2 Measure and draw.
Use a ruler to measure $\overline{MN}$. MN appears to be 3.1 cm. Use a ruler and draw $\overline{XY}$ to have length 3.1 cm.

Step 3 Construct and compare.
Use a compass and straightedge to construct $\overline{ST}$ congruent to $\overline{MN}$.

A ruler shows that $\overline{PQ}$ and $\overline{XY}$ are approximately the same length as $\overline{MN}$, but $\overline{ST}$ is precisely the same length.

CHECK IT OUT!

2. Sketch, draw, and construct a segment congruent to $\overline{JK}$.

In order for you to say that a point B is **between** two points A and C, all three of the points must lie on the same line, and AB + BC = AC.

Postulate 19-1-2   Segment Addition Postulate

If B is between A and C, then AB + BC = AC.

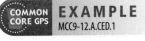

EXAMPLE **3** **Using the Segment Addition Postulate**

MCC9-12.A.CED.1

A B is between A and C, $AC = 14$, and $BC = 11.4$. Find AB.

$AC = AB + BC$	*Seg. Add. Post.*
$14 = AB + 11.4$	*Substitute 14 for AC and 11.4 for BC.*
$\underline{-11.4 \qquad -11.4}$	*Subtract 11.4 from both sides.*
$2.6 = AB$	*Simplify.*

B S is between R and T. Find RT.

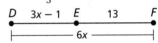

$RT = RS + ST$	*Seg. Add. Post.*
$4x = (2x + 7) + 28$	*Substitute the given values.*
$4x = 2x + 35$	*Simplify.*
$\underline{-2x \qquad -2x}$	*Subtract 2x from both sides.*
$2x = 35$	*Simplify.*
$\dfrac{2x}{2} = \dfrac{35}{2}$	*Divide both sides by 2.*
$x = \dfrac{35}{2}$, or 17.5	*Simplify.*
$RT = 4x$	
$\quad = 4(17.5) = 70$	*Substitute 17.5 for x.*

 3a. Y is between X and Z, $XZ = 3$, and $XY = 1\frac{1}{3}$. Find YZ.

3b. E is between D and F. Find DF.

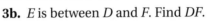

The **midpoint** M of $\overline{AB}$ is the point that **bisects**, or divides, the segment into two congruent segments. If M is the midpoint of $\overline{AB}$, then $AM = MB$. So if $AB = 6$, then $AM = 3$ and $MB = 3$.

EXAMPLE **4** ***Recreation Application***

MCC9-12.A.CED.1

The map shows the route for a race. You are 365 m from drink station R and 2 km from drink station S. The first-aid station is located at the midpoint of the two drink stations. How far are you from the first-aid station?

Let your current location be X and the location of the first-aid station be Y.

$XR + RS = XS$	*Seg. Add. Post.*
$365 + RS = 2000$	*Substitute 365 for XR and 2000 for XS.*
$\underline{-365 \qquad\quad -365}$	*Subtract 365 from both sides.*
$RS = 1635$	*Simplify.*
$RY = 817.5$	*Y is the mdpt. of $\overline{RS}$, so $RY = \frac{1}{2}RS$.*
$XY = XR + RY$	
$\quad = 365 + 817.5 = 1182.5$ m	*Substitute 365 for XR and 817.5 for RY.*

You are 1182.5 m from the first-aid station.

 4. What is the distance to a drink station located at the midpoint between your current location and the first-aid station?

A **segment bisector** is any ray, segment, or line that intersects a segment at its midpoint. It divides the segment into two equal parts at its midpoint.

Construction Segment Bisector

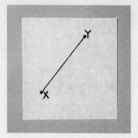

❶ Draw $\overline{XY}$ on a sheet of paper.

❷ Fold the paper so that Y is on top of X.

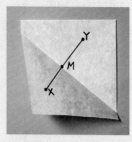

❸ Unfold the paper. The line represented by the crease bisects $\overline{XY}$. Label the midpoint M.

$XM = MY$

 COMMON CORE GPS
MCC9-12.A.CED.1

EXAMPLE 5

Using Midpoints to Find Lengths

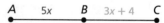

B is the midpoint of $\overline{AC}$, $AB = 5x$, and $BC = 3x + 4$. Find AB, BC, and AC.

my.hrw.com

Online Video Tutor

Step 1 Solve for x.

$AB = BC$	*B is the mdpt. of $\overline{AC}$.*
$5x = 3x + 4$	*Substitute 5x for AB and 3x + 4 for BC.*
$\underline{-3x \qquad -3x}$	*Subtract 3x from both sides.*
$2x = 4$	*Simplify.*
$\dfrac{2x}{2} = \dfrac{4}{2}$	*Divide both sides by 2.*
$x = 2$	*Simplify.*

Step 2 Find AB, BC, and AC.

$AB = 5x$	$BC = 3x + 4$	$AC = AB + BC$
$= 5(2) = 10$	$= 3(2) + 4 = 10$	$= 10 + 10 = 20$

CHECK IT OUT!

5. S is the midpoint of $\overline{RT}$, $RS = -2x$, and $ST = -3x - 2$. Find RS, ST, and RT.

MCC.MP.2  MATHEMATICAL PRACTICES

THINK AND DISCUSS

1. Suppose R is the midpoint of $\overline{ST}$. Explain how SR and ST are related.

2. GET ORGANIZED Copy and complete the graphic organizer. Make a sketch and write an equation to describe each relationship.

	B is between A and C.	B is the midpoint of $\overline{AC}$.
Sketch		
Equation		

(tl) (tc) (tr), Andy Christiansen/HMH Photo

GUIDED PRACTICE

Vocabulary Apply the vocabulary from this lesson to answer each question.

1. Line ℓ bisects $\overline{XY}$ at M and divides $\overline{XY}$ into two equal parts. Name a pair of congruent segments.

2. ___?___ is the amount of space between two points on a line. It is always expressed as a nonnegative number. (*distance* or *midpoint*)

SEE EXAMPLE 1 Find each length.

3. AB 4. BC

SEE EXAMPLE 2

5. Sketch, draw, and construct a segment congruent to $\overline{RS}$.

R   S

SEE EXAMPLE 3

6. B is between A and C, $AC = 15.8$, and $AB = 9.9$. Find BC.

7. Find MP.

M   17   N   3y   P

├──── $5y + 9$ ────┤

SEE EXAMPLE 4

8. **Travel** If a picnic area is located at the midpoint between Sacramento and Oakland, find the distance to the picnic area from the road sign.

Roseville	5
Sacramento	23
Oakland	110

SEE EXAMPLE 5

9. **Multi-Step** K is the midpoint of $\overline{JL}$, $JL = 4x - 2$, and $JK = 7$. Find x, KL, and JL.

10. E bisects $\overline{DF}$, $DE = 2y$, and $EF = 8y - 3$. Find DE, EF, and DF.

PRACTICE AND PROBLEM SOLVING

Independent Practice	
For Exercises	See Example
11–12	1
13	2
14–15	3
16	4
17–18	5

my.hrw.com

Online Extra Practice

Find each length.

11. DB 12. CD

13. Sketch, draw, and construct a segment twice the length of $\overline{AB}$.

A   B

14. D is between C and E, $CE = 17.1$, and $DE = 8$. Find CD.

15. Find MN.

M   2.5x   N   x   R

├──── $5x - 3$ ────┤

16. **Sports** During a football game, a quarterback standing at the 9-yard line passes the ball to a receiver at the 24-yard line. The receiver then runs with the ball halfway to the 50-yard line. How many total yards (passing plus running) did the team gain on the play?

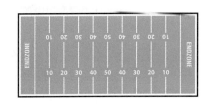

17. **Multi-Step** E is the midpoint of $\overline{DF}$, $DE = 2x + 4$, and $EF = 3x - 1$. Find DE, EF, and DF.

18. Q bisects $\overline{PR}$, $PQ = 3y$, and $PR = 42$. Find y and QR.

Real-World Connections

19. Prep. Archaeologists at Valley Forge were eager to find what remained of the winter camp that soldiers led by George Washington called home for several months. The diagram represents one of the restored log cabins.

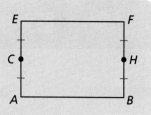

   a. How is C related to $\overline{AE}$?

   b. If $AC = 7$ ft, $EF = 2(AC) + 2$, and $AB = 2(EF) - 16$, what are AB and EF?

Use the diagram for Exercises 20–23.

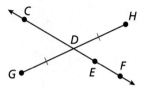

20. $GD = 4\frac{2}{3}$. Find GH.

21. $\overline{CD} \cong \overline{DF}$, E bisects $\overline{DF}$, and $CD = 14.2$. Find EF.

22. $GH = 4x - 1$, and $DH = 8$. Find x.

23. $\overline{GH}$ bisects $\overline{CF}$, $CF = 2y - 2$, and $CD = 3y - 11$. Find CD.

H.O.T. **Tell whether each statement is sometimes, always, or never true. Support each of your answers with a sketch.**

24. Two segments that have the same length must be congruent.

25. If M is between A and B, then M bisects $\overline{AB}$.

26. If Y is between X and Z, then X, Y, and Z are collinear.

27. ///**ERROR ANALYSIS**/// Below are two statements about the midpoint of $\overline{AB}$. Which is incorrect? Explain the error.

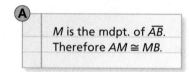

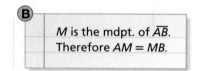

H.O.T. **28.** **Carpentry** A carpenter has a wooden dowel that is 72 cm long. She wants to cut it into two pieces so that one piece is 5 times as long as the other. What are the lengths of the two pieces?

29. The coordinate of M is 2.5, and $MN = 4$. What are the possible coordinates for N?

30. Draw three collinear points where E is between D and F. Then write an equation using these points and the Segment Addition Postulate.

Suppose S is between R and T. Use the Segment Addition Postulate to solve for each variable.

31. $RS = 7y - 4$
   $ST = y + 5$
   $RT = 28$

32. $RS = 3x + 1$
   $ST = \frac{1}{2}x + 3$
   $RT = 18$

33. $RS = 2z + 6$
   $ST = 4z - 3$
   $RT = 5z + 12$

34. **Write About It** In the diagram, B is not between A and C. Explain.

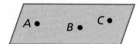

35. **Construction** Use a compass and straightedge to construct a segment whose length is $AB + CD$.

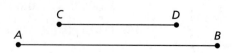

Photodisc Royalty Free

TEST PREP

36. Q is between P and R. S is between Q and R, and R is between Q and T. $PT = 34$, $QR = 8$, and $PQ = SQ = SR$. What is the length of $\overline{RT}$?

Ⓐ 9 　　　　 Ⓑ 10 　　　　 Ⓒ 18 　　　　 Ⓓ 22

37. C is the midpoint of $\overline{AD}$. B is the midpoint of $\overline{AC}$. $BC = 12$. What is the length of $\overline{AD}$?

Ⓕ 12 　　　　 Ⓖ 24 　　　　 Ⓗ 36 　　　　 Ⓙ 48

38. Which expression correctly states that $\overline{XY}$ is congruent to $\overline{VW}$?

Ⓐ $XY \cong VW$ 　　 Ⓑ $\overline{XY} \cong \overline{VW}$ 　　 Ⓒ $\overline{XY} = \overline{VW}$ 　　 Ⓓ $XY = VW$

39. A, B, C, D, and E are collinear points. $AE = 34$, $BD = 16$, and $AB = BC = CD$. What is the length of $\overline{CE}$?

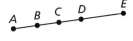

Ⓕ 10 　　　　 Ⓖ 16 　　　　 Ⓗ 18 　　　　 Ⓙ 24

CHALLENGE AND EXTEND

40. HJ is twice JK. J is between H and K. If $HJ = 4x$ and $HK = 78$, find JK.

41. A, D, N, and X are collinear points. D is between N and A. $NA + AX = NX$. Draw a diagram that represents this information.

Sports Use the following information for Exercises 42 and 43.

The table shows regulation distances between hurdles in women's and men's races. In both the women's and men's events, the race consists of a straight track with 10 equally spaced hurdles.

Event	Distance of Race	Distance from Start to First Hurdle	Distance Between Hurdles	Distance from Last Hurdle to Finish
Women's	100 m	13.00 m	8.50 m	
Men's	110 m	13.72 m	9.14 m	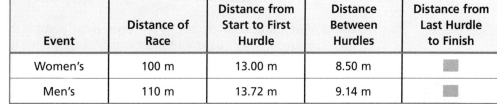

42. Find the distance from the last hurdle to the finish line for the women's race.

43. Find the distance from the last hurdle to the finish line for the men's race.

H.O.T. 44. Critical Thinking Given that J, K, and L are collinear and that K is between J and L, is it possible that $JK = JL$? If so, draw an example. If not, explain.

FOCUS ON MATHEMATICAL PRACTICES

H.O.T. 45. Number Sense Kendra said that when you compare the lengths of two segments, there are three possible relationships. Is Kendra correct? If so, what are the three relationships?

H.O.T. 46. Analysis Can you use the method for constructing a segment bisector to construct a line bisector? Explain why or why not.

H.O.T. 47. Precision Zuzu said tick marks indicate congruent segments. Josh said tick marks indicate segments with equal measures. Who is correct? Explain.

Sports

Joanna Hayes, of the United States, clears a hurdle on her way to winning the gold medal in the women's 100 m hurdles during the 2004 Olympic Games.

Gabriel Bouys/AFP/Getty Images

19-2 Measuring and Constructing Angles

? Essential Question: How can you measure, construct, and describe angles?

Objectives
Name and classify angles.

Measure and construct angles and angle bisectors.

Vocabulary
angle
vertex
interior of an angle
exterior of an angle
measure
degree
acute angle
right angle
obtuse angle
straight angle
congruent angles
angle bisector

Who uses this?
Surveyors use angles to help them measure and map the earth's surface. (See Exercise 27.)

A transit is a tool for measuring angles. It consists of a telescope that swivels horizontally and vertically. Using a transit, a surveyor can measure the *angle* formed by his or her location and two distant points.

An **angle** is a figure formed by two rays, or sides, with a common endpoint called the **vertex** (plural: *vertices*). You can name an angle several ways: by its vertex, by a point on each ray and the vertex, or by a number.

The set of all points between the sides of the angle is the **interior of an angle**. The **exterior of an angle** is the set of all points outside the angle.

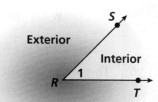

Angle Name

∠R, ∠SRT, ∠TRS, or ∠1

You cannot name an angle just by its vertex if the point is the vertex of more than one angle. In this case, you must use all three points to name the angle, and the middle point is always the vertex.

EXAMPLE 1 Naming Angles
MCC9-12.G.CO.1

A surveyor recorded the angles formed by a transit (point *T*) and three distant points, *Q*, *R*, and *S*. Name three of the angles.

∠QTR, ∠QTS, and ∠RTS

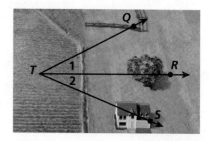

my.hrw.com

Online Video Tutor

 1. Write the different ways you can name the angles in the diagram.

The **measure** of an angle is usually given in degrees. Since there are 360° in a circle, one **degree** is $\frac{1}{360}$ of a circle. When you use a protractor to measure angles, you are applying the following postulate.

Postulate 19-2-1 | **Protractor Postulate**

Given $\overrightarrow{AB}$ and a point *O* on $\overrightarrow{AB}$, all rays that can be drawn from *O* can be put into a one-to-one correspondence with the real numbers from 0 to 180.

Gary Conner/Photo Edit

Using a Protractor

Most protractors have two sets of numbers around the edge. When I measure an angle and need to know which number to use, I first ask myself whether the angle is acute, right, or obtuse. For example, ∠RST looks like it is obtuse, so I know its measure must be 110°, not 70°.

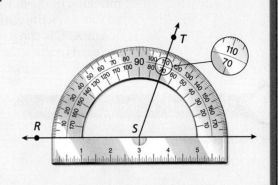

You can use the Protractor Postulate to help you classify angles by their measure. The measure of an angle is the absolute value of the difference of the real numbers that the rays correspond with on a protractor. If $\overrightarrow{OC}$ corresponds with c and $\overrightarrow{OD}$ corresponds with d, $m\angle DOC = |d - c|$ or $|c - d|$.

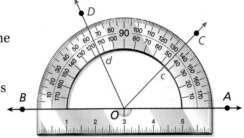

Types of Angles

Acute Angle	Right Angle	Obtuse Angle	Straight Angle
			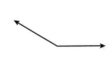
Measures greater than 0° and less than 90°	Measures 90°	Measures greater than 90° and less than 180°	Formed by two opposite rays and measures 180°

EXAMPLE 2 Measuring and Classifying Angles

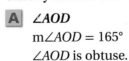
Find the measure of each angle. Then classify each as acute, right, or obtuse.

A ∠AOD
m∠AOD = 165°
∠AOD is obtuse.

B ∠COD
m∠COD = |165 − 75| = 90°
∠COD is a right angle.

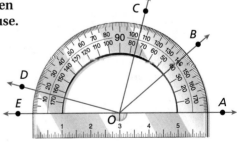

CHECK IT OUT! Use the diagram to find the measure of each angle. Then classify each as acute, right, or obtuse.

2a. ∠BOA   **2b.** ∠DOB   **2c.** ∠EOC

Congruent angles are angles that have the same measure. In the diagram, m∠ABC = m∠DEF, so you can write ∠ABC ≅ ∠DEF. This is read as "angle ABC is congruent to angle DEF." *Arc marks* are used to show that the two angles are congruent.

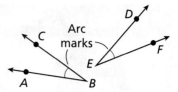

Construction   Congruent Angle

Construct an angle congruent to ∠A.

❶

Use a straightedge to draw a ray with endpoint *D*.

❷

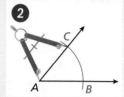

Place the compass point at *A* and draw an arc that intersects both sides of ∠A. Label the intersection points *B* and *C*.

❸

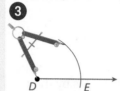

Using the same compass setting, place the compass point at *D* and draw an arc that intersects the ray. Label the intersection *E*.

❹

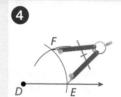

Place the compass point at *B* and open it to the distance *BC*. Place the point of the compass at *E* and draw an arc. Label its intersection with the first arc *F*.

❺

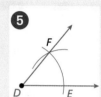

Use a straightedge to draw $\overrightarrow{DF}$.

∠D ≅ ∠A

The Angle Addition Postulate is very similar to the Segment Addition Postulate that you learned in the previous lesson.

Postulate 19-2-2   Angle Addition Postulate

If *S* is in the interior of ∠PQR, then
m∠PQS + m∠SQR = m∠PQR.
(∠ Add. Post.)

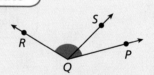

EXAMPLE 3
MCC9-12.A.CED.1

Using the Angle Addition Postulate

m∠ABD = 37° and m∠ABC = 84°. Find m∠DBC.

m∠ABC = m∠ABD + m∠DBC	∠ Add. Post.
84° = 37° + m∠DBC	Substitute the given values.
−37 −37	Subtract 37 from both sides.
47° = m∠DBC	Simplify.

Online Video Tutor

CHECK IT OUT!

3. m∠XWZ = 121° and m∠XWY = 59°. Find m∠YWZ.

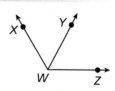

An **angle bisector** is a ray that divides an angle into two congruent angles. $\overrightarrow{JK}$ bisects $\angle LJM$; thus $\angle LJK \cong \angle KJM$.

Construction   Angle Bisector

Construct the bisector of ∠A.

1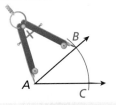

2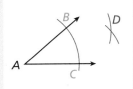

3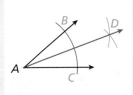

Place the point of the compass at *A* and draw an arc. Label its points of intersection with ∠*A* as *B* and *C*.

Without changing the compass setting, draw intersecting arcs from *B* and *C*. Label the intersection of the arcs as *D*.

Use a straightedge to draw $\overrightarrow{AD}$.

$\overrightarrow{AD}$ bisects ∠*A*.

COMMON CORE GPS

 **EXAMPLE** **4**
MCC9-12.A.CED.1

my.hrw.com

Online Video Tutor

Finding the Measure of an Angle

$\overrightarrow{BD}$ bisects $\angle ABC$, $m\angle ABD = (6x + 3)^\circ$, and $m\angle DBC = (8x - 7)^\circ$. Find $m\angle ABD$.

Step 1 Find x.

$m\angle ABD = m\angle DBC$	*Def. of ∠ bisector*
$(6x + 3)^\circ = (8x - 7)^\circ$	*Substitute the given values.*
$\underline{+7+7}$	*Add 7 to both sides.*
$6x + 10 = 8x$	*Simplify.*
$\underline{-6x-6x}$	*Subtract 6x from both sides.*
$10 = 2x$	*Simplify.*
$\dfrac{10}{2} = \dfrac{2x}{2}$	*Divide both sides by 2.*
$5 = x$	*Simplify.*

Step 2 Find $m\angle ABD$.

$$m\angle ABD = 6x + 3$$
$$= 6(5) + 3 \qquad \textit{Substitute 5 for x.}$$
$$= 33^\circ \qquad \textit{Simplify.}$$

Find the measure of each angle.

4a. $\overrightarrow{QS}$ bisects $\angle PQR$, $m\angle PQS = (5y - 1)^\circ$, and $m\angle PQR = (8y + 12)^\circ$. Find $m\angle PQS$.

4b. $\overrightarrow{JK}$ bisects $\angle LJM$, $m\angle LJK = (-10x + 3)^\circ$, and $m\angle KJM = (-x + 21)^\circ$. Find $m\angle LJM$.

19-2 Measuring and Constructing Angles   **541**

THINK AND DISCUSS

1. Explain why any two right angles are congruent.

2. $\overrightarrow{BD}$ bisects $\angle ABC$. How are m$\angle ABC$, m$\angle ABD$, and m$\angle DBC$ related?

3. GET ORGANIZED Copy and complete the graphic organizer. In the cells sketch, measure, and name an example of each angle type.

	Diagram	Measure	Name
Acute Angle			
Right Angle			
Obtuse Angle			
Straight Angle			

19-2 Exercises

my.hrw.com
Homework Help

GUIDED PRACTICE

Vocabulary Apply the vocabulary from this lesson to answer each question.

1. $\angle A$ is an acute angle. $\angle O$ is an obtuse angle. $\angle R$ is a right angle. Put $\angle A$, $\angle O$, and $\angle R$ in order from least to greatest by measure.

2. Which point is the vertex of $\angle BCD$? Which rays form the sides of $\angle BCD$?

SEE EXAMPLE 1

3. Music Musicians use a metronome to keep time as they play. The metronome's needle swings back and forth in a fixed amount of time. Name all of the angles in the diagram.

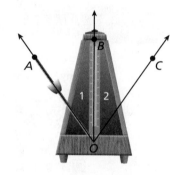

SEE EXAMPLE 2

Use the protractor to find the measure of each angle. Then classify each as acute, right, or obtuse.

4. $\angle VXW$

5. $\angle TXW$

6. $\angle RXU$

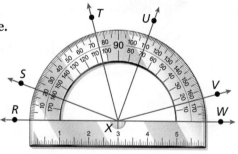

SEE EXAMPLE 3

L is in the interior of $\angle JKM$. Find each of the following.

7. m$\angle JKM$ if m$\angle JKL = 42°$ and m$\angle LKM = 28°$

8. m$\angle LKM$ if m$\angle JKL = 56.4°$ and m$\angle JKM = 82.5°$

SEE EXAMPLE 4

Multi-Step $\overrightarrow{BD}$ bisects $\angle ABC$. Find each of the following.

9. m$\angle ABD$ if m$\angle ABD = (6x + 4)°$ and m$\angle DBC = (8x - 4)°$

10. m$\angle ABC$ if m$\angle ABD = (5y - 3)°$ and m$\angle DBC = (3y + 15)°$

PRACTICE AND PROBLEM SOLVING

Independent Practice

For Exercises	See Example
11	1
12–14	2
15–16	3
17–18	4

my.hrw.com

Online Extra Practice

11. Physics Pendulum clocks have been used since 1656 to keep time. The pendulum swings back and forth once or twice per second. Name all of the angles in the diagram.

Use the protractor to find the measure of each angle. Then classify each as acute, right, or obtuse.

12. ∠CGE   **13.** ∠BGD   **14.** ∠AGB

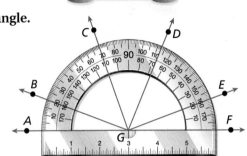

T is in the interior of ∠RSU. Find each of the following.

15. m∠RSU if m∠RST = 38° and m∠TSU = 28.6°

16. m∠RST if m∠TSU = 46.7° and m∠RSU = 83.5°

H.O.T. Multi-Step $\overrightarrow{SP}$ bisects ∠RST. Find each of the following.

17. m∠RST if m∠RSP = $(3x - 2)°$ and m∠PST = $(9x - 26)°$

18. m∠RSP if m∠RST = $\frac{5}{2}y°$ and m∠PST = $(y + 5)°$

Estimation Use the following information for Exercises 19–22.

Assume the corner of a sheet of paper is a right angle. Use the corner to estimate the measure and classify each angle in the diagram.

19. ∠BOA   **20.** ∠COA

21. ∠EOD   **22.** ∠EOB

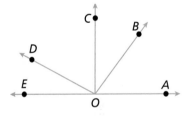

Use a protractor to draw an angle with each of the following measures.

23. 33°   **24.** 142°   **25.** 90°   **26.** 168°

27. Surveying A surveyor at point *S* discovers that the angle between peaks *A* and *B* is 3 times as large as the angle between peaks *B* and *C*. The surveyor knows that ∠ASC is a right angle. Find m∠ASB and m∠BSC.

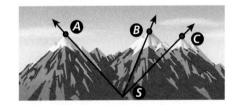

28. Math History As far back as the 5th century B.C., mathematicians have been fascinated by the problem of trisecting an angle. It is possible to construct an angle with $\frac{1}{4}$ the measure of a given angle. Explain how to do this.

Find the value of *x*.

29. m∠AOC = 7x - 2, m∠DOC = 2x + 8, m∠EOD = 27

30. m∠AOB = 4x - 2, m∠BOC = 5x + 10, m∠COD = 3x - 8

31. m∠AOB = 6x + 5, m∠BOC = 4x - 2, m∠AOC = 8x + 21

H.O.T. 32. Multi-Step *Q* is in the interior of right ∠PRS. If m∠PRQ is 4 times as large as m∠QRS, what is m∠PRQ?

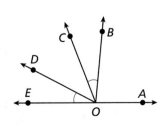

Real-World Connections

33. An archaeologist standing at *O* looks for clues on where to dig for artifacts.

    a. What value of *x* will make the angle between the pottery and the arrowhead measure 57°?

    b. What value of *x* makes ∠LOJ ≅ ∠JOK?

    c. What values of *x* make ∠LOK an acute angle?

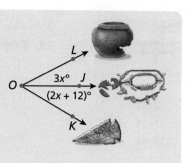

Data Analysis Use the circle graph for Exercises 34–36.

34. Find m∠AOB, m∠BOC, m∠COD, and m∠DOA. Classify each angle as acute, right, or obtuse.

35. What if...? Next year, the music store will use some of the shelves currently holding jazz music to double the space for rap. What will m∠COD and m∠BOC be next year?

36. Suppose a fifth type of music, salsa, is added. If the space is divided equally among the five types, what will be the angle measure for each type of music in the circle graph?

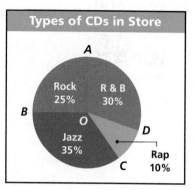

37. Critical Thinking Can an obtuse angle be congruent to an acute angle? Why or why not?

38. The measure of an obtuse angle is (5*x* + 45)°. What is the largest value for *x*?

39. Write About It $\overrightarrow{FH}$ bisects ∠EFG. Use the Angle Addition Postulate to explain why m∠EFH = ½m∠EFG.

40. Multi-Step Use a protractor to draw a 70° angle. Then use a compass and straightedge to bisect the angle. What do you think will be the measure of each angle formed? Use a protractor to support your answer.

TEST PREP

41. m∠UOW = 50°, and $\overrightarrow{OV}$ bisects ∠UOW. What is m∠VOY?

    Ⓐ 25°   Ⓒ 130°

    Ⓑ 65°   Ⓓ 155°

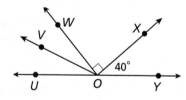

42. What is m∠UOX?

    Ⓕ 50°   Ⓖ 115°   Ⓗ 140°   Ⓙ 165°

43. $\overrightarrow{BD}$ bisects ∠ABC, m∠ABC = (4*x* + 5)°, and m∠ABD = (3*x* − 1)°. What is the value of *x*?

    Ⓐ 2.2   Ⓑ 3   Ⓒ 3.5   Ⓓ 7

44. If an angle is bisected and then 30° is added to the measure of the bisected angle, the result is the measure of a right angle. What is the measure of the original angle?

    Ⓕ 30°   Ⓖ 60°   Ⓗ 75°   Ⓙ 120°

H.O.T. 45. Short Response If an obtuse angle is bisected, are the resulting angles acute or obtuse? Explain.

CHALLENGE AND EXTEND

46. Find the measure of the angle formed by the hands of a clock when it is 7:00.

47. $\overrightarrow{QS}$ bisects $\angle PQR$, m$\angle PQR = (x^2)°$, and m$\angle PQS = (2x + 6)°$. Find all the possible measures for $\angle PQR$.

48. For more precise measurements, a degree can be divided into 60 minutes, and each minute can be divided into 60 seconds. An angle measure of 42 degrees, 30 minutes, and 10 seconds is written as $42°30'10''$. Subtract this angle measure from the measure $81°24'15''$.

49. If 1 degree equals 60 minutes and 1 minute equals 60 seconds, how many seconds are in 2.25 degrees?

50. $\angle ABC \cong \angle DBC$. m$\angle ABC = \left(\frac{3x}{2} + 4\right)°$ and m$\angle DBC = \left(2x - 27\frac{1}{4}\right)°$. Is $\angle ABD$ a straight angle? Explain.

FOCUS ON MATHEMATICAL PRACTICES

51. Estimation Flo says she can use the corner of a piece of paper to accurately estimate the measures of common angles such as 30°, 45°, 60°, and 90°. Explain how Flo can make these estimates.

52. Analysis Some textbooks state the Angle Addition Postulate separately for straight angles. What makes straight angles a special case of the Angle Addition Postulate?

53. Constructions Explain how to construct an angle that is exactly twice the measure of another angle.

Using Technology Segment and Angle Bisectors

1. Construct the bisector of $\overline{MN}$.

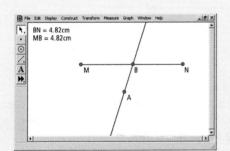

a. Draw $\overline{MN}$ and construct the midpoint B.

b. Construct a point A not on the segment.

c. Construct bisector $\overleftrightarrow{AB}$ and measure $\overline{MB}$ and $\overline{NB}$.

d. Drag M and N and observe MB and NB.

2. Construct the bisector of $\angle BAC$.

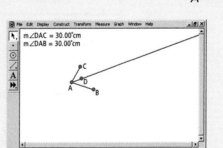

a. Draw $\angle BAC$.

b. Construct the angle bisector $\overrightarrow{AD}$ and measure $\angle DAC$ and $\angle DAB$.

c. Drag the angle and observe m$\angle DAB$ and m$\angle DAC$.

19-3 Using Inductive Reasoning to Make Conjectures

 Essential Question: How can you make and disprove conjectures?

Objectives
Use inductive reasoning to identify patterns and make conjectures.

Find counterexamples to disprove conjectures.

Vocabulary
inductive reasoning
conjecture
counterexample

Who uses this?
Biologists use inductive reasoning to develop theories about migration patterns.

Biologists studying the migration patterns of California gray whales developed two theories about the whales' route across Monterey Bay. The whales either swam directly across the bay or followed the shoreline.

 EXAMPLE 1 MCC.MP.3 | **1** | **Identifying a Pattern**

Find the next item in each pattern.

my.hrw.com

Online Video Tutor

A Monday, Wednesday, Friday, …
Alternating days of the week make up the pattern.
The next day is Sunday.

B 3, 6, 9, 12, 15, …
Multiples of 3 make up the pattern. The next multiple is 18.

C ←, ↖, ↑, …
In this pattern, the figure rotates 45° clockwise each time.
The next figure is ↗.

 1. Find the next item in the pattern 0.4, 0.04, 0.004, …

When several examples form a pattern and you assume the pattern will continue, you are applying *inductive reasoning*. **Inductive reasoning** is the process of reasoning that a rule or statement is true because specific cases are true. You may use inductive reasoning to draw a conclusion from a pattern. A statement you believe to be true based on inductive reasoning is called a **conjecture**.

 EXAMPLE 2 MCC.MP.3 | **2** | **Making a Conjecture**

Complete each conjecture.

A The product of an even number and an odd number is __?__ .
List some examples and look for a pattern.
$(2)(3) = 6$ $(2)(5) = 10$ $(4)(3) = 12$ $(4)(5) = 20$
The product of an even number and an odd number is even.

546   Module 19 Tools of Geometry

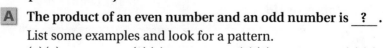

© Francois Gohier/Photo Researchers, Inc.

my.hrw.com

Online Video Tutor

Complete each conjecture.

B The number of segments formed by *n* collinear points is __?__ .

Draw a segment. Mark points on the segment, and count the number of individual segments formed. Be sure to include overlapping segments.

Points	Segments
2	1
3	2 + 1 = 3
4	3 + 2 + 1 = 6
5	4 + 3 + 2 + 1 = 10

The number of segments formed by *n* collinear points is the sum of the whole numbers less than *n*.

2. Complete the conjecture: The product of two odd numbers is __?__ .

COMMON CORE GPS
EXAMPLE 3
MCC.MP.3

my.hrw.com

Online Video Tutor

Biology Application

To learn about the migration behavior of California gray whales, biologists observed whales along two routes. For seven days they counted the numbers of whales seen along each route. Make a conjecture based on the data.

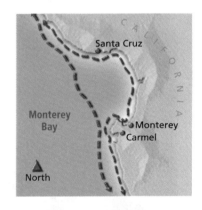

Numbers of Whales Each Day							
Direct Route	1	3	0	2	1	1	0
Shore Route	7	9	5	8	8	6	7

More whales were seen along the shore route each day. The data supports the conjecture that most California gray whales migrate along the shoreline.

3. Make a conjecture about the lengths of male and female whales based on the data.

Average Whale Lengths						
Length of Female (ft)	49	51	50	48	51	47
Length of Male (ft)	47	45	44	46	48	48

To show that a conjecture is always true, you must prove it.
To show that a conjecture is false, you have to find only one example in which the conjecture is not true. This case is called a **counterexample**.
A counterexample can be a drawing, a statement, or a number.

Inductive Reasoning
1. Look for a pattern
2. Make a conjecture.
3. Prove the conjecture or find a counterexample.

19-3 Using Inductive Reasoning to Make Conjectures **547**

COMMON CORE GPS MCC.MP.3 | **EXAMPLE** | **4** | **Finding a Counterexample**

my.hrw.com

Online Video Tutor

Show that each conjecture is false by finding a counterexample.

A For all positive numbers n, $\frac{1}{n} \le n$.

Pick positive values for n and substitute them into the equation to see if the conjecture holds.

Let $n = 1$. Since $\frac{1}{n} = 1$ and $1 \le 1$, the conjecture holds.

Let $n = 2$. Since $\frac{1}{n} = \frac{1}{2}$ and $\frac{1}{2} \le 2$, the conjecture holds.

Let $n = \frac{1}{2}$. Since $\frac{1}{n} = \frac{1}{\frac{1}{2}} = 2$ and $2 \nleq \frac{1}{2}$, the conjecture is false.

$n = \frac{1}{2}$ is a counterexample.

B For any three points in a plane, there are three different lines that contain two of the points.

 *Draw three collinear points.*

If the three points are collinear, the conjecture is false.

C The temperature in Abilene, Texas, never exceeds 100°F during the spring months (March, April, and May).

Monthly High Temperatures (°F) in Abilene, Texas											
Jan	Feb	Mar	Apr	May	Jun	Jul	Aug	Sep	Oct	Nov	Dec
88	89	97	99	107	109	110	107	106	103	92	89

The temperature in May was 107°F, so the conjecture is false.

 CHECK IT OUT! Show that each conjecture is false by finding a counterexample.

4a. For any real number x, $x^2 \ge x$.

4b. Supplementary angles are adjacent.

4c. The radius of every planet in the solar system is less than 50,000 km.

Planets' Diameters (km)							
Mercury	Venus	Earth	Mars	Jupiter	Saturn	Uranus	Neptune
4880	12,100	12,800	6790	143,000	121,000	51,100	49,500

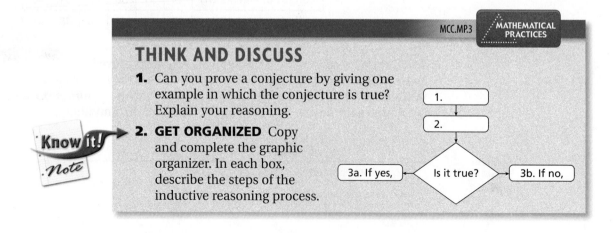

MCC.MP.3 | **MATHEMATICAL PRACTICES**

THINK AND DISCUSS

1. Can you prove a conjecture by giving one example in which the conjecture is true? Explain your reasoning.

2. GET ORGANIZED Copy and complete the graphic organizer. In each box, describe the steps of the inductive reasoning process.

Know it! Note

1.

2.

Is it true? → 3a. If yes, / 3b. If no,

548 *Module 19 Tools of Geometry*

NASA Images

19-3 Exercises

my.hrw.com
Homework Help

GUIDED PRACTICE

1. **Vocabulary** Explain why a *conjecture* may be true or false.

SEE EXAMPLE **1** Find the next item in each pattern.

2. March, May, July, …   3. $\frac{1}{3}, \frac{2}{4}, \frac{3}{5}, …$ 4. $|\circ|, \overline{\underline{\circ}}, |\circ|\circ|, …$

SEE EXAMPLE **2** Complete each conjecture.

5. The product of two even numbers is   ?   .

6. A rule in terms of n for the sum of the first n odd positive integers is   ?   .

SEE EXAMPLE **3**

7. **Biology** A laboratory culture contains 150 bacteria. After twenty minutes, the culture contains 300 bacteria. After one hour, the culture contains 1200 bacteria. Make a conjecture about the rate at which the bacteria increases.

SEE EXAMPLE **4** Show that each conjecture is false by finding a counterexample.

8. Kennedy is the youngest U.S. president to be inaugurated.

9. Three points on a plane always form a triangle.

10. For any real number x, if $x^2 \geq 1$, then $x \geq 1$.

President	Age at Inauguration
Washington	57
T. Roosevelt	42
Truman	60
Kennedy	43
Clinton	46

PRACTICE AND PROBLEM SOLVING

Independent Practice	
For Exercises	See Example
11–13	1
14–15	2
16	3
17–19	4

my.hrw.com

Online Extra Practice

Find the next item in each pattern.

11. 8 A.M., 11 A.M., 2 P.M., …   12. 75, 64, 53, …   13. △, □, ⬠, …

Complete each conjecture.

14. A rule in terms of n for the sum of the first n even positive integers is   ?   .

15. The number of nonoverlapping segments formed by n collinear points is   ?   .

16. **Industrial Arts** About 5% of the students at Lincoln High School usually participate in the robotics competition. There are 526 students in the school this year. Make a conjecture about the number of students who will participate in the robotics competition this year.

Show that each conjecture is false by finding a counterexample.

17. If $1 - y > 0$, then $0 < y < 1$.

18. For any real number x, $x^3 \geq x^2$.

19. Every pair of supplementary angles includes one obtuse angle.

Make a conjecture about each pattern. Write the next two items.

20. 2, 4, 16, …   21. $\frac{1}{2}, \frac{1}{4}, \frac{1}{8}, …$ 22. –3, 6, –9, 12, …

23. Draw a square of dots. Make a conjecture about the number of dots needed to increase the size of the square from $n \times n$ to $(n + 1) \times (n + 1)$.

19-3 Using Inductive Reasoning to Make Conjectures **549**

Determine if each conjecture is true. If not, write or draw a counterexample.

24. Points X, Y, and Z are coplanar.

25. If n is an integer, then $-n$ is positive.

26. In a triangle with one right angle, two of the sides are congruent.

27. If $\overrightarrow{BD}$ bisects $\angle ABC$, then $m\angle ABD = m\angle CBD$.

28. Estimation The Westside High School band is selling coupon books to raise money for a trip. The table shows the amount of money raised for the first four days of the sale. If the pattern continues, estimate the amount of money raised during the sixth day.

Day	Money Raised ($)
1	146.25
2	195.75
3	246.25
4	295.50

29. Write each fraction in the pattern $\frac{1}{11}$, $\frac{2}{11}$, $\frac{3}{11}$, ... as a repeating decimal. Then write a description of the fraction pattern and the resulting decimal pattern.

30. Math History Remember that a prime number is a whole number greater than 1 that has exactly two factors, itself and 1. Goldbach's conjecture states that every even number greater than 2 can be written as the sum of two primes. For example, $4 = 2 + 2$. Write the next five even numbers as the sum of two primes.

31. The pattern 1, 1, 2, 3, 5, 8, 13, 21, ... is known as the *Fibonacci sequence*. Find the next three terms in the sequence and write a conjecture for the pattern.

32. Look at a monthly calendar and pick any three squares in a row—across, down, or diagonal. Make a conjecture about the number in the middle.

12	13	14
19	20	21
26	27	28

33. Make a conjecture about the value of $2n - 1$ when n is an integer.

H.O.T. 34. Critical Thinking The turnaround date for migrating gray whales occurs when the number of northbound whales exceeds the number of southbound whales. Make a conjecture about the turnaround date, based on the table below. What factors might affect the validity of your conjecture in the future?

Migration Direction of Gray Whales							
	Feb. 16	Feb. 17	Feb. 18	Feb. 19	Feb. 20	Feb. 21	Feb. 22
Southbound	0	2	3	0	1	1	0
Northbound	0	0	2	5	3	2	1

H.O.T. 35. Write About It Explain why a true conjecture about even numbers does not necessarily hold for all numbers. Give an example to support your answer.

Real-World Connections

36. a. For how many hours did the Mock Turtle do lessons on the third day?

b. On what day did the Mock Turtle do 1 hour of lessons?

"And how many hours a day did you do lessons?" said Alice, in a hurry to change the subject.

"Ten hours the first day," said the Mock Turtle: "nine the next, and so on."

(c) North Wind Picture Archive/Alamy; (bl) Victoria Smith/HMH; (br) The Granger Collection

37. Which of the following conjectures is false?
    Ⓐ If x is odd, then $x + 1$ is even.
    Ⓑ The sum of two odd numbers is even.
    Ⓒ The difference of two even numbers is positive.
    Ⓓ If x is positive, then $-x$ is negative.

38. A student conjectures that if x is a prime number, then $x + 1$ is not prime. Which of the following is a counterexample?
    Ⓕ $x = 11$ Ⓖ $x = 6$ Ⓗ $x = 3$ Ⓙ $x = 2$

39. The class of 2004 holds a reunion each year. In 2005, 87.5% of the 120 graduates attended. In 2006, 90 students went, and in 2007, 75 students went. About how many students do you predict will go to the reunion in 2010?
    Ⓐ 12   Ⓑ 15   Ⓒ 24   Ⓓ 30

CHALLENGE AND EXTEND

H.O.T. 40. **Multi-Step** Make a table of values for the rule $x^2 + x + 11$ when x is an integer from 1 to 8. Make a conjecture about the type of number generated by the rule. Continue your table. What value of x generates a counterexample?

41. **Political Science** Presidential elections are held every four years. U.S. senators are elected to 6-year terms, but only $\frac{1}{3}$ of the Senate is up for election every two years. If $\frac{1}{3}$ of the Senate is elected during a presidential election year, how many years must pass before these same senate seats are up for election during another presidential election year?

H.O.T. 42. **Physical Fitness** Rob is training for the President's Challenge physical fitness program. During his first week of training, Rob does 15 sit-ups each day. He will add 20 sit-ups to his daily routine each week. His goal is to reach 150 sit-ups per day.
    a. Make a table of the number of sit-ups Rob does each week from week 1 through week 10.
    b. During which week will Rob reach his goal?
    c. Write a conjecture for the number of sit-ups Rob does during week n.

43. **Construction** Draw $\overline{AB}$. Then construct point C so that it is not on $\overline{AB}$ and is the same distance from A and B. Construct $\overline{AC}$ and $\overline{BC}$. Compare m∠CAB and m∠CBA and compare AC and CB. Make a conjecture.

FOCUS ON MATHEMATICAL PRACTICES

H.O.T. 44. **Modeling** Every cut of a round pizza divides it along a diameter. There are two pieces of pizza after one cut, four pieces after two cuts, and so on. How many pieces do n cuts create?

H.O.T. 45. **Counterexamples** Teri says that the sum of the measures of any two vertical angles is less than or equal to 180°. Describe all possible counterexamples to the statement "The sum of the measures of any two vertical angles is less than or equal to 180°."

H.O.T. 46. **Analysis** Consider the statement "If the sun is not visible, then it is raining." Describe three scenarios besides raining where the sun is not visible.

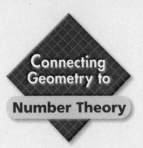

Connecting
Geometry to

Number Theory

Venn Diagrams

Recall that in a Venn diagram, ovals are used to represent each set. The ovals can overlap if the sets share common elements.

The real number system contains an infinite number of subsets. The following chart shows some of them. Other examples of subsets are even numbers, multiples of 3, and numbers less than 6.

Set	Description	Examples
Natural numbers	The counting numbers	1, 2, 3, 4, 5, …
Whole numbers	The set of natural numbers and 0	0, 1, 2, 3, 4, …
Integers	The set of whole numbers and their opposites	…, −2, −1, 0, 1, 2, …
Rational numbers	The set of numbers that can be written as a ratio of integers	$-\frac{3}{4}$, 5, −2, 0.5, 0
Irrational numbers	The set of numbers that cannot be written as a ratio of integers	$\pi, \sqrt{10}, 8 + \sqrt{2}$

Example

Draw a Venn diagram to show the relationship between the set of even numbers and the set of natural numbers.

The set of even numbers includes all numbers that are divisible by 2. This includes natural numbers such as 2, 4, and 6. But even numbers such as −4 and −10 are not natural numbers.

So the set of even numbers includes some, but not all, elements in the set of natural numbers. Similarly, the set of natural numbers includes some, but not all, even numbers.

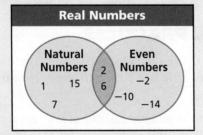

Draw a rectangle to represent all real numbers.

Draw overlapping ovals to represent the sets of even and natural numbers. You may write individual elements in each region.

Try This

Draw a Venn diagram to show the relationship between the given sets.

1. natural numbers, whole numbers

2. odd numbers, whole numbers

3. irrational numbers, integers

552   *Module 19 Tools of Geometry*

Conditional Statements

 Essential Question: How can you express and symbolize if-then statements?

Objectives
Identify, write, and analyze the truth value of conditional statements.

Write the inverse, converse, and contrapositive of a conditional statement.

Vocabulary
conditional statement
hypothesis
conclusion
truth value
negation
converse
inverse
contrapositive
logically equivalent
  statements

Why learn this?

To identify a species of butterfly, you must know what characteristics one butterfly species has that another does not.

It is thought that the viceroy butterfly mimics the bad-tasting monarch butterfly to avoid being eaten by birds. By comparing the appearance of the two butterfly species, you can make the following conjecture:

If a butterfly has a curved black line on its hind wing, then it is a viceroy.

Conditional Statements

DEFINITION	SYMBOLS	VENN DIAGRAM
A **conditional statement** is a statement that can be written in the form "if *p,* then *q.*"	$p \rightarrow q$	
The **hypothesis** is the part *p* of a conditional statement following the word *if.*		
The **conclusion** is the part *q* of a conditional statement following the word *then.*		

By phrasing a conjecture as an if-then statement, you can quickly identify its hypothesis and conclusion.

COMMON CORE GPS

EXAMPLE 1 | Identifying the Parts of a Conditional Statement
MCC.MP.3

Identify the hypothesis and conclusion of each conditional.

A **If a butterfly has a curved black line on its hind wing, then it is a viceroy.**

Hypothesis: A butterfly has a curved black line on its hind wing.
Conclusion: The butterfly is a Viceroy.

my.hrw.com

Online Video Tutor

B **A number is an integer if it is a natural number.**

Hypothesis: A number is a natural number.
Conclusion: The number is an integer.

Writing Math

"If *p,* then *q*" can also be written as "if *p, q,*" "*q,* if *p,*" "*p* implies *q,*" and "*p* only if *q.*"

CHECK IT OUT!

1. Identify the hypothesis and conclusion of the statement "A number is divisible by 3 if it is divisible by 6."

Many sentences without the words *if* and *then* can be written as conditionals. To do so, identify the sentence's hypothesis and conclusion by figuring out which part of the statement depends on the other.

EXAMPLE 2 Writing a Conditional Statement

MCC.MP.3

Write a conditional statement from each of the following.

A **The midpoint *M* of a segment bisects the segment.**

The midpoint *M* of a segment bisects the segment.   *Identify the hypothesis and conclusion.*

Conditional: If *M* is the midpoint of a segment, then *M* bisects the segment.

B

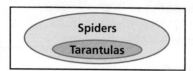

The **inner** oval represents the **hypothesis**, and the **outer** oval represents the **conclusion**.

Conditional: If an animal is a tarantula, then it is a spider.

  2. Write a conditional statement from the sentence "Two angles that are complementary are acute."

A conditional statement has a **truth value** of either true (T) or false (F). It is false only when the hypothesis is true and the conclusion is false. Consider the conditional "If I get paid, I will take you to the movie." If I don't get paid, I haven't broken my promise. So the statement is still true.

To show that a conditional statement is false, you need to find only one counterexample where the hypothesis is true and the conclusion is false.

EXAMPLE 3 Analyzing the Truth Value of a Conditional Statement

MCC.MP.3

Determine if each conditional is true. If false, give a counterexample.

A **If today is Sunday, then tomorrow is Monday.**

When the hypothesis is true, the conclusion is also true because Monday follows Sunday. So the conditional is true.

B **If an angle is obtuse, then it has a measure of 100°.**

You can draw an obtuse angle whose measure is not 100°. In this case, the hypothesis is true, but the conclusion is false. Since you can find a counterexample, the conditional is false.

C **If an odd number is divisible by 2, then 8 is a perfect square.**

An odd number is never divisible by 2, so the hypothesis is false. The number 8 is not a perfect square, so the conclusion is false. However, the conditional is true because the hypothesis is false.

> **Remember!**
>
> If the hypothesis is false, the conditional statement is true, regardless of the truth value of the conclusion.

  3. Determine if the conditional "If a number is odd, then it is divisible by 3" is true. If false, give a counterexample.

The **negation** of statement *p* is "not *p*," written as ~*p*. The negation of the statement "*M* is the midpoint of $\overline{AB}$" is "*M* is *not* the midpoint of $\overline{AB}$." The negation of a true statement is false, and the negation of a false statement is true. Negations are used to write related conditional statements.

Related Conditionals

DEFINITION	SYMBOLS
A conditional is a statement that can be written in the form "If p, then q."	$p \rightarrow q$
The **converse** is the statement formed by exchanging the hypothesis and conclusion.	$q \rightarrow p$
The **inverse** is the statement formed by negating the hypothesis and the conclusion.	$\sim p \rightarrow \sim q$
The **contrapositive** is the statement formed by both exchanging and negating the hypothesis and conclusion.	$\sim q \rightarrow \sim p$

COMMON CORE GPS
MCC.MP.3

EXAMPLE 4

Biology Application

Write the converse, inverse, and contrapositive of the conditional statement. Use the photos to find the truth value of each.

my.hrw.com

Online Video Tutor

If an insect is a butterfly, then it has four wings.
If an insect is a butterfly, then it has four wings.

Converse: If an insect has four wings, then it is a butterfly.
A moth also is an insect with four wings. So the converse is false.

Inverse: If an insect is not a butterfly, then it does not have four wings.
A moth is not a butterfly, but it has four wings. So the inverse is false.

Contrapositive: If an insect does not have four wings, then it is not a butterfly.
Butterflies must have four wings. So the contrapositive is true.

Butterfly

Moth

4. Write the converse, inverse, and contrapositive of the conditional statement "If an animal is a cat, then it has four paws." Find the truth value of each.

Helpful Hint

The logical equivalence of a conditional and its contrapositive is known as the Law of Contrapositive.

In the example above, the conditional statement and its contrapositive are both true, and the converse and inverse are both false. Related conditional statements that have the same truth value are called **logically equivalent statements**. A conditional and its contrapositive are logically equivalent, and so are the converse and inverse.

Statement	Example	Truth Value
Conditional	If $m\angle A = 95°$, then $\angle A$ is obtuse.	T
Converse	If $\angle A$ is obtuse, then $m\angle A = 95°$.	F
Inverse	If $m\angle A \neq 95°$, then $\angle A$ is not obtuse.	F
Contrapositive	If $\angle A$ is not obtuse, then $m\angle A \neq 95°$.	T

However, the converse of a true conditional is not necessarily false. All four related conditionals can be true, or all four can be false, depending on the statement.

THINK AND DISCUSS

1. If a conditional statement is false, what are the truth values of its hypothesis and conclusion?

2. What is the truth value of a conditional whose hypothesis is false?

3. Can a conditional statement and its converse be logically equivalent? Support your answer with an example.

4. **GET ORGANIZED** Copy and complete the graphic organizer. In each box, write the definition and give an example.

19-4 Exercises

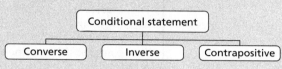

my.hrw.com
Homework Help

GUIDED PRACTICE

Vocabulary Apply the vocabulary from this lesson to answer each question.

1. The __?__ of a *conditional statement* is formed by exchanging the hypothesis and conclusion. (*converse, inverse,* or *contrapositive*)

2. A *conditional* and its *contrapositive* are __?__ because they have the same truth value. (*logically equivalent* or *converses*)

SEE EXAMPLE 1 Identify the hypothesis and conclusion of each conditional.

3. If a person is at least 16 years old, then the person can drive a car.

4. A figure is a parallelogram if it is a rectangle.

5. The statement $a - b < a$ implies that b is a positive number.

SEE EXAMPLE 2 Write a conditional statement from each of the following.

6. Eighteen-year-olds are eligible to vote.

7. $\left(\dfrac{a}{b}\right)^2 < \dfrac{a}{b}$ when $0 < a < b$.

8.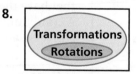

SEE EXAMPLE 3 Determine if each conditional is true. If false, give a counterexample.

9. If three points form the vertices of a triangle, then they lie in the same plane.

10. If $x > y$, then $|x| > |y|$.

11. If the season is spring, then the month is March.

SEE EXAMPLE 4 12. **Travel** Write the converse, inverse, and contrapositive of the following conditional statement. Find the truth value of each.

If Brielle drives at exactly 30 mi/h, then she travels 10 mi in 20 min.

PRACTICE AND PROBLEM SOLVING

Independent Practice

For Exercises	See Example
13–15	1
16–18	2
19–21	3
22–23	4

my.hrw.com

Online Extra Practice

Identify the hypothesis and conclusion of each conditional.

13. If an animal is a tabby, then it is a cat.

14. Four angles are formed if two lines intersect.

15. If 8 ounces of cereal cost $2.99, then 16 ounces of cereal cost $5.98.

Write a conditional statement from each sentence.

16. You should monitor the heart rate of a patient who is ill.

17. After three strikes, the batter is out.

18. Congruent segments have equal measures.

Determine if each conditional is true. If false, give a counterexample.

19. If you subtract -2 from -6, then the result is -4.

20. If two planes intersect, then they intersect in exactly one point.

21. If a cat is a bird, then today is Friday.

H.O.T. **Write the converse, inverse, and contrapositive of each conditional statement. Find the truth value of each.**

22. **Probability** If the probability of an event is 0.1, then the event is unlikely to occur.

23. **Meteorology** If freezing rain is falling, then the air temperature is 32°F or less. (*Hint:* The freezing point of water is 32°F.)

Find the truth value of each statement.

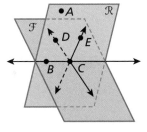

24. E lies in plane $\mathcal{R}$.

25. $\overleftrightarrow{CD}$ lies in plane $\mathcal{F}$.

26. C, E, and D are coplanar.

27. Plane $\mathcal{F}$ contains $\overrightarrow{ED}$.

28. B and E are collinear.

29. $\overleftrightarrow{BC}$ contains $\mathcal{F}$ and $\mathcal{R}$.

Draw a Venn diagram.

30. All integers are rational numbers.

31. All natural numbers are real.

32. All rectangles are quadrilaterals.

33. Plane is an undefined term.

Write a conditional statement from each Venn diagram.

34.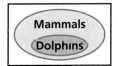

35.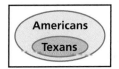

36.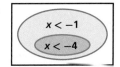

37. a. Identify the hypothesis and conclusion in the Duchess's statement.

b. Rewrite the Duchess's claim as a conditional statement.

"Tut, tut, child!" said the Duchess. "Everything's got a moral, if only you can find it." And she squeezed herself up closer to Alice's side as she spoke.

(bl) Victoria Smith/HMH; (br) Corbis

Find a counterexample to show that the converse of each conditional is false.

38. If $x = -5$, then $x^2 = 25$.

39. If two angles are vertical angles, then they are congruent.

40. If two angles are adjacent, then they share a vertex.

41. If you use sunscreen, then you will not get sunburned.

Geology Mohs' scale is used to identify minerals. A mineral with a higher number is harder than a mineral with a lower number.

Use the table and the statements below for Exercises 42–47. Write each conditional and find its truth value.

p: calcite $\qquad\qquad$ q: not apatite

r: a hardness of 3 $\qquad\qquad$ s: a hardness less than 5

42. $p \to r$ $\qquad$ **43.** $s \to q$ $\qquad$ **44.** $q \to s$

45. $q \to p$ $\qquad$ **46.** $r \to q$ $\qquad$ **47.** $p \to s$

Mohs' Scale	
Hardness	**Mineral**
1	Talc
2	Gypsum
3	Calcite
4	Fluorite
5	Apatite
6	Orthoclase
7	Quartz
8	Topaz
9	Corundum
10	Diamond

H.O.T. 48. Critical Thinking Consider the conditional "If two angles are congruent, then they have the same measure." Write the converse, inverse, and contrapositive and find the truth value of each. Use the related conditionals to draw a Venn diagram that represents the relationship between congruent angles and their measures.

H.O.T. 49. Write About It When is a conditional statement false? Explain why a true conditional statement can have a hypothesis that is false.

TEST PREP

50. What is the inverse of "If it is Saturday, then it is the weekend"?

Ⓐ If it is the weekend, then it is Saturday.

Ⓑ If it is not Saturday, then it is the weekend.

Ⓒ If it is not Saturday, then it is not the weekend.

Ⓓ If it is not the weekend, then it is not Saturday.

51. Let a represent "Two lines are parallel to the same line," and let b represent "The two lines are parallel." Which symbolic statement represents the conditional "If two lines are NOT parallel, then they are parallel to the same line"?

Ⓕ $a \to b$ $\qquad$ Ⓖ $b \to a$ $\qquad$ Ⓗ $\sim b \to a$ $\qquad$ Ⓙ $b \to \sim a$

52. Which statement is a counterexample for the conditional statement "If $f(x) = \sqrt{25 - x^2}$, then $f(x)$ is positive"?

Ⓐ $x = 0$ $\qquad$ Ⓑ $x = 3$ $\qquad$ Ⓒ $x = 4$ $\qquad$ Ⓓ $x = 5$

53. Which statement has the same truth value as its converse?

Ⓕ If a triangle has a right angle, its side lengths are 3 centimeters, 4 centimeters, and 5 centimeters.

Ⓖ If an angle measures 104°, then the angle is obtuse.

Ⓗ If a number is an integer, then it is a natural number.

Ⓙ If an angle measures 90°, then it is an acute angle.

CHALLENGE AND EXTEND

For each Venn diagram, write two statements beginning with *Some, All,* or *No.*

54.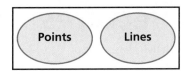

55.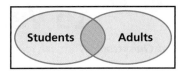

56. Given: If a figure is a square, then it is a rectangle. Figure *A* is not a rectangle.
    Conclusion: Figure *A* is not a square.

    a. Draw a Venn diagram to represent the given conditional statement.
       Use the Venn diagram to explain why the conclusion is valid.

    b. Write the contrapositive of the given conditional. How can you use the
       contrapositive to justify the conclusion?

57. **Multi-Step** How many true conditionals can you write using the statements below?

    p: *n* is an integer.   *q*: *n* is a whole number.   *r*: *n* is a natural number.

FOCUS ON MATHEMATICAL PRACTICES

H.O.T. 58. **Analysis** Write a conditional statement about money for which the converse,
    inverse, and contrapositive statements are all false. Write each statement.

H.O.T. 59. **Justify** Explain why the statement "If the contrapositive of a conditional statement
    is false, then the conditional statement is false" is true.

H.O.T. 60. **Reasoning** Vivian says that if a conditional and its inverse are both true, then the
    contrapositive and converse are false. Is she correct? Explain.

Career Path

Stephanie Poulin
Desktop Publisher
Daily Reporter

Q: What high school math classes did you take?

A: I took three years of math: Pre-Algebra, Algebra, and Geometry.

Q: What training do you need to be a desktop publisher?

A: Most of my training was done on the job. The computer science and
typing classes I took in high school have been helpful.

Q: How do you use math?

A: Part of my job is to make sure all the text, charts, and photographs
are formatted to fit the layout of each page. I have to manipulate
things by comparing ratios, calculating areas, and using estimation.

Q: What future plans do you have?

A: My goal is to start my own business as a freelance graphic artist.

19-5 Using Deductive Reasoning to Verify Conjectures

 Essential Question: What are some valid forms of deductive reasoning?

Objective
Apply the Law of Detachment and the Law of Syllogism in logical reasoning.

Vocabulary
deductive reasoning

Why learn this?
You can use inductive and deductive reasoning to decide whether a common myth is accurate.

You have learned that one counterexample is enough to disprove a conjecture. But to prove that a conjecture is true, you must use *deductive reasoning*. **Deductive reasoning** is the process of using logic to draw conclusions from given facts, definitions, and properties.

EXAMPLE **1** *Media Application*
MCC.MP.3

Online Video Tutor

Urban legends and modern myths spread quickly through the media. Many Web sites and television shows are dedicated to confirming or disproving such myths. Is each conclusion a result of inductive or deductive reasoning?

A There is a myth that toilets and sinks drain in opposite directions in the Southern and Northern Hemispheres. However, if you were to observe sinks draining in the two hemispheres, you would see that this myth is false.

Since the conclusion is based on a pattern of observation, it is a result of inductive reasoning.

B There is a myth that you should not touch a baby bird that has fallen from its nest because the mother bird will disown the baby if she detects human scent. However, biologists have shown that birds cannot detect human scent. Therefore, the myth cannot be true.

The conclusion is based on logical reasoning from scientific research. It is a result of deductive reasoning.

1. There is a myth that an eelskin wallet will demagnetize credit cards because the skin of the electric eels used to make the wallet holds an electric charge. However, eelskin products are not made from electric eels. Therefore, the myth cannot be true. Is this conclusion a result of inductive or deductive reasoning?

In deductive reasoning, if the given facts are true and you apply the correct logic, then the conclusion must be true. The Law of Detachment is one valid form of deductive reasoning.

(cr) Alamy Images; (br) Taxi/Getty Images

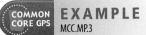 **Law of Detachment**

If $p \rightarrow q$ is a true statement and p is true, then q is true.

COMMON CORE GPS **EXAMPLE** **2**
MCC.MP.3

🌐 my.hrw.com

Online Video Tutor

Verifying Conjectures by Using the Law of Detachment

Determine if each conjecture is valid by the Law of Detachment.

A Given: If two segments are congruent, then they have the same length. $\overline{AB} \cong \overline{XY}$.

Conjecture: $AB = XY$

Identify the hypothesis and conclusion in the given conditional.

If **two segments are congruent**, then **they have the same length**.

The given statement $\overline{AB} \cong \overline{XY}$ matches the hypothesis of a true conditional. By the Law of Detachment $AB = XY$. The conjecture is valid.

B Given: If you are tardy 3 times, you must go to detention.
Shea is in detention.

Conjecture: Shea was tardy at least 3 times.

Identify the hypothesis and conclusion in the given conditional.

If **you are tardy 3 times**, you must **go to detention**.

The given statement "Shea is in detention" matches the conclusion of a true conditional. But this does not mean the hypothesis is true. Shea could be in detention for another reason. The conjecture is not valid.

 2. Determine if the conjecture is valid by the Law of Detachment.
Given: If a student passes his classes, the student is eligible to play sports. Ramon passed his classes.
Conjecture: Ramon is eligible to play sports.

Another valid form of deductive reasoning is the Law of Syllogism. It allows you to draw conclusions from two conditional statements when the conclusion of one is the hypothesis of the other.

 **Law of Syllogism**

If $p \rightarrow q$ and $q \rightarrow r$ are true statements, then $p \rightarrow r$ is a true statement.

COMMON CORE GPS **EXAMPLE** **3**
MCC.MP.3

🌐 my.hrw.com

Online Video Tutor

Verifying Conjectures by Using the Law of Syllogism

Determine if each conjecture is valid by the Law of Syllogism.

A Given: If $m\angle A < 90°$, then $\angle A$ is acute. If $\angle A$ is acute, then it is not a right angle.

Conjecture: If $m\angle A < 90°$, then it is not a right angle.

Let p, q, and r represent the following.

p: The measure of an angle is less than $90°$.

q: The angle is acute.

r: The angle is not a right angle.

You are given that $p \rightarrow q$ and $q \rightarrow r$. Since q is the conclusion of the first conditional and the hypothesis of the second conditional, you can conclude that $p \rightarrow r$. The conjecture is valid by the Law of Syllogism.

Determine if each conjecture is valid by the Law of Syllogism.

B Given: If a number is divisible by 4, then it is divisible by 2.
If a number is even, then it is divisible by 2.

Conjecture: If a number is divisible by 4, then it is even.

Let x, y, and z represent the following.

x: A number is divisible by 4.

y: A number is divisible by 2.

z: A number is even.

You are given that $x \rightarrow y$ and $z \rightarrow y$. The Law of Syllogism cannot be used to draw a conclusion since y is the conclusion of both conditionals. Even though the conjecture $x \rightarrow z$ is true, the logic used to draw the conclusion is not valid.

 3. Determine if the conjecture is valid by the Law of Syllogism.
Given: If an animal is a mammal, then it has hair.
If an animal is a dog, then it is a mammal.
Conjecture: If an animal is a dog, then it has hair.

my.hrw.com

Online Video Tutor

EXAMPLE 4 Applying the Laws of Deductive Reasoning

Draw a conclusion from the given information.

A Given: If a team wins 10 games, then they play in the finals. If a team plays in the finals, then they travel to Boston. The Ravens won 10 games.

Conclusion: The Ravens will travel to Boston.

B Given: If two angles form a linear pair, then they are adjacent. If two angles are adjacent, then they share a side. ∠1 and ∠2 form a linear pair.

Conclusion: ∠1 and ∠2 share a side.

 **4.** Draw a conclusion from the given information.
Given: If a polygon is a triangle, then it has three sides. If a polygon has three sides, then it is not a quadrilateral. Polygon P is a triangle.

MCC.MP.2 **MATHEMATICAL PRACTICES**

THINK AND DISCUSS

1. Could "A square has exactly two sides" be the conclusion of a valid argument? If so, what do you know about the truth value of the given information?

2. Explain why writing conditional statements as symbols might help you evaluate the validity of an argument.

 3. GET ORGANIZED Copy and complete the graphic organizer. Write each law in your own words and give an example of each.

```
            Deductive Reasoning
             /            \
Law of Detachment    Law of Syllogism
```

19-5 Exercises

my.hrw.com
Homework Help

GUIDED PRACTICE

1. **Vocabulary** Explain how *deductive reasoning* differs from inductive reasoning.

SEE EXAMPLE 1 — **Does each conclusion use inductive or deductive reasoning?**

2. At Bell High School, students must take Biology before they take Chemistry. Sam is in Chemistry, so Marcia concludes that he has taken Biology.

3. A detective learns that his main suspect was out of town the day of the crime. He concludes that the suspect is innocent.

SEE EXAMPLE 2 — **Determine if each conjecture is valid by the Law of Detachment.**

4. Given: If you want to go on a field trip, you must have a signed permission slip. Zola has a signed permission slip.
Conjecture: Zola wants to go on a field trip.

5. Given: If the side lengths of a rectangle are 3 ft and 4 ft, then its area is 12 ft². A rectangle has side lengths of 3 ft and 4 ft.
Conjecture: The area of the rectangle is 12 ft².

SEE EXAMPLE 3 — **Determine if each conjecture is valid by the Law of Syllogism.**

6. Given: If you fly from Texas to California, you travel from the central to the Pacific time zone. If you travel from the central to the Pacific time zone, then you gain two hours.
Conjecture: If you fly from Texas to California, you gain two hours.

7. Given: If a figure is a **square**, then the figure is a **rectangle**. If a figure is a **square**, then it is a parallelogram.
Conjecture: If a figure is a parallelogram, then it is a **rectangle**.

SEE EXAMPLE 4

8. Draw a conclusion from the given information.
Given: If you leave your car lights on overnight, then your car battery will drain. If your battery is drained, your car might not start. Alex left his car lights on last night.

PRACTICE AND PROBLEM SOLVING

Does each conclusion use inductive or deductive reasoning?

9. The sum of the angle measures of a triangle is 180°. Two angles of a triangle measure 40° and 60°, so Kandy concludes that the third angle measures 80°.

10. All of the students in Henry's Geometry class are juniors. Alexander takes Geometry, but has another teacher. Henry concludes that Alexander is also a junior.

11. Determine if the conjecture is valid by the Law of Detachment.
Given: If one integer is odd and another integer is even, their product is even. The product of two integers is 24.
Conjecture: One of the two integers is odd.

For Exercises	See Example
9–10	1
11	2
12	3
13	4

my.hrw.com

Online Extra Practice

19-5 Using Deductive Reasoning to Verify Conjectures **563**

12. Science Determine if the conjecture is valid by the Law of Syllogism.
Given: If an element is an alkali metal, then it reacts with water. If an element is in the first column of the periodic table, then it is an alkali metal.
Conjecture: If an element is in the first column of the periodic table, then it reacts with water.

H.O.T. 13. Draw a conclusion from the given information.
Given: If Dakota watches the news, she is informed about current events.
If Dakota knows about current events, she gets better grades in Social Studies.
Dakota watches the news.

14. Technology Joseph downloads a file in 18 minutes with a dial-up modem. How long would it take to download the file with a Cheetah-Net cable modem?

CHEETAH-NET CABLE
75 Times As Fast As Dial-Up

Recreation

When the Gemini roller coaster opened in Cedar Point in 1978, it was the fastest roller coaster in the world. It no longer holds this title, but it is still a popular attraction.

Recreation Use the true statements below for Exercises 15–18. Determine whether each conclusion is valid.

    I. The Gemini is at Cedar Point amusement park in Sandusky, OH.

    II. Carter and Mary go to Cedar Point.

    III. The Gemini roller coaster reaches speeds of 60 mi/h.

    IV. When Carter goes to an amusement park, he rides all the roller coasters.

15. Carter went to Sandusky, OH.

16. Mary rode the Gemini.

17. Carter rode a roller coaster that travels 60 mi/h.

18. Mary rode a roller coaster that travels 60 mi/h.

19. Critical Thinking Is the argument below a valid application of the Law of Syllogism? Is the conclusion true? Explain your answers.
If $3 - x < 5$, then $x < -2$. If $x < -2$, then $-5x > 10$. Thus, if $3 - x < 5$, then $-5x > 10$.

H.O.T. 20. **///ERROR ANALYSIS///** Below are two conclusions. Which is incorrect? Explain the error.

If two angles are complementary, their measures add to 90°. If an angle measures 90°, then it is a right angle. $\angle A$ and $\angle B$ are complementary.

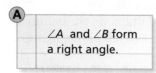
A
$\angle A$ and $\angle B$ form a right angle.

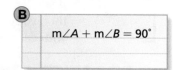
B
$m\angle A + m\angle B = 90°$

H.O.T. 21. **Write About It** Write one example of a real-life logical argument that uses the Law of Detachment and one that uses the Law of Syllogism. Explain why the conclusions are valid.

Real-World Connections

22. When Alice meets the Pigeon in Wonderland, the Pigeon thinks she is a serpent. The Pigeon reasons that serpents eat eggs, and Alice confirms that she has eaten eggs.

    a. Write "Serpents eat eggs" as a conditional statement.

    b. Is the Pigeon's conclusion that Alice is a serpent valid? Explain your reasoning.

TEST PREP

23. The Supershots scored over 75 points in each of ten straight games. The newspaper predicts that they will score more than 75 points tonight. Which form of reasoning is this conclusion based on?

Ⓐ Deductive reasoning, because the conclusion is based on logic

Ⓑ Deductive reasoning, because the conclusion is based on a pattern

Ⓒ Inductive reasoning, because the conclusion is based on logic

Ⓓ Inductive reasoning, because the conclusion is based on a pattern

24. $\overrightarrow{HF}$ bisects $\angle EHG$. Which conclusion is NOT valid?

Ⓕ E, F, and G are coplanar.

Ⓖ $\angle EHF \cong \angle FHG$

Ⓗ $\overline{EF} \cong \overline{FG}$

Ⓘ $m\angle EHF = m\angle FHG$

25. **Gridded Response** If Whitney plays a low G on her piano, the frequency of the note is 24.50 hertz. The frequency of a note doubles with each octave. What is the frequency in hertz of a G note that is 3 octaves above low G?

CHALLENGE AND EXTEND

H.O.T. 26. Political Science To be eligible to hold the office of the president of the United States, a person must be at least 35 years old, be a natural-born U.S. citizen, and have been a U.S. resident for at least 14 years. Given this information, what conclusion, if any, can be drawn from the statements below? Explain your reasoning.

Andre is not eligible to be the president of the United States.
Andre has lived in the United States for 16 years.

H.O.T. 27. Multi-Step Consider the two conditional statements below.
If you live in San Diego, then you live in California.
If you live in California, then you live in the United States.

a. Draw a conclusion from the given conditional statements.

b. Write the contrapositive of each conditional statement.

c. Draw a conclusion from the two contrapositives.

d. How does the conclusion in part **a** relate to the conclusion in part **c**?

28. If Cassie goes to the skate park, Hanna and Amy will go. If Hanna or Amy goes to the skate park, then Marc will go. If Marc goes to the skate park, then Dallas will go. If only two of the five people went to the skate park, who were they?

FOCUS ON MATHEMATICAL PRACTICES

H.O.T. 29. Analysis Find the missing statement so that the following conjecture is true:
If the mountains are to my left, then I'm driving to visit a friend.

Given: If I am going to Ingleton, then I'm driving to visit a friend.
If the mountains are to my left, then I am driving north.

H.O.T. 30. Reasoning Rewrite each statement in symbolic form. Explain the validity of the following conjecture: If Gavin likes geometry, then Alice and Gavin will study math together.

I. If Gavin likes geometry, then he likes math.

II. If Alice likes Gavin, then they will study math together.

III. If Alice doesn't like Gavin, then Gavin doesn't like math.

Ready to Go On?

my.hrw.com
Assessment and Intervention

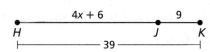

19-1 Measuring and Constructing Segments

Find the length of each segment.

1. $\overline{SV}$ **2.** $\overline{TR}$ **3.** $\overline{ST}$

4. The diagram represents a straight highway with three towns, Henri, Joaquin, and Kenard. Find the distance from Henri H to Joaquin J.

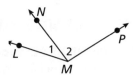

5. Sketch, draw, and construct a segment congruent to $\overline{CD}$.

6. Q is the midpoint of $\overline{PR}$, $PQ = 2z$, and $PR = 8z - 12$. Find z, PQ, and PR.

19-2 Measuring and Constructing Angles

7. Name all the angles in the diagram.

Classify each angle by its measure.

8. $m\angle PVQ = 21°$ **9.** $m\angle RVT = 96°$ **10.** $m\angle PVS = 143°$

11. $\overrightarrow{RS}$ bisects $\angle QRT$, $m\angle QRS = (3x + 8)°$, and $m\angle SRT = (9x - 4)°$. Find $m\angle SRT$.

12. Use a protractor and straightedge to draw a 130° angle. Then bisect the angle.

19-3 Using Inductive Reasoning to Make Conjectures

Find the next item in each pattern.

13. 1, 10, 18, 25, …   **14.** July, May, March, …   **15.** $\frac{1}{8}, -\frac{1}{4}, \frac{1}{2}, …$ **16.** |, +, ‖, …

17. A biologist recorded the following data about the weight of male lions in a wildlife park in Africa. Use the table to make a conjecture about the average weight of a male lion.

18. Complete the conjecture "The sum of two negative numbers is ___?___."

19. Show that the conjecture "If an even number is divided by 2, then the result is an even number" is false by finding a counterexample.

ID Number	Weight (lb)
A1902SM	387.2
A1904SM	420.5
A1920SM	440.6
A1956SM	398.7
A1974SM	415.0

19-4 Conditional Statements

20. Identify the hypothesis and conclusion of the conditional statement "An angle is obtuse if its measure is 107°."

Write a conditional statement from each of the following.

21. A whole number is an integer.

22.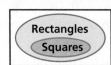

23. The diagonals of a square are congruent.

Determine if each conditional is true. If false, give a counterexample.

24. If an angle is acute, then it has a measure of 30°.

25. If $9x - 11 = 2x + 3$, then $x = 2$.

26. Write the converse, inverse, and contrapositive of the statement "If a number is even, then it is divisible by 4." Find the truth value of each.

✓ 19-5 Using Deductive Reasoning to Verify Conjectures

27. Determine if the following conjecture is valid by the Law of Detachment.
Given: If Sue finishes her science project, she can go to the movie. Sue goes to the movie.
Conjecture: Sue finished her science project.

28. Use the Law of Syllogism to draw a conclusion from the given information.
Given: If one angle of a triangle is 90°, then the triangle is a right triangle. If a triangle is a right triangle, then its acute angle measures are complementary.

PARCC Assessment Readiness

COMMON CORE GPS

Selected Response

1. Identify the hypothesis and conclusion of the conditional statement.

   If it is raining then it is cloudy.

   (A) Hypothesis: It is raining.
   Conclusion: It is cloudy.

   (B) Hypothesis: It is cloudy.
   Conclusion: It is raining.

   (C) Hypothesis: Clouds make rain.
   Conclusion: Rain does not make clouds.

   (D) Hypothesis: Rain and clouds happen together.
   Conclusion: Rain and clouds do not happen together.

2. Complete the conjecture.

   The sum of two odd numbers is _____.

   (F) even

   (G) odd

   (H) sometimes odd, sometimes even

   (J) even most of the time

3. Find the length of $\overline{BC}$.

   (A) $BC = -7$

   (B) $BC = -9$

   (C) $BC = 7$

   (D) $BC = 8$

4. Determine if the conjecture is valid by the Law of Detachment.

   Given: If Tommy makes cookies tonight, then Tommy must have an oven. Tommy has an oven.

   Conjecture: Tommy made cookies tonight.

   (F) The conjecture is valid, because if Tommy didn't have an oven then he didn't make cookies tonight.

   (G) The conjecture is not valid, because if Tommy didn't have an oven then he didn't make cookies tonight.

   (H) The conjecture is valid, because Tommy could have an oven but he could make something besides cookies tonight.

   (J) The conjecture is not valid, because Tommy could have an oven but he could make something besides cookies tonight.

Mini-Tasks

5. $\overrightarrow{BD}$ bisects $\angle ABC$, $m\angle ABD = (7x - 1)°$, and $m\angle DBC = (4x + 8)°$. Find $m\angle ABD$.

6. Point C is the midpoint of $\overline{AB}$ and point D is the midpoint of $\overline{CB}$. If $AB = 20$, what is AD?

UNIT 7

Module

20 Algebraic and Geometric Proofs

Contents

MATHEMATICAL PRACTICES   The Common Core Georgia Performance Standards for Mathematical Practice describe varieties of expertise that all students should seek to develop. Opportunities to develop these practices are integrated throughout this program.

1 Make sense of problems and persevere in solving them.

2 Reason abstractly and quantitatively.

3 Construct viable arguments and critique the reasoning of others.

4 Model with mathematics.

5 Use appropriate tools strategically.

6 Attend to precision.

7 Look for and make use of structure.

8 Look for and express regularity in repeated reasoning.

Unpacking the Standards

Understanding the standards and the vocabulary terms in the standards will help you know exactly what you are expected to learn in this chapter.

 MCC9-12.G.CO.9

Prove theorems about lines and angles.

Key Vocabulary

proof (demostración)
An argument that uses logic to show that a conclusion is true.

theorem (teorema)
A statement that has been proven.

line (línea)
An undefined term in geometry, a line is a straight path that has no thickness and extends forever.

angle (ángulo)
A figure formed by two rays with a common endpoint.

What It Means For You

With just a few definitions, properties, and postulates, you can begin to prove simple theorems about line segments, linear pairs, right angles, vertical angles, and complementary or supplementary angles.

EXAMPLE

Given: ∠1 and ∠3 are vertical angles.
Prove: ∠1 ≅ ∠3

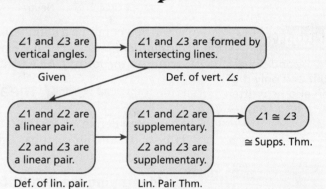

20-1 Biconditional Statements and Definitions

? Essential Question: How can definitions be written as biconditional statements?

Objective
Write and analyze biconditional statements.

Vocabulary
biconditional statement
definition
polygon
triangle
quadrilateral

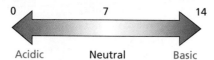

Who uses this?
A gardener can plan the color of the hydrangeas she plants by checking the pH of the soil.

The pH of a solution is a measure of the concentration of hydronium ions in the solution. If a solution has a pH less than 7, it is an acid. Also, if a solution is an acid, it has a pH less than 7.

Acidic   Neutral   Basic

Writing Math

The biconditional "p if and only if q" can also be written as "p iff q" or $p \leftrightarrow q$.

When you combine a conditional statement and its converse, you create a *biconditional statement.* A **biconditional statement** is a statement that can be written in the form "p if and only if q." This means "if p, then q" and "if q, then p."

$$p \longleftrightarrow q \text{ means } p \longrightarrow q \text{ and } q \longrightarrow p$$

So you can define an acid with the following biconditional statement: A solution is an acid if and only if it has a pH less than 7.

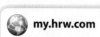

EXAMPLE 1 Prep for MCC9-12.G.CO.9

my.hrw.com

Online Video Tutor

Identifying the Conditionals within a Biconditional Statement

Write the conditional statement and converse within each biconditional.

A Two angles are congruent if and only if their measures are equal.
    Let p and q represent the following.
       p: Two angles are congruent.
       q: Two angle measures are equal.
    The two parts of the biconditional $p \leftrightarrow q$ are $p \rightarrow q$ and $q \rightarrow p$.
    Conditional: If two angles are congruent, then their measures are equal.
    Converse: If two angle measures are equal, then the angles are congruent.

B A solution is a base $\leftrightarrow$ it has a pH greater than 7.
    Let x and y represent the following.
       x: A solution is a base.
       y: A solution has a pH greater than 7.
    The two parts of the biconditional $x \leftrightarrow y$ are $x \rightarrow y$ and $y \rightarrow x$.
    Conditional: If a solution is a base, then it has a pH greater than 7.
    Converse: If a solution has a pH greater than 7, then it is a base.

Write the conditional statement and converse within each biconditional.

  1a. An angle is acute iff its measure is greater than 0° and less than 90°.
  1b. Cho is a member if and only if he has paid the $5 dues.

© Steffan Hauser/botanikfoto/Alamy

EXAMPLE Prep for MCC9-12.G.CO.9

2

Writing a Biconditional Statement

For each conditional, write the converse and a biconditional statement.

A If $2x + 5 = 11$, then $x = 3$.

Converse: If $x = 3$, then $2x + 5 = 11$.

Biconditional: $2x + 5 = 11$ if and only if $x = 3$.

B If a point is a midpoint, then it divides the segment into two congruent segments.

Converse: If a point divides a segment into two congruent segments, then the point is a midpoint.

Biconditional: A point is a midpoint if and only if it divides the segment into two congruent segments.

 For each conditional, write the converse and a biconditional statement.

2a. If the date is July 4th, then it is Independence Day.

2b. If points lie on the same line, then they are collinear.

For a biconditional statement to be true, both the conditional statement and its converse must be true. If either the conditional or the converse is false, then the biconditional statement is false.

EXAMPLE MCC.MP.3

3

Analyzing the Truth Value of a Biconditional Statement

Determine if each biconditional is true. If false, give a counterexample.

A A square has a side length of 5 if and only if it has an area of 25.

Conditional: If a square has a side length of 5, then it has an area of 25.   *The conditional is true.*

Converse: If a square has an area of 25, then it has a side length of 5.   *The converse is true.*

Since the conditional and its converse are true, the biconditional is true.

B The number n is a positive integer $\leftrightarrow 2n$ is a natural number.

Conditional: If n is a positive integer, then $2n$ is a natural number.   *The conditional is true.*

Converse: If $2n$ is a natural number, then n is a positive integer.   *The converse is false.*

If $2n = 1$, then $n = \frac{1}{2}$, which is not an integer. Because the converse is false, the biconditional is false.

 Determine if each biconditional is true. If false, give a counterexample.

3a. An angle is a right angle iff its measure is 90°.

3b. $y = -5 \leftrightarrow y^2 = 25$

In geometry, biconditional statements are used to write *definitions*. A **definition** is a statement that describes a mathematical object and can be written as a true biconditional. Most definitions in the glossary are not written as biconditional statements, but they can be. The "if and only if" is implied.

In the glossary, a **polygon** is defined as a closed plane figure formed by three or more line segments. Each segment intersects exactly two other segments only at their endpoints, and no two segments with a common endpoint are collinear.

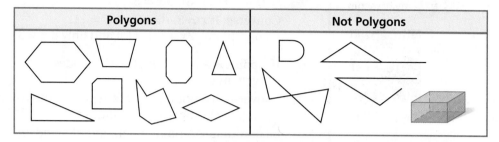

Polygons	Not Polygons

A **triangle** is defined as a three-sided polygon, and a **quadrilateral** is a four-sided polygon.

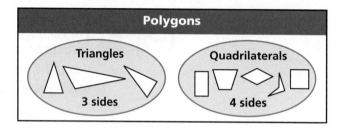

Polygons

Triangles
3 sides

Quadrilaterals
4 sides

Helpful Hint

Think of definitions as being reversible. Postulates, however, are not necessarily true when reversed.

A good, precise definition can be used forward and backward. For example, if a figure is a quadrilateral, then it is a four-sided polygon. If a figure is a four-sided polygon, then it is a quadrilateral. To make sure a definition is precise, it helps to write it as a biconditional statement.

COMMON CORE GPS
EXAMPLE 4
MCC.MP.6

my.hrw.com

Online Video Tutor

Writing Definitions as Biconditional Statements

Write each definition as a biconditional.

A A triangle is a three-sided polygon.

A figure is a triangle if and only if it is a three-sided polygon.

B A segment bisector is a ray, segment, or line that divides a segment into two congruent segments.

A ray, segment, or line is a segment bisector if and only if it divides a segment into two congruent segments.

CHECK IT OUT!

Write each definition as a biconditional.

4a. A quadrilateral is a four-sided polygon.

4b. The measure of a straight angle is 180°.

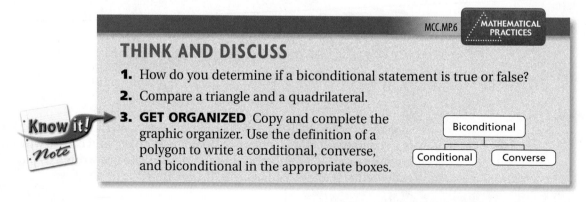

MCC.MP.6 MATHEMATICAL PRACTICES

THINK AND DISCUSS

1. How do you determine if a biconditional statement is true or false?

2. Compare a triangle and a quadrilateral.

3. GET ORGANIZED Copy and complete the graphic organizer. Use the definition of a polygon to write a conditional, converse, and biconditional in the appropriate boxes.

Know it! Note

Biconditional

Conditional   Converse

GUIDED PRACTICE

1. **Vocabulary** How is a *biconditional statement* different from a conditional statement?

SEE EXAMPLE 1 Write the conditional statement and converse within each biconditional.

2. Perry can paint the entire living room if and only if he has enough paint.

3. Your medicine will be ready by 5 P.M. if and only if you drop your prescription off by 8 A.M.

SEE EXAMPLE 2 For each conditional, write the converse and a biconditional statement.

4. If a student is a sophomore, then the student is in the tenth grade.

5. If two segments have the same length, then they are congruent.

SEE EXAMPLE 3 **Multi-Step** Determine if each biconditional is true. If false, give a counterexample.

6. $xy = 0 \leftrightarrow x = 0$ or $y = 0$.

7. A figure is a quadrilateral if and only if it is a polygon.

SEE EXAMPLE 4 Write each definition as a biconditional.

8. Parallel lines are two coplanar lines that never intersect.

9. A hummingbird is a tiny, brightly colored bird with narrow wings, a slender bill, and a long tongue.

PRACTICE AND PROBLEM SOLVING

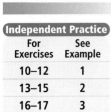

Independent Practice	
For Exercises	See Example
10–12	1
13–15	2
16–17	3
18–19	4

my.hrw.com

Online Extra Practice

Write the conditional statement and converse within each biconditional.

10. Three points are coplanar if and only if they lie in the same plane.

11. A parallelogram is a rectangle if and only if it has four right angles.

12. A lunar eclipse occurs if and only if Earth is between the Sun and the Moon.

For each conditional, write the converse and a biconditional statement.

13. If today is Saturday or Sunday, then it is the weekend.

14. If Greg has the fastest time, then he wins the race.

15. If a triangle contains a right angle, then it is a right triangle.

Multi-Step Determine if each biconditional is true. If false, give a counterexample.

16. Felipe is a swimmer if and only if he is an athlete.

17. The number $2n$ is even if and only if n is an integer.

Write each definition as a biconditional.

18. A circle is the set of all points in a plane that are a fixed distance from a given point.

19. A catcher is a baseball player who is positioned behind home plate and who catches throws from the pitcher.

Algebra Determine if a true biconditional can be written from each conditional statement. If not, give a counterexample.

20. If $a = b$, then $|a| = |b|$.

21. If $3x - 2 = 13$, then $\frac{4}{5}x + 8 = 12$.

22. If $y^2 = 64$, then $3y = 24$.

23. If $x > 0$, then $x^2 > 0$.

Use the diagrams to write a definition for each figure.

24.

Equilateral triangle Not an equilateral triangle

25.

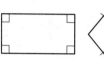

Square Not squares

26. **Biology** White blood cells are cells that defend the body against invading organisms by engulfing them or by releasing chemicals called *antibodies*. Write the definition of a white blood cell as a biconditional statement.

Explain why the given statement is not a definition.

27. An automobile is a vehicle that moves along the ground.

28. A calculator is a machine that performs computations with numbers.

29. An angle is a geometric object formed by two rays.

H.O.T. **Chemistry** Use the table for Exercises 30–32. Determine if a true biconditional statement can be written from each conditional.

30. If a solution has a pH of 4, then it is tomato juice.

31. If a solution is bleach, then its pH is 13.

32. If a solution has a pH greater than 7, then it is not battery acid.

pH	Examples
0	Battery Acid
4	Acid rain, tomato juice
6	Saliva
8	Sea water
13	Bleach, oven cleaner
14	Drain cleaner

Complete each statement to form a true biconditional.

33. The circumference of a circle is 10π if and only if its radius is __?__ .

34. Four points in a plane form a __?__ if and only if no three of them are collinear.

H.O.T. **35.** **Critical Thinking** Write the definition of a biconditional statement as a biconditional statement. Use the conditional and converse within the statement to explain why your biconditional is true.

36. **Write About It** Use the definition of an angle bisector to explain what is meant by the statement "A good definition is reversible."

Real-World Connections

37. a. Write "I say what I mean" and "I mean what I say" as conditionals.

b. Explain why the biconditional statement implied by Alice is false.

"Then you should say what you mean," the March Hare went on.

"I do," Alice hastily replied; "at least—at least I mean what I say—that's the same thing, you know."

Biology

White blood cells live less than a few weeks. A drop of blood can contain anywhere from 7000 to 25,000 white blood cells.

TEST PREP

38. Which is a counterexample for the biconditional "An angle measures 80° if and only if the angle is acute"?

Ⓐ m∠S = 60° Ⓑ m∠S = 115° Ⓒ m∠S = 90° Ⓓ m∠S = 360°

39. Which biconditional is equivalent to the spelling phrase "*I* before *E* except after *C*"?

Ⓕ The letter *I* comes before *E* if and only if *I* follows *C*.

Ⓖ The letter *E* comes before *I* if and only if *E* follows *C*.

Ⓗ The letter *E* comes before *I* if and only if *E* comes before *C*.

Ⓙ The letter *I* comes before *E* if and only if *I* comes before *C*.

40. Which conditional statement can be used to write a true biconditional?

Ⓐ If a number is divisible by 4, then it is even.

Ⓑ If a ratio compares two quantities measured in different units, the ratio is a rate.

Ⓒ If two angles are supplementary, then they are adjacent.

Ⓓ If an angle is right, then it is not acute.

H.O.T. 41. Short Response Write the two conditional statements that make up the biconditional "You will get a traffic ticket if and only if you are speeding." Is the biconditional true or false? Explain your answer.

CHALLENGE AND EXTEND

H.O.T. 42. Critical Thinking Describe what the Venn diagram of a true biconditional statement looks like. How does this support the idea that a definition can be written as a true biconditional?

43. Consider the conditional "If an angle measures 105°, then the angle is obtuse."

a. Write the inverse of the conditional statement.

b. Write the converse of the inverse.

c. How is the converse of the inverse related to the original conditional?

d. What is the truth value of the biconditional statement formed by the inverse of the original conditional and the converse of the inverse? Explain.

44. Suppose *A*, *B*, *C*, and *D* are coplanar, and *A*, *B*, and *C* are not collinear. What is the truth value of the biconditional formed from the true conditional "If m∠ABD + m∠DBC = m∠ABC, then *D* is in the interior of ∠ABC"? Explain.

45. Find a counterexample for "*n* is divisible by 4 if and only if n^2 is even."

FOCUS ON MATHEMATICAL PRACTICES

H.O.T. 46. Error Analysis Blake wrote, "An angle is obtuse if and only if it is not an acute angle." What did Blake overlook? Complete this statement: "An angle is obtuse if and only if ? ."

H.O.T. 47. Precision Is the following a good, precise definition? Explain. *If a polygon has exactly three acute angles, then it is a triangle.*

H.O.T. 48. Justify A conditional statement is true, and so is its inverse. Explain why the conditional statement is a valid biconditional statement.

20-2 Algebraic Proof

? **Essential Question:** What kinds of justifications can you use in writing algebraic and geometric proofs?

Objectives
Review properties of equality and use them to write algebraic proofs.

Identify properties of equality and congruence.

Vocabulary
proof

Who uses this?
Game designers and animators solve equations to simulate motion. (See Example 2.)

A **proof** is an argument that uses logic, definitions, properties, and previously proven statements to show that a conclusion is true.

If you've ever solved an equation in Algebra, then you've already done a proof! An algebraic proof uses algebraic properties such as the properties of equality and the Distributive Property.

Remember!

The Distributive Property states that $a(b + c) = ab + ac$.

Properties of Equality

Addition Property of Equality	If $a = b$, then $a + c = b + c$.
Subtraction Property of Equality	If $a = b$, then $a - c = b - c$.
Multiplication Property of Equality	If $a = b$, then $ac = bc$.
Division Property of Equality	If $a = b$ and $c \neq 0$, then $\frac{a}{c} = \frac{b}{c}$.
Reflexive Property of Equality	$a = a$
Symmetric Property of Equality	If $a = b$, then $b = a$.
Transitive Property of Equality	If $a = b$ and $b = c$, then $a = c$.
Substitution Property of Equality	If $a = b$, then b can be substituted for a in any expression.

As you have learned, if you start with a true statement and each logical step is valid, then your conclusion is valid.

An important part of writing a proof is giving justifications to show that every step is valid. For each justification, you can use a definition, postulate, property, or a piece of information that is given.

COMMON CORE GPS MCC9-12.A.REI.1

EXAMPLE 1 Solving an Equation in Algebra

Solve the equation $-5 = 3n + 1$. Write a justification for each step.

my.hrw.com

Online Video Tutor

$-5 = 3n + 1$	Given equation
$\underline{-1 \qquad -1}$	Subtraction Property of Equality
$-6 = 3n$	Simplify.
$\dfrac{-6}{3} = \dfrac{3n}{3}$	Division Property of Equality
$-2 = n$	Simplify.
$n = -2$	Symmetric Property of Equality

 1. Solve the equation $\frac{1}{2}t = -7$. Write a justification for each step.

© Getty Images

EXAMPLE 2
MCC9-12.A.REI.1

my.hrw.com

Online Video Tutor

Make sense of problems and persevere in solving them.

Problem-Solving Application

To simulate the motion of an object in a computer game, the designer uses the formula $sr = 3.6p$ to find the number of pixels the object must travel during each second of animation. In the formula, s is the desired speed of the object in kilometers per hour, r is the scale of pixels per meter, and p is the number of pixels traveled per second.

The graphics in a game are based on a scale of 6 pixels per meter. The designer wants to simulate a vehicle moving at 75 km/h. How many pixels must the vehicle travel each second? Solve the equation for p and justify each step.

1 Understand the Problem

The **answer** will be the number of pixels traveled per second.

List the important information:

- $sr = 3.6p$
- p: pixels traveled per second
- $s = 75$ km/h
- $r = 6$ pixels per meter

2 Make a Plan

Substitute the given information into the formula and solve.

3 Solve

$sr = 3.6p$	Given equation
$(75)(6) = 3.6p$	Substitution Property of Equality
$450 = 3.6p$	Simplify.
$\dfrac{450}{3.6} = \dfrac{3.6p}{3.6}$	Division Property of Equality
$125 = p$	Simplify.
$p = 125$ pixels	Symmetric Property of Equality

4 Look Back

Check your answer by substituting it back into the original formula.

$$sr = 3.6p$$
$$(75)(6) = 3.6(125)$$
$$450 = 450 \quad \checkmark$$

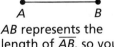

$A \bullet \qquad \bullet B$

AB represents the length of $\overline{AB}$, so you can think of AB as a variable representing a number.

 CHECK IT OUT!

2. What is the temperature in degrees Celsius C when it is 86°F? Solve the equation $C = \dfrac{5}{9}(F - 32)$ for C and justify each step.

Like algebra, geometry also uses numbers, variables, and operations. For example, segment lengths and angle measures are numbers. So you can use these same properties of equality to write algebraic proofs in geometry.

 EXAMPLE **3**
Prep for MCC9-12.G.CO.9

Solving an Equation in Geometry

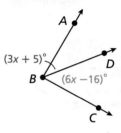

Write a justification for each step.

 my.hrw.com

Online Video Tutor

$KM = KL + LM$	Segment Addition Postulate
$5x - 4 = (x + 3) + (2x - 1)$	Substitution Property of Equality
$5x - 4 = 3x + 2$	Simplify.
$2x - 4 = 2$	Subtraction Property of Equality
$2x = 6$	Addition Property of Equality
$x = 3$	Division Property of Equality

 3. Write a justification for each step.

$$m\angle ABC = m\angle ABD + m\angle DBC$$
$$8x° = (3x + 5)° + (6x - 16)°$$
$$8x = 9x - 11$$
$$-x = -11$$
$$x = 11$$

$(3x + 5)°$ $(6x - 16)°$

$m\angle ABC = 8x°$

You have learned that segments with equal lengths are congruent and angles with equal measures are congruent. So the Reflexive, Symmetric, and Transitive Properties of Equality have corresponding properties of congruence.

 Know it! Note

Properties of Congruence

SYMBOLS	EXAMPLE
Reflexive Property of Congruence figure $A \cong$ figure A (Reflex. Prop. of $\cong$)	$\overline{EF} \cong \overline{EF}$
Symmetric Property of Congruence If figure $A \cong$ figure B, then figure $B \cong$ figure A. (Sym. Prop. of $\cong$)	If $\angle 1 \cong \angle 2$, then $\angle 2 \cong \angle 1$.
Transitive Property of Congruence If figure $A \cong$ figure B and figure $B \cong$ figure C, then figure $A \cong$ figure C. (Trans. Prop. of $\cong$)	If $\overline{PQ} \cong \overline{RS}$ and $\overline{RS} \cong \overline{TU}$, then $\overline{PQ} \cong \overline{TU}$.

Remember!

Numbers are equal (=) and figures are congruent ($\cong$).

 EXAMPLE **4**
Prep for MCC9-12.G.CO.9

Identifying Properties of Equality and Congruence

Identify the property that justifies each statement.

 my.hrw.com

Online Video Tutor

A $m\angle 1 = m\angle 1$ Reflex. Prop. of =

B $\overline{XY} \cong \overline{VW}$, so $\overline{VW} \cong \overline{XY}$. Sym. Prop. of $\cong$

C $\angle ABC \cong \angle ABC$ Reflex. Prop. of $\cong$

D $\angle 1 \cong \angle 2$, and $\angle 2 \cong \angle 3$. So $\angle 1 \cong \angle 3$. Trans. Prop. of $\cong$

 Identify the property that justifies each statement.

4a. $DE = GH$, so $GH = DE$.   **4b.** $94° = 94°$

4c. $0 = a$, and $a = x$. So $0 = x$.   **4d.** $\angle A \cong \angle Y$, so $\angle Y \cong \angle A$.

THINK AND DISCUSS

1. Tell what property you would use to solve the equation $\frac{k}{6} = 3.5$.

2. Explain when to use a congruence symbol instead of an equal sign.

3. GET ORGANIZED Copy and complete the graphic organizer. In each box, write an example of the property, using the correct symbol.

Property	Equality	Congruence
Reflexive		
Symmetric		
Transitive		

20-2 Exercises

my.hrw.com
Homework Help

GUIDED PRACTICE

1. Vocabulary Write the definition of *proof* in your own words.

SEE EXAMPLE 1 **Multi-Step** Solve each equation. Write a justification for each step.

2. $y + 1 = 5$

3. $t - 3.2 = -8.3$

4. $2p - 30 = -4p + 6$

5. $\frac{x + 3}{-2} = 8$

6. $\frac{1}{2}n = \frac{3}{4}$

7. $0 = 2(r - 3) + 4$

SEE EXAMPLE 2 **8. Nutrition** Amy's favorite breakfast cereal has 102 Calories per serving. The equation $C = 9f + 90$ relates the grams of fat f in one serving to the Calories C in one serving. How many grams of fat are in one serving of the cereal? Solve the equation for f and justify each step.

9. Movie Rentals The equation $C = \$5.75 + \$0.89m$ relates the number of movie rentals m to the monthly cost C of a movie club membership. How many movies did Elias rent this month if his membership cost $11.98? Solve the equation for m and justify each step.

SEE EXAMPLE 3 Write a justification for each step.

10.

$5y + 6$ $2y + 21$

A   B   C

$AB = BC$

$5y + 6 = 2y + 21$

$3y + 6 = 21$

$3y = 15$

$y = 5$

11.

$9n - 5$

P $3n$ Q 25 R

$PQ + QR = PR$

$3n + 25 = 9n - 5$

$25 = 6n - 5$

$30 = 6n$

$5 = n$

SEE EXAMPLE 4 Identify the property that justifies each statement.

12. $\overline{AB} \cong \overline{AB}$

13. $m\angle 1 = m\angle 2$, and $m\angle 2 = m\angle 4$. So $m\angle 1 = m\angle 4$.

14. $x = y$, so $y = x$.

15. $\overline{ST} \cong \overline{YZ}$, and $\overline{YZ} \cong \overline{PR}$. So $\overline{ST} \cong \overline{PR}$.

PRACTICE AND PROBLEM SOLVING

Independent Practice

For Exercises	See Example
16–21	1
22	2
23–24	3
25–28	4

my.hrw.com

Online Extra Practice

Multi-Step Solve each equation. Write a justification for each step.

16. $5x - 3 = 4(x + 2)$ **17.** $1.6 = 3.2n$ **18.** $\frac{z}{3} - 2 = -10$

19. $-(h + 3) = 72$ **20.** $9y + 17 = -19$ **21.** $\frac{1}{2}(p - 16) = 13$

22. Ecology The equation $T = 0.03c + 0.05b$ relates the numbers of cans c and bottles b collected in a recycling rally to the total dollars T raised. How many cans were collected if \$147 was raised and 150 bottles were collected? Solve the equation for c and justify each step.

Write a justification for each step.

23. $m\angle XYZ = m\angle 2 + m\angle 3$
$4n - 6 = 58 + (2n - 12)$
$4n - 6 = 2n + 46$
$2n - 6 = 46$
$2n = 52$
$n = 26$

24. $m\angle WYV = m\angle 1 + m\angle 2$
$5n = 3(n - 2) + 58$
$5n = 3n - 6 + 58$
$5n = 3n + 52$
$2n = 52$
$n = 26$

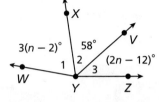

$m\angle WYV = 5n°$
$m\angle XYZ = (4n - 6)°$

Identify the property that justifies each statement.

25. $\overline{KL} \cong \overline{PR}$, so $\overline{PR} \cong \overline{KL}$.   **26.** $412 = 412$

27. If $a = b$ and $b = 0$, then $a = 0$.   **28.** figure $A \cong$ figure A

29. Estimation Round the numbers in the equation $2(3.1x - 0.87) = 94.36$ to the nearest whole number and estimate the solution. Then solve the equation, justifying each step. Compare your estimate to the exact solution.

Use the indicated property to complete each statement.

30. Reflexive Property of Equality: $3x - 1 = \underline{\ ?\ }$

31. Transitive Property of Congruence: If $\angle A \cong \angle X$ and $\angle X \cong \angle T$, then $\underline{\ ?\ }$.

32. Symmetric Property of Congruence: If $\overline{BC} \cong \overline{NP}$, then $\underline{\ ?\ }$.

33. Recreation The north campground is midway between the Northpoint Overlook and the waterfall. Use the midpoint formula to find the values of x and y, and justify each step.

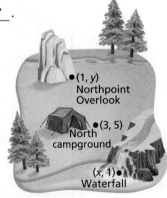

H.O.T. 34. Business A computer repair technician charges \$35 for each job plus \$21 per hour of labor and 110% of the cost of parts. The total charge for a 3-hour job was \$169.50. What was the cost of parts for this job? Write and solve an equation and justify each step in the solution.

H.O.T. 35. Finance Morgan spent a total of \$1,733.65 on her car last year. She spent \$92.50 on registration, \$79.96 on maintenance, and \$983 on insurance. She spent the remaining money on gas. She drove a total of 10,820 miles.

   a. How much on average did the gas cost per mile? Write and solve an equation and justify each step in the solution.

   b. What if...? Suppose Morgan's car averages 32 miles per gallon of gas. How much on average did Morgan pay for a gallon of gas?

H.O.T. 36. Critical Thinking Use the definition of segment congruence and the properties of equality to show that all three properties of congruence are true for segments.

Real-World Connections

37. Recall from Algebra 1 that the Multiplication and Division Properties of Inequality tell you to reverse the inequality sign when multiplying or dividing by a negative number.

   a. Solve the inequality $x + 15 \leq 63$ and write a justification for each step.

   b. Solve the inequality $-2x > 36$ and write a justification for each step.

38. **Write About It** Compare the conclusion of a deductive proof and a conjecture based on inductive reasoning.

TEST PREP

39. Which could NOT be used to justify the statement $\overline{AB} \cong \overline{CD}$?

   Ⓐ Definition of congruence

   Ⓑ Reflexive Property of Congruence

   Ⓒ Symmetric Property of Congruence

   Ⓓ Transitive Property of Congruence

40. A club membership costs $35 plus $3 each time t the member uses the pool. Which equation represents the total cost C of the membership?

   Ⓕ $35 = C + 3t$ Ⓖ $C + 35 = 3t$ Ⓗ $C = 35 + 3t$ Ⓙ $C = 35t + 3$

41. Which statement is true by the Reflexive Property of Equality?

   Ⓐ $x = 35$ Ⓑ $\overline{CD} = \overline{CD}$ Ⓒ $\overline{RT} \cong \overline{TR}$ Ⓓ $CD = CD$

42. **Gridded Response** In the triangle, $m\angle 1 + m\angle 2 + m\angle 3 = 180°$. If $m\angle 3 = 2m\angle 1$ and $m\angle 1 = m\angle 2$, find $m\angle 3$ in degrees.

CHALLENGE AND EXTEND

43. In the gate, $PA = QB$, $QB = RA$, and $PA = 18$ in. Find PR, and justify each step.

44. **Critical Thinking** Explain why there is no Addition Property of Congruence.

H.O.T. **45.** **Algebra** Justify each step in the solution of the inequality $7 - 3x > 19$.

FOCUS ON MATHEMATICAL PRACTICES

MATHEMATICAL PRACTICES

H.O.T. **46.** **Reasoning** Petra is writing an algebraic proof. She states that $2x = 9$ is true because of the Symmetric Property of Equality. What was her statement just prior to that? Explain.

H.O.T. **47.** **Draw Conclusions** Students are asked to prove that $n = 1.5$ is a solution of $12n - 3 = 15$. Kevyn used the Addition Property of Equality followed by the Division Property of Equality. Carla used the Substitution Property of Equality and simplified the expression. Are both proofs valid? Explain.

20-3 Geometric Proof

Essential Question: How can you organize the deductive reasoning of a geometric proof?

Objectives
Write two-column proofs.

Prove geometric theorems by using deductive reasoning.

Vocabulary
theorem
two-column proof

Who uses this?
To persuade your parents to increase your allowance, your argument must be presented logically and precisely.

When writing a geometric proof, you use deductive reasoning to create a chain of logical steps that move from the hypothesis to the conclusion of the conjecture you are proving. By proving that the conclusion is true, you have proven that the original conjecture is true.

Hypothesis → • Definitions • Postulates • Properties • Theorems → Conclusion

When writing a proof, it is important to justify each logical step with a reason. You can use symbols and abbreviations, but they must be clear enough so that anyone who reads your proof will understand them.

COMMON CORE GPS
MCC9-12.G.CO.9

EXAMPLE 1 Writing Justifications

my.hrw.com

Online Video Tutor

Write a justification for each step, given that $\angle A$ and $\angle B$ are complementary and $\angle A \cong \angle C$.

1. $\angle A$ and $\angle B$ are complementary.	Given information
2. $m\angle A + m\angle B = 90°$	Def. of comp. ∡
3. $\angle A \cong \angle C$	Given information
4. $m\angle A = m\angle C$	Def. of ≅ ∡
5. $m\angle C + m\angle B = 90°$	Subst. Prop. of = *Steps 2, 4*
6. $\angle C$ and $\angle B$ are complementary.	Def. of comp. ∡

CHECK IT OUT! 1. Write a justification for each step, given that B is the midpoint of $\overline{AC}$ and $\overline{AB} \cong \overline{EF}$.
   1. B is the midpoint of $\overline{AC}$.
   2. $\overline{AB} \cong \overline{BC}$
   3. $\overline{AB} \cong \overline{EF}$
   4. $\overline{BC} \cong \overline{EF}$

A **theorem** is any statement that you can prove. Once you have proven a theorem, you can use it as a reason in later proofs.

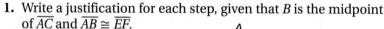
Theorem

	THEOREM	HYPOTHESIS	CONCLUSION
20-3-1	**Linear Pair Theorem** If two angles form a linear pair, then they are supplementary.	$\angle A$ and $\angle B$ form a linear pair.	$\angle A$ and $\angle B$ are supplementary.

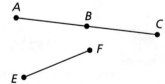

Theorem

THEOREM	HYPOTHESIS	CONCLUSION
20-3-2 **Congruent Supplements Theorem** If two angles are supplementary to the same angle (or to two congruent angles), then the two angles are congruent.	∠1 and ∠2 are supplementary. ∠2 and ∠3 are supplementary.	∠1 ≅ ∠3

A geometric proof begins with *Given* and *Prove* statements, which restate the hypothesis and conclusion of the conjecture. In a **two-column proof**, you list the steps of the proof in the left column. You write the matching reason for each step in the right column.

Online Video Tutor

EXAMPLE 2   Completing a Two-Column Proof

Fill in the blanks to complete a two-column proof of the Linear Pair Theorem.

Given: ∠1 and ∠2 form a linear pair.
Prove: ∠1 and ∠2 are supplementary.
Proof:

Statements	Reasons
1. ∠1 and ∠2 form a linear pair.	**1.** Given
2. $\overrightarrow{BA}$ and $\overrightarrow{BC}$ form a line.	**2.** Def. of lin. pair
3. m∠ABC = 180°	**3.** Def. of straight ∠
4. a. ___?___	**4.** ∠ Add. Post.
5. b. ___?___	**5.** Subst. *Steps 3, 4*
6. ∠1 and ∠2 are supplementary.	**6. c.** ___?___

Use the existing statements and reasons in the proof to fill in the blanks.

   a. m∠1 + m∠2 = m∠ABC   *The ∠ Add. Post. is given as the reason.*
   b. m∠1 + m∠2 = 180°   *Substitute 180° for m∠ABC.*
   c. Def. of supp. ∠   *The measures of supp. ∠ add to 180° by def.*

Remember!

A *linear pair* of angles is a pair of angles in the same plane that have a common vertex and a common side, no common interior points, and noncommon sides that are opposite rays.

2. Fill in the blanks to complete a two-column proof of one case of the Congruent Supplements Theorem.

   Given: ∠1 and ∠2 are supplementary, and ∠2 and ∠3 are supplementary.

   Prove: ∠1 ≅ ∠3

   Proof:

Statements	Reasons
1. a. ___?___	**1.** Given
2. m∠1 + m∠2 = 180° m∠2 + m∠3 = 180°	**2.** Def. of supp. ∠
3. b. ___?___	**3.** Subst.
4. m∠2 = m∠2	**4.** Reflex. Prop. of =
5. m∠1 = m∠3	**5. c.** ___?___
6. d. ___?___	**6.** Def. of ≅ ∠

Before you start writing a proof, you should plan out your logic. Sometimes you will be given a plan for a more challenging proof. This plan will detail the major steps of the proof for you.

Theorems

	THEOREM	HYPOTHESIS	CONCLUSION
20-3-3	**Right Angle Congruence Theorem** All right angles are congruent.	∠A and ∠B are right angles.	∠A ≅ ∠B
20-3-4	**Congruent Complements Theorem** If two angles are complementary to the same angle (or to two congruent angles), then the two angles are congruent.	∠1 and ∠2 are complementary. ∠2 and ∠3 are complementary.	∠1 ≅ ∠3

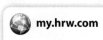

COMMON CORE GPS **EXAMPLE 3** MCC9-12.G.CO.9

my.hrw.com

Online Video Tutor

Writing a Two-Column Proof from a Plan

Use the given plan to write a two-column proof of the Right Angle Congruence Theorem.
Given: ∠1 and ∠2 are right angles.
Prove: ∠1 ≅ ∠2

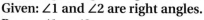

Plan: Use the definition of a right angle to write the measure of each angle. Then use the Transitive Property and the definition of congruent angles.

Proof:

Statements	Reasons
1. ∠1 and ∠2 are right angles.	**1.** Given
2. m∠1 = 90°, m∠2 = 90°	**2.** Def. of rt. ∠
3. m∠1 = m∠2	**3.** Trans. Prop. of =
4. ∠1 ≅ ∠2	**4.** Def. of ≅ ∠

 3. Use the given plan to write a two-column proof of one case of the Congruent Complements Theorem.

Given: ∠1 and ∠2 are complementary, and ∠2 and ∠3 are complementary.

Prove: ∠1 ≅ ∠3

Plan: The measures of complementary angles add to 90° by definition. Use substitution to show that the sums of both pairs are equal. Use the Subtraction Property and the definition of congruent angles to conclude that ∠1 ≅ ∠3.

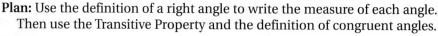

The Proof Process
1. Write the conjecture to be proven.
2. Draw a diagram to represent the hypothesis of the conjecture.
3. State the given information and mark it on the diagram.
4. State the conclusion of the conjecture in terms of the diagram.
5. Plan your argument and prove the conjecture.

THINK AND DISCUSS

1. Which step in a proof should match the Prove statement?

2. Why is it important to include every logical step in a proof?

3. List four things you can use to justify a step in a proof.

4. **GET ORGANIZED** Copy and complete the graphic organizer. In each box, describe the steps of the proof process.

1. ⟶ 2. ⟶ 3. ⟶ 4. ⟶ 5.

20-3 Exercises

my.hrw.com
Homework Help

GUIDED PRACTICE

Vocabulary Apply the vocabulary from this lesson to answer each question.

1. In a *two-column proof*, you list the ___?___ in the left column and the ___?___ in the right column. (*statements* or *reasons*)

2. A ___?___ is a statement you can prove. (*postulate* or *theorem*)

SEE EXAMPLE **1**

3. Write a justification for each step, given that $m\angle A = 60°$ and $m\angle B = 2m\angle A$.

   1. $m\angle A = 60°$, $m\angle B = 2m\angle A$
   2. $m\angle B = 2(60°)$
   3. $m\angle B = 120°$
   4. $m\angle A + m\angle B = 60° + 120°$
   5. $m\angle A + m\angle B = 180°$
   6. $\angle A$ and $\angle B$ are supplementary.

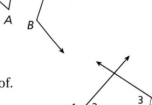

SEE EXAMPLE **2**

4. Fill in the blanks to complete the two-column proof.

   Given: $\angle 2 \cong \angle 3$
   Prove: $\angle 1$ and $\angle 3$ are supplementary.
   Proof:

Statements	Reasons
1. $\angle 2 \cong \angle 3$	1. Given
2. $m\angle 2 = m\angle 3$	2. a. ___?___
3. b. ___?___	3. Lin. Pair Thm.
4. $m\angle 1 + m\angle 2 = 180°$	4. Def. of supp. ∠
5. $m\angle 1 + m\angle 3 = 180°$	5. c. ___?___ *Steps 2, 4*
6. d. ___?___	6. Def. of supp. ∠

SEE EXAMPLE **3**

5. Use the given plan to write a two-column proof.

   Given: X is the midpoint of $\overline{AY}$, and Y is the midpoint of $\overline{XB}$.
   Prove: $\overline{AX} \cong \overline{YB}$

   Plan: By the definition of midpoint, $\overline{AX} \cong \overline{XY}$, and $\overline{XY} \cong \overline{YB}$. Use the Transitive Property to conclude that $\overline{AX} \cong \overline{YB}$.

PRACTICE AND PROBLEM SOLVING

Independent Practice

For Exercises	See Example
6	1
7–8	2
9–10	3

my.hrw.com

Online Extra Practice

6. Write a justification for each step, given that $\overrightarrow{BX}$ bisects $\angle ABC$ and m$\angle XBC = 45°$.

1. $\overrightarrow{BX}$ bisects $\angle ABC$.
2. $\angle ABX \cong \angle XBC$
3. m$\angle ABX =$ m$\angle XBC$
4. m$\angle XBC = 45°$
5. m$\angle ABX = 45°$
6. m$\angle ABX +$ m$\angle XBC =$ m$\angle ABC$
7. $45° + 45° =$ m$\angle ABC$
8. $90° =$ m$\angle ABC$
9. $\angle ABC$ is a right angle.

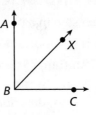

Fill in the blanks to complete each two-column proof.

7. Given: $\angle 1$ and $\angle 2$ are supplementary, and
$\angle 3$ and $\angle 4$ are supplementary.
$\angle 2 \cong \angle 3$
Prove: $\angle 1 \cong \angle 4$

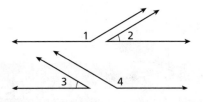

Proof:

Statements	Reasons
1. $\angle 1$ and $\angle 2$ are supplementary. $\angle 3$ and $\angle 4$ are supplementary.	1. Given
2. a. ___?___	2. Def. of supp. ∠
3. m$\angle 1 +$ m$\angle 2 =$ m$\angle 3 +$ m$\angle 4$	3. b. ___?___
4. $\angle 2 \cong \angle 3$	4. Given
5. m$\angle 2 =$ m$\angle 3$	5. Def. of $\cong$ ∠
6. c. ___?___	6. Subtr. Prop. of = *Steps 3, 5*
7. $\angle 1 \cong \angle 4$	7. d. ___?___

8. Given: $\angle BAC$ is a right angle. $\angle 2 \cong \angle 3$
Prove: $\angle 1$ and $\angle 3$ are complementary.

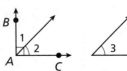

Proof:

Statements	Reasons
1. $\angle BAC$ is a right angle.	1. Given
2. m$\angle BAC = 90°$	2. a. ___?___
3. b. ___?___	3. $\angle$ Add. Post.
4. m$\angle 1 +$ m$\angle 2 = 90°$	4. Subst. *Steps 2, 3*
5. $\angle 2 \cong \angle 3$	5. Given
6. c. ___?___	6. Def. of $\cong$ ∠
7. m$\angle 1 +$ m$\angle 3 = 90°$	7. d. ___?___ *Steps 4, 6*
8. e. ___?___	8. Def. of comp. ∠

Use the given plan to write a two-column proof.

9. Given: $\overline{BE} \cong \overline{CE}$, $\overline{DE} \cong \overline{AE}$
Prove: $\overline{AB} \cong \overline{CD}$

Plan: Use the definition of congruent segments to write the given information in terms of lengths. Then use the Segment Addition Postulate to show that $AB = CD$ and thus $\overline{AB} \cong \overline{CD}$.

Use the given plan to write a two-column proof.

10. Given: ∠1 and ∠3 are complementary, and ∠2 and ∠4 are complementary. ∠3 ≅ ∠4

   Prove: ∠1 ≅ ∠2

   Plan: Since ∠1 and ∠3 are complementary and ∠2 and ∠4 are complementary, both pairs of angle measures add to 90°. Use substitution to show that the sums of both pairs are equal. Since ∠3 ≅ ∠4, their measures are equal. Use the Subtraction Property of Equality and the definition of congruent angles to conclude that ∠1 ≅ ∠2.

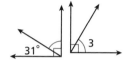

Find each angle measure.

11. m∠1

12. m∠2

13. m∠3

14. Engineering The Oresund Bridge, which connects the countries of Denmark and Sweden, was completed in 1999. If ∠1 ≅ ∠2, which theorem can you use to conclude that ∠3 ≅ ∠4?

15. Critical Thinking Explain why there are two cases to consider when proving the Congruent Supplements Theorem and the Congruent Complements Theorem.

Tell whether each statement is sometimes, always, or never true.

16. An angle and its complement are congruent.

17. A pair of right angles forms a linear pair.

18. An angle and its complement form a right angle.

19. A linear pair of angles is complementary.

Algebra Find the value of each variable.

20.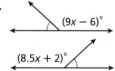

$(4n + 5)°$ $(8n - 5)°$

21.

$(9x - 6)°$
$(8.5x + 2)°$

22.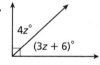

$4z°$
$(3z + 6)°$

H.O.T. 23. Write About It How are a theorem and a postulate alike? How are they different?

Real-World Connections

24. Sometimes you may be asked to write a proof without a specific statement of the Given and Prove information being provided for you. For each of the following situations, use the triangle to write a Given and Prove statement.

   a. The segment connecting the midpoints of two sides of a triangle is half as long as the third side.

   b. The acute angles of a right triangle are complementary.

   c. In a right triangle, the sum of the squares of the legs is equal to the square of the hypotenuse.

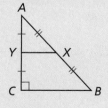

TEST PREP

25. Which theorem justifies the conclusion that $\angle 1 \cong \angle 4$?

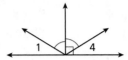

    (A) Linear Pair Theorem

    (B) Congruent Supplements Theorem

    (C) Congruent Complements Theorem

    (D) Right Angle Congruence Theorem

26. What can be concluded from the statement $m\angle 1 + m\angle 2 = 180°$?

    (F) $\angle 1$ and $\angle 2$ are congruent.   (H) $\angle 1$ and $\angle 2$ are complementary.

    (G) $\angle 1$ and $\angle 2$ are supplementary.   (J) $\angle 1$ and $\angle 2$ form a linear pair.

27. Given: Two angles are complementary. The measure of one angle is 10° less than the measure of the other angle. Conclusion: The measures of the angles are 85° and 95°. Which statement is true?

    (A) The conclusion is correct because 85° is 10° less than 95°.

    (B) The conclusion is verified by the first statement given.

    (C) The conclusion is invalid because the angles are not congruent.

    (D) The conclusion is contradicted by the first statement given.

CHALLENGE AND EXTEND

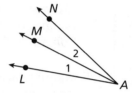

28. Write a two-column proof.

    Given: $m\angle LAN = 30°$, $m\angle 1 = 15°$

    Prove: $\overrightarrow{AM}$ bisects $\angle LAN$.

H.O.T. Multi-Step Find the value of the variable and the measure of each angle.

29.

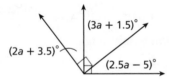

30.

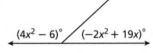

FOCUS ON MATHEMATICAL PRACTICES

H.O.T. 31. Proof The left side of a two-column proof is shown along with the supporting figure. Identify any given. Justify your choices.

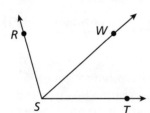

Statements
1. $m\angle WST = 46°$
2. $m\angle RSW = 64°$
3. $m\angle RST = 110°$
4. $\angle WST$ is an acute angle.

H.O.T. 32. Communication Lynne wants to prove that if two angles form a linear pair, then they are supplementary. Can she use the Linear Pair Theorem as a reason to justify the statement? Why or why not?

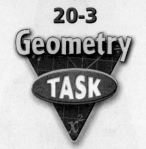

20-3

Geometry TASK

Use with Geometric Proof

Design Plans for Proofs

Sometimes the most challenging part of writing a proof is planning the logical steps that will take you from the Given statement to the Prove statement. Like working a jigsaw puzzle, you can start with any piece. Write down everything you know from the Given statement. If you don't see the connection right away, start with the Prove statement and work backward. Then connect the pieces into a logical order.

MATHEMATICAL PRACTICES

Construct viable arguments and critique the reasoning of others.

MCC9-12.G.CO.9 Prove theorems about lines and angles.

Activity

Prove the Common Angles Theorem.
Given: $\angle AXB \cong \angle CXD$
Prove: $\angle AXC \cong \angle BXD$

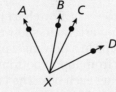

1 Start by considering the difference in the Given and Prove statements. How does $\angle AXB$ compare to $\angle AXC$? How does $\angle CXD$ compare to $\angle BXD$?

In both cases, $\angle BXC$ is combined with the first angle to get the second angle.

2 The situation involves combining adjacent angle measures, so list any definitions, properties, postulates, and theorems that might be helpful.

Definition of congruent angles, Angle Addition Postulate, properties of equality, and Reflexive, Symmetric, and Transitive Properties of Congruence

3 Start with what you are given and what you are trying to prove and then work toward the middle.

$\angle AXB \cong \angle CXD$	The first reason will be "Given."
$m\angle AXB = m\angle CXD$	Def. of $\cong$ $\angle$s
???	???
$m\angle AXC = m\angle BXD$	???
$\angle AXC \cong \angle BXD$	The last statement will be the Prove statement.

4 Based on Step 1, $\angle BXC$ is the missing piece in the middle of the logical flow. So write down what you know about $\angle BXC$.

$\angle BXC \cong \angle BXC$	Reflex. Prop. of $\cong$
$m\angle BXC = m\angle BXC$	Reflex. Prop. of $=$

5 Now you can see that the Angle Addition Postulate needs to be used to complete the proof.

$m\angle AXB + m\angle BXC = m\angle AXC$	$\angle$ Add. Post.
$m\angle BXC + m\angle CXD = m\angle BXD$	$\angle$ Add. Post.

6 Use the pieces to write a complete two-column proof of the Common Angles Theorem.

Try This

1. Describe how a plan for a proof differs from the actual proof.

2. Write a plan and a two-column proof.
   Given: $\overrightarrow{BD}$ bisects $\angle ABC$.
   Prove: $2m\angle 1 = m\angle ABC$

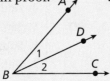

3. Write a plan and a two-column proof.
   Given: $\angle LXN$ is a right angle.
   Prove: $\angle 1$ and $\angle 2$ are complementary.

20-4 Flowchart and Paragraph Proofs

? Essential Question: What are some formats you can use to organize geometric proofs?

Objectives
Write flowchart and paragraph proofs.

Prove geometric theorems by using deductive reasoning.

Vocabulary
flowchart proof
paragraph proof

Why learn this?
Flowcharts make it easy to see how the steps of a process are linked together.

A second style of proof is a **flowchart proof**, which uses boxes and arrows to show the structure of the proof. The steps in a flowchart proof move from left to right or from top to bottom, shown by the arrows connecting each box. The justification for each step is written below the box.

Theorem 20-4-1	**Common Segments Theorem**	
THEOREM	**HYPOTHESIS**	**CONCLUSION**
Given collinear points A, B, C, and D arranged as shown, if $\overline{AB} \cong \overline{CD}$, then $\overline{AC} \cong \overline{BD}$. A B C D	$\overline{AB} \cong \overline{CD}$	$\overline{AC} \cong \overline{BD}$

COMMON CORE GPS MCC9-12.G.CO.9

EXAMPLE 1

my.hrw.com

Online Video Tutor

Animated Math

Reading a Flowchart Proof

Use the given flowchart proof to write a two-column proof of the Common Segments Theorem.

Given: $\overline{AB} \cong \overline{CD}$
Prove: $\overline{AC} \cong \overline{BD}$

A B C D

Flowchart proof:

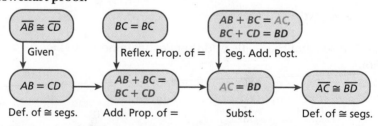

Two-column proof:

Statements	**Reasons**
1. $\overline{AB} \cong \overline{CD}$	1. Given
2. $AB = CD$	2. Def. of $\cong$ segs.
3. $BC = BC$	3. Reflex. Prop. of $=$
4. $AB + BC = BC + CD$	4. Add. Prop. of $=$
5. $AB + BC = AC,\ BC + CD = BD$	5. Seg. Add. Post.
6. $AC = BD$	6. Subst.
7. $\overline{AC} \cong \overline{BD}$	7. Def. of $\cong$ segs.

© HRW Photo

1. Use the given flowchart proof to write a two-column proof.

Given: $RS = UV$, $ST = TU$

Prove: $\overline{RT} \cong \overline{TV}$

Flowchart proof:

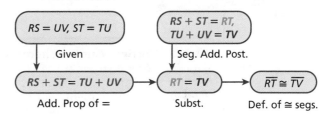

EXAMPLE 2 MCC9-12.G.CO.9

Writing a Flowchart Proof

Use the given two-column proof to write a flowchart proof of the Converse of the Common Segments Theorem.

Given: $\overline{AC} \cong \overline{BD}$

Prove: $\overline{AB} \cong \overline{CD}$

Two-column proof:

Online Video Tutor

my.hrw.com

Statements	Reasons
1. $\overline{AC} \cong \overline{BD}$	1. Given
2. $AC = BD$	2. Def. of $\cong$ segs.
3. $AB + BC = AC$, $BC + CD = BD$	3. Seg. Add. Post.
4. $AB + BC = BC + CD$	4. Subst. *Steps 2, 3*
5. $BC = BC$	5. Reflex. Prop. of $=$
6. $AB = CD$	6. Subtr. Prop. of $=$
7. $\overline{AB} \cong \overline{CD}$	7. Def. of $\cong$ segs.

Helpful Hint

Like the converse of a conditional statement, the converse of a theorem is found by switching the hypothesis and conclusion.

Flowchart proof:

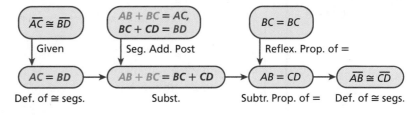

2. Use the given two-column proof to write a flowchart proof.

Given: $\angle 2 \cong \angle 4$

Prove: $m\angle 1 = m\angle 3$

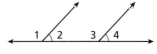

Two-column proof:

Statements	Reasons
1. $\angle 2 \cong \angle 4$	1. Given
2. $\angle 1$ and $\angle 2$ are supplementary. $\angle 3$ and $\angle 4$ are supplementary.	2. Lin. Pair Thm.
3. $\angle 1 \cong \angle 3$	3. $\cong$ Supps. Thm.
4. $m\angle 1 = m\angle 3$	4. Def. of $\cong \angle$

A **paragraph proof** is a style of proof that presents the steps of the proof and their matching reasons as sentences in a paragraph. Although this style of proof is less formal than a two-column proof, you still must include every step.

Theorems

THEOREM	HYPOTHESIS	CONCLUSION
20-4-2 Vertical Angles Theorem Vertical angles are congruent.	$\angle A$ and $\angle B$ are vertical angles.	$\angle A \cong \angle B$
20-4-3 If two congruent angles are supplementary, then each angle is a right angle. ($\cong \angle$ supp. → rt. $\angle$)	$\angle 1 \cong \angle 2$ $\angle 1$ and $\angle 2$ are supplementary.	$\angle 1$ and $\angle 2$ are right angles.

COMMON CORE GPS MCC9-12.G.CO.9

EXAMPLE 3

my.hrw.com

Online Video Tutor

Reading a Paragraph Proof

Use the given paragraph proof to write a two-column proof of the Vertical Angles Theorem.

Given: $\angle 1$ and $\angle 3$ are vertical angles.
Prove: $\angle 1 \cong \angle 3$

Paragraph proof: $\angle 1$ and $\angle 3$ are vertical angles, so they are formed by intersecting lines. Therefore $\angle 1$ and $\angle 2$ are a linear pair, and $\angle 2$ and $\angle 3$ are a linear pair. By the Linear Pair Theorem, $\angle 1$ and $\angle 2$ are supplementary, and $\angle 2$ and $\angle 3$ are supplementary. So by the Congruent Supplements Theorem, $\angle 1 \cong \angle 3$.

Two-column proof:

Statements	Reasons
1. $\angle 1$ and $\angle 3$ are vertical angles.	1. Given
2. $\angle 1$ and $\angle 3$ are formed by intersecting lines.	2. Def. of vert. $\angle$
3. $\angle 1$ and $\angle 2$ are a linear pair. $\angle 2$ and $\angle 3$ are a linear pair.	3. Def. of lin. pair
4. $\angle 1$ and $\angle 2$ are supplementary. $\angle 2$ and $\angle 3$ are supplementary.	4. Lin. Pair Thm.
5. $\angle 1 \cong \angle 3$	5. $\cong$ Supps. Thm.

Remember!

Vertical angles are angles formed by intersecting lines that share a vertex but do not have common sides.

3. Use the given paragraph proof to write a two-column proof.

Given: $\angle WXY$ is a right angle. $\angle 1 \cong \angle 3$
Prove: $\angle 1$ and $\angle 2$ are complementary.

Paragraph proof: Since $\angle WXY$ is a right angle, m$\angle WXY = 90°$ by the definition of a right angle. By the Angle Addition Postulate, m$\angle WXY =$ m$\angle 2 +$ m$\angle 3$. By substitution, m$\angle 2 +$ m$\angle 3 = 90°$. Since $\angle 1 \cong \angle 3$, m$\angle 1 =$ m$\angle 3$ by the definition of congruent angles. Using substitution, m$\angle 2 +$ m$\angle 1 = 90°$. Thus by the definition of complementary angles, $\angle 1$ and $\angle 2$ are complementary.

© Alamy Images

Student to Student

Writing a Proof

When I have to write a proof and I don't see how to start, I look at what I'm supposed to be proving and see if it makes sense. If it does, I ask myself why. Sometimes this helps me to see what the reasons in the proof might be. If all else fails, I just start writing down everything I know based on the diagram and the given statement. By brainstorming like this, I can usually figure out the steps of the proof. You can even write each thing on a separate piece of paper and arrange the pieces of paper like a flowchart.

Claire Jeffords
Riverbend High School

COMMON CORE GPS

EXAMPLE 4
MCC9-12.G.CO.9

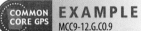

my.hrw.com

Online Video Tutor

Writing a Paragraph Proof

Use the given two-column proof to write a paragraph proof of Theorem 20-4-3.

Given: $\angle 1$ and $\angle 2$ are supplementary. $\angle 1 \cong \angle 2$
Prove: $\angle 1$ and $\angle 2$ are right angles.

Two-column proof:

Statements	Reasons
1. $\angle 1$ and $\angle 2$ are supplementary. $\angle 1 \cong \angle 2$	**1.** Given
2. $m\angle 1 + m\angle 2 = 180°$	**2.** Def. of supp. $\angle$
3. $m\angle 1 = m\angle 2$	**3.** Def. of $\cong$ $\angle$ *Step 1*
4. $m\angle 1 + m\angle 1 = 180°$	**4.** Subst. *Steps 2, 3*
5. $2m\angle 1 = 180°$	**5.** Simplification
6. $m\angle 1 = 90°$	**6.** Div. Prop. of $=$
7. $m\angle 2 = 90°$	**7.** Trans. Prop. of $=$ *Steps 3, 6*
8. $\angle 1$ and $\angle 2$ are right angles.	**8.** Def. of rt. $\angle$

Paragraph proof: $\angle 1$ and $\angle 2$ are supplementary, so $m\angle 1 + m\angle 2 = 180°$ by the definition of supplementary angles. They are also congruent, so their measures are equal by the definition of congruent angles. By substitution, $m\angle 1 + m\angle 1 = 180°$, so $m\angle 1 = 90°$ by the Division Property of Equality. Because $m\angle 1 = m\angle 2$, $m\angle 2 = 90°$ by the Transitive Property of Equality. So both are right angles by the definition of a right angle.

4. Use the given two-column proof to write a paragraph proof.

Given: $\angle 1 \cong \angle 4$
Prove: $\angle 2 \cong \angle 3$

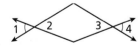

Two-column proof:

Statements	Reasons
1. $\angle 1 \cong \angle 4$	**1.** Given
2. $\angle 1 \cong \angle 2$, $\angle 3 \cong \angle 4$	**2.** Vert. $\angle$ Thm.
3. $\angle 2 \cong \angle 4$	**3.** Trans. Prop. of $\cong$ *Steps 1, 2*
4. $\angle 2 \cong \angle 3$	**4.** Trans. Prop. of $\cong$ *Steps 2, 3*

THINK AND DISCUSS

1. Explain why there might be more than one correct way to write a proof.

2. Describe the steps you take when writing a proof.

3. GET ORGANIZED
Copy and complete the graphic organizer. In each box, describe the proof style in your own words.

```
              Proof Styles
        ┌──────────┼──────────┐
   Two-column   Flowchart   Paragraph
```

20-4 Exercises

my.hrw.com
Homework Help

GUIDED PRACTICE

Vocabulary Apply the vocabulary from this lesson to answer each question.

1. In a ___?___ proof, the logical order is represented by arrows that connect each step. (*flowchart* or *paragraph*)

2. The steps and reasons of a ___?___ proof are written out in sentences. (*flowchart* or *paragraph*)

SEE EXAMPLE 1

3. Use the given flowchart proof to write a two-column proof.

Given: ∠1 ≅ ∠2
Prove: ∠1 and ∠2 are right angles.

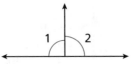

Flowchart proof:

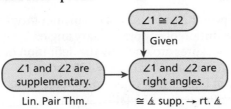

```
                    ┌─────────┐
                    │ ∠1 ≅ ∠2 │
                    └────┬────┘
                       Given
                         │
                         ▼
 ┌────────────────┐   ┌────────────────┐
 │ ∠1 and ∠2 are  │──▶│ ∠1 and ∠2 are  │
 │ supplementary. │   │ right angles.  │
 └────────────────┘   └────────────────┘
   Lin. Pair Thm.     ≅ ⦞ supp. → rt. ⦞
```

SEE EXAMPLE 2

4. Use the given two-column proof to write a flowchart proof.

Given: ∠2 and ∠4 are supplementary.
Prove: m∠2 = m∠3

Two-column proof:

Statements	Reasons
1. ∠2 and ∠4 are supplementary.	**1.** Given
2. ∠3 and ∠4 are supplementary.	**2.** Lin. Pair Thm.
3. ∠2 ≅ ∠3	**3.** ≅ Supps. Thm. *Steps 1, 2*
4. m∠2 = m∠3	**4.** Def. of ≅ ⦞

SEE EXAMPLE 3

5. Use the given paragraph proof to write a two-column proof.

Given: $\angle 2 \cong \angle 4$
Prove: $\angle 1 \cong \angle 3$

Paragraph proof:

By the Vertical Angles Theorem, $\angle 1 \cong \angle 2$, and $\angle 3 \cong \angle 4$. It is given that $\angle 2 \cong \angle 4$. By the Transitive Property of Congruence, $\angle 1 \cong \angle 4$, and thus $\angle 1 \cong \angle 3$.

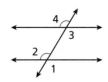

SEE EXAMPLE 4

6. Use the given two-column proof to write a paragraph proof.

Given: $\overrightarrow{BD}$ bisects $\angle ABC$.
Prove: $\overrightarrow{BG}$ bisects $\angle FBH$.

Two-column proof:

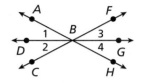

Statements	Reasons
1. $\overrightarrow{BD}$ bisects $\angle ABC$.	**1.** Given
2. $\angle 1 \cong \angle 2$	**2.** Def. of $\angle$ bisector
3. $\angle 1 \cong \angle 4, \angle 2 \cong \angle 3$	**3.** Vert. $\angle$ Thm.
4. $\angle 4 \cong \angle 2$	**4.** Trans. Prop. of $\cong$ *Steps 2, 3*
5. $\angle 4 \cong \angle 3$	**5.** Trans. Prop. of $\cong$ *Steps 3, 4*
6. $\overrightarrow{BG}$ bisects $\angle FBH$.	**6.** Def. of $\angle$ bisector

PRACTICE AND PROBLEM SOLVING

Independent Practice

For Exercises	See Example
7	1
8	2
9	3
10	4

my.hrw.com

Online Extra Practice

7. Use the given flowchart proof to write a two-column proof.

Given: B is the midpoint of $\overline{AC}$.
$AD = EC$
Prove: $DB = BE$

Flowchart proof:

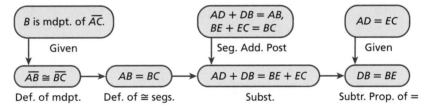

8. Use the given two-column proof to write a flowchart proof.

Given: $\angle 3$ is a right angle.
Prove: $\angle 4$ is a right angle.

Two-column proof:

Statements	Reasons
1. $\angle 3$ is a right angle.	**1.** Given
2. $m\angle 3 = 90°$	**2.** Def. of rt. $\angle$
3. $\angle 3$ and $\angle 4$ are supplementary.	**3.** Lin. Pair Thm.
4. $m\angle 3 + m\angle 4 = 180°$	**4.** Def. of supp. $\angle$
5. $90° + m\angle 4 = 180°$	**5.** Subst. *Steps 2, 4*
6. $m\angle 4 = 90°$	**6.** Subtr. Prop. of $=$
7. $\angle 4$ is a right angle.	**7.** Def. of rt. $\angle$

9. Use the given paragraph proof to write a two-column proof.

Given: $\angle 1 \cong \angle 4$
Prove: $\angle 2$ and $\angle 3$ are supplementary.

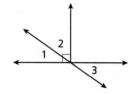

Paragraph proof:

$\angle 4$ and $\angle 3$ form a linear pair, so they are supplementary by the Linear Pair Theorem. Therefore, $m\angle 4 + m\angle 3 = 180°$. Also, $\angle 1$ and $\angle 2$ are vertical angles, so $\angle 1 \cong \angle 2$ by the Vertical Angles Theorem. It is given that $\angle 1 \cong \angle 4$. So by the Transitive Property of Congruence, $\angle 4 \cong \angle 2$, and by the definition of congruent angles, $m\angle 4 = m\angle 2$. By substitution, $m\angle 2 + m\angle 3 = 180°$, so $\angle 2$ and $\angle 3$ are supplementary by the definition of supplementary angles.

10. Use the given two-column proof to write a paragraph proof.

Given: $\angle 1$ and $\angle 2$ are complementary.
Prove: $\angle 2$ and $\angle 3$ are complementary.

Two-column proof:

Statements	Reasons
1. $\angle 1$ and $\angle 2$ are complementary.	1. Given
2. $m\angle 1 + m\angle 2 = 90°$	2. Def. of comp. ∡
3. $\angle 1 \cong \angle 3$	3. Vert. ∡ Thm.
4. $m\angle 1 = m\angle 3$	4. Def. of ≅ ∡
5. $m\angle 3 + m\angle 2 = 90°$	5. Subst. *Steps 2, 4*
6. $\angle 2$ and $\angle 3$ are complementary.	6. Def. of comp. ∡

H.O.T. **Find each measure and name the theorem that justifies your answer.**

11. AB

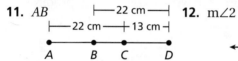

12. $m\angle 2$

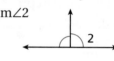

13. $m\angle 3$

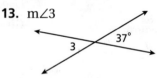

Algebra Find the value of each variable.

14.

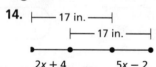

15.

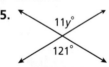

16.

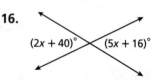

H.O.T. **17.** ///ERROR ANALYSIS/// Below are two drawings for the given proof. Which is incorrect? Explain the error.

Given: $\overline{AB} \cong \overline{BC}$
Prove: $\angle A \cong \angle C$

A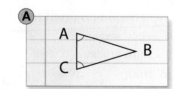

B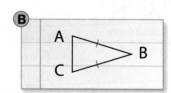

Real-World Connections

18. Rearrange the pieces to create a flowchart proof.

$m\angle 1 + m\angle 2 = 180°$	$m\angle 1 = 117°$	$\angle 1$ and $\angle 2$ are supplementary.	$m\angle 2 = 63°$	$m\angle 1 + 63° = 180°$
Def. of supp. ∡	Subtr. Prop. of =	Lin. Pair Thm.	Given	Subst.

19. Critical Thinking Two lines intersect, and one of the angles formed is a right angle. Explain why all four angles are congruent.

20. Write About It Which style of proof do you find easiest to write? to read?

TEST PREP

21. Which pair of angles in the diagram must be congruent?

   Ⓐ ∠1 and ∠5   Ⓒ ∠5 and ∠8

   Ⓑ ∠3 and ∠4   Ⓓ None of the above

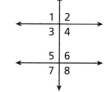

22. What is the measure of ∠2?

   Ⓕ 38°   Ⓗ 128°

   Ⓖ 52°   Ⓙ 142°

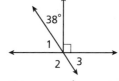

23. Which statement is NOT true if ∠2 and ∠6 are supplementary?

   Ⓐ m∠2 + m∠6 = 180°

   Ⓑ ∠2 and ∠3 are supplementary.

   Ⓒ ∠1 and ∠6 are supplementary.

   Ⓓ m∠1 + m∠4 = 180°

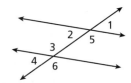

CHALLENGE AND EXTEND

24. Textiles Use the woven pattern to write a flowchart proof.

   Given: ∠1 ≅ ∠3
   Prove: m∠4 + m∠5 = m∠6

25. Write a two-column proof.

   Given: ∠AOC ≅ ∠BOD
   Prove: ∠AOB ≅ ∠COD

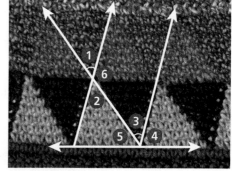

26. Write a paragraph proof.

   Given: ∠2 and ∠5 are right angles.
         m∠1 + m∠2 + m∠3 = m∠4 + m∠5 + m∠6
   Prove: ∠1 ≅ ∠4

H.O.T. 27. Multi-Step Find the value of each variable and the measures of all four angles.

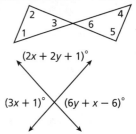

FOCUS ON MATHEMATICAL PRACTICES

H.O.T. 28. Reasoning One of the statements within a proof with the diagram shown at the right is ∠PRS ≅ ∠SRT, and the Transitive Property of Congruence is given as the reason. What other statement or statements may also be in the proof? Why?

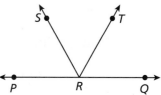

H.O.T. 29. Communication Compare a flowchart proof to a two-column proof. In what ways are they similar? In what ways are they different?

Ready to Go On?

my.hrw.com
Assessment and Intervention

✓ 20-1 Biconditional Statements and Definitions

1. For the conditional "If two angles are supplementary, the sum of their measures is 180°," write the converse and a biconditional statement.

2. Determine if the biconditional "$\sqrt{x} = 4$ if and only if $x = 16$" is true. If false, give a counterexample.

✓ 20-2 Algebraic Proof

Solve each equation. Write a justification for each step.

3. $m - 8 = 13$ 4. $4y - 1 = 27$ 5. $-\dfrac{x}{3} = 2$

Identify the property that justifies each statement.

6. $m\angle XYZ = m\angle PQR$, so $m\angle PQR = m\angle XYZ$.

7. $\overline{AB} \cong \overline{AB}$

8. $\angle 4 \cong \angle A$, and $\angle A \cong \angle 1$. So $\angle 4 \cong \angle 1$.

9. $k = 7$, and $m = 7$. So $k = m$.

✓ 20-3 Geometric Proof

10. Fill in the blanks to complete the two-column proof.
    Given: $m\angle 1 + m\angle 3 = 180°$
    Prove: $\angle 1 \cong \angle 4$

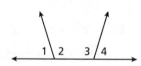

Proof:

Statements	Reasons
1. $m\angle 1 + m\angle 3 = 180°$	1. a. ___?___
2. b. ___?___	2. Def. of supp. ∠
3. $\angle 3$ and $\angle 4$ are supplementary.	3. Lin. Pair Thm.
4. $\angle 3 \cong \angle 3$	4. c. ___?___
5. d. ___?___	5. ≅ Supps. Thm.

11. Use the given plan to write a two-column proof of the Symmetric Property of Congruence.

    Given: $\overline{AB} \cong \overline{EF}$
    Prove: $\overline{EF} \cong \overline{AB}$

    Plan: Use the definition of congruent segments to write $\overline{AB} \cong \overline{EF}$ as a statement of equality. Then use the Symmetric Property of Equality to show that $EF = AB$. So $\overline{EF} \cong \overline{AB}$ by the definition of congruent segments.

20-4 Flowchart and Paragraph Proofs

Use the given two-column proof to write the following.

Given: $\angle 1 \cong \angle 3$
Prove: $\angle 2 \cong \angle 4$

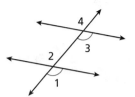

Proof:

Statements	Reasons
1. $\angle 1 \cong \angle 3$	1. Given
2. $\angle 1 \cong \angle 2$, $\angle 3 \cong \angle 4$	2. Vert. $\angle$ Thm.
3. $\angle 2 \cong \angle 3$	3. Trans. Prop. of $\cong$
4. $\angle 2 \cong \angle 4$	4. Trans. Prop. of $\cong$

12. a flowchart proof

13. a paragraph proof

PARCC Assessment Readiness

COMMON CORE GPS

Selected Response

1. Write the conditional statement and converse within the biconditional.

A rectangle is a square if and only if all four sides of the rectangle have equal lengths.

(A) Conditional: If all four sides of the rectangle have equal lengths, then it is a square.
Converse: If a rectangle is a square, then its four sides have equal lengths.

(B) Conditional: If a rectangle is a square, then it is also a rhombus.
Converse: If a rectangle is a rhombus, then it is also a square.

(C) Conditional: If all four sides have equal lengths, then all four angles are 90°.
Converse: If all four angles are 90°, then all four sides have equal lengths.

(D) Conditional: If a rectangle is not a square, then its sides are of different lengths.
Converse: If the sides are of different lengths, then the rectangle is not a square.

2. Give the missing justifications in the solution of $4x - 6 = 34$ shown below.

$4x - 6 = 34$	Given equation
$\underline{+6 \quad +6}$	[1]
$4x = 40$	Simplify.
$\dfrac{4x}{4} = \dfrac{40}{4}$	[2]
$x = 10$	Simplify.

(F) [1] Substitution Property of Equality;
[2] Division Property of Equality

(G) [1] Addition Property of Equality;
[2] Division Property of Equality

(H) [1] Division Property of Equality;
[2] Subtraction Property of Equality

(J) [1] Addition Property of Equality;
[2] Reflexive Property of Equality

Mini-Task

3. Two angles with measures $(5x + 35)°$ and $(7x + 85)°$ are supplementary. Find the value of x and the measure of each angle.

21 Proving Theorems about Lines and Angles

COMMON
CORE GPS

Contents

MATHEMATICAL PRACTICES   The Common Core Georgia Performance Standards for Mathematical Practice describe varieties of expertise that all students should seek to develop. Opportunities to develop these practices are integrated throughout this program.

1 Make sense of problems and persevere in solving them.

2 Reason abstractly and quantitatively.

3 Construct viable arguments and critique the reasoning of others.

4 Model with mathematics.

5 Use appropriate tools strategically.

6 Attend to precision.

7 Look for and make use of structure.

8 Look for and express regularity in repeated reasoning.

Unpacking the Standards

Understanding the standards and the vocabulary terms in the standards will help you know exactly what you are expected to learn in this chapter.

 MCC9-12.G.CO.9

Prove theorems about lines and angles.

Key Vocabulary

proof (demostración)
An argument that uses logic to show that a conclusion is true.

theorem (teorema)
A statement that has been proven.

line (línea)
An undefined term in geometry, a line is a straight path that has no thickness and extends forever.

angle (ángulo)
A figure formed by two rays with a common endpoint.

What It Means For You

A line crossing a pair of parallel lines forms pairs of angles that are either congruent or supplementary. You can use simple proofs to show these relationships.

EXAMPLE

In the diagram, line p is parallel to line q.

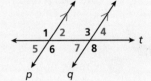

You can show that:

(1) Any pair of black numbered angles is a pair of congruent angles.

(2) Any pair of blue numbered angles is a pair of congruent angles.

(3) Any pair of one black and one blue numbered angle is a pair of supplementary angles.

Explore Parallel Lines and Transversals

Geometry software can help you explore angles that are formed when a transversal intersects a pair of parallel lines.

Use with Angles Formed by Parallel Lines and Transversals

Use appropriate tools strategically.

MCC9-12.G.CO.9 Prove theorems about lines and angles.

Activity

1 Construct a line and label two points on the line A and B.

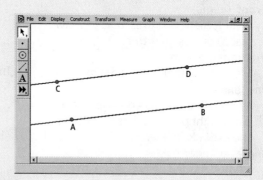

2 Create point C not on $\overleftrightarrow{AB}$. Construct a line parallel to $\overleftrightarrow{AB}$ through point C. Create another point on this line and label it D.

3 Create two points outside the two parallel lines and label them E and F. Construct transversal $\overleftrightarrow{EF}$. Label the points of intersection G and H.

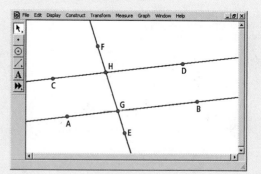

4 Measure the angles formed by the parallel lines and the transversal. Write the angle measures in a chart like the one below. Drag point E or F and chart with the new angle measures. What relationships do you notice about the angle measures? What conjectures can you make?

Angle	∠AGE	∠BGE	∠AGH	∠BGH	∠CHG	∠DHG	∠CHF	∠DHF
Measure								
Measure								

Try This

1. Identify the pairs of corresponding angles in the diagram. What conjecture can you make about their angle measures? Drag a point in the figure to confirm your conjecture.

2. Repeat steps in the previous problem for alternate interior angles, alternate exterior angles, and same-side interior angles.

3. Try dragging point C to change the distance between the parallel lines. What happens to the angle measures in the figure? Why do you think this happens?

21-1 Angles Formed by Parallel Lines and Transversals

Essential Question: How can you prove and use theorems about angles formed by transversals that intersect parallel lines?

Objective
Prove and use theorems about the angles formed by parallel lines and a transversal.

Who uses this?
Piano makers use parallel strings for the higher notes. The longer strings used to produce the lower notes can be viewed as transversals. (See Example 3.)

When parallel lines are cut by a transversal, the angle pairs formed are either congruent or supplementary.

Postulate 21-1-1 (**Corresponding Angles Postulate**)

POSTULATE	HYPOTHESIS	CONCLUSION
If two parallel lines are cut by a transversal, then the pairs of corresponding angles are congruent.		$\angle 1 \cong \angle 3$ $\angle 2 \cong \angle 4$ $\angle 5 \cong \angle 7$ $\angle 6 \cong \angle 8$

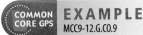

EXAMPLE MCC9-12.G.CO.9

1 **Using the Corresponding Angles Postulate**

Find each angle measure.

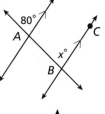

A m∠ABC

$$x = 80 \qquad \textit{Corr. } \angle \textit{ Post.}$$
$$m\angle ABC = 80°$$

B m∠DEF

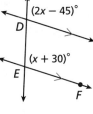

$$(2x - 45)° = (x + 30)° \qquad \textit{Corr. } \angle \textit{ Post.}$$
$$x - 45 = 30 \qquad \textit{Subtract x from both sides.}$$
$$x = 75 \qquad \textit{Add 45 to both sides.}$$
$$m\angle DEF = x + 30$$
$$= 75 + 30 \qquad \textit{Substitute 75 for x.}$$
$$= 105°$$

1. Find m∠QRS.

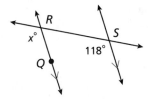

Remember that postulates are statements that are accepted without proof. Since the Corresponding Angles Postulate is given as a postulate, it can be used to prove the next three theorems.

Theorems | Parallel Lines and Angle Pairs

	THEOREM	HYPOTHESIS	CONCLUSION
21-1-2	**Alternate Interior Angles Theorem** If two parallel lines are cut by a transversal, then the pairs of alternate interior angles are congruent.		$\angle 1 \cong \angle 3$ $\angle 2 \cong \angle 4$
21-1-3	**Alternate Exterior Angles Theorem** If two parallel lines are cut by a transversal, then the two pairs of alternate exterior angles are congruent.		$\angle 5 \cong \angle 7$ $\angle 6 \cong \angle 8$
21-1-4	**Same-Side Interior Angles Theorem** If two parallel lines are cut by a transversal, then the two pairs of same-side interior angles are supplementary.		$m\angle 1 + m\angle 4 = 180°$ $m\angle 2 + m\angle 3 = 180°$

Helpful Hint

If a transversal is perpendicular to two parallel lines, all eight angles are congruent.

You will prove Theorems 21-1-3 and 21-1-4 in Exercises 25 and 26.

PROOF **Alternate Interior Angles Theorem**

Given: $\ell \parallel m$
Prove: $\angle 2 \cong \angle 3$
Proof:

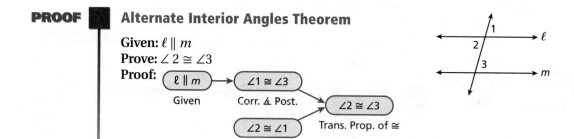

COMMON CORE GPS **EXAMPLE** **2**
MCC9-12.G.CO.9

Finding Angle Measures

Find each angle measure.

my.hrw.com

Online Video Tutor

A **m∠EDF**

$x = 125$
$m\angle EDF = 125°$ *Alt. Ext. ∠ Thm.*

B **m∠TUS**

$13x° + 23x° = 180°$ *Same-Side Int. ∠ Thm.*
$36x = 180$ *Combine like terms.*
$x = 5$ *Divide both sides by 36.*
$m\angle TUS = 23(5) = 115°$ *Substitute 5 for x.*

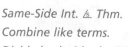

CHECK IT OUT! **2.** Find m∠ABD.

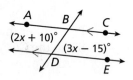

Student to Student

Parallel Lines and Transversals

Nancy Martin
East Branch
High School

When I solve problems with parallel lines and transversals, I remind myself that every pair of angles is either congruent or supplementary.

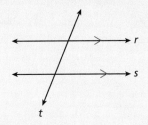

If r ∥ s, all the acute angles are congruent and all the obtuse angles are congruent. The acute angles are supplementary to the obtuse angles.

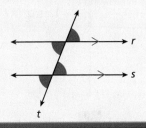

COMMON CORE GPS

EXAMPLE 3
MCC9-12.G.CO.9

my.hrw.com

Online Video Tutor

Music Application

The treble strings of a grand piano are parallel. Viewed from above, the bass strings form transversals to the treble strings. Find x and y in the diagram.

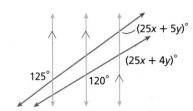

Bass strings   Treble strings

By the Alternate Exterior Angles Theorem, $(25x + 5y)° = 125°$.

By the Corresponding Angles Postulate, $(25x + 4y)° = 120°$.

$$25x + 5y = 125$$
$$-(25x + 4y = 120)$$
$$\overline{y = 5}$$

Subtract the second equation from the first equation.

$$25x + 5(5) = 125$$

Substitute 5 for y in 25x + 5y = 125. Simplify and solve for x.

$$x = 4, y = 5$$

3. Find the measures of the acute angles in the diagram.

MCC.MP.1

MATHEMATICAL PRACTICES

THINK AND DISCUSS

1. Explain why a transversal that is perpendicular to two parallel lines forms eight congruent angles.

2. GET ORGANIZED Copy the diagram and graphic organizer. Complete the graphic organizer by explaining why each of the three theorems is true.

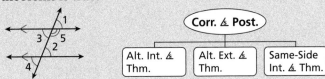

GUIDED PRACTICE

SEE EXAMPLE 1 Find each angle measure.

1. m∠JKL

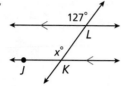

2. m∠BEF

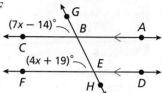

SEE EXAMPLE 2 **3.** m∠1

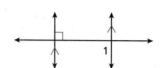

4. m∠CBY

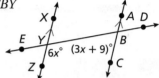

SEE EXAMPLE 3 **5. Safety** The railing of a wheelchair ramp is parallel to the ramp. Find x and y in the diagram.

PRACTICE AND PROBLEM SOLVING

Find each angle measure.

Independent Practice	
For Exercises	See Example
6–7	1
8–11	2
12	3

my.hrw.com

Online Extra Practice

6. m∠KLM

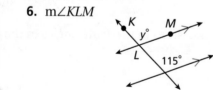

7. m∠VYX

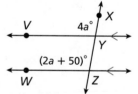

8. m∠ABC

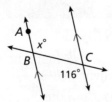

9. m∠EFG

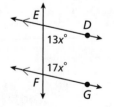

10. m∠PQR

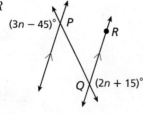

11. m∠STU

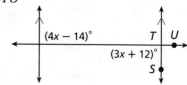

12. **Parking** In the parking lot shown, the lines that mark the width of each space are parallel.
$m\angle 1 = (2x - 3y)°$
$m\angle 2 = (x + 3y)°$
Find x and y.

Find each angle measure. Justify each answer with a postulate or theorem.

13. $m\angle 1$ 14. $m\angle 2$ 15. $m\angle 3$

16. $m\angle 4$ 17. $m\angle 5$ 18. $m\angle 6$

19. $m\angle 7$

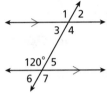

Algebra State the theorem or postulate that is related to the measures of the angles in each pair. Then find the angle measures.

20. $m\angle 1 = (7x + 15)°$, $m\angle 2 = (10x - 9)°$

21. $m\angle 3 = (23x + 11)°$, $m\angle 4 = (14x + 21)°$

22. $m\angle 4 = (37x - 15)°$, $m\angle 5 = (44x - 29)°$

23. $m\angle 1 = (6x + 24)°$, $m\angle 4 = (17x - 9)°$

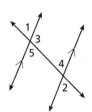

24. **Architecture** The Luxor Hotel in Las Vegas, Nevada, is a 30-story pyramid. The hotel uses an elevator called an inclinator to take people up the side of the pyramid. The inclinator travels at a 39° angle. Which theorem or postulate best illustrates the angles formed by the path of the inclinator and each parallel floor? (*Hint:* Draw a picture.)

25. **Complete the two-column proof of the Alternate Exterior Angles Theorem.**
   Given: $\ell \parallel m$
   Prove: $\angle 1 \cong \angle 2$
   Proof:

Statements	Reasons
1. $\ell \parallel m$	1. Given
2. a. ?	2. Vert. $\angle$s Thm.
3. $\angle 3 \cong \angle 2$	3. b. ?
4. c. ?	4. d. ?

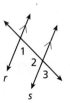

H.O.T. 26. Write a paragraph proof of the Same-Side Interior Angles Theorem.
   Given: $r \parallel s$
   Prove: $m\angle 1 + m\angle 2 = 180°$

H.O.T. Draw the given situation or tell why it is impossible.

27. Two parallel lines are intersected by a transversal so that the corresponding angles are supplementary.

28. Two parallel lines are intersected by a transversal so that the same-side interior angles are complementary.

29. In the diagram, which represents the side view of a mystery spot, m∠SRT = 25°. $\overleftrightarrow{RT}$ is a transversal to $\overleftrightarrow{PS}$ and $\overleftrightarrow{QR}$.

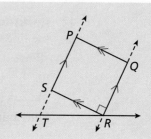

    a. What type of angle pair is ∠QRT and ∠STR?

    b. Find m∠STR. Use a theorem or postulate to justify your answer.

H.O.T. 30. Land Development A piece of property lies between two parallel streets as shown. m∠1 = $(2x + 6)°$, and m∠2 = $(3x + 9)°$. What is the relationship between the angles? What are their measures?

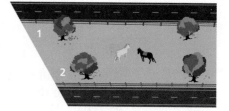

H.O.T. 31. ///**ERROR ANALYSIS**/// In the figure, m∠ABC = $(15x + 5)°$, and m∠BCD = $(10x + 25)°$. Which value of *m∠BCD* is incorrect? Explain.

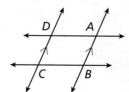

Ⓐ

$$15x + 5 = 10x + 25$$
$$\underline{-10x \qquad -10x}$$
$$5x + 5 = 25$$
$$\underline{-5 \qquad -5}$$
$$5x = 20$$
$$x = 4$$

m∠BCD = 10(4) + 25 = 65°

Ⓑ

$$(15x + 5) + (10x + 25) = 180$$
$$25x + 30 = 180$$
$$\underline{-30 \quad -30}$$
$$25x = 150$$
$$x = 6$$

m∠BCD = 10(6) + 25 = 85°

32. Critical Thinking In the diagram, ℓ ∥ m. Explain why $\frac{x}{y} = 1$.

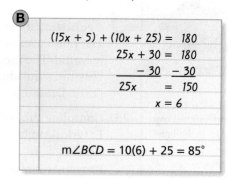

H.O.T. 33. Write About It Suppose that lines ℓ and m are intersected by transversal *p*. One of the angles formed by ℓ and *p* is congruent to every angle formed by *m* and *p*. Draw a diagram showing lines ℓ, *m*, and *p*, mark any congruent angles that are formed, and explain what you know is true.

TEST PREP

34. m∠RST = $(x + 50)°$, and m∠STU = $(3x + 20)°$. Find m∠RVT.

    Ⓐ 15°   **Ⓒ** 65°

    Ⓑ 27.5°   **Ⓓ** 77.5°

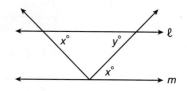

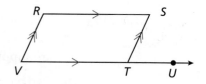

35. For two parallel lines and a transversal, m∠1 = 83°. For which pair of angle measures is the sum the least?

  (F) ∠1 and a corresponding angle

  (G) ∠1 and a same-side interior angle

  (H) ∠1 and its supplement

  (J) ∠1 and its complement

36. **Short Response** Given a ∥ b with transversal t, explain why ∠1 and ∠3 are supplementary.

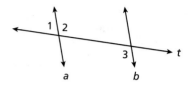

CHALLENGE AND EXTEND

Multi-Step Find m∠1 in each diagram. (*Hint:* Draw a line parallel to the given parallel lines.)

37.

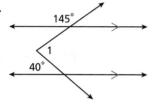

38.

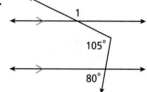

39. Find x and y in the diagram. Justify your answer.

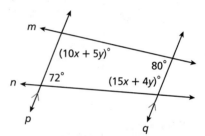

H.O.T. 40. Two lines are parallel. The measures of two corresponding angles are $a°$ and $2b°$, and the measures of two same-side interior angles are $a°$ and $b°$. Find the value of a.

MATHEMATICAL PRACTICES

FOCUS ON MATHEMATICAL PRACTICES

H.O.T. 41. **Error Analysis** Sarah found that m∠D = 70° and m∠B = 70°. Explain her error.

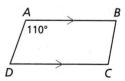

H.O.T. 42. **Reasonableness** Write a convincing argument that ∠1 is congruent to ∠15 in the figure.

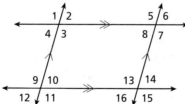

H.O.T. 43. **Problem Solving** 18th Street and 20th Street both cross the canal as shown in the figure. Find x and y. Show your work.

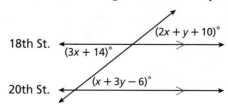

21-1 Angles Formed by Parallel Lines and Transversals   **609**

21-2 Proving Lines Parallel

Essential Question: How can you prove lines are parallel?

Objective
Use the angles formed by a transversal to prove two lines are parallel.

Who uses this?
Rowers have to keep the oars on each side parallel in order to travel in a straight line. (See Example 4.)

Recall that the converse of a theorem is found by exchanging the hypothesis and conclusion. The converse of a theorem is not automatically true. If it is true, it must be stated as a postulate or proved as a separate theorem.

Know it!
Note

Postulate 21-2-1 ⟨ **Converse of the Corresponding Angles Postulate** ⟩

POSTULATE	HYPOTHESIS	CONCLUSION
If two coplanar lines are cut by a transversal so that a pair of corresponding angles are congruent, then the two lines are parallel.	$\angle 1 \cong \angle 2$ 	$m \parallel n$

COMMON CORE GPS

EXAMPLE 1 MCC9-12.G.CO.9

Using the Converse of the Corresponding Angles Postulate

my.hrw.com

Online Video Tutor

Use the Converse of the Corresponding Angles Postulate and the given information to show that $\ell \parallel m$.

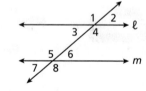

A $\angle 1 \cong \angle 5$

$\angle 1 \cong \angle 5$ *$\angle 1$ and $\angle 5$ are corresponding angles.*

$\ell \parallel m$ *Conv. of Corr. $\angle$s Post.*

B $m\angle 4 = (2x + 10)^\circ$, $m\angle 8 = (3x - 55)^\circ$, $x = 65$

$m\angle 4 = 2(65) + 10 = 140$ *Substitute 65 for x.*

$m\angle 8 = 3(65) - 55 = 140$ *Substitute 65 for x.*

$m\angle 4 = m\angle 8$ *Trans. Prop. of Equality*

$\angle 4 \cong \angle 8$ *Def. of $\cong$ $\angle$s*

$\ell \parallel m$ *Conv. of Corr. $\angle$s Post.*

CHECK IT OUT!

Use the Converse of the Corresponding Angles Postulate and the given information to show that $\ell \parallel m$.

1a. $m\angle 1 = m\angle 3$

1b. $m\angle 7 = (4x + 25)^\circ$, $m\angle 5 = (5x + 12)^\circ$, $x = 13$

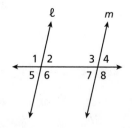

Ken Hawkins/Mira.com

Postulate 21-2-2 (Parallel Postulate)

Through a point *P* not on line ℓ, there is exactly one line parallel to ℓ.

The Converse of the Corresponding Angles Postulate is used to construct parallel lines. The Parallel Postulate guarantees that for any line ℓ, you can always construct a parallel line through a point that is not on ℓ.

Construction Parallel Lines

1 Draw a line ℓ and a point *P* that is not on ℓ.

2 Draw a line *m* through *P* that intersects ℓ. Label the angle 1.

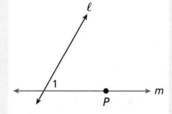

3 Construct an angle congruent to ∠1 at *P*. By the converse of the Corresponding Angles Postulate, ℓ ∥ *n*.

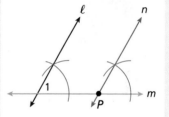

Theorems (Proving Lines Parallel)

	THEOREM	HYPOTHESIS	CONCLUSION
21-2-3	**Converse of the Alternate Interior Angles Theorem** If two coplanar lines are cut by a transversal so that a pair of alternate interior angles are congruent, then the two lines are parallel.	∠1 ≅ ∠2	*m* ∥ *n*
21-2-4	**Converse of the Alternate Exterior Angles Theorem** If two coplanar lines are cut by a transversal so that a pair of alternate exterior angles are congruent, then the two lines are parallel.	∠3 ≅ ∠4	*m* ∥ *n*
21-2-5	**Converse of the Same-Side Interior Angles Theorem** If two coplanar lines are cut by a transversal so that a pair of same-side interior angles are supplementary, then the two lines are parallel.	$m\angle 5 + m\angle 6 = 180°$	*m* ∥ *n*

You will prove Theorems 21-2-3 and 21-2-5 in Exercises 38 and 39.

PROOF | **Converse of the Alternate Exterior Angles Theorem**

Given: ∠1 ≅ ∠2
Prove: ℓ ∥ m
Proof: It is given that ∠1 ≅ ∠2. Vertical angles are congruent, so ∠1 ≅ ∠3. By the Transitive Property of Congruence, ∠2 ≅ ∠3. So ℓ ∥ m by the Converse of the Corresponding Angles Postulate.

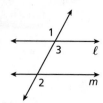

EXAMPLE 2

Determining Whether Lines are Parallel

Use the given information and the theorems you have learned to show that $r \parallel s$.

A ∠2 ≅ ∠6

∠2 ≅ ∠6   ∠2 and ∠6 are alternate interior angles.
$r \parallel s$ Conv. of Alt. Int. ∠ Thm.

B m∠6 = $(6x + 18)°$, m∠7 = $(9x + 12)°$, $x = 10$

m∠6 = $6x + 18$
    = $6(10) + 18 = 78°$ Substitute 10 for x.
m∠7 = $9x + 12$
    = $9(10) + 12 = 102°$ Substitute 10 for x.
m∠6 + m∠7 = $78° + 102°$
      = $180°$ ∠6 and ∠7 are same-side interior angles.
$r \parallel s$ Conv. of Same-Side Int. ∠ Thm.

CHECK IT OUT! Refer to the diagram above. Use the given information and the theorems you have learned to show that $r \parallel s$.

2a. m∠4 = m∠8   **2b.** m∠3 = $2x°$, m∠7 = $(x + 50)°$, $x = 50$

EXAMPLE 3

Proving Lines Parallel

Given: $\ell \parallel m$, ∠1 ≅ ∠3
Prove: $r \parallel p$

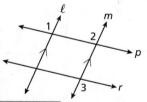

Proof:

Statements	Reasons
1. $\ell \parallel m$	1. Given
2. ∠1 ≅ ∠2	2. Corr. ∠ Post.
3. ∠1 ≅ ∠3	3. Given
4. ∠2 ≅ ∠3	4. Trans. Prop. of ≅
5. $r \parallel p$	5. Conv. of Alt. Ext. ∠ Thm.

CHECK IT OUT! **3. Given:** ∠1 ≅ ∠4, ∠3 and ∠4 are supplementary.
Prove: $\ell \parallel m$

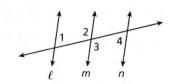

COMMON CORE GPS MCC9-12.G.CO.9

EXAMPLE **4**

Sports Application

During a race, all members of a rowing team should keep the oars parallel on each side. If $m\angle 1 = (3x + 13)°$, $m\angle 2 = (5x - 5)°$, and $x = 9$, show that the oars are parallel.

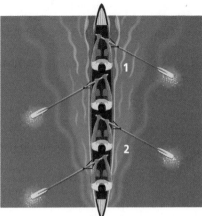

A line through the center of the boat forms a transversal to the two oars on each side of the boat.

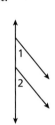

$\angle 1$ and $\angle 2$ are corresponding angles. If $\angle 1 \cong \angle 2$, then the oars are parallel.

Substitute 9 for x in each expression:

$m\angle 1 = 3x + 13$
$\qquad = 3(9) + 13 = 40°$ *Substitute 9 for x in each expression.*

$m\angle 2 = 5x - 5$
$\qquad = 5(9) - 5 = 40°$ *$m\angle 1 = m\angle 2$, so $\angle 1 \cong \angle 2$.*

The corresponding angles are congruent, so the oars are parallel by the Converse of the Corresponding Angles Postulate.

4. What if...? Suppose the corresponding angles on the opposite side of the boat measure $(4y - 2)°$ and $(3y + 6)°$, where $y = 8$. Show that the oars are parallel.

MCC.MP.3

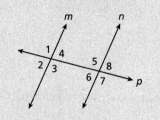
MATHEMATICAL PRACTICES

THINK AND DISCUSS

1. Explain three ways of proving that two lines are parallel.

2. If you know $m\angle 1$, how could you use the measures of $\angle 5$, $\angle 6$, $\angle 7$, or $\angle 8$ to prove $m \parallel n$?

3. GET ORGANIZED Copy and complete the graphic organizer. Use it to compare the Corresponding Angles Postulate with the Converse of the Corresponding Angles Postulate.

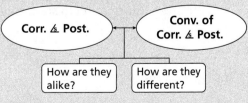

GUIDED PRACTICE

SEE EXAMPLE **1** Use the Converse of the Corresponding Angles Postulate and the given information to show that $p \parallel q$.
1. $\angle 4 \cong \angle 5$

2. $m\angle 1 = (4x + 16)°$, $m\angle 8 = (5x - 12)°$, $x = 28$

3. $m\angle 4 = (6x - 19)°$, $m\angle 5 = (3x + 14)°$, $x = 11$

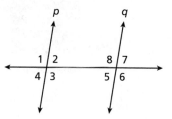

SEE EXAMPLE **2** Use the theorems and given information to show that $r \parallel s$.
4. $\angle 1 \cong \angle 5$

5. $m\angle 3 + m\angle 4 = 180°$

6. $\angle 3 \cong \angle 7$

7. $m\angle 4 = (13x - 4)°$, $m\angle 8 = (9x + 16)°$, $x = 5$

8. $m\angle 8 = (17x + 37)°$, $m\angle 7 = (9x - 13)°$, $x = 6$

9. $m\angle 2 = (25x + 7)°$, $m\angle 6 = (24x + 12)°$, $x = 5$

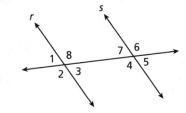

SEE EXAMPLE **3** 10. Complete the following two-column proof.
Given: $\angle 1 \cong \angle 2$, $\angle 3 \cong \angle 1$
Prove: $\overline{XY} \parallel \overline{WV}$
Proof:

Statements	Reasons
1. $\angle 1 \cong \angle 2$, $\angle 3 \cong \angle 1$	**1.** Given
2. $\angle 2 \cong \angle 3$	**2. a.** _____?_____
3. b. _____?_____	**3. c.** _____?_____

SEE EXAMPLE **4** 11. **Architecture** In the fire escape, $m\angle 1 = (17x + 9)°$, $m\angle 2 = (14x + 18)°$, and $x = 3$. Show that the two landings are parallel.

PRACTICE AND PROBLEM SOLVING

Use the Converse of the Corresponding Angles Postulate and the given information to show that $\ell \parallel m$.

12. $\angle 3 \cong 7$

13. $m\angle 4 = 54°$, $m\angle 8 = (7x + 5)°$, $x = 7$

14. $m\angle 2 = (8x + 4)°$, $m\angle 6 = (11x - 41)°$, $x = 15$

15. $m\angle 1 = (3x + 19)°$, $m\angle 5 = (4x + 7)°$, $x = 12$

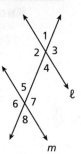

Independent Practice

For Exercises	See Example
12–15	1
16–21	2
22	3
23	4

my.hrw.com

Online Extra Practice

Use the theorems and given information to show that $n \parallel p$.

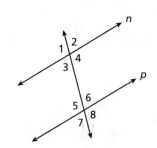

16. $\angle 3 \cong \angle 6$

17. $\angle 2 \cong \angle 7$

18. $m\angle 4 + m\angle 6 = 180°$

19. $m\angle 1 = (8x - 7)°$, $m\angle 8 = (6x + 21)°$, $x = 14$

20. $m\angle 4 = (4x + 3)°$, $m\angle 5 = (5x - 22)°$, $x = 25$

21. $m\angle 3 = (2x + 15)°$, $m\angle 5 = (3x + 15)°$, $x = 30$

22. Complete the following two-column proof.
Given: $\overline{AB} \parallel \overline{CD}$, $\angle 1 \cong \angle 2$, $\angle 3 \cong \angle 4$
Prove: $\overline{BC} \parallel \overline{DE}$

Proof:

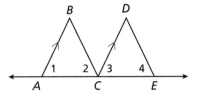

Statements	Reasons
1. $\overline{AB} \parallel \overline{CD}$	1. Given
2. $\angle 1 \cong \angle 3$	2. a. _____?_____
3. $\angle 1 \cong \angle 2$, $\angle 3 \cong \angle 4$	3. b. _____?_____
4. $\angle 2 \cong \angle 4$	4. c. _____?_____
5. d. _____?_____	5. e. _____?_____

H.O.T. **23. Art** Edmund Dulac used perspective when drawing the floor titles in an illustration for *The Wind's Tale* by Hans Christian Andersen. Show that $\overline{DJ} \parallel \overline{EK}$ if $m\angle 1 = (3x + 2)°$, $m\angle 2 = (5x - 10)°$, and $x = 6$.

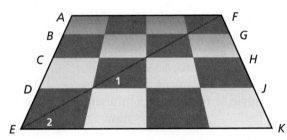

Name the postulate or theorem that proves that $\ell \parallel m$.

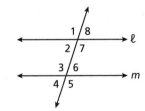

24. $\angle 8 \cong \angle 6$ **25.** $\angle 8 \cong \angle 4$

26. $\angle 2 \cong \angle 6$ **27.** $\angle 7 \cong \angle 5$

28. $\angle 3 \cong \angle 7$ **29.** $m\angle 2 + m\angle 3 = 180°$

For the given information, tell which pair of lines must be parallel. Name the postulate or theorem that supports your answer.

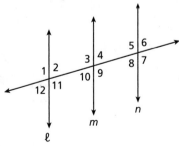

30. $m\angle 2 = m\angle 10$ **31.** $m\angle 8 + m\angle 9 = 180°$

32. $\angle 1 \cong \angle 7$ **33.** $m\angle 10 = m\angle 6$

34. $\angle 11 \cong \angle 5$ **35.** $m\angle 2 + m\angle 5 = 180°$

36. Multi-Step Two lines are intersected by a transversal so that $\angle 1$ and $\angle 2$ are corresponding angles, $\angle 1$ and $\angle 3$ are alternate exterior angles, and $\angle 3$ and $\angle 4$ are corresponding angles. If $\angle 2 \cong \angle 4$, what theorem or postulate can be used to prove the lines parallel?

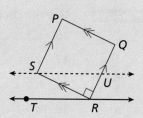

Real-World Connections

37. In the diagram, which represents the side view of a mystery spot, m∠SRT = 25°, and m∠SUR = 65°.

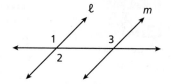

a. Name a same-side interior angle of ∠SUR for lines $\overleftrightarrow{SU}$ and $\overleftrightarrow{RT}$ with transversal $\overline{RU}$. What is its measure? Explain your reasoning.

b. Prove that $\overleftrightarrow{SU}$ and $\overleftrightarrow{RT}$ are parallel.

38. Complete the flowchart proof of the Converse of the Alternate Interior Angles Theorem.

Given: ∠2 ≅ ∠3
Prove: ℓ ∥ m
Proof:

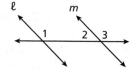

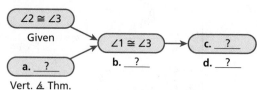

39. Use the diagram to write a paragraph proof of the Converse of the Same-Side Interior Angles Theorem.

Given: ∠1 and ∠2 are supplementary.
Prove: ℓ ∥ m

H.O.T. 40. Carpentry A *plumb bob* is a weight hung at the end of a string, called a *plumb line*. The weight pulls the string down so that the plumb line is perfectly vertical. Suppose that the angle formed by the wall and the roof is 123° and the angle formed by the plumb line and the roof is 123°. How does this show that the wall is perfectly vertical?

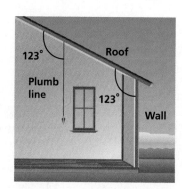

H.O.T. 41. Critical Thinking Are the Reflexive, Symmetric, and Transitive Properties true for parallel lines? Explain why or why not.

Reflexive: ℓ ∥ ℓ
Symmetric: If ℓ ∥ m, then m ∥ ℓ.
Transitive: If ℓ ∥ m and m ∥ n, then ℓ ∥ n.

H.O.T. 42. Write About It Does the information given in the diagram allow you to conclude that a ∥ b? Explain.

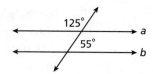

TEST PREP

43. Which postulate or theorem can be used to prove ℓ ∥ m?

Ⓐ Converse of the Corresponding Angles Postulate
Ⓑ Converse of the Alternate Interior Angles Theorem
Ⓒ Converse of the Alternate Exterior Angles Theorem
Ⓓ Converse of the Same-Side Interior Angles Theorem

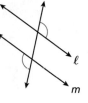

44. Two coplanar lines are cut by a transversal. Which condition does NOT guarantee that the two lines are parallel?

Ⓐ A pair of alternate interior angles are congruent.

Ⓑ A pair of same-side interior angles are supplementary.

Ⓒ A pair of corresponding angles are congruent.

Ⓓ A pair of alternate exterior angles are complementary.

45. Gridded Response Find the value of x so that $\ell \parallel m$.

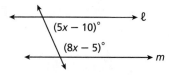

CHALLENGE AND EXTEND

Determine which lines, if any, can be proven parallel using the given information. Justify your answers.

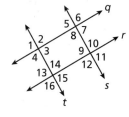

46. $\angle 1 \cong \angle 15$

47. $\angle 8 \cong \angle 14$

48. $\angle 3 \cong \angle 7$

49. $\angle 8 \cong \angle 10$

50. $\angle 6 \cong \angle 8$

51. $\angle 13 \cong \angle 11$

52. $m\angle 12 + m\angle 15 = 180°$

53. $m\angle 5 + m\angle 8 = 180°$

H.O.T. 54. Write a paragraph proof that $\overline{AE} \parallel \overline{BD}$.

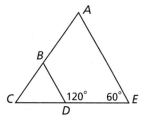

Use the diagram for Exercises 55 and 56.

55. Given: $m\angle 2 + m\angle 3 = 180°$
Prove: $\ell \parallel m$

56. Given: $m\angle 2 + m\angle 5 = 180°$
Prove: $\ell \parallel n$

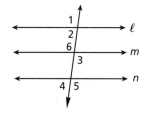

FOCUS ON MATHEMATICAL PRACTICES

H.O.T. 57. Communication Explain when the Alternate Interior Angles Theorem can be applied, and when the Converse of the Alternate Interior Angles Theorem can be applied.

H.O.T. 58. Reasoning In the figure, line a is parallel to line b. Is line c parallel to line d? Justify your answer.

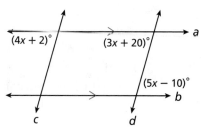

H.O.T. 59. Justify June named $\angle 5$ and $\angle 8$ same-side exterior angles. How are their measures related if the lines p and q are parallel? Support your answer.

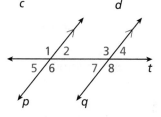

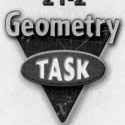

21-2
Geometry
TASK

*Use with Proving
Lines Parallel*

Construct Parallel Lines

You have learned one method of constructing parallel lines using a compass and straightedge. Another method, called the rhombus method, uses a property of a figure called a *rhombus*. The rhombus method is shown below.

MATHEMATICAL PRACTICES

Use appropriate tools strategically.

MCC9-12.G.CO.12 Make formal geometric constructions with a variety of tools and methods …

Activity 1

1 Draw a line ℓ and a point P not on the line.

P •

ℓ

2 Choose a point Q on the line. Place your compass point at Q and draw an arc through P that intersects ℓ. Label the intersection R.

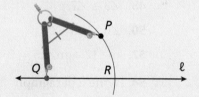

3 Using the same compass setting as the first arc, draw two more arcs: one from P, the other from R. Label the intersection of the two arcs S.

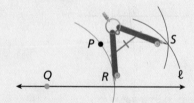

4 Draw $\overleftrightarrow{PS} \parallel \ell$.

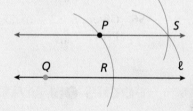

Try This

1. Repeat Activity 1 using a different point not on the line. Are your results the same?

2. Using the lines you constructed in Problem 1, draw transversal $\overleftrightarrow{PQ}$. Verify that the lines are parallel by using a protractor to measure alternate interior angles.

3. What postulate ensures that this construction is always possible?

4. A *rhombus* is a quadrilateral with four congruent sides. Explain why this method is called the rhombus method.

Activity 2

1 Draw a line ℓ and point P on a piece of patty paper.

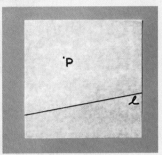

2 Fold the paper through P so that both sides of line ℓ match up

3 Crease the paper to form line m. P should be on line m.

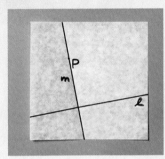

4 Fold the paper again through P so that both sides of line m match up.

5 Crease the paper to form line n. Line n is parallel to line ℓ through P.

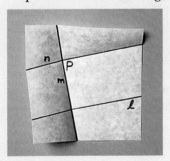

Try This

5. Repeat Activity 2 using a point in a different place not on the line. Are your results the same?

6. Use a protractor to measure corresponding angles. How can you tell that the lines are parallel?

7. Draw a triangle and construct a line parallel to one side through the vertex that is not on that side.

8. Line m is perpendicular to both ℓ and n. Use this statement to complete the following conjecture: If two lines in a plane are perpendicular to the same line, then _____?_____ .

21-3 Perpendicular Lines

Essential Question: How can you prove and use theorems about perpendicular lines?

Objective
Prove and apply theorems about perpendicular lines.

Vocabulary
perpendicular bisector
distance from a point to a line

The **perpendicular bisector** of a segment is a line perpendicular to a segment at the segment's midpoint. A construction of a perpendicular bisector is shown below.

Construction Perpendicular Bisector of a Segment

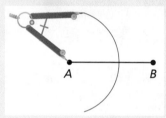 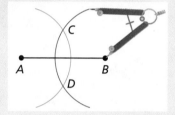 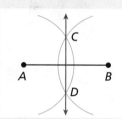

1 Draw $\overline{AB}$. Open the compass wider than half of AB and draw an arc centered at A.

2 Using the same compass setting, draw an arc centered at B that intersects the first arc at C and D.

3 Draw $\overleftrightarrow{CD}$. $\overleftrightarrow{CD}$ is the perpendicular bisector of $\overline{AB}$.

The shortest segment from a point to a line is perpendicular to the line. This fact is used to define the **distance from a point to a line** as the length of the perpendicular segment from the point to the line.

EXAMPLE MCC9-12.A.REI.3

1 **Distance From a Point to a Line**

Online Video Tutor

A Name the shortest segment from P to $\overleftrightarrow{AC}$.

The shortest distance from a point to a line is the length of the perpendicular segment, so $\overline{PB}$ is the shortest segment from P to $\overleftrightarrow{AC}$.

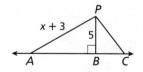

B Write and solve an inequality for x.

$$PA > PB \qquad \text{\textit{$\overline{PB}$ is the shortest segment.}}$$
$$x + 3 > \quad 5 \qquad \text{\textit{Substitute $x + 3$ for PA and 5 for PB.}}$$
$$\underline{-3 \quad -3} \qquad \text{\textit{Subtract 3 from both sides of the inequality.}}$$
$$x > \quad 2$$

CHECK IT OUT!

1a. Name the shortest segment from A to $\overleftrightarrow{BC}$.

1b. Write and solve an inequality for x.

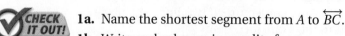

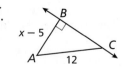

Alamy Images

	THEOREM	HYPOTHESIS	CONCLUSION
21-3-1	If two intersecting lines form a linear pair of congruent angles, then the lines are perpendicular. (2 intersecting lines form lin. pair of ≅ ∡ → lines ⊥.)		$\ell \perp m$
21-3-2	**Perpendicular Transversal Theorem** In a plane, if a transversal is perpendicular to one of two parallel lines, then it is perpendicular to the other line.		$q \perp p$
21-3-3	If two coplanar lines are perpendicular to the same line, then the two lines are parallel to each other. (2 lines ⊥ to same line → 2 lines ∥.)		$r \parallel s$

You will prove Theorems 21-3-1 and 21-3-3 in Exercises 37 and 38.

PROOF **Perpendicular Transversal Theorem**

Given: $\overleftrightarrow{BC} \parallel \overleftrightarrow{DE}$, $\overleftrightarrow{AB} \perp \overleftrightarrow{BC}$

Prove: $\overleftrightarrow{AB} \perp \overleftrightarrow{DE}$

Proof:

It is given that $\overleftrightarrow{BC} \parallel \overleftrightarrow{DE}$, so $\angle ABC \cong \angle BDE$ by the Corresponding Angles Postulate. It is also given that $\overleftrightarrow{AB} \perp \overleftrightarrow{BC}$, so m$\angle ABC = 90°$. By the definition of congruent angles, m$\angle ABC =$ m$\angle BDE$, so m$\angle BDE = 90°$ by the Transitive Property of Equality. By the definition of perpendicular lines, $\overleftrightarrow{AB} \perp \overleftrightarrow{DE}$.

EXAMPLE **2** **Proving Properties of Lines**

Write a two-column proof.

Given: $\overleftrightarrow{AD} \parallel \overleftrightarrow{BC}$, $\overleftrightarrow{AD} \perp \overleftrightarrow{AB}$, $\overleftrightarrow{BC} \perp \overleftrightarrow{DC}$

Prove: $\overleftrightarrow{AB} \parallel \overleftrightarrow{DC}$

Proof:

Online Video Tutor

Statements	Reasons
1. $\overleftrightarrow{AD} \parallel \overleftrightarrow{BC}$, $\overleftrightarrow{BC} \perp \overleftrightarrow{DC}$	1. Given
2. $\overleftrightarrow{AD} \perp \overleftrightarrow{DC}$	2. ⊥ Transv. Thm.
3. $\overleftrightarrow{AD} \perp \overleftrightarrow{AB}$	3. Given
4. $\overleftrightarrow{AB} \parallel \overleftrightarrow{DC}$	4. 2 lines ⊥ to same line → 2 lines ∥.

2. Write a two-column proof.

Given: $\angle EHF \cong \angle HFG$, $\overleftrightarrow{FG} \perp \overleftrightarrow{GH}$

Prove: $\overleftrightarrow{EH} \perp \overleftrightarrow{GH}$

Oceanography Application

my.hrw.com

Online Video Tutor

Rip currents may be caused by a sandbar parallel to the shoreline. Waves cause a buildup of water between the sandbar and the shoreline. When this water breaks through the sandbar, it flows out in a direction perpendicular to the sandbar. Why must the rip current be perpendicular to the shoreline?

The rip current forms a transversal to the shoreline and the sandbar.

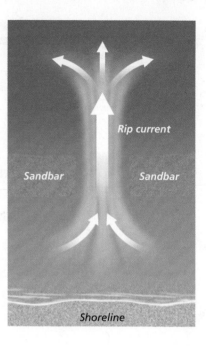

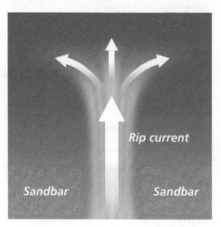

The shoreline and the sandbar are parallel, and the rip current is perpendicular to the sandbar. So by the Perpendicular Transversal Theorem, the rip current is perpendicular to the shoreline.

CHECK IT OUT!

3. A swimmer who gets caught in a rip current should swim in a direction perpendicular to the current. Why should the path of the swimmer be parallel to the shoreline?

THINK AND DISCUSS

1. Describe what happens if two intersecting lines form a linear pair of congruent angles.

2. Explain why a transversal that is perpendicular to two parallel lines forms eight congruent angles.

3. GET ORGANIZED Copy and complete the graphic organizer. Use the diagram and the theorems from this lesson to complete the table.

Diagram	If you are given . . .	Then you can conclude . . .
	$m\angle 1 = m\angle 2$	
	$m\angle 2 = 90°$ $m\angle 3 = 90°$	
	$m\angle 2 = 90°$ $m \parallel n$	

my.hrw.com
Homework Help

GUIDED PRACTICE

1. **Vocabulary** $\overleftrightarrow{CD}$ is the *perpendicular bisector* of $\overline{AB}$. $\overleftrightarrow{CD}$ intersects $\overline{AB}$ at C. What can you say about $\overline{AB}$ and $\overleftrightarrow{CD}$? What can you say about $\overline{AC}$ and $\overline{BC}$?

SEE EXAMPLE 1

2. Name the shortest segment from point E to $\overleftrightarrow{AD}$.

3. Write and solve an inequality for x.

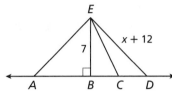

SEE EXAMPLE 2

4. Complete the two-column proof.
   Given: $\angle ABC \cong \angle CBE$, $\overleftrightarrow{DE} \perp \overleftrightarrow{AF}$
   Prove: $\overleftrightarrow{CB} \parallel \overleftrightarrow{DE}$
   Proof:

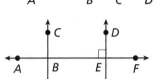

Statements	Reasons
1. $\angle ABC \cong \angle CBE$	1. Given
2. $\overleftrightarrow{CB} \perp \overleftrightarrow{AF}$	2. a. ____?____
3. b. ____?____	3. Given
4. $\overleftrightarrow{CB} \parallel \overleftrightarrow{DE}$	4. c. ____?____

SEE EXAMPLE 3

5. **Sports** The center line in a tennis court is perpendicular to both service lines. Explain why the service lines must be parallel to each other.

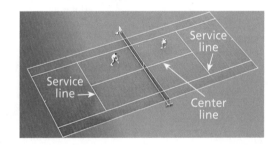

Service line

Service line

Center line

PRACTICE AND PROBLEM SOLVING

my.hrw.com

Online Extra Practice

6. Name the shortest segment from point W to $\overline{XZ}$.

7. Write and solve an inequality for x.

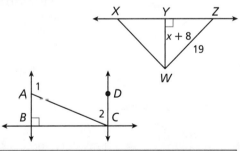

8. Complete the two-column proof below.
   Given: $\overleftrightarrow{AB} \perp \overleftrightarrow{BC}$, $m\angle 1 + m\angle 2 = 100°$
   Prove: $\overleftrightarrow{BC} \perp \overleftrightarrow{CD}$
   Proof:

Statements	Reasons
1. $\overleftrightarrow{AB} \perp \overleftrightarrow{BC}$	1. Given
2. $m\angle 1 + m\angle 2 = 180°$	2. a. ____?____
3. $\angle 1$ and $\angle 2$ are supplementary.	3. Def. of supplementary
4. b. ____?____	4. Converse of the Same-Side Interior Angles Theorem
5. $\overleftrightarrow{BC} \perp \overleftrightarrow{CD}$	5. c. ____?____

9. **Music** The *frets* on a guitar are all perpendicular to one of the strings. Explain why the frets must be parallel to each other.

String

Fret

For each diagram, write and solve an inequality for *x*.

10.

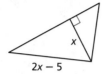

x

$2x - 5$

11.

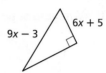

$6x + 5$

$9x - 3$

Multi-Step Solve to find *x* and *y* in each diagram.

12.

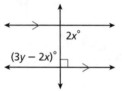

$2x°$

$(3y - 2x)°$

13.

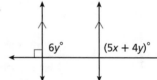

$6y°$

$(5x + 4y)°$

14.

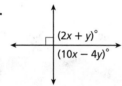

$(2x + y)°$

$(10x - 4y)°$

15.

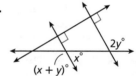

$2y°$

$x°$

$(x + y)°$

Determine if there is enough information given in the diagram to prove each statement.

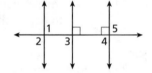

16. $\angle 1 \cong \angle 2$ 17. $\angle 1 \cong \angle 3$

18. $\angle 2 \cong \angle 3$ 19. $\angle 2 \cong \angle 4$

20. $\angle 3 \cong \angle 4$ 21. $\angle 3 \cong \angle 5$

H.O.T. 22. **Critical Thinking** Are the Reflexive, Symmetric, and Transitive Properties true for perpendicular lines? Explain why or why not.
Reflexive: $\ell \perp \ell$
Symmetric: If $\ell \perp m$, then $m \perp \ell$.
Transitive: If $\ell \perp m$ and $m \perp n$, then $\ell \perp n$.

Real-World Connections

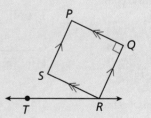

Demonstrating the Creeping Ball

23. In the diagram, which represents the side view of a mystery spot, $\overline{QR} \perp \overline{PQ}$, $\overline{PQ} \parallel \overline{RS}$, and $\overline{PS} \parallel \overline{QR}$.

   a. Prove $\overline{QR} \perp \overline{RS}$ and $\overline{PS} \perp \overline{RS}$.

   b. Prove $\overline{PQ} \perp \overline{PS}$.

P

Q

S

T

R

24. **Geography** Felton Avenue, Arlee Avenue, and Viehl Avenue are all parallel. Broadway Street is perpendicular to Felton Avenue. Use the satellite photo and the given information to determine the values of *x* and *y*.

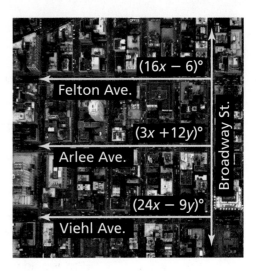

Felton Ave.
(16x − 6)°
(3x + 12y)°
Arlee Ave.
(24x − 9y)°
Viehl Ave.
Broadway St.

25. **Estimation** Copy the diagram onto a grid with 1 cm by 1 cm squares. Estimate the distance from point *P* to line ℓ.

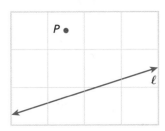

P •
ℓ

H.O.T. 26. **Critical Thinking** Draw a figure to show that Theorem 21-3-3 is not true if the lines are not in the same plane.

27. Draw a figure in which $\overline{AB}$ is a perpendicular bisector of $\overline{XY}$ but $\overline{XY}$ is not a perpendicular bisector of $\overline{AB}$.

H.O.T. 28. **Write About It** A ladder is formed by rungs that are perpendicular to the sides of the ladder. Explain why the rungs of the ladder are parallel.

Construction Construct a segment congruent to each given segment and then construct its perpendicular bisector.

29.    30.

TEST PREP

31. Which inequality is correct for the given diagram?

    (A) $2x + 5 < 3x$ (C) $2x + 5 > 3x$
    (B) $x > 1$ (D) $x > 5$

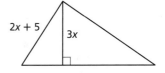

2x + 5   3x

32. In the diagram, $ℓ \perp m$. Find *x* and *y*.

    (F) $x = 5, y = 7$
    (G) $x = 7, y = 5$
    (H) $x = 90, y = 90$
    (J) $x = 10, y = 5$

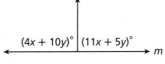

ℓ
(4x + 10y)° (11x + 5y)°
m

33. If $ℓ \perp m$, which statement is NOT correct?

    (A) $m\angle 2 = 90°$
    (B) $m\angle 1 + m\angle 2 = 180°$
    (C) $\angle 1 \cong \angle 2$
    (D) $\angle 1 \perp \angle 2$

ℓ
1 2
m

34. In a plane, both lines *m* and *n* are perpendicular to both lines *p* and *q*. Which conclusion CANNOT be made?

    Ⓐ *p* ∥ *q*

    Ⓑ *m* ∥ *n*

    Ⓒ *p* ⊥ *q*

    Ⓓ All angles formed by lines *m*, *n*, *p*, and *q* are congruent.

H.O.T. 35. Extended Response Lines *m* and *n* are parallel. Line *p* intersects line *m* at *A* and line *n* at *B*, and is perpendicular to line *m*.

    a. What is the relationship between line *n* and line *p*? Draw a diagram to support your answer.

    b. What is the distance from point *A* to line *n*? What is the distance from point *B* to line *m*? Explain.

    c. How would you define the distance between two parallel lines in a plane?

CHALLENGE AND EXTEND

H.O.T. 36. Multi-Step Find m∠1 in the diagram. (*Hint:* Draw a line parallel to the given parallel lines.)

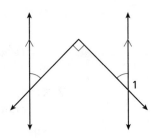

37. Prove Theorem 21-3-1: If two intersecting lines form a linear pair of congruent angles, then the two lines are perpendicular.

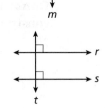

38. Prove Theorem 21-3-3: If two coplanar lines are perpendicular to the same line, then the two lines are parallel to each other.

FOCUS ON MATHEMATICAL PRACTICES

H.O.T. 39. Modeling Korey said that two lines parallel to the same line are perpendicular. Draw a figure to prove or disprove his statement.

H.O.T. 40. Reasoning $\overline{CD}$ is the perpendicular bisector of $\overline{AB}$ and intersects it at point *E*. $AE = 2x + 6$, $BE = 5x - 12$, $CE = 4x + 9$, and $DE = 6x - 3$. Is $\overline{AB}$ the perpendicular bisector of $\overline{CD}$? Justify your answer.

H.O.T. 41. Communication Explain how you know that the distance from the origin to the line shown is less than 3.

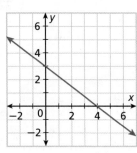

21-3
Geometry
TASK

Use with Perpendicular Lines

Construct Perpendicular Lines

You have learned to construct the perpendicular bisector of a segment. This is the basis of the construction of a line perpendicular to a given line through a given point. The steps in the construction are the same whether the point is on or off the line.

Use appropriate tools strategically.

MCC9-12.G.CO.12 Make formal geometric constructions with a variety of tools and methods ...

Activity

Copy the given line ℓ and point P.

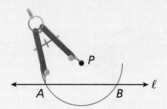

① Place the compass point on P and draw an arc that intersects ℓ at two points. Label the points A and B.

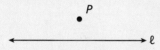

② Construct the perpendicular bisector of $\overline{AB}$.

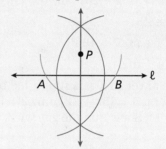

Try This

Copy each diagram and construct a line perpendicular to line ℓ through point P. Use a protractor to verify that the lines are perpendicular.

1.   2.

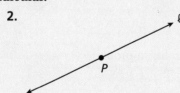

3. Follow the steps below to construct two parallel lines. Explain why ℓ ∥ n.

Step 1 Given a line ℓ, draw a point P not on ℓ.

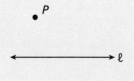

Step 2 Construct line m perpendicular to ℓ through P.

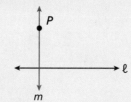

Step 3 Construct line n perpendicular to m through P.

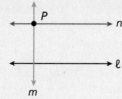

Ready to Go On?

my.hrw.com
Assessment and Intervention

✓ 21-1 Angles Formed by Parallel Lines and Transversals

Find each angle measure.

1.

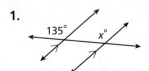

2.

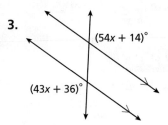

3.

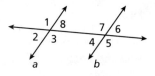

✓ 21-2 Proving Lines Parallel

Use the given information and the theorems and postulates you have learned to show that $a \parallel b$.

4. $m\angle 8 = (13x + 20)°$, $m\angle 6 = (7x + 38)°$, $x = 3$

5. $\angle 1 \cong \angle 5$

6. $m\angle 8 + m\angle 7 = 180°$

7. $m\angle 8 = m\angle 4$

8. The tower shown is supported by guy wires such that $m\angle 1 = (3x + 12)°$, $m\angle 2 = (4x - 2)°$, and $x = 14$. Show that the guy wires are parallel.

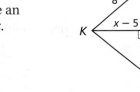

✓ 21-3 Perpendicular Lines

9. Name the shortest segment from point K to $\overline{LN}$.

10. Write and solve an inequality for x.

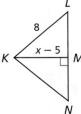

11. Write a two-column proof.
   Given: $\angle 1 \cong \angle 2$, $\ell \perp n$
   Prove: $\ell \perp p$

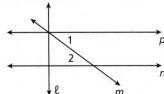

PARCC Assessment Readiness

Selected Response

1. Find m∠RST.

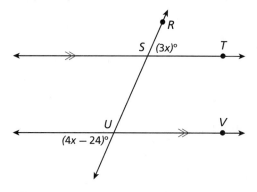

- (A) m∠RST = 108°
- (C) m∠RST = 156°
- (B) m∠RST = 24°
- (D) m∠RST = 72°

2. From the ocean, salmon swim perpendicularly toward the shore to lay their eggs in rivers. Waves in the ocean are parallel to the shore. Why must the salmon swim perpendicularly to the waves?

- (F) Swimming salmon form a transversal to the shore and the waves. The shore and the waves are parallel, and the swimming salmon are perpendicular to the shore. So by the Perpendicular Transversal Theorem, the salmon are perpendicular to the waves.

- (G) Swimming salmon form a transversal to the shore and the waves. The shore and the waves are perpendicular, and the swimming salmon are parallel to the shore. So by the Perpendicular Transversal Theorem, the salmon are perpendicular to the waves.

- (H) Swimming salmon form a transversal to the shore and the waves. The shore and the waves are parallel, and the swimming salmon are parallel to the shore. So by the Perpendicular Transversal Theorem, the salmon are perpendicular to the waves.

- (J) Swimming salmon form a transversal to the shore and the waves. The shore and the waves are parallel, and the swimming salmon are perpendicular to the shore. So by the Parallel Transversal Theorem, the salmon are perpendicular to the waves.

Mini-Tasks

3. In a swimming pool, two lanes are represented by lines l and m. If a string of flags strung across the lanes is represented by transversal t, and $x = 10$, show that the lanes are parallel.

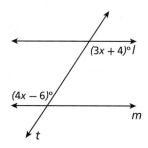

4. **Given:** $\overline{AD} \parallel \overline{BC}$, $\overline{AD} \perp \overline{AB}$, $\overline{DC} \perp \overline{BC}$
   Prove: $\overline{AB} \parallel \overline{CD}$

5. **Given:** $m \perp p$, ∠1 and ∠2 are complementary.
   Prove: $p \parallel q$

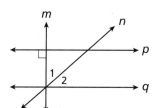

UNIT 7

Module

22

Congruence and Triangles

Contents

 The Common Core Georgia Performance Standards for Mathematical Practice describe varieties of expertise that all students should seek to develop. Opportunities to develop these practices are integrated throughout this program.

1 Make sense of problems and persevere in solving them.

2 Reason abstractly and quantitatively.

3 Construct viable arguments and critique the reasoning of others.

4 Model with mathematics.

5 Use appropriate tools strategically.

6 Attend to precision.

7 Look for and make use of structure.

8 Look for and express regularity in repeated reasoning.

Unpacking the Standards

my.hrw.com
Multilingual Glossary

Understanding the standards and the vocabulary terms in the standards will help you know exactly what you are expected to learn in this chapter.

 MCC9-12.G.CO.10

Prove theorems about triangles.

Key Vocabulary

proof (demostración)
An argument that uses logic to show that a conclusion is true.

theorem (teorema)
A statement that has been proven.

What It Means For You

There are theorems about angle measures involved with triangles, about sides and angles in special types of triangles, and about side and angle relationships that identify when triangles are congruent. Proving these theorems makes them available for solving new problems.

EXAMPLE — **Exterior Angle Theorem**

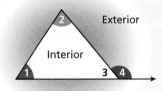

$$m\angle 4 = m\angle 1 + m\angle 2$$

EXAMPLE — **Isosceles Triangle Theorem**

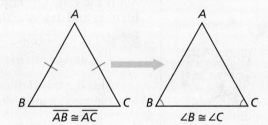

$$\overline{AB} \cong \overline{AC} \qquad \angle B \cong \angle C$$

22-1 Congruence and Transformations

Essential Question: How can you use properties of transformations to determine whether figures are congruent?

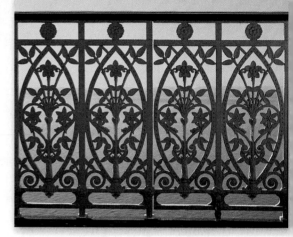

Objectives
Draw, identify, and describe transformations in the coordinate plane.

Use properties of rigid motions to determine whether figures are congruent and to prove figures congruent.

Vocabulary
dilation
isometry
rigid transformation

Why learn this?

Transformations can be used to create frieze patterns in art and architecture, such as in this cast iron gate.

A transformation is a change in the position, shape, or size of a figure. Some types of transformations are translations (slides), reflections (flips), rotations (turns), and *dilations*.

A **dilation** with scale factor $k > 0$ and center $(0, 0)$ maps (x, y) to (kx, ky).

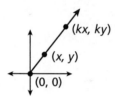

MCC9-12.G.CO.5

Drawing and Identifying Transformations

Apply the transformation M to the polygon with the given vertices. Identify and describe the transformation.

my.hrw.com

Online Video Tutor

A $M : (x, y) \rightarrow (x + 2, y - 5)$
$P(1, 2), Q(4, 4), R(4, 2)$

This is a translation 2 units right and 5 units down.

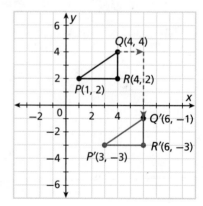

Remember!

In a transformation, the original figure is the preimage. The resulting figure is the image.

B $M : (x, y) \rightarrow (-x, y)$
$A(1, 1), B(3, 2), C(3, 5)$

This is a reflection across the y-axis.

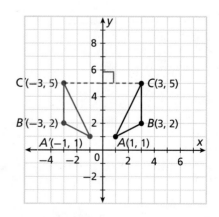

© Allan Baxter/Getty Images

C $M: (x, y) \rightarrow (-y, x)$
$R(1, 2), E(1, 4), C(5, 4), T(5, 2)$

This is a 90° rotation counterclockwise with center of rotation (0, 0).

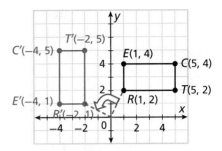

D $M: (x, y) \rightarrow (2x, 2y)$
$K(-1, 2), L(2, 2), N(1, 3)$

This is a dilation with scale factor 2 and center (0, 0).

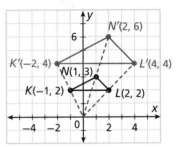

 1. Apply the transformation $M: (x, y) \rightarrow (3x, 3y)$ to the polygon with vertices $D(1, 3), E(1, -2),$ and $F(3, 0)$. Name the coordinates of the image points. Identify and describe the transformation.

Representing Transformations in the Coordinate Plane

TRANSFORMATION	COORDINATE MAPPING AND DESCRIPTION
Translation	$(x, y) \rightarrow (x + a, y + b)$ — Translation a units horizontally and b units vertically
Reflection	$(x, y) \rightarrow (-x, y)$ — Reflection across y-axis
	$(x, y) \rightarrow (x, -y)$ — Reflection across x-axis
Rotation	$(x, y) \rightarrow (y, -x)$ — Rotation about (0, 0), 90° clockwise
	$(x, y) \rightarrow (-y, x)$ — Rotation about (0, 0), 90° counterclockwise
	$(x, y) \rightarrow (-x, -y)$ — Rotation about (0, 0), 180°
Dilation	$(x, y) \rightarrow (kx, ky), k > 0$ — Dilation with scale factor k and center (0, 0)

An **isometry** is a transformation that preserves length, angle measure, and area. Because of these properties, an isometry produces an image that is congruent to the preimage. A **rigid transformation** is another name for an isometry.

Helpful Hint

Translations, reflections, and rotations can be called congruence transformations.

Transformations and Congruence

Translations, reflections, and rotations produce images that are congruent to their preimages.

Dilations with scale factor $k \neq 1$ produce images that are not congruent to their preimages.

You can determine whether some figures are congruent by determining what type of transformation(s) can be applied to one figure to produce the other figure.

EXAMPLE 2

Determining Whether Figures are Congruent

Determine whether the polygons with the given vertices are congruent.

A $A(1, 1)$, $B(4, 1)$, $C(4, 3)$
$P(-4, 2)$, $Q(-1, 2)$, $R(-1, 4)$

The triangles are congruent because $\triangle ABC$ can be mapped to $\triangle PQR$ by a translation:

$(x, y) \rightarrow (x - 5, y + 1)$.

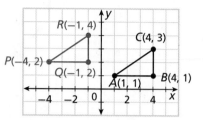

B $A(2, 2)$, $B(-4, 4)$, $C(2, 4)$
$P(3, 3)$, $Q(-6, 6)$, $R(3, 6)$

The triangles are not congruent because $\triangle ABC$ can be mapped to $\triangle PQR$ by a dilation with scale factor $k \neq 1$:

$(x, y) \rightarrow (1.5x, 1.5y)$.

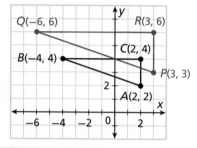

CHECK IT OUT!

2. Determine whether the polygons with the given vertices are congruent. Support your answer by describing a transformation: $A(2, -1)$, $B(3, 0)$, $C(2, 3)$ and $P(1, 2)$, $Q(0, 3)$, $R(-3, 2)$.

You can prove two figures are congruent by showing there are one or more translations, reflections, or rotations that map one figure to the other.

EXAMPLE 3

Applying Transformations

Prove that the polygons with the given vertices are congruent.

$A(3, 1)$, $B(2, -1)$, $C(7, -1)$
$P(-3, -2)$, $Q(-5, -1)$, $R(-5, -6)$

Graph the triangles. There is no apparent single transformation that maps $\triangle ABC$ to $\triangle PQR$. Look for a combination of congruence transformations that map $\triangle ABC$ to $\triangle PQR$.

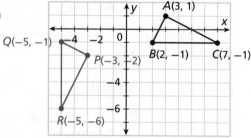

The triangles are congruent because $\triangle ABC$ can be mapped to $\triangle A'B'C'$ by a translation:

$(x, y) \rightarrow (x - 1, y - 4)$; and $\triangle A'B'C'$ can then be mapped to $\triangle PQR$ by a rotation:

$(x, y) \rightarrow (y, -x)$.

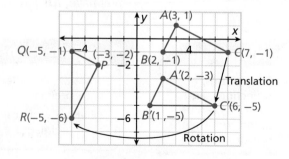

3. Prove that the polygons with the given vertices are congruent: $A(-4, -2)$, $B(-2, 1)$, $C(-2, -2)$ and $P(1, 0)$, $Q(3, -3)$, $R(3, 0)$.

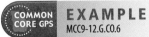
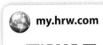

Architecture Application

What transformation is used to create the frieze pattern in this cast iron gate? Are sections of the gate congruent? Explain your answer.

Repeated horizontal translations create the frieze pattern. A translation of any section either to the left or to the right by a distance equal to the width of the section produces an image that is congruent to the preimage.

 4. Sketch a frieze pattern that can be produced by using reflections.

MCC.MP.2 | **MATHEMATICAL PRACTICES**

THINK AND DISCUSS

1. Think of the transformation mapping $(x, y) \rightarrow (x + 5, y - 2)$ as a function with input (x, y). What is the output of the function? If the transformation is applied to a polygon, describe the size, shape, and position of the image compared to the preimage.

2. What type of transformation preserves angle but does not preserve distance?

3. Describe a dilation with center $(0, 0)$ that would produce an image such that every image point is closer to $(0, 0)$ than its corresponding preimage point.

4. GET ORGANIZED
Copy and complete the graphic organizer, including coordinate transformation rules.

> **Congruence Transformations** | **Not Congruence Transformations**

22-1 ## Exercises

GUIDED PRACTICE

Vocabulary Apply the vocabulary from this lesson to answer each question.

1. Dilations with scale factor $k \neq 1$ produce images that ____?____ (*are, are not*) congruent to their preimages.

2. An ____?____ (*isometry, image*) is a transformation that preserves length, angle, and area; it is also called a ____?____ (*translation, rigid transformation*).

©Allan Baxter/Getty Images

SEE EXAMPLE 1

Apply the transformation *M* to the polygon with the given vertices. Name the coordinates of the image points. Identify and describe the transformation.

3. *M*: $(x, y) \rightarrow (x, -y)$
  A(2, 1), *B*(5, 4), *C*(5, 1)

4. *M*: $(x, y) \rightarrow (3x, 3y)$
  P(−2, 1), *Q*(−1, 2), *R*(0, 1)

5. *M*: $(x, y) \rightarrow (y, -x)$
  L(3, 1), *M*(3, 4), *N*(5, 4), *O*(5, 1)

6. *M*: $(x, y) \rightarrow (x - 3, y + 2)$
  D(4, −1), *E*(7, 3), *F*(7, −1)

SEE EXAMPLE 2

Determine whether the polygons with the given vertices are congruent. Support your answer by describing a transformation.

7. *A*(−4, 4), *B*(−4, 6), *C*(2, 6), *D*(2, 4) and *W*(−2, 2), *X*(−2, 3), *Y*(1, 3), *Z*(1, 2)

8. *A*(−2, −2), *B*(−4, −1), *C*(−1, −1) and *T*(2, 2), *U*(4, 1), *V*(1, 1)

SEE EXAMPLE 3

Prove that the polygons with the given vertices are congruent.

9. *J*(−5, 2), *K*(−2, 5), *L*(−2, 2) and *M*(5, 0), *N*(2, 3), *O*(2, 0)

10. *D*(−1, −5), *E*(−4, −4), *F*(−1, −2) and *X*(3, 4), *Y*(6, 3), *Z*(3, 1)

SEE EXAMPLE 4

11. Victorian Crafts What transformation is used to create the frieze pattern in the wallpaper shown? Are there any congruent sections of the wallpaper? Explain your answer.

12. Sketch a frieze pattern that can be produced by using reflections and/or translations.

PRACTICE AND PROBLEM SOLVING

Independent Practice	
For Exercises	See Example
13–18	1
19–21	2
22–24	3
25	4

my.hrw.com

Online Extra Practice

Apply the transformation *M* to the polygon with the given vertices. Name the coordinates of the image points. Identify and describe the transformation.

13. *M*: $(x, y) \rightarrow (x + 5, y - 4)$
  G(4, −1), *H*(7, 3), *I*(7, −1)

14. *M*: $(x, y) \rightarrow (-x, y)$
  P(3, 2), *Q*(6, 2), *R*(3, 5)

15. *M*: $(x, y) \rightarrow (1.5x, 1.5y)$
  L(−1, 4), *M*(−4, 4), *N*(−4, 3)

16. *M*: $(x, y) \rightarrow (-y, x)$
  A(−7, 6), *B*(−7, 4), *C*(−4, 6), *D*(−4, 4)

17. *M*: $(x, y) \rightarrow (x - 1, y + 1)$
  N(1, −2), *O*(0, 4), *P*(2, 4)

18. *M*: $(x, y) \rightarrow (-x, -y)$
  W(5, 2), *X*(2, 2), *Y*(5, 5)

Determine whether the polygons with the given vertices are congruent. Support your answer by describing a transformation.

19. *J*(−4, 4), *K*(−4, 6), *L*(2, 6), *M*(2, 4) and *A*(4, 4), *B*(6, 4), *C*(6, −2), *D*(4, −2)

20. *P*(−2, −2), *Q*(−4, −1), *R*(−1, −1) and *X*(2, 2), *Y*(4, 1), *Z*(1, 1)

21. *E*(−1, −1), *F*(2, 2), *G*(−3, 3) and *U*(−1, 2), *V*(2, 5), *W*(−3, 6)

Prove that the polygons with the given vertices are congruent.

22. *D*(−5, −1), *E*(−2, 1), *F*(2, −1) and *X*(−1, 1), *Y*(2, −1), *Z*(6, 1)

23. *A*(2, −1), *B*(4, −2), *C*(6, 0) and *D*(−3, −2), *E*(−4, −4), *F*(−2, −6)

24. *P*(−7, 3), *Q*(−8, 7), *R*(−4, 7) and *G*(4, −3), *H*(5, −7), *I*(1, −7)

H.O.T. 25. Quilting Jennifer is designing a quilt. She made this diagram to follow when making her quilt.

  a. What transformation or combination of transformations is used to create the pattern in this quilt design?

  b. Are sections of the quilt congruent? Explain your answer.

  c. What if ... ? How might the design look different if she had used 180° rotations instead?

Apply the transformation M to the polygon with the given vertices. Name the coordinates of the image points. Identify and describe the transformation.

26. $M: (x, y) \rightarrow (x - 3, y + 2)$

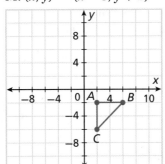

27. $M: (x, y) \rightarrow (y, -x)$

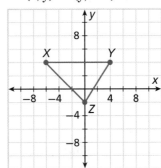

28. Logo Design Eli made this logo design for a company letterhead. What transformation(s) did he use to make the design? Are there any congruent shapes in the design?

Apply the transformations M to the polygon with the given vertices. Name the coordinates of the image points. Identify and describe the transformations.

29. $M: (x, y) \rightarrow (x, -y) \rightarrow (x + 3, y)$

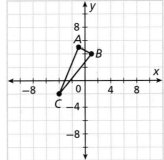

30. $M: (x, y) \rightarrow (3x, 3y) \rightarrow (-y, x)$

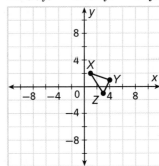

31. **Tessellations** Frank developed a tessellating shape to use in a repeating design. Describe the series of transformations he used to create this square design of his tessellated shape.

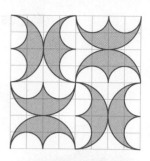

32. **Signal Flags** Seth is going to recreate this signal flag out of fabric. He has light blue and dark blue fabric. What transformations will he perform on the light blue triangles to position them correctly, if he starts in the upper left corner?

H.O.T. 33. ///ERROR ANALYSIS/// Erin and Dave are looking at the triangles on the coordinate plane shown. They are each trying to prove that the triangles are congruent. Who has the correct answer? Explain why.

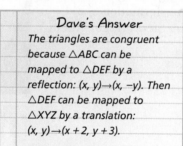

Erin's Answer
The triangles are congruent because △ABC can be mapped to △DEF by a rotation: $(x, y) \rightarrow (-y, x)$. Then △DEF can be mapped to △XYZ by a translation: $(x, y) \rightarrow (x + 2, y + 3)$.

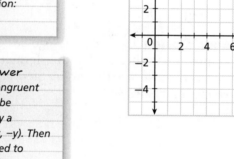

Dave's Answer
The triangles are congruent because △ABC can be mapped to △DEF by a reflection: $(x, y) \rightarrow (x, -y)$. Then △DEF can be mapped to △XYZ by a translation: $(x, y) \rightarrow (x + 2, y + 3)$.

34. **Write About It** Describe the differences in reflecting a polygon and rotating a polygon in terms of the coordinate mapping directions.

H.O.T. 35. **Critical Thinking** How does a dilation of a figure with scale factor 0.5 compare to a dilation of the figure with scale factor 2? Explain.

TEST PREP

36. Alex is trying two transformations that will map the preimage to the image.
    $D(-5, -2), E(-2, -2), F(-4, -5)$ and $X(10, -4), Y(4, -4), Z(8, -10)$
    Which two transformations should he choose?
    A translation and reflection
    B dilation and reflection
    C reflection and rotatoin
    D rotation and dilation

37. Bill applied the transformation M to the polygon. What are the coordinates of the image points for the polygon?

$M: (x, y) \rightarrow (x, -y)$

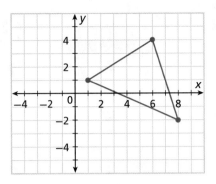

- Ⓐ $A'(1, 1)$, $B'(6, 4)$, $C'(8, -2)$
- Ⓑ $A'(-1, 1)$, $B'(-6, 4)$, $C'(-8, -2)$
- Ⓒ $A'(-1, -1)$, $B'(-6, -4)$, $C'(-8, 2)$
- Ⓓ $A'(1, -1)$, $B'(6, -4)$, $C'(8, 2)$

CHALLENGE AND EXTEND

38. Architecture Steve was visiting the ruins at Mitla, an archeological site in Mexico. He saw this frieze design.

- **a.** Does the frieze have congruent shapes? What transformation or combination of tranformations are used to create the pattern in this frieze design?

- **b. What if ... ?** How might the design have looked if the designers had rotated the S-shapes 90 degrees clockwise and then translated an entire row to make the next row? Sketch your answer.

MATHEMATICAL PRACTICES

FOCUS ON MATHEMATICAL PRACTICES

H.O.T. **39. Communication** Given the coordinates of the vertices of a polygon and the corresponding coordinates of a second polygon, explain how to determine whether one polygon is a dilation of the other with center $(0, 0)$.

H.O.T. **40. Patterns** An arrow in Quadrant I is pointing to the right. It is reflected repeatedly across the x-axis and y-axis until there is an image in every quadrant. What direction does the arrow point in each of the other three quadrants? How would you answer this question if the arrow in Quadrant I is pointing down?

H.O.T. **41. Analysis** The vertices of a triangle are $K(-4, 9)$, $L(2, 0)$, and $M(8, -1)$. After a transformation, two of the image vertices are $L'(-2, 0)$ and $M'(-8, 1)$. What are the coordinates of K'? Describe the transformation.

H.O.T. **42. Proof** Given that $(x, y) \rightarrow (-y, x)$ represents a 90° counterclockwise rotation about $(0, 0)$, prove that $(x, y) \rightarrow (-x, -y)$ represents a 180° rotation about $(0, 0)$.

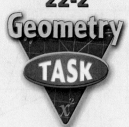

22-2
Geometry TASK

Develop the Triangle Sum Theorem

In this task, you will use patty paper to discover a relationship between the measures of the interior angles of a triangle.

Use with *Angle Relationships in Triangles*

Look for and express regularity in repeated reasoning.

MCC9-12.G.CO.10 Prove theorems about triangles.

Activity

1 Draw and label △*ABC* on a sheet of notebook paper.

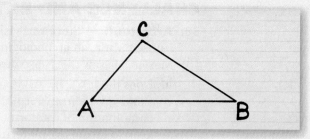

2 On patty paper draw a line ℓ and label a point *P* on the line.

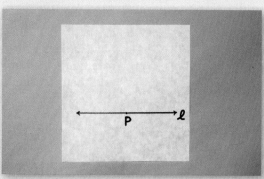

3 Place the patty paper on top of the triangle you drew. Align the papers so that $\overline{AB}$ is on line ℓ and *P* and *B* coincide. Trace ∠*B*. Rotate the triangle and trace ∠*C* adjacent to ∠*B*. Rotate the triangle again and trace ∠*A* adjacent to ∠*C*. The diagram shows your final step.

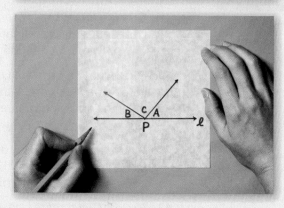

Try This

1. What do you notice about the three angles of the triangle that you traced?

2. Repeat the activity two more times using two different triangles. Do you get the same results each time?

3. Write an equation describing the relationship among the measures of the angles of △*ABC*.

4. Use inductive reasoning to write a conjecture about the sum of the measures of the angles of a triangle.

22-2 Angle Relationships in Triangles

? *Essential Question:* What are some theorems about the measures of angles in triangles?

Objectives
Find the measures of interior and exterior angles of triangles.

Apply theorems about the interior and exterior angles of triangles.

Vocabulary
auxiliary line
corollary
interior
exterior
interior angle
exterior angle
remote interior angle

Who uses this?
Surveyors use triangles to make measurements and create boundaries. (See Example 1.)

Triangulation is a method used in surveying. Land is divided into adjacent triangles. By measuring the sides and angles of one triangle and applying properties of triangles, surveyors can gather information about adjacent triangles.

This engraving shows the county surveyor and commissioners laying out the town of Baltimore in 1730.

Theorem 22-2-1 **Triangle Sum Theorem**

The sum of the angle measures of a triangle is 180°.

$$m\angle A + m\angle B + m\angle C = 180°$$

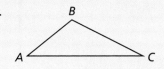

The proof of the Triangle Sum Theorem uses an *auxiliary line*. An **auxiliary line** is a line that is added to a figure to aid in a proof.

PROOF **Triangle Sum Theorem**

Given: △*ABC*
Prove: m∠1 + m∠2 + m∠3 = 180°

Proof:

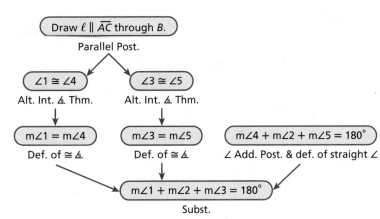

Alamy/PhotoCongress/CORBIS

EXAMPLE 1
MCC9-12.G.MG.1

COMMON CORE GPS

Surveying Application

The map of France commonly used in the 1600s was significantly revised as a result of a triangulation land survey. The diagram shows part of the survey map. Use the diagram to find the indicated angle measures.

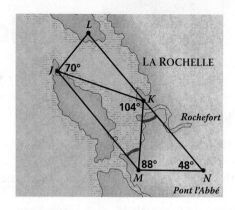

A m∠NKM

m∠KMN + m∠MNK + m∠NKM = 180°	△ Sum Thm.
88 + 48 + m∠NKM = 180	Substitute 88 for m∠KMN and 48 for m∠MNK.
136 + m∠NKM = 180	Simplify.
m∠NKM = 44°	Subtract 136 from both sides.

B m∠JLK

Step 1 Find m∠JKL.

m∠NKM + m∠MKJ + m∠JKL = 180°	Lin. Pair Thm. & ∠ Add. Post.
44 + 104 + m∠JKL = 180	Substitute 44 for m∠NKM and 104 for m∠MKJ.
148 + m∠JKL = 180	Simplify.
m∠JKL = 32°	Subtract 148 from both sides.

Step 2 Use substitution and then solve for m∠JLK.

m∠JLK + m∠JKL + m∠KJL = 180°	△ Sum Thm.
m∠JLK + 32 + 70 = 180	Substitute 32 for m∠JKL and 70 for m∠KJL.
m∠JLK + 102 = 180	Simplify.
m∠JLK = 78°	Subtract 102 from both sides.

CHECK IT OUT! **1.** Use the diagram to find m∠MJK.

A **corollary** is a theorem whose proof follows directly from another theorem. Here are two corollaries to the Triangle Sum Theorem.

Know it! Note

Corollaries

COROLLARY	HYPOTHESIS	CONCLUSION
22-2-2 The acute angles of a right triangle are complementary.	*(triangle with vertices D, F, E; right angle at F)*	∠D and ∠E are complementary. m∠D + m∠E = 90°
22-2-3 The measure of each angle of an equiangular triangle is 60°.	*(triangle with vertices A, B, C)*	m∠A = m∠B = m∠C = 60°

You will prove Corollaries 22-2-2 and 22-2-3 in Exercises 24 and 25.

Online Video Tutor

EXAMPLE 2 Finding Angle Measures in Right Triangles

MCC9-12.A.CED.1

One of the acute angles in a right triangle measures 22.9°. What is the measure of the other acute angle?

Let the acute angles be $\angle M$ and $\angle N$, with $m\angle M = 22.9°$.

$m\angle M + m\angle N = 90$	Acute $\angle$ of rt. $\triangle$ are comp.
$22.9 + m\angle N = 90$	Substitute 22.9 for $m\angle M$.
$m\angle N = 67.1°$	Subtract 22.9 from both sides.

 CHECK IT OUT! The measure of one of the acute angles in a right triangle is given. What is the measure of the other acute angle?

2a. $63.7°$ **2b.** $x°$ **2c.** $48\frac{2}{5}°$

The **interior** is the set of all points inside the figure. The **exterior** is the set of all points outside the figure. An **interior angle** is formed by two sides of a triangle. An **exterior angle** is formed by one side of the triangle and the extension of an adjacent side. Each exterior angle has two *remote interior angles*. A **remote interior angle** is an interior angle that is not adjacent to the exterior angle.

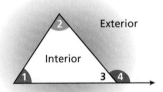

$\angle 4$ is an exterior angle. Its remote interior angles are $\angle 1$ and $\angle 2$.

Theorem 22-2-4   **Exterior Angle Theorem**

The measure of an exterior angle of a triangle is equal to the sum of the measures of its remote interior angles.

$$m\angle 4 = m\angle 1 + m\angle 2$$

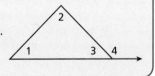

You will prove Theorem 22-2-4 in Exercise 28.

Online Video Tutor

EXAMPLE 3 Applying the Exterior Angle Theorem

MCC9-12.A.CED.1

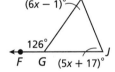

Find $m\angle J$.

$m\angle J + m\angle H = m\angle FGH$	Ext. $\angle$ Thm.
$5x + 17 + 6x - 1 = 126$	Substitute $5x + 17$ for $m\angle J$, $6x - 1$ for $m\angle H$, and 126 for $m\angle FGH$.
$11x + 16 = 126$	Simplify.
$11x = 110$	Subtract 16 from both sides.
$x = 10$	Divide both sides by 11.

$m\angle J = 5x + 17 = 5(10) + 17 = 67°$

 CHECK IT OUT! **3.** Find $m\angle ACD$.

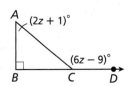

Theorem 22-2-5 **Third Angles Theorem**

THEOREM	HYPOTHESIS	CONCLUSION
If two angles of one triangle are congruent to two angles of another triangle, then the third pair of angles are congruent.	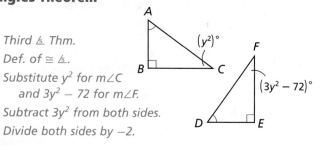	$\angle N \cong \angle T$

You will prove Theorem 22-2-5 in Exercise 27.

EXAMPLE 4
MCC9-12.A.CED.1

my.hrw.com

Online Video Tutor

Applying the Third Angles Theorem

Find m$\angle C$ and m$\angle F$.

$\angle C \cong \angle F$	*Third $\angle$s Thm.*
m$\angle C =$ m$\angle F$	*Def. of $\cong$ $\angle$s.*
$y^2 = 3y^2 - 72$	*Substitute y^2 for m$\angle C$ and $3y^2 - 72$ for m$\angle F$.*
$-2y^2 = -72$	*Subtract $3y^2$ from both sides.*
$y^2 = 36$	*Divide both sides by -2.*

So m$\angle C = 36°$.
Since m$\angle F =$ m$\angle C$, m$\angle F = 36°$.

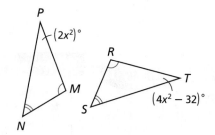

CHECK IT OUT!

4. Find m$\angle P$ and m$\angle T$.

MCC.MP.3 **MATHEMATICAL PRACTICES**

THINK AND DISCUSS

1. Use the Triangle Sum Theorem to explain why the supplement of one of the angles of a triangle equals in measure the sum of the other two angles of the triangle. Support your answer with a sketch.

2. Sketch a triangle and draw all of its exterior angles. How many exterior angles are there at each vertex of the triangle? How many total exterior angles does the triangle have?

3. GET ORGANIZED Copy and complete the graphic organizer. In each box, write each theorem in words and then draw a diagram to represent it.

Theorem	Words	Diagram
Triangle Sum Theorem		
Exterior Angle Theorem		
Third Angles Theorem		

GUIDED PRACTICE

Vocabulary Apply the vocabulary from this lesson to answer each question.

1. To remember the meaning of *remote interior angle*, think of a television remote control. What is another way to remember the term *remote*?

2. An *exterior angle* is drawn at vertex E of $\triangle DEF$. What are its *remote interior angles*?

3. What do you call segments, rays, or lines that are added to a given diagram?

SEE EXAMPLE 1
Astronomy Use the following information for Exercises 4 and 5.

An *asterism* is a group of stars that is easier to recognize than a constellation. One popular asterism is the Summer Triangle, which is composed of the stars Deneb, Altair, and Vega.

4. What is the value of y?

5. What is the measure of each angle in the Summer Triangle?

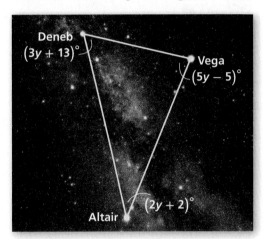

Deneb $(3y + 13)°$

Vega $(5y - 5)°$

$(2y + 2)°$

Altair

SEE EXAMPLE 2
The measure of one of the acute angles in a right triangle is given. What is the measure of the other acute angle?

6. $20.8°$ 7. $y°$ 8. $24\frac{2}{3}°$

SEE EXAMPLE 3
Find each angle measure.

9. $m\angle M$

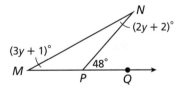

N
$(2y + 2)°$
$(3y + 1)°$
M $48°$ P Q

10. $m\angle L$

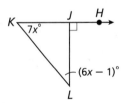

K $7x°$ J H
$(6x - 1)°$
L

11. In $\triangle ABC$, $m\angle A = 65°$, and the measure of an exterior angle at C is $117°$. Find $m\angle B$ and the $m\angle BCA$.

SEE EXAMPLE 4
12. $m\angle C$ and $m\angle F$

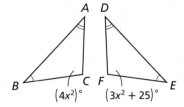

A D
B C F E
$(4x^2)°$ $(3x^2 + 25)°$

13. $m\angle S$ and $m\angle U$

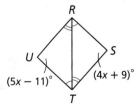

R
U S
$(5x - 11)°$ $(4x + 9)°$
T

14. For $\triangle ABC$ and $\triangle XYZ$, $m\angle A = m\angle X$ and $m\angle B = m\angle Y$. Find the measures of $\angle C$ and $\angle Z$ if $m\angle C = 4x + 7$ and $m\angle Z = 3(x + 5)$.

Eckhard Slawik/Photo Researchers

PRACTICE AND PROBLEM SOLVING

Independent Practice

For Exercises	See Example
15	1
16–18	2
19–20	3
21–22	4

my.hrw.com

Online Extra Practice

15. Navigation A sailor on ship A measures the angle between ship B and the pier and finds that it is 39°. A sailor on ship B measures the angle between ship A and the pier and finds that it is 57°. What is the measure of the angle between ships A and B?

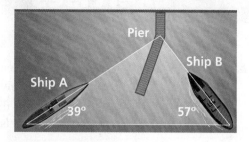

The measure of one of the acute angles in a right triangle is given. What is the measure of the other acute angle?

16. $76\frac{1}{4}°$

17. $2x°$

18. $56.8°$

Find each angle measure.

19. m∠XYZ

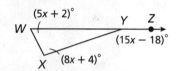

20. m∠C

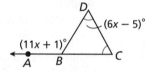

21. m∠N and m∠P

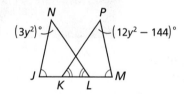

22. m∠Q and m∠S

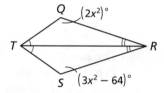

H.O.T. 23. Multi-Step The measures of the angles of a triangle are in the ratio 1:4:7. What are the measures of the angles? (*Hint:* Let x, $4x$, and $7x$ represent the angle measures.)

24. Complete the proof of Corollary 22-2-2.

Given: △DEF with right ∠F
Prove: ∠D and ∠E are complementary.
Proof:

Statements	Reasons
1. △DEF with rt. ∠F	1. a. __?__
2. b. __?__	2. Def. of rt. ∠
3. m∠D + m∠E + m∠F = 180°	3. c. __?__
4. m∠D + m∠E + 90° = 180°	4. d. __?__
5. e. __?__	5. Subtr. Prop.
6. ∠D and ∠E are comp.	6. f. __?__

H.O.T. 25. Prove Corollary 22-2-3 using two different methods of proof.

Given: △ABC is equiangular.
Prove: m∠A = m∠B = m∠C = 60°

H.O.T. 26. Multi-Step The measure of one acute angle in a right triangle is $1\frac{1}{4}$ times the measure of the other acute angle. What is the measure of the larger acute angle?

27. Write a two-column proof of the Third Angles Theorem.

28. Prove the Exterior Angle Theorem.

Given: △ABC with exterior angle ∠ACD
Prove: m∠ACD = m∠A + m∠B
(*Hint:* ∠BCA and ∠DCA form a linear pair.)

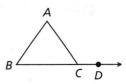

Find each angle measure.

29. ∠UXW

30. ∠UWY

31. ∠WZX

32. ∠XYZ

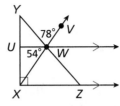

33. Critical Thinking What is the measure of any exterior angle of an equiangular triangle? What is the sum of the exterior angle measures?

34. Find m∠SRQ, given that ∠P ≅ ∠U, ∠Q ≅ ∠T, and m∠RST = 37.5°.

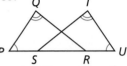

35. Multi-Step In a right triangle, one acute angle measure is 4 times the other acute angle measure. What is the measure of the smaller angle?

36. Aviation To study the forces of lift and drag, the Wright brothers built a glider, attached two ropes to it, and flew it like a kite. They modeled the two wind forces as the legs of a right triangle.

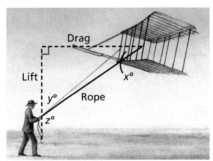

  a. What part of a right triangle is formed by each rope?

  b. Use the Triangle Sum Theorem to write an equation relating the angle measures in the right triangle.

  c. Simplify the equation from part **b**. What is the relationship between *x* and *y*?

  d. Use the Exterior Angle Theorem to write an expression for *z* in terms of *x*.

  e. If *x* = 37°, use your results from parts **c** and **d** to find *y* and *z*.

37. Estimation Draw a triangle and two exterior angles at each vertex. Estimate the measure of each angle. How are the exterior angles at each vertex related? Explain.

38. Given: $\overline{AB} \perp \overline{BD}$, $\overline{BD} \perp \overline{DC}$, ∠A ≅ ∠C
    Prove: $\overline{AD} \parallel \overline{CB}$

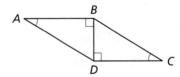

H.O.T. 39. Write About It A triangle has angle measures of 115°, 40°, and 25°. Explain how to find the measures of the triangle's exterior angles. Support your answer with a sketch.

Real-World Connections

40. One of the steps in making an origami crane involves folding a square sheet of paper into the shape shown.

  a. ∠DCE is a right angle. $\overline{FC}$ bisects ∠DCE, and $\overline{BC}$ bisects ∠FCE. Find m∠FCB.

  b. Use the Triangle Sum Theorem to find m∠CBE.

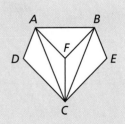

TEST PREP

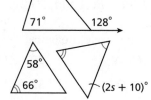

41. What is the value of *x*?

    Ⓐ 19   Ⓒ 57

    Ⓑ 52   Ⓓ 71

42. Find the value of *s*.

    Ⓕ 23   Ⓗ 34

    Ⓖ 28   Ⓙ 56

43. $\angle A$ and $\angle B$ are the remote interior angles of $\angle BCD$ in $\triangle ABC$. Which of these equations must be true?

    Ⓐ $m\angle A - 180° = m\angle B$ Ⓒ $m\angle BCD = m\angle BCA - m\angle A$

    Ⓑ $m\angle A = 90° - m\angle B$ Ⓓ $m\angle B = m\angle BCD - m\angle A$

H.O.T. 44. Extended Response The measures of the angles in a triangle are in the ratio 2:3:4. Describe how to use algebra to find the measures of these angles. Then find the measure of each angle and classify the triangle.

CHALLENGE AND EXTEND

45. An exterior angle of a triangle measures 117°. Its remote interior angles measure $\left(2y^2 + 7\right)°$ and $\left(61 - y^2\right)°$. Find the value of *y*.

H.O.T. 46. Two parallel lines are intersected by a transversal. What type of triangle is formed by the intersection of the angle bisectors of two same-side interior angles? Explain. (*Hint:* Use geometry software or construct a diagram of the angle bisectors of two same-side interior angles.)

47. Critical Thinking Explain why an exterior angle of a triangle cannot be congruent to a remote interior angle.

48. Probability The measure of each angle in a triangle is a multiple of 30°. What is the probability that the triangle has at least two congruent angles?

49. In $\triangle ABC$, $m\angle B$ is 5° less than $1\frac{1}{2}$ times $m\angle A$. $m\angle C$ is 5° less than $2\frac{1}{2}$ times $m\angle A$. What is $m\angle A$ in degrees?

FOCUS ON MATHEMATICAL PRACTICES

H.O.T. 50. Modeling Sketch a scalene triangle with a 90° exterior angle.

H.O.T. 51. Justify A right triangle has an acute angle of 63°. A second right triangle has an acute angle of 27°. How many pairs of congruent angles do the two triangles have? Justify your answer.

H.O.T. 52. Analysis Explain why a triangle can have, at most, one obtuse angle.

H.O.T. 53. Make a Conjecture Given that the exterior angle measure of a triangle equals the sum of the two remote interior angle measures, what must be the sum of three exterior angle measures (one at each vertex)? Justify your answer.

22-3 Congruent Triangles

Essential Question: How can you use corresponding sides and corresponding angles to show that triangles are congruent?

Objectives
Use properties of congruent triangles.

Prove triangles congruent by using the definition of congruence.

Vocabulary
corresponding angles
corresponding sides
congruent polygons

Animated Math

Who uses this?
Machinists used triangles to construct a model of the International Space Station's support structure.

Geometric figures are congruent if they are the same size and shape.
Corresponding angles and **corresponding sides** are in the same position in polygons with an equal number of sides. Two polygons are **congruent polygons** if and only if their corresponding angles and sides are congruent. Thus triangles that are the same size and shape are congruent.

Know it! Note

Properties of Congruent Polygons

Helpful Hint

Two vertices that are the endpoints of a side are called consecutive vertices. For example, P and Q are consecutive vertices.

DIAGRAM	CORRESPONDING ANGLES	CORRESPONDING SIDES
$\triangle ABC \cong \triangle DEF$	$\angle A \cong \angle D$ $\angle B \cong \angle E$ $\angle C \cong \angle F$	$\overline{AB} \cong \overline{DE}$ $\overline{BC} \cong \overline{EF}$ $\overline{AC} \cong \overline{DF}$
polygon $PQRS \cong$ polygon $WXYZ$	$\angle P \cong \angle W$ $\angle Q \cong \angle X$ $\angle R \cong \angle Y$ $\angle S \cong \angle Z$	$\overline{PQ} \cong \overline{WX}$ $\overline{QR} \cong \overline{XY}$ $\overline{RS} \cong \overline{YZ}$ $\overline{PS} \cong \overline{WZ}$

To name a polygon, write the vertices in consecutive order. For example, you can name polygon $PQRS$ as $QRSP$ or $SRQP$, but **not** as $PRQS$. In a congruence statement, the order of the vertices indicates the corresponding parts.

COMMON CORE GPS
MCC9-12.G.CO.7

EXAMPLE 1

my.hrw.com

Online Video Tutor

Naming Congruent Corresponding Parts

$\triangle RST$ and $\triangle XYZ$ represent the triangles of the space station's support structure. If $\triangle RST \cong \triangle XYZ$, identify all pairs of congruent corresponding parts.

Angles: $\angle R \cong \angle X$, $\angle S \cong \angle Y$, $\angle T \cong \angle Z$
Sides: $\overline{RS} \cong \overline{XY}$, $\overline{ST} \cong \overline{YZ}$, $\overline{RT} \cong \overline{XZ}$

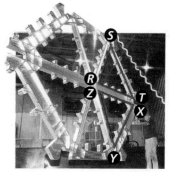

CHECK IT OUT!

1. If polygon $LMNP \cong$ polygon $EFGH$, identify all pairs of corresponding congruent parts.

EXAMPLE MCC9-12.A.CED.1 **2**

Using Corresponding Parts of Congruent Triangles

Given: $\triangle EFH \cong \triangle GFH$

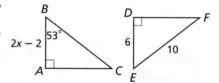

A Find the value of x.

$\angle FHE$ and $\angle FHG$ are rt. $\angle$s.	Def. of $\perp$ lines
$\angle FHE \cong \angle FHG$	Rt. $\angle \cong$ Thm.
$m\angle FHE = m\angle FHG$	Def. of $\cong \angle$s
$(6x - 12)° = 90°$	Substitute values for $m\angle FHE$ and $m\angle FHG$.
$6x = 102$	Add 12 to both sides.
$x = 17$	Divide both sides by 6.

B Find $m\angle GFH$.

$m\angle EFH + m\angle FHE + m\angle E = 180°$	$\triangle$ Sum Thm.
$m\angle EFH + 90 + 21.6 = 180$	Substitute values for $m\angle FHE$ and $m\angle E$.
$m\angle EFH + 111.6 = 180$	Simplify.
$m\angle EFH = 68.4$	Subtract 111.6 from both sides.
$\angle GFH \cong \angle EFH$	Corr. $\angle$s of $\cong$ $\triangle$s are $\cong$.
$m\angle GFH = m\angle EFH$	Def. of $\cong \angle$s
$m\angle GFH = 68.4°$	Trans. Prop. of $=$

Given: $\triangle ABC \cong \triangle DEF$

2a. Find the value of x.

2b. Find $m\angle F$.

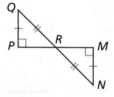

EXAMPLE MCC9-12.G.CO.10 **3**

Proving Triangles Congruent

Given: $\angle P$ and $\angle M$ are right angles.
R is the midpoint of $\overline{PM}$.
$\overline{PQ} \cong \overline{MN}$, $\overline{QR} \cong \overline{NR}$

Prove: $\triangle PQR \cong \triangle MNR$

Proof:

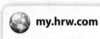
Statements	Reasons
1. $\angle P$ and $\angle M$ are rt. $\angle$s	**1.** Given
2. $\angle P \cong \angle M$	**2.** Rt. $\angle \cong$ Thm.
3. $\angle PRQ \cong \angle MRN$	**3.** Vert. $\angle$s Thm.
4. $\angle Q \cong \angle N$	**4.** Third $\angle$ Thm.
5. R is the mdpt. of $\overline{PM}$.	**5.** Given
6. $\overline{PR} \cong \overline{MR}$	**6.** Def. of mdpt.
7. $\overline{PQ} \cong \overline{MN}$; $\overline{QR} \cong \overline{NR}$	**7.** Given
8. $\triangle PQR \cong \triangle MNR$	**8.** Def. of $\cong$ $\triangle$s

3. Given: $\overline{AD}$ bisects $\overline{BE}$.
$\overline{BE}$ bisects $\overline{AD}$.
$\overline{AB} \cong \overline{DE}$, $\angle A \cong \angle D$

Prove: $\triangle ABC \cong \triangle DEC$

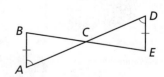

Overlapping Triangles

Cecelia Medina
Lamar High School

"With overlapping triangles, it helps me to redraw the triangles separately. That way I can mark what I know about one triangle without getting confused by the other one."

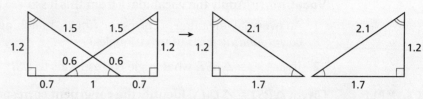

EXAMPLE MCC9-12.G.CO.10 **4**

my.hrw.com

Online Video Tutor

Engineering Application

The bars that give structural support to a roller coaster form triangles. Since the angle measures and the lengths of the corresponding sides are the same, the triangles are congruent.

Given: $\overline{JK} \perp \overline{KL}$, $\overline{ML} \perp \overline{KL}$, $\angle KLJ \cong \angle LKM$, $\overline{JK} \cong \overline{ML}$, $\overline{JL} \cong \overline{MK}$

Prove: $\triangle JKL \cong \triangle MLK$

Proof:

Statements	Reasons
1. $\overline{JK} \perp \overline{KL}$, $\overline{ML} \perp \overline{KL}$	1. Given
2. $\angle JKL$ and $\angle MLK$ are rt. ∡.	2. Def. of ⊥ lines
3. $\angle JKL \cong \angle MLK$	3. Rt. ∠ ≅ Thm.
4. $\angle KLJ \cong \angle LKM$	4. Given
5. $\angle KJL \cong \angle LMK$	5. Third ∡ Thm.
6. $\overline{JK} \cong \overline{ML}$, $\overline{JL} \cong \overline{MK}$	6. Given
7. $\overline{KL} \cong \overline{LK}$	7. Reflex. Prop. of ≅
8. $\triangle JKL \cong \triangle MLK$	8. Def. of ≅ ▲

Helpful Hint

When you write a statement such as $\triangle JKL \cong \triangle MLK$, you are also stating which parts are congruent.

 CHECK IT OUT!

4. Use the diagram to prove the following.
Given: $\overline{MK}$ bisects $\overline{JL}$. $\overline{JL}$ bisects $\overline{MK}$. $\overline{JK} \cong \overline{ML}$, $\overline{JK} \parallel \overline{ML}$
Prove: $\triangle JKN \cong \triangle LMN$

MCC.MP.4 **MATHEMATICAL PRACTICES**

THINK AND DISCUSS

1. A roof truss is a triangular structure that supports a roof. How can you be sure that two roof trusses are the same size and shape?

2. **GET ORGANIZED** Copy and complete the graphic organizer. In each box, name the congruent corresponding parts.

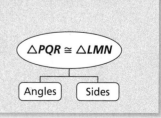

$\triangle PQR \cong \triangle LMN$

Angles | Sides

GUIDED PRACTICE

Vocabulary Apply the vocabulary from this lesson to answer each question.

1. An everyday meaning of *corresponding* is "matching." How can this help you find the *corresponding* parts of two triangles?

2. If △ABC ≅ △RST, what angle corresponds to ∠S?

SEE EXAMPLE 1 **Given:** △RST ≅ △LMN. **Identify the congruent corresponding parts.**

3. $\overline{RS}$ ≅ ___?___   4. $\overline{LN}$ ≅ ___?___   5. ∠S ≅ ___?___

6. $\overline{TS}$ ≅ ___?___   7. ∠L ≅ ___?___   8. ∠N ≅ ___?___

SEE EXAMPLE 2 **Given:** △FGH ≅ △JKL. **Find each value.**

9. KL   10. x

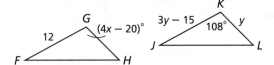

SEE EXAMPLE 3 11. **Given:** E is the midpoint of $\overline{AC}$ and $\overline{BD}$.
$\overline{AB} \cong \overline{CD}$, $\overline{AB} \parallel \overline{CD}$
Prove: △ABE ≅ △CDE

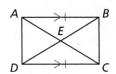

Proof:

Statements	Reasons
1. $\overline{AB} \parallel \overline{CD}$	1. a. ___?___
2. ∠ABE ≅ ∠CDE, ∠BAE ≅ ∠DCE	2. b. ___?___
3. $\overline{AB} \cong \overline{CD}$	3. c. ___?___
4. E is the mdpt. of $\overline{AC}$ and $\overline{BD}$.	4. d. ___?___
5. e. ___?___	5. Def. of mdpt.
6. ∠AEB ≅ ∠CED	6. f. ___?___
7. △ABE ≅ △CDE	7. g. ___?___

SEE EXAMPLE 4 12. **Engineering** The geodesic dome shown is a 14-story building that models Earth. Use the given information to prove that the triangles that make up the sphere are congruent.

Given: $\overline{SU} \cong \overline{ST} \cong \overline{SR}$, $\overline{TU} \cong \overline{TR}$, ∠UST ≅ ∠RST, and ∠U ≅ ∠R
Prove: △RTS ≅ △UTS

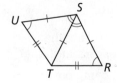

PRACTICE AND PROBLEM SOLVING

Independent Practice

For Exercises	See Example
13–16	1
17–18	2
19	3
20	4

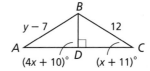
my.hrw.com

Online Extra Practice

Given: Polygon $CDEF \cong$ polygon $KLMN$. Identify the congruent corresponding parts.

13. $\overline{DE} \cong$ ___?___

14. $\overline{KN} \cong$ ___?___

15. $\angle F \cong$ ___?___

16. $\angle L \cong$ ___?___

Given: $\triangle ABD \cong \triangle CBD$. Find each value.

17. $m\angle C$ 18. y

19. **Given:** $\overline{MP}$ bisects $\angle NMR$. P is the midpoint of $\overline{NR}$. $\overline{MN} \cong \overline{MR}$, $\angle N \cong \angle R$
   Prove: $\triangle MNP \cong \triangle MRP$

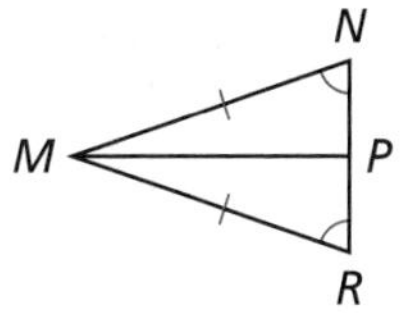

   Proof:

Statements	Reasons
1. $\angle N \cong \angle R$	1. a. ___?___
2. $\overline{MP}$ bisects $\angle NMR$.	2. b. ___?___
3. c. ___?___	3. Def. of $\angle$ bisector
4. d. ___?___	4. Third $\angle$ Thm.
5. P is the mdpt. of $\overline{NR}$.	5. e. ___?___
6. f. ___?___	6. Def. of mdpt.
7. $\overline{MN} \cong \overline{MR}$	7. g. ___?___
8. $\overline{MP} \cong \overline{MP}$	8. h. ___?___
9. $\triangle MNP \cong \triangle MRP$	9. Def. of $\cong$ $\triangle$

H.O.T. 20. **Hobbies** In a garden, triangular flower beds are separated by straight rows of grass as shown.

   Given: $\angle ADC$ and $\angle BCD$ are right angles. $\overline{AC} \cong \overline{BD}$, $\overline{AD} \cong \overline{BC}$ $\angle DAC \cong \angle CBD$

   Prove: $\triangle ADC \cong \triangle BCD$

21. For two triangles, the following corresponding parts are given: $\overline{GS} \cong \overline{KP}$, $\overline{GR} \cong \overline{KH}$, $\overline{SR} \cong \overline{PH}$, $\angle S \cong \angle P$, $\angle G \cong \angle K$, and $\angle R \cong \angle H$. Write three different congruence statements.

22. The two polygons in the diagram are congruent. Complete the following congruence statement for the polygons. polygon R ___?___ $\cong$ polygon V ___?___

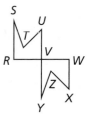

Write and solve an equation for each of the following.

23. $\triangle ABC \cong \triangle DEF$. $AB = 2x - 10$, and $DE = x + 20$. Find the value of x and AB.

24. $\triangle JKL \cong \triangle MNP$. $m\angle L = \left(x^2 + 10\right)^\circ$, and $m\angle P = \left(2x^2 + 1\right)^\circ$. What is $m\angle L$?

25. Polygon $ABCD \cong$ polygon $PQRS$. $BC = 6x + 5$, and $QR = 5x + 7$. Find the value of x and BC.

Real-World Connections

26. Many origami models begin with a square piece of paper, *JKLM*, that is folded along both diagonals to make the creases shown. $\overline{JL}$ and $\overline{MK}$ are perpendicular bisectors of each other, and $\angle NML \cong \angle NKL$.

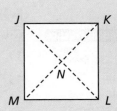

a. Explain how you know that $\overline{KL}$ and $\overline{ML}$ are congruent.

b. Prove $\triangle NML \cong \triangle NKL$.

H.O.T. 27. Draw a diagram and then write a proof.
Given: $\overline{BD} \perp \overline{AC}$. *D* is the midpoint of $\overline{AC}$. $\overline{AB} \cong \overline{CB}$, and $\overline{BD}$ bisects $\angle ABC$.
Prove: $\triangle ABD \cong \triangle CBD$

28. Critical Thinking Draw two triangles that are not congruent but have an area of 4 cm^2 each.

29. ///**ERROR ANALYSIS**/// Given $\triangle MPQ \cong \triangle EDF$. Two solutions for finding m$\angle E$ are shown. Which is incorrect? Explain the error.

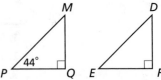

A
Since corr. parts of ≅ △ are ≅, $\angle E \cong \angle P$. So m$\angle E =$ m$\angle P = 44°$.

B
Since the acute ∡ of a rt. △ are comp., m$\angle M = 46°$. $\angle E \cong \angle M$, so m$\angle E = 46°$.

H.O.T. 30. Write About It Given the diagram of the triangles, is there enough information to prove that $\triangle HKL$ is congruent to $\triangle YWX$? Explain.

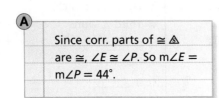

TEST PREP

31. Which congruence statement correctly indicates that the two given triangles are congruent?

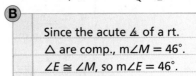

Ⓐ $\triangle ABC \cong \triangle EFD$ Ⓒ $\triangle ABC \cong \triangle DEF$

Ⓑ $\triangle ABC \cong \triangle FDE$ Ⓓ $\triangle ABC \cong \triangle FED$

32. $\triangle MNP \cong \triangle RST$. What are the values of *x* and *y*?

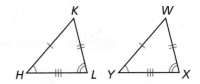

Ⓕ $x = 26$, $y = 21\frac{1}{3}$ Ⓗ $x = 25$, $y = 20\frac{2}{3}$

Ⓖ $x = 27$, $y = 20$ Ⓙ $x = 30\frac{1}{3}$, $y = 16\frac{2}{3}$

33. $\triangle ABC \cong \triangle XYZ$. m$\angle A = 47.1°$, and m$\angle C = 13.8°$. Find m$\angle Y$.

Ⓐ 13.8 Ⓒ 76.2

Ⓑ 42.9 Ⓓ 119.1

34. $\triangle MNR \cong \triangle SPQ$, $NL = 18$, $SP = 33$, $SR = 10$, $RQ = 24$, and $QP = 30$. What is the perimeter of $\triangle MNR$?

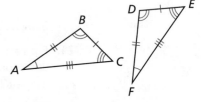

Ⓕ 79 Ⓗ 87

Ⓖ 85 Ⓙ 97

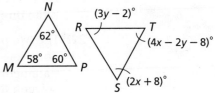

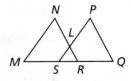

Andy Christiansen/HMH

CHALLENGE AND EXTEND

H.O.T. **35. Multi-Step** Given that the perimeter of *TUVW* is 149 units, find the value of *x*. Is △*TUV* ≅ △*TWV*? Explain.

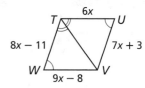

H.O.T. **36. Multi-Step** Polygon *ABCD* ≅ polygon *EFGH*. ∠*A* is a right angle. m∠*E* = $(y^2 - 10)°$, and m∠*H* = $(2y^2 - 132)°$. Find m∠*D*.

37. Given: $\overline{RS} \cong \overline{RT}$, ∠*S* ≅ ∠*T*
Prove: △*RST* ≅ △*RTS*

MATHEMATICAL PRACTICES

FOCUS ON MATHEMATICAL PRACTICES

H.O.T. **38. Analysis** Two triangles are congruent. Are their perimeters necessarily equal? Explain why or why not.

H.O.T. **39. Justify** △*ABC* is an isosceles right triangle with *AB* = 3 and *BC* = 3. △*PQR* is also an isosceles right triangle with *PR* = 3. Is △*ABC* ≅ △*PQR*? Justify your answer.

H.O.T. **40. Problem Solving** △*SFT* ≅ △*MKD*, m∠*M* = 54°, and m∠*T* = 58°. Find m∠*S* + m∠*F*. Explain.

Career Path

Jordan Carter
Emergency Medical
Services Program

Q: What math classes did you take in high school?
A: Algebra 1 and 2, Geometry, Precalculus

Q: What kind of degree or certification will you receive?
A: I will receive an associate's degree in applied science. Then I will take an exam to be certified as an EMT or paramedic.

Q: How do you use math in your hands-on training?
A: I calculate dosages based on body weight and age. I also calculate drug doses in milligrams per kilogram per hour or set up an IV drip to deliver medications at the correct rate.

Q: What are your future career plans?
A: When I am certified, I can work for a private ambulance service or with a fire department. I could also work in a hospital, transporting critically ill patients by ambulance or helicopter.

Ready to Go On?

my.hrw.com
Assessment and Intervention

22-1 Congruence and Transformations

Apply the transformation *M* to the polygon with vertices *A*(5, 2), *B*(–3, 4), and *C*(–1, –6). Identify and describe the transformation.

1. $M : (x, y) \rightarrow (x - 2, y + 3)$

2. $M : (x, y) \rightarrow (x, -y)$

3. $M : (x, y) \rightarrow (-y, x)$

4. $M : (x, y) \rightarrow (3x, 3y)$

22-2 Angle Relationships in Triangles

Find each angle measure.

5. m∠*M*

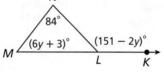

6. m∠*ABC*

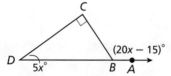

22-3 Congruent Triangles

Given: △*JKL* ≅ △*DEF*. Identify the congruent corresponding parts.

7. $\overline{KL} \cong$ _____?_____

8. $\overline{DF} \cong$ _____?_____

9. ∠*K* ≅ _____?_____

10. ∠*F* ≅ _____?_____

Given: △*ABC* ≅ △*CDA*. Find each value.

11. *x*

12. *CD*

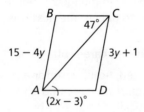

13. Given: $\overleftrightarrow{AB} \parallel \overleftrightarrow{CD}$, $\overline{AB} \cong \overline{CD}$, $\overline{AC} \cong \overline{BD}$, $\overline{AC} \perp \overline{CD}$, $\overline{DB} \perp \overline{AB}$

Prove: $\triangle ACD \cong \triangle DBA$

Proof:

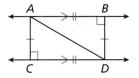

Statements	Reasons
1. $\overleftrightarrow{AB} \parallel \overleftrightarrow{CD}$	1. a. ____?____
2. $\angle BAD \cong \angle CDA$	2. b. ____?____
3. $\overline{AC} \perp \overline{CD}$, $\overline{DB} \perp \overline{AB}$	3. c. ____?____
4. $\angle ACD$ and $\angle DBA$ are rt. $\angle$	4. d. ____?____
5. e. ____?____	5. Rt. $\angle \cong$ Thm.
6. f. ____?____	6. Third $\angle$ Thm.
7. $\overline{AB} \cong \overline{CD}$, $\overline{AC} \cong \overline{BD}$	7. g. ____?____
8. h. ____?____	8. Reflex Prop. of $\cong$
9. $\triangle ACD \cong \triangle DBA$	9. i. ____?____

PARCC Assessment Readiness

Selected Response

1. Prove that the triangles with the given vertices are congruent.

$A(3, 1)$, $B(4, 5)$, $C(2, 3)$
$D(-1, -3)$, $E(-5, -4)$, $F(-3, -2)$

(A) The triangles are congruent because $\triangle ABC$ can be mapped onto $\triangle DEF$ by a rotation: $(x, y) \rightarrow (y, -x)$, followed by a reflection: $(x, y) \rightarrow (x, -y)$.

(B) The triangles are congruent because $\triangle ABC$ can be mapped onto $\triangle DEF$ by a reflection: $(x, y) \rightarrow (-x, y)$, followed by a rotation: $(x, y) \rightarrow (y, -x)$.

(C) The triangles are congruent because $\triangle ABC$ can be mapped onto $\triangle DEF$ by a translation: $(x, y) \rightarrow (x - 4, y)$, followed by another translation: $(x, y) \rightarrow (x, y - 6)$.

(D) The triangles are congruent because $\triangle ABC$ can be mapped onto $\triangle DEF$ by a rotation: $(x, y) \rightarrow (-y, x)$, followed by a reflection: $(x, y) \rightarrow (x, -y)$.

2. Find m$\angle K$.

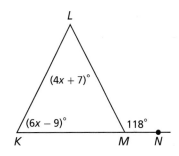

(F) m$\angle K = 63°$ **(H)** m$\angle K = 79°$

(G) m$\angle K = 55°$ **(J)** m$\angle K = 39°$

Mini-Task

3. Given: $\triangle ABC \cong \triangle MNO$

Identify all pairs of congruent corresponding parts.

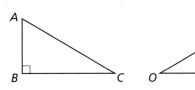

Proving Triangles Congruent

COMMON
CORE GPS

Contents

MATHEMATICAL
PRACTICES
The Common Core Georgia Performance Standards for Mathematical Practice describe varieties of expertise that all students should seek to develop. Opportunities to develop these practices are integrated throughout this program.

1 Make sense of problems and persevere in solving them.

2 Reason abstractly and quantitatively.

3 Construct viable arguments and critique the reasoning of others.

4 Model with mathematics.

5 Use appropriate tools strategically.

6 Attend to precision.

7 Look for and make use of structure.

8 Look for and express regularity in repeated reasoning.

Unpacking the Standards

Understanding the standards and the vocabulary terms in the standards will help you know exactly what you are expected to learn in this chapter.

 MCC9-12.G.SRT.5

Use congruence ... criteria for triangles to solve problems and to prove relationships in geometric figures.

Key Vocabulary

congruent (congruente)
  Having the same size and shape, denoted by ≅.
triangle (triángulo)
  A three-sided polygon.

What It Means For You

When two triangles are *congruent,* it means that matching sides have the same measure and matching angles have the same measure. You can use this fact to help you solve problems.

EXAMPLE

You can use congruent triangles to find the distance across a canyon by measuring distances on only one side of the canyon.

Walk from D perpendicular to $\overline{BD}$ until you are in line with C and A. Call this point E. The distance DE is the same as the distance AB across the canyon.

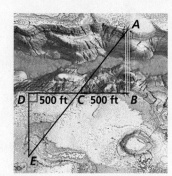

Geometry
TASK

x^2

**Use with *Triangle
Congruence: SSS and SAS***

Explore SSS and SAS Triangle Congruence

You have used the definition of congruent triangles to prove triangles congruent. To use the definition, you need to prove that all three pairs of corresponding sides and all three pairs of corresponding angles are congruent.

In this task, you will discover some shortcuts for proving triangles congruent.

**MATHEMATICAL
PRACTICES**

**Use appropriate
tools strategically.**

MCC9-12.G.CO.8 Explain how the criteria for triangle congruence … follow from … rigid motions.

Activity 1

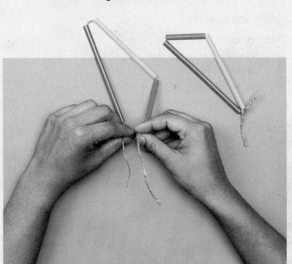

① Measure and cut six pieces from the straws: two that are 2 inches long, two that are 4 inches long, and two that are 5 inches long.

② Cut two pieces of string that are each about 20 inches long.

③ Thread one piece of each size of straw onto a piece of string. Tie the ends of the string together so that the pieces of straw form a triangle.

④ Using the remaining pieces, try to make another triangle with the same side lengths that is *not* congruent to the first triangle.

Try This

1. Repeat Activity 1 using side lengths of your choice. Are your results the same?

2. Do you think it is possible to make two triangles that have the same side lengths but that are not congruent? Why or why not?

3. How does your answer to Problem 2 provide a shortcut for proving triangles congruent?

4. Complete the following conjecture based on your results. Two triangles are congruent if _____?_____.

Sam Dudgeon/HMH

Activity 2

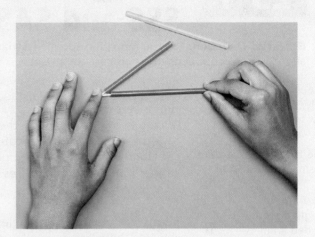

1 Measure and cut two pieces from the straws: one that is 4 inches long and one that is 5 inches long.

2 Use a protractor to help you bend a paper clip to form a 30° angle.

3 Place the pieces of straw on the sides of the 30° angle. The straws will form two sides of your triangle.

4 Without changing the angle formed by the paper clip, use a piece of straw to make a third side for your triangle, cutting it to fit as necessary. Use additional paper clips or string to hold the straws together in a triangle.

Try This

5. Repeat Activity 2 using side lengths and an angle measure of your choice. Are your results the same?

6. Suppose you know two side lengths of a triangle and the measure of the angle between these sides. Can the length of the third side be any measure? Explain.

7. How does your answer to Problem 6 provide a shortcut for proving triangles congruent?

8. Use the two given sides and the given angle from Activity 2 to form a triangle that is not congruent to the triangle you formed. (*Hint:* One of the given sides does not have to be adjacent to the given angle.)

9. Complete the following conjecture based on your results.
Two triangles are congruent if _____ ? _____.

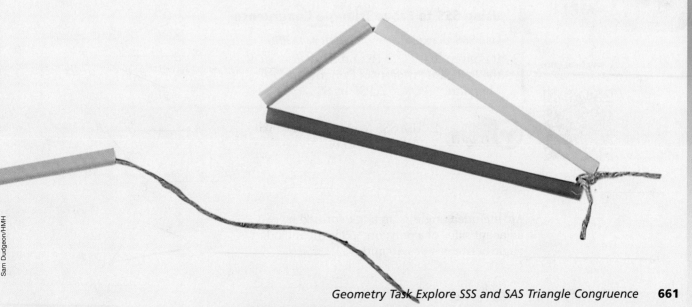

23-1 Triangle Congruence: SSS and SAS

? Essential Question: What information about two triangles allows you to conclude the triangles are congruent?

Objectives
Apply SSS and SAS to construct triangles and to solve problems.

Prove triangles congruent by using SSS and SAS.

Vocabulary
triangle rigidity
included angle

Who uses this?
Engineers used the property of triangle rigidity to design the internal support for the Statue of Liberty and to build bridges, towers, and other structures. (See Example 2.)

Recall that you proved triangles congruent by showing that all six pairs of corresponding parts were congruent.

The property of **triangle rigidity** gives you a shortcut for proving two triangles congruent. It states that if the side lengths of a triangle are given, the triangle can have only one shape.

For example, you only need to know that two triangles have three pairs of congruent corresponding sides. This can be expressed as the following postulate.

Postulate 23-1-1 | **Side-Side-Side (SSS) Congruence**

POSTULATE	HYPOTHESIS	CONCLUSION
If three sides of one triangle are congruent to three sides of another triangle, then the triangles are congruent.	*A* 4 cm, 7 cm, *B* 6 cm *C* — *D* 4 cm, *F* 6 cm, 7 cm *E*	△*ABC* ≅ △*FDE*

COMMON CORE GPS MCC9-12.G.SRT.5

 **EXAMPLE 1** **Using SSS to Prove Triangle Congruence**

Use SSS to explain why △*PQR* ≅ △*PSR*.

It is given that $\overline{PQ} \cong \overline{PS}$ and that $\overline{QR} \cong \overline{SR}$. By the Reflexive Property of Congruence, $\overline{PR} \cong \overline{PR}$. Therefore △*PQR* ≅ △*PSR* by SSS.

 **my.hrw.com**

Online Video Tutor

✓ CHECK IT OUT! **1.** Use SSS to explain why △*ABC* ≅ △*CDA*.

An **included angle** is an angle formed by two adjacent sides of a polygon. ∠*B* is the included angle between sides $\overline{AB}$ and $\overline{BC}$.

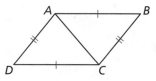
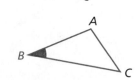

It can also be shown that only two pairs of congruent corresponding sides are needed to prove the congruence of two triangles if the included angles are also congruent.

Postulate 23-1-2 | **Side-Angle-Side (SAS) Congruence**

POSTULATE	HYPOTHESIS	CONCLUSION
If two sides and the included angle of one triangle are congruent to two sides and the included angle of another triangle, then the triangles are congruent.	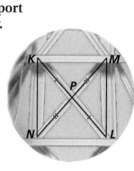	△ABC ≅ △EFD

EXAMPLE 2 MCC9-12.G.SRT.5

Engineering Application

Online Video Tutor

The figure shows part of the support structure of the Statue of Liberty. Use SAS to explain why △KPN ≅ △LPM.

It is given that $\overline{KP} \cong \overline{LP}$ and that $\overline{NP} \cong \overline{MP}$. By the Vertical Angles Theorem, ∠KPN ≅ ∠LPM. Therefore △KPN ≅ △LPM by SAS.

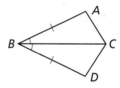

CHECK IT OUT!

2. Use SAS to explain why △ABC ≅ △DBC.

The SAS Postulate guarantees that if you are given the lengths of two sides and the measure of the included angle, you can construct one and only one triangle.

Construction Congruent Triangles Using SAS

Use a straightedge to draw two segments and one angle, or copy the given segments and angle.

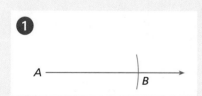

1

Construct $\overline{AB}$ congruent to one of the segments.

2

Construct ∠A congruent to the given angle.

3

Construct $\overline{AC}$ congruent to the other segment. Draw $\overline{CB}$ to complete △ABC.

23-1 Triangle Congruence: SSS and SAS **663**

EXAMPLE 3 MCC9-12.A.CED.1

Verifying Triangle Congruence

Show that the triangles are congruent for the given value of the variable.

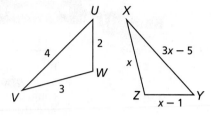

A $\triangle UVW \cong \triangle YXZ, x = 3$

$ZY = x - 1$
$\quad = 3 - 1 = 2$
$XZ = x = 3$
$XY = 3x - 5$
$\quad = 3(3) - 5 = 4$

$\overline{UV} \cong \overline{YX}. \overline{VW} \cong \overline{XZ}$, and $\overline{UW} \cong \overline{YZ}$.
So $\triangle UVW \cong \triangle YXZ$ by SSS.

Caution!

The letters SAS are written in that order because the congruent angles must be between pairs of congruent corresponding sides.

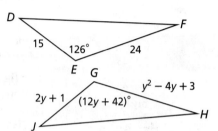

B $\triangle DEF \cong \triangle JGH, y = 7$

$JG = 2y + 1$
$\quad = 2(7) + 1$
$\quad = 15$
$GH = y^2 - 4y + 3$
$\quad = (7)^2 - 4(7) + 3$
$\quad = 24$
$m\angle G = 12y + 42$
$\quad = 12(7) + 42$
$\quad = 126°$

$\overline{DE} \cong \overline{JG}. \overline{EF} \cong \overline{GH}$, and $\angle E \cong \angle G$.
So $\triangle DEF \cong \triangle JGH$ by SAS.

CHECK IT OUT!

3. Show that $\triangle ADB \cong \triangle CDB$ when $t = 4$.

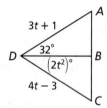

EXAMPLE 4 MCC9-12.G.SRT.5

Proving Triangles Congruent

Given: $\ell \parallel m, \overline{EG} \cong \overline{HF}$
Prove: $\triangle EGF \cong \triangle HFG$
Proof:

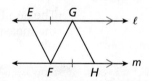

Statements	Reasons
1. $\overline{EG} \cong \overline{HF}$	1. Given
2. $\ell \parallel m$	2. Given
3. $\angle EGF \cong \angle HFG$	3. Alt. Int. ∠ Thm.
4. $\overline{FG} \cong \overline{GF}$	4. Reflex Prop. of $\cong$
5. $\triangle EGF \cong \triangle HFG$	5. SAS *Steps 1, 3, 4*

CHECK IT OUT!

4. Given: $\overrightarrow{QP}$ bisects $\angle RQS$. $\overline{QR} \cong \overline{QS}$
Prove: $\triangle RQP \cong \triangle SQP$

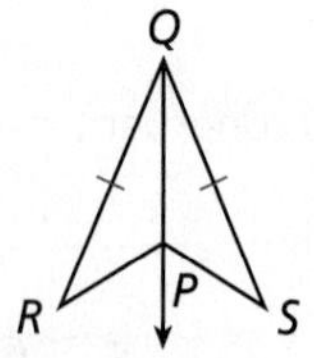

THINK AND DISCUSS

1. Describe three ways you could prove that $\triangle ABC \cong \triangle DEF$.

2. Explain why the SSS and SAS Postulates are shortcuts for proving triangles congruent.

3. **GET ORGANIZED** Copy and complete the graphic organizer. Use it to compare the SSS and SAS postulates.

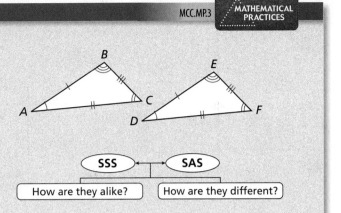

SSS — SAS

How are they alike? | How are they different?

23-1 Exercises

GUIDED PRACTICE

1. **Vocabulary** In $\triangle RST$ which angle is the included angle of sides $\overline{ST}$ and $\overline{TR}$?

SEE EXAMPLE 1

Use SSS to explain why the triangles in each pair are congruent.

2. $\triangle ABD \cong \triangle CDB$

3. $\triangle MNP \cong \triangle MQP$

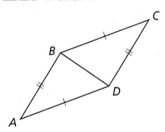

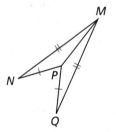

SEE EXAMPLE 2

4. **Sailing** Signal flags are used to communicate messages when radio silence is required. The Zulu signal flag means, "I require a tug." $GJ = GH = GL = GK = 20$ in. Use SAS to explain why $\triangle JGK \cong \triangle LGH$.

SEE EXAMPLE 3

Show that the triangles are congruent for the given value of the variable.

5. $\triangle GHJ \cong \triangle IHJ$, $x = 4$

6. $\triangle RST \cong \triangle TUR$, $x = 18$

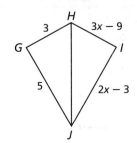

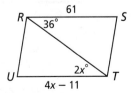

7. Given: $\overline{JK} \cong \overline{ML}$, $\angle JKL \cong \angle MLK$
Prove: $\triangle JKL \cong \triangle MLK$

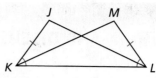

Proof:

Statements	Reasons
1. $\overline{JK} \cong \overline{ML}$	1. a. ___?___
2. b. ___?___	2. Given
3. $\overline{KL} \cong \overline{LK}$	3. c. ___?___
4. $\triangle JKL \cong \triangle MLK$	4. d. ___?___

PRACTICE AND PROBLEM SOLVING

Independent Practice

For Exercises	See Example
8–9	1
10	2
11–12	3
13	4

my.hrw.com

Online Extra Practice

Use SSS to explain why the triangles in each pair are congruent.

8. $\triangle BCD \cong \triangle EDC$

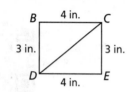

9. $\triangle GJK \cong \triangle GJL$

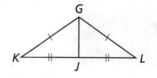

10. Theater The lights shining on a stage appear to form two congruent right triangles. Given $\overline{EC} \cong \overline{DB}$, use SAS to explain why $\triangle ECB \cong \triangle DBC$.

Show that the triangles are congruent for the given value of the variable.

11. $\triangle MNP \cong \triangle QNP$, $y = 3$

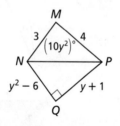

12. $\triangle XYZ \cong \triangle STU$, $t = 5$

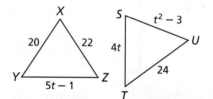

13. Given: B is the midpoint of $\overline{DC}$. $\overline{AB} \perp \overline{DC}$
Prove: $\triangle ABD \cong \triangle ABC$

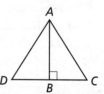

Proof:

Statements	Reasons
1. B is the mdpt. of $\overline{DC}$.	1. a. ___?___
2. b. ___?___	2. Def. of mdpt.
3. c. ___?___	3. Given
4. $\angle ABD$ and $\angle ABC$ are rt. $\angle$.	4. d. ___?___
5. $\angle ABD \cong \angle ABC$	5. e. ___?___
6. f. ___?___	6. Reflex. Prop. of $\cong$
7. $\triangle ABD \cong \triangle ABC$	7. g. ___?___

Which postulate, if any, can be used to prove the triangles congruent?

14.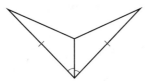

15.

16.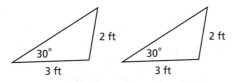

17.

18. Explain what additional information, if any, you would need to prove $\triangle ABC \cong \triangle DEC$ by each postulate.
  a. SSS   **b.** SAS

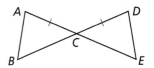

H.O.T. **Multi-Step** Graph each triangle. Then use the Distance Formula and the SSS Postulate to determine whether the triangles are congruent.

19. $\triangle QRS$ and $\triangle TUV$
  $Q(-2, 0), R(1, -2), S(-3, -2)$
  $T(5, 1), U(3, -2), V(3, 2)$

20. $\triangle ABC$ and $\triangle DEF$
  $A(2, 3), B(3, -1), C(7, 2)$
  $D(-3, 1), E(1, 2), F(-3, 5)$

21. Given: $\angle ZVY \cong \angle WYV$,
  $\angle ZVW \cong \angle WYZ$,
  $\overline{VW} \cong \overline{YZ}$
  Prove: $\triangle ZVY \cong \triangle WYV$
  Proof:

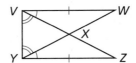

Statements	Reasons
1. $\angle ZVY \cong \angle WYV$, $\angle ZVW \cong WYZ$	1. a. ___?___
2. $m\angle ZVY = m\angle WYV$, $m\angle ZVW = m\angle WYZ$	2. b. ___?___
3. $m\angle ZVY + m\angle ZVW = m\angle WYV + m\angle WYZ$	3. Add. Prop. of =
4. c. ___?___	4. $\angle$ Add. Post.
5. $\angle WVY \cong \angle ZYV$	5. d. ___?___
6. $\overline{VW} \cong \overline{YZ}$	6. e. ___?___
7. f. ___?___	7. Reflex. Prop. of $\cong$
8. $\triangle ZVY \cong \triangle WYV$	8. g. ___?___

Real-World Connections

22. The diagram shows two triangular trusses that were built for the roof of a doghouse.

  a. You can use a protractor to check that $\angle A$ and $\angle D$ are right angles. Explain how you could make just two additional measurements on each truss to ensure that the trusses are congruent.

  b. You verify that the trusses are congruent and find that $AB = AC = 2.5$ ft. Find the length of $\overline{EF}$ to the nearest tenth. Explain.

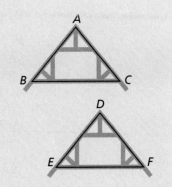

© GK Hart/Vikki Hart/Getty Images

23-1 Triangle Congruence: SSS and SAS   **667**

23. **Critical Thinking** Draw two isosceles triangles that are not congruent but that have a perimeter of 15 cm each.

24. $\triangle ABC \cong \triangle ADC$ for what value of x? Explain why the SSS Postulate can be used to prove the two triangles congruent.

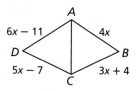

25. **Ecology** A *wing deflector* is a triangular structure made of logs that is filled with large rocks and placed in a stream to guide the current or prevent erosion. Wing deflectors are often used in pairs. Suppose an engineer wants to build two wing deflectors. The logs that form the sides of each wing deflector are perpendicular. How can the engineer make sure that the two wing deflectors are congruent?

26. **Write About It** If you use the same two sides and included angle to repeat the construction of a triangle, are your two constructed triangles congruent? Explain.

27. **H.O.T. Construction** Use three segments (SSS) to construct a scalene triangle. Suppose you then use the same segments in a different order to construct a second triangle. Will the result be the same? Explain.

TEST PREP

28. Which of the three triangles below can be proven congruent by SSS or SAS?

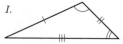   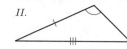   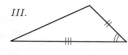

    Ⓐ I and II   Ⓑ II and III   Ⓒ I and III   Ⓓ I, II, and III

29. What is the perimeter of polygon *ABCD*?

    Ⓕ 29.9 cm   Ⓗ 49.8 cm

    Ⓖ 39.8 cm   Ⓙ 59.8 cm

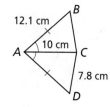

30. Jacob wants to prove that $\triangle FGH \cong \triangle JKL$ using SAS. He knows that $\overline{FG} \cong \overline{JK}$ and $\overline{FH} \cong \overline{JL}$. What additional piece of information does he need?

    Ⓐ $\angle F \cong \angle J$ Ⓒ $\angle H \cong \angle L$

    Ⓑ $\angle G \cong \angle K$ Ⓓ $\angle F \cong \angle G$

31. What must the value of x be in order to prove that $\triangle EFG \cong \triangle EHG$ by SSS?

    Ⓕ 1.5   Ⓗ 4.67

    Ⓖ 4.25   Ⓙ 5.5

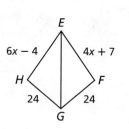

CHALLENGE AND EXTEND

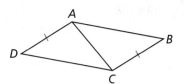

H.O.T. **32.** **Given:** ∠ADC and ∠BCD are
supplementary. $\overline{AD} \cong \overline{CB}$

Prove: △ADB ≅ △CBD
(*Hint:* Draw an auxiliary line.)

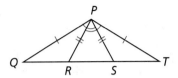

H.O.T. **33.** **Given:** ∠QPS ≅ ∠TPR, $\overline{PQ} \cong \overline{PT}$, $\overline{PR} \cong \overline{PS}$

Prove: △PQR ≅ △PTS

Algebra **Use the following information for Exercises 34 and 35.**
Find the value of *x*. Then use SSS or SAS to write a paragraph
proof showing that two of the triangles are congruent.

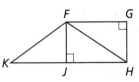

34. m∠FKJ = 2*x*°
m∠KFJ = $(3x + 10)°$
KJ = 4*x* + 8
HJ = 6(*x* − 4)

35. $\overline{FJ}$ bisects ∠KFH.
m∠KFJ = $(2x + 6)°$
m∠HFJ = $(3x − 21)°$
FK = 8*x* − 45
FH = 6*x* + 9

MATHEMATICAL PRACTICES

FOCUS ON MATHEMATICAL PRACTICES

H.O.T. **36.** **Modeling** The vertices of △ABC are A(−1, 5), B(−1, −1), and C(3, −1).
Consider points M(2, 1) and N(2, −5). At which location, or locations,
for P is △MNP ≅ △ABC by SSS?

H.O.T. **37.** **Proof** **Given:** △XYZ is an equilateral triangle.

$\overrightarrow{XM}$ bisects ∠X and intersects $\overline{YZ}$ at M.

Prove: △XMY ≅ △XMZ

Using Technology

Use geometry software to complete the following.

1. Draw a triangle and label the vertices *A*, *B*, and *C*.
Draw a point and label it *D*. Mark a vector from *A* to *B*
and translate *D* by the marked vector. Label the image *E*.
Draw $\overleftrightarrow{DE}$. Mark ∠BAC and rotate $\overleftrightarrow{DE}$ about *D* by the
marked angle. Mark ∠ABC and rotate $\overleftrightarrow{DE}$ about *E* by
the marked angle. Label the intersection *F*.

2. Drag *A*, *B*, and *C* to different locations.
What do you notice about the two triangles?

3. Write a conjecture about △ABC and △DEF.

4. Test your conjecture by measuring the sides and angles of △ABC and △DEF.

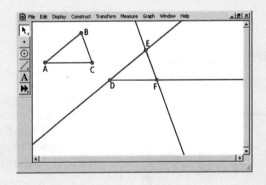

Triangle Congruence: ASA, AAS, and HL

? **Essential Question:** What information about two triangles allows you to conclude the triangles are congruent?

Objectives
Apply ASA, AAS, and HL to construct triangles and to solve problems.

Prove triangles congruent by using ASA, AAS, and HL.

Vocabulary
included side

Why use this?
Bearings are used to convey direction, helping people find their way to specific locations.

Participants in an *orienteering* race use a map and a compass to find their way to checkpoints along an unfamiliar course. Directions are given by *bearings*, which are based on compass headings. For example, to travel along the bearing S 43° E, you face south and then turn 43° to the east.

An **included side** is the common side of two consecutive angles in a polygon. The following postulate uses the idea of an *included side*.

$\overline{PQ}$ is the included side of ∠*P* and ∠*Q*.

Postulate 23-2-1	Angle-Side-Angle (ASA) Congruence	
POSTULATE	**HYPOTHESIS**	**CONCLUSION**
If two angles and the included side of one triangle are congruent to two angles and the included side of another triangle, then the triangles are congruent.		△*ABC* ≅ △*DEF*

COMMON CORE GPS
MCC9-12.G.MG.1

EXAMPLE 1

my.hrw.com

Online Video Tutor

Problem-Solving Application

Organizers of an orienteering race are planning a course with checkpoints *A*, *B*, and *C*. Does the table give enough information to determine the location of the checkpoints?

	Bearing	Distance
A to B	N 55° E	7.6 km
B to C	N 26° W	
C to A	S 20° W	

1 **Understand the Problem**

The **answer** is whether the information in the table can be used to find the position of checkpoints *A*, *B*, and *C*. List the **important information:** The bearing from *A* to *B* is N 55° E. From *B* to *C* is N 26° W, and from *C* to *A* is S 20° W. The distance from *A* to *B* is 7.6 km.

(tr), ©Steve Skjold/Alamy Photos; (cr), Stockbyte Royalty-Free Images/HMH Library

MATHEMATICAL PRACTICES

Make sense of problems and persevere in solving them.

 Make a Plan

Draw the course using vertical lines to show north-south directions. Then use these parallel lines and the alternate interior angles to help find angle measures of $\triangle ABC$.

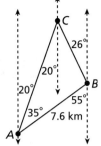

3 **Solve**

$m\angle CAB = 55° - 20° = 35°$

$m\angle CBA = 180° - (26° + 55°) = 99°$

You know the measures of $\angle CAB$ and $\angle CBA$ and the length of the included side $\overline{AB}$. Therefore by ASA, a unique triangle ABC is determined.

 Look Back

One and only one triangle can be made using the information in the table, so the table does give enough information to determine the location of all the checkpoints.

✔ CHECK IT OUT!

1. What if...? If 7.6 km is the distance from B to C, is there enough information to determine the location of all the checkpoints? Explain.

COMMON CORE GPS MCC9-12.G.SRT.5

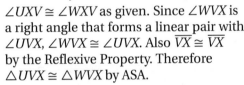

Applying ASA Congruence

Determine if you can use ASA to prove $\triangle UVX \cong \triangle WVX$. Explain.

$\angle UXV \cong \angle WXV$ as given. Since $\angle WVX$ is a right angle that forms a linear pair with $\angle UVX$, $\angle WVX \cong \angle UVX$. Also $\overline{VX} \cong \overline{VX}$ by the Reflexive Property. Therefore $\triangle UVX \cong \triangle WVX$ by ASA.

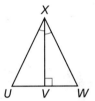

 my.hrw.com

Online Video Tutor

✔ CHECK IT OUT!

2. Determine if you can use ASA to prove $\triangle NKL \cong \triangle LMN$. Explain.

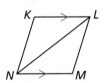

Construction Congruent Triangles Using ASA

Use a straightedge to draw a segment and two angles, or copy the given segment and angles.

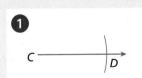

Construct $\overline{CD}$ congruent to the given segment.

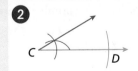

Construct $\angle C$ congruent to one of the angles.

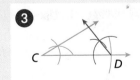

Construct $\angle D$ congruent to the other angle.

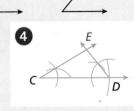

$\triangle CDE$

Label the intersection of the rays as E.

You can use the Third Angles Theorem to prove another congruence relationship based on ASA. This theorem is Angle-Angle-Side (AAS).

Theorem 23-2-2 **Angle-Angle-Side (AAS) Congruence**

THEOREM	HYPOTHESIS	CONCLUSION
If two angles and a nonincluded side of one triangle are congruent to the corresponding angles and nonincluded side of another triangle, then the triangles are congruent.	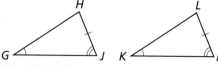	$\triangle GHJ \cong \triangle KLM$

PROOF **Angle-Angle-Side Congruence**

Given: $\angle G \cong \angle K$, $\angle J \cong \angle M$, $\overline{HJ} \cong \overline{LM}$
Prove: $\triangle GHJ \cong \triangle KLM$

Proof:

Statements	Reasons
1. $\angle G \cong \angle K$, $\angle J \cong \angle M$	**1.** Given
2. $\angle H \cong \angle L$	**2.** Third ∠ Thm.
3. $\overline{HJ} \cong \overline{LM}$	**3.** Given
4. $\triangle GHJ \cong \triangle KLM$	**4.** ASA *Steps 1, 3, and 2*

COMMON CORE GPS
MCC9-12.G.SRT.5

EXAMPLE 3 **Using AAS to Prove Triangles Congruent**

my.hrw.com

Online Video Tutor

Use AAS to prove the triangles congruent.
Given: $\overline{AB} \parallel \overline{ED}$, $\overline{BC} \cong \overline{DC}$
Prove: $\triangle ABC \cong \triangle EDC$
Proof:

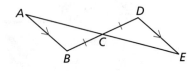

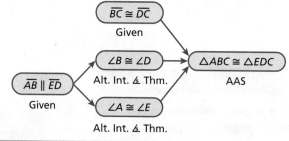

CHECK IT OUT!

3. Use AAS to prove the triangles congruent.
   Given: $\overline{JL}$ bisects $\angle KLM$. $\angle K \cong \angle M$
   Prove: $\triangle JKL \cong \triangle JML$

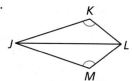

There are four theorems for right triangles that are not used for acute or obtuse triangles. They are Leg-Leg (LL), Hypotenuse-Angle (HA), Leg-Angle (LA), and Hypotenuse-Leg (HL). You will prove LL, HA, and LA in Exercises 21, 23, and 33.

THEOREM	HYPOTHESIS	CONCLUSION
If the hypotenuse and a leg of a right triangle are congruent to the hypotenuse and a leg of another right triangle, then the triangles are congruent.	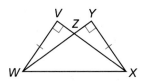	$\triangle ABC \cong \triangle DEF$

You will prove the Hypotenuse-Leg Theorem in Lesson 23-4, Exercise 41.

COMMON CORE GPS   **EXAMPLE** **4**   MCC.MP.3

my.hrw.com

Online Video Tutor

Applying HL Congruence

Determine if you can use the HL Congruence Theorem to prove the triangles congruent. If not, tell what else you need to know.

A $\triangle VWX$ and $\triangle YXW$

According to the diagram, $\triangle VWX$ and $\triangle YXW$ are right triangles that share hypotenuse $\overline{WX}$. $\overline{WX} \cong \overline{XW}$ by the Reflexive Property. It is given that $\overline{WV} \cong \overline{XY}$, therefore $\triangle VWX \cong \triangle YXW$ by HL.

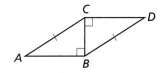

B $\triangle VWZ$ and $\triangle YXZ$

This conclusion cannot be proved by HL. According to the diagram, $\triangle VWZ$ and $\triangle YXZ$ are right triangles, and $\overline{WV} \cong \overline{XY}$. You do not know that hypotenuse $\overline{WZ}$ is congruent to hypotenuse $\overline{XZ}$.

CHECK IT OUT!

4. Determine if you can use the HL Congruence Theorem to prove $\triangle ABC \cong \triangle DCB$. If not, tell what else you need to know.

MCC.MP.7   MATHEMATICAL PRACTICES

THINK AND DISCUSS

1. Could you use AAS to prove that these two triangles are congruent? Explain.

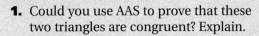

2. The arrangement of the letters in ASA matches the arrangement of what parts of congruent triangles? Include a sketch to support your answer.

3. GET ORGANIZED Copy and complete the graphic organizer. In each column, write a description of the method and then sketch two triangles, marking the appropriate congruent parts.

Proving Triangles Congruent						
	Def. of △ ≅	SSS	SAS	ASA	AAS	HL
Words						
Pictures						

GUIDED PRACTICE

1. **Vocabulary** A triangle contains ∠ABC and ∠ACB with $\overline{BC}$ "closed in" between them. How would this help you remember the definition of *included side*?

SEE EXAMPLE 1

Surveying Use the table for Exercises 2 and 3.
A landscape designer surveyed the boundaries of a triangular park. She made the following table for the dimensions of the land.

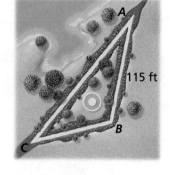

115 ft

	A to B	B to C	C to A
Bearing	E	S 25° E	N 62° W
Distance	115 ft	?	?

2. Draw the plot of land described by the table. Label the measures of the angles in the triangle.

3. Does the table have enough information to determine the locations of points *A*, *B*, and *C*? Explain.

SEE EXAMPLE 2

Determine if you can use ASA to prove the triangles congruent. Explain.

4. △VRS and △VTS, given that $\overline{VS}$ bisects ∠RST and ∠RVT

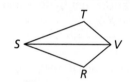

5. △DEH and △FGH

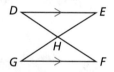

SEE EXAMPLE 3

6. Use AAS to prove the triangles congruent.

Given: ∠R and ∠P are right angles.
$\overline{QR} \parallel \overline{SP}$
Prove: △QPS ≅ △SRQ
Proof:

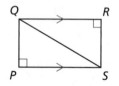

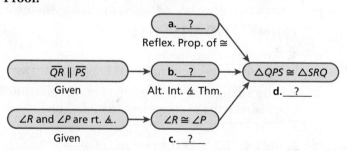

SEE EXAMPLE 4

Determine if you can use the HL Congruence Theorem to prove the triangles congruent. If not, tell what else you need to know.

7. △ABC and △CDA

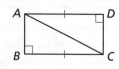

8. △XYV and △ZYV

PRACTICE AND PROBLEM SOLVING

Independent Practice

For Exercises	See Example
9–10	1
11–12	2
13	3
14–15	4

my.hrw.com

Online Extra Practice

Surveying Use the table for Exercises 9 and 10.

From two different observation towers a fire is sighted. The locations of the towers are given in the following table.

	X to Y	X to F	Y to F
Bearing	E	N 53° E	N 16° W
Distance	6 km	?	?

9. Draw the diagram formed by observation tower *X*, observation tower *Y*, and the fire *F*. Label the measures of the angles.

10. Is there enough information given in the table to pinpoint the location of the fire? Explain.

Determine if you can use ASA to prove the triangles congruent. Explain.

11. △*MKJ* and △*MKL*

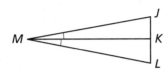

12. △*RST* and △*TUR*

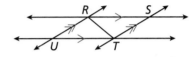

13. **Given:** $\overline{AB} \cong \overline{DE}$, $\angle C \cong \angle F$
   Prove: △*ABC* ≅ △*DEF*

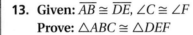

Proof:

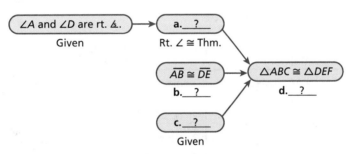

Math History

Euclid wrote the mathematical text *The Elements* around 2300 years ago. It may be the second most reprinted book in history.

Determine if you can use the HL Congruence Theorem to prove the triangles congruent. If not, tell what else you need to know.

14. △*GHJ* and △*JKG*

15. △*ABE* and △*DCE*, given that *E* is the midpoint of $\overline{AD}$ and $\overline{BC}$

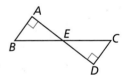

H.O.T. Multi-Step For each pair of triangles write a triangle congruence statement. Identify the transformation that moves one triangle to the position of the other triangle.

16.

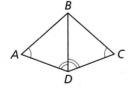

17.

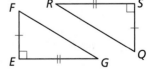

H.O.T. 18. **Critical Thinking** Side-Side-Angle (SSA) cannot be used to prove two triangles congruent. Draw a diagram that shows why this is true.

Real-World Connections

19. A carpenter built a truss to support the roof of a doghouse.

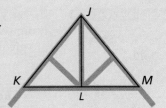

a. The carpenter knows that $\overline{KJ} \cong \overline{MJ}$. Can the carpenter conclude that $\triangle KJL \cong \triangle MJL$? Why or why not?

b. Suppose the carpenter also knows that $\angle JLK$ is a right angle. Which theorem can be used to show that $\triangle KJL \cong \triangle MJL$?

20. **///ERROR ANALYSIS///** Two proofs that $\triangle EFH \cong \triangle GHF$ are given. Which is incorrect? Explain the error.

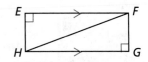

A

It is given that $\overline{EF} \parallel \overline{GH}$. By the Alt. Int. ∡ Thm., $\angle EFH \cong \angle GHF$. $\angle E \cong \angle G$ by the Rt. $\angle$ Thm. By the Reflex. Prop. of $\cong$, $\overline{HF} \cong \overline{HF}$. So by AAS, $\triangle EFH \cong \triangle GHF$.

B

$\overline{HF}$ is the hyp. of both rt. ▵. $\overline{HF} \cong \overline{HF}$ by the Reflex. Prop. of $\cong$. Since the opp. sides of a rect. are $\cong$, $\overline{EF} \cong \overline{GH}$. So by HL, $\triangle EFH \cong \triangle FHG$.

H.O.T. 21. Write a paragraph proof of the Leg-Leg (LL) Congruence Theorem. If the legs of one right triangle are congruent to the corresponding legs of another right triangle, the triangles are congruent.

22. Use AAS to prove the triangles congruent.

Given: $\overline{AD} \parallel \overline{BC}$, $\overline{AD} \cong \overline{CB}$
Prove: $\triangle AED \cong \triangle CEB$

Proof:

Statements	Reasons
1. $\overline{AD} \parallel \overline{BC}$	1. a. ___?___
2. $\angle DAE \cong \angle BCE$	2. b. ___?___
3. c. ___?___	3. Vert. ∡ Thm.
4. d. ___?___	3. Given
5. e. ___?___	4. f. ___?___

23. Prove the Hypotenuse-Angle (HA) Theorem.
Given: $\overline{KM} \perp \overline{JL}$, $\overline{JM} \cong \overline{LM}$, $\angle JMK \cong \angle LMK$
Prove: $\triangle JKM \cong \triangle LKM$

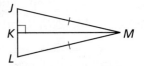

24. **Write About It** The legs of both right $\triangle DEF$ and right $\triangle RST$ are 3 cm and 4 cm. They each have a hypotenuse 5 cm in length. Describe two different ways you could prove that $\triangle DEF \cong \triangle RST$.

H.O.T. 25. **Construction** Use the method for constructing perpendicular lines to construct a right triangle.

TEST PREP

26. What additional congruence statement is necessary to prove $\triangle XWY \cong \triangle XVZ$ by ASA?

Ⓐ $\angle XVZ \cong \angle XWY$

Ⓑ $\angle VUY \cong \angle WUZ$

Ⓒ $\overline{VZ} \cong \overline{WY}$

Ⓓ $\overline{XZ} \cong \overline{XY}$

27. Which postulate or theorem justifies the congruence statement △STU ≅ △VUT?

    ⒻASA   ⒽHL

    ⒼSSS   ⒿSAS

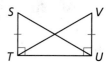

28. Which of the following congruence statements is true?

    Ⓐ ∠A ≅ ∠B   Ⓒ △AED ≅ △CEB

    Ⓑ $\overline{CE} \cong \overline{DE}$ Ⓓ △AED ≅ △BEC

29. In △RST, RT = 6y − 2. In △UVW, UW = 2y + 7. ∠R ≅ ∠U, and ∠S ≅ ∠V. What must be the value of y in order to prove that △RST ≅ △UVW?

    Ⓕ 1.25   Ⓖ 2.25   Ⓗ 9.0   Ⓙ 11.5

30. Extended Response Draw a triangle. Construct a second triangle that has the same angle measures but is not congruent. Compare the lengths of each pair of corresponding sides. Consider the relationship between the lengths of the sides and the measures of the angles. Explain why Angle-Angle-Angle (AAA) is not a congruence principle.

CHALLENGE AND EXTEND

H.O.T. 31. Sports This bicycle frame includes △VSU and △VTU, which lie in intersecting planes. From the given angle measures, can you conclude that △VSU ≅ △VTU? Explain.

$$m\angle VUS = (7y - 2)^\circ \quad m\angle VUT = \left(5\tfrac{1}{2}x - \tfrac{1}{2}\right)^\circ$$

$$m\angle USV = 5\tfrac{2}{3}y^\circ \quad m\angle UTV = (4x + 8)^\circ$$

$$m\angle SVU = (3y - 6)^\circ \quad m\angle TVU = 2x^\circ$$

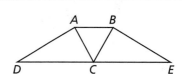

32. Given: △ABC is equilateral. C is the midpoint of $\overline{DE}$. ∠DAC and ∠EBC are congruent and supplementary.

Prove: △DAC ≅ △EBC

H.O.T. 33. Write a two-column proof of the Leg-Angle (LA) Congruence Theorem. If a leg and an acute angle of one right triangle are congruent to the corresponding parts of another right triangle, the triangles are congruent. (*Hint:* There are two cases to consider.)

34. If two triangles are congruent by ASA, what theorem could you use to prove that the triangles are also congruent by AAS? Explain.

FOCUS ON MATHEMATICAL PRACTICES

H.O.T. 35. Analysis In the figure, ∠VWL ≅ ∠VRL, $\overline{WG}$ bisects ∠VWL, $\overline{RG}$ bisects ∠VRL, $\overline{VW} \cong \overline{VR}$, and $\overline{VL} \perp \overline{WR}$ at L. Clarita says △GWL ≅ △GRL by AAS. Is she correct? Explain.

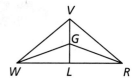

H.O.T. 36. Reasoning Two right triangles share a side. A leg of one triangle, which is not the shared side, is congruent to a leg of the second triangle, which is also not the shared side. Are the two triangles necessarily congruent? Explain.

23-3 Triangle Congruence: CPCTC

? Essential Question: If you know two figures are congruent, what can you conclude about corresponding sides and corresponding angles?

Objective
Use CPCTC to prove parts of triangles are congruent.

Vocabulary
CPCTC

Why learn this?
You can use congruent triangles to estimate distances.

CPCTC is an abbreviation for the phrase "Corresponding Parts of Congruent Triangles are Congruent." It can be used as a justification in a proof after you have proven two triangles congruent.

EXAMPLE 1
MCC9-12.G.CO.7

Online Video Tutor

Engineering Application

To design a bridge across a canyon, you need to find the distance from A to B. Locate points C, D, and E as shown in the figure. If $DE = 600$ ft, what is AB?

$\angle D \cong \angle B$, because they are both right angles.
$\overline{DC} \cong \overline{CB}$, because $DC = CB = 500$ ft.
$\angle DCE \cong \angle BCA$, because vertical angles are congruent. Therefore $\triangle DCE \cong \triangle BCA$ by ASA or LA. By CPCTC, $\overline{ED} \cong \overline{AB}$, so $AB = ED = 600$ ft.

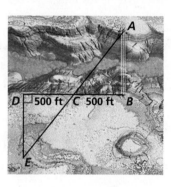

CHECK IT OUT! **1.** A landscape architect sets up the triangles shown in the figure to find the distance JK across a pond. What is JK?

EXAMPLE 2
MCC9-12.G.SRT.5

Online Video Tutor

Proving Corresponding Parts Congruent

Given: $\overline{AB} \cong \overline{DC}$, $\angle ABC \cong \angle DCB$
Prove: $\angle A \cong \angle D$
Proof:

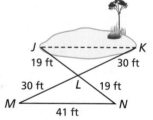

```
 ( AB ≅ DC )
   Given
                  \
 ( ∠ABC ≅ ∠DCB )   → ( △ABC ≅ △DCB ) → ( ∠A ≅ ∠D )
   Given                  SAS              CPCTC
                  /
 ( BC ≅ CB )
 Reflex. Prop. of ≅
```

CHECK IT OUT! **2. Given:** $\overline{PR}$ bisects $\angle QPS$ and $\angle QRS$.
Prove: $\overline{PQ} \cong \overline{PS}$

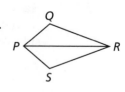

EXAMPLE 3 Using CPCTC in a Proof
MCC9-12.G.CO.10

Given: $\overline{EG} \parallel \overline{DF}$, $\overline{EG} \cong \overline{DF}$
Prove: $\overline{ED} \parallel \overline{GF}$

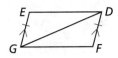

Proof:

Statements	Reasons
1. $\overline{EG} \cong \overline{DF}$	1. Given
2. $\overline{EG} \parallel \overline{DF}$	2. Given
3. $\angle EGD \cong \angle FDG$	3. Alt. Int. ∠ Thm.
4. $\overline{GD} \cong \overline{DG}$	4. Reflex. Prop. of ≅
5. $\triangle EGD \cong \triangle FDG$	5. SAS *Steps 1, 3, and 4*
6. $\angle EDG \cong \angle FGD$	6. CPCTC
7. $\overline{ED} \parallel \overline{GF}$	7. Converse of Alt. Int. ∠ Thm.

Helpful Hint

Work backward when planning a proof. To show that $\overline{KL} \parallel \overline{MN}$, look for a pair of angles that are congruent. Then look for triangles that contain these angles.

 3. Given: J is the midpoint of $\overline{KM}$ and $\overline{NL}$.
Prove: $\overline{KL} \parallel \overline{MN}$

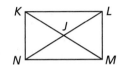

You can also use CPCTC when triangles are on a coordinate plane.
You use the Distance Formula to find the lengths of the sides of each triangle.
Then, after showing that the triangles are congruent, you can
make conclusions about their corresponding parts.

EXAMPLE 4 Using CPCTC in the Coordinate Plane
MCC9-12.G.GPE.4

Given: $A(2, 3)$, $B(5, -1)$, $C(1, 0)$,
$D(-4, -1)$, $E(0, 2)$, $F(-1, -2)$
Prove: $\angle ABC \cong \angle DEF$

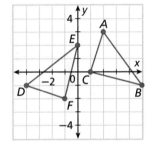

Step 1 Plot the points on a coordinate plane.

Step 2 Use the Distance Formula to find the lengths of the sides of each triangle.

$$D = \sqrt{(x_2 - x_1)^2 + (y_2 - y_1)^2}$$

$$AB = \sqrt{(5-2)^2 + (-1-3)^2} \qquad DE = \sqrt{(0-(-4))^2 + (2-(-1))^2}$$
$$= \sqrt{9 + 16} = \sqrt{25} = 5 \qquad\qquad = \sqrt{16 + 9} = \sqrt{25} = 5$$

$$BC = \sqrt{(1-5)^2 + (0-(-1))^2} \qquad EF = \sqrt{(-1-0)^2 + (-2-2)^2}$$
$$= \sqrt{16 + 1} = \sqrt{17} \qquad\qquad = \sqrt{1 + 16} = \sqrt{17}$$

$$AC = \sqrt{(1-2)^2 + (0-3)^2} \qquad DF = \sqrt{(-1-(-4))^2 + (-2-(-1))^2}$$
$$= \sqrt{1 + 9} = \sqrt{10} \qquad\qquad = \sqrt{9 + 1} = \sqrt{10}$$

Remember!

SSS, SAS, ASA, AAS, and HL use corresponding parts to prove triangles congruent. CPCTC uses congruent triangles to prove corresponding parts congruent.

So $\overline{AB} \cong \overline{DE}$, $\overline{BC} \cong \overline{EF}$, and $\overline{AC} \cong \overline{DF}$. Therefore $\triangle ABC \cong \triangle DEF$ by SSS, and $\angle ABC \cong \angle DEF$ by CPCTC.

 4. Given: $J(-1, -2)$, $K(2, -1)$, $L(-2, 0)$, $R(2, 3)$, $S(5, 2)$, $T(1, 1)$
Prove: $\angle JKL \cong \angle RST$

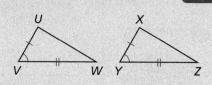

THINK AND DISCUSS

1. In the figure, $\overline{UV} \cong \overline{XY}$, $\overline{VW} \cong \overline{YZ}$, and $\angle V \cong \angle Y$. Explain why $\triangle UVW \cong \triangle XYZ$. By CPCTC, which additional parts are congruent?

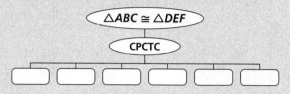

Know it! Note

2. **GET ORGANIZED** Copy and complete the graphic organizer. Write all conclusions you can make using CPCTC.

$\triangle ABC \cong \triangle DEF$

CPCTC

23-3 Exercises

GUIDED PRACTICE

1. **Vocabulary** You use CPCTC after proving triangles are congruent. Which parts of congruent triangles are referred to as corresponding parts?

SEE EXAMPLE 1

2. **Archaeology** An archaeologist wants to find the height AB of a rock formation. She places a marker at C and steps off the distance from C to B. Then she walks the same distance from C and places a marker at D. If $DE = 6.3$ m, what is AB?

SEE EXAMPLE 2

3. **Given:** X is the midpoint of $\overline{ST}$. $\overline{RX} \perp \overline{ST}$

   Prove: $\overline{RS} \cong \overline{RT}$

   Proof:

   | $\overline{RX} \perp \overline{ST}$ | $\rightarrow$ | $\angle RXS$ and $\angle RXT$ are rt. $\angle$. | $\rightarrow$ | $\angle RXS \cong \angle RXT$ |
   Given | | a. ___?___ | | b. ___?___ |

   $\overline{RX} \cong \overline{RX}$
   c. ___?___

   X is the mdpt. of $\overline{ST}$.
   Given

   $\overline{SX} \cong \overline{TX}$
   d. ___?___

   e. ___?___
   SAS

   $\overline{RS} \cong \overline{RT}$
   f. ___?___

SEE EXAMPLE 3

4. Given: $\overline{AC} \cong \overline{AD}$, $\overline{CB} \cong \overline{DB}$
Prove: $\overline{AB}$ bisects $\angle CAD$.

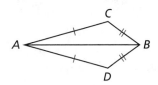

Proof:

Statements	Reasons
1. $\overline{AC} \cong \overline{AD}$, $\overline{CB} \cong \overline{DB}$	1. a. ?
2. b. ?	2. Reflex. Prop. of $\cong$
3. $\triangle ACB \cong \triangle ADB$	3. c. ?
4. $\angle CAB \cong \angle DAB$	4. d. ?
5. $\overline{AB}$ bisects $\angle CAD$	5. e. ?

SEE EXAMPLE 4

Multi-Step Use the given set of points to prove each congruence statement.

5. $E(-3, 3)$, $F(-1, 3)$, $G(-2, 0)$, $J(0, -1)$, $K(2, -1)$, $L(1, 2)$; $\angle EFG \cong \angle JKL$

6. $A(2, 3)$, $B(4, 1)$, $C(1, -1)$, $R(-1, 0)$, $S(-3, -2)$, $T(0, -4)$; $\angle ACB \cong \angle RTS$

PRACTICE AND PROBLEM SOLVING

Independent Practice

For Exercises	See Example
7	1
8–9	2
10–11	3
12–13	4

my.hrw.com

Online Extra Practice

7. Surveying To find the distance AB across a river, a surveyor first locates point C. He measures the distance from C to B. Then he locates point D the same distance east of C. If $DE = 420$ ft, what is AB?

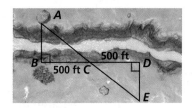

8. Given: M is the midpoint of $\overline{PQ}$ and $\overline{RS}$.
Prove: $\overline{QR} \cong \overline{PS}$

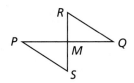

9. Given: $\overline{WX} \cong \overline{XY} \cong \overline{YZ} \cong \overline{ZW}$
Prove: $\angle W \cong \angle Y$

10. Given: G is the midpoint of $\overline{FH}$.
$\overline{EF} \cong \overline{EH}$
Prove: $\angle 1 \cong \angle 2$

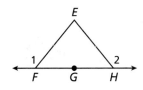

11. Given: $\overline{LM}$ bisects $\angle JLK$. $\overline{JL} \cong \overline{KL}$
Prove: M is the midpoint of $\overline{JK}$.

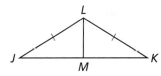

H.O.T. Multi-Step Use the given set of points to prove each congruence statement.

12. $R(0, 0)$, $S(2, 4)$, $T(-1, 3)$, $U(-1, 0)$, $V(-3, -4)$, $W(-4, -1)$; $\angle RST \cong \angle UVW$

13. $A(-1, 1)$, $B(2, 3)$, $C(2, -2)$, $D(2, -3)$, $E(-1, -5)$, $F(-1, 0)$; $\angle BAC \cong \angle EDF$

14. Given: $\triangle QRS$ is adjacent to $\triangle QTS$. $\overline{QS}$ bisects $\angle RQT$. $\angle R \cong \angle T$
Prove: $\overline{QS}$ bisects $\overline{RT}$.

15. Given: $\triangle ABE$ and $\triangle CDE$ with E the midpoint of $\overline{AC}$ and $\overline{BD}$
Prove: $\overline{AB} \parallel \overline{CD}$

Real-World Connections

16. The front of a doghouse has the dimensions shown.
    a. How can you prove that △ADB ≅ △ADC?
    b. Prove that $\overline{BD} \cong \overline{CD}$.
    c. What is the length of $\overline{BD}$ and $\overline{BC}$ to the nearest tenth?

Multi-Step Find the value of *x*.

H.O.T. 17.

$x + 11$ $2x - 3$

18.

$(4x + 1)°$ $(6x - 41)°$

Use the diagram for Exercises 19–21.

19. **Given:** $PS = RQ$, m∠1 = m∠4
    Prove: m∠3 = m∠2

20. **Given:** m∠1 = m∠2, m∠3 = m∠4
    Prove: $PS = RS$

21. **Given:** $PS = RQ$, $PQ = RS$
    Prove: $\overline{PQ} \parallel \overline{RS}$

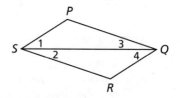

22. **Critical Thinking** Does the diagram contain
    enough information to allow you to conclude
    that $\overline{JK} \parallel \overline{ML}$? Explain.

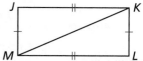

H.O.T. 23. **Write About It** Draw a diagram and explain how a surveyor can set up triangles
    to find the distance across a lake. Label each part of your diagram. List which
    sides or angles must be congruent.

TEST PREP

24. Which of these will NOT be used as a reason in a proof
    of $\overline{AC} \cong \overline{AD}$?

    Ⓐ SAS   Ⓒ ASA
    Ⓑ CPCTC   Ⓓ Reflexive Property

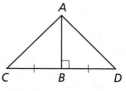

25. Given the points $K(1, 2)$, $L(0, -4)$, $M(-2, -3)$, and $N(-1, 3)$,
    which of these is true?

    Ⓕ ∠KNL ≅ ∠MNL   Ⓗ ∠MLN ≅ ∠KLN
    Ⓖ ∠LNK ≅ ∠NLM   Ⓙ ∠MNK ≅ ∠NKL

26. What is the value of *y*?

    Ⓐ 10   Ⓒ 35
    Ⓑ 20   Ⓓ 85

$6x$ $40°$ $(10x + y)°$ $x + \frac{5}{2}$

27. Which of these are NOT used to prove angles congruent?

    Ⓕ congruent triangles   Ⓗ parallel lines
    Ⓖ noncorresponding parts   Ⓙ perpendicular lines

28. Which set of coordinates represents the vertices of a triangle congruent to △RST? (*Hint:* Find the lengths of the sides of △RST.)

(A) (3, 4), (3, 0), (0, 0)   (C) (3, 1), (3, 3), (4, 6)
(B) (3, 3), (0, 4), (0, 0)   (D) (3, 0), (4, 4), (0, 6)

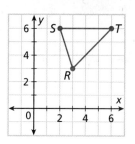

CHALLENGE AND EXTEND

H.O.T. **29.** All of the edges of a cube are congruent. All of the angles on each face of a cube are right angles. Use CPCTC to explain why any two diagonals on the faces of a cube (for example, $\overline{AC}$ and $\overline{AF}$) must be congruent.

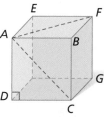

30. **Given:** $\overline{JK} \cong \overline{ML}, \overline{JM} \cong \overline{KL}$
Prove: $\angle J \cong \angle L$
(*Hint:* Draw an auxiliary line.)

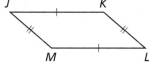

31. **Given:** *R* is the midpoint of $\overline{AB}$.
S is the midpoint of $\overline{DC}$.
$\overline{RS} \perp \overline{AB}, \angle ASD \cong \angle BSC$
Prove: △ASD ≅ △BSC

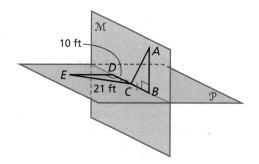

H.O.T. **32.** △ABC is in plane ℳ. △CDE is in plane 𝒫. Both planes have *C* in common and $\angle A \cong \angle E$. What is the height *AB* to the nearest foot?

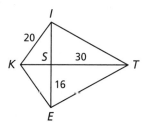

FOCUS ON MATHEMATICAL PRACTICES

H.O.T. **33.** **Problem Solving** In the figure, $\overrightarrow{KT}$ bisects $\angle IKE$, $\overline{KI} \cong \overline{KE}$, $ST = 30$, $KI = 20$, and $ES = 16$. Use this information to find the perimeter of △KIT. Explain your steps.

H.O.T. **34.** **Make a Conjecture** Two congruent right triangles share a hypotenuse. An auxiliary segment has endpoints on the vertex of each right angle. Under what conditions is the auxiliary segment perpendicular to the shared hypotenuse?

H.O.T. **35.** **Proof** In the figure, △PTQ ≅ △RTS. Prove that $\overline{PS} \parallel \overline{QR}$.

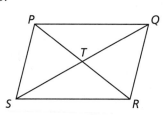

Proving Constructions Valid

? **Essential Question:** How can triangle congruence criteria be used to prove the validity of some geometric constructions?

Objective
Use congruent triangles to prove constructions valid.

When performing a compass and straight edge construction, the compass setting remains the same width until you change it. This fact allows you to construct a segment congruent to a given segment. You can assume that two distances constructed with the same compass setting are congruent.

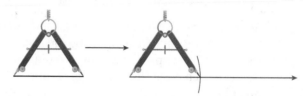

The steps in the construction of a figure can be justified by combining the assumptions of compass and straightedge constructions and the postulates and theorems that are used for proving triangles congruent.

You have learned that there exists exactly one midpoint on any line segment. The proof below justifies the construction of a midpoint.

EXAMPLE 1 **Proving the Construction of a Midpoint**

Given: diagram showing the steps in the construction
Prove: M is the midpoint of $\overline{AB}$.

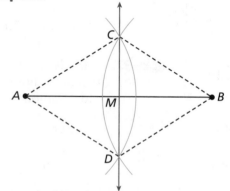

Remember!

To construct a midpoint, see the construction of a perpendicular bisector in *Perpendicular Lines*.

Proof:

Statements	Reasons
1. Draw $\overline{AC}$, $\overline{BC}$, $\overline{AD}$, and $\overline{BD}$.	1. Through any two pts. there is exactly one line.
2. $\overline{AC} \cong \overline{BC} \cong \overline{AD} \cong \overline{BD}$	2. Same compass setting used
3. $\overline{CD} \cong \overline{CD}$	3. Reflex. Prop. of $\cong$
4. $\triangle ACD \cong \triangle BCD$	4. SSS *Steps 2, 3*
5. $\angle ACD \cong \angle BCD$	5. CPCTC
6. $\overline{CM} \cong \overline{CM}$	6. Reflex. Prop. of $\cong$
7. $\triangle ACM \cong \triangle BCM$	7. SAS *Steps 2, 5, 6*
8. $\overline{AM} \cong \overline{BM}$	8. CPCTC
9. M is the midpt. of $\overline{AB}$.	9. Def. of mdpt.

 CHECK IT OUT!
1. **Given:** above diagram
Prove: $\overleftrightarrow{CD}$ is the perpendicular bisector of $\overline{AB}$.

EXAMPLE MCC9-12.G.SRT.5 **2** **Proving the Construction of an Angle**

Given: diagram showing the steps in the construction

Prove: $\angle A \cong \angle D$

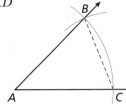
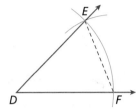

Remember!

To review the construction of an angle congruent to another angle, see *Measuring and Constructing Angles*.

Proof: Since there is a straight line through any two points, you can draw $\overline{BC}$ and $\overline{EF}$. The same compass setting was used to construct $\overline{AC}$, $\overline{AB}$, $\overline{DF}$, and $\overline{DE}$, so $\overline{AC} \cong \overline{AB} \cong \overline{DF} \cong \overline{DE}$. The same compass setting was used to construct $\overline{BC}$ and $\overline{EF}$, so $\overline{BC} \cong \overline{EF}$. Therefore $\triangle BAC \cong \triangle EDF$ by SSS, and $\angle A \cong \angle D$ by CPCTC.

CHECK IT OUT! **2.** Prove the construction for bisecting an angle.

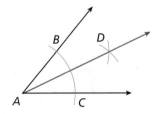

EXTENSION

Exercises

my.hrw.com
Homework Help

Use each diagram to prove the construction valid.

1. parallel lines

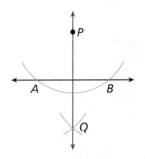

2. a perpendicular through a point not on the line

3. constructing a triangle using SAS

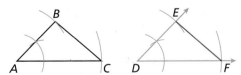

4. constructing a triangle using ASA

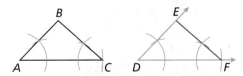

Mastering the Standards

for Mathematical Practice

The topics described in the Standards for Mathematical Content will vary from year to year. However, the *way* in which you learn, study, and think about mathematics will not. The Standards for Mathematical Practice describe skills that you will use in all of your math courses.

Mathematical Practices

1. *Make sense of problems and persevere in solving them.*
2. *Reason abstractly and quantitatively.*
3. *Construct viable arguments and critique the reasoning of others.*
4. *Model with mathematics.*
5. *Use appropriate tools strategically.*
6. *Attend to precision.*
7. *Look for and make use of structure.*
8. *Look for and express regularity in repeated reasoning.*

① Make sense of problems and persevere in solving them.

Mathematically proficient students start by explaining to themselves the meaning of a problem... They analyze givens, constraints, relationships, and goals. They make conjectures about the form... of the solution and plan a solution pathway...

In your book

Focus on Problem Solving describes a four-step plan for problem solving. The plan is introduced at the beginning of your book, and practice with the plan appears throughout the book.

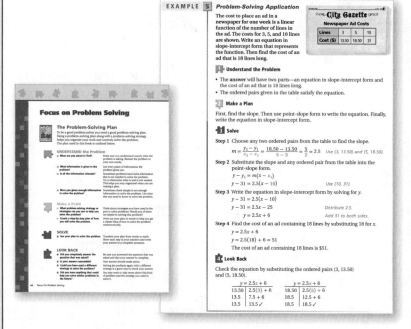

23-4 Isosceles and Equilateral Triangles

Essential Question: What special relationships exist among the sides and angles of isosceles and equilateral triangles?

Objectives
Prove theorems about isosceles and equilateral triangles.

Apply properties of isosceles and equilateral triangles.

Vocabulary
legs of an isosceles triangle
vertex angle
base
base angles

Who uses this?

Astronomers use geometric methods. (See Example 1.)

Recall that an isosceles triangle has at least two congruent sides. The congruent sides are called the **legs** . The **vertex angle** is the angle formed by the legs. The side opposite the vertex angle is called the **base** , and the **base angles** are the two angles that have the base as a side.

∠3 is the vertex angle.
∠1 and ∠2 are the base angles.

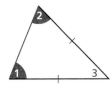

Theorems   Isosceles Triangle

THEOREM	HYPOTHESIS	CONCLUSION
23-4-1 **Isosceles Triangle Theorem** If two sides of a triangle are congruent, then the angles opposite the sides are congruent.	*A* *B* *C*	∠B ≅ ∠C
23-4-2 **Converse of Isosceles Triangle Theorem** If two angles of a triangle are congruent, then the sides opposite those angles are congruent.	*D* *E* *F*	$\overline{DE} \cong \overline{DF}$

Theorem 23-4-1 is proven below. You will prove Theorem 23-4-2 in Exercise 35.

PROOF   Isosceles Triangle Theorem

Given: $\overline{AB} \cong \overline{AC}$
Prove: ∠B ≅ ∠C
Proof:

Reading Math

The Isosceles Triangle Theorem is sometimes stated as "Base angles of an isosceles triangle are congruent."

Statements	Reasons
1. Draw *X*, the mdpt. of $\overline{BC}$.	**1.** Every seg. has a unique mdpt.
2. Draw the auxiliary line $\overline{AX}$.	**2.** Through two pts. there is exactly one line.
3. $\overline{BX} \cong \overline{CX}$	**3.** Def. of mdpt.
4. $\overline{AB} \cong \overline{AC}$	**4.** Given
5. $\overline{AX} \cong \overline{AX}$	**5.** Reflex. Prop. of ≅
6. △ABX ≅ △ACX	**6.** SSS *Steps 3, 4, 5*
7. ∠B ≅ ∠C	**7.** CPCTC

Jason T. Ware/ Photo Researchers, Inc.

Animated Math

Know it! Note

EXAMPLE **1**
MCC9-12.G.MG.1

my.hrw.com

Online Video Tutor

Astronomy Application

The distance from Earth to nearby stars can be measured using the parallax method, which requires observing the positions of a star 6 months apart. If the distance LM to a star in July is 4.0×10^{13} km, explain why the distance LK to the star in January is the same. (Assume the distance from Earth to the Sun does not change.)

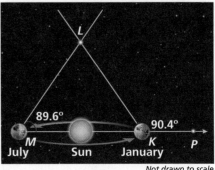

Not drawn to scale

$m\angle LKM = 180 - 90.4$, so $m\angle LKM = 89.6°$. Since $\angle LKM \cong \angle M$, $\triangle LMK$ is isosceles by the Converse of the Isosceles Triangle Theorem. Thus $LK = LM = 4.0 \times 10^{13}$ km.

1. If the distance from Earth to a star in September is 4.2×10^{13} km, what is the distance from Earth to the star in March? Explain.

EXAMPLE **2**
MCC9-12.A.CED.1

my.hrw.com

Online Video Tutor

Finding the Measure of an Angle

Find each angle measure.

$m\angle C = m\angle B = x°$	*Isosc. △ Thm.*
$m\angle C + m\angle B + m\angle A = 180$	*△ Sum Thm.*
$x + x + 38 = 180$	*Substitute the given values.*
$2x = 142$	*Simplify and subtract 38 from both sides.*
$x = 71$	*Divide both sides by 2.*

Thus $m\angle C = 71°$.

 m∠S

$m\angle S = m\angle R$	*Isosc. △ Thm.*
$2x° = (x + 30)°$	*Substitute the given values.*
$x = 30$	*Subtract x from both sides.*

Thus $m\angle S = 2x° = 2(30) = 60°$.

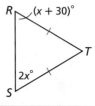

Find each angle measure.
2a. $m\angle H$ **2b.** $m\angle N$

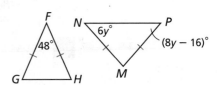

The following corollary and its converse show the connection between equilateral triangles and equiangular triangles.

Corollary 23-4-3 | Equilateral Triangle

COROLLARY	HYPOTHESIS	CONCLUSION
If a triangle is equilateral, then it is equiangular. (equilateral △ → equiangular △)	*A* *B* *C*	$\angle A \cong \angle B \cong \angle C$

You will prove Corollary 23-4-3 in Exercise 36.

Corollary 23-4-4 | **Equiangular Triangle**

COROLLARY	HYPOTHESIS	CONCLUSION
If a triangle is equiangular, then it is equilateral. (equiangular △ → equilateral △)		$\overline{DE} \cong \overline{DF} \cong \overline{EF}$

You will prove Corollary 23-4-4 in Exercise 37.

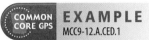

EXAMPLE 3

MCC9-12.A.CED.1

Online Video Tutor

Using Properties of Equilateral Triangles

Find each value.

A x

$\triangle ABC$ is equiangular.

$(3x + 15)° = 60°$ *Equilateral △ → equiangular △*

                      The measure of each ∠ of
                         an equiangular △ is 60°.

         $3x = 45$ *Subtract 15 from both sides.*

           $x = 15$ *Divide both sides by 3.*

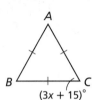

B t

$\triangle JKL$ is equilateral.

$4t - 8 = 2t + 1$ *Equiangular △ → equilateral △*
                       Def. of equilateral △

       $2t = 9$ *Subtract 2t and add 8 to*
                      both sides.

         $t = 4.5$ *Divide both sides by 2.*

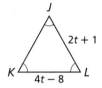

 3. Use the diagram to find *JL*.

EXAMPLE 4

MCC9-12.G.GPE.4

Online Video Tutor

Using Coordinate Proof

Prove that the triangle whose vertices are the midpoints of the sides of an isosceles triangle is also isosceles.

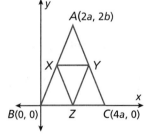

Given: $\triangle ABC$ is isosceles. X is the mdpt. of $\overline{AB}$.
         Y is the mdpt. of $\overline{AC}$. Z is the mdpt. of $\overline{BC}$.
Prove: $\triangle XYZ$ is isosceles.

Proof:

Draw a diagram and place the coordinates of $\triangle ABC$ and $\triangle XYZ$ as shown.

By the Midpoint Formula, the coordinates of X are $\left(\frac{2a+0}{2}, \frac{2b+0}{2}\right) = (a, b)$,

the coordinates of Y are $\left(\frac{2a+4a}{2}, \frac{2b+0}{2}\right) = (3a, b)$, and the coordinates of Z

are $\left(\frac{4a+0}{2}, \frac{0+0}{2}\right) = (2a, 0)$.

By the Distance Formula, $XZ = \sqrt{(2a-a)^2 + (0-b)^2} = \sqrt{a^2 + b^2}$, and

$YZ = \sqrt{(2a-3a)^2 + (0-b)^2} = \sqrt{a^2 + b^2}$.

Since $XZ = YZ$, $\overline{XZ} \cong \overline{YZ}$ by definition. So $\triangle XYZ$ is isosceles.

 4. What if...? The coordinates of $\triangle ABC$ are $A(0, 2b)$, $B(-2a, 0)$, and $C(2a, 0)$. Prove $\triangle XYZ$ is isosceles.

THINK AND DISCUSS

1. Explain why each of the angles in an equilateral triangle measures 60°.

2. **GET ORGANIZED** Copy and complete the graphic organizer. In each box, draw and mark a diagram for each type of triangle.

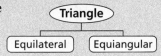

23-4 Exercises

my.hrw.com
Homework Help

GUIDED PRACTICE

1. **Vocabulary** Draw isosceles △*JKL* with ∠*K* as the vertex angle. Name the legs, base, and base angles of the triangle.

SEE EXAMPLE 1

2. **Surveying** To find the distance *QR* across a river, a surveyor locates three points *Q*, *R*, and *S*. *QS* = 41 m, and m∠*S* = 35°. The measure of exterior ∠*PQS* = 70°. Draw a diagram and explain how you can find *QR*.

SEE EXAMPLE 2

Find each angle measure.

3. m∠*ECD*

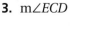

4. m∠*K*

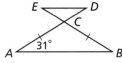

5. m∠*X*

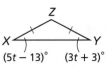

6. m∠*A*

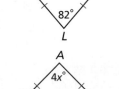

SEE EXAMPLE 3

Find each value.

7. *y*

8. *x*

9. *BC*

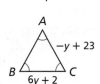

10. *JK*

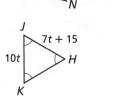

SEE EXAMPLE 4

11. **Given:** △*ABC* is right isosceles. *X* is the midpoint of $\overline{AC}$. $\overline{AB} \cong \overline{BC}$

Prove: △*AXB* is isosceles.

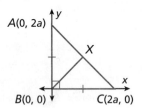

PRACTICE AND PROBLEM SOLVING

Independent Practice

For Exercises	See Example
12	1
13–16	2
17–20	3
21	4

my.hrw.com

Online Extra Practice

12. Aviation A plane is flying parallel to the ground along $\overrightarrow{AC}$. When the plane is at A, an air-traffic controller in tower T measures the angle to the plane as 40°. After the plane has traveled 2.4 mi to B, the angle to the plane is 80°. How can you find BT?

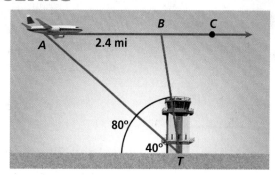

Find each angle measure.

13. m∠E

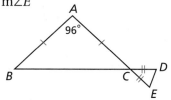

14. m∠TRU

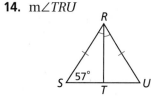

15. m∠F

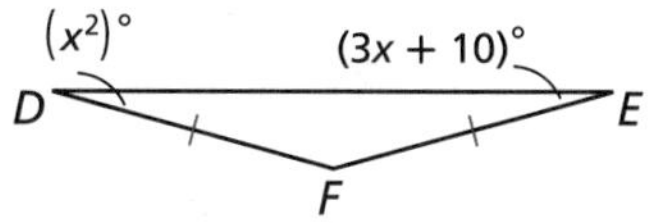

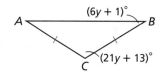

16. m∠A

Find each value.

17. z

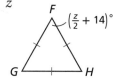

18. y

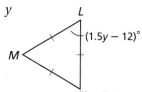

19. BC

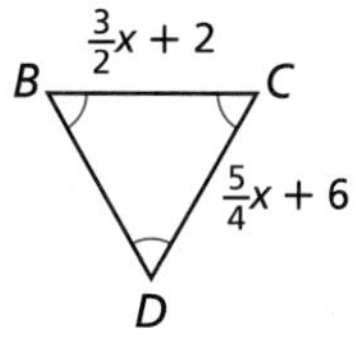

20. XZ

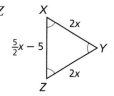

21. Given: △ABC is isosceles. P is the midpoint of $\overline{AB}$. Q is the midpoint of $\overline{AC}$.
$\overline{AB} \cong \overline{AC}$
Prove: $\overline{PC} \cong \overline{QB}$

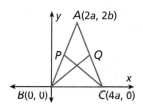

H.O.T. Tell whether each statement is sometimes, always, or never true. Support your answer with a sketch.

22. An equilateral triangle is an isosceles triangle.

23. The vertex angle of an isosceles triangle is congruent to the base angles.

24. An isosceles triangle is a right triangle.

25. An equilateral triangle and an obtuse triangle are congruent.

H.O.T. 26. Critical Thinking Can a base angle of an isosceles triangle be an obtuse angle? Why or why not?

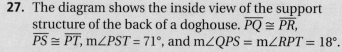

27. The diagram shows the inside view of the support structure of the back of a doghouse. $\overline{PQ} \cong \overline{PR}$, $\overline{PS} \cong \overline{PT}$, m∠PST = 71°, and m∠QPS = m∠RPT = 18°.

a. Find m∠SPT.

b. Find m∠PQR and m∠PRQ.

Multi-Step Find the measure of each numbered angle.

28.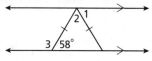

29.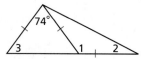

30. Write a coordinate proof.

Given: ∠B is a right angle in isosceles right △ABC. X is the midpoint of $\overline{AC}$. $\overline{BA} \cong \overline{BC}$
Prove: △AXB ≅ △CXB

31. Estimation Draw the figure formed by (−2, 1), (5, 5), and (−1, −7). Estimate the measure of each angle and make a conjecture about the classification of the figure. Then use a protractor to measure each angle. Was your conjecture correct? Why or why not?

H.O.T. 32. How many different isosceles triangles have a perimeter of 18 and sides whose lengths are natural numbers? Explain.

Multi-Step Find the value of the variable in each diagram.

33.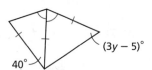

34.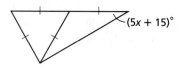

35. Prove the Converse of the Isosceles Triangle Theorem.

36. Complete the proof of Corollary 23-4-3.

Given: $\overline{AB} \cong \overline{AC} \cong \overline{BC}$
Prove: ∠A ≅ ∠B ≅ ∠C

Proof: Since $\overline{AB} \cong \overline{AC}$, **a.** ___?___ by the Isosceles Triangle Theorem. Since $\overline{AC} \cong \overline{BC}$, ∠A ≅ ∠B by **b.** ___?___ . Therefore ∠A ≅ ∠C by **c.** ___?___ . By the Transitive Property of ≅, ∠A ≅ ∠B ≅ ∠C.

37. Prove Corollary 23-4-4.

Navigation

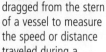

The taffrail log is dragged from the stern of a vessel to measure the speed or distance traveled during a voyage. The log consists of a rotator, recording device, and governor.

38. Navigation The captain of a ship traveling along $\overrightarrow{AB}$ sights an island C at an angle of 45°. The captain measures the distance the ship covers until it reaches B, where the angle to the island is 90°. Explain how to find the distance BC to the island.

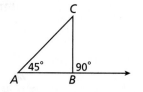

39. Given: △ABC ≅ △CBA
Prove: △ABC is isosceles.

40. Write About It Write the Isosceles Triangle Theorem and its converse as a biconditional.

41. Rewrite the paragraph proof of the Hypotenuse-Leg (HL) Congruence Theorem as a two-column proof.

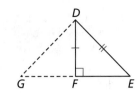

Given: $\triangle ABC$ and $\triangle DEF$ are right triangles. $\angle C$ and $\angle F$ are right angles. $\overline{AC} \cong \overline{DF}$, and $\overline{AB} \cong \overline{DE}$.

Prove: $\triangle ABC \cong \triangle DEF$

Proof: On $\triangle DEF$ draw $\overrightarrow{EF}$. Mark G so that $FG = CB$. Thus $\overline{FG} \cong \overline{CB}$. From the diagram, $\overline{AC} \cong \overline{DF}$ and $\angle C$ and $\angle F$ are right angles. $\overline{DF} \perp \overline{EG}$ by definition of perpendicular lines. Thus $\angle DFG$ is a right angle, and $\angle DFG \cong \angle C$. $\triangle ABC \cong \triangle DGF$ by SAS. $\overline{DG} \cong \overline{AB}$ by CPCTC. $\overline{AB} \cong \overline{DE}$ as given. $\overline{DG} \cong \overline{DE}$ by the Transitive Property. By the Isosceles Triangle Theorem $\angle G \cong \angle E$. $\angle DFG \cong \angle DFE$ since right angles are congruent. So $\triangle DGF \cong \triangle DEF$ by AAS. Therefore $\triangle ABC \cong \triangle DEF$ by the Transitive Property.

TEST PREP

42. Lorena is designing a window so that $\angle R$, $\angle S$, $\angle T$, and $\angle U$ are right angles, $\overline{VU} \cong \overline{VT}$, and $m\angle UVT = 20°$. What is $m\angle RUV$?

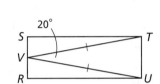

- (A) 10°
- (C) 20°
- (B) 70°
- (D) 80°

43. Which of these values of y makes $\triangle ABC$ isosceles?

- (F) $1\frac{1}{4}$
- (H) $7\frac{1}{2}$
- (G) $2\frac{1}{2}$
- (J) $15\frac{1}{2}$

44. Gridded Response The vertex angle of an isosceles triangle measures $(6t - 9)°$, and one of the base angles measures $(4t)°$. Find t.

CHALLENGE AND EXTEND

H.O.T. 45. In the figure, $\overline{JK} \cong \overline{JL}$, and $\overline{KM} \cong \overline{KL}$. Let $m\angle J = x°$. Prove $m\angle MKL$ must also be $x°$.

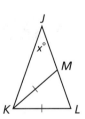

H.O.T. 46. An equilateral $\triangle ABC$ is placed on a coordinate plane. Each side length measures $2a$. B is at the origin, and C is at $(2a, 0)$. Find the coordinates of A.

47. An isosceles triangle has coordinates $A(0, 0)$ and $B(a, b)$. What are all possible coordinates of the third vertex?

FOCUS ON MATHEMATICAL PRACTICES

H.O.T. 48. Draw Conclusions In the figure, $\overline{RS} \parallel \overline{TW}$, and $\overrightarrow{TW}$ bisects $\angle RTU$. Classify $\triangle RST$. Justify your answer.

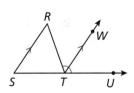

H.O.T. 49. Analysis In the figure, $\angle R \cong \angle K$, $\angle PGK \cong \angle JHR$, and $\overline{JM} \cong \overline{PM}$. Is this enough to prove $\triangle JRH \cong \triangle PKG$? Explain.

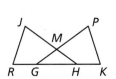

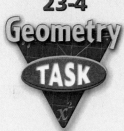

23-4
Geometry
TASK

Construct Regular Polygons

An equilateral triangle is a triangle with three congruent sides. You also learned that an equilateral triangle is equiangular, meaning that all its angles are congruent.

In this task, you will construct polygons that are both equilateral and equiangular by inscribing them in circles.

Use appropriate tools strategically.

MCC9-12.G.CO.13 Construct an equilateral triangle, a square, and a regular hexagon inscribed in a circle.

Activity 1

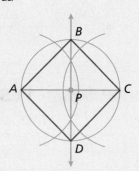

1 Construct circle *P*. Draw a diameter $\overline{AC}$.

2 Construct the perpendicular bisector of $\overline{AC}$. Label the intersections of the bisector and the circle as *B* and *D*.

3 Draw $\overline{AB}$, $\overline{BC}$, $\overline{CD}$, and $\overline{DA}$. The polygon *ABCD* is a *regular quadrilateral*. This means it is a four-sided polygon that has four congruent sides and four congruent angles.

Try This

1. Describe a different method for constructing a regular quadrilateral.

2. The regular quadrilateral in Activity 1 is inscribed in the circle. What is the relationship between the circle and the regular quadrilateral?

3. A *regular octagon* is an eight-sided polygon that has eight congruent sides and eight congruent angles. Use angle bisectors to construct a regular octagon from a regular quadrilateral.

Activity 2

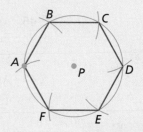

1 Construct circle *P*. Draw a point *A* on the circle.

2 Use the same compass setting. Starting at *A*, draw arcs to mark off equal parts along the circle. Label the other points where the arcs intersect the circle as *B*, *C*, *D*, *E*, and *F*.

3 Draw $\overline{AB}$, $\overline{BC}$, $\overline{CD}$, $\overline{DE}$, $\overline{EF}$, and $\overline{FA}$. The polygon *ABCDEF* is a *regular hexagon*. This means it is a six-sided polygon that has six congruent sides and six congruent angles.

Try This

4. Justify the conclusion that *ABCDEF* is a regular hexagon. (*Hint:* Draw diameters $\overline{AD}$, $\overline{BE}$, and $\overline{CF}$. What types of triangles are formed?)

5. A *regular dodecagon* is a 12-sided polygon that has 12 congruent sides and 12 congruent angles. Use the construction of a regular hexagon to construct a regular dodecagon. Explain your method.

Activity 3

1 Construct circle *P*. Draw a diameter $\overline{AB}$.

2 Construct the perpendicular bisector of $\overline{AB}$. Label one point where the bisector intersects the circle as point *E*.

3 Construct the midpoint of radius $\overline{PB}$. Label it as point *C*.

4 Set your compass to the length *CE*. Place the compass point at *C* and draw an arc that intersects $\overline{AB}$. Label the point of intersection *D*.

5 Set the compass to the length *ED*. Starting at *E*, draw arcs to mark off equal parts along the circle. Label the other points where the arcs intersect the circle as *F*, *G*, *H*, and *J*.

6 Draw $\overline{EF}$, $\overline{FG}$, $\overline{GH}$, $\overline{HJ}$, and $\overline{JE}$. The polygon *EFGHJ* is a *regular pentagon*. This means it is a five-sided polygon that has five congruent sides and five congruent angles.

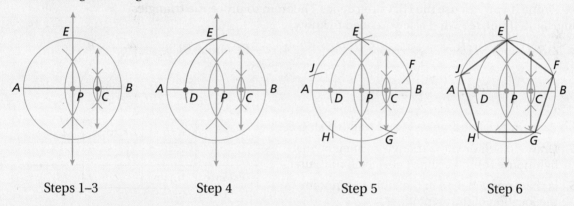

Steps 1–3   Step 4   Step 5   Step 6

Try This

6. A *regular decagon* is a ten-sided polygon that has ten congruent sides and ten congruent angles. Use the construction of a regular pentagon to construct a regular decagon. Explain your method.

7. Measure each angle of the regular polygons in Activities 1–3 and complete the following table.

REGULAR POLYGONS				
Number of Sides	3	4	5	6
Measure of Each Angle	60°			
Sum of Angle Measures	180°			

8. Make a Conjecture What is a general rule for finding the sum of the angle measures in a regular polygon with *n* sides?

9. Make a Conjecture What is a general rule for finding the measure of each angle in a regular polygon with *n* sides?

Ready to Go On?

my.hrw.com
Assessment and Intervention

✓ 23-1 Triangle Congruence: SSS and SAS

1. The figure shows one tower and the cables of a suspension bridge. Given that $\overline{AC} \cong \overline{BC}$, use SAS to explain why $\triangle ACD \cong \triangle BCD$.

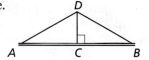

2. **Given:** $\overline{JK}$ bisects $\angle MJN$. $\overline{MJ} \cong \overline{NJ}$
   Prove: $\triangle MJK \cong \triangle NJK$

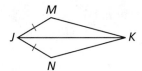

✓ 23-2 Triangle Congruence: ASA, AAS, and HL

Determine if you can use the HL Congruence Theorem to prove the triangles congruent. If not, tell what else you need to know.

3. $\triangle RSU$ and $\triangle TUS$

4. $\triangle ABC$ and $\triangle DCB$

Observers in two lighthouses K and L spot a ship S.

5. Draw a diagram of the triangle formed by the lighthouses and the ship. Label each measure.

6. Is there enough data in the table to pinpoint the location of the ship? Why?

	K to L	K to S	L to S
Bearing	E	N 58° E	N 77° W
Distance	12 km	?	?

✓ 23-3 Triangle Congruence: CPCTC

7. **Given:** $\overline{CD} \parallel \overline{BE}$, $\overline{DE} \parallel \overline{CB}$
   Prove: $\angle D \cong \angle B$

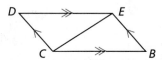

8. **Given:** $\overline{PQ} \cong \overline{RQ}$, $\overline{PS} \cong \overline{RS}$
   Prove: $\overline{QS}$ bisects $\angle PQR$.

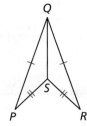

✓ 23-4 Isosceles and Equilateral Triangles

Find each value.

9. m∠C

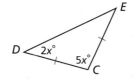

10. ST

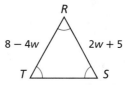

11. **Given:** Isosceles △JKL has coordinates J(0, 0), K(2a, 2b), and L(4a, 0).
M is the midpoint of $\overline{JK}$, and N is the midpoint of $\overline{KL}$.
Prove: △KMN is isosceles.

PARCC Assessment Readiness

Selected Response

1. A pilot uses triangles to find the angle of elevation ∠A from the ground to her plane. How can she find m∠A?

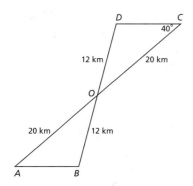

(A) △ABO ≅ △CDO by SAS and ∠A ≅ ∠C by CPCTC, so m∠A = 40° by substitution.

(B) △ABO ≅ △CDO by CPCTC and ∠A ≅ ∠C by SAS, so m∠A = 40° by substitution.

(C) △ABO ≅ △CDO by ASA and ∠A ≅ ∠C by CPCTC, so m∠A = 40° by substitution.

(D) △ABO ≅ △CDO by CPCTC and ∠A ≅ ∠C by ASA, so m∠A = 40° by substitution.

2. Given the lengths marked on the figure and that $\overline{AD}$ bisects $\overline{BE}$, use SSS to explain why △ABC ≅ △DEC.

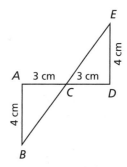

(F) $\overline{AC} \cong \overline{CD}$, $\overline{AB} \cong \overline{ED}$, $\overline{BC} \cong \overline{CE}$

(G) $\overline{AC} \cong \overline{CD}$, $\overline{AB} \cong \overline{ED}$, $\overline{BC} \cong \overline{BC}$

(H) $\overline{AC} \cong \overline{CB}$, $\overline{AB} \cong \overline{ED}$, $\overline{CD} \cong \overline{CE}$

(J) The triangles are not congruent.

Mini-Task

3. Determine if you can use ASA to prove △CBA ≅ △CED. Explain.

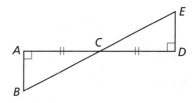

24 Special Points and Segments in Triangles

COMMON
CORE GPS

Contents

MATHEMATICAL PRACTICES   The Common Core Georgia Performance Standards for Mathematical Practice describe varieties of expertise that all students should seek to develop. Opportunities to develop these practices are integrated throughout this program.

1 Make sense of problems and persevere in solving them.

2 Reason abstractly and quantitatively.

3 Construct viable arguments and critique the reasoning of others.

4 Model with mathematics.

5 Use appropriate tools strategically.

6 Attend to precision.

7 Look for and make use of structure.

8 Look for and express regularity in repeated reasoning.

Unpacking the Standards

Understanding the standards and the vocabulary terms in the standards will help you know exactly what you are expected to learn in this chapter.

 MCC9-12.G.CO.9

Prove theorems about lines and angles.

Key Vocabulary

proof (demostración)
An argument that uses logic to show that a conclusion is true.

theorem (teorema)
A statement that has been proven.

line (línea)
An undefined term in geometry, a line is a straight path that has no thickness and extends forever.

angle (ángulo)
A figure formed by two rays with a common endpoint.

What It Means For You

Many segments associated with triangles, such as those that bisect angles or sides, are perpendiculars, connect midpoints, and so on, have special properties that you can prove.

EXAMPLE

Medians $\overline{AY}$, $\overline{CX}$, and $\overline{BZ}$ meet in a single point P.

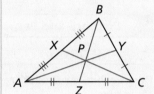

Midsegment $\overline{DE}$ is parallel to side $\overline{AC}$.

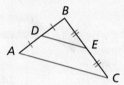

 MCC9-12.G.CO.10

Prove theorems about triangles.

Key Vocabulary

proof (demostración)
An argument that uses logic to show that a conclusion is true.

theorem (teorema)
A statement that has been proven.

triangle (triángulo)
A three-sided polygon.

What It Means For You

You can prove theorems about the relationships among side lengths and angle measures within a single triangle and between two or more triangles.

EXAMPLE   **Relationships within a triangle**

Because m$\angle PSQ = 51°$ by the Triangle Sum Theorem, it is the smallest angle in $\triangle PSQ$. So, the opposite side, $\overline{PQ}$, is the shortest side of $\triangle PSQ$.

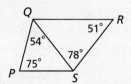

EXAMPLE   **Relationships between triangles**

By the Hinge Theorem, if $m\angle B > m\angle E$ in the two triangles shown with congruent sides as marked, then $AC > DF$.

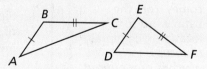

24-1 Perpendicular and Angle Bisectors

? Essential Question: How can you describe the set of points equidistant from the endpoints of a segment or from the sides of an angle?

Objectives
Prove and apply theorems about perpendicular bisectors.

Prove and apply theorems about angle bisectors.

Vocabulary
equidistant
locus

Who uses this?
The suspension and steering lines of a parachute keep the sky diver centered under the parachute. (See Example 3.)

When a point is the same distance from two or more objects, the point is said to be **equidistant** from the objects. Triangle congruence theorems can be used to prove theorems about equidistant points.

Know it! Note

Animated Math

Theorems	**Distance and Perpendicular Bisectors**		
THEOREM		**HYPOTHESIS**	**CONCLUSION**
24-1-1 Perpendicular Bisector Theorem If a point is on the perpendicular bisector of a segment, then it is equidistant from the endpoints of the segment.		$\overline{XY} \perp \overline{AB}$ $\overline{YA} \cong \overline{YB}$	$XA = XB$
24-1-2 Converse of the Perpendicular Bisector Theorem If a point is equidistant from the endpoints of a segment, then it is on the perpendicular bisector of the segment.		$XA = XB$	$\overline{XY} \perp \overline{AB}$ $\overline{YA} \cong \overline{YB}$

You will prove Theorem 24-1-2 in Exercise 30.

PROOF **Perpendicular Bisector Theorem**

Reading Math

The word *locus* comes from the Latin word for location. The plural of *locus* is *loci*, which is pronounced LOW-sigh.

Given: ℓ is the perpendicular bisector of $\overline{AB}$.
Prove: $XA = XB$

Proof:
Since ℓ is the perpendicular bisector of $\overline{AB}$, $\ell \perp \overline{AB}$ and Y is the midpoint of $\overline{AB}$. By the definition of perpendicular, $\angle AYX$ and $\angle BYX$ are right angles and $\angle AYX \cong \angle BYX$. By the definition of midpoint, $\overline{AY} \cong \overline{BY}$. By the Reflexive Property of Congruence, $\overline{XY} \cong \overline{XY}$. So $\triangle AYX \cong \triangle BYX$ by SAS, and $\overline{XA} \cong \overline{XB}$ by CPCTC. Therefore $XA = XB$ by the definition of congruent segments.

A **locus** is a set of points that satisfies a given condition. The perpendicular bisector of a segment can be defined as the locus of points in a plane that are equidistant from the endpoints of the segment.

EXAMPLE 1 **Applying the Perpendicular Bisector Theorem and Its Converse**

Find each measure.

A *YW*

$YW = XW$ ⊥ *Bisector Thm.*

$YW = 7.3$ *Substitute 7.3 for XW.*

B *BC*

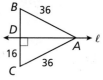

Since $AB = AC$ and $\ell \perp \overline{BC}$, ℓ is the perpendicular bisector of $\overline{BC}$ by the Converse of the Perpendicular Bisector Theorem.

$BC = 2CD$ *Def. of seg. bisector*

$BC = 2(16) = 32$ *Substitute 16 for CD.*

C *PR*

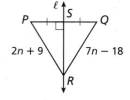

$PR = RQ$ ⊥ *Bisector Thm.*

$2n + 9 = 7n - 18$ *Substitute the given values.*

$9 = 5n - 18$ *Subtract 2n from both sides.*

$27 = 5n$ *Add 18 to both sides.*

$5.4 = n$ *Divide both sides by 5.*

So $PR = 2(5.4) + 9 = 19.8$.

Find each measure.

1a. Given that line ℓ is the perpendicular bisector of $\overline{DE}$ and $EG = 14.6$, find DG.

1b. Given that $DE = 20.8$, $DG = 36.4$, and $EG = 36.4$, find EF.

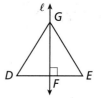

Remember that the distance between a point and a line is the length of the perpendicular segment from the point to the line.

Theorems | **Distance and Angle Bisectors**

THEOREM	HYPOTHESIS	CONCLUSION
24-1-3 **Angle Bisector Theorem** If a point is on the bisector of an angle, then it is equidistant from the sides of the angle.	∠APC ≅ ∠BPC	AC = BC
24-1-4 **Converse of the Angle Bisector Theorem** If a point in the interior of an angle is equidistant from the sides of the angle, then it is on the bisector of the angle.	AC = BC	∠APC ≅ ∠BPC

You will prove these theorems in Exercises 31 and 40.

Based on these theorems, an angle bisector can be defined as the locus of all points in the interior of the angle that are equidistant from the sides of the angle.

EXAMPLE 2
MCC9-12.A.CED.1

Applying the Angle Bisector Theorems

Find each measure.

A *LM*

$LM = JM$ *∠ Bisector Thm.*

$LM = 12.8$ *Substitute 12.8 for JM.*

B m∠*ABD*, given that m∠*ABC* = 112°

Since $AD = DC$, $\overline{AD} \perp \overline{BA}$, and $\overline{DC} \perp \overline{BC}$, $\overrightarrow{BD}$ bisects ∠*ABC* by the Converse of the Angle Bisector Theorem.

$m\angle ABD = \frac{1}{2}m\angle ABC$ *Def. of ∠ bisector*

$m\angle ABD = \frac{1}{2}(112°) = 56°$ *Substitute 112° for m∠ABC.*

C m∠*TSU*

Since $RU = UT$, $\overline{RU} \perp \overline{SR}$, and $\overline{UT} \perp \overline{ST}$, $\overrightarrow{SU}$ bisects ∠*RST* by the Converse of the Angle Bisector Theorem.

$m\angle RSU = m\angle TSU$ *Def. of ∠ bisector*

$6z + 14 = 5z + 23$ *Substitute the given values.*

$z + 14 = 23$ *Subtract 5z from both sides.*

$z = 9$ *Subtract 14 from both sides.*

So $m\angle TSU = \left[5(9) + 23\right]° = 68°$.

CHECK IT OUT!

Find each measure.

2a. Given that $\overrightarrow{YW}$ bisects ∠*XYZ* and $WZ = 3.05$, find *WX*.

2b. Given that m∠*WYZ* = 63°, $XW = 5.7$, and $ZW = 5.7$, find m∠*XYZ*.

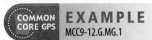

EXAMPLE 3
MCC9-12.G.MG.1

Parachute Application

Each pair of suspension lines on a parachute are the same length and are equally spaced from the center of the chute. How do these lines keep the sky diver centered under the parachute?

It is given that $\overline{PQ} \cong \overline{RQ}$. So Q is on the perpendicular bisector of $\overline{PR}$ by the Converse of the Perpendicular Bisector Theorem. Since S is the midpoint of $\overline{PR}$, $\overline{QS}$ is the perpendicular bisector of $\overline{PR}$. Therefore the sky diver remains centered under the chute.

3. *S* is equidistant from each pair of suspension lines. What can you conclude about $\overrightarrow{QS}$?

EXAMPLE **4**
MCC9-12.G.GPE.5

Online Video Tutor

Writing Equations of Bisectors in the Coordinate Plane

Write an equation in point-slope form for the perpendicular bisector of the segment with endpoints $A(-1, 6)$ and $B(3, 4)$.

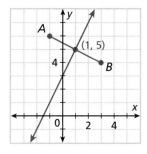

Step 1 Graph $\overline{AB}$.

The perpendicular bisector of $\overline{AB}$ is perpendicular to $\overline{AB}$ at its midpoint.

Step 2 Find the midpoint of $\overline{AB}$.

$$\left(\frac{x_1 + x_2}{2}, \frac{y_1 + y_2}{2}\right) \quad \textit{Midpoint formula}$$

$$\text{mdpt. of } \overline{AB} = \left(\frac{-1 + 3}{2}, \frac{6 + 4}{2}\right) = (1, 5)$$

Step 3 Find the slope of the perpendicular bisector.

$$\text{slope} = \frac{y_2 - y_1}{x_2 - x_1} \quad \textit{Slope formula}$$

$$\text{slope of } \overline{AB} = \frac{4 - 6}{3 - (-1)} = \frac{-2}{4} = -\frac{1}{2}$$

Since the slopes of perpendicular lines are opposite reciprocals, the slope of the perpendicular bisector is 2.

Step 4 Use point-slope form to write an equation.

The perpendicular bisector of $\overline{AB}$ has slope 2 and passes through $(1, 5)$.

$$y - y_1 = m(x - x_1) \quad \textit{Point-slope form}$$
$$y - 5 = 2(x - 1) \quad \textit{Substitute 5 for } y_1, 2 \text{ for } m, \text{ and 1 for } x_1.$$

4. Write an equation in point-slope form for the perpendicular bisector of the segment with endpoints $P(5, 2)$ and $Q(1, -4)$.

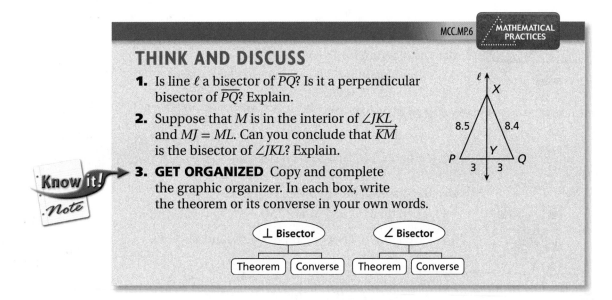

MCC.MP.6   **MATHEMATICAL PRACTICES**

THINK AND DISCUSS

1. Is line ℓ a bisector of $\overline{PQ}$? Is it a perpendicular bisector of $\overline{PQ}$? Explain.

2. Suppose that M is in the interior of $\angle JKL$ and $MJ = ML$. Can you conclude that $\overrightarrow{KM}$ is the bisector of $\angle JKL$? Explain.

3. GET ORGANIZED Copy and complete the graphic organizer. In each box, write the theorem or its converse in your own words.

⊥ Bisector | ∠ Bisector
Theorem | Converse | Theorem | Converse

GUIDED PRACTICE

1. **Vocabulary** A ___?___ is the *locus* of all points in a plane that are *equidistant* from the endpoints of a segment. *(perpendicular bisector or angle bisector)*

SEE EXAMPLE 1 **Use the diagram for Exercises 2–4.**

2. Given that $PS = 53.4$, $QT = 47.7$, and $QS = 53.4$, find PQ.

3. Given that m is the perpendicular bisector of $\overline{PQ}$ and $SQ = 25.9$, find SP.

4. Given that m is the perpendicular bisector of $\overline{PQ}$, $PS = 4a$, and $QS = 2a + 26$, find QS.

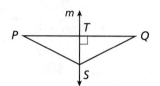

SEE EXAMPLE 2 **Use the diagram for Exercises 5–7.**

5. Given that $\overrightarrow{BD}$ bisects $\angle ABC$ and $CD = 21.9$, find AD.

6. Given that $AD = 61$, $CD = 61$, and $m\angle ABC = 48°$, find $m\angle CBD$.

7. Given that $DA = DC$, $m\angle DBC = (10y + 3)°$, and $m\angle DBA = (8y + 10)°$, find $m\angle DBC$.

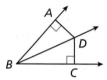

SEE EXAMPLE 3

8. **Carpentry** For a king post truss to be constructed correctly, P must lie on the bisector of $\angle JLN$. How can braces $\overline{PK}$ and $\overline{PM}$ be used to ensure that P is in the proper location?

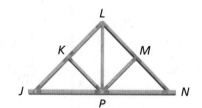

SEE EXAMPLE 4 **Write an equation in point-slope form for the perpendicular bisector of the segment with the given endpoints.**

9. $M(-5, 4)$, $N(1, -2)$ 10. $U(2, -6)$, $V(4, 0)$ 11. $J(-7, 5)$, $K(1, -1)$

PRACTICE AND PROBLEM SOLVING

Use the diagram for Exercises 12–14.

12. Given that line t is the perpendicular bisector of $\overline{JK}$ and $GK = 8.25$, find GJ.

13. Given that line t is the perpendicular bisector of $\overline{JK}$, $JG = x + 12$, and $KG = 3x - 17$, find KG.

14. Given that $GJ = 70.2$, $JH = 26.5$, and $GK = 70.2$, find JK.

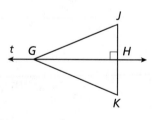

Use the diagram for Exercises 15–17.

15. Given that $m\angle RSQ = m\angle TSQ$ and $TQ = 1.3$, find RQ.

16. Given that $m\angle RSQ = 58°$, $RQ = 49$, and $TQ = 49$, find $m\angle RST$.

17. Given that $RQ = TQ$, $m\angle QSR = (9a + 48)°$, and $m\angle QST = (6a + 50)°$, find $m\angle QST$.

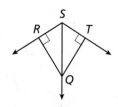

18. City Planning The planners for a new section of the city want every location on Main Street to be equidistant from Elm Street and Grove Street. How can the planners ensure that this is the case?

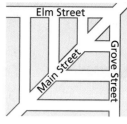

Write an equation in point-slope form for the perpendicular bisector of the segment with the given endpoints.

19. $E(-4, -7), F(0, 1)$ **20.** $X(-7, 5), Y(-1, -1)$ **21.** $M(-3, -1), N(7, -5)$

22. $\overline{PQ}$ is the perpendicular bisector of $\overline{ST}$. Find the values of m and n.

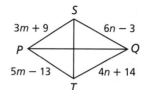

Shuffleboard Use the diagram of a shuffleboard and the following information to find each length in Exercises 23–28.

$\overline{KZ}$ is the perpendicular bisector of $\overline{GN}$, $\overline{HM}$, and $\overline{JL}$.

23. JK **24.** GN **25.** ML

26. HY **27.** JL **28.** NM

One of the first recorded shuffleboard games was played in England in 1532. In this game, Henry VIII supposedly lost £9 to Lord William.

29. Multi-Step The endpoints of $\overline{AB}$ are $A(-2, 1)$ and $B(4, -3)$. Find the coordinates of a point C other than the midpoint of $\overline{AB}$ that is on the perpendicular bisector of $\overline{AB}$. How do you know it is on the perpendicular bisector?

30. Write a paragraph proof of the Converse of the Perpendicular Bisector Theorem.

Given: $AX = BX$
Prove: X is on the perpendicular bisector of $\overline{AB}$.

Plan: Draw ℓ perpendicular to $\overline{AB}$ through X. Show that $\triangle AYX \cong \triangle BYX$ and thus $\overline{AY} \cong \overline{BY}$. By definition, ℓ is the perpendicular bisector of $\overline{AB}$.

31. Write a two-column proof of the Angle Bisector Theorem.
Given: $\overrightarrow{PS}$ bisects $\angle QPR$. $\overline{SQ} \perp \overrightarrow{PQ}$, $\overline{SR} \perp \overrightarrow{PR}$
Prove: $SQ = SR$

Plan: Use the definitions of angle bisector and perpendicular to identify two pairs of congruent angles. Show that $\triangle PQS \cong \triangle PRS$ and thus $\overline{SQ} \cong \overline{SR}$.

H.O.T. 32. Critical Thinking In the Converse of the Angle Bisector Theorem, why is it important to say that the point must be in the interior of the angle?

Real-World Connections

33. A music company has stores in Abby $(-3, -2)$ and Cardenas $(3, 6)$. Each unit in the coordinate plane represents 1 mile.

a. The company president wants to build a warehouse that is equidistant from the two stores. Write an equation that describes the possible locations.

b. A straight road connects Abby and Cardenas. The warehouse will be located exactly 4 miles from the road. How many locations are possible?

c. To the nearest tenth of a mile, how far will the warehouse be from each store?

H.O.T **34. Write About It** How is the construction of the perpendicular bisector of a segment related to the Converse of the Perpendicular Bisector Theorem?

TEST PREP

35. If $\overleftrightarrow{JK}$ is perpendicular to $\overline{XY}$ at its midpoint M, which statement is true?

    Ⓐ $JX = KY$ Ⓑ $JX = KX$ Ⓒ $JM = KM$ Ⓓ $JX = JY$

36. What information is needed to conclude that $\overrightarrow{EF}$ is the bisector of $\angle DEG$?

    Ⓕ $m\angle DEF = m\angle DEG$ Ⓗ $m\angle GED = m\angle GEF$

    Ⓖ $m\angle FEG = m\angle DEF$ Ⓙ $m\angle DEF = m\angle EFG$

37. Short Response The city wants to build a visitor center in the park so that it is equidistant from Park Street and Washington Avenue. They also want the visitor center to be equidistant from the museum and the library. Find the point V where the visitor center should be built. Explain your answer.

CHALLENGE AND EXTEND

H.O.T **38.** Consider the points $P(2, 0)$, $A(-4, 2)$, $B(0, -6)$, and $C(6, -3)$.

    a. Show that P is on the bisector of $\angle ABC$.

    b. Write an equation of the line that contains the bisector of $\angle ABC$.

39. Find the locus of points that are equidistant from the x-axis and y-axis.

H.O.T **40.** Write a two-column proof of the Converse of the Angle Bisector Theorem.

    Given: $\overline{VX} \perp \overrightarrow{YX}$, $\overline{VZ} \perp \overrightarrow{YZ}$, $VX = VZ$
    Prove: $\overrightarrow{YV}$ bisects $\angle XYZ$.

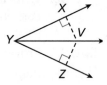

H.O.T **41.** Write a paragraph proof.

    Given: $\overline{KN}$ is the perpendicular bisector of $\overline{JL}$.
              $\overline{LN}$ is the perpendicular bisector of $\overline{KM}$.
              $\overline{JR} \cong \overline{MT}$
    Prove: $\angle JKM \cong \angle MLJ$

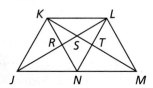

FOCUS ON MATHEMATICAL PRACTICES

H.O.T **42. Communication** In the figure, $TX = TY$ and $XV = YV$. Explain how you can prove that $WX = WY$ without proving pairs of triangles congruent.

H.O.T **43. Problem Solving** $\overline{AB}$ has endpoints $A(1, -4)$ and $B(x, y)$. The line $y = -\frac{1}{2}x + 4$ is the perpendicular bisector of $\overline{AB}$.

    a. Write an equation for the line that contains $\overline{AB}$.

    b. Find the intersection of the two lines.

    c. Find the change in x-values from point A to the intersection of the two lines. Do the same for the change in y-values.

    d. Use the changes in x and y to locate point B.

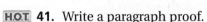

24-2 Bisectors of Triangles

Essential Question: How can you construct the circumcircle and incircle of any triangle?

Objectives
Prove and apply properties of perpendicular bisectors of a triangle.

Prove and apply properties of angle bisectors of a triangle.

Vocabulary
concurrent
point of concurrency
circumcenter of a triangle
circumscribed
incenter of a triangle
inscribed

Who uses this?
An event planner can use perpendicular bisectors of triangles to find the best location for a fireworks display. (See Example 4.)

Since a triangle has three sides, it has three perpendicular bisectors. When you construct the perpendicular bisectors, you find that they have an interesting property.

Helpful Hint

The perpendicular bisector of a side of a triangle does not always pass through the opposite vertex.

Construction Circumcenter of a Triangle

1
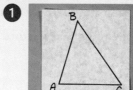
Draw a large scalene acute triangle *ABC* on a piece of patty paper.

2
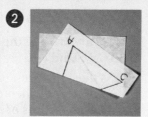
Fold the perpendicular bisector of each side.

3
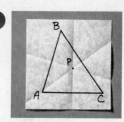
Label the point where the three perpendicular bisectors intersect as *P*.

When three or more lines intersect at one point, the lines are said to be **concurrent**. The **point of concurrency** is the point where they intersect. In the construction, you saw that the three perpendicular bisectors of a triangle are concurrent. This point of concurrency is the **circumcenter of the triangle**.

Know it!
Note

Theorem 24-2-1 Circumcenter Theorem

The circumcenter of a triangle is equidistant from the vertices of the triangle.

$$PA = PB = PC$$

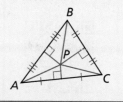

The circumcenter can be inside the triangle, outside the triangle, or on the triangle.

Acute triangle

Obtuse triangle

Right triangle

The circumcenter of $\triangle ABC$ is the center of its *circumscribed* circle. A circle that contains all the vertices of a polygon is **circumscribed** about the polygon.

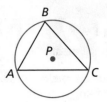

PROOF ■ **Circumcenter Theorem**

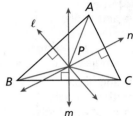

Given: Lines ℓ, m, and n are the perpendicular bisectors of $\overline{AB}$, $\overline{BC}$, and $\overline{AC}$, respectively.

Prove: $PA = PB = PC$

Proof:

P is the circumcenter of $\triangle ABC$. Since P lies on the perpendicular bisector of $\overline{AB}$, $PA = PB$ by the Perpendicular Bisector Theorem. Similarly, P also lies on the perpendicular bisector of $\overline{BC}$, so $PB = PC$. Therefore $PA = PB = PC$ by the Transitive Property of Equality.

EXAMPLE 1 Using Properties of Perpendicular Bisectors

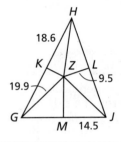

$\overline{KZ}$, $\overline{LZ}$, and $\overline{MZ}$ are the perpendicular bisectors of $\triangle GHJ$. Find HZ.

Z is the circumcenter of $\triangle GHJ$. By the Circumcenter Theorem, Z is equidistant from the vertices of $\triangle GHJ$.

$HZ = GZ$ *Circumcenter Thm.*

$HZ = 19.9$ *Substitute 19.9 for GZ.*

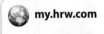

✓ CHECK IT OUT! Use the diagram above. Find each length.

1a. GM **1b.** GK **1c.** JZ

EXAMPLE 2 Finding the Circumcenter of a Triangle

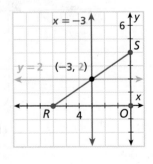

Find the circumcenter of $\triangle RSO$ with vertices $R(-6, 0)$, $S(0, 4)$, and $O(0, 0)$.

Step 1 Graph the triangle.

Step 2 Find equations for two perpendicular bisectors.

Since two sides of the triangle lie along the axes, use the graph to find the perpendicular bisectors of these two sides. The perpendicular bisector of $\overline{RO}$ is $x = -3$, and the perpendicular bisector of $\overline{OS}$ is $y = 2$.

Step 3 Find the intersection of the two equations.

The lines $x = -3$ and $y = 2$ intersect at $(-3, 2)$, the circumcenter of $\triangle RSO$.

2. Find the circumcenter of △*GOH* with vertices *G*(0, −9), *O*(0, 0), and *H*(8, 0).

A triangle has three angles, so it has three angle bisectors. The angle bisectors of a triangle are also concurrent. This point of concurrency is the **incenter of the triangle** .

Theorem 24-2-2 (**Incenter Theorem**)

The incenter of a triangle is equidistant from the sides of the triangle.

PX = *PY* = *PZ*

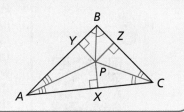

You will prove Theorem 24-2-2 in Exercise 35.

Remember!

The distance between a point and a line is the length of the perpendicular segment from the point to the line.

Unlike the circumcenter, the incenter is always inside the triangle.

Acute triangle

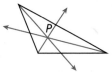

Obtuse triangle

Right triangle

The incenter is the center of the triangle's *inscribed circle*. A circle **inscribed** in a polygon intersects each line that contains a side of the polygon at exactly one point.

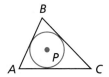

EXAMPLE 3
MCC9-12.G.C.3

my.hrw.com

Online Video Tutor

Using Properties of Angle Bisectors

$\overline{JV}$ and $\overline{KV}$ are angle bisectors of △*JKL*. Find each measure.

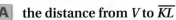

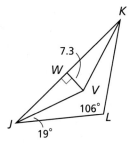

A the distance from *V* to $\overline{KL}$

V is the incenter of △*JKL*. By the Incenter Theorem, *V* is equidistant from the sides of △*JKL*.
The distance from *V* to $\overline{JK}$ is 7.3.
So the distance from *V* to $\overline{KL}$ is also 7.3.

B m∠*VKL*

m∠*KJL* = 2m∠*VJL*	$\overline{JV}$ *is the bisector of* ∠*KJL*.
m∠*KJL* = 2(19°) = 38°	*Substitute 19° for* m∠*VJL*.
m∠*KJL* + m∠*JLK* + m∠*JKL* = 180°	△ *Sum Thm.*
38 + 106 + m∠*JKL* = 180	*Substitute the given values.*
m∠*JKL* = 36°	*Subtract 144° from both sides.*
m∠*VKL* = $\frac{1}{2}$m∠*JKL*	$\overline{KV}$ *is the bisector of* ∠*JKL*.
m∠*VKL* = $\frac{1}{2}$(36°) = 18°	*Substitute 36° for* m∠*JKL*.

$\overline{QX}$ and $\overline{RX}$ are angle bisectors of $\triangle PQR$. Find each measure.

3a. the distance from X to $\overline{PQ}$

3b. m$\angle PQX$

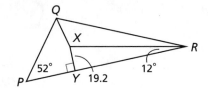

EXAMPLE **4**

Community Application

Online Video Tutor

For the next Fourth of July, the towns of Ashton, Bradford, and Clearview will launch a fireworks display from a boat in the lake. Draw a sketch to show where the boat should be positioned so that it is the same distance from all three towns. Justify your sketch.

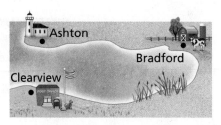

Let the three towns be vertices of a triangle. By the Circumcenter Theorem, the circumcenter of the triangle is equidistant from the vertices.

Trace the outline of the lake. Draw the triangle formed by the towns. To find the circumcenter, find the perpendicular bisectors of each side. The position of the boat is the circumcenter, F.

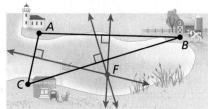

 4. A city plans to build a firefighters' monument in the park between three streets. Draw a sketch to show where the city should place the monument so that it is the same distance from all three streets. Justify your sketch.

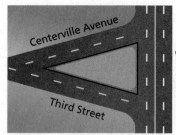

THINK AND DISCUSS

1. Sketch three lines that are concurrent.

2. P and Q are the circumcenter and incenter of $\triangle RST$, but not necessarily in that order. Which point is the circumcenter? Which point is the incenter? Explain how you can tell without constructing any of the bisectors.

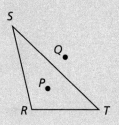

Know it! Note

3. GET ORGANIZED Copy and complete the graphic organizer. Fill in the blanks to make each statement true.

	Circumcenter	Incenter
Definition	The point of concurrency of the _?_	The point of concurrency of the _?_
Distance	Equidistant from the _?_	Equidistant from the _?_
Location (Inside, Outside, or On)	Can be _?_ the triangle	_?_ the triangle

GUIDED PRACTICE

Vocabulary Apply the vocabulary from this lesson to answer each question.

1. Explain why lines ℓ, *m*, and *n* are NOT *concurrent*.

2. A circle that contains all the vertices of a polygon is ___?___ the polygon. (*circumscribed about* or *inscribed in*)

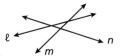

SEE EXAMPLE 1 $\overline{SN}$, $\overline{TN}$, and $\overline{VN}$ are the perpendicular bisectors of △*PQR*. Find each length.

3. *NR*   4. *RV*

5. *TR*   6. *QN*

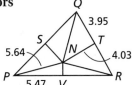

SEE EXAMPLE 2 **Multi-Step** Find the circumcenter of a triangle with the given vertices.

7. $O(0, 0)$, $K(0, 12)$, $L(4, 0)$

8. $A(-7, 0)$, $O(0, 0)$, $B(0, -10)$

SEE EXAMPLE 3 $\overline{CF}$ and $\overline{EF}$ are angle bisectors of △*CDE*. Find each measure.

9. the distance from *F* to $\overline{CD}$

10. m∠*FED*

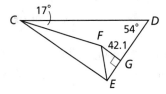

SEE EXAMPLE 4 11. **Design** The designer of the Newtown High School pennant wants the circle around the bear emblem to be as large as possible. Draw a sketch to show where the center of the circle should be located. Justify your sketch.

PRACTICE AND PROBLEM SOLVING

Independent Practice	
For Exercises	See Example
12–15	1
16–17	2
18–19	3
20	4

$\overline{DY}$, $\overline{EY}$, and $\overline{FY}$ are the perpendicular bisectors of △*ABC*. Find each length.

12. *CF*   13. *YC*

14. *DB*   15. *AY*

Multi-Step Find the circumcenter of a triangle with the given vertices.

16. $M(-5, 0)$, $N(0, 14)$, $O(0, 0)$ 17. $O(0, 0)$, $V(0, 19)$, $W(-3, 0)$

$\overline{TJ}$ and $\overline{SJ}$ are angle bisectors of △*RST*. Find each measure.

18. the distance from *J* to $\overline{RS}$

19. m∠*RTJ*

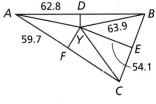
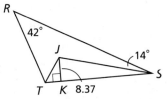

H.O.T. **20. Business** A company repairs photocopiers in Harbury, Gaspar, and Knowlton. Draw a sketch to show where the company should locate its office so that it is the same distance from each city. Justify your sketch.

21. Critical Thinking If *M* is the incenter of △*JKL*, explain why ∠*JML* cannot be a right angle.

Tell whether each segment lies on a perpendicular bisector, an angle bisector, or neither. Justify your answer.

22. $\overline{AE}$ **23.** $\overline{DG}$ **24.** $\overline{BG}$

25. $\overline{CR}$ **26.** $\overline{FR}$ **27.** $\overline{DR}$

Tell whether each statement is sometimes, always, or never true. Support your answer with a sketch.

28. The angle bisectors of a triangle intersect at a point outside the triangle.

29. An angle bisector of a triangle bisects the opposite side.

30. A perpendicular bisector of a triangle passes through the opposite vertex.

31. The incenter of a right triangle is on the triangle.

32. The circumcenter of a scalene triangle is inside the triangle.

H.O.T. **Algebra** Find the circumcenter of the triangle with the given vertices.

33. $O(0, 0)$, $A(4, 8)$, $B(8, 0)$ **34.** $O(0, 0)$, $Y(0, 12)$, $Z(6, 6)$

H.O.T. **35.** Complete this proof of the Incenter Theorem by filling in the blanks.

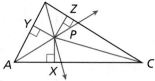

Given: $\overrightarrow{AP}$, $\overrightarrow{BP}$, and $\overrightarrow{CP}$ bisect ∠*A*, ∠*B*, and ∠*C*, respectively.
$\overline{PX} \perp \overline{AC}$, $\overline{PY} \perp \overline{AB}$, $\overline{PZ} \perp \overline{BC}$

Prove: $PX = PY = PZ$

Proof: Let *P* be the incenter of △*ABC*. Since *P* lies on the bisector of ∠*A*, $PX = PY$ by **a.** __?__ . Similarly, *P* also lies on **b.** __?__ , so $PY = PZ$. Therefore **c.** __?__ by the Transitive Property of Equality.

H.O.T. **36.** Prove that the bisector of the vertex angle of an isosceles triangle is the perpendicular bisector of the base.

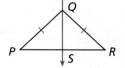

Given: $\overleftrightarrow{QS}$ bisects ∠*PQR*. $\overline{PQ} \cong \overline{RQ}$

Prove: $\overleftrightarrow{QS}$ is the perpendicular bisector of $\overline{PR}$.

Plan: Show that △*PQS* ≅ △*RQS*. Then use CPCTC to show that *S* is the midpoint of $\overline{PR}$ and that $\overleftrightarrow{QS} \perp \overline{PR}$.

Real-World Connections

37. A music company has stores at $A(0, 0)$, $B(8, 0)$, and $C(4, 3)$, where each unit of the coordinate plane represents one mile.

   a. A new store will be built so that it is equidistant from the three existing stores. Find the coordinates of the new store's location.

   b. Where will the new store be located in relation to △*ABC*?

   c. To the nearest tenth of a mile, how far will the new store be from each of the existing stores?

Module 24 Special Points and Segments in Triangles

38. Write About It How are the inscribed circle and the circumscribed circle of a triangle alike? How are they different?

39. Construction Draw a large scalene acute triangle.

a. Construct the angle bisectors to find the incenter. Inscribe a circle in the triangle.

b. Construct the perpendicular bisectors to find the circumcenter. Circumscribe a circle around the triangle.

TEST PREP

40. *P* is the incenter of △*ABC*. Which must be true?

Ⓐ *PA* = *PB*   Ⓒ *YA* = *YB*

Ⓑ *PX* = *PY*   Ⓓ *AX* = *BZ*

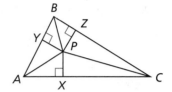

41. Lines *r*, *s*, and *t* are concurrent. The equation of line *r* is $x = 5$, and the equation of line *s* is $y = -2$. Which could be the equation of line *t*?

Ⓕ $y = x - 7$ Ⓗ $y = x + 3$

Ⓖ $y = x - 3$ Ⓙ $y = x + 7$

42. Gridded Response Lines *a*, *b*, and *c* are the perpendicular bisectors of △*KLM*. Find *LN*.

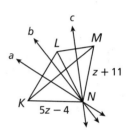

CHALLENGE AND EXTEND

43. Use the right triangle with the given coordinates.

a. Prove that the midpoint of the hypotenuse of a right triangle is equidistant from all three vertices.

b. Make a conjecture about the circumcenter of a right triangle.

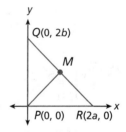

Design

The trefoil shape, as seen in this stained glass window, has been used in design for centuries.

44. Design A *trefoil* is created by constructing three overlapping circles. In the figure, an equilateral triangle is inscribed inside a trefoil, and $\overline{AB}$ is a perpendicular bisector of the triangle. If the distance from one vertex to the circumcenter is 28 cm, what is the distance *AB* across the trefoil?

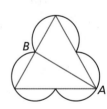

FOCUS ON MATHEMATICAL PRACTICES

H.O.T. 45. Reasoning For every triangle, a line exists such that every point on the line is equidistant from each vertex of the triangle. Describe this line.

H.O.T. 46. Problem Solving Point *I* is the incenter of △*RST*. $IL = LS = 10$. ∠*S* is a right angle, and $RS = 30$.

a. Why is $LS = NS = IL = IN = 10$?

b. Find *RL*. Explain why $RL = RM$ and $MT = NT$.

c. Let $x = MT = NT$. Use the Pythagorean Theorem to find the value of *x*.

d. Find *ST* and *RT*.

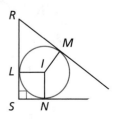

24-2 Bisectors of Triangle.

24-3 Medians and Altitudes of Triangles

Essential Question: How can you find the balancing point in the interior of any triangle?

Objectives
Apply properties of medians of a triangle.

Apply properties of altitudes of a triangle.

Vocabulary
median of a triangle
centroid of a triangle
altitude of a triangle
orthocenter of a triangle

Who uses this?

Sculptors who create mobiles of moving objects can use centers of gravity to balance the objects. (See Example 2.)

A **median of a triangle** is a segment whose endpoints are a vertex of the triangle and the midpoint of the opposite side.

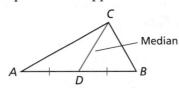

Every triangle has three medians, and the medians are concurrent, as shown in the construction below.

Construction Centroid of a Triangle

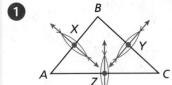

① Draw △ABC. Construct the midpoints of $\overline{AB}$, $\overline{BC}$, and $\overline{AC}$. Label the midpoints of the sides X, Y, and Z, respectively.

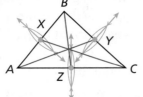

② Draw $\overline{AY}$, $\overline{BZ}$, and $\overline{CX}$. These are the three medians of △ABC.

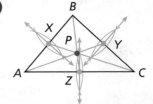

③ Label the point where $\overline{AY}$, $\overline{BZ}$, and $\overline{CX}$ intersect as P.

The point of concurrency of the medians of a triangle is the **centroid of the triangle**. The centroid is always inside the triangle. The centroid is also called the *center of gravity* because it is the point where a triangular region will balance.

Know it!
Note

Theorem 24-3-1 Centroid Theorem

The centroid of a triangle is located $\frac{2}{3}$ of the distance from each vertex to the midpoint of the opposite side.

$$AP = \frac{2}{3}AY \qquad BP = \frac{2}{3}BZ \qquad CP = \frac{2}{3}CX$$

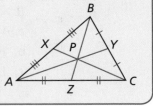

COMMON CORE GPS
MCC9-12.G.CO.10

EXAMPLE **1** | **Using the Centroid to Find Segment Lengths**

In $\triangle ABC$, $AF = 9$, and $GE = 2.4$. Find each length.

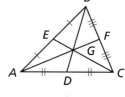

A AG

$AG = \dfrac{2}{3}AF$ *Centroid Thm.*

$AG = \dfrac{2}{3}(9)$ *Substitute 9 for AF.*

$AG = 6$ *Simplify.*

B CE

$CG = \dfrac{2}{3}CE$ *Centroid Thm.*

$CG + GE = CE$ *Seg. Add. Post.*

$\dfrac{2}{3}CE + GE = CE$ *Substitute $\frac{2}{3}$CE for CG.*

$GE = \dfrac{1}{3}CE$ *Subtract $\frac{2}{3}$CE from both sides.*

$2.4 = \dfrac{1}{3}CE$ *Substitute 2.4 for GE.*

$7.2 = CE$ *Multiply both sides by 3.*

 In $\triangle JKL$, $ZW = 7$, and $LX = 8.1$.
Find each length.

1a. KW

1b. LZ

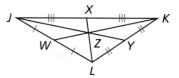

COMMON CORE GPS
MCC9-12.G.GPE.4

EXAMPLE **2** | *Problem-Solving Application*

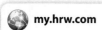

Make sense of problems and
persevere in solving them.

The diagram shows the plan for a triangular
piece of a mobile. Where should the
sculptor attach the support so that the
triangle is balanced?

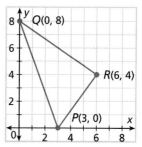

 Understand the Problem

The **answer** will be the coordinates of
the centroid of $\triangle PQR$. The **important
information** is the location of the vertices,
$P(3, 0)$, $Q(0, 8)$, and $R(6, 4)$.

2 **Make a Plan**

The centroid of the triangle is the point of intersection of
the three medians. So write the equations for two medians
and find their point of intersection.

3 **Solve**

Let M be the midpoint of $\overline{QR}$ and N be the midpoint of $\overline{QP}$.

$$M = \left(\frac{0+6}{2}, \frac{8+4}{2}\right) = (3, 6) \qquad N = \left(\frac{0+3}{2}, \frac{8+0}{2}\right) = (1.5, 4)$$

$\overline{PM}$ is vertical. Its equation is $x = 3$. $\overline{RN}$ is horizontal.
Its equation is $y = 4$. The coordinates of the centroid are $S(3, 4)$.

Look Back

Let L be the midpoint of $\overline{PR}$. The equation for $\overleftrightarrow{QL}$ is $y = -\frac{4}{3}x + 8$, which intersects $x = 3$ at $S(3, 4)$.

CHECK IT OUT! **2.** Find the average of the x-coordinates and the average of the y-coordinates of the vertices of $\triangle PQR$. Make a conjecture about the centroid of a triangle.

The height of a triangle is the length of an altitude.

An **altitude of a triangle** is a perpendicular segment from a vertex to the line containing the opposite side. Every triangle has three altitudes. An altitude can be inside, outside, or on the triangle.

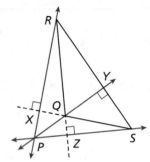

In $\triangle QRS$, altitude $\overline{QY}$ is inside the triangle, but $\overline{RX}$ and $\overline{SZ}$ are not. Notice that the lines containing the altitudes are concurrent at P. This point of concurrency is the **orthocenter of the triangle**.

COMMON CORE GPS MCC9-12.G.GPE.5

EXAMPLE **3**

 my.hrw.com

Online Video Tutor

Finding the Orthocenter

Find the orthocenter of $\triangle JKL$ with vertices $J(-4, 2)$, $K(-2, 6)$, and $L(2, 2)$.

Step 1 Graph the triangle.

Step 2 Find an equation of the line containing the altitude from K to $\overline{JL}$.

Since $\overleftrightarrow{JL}$ is horizontal, the altitude is vertical. The line containing it must pass through $K(-2, 6)$, so the equation of the line is $x = -2$.

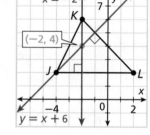

Step 3 Find an equation of the line containing the altitude from J to $\overline{KL}$.

$$\text{slope of } \overleftrightarrow{KL} = \frac{2 - 6}{2 - (-2)} = -1$$

The slope of a line perpendicular to $\overleftrightarrow{KL}$ is 1. This line must pass through $J(-4, 2)$.

$y - y_1 = m(x - x_1)$ *Point-slope form*

$y - 2 = 1[x - (-4)]$ *Substitute 2 for y_1, 1 for m, and -4 for x_1.*

$y - 2 = x + 4$ *Distribute 1.*

$y = x + 6$ *Add 2 to both sides.*

Step 4 Solve the system to find the coordinates of the orthocenter.

$$\begin{cases} x = -2 \\ y = x + 6 \end{cases}$$

$y = -2 + 6 = 4$ *Substitute -2 for x.*

The coordinates of the orthocenter are $(-2, 4)$.

CHECK IT OUT! **3.** Show that the altitude to $\overline{JK}$ passes through the orthocenter of $\triangle JKL$.

THINK AND DISCUSS

1. Draw a triangle in which a median and an altitude are the same segment. What type of triangle is it?

2. Draw a triangle in which an altitude is also a side of the triangle. What type of triangle is it?

3. The centroid of a triangle divides each median into two segments. What is the ratio of the two lengths of each median?

4. **GET ORGANIZED** Copy and complete the graphic organizer. Fill in the blanks to make each statement true.

	Centroid	Orthocenter
Definition	The point of concurrency of the ?	The point of concurrency of the ?
Location (Inside, Outside, or On)	? the triangle	Can be ? the triangle

24-3 Exercises

my.hrw.com
Homework Help

GUIDED PRACTICE

Vocabulary Apply the vocabulary from this lesson to answer each question.

1. The ___?___ of a triangle is located $\frac{2}{3}$ of the distance from each vertex to the midpoint of the opposite side. (*centroid* or *orthocenter*)

2. The ___?___ of a triangle is perpendicular to the line containing a side. (*altitude* or *median*)

SEE EXAMPLE 1 $VX = 204$, and $RW = 104$. Find each length.

3. VW 　　　4. WX

5. RY 　　　6. WY

SEE EXAMPLE 2

7. **Design** The diagram shows a plan for a piece of a mobile. A chain will hang from the centroid of the triangle. At what coordinates should the artist attach the chain?

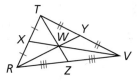

SEE EXAMPLE 3   **Multi-Step** Find the orthocenter of a triangle with the given vertices.

8. $K(2, -2)$, $L(4, 6)$, $M(8, -2)$

9. $U(-4, -9)$, $V(-4, 6)$, $W(5, -3)$

10. $P(-5, 8)$, $Q(4, 5)$, $R(-2, 5)$

11. $C(-1, -3)$, $D(-1, 2)$, $E(9, 2)$

PRACTICE AND PROBLEM SOLVING

Independent Practice

For Exercises	See Example
12–15	1
16	2
17–20	3

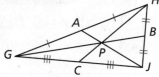

my.hrw.com

Online Extra Practice

$PA = 2.9$, and $HC = 10.8$. Find each length.

12. PC **13.** HP

14. JA **15.** JP

16. Design In the plan for a table, the triangular top has coordinates $(0, 10)$, $(4, 0)$, and $(8, 14)$. The tabletop will rest on a single support placed beneath it. Where should the support be attached so that the table is balanced?

Multi-Step Find the orthocenter of a triangle with the given vertices.

17. $X(-2, -2)$, $Y(6, 10)$, $Z(6, -6)$ **18.** $G(-2, 5)$, $H(6, 5)$, $J(4, -1)$

19. $R(-8, 9)$, $S(-2, 9)$, $T(-2, 1)$ **20.** $A(4, -3)$, $B(8, 5)$, $C(8, -8)$

Find each measure.

21. GL **22.** PL

23. HL **24.** GJ

25. perimeter of $\triangle GHJ$ **26.** area of $\triangle GHJ$

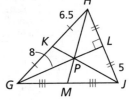

H.O.T. **Algebra** Find the centroid of a triangle with the given vertices.

27. $A(0, -4)$, $B(14, 6)$, $C(16, -8)$ **28.** $X(8, -1)$, $Y(2, 7)$, $Z(5, -3)$

Find each length.

29. PZ **30.** PX

31. QZ **32.** YZ

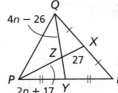

33. Critical Thinking Draw an isosceles triangle and its line of symmetry. What are four other names for this segment?

Tell whether each statement is sometimes, always, or never true. Support your answer with a sketch.

34. A median of a triangle bisects one of the angles.

35. If one altitude of a triangle is in the triangle's exterior, then a second altitude is also in the triangle's exterior.

36. The centroid of a triangle lies in its exterior.

37. In an isosceles triangle, the altitude and median from the vertex angle are the same line as the bisector of the vertex angle.

38. Write a two-column proof.

   Given: $\overline{PS}$ and $\overline{RT}$ are medians of $\triangle PQR$. $\overline{PS} \cong \overline{RT}$
   Prove: $\triangle PQR$ is an isosceles triangle.

   Plan: Show that $\triangle PTR \cong \triangle RSP$ and use CPCTC to conclude that $\angle QPR \cong \angle QRP$.

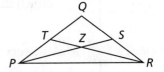

39. Write About It Draw a large triangle on a sheet of paper and cut it out. Find the centroid by paper folding. Try to balance the shape on the tip of your pencil at a point other than the centroid. Now try to balance the shape at its centroid. Explain why the centroid is also called the center of gravity.

Corbis Images

Real-World Connections

40. The towns of Davis, El Monte, and Fairview have the coordinates shown in the table, where each unit of the coordinate plane represents one mile. A music company has stores in each city and a distribution warehouse at the centroid of $\triangle DEF$.

City	Location
Davis	$D(0, 0)$
El Monte	$E(0, 8)$
Fairview	$F(8, 0)$

   a. What are the coordinates of the warehouse?

   b. Find the distance from the warehouse to the Davis store. Round your answer to the nearest tenth of a mile.

   c. A straight road connects El Monte and Fairview. What is the distance from the warehouse to the road?

TEST PREP

41. $\overline{QT}$, $\overline{RV}$, and $\overline{SW}$ are medians of $\triangle QRS$. Which statement is NOT necessarily true?

   (A) $QP = \frac{2}{3}QT$ (C) $RT = ST$

   (B) $RP = 2PV$ (D) $QT = SW$

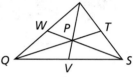

42. Suppose that the orthocenter of a triangle lies outside the triangle. Which points of concurrency are inside the triangle?

   I. incenter   **II.** circumcenter   **III.** centroid

   (F) I and II only   (H) II and III only

   (G) I and III only   (J) I, II, and III

43. In the diagram, which of the following correctly describes $\overline{LN}$?

   (A) Altitude   (C) Median

   (B) Angle bisector   (D) Perpendicular bisector

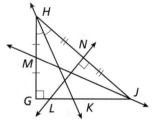

CHALLENGE AND EXTEND

H.O.T. **44.** Draw an equilateral triangle.

   a. Explain why the perpendicular bisector of any side contains the vertex opposite that side.

   b. Explain why the perpendicular bisector through any vertex also contains the median, the altitude, and the angle bisector through that vertex.

   c. Explain why the incenter, circumcenter, centroid, and orthocenter are the same point.

H.O.T. **45.** Use coordinates to show that the lines containing the altitudes of a triangle are concurrent.

   a. Find the slopes of $\overline{RS}$, $\overline{ST}$, and $\overline{RT}$.

   b. Find the slopes of lines ℓ, m, and n.

   c. Write equations for lines ℓ, m, and n.

   d. Solve a system of equations to find the point P where lines ℓ and m intersect.

   e. Show that line n contains P.

   f. What conclusion can you draw?

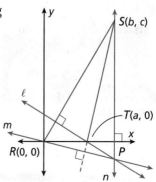

24-3 Medians and Altitudes of Triangles **719**

Creatas/Punchstock.com

H.O.T. **46. Reasoning** Classify the triangle for which the circumcenter, incenter, centroid, and orthocenter all lie inside the triangle.

H.O.T. **47. Communication** The orthocenter of a triangle is outside the triangle. Is its circumcenter also outside the triangle? Explain.

H.O.T. **48. Draw Conclusions** △*ABC* is an equilateral triangle. A circle is inscribed in △*ABC* and another circle is circumscribed about △*ABC*.

    a. The radius of the inscribed circle is *r*. What is the radius of the circumscribed circle?

    b. For an equilateral triangle, what is the ratio of the radius of the inscribed circle to the radius of the circumscribed circle?

Construction Orthocenter of a Triangle

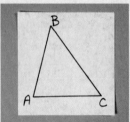

❶ Draw a large scalene acute triangle *ABC* on a piece of patty paper.

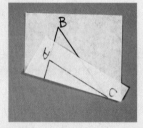

❷ Find the altitude of each side by folding the side so that it overlaps itself and so that the fold intersects the opposite vertex.

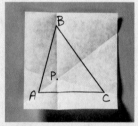

❸ Mark the point where the three lines containing the altitudes intersect and label it *P*. *P* is the orthocenter of △*ABC*.

1. Repeat the construction for a scalene obtuse triangle and a scalene right triangle.

2. Make a conjecture about the location of the orthocenter in an acute, an obtuse, and a right triangle.

Career Path

Alex Peralta
Electrician

Q: What high school math classes did you take?

A: Algebra 1, Geometry, and Statistics.

Q: What type of training did you receive?

A: In high school, I took classes in electricity, electronics, and drafting. I began an apprenticeship program last year to prepare for the exam to get my license.

Q: How do you use math?

A: Determining the locations of outlets and circuits on blueprints requires good spatial sense. I also use ratios and proportions, calculate distances, work with formulas, and estimate job costs.

24-3

Technology TASK

Special Points in Triangles

In this task, you will use geometry software to explore properties of the four points of concurrency you have studied.

Use with Medians and Altitudes of Triangles

Use appropriate tools strategically.

MCC9-12.G.CO.10 Prove theorems about triangles.

Activity

1 Construct a triangle.

2 Construct the perpendicular bisector of each side of the triangle. Construct the point of intersection of these three lines. This is the circumcenter of the triangle. Label it *U* and hide the perpendicular bisectors.

3 In the same triangle, construct the bisector of each angle. Construct the point of intersection of these three lines. This is the incenter of the triangle. Label it *I* and hide the angle bisectors.

4 In the same triangle, construct the midpoint of each side. Then construct the three medians. Construct the point of intersection of these three lines. Label the centroid *C* and hide the medians.

5 In the same triangle, construct the altitude to each side. Construct the point of intersection of these three lines. Label the orthocenter *O* and hide the altitudes.

6 Move a vertex of the triangle and observe the positions of the four points of concurrency. In 1765, Swiss mathematician Leonhard Euler showed that three of these points are always collinear. The line containing them is called the *Euler line*.

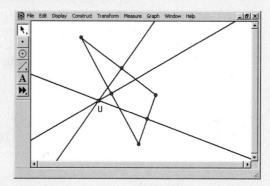

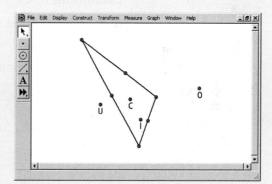

Try This

1. Which three points of concurrency lie on the Euler line?

2. Make a Conjecture Which point on the Euler line is always between the other two? Measure the distances between the points. Make a conjecture about the relationship of the distances between these three points.

3. Make a Conjecture Move a vertex of the triangle until all four points of concurrency are collinear. In what type of triangle are all four points of concurrency on the Euler line?

4. Make a Conjecture Find a triangle in which all four points of concurrency coincide. What type of triangle has this special property?

24-4 The Triangle Midsegment Theorem

Essential Question: What are properties of the triangle whose vertices are the midpoints of the three sides of a triangle?

Objective
Prove and use properties of triangle midsegments.

Vocabulary
midsegment of a triangle

Why learn this?
You can use triangle midsegments to make indirect measurements of distances, such as the distance across a volcano. (See Example 3.)

A **midsegment of a triangle** is a segment that joins the midpoints of two sides of the triangle. Every triangle has three midsegments, which form the *midsegment triangle*.

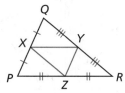

Midsegments: $\overline{XY}, \overline{YZ}, \overline{ZX}$
Midsegment triangle: $\triangle XYZ$

EXAMPLE 1
MCC9-12.G.GPE.4

Online Video Tutor

Examining Midsegments in the Coordinate Plane

In $\triangle GHJ$, show that midsegment $\overline{KL}$ is parallel to $\overline{GJ}$ and that $KL = \frac{1}{2}GJ$.

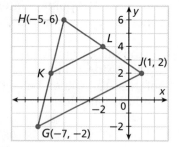

Step 1 Find the coordinates of K and L.

$$\text{mdpt. of } \overline{GH} = \left(\frac{-7 + (-5)}{2}, \frac{-2 + 6}{2}\right)$$
$$= (-6, 2)$$

$$\text{mdpt. of } \overline{HJ} = \left(\frac{-5 + 1}{2}, \frac{6 + 2}{2}\right) = (-2, 4)$$

Step 2 Compare the slopes of $\overline{KL}$ and $\overline{GJ}$.

$$\text{slope of } \overline{KL} = \frac{4 - 2}{-2 - (-6)} = \frac{1}{2} \qquad \text{slope of } \overline{GJ} = \frac{2 - (-2)}{1 - (-7)} = \frac{1}{2}$$

Since the slopes are the same, $\overline{KL} \parallel \overline{GJ}$.

Step 3 Compare the lengths of $\overline{KL}$ and $\overline{GJ}$.

$$KL = \sqrt{[-2 - (-6)]^2 + (4 - 2)^2} = 2\sqrt{5}$$
$$GJ = \sqrt{[1 - (-7)]^2 + [2 - (-2)]^2} = 4\sqrt{5}$$
Since $2\sqrt{5} = \frac{1}{2}(4\sqrt{5})$, $KL = \frac{1}{2}GJ$.

1. The vertices of $\triangle RST$ are $R(-7, 0)$, $S(-3, 6)$, and $T(9, 2)$. M is the midpoint of $\overline{RT}$, and N is the midpoint of $\overline{ST}$. Show that $\overline{MN} \parallel \overline{RS}$ and $MN = \frac{1}{2}RS$.

The relationship shown in Example 1 is true for the three midsegments of every triangle.

Theorem 24-4-1 (**Triangle Midsegment Theorem**)

A midsegment of a triangle is parallel to a side of the triangle, and its length is half the length of that side.

$$\overline{DE} \parallel \overline{AC}, DE = \frac{1}{2}AC$$

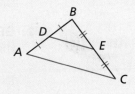

You will prove Theorem 24-4-1 in Exercise 38.

EXAMPLE 2 **Using the Triangle Midsegment Theorem**

Find each measure.

Online Video Tutor

A *UW*

$UW = \frac{1}{2}ST$ △ *Midsegment Thm.*

$UW = \frac{1}{2}(7.4)$ *Substitute 7.4 for ST.*

$UW = 3.7$ *Simplify.*

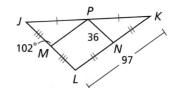

B m∠*SVU*

$\overline{UW} \parallel \overline{ST}$ △ *Midsegment Thm.*

m∠*SVU* = m∠*VUW*   *Alt. Int. ∠ Thm.*

m∠*SVU* = 41°   *Substitute 41° for m∠VUW.*

 CHECK IT OUT!   **Find each measure.**

2a. *JL*   **2b.** *PM*   **2c.** m∠*MLK*

EXAMPLE 3 *Indirect Measurement Application*

Anna wants to find the distance across the base of Capulin Volcano, an extinct volcano in New Mexico. She measures a triangle at one side of the volcano as shown in the diagram. What is *AE*?

Online Video Tutor

$BD = \frac{1}{2}AE$ △ *Midsegment Thm.*

$775 = \frac{1}{2}AE$ *Substitute 775 for BD.*

$1550 = AE$ *Multiply both sides by 2.*

The distance *AE* across the base of the volcano is about 1550 meters.

 CHECK IT OUT!

3. What if...? Suppose Anna's result in Example 3 is correct. To check it, she measures a second triangle. How many meters will she measure between *H* and *F*?

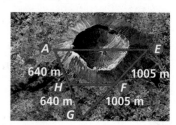

THINK AND DISCUSS

1. Explain why $\overline{XY}$ is NOT a midsegment of the triangle.

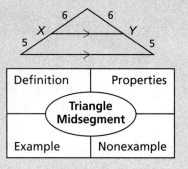

2. GET ORGANIZED Copy and complete the graphic organizer. Write the definition of a triangle midsegment and list its properties. Then draw an example and a nonexample.

Definition	Properties
Example	Nonexample

Triangle Midsegment

24-4 Exercises

my.hrw.com
Homework Help

GUIDED PRACTICE

1. Vocabulary The *midsegment of a triangle* joins the ___?___ of two sides of the triangle. (*endpoints* or *midpoints*)

SEE EXAMPLE **1**

2. The vertices of $\triangle PQR$ are $P(-4, -1)$, $Q(2, 9)$, and $R(6, 3)$. S is the midpoint of $\overline{PQ}$, and T is the midpoint of $\overline{QR}$. Show that $\overline{ST} \parallel \overline{PR}$ and $ST = \frac{1}{2}PR$.

SEE EXAMPLE **2**

Find each measure.

3. NM
4. XZ
5. NZ
6. $m\angle LMN$
7. $m\angle YXZ$
8. $m\angle XLM$

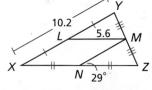

SEE EXAMPLE **3**

9. Architecture In this A-frame house, the width of the first floor $\overline{XZ}$ is 30 feet. The second floor $\overline{CD}$ is slightly above and parallel to the midsegment of $\triangle XYZ$. Is the width of the second floor more or less than 5 yards? Explain.

PRACTICE AND PROBLEM SOLVING

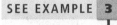

For Exercises	See Example
10	1
11–16	2
17	3

10. The vertices of $\triangle ABC$ are $A(-6, 11)$, $B(6, -3)$, and $C(-2, -5)$. D is the midpoint of $\overline{AC}$, and E is the midpoint of $\overline{AB}$. Show that $\overline{DE} \parallel \overline{CB}$ and $DE = \frac{1}{2}CB$.

Find each measure.

11. GJ
12. RQ
13. RJ
14. $m\angle PQR$
15. $m\angle HGJ$
16. $m\angle GPQ$

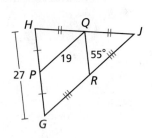

Online Extra Practice

17. Carpentry In each support for the garden swing, the crossbar $\overline{DE}$ is attached at the midpoints of legs $\overline{BA}$ and $\overline{BC}$. The distance AC is $4\frac{1}{2}$ feet. The carpenter has a timber that is 30 inches long. Is this timber long enough to be used as one of the crossbars? Explain.

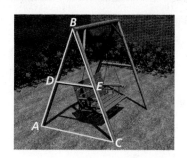

△KLM is the midsegment triangle of △GHJ.

18. What is the perimeter of △GHJ?

19. What is the perimeter of △KLM?

20. What is the relationship between the perimeter of △GHJ and the perimeter of △KLM?

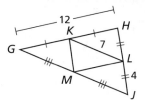

Algebra Find the value of *n* in each triangle.

21.
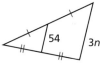

22.
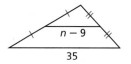

23.
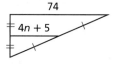

24.
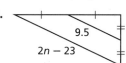

25.
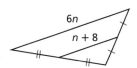

26.
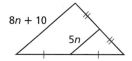

27. ///ERROR ANALYSIS/// Below are two solutions for finding *BC*. Which is incorrect? Explain the error.

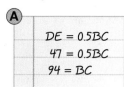

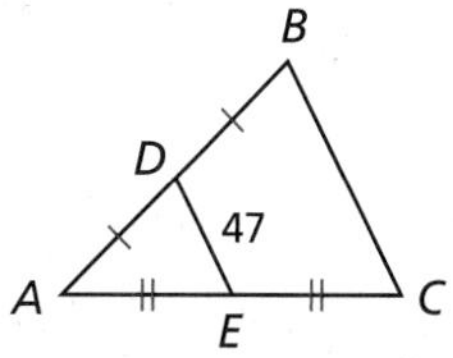

Ⓐ

DE = 0.5BC
47 = 0.5BC
94 = BC

Ⓑ

BC = 0.5DE
BC = 0.5(47)
BC = 23.5

28. Critical Thinking Draw scalene △DEF. Label *X* as the midpoint of $\overline{DE}$, *Y* as the midpoint of $\overline{EF}$, and *Z* as the midpoint of $\overline{DF}$. Connect the three midpoints. List all of the congruent angles in your drawing.

H.O.T. 29. Estimation The diagram shows the sketch for a new street. Parallel parking spaces will be painted on both sides of the street. Each parallel parking space is 23 feet long. About how many parking spaces can the city accommodate on both sides of the new street? Explain your answer.

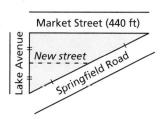

$\overline{CG}$, $\overline{EH}$, and $\overline{FJ}$ are midsegments of △ABD, △GCD, and △GHE, respectively. Find each measure.

30. *CG*

31. *EH*

32. *FJ*

33. m∠DCG

34. m∠GHE

35. m∠FJH

H.O.T. 36. Write About It An isosceles triangle has two congruent sides. Does it also have two congruent midsegments? Explain.

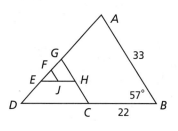

37. The figure shows the roads connecting towns A, B, and C. A music company has a store in each town and a distribution warehouse W at the midpoint of road $\overline{XY}$.

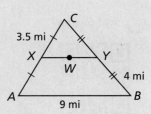

  a. What is the distance from the warehouse to point X?

  b. A truck starts at the warehouse, delivers instruments to the stores in towns A, B, and C (in this order) and then returns to the warehouse. What is the total length of the trip, assuming the driver takes the shortest possible route?

38. Use coordinates to prove the Triangle Midsegment Theorem.

  a. M is the midpoint of $\overline{PQ}$. What are its coordinates?

  b. N is the midpoint of $\overline{QR}$. What are its coordinates?

  c. Find the slopes of $\overline{PR}$ and $\overline{MN}$. What can you conclude?

  d. Find PR and MN. What can you conclude?

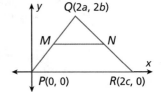

TEST PREP

39. $\overline{PQ}$ is a midsegment of △RST. What is the length of $\overline{RT}$?

  Ⓐ 9 meters

  Ⓑ 21 meters

  Ⓒ 45 meters

  Ⓓ 63 meters

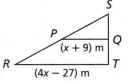

40. In △UVW, M is the midpoint of $\overline{VU}$, and N is the midpoint of $\overline{VW}$. Which statement is true?

  Ⓕ VM = VN   Ⓗ VU = 2VM

  Ⓖ MN = UV   Ⓙ $VW = \frac{1}{2}VN$

41. △XYZ is the midsegment triangle of △JKL, XY = 8, YK = 14, and m∠YKZ = 67°. Which of the following measures CANNOT be determined?

  Ⓐ KL   Ⓒ m∠XZL

  Ⓑ JY   Ⓓ m∠KZY

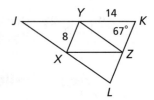

CHALLENGE AND EXTEND

42. Multi-Step The midpoints of the sides of a triangle are $A(-6, 3)$, $B(2, 1)$, and $C(0, -3)$. Find the coordinates of the vertices of the triangle.

43. Critical Thinking Classify the midsegment triangle of an equilateral triangle by its side lengths and angle measures.

 Algebra Find the value of n in each triangle.

44.

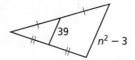

45.

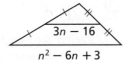

46. △*XYZ* is the midsegment triangle of △*PQR*. Write a congruence statement involving all four of the smaller triangles. What is the relationship between the area of △*XYZ* and △*PQR*?

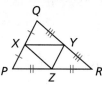

47. $\overline{AB}$ is a midsegment of △*XYZ*. $\overline{CD}$ is a midsegment of △*ABZ*. $\overline{EF}$ is a midsegment of △*CDZ*, and $\overline{GH}$ is a midsegment of △*EFZ*.

a. Copy and complete the table.

Number of Midsegment	1	2	3	4
Length of Midsegment	▨	▨	▨	▨

b. If this pattern continues, what will be the length of midsegment 8?

c. Write an algebraic expression to represent the length of midsegment *n*. (*Hint*: Think of the midsegment lengths as powers of 2.)

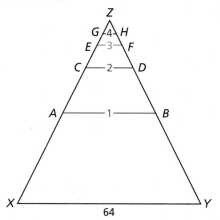

FOCUS ON MATHEMATICAL PRACTICES

H.O.T. **48. Problem Solving** △*FGH* is an equilateral triangle. The perimeter of the midsegment triangle of △*FGH* is 60 centimeters. Find *FH*.

H.O.T. **49. Communication** What information about measures of angles and segments does a midsegment imply that can be used in a proof?

H.O.T. **50. Precision** In △*ABC*, *AB* = 6, *AC* = 8, and *BC* = 10. A midsegment $\overline{MN}$ of the triangle measures 4. What sides contain the endpoints of $\overline{MN}$?

H.O.T. **51. Modeling** The midsegment of a triangle divides the triangle into two regions, a triangle and a trapezoid. What is the ratio of their areas?

Construction Midsegment of a Triangle

 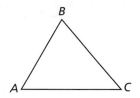

 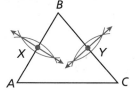

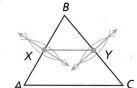

Draw a large triangle. Label the vertices *A*, *B*, and *C*.

Construct the midpoints of $\overline{AB}$ and $\overline{BC}$. Label the midpoints *X* and *Y*, respectively.

Draw the midsegment $\overline{XY}$.

1. Using a ruler, measure $\overline{XY}$ and $\overline{AC}$. How are the two lengths related?

2. How can you use a protractor to verify that $\overline{XY}$ is parallel to $\overline{AC}$?

Ready to Go On?

24-1 Perpendicular and Angle Bisectors

Find each measure.

1. PQ

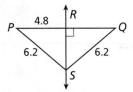

2. JM

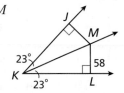

3. AC

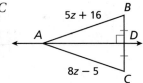

4. Write an equation in point-slope form for the perpendicular bisector of the segment with endpoints $M(-1, -3)$ and $N(7, 1)$.

24-2 Bisectors of Triangles

5. $\overline{PX}$, $\overline{PY}$, and $\overline{PZ}$ are the perpendicular bisectors of $\triangle RST$. Find PS and XT.

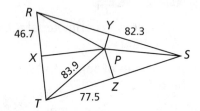

6. $\overline{JK}$ and $\overline{HK}$ are angle bisectors of $\triangle GHJ$. Find m$\angle GJK$ and the distance from K to $\overline{HJ}$.

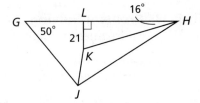

7. Find the circumcenter of $\triangle TVO$ with vertices $T(9, 0)$, $V(0, -4)$, and $O(0, 0)$.

24-3 Medians and Altitudes of Triangles

8. In $\triangle DEF$, $BD = 87$, and $WE = 38$. Find BW, CW, and CE.

9. Paula cuts a triangle with vertices at coordinates $(0, 4)$, $(8, 0)$, and $(10, 8)$ from grid paper. At what coordinates should she place the tip of a pencil to balance the triangle?

10. Find the orthocenter of $\triangle PSV$ with vertices $P(2, 4)$, $S(8, 4)$, and $V(4, 0)$.

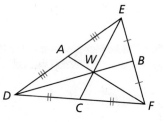

24-4 The Triangle Midsegment Theorem

11. Find ZV, PM, and m$\angle RZV$ in $\triangle JMP$.

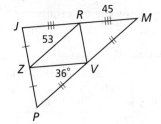

12. What is the distance XZ across the pond?

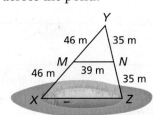

Selected Response

1. Find the measures BC and AC.

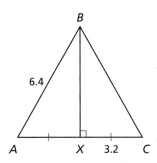

- Ⓐ BC = 6.4, AC = 6.4
- Ⓑ BC = 3.2, AC = 6.4
- Ⓒ BC = 6.4, AC = 3.2
- Ⓓ BC = 3.2, AC = 3.2

2. Write an equation in point-slope form for the perpendicular bisector of the segment with endpoints X(3, 2) and Y(5, 10).

- Ⓕ $y - 6 = 4(x - 4)$
- Ⓖ $y - 6 = -0.25(x - 4)$
- Ⓗ $y + 6 = 0.25(x + 4)$
- Ⓙ $y - 12 = -0.25(x - 8)$

3. The distance from A to each of the three sides of the triangle shown is 18. Find the measure of ∠AVW.

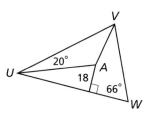

- Ⓐ 20°
- Ⓑ 24°
- Ⓒ 33°
- Ⓓ 37°

4. Point O is the centroid of △ABC, and CO = 18. Find CZ.

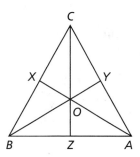

- Ⓕ 24
- Ⓖ 27
- Ⓗ 30
- Ⓙ 36

5. Given △ABC with midsegment $\overline{XY}$, AB = 3, BY = 3.3, and AX = 3.8. Find XY.

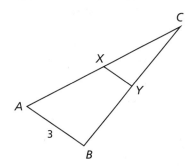

- Ⓐ 1.5
- Ⓑ 1.65
- Ⓒ 1.9
- Ⓓ 2.0

Mini-Tasks

6. Write an equation for the perpendicular bisector of the segment with endpoints A(−4, 5) and B(6, −5).

7. Find the circumcenter of △ABC with vertices A(−2, 4), B(−2, −2), and C(4, −2).

8. The coordinates of the vertices of a triangular piece of a mobile are (0, 4), (3, 8), and (6, 0). The piece will hang from a chain that is attached at the intersection of the medians of the triangle. At what coordinates should the chain be attached?

9. The vertices of △GHJ are G(−4, −7), H(2, 5), and J(10, −3). V is the midpoint of $\overline{GH}$, and W is the midpoint of $\overline{HJ}$. Show that $\overline{VW} \parallel \overline{GJ}$ and $VW = \frac{1}{2}GJ$.

COMMON
CORE GPS

Contents

MATHEMATICAL
PRACTICES
The Common Core Georgia Performance Standards for Mathematical Practice describe varieties of expertise that all students should seek to develop. Opportunities to develop these practices are integrated throughout this program.

1 Make sense of problems and persevere in solving them.

2 Reason abstractly and quantitatively.

3 Construct viable arguments and critique the reasoning of others.

4 Model with mathematics.

5 Use appropriate tools strategically.

6 Attend to precision.

7 Look for and make use of structure.

8 Look for and express regularity in repeated reasoning.

Unpacking the Standards

Understanding the standards and the vocabulary terms in the standards will help you know exactly what you are expected to learn in this chapter.

 MCC9-12.G.CO.11

Prove theorems about parallelograms.

Key Vocabulary

parallelogram (paralelogramo)
A quadrilateral with two pairs of parallel sides.

What It Means For You

Parallelograms, including rectangles and squares, are everywhere around you. You can prove the many special relationships about their sides and angles that make them so important.

EXAMPLE

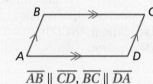

$\overline{AB} \parallel \overline{CD}, \overline{BC} \parallel \overline{DA}$

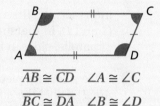

$\overline{AB} \cong \overline{CD} \quad \angle A \cong \angle C$

$\overline{BC} \cong \overline{DA} \quad \angle B \cong \angle D$

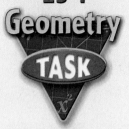

25-1 Geometry TASK

Use with Properties of Parallelograms

Explore Properties of Parallelograms

In this task, you will investigate the relationships among the angles and sides of a special type of quadrilateral called a *parallelogram*. You will need to apply the Transitive Property of Congruence. That is, if figure *A* ≅ figure *B* and figure *B* ≅ figure *C*, then figure *A* ≅ figure *C*.

 Use appropriate tools strategically.

MCC9-12.G.CO.11 Prove theorems about parallelograms.

Activity

1. Use opposite sides of an index card to draw a set of parallel lines on a piece of patty paper. Then use opposite sides of a ruler to draw a second set of parallel lines that intersects the first. Label the points of intersection *A*, *B*, *C*, and *D*, in that order. Quadrilateral *ABCD* has two pairs of parallel sides. It is a *parallelogram*.

2. Place a second piece of patty paper over the first and trace *ABCD*. Label the points that correspond to *A*, *B*, *C*, and *D* as *Q*, *R*, *S*, and *T*, in that order. The parallelograms *ABCD* and *QRST* are congruent. Name all the pairs of congruent corresponding sides and angles.

3. Lay *ABCD* over *QRST* so that $\overline{AB}$ overlays $\overline{ST}$. What do you notice about their lengths? What does this tell you about $\overline{AB}$ and $\overline{CD}$? Now move *ABCD* so that $\overline{DA}$ overlays $\overline{RS}$. What do you notice about their lengths? What does this tell you about $\overline{DA}$ and $\overline{BC}$?

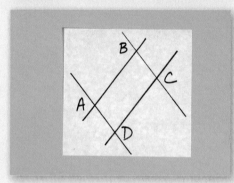

4. Lay *ABCD* over *QRST* so that ∠*A* overlays ∠*S*. What do you notice about their measures? What does this tell you about ∠*A* and ∠*C*? Now move *ABCD* so that ∠*B* overlays ∠*T*. What do you notice about their measures? What does this tell you about ∠*B* and ∠*D*?

5. Arrange the pieces of patty paper so that $\overline{RS}$ overlays $\overline{AD}$. What do you notice about $\overline{QR}$ and $\overline{AB}$? What does this tell you about ∠*A* and ∠*R*? What can you conclude about ∠*A* and ∠*B*?

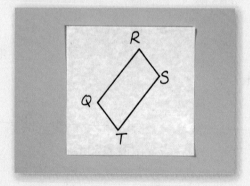

6. Draw diagonals $\overline{AC}$ and $\overline{BD}$. Fold *ABCD* so that *A* matches *C*, making a crease. Unfold the paper and fold it again so that *B* matches *D*, making another crease. What do you notice about the creases? What can you conclude about the diagonals?

Try This

1. Repeat the above steps with a different parallelogram. Do you get the same results?

2. **Make a Conjecture** How do you think the sides of a parallelogram are related to each other? the angles? the diagonals? Write your conjectures as conditional statements.

© HMH

25-1 Properties of Parallelograms

? ***Essential Question:*** If a quadrilateral is a parallelogram, what are some conclusions you can make about its angles, sides, and diagonals?

Objectives
Prove and apply properties of parallelograms.

Use properties of parallelograms to solve problems.

Vocabulary
parallelogram

Who uses this?
Race car designers can use a parallelogram-shaped linkage to keep the wheels of the car vertical on uneven surfaces. (See Example 1.)

Any polygon with four sides is a quadrilateral. However, some quadrilaterals have special properties. These *special quadrilaterals* are given their own names.

Helpful Hint

Opposite sides of a quadrilateral do not share a vertex. Opposite angles do not share a side.

A quadrilateral with two pairs of parallel sides is a **parallelogram**. To write the name of a parallelogram, you use the symbol ▱.

Parallelogram *ABCD*
▱*ABCD*

$\overline{AB} \parallel \overline{CD}$, $\overline{BC} \parallel \overline{DA}$

Theorem 25-1-1	**Properties of Parallelograms**	
THEOREM	**HYPOTHESIS**	**CONCLUSION**
If a quadrilateral is a parallelogram, then its opposite sides are congruent. (▱ → opp. sides ≅)		$\overline{AB} \cong \overline{CD}$ $\overline{BC} \cong \overline{DA}$

PROOF ▮ **Theorem 25-1-1**

Given: *JKLM* is a parallelogram.
Prove: $\overline{JK} \cong \overline{LM}$, $\overline{KL} \cong \overline{MJ}$

Proof:

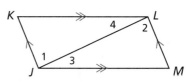

Statements	Reasons
1. *JKLM* is a parallelogram.	**1.** Given
2. $\overline{JK} \parallel \overline{LM}$, $\overline{KL} \parallel \overline{MJ}$	**2.** Def. of ▱
3. ∠1 ≅ ∠2, ∠3 ≅ ∠4	**3.** Alt. Int. ∠ Thm.
4. $\overline{JL} \cong \overline{JL}$	**4.** Reflex. Prop. of ≅
5. △*JKL* ≅ △*LMJ*	**5.** ASA *Steps 3, 4*
6. $\overline{JK} \cong \overline{LM}$, $\overline{KL} \cong \overline{MJ}$	**6.** CPCTC

Theorems (**Properties of Parallelograms**)

THEOREM	HYPOTHESIS	CONCLUSION
25-1-2 If a quadrilateral is a parallelogram, then its opposite angles are congruent. ($\square \rightarrow$ opp. $\angle s \cong$)		$\angle A \cong \angle C$ $\angle B \cong \angle D$
25-1-3 If a quadrilateral is a parallelogram, then its consecutive angles are supplementary. ($\square \rightarrow$ cons. $\angle s$ supp.)		$m\angle A + m\angle B = 180°$ $m\angle B + m\angle C = 180°$ $m\angle C + m\angle D = 180°$ $m\angle D + m\angle A = 180°$
25-1-4 If a quadrilateral is a parallelogram, then its diagonals bisect each other. ($\square \rightarrow$ diags. bisect each other)		$\overline{AZ} \cong \overline{CZ}$ $\overline{BZ} \cong \overline{DZ}$

You will prove Theorems 25-1-3 and 25-1-4 in Exercises 45 and 44.

COMMON CORE GPS
MCC9-12.G.MG.1

EXAMPLE **1**

Racing Application

my.hrw.com

Online Video Tutor

The diagram shows the parallelogram-shaped linkage that joins the frame of a race car to one wheel of the car. In $\square PQRS$, $QR = 48$ cm, $RT = 30$ cm, and $m\angle QPS = 73°$. Find each measure.

A *PS*

$\overline{PS} \cong \overline{QR}$ $\square \rightarrow$ opp. sides $\cong$

$PS = QR$ Def. of $\cong$ segs.

$PS = 48$ cm   Substitute 48 for QR.

B $m\angle PQR$

$m\angle PQR + m\angle QPS = 180°$ $\square \rightarrow$ cons. $\angle s$ supp.

$m\angle PQR + 73 = 180$ Substitute 73 for m∠QPS.

$m\angle PQR = 107°$ Subtract 73 from both sides.

C *PT*

$\overline{PT} \cong \overline{RT}$ $\square \rightarrow$ diags. bisect each other

$PT = RT$ Def. of $\cong$ segs.

$PT = 30$ cm   Substitute 30 for RT.

CHECK IT OUT!

In $\square KLMN$, $LM = 28$ in., $LN = 26$ in., and $m\angle LKN = 74°$. Find each measure.

1a. *KN*

1b. $m\angle NML$

1c. *LO*

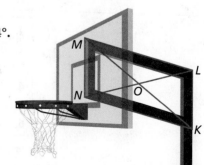

EXAMPLE 2
MCC9-12.A.CED.1

Using Properties of Parallelograms to Find Measures

ABCD is a parallelogram. Find each measure.

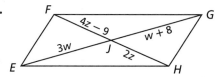

A *AD*

$\overline{AD} \cong \overline{BC}$ $\square \to$ opp. sides $\cong$

$AD = BC$ Def. of $\cong$ segs.

$7x = 5x + 19$ Substitute the given values.

$2x = 19$ Subtract 5x from both sides.

$x = 9.5$ Divide both sides by 2.

$AD = 7x = 7(9.5) = 66.5$

B $m\angle B$

$m\angle A + m\angle B = 180°$ $\square \to$ cons. $\angle$ supp.

$(10y - 1) + (6y + 5) = 180$ Substitute the given values.

$16y + 4 = 180$ Combine like terms.

$16y = 176$ Subtract 4 from both sides.

$y = 11$ Divide both sides by 16.

$m\angle B = (6y + 5)° = [6(11) + 5]° = 71°$

 EFGH is a parallelogram. Find each measure.

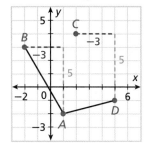

2a. *JG*

2b. *FH*

EXAMPLE 3
MCC9-12.G.GPE.4

Parallelograms in the Coordinate Plane

Three vertices of $\square ABCD$ are $A(1, -2)$, $B(-2, 3)$, and $D(5, -1)$. Find the coordinates of vertex *C*.

Since *ABCD* is a parallelogram, both pairs of opposite sides must be parallel.

Step 1 Graph the given points.

Step 2 Find the slope of $\overline{AB}$ by counting the units from *A* to *B*.
The rise from -2 to 3 is 5.
The run from 1 to -2 is -3.

Step 3 Start at *D* and count the same number of units.
A rise of 5 from -1 is 4.
A run of -3 from 5 is 2. Label $(2, 4)$ as vertex *C*.

Step 4 Use the slope formula to verify that $\overline{BC} \parallel \overline{AD}$.

slope of $\overline{BC} = \dfrac{4 - 3}{2 - (-2)} = \dfrac{1}{4}$

slope of $\overline{AD} = \dfrac{-1 - (-2)}{5 - 1} = \dfrac{1}{4}$

The coordinates of vertex *C* are $(2, 4)$.

Remember!

When you are drawing a figure in the coordinate plane, the name *ABCD* gives the order of the vertices.

 3. Three vertices of $\square PQRS$ are $P(-3, -2)$, $Q(-1, 4)$, and $S(5, 0)$. Find the coordinates of vertex *R*.

EXAMPLE 4 MCC9-12.G.CO.11

Using Properties of Parallelograms in a Proof

Write a two-column proof.

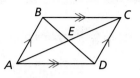

A Theorem 25-1-2

Given: *ABCD* is a parallelogram.

Prove: ∠*BAD* ≅ ∠*DCB*, ∠*ABC* ≅ ∠*CDA*

Proof:

Statements	Reasons
1. *ABCD* is a parallelogram.	1. Given
2. $\overline{AB} \cong \overline{CD}$, $\overline{DA} \cong \overline{BC}$	2. ▱ → opp. sides ≅
3. $\overline{BD} \cong \overline{BD}$	3. Reflex. Prop. of ≅
4. △*BAD* ≅ △*DCB*	4. SSS *Steps 2, 3*
5. ∠*BAD* ≅ ∠*DCB*	5. CPCTC
6. $\overline{AC} \cong \overline{AC}$	6. Reflex. Prop. of ≅
7. △*ABC* ≅ △*CDA*	7. SSS *Steps 2, 6*
8. ∠*ABC* ≅ ∠*CDA*	8. CPCTC

B **Given:** *GHJN* and *JKLM* are parallelograms. *H* and *M* are collinear. *N* and *K* are collinear.

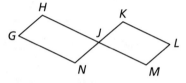

Prove: ∠*G* ≅ ∠*L*

Proof:

Statements	Reasons
1. *GHJN* and *JKLM* are parallelograms.	1. Given
2. ∠*HJN* ≅ ∠*G*, ∠*MJK* ≅ ∠*L*	2. ▱ → opp. ∡ ≅
3. ∠*HJN* ≅ ∠*MJK*	3. Vert. ∡ Thm.
4. ∠*G* ≅ ∠*L*	4. Trans. Prop. of ≅

4. Use the figure in Example 4B to write a two-column proof.
Given: *GHJN* and *JKLM* are parallelograms.
          H and *M* are collinear. *N* and *K* are collinear.

Prove: ∠*N* ≅ ∠*K*

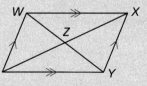

MCC.MP.3   MATHEMATICAL PRACTICES

THINK AND DISCUSS

1. The measure of one angle of a parallelogram is 71°. What are the measures of the other angles?

2. In ▱*VWXY*, *VW* = 21, and *WY* = 36. Find as many other measures as you can. Justify your answers.

3. GET ORGANIZED Copy and complete the graphic organizer. In each cell, draw a figure with markings that represents the given property.

Properties of Parallelograms				
Opp. sides ‖	Opp. sides ≅	Opp. ∡ ≅	Cons. ∡ supp.	Diags. bisect each other.

GUIDED PRACTICE

Vocabulary Apply the vocabulary from this lesson to answer each question.

1. Explain why the figure at right is NOT a *parallelogram*.

2. Draw ▱*PQRS*. Name the opposite sides and opposite angles.

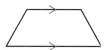

SEE EXAMPLE **1**

Safety The handrail is made from congruent parallelograms. In ▱*ABCD*, *AB* = 17.5, *DE* = 18, and m∠*BCD* = 110°. Find each measure.

3. *BD*   4. *CD*

5. *BE*   6. m∠*ABC*

7. m∠*ADC*   8. m∠*DAB*

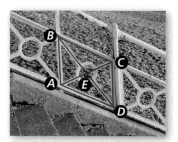

SEE EXAMPLE **2**

JKLM is a parallelogram. Find each measure.

9. *JK*   10. *LM*

11. m∠*L*   12. m∠*M*

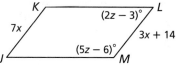

SEE EXAMPLE **3**

13. **Multi-Step** Three vertices of ▱*DFGH* are $D(-9, 4)$, $F(-1, 5)$, and $G(2, 0)$. Find the coordinates of vertex *H*.

SEE EXAMPLE **4**

14. Write a two-column proof.
    Given: *PSTV* is a parallelogram. $\overline{PQ} \cong \overline{RQ}$
    Prove: ∠*STV* ≅ ∠*R*

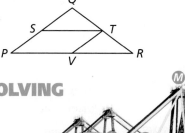

PRACTICE AND PROBLEM SOLVING

Independent Practice

For Exercises	See Example
15–20	1
21–24	2
25	3
26	4

my.hrw.com

Online Extra Practice

Shipping Cranes can be used to load cargo onto ships. In ▱*JKLM*, *JL* = 165.8, *JK* = 110, and m∠*JML* = 50°. Find the measure of each part of the crane.

15. *JN*   16. *LM*

17. *LN*   18. m∠*JKL*

19. m∠*KLM*   20. m∠*MJK*

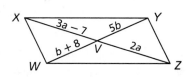

WXYZ is a parallelogram. Find each measure.

21. *WV*   22. *YW*

23. *XZ*   24. *ZV*

25. **Multi-Step** Three vertices of ▱*PRTV* are $P(-4, -4)$, $R(-10, 0)$, and $V(5, -1)$. Find the coordinates of vertex *T*.

26. Write a two-column proof.
    Given: *ABCD* and *AFGH* are parallelograms.
    Prove: ∠*C* ≅ ∠*G*

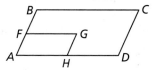

Algebra The perimeter of ▱*PQRS* is 84. Find the length of each side of ▱*PQRS* under the given conditions.

27. $PQ = QR$　　**28.** $QR = 3(RS)$　　**29.** $RS = SP - 7$　　**30.** $SP = RS^2$

31. Cars To repair a large truck, a mechanic might use a *parallelogram lift*. In the lift, $\overline{FG} \cong \overline{GH} \cong \overline{LK} \cong \overline{KJ}$, and $\overline{FL} \cong \overline{GK} \cong \overline{HJ}$.

　　a. Which angles are congruent to ∠1? Justify your answer.

　　b. What is the relationship between ∠1 and each of the remaining labeled angles? Justify your answer.

Complete each statement about ▱*KMPR*. Justify your answer.

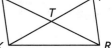

32. $\angle MPR \cong$ ___?___　　**33.** $\angle PRK \cong$ ___?___　　**34.** $\overline{MT} \cong$ ___?___

35. $\overline{PR} \cong$ ___?___　　**36.** $\overline{MP} \parallel$ ___?___　　**37.** $\overline{MK} \parallel$ ___?___

38. $\angle MPK \cong$ ___?___　　**39.** $\angle MTK \cong$ ___?___　　**40.** $m\angle MKR + m\angle PRK =$ ___?___

Find the values of *x, y,* and *z* in each parallelogram.

41. 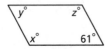　　**42.** 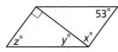　　**43.**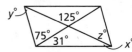

44. Complete the paragraph proof of Theorem 25-1-4 by filling in the blanks.

　　Given: *ABCD* is a parallelogram.
　　Prove: $\overline{AC}$ and $\overline{BD}$ bisect each other at *E*.

　　Proof: It is given that *ABCD* is a parallelogram. By the definition of a parallelogram, $\overline{AB} \parallel$ **a.** ___?___ . By the Alternate Interior Angles Theorem, $\angle 1 \cong$ **b.** ___?___ , and $\angle 3 \cong$ **c.** ___?___ . $\overline{AB} \cong \overline{CD}$ because **d.** ___?___ . This means that $\triangle ABE \cong \triangle CDE$ by **e.** ___?___ . So by **f.** ___?___ , $\overline{AE} \cong \overline{CE}$, and $\overline{BE} \cong \overline{DE}$. Therefore $\overline{AC}$ and $\overline{BD}$ bisect each other at *E* by the definition of **g.** ___?___ .

H.O.T. 45. Write a two-column proof of Theorem 25-1-3: If a quadrilateral is a parallelogram, then its consecutive angles are supplementary.

Algebra Find the values of *x* and *y* in each parallelogram.

46. 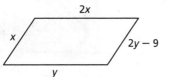　　　　**47.**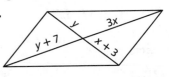

Real-World Connections

48. In this calcite crystal, the face *ABCD* is a parallelogram.

　　a. In ▱*ABCD*, $m\angle B = (6x + 12)°$, and $m\angle D = (9x - 33)°$. Find $m\angle B$.

　　b. Find $m\angle A$ and $m\angle C$. Which theorem or theorems did you use to find these angle measures?

H.O.T. 49. Critical Thinking Draw any parallelogram. Draw a second parallelogram whose corresponding sides are congruent to the sides of the first parallelogram but whose corresponding angles are not congruent to the angles of the first.

    a. Is there an SSSS congruence postulate for parallelograms? Explain.

    b. Remember the meaning of triangle rigidity. Is a parallelogram rigid? Explain.

50. Write About It Explain why every parallelogram is a quadrilateral but every quadrilateral is not necessarily a parallelogram.

TEST PREP

51. What is the value of x in $\square PQRS$?

    Ⓐ 15   Ⓒ 30

    Ⓑ 20   Ⓓ 70

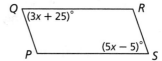

52. The diagonals of $\square JKLM$ intersect at Z. Which statement is true?

    Ⓕ $JL = KM$ Ⓖ $JL = \frac{1}{2}KM$ Ⓗ $JL = \frac{1}{2}JZ$ Ⓙ $JL = 2JZ$

53. Gridded Response In $\square ABCD$, $BC = 8.2$, and $CD = 5$. What is the perimeter of $\square ABCD$?

CHALLENGE AND EXTEND

H.O.T. The coordinates of three vertices of a parallelogram are given. Give the coordinates for all possible locations of the fourth vertex.

54. $(0, 5), (4, 0), (8, 5)$ **55.** $(-2, 1), (3, -1), (-1, -4)$

H.O.T. 56. The feathers on an arrow form two congruent parallelograms that share a common side. Each parallelogram is the reflection of the other across the line they share. Show that $y = 2x$.

H.O.T. 57. Prove that the bisectors of two consecutive angles of a parallelogram are perpendicular.

FOCUS ON MATHEMATICAL PRACTICES

H.O.T. 58. Problem Solving A fence uses a pattern of quadrilaterals that are parallelograms like the one shown at the right. Find the value of x and the angle measures of the parallelogram.

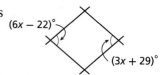

H.O.T. 59. Modeling A parallelogram has one right angle. What is a more specific name for the parallelogram? Justify your answer.

H.O.T. 60. Error Analysis Tony said the diagonals of a parallelogram are always congruent. Do you agree with Tony? If you disagree, correct his statement.

25-2 Conditions for Parallelograms

? *Essential Question:* What information about the angles, sides, or diagonals of a quadrilateral allows you to conclude it is a parallelogram?

Objective
Prove that a given quadrilateral is a parallelogram.

Who uses this?

A bird watcher can use a *parallelogram mount* to adjust the height of a pair of binoculars without changing the viewing angle. (See Example 4.)

You have learned to identify the properties of a parallelogram. Now you will be given the properties of a quadrilateral and will have to tell if the quadrilateral is a parallelogram. To do this, you can use the definition of a parallelogram or the conditions below.

Know it!
Note

Theorems (Conditions for Parallelograms)

THEOREM	EXAMPLE
25-2-1 If one pair of opposite sides of a quadrilateral are parallel and congruent, then the quadrilateral is a parallelogram. (quad. with pair of opp. sides ∥ and ≅ → ▱)	
25-2-2 If both pairs of opposite sides of a quadrilateral are congruent, then the quadrilateral is a parallelogram. (quad. with opp. sides ≅ → ▱)	
25-2-3 If both pairs of opposite angles of a quadrilateral are congruent, then the quadrilateral is a parallelogram. (quad. with opp. ∠ ≅ → ▱)	

Remember!

In the converse of a theorem, the hypothesis and conclusion are exchanged.

You will prove Theorems 25-2-2 and 25-2-3 in Exercises 26 and 29.

PROOF ■ **Theorem 25-2-1**

Given: $\overline{KL} \parallel \overline{MJ}$, $\overline{KL} \cong \overline{MJ}$
Prove: *JKLM* is a parallelogram.

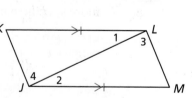

Proof:
It is given that $\overline{KL} \cong \overline{MJ}$. Since $\overline{KL} \parallel \overline{MJ}$, $\angle 1 \cong \angle 2$ by the Alternate Interior Angles Theorem. By the Reflexive Property of Congruence, $\overline{JL} \cong \overline{JL}$. So $\triangle JKL \cong \triangle LMJ$ by SAS. By CPCTC, $\angle 3 \cong \angle 4$, and $\overline{JK} \parallel \overline{LM}$ by the Converse of the Alternate Interior Angles Theorem. Since the opposite sides of *JKLM* are parallel, *JKLM* is a parallelogram by definition.

HMH Photo by Sam Dudgeon

The two theorems below can also be used to show that a given quadrilateral is a parallelogram.

Theorems — Conditions for Parallelograms

THEOREM	EXAMPLE
25-2-4 If an angle of a quadrilateral is supplementary to both of its consecutive angles, then the quadrilateral is a parallelogram. (quad. with ∠ supp. to cons. ∠ → ▱)	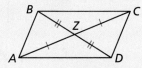
25-2-5 If the diagonals of a quadrilateral bisect each other, then the quadrilateral is a parallelogram. (quad. with diags. bisecting each other → ▱)	

You will prove Theorems 25-2-4 and 25-2-5 in Exercises 27 and 30.

EXAMPLE 1
MCC9-12.A.CED.1

Verifying Figures are Parallelograms

A Show that *ABCD* is a parallelogram for $x = 7$ and $y = 4$.

Step 1 Find *BC* and *DA*.

$BC = x + 14$ *Given* $DA = 3x$

$BC = 7 + 14 = 21$ *Substitute and simplify.* $DA = 3x = 3(7) = 21$

Step 2 Find *AB* and *CD*.

$AB = 5y - 4$ *Given* $CD = 2y + 8$

$AB = 5(4) - 4 = 16$ *Substitute and simplify.* $CD = 2(4) + 8 = 16$

Since $BC = DA$ and $AB = CD$, *ABCD* is a parallelogram by Theorem 25-2-2.

B Show that *EFGH* is a parallelogram for $z = 11$ and $w = 4.5$.

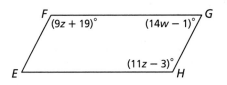

$m\angle F = (9z + 19)°$ *Given*

$m\angle F = [9(11) + 19]° = 118°$ *Substitute 11 for z and simplify.*

$m\angle H = (11z - 3)°$ *Given*

$m\angle H = [11(11) - 3]° = 118°$ *Substitute 11 for z and simplify.*

$m\angle G = (14w - 1)°$ *Given*

$m\angle G = [14(4.5) - 1]° = 62°$ *Substitute 4.5 for w and simplify.*

Since $118° + 62° = 180°$, $\angle G$ is supplementary to both $\angle F$ and $\angle H$. *EFGH* is a parallelogram by Theorem 25-2-4.

1. Show that *PQRS* is a parallelogram for $a = 2.4$ and $b = 9$.

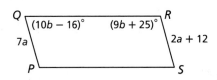

 EXAMPLE 2   Applying Conditions for Parallelograms

Determine if each quadrilateral must be a parallelogram. Justify your answer.

A
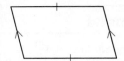

No. One pair of opposite sides are parallel. A different pair of opposite sides are congruent. The conditions for a parallelogram are not met.

B
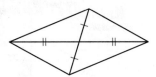

Yes. The diagonals bisect each other. By Theorem 25-2-5, the quadrilateral is a parallelogram.

CHECK IT OUT! Determine if each quadrilateral must be a parallelogram. Justify your answer.

2a.
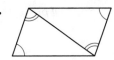

2b.

 EXAMPLE 3   Proving Parallelograms in the Coordinate Plane

Show that quadrilateral *ABCD* is a parallelogram by using the given definition or theorem.

A $A(-3, 2), B(-2, 7), C(2, 4), D(1, -1)$; definition of parallelogram

Find the slopes of both pairs of opposite sides.

$$\text{slope of } \overline{AB} = \frac{7-2}{-2-(-3)} = \frac{5}{1} = 5$$

$$\text{slope of } \overline{CD} = \frac{-1-4}{1-2} = \frac{-5}{-1} = 5$$

$$\text{slope of } \overline{BC} = \frac{4-7}{2-(-2)} = \frac{-3}{4} = -\frac{3}{4}$$

$$\text{slope of } \overline{DA} = \frac{2-(-1)}{-3-1} = \frac{3}{-4} = -\frac{3}{4}$$

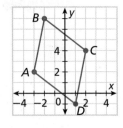

Since both pairs of opposite sides are parallel, *ABCD* is a parallelogram by definition.

Helpful Hint

To say that a quadrilateral is a parallelogram *by definition*, you must show that both pairs of opposite sides are parallel.

B $F(-4, -2), G(-2, 2), H(4, 3), J(2, -1)$; Theorem 25-2-1

Find the slopes and lengths of one pair of opposite sides.

$$\text{slope of } \overline{GH} = \frac{3-2}{4-(-2)} = \frac{1}{6}$$

$$\text{slope of } \overline{JF} = \frac{-2-(-1)}{-4-2} = \frac{-1}{-6} = \frac{1}{6}$$

$$GH = \sqrt{[4-(-2)]^2 + (3-2)^2} = \sqrt{37}$$

$$JF = \sqrt{(-4-2)^2 + [-2-(-1)]^2} = \sqrt{37}$$

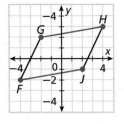

$\overline{GH}$ and $\overline{JF}$ have the same slope, so $\overline{GH} \parallel \overline{JF}$. Since $GH = JF$, $\overline{GH} \cong \overline{JF}$. So by Theorem 25-2-1, *FGHJ* is a parallelogram.

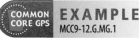

3. Use the definition of a parallelogram to show that the quadrilateral with vertices $K(-3, 0)$, $L(-5, 7)$, $M(3, 5)$, and $N(5, -2)$ is a parallelogram.

You have learned several ways to determine whether a quadrilateral is a parallelogram. You can use the given information about a figure to decide which condition is best to apply.

Conditions for Parallelograms
Both pairs of opposite sides are parallel. (definition)
One pair of opposite sides are parallel and congruent. (Theorem 25-2-1)
Both pairs of opposite sides are congruent. (Theorem 25-2-2)
Both pairs of opposite angles are congruent. (Theorem 25-2-3)
One angle is supplementary to both of its consecutive angles. (Theorem 25-2-4)
The diagonals bisect each other. (Theorem 25-2-5)

my.hrw.com

Online Video Tutor

COMMON CORE GPS **EXAMPLE** **4**
MCC9-12.G.MG.1

Bird-Watching Application

In the parallelogram mount, there are bolts at *P*, *Q*, *R*, and *S* such that *PQ* = *RS* and *QR* = *SP*. The frame *PQRS* moves when you raise or lower the binoculars. Why is *PQRS* always a parallelogram?

When you move the binoculars, the angle measures change, but *PQ*, *QR*, *RS*, and *SP* stay the same. So it is always true that *PQ* = *RS* and *QR* = *SP*. Since both pairs of opposite sides of the quadrilateral are congruent, *PQRS* is always a parallelogram.

4. The frame is attached to the tripod at points *A* and *B* such that *AB* = *RS* and *BR* = *SA*. So *ABRS* is also a parallelogram. How does this ensure that the angle of the binoculars stays the same?

MCC.MP.2 **MATHEMATICAL PRACTICES**

THINK AND DISCUSS

1. What do all the theorems in this lesson have in common?

2. How are the theorems in this lesson different from the theorems in the lesson *Properties of Parallelograms*?

3. **GET ORGANIZED** Copy and complete the graphic organizer. In each box, write one of the six conditions for a parallelogram. Then sketch a parallelogram and label it to show how it meets the condition.

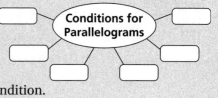

Conditions for Parallelograms

HMH Photo by Sam Dudgeon W

GUIDED PRACTICE

SEE EXAMPLE 1

1. Show that *EFGH* is a parallelogram for $s = 5$ and $t = 6$.

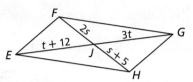

2. Show that *KLPQ* is a parallelogram for $m = 14$ and $n = 12.5$.

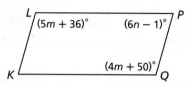

SEE EXAMPLE 2

Determine if each quadrilateral must be a parallelogram. Justify your answer.

3.

4.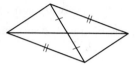

5.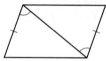

SEE EXAMPLE 3

Show that the quadrilateral with the given vertices is a parallelogram.

6. $W(-5, -2)$, $X(-3, 3)$, $Y(3, 5)$, $Z(1, 0)$

7. $R(-1, -5)$, $S(-2, -1)$, $T(4, -1)$, $U(5, -5)$

SEE EXAMPLE 4

8. **Navigation** A parallel rule can be used to plot a course on a navigation chart. The tool is made of two rulers connected at hinges to two congruent crossbars $\overline{AD}$ and $\overline{BC}$. You place the edge of one ruler on your desired course and then move the second ruler over the compass rose on the chart to read the bearing for your course. If $\overline{AD} \parallel \overline{BC}$, why is $\overline{AB}$ always parallel to $\overline{CD}$?

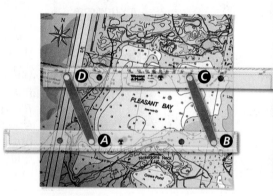

PRACTICE AND PROBLEM SOLVING

Independent Practice

For Exercises	See Example
9–10	1
11–13	2
14–15	3
16	4

9. Show that *BCGH* is a parallelogram for $x = 3.2$ and $y = 7$.

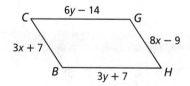

10. Show that *TUVW* is a parallelogram for for $a = 19.5$ and $b = 22$.

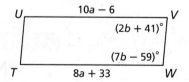

my.hrw.com

Online Extra Practice

Determine if each quadrilateral must be a parallelogram. Justify your answer.

11.

12.

13.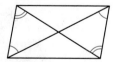

Show that the quadrilateral with the given vertices is a parallelogram.

14. $J(-1, 0)$, $K(-3, 7)$, $L(2, 6)$, $M(4, -1)$

15. $P(-8, -4)$, $Q(-5, 1)$, $R(1, -5)$, $S(-2, -10)$

16. Design The toolbox has cantilever trays that pull away from the box so that you can reach the items beneath them. Two congruent brackets connect each tray to the box. Given that $AD = BC$, how do the brackets $\overline{AB}$ and $\overline{CD}$ keep the tray horizontal?

Determine if each quadrilateral must be a parallelogram. Justify your answer.

17.

18.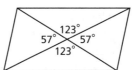

19.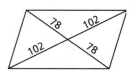

H.O.T. **Algebra** Find the values of a and b that would make the quadrilateral a parallelogram.

20.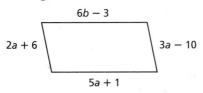

21.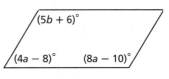

22.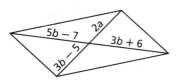

23.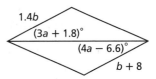

24. Critical Thinking Draw a quadrilateral that has congruent diagonals but is not a parallelogram. What can you conclude about using congruent diagonals as a condition for a parallelogram?

25. Social Studies The angles at the corners of the flag of the Republic of the Congo are right angles. The red and green triangles are congruent isosceles right triangles. Why is the shape of the yellow stripe a parallelogram?

26. Complete the two-column proof of Theorem 25-2-2 by filling in the blanks.

Given: $\overline{AB} \cong \overline{CD}$, $\overline{BC} \cong \overline{DA}$

Prove: $ABCD$ is a parallelogram.

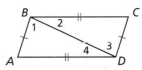

Proof:

Statements	Reasons
1. $\overline{AB} \cong \overline{CD}$, $\overline{BC} \cong \overline{DA}$	**1.** Given
2. $\overline{BD} \cong \overline{BD}$	**2. a.** ___?___
3. $\triangle DAB \cong$ **b.** ___?___	**3. c.** ___?___
4. $\angle 1 \cong$ **d.** ___?___, $\angle 4 \cong$ **e.** ___?___	**4.** CPCTC
5. $\overline{AB} \parallel \overline{CD}$, $\overline{BC} \parallel \overline{DA}$	**5. f.** ___?___
6. $ABCD$ is a parallelogram.	**6. g.** ___?___

27. Complete the paragraph proof of Theorem 25-2-4
by filling in the blanks.
Given: ∠P is supplementary to ∠Q.
  ∠P is supplementary to ∠S.
Prove: PQRS is a parallelogram.

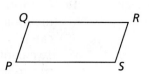

Proof:
It is given that ∠P is supplementary to **a.** ___?___ and **b.** ___?___ .
By the Converse of the Same-Side Interior Angles Theorem,
$\overline{QR} \parallel$ **c.** ___?___ and $\overline{PQ} \parallel$ **d.** ___?___ . So PQRS is a parallelogram
by the definition of **e.** ___?___ .

28. Measurement In the eighteenth century,
Gilles Personne de Roberval designed a scale
with two beams and two hinges. In ▱ABCD,
E is the midpoint of $\overline{AB}$, and F is the midpoint
of $\overline{CD}$. Write a paragraph proof that AEFD and
EBCF are parallelograms.

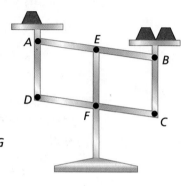

Prove each theorem.

29. Theorem 25-2-3
Given: ∠E ≅ ∠G, ∠F ≅ ∠H
Prove: EFGH is a parallelogram.

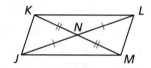

Plan: Show that the sum of the interior angles of EFGH
is 360°. Then apply properties of equality to show that
m∠E + m∠F = 180° and m∠E + m∠H = 180°.
Then you can conclude that $\overline{EF} \parallel \overline{GH}$ and $\overline{FG} \parallel \overline{HE}$.

30. Theorem 25-2-5
Given: $\overline{JL}$ and $\overline{KM}$ bisect each other.
Prove: JKLM is a parallelogram.

Plan: Show that △JNK ≅ △LNM and
△KNL ≅ △MNJ. Then use the fact that
the corresponding angles are congruent to show $\overline{JK} \parallel \overline{LM}$ and $\overline{KL} \parallel \overline{MJ}$.

H.O.T. 31. Prove that the figure formed by two midsegments of a triangle and their
corresponding bases is a parallelogram.

32. Write About It Use the theorems about properties of parallelograms to write three
biconditional statements about parallelograms.

H.O.T. 33. Construction Explain how you can construct a parallelogram based on the
conditions of Theorem 25-2-1. Use your method to construct a parallelogram.

34. A geologist made the following observations
while examining this amethyst crystal.
Tell whether each set of observations allows
the geologist to conclude that PQRS is a
parallelogram. If so, explain why.

a. $\overline{PQ} \cong \overline{SR}$, and $\overline{PS} \parallel \overline{QR}$.

b. ∠S and ∠R are supplementary, and $\overline{PS} \cong \overline{QR}$.

c. ∠S ≅ ∠Q, and $\overline{PQ} \parallel \overline{SR}$.

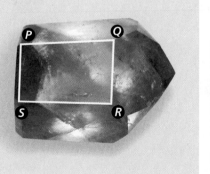

TEST PREP

35. What additional information would allow you to conclude that *WXYZ* is a parallelogram?

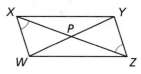

(A) $\overline{XY} \cong \overline{ZW}$ (C) $\overline{WY} \cong \overline{WZ}$

(B) $\overline{WX} \cong \overline{YZ}$ (D) $\angle XWY \cong \angle ZYW$

36. Which could be the coordinates of the fourth vertex of $\square ABCD$ with $A(-1, -1)$, $B(1, 3)$, and $C(6, 1)$?

(F) $D(8, 5)$ (G) $D(4, -3)$ (H) $D(13, 3)$ (J) $D(3, 7)$

37. Short Response The vertices of quadrilateral *RSTV* are $R(-5, 0)$, $S(-1, 3)$, $T(5, 1)$, and $V(2, -2)$. Is *RSTV* a parallelogram? Justify your answer.

CHALLENGE AND EXTEND

38. Write About It As the upper platform of the movable staircase is raised and lowered, the height of each step changes. How does the upper platform remain parallel to the ground?

H.O.T. 39. Multi-Step The diagonals of a parallelogram intersect at $(-2, 1.5)$. Two vertices are located at $(-7, 2)$ and $(2, 6.5)$. Find the coordinates of the other two vertices.

H.O.T. 40. Given: *D* is the midpoint of $\overline{AC}$, and *E* is the midpoint of $\overline{BC}$.

Prove: $\overline{DE} \parallel \overline{AB}$, $DE = \frac{1}{2}AB$

(*Hint:* Extend $\overline{DE}$ to form $\overline{DF}$ so that $\overline{EF} \cong \overline{DE}$. Then show that *DFBA* is a parallelogram.)

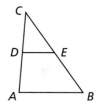

FOCUS ON MATHEMATICAL PRACTICES

H.O.T. 41. Proof A precision ice skating team with 10 members formed the figure shown. The skaters positioned themselves along four lines, and the space between each pair of adjacent skaters was 3 feet. Prove that the skaters formed a parallelogram.

H.O.T. 42. Problem Solving The figure shows a parallelogram.

a. Find the coordinates of the fourth vertex.

b. Find the midpoints of the sides of the parallelogram.

c. Show that the quadrilateral formed by connecting the midpoints of adjacent sides is also a parallelogram.

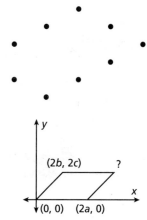

25-3 Properties of Special Parallelograms

Essential Question: What are the geometric properties of rectangles, rhombuses, and squares?

Objectives
Prove and apply properties of rectangles, rhombuses, and squares.

Use properties of rectangles, rhombuses, and squares to solve problems.

Vocabulary
rectangle
rhombus
square

Who uses this?
Artists who work with stained glass can use properties of rectangles to cut materials to the correct sizes.

A second type of special quadrilateral is a *rectangle*. A **rectangle** is a quadrilateral with four right angles.

Rectangle *ABCD*

Theorems | **Properties of Rectangles**

THEOREM	HYPOTHESIS	CONCLUSION
25-3-1 If a quadrilateral is a rectangle, then it is a parallelogram. (rect. → ▱)		*ABCD* is a parallelogram.
25-3-2 If a parallelogram is a rectangle, then its diagonals are congruent. (rect. → diags. ≅)		$\overline{AC} \cong \overline{BD}$

You will prove Theorems 25-3-1 and 25-3-2 in Exercises 38 and 35.

Since a rectangle is a parallelogram by Theorem 25-3-1, a rectangle "inherits" all the properties of parallelograms.

COMMON CORE GPS MCC9-12.G.MG.1

EXAMPLE 1 | Craft Application

my.hrw.com

Online Video Tutor

An artist connects stained glass pieces with lead strips. In this rectangular window, the strips are cut so that $FG = 24$ in. and $FH = 34$ in. Find JG.

$\overline{EG} \cong \overline{FH}$	*Rect. → diags. ≅*
$EG = FH = 34$	*Def. of ≅ segs.*
$JG = \frac{1}{2}EG$	*▱ → diags. bisect each other*
$JG = \frac{1}{2}(34) = 17$ in.	*Substitute and simplify.*

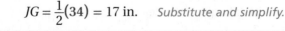

CHECK IT OUT! **Carpentry** The rectangular gate has diagonal braces. Find each length.

1a. *HJ*

1b. *HK*

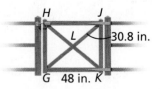

Courtesy of Wimberley Stain Glass/HMH Photo by Peter Van Steen

A *rhombus* is another special quadrilateral. A **rhombus** is a quadrilateral with four congruent sides.

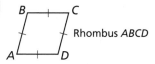

Rhombus *ABCD*

Theorems   **Properties of Rhombuses**

THEOREM	HYPOTHESIS	CONCLUSION
25-3-3 If a quadrilateral is a rhombus, then it is a parallelogram. (rhombus → ▱)		*ABCD* is a parallelogram.
25-3-4 If a parallelogram is a rhombus, then its diagonals are perpendicular. (rhombus → diags. ⊥)		$\overline{AC} \perp \overline{BD}$
25-3-5 If a parallelogram is a rhombus, then each diagonal bisects a pair of opposite angles. (rhombus → each diag. bisects opp. ∡)		$\angle 1 \cong \angle 2$ $\angle 3 \cong \angle 4$ $\angle 5 \cong \angle 6$ $\angle 7 \cong \angle 8$

You will prove Theorems 25-3-3 and 25-3-4 in Exercises 34 and 37.

PROOF   **Theorem 25-3-5**

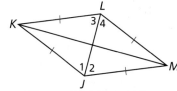

Given: *JKLM* is a rhombus.
Prove: $\overline{JL}$ bisects ∠*KJM* and ∠*KLM*.
        $\overline{KM}$ bisects ∠*JKL* and ∠*JML*.

Proof:
Since *JKLM* is a rhombus, $\overline{JK} \cong \overline{JM}$, and $\overline{KL} \cong \overline{ML}$ by the definition of a rhombus. By the Reflexive Property of Congruence, $\overline{JL} \cong \overline{JL}$. Thus △*JKL* ≅ △*JML* by SSS. Then ∠1 ≅ ∠2, and ∠3 ≅ ∠4 by CPCTC. So $\overline{JL}$ bisects ∠*KJM* and ∠*KLM* by the definition of an angle bisector. By similar reasoning, $\overline{KM}$ bisects ∠*JKL* and ∠*JML*.

Like a rectangle, a rhombus is a parallelogram. So you can apply the properties of parallelograms to rhombuses.

COMMON CORE GPS
MCC9-12.A.CED.1

EXAMPLE   **2**   **Using Properties of Rhombuses to Find Measures**

RSTV is a rhombus. Find each measure.

my.hrw.com

Online Video Tutor

A   *VT*

$$ST = SR$$ *Def. of rhombus*
$$4x + 7 = 9x - 11$$ *Substitute the given values.*
$$18 = 5x$$ *Subtract 4x from both sides and add 11 to both sides.*
$$3.6 = x$$ *Divide both sides by 5.*
$$VT = ST$$ *Def. of rhombus*
$$VT = 4x + 7$$ *Substitute 4x + 7 for ST.*
$$VT = 4(3.6) + 7 = 21.4$$ *Substitute 3.6 for x and simplify.*

RSTV is a rhombus. Find each measure.

B m∠*WSR*

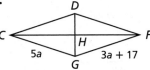

m∠*SWT* = 90°	*Rhombus → diags.* ⊥
2*y* + 10 = 90	*Substitute 2y + 10 for m∠SWT.*
y = 40	*Subtract 10 from both sides and divide both sides by 2.*

m∠*WSR* = m∠*TSW*	*Rhombus → each diag. bisects opp. ∠s*
m∠*WSR* = (*y* + 2)°	*Substitute y + 2 for m∠TSW.*
m∠*WSR* = (40 + 2)° = 42°	*Substitute 40 for y and simplify.*

 CHECK IT OUT!

CDFG is a rhombus. Find each measure.

2a. *CD*

2b. m∠*GCH* if m∠*GCD* = (*b* + 3)° and m∠*CDF* = (6*b* − 40)°

Helpful Hint

Rectangles, rhombuses, and squares are sometimes referred to as *special parallelograms*.

A **square** is a quadrilateral with four right angles and four congruent sides. In the exercises, you will show that a square is a parallelogram, a rectangle, and a rhombus. So a square has the properties of all three.

Square *ABCD*

COMMON CORE GPS MCC9-12.G.GPE.4

EXAMPLE 3

Verifying Properties of Squares

my.hrw.com

Online Video Tutor

Show that the diagonals of square *ABCD* are congruent perpendicular bisectors of each other.

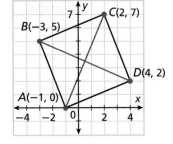

Step 1 Show that $\overline{AC}$ and $\overline{BD}$ are congruent.

$$AC = \sqrt{[2 - (-1)]^2 + (7 - 0)^2} = \sqrt{58}$$

$$BD = \sqrt{[4 - (-3)]^2 + (2 - 5)^2} = \sqrt{58}$$

Since $AC = BD$, $\overline{AC} \cong \overline{BD}$.

Step 2 Show that $\overline{AC}$ and $\overline{BD}$ are perpendicular.

$$\text{slope of } \overline{AC} = \frac{7 - 0}{2 - (-1)} = \frac{7}{3}$$

$$\text{slope of } \overline{BD} = \frac{2 - 5}{4 - (-3)} = \frac{-3}{7} = -\frac{3}{7}$$

Since $\left(\frac{7}{3}\right)\left(-\frac{3}{7}\right) = -1$, $\overline{AC} \perp \overline{BD}$.

Step 3 Show that $\overline{AC}$ and $\overline{BD}$ bisect each other.

$$\text{mdpt. of } \overline{AC}: \left(\frac{-1 + 2}{2}, \frac{0 + 7}{2}\right) = \left(\frac{1}{2}, \frac{7}{2}\right)$$

$$\text{mdpt. of } \overline{BD}: \left(\frac{-3 + 4}{2}, \frac{5 + 2}{2}\right) = \left(\frac{1}{2}, \frac{7}{2}\right)$$

Since $\overline{AC}$ and $\overline{BD}$ have the same midpoint, they bisect each other. The diagonals are congruent perpendicular bisectors of each other.

 CHECK IT OUT!

3. The vertices of square *STVW* are *S*(−5, −4), *T*(0, 2), *V*(6, −3), and *W*(1, −9). Show that the diagonals of square *STVW* are congruent perpendicular bisectors of each other.

Special Parallelograms

*To remember the properties of rectangles, rhombuses, and squares, I start with a **square**, which has all the properties of the others.*

*To get a **rectangle** that is not a square, I stretch the square in one direction. Its diagonals are still congruent, but they are no longer perpendicular.*

*To get a **rhombus** that is not a square, I go back to the square and slide the top in one direction. Its diagonals are still perpendicular and bisect the opposite angles, but they aren't congruent.*

EXAMPLE **4**
MCC9-12.G.CO.11

my.hrw.com

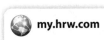

Online Video Tutor

Using Properties of Special Parallelograms in Proofs

Given: *EFGH* is a rectangle. *J* is the midpoint of $\overline{EH}$.
Prove: △*FJG* is isosceles.

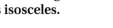

Proof:

Statements	Reasons
1. *EFGH* is a rectangle. *J* is the midpoint of $\overline{EH}$.	1. Given
2. ∠*E* and ∠*H* are right angles.	2. Def. of rect.
3. ∠*E* ≅ ∠*H*	3. Rt. ∠ ≅ Thm.
4. *EFGH* is a parallelogram.	4. Rect. → ▱
5. $\overline{EF} \cong \overline{HG}$	5. ▱ → opp. sides ≅
6. $\overline{EJ} \cong \overline{HJ}$	6. Def. of mdpt.
7. △*FJE* ≅ △*GJH*	7. SAS *Steps 3, 5, 6*
8. $\overline{FJ} \cong \overline{GJ}$	8. CPCTC
9. △*FJG* is isosceles.	9. Def. of isosc. △

 4. Given: *PQTS* is a rhombus with diagonal $\overline{PR}$.
     Prove: $\overline{RQ} \cong \overline{RS}$

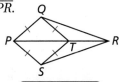

MCC.MP.7   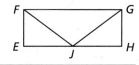 MATHEMATICAL PRACTICES

THINK AND DISCUSS

1. Which theorem means "The diagonals of a rectangle are congruent"? Why do you think the theorem is written as a conditional?

2. What properties of a rhombus are the same as the properties of all parallelograms? What special properties does a rhombus have?

3. GET ORGANIZED Copy and complete the graphic organizer. Write the missing terms in the three unlabeled sections. Then write a definition of each term.

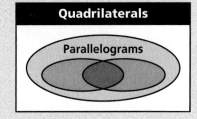

Quadrilaterals
Parallelograms

GUIDED PRACTICE

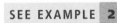

1. **Vocabulary** What is another name for an *equilateral quadrilateral*? an *equiangular quadrilateral*? a *regular quadrilateral*?

SEE EXAMPLE **1** **Engineering** The braces of the bridge support lie along the diagonals of rectangle *PQRS*. *RS* = 160 ft, and *QS* = 380 ft. Find each length.

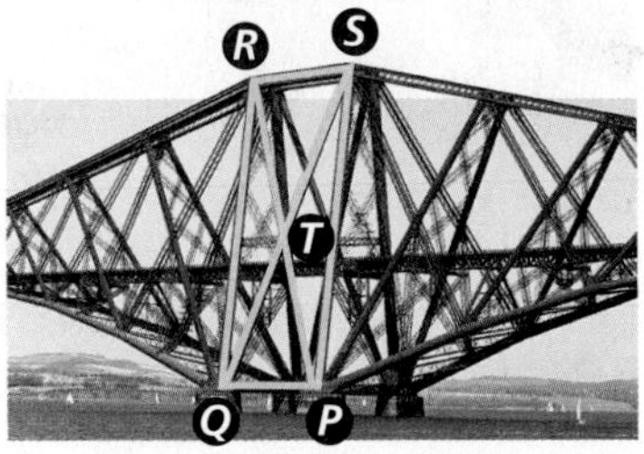

2. *TQ*   3. *PQ*

4. *ST*   5. *PR*

SEE EXAMPLE **2** *ABCD* is a rhombus. Find each measure.

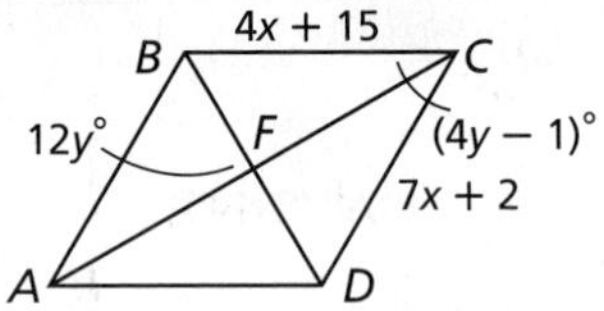

6. *AB*   7. m∠*ABC*

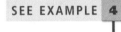

SEE EXAMPLE **3** 8. **Multi-Step** The vertices of square *JKLM* are *J*(−3, −5), *K*(−4, 1), *L*(2, 2), and *M*(3, −4). Show that the diagonals of square *JKLM* are congruent perpendicular bisectors of each other.

SEE EXAMPLE **4** 9. **Given:** *RECT* is a rectangle. $\overline{RX} \cong \overline{TY}$
   Prove: $\triangle REY \cong \triangle TCX$

PRACTICE AND PROBLEM SOLVING

Independent Practice	
For Exercises	See Example
10–13	1
14–15	2
16	3
17	4

Carpentry A carpenter measures the diagonals of a piece of wood. In rectangle *JKLM*, *JM* = 25 in., and *JP* = $14\frac{1}{2}$ in. Find each length.

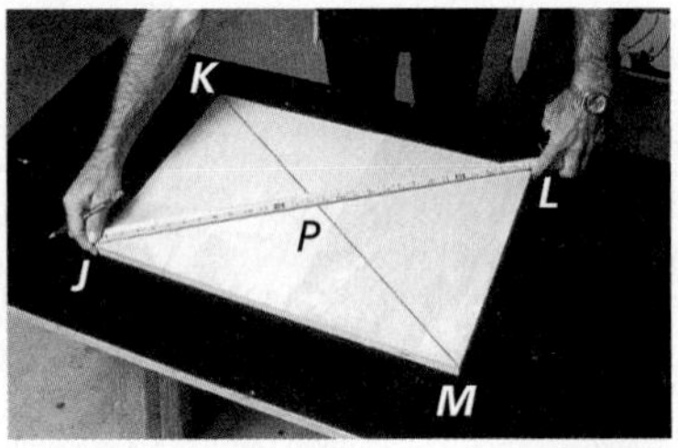

10. *JL*   11. *KL*

12. *KM*   13. *MP*

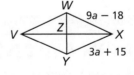

VWXY is a rhombus. Find each measure.

14. *VW*

15. m∠*VWX* and m∠*WYX* if m∠*WVY* = $(4b + 10)°$ and m∠*XZW* = $(10b − 5)°$

H.O.T. 16. **Multi-Step** The vertices of square *PQRS* are *P*(−4, 0), *Q*(4, 3), *R*(7, −5), and *S*(−1, −8). Show that the diagonals of square *PQRS* are congruent perpendicular bisectors of each other.

17. **Given:** *RHMB* is a rhombus with diagonal $\overline{HB}$.
    Prove: ∠*HMX* ≅ ∠*HRX*

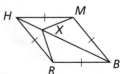

Find the measures of the numbered angles in each rectangle.

18. 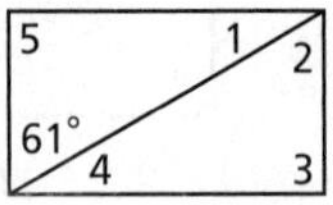   19. 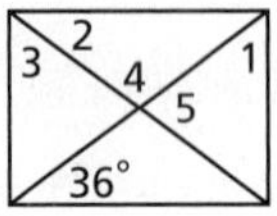   20.

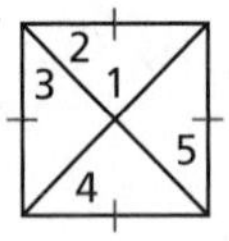

Find the measures of the numbered angles in each rhombus.

21.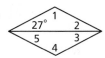

22.

23.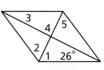

Tell whether each statement is sometimes, always, or never true.
(*Hint:* Refer to your graphic organizer for this lesson.)

24. A rectangle is a parallelogram.

25. A rhombus is a square.

26. A parallelogram is a rhombus.

27. A rhombus is a rectangle.

28. A square is a rhombus.

29. A rectangle is a quadrilateral.

30. A square is a rectangle.

31. A rectangle is a square.

H.O.T. 32. **Critical Thinking** A triangle is equilateral if and only if the triangle is equiangular. Can you make a similar statement about a quadrilateral? Explain your answer.

33. **History** There are five shapes of clay tiles in this tile mosaic from the ruins of Pompeii.

   a. Make a sketch of each shape of tile and tell whether the shape is a polygon.

   b. Name each polygon by its number of sides. Does each shape appear to be regular or irregular?

   c. Do any of the shapes appear to be special parallelograms? If so, identify them by name.

   d. Find the measure of each interior angle of the center polygon.

H.O.T. 34. ///ERROR ANALYSIS/// Find and correct the error in this proof of Theorem 25-3-3.

Given: *JKLM* is a rhombus.
Prove: *JKLM* is a parallelogram.

Proof:
   It is given that *JKLM* is a rhombus. So by the definition of a rhombus, $\overline{JK} \cong \overline{LM}$, and $\overline{KL} \cong \overline{MJ}$. If a quadrilateral is a parallelogram, then its opposite sides are congruent. So *JKLM* is a parallelogram.

35. Complete the two-column proof of Theorem 25-3-2 by filling in the blanks.

Given: *EFGH* is a rectangle.
Prove: $\overline{FH} \cong \overline{GE}$

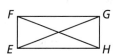

Proof:

Statements	Reasons
1. *EFGH* is a rectangle.	1. Given
2. *EFGH* is a parallelogram.	2. a. ___?___
3. $\overline{EF} \cong$ b. ___?___	3. ▱ → opp. sides ≅
4. $\overline{EH} \cong \overline{EH}$	4. c. ___?___
5. ∠*FEH* and ∠*GHE* are right angles.	5. d. ___?___
6. ∠*FEH* ≅ e. ___?___	6. Rt. ∠ ≅ Thm.
7. △*FEH* ≅ △*GHE*	7. f. ___?___
8. $\overline{FH} \cong \overline{GE}$	8. g. ___?___

Real-World Connections

36. The organizers of a fair plan to fence off a plot of land given by the coordinates $A(2, 4)$, $B(4, 2)$, $C(-1, -3)$, and $D(-3, -1)$.

  a. Find the slope of each side of quadrilateral $ABCD$.

  b. What type of quadrilateral is formed by the fences? Justify your answer.

  c. The organizers plan to build a straight path connecting A and C and another path connecting B and D. Explain why these two paths will have the same length.

37. Use this plan to write a proof of Theorem 25-3-4.

  Given: $VWXY$ is a rhombus.

  Prove: $\overline{VX} \perp \overline{WY}$

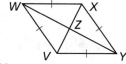

  Plan: Use the definition of a rhombus and the properties of parallelograms to show that $\triangle WZX \cong \triangle YZX$. Then use CPCTC to show that $\angle WZX$ and $\angle YZX$ are right angles.

38. Write a paragraph proof of Theorem 25-3-1.

  Given: $ABCD$ is a rectangle.

  Prove: $ABCD$ is a parallelogram.

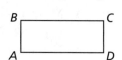

39. Write a two-column proof.

  Given: $ABCD$ is a rhombus. E, F, G, and H are the midpoints of the sides.

  Prove: $EFGH$ is a parallelogram.

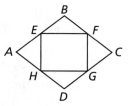

H.O.T. **Multi-Step** Find the perimeter and area of each figure. Round to the nearest hundredth, if necessary.

40.

41.

42.

H.O.T. **43. Write About It** Explain why each of these conditional statements is true.

  a. If a quadrilateral is a square, then it is a parallelogram.

  b. If a quadrilateral is a square, then it is a rectangle.

  c. If a quadrilateral is a square, then it is a rhombus.

44. Write About It List the properties that a square "inherits" because it is (1) a parallelogram, (2) a rectangle, and (3) a rhombus.

TEST PREP

45. Which expression represents the measure of $\angle J$ in rhombus $JKLM$?

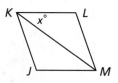

  Ⓐ $x°$

  Ⓑ $2x°$

  Ⓒ $(180 - x)°$

  Ⓓ $(180 - 2x)°$

46. Short Response The diagonals of rectangle $QRST$ intersect at point P. If $QR = 1.8$ cm, $QP = 1.5$ cm, and $QT = 2.4$ cm, find the perimeter of $\triangle RST$. Explain how you found your answer.

47. Which statement is NOT true of a rectangle?

  Ⓕ Both pairs of opposite sides are congruent and parallel.

  Ⓖ Both pairs of opposite angles are congruent and supplementary.

  Ⓗ All pairs of consecutive sides are congruent and perpendicular.

  Ⓙ All pairs of consecutive angles are congruent and supplementary.

CHALLENGE AND EXTEND

48. Algebra Find the value of x in the rhombus.

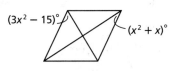

H.O.T. 49. Prove that the segment joining the midpoints of two consecutive sides of a rhombus is perpendicular to one diagonal and parallel to the other.

50. Extend the definition of a triangle midsegment to write a definition for the midsegment of a rectangle. Prove that a midsegment of a rectangle divides the rectangle into two congruent rectangles.

51. The figure is formed by joining eleven congruent squares. How many rectangles are in the figure?

FOCUS ON MATHEMATICAL PRACTICES

H.O.T. 52. Reasoning Explain the relationship between the two labeled angles in the rhombus shown and their relationship to $\angle BAD$, then find the value of x and m$\angle BAD$.

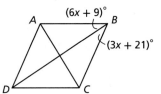

H.O.T. 53. Problem Solving $ABCD$ is a rhombus. Find x and m$\angle DAC$. Show your work.

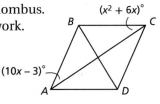

Construction Rhombus

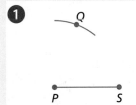

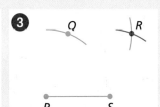

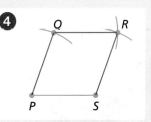

Draw $\overline{PS}$. Set the compass to the length of $\overline{PS}$. Place the compass point at P and draw an arc above $\overline{PS}$. Label a point Q on the arc.

Place the compass point at Q and draw an arc to the right of Q.

Place the compass point at S and draw an arc that intersects the arc drawn from Q. Label the point of intersection R.

Draw $\overline{PQ}$, $\overline{QR}$, and $\overline{RS}$.

25-4 Technology TASK

Predict Conditions for Special Parallelograms

In this task, you will use geometry software to predict the conditions that are sufficient to prove that a parallelogram is a rectangle, rhombus, or square.

Use with *Conditions for Special Parallelograms*

 Use appropriate tools strategically.

MCC9-12.G.CO.11 Prove theorems about parallelograms.

Activity 1

1 Construct $\overline{AB}$ and $\overline{AD}$ with a common endpoint A. Construct a line through D parallel to $\overline{AB}$. Construct a line through B parallel to $\overline{AD}$.

2 Construct point C at the intersection of the two lines. Hide the lines and construct $\overline{BC}$ and $\overline{CD}$ to complete the parallelogram.

3 Measure the four sides and angles of the parallelogram.

4 Move A so that m∠ABC = 90°. What type of special parallelogram results?

5 Move A so that m∠ABC ≠ 90°.

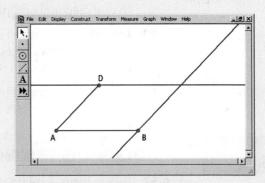

6 Construct $\overline{AC}$ and $\overline{BD}$ and measure their lengths. Move A so that $AC = BD$. What type of special parallelogram results?

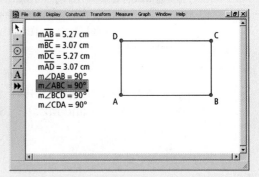

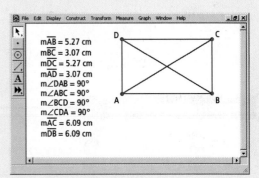

Try This

1. How does the method of constructing $ABCD$ in Steps 1 and 2 guarantee that the quadrilateral is a parallelogram?

2. **Make a Conjecture** What are two conditions for a rectangle? Write your conjectures as conditional statements.

Activity 2

1 Use the parallelogram you constructed in Activity 1. Move *A* so that *AB* = *BC*. What type of special parallelogram results?

2 Move *A* so that *AB* ≠ *BC*.

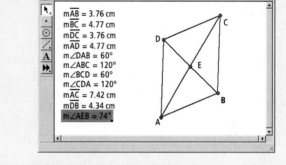

3 Label the intersection of the diagonals as *E*. Measure ∠*AEB*.

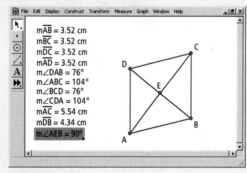

4 Move *A* so that m∠*AEB* = 90°. What type of special parallelogram results?

5 Move *A* so that m∠*AEB* ≠ 90°.

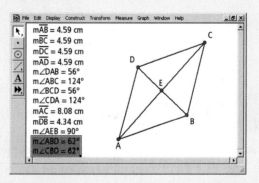

6 Measure ∠*ABD* and ∠*CBD*. Move *A* so that m∠*ABD* = m∠*CBD*. What type of special parallelogram results?

Try This

3. Make a Conjecture What are three conditions for a rhombus? Write your conjectures as conditional statements.

4. Make a Conjecture A square is both a rectangle and a rhombus. What conditions do you think must hold for a parallelogram to be a square?

Conditions for Special Parallelograms

Essential Question: What information about a parallelogram allows you to conclude it is a rectangle, rhombus, or square?

Objective
Prove that a given quadrilateral is a rectangle, rhombus, or square.

Who uses this?
Building contractors and carpenters can use the conditions for rectangles to make sure the frame for a house has the correct shape.

When you are given a parallelogram with certain properties, you can use the theorems below to determine whether the parallelogram is a rectangle.

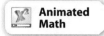
Animated Math

Know it!
Note

Theorems	**Conditions for Rectangles**

THEOREM	EXAMPLE
25-4-1 If one angle of a parallelogram is a right angle, then the parallelogram is a rectangle. ($\square$ with one rt. $\angle$ → rect.)	*diagram: parallelogram with vertices B, C, A, D and right angle at A*
25-4-2 If the diagonals of a parallelogram are congruent, then the parallelogram is a rectangle. ($\square$ with diags. $\cong$ → rect.)	*diagram: parallelogram with vertices B, C, A, D with diagonals* $\overline{AC} \cong \overline{BD}$

You will prove Theorems 25-4-1 and 25-4-2 in Exercises 31 and 28.

COMMON CORE GPS
EXAMPLE 1
MCC9-12.G.MG.1

Carpentry Application

my.hrw.com

Online Video Tutor

A contractor built a wood frame for the side of a house so that $\overline{XY} \cong \overline{WZ}$ and $\overline{XW} \cong \overline{YZ}$. Using a tape measure, the contractor found that $XZ = WY$. Why must the frame be a rectangle?

Both pairs of opposite sides of $WXYZ$ are congruent, so $WXYZ$ is a parallelogram. Since $XZ = WY$, the diagonals of $\square WXYZ$ are congruent. Therefore the frame is a rectangle by Theorem 25-4-2.

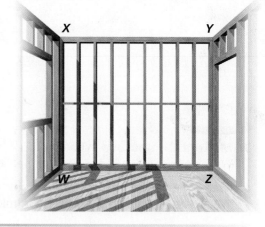

David Papazian/Getty Images

1. A carpenter's square can be used to test that an angle is a right angle. How could the contractor use a carpenter's square to check that the frame is a rectangle?

Below are some conditions you can use to determine whether a parallelogram is a rhombus.

Theorems **Conditions for Rhombuses**

THEOREM	EXAMPLE
25-4-3 If one pair of consecutive sides of a parallelogram are congruent, then the parallelogram is a rhombus. (□ with one pair cons. sides ≅ → rhombus)	
25-4-4 If the diagonals of a parallelogram are perpendicular, then the parallelogram is a rhombus. (□ with diags. ⊥ → rhombus)	
25-4-5 If one diagonal of a parallelogram bisects a pair of opposite angles, then the parallelogram is a rhombus. (□ with diag. bisecting opp. ⦞ → rhombus)	

Caution!

In order to apply Theorems 25-5-1 through 25-5-5, the quadrilateral must be a parallelogram.

You will prove Theorems 25-4-3 and 25-4-4 in Exercises 32 and 30.

PROOF **Theorem 25-4-5**

Given: *JKLM* is a parallelogram.
$\overline{JL}$ bisects ∠*KJM* and ∠*KLM*.
Prove: *JKLM* is a rhombus.

Proof:

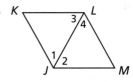

Statements	Reasons
1. *JKLM* is a parallelogram. $\overline{JL}$ bisects ∠*KJM* and ∠*KLM*.	1. Given
2. ∠1 ≅ ∠2, ∠3 ≅ ∠4	2. Def. of ∠ bisector
3. $\overline{JL} \cong \overline{JL}$	3. Reflex. Prop. of ≅
4. △*JKL* ≅ △*JML*	4. ASA *Steps 2, 3*
5. $\overline{JK} \cong \overline{JM}$	5. CPCTC
6. *JKLM* is a rhombus.	6. □ with one pair cons. sides ≅ → rhombus

To prove that a given quadrilateral is a square, it is sufficient to show that the figure is both a rectangle and a rhombus. You will explain why this is true in Exercise 43.

EXAMPLE **2**
MCC9-12.G.CO.11

my.hrw.com

Online Video Tutor

Applying Conditions for Special Parallelograms

Determine if the conclusion is valid. If not, tell what additional information is needed to make it valid.

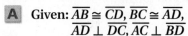

A Given: $\overline{AB} \cong \overline{CD}, \overline{BC} \cong \overline{AD},$
$\overline{AD} \perp \overline{DC}, \overline{AC} \perp \overline{BD}$
Conclusion: *ABCD* is a square.

Step 1 Determine if *ABCD* is a parallelogram.

$\overline{AB} \cong \overline{CD}, \overline{BC} \cong \overline{AD}$ *Given*

ABCD is a parallelogram.   *Quad. with opp. sides* $\cong \to \square$

Step 2 Determine if *ABCD* is a rectangle.

$\overline{AD} \perp \overline{DC}$, so $\angle ADC$ is a right angle.   *Def. of* $\perp$

ABCD is a rectangle. $\square$ *with one rt.* $\angle \to$ *rect.*

Step 3 Determine if *ABCD* is a rhombus.

$\overline{AC} \perp \overline{BD}$ *Given*

ABCD is a rhombus. $\square$ *with diags.* $\perp \to$ *rhombus*

Step 4 Determine if *ABCD* is a square.

Since *ABCD* is a rectangle and a rhombus, it has four right angles and four congruent sides. So *ABCD* is a square by definition. The conclusion is valid.

B Given: $\overline{AB} \cong \overline{BC}$
Conclusion: *ABCD* is a rhombus.

The conclusion is not valid. By Theorem 25-4-3, if one pair of consecutive sides of a parallelogram are congruent, then the parallelogram is a rhombus. To apply this theorem, you must first know that *ABCD* is a parallelogram.

2. Determine if the conclusion is valid. If not, tell what additional information is needed to make it valid.
Given: $\angle ABC$ is a right angle.
Conclusion: *ABCD* is a rectangle.

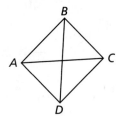

Remember!

You can also prove that a given quadrilateral is a rectangle, rhombus, or square by using the definitions of the special quadrilaterals.

EXAMPLE **3**
MCC9-12.G.GPE.5

my.hrw.com

Online Video Tutor

Identifying Special Parallelograms in the Coordinate Plane

Use the diagonals to determine whether a parallelogram with the given vertices is a rectangle, rhombus, or square. Give all the names that apply.

A $A(0, 2), B(3, 6), C(8, 6), D(5, 2)$

Step 1 Graph $\square ABCD$.

Step 2 Determine if *ABCD* is a rectangle.

$$AC = \sqrt{(8-0)^2 + (6-2)^2}$$
$$= \sqrt{80} = 4\sqrt{5}$$

$$BD = \sqrt{(5-3)^2 + (2-6)^2}$$
$$= \sqrt{20} = 2\sqrt{5}$$

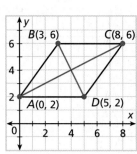

Since $4\sqrt{5} \neq 2\sqrt{5}$, *ABCD* is not a rectangle.
Thus *ABCD* is not a square.

Step 3 Determine if *ABCD* is a rhombus.

slope of $\overline{AC} = \frac{6-2}{8-0} = \frac{1}{2}$ 　　slope of $\overline{BD} = \frac{2-6}{5-3} = -2$

Since $\left(\frac{1}{2}\right)(-2) = -1$, $\overline{AC} \perp \overline{BD}$. *ABCD* is a rhombus.

B $E(-4, -1), F(-3, 2), G(3, 0), H(2, -3)$

Step 1 Graph $\square EFGH$.

Step 2 Determine if *EFGH* is a rectangle.

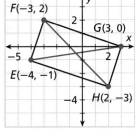

$$EG = \sqrt{[3 - (-4)]^2 + [0 - (-1)]^2}$$
$$= \sqrt{50} = 5\sqrt{2}$$

$$FH = \sqrt{[2 - (-3)]^2 + (-3 - 2)^2}$$
$$= \sqrt{50} = 5\sqrt{2}$$

Since $5\sqrt{2} = 5\sqrt{2}$, the diagonals are congruent.
EFGH is a rectangle.

Step 3 Determine if *EFGH* is a rhombus.

slope of $\overline{EG} = \frac{0 - (-1)}{3 - (-4)} = \frac{1}{7}$

slope of $\overline{FH} = \frac{-3 - 2}{2 - (-3)} = \frac{-5}{5} = -1$

Since $\left(\frac{1}{7}\right)(-1) \neq -1$, $\overline{EG} \not\perp \overline{FH}$.

So *EFGH* is a not a rhombus and cannot be a square.

 Use the diagonals to determine whether a parallelogram with the given vertices is a rectangle, rhombus, or square. Give all the names that apply.

3a. $K(-5, -1), L(-2, 4), M(3, 1), N(0, -4)$

3b. $P(-4, 6), Q(2, 5), R(3, -1), S(-3, 0)$

MCC.MP.6　**MATHEMATICAL PRACTICES**

THINK AND DISCUSS

1. What special parallelogram is formed when the diagonals of a parallelogram are congruent? when the diagonals are perpendicular? when the diagonals are both congruent and perpendicular?

2. Draw a figure that shows why this statement is not necessarily true: If one angle of a quadrilateral is a right angle, then the quadrilateral is a rectangle.

3. A rectangle can also be defined as a parallelogram with a right angle. Explain why this definition is accurate.

4. GET ORGANIZED Copy and complete the graphic organizer. In each box, write at least three conditions for the given parallelogram.

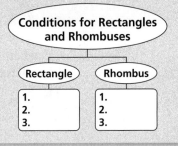

GUIDED PRACTICE

SEE EXAMPLE 1

1. **Gardening** A city garden club is planting a square garden. They drive pegs into the ground at each corner and tie strings between each pair. The pegs are spaced so that $\overline{WX} \cong \overline{XY} \cong \overline{YZ} \cong \overline{ZW}$. How can the garden club use the diagonal strings to verify that the garden is a square?

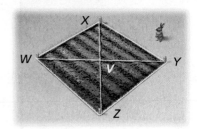

SEE EXAMPLE 2

Determine if the conclusion is valid. If not, tell what additional information is needed to make it valid.

2. Given: $\overline{AC} \cong \overline{BD}$
   Conclusion: *ABCD* is a rectangle.

3. Given: $\overline{AB} \parallel \overline{CD}, \overline{AB} \cong \overline{CD}, \overline{AB} \perp \overline{BC}$
   Conclusion: *ABCD* is a rectangle.

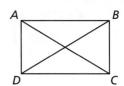

SEE EXAMPLE 3

Multi-Step Use the diagonals to determine whether a parallelogram with the given vertices is a rectangle, rhombus, or square. Give all the names that apply.

4. $P(-5, 2), Q(4, 5), R(6, -1), S(-3, -4)$

5. $W(-6, 0), X(1, 4), Y(2, -4), Z(-5, -8)$

PRACTICE AND PROBLEM SOLVING

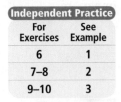

For Exercises	See Example
6	1
7–8	2
9–10	3

Online Extra Practice

6. **Crafts** A framer uses a clamp to hold together the pieces of a picture frame. The pieces are cut so that $\overline{PQ} \cong \overline{RS}$ and $\overline{QR} \cong \overline{SP}$. The clamp is adjusted so that *PZ*, *QZ*, *RZ*, and *SZ* are all equal. Why must the frame be a rectangle?

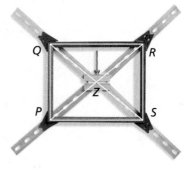

Determine if the conclusion is valid. If not, tell what additional information is needed to make it valid.

7. Given: $\overline{EG}$ and $\overline{FH}$ bisect each other. $\overline{EG} \perp \overline{FH}$
   Conclusion: *EFGH* is a rhombus.

8. Given: $\overline{FH}$ bisects $\angle EFG$ and $\angle EHG$.
   Conclusion: *EFGH* is a rhombus.

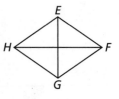

Multi-Step Use the diagonals to determine whether a parallelogram with the given vertices is a rectangle, rhombus, or square. Give all the names that apply.

9. $A(-10, 4), B(-2, 10), C(4, 2), D(-4, -4)$

10. $J(-9, -7), K(-4, -2), L(3, -3), M(-2, -8)$

Tell whether each quadrilateral is a parallelogram, rectangle, rhombus, or square. Give all the names that apply.

11.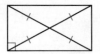

12.

13.

Peter Van Steen/HMH Photo

Tell whether each quadrilateral is a parallelogram, rectangle, rhombus, or square. Give all the names that apply.

14.   **15.**   **16.**

17. ///**ERROR ANALYSIS**/// In □ABCD, $\overline{AC} \cong \overline{BD}$. Which conclusion is incorrect? Explain the error.

   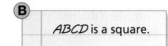

H.O.T. Give one characteristic of the diagonals of each figure that would make the conclusion valid.

18. Conclusion: *JKLM* is a rhombus.

19. Conclusion: *PQRS* is a square.

The coordinates of three vertices of □ABCD are given. Find the coordinates of *D* so that the given type of figure is formed.

20. $A(4, -2)$, $B(-5, -2)$, $C(4, 4)$; rectangle

21. $A(-5, 5)$, $B(0, 0)$, $C(7, 1)$; rhombus

22. $A(0, 2)$, $B(4, -2)$, $C(0, -6)$; square

23. $A(2, 1)$, $B(-1, 5)$, $C(-5, 2)$; square

Find the value of *x* that makes each parallelogram the given type.

24. rectangle

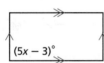

25. rhombus

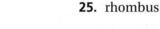 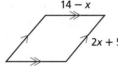

26. square

 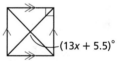

27. Critical Thinking The diagonals of a quadrilateral are perpendicular bisectors of each other. What is the best name for this quadrilateral? Explain your answer.

28. Complete the two-column proof of Theorem 25-4-2 by filling in the blanks.

Given: *EFGH* is a parallelogram.
$\overline{EG} \cong \overline{HF}$
Prove: *EFGH* is a rectangle.

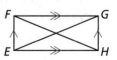

Proof:

Statements	Reasons
1. *EFGH* is a parallelogram. $\overline{EG} \cong \overline{HF}$	**1.** Given
2. $\overline{EF} \cong \overline{HG}$	**2. a.** ___?___
3. b. ___?___	**3.** Reflex. Prop. of $\cong$
4. $\triangle EFH \cong \triangle HGE$	**4. c.** ___?___
5. $\angle FEH \cong$ **d.** ___?___	**5. e.** ___?___
6. $\angle FEH$ and $\angle GHE$ are supplementary.	**6. f.** ___?___
7. g. ___?___	**7.** $\cong \angle$ supp. → rt. $\angle$
8. *EFGH* is a rectangle.	**8. h.** ___?___

29. A state fair takes place on a plot of land given by the coordinates $A(-2, 3)$, $B(1, 2)$, $C(2, -1)$, and $D(-1, 0)$.

  a. Show that the opposite sides of quadrilateral $ABCD$ are parallel.

  b. A straight path connects A and C, and another path connects B and D. Use slopes to prove that these two paths are perpendicular.

  c. What can you conclude about $ABCD$? Explain your answer.

30. Complete the paragraph proof of Theorem 25-4-4 by filling in the blanks.

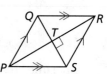

Given: $PQRS$ is a parallelogram. $\overline{PR} \perp \overline{QS}$
Prove: $PQRS$ is a rhombus.

Proof:

It is given that $PQRS$ is a parallelogram. The diagonals of a parallelogram bisect each other, so $\overline{PT} \cong$ **a.** ___?___ . By the Reflexive Property of Congruence, $\overline{QT} \cong$ **b.** ___?___ . It is given that $\overline{PR} \perp \overline{QS}$, so $\angle QTP$ and $\angle QTR$ are right angles by the definition of **c.** ___?___ . Then $\angle QTP \cong \angle QTR$ by the **d.** ___?___ . So $\triangle QTP \cong \triangle QTR$ by **e.** ___?___ , and $\overline{QP} \cong$ **f.** ___?___ , by CPCTC. By Theorem 25-4-3, if one pair of consecutive sides of a parallelogram are congruent, then the parallelogram is a **g.** ___?___ . Therefore $PQRS$ is rhombus.

H.O.T. 31. Write a two-column proof of Theorem 25-4-1.

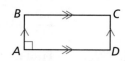

  Given: $ABCD$ is a parallelogram. $\angle A$ is a right angle.
  Prove: $ABCD$ is a rectangle.

H.O.T. 32. Write a paragraph proof of Theorem 25-4-3.

  Given: $JKLM$ is a parallelogram. $\overline{JK} \cong \overline{KL}$
  Prove: $JKLM$ is a rhombus.

H.O.T. 33. Algebra Four lines are represented by the equations below.

  $\ell: y = -x + 1$ $m: y = -x + 7$ $n: y = 2x + 1$ $p: y = 2x + 7$

  a. Graph the four lines in the coordinate plane.

  b. Classify the quadrilateral formed by the lines.

  c. What if...? Suppose the slopes of lines n and p change to 1. Reclassify the quadrilateral.

H.O.T. 34. Write a two-column proof.

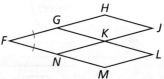

  Given: $FHJN$ and $GLMF$ are parallelograms. $\overline{FG} \cong \overline{FN}$
  Prove: $FGKN$ is a rhombus.

35. Write About It Write a biconditional statement based on the theorems about the diagonals of rectangles. Write a biconditional statement based on the theorems about the diagonals of rhombuses. Can you write a biconditional statement based on the theorems about opposite angles in parallelograms? Explain your answer.

Construction Use the diagonals to construct each figure. Then use the theorems from this lesson to explain why your method works.

36. rectangle   **37.** rhombus   **38.** square

39. In ▱*PQRS*, $\overline{PR}$ and $\overline{QS}$ intersect at *T*. What additional information is needed to conclude that *PQRS* is a rectangle?

Ⓐ $\overline{PT} \cong \overline{QT}$ Ⓒ $\overline{PT} \perp \overline{QT}$

Ⓑ $\overline{PT} \cong \overline{RT}$ Ⓓ $\overline{PT}$ bisects ∠*QPS*.

40. Which of the following is the best name for figure *WXYZ* with vertices *W*(−3, 1), *X*(1, 5), *Y*(8, −2), and *Z*(4, −6)?

Ⓕ Parallelogram   Ⓖ Rectangle   Ⓗ Rhombus   Ⓙ Square

41. **Extended Response**

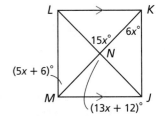

a. Write and solve an equation to find the value of *x*.

b. Is *JKLM* a parallelogram? Explain.

c. Is *JKLM* a rectangle? Explain.

d. Is *JKLM* a rhombus? Explain.

42. **Given:** $\overline{AC} \cong \overline{DF}, \overline{AB} \cong \overline{DE}, \overline{AB} \perp \overline{BC}, \overline{DE} \perp \overline{EF},$
$\overline{BE} \perp \overline{EF}, \overline{BC} \parallel \overline{EF}$
Prove: *EBCF* is a rectangle.

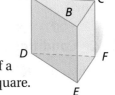

43. **Critical Thinking** Consider the following statement: If a quadrilateral is a rectangle and a rhombus, then it is a square.

a. Explain why the statement is true.

b. If a quadrilateral is a rectangle, is it necessary to show that all four sides are congruent in order to conclude that it is a square? Explain.

c. If a quadrilateral is a rhombus, is it necessary to show that all four angles are right angles in order to conclude that it is a square? Explain.

44. **Cars** As you turn the crank of a car jack, the platform that supports the car rises. Use the diagonals of the parallelogram to explain whether the jack forms a rectangle, rhombus, or square.

FOCUS ON MATHEMATICAL PRACTICES

H.O.T. 45. **Properties** Give the most specific name for the parallelogram with the given properties.

a. diagonals are congruent and perpendicular

b. diagonals bisect each other and are congruent

c. diagonals are perpendicular

H.O.T. 46. **Justify** Coco made a skating rink in her back yard. The rink is a quadrilateral *PQRS* where $\overline{PQ}$ is parallel to $\overline{RS}$, $\overline{PQ}$ is congruent to $\overline{RS}$, and $\overline{PR}$ is congruent to $\overline{QS}$. What type of quadrilateral is her rink? Justify your answer.

Ready to Go On?

my.hrw.com
Assessment and Intervention

25-1 Properties of Parallelograms

A pantograph is used to copy drawings. Its legs form a parallelogram. In $\square JKLM$, $LM = 17$ cm, $KN = 13.5$ cm, and m$\angle KJM = 102°$. Find each measure.

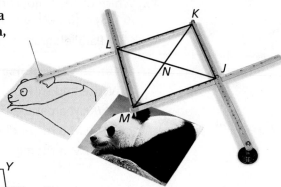

1. KM 2. KJ 3. MN

4. m$\angle JKL$ 5. m$\angle JML$ 6. m$\angle KLM$

7. Three vertices of $\square ABCD$ are $A(-3, 1)$, $B(5, 7)$, and $C(6, 2)$. Find the coordinates of vertex D.

$WXYZ$ is a parallelogram. Find each measure.

8. WX 9. YZ

10. m$\angle X$ 11. m$\angle W$

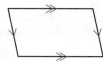

25-2 Conditions for Parallelograms

12. Show that $RSTV$ is a parallelogram for $x = 6$ and $y = 4.5$.

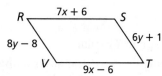

13. Show that $GHJK$ is a parallelogram for $m = 12$ and $n = 9.5$.

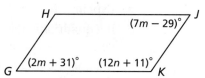

Determine if each quadrilateral must be a parallelogram. Justify your answer.

14.   15.   16.

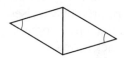

17. Show that a quadrilateral with vertices $C(-9, 4)$, $D(-4, 8)$, $E(2, 6)$, and $F(-3, 2)$ is a parallelogram.

25-3 Properties of Special Parallelograms

The flag of Jamaica is a rectangle with stripes along the diagonals. In rectangle $QRST$, $QS = 80.5$, and $RS = 36$. Find each length.

18. SP 19. QT 20. TR 21. TP

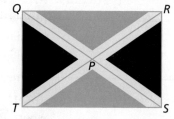

$GHJK$ is a rhombus. Find each measure.

22. HJ

23. m$\angle HJG$ and m$\angle GHJ$ if m$\angle JLH = (4b - 6)°$ and m$\angle JKH = (2b + 11)°$

24. **Given:** $QSTV$ is a rhombus. $\overline{PT} \cong \overline{RT}$
    Prove: $\overline{PQ} \cong \overline{RQ}$

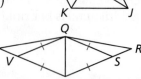

✓ 25-4 Conditions for Special Parallelograms

Determine if the conclusion is valid. If not, tell what additional information is needed to make it valid.

25. Given: $\overline{AC} \perp \overline{BD}$
Conclusion: *ABCD* is a rhombus.

26. Given: $\overline{AB} \cong \overline{CD}$, $\overline{AC} \cong \overline{BD}$, $\overline{AB} \parallel \overline{CD}$
Conclusion: *ABCD* is a rectangle.

Use the diagonals to determine whether a parallelogram with the given vertices is a rectangle, rhombus, or square. Give all the names that apply.

27. $W(-2, 2)$, $X(1, 5)$, $Y(7, -1)$, $Z(4, -4)$ **28.** $M(-4, 5)$, $N(1, 7)$, $P(3, 2)$, $Q(-2, 0)$

29. Given: $\overline{VX}$ and $\overline{ZX}$ are midsegments of $\triangle TWY$. $\overline{TW} \cong \overline{TY}$
Prove: *TVXZ* is a rhombus.

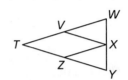

PARCC Assessment Readiness

COMMON CORE GPS

Selected Response

1. The diagram shows the parallelogram-shaped component that attaches a car's rearview mirror to the car. In parallelogram *RSTU*, $UR = 25$, $RX = 16$, and $m\angle STU = 42.4°$. Find *ST*, *XT*, and $m\angle RST$.

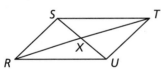

- **A** $ST = 16$, $XT = 25$, $m\angle RST = 42.4°$
- **B** $ST = 25$, $XT = 16$, $m\angle RST = 47.8°$
- **C** $ST = 25$, $XT = 16$, $m\angle RST = 137.6°$
- **D** $ST = 5$, $XT = 4$, $m\angle RST = 137.6°$

2. Use the diagonals to determine whether a parallelogram with vertices $A(-1, -2)$, $B(-2, 0)$, $C(0, 1)$, and $D(1, -1)$ is a rectangle, rhombus, or square. Give all the names that apply.

- **F** rectangle, rhombus, square
- **G** rectangle, rhombus
- **H** rectangle
- **J** square

3. An artist designs a rectangular quilt piece with different types of ribbon that go from the corner to the center of the quilt. The dimensions of the rectangle are $AB = 10$ inches and $AC = 14$ inches. Find *BX*.

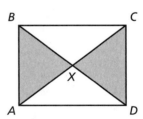

- **A** $BX = 7$ inches
- **C** $BX = 5$ inches
- **B** $BX = 10$ inches
- **D** $BX = 14$ inches

Mini-Task

4. Two vertices of a parallelogram are $A(2, 3)$ and $B(8, 11)$, and the intersection of the diagonals is $X(7, 6)$. Find the coordinates of the other two vertices.

COMMON
CORE GPS

MATHEMATICAL
PRACTICES
The Common Core Georgia Performance Standards for Mathematical Practice describe varieties of expertise that all students should seek to develop. Opportunities to develop these practices are integrated throughout this program.

1 Make sense of problems and persevere in solving them.

2 Reason abstractly and quantitatively.

3 Construct viable arguments and critique the reasoning of others.

4 Model with mathematics.

5 Use appropriate tools strategically.

6 Attend to precision.

7 Look for and make use of structure.

8 Look for and express regularity in repeated reasoning.

Unpacking the Standards

Understanding the standards and the vocabulary terms in the standards will help you know exactly what you are expected to learn in this chapter.

 MCC9-12.G.SRT.2

Given two figures, ... decide if they are similar; explain using similarity transformations the meaning of similarity for triangles as the equality of all corresponding pairs of angles and the proportionality of all corresponding pairs of sides.

Key Vocabulary

similar polygons (polígonos semejantes) Two polygons whose corresponding angles are congruent and whose corresponding side lengths are proportional.

similarity transformation (transformación de semejanza) A transformation that produces similar figures.

triangle (triángulo) A three-sided polygon.

corresponding angles of polygons (ángulos correspondientes de los polígonos) Angles in the same position in two different polygons that have the same number of angles.

corresponding sides of polygons (lados correspondientes de los polígonos) Sides in the same position in two different polygons that have the same number of sides.

What It Means For You

Two figures are similar if they have the same shape but not necessarily the same size. When two figures are similar, you can dilate one of them and then slide, flip, and/or rotate it so that it coincides with the other. As a result, corresponding angles of similar figures are congruent and corresponding side lengths are proportional.

EXAMPLE **Similar figures**

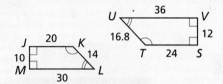

The figures are similar because you can multiply all the side lengths of the smaller figure by 1.2, rotate it 180°, and slide it so that it coincides with the larger figure.

NON-EXAMPLE **Non-similar figures**

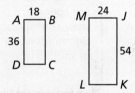

The rectangles are not similar. There is no combination of dilations, slides, flips, and/or rotations that will cause the two figures to coincide.

26-1 Ratios in Similar Polygons

 Essential Question: How are ratios and corresponding parts used to solve problems about similar polygons?

Objectives
Identify similar polygons.

Apply properties of similar polygons to solve problems.

Vocabulary
similar
similar polygons
similarity ratio

Why learn this?

Similar polygons are used to build models of actual objects. (See Example 3.)

Figures that are **similar** (~) have the same shape but not necessarily the same size.

△1 is similar to △2(△1 ~ △2).   △1 is not similar to △3(△1 ≁ △3).

 Similar Polygons

DEFINITION	DIAGRAM	STATEMENTS
Two polygons are **similar polygons** if and only if their corresponding angles are congruent and their corresponding side lengths are proportional.	A 6 B 5 5.4 D 4 C E 12 F 10 10.8 H 8 G $ABCD \sim EFGH$	$\angle A \cong \angle E$ $\angle B \cong \angle F$ $\angle C \cong \angle G$ $\angle D \cong \angle H$ $\frac{AB}{EF} = \frac{BC}{FG} = \frac{CD}{GH} = \frac{DA}{HE} = \frac{1}{2}$

COMMON CORE GPS **EXAMPLE 1** MCC9-12.G.SRT.2

Describing Similar Polygons

Identify the pairs of congruent angles and corresponding sides.

$\angle Z \cong \angle R$ and $\angle Y \cong \angle Q$. By the Third Angles Theorem, $\angle X \cong \angle S$.

$\frac{XY}{SQ} = \frac{6}{9} = \frac{2}{3}$, $\frac{YZ}{QR} = \frac{12}{18} = \frac{2}{3}$,

$\frac{XZ}{SR} = \frac{9}{13.5} = \frac{2}{3}$

 my.hrw.com

Online Video Tutor

 CHECK IT OUT! 1. Identify the pairs of congruent angles and corresponding sides.

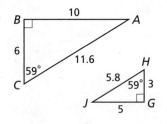

Jens Meyer/AP/Wide World Photos

A **similarity ratio** is the ratio of the lengths of the corresponding sides of two similar polygons. The similarity ratio of $\triangle ABC$ to $\triangle DEF$ is $\frac{3}{6}$, or $\frac{1}{2}$.
The similarity ratio of $\triangle DEF$ to $\triangle ABC$ is $\frac{6}{3}$, or 2.

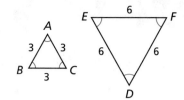

EXAMPLE 2
MCC9-12.G.SRT.2

my.hrw.com

Online Video Tutor

Identifying Similar Polygons

Determine whether the polygons are similar. If so, write the similarity ratio and a similarity statement.

A rectangles $PQRS$ and $TUVW$

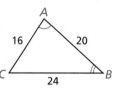

Step 1 Identify pairs of congruent angles.
$\angle P \cong \angle T$, $\angle Q \cong \angle U$,
$\angle R \cong \angle V$, and $\angle S \cong \angle W$ *All ∠ of a rect. are rt. ∠ and are ≅.*

Step 2 Compare corresponding sides.
$$\frac{PQ}{TU} = \frac{12}{16} = \frac{3}{4}, \quad \frac{PS}{TW} = \frac{4}{6} = \frac{2}{3}$$

Since corresponding sides are not proportional, the rectangles are not similar.

B $\triangle ABC$ and $\triangle DEF$

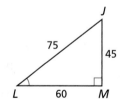

Step 1 Identify pairs of congruent angles.
$\angle A \cong \angle D$, $\angle B \cong \angle E$ *Given*
$\angle C \cong \angle F$ *Third ∠ Thm.*

Step 2 Compare corresponding sides.
$$\frac{AB}{DE} = \frac{20}{15} = \frac{4}{3}, \quad \frac{BC}{EF} = \frac{24}{18} = \frac{4}{3}, \quad \frac{AC}{DF} = \frac{16}{12} = \frac{4}{3}$$

Thus the similarity ratio is $\frac{4}{3}$, and $\triangle ABC \sim \triangle DEF$.

Writing a similarity statement is like writing a congruence statement—be sure to list corresponding vertices in the same order.

CHECK IT OUT!

2. Determine if $\triangle JLM \sim \triangle NPS$. If so, write the similarity ratio and a similarity statement.

Student to Student   *Proportions with Similar Figures*

Anna Woods
Westwood High School

When I set up a proportion, I make sure each ratio compares the figures in the same order. To find x, I wrote $\frac{10}{4} = \frac{6}{x}$. This will work because the first ratio compares the lengths starting with rectangle ABCD. The second ratio compares the widths, also starting with rectangle ABCD.

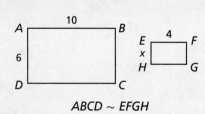

$ABCD \sim EFGH$

EXAMPLE **3**
MCC9-12.G.MG.1

Hobby Application

A Railbox boxcar can be used to transport auto parts. If the length of the actual boxcar is 50 ft, find the width of the actual boxcar to the nearest tenth of a foot.

Online Video Tutor

Let x be the width of the actual boxcar in feet. The rectangular model of a boxcar is similar to the rectangular boxcar, so the corresponding lengths are proportional.

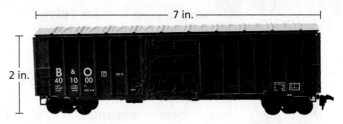

$$\frac{\text{length of boxcar}}{\text{length of model}} = \frac{\text{width of boxcar}}{\text{width of model}}$$

$$\frac{50}{7} = \frac{x}{2}$$

$7x = (50)(2)$ *Cross Products Prop.*

$7x = 100$ *Simplify.*

$x \approx 14.3$ *Divide both sides by 7.*

The width of the model is approximately 14.3 ft.

Helpful Hint

When you work with proportions, be sure the ratios compare corresponding measures.

3. A boxcar has the dimensions shown. A model of the boxcar is 1.25 in. wide. Find the length of the model to the nearest inch.

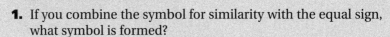

36.25 ft

9 ft | Boxcar

x in.

Model | 1.25 in.

THINK AND DISCUSS

1. If you combine the symbol for similarity with the equal sign, what symbol is formed?

2. The similarity ratio of rectangle *ABCD* to rectangle *EFGH* is $\frac{1}{9}$. How do the side lengths of rectangle *ABCD* compare to the corresponding side lengths of rectangle *EFGH*?

3. What shape(s) are always similar?

4. GET ORGANIZED Copy and complete the graphic organizer. Write the definition of similar polygons, and a similarity statement. Then draw examples and nonexamples of similar polygons.

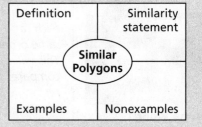

Definition	Similarity statement
	Similar Polygons
Examples	Nonexamples

©Nathan Keay/HMH

GUIDED PRACTICE

1. **Vocabulary** Give an example of similar figures in your classroom.

SEE EXAMPLE **1**   Identify the pairs of congruent angles and corresponding sides.

2.

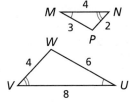

3.

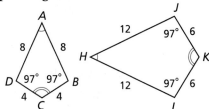

SEE EXAMPLE **2**   **Multi-Step** Determine whether the polygons are similar. If so, write the similarity ratio and a similarity statement.

4. rectangles *ABCD* and *EFGH*

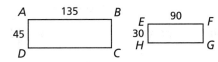

5. △*RMP* and △*UWX*

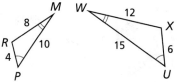

SEE EXAMPLE **3**   6. **Art** The town of Goodland, Kansas, claims that it has one of the world's largest easels. It holds an enlargement of a van Gogh painting that is 24 ft wide. The original painting is 58 cm wide and 73 cm tall. If the reproduction is similar to the original, what is the height of the reproduction to the nearest foot?

PRACTICE AND PROBLEM SOLVING

Identify the pairs of congruent angles and corresponding sides.

Independent Practice	
For Exercises	See Example
7–8	1
9–10	2
11	3

my.hrw.com

Online Extra Practice

7.

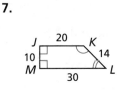

8.

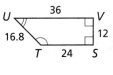

Multi-Step Determine whether the polygons are similar. If so, write the similarity ratio and a similarity statement.

9. △*RSQ* and △*UXZ*

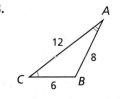

10. rectangles *ABCD* and *JKLM*

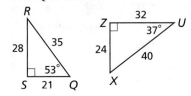

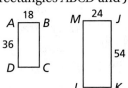

H.O.T. **11. Hobbies** The ratio of the model car's dimensions to the actual car's dimensions is $\frac{1}{56}$. The model has a length of 3 in. What is the length of the actual car?

12. Square *ABCD* has an area of 4 m². Square *PQRS* has an area of 36 m². What is the similarity ratio of square *ABCD* to square *PQRS*? What is the similarity ratio of square *PQRS* to square *ABCD*?

Tell whether each statement is sometimes, always, or never true.

13. Two right triangles are similar.

14. Two squares are similar.

15. A parallelogram and a trapezoid are similar.

16. If two polygons are congruent, they are also similar.

17. If two polygons are similar, they are also congruent.

18. Critical Thinking Explain why any two regular polygons having the same number of sides are similar.

Find the value of x.

19. *ABCD ~ EFGH*

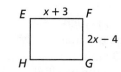

20. $\triangle MNP \sim \triangle XYZ$

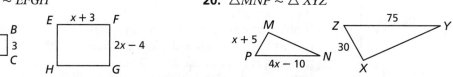

Monument

The height of the Statue of Liberty from the foundation of the pedestal to the torch is 305 ft. Her index finger measures 8 ft, and the fingernail is 13 in. by 10 in.

Source: libertystatepark.org

21. Estimation The Statue of Liberty's hand is 16.4 ft long. Assume that your own body is similar to that of the Statue of Liberty and estimate the length of the Statue of Liberty's nose. (*Hint:* Use a ruler to measure your own hand and nose. Then set up a proportion.)

22. Write the definition of similar polygons as two conditional statements.

23. ▱*JKLM ~* ▱*NOPQ*. If m∠*K* = 75°, name two 75° angles in ▱*NOPQ*.

24. A dining room is 18 ft long and 14 ft wide. On a blueprint for the house, the dining room is 3.5 in. long. To the nearest tenth of an inch, what is the width of the dining room on the blueprint?

H.O.T. **25. Write About It** Two similar polygons have a similarity ratio of 1 : 1. What can you say about the two polygons? Explain.

Real-World Connections

26. A stage set consists of a painted backdrop with some wooden flats in front of it. One of the flats shows a tree that has a similarity ratio of $\frac{1}{2}$ to an actual tree. To give an illusion of distance, the backdrop includes a small painted tree that has a similarity ratio of $\frac{1}{10}$ to the tree on the flat.

   a. The tree on the backdrop is 0.9 ft tall. What is the height of the tree on the flat?

   b. What is the height of the actual tree?

   c. Find the similarity ratio of the tree on the backdrop to the actual tree.

27. Which value of *y* makes the two rectangles similar?

    Ⓐ 3   Ⓒ 25.2

    Ⓑ 8.2   Ⓓ 28.8

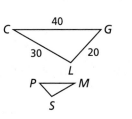

28. △CGL ~ △MPS. The similarity ratio of △CGL to △MPS is $\frac{5}{2}$. What is the length of $\overline{PS}$?

    Ⓕ 8   Ⓗ 50

    Ⓖ 12   Ⓙ 75

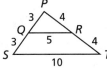

29. **Short Response** Explain why 1.5, 2.5, 3.5 and 6, 10, 12 cannot be corresponding sides of similar triangles.

CHALLENGE AND EXTEND

30. **Architecture** An architect is designing a building that is 200 ft long and 140 ft wide. She builds a model so that the similarity ratio of the model to the building is $\frac{1}{500}$. What is the length and width of the model in inches?

H.O.T. 31. Write a paragraph proof.

    Given: $\overline{QR} \parallel \overline{ST}$

    Prove: △PQR ~ △PST

H.O.T. 32. In the figure, *D* is the midpoint of $\overline{AC}$.

    a. Find *AC*, *DC*, and *DB*.

    b. Use your results from part **a** to help you explain why △ABC ~ △CDB.

H.O.T. 33. A golden rectangle has the following property: If a square is cut from one end of the rectangle, the rectangle that remains is similar to the original rectangle.

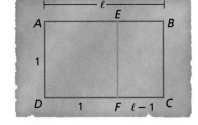

    a. Rectangle *ABCD* is a golden rectangle. Write a similarity statement for rectangle *ABCD* and rectangle *BCFE*.

    b. Write a proportion using the corresponding sides of these rectangles.

    c. Solve the proportion for ℓ. (*Hint:* Use the Quadratic Formula.)

    d. The value of ℓ is known as the golden ratio. Use a calculator to find ℓ to the nearest tenth.

FOCUS ON MATHEMATICAL PRACTICES

H.O.T. 34. **Precision** △MNO ~ △XYZ, and $\overline{XY}$ is the hypotenuse of a right triangle. Name two acute angles in △MNO.

H.O.T. 35. **Reasoning** △FGH ~ △RST. The similarity ratio of △FGH to △RST is $\frac{2}{5}$. The area of △RST is 275 square units. Find the area of △FGH and explain your work.

H.O.T. 36. **Problem Solving** Rectangle *EFGH* has side lengths of 2 and 7. The longer side of rectangle *QRST* has a length of $3y - 22$ and the shorter side has a length of $2x + 4$. Describe the relation of *y* in terms of *x* that will make the two rectangles similar. If the rectangles are similar and $x = 6$, what are the two side lengths of rectangle *QRST*?

26-2 # Similarity and Transformations

Essential Question: How can you use properties of transformations to determine whether figures are similar?

Objectives
Draw and describe similarity transformations in the coordinate plane.

Use properties of similarity transformations to determine whether polygons are similar and to prove circles are similar.

Vocabulary
dilation
scale factor
similarity transformation

A transformation that maps (x, y) to (kx, ky), where $k > 0$, is a **dilation** with center $(0, 0)$ and **scale factor** k. If $0 < k < 1$, the dilation is a *reduction*. If $k > 1$, the dilation is an *enlargement*.

 EXAMPLE MCC9-12.G.SRT.1 **1** **Drawing and Describing Dilations**

my.hrw.com

Online Video Tutor

Apply the dilation D to the polygon with the given vertices. Describe the dilation.

A $D: (x, y) \rightarrow (2x, 2y)$

$A(2, 1)$, $B(2, 3)$, $C(5, 1)$

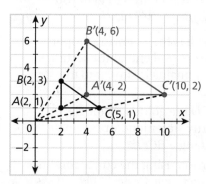

This is a dilation with center $(0, 0)$ and scale factor 2.

B $D: (x, y) \rightarrow \left(\frac{2}{3}x, \frac{2}{3}y\right)$

$P(-6, 3)$, $Q(-3, 9)$, $R(3, 6)$

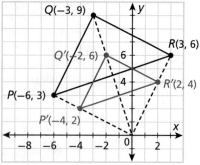

This is a dilation with center $(0, 0)$ and scale factor $\frac{2}{3}$.

 1. Apply the dilation $D: (x, y) \rightarrow \left(\frac{1}{4}x, \frac{1}{4}y\right)$ to the polygon with vertices $D(-8, 0)$, $E(-8, -4)$, and $F(-4, -8)$. Name the coordinates of the image points. Describe the dilation.

Remember!

Translations, reflections, and rotations are congruence transformations.

In a dilation, the image and the preimage are similar because they have the same shape. When the figures in a dilation are polygons, the image and preimage are similar polygons, so corresponding side lengths are proportional and corresponding angles are congruent. That is, dilations preserve angle measure.

A transformation that produces similar figures is a *similarity transformation*. A **similarity transformation** is a dilation or a composite of one or more dilations and one or more congruence transformations. Two figures are similar if and only if there is a similarity transformation that maps one figure to the other figure.

EXAMPLE **2**
MCC9-12.G.SRT.2

my.hrw.com

Online Video Tutor

Determining Whether Polygons are Similar

Determine whether the polygons with the given vertices are similar.

A $A(-3, -3)$, $B(-3, 6)$, $C(6, 6)$, $D(6, -3)$
$H(-2, -2)$, $J(-2, 4)$, $K(4, 4)$, $L(4, -2)$

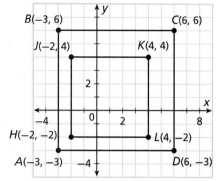

Yes; *ABCD* can be mapped to *HJKL*
by a dilation: $(x, y) \rightarrow \left(\frac{2}{3}x, \frac{2}{3}y\right)$.

B $P(2, 2)$, $Q(2, 4)$, $R(6, 4)$, $S(6, 2)$
$W(5, 5)$, $X(5, 9)$, $Y(12, 9)$,
$Z(12, 5)$

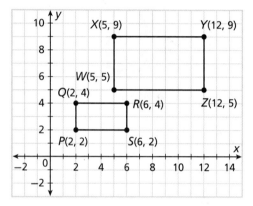

No;

The rule $(x, y) \rightarrow (2.5x, 2.5y)$
maps *P* to *W*, but not *Q* to *X*.
No similarity transformation
maps *PQRS* to *WXYZ*.

C $A(2, 1)$, $B(4, 2)$, $C(4, 1)$
$D(-9, 6)$, $E(-3, 6)$, $F(-3, 9)$

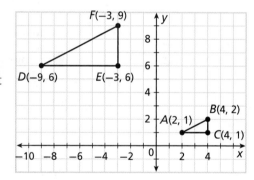

Yes; Translate $\triangle ABC$ to the left
and up. Then enlarge the
image to obtain $\triangle DFE$.

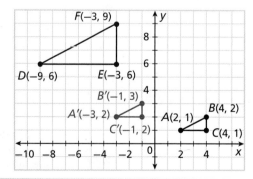

Yes; $\triangle ABC$ can be mapped to
$\triangle A'B'C'$ by a translation:
$(x, y) \rightarrow (x - 5, y + 1)$. Then
$\triangle A'B'C'$ can be mapped to
$\triangle DFE$ by a dilation:
$(x, y) \rightarrow (3x, 3y)$.

2. Determine whether the polygons with the given vertices are similar: $A(2, -1)$, $B(3, -1)$, $C(3, -4)$ and $P(3, 6)$, $Q(3, 9)$, $R(12, 9)$.

All circles are similar because they all have the same shape. To prove this, it is helpful to use a dilation whose center is not $(0, 0)$. In general, a dilation with center C and scale factor k maps P to P' so that P' is on $\overline{CP}$ and $CP' = k \cdot CP$.

EXAMPLE 3

MCC9-12.G.C.1

Proving Circles Similar

A Prove that circle *A* with center $(0, 0)$ and radius 1 is similar to circle *B* with center $(5, 0)$ and radius 2.

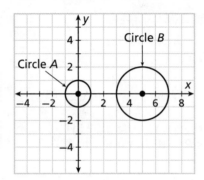
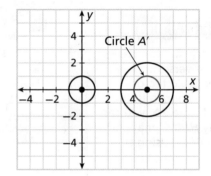

Circle *A* can be mapped to circle *A'* by a translation: $(x, y) \rightarrow (x + 5, y)$. Circle *A'* and circle *B* both have center $(5, 0)$. Then circle *A'* can be mapped to circle *B* by a dilation with center $(5, 0)$ and scale factor 2. So circles *A* and *B* are similar.

B Prove that circle *C* with center $(-2, 0)$ and radius 2 is similar to circle *D* with center $(4, 1)$ and radius 3.

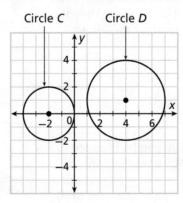
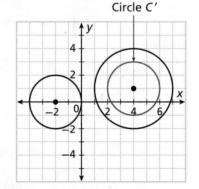

Circle *C* can be mapped to circle *C'* by a translation: $(x, y) \rightarrow (x + 6, y + 1)$. Circle *C'* and circle *D* both have center $(4, 1)$. Then circle *C'* can be mapped to circle *D* by a dilation with center $(4, 1)$ and scale factor $\frac{3}{2}$. So circles *C* and *D* are similar.

3. Prove that circle *A* with center $(2, 1)$ and radius 4 is similar to circle *B* with center $(-1, -1)$ and radius 2.

EXAMPLE 4
MCC9-12.G.CO.2

Business Application

Tia makes signs and banners. She is making a banner that shows five Texas flags. The middle flag is 3 times the size of each of the other flags. Tia will first draw the lower left flag and then the middle flag. How can she draw those flags?

Place the lower left flag on a coordinate plane in a convenient position, such as that shown by rectangle *ABCD*.

Apply the dilation with center (0, 0) and scale factor 3: $(x, y) \rightarrow (3x, 3y)$.

The image, *A'B'C'D'*, represents the middle flag.

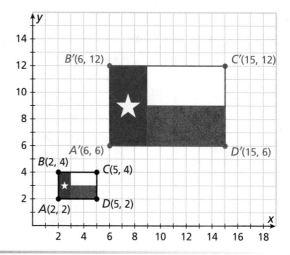

CHECK IT OUT!

4. What if...? How could Tia draw the middle flag to make it 4 times the size of each of the other flags?

MCC.MP.1

MATHEMATICAL PRACTICES

THINK AND DISCUSS

1. Consider this dilation applied to a polygon: $(x, y) \rightarrow (1.5x, 1.5y)$. Describe the corresponding side lengths, corresponding angle measures, and position of the image compared to the preimage.

2. Explain why the rules $(x, y) \rightarrow (y, -x)$ and then $(x, y) \rightarrow (2x, 2y)$ form a similarity transformation.

3. GET ORGANIZED Copy and complete the graphic organizer.

Determining if polygons are similar	
Proving circles are similar	

GUIDED PRACTICE

Vocabulary Apply the vocabulary from this lesson to answer each question.

1. A(n) ____?____ transformation produces figures that are similar. (*similarity, congruence,* or *scale factor*)

2. If the scale factor k in a dilation is a value between 0 and 1, the dilation is a(n) ____?____ . (*enlargement, reduction,* or *translation*)

SEE EXAMPLE 1 Apply the dilation D to the polygon with the given vertices. Name the coordinates of the image points. Identify and describe the transformation.

3. $D: (x, y) \rightarrow (4x, 4y)$

   $A(-1, -1), B(2, 1), C(-2, 1)$

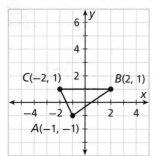

4. $D: (x, y) \rightarrow \left(\frac{1}{3}x, \frac{1}{3}y\right)$

   $A(3, 9), B(-6, 3), C(3, -3)$

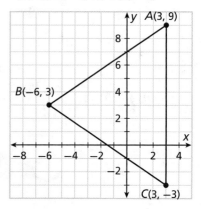

5. $D: (x, y) \rightarrow (2.5x, 2.5y)$

   $A(2, 3), B(5, -2), C(-4, -2)$

6. $D: (x, y) \rightarrow \left(\frac{3}{4}x, \frac{3}{4}y\right)$

   $A(4, 8), B(-8, 4), C(8, -4)$

SEE EXAMPLE 2 Determine whether the polygons with the given vertices are similar. Support your answer by describing a transformation.

7. $L(1, -4), M(1, -9), N(5, -2), O(9, -5)$
   $P(2, 5), Q(2, -5), R(10, 9), S(18, 3)$

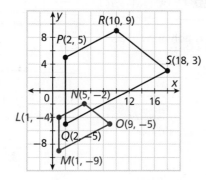

8. $W(-4, 2), X(-4, 6), Y(6, 2), Z(6, 6)$
   $D(-2, 1), E(-8, 12), F(3, 10), G(3, 3)$

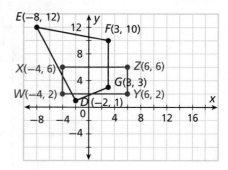

9. $A(3, 0), B(3, 6), C(9, 6)$
   $X(4, 0), Y(4, -8), Z(12, -8)$

10. $L(-10, 5), M(-5, 0), N(0, 0), O(5, 5)$
    $D(4, 2), E(2, 0), F(0, 0), G(-2, 2)$

SEE EXAMPLE 3

11. Prove that circle *A* with center (4, 0) and radius 5 is similar to circle *B* with center (−6, −3) and radius 3.

12. Prove that circle *A* with center (6, −9) and radius 4 is similar to circle *B* with center (3, −8) and radius 5.

SEE EXAMPLE 4

13. Hector is making an art project by cutting and gluing shapes to a wooden board. His design includes two similar triangles, with one 4 times the size of the other. He cuts and traces the small triangle first onto grid paper. Describe how he can use the tracing to make a pattern for the large fabric triangle.

PRACTICE AND PROBLEM SOLVING

Independent Practice	
For Exercises	See Example
14–15	1
16–17	2
22	3
23	4

my.hrw.com

Online Extra Practice

Apply the dilation *D* to the polygon with the given vertices. Name the coordinates of the image points. Identify and describe the transformation.

14. $D : (x, y) \rightarrow (0.5x, 0.5y)$

$A(1, -2), B(1, -4), C(5, -2) \, D(5, -4)$

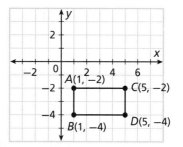

15. $D : (x, y) \rightarrow \left(\dfrac{3}{10}x, \dfrac{3}{10}y \right)$

$A(20, 10), B(0, -20), C(10, 30)$

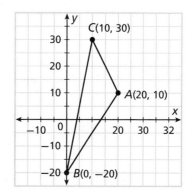

H.O.T. **Determine whether the polygons with the given vertices are similar. Support your answer by describing a transformation.**

16. $V(3, 2), W(8, 2), X(1, 5)$

$R(6, 4), S(16, 4), T(3, 15)$

17. $A(-2, -3), B(-2, 0), C(10, -3)$

$P(-4, 2), Q(-4, 4), R(4, 2)$

18. **Write About It** Triangle *ABC* is dilated by a scale factor of 5. The image is *A′B′C′*. Compare the angle measures and side lengths of the original triangle and its image after dilation.

Determine whether the polygons shown are similar. If they are similar, describe the transformation in two different ways, from the larger to the smaller figure, and from the smaller to the larger figure.

19.

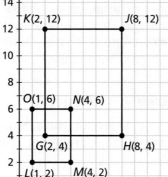

20.

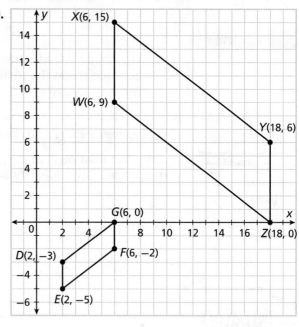

21. **///ERROR ANALYSIS///** Triangle *ABC* has vertices at $A(-12, -6)$, $B(-6, 12)$, and $C(6, 12)$. The images of *A* and *B* after the similarity transformation *D* are $A'(-8, -4)$ and $B'(-4, 8)$. Reggie and Hillary find different coordinates for *C'*, the image of *C*. Their work is shown below. Who made an error? Describe the error.

Hillary's Work	Reggie's Work
$C': (6, 12) \rightarrow \left(\frac{2}{3} \cdot 6, \frac{2}{3} \cdot 12\right)$ $\rightarrow (4, 8)$	$C': (6, 12) \rightarrow \left(\frac{3}{2} \cdot 6, \frac{3}{2} \cdot 12\right)$ $\rightarrow (9, 18)$

H.O.T. 22. A baby pool with radius 2 meters is being built near a larger pool with radius 4 meters at a recreation center. The plans for the construction are laid out on the coordinate system shown. Prove that the baby pool is similar to the larger pool.

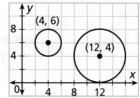

23. **Architecture** An architect is making a scale drawing of two buildings whose floor plans are to be similar rectangles. He has already drawn the smaller building. The larger building will be located to the upper right and will have dimensions 5 times those of the smaller building. How can he draw the larger building?

H.O.T. 24. **Critical Thinking** To map a figure *A* to a similar figure *B*, first *A* is mapped to *A'* by a dilation: $(x, y) \rightarrow \left(\frac{5}{3}x, \frac{5}{3}y\right)$. Then *A'* is mapped to *B* by a translation $(x, y) \rightarrow (x - 2, y + 1)$. The vertices of *A'* are $W(-10, 0)$, $X(-5, 10)$, $Y(5, 10)$, and $Z(-5, 0)$. Find the vertices of *A* and *B*.

25. Triangle *ABC* undergoes a transformation *T* to produce the image *EFG*. Given the vertices of the triangles below, which is a true statement about *T*?

A(4, 8), B(0, 4), C(4, 0)
E(3, 6), F(0, 3), G(3, 0)

Ⓐ *T* is a similarity transformation in which *ABC* is dilated by a scale factor of $\frac{3}{4}$.

Ⓑ *T* is a congruence transformation in which *ABC* is dilated by a scale factor of $\frac{3}{4}$.

Ⓒ *T* is a similarity transformation in which *ABC* is dilated by a scale factor of of $\frac{4}{3}$.

Ⓓ *T* is a congruence transformation in which *ABC* is dilated by a scale factor of $\frac{4}{3}$.

26. Figure *ABCD* with the vertices given below is translated 6 units left and 7 units down. It is then dilated to produce the similar figure *EFGH* with the vertices given below. By what scale is the figure dilated?

A(10, 15), B(14, 7), C(6, 7), D(6, 11)
E(5, 10), F(10, 0), G(0, 0), H(0, 5)

Ⓐ 0.5

Ⓑ 0.8

Ⓒ 1.25

Ⓓ 1.5

CHALLENGE AND EXTEND

27. The area of a square is 16 square units. Its sides are horizontal and vertical, and its lower left vertex is (2, 0). After a similarity transformation, the image of the lower left vertex is (−8, 0). Name the other three vertices of the image and find its area.

H.O.T. 28. The hypotenuse of a right triangle *ABC* in a coordinate plane is $\overline{AB}$, with *A* at (1, 2) and *B* at (3, 6). The image of the hypotenuse after a rotation of 180° and a dilation is $\overline{A'B'}$, with *A'* at (−3.5, −7) and *B'* at (−10.5, −21). Give two possible locations of *C'*, the image of *C*.

FOCUS ON MATHEMATICAL PRACTICES

H.O.T. 29. Reasoning A circle has center (3, −4) and radius 2. The circle undergoes a dilation with center (3, −4) so that the image passes through the origin.

    a. Is the dilation an enlargement or a reduction? Explain your answer.

    b. What is the scale factor of the dilation?

H.O.T. 30. Justify A triangle undergoes a 180° rotation about the origin. It is then translated 4 units to the left and 6 units upward. Finally the triangle is dilated with center (0, 0) and scale factor 2.5. Is the net result a similarity transformation? Describe how the transformations change the triangle's appearance.

H.O.T. 31. Analysis A square with vertices *A*(1, 1), *B*(1, 3), *C*(3, 3), and *D*(3, 1) undergoes a congruence transformation followed by a dilation with center (0, 0) and scale factor 3. The resulting square has vertices *A'*(−3, 3), *B'*(−9, 3), *C'*(−9, 9), and *D'*(−3, 9). What is the congruence transformation?

26-3

Predict Triangle Similarity Relationships

You have found shortcuts for determining that two triangles are congruent. Now you will use geometry software to find ways to determine that triangles are similar.

Use with Triangle Similarity: AA, SSS, and SAS

 Use appropriate tools strategically.

MCC9-12.G.SRT.3 Use the properties of similarity transformations to establish the AA criterion for two triangles to be similar.

Activity 1

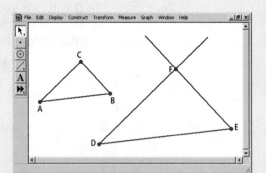

1 Construct △ABC. Construct $\overline{DE}$ longer than any of the sides of △ABC. Rotate $\overline{DE}$ around D by rotation ∠BAC. Rotate $\overline{DE}$ around E by rotation ∠ABC. Label the intersection point of the two rotated segments as F.

2 Measure angles to confirm that ∠BAC ≅ ∠EDF and ∠ABC ≅ ∠DEF. Drag a vertex of △ABC or an endpoint of $\overline{DE}$ to show that the two triangles have two pairs of congruent angles.

3 Measure the side lengths of both triangles. Divide each side length of △ABC by the corresponding side length of △DEF. Compare the resulting ratios. What do you notice?

Try This

1. What theorem guarantees that the third pair of angles in the triangles are also congruent?

2. Will the ratios of corresponding sides found in Step 3 always be equal? Drag a vertex of △ABC or an endpoint of $\overline{DE}$ to investigate this question. State a conjecture based on your results.

Activity 2

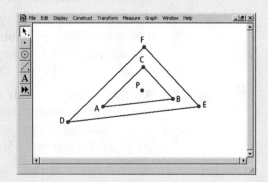

1 Construct a new △ABC. Create P in the interior of the triangle. Create △DEF by enlarging △ABC around P by a multiple of 2 using the Dilation command. Drag P outside of △ABC to separate the triangles.

784 *Module 26 Similarity*

2 Measure the side lengths of △DEF to confirm that each side is twice as long as the corresponding side of △ABC. Drag a vertex of △ABC to verify that this relationship is true.

3 Measure the angles of both triangles. What do you notice?

Try This

3. Did the construction of the triangles with three pairs of sides in the same ratio guarantee that the corresponding angles would be congruent? State a conjecture based on these results.

4. Compare your conjecture to the SSS Congruence Theorem. How are they similar and how are they different?

Activity 3

1 Construct a different △ABC. Create P in the interior of the triangle. Expand $\overline{AB}$ and $\overline{AC}$ around P by a multiple of 2 using the Dilation command. Create an angle congruent to ∠BAC with sides that are each twice as long as $\overline{AB}$ and $\overline{AC}$.

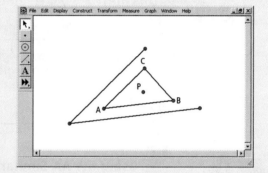

2 Use a segment to create the third side of a new triangle and label it △DEF. Drag P outside of △ABC to separate the triangles.

3 Measure each side length and determine the relationship between corresponding sides of △ABC and △DEF.

4 Measure the angles of both triangles. What do you notice?

Try This

5. Tell whether △ABC is similar to △DEF. Explain your reasoning.

6. Write a conjecture based on the activity. What congruency theorem is related to your conjecture?

26-3 Triangle Similarity: AA, SSS, and SAS

Essential Question: What information about the sides and angles in two triangles allows you to conclude the triangles are similar?

Objectives
Prove certain triangles are similar by using AA, SSS, and SAS.

Use triangle similarity to solve problems.

Who uses this?
Engineers use similar triangles when designing buildings, such as the Pyramid Building in San Diego, California. (See Example 5.)

There are several ways to prove certain triangles are similar. The following postulate, as well as the SSS and SAS Similarity Theorems, will be used in proofs just as SSS, SAS, ASA, HL, and AAS were used to prove triangles congruent.

Postulate 26-3-1 | **Angle-Angle (AA) Similarity**

POSTULATE	HYPOTHESIS	CONCLUSION
If two angles of one triangle are congruent to two angles of another triangle, then the triangles are similar.		$\triangle ABC \sim \triangle DEF$

COMMON CORE GPS
MCC9-12.G.SRT.5

EXAMPLE 1

Using the AA Similarity Postulate

my.hrw.com

Online Video Tutor

Explain why the triangles are similar and write a similarity statement.

Since $\overline{PT} \parallel \overline{SR}$, $\angle P \cong \angle R$, and $\angle T \cong \angle S$ by the Alternate Interior Angles Theorem. Therefore $\triangle PQT \sim \triangle RQS$ by AA $\sim$.

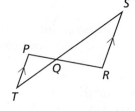

1. Explain why the triangles are similar and write a similarity statement.

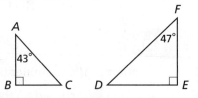

Theorem 26-3-2 | **Side-Side-Side (SSS) Similarity**

THEOREM	HYPOTHESIS	CONCLUSION
If the three sides of one triangle are proportional to the three corresponding sides of another triangle, then the triangles are similar.		$\triangle ABC \sim \triangle DEF$

You will prove Theorem 26-3-2 in Exercise 38.

Theorem 26-3-3 Side-Angle-Side (SAS) Similarity

THEOREM	HYPOTHESIS	CONCLUSION
If two sides of one triangle are proportional to two sides of another triangle and their included angles are congruent, then the triangles are similar.	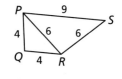 $\angle B \cong \angle E$	$\triangle ABC \sim \triangle DEF$

You will prove Theorem 26-3-3 in Exercise 39.

EXAMPLE 2
MCC9-12.G.SRT.5

my.hrw.com

Online Video Tutor

Verifying Triangle Similarity

Verify that the triangles are similar.

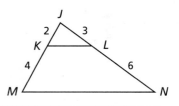

A $\triangle PQR$ and $\triangle PRS$

$\dfrac{PQ}{PR} = \dfrac{4}{6} = \dfrac{2}{3}, \dfrac{QR}{RS} = \dfrac{4}{6} = \dfrac{2}{3}, \dfrac{PR}{PS} = \dfrac{6}{9} = \dfrac{2}{3}$

Therefore $\triangle PQR \sim \triangle PRS$ by SSS ~.

B $\triangle JKL$ and $\triangle JMN$

$\angle J \cong \angle J$ by the Reflexive Property of $\cong$.

$\dfrac{JK}{JM} = \dfrac{2}{6} = \dfrac{1}{3}, \dfrac{JL}{JN} = \dfrac{3}{9} = \dfrac{1}{3}$

Therefore $\triangle JKL \sim \triangle JMN$ by SAS ~.

2. Verify that $\triangle TXU \sim \triangle VXW$.

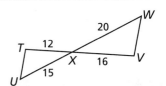

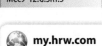
EXAMPLE 3
MCC9-12.G.SRT.5

my.hrw.com

Online Video Tutor

Finding Lengths in Similar Triangles

Explain why $\triangle ABC \sim \triangle DBE$ and then find BE.

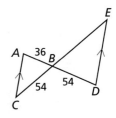

Step 1 Prove triangles are similar.

As shown $\overline{AC} \parallel \overline{ED}$, $\angle A \cong \angle D$, and $\angle C \cong \angle E$ by the Alternate Interior Angles Theorem. Therefore $\triangle ABC \sim \triangle DBE$ by AA ~.

Step 2 Find BE.

$\dfrac{AB}{DB} = \dfrac{BC}{BE}$ *Corr. sides are proportional.*

$\dfrac{36}{54} = \dfrac{54}{BE}$ *Substitute 36 for AB, 54 for DB, and 54 for BC.*

$36(BE) = 54^2$ *Cross Products Prop.*

$36(BE) = 2916$ *Simplify.*

$BE = 81$ *Divide both sides by 36.*

3. Explain why $\triangle RSV \sim \triangle RTU$ and then find RT.

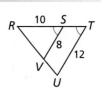

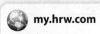

EXAMPLE 4
MCC9-12.G.SRT.4

Writing Proofs with Similar Triangles

Given: *A* is the midpoint of $\overline{BC}$.
$\qquad$ *D* is the midpoint of $\overline{BE}$.

Prove: $\triangle BDA \sim \triangle BEC$

Proof:

Statements	Reasons
1. *A* is the mdpt. of $\overline{BC}$. *D* is the mdpt. of $\overline{BE}$.	1. Given
2. $\overline{BA} \cong \overline{AC}, \overline{BD} \cong \overline{DE}$	2. Def. of mdpt.
3. $BA = AC, BD = DE$	3. Def. of $\cong$ seg.
4. $BC = BA + AC, BE = BD + DE$	4. Seg. Add. Post.
5. $BC = BA + BA, BE = BD + BD$	5. Subst. Prop.
6. $BC = 2BA, BE = 2BD$	6. Simplify.
7. $\dfrac{BC}{BA} = 2, \dfrac{BE}{BD} = 2$	7. Div. Prop. of $=$
8. $\dfrac{BC}{BA} = \dfrac{BE}{BD}$	8. Trans. Prop. of $=$
9. $\angle B \cong \angle B$	9. Reflex. Prop. of $\cong$
10. $\triangle BDA \sim \triangle BEC$	10. SAS $\sim$ *Steps 8, 9*

CHECK IT OUT!

4. Given: *M* is the midpoint of $\overline{JK}$.
$\qquad$ *N* is the midpoint of $\overline{KL}$,
$\qquad$ and *P* is the midpoint of $\overline{JL}$.

$\qquad$ **Prove:** $\triangle JKL \sim \triangle NPM$
$\qquad$ (*Hint:* Use the Triangle
$\qquad$ Midsegment Theorem and SSS $\sim$.)

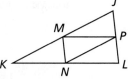

EXAMPLE 5
MCC9-12.G.MG.1

Engineering Application

The photo shows a gable roof. $\overline{AC} \parallel \overline{FG}$. Use similar triangles to prove $\triangle ABC \sim \triangle FBG$ and then find *BF* to the nearest tenth of a foot.

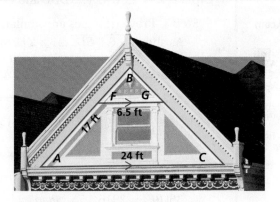

Step 1 Prove the triangles are similar.

$\overline{AC} \parallel \overline{FG}$ $\qquad\qquad$ *Given*

$\angle BFG \cong \angle BAC$ $\qquad$ *Corr. $\angle$ Thm.*

$\angle B \cong \angle B$ $\qquad\qquad$ *Reflex. Prop. of $\cong$*

Therefore $\triangle ABC \sim \triangle FBG$ by AA $\sim$.

PhotoDisc/gettyimages

Step 2 Find *BF*.

$$\frac{BA}{AC} = \frac{BF}{FG}$$ *Corr. sides are proportional.*

$$\frac{x + 17}{24} = \frac{x}{6.5}$$ *Substitute the given values.*

$$6.5(x + 17) = 24x$$ *Cross Products Prop.*

$$6.5x + 110.5 = 24x$$ *Distrib. Prop.*

$$110.5 = 17.5x$$ *Subtract 6.5x from both sides.*

$$6.3 \approx x \text{ or } BF$$ *Divide both sides by 17.5.*

 5. What if...? If $AB = 4x$, $AC = 5x$, and $BF = 4$, find *FG*.

The Reflexive, Symmetric, and Transitive Properties of Equality have corresponding properties of congruence. These properties also hold true for similarity of triangles.

Properties of Similarity

Reflexive Property of Similarity

$\triangle ABC \sim \triangle ABC$ (Reflex. Prop. of $\sim$)

Symmetric Property of Similarity

If $\triangle ABC \sim \triangle DEF$, then $\triangle DEF \sim \triangle ABC$. (Sym. Prop. of $\sim$)

Transitive Property of Similarity

If $\triangle ABC \sim \triangle DEF$ and $\triangle DEF \sim \triangle XYZ$, then $\triangle ABC \sim \triangle XYZ$. (Trans. Prop. of $\sim$)

MCC.MP.3 | MATHEMATICAL PRACTICES

THINK AND DISCUSS

1. What additional information, if any, would you you need in order to show that $\triangle ABC \sim \triangle DEF$ by the AA Similarity Postulate?

2. What additional information, if any, would you you need in order to show that $\triangle ABC \sim \triangle DEF$ by the SAS Similarity Theorem?

3. Do corresponding sides of similar triangles need to be proportional and congruent? Explain.

 4. GET ORGANIZED Copy and complete the graphic organizer. If possible, write a congruence or similarity theorem or postulate in each section of the table. Include a marked diagram for each.

	Congruence	Similarity
SSS		
SAS		
AA		

GUIDED PRACTICE

SEE EXAMPLE 1 Explain why the triangles are similar and write a similarity statement.

1.

2.

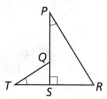

SEE EXAMPLE 2 Verify that the triangles are similar.

3. △DEF and △JKL

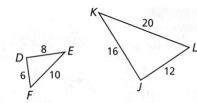

4. △MNP and △MRQ

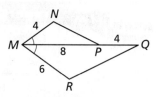

SEE EXAMPLE 3 **Multi-Step** Explain why the triangles are similar and then find each length.

5. AB

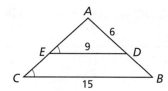

6. WY

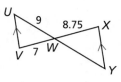

SEE EXAMPLE 4

7. Given: $\overleftrightarrow{MN} \parallel \overline{KL}$
Prove: △JMN ~ △JKL

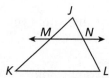

8. Given: $SQ = 2QP$, $TR = 2RP$
Prove: △PQR ~ △PST

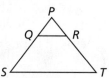

9. The coordinates of A, B, and C are A(0, 0), B(2, 6), and C(8, −2). What theorem or postulate justifies the statement △ABC ~ △ADE, if the coordinates of D and E are twice the coordinates of B and C?

SEE EXAMPLE 5 **10. Surveying** In order to measure the distance AB across the meteorite crater, a surveyor at S locates points A, B, C, and D as shown. What is AB to the nearest meter? nearest kilometer?

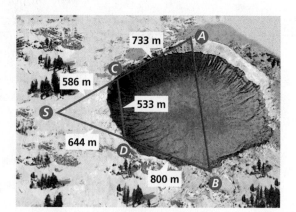

PRACTICE AND PROBLEM SOLVING

Independent Practice

For Exercises	See Example
11–12	1
13–14	2
15–16	3
17–18	4
19	5

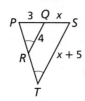

Online Extra Practice

my.hrw.com

Explain why the triangles are similar and write a similarity statement.

11.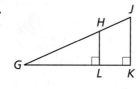

12.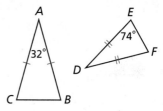

Verify that the given triangles are similar.

13. $\triangle KLM$ and $\triangle KNL$

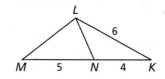

14. $\triangle UVW$ and $\triangle XYZ$

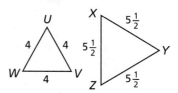

Multi-Step **Explain why the triangles are similar and then find each length.**

15. AB

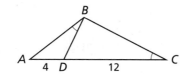

16. PS

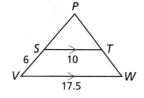

17. **Given:** $CD = 3AC$, $CE = 3BC$

Prove: $\triangle ABC \sim \triangle DEC$

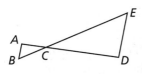

18. **Given:** $\dfrac{PR}{MR} = \dfrac{QR}{NR}$

Prove: $\angle 1 \cong \angle 2$

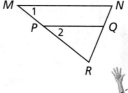

19. **Photography** The picture shows a person taking a pinhole photograph of himself. Light entering the opening reflects his image on the wall, forming similar triangles. What is the height of the image to the nearest tenth of a foot?

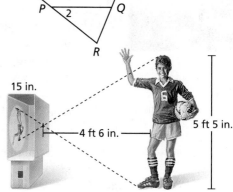

Draw $\triangle JKL$ and $\triangle MNP$. Determine if you can conclude that $\triangle JKL \sim \triangle MNP$ based on the given information. If so, which postulate or theorem justifies your response?

20. $\angle K \cong \angle N$, $\dfrac{JK}{MN} = \dfrac{KL}{NP}$

21. $\dfrac{JK}{MN} = \dfrac{KL}{NP} = \dfrac{JL}{MP}$

22. $\angle J \cong \angle M$, $\dfrac{JL}{MP} = \dfrac{KL}{NP}$

Find the value of x.

23.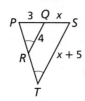

24.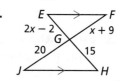

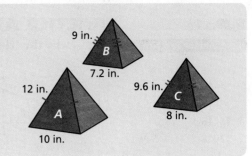

25. The set for an animated film includes three small triangles that represent pyramids.
    a. Which pyramids are similar? Why?
    b. What is the similarity ratio of the similar pyramids?

H.O.T. 26. Critical Thinking △*ABC* is not similar to △*DEF*, and △*DEF* is not similar to △*XYZ*. Could △*ABC* be similar to △*XYZ*? Why or why not? Make a sketch to support your answer.

27. **Recreation** To play shuffleboard, two teams take turns sliding disks on a court. The dimensions of the scoring area for a standard shuffleboard court are shown. What are *JK* and *MN*?

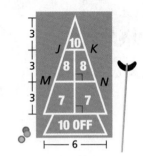

28. Prove the Transitive Property of Similarity.
    Given: △*ABC* ~ △*DEF*,
    △*DEF* ~ △*XYZ*
    Prove: △*ABC* ~ △*XYZ*

29. Draw and label △*PQR* and △*STU* such that $\frac{PQ}{ST} = \frac{QR}{TU}$ but △*PQR* is NOT similar to △*STU*.

30. **Given:** △*KNJ* is isosceles with ∠*N* as the vertex angle.
    ∠*H* ≅ ∠*L*
    Prove: △*GHJ* ~ △*MLK*

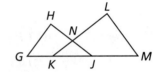

31. **Meteorology** Satellite photography makes it possible to measure the diameter of a hurricane. The figure shows that a camera's aperture *YX* is 35 mm and its focal length *WZ* is 50 mm. The satellite *W* holding the camera is 150 mi above the hurricane, centered at *C*.
    a. Why is △*XYZ* ~ △*ABZ*? What assumption must you make about the position of the camera in order to make this conclusion?
    b. What other triangles in the figure must be similar? Why?
    c. Find the diameter *AB* of the hurricane.

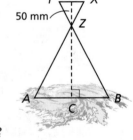

Meteorology

A tropical storm is classified as a hurricane if its winds reach a speed of at least 74 mi/h.
Source: http://www.nhc.noaa.gov

32. **///ERROR ANALYSIS///** Which solution for the value of *y* is incorrect? Explain the error.

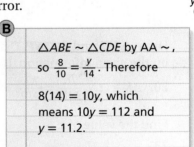

A	B
△*ABE* ~ △*CDE* by AA ~ , so $\frac{14}{8+y} = \frac{10}{8}$. Then 10(8 + *y*) = 8(14), or 80 + 10*y* = 112. So 10*y* = 32 and *y* = 3.2.	△*ABE* ~ △*CDE* by AA ~ , so $\frac{8}{10} = \frac{y}{14}$. Therefore 8(14) = 10*y*, which means 10*y* = 112 and *y* = 11.2.

H.O.T. 33. Write About It Two isosceles triangles have congruent vertex angles. Explain why the two triangles must be similar.

TEST PREP

34. What is the length of $\overline{TU}$?

    (A) 36   (C) 48

    (B) 40   (D) 90

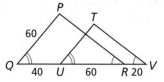

35. Which dimensions guarantee that $\triangle BCD \sim \triangle FGH$?

    (F) $FG = 11.6$, $GH = 8.4$

    (G) $FG = 12$, $GH = 14$

    (H) $FG = 11.4$, $GH = 11.4$

    (J) $FG = 10.5$, $GH = 14.5$

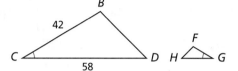

36. $\square ABCD \sim \square EFGH$. Which similarity postulate or theorem lets you conclude that $\triangle BCD \sim \triangle FGH$?

    (A) AA   (C) SAS

    (B) SSS   (D) None of these

37. Gridded Response If 6, 8, and 12 and 15, 20, and x are the lengths of the corresponding sides of two similar triangles, what is the value of x?

CHALLENGE AND EXTEND

H.O.T. 38. Prove the SSS Similarity Theorem.

    Given: $\dfrac{AB}{DE} = \dfrac{BC}{EF} = \dfrac{AC}{DF}$

    Prove: $\triangle ABC \sim \triangle DEF$

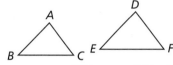

    (*Hint:* Assume that $AB < DE$ and choose point X on $\overline{DE}$ so that $\overline{AB} \cong \overline{DX}$. Then choose point Y on $\overline{DF}$ so that $\overleftrightarrow{XY} \parallel \overline{EF}$. Show that $\triangle DXY \sim \triangle DEF$ and that $\triangle ABC \cong \triangle DXY$.)

H.O.T. 39. Prove the SAS Similarity Theorem.

    Given: $\angle B \cong \angle E$, $\dfrac{AB}{DE} = \dfrac{BC}{EF}$

    Prove: $\triangle ABC \sim \triangle DEF$

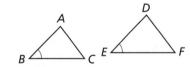

    (*Hint:* Assume that $AB < DE$ and choose point X on $\overline{DE}$ so that $\overline{EX} \cong \overline{BA}$. Then choose point Y on $\overline{EF}$ so that $\angle EXY \cong \angle EDF$. Show that $\triangle XEY \sim \triangle DEF$ and that $\triangle ABC \cong \triangle XEF$.)

H.O.T. 40. Given $\triangle ABC \sim \triangle XYZ$, $m\angle A = 50°$, $m\angle X = (2x + 5y)°$, $m\angle Z = (5x + y)°$, and that $m\angle B = (102 - x)°$, find $m\angle Z$.

FOCUS ON MATHEMATICAL PRACTICES

MATHEMATICAL PRACTICES

H.O.T. 41. Reasoning Explain why angle-side-angle (ASA) is not given as a relationship that proves two triangles are similar.

H.O.T. 42. Justify $\triangle ABC$ and $\triangle JKL$ are isosceles triangles with congruent legs. $\angle B$ and $\angle K$ are both 40° angles. Must the two triangles be similar? Explain.

H.O.T. 43. Problem Solving $\triangle EFG \sim \triangle PQR$. The following side lengths are given: $PQ = 3$, $QR = 5$, and $EG = 24$. The perimeter of $\triangle EFG$ is 56. Find the unknown side lengths of each triangle.

EXTENSION

Proving the Pythagorean Theorem

? *Essential Question:* How can similar triangles be used in a proof of the Pythagorean Theorem?

Objective
Prove the Pythagorean
Theorem using similar
triangles.

The Pythagorean Theorem is one of the most widely used and well-known mathematical theorems. The theorem has been proven in many different ways, some of which involve subdividing the triangle in some way. The following proof uses similar triangles.

COMMON CORE GPS EXAMPLE **1**
MCC9-12.G.SRT.4

Proving the Pythagorean Theorem Using Similar Triangles

Prove the Pythagorean Theorem using similar triangles.
Given: $\triangle ABC$ with right $\angle C$
Prove: $a^2 + b^2 = c^2$

Proof: Draw an altitude from vertex C to side c as shown. By the Reflexive Property of Congruence, $\angle A \cong \angle A$ and $\angle B \cong \angle B$. All right angles are congruent, so $\angle ADC \cong \angle ACB$ and $\angle BDC \cong \angle ACB$. Therefore, $\triangle ACD \sim \triangle ABC$ and $\triangle CBD \sim \triangle ABC$ by the AA Similarity Postulate.

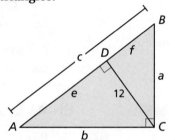

By the Transitive Property of Similarity, $\triangle ACD \sim \triangle CBD$.

Corresponding sides of similar triangles are proportional, so $\dfrac{c}{a} = \dfrac{a}{f}$ and $\dfrac{c}{b} = \dfrac{b}{e}$.

$\dfrac{c}{a} = \dfrac{a}{f}$	$\dfrac{c}{b} = \dfrac{b}{e}$	
$cf = a^2$	$ce = b^2$	*Cross-multiply.*
	$a^2 + ce = a^2 + b^2$	*Add a^2 to both sides.*
	$cf + ce = a^2 + b^2$	*$cf = a^2$*
	$c(f + e) = a^2 + b^2$	*Factor.*
	$c^2 = a^2 + b^2$	*$c = e + f$ (Segment Addition)*

1. In the figure, find c, e, and f.

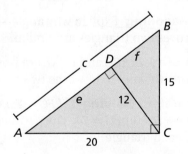

EXAMPLE 2 | **Applying the Pythagorean Theorem**
MCC9-12.G.SRT.8

Mike places a 20-foot ladder diagonally against the wall of the building. The bottom of the ladder is 3.5 feet from the building. The top of the ladder reaches how many feet above the ground?

Use the Pythagorean Theorem. The ladder is the hypotenuse of the triangle.

$$a^2 + b^2 = c^2$$
$$3.5^2 + b^2 = 20^2$$
$$12.25 + b^2 = 400$$
$$b^2 = 387.75$$
$$b \approx 19.7$$

The ladder reaches approximately 19.7 ft above the ground.

 2. Jackie drives 5 miles east and 3 miles north from home to school. What is the shortest distance from Jackie's home to school?

EXTENSION

Exercises

my.hrw.com
Homework Help

Find the unknown values in each figure. Give your answers in simplest radical form.

1.

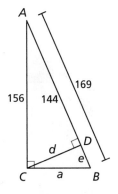

2.

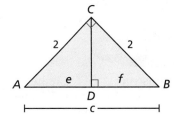

3. Critical Thinking Explain why any triple a, $2a$, $a\sqrt{3}$ are possible side lengths of a right triangle for any constant a.

4. The figure shows a loading dock with a ramp used to unload packages. What is the length of the ramp?

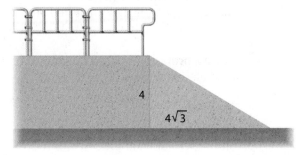

26-4
Technology TASK

Investigate Angle Bisectors of a Triangle

In a triangle, an angle bisector divides the opposite side into two segments. You will use geometry software to explore the relationships between these segments.

Use with *Applying Properties of Similar Triangles*

 Use appropriate tools strategically.

Activity 1

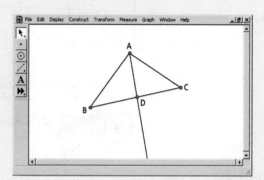

❶ Construct △*ABC*. Bisect ∠*BAC* and create the point of intersection of the angle bisector and $\overline{BC}$. Label the intersection *D*.

❷ Measure $\overline{AB}$, $\overline{AC}$, $\overline{BD}$, and $\overline{CD}$. Use these measurements to write ratios. What are the results? Drag a vertex of △*ABC* and examine the ratios again. What do you notice?

Try This

1. Choose Tabulate and create a table using the four lengths and the ratios from Step 2. Drag a vertex of △*ABC* and add the new measurements to the table. What conjecture can you make about the segments created by an angle bisector?

2. Write a proportion based on your conjecture.

Activity 2

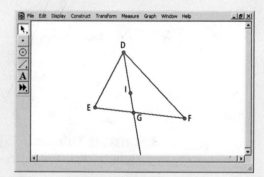

❶ Construct △*DEF*. Create the *incenter* of the triangle and label it *I*. Hide the angle bisectors of ∠*E* and ∠*F*. Find the point of intersection of $\overline{EF}$ and the bisector of ∠*D*. Label the intersection *G*.

❷ Find *DI*, *DG*, and the perimeter of △*DEF*.

❸ Divide the length of $\overline{DI}$ by the length of *DG*. Add the lengths of $\overline{DE}$ and $\overline{DF}$. Then divide this sum by the perimeter of △*DEF*. Compare the two quotients. Drag a vertex of △*DEF* and examine the quotients again. What do you notice?

❹ Write a proportion based on your quotients. What conjecture can you make about this relationship?

Try This

3. Show the hidden angle bisector of ∠*E* or ∠*F*. Confirm that your conjecture is true for this bisector. Drag a vertex of △*DEF* and observe the results.

4. Choose Tabulate and create a table with the measurements you used in your proportion in Step 4.

26-4 Applying Properties of Similar Triangles

Essential Question: What proportional relationships are formed when parallel lines or segments intersect other lines or segments?

Objectives
Use properties of similar triangles to find segment lengths.

Apply proportionality and triangle angle bisector theorems.

Who uses this?
Artists use similarity and proportionality to give paintings an illusion of depth. (See Example 3.)

Artists use mathematical techniques to make two-dimensional paintings appear three-dimensional. The invention of *perspective* was based on the observation that far away objects look smaller and closer objects look larger.

Mathematical theorems like the Triangle Proportionality Theorem are important in making perspective drawings.

Know it! Note

Theorem 26-4-1 | Triangle Proportionality Theorem

THEOREM	HYPOTHESIS	CONCLUSION
If a line parallel to a side of a triangle intersects the other two sides, then it divides those sides proportionally.	$\overleftrightarrow{EF} \parallel \overline{BC}$	$\dfrac{AE}{EB} = \dfrac{AF}{FC}$

You can use a compass-and-straightedge construction to verify this theorem. Although the construction is not a proof, it should help convince you that the theorem is true. After you have completed the construction, use a ruler to measure $\overline{AE}$, $\overline{EB}$, $\overline{AF}$, and $\overline{FC}$ to see that $\frac{AE}{EB} = \frac{AF}{FC}$.

Construction Triangle Proportionality Theorem

Construct a line parallel to a side of a triangle.

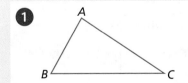

❶ Use a straightedge to draw △ABC.

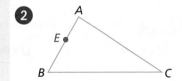

❷ Label *E* on *AB*.

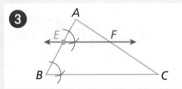

❸ Construct ∠E ≅ ∠B. Label the intersection of $\overleftrightarrow{EF}$ and $\overline{AC}$ as *F*. $\overleftrightarrow{EF} \parallel \overline{BC}$ by the Converse of the Corresponding Angles Postulate.

EXAMPLE 1
MCC9-12.G.SRT.5

my.hrw.com

Online Video Tutor

Finding the Length of a Segment

Find CY.

It is given that $\overline{XY} \parallel \overline{BC}$, so $\frac{AX}{XB} = \frac{AY}{YC}$
by the Triangle Proportionality Theorem.

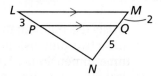

$$\frac{9}{4} = \frac{10}{CY} \qquad \textit{Substitute 9 for AX, 4 for XB, and 10 for AY.}$$

$$9(CY) = 40 \qquad \textit{Cross Products Prop.}$$

$$CY = \frac{40}{9}, \text{ or } 4\frac{4}{9} \qquad \textit{Divide both sides by 9.}$$

CHECK IT OUT! **1.** Find *PN*.

Know it!
Note

Theorem 26-4-2 **Converse of the Triangle Proportionality Theorem**

THEOREM	HYPOTHESIS	CONCLUSION
If a line divides two sides of a triangle proportionally, then it is parallel to the third side.	$\frac{AE}{EB} = \frac{AF}{FC}$	$\overleftrightarrow{EF} \parallel \overline{BC}$

You will prove Theorem 26-4-2 in Exercise 23.

EXAMPLE 2
MCC9-12.G.SRT.5

my.hrw.com

Online Video Tutor

Verifying Segments are Parallel

Verify that $\overline{MN} \parallel \overline{KL}$.

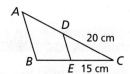

$$\frac{JM}{MK} = \frac{42}{21} = 2$$

$$\frac{JN}{NL} = \frac{30}{15} = 2$$

Since $\frac{JM}{MK} = \frac{JN}{NL}$, $\overline{MN} \parallel \overline{KL}$ by the Converse of the
Triangle Proportionality Theorem.

CHECK IT OUT! **2.** $AC = 36$ cm, and $BC = 27$ cm.
Verify that $\overline{DE} \parallel \overline{AB}$.

Know it!
Note

Corollary 26-4-3 **Two-Transversal Proportionality**

COROLLARY	HYPOTHESIS	CONCLUSION
If three or more parallel lines intersect two transversals, then they divide the transversals proportionally.		$\frac{AC}{CE} = \frac{BD}{DF}$

You will prove Corollary 26-4-3 in Exercise 24.

EXAMPLE 3 MCC9-12.G.CO.9

Art Application

An artist used perspective to draw guidelines to help her sketch a row of parallel trees. She then checked the drawing by measuring the distances between the trees. What is LN?

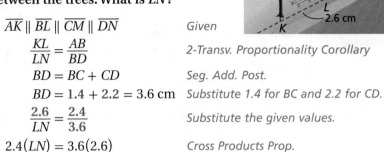

$\overline{AK} \parallel \overline{BL} \parallel \overline{CM} \parallel \overline{DN}$ *Given*

$\dfrac{KL}{LN} = \dfrac{AB}{BD}$ *2-Transv. Proportionality Corollary*

$BD = BC + CD$ *Seg. Add. Post.*

$BD = 1.4 + 2.2 = 3.6$ cm   *Substitute 1.4 for BC and 2.2 for CD.*

$\dfrac{2.6}{LN} = \dfrac{2.4}{3.6}$ *Substitute the given values.*

$2.4(LN) = 3.6(2.6)$ *Cross Products Prop.*

$LN = 3.9$ cm   *Divide both sides by 2.4.*

3. Use the diagram to find LM and MN to the nearest tenth.

The previous theorems and corollary lead to the following conclusion.

Theorem 26-4-4   Triangle Angle Bisector Theorem

THEOREM	HYPOTHESIS	CONCLUSION
An angle bisector of a triangle divides the opposite side into two segments whose lengths are proportional to the lengths of the other two sides. (△ ∠ Bisector Thm.)	*diagram of triangle ABC with vertex A, base BC, point D on base*	$\dfrac{BD}{DC} = \dfrac{AB}{AC}$

You will prove Theorem 26-4-4 in Exercise 38.

EXAMPLE 4 MCC9-12.A.CED.1

Using the Triangle Angle Bisector Theorem

Find RV and VT.

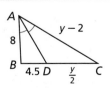

$\dfrac{RV}{VT} = \dfrac{SR}{ST}$ by the △ ∠ Bisector Thm.

$\dfrac{x+2}{2x+1} = \dfrac{10}{14}$ *Substitute the given values.*

$14(x+2) = 10(2x+1)$ *Cross Products Prop.*

$14x + 28 = 20x + 10$ *Dist. Prop.*

$18 = 6x$ *Simplify.*

$x = 3$ *Divide both sides by 6.*

$RV = x + 2$ $VT = 2x + 1$ *Substitute 3 for x.*

$= 3 + 2 = 5$ $= 2(3) + 1 = 7$

4. Find AC and DC.

26-4 Applying Properties of Similar Triangles   **799**

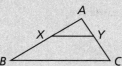

THINK AND DISCUSS

1. $\overline{XY} \parallel \overline{BC}$. Use what you know about similarity and proportionality to state as many different proportions as possible.

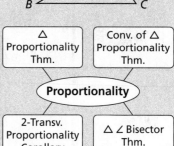

2. GET ORGANIZED Copy and complete the graphic organizer. Draw a figure for each proportionality theorem or corollary and then measure it. Use your measurements to write an if-then statement about each figure.

26-4 Exercises

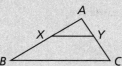

my.hrw.com
Homework Help

GUIDED PRACTICE

SEE EXAMPLE 1

Find the length of each segment.

1. $\overline{DG}$

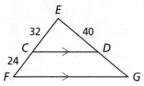

2. $\overline{RN}$

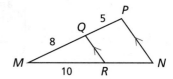

SEE EXAMPLE 2

Verify that the given segments are parallel.

3. $\overline{AB}$ and $\overline{CD}$

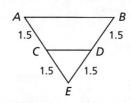

4. $\overline{TU}$ and $\overline{RS}$

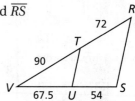

SEE EXAMPLE 3

5. Travel The map shows the area around Herald Square in Manhattan, New York, and the approximate length of several streets. If the numbered streets are parallel, what is the length of Broadway between 34th St. and 35th St. to the nearest foot?

800 *Module 26 Similarity*

Find the length of each segment.

6. $\overline{QR}$ and $\overline{RS}$

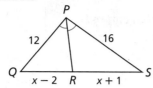

7. $\overline{CD}$ and $\overline{AD}$

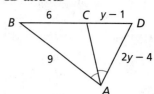

PRACTICE AND PROBLEM SOLVING

my.hrw.com

Online Extra Practice

Find the length of each segment.

8. $\overline{KL}$

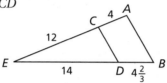

9. $\overline{XZ}$

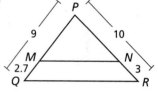

Verify that the given segments are parallel.

10. $\overline{AB}$ and $\overline{CD}$

11. $\overline{MN}$ and $\overline{QR}$

12. Architecture The wooden treehouse has horizontal siding that is parallel to the base. What are LM and MN to the nearest hundredth?

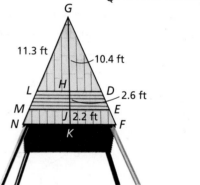

Find the length of each segment.

13. $\overline{BC}$ and $\overline{CD}$

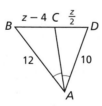

14. $\overline{ST}$ and $\overline{TU}$

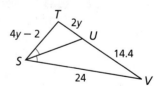

In the figure, $\overleftrightarrow{BC} \parallel \overleftrightarrow{DE} \parallel \overleftrightarrow{FG}$. Complete each proportion.

15. $\dfrac{AB}{BD} = \dfrac{AC}{\blacksquare}$

16. $\dfrac{\blacksquare}{DF} = \dfrac{AE}{EG}$

17. $\dfrac{DF}{\blacksquare} = \dfrac{EG}{CE}$

18. $\dfrac{AF}{AB} = \dfrac{\blacksquare}{AC}$

19. $\dfrac{BD}{CE} = \dfrac{\blacksquare}{EG}$

20. $\dfrac{AB}{AC} = \dfrac{BF}{\blacksquare}$

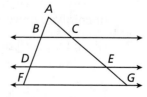

21. The bisector of an angle of a triangle divides the opposite side of the triangle into segments that are 12 in. and 16 in. long. Another side of the triangle is 20 in. long. What are two possible lengths for the third side?

Real-World Connections

22. Jaclyn is building a slide rail, the narrow, slanted beam found in skateboard parks.

   a. Write a proportion that Jaclyn can use to calculate the length of $\overline{CE}$.

   b. Find *CE*.

   c. What is the overall length of the slide rail *AJ*?

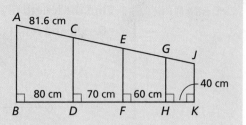

H.O.T 23. Prove the Converse of the Triangle Proportionality Theorem.

   Given: $\dfrac{AE}{EB} = \dfrac{AF}{FC}$

   Prove: $\overleftrightarrow{EF} \parallel \overline{BC}$

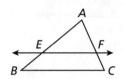

H.O.T 24. Prove the Two-Transversal Proportionality Corollary.

   Given: $\overleftrightarrow{AB} \parallel \overleftrightarrow{CD}, \overleftrightarrow{CD} \parallel \overleftrightarrow{EF}$

   Prove: $\dfrac{AC}{CE} = \dfrac{BD}{DF}$

   (*Hint:* Draw $\overleftrightarrow{BE}$ through *X*.)

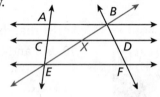

25. Given that $\overleftrightarrow{PQ} \parallel \overleftrightarrow{RS} \parallel \overleftrightarrow{TU}$

   a. Find *PR*, *RT*, *QS*, and *SU*.

   b. Use your results from part **b** to write a proportion relating the segment lengths.

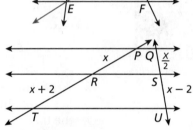

H.O.T Find the length of each segment.

26. $\overline{EF}$

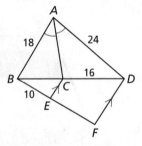

27. $\overline{ST}$

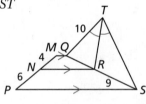

H.O.T 28. **Real Estate** A developer is laying out lots along Grant Rd. whose total width is 500 ft. Given the width of each lot along Chavez St., what is the width of each of the lots along Grant Rd. to the nearest foot?

29. **Critical Thinking** Explain how to use a sheet of lined notebook paper to divide a segment into five congruent segments. Which theorem or corollary do you use?

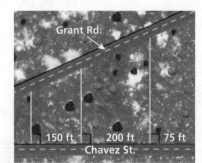

30. Given that $\overline{DE} \parallel \overline{BC}, \overline{XY} \parallel \overline{AD}$ Find *EC*.

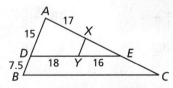

31. **Write About It** In $\triangle ABC$, $\overrightarrow{AD}$ bisects $\angle BAC$. Write a proportionality statement for the triangle. What theorem supports your conclusion?

Royalty-Free/Comstock

TEST PREP

32. Which dimensions let you conclude that $\overline{UV} \parallel \overline{ST}$?

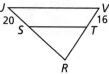

   Ⓐ $SR = 12$, $TR = 9$ Ⓒ $SR = 35$, $TR = 28$

   Ⓑ $SR = 16$, $TR = 20$ Ⓓ $SR = 50$, $TR = 48$

33. In $\triangle ABC$, the bisector of $\angle A$ divides $\overline{BC}$ into segments with lengths 16 and 20. $AC = 25$. Which of these could be the length of $\overline{AB}$?

   Ⓕ 12.8   Ⓖ 16   Ⓗ 18.75   Ⓙ 20

34. On the map, 1st St. and 2nd St. are parallel. What is the distance from City Hall to 2nd St. along Cedar Rd.?

   Ⓐ 1.8 mi   Ⓒ 4.2 mi

   Ⓑ 3.2 mi   Ⓓ 5.6 mi

H.O.T. **35. Extended Response** Two segments are divided proportionally. The first segment is divided into lengths 20, 15, and x. The corresponding lengths in the second segment are 16, y, and 24. Find the value of x and y. Use these values and write six proportions.

CHALLENGE AND EXTEND

36. The perimeter of $\triangle ABC$ is 29 cm. $\overline{AD}$ bisects $\angle A$. Find AB and AC.

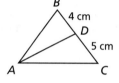

H.O.T. **37.** Prove that if two triangles are similar, then the ratio of their corresponding angle bisectors is the same as the ratio of their corresponding sides.

H.O.T. **38.** Prove the Triangle Angle Bisector Theorem.

   Given: In $\triangle ABC$, $\overline{AD}$ bisects $\angle A$.

   Prove: $\dfrac{BD}{DC} = \dfrac{AB}{AC}$

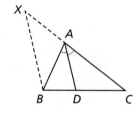

   Plan: Draw $\overline{BX} \parallel \overline{AD}$ and extend $\overline{AC}$ to X. Use properties of parallel lines and the Converse of the Isosceles Triangle Theorem to show that $\overline{AX} \cong \overline{AB}$. Then apply the Triangle Proportionality Theorem.

39. Construction Construct three parallel lines cut by a transversal. Construct a second transversal that forms line segments twice the length of the corresponding segments on the first transversal.

FOCUS ON MATHEMATICAL PRACTICES

H.O.T. **40. Justify** In the figure shown, does $\overline{KM}$ bisect $\angle LKN$? If not, which is larger, m$\angle LKM$ or m$\angle MKN$? Justify your answer.

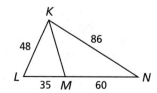

H.O.T. **41. Problem Solving** $\triangle WXY$ is isosceles with $\angle X$ as its vertex angle. Find YZ and WX. Show your work.

26-5 Dilations and Similarity in the Coordinate Plane

Essential Question: How can you use dilations to draw similar figures in a coordinate plane?

Objectives
Apply similarity properties in the coordinate plane.

Use coordinate proof to prove figures similar.

Vocabulary
dilation
scale factor

Who uses this?
Computer programmers use coordinates to enlarge or reduce images.

Many photographs on the Web are in JPEG format, which is short for Joint Photographic Experts Group. When you drag a corner of a JPEG image in order to enlarge it or reduce it, the underlying program uses coordinates and similarity to change the image's size.

A **dilation** is a transformation that changes the size of a figure but not its shape. The preimage and the image are always similar. A **scale factor** describes how much the figure is enlarged or reduced. For a dilation with scale factor k, you can find the image of a point by multiplying each coordinate by k: $(a, b) \rightarrow (ka, kb)$.

EXAMPLE 1
MCC9-12.G.CO.2

Computer Graphics Application

my.hrw.com

Online Video Tutor

The figure shows the position of a JPEG photo. Draw the border of the photo after a dilation with scale factor $\frac{3}{2}$.

Step 1 Multiply the vertices of the photo $A(0, 0)$, $B(0, 4)$, $C(3, 4)$, and $D(3, 0)$ by $\frac{3}{2}$.

Rectangle ABCD	Rectangle A'B'C'D'

$$A(0, 0) \rightarrow A'\left(0 \cdot \frac{3}{2}, 0 \cdot \frac{3}{2}\right) \rightarrow A'(0, 0)$$

$$B(0, 4) \rightarrow B'\left(0 \cdot \frac{3}{2}, 4 \cdot \frac{3}{2}\right) \rightarrow B'(0, 6)$$

$$C(3, 4) \rightarrow C'\left(3 \cdot \frac{3}{2}, 4 \cdot \frac{3}{2}\right) \rightarrow C'(4.5, 6)$$

$$D(3, 0) \rightarrow D'\left(3 \cdot \frac{3}{2}, 0 \cdot \frac{3}{2}\right) \rightarrow D'(4.5, 0)$$

Step 2 Plot points $A'(0, 0)$, $B'(0, 6)$, $C'(4.5, 6)$, and $D'(4.5, 0)$. Draw the rectangle.

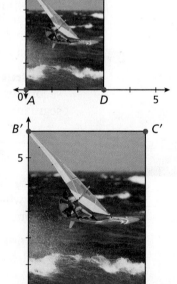

Helpful Hint

If the scale factor of a dilation is greater than 1 ($k > 1$), it is an *enlargement*. If the scale factor is less than 1 ($k < 1$), it is a *reduction*.

1. What if...? Draw the border of the original photo after a dilation with scale factor $\frac{1}{2}$.

EXAMPLE **2** Finding Coordinates of Similar Triangles

Given that $\triangle AOB \sim \triangle COD$, find the coordinates of D and the scale factor.

Since $\triangle AOB \sim \triangle COD$,

$$\frac{AO}{CO} = \frac{OB}{OD}$$

$$\frac{2}{4} = \frac{3}{OD}$$ *Substitute 2 for AO, 4 for CO, and 3 for OB.*

$$2OD = 12$$ *Cross Products Prop.*

$$OD = 6$$ *Divide both sides by 2.*

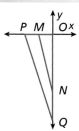

D lies on the x-axis, so its y-coordinate is 0. Since $OD = 6$, its x-coordinate must be 6. The coordinates of D are $(6, 0)$.

$(3, 0) \rightarrow (3 \cdot 2, 0 \cdot 2) \rightarrow (6, 0)$, so the scale factor is 2.

 2. Given that $\triangle MON \sim \triangle POQ$ and coordinates $P(-15, 0)$, $M(-10, 0)$, and $Q(0, -30)$, find the coordinates of N and the scale factor.

EXAMPLE **3** Proving Triangles Are Similar

Given: $A(1, 5)$, $B(-1, 3)$, $C(3, 4)$, $D(-3, 1)$, and $E(5, 3)$

Prove: $\triangle ABC \sim \triangle ADE$

Step 1 Plot the points and draw the triangles.

Step 2 Use the Distance Formula to find the side lengths.

$$AB = \sqrt{(-1 - 1)^2 + (3 - 5)^2} \qquad AC = \sqrt{(3 - 1)^2 + (4 - 5)^2}$$

$$= \sqrt{8} = 2\sqrt{2} \qquad\qquad = \sqrt{5}$$

$$AD = \sqrt{(-3 - 1)^2 + (1 - 5)^2} \qquad AE = \sqrt{(5 - 1)^2 + (3 - 5)^2}$$

$$= \sqrt{32} = 4\sqrt{2} \qquad\qquad = \sqrt{20} = 2\sqrt{5}$$

Step 3 Find the similarity ratio.

$$\frac{AB}{AD} = \frac{2\sqrt{2}}{4\sqrt{2}} \qquad\qquad \frac{AC}{AE} = \frac{\sqrt{5}}{2\sqrt{5}}$$

$$= \frac{2}{4} \qquad\qquad\qquad = \frac{1}{2}$$

$$= \frac{1}{2}$$

Since $\frac{AB}{AD} = \frac{AC}{AE}$ and $\angle A \cong \angle A$ by the Reflexive Property, $\triangle ABC \sim \triangle ADE$ by SAS $\sim$.

 3. Given: $R(-2, 0)$, $S(-3, 1)$, $T(0, 1)$, $U(-5, 3)$, and $V(4, 3)$
Prove: $\triangle RST \sim \triangle RUV$

EXAMPLE 4
MCC9-12.G.SRT.5

my.hrw.com

Online Video Tutor

Using the SSS Similarity Theorem

Graph the image of $\triangle ABC$ after a dilation with scale factor 2. Verify that $\triangle A'B'C' \sim \triangle ABC$.

Step 1 Multiply each coordinate by 2 to find the coordinates of the vertices of $\triangle A'B'C'$.

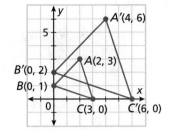

$$A(2, 3) \rightarrow A'(2\cdot2, 3\cdot2) = A'(4, 6)$$
$$B(0, 1) \rightarrow B'(0\cdot2, 1\cdot2) = B'(0, 2)$$
$$C(3, 0) \rightarrow C'(3\cdot2, 0\cdot2) = C'(6, 0)$$

Step 2 Graph $\triangle A'B'C'$.

Step 3 Use the Distance Formula to find the side lengths.

$$AB = \sqrt{(2 - 0)^2 + (3 - 1)^2} \qquad A'B' = \sqrt{(4 - 0)^2 + (6 - 2)^2}$$
$$= \sqrt{8} = 2\sqrt{2} \qquad\qquad = \sqrt{32} = 4\sqrt{2}$$

$$BC = \sqrt{(3 - 0)^2 + (0 - 1)^2} \qquad B'C' = \sqrt{(6 - 0)^2 + (0 - 2)^2}$$
$$= \sqrt{10} \qquad\qquad\qquad = \sqrt{40} = 2\sqrt{10}$$

$$AC = \sqrt{(3 - 2)^2 + (0 - 3)^2} \qquad A'C' = \sqrt{(6 - 4)^2 + (0 - 6)^2}$$
$$= \sqrt{10} \qquad\qquad\qquad = \sqrt{40} = 2\sqrt{10}$$

Step 4 Find the similarity ratio.

$$\frac{A'B'}{AB} = \frac{4\sqrt{2}}{2\sqrt{2}} = 2, \frac{B'C'}{BC} = \frac{2\sqrt{10}}{\sqrt{10}} = 2, \frac{A'C'}{AC} = \frac{2\sqrt{10}}{\sqrt{10}} = 2$$

Since $\dfrac{A'B'}{AB} = \dfrac{B'C'}{BC} = \dfrac{A'C'}{AC}$, $\triangle ABC \sim \triangle A'B'C'$ by SSS ~.

CHECK IT OUT!

4. Graph the image of $\triangle MNP$ after a dilation with scale factor 3. Verify that $\triangle M'N'P' \sim \triangle MNP$.

MCC.MP.8

Know it!
Note

THINK AND DISCUSS

1. $\triangle JKL$ has coordinates $J(0, 0)$, $K(0, 2)$, and $L(3, 0)$. Its image after a dilation has coordinates $J'(0, 0)$, $K'(0, 8)$, and $L'(12, 0)$. Explain how to find the scale factor of the dilation.

2. **GET ORGANIZED** Copy and complete the graphic organizer. Write the definition of a dilation, a property of dilations, and an example and nonexample of a dilation.

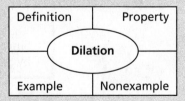

MATHEMATICAL PRACTICES

Exercises

GUIDED PRACTICE

Vocabulary Apply the vocabulary from this lesson to answer each question.

1. A ___?___ is a transformation that proportionally reduces or enlarges a figure, such as the pupil of an eye. (*dilation* or *scale factor*)

2. A ratio that describes or determines the dimensional relationship of a figure to that which it represents, such as a map scale of 1 in. : 45 ft, is called a ___?___ . (*dilation* or *scale factor*)

SEE EXAMPLE 1

3. **Graphic Design** A designer created this logo for a real estate agent but needs to make the logo twice as large for use on a sign. Draw the logo after a dilation with scale factor 2.

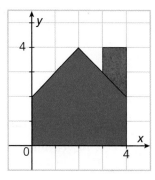

SEE EXAMPLE 2

4. Given that $\triangle AOB \sim \triangle COD$, find the coordinates of C and the scale factor.

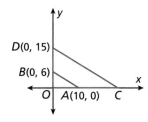

5. Given that $\triangle ROS \sim \triangle POQ$, find the coordinates of S and the scale factor.

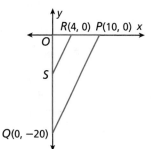

SEE EXAMPLE 3

6. **Given:** $A(0, 0)$, $B(-1, 1)$, $C(3, 2)$, $D(-2, 2)$, and $E(6, 4)$
   Prove: $\triangle ABC \sim \triangle ADE$

7. **Given:** $J(-1, 0)$, $K(-3, -4)$, $L(3, -2)$, $M(-4, -6)$, and $N(5, -3)$
   Prove: $\triangle JKL \sim \triangle JMN$

SEE EXAMPLE 4

Multi-Step Graph the image of each triangle after a dilation with the given scale factor. Then verify that the image is similar to the given triangle.

8. scale factor 2

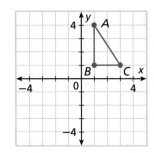

9. scale factor $\frac{3}{2}$

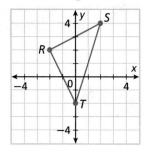

Independent Practice

For Exercises	See Example
10	1
11–12	2
13–14	3
15–16	4

my.hrw.com

Online Extra Practice

10. **Advertising** A promoter produced this design for a street festival. She now wants to make the design smaller to use on postcards. Sketch the design after a dilation with scale factor $\frac{1}{2}$.

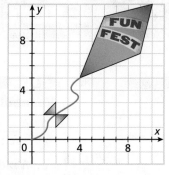

11. Given that $\triangle UOV \sim \triangle XOY$, find the coordinates of X and the scale factor.

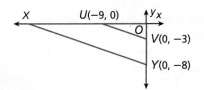

12. Given that $\triangle MON \sim \triangle KOL$, find the coordinates of K and the scale factor.

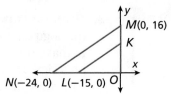

13. **Given:** $D(-1, 3)$, $E(-3, -1)$, $F(3, -1)$, $G(-4, -3)$, and $H(5, -3)$
    Prove: $\triangle DEF \sim \triangle DGH$

14. **Given:** $M(0, 10)$, $N(5, 0)$, $P(15, 15)$, $Q(10, -10)$, and $R(30, 20)$
    Prove: $\triangle MNP \sim \triangle MQR$

H.O.T. **Multi-Step** Graph the image of each triangle after a dilation with the given scale factor. Then verify that the image is similar to the given triangle.

15. $J(-2, 0)$ and $K(-1, -1)$, and $L(-3, -2)$ with scale factor 3

16. $M(0, 4)$, $N(4, 2)$, and $P(2, -2)$ with scale factor $\frac{1}{2}$

H.O.T. 17. **Critical Thinking** Consider the transformation given by the mapping $(x, y) \rightarrow (2x, 4y)$. Is this transformation a dilation? Why or why not?

18. **///ERROR ANALYSIS///** Which solution to find the scale factor of the dilation that maps $\triangle RST$ to $\triangle UVW$ is incorrect? Explain the error.

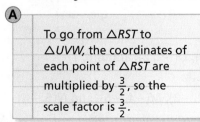

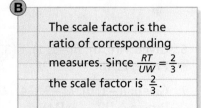

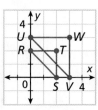

H.O.T. 19. **Write About It** A dilation maps $\triangle ABC$ to $\triangle A'B'C'$. How is the scale factor of the dilation related to the similarity ratio of $\triangle ABC$ to $\triangle A'B'C'$? Explain.

Real-World Connections

20. a. In order to build a skateboard ramp, Miles draws $\triangle JKL$ on a coordinate plane. One unit on the drawing represents 60 cm of actual distance. Explain how he should assign coordinates for the vertices of $\triangle JKL$.

   b. Graph the image of $\triangle JKL$ after a dilation with scale factor 3.

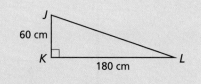

TEST PREP

21. Which coordinates for C make $\triangle COD$ similar to $\triangle AOB$?

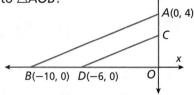

- Ⓐ $(0, 2.4)$
- Ⓒ $(0, 3)$
- Ⓑ $(0, 2.5)$
- Ⓓ $(0, 3.6)$

22. A dilation with scale factor 2 maps $\triangle RST$ to $\triangle R'S'T'$. The perimeter of $\triangle RST$ is 60. What is the perimeter of $\triangle R'S'T'$?

- Ⓕ 30
- Ⓖ 60
- Ⓗ 120
- Ⓙ 240

23. Which triangle with vertices D, E, and F is similar to $\triangle ABC$?

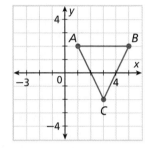

- Ⓐ $D(1, 2)$, $E(3, 2)$, $F(2, 0)$
- Ⓑ $D(-1, -2)$, $E(2, -2)$, $F(1, -5)$
- Ⓒ $D(1, 2)$, $E(5, 2)$, $F(3, 0)$
- Ⓓ $D(-2, -2)$, $E(0, 2)$, $F(-1, 0)$

24. Gridded Resonse $\overline{AB}$ with endpoints $A(3, 2)$ and $B(7, 5)$ is dilated by a scale factor of 3. Find the length of $\overline{A'B'}$.

CHALLENGE AND EXTEND

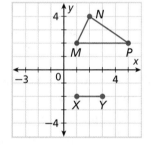

25. How many different triangles having $\overline{XY}$ as a side are similar to $\triangle MNP$?

26. $\triangle XYZ \sim \triangle MPN$. Find the coordinates of Z.

27. A rectangle has two of its sides on the x- and y-axes, a vertex at the origin, and a vertex on the line $y = 2x$. Prove that any two such rectangles are similar.

28. $\triangle ABC$ has vertices $A(0, 1)$, $B(3, 1)$, and $C(1, 3)$. $\triangle DEF$ has vertices $D(1, -1)$ and $E(7, -1)$. Find two different locations for vertex F so that $\triangle ABC \sim \triangle DEF$.

FOCUS ON MATHEMATICAL PRACTICES

29. Error Analysis Jonah says that $\triangle RST$ shown is similar to a triangle in the coordinate plane with vertices $D(6, 6)$, $E(1, 6)$, and $F(1, 10)$. Charles says that the two triangles are not similar. Who is correct? Explain your answer.

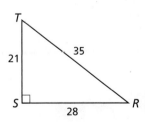

30. Problem Solving $\overline{JK}$ has length 10. $\overline{J'K'}$ is a dilation of $\overline{JK}$ and has endpoints $J'(5, 16)$ and $K'(12, -8)$. Find the scale factor of the dilation and show your work. Is the dilation an enlargement or a reduction? How do you know?

Ready to Go On?

my.hrw.com
Assessment and Intervention

✓ 26-1 Ratios in Similar Polygons

Determine whether the two polygons are similar. If so, write the similarity ratio and a similarity statement.

1. rectangles *ABCD* and *WXYZ*

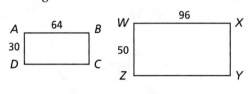

2. △*JMR* and △*NPK*

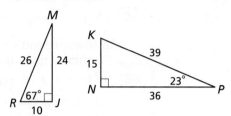

3. Leonardo da Vinci's famous portrait the *Mona Lisa* is 30 in. long and 21 in. wide. Janelle has a refrigerator magnet of the painting that is 3.5 cm wide. What is the length of the magnet?

✓ 26-2 Similarity and Transformations

Apply the dilation to the polygon with the given vertices. Name the coordinates of the points. Identify and describe the transformation.

4. $D : (x, y) \rightarrow (3x, 3y)$; $A(0, 0)$, $B(1, 2)$, $C(3, -2)$

5. $D : (x, y) \rightarrow (0.5x, 0.5y)$; $A(10, 6)$, $B(8, -4)$, $C(-2, 0)$

Determine whether the polygons with the given vertices are similar. Support your answer by describing a transformation.

6. $A(0, 0)$, $B(-2, 0)$, $C(-2, 1)$
   $X(10, 0)$, $Y(6, 0)$, $Z(6, 2)$

7. $A(0, 0)$, $B(1, 3)$, $C(-1, 4)$
   $X(0, 0)$, $Y(3, 9)$, $Z(-2, 8)$

✓ 26-3 Triangle Similarity: AA, SSS, and SAS

8. Given: ▱*ABCD*
   Prove: △*EDG* ~ △*FBG*

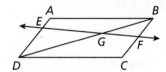

9. Given: $MQ = \frac{1}{3}MN$, $MR = \frac{1}{3}MP$
   Prove: △*MQR* ~ △*MNP*

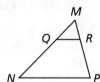

✓ 26-4 Applying Properties of Similar Triangles

Find the length of each segment.

10. $\overline{ST}$

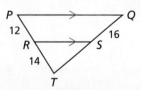

11. $\overline{AB}$ and $\overline{AC}$

✅ 26-5 Dilations and Similarity in the Coordinate Plane

12. **Given:** $A(-1, 2)$, $B(-3, -2)$, $C(3, 0)$, $D(-2, 0)$, and $E(1, 1)$
    Prove: $\triangle ADE \sim \triangle ABC$

13. **Given:** $R(0, 0)$, $S(-2, -1)$, $T(0, -3)$, $U(4, 2)$, and $V(0, 6)$
    Prove: $\triangle RST \sim \triangle RUV$

Graph the image of each triangle after a dilation with the given scale factor. Then verify that the image is similar to the given triangle.

14. scale factor 3

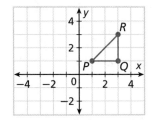

15. scale factor 1.5

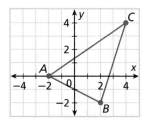

PARCC Assessment Readiness

COMMON CORE GPS

Selected Response

1. A video game designer is modeling a tower that is 320 ft high and 260 ft wide. She creates a model so that the similarity ratio of the model to the tower is $\dfrac{1}{500}$. What are the height and the width of the model in inches?

   (A) height = 0.64 in.; width = 0.52 in.

   (B) height = 3840 in.; width = 3120 in.

   (C) height = 7.68 in.; width = 6.24 in.

   (D) height = 160,000 in.; width = 130,000 in.

2. Find *NP*.

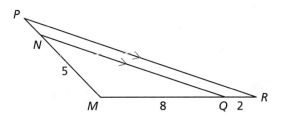

   (F) *NP* = 1

   (G) *NP* = 1.25

   (H) *NP* = 1.6

   (J) *NP* = 2

Mini-Tasks

3. **Given:** $\overline{BD} \parallel \overline{CE}$
   Prove: $AB(CE) = AC(BD)$

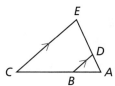

4. Apply the dilation *D* to the polygon with the given vertices. Name the coordinates of the image points. Identify and describe the transformation.

   $D:(x, y) \rightarrow (4x, 4y)$

   $A(2, 1)$, $B(4, 1)$, $C(4, -3)$

PARCC Assessment Readiness

COMMON CORE GPS

Selected Response

1. $\triangle ABC \cong \triangle DEF$, $EF = x^2 - 7$, and $BC = 4x - 2$. Find the values of x.

   (A) −1 and 5 (C) 1 and 5
   (B) −1 and 6 (D) 2 and 3

2. For two lines and a transversal, $\angle 1$ and $\angle 2$ are same-side interior angles, $\angle 2$ and $\angle 3$ are vertical angles, and $\angle 3$ and $\angle 4$ are alternate exterior angles. Which classification best describes the angle pair $\angle 2$ and $\angle 4$?

   (F) Adjacent angles
   (G) Alternate interior angles
   (H) Corresponding angles
   (J) Vertical angles

3. If $\triangle ABC \cong \triangle PQR$ and $\triangle RPQ \cong \triangle XYZ$, which of the following angles is congruent to $\angle CAB$?

   (A) $\angle QRP$ (C) $\angle YXZ$
   (B) $\angle XZY$ (D) $\angle XYZ$

4. For $\triangle ABC$ and $\triangle DEF$, $\angle A \cong \angle F$, and $\overline{AC} \cong \overline{EF}$. Which of the following would allow you to conclude that these triangles are congruent by AAS?

   (F) $\angle ABC \cong \angle EDF$
   (G) $\angle ACB \cong \angle EDF$
   (H) $\angle BAC \cong \angle FDE$
   (J) $\angle CBA \cong \angle FED$

5. The measure of $\angle 1$ is 4 times the measure of its supplement. What is the measure, in degrees, of $\angle 1$?

   (A) 36 (C) 135
   (B) 45 (D) 144

6. R has coordinates $(-4, 9)$. S has coordinates $(4, -6)$. What is RS?

   (F) 8 (H) 17
   (G) 15 (J) 23

Use the figure below for Items 7 and 8.

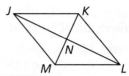

7. If $\overline{JK} \parallel \overline{ML}$, what additional information do you need to prove that quadrilateral $JKLM$ is a parallelogram?

   (A) $\overline{JM} \cong \overline{KL}$
   (B) $\overline{MN} \cong \overline{LN}$
   (C) $\angle MLK$ and $\angle LKJ$ are right angles.
   (D) $\angle JML$ and $\angle KLM$ are supplementary.

8. Given that $JKLM$ is a parallelogram and that $m\angle KLN = 25°$, $m\angle JMN = 65°$, and $m\angle JML = 130°$, which term best describes quadrilateral $JKLM$?

   (F) Rectangle
   (G) Rhombus
   (H) Square
   (J) Trapezoid

9. The vertices of $\square ABCD$ are $A(1, 4)$, $B(4, y)$, $C(3, -2)$, and $D(0, -3)$. What is the value of y?

   (A) 3 (C) 5
   (B) 4 (D) 6

10. Quadrilateral $RSTU$ is a kite. What is the length of $\overline{RV}$?

   (F) 4 inches (H) 6 inches
   (G) 5 inches (J) 13 inches

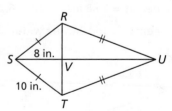

11. Which of the following is NOT valid for proving that triangles are congruent?

(A) AAA   (C) SAS

(B) ASA   (D) HL

12. Which condition guarantees that $r \parallel s$?

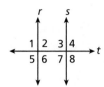

(F) $\angle 1 \cong \angle 2$ (H) $\angle 2 \cong \angle 3$

(G) $\angle 2 \cong \angle 7$ (J) $\angle 1 \cong \angle 4$

13. Two lines a and b are cut by a transversal so that $\angle 1$ and $\angle 2$ are same-side interior angles. If m$\angle 1 = (2x + 30)^\circ$ and m$\angle 2 = (4x - 75)^\circ$, what value of x proves that $a \parallel b$?

(A) 22.5   (C) 45

(B) 37.5   (D) 67.5

14. Heather is 1.6 m tall and casts a shadow of 3.5 m. At the same time, a barn casts a shadow of 17.5 m. Find the height of the barn in meters.

(F) 5   (H) 14

(G) 8   (J) 38

15. What is the measure, in degrees, of $\angle H$?

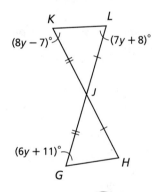

(A) 17   (C) 65

(B) 44   (D) 71

16. $\triangle JKL \cong \triangle XYZ$, and $JK = 10 - 2n$. $XY = 2$, and $YZ = n^2$. What is KL?

(F) 2   (H) 8

(G) 4   (J) 16

Use the diagram for Items 17 and 18.

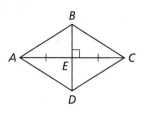

17. Which of these congruence statements can be proved from the information given in the figure?

(A) $\triangle AEB \cong \triangle CED$

(B) $\triangle BAC \cong \triangle DAC$

(C) $\triangle ABD \cong \triangle BCA$

(D) $\triangle DEC \cong \triangle DEA$

18. What other information is needed to prove that $\triangle CEB \cong \triangle AED$ by the HL Congruence Theorem?

(F) $\overline{AD} \cong \overline{AB}$

(G) $\overline{BE} \cong \overline{AE}$

(H) $\overline{CB} \cong \overline{AD}$

(J) $\overline{DE} \cong \overline{CE}$

19. What is the measure of $\angle ACD$?

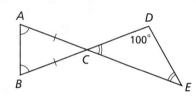

(A) 40°   (C) 100°

(B) 80°   (D) 140°

20. Congruent segments have equal measures. A segment bisector divides a segment into two congruent segments. $\overrightarrow{XY}$ intersects $\overline{DE}$ at X and bisects $\overline{DE}$. Which conjecture is valid?

(F) m$\angle YXD = $ m$\angle YXE$

(G) Y is between D and E.

(H) $DX = XE$

(J) $DE = YE$

21. $\overline{GJ}$ is a midsegment of $\triangle DEF$, and $\overline{HK}$ is a midsegment of $\triangle GFJ$. What is the length of $\overline{HK}$?

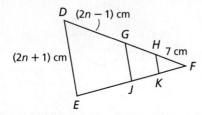

    (A) 2.25 centimeters

    (B) 4 centimeters

    (C) 7.5 centimeters

    (D) 9 centimeters

22. In $\triangle ABC$ and $\triangle DEF$, $\overline{AC} \cong \overline{DE}$, and $\angle A \cong \angle E$. Which of the following would allow you to conclude by SAS that these triangles are congruent?

    (F) $\overline{AB} \cong \overline{DF}$

    (G) $\overline{AC} \cong \overline{EF}$

    (H) $\overline{BA} \cong \overline{FE}$

    (J) $\overline{CB} \cong \overline{DF}$

23. The coordinates of the vertices of quadrilateral $RSTU$ are $R(1, 3)$, $S(2, 7)$, $T(10, 5)$, and $U(9, 1)$. Which term best describes quadrilateral $RSTU$?

    (A) Parallelogram   (C) Rhombus

    (B) Rectangle   (D) Trapezoid

24. If quadrilateral $MNPQ$ is a parallelogram, what is the value of x?

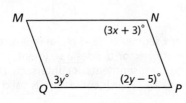

    (F) 36   (H) 38

    (G) 37   (J) 72

25. Quadrilateral $RSTU$ is a rectangle with diagonals $\overline{RT}$ and $\overline{SU}$. If $RT = 4a + 2$ and $SU = 6a - 25$, what is the value of a?

    (A) 2.7   (C) 13.5

    (B) 11.5   (D) 20.5

Use the diagram for Items 26 and 27.

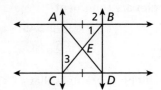

26. Given that $\overline{AB} \cong \overline{CD}$, which additional information would be sufficient to prove that $ABCD$ is a parallelogram?

    (F) $\overline{AB} \parallel \overline{CD}$

    (G) $\overline{AC} \parallel \overline{BD}$

    (H) $\angle CAB \cong \angle CDB$

    (J) E is the midpoint of $\overline{AD}$.

27. If $\overleftrightarrow{AC}$ is parallel to $\overleftrightarrow{BD}$ and $m\angle 1 + m\angle 2 = 140°$, what is the measure of $\angle 3$?

    (A) 20°   (C) 50°

    (B) 40°   (D) 70°

Mini-Tasks

28. $\triangle ABC$ has vertices $A(-2, 0)$, $B(2, 2)$, and $C(2, -2)$. $\triangle DEC$ has vertices $D(0, -1)$, $E(2, 0)$, and $C(2, -2)$. Prove that $\triangle ABC \sim \triangle DEC$.

29. $\triangle ABC$ and $\triangle ABD$ share side $\overline{AB}$. Given that $\triangle ABC \sim \triangle ABD$, use AAS to explain why these two triangles must also be congruent.

30. Given $\ell \parallel m$ with transversal t, explain why $\angle 1$ and $\angle 8$ are supplementary.

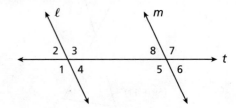

31. In $\triangle RST$, S is on the perpendicular bisector of $\overline{RT}$, $m\angle S = (4n + 16)°$, and $m\angle R = (3n - 18)°$. Find $m\angle R$. Show your work and explain how you determined your answer.

32. Use the given two-column proof to write a flowchart proof.

Given: $\overline{DE} \cong \overline{FH}$
Prove: $DE = FG + GH$

Two-column proof:

Statements	Reasons
1. $\overline{DE} \cong \overline{FH}$	1. Given
2. $DE = FH$	2. Def. of $\cong$ segs.
3. $FG + GH = FH$	3. Seg. Add. Post.
4. $DE = FG + GH$	4. Subst.

Performance Tasks

33. a. Complete the following proof by filling in the missing statements and reasons.

Given: $\overline{WY}$ bisects $\angle XWZ$,
  $\overline{WX} \cong \overline{WZ}$
Prove: $\overline{WY}$ bisects $\overline{XZ}$

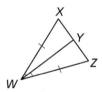

Statements	Reasons
1. ___?___	1. Given
2. $\overline{WX} \cong \overline{WZ}$	2. ___?___
3. $\overline{WY} \cong \overline{WY}$	3. ___?___
4. $\angle XWY \cong \angle ZWY$	4. Def. of angle bisector
5. ___?___	5. SAS
6. $\overline{XY} \cong \overline{ZY}$	6. ___?___
7. ___?___	7. ___?___

b. Another student claims that you don't need SAS to prove this result. Is the student correct? Which congruence theorem could you use? Rewrite the proof using that theorem.

34. Abstract Furnishings is a company that specializes in designing and making unusual furniture. The diagram shows one of their bookshelf designs.

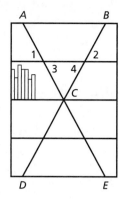

a. Complete the two-column proof.

Given: $\angle 1 \cong \angle 2$
Prove: $\angle 3 \cong \angle 4$

Statements	Reasons
1. $\angle 1 \cong \angle 2$	1. Given
2. $m\angle 1 = m\angle 2$	2. Def. of $\cong \angle$s
3. $\angle 1 \cong$ ___?___	3. Vert. $\angle$s Thm.
4. $m\angle 1 = m\angle 3$	4. Def. of $\cong \angle$s
5. $\angle 2 \cong \angle 4$	5. ___?___
6. $m\angle 2 = m\angle 4$	6. Def. of $\cong \angle$s
7. $m\angle 1 = m\angle 4$	7. ___?___
8. $m\angle 3 =$ ___?___	8. Substitution
9. $\angle 3 \cong \angle 4$	9. Def. of $\cong \angle$s

b. The designer wants to change the design so that AB is smaller, while keeping C fixed in place. How will this affect the numbered angle measures? Include a sketch with your answer.

c. If $\angle 1 \cong \angle 2$ is still true in the new design, can you still conclude $\angle 3 \cong \angle 4$? Explain why or why not.

my.hrw.com
Online Assessment
Go online for updated, PARCC-aligned assessment readiness.

Are You Ready?

my.hrw.com
Assessment and Intervention

✓ Vocabulary

Match each term on the left with a definition on the right.

1. angle bisector

2. conclusion

3. hypotenuse

4. leg of a right triangle

5. perpendicular bisector of a segment

A. the side opposite the right angle in a right triangle

B. a line that is perpendicular to a segment at its midpoint

C. the phrase following the word *then* in a conditional statement

D. one of the two sides that form the right angle in a right triangle

E. a line or ray that divides an angle into two congruent angles

F. the phrase following the word *if* in a conditional statement

✓ Classify Triangles

Tell whether each triangle is acute, right, or obtuse.

6.
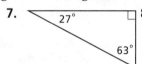

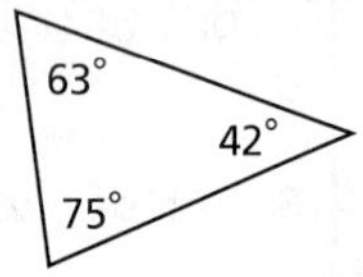

7.
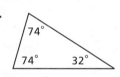

8.
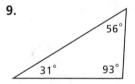

9.

✓ Squares and Square Roots

Simplify each expression.

10. 8^2

11. $(-12)^2$

12. $\sqrt{49}$

13. $-\sqrt{36}$

✓ Simplify Radical Expressions

Simplify each expression.

14. $\sqrt{9 + 16}$

15. $\sqrt{100 - 36}$

16. $\sqrt{\dfrac{81}{25}}$

17. $\sqrt{2^2}$

Career Readiness Air Traffic Controllers

Air traffic controllers coordinate movement of air traffic using radar and visual observation. They observe takeoffs and landings (including angles of elevation and depression), handle flight data, and monitor the movement of all planes for which they are responsible. Training of air traffic controllers varies but includes certification by the Federal Aviation Administration (FAA). Air traffic controllers may be employed by the FAA, the Department of Defense, or private air traffic control companies.

UNIT

8

Right Triangle Trigonometry

Online Edition

my.hrw.com

Access the complete online textbook, interactive features, and additional resources.

Animated Math

Interactively explore key concepts with these online tutorials.

Homework Help

Get instant help with tutorial videos, practice problems, and step-by-step solutions.

Portable Devices

On the Spot

Watch video tutorials anywhere, anytime with this app for iPhone® and iPad®.

HMH Fuse

Make your learning experience completely portable and interactive with this app for iPad®.

Chapter Resources

Scan with your smart phone to jump directly to the online edition.

Use a computer or handheld to explore special right triangles with TI-Nspire™ activities.

27 Right Triangles

COMMON CORE GPS

Contents

MATHEMATICAL PRACTICES The Common Core Georgia Performance Standards for Mathematical Practice describe varieties of expertise that all students should seek to develop. Opportunities to develop these practices are integrated throughout this program.

1 Make sense of problems and persevere in solving them.

2 Reason abstractly and quantitatively.

3 Construct viable arguments and critique the reasoning of others.

4 Model with mathematics.

5 Use appropriate tools strategically.

6 Attend to precision.

7 Look for and make use of structure.

8 Look for and express regularity in repeated reasoning.

Unpacking the Standards

Understanding the standards and the vocabulary terms in the standards will help you know exactly what you are expected to learn in this chapter.

 MCC9-12.G.SRT.8

Use … the Pythagorean Theorem to solve right triangles in applied problems.

Key Vocabulary

Pythagorean Theorem (Teorema de Pitágoras) If a right triangle has legs of lengths a and b and a hypotenuse of length c, then $a^2 + b^2 = c^2$.

right triangle (triángulo rectángulo) A triangle with one right angle.

What It Means For You

You can use the relationship between the side lengths of a right triangle to solve real-world problems.

EXAMPLE

The diagram shows the recommended position for placing a ladder. Given the length L of the ladder, you can use the Pythagorean Theorem to find x, the distance from the base of the wall to place the foot of the ladder.

$$L^2 = x^2 + (4x)^2$$
$$L^2 = 17x^2$$
$$\frac{L^2}{17} = x^2$$
$$\frac{L}{\sqrt{17}} = x$$

27-1 The Pythagorean Theorem

Essential Question: How can you use side lengths to determine whether a triangle is acute, right, or obtuse?

Objectives
Use the Pythagorean Theorem and its converse to solve problems.

Use Pythagorean inequalities to classify triangles.

Vocabulary
Pythagorean triple

Why learn this?

You can use the Pythagorean Theorem to determine whether a ladder is in a safe position. (See Example 2.)

The Pythagorean Theorem is probably the most famous mathematical relationship. The theorem states that in a right triangle, the sum of the squares of the lengths of the legs equals the square of the length of the hypotenuse.

$$a^2 + b^2 = c^2$$

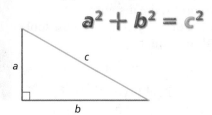

The Pythagorean Theorem is named for the Greek mathematician Pythagoras, who lived in the sixth century B.C.E. However, this relationship was known to earlier people, such as the Babylonians, Egyptians, and Chinese.

There are many different proofs of the Pythagorean Theorem. The one below uses area and algebra.

PROOF

Pythagorean Theorem

Given: A right triangle with leg lengths a and b and hypotenuse of length c
Prove: $a^2 + b^2 = c^2$

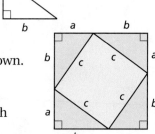

Remember!

The area A of a square with side length s is given by the formula $A = s^2$.

The area A of a triangle with base b and height h is given by the formula $A = \frac{1}{2}bh$.

Proof: Arrange four copies of the triangle as shown. The sides of the triangles form two squares.

The area of the outer square is $(a + b)^2$. The area of the inner square is c^2. The area of each blue triangle is $\frac{1}{2}ab$.

area of outer square = area of 4 blue triangles + area of inner square

$$(a + b)^2 = 4\left(\frac{1}{2}ab\right) + c^2 \qquad \textit{Substitute the areas.}$$

$$a^2 + 2ab + b^2 = 2ab + c^2 \qquad \textit{Simplify.}$$

$$a^2 + b^2 = c^2 \qquad \textit{Subtract 2ab from both sides.}$$

The Pythagorean Theorem gives you a way to find unknown side lengths when you know a triangle is a right triangle.

Online Video Tutor

EXAMPLE 1 MCC9-12.G.SRT.8

Using the Pythagorean Theorem

Find the value of x. Give your answer in simplest radical form.

A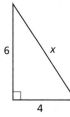

$$a^2 + b^2 = c^2 \qquad \textit{Pythagorean Theorem}$$
$$6^2 + 4^2 = x^2 \qquad \textit{Substitute 6 for a, 4 for b, and x for c.}$$
$$52 = x^2 \qquad \textit{Simplify.}$$
$$\sqrt{52} = x \qquad \textit{Find the positive square root.}$$
$$x = \sqrt{(4)(13)} = 2\sqrt{13} \qquad \textit{Simplify the radical.}$$

B

$$a^2 + b^2 = c^2 \qquad \textit{Pythagorean Theorem}$$
$$5^2 + (x-1)^2 = x^2 \qquad \textit{Substitute 5 for a, x − 1 for b, and x for c.}$$
$$25 + x^2 - 2x + 1 = x^2 \qquad \textit{Multiply.}$$
$$-2x + 26 = 0 \qquad \textit{Combine like terms.}$$
$$26 = 2x \qquad \textit{Add 2x to both sides.}$$
$$x = 13 \qquad \textit{Divide both sides by 2.}$$

Find the value of x. Give your answer in simplest radical form.

1a.

1b.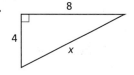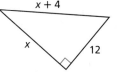

Online Video Tutor

EXAMPLE 2 MCC9-12.G.SRT.8

Safety Application

To prevent a ladder from shifting, safety experts recommend that the ratio of $a:b$ be $4:1$. How far from the base of the wall should you place the foot of a 10-foot ladder? Round to the nearest inch.

Let x be the distance in feet from the foot of the ladder to the base of the wall. Then $4x$ is the distance in feet from the top of the ladder to the base of the wall.

$$a^2 + b^2 = c^2 \qquad \textit{Pythagorean Theorem}$$
$$(4x)^2 + x^2 = 10^2 \qquad \textit{Substitute.}$$
$$17x^2 = 100 \qquad \textit{Multiply and combine like terms.}$$
$$x^2 = \frac{100}{17} \qquad \textit{Divide both sides by 17.}$$
$$x = \sqrt{\frac{100}{17}} \approx 2 \text{ ft } 5 \text{ in.} \qquad \textit{Find the positive square root and round it.}$$

2. What if...? According to the recommended ratio, how high will a 30-foot ladder reach when placed against a wall? Round to the nearest inch.

A set of three nonzero whole numbers a, b, and c such that $a^2 + b^2 = c^2$ is called a **Pythagorean triple**.

Common Pythagorean Triples			
3, 4, 5	5, 12, 13	8, 15, 17	7, 24, 25

EXAMPLE **3** Identifying Pythagorean Triples

MCC9-12.A.REI.4b

Find the missing side length. Tell if the side lengths form a Pythagorean triple. Explain.

A

$$a^2 + b^2 = c^2$$ *Pythagorean Theorem*
$$12^2 + b^2 = 15^2$$ *Substitute 12 for a and 15 for c.*
$$b^2 = 81$$ *Multiply and subtract 144 from both sides.*
$$b = 9$$ *Find the positive square root.*

The side lengths are nonzero whole numbers that satisfy the equation $a^2 + b^2 = c^2$, so they form a Pythagorean triple.

B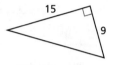

$$a^2 + b^2 = c^2$$ *Pythagorean Theorem*
$$9^2 + 15^2 = c^2$$ *Substitute 9 for a and 15 for b.*
$$306 = c^2$$ *Multiply and add.*
$$c = \sqrt{306} = 3\sqrt{34}$$ *Find the positive square root and simplify.*

The side lengths do not form a Pythagorean triple because $3\sqrt{34}$ is not a whole number.

CHECK IT OUT! **Find the missing side length. Tell if the side lengths form a Pythagorean triple. Explain.**

3a.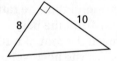

3b.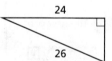

3c.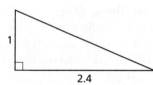

3d.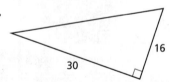

The converse of the Pythagorean Theorem gives you a way to tell if a triangle is a right triangle when you know the side lengths.

Know it! Note

Theorems 27-1-1	**Converse of the Pythagorean Theorem**	
THEOREM	**HYPOTHESIS**	**CONCLUSION**
If the sum of the squares of the lengths of two sides of a triangle is equal to the square of the length of the third side, then the triangle is a right triangle.	 $$a^2 + b^2 = c^2$$	$\triangle ABC$ is a right triangle.

You will prove Theorem 27-1-1 in Exercise 45.

You can also use side lengths to classify a triangle as acute or obtuse.

Theorems 27-1-2 (**Pythagorean Inequalities Theorem**)

In $\triangle ABC$, c is the length of the longest side.

If $c^2 > a^2 + b^2$, then $\triangle ABC$ is an **obtuse** triangle.

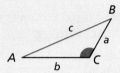

If $c^2 < a^2 + b^2$, then $\triangle ABC$ is an **acute** triangle.

To understand why the Pythagorean inequalities are true, consider $\triangle ABC$.

If $c^2 = a^2 + b^2$, then $\triangle ABC$ is a right triangle by the Converse of the Pythagorean Theorem. So $m\angle C = 90°$.

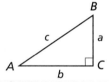

If $c^2 > a^2 + b^2$, then c has increased. By the Converse of the Hinge Theorem, $m\angle C$ has also increased. So $m\angle C > 90°$.

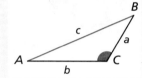

If $c^2 < a^2 + b^2$, then c has decreased. By the Converse of the Hinge Theorem, $m\angle C$ has also decreased. So $m\angle C < 90°$.

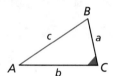

 **EXAMPLE** **4**
MCC9-12.A.CED.3

 my.hrw.com

Online Video Tutor

Classifying Triangles

Tell if the measures can be the side lengths of a triangle. If so, classify the triangle as acute, obtuse, or right.

A 8, 11, 13

Step 1 Determine if the measures form a triangle.

By the Triangle Inequality Theorem, 8, 11, and 13 can be the side lengths of a triangle.

Step 2 Classify the triangle.

$$c^2 \overset{?}{=} a^2 + b^2 \qquad \textit{Compare } c^2 \textit{ to } a^2 + b^2.$$
$$13^2 \overset{?}{=} 8^2 + 11^2 \qquad \textit{Substitute the longest side length for c.}$$
$$169 \overset{?}{=} 64 + 121 \qquad \textit{Multiply.}$$
$$169 < 185 \qquad \textit{Add and compare.}$$

Since $c^2 < a^2 + b^2$, the triangle is **acute**.

B 5.8, 9.3, 15.6

Step 1 Determine if the measures form a triangle.

Since $5.8 + 9.3 = 15.1$ and $15.1 \not> 15.6$, these cannot be the side lengths of a triangle.

 CHECK IT OUT! **Tell if the measures can be the side lengths of a triangle. If so, classify the triangle as acute, obtuse, or right.**

4a. 7, 12, 16   **4b.** 11, 18, 34   **4c.** 3.8, 4.1, 5.2

THINK AND DISCUSS

1. How do you know which numbers to substitute for *c*, *a*, and *b* when using the Pythagorean Inequalities?

2. Explain how the figure at right demonstrates the Pythagorean Theorem.

3. List the conditions that a set of three numbers must satisfy in order to form a Pythagorean triple.

4. **GET ORGANIZED** Copy and complete the graphic organizer. In each box, summarize the Pythagorean relationship.

Pythagorean Relationships
- Pythagorean Theorem
- Converse of the Pythagorean Theorem
- Pythagorean Inequalities Theorem

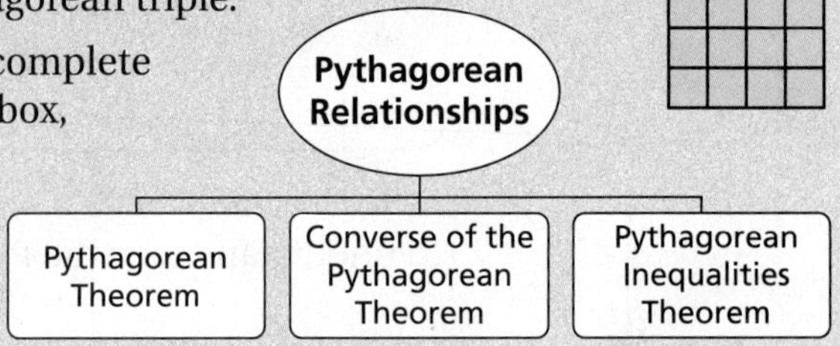

27-1 Exercises

my.hrw.com
Homework Help

GUIDED PRACTICE

1. Vocabulary Do the numbers 2.7, 3.6, and 4.5 form a *Pythagorean triple*? Explain why or why not.

SEE EXAMPLE 1 Find the value of *x*. Give your answer in simplest radical form.

2.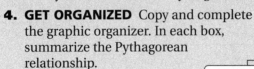

3.

4.

SEE EXAMPLE 2 **5. Computers** The size of a computer monitor is usually given by the length of its diagonal. A monitor's aspect ratio is the ratio of its width to its height. This monitor has a diagonal length of 19 inches and an aspect ratio of 5 : 4. What are the width and height of the monitor? Round to the nearest tenth of an inch.

19 in.

SEE EXAMPLE 3 Find the missing side length. Tell if the side lengths form a Pythagorean triple. Explain.

6.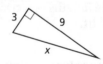

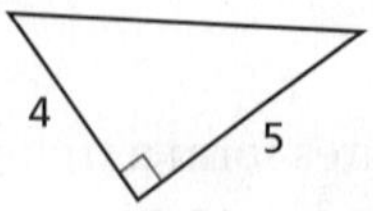

7.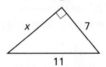

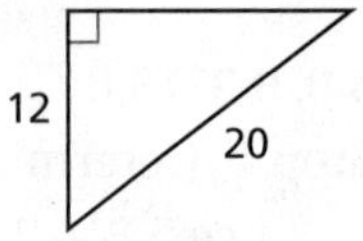

8.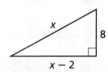

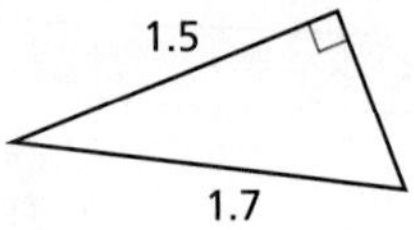

SEE EXAMPLE 4 **Multi-Step** Tell if the measures can be the side lengths of a triangle. If so, classify the triangle as acute, obtuse, or right.

9. 7, 10, 12

10. 9, 11, 15

11. 9, 40, 41

12. $1\frac{1}{2}$, $1\frac{3}{4}$, $3\frac{1}{4}$

13. 5.9, 6, 8.4

14. 11, 13, $7\sqrt{6}$

PRACTICE AND PROBLEM SOLVING

Independent Practice

For Exercises	See Example
15–17	1
18	2
19–21	3
22–27	4

my.hrw.com

Online Extra Practice

Find the value of *x*. Give your answer in simplest radical form.

15.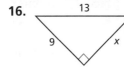

16.

17.

18. **Safety** The safety rules for a playground state that the height of the slide and the distance from the base of the ladder to the front of the slide must be in a ratio of 3:5. If a slide is about 8 feet long, what are the height of the slide and the distance from the base of the ladder to the front of the slide? Round to the nearest inch.

Find the missing side length. Tell if the side lengths form a Pythagorean triple. Explain.

19.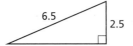

20.

21.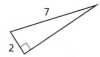

Multi-Step Tell if the measures can be the side lengths of a triangle. If so, classify the triangle as acute, obtuse, or right.

22. 10, 12, 15

23. 8, 13, 23

24. 9, 14, 17

25. $1\frac{1}{2}, 2, 2\frac{1}{2}$

26. 0.7, 1.1, 1.7

27. $7, 12, 6\sqrt{5}$

28. **Surveying** It is believed that surveyors in ancient Egypt laid out right angles using a rope divided into twelve sections by eleven equally spaced knots. How could the surveyors use this rope to make a right angle?

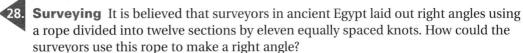

29. ///**ERROR ANALYSIS**/// Below are two solutions for finding *x*. Which is incorrect? Explain the error.

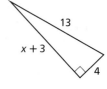

A
$$a^2 + 4^2 = 13^2$$
$$a^2 = 169 - 16 = 153$$
$$a \approx 12.4$$
$$x + 3 \approx 12.4$$
$$x \approx 9.4$$

B
$$(x + 3)^2 + 4^2 = 13^2$$
$$x^2 + 9 + 16 = 169$$
$$x^2 = 144$$
$$x = 12$$

Find the value of *x*. Give your answer in simplest radical form.

30.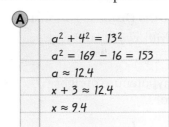

31.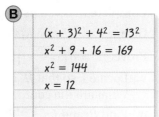

32.

33.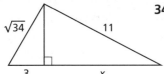

34.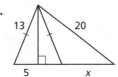

35.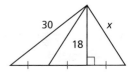

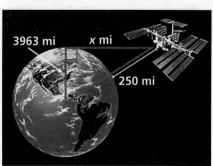

Not drawn to scale

H.O.T. 36. **Space Exploration** The International Space Station orbits at an altitude of about 250 miles above Earth's surface. The radius of Earth is approximately 3963 miles. How far can an astronaut in the space station see to the horizon? Round to the nearest mile.

37. **Critical Thinking** In the proof of the Pythagorean Theorem on the first page of this lesson, how do you know the outer figure is a square? How do you know the inner figure is a square?

Multi-Step Find the perimeter and the area of each figure. Give your answer in simplest radical form.

38.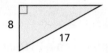

39.

40.

41.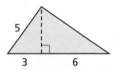

42.

43.

44. **Write About It** When you apply both the Pythagorean Theorem and its converse, you use the equation $a^2 + b^2 = c^2$. Explain in your own words how the two theorems are different.

45. Use this plan to write a paragraph proof of the Converse of the Pythagorean Theorem.

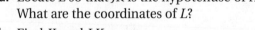

Given: $\triangle ABC$ with $a^2 + b^2 = c^2$
Prove: $\triangle ABC$ is a right triangle.

Plan: Draw $\triangle PQR$ with $\angle R$ as the right angle, leg lengths of a and b, and a hypotenuse of length x. By the Pythagorean Theorem, $a^2 + b^2 = x^2$. Use substitution to compare x and c. Show that $\triangle ABC \cong \triangle PQR$ and thus $\angle C$ is a right angle.

H.O.T. 46. Complete these steps to prove the Distance Formula.

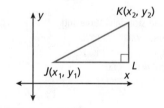

Given: $J(x_1, y_1)$ and $K(x_2, y_2)$ with $x_1 \neq x_2$ and $y_1 \neq y_2$
Prove: $JK = \sqrt{(x_2 - x_1)^2 + (y_2 - y_1)^2}$

   a. Locate L so that $\overline{JK}$ is the hypotenuse of right $\triangle JKL$. What are the coordinates of L?

   b. Find JL and LK.

   c. By the Pythagorean Theorem, $JK^2 = JL^2 + LK^2$. Find JK.

Real-World Connections

47. The figure shows an airline's routes between four cities.

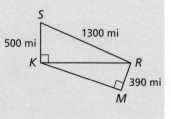

   a. A traveler wants to go from Sanak (*S*) to Manitou (*M*). To minimize the total number of miles traveled, should she first fly to King City (*K*) or to Rice Lake (*R*)?

   b. The airline decides to offer a direct flight from Sanak (*S*) to Manitou (*M*). Given that the length of this flight is more than 1360 mi, what can you say about m$\angle SRM$?

TEST PREP

48. Gridded Response $\overline{KX}$, $\overline{LX}$, and $\overline{MX}$ are the perpendicular bisectors of $\triangle GHJ$. Find GJ to the nearest tenth of a unit.

49. Which number forms a Pythagorean triple with 24 and 25?

    (A) 1   (B) 7   (C) 26   (D) 49

50. The lengths of two sides of an obtuse triangle are 7 meters and 9 meters. Which could NOT be the length of the third side?

    (F) 4 meters   (G) 5 meters   (H) 11 meters   (J) 12 meters

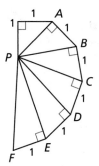

H.O.T. 51. Extended Response The figure shows the first six triangles in a pattern of triangles.

    a. Find *PA*, *PB*, *PC*, *PD*, *PE*, and *PF* in simplest radical form.

    b. If the pattern continues, what would be the length of the hypotenuse of the ninth triangle? Explain your answer.

    c. Write a rule for finding the length of the hypotenuse of the *n*th triangle in the pattern. Explain your answer.

CHALLENGE AND EXTEND

52. Algebra Find all values of k so that $(-1, 2)$, $(-10, 5)$, and $(-4, k)$ are the vertices of a right triangle.

H.O.T. 53. Critical Thinking Use a diagram of a right triangle to explain why $a + b > \sqrt{a^2 + b^2}$ for any positive numbers a and b.

54. In a right triangle, the leg lengths are a and b, and the length of the altitude to the hypotenuse is h. Write an expression for h in terms of a and b. (*Hint:* Think of the area of the triangle.)

H.O.T. 55. Critical Thinking Suppose the numbers a, b, and c form a Pythagorean triple. Is each of the following also a Pythagorean triple? Explain.

    a. $a + 1, b + 1, c + 1$ **b.** $2a, 2b, 2c$

    c. a^2, b^2, c^2 **d.** $\sqrt{a}, \sqrt{b}, \sqrt{c}$

FOCUS ON MATHEMATICAL PRACTICES

H.O.T. 56. Reasoning Joe rides his bicycle 9 blocks north, then 22 blocks east, then 3 blocks north, and then 12 blocks east. The blocks are square.

    a. How many blocks north did Joe ride? How many blocks east?

    b. Each block is 0.5 mile long. To the nearest tenth of a mile, how far is Joe from his starting point?

H.O.T. 57. Problem Solving A dog pen in the shape of a right isosceles triangle will be placed in the corner of a yard. The owner wants the pen to have an area of 200 square feet. About how much fencing will the owner need?

H.O.T. 58. Analysis $BC = 120$ and the perimeter of *ABCD* is 458.

    a. Find *AB*.

    b. Explain why $\triangle AXD$ is a right triangle.

    c. Find the perimeter of $\triangle AXD$.

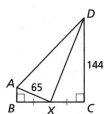

Applying Special Right Triangles

Essential Question: What are the proportions of the side lengths in 30°-60°-90° triangles and 45°-45°-90° triangles?

Objectives
Justify and apply properties of 45°-45°-90° triangles.

Justify and apply properties of 30°-60°-90° triangles.

Who uses this?
You can use properties of special right triangles to calculate the correct size of a bandana for your dog. (See Example 2.)

A diagonal of a square divides it into two congruent isosceles right triangles. Since the base angles of an isosceles triangle are congruent, the measure of each acute angle is 45°. So another name for an isosceles right triangle is a 45°-45°-90° triangle.

 Animated Math

A 45°-45°-90° triangle is one type of *special right triangle*. You can use the Pythagorean Theorem to find a relationship among the side lengths of a 45°-45°-90° triangle.

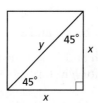

$$a^2 + b^2 = c^2 \quad \text{Pythagorean Theorem}$$
$$x^2 + x^2 = y^2 \quad \text{Substitute the given values.}$$
$$2x^2 = y^2 \quad \text{Simplify.}$$
$$\sqrt{2x^2} = \sqrt{y^2} \quad \text{Find the square root of both sides.}$$
$$x\sqrt{2} = y \quad \text{Simplify.}$$

Theorem 27-2-1 (**45°-45°-90° Triangle Theorem**)

In a 45°-45°-90° triangle, both legs are congruent, and the length of the hypotenuse is the length of a leg times $\sqrt{2}$.

$$AC = BC = \ell \qquad AB = \ell\sqrt{2}$$

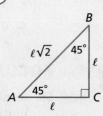

COMMON CORE GPS
MCC9-12.G.SRT.6

EXAMPLE 1 **Finding Side Lengths in a 45°-45°-90° Triangle**

Find the value of *x*. Give your answer in simplest radical form.

A

By the Triangle Sum Theorem, the measure of the third angle of the triangle is 45°. So it is a 45°-45°-90° triangle with a leg length of 7.

$$x = 7\sqrt{2} \qquad \textit{Hypotenuse} = \textit{leg}\sqrt{2}$$

Find the value of *x*. Give your answer in simplest radical form.

The triangle is an isosceles right triangle, which is a 45°-45°-90° triangle. The length of the hypotenuse is 3.

$3 = x\sqrt{2}$ *Hypotenuse = leg$\sqrt{2}$*

$\dfrac{3}{\sqrt{2}} = x$ *Divide both sides by $\sqrt{2}$.*

$\dfrac{3\sqrt{2}}{2} = x$ *Rationalize the denominator.*

CHECK IT OUT! **Find the value of *x*. Give your answer in simplest radical form.**

1a.

1b.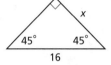

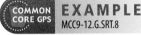

COMMON CORE GPS MCC9-12.G.SRT.8 **EXAMPLE 2**

 my.hrw.com

Online Video Tutor

Craft Application

Tessa wants to make a bandana for her dog by folding a square of cloth into a 45°-45°-90° triangle. Her dog's neck has a circumference of about 32 cm. The folded bandana needs to be an extra 16 cm long so Tessa can tie it around her dog's neck. What should the side length of the square be? Round to the nearest centimeter.

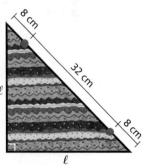

Tessa needs a 45°-45°-90° triangle with a hypotenuse of 48 cm.

$48 = \ell\sqrt{2}$ *Hypotenuse = leg$\sqrt{2}$*

$\ell = \dfrac{48}{\sqrt{2}} \approx 34 \text{ cm}$ *Divide by $\sqrt{2}$ and round.*

CHECK IT OUT! **2. What if...?** Tessa's other dog is wearing a square bandana with a side length of 42 cm. What would you expect the circumference of the other dog's neck to be? Round to the nearest centimeter.

A 30°-60°-90° triangle is another special right triangle. You can use an equilateral triangle to find a relationship between its side lengths.

Draw an altitude in $\triangle PQR$. Since $\triangle PQS \cong \triangle RQS$, $\overline{PS} \cong \overline{RS}$. Label the side lengths in terms of *x*, and use the Pythagorean Theorem to find *y*.

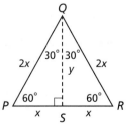

$a^2 + b^2 = c^2$ *Pythagorean Theorem*

$x^2 + y^2 = (2x)^2$ *Substitute x for a, y for b, and 2x for c.*

$y^2 = 3x^2$ *Multiply and combine like terms.*

$\sqrt{y^2} = \sqrt{3x^2}$ *Find the square root of both sides.*

$y = x\sqrt{3}$ *Simplify.*

Theorem 27-2-2 (**30°-60°-90° Triangle Theorem**)

In a 30°-60°-90° triangle, the length of the hypotenuse is is 2 times the length of the shorter leg, and the length of the longer leg is the length of the shorter leg times $\sqrt{3}$.

$$AC = s \qquad AB = 2s \qquad BC = s\sqrt{3}$$

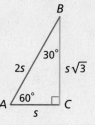

EXAMPLE MCC9-12.G.SRT.6 **3**

Finding Side Lengths in a 30°-60°-90° Triangle

Find the values of x and y. Give your answers in simplest radical form.

Online Video Tutor

A

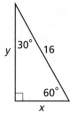

$16 = 2x$	*Hypotenuse = 2(shorter leg)*
$8 = x$	*Divide both sides by 2.*
$y = x\sqrt{3}$	*Longer leg = (shorter leg)$\sqrt{3}$*
$y = 8\sqrt{3}$	*Substitute 8 for x.*

B

$11 = x\sqrt{3}$	*Longer leg = (shorter leg)$\sqrt{3}$*
$\dfrac{11}{\sqrt{3}} = x$	*Divide both sides by $\sqrt{3}$.*
$\dfrac{11\sqrt{3}}{3} = x$	*Rationalize the denominator.*
$y = 2x$	*Hypotenuse = 2(shorter leg)*
$y = 2\left(\dfrac{11\sqrt{3}}{3}\right)$	*Substitute $\dfrac{11\sqrt{3}}{3}$ for x.*
$y = \dfrac{22\sqrt{3}}{3}$	*Simplify.*

Remember!

If two angles of a triangle are not congruent, the shorter side lies opposite the smaller angle.

CHECK IT OUT! Find the values of x and y. Give your answers in simplest radical form.

3a.
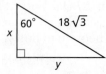

3b.
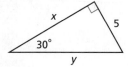

3c.
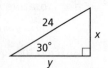

3d.
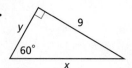

30°-60°-90° Triangles

Marcus Maiello
Johnson High School

To remember the side relationships in a 30°-60°-90° triangle, I draw a simple "1-2-√3" triangle like this.

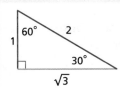

$2 = 2(1)$, so
hypotenuse $= 2$(*shorter leg*).

$\sqrt{3} = \sqrt{3}(1)$, so
longer leg $= \sqrt{3}$(*shorter leg*).

EXAMPLE 4
MCC9-12.G.SRT.8

my.hrw.com

Online Video Tutor

Using the 30°-60°-90° Triangle Theorem

The frame of the clock shown is an equilateral triangle. The length of one side of the frame is 20 cm. Will the clock fit on a shelf that is 18 cm below the shelf above it?

Step 1 Divide the equilateral triangle into two 30°-60°-90° triangles.

The height of the frame is the length of the longer leg.

Step 2 Find the length x of the shorter leg.

$20 = 2x$ *Hypotenuse* = 2(*shorter leg*)

$10 = x$ *Divide both sides by 2.*

Step 3 Find the length h of the longer leg.

$h = 10\sqrt{3} \approx 17.3$ cm   *Longer leg* = (*shorter leg*) $\sqrt{3}$

The frame is approximately 17.3 centimeters tall.
So the clock will fit on the shelf.

CHECK IT OUT!

4. What if...? A manufacturer wants to make a larger clock with a height of 30 centimeters. What is the length of each side of the frame? Round to the nearest tenth.

MCC.MP.6   **MATHEMATICAL PRACTICES**

THINK AND DISCUSS

1. Explain why an isosceles right triangle is a 45°-45°-90° triangle.

2. Describe how finding x in triangle I is different from finding x in triangle II.

I. 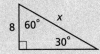   **II.**

3. GET ORGANIZED Copy and complete the graphic organizer. In each box, sketch the special right triangle and label its side lengths in terms of s.

Special Right Triangles

45°–45°–90° triangle   30°–60°–90° triangle

GUIDED PRACTICE

SEE EXAMPLE 1 · Find the value of *x*. Give your answer in simplest radical form.

1.

2.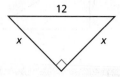

3.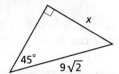

SEE EXAMPLE 2 · **4. Transportation** The two arms of the railroad sign are perpendicular bisectors of each other. In Pennsylvania, the lengths marked in red must be 19.5 inches. What is the distance labeled *d*? Round to the nearest tenth of an inch.

SEE EXAMPLE 3 · Find the values of *x* and *y*. Give your answers in simplest radical form.

5.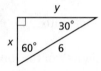

6.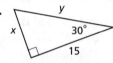

7.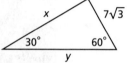

SEE EXAMPLE 4 · **8. Entertainment** Regulation billiard balls are $2\frac{1}{4}$ inches in diameter. The rack used to group 15 billiard balls is in the shape of an equilateral triangle. What is the approximate height of the triangle formed by the rack? Round to the nearest quarter of an inch.

PRACTICE AND PROBLEM SOLVING

Independent Practice	
For Exercises	See Example
9–11	1
12	2
13–15	3
16	4

my.hrw.com

Online Extra Practice

Find the value of *x*. Give your answer in simplest radical form.

9.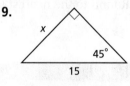

10.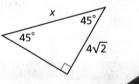

11.

12. Design This tabletop is an isosceles right triangle. The length of the front edge of the table is 48 inches. What is the length *w* of each side edge? Round to the nearest tenth of an inch.

Find the value of *x* and *y*. Give your answers in simplest radical form.

13.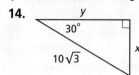

14.

15.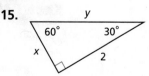

16. **Pets** A dog walk is used in dog agility competitions. In this dog walk, each ramp makes an angle of 30° with the ground.

    a. How long is one ramp?

    b. How long is the entire dog walk, including both ramps?

Multi-Step Find the perimeter and area of each figure. Give your answers in simplest radical form.

17. a 45°-45°-90° triangle with hypotenuse length 12 inches

18. a 30°-60°-90° triangle with hypotenuse length 28 centimeters

19. a square with diagonal length 18 meters

20. an equilateral triangle with side length 4 feet

21. an equilateral triangle with height 30 yards

H.O.T. 22. **Estimation** The triangle loom is made from wood strips shaped into a 45°-45°-90° triangle. Pegs are placed every $\frac{1}{2}$ inch along the hypotenuse and every $\frac{1}{4}$ inch along each leg. Suppose you make a loom with an 18-inch hypotenuse. Approximately how many pegs will you need?

H.O.T. 23. **Critical Thinking** The angle measures of a triangle are in the ratio 1 : 2 : 3. Are the side lengths also in the ratio 1 : 2 : 3? Explain your answer.

Find the coordinates of point *P* under the given conditions. Give your answers in simplest radical form.

24. △*PQR* is a 45°-45°-90° triangle with vertices *Q*(4, 6) and *R*(−6, −4), and m∠*P* = 90°. *P* is in Quadrant II.

25. △*PST* is a 45°-45°-90° triangle with vertices *S*(4, −3) and *T*(−2, 3), and m∠*S* = 90°. *P* is in Quadrant I.

26. △*PWX* is a 30°-60°-90° triangle with vertices *W*(−1, −4) and *X*(4, −4), and m∠*W* = 90°. *P* is in Quadrant II.

27. △*PYZ* is a 30°-60°-90° triangle with vertices *Y*(−7, 10) and *Z*(5, 10), and m∠*Z* = 90°. *P* is in Quadrant IV.

28. **Write About It** Why do you think 30°-60°-90° triangles and 45°-45°-90° triangles are called *special right triangles*?

Real-World Connections

29. The figure shows an airline's routes among four cities. The airline offers one frequent-flier mile for each mile flown (rounded to the nearest mile). How many frequent-flier miles do you earn for each flight?

    a. Nelson (*N*) to Belton (*B*)

    b. Idria (*I*) to Nelson (*N*)

    c. Belton (*B*) to Idria (*I*)

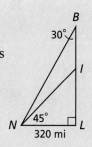

30. Which is a true statement?

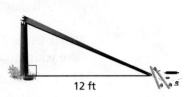

Ⓐ $AB = BC\sqrt{2}$ Ⓒ $AC = BC\sqrt{3}$

Ⓑ $AB = BC\sqrt{3}$ Ⓓ $AC = AB\sqrt{2}$

31. An 18-foot pole is broken during a storm. The top of the pole touches the ground 12 feet from the base of the pole. How tall is the part of the pole left standing?

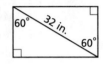

Ⓕ 5 feet   Ⓗ 13 feet

Ⓖ 6 feet   Ⓙ 22 feet

32. The length of the hypotenuse of an isosceles right triangle is 24 inches. What is the length of one leg of the triangle, rounded to the nearest tenth of an inch?

Ⓐ 13.9 inches   Ⓒ 33.9 inches

Ⓑ 17.0 inches   Ⓓ 41.6 inches

33. **Gridded Response** Find the area of the rectangle to the nearest tenth of a square inch.

CHALLENGE AND EXTEND

H.O.T. **Multi-Step** Find the value of x in each figure.

34.

35.

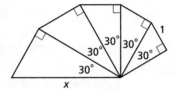

36. Each edge of the cube has length e.

a. Find the diagonal length d when $e = 1$, $e = 2$, and $e = 3$. Give the answers in simplest radical form.

b. Write a formula for d for any positive value of e.

H.O.T. 37. Write a paragraph proof to show that the altitude to the hypotenuse of a 30°-60°-90° triangle divides the hypotenuse into two segments, one of which is 3 times as long as the other.

FOCUS ON MATHEMATICAL PRACTICES

H.O.T. 38. **Number Sense** The lengths of the sides of a triangle, rounded to the nearest ten, are 60 cm, 100 cm, and 120 cm. Could the triangle be a special right triangle? If so, which one could it be?

H.O.T. 39. **Make a Conjecture** Three clocks with identical heights are shaped like isosceles triangles. They have base angles of 30°, 45°, and 60°. Order the lengths of the bases from least to greatest. Make a conjecture about the relationship between the measures of the base angles and the lengths of the bases of isosceles triangles with equal heights.

H.O.T. 40. **Reasoning** The perimeter of a 45°-45°-90° triangle is P. Write an expression for the length of one leg in terms of P.

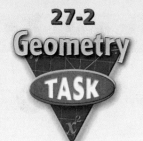

27-2
Geometry TASK

Graph Irrational Numbers

Numbers such as $\sqrt{2}$ and $\sqrt{3}$ are irrational. That is, they cannot be written as the ratio of two integers. In decimal form, they are infinite nonrepeating decimals. You can round the decimal form to estimate the location of these numbers on a number line, or you can use right triangles to construct their locations exactly.

Use with Applying Special Right Triangles

MATHEMATICAL PRACTICES Use appropriate tools strategically.

Activity

① Draw a line. Mark two points near the left side of the line and label them 0 and 1. The distance from 0 to 1 is 1 unit.

② Set your compass to 1 unit and mark increments at 2, 3, 4, and 5 units to construct a number line.

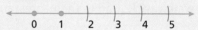

③ Construct a perpendicular to the line through 1.

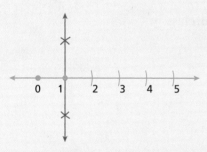

④ Using your compass, mark 1 unit up from the number line and then draw a right triangle. The legs both have length 1, so by the Pythagorean Theorem, the hypotenuse has a length of $\sqrt{2}$.

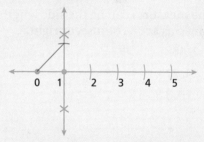

⑤ Set your compass to the length of the hypotenuse. Draw an arc centered at 0 that intersects the number line at $\sqrt{2}$.

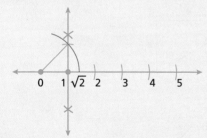

⑥ Repeat Steps 3 through 5, starting at $\sqrt{2}$, to construct a segment of length $\sqrt{3}$.

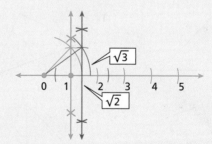

Try This

1. Sketch the two right triangles from Step 6. Label the side lengths and use the Pythagorean Theorem to show why the construction is correct.

2. Construct $\sqrt{4}$ and verify that it is equal to 2.

3. Construct $\sqrt{5}$ through $\sqrt{9}$ and verify that $\sqrt{9}$ is equal to 3.

4. Set your compass to the length of the segment from 0 to $\sqrt{2}$. Mark off another segment of length $\sqrt{2}$ to show that $\sqrt{8}$ is equal to $2\sqrt{2}$.

Ready to Go On?

my.hrw.com
Assessment and Intervention

✓ **27-1** **The Pythagorean Theorem**

1. Find the value of *x*. Give the answer in simplest radical form.

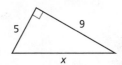

2. Find the missing side length. Tell if the side lengths form a Pythagorean triple. Explain.

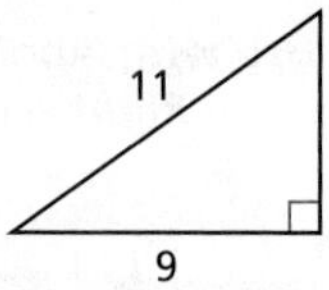

3. Tell if the measures 10, 12, and 16 can be the side lengths of a triangle. If so, classify the triangle as acute, obtuse, or right.

4. A landscaper wants to place a stone walkway from one corner of the rectangular lawn to the opposite corner. What will be the length of the walkway? Round to the nearest inch.

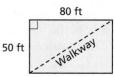

Find the missing side length. Tell if the sides form a Pythagorean triple. Explain.

5.

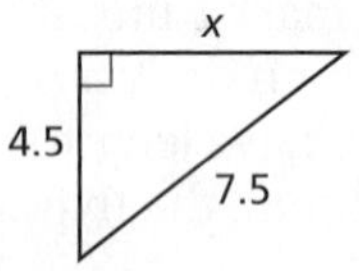

6.
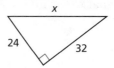

Tell if the measures can be the side lengths of a triangle. If so, classify the triangle as acute, obtuse, or right.

7. 9, 12, 16

8. 11, 14, 27

9. 1.5, 3.6, 3.9

10. 2, 3.7, 4.1

✓ **27-2** **Applying Special Right Triangles**

Find the values of the variables. Give your answers in simplest radical form.

11.

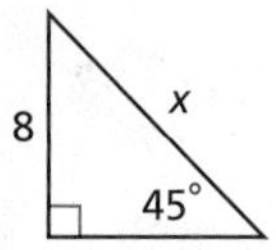

12.

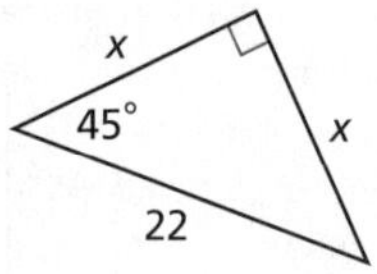

13.
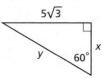

14.

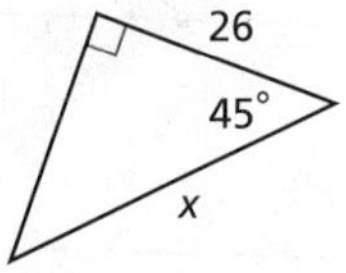

15.

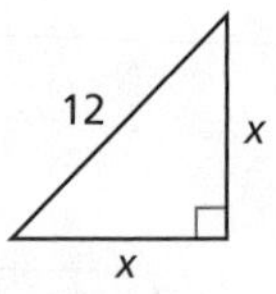

16.

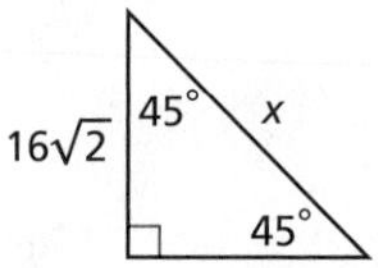

17.
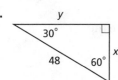

18.
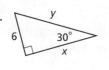

19.
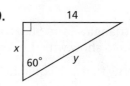

PARCC Assessment Readiness

Selected Response

1. Find the value of *x*. Express your answer in simplest radical form.

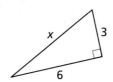

Ⓐ $x = 3\sqrt{5}$ Ⓒ $x = 3\sqrt{3}$

Ⓑ $x = 9\sqrt{5}$ Ⓓ $x = 5\sqrt{3}$

2. Find the value of *x*. Express your answer in simplest radical form.

Ⓕ $x = 11$ Ⓗ $x = 2\sqrt{65}$

Ⓖ $x = 2\sqrt{33}$ Ⓙ $x = 12\sqrt{11}$

3. Tell if the measures 9, 11, and 15 can be side lengths of a triangle. If so, classify the triangle as acute, right, or obtuse.

Ⓐ Yes; acute triangle

Ⓑ Yes; right triangle

Ⓒ Yes; obtuse triangle

Ⓓ No; the measures cannot be side lengths of a triangle.

4. The length of the hypotenuse of a right triangle is three times the length of the shorter leg. The length of the longer leg is 12. What is the length of the shorter leg?

Ⓕ $2\sqrt{3}$ Ⓗ $3\sqrt{2}$

Ⓖ $\sqrt{14.4}$ Ⓙ $6\sqrt{2}$

5. What is an expression in simplest form for the perimeter of the 30°-60°-90° triangle shown?

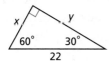

Ⓐ $22 + 22\sqrt{2}$ Ⓒ $44\sqrt{3}$

Ⓑ $33 + 22\sqrt{3}$ Ⓓ $33 + 11\sqrt{3}$

6. Each triangle is a 45°-45°-90° triangle. Find the value of *x*.

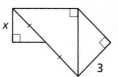

Ⓕ $x = \dfrac{3\sqrt{2}}{2}$ Ⓗ $x = 3\sqrt{2}$

Ⓖ $x = \dfrac{3}{2}$ Ⓙ $x = \dfrac{3\sqrt{3}}{2}$

7. The size of a TV screen is given by the length of its diagonal. The screen aspect ratio is the ratio of its width to its height. The screen aspect ratio of a standard TV screen is 4:3. What are the width and height of a 27″ TV screen?

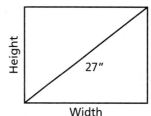

Ⓐ width: 21.6 in., height: 16.2 in.

Ⓑ width: 16.2 in., height: 21.6 in.

Ⓒ width: 21.6 in., height: 5.4 in.

Ⓓ width: 5.4 in., height: 21.6 in.

Mini-Task

8. The yield sign has the shape of an equilateral triangle with a side length of 36 inches. What is the height of the sign? Will a rectangular metal sheet 36 inches wide and 32 inches tall be big enough to make one sign?

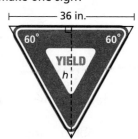

28 Trigonometry

COMMON
CORE GPS

Contents

MATHEMATICAL
PRACTICES   The Common Core Georgia Performance Standards for Mathematical Practice describe varieties of expertise that all students should seek to develop. Opportunities to develop these practices are integrated throughout this program.

1 Make sense of problems and persevere in solving them.

2 Reason abstractly and quantitatively.

3 Construct viable arguments and critique the reasoning of others.

4 Model with mathematics.

5 Use appropriate tools strategically.

6 Attend to precision.

7 Look for and make use of structure.

8 Look for and express regularity in repeated reasoning.

Unpacking the Standards

my.hrw.com
Multilingual Glossary

Understanding the standards and the vocabulary terms in the standards will help you know exactly what you are expected to learn in this chapter.

 MCC9-12.G.SRT.6

Understand that by similarity, side ratios in right triangles are properties of the angles in the triangle, leading to definitions of trigonometric ratios for acute angles.

Key Vocabulary

similar (semejantes)
 Two figures are similar if they have the same shape but not necessarily the same size.

ratio (razón)
 A comparison of two quantities by division.

right triangle (triángulo rectángulo)
 A triangle with one right (90°) angle.

angle (ángulo)
 A figure formed by two rays with a common endpoint.

trigonometric ratio (razón trigonométrica)
 A ratio of two sides of a right triangle.

acute angle (ángulo agudo)
 An angle that measures greater than 0° and less than 90°.

What It Means For You

All right triangles with the same angle measures are similar, and similar triangles have proportional side lengths. So the measures of the acute angles in a given right triangle determine the ratios of the side lengths of that triangle and of all similar triangles. These ratios, called *trigonometric ratios*, can be used to solve problems.

EXAMPLE

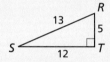

The sine of $\angle R$ is $\dfrac{\text{opposite leg}}{\text{hypotenuse}} = \dfrac{12}{13}$.

The cosine of $\angle R$ is $\dfrac{\text{adjacent leg}}{\text{hypotenuse}} = \dfrac{5}{13}$.

The tangent of $\angle R$ is $\dfrac{\text{opposite leg}}{\text{adjacent leg}} = \dfrac{12}{5}$.

28-1 Technology TASK

Explore Trigonometric Ratios

In a right triangle, the ratio of two side lengths is known as a *trigonometric ratio*.

Use with Trigonometric Ratios

Use appropriate tools strategically.

MCC9-12.G.SRT.6 Understand that … side ratios in right triangles are properties of the angles in the triangle, leading to definitions of trigonometric ratios …

Activity

1 Construct three points and label them *A*, *B*, and *C*. Construct rays $\vec{AB}$ and $\vec{AC}$ with common endpoint *A*. Move *C* so that ∠*A* is an acute angle.

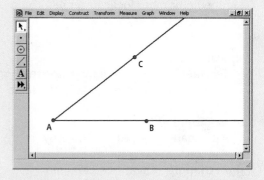

2 Construct point *D* on $\vec{AC}$. Construct a line through *D* perpendicular to $\vec{AB}$. Label the intersection of the perpendicular line and $\vec{AB}$ as *E*.

3 Measure ∠*A*. Measure *DE*, *AE*, and *AD*, the side lengths of △*AED*.

4 Calculate the ratios $\frac{DE}{AD}$, $\frac{AE}{AD}$, and $\frac{DE}{AE}$.

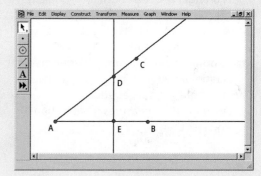

Try This

1. Drag *D* along $\vec{AC}$. What happens to the measure of ∠*A* as *D* moves? What postulate or theorem guarantees that the different triangles formed are similar to each other?

2. As you move *D*, what happens to the values of the three ratios you calculated? Use the properties of similar triangles to explain this result.

3. Move *C*. What happens to the measure of ∠*A*? With a new value for m∠*A*, note the values of the three ratios. What happens to the ratios if you drag *D*?

4. Move *C* until $\frac{DE}{AD} = \frac{AE}{AD}$. What is the value of $\frac{DE}{AE}$? What is the measure of ∠*A*? Use the properties of special right triangles to justify this result.

28-1 Trigonometric Ratios

Essential Question: How do side ratios in right triangles define trigonometric ratios?

Objectives
Find the sine, cosine, and tangent of an acute angle.

Use trigonometric ratios to find side lengths in right triangles and to solve real-world problems.

Vocabulary
trigonometric ratio
sine
cosine
tangent

Animated Math

Who uses this?
Contractors use trigonometric ratios to build ramps that meet legal requirements.

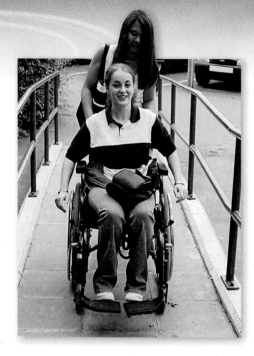

According to the Americans with Disabilities Act (ADA), the maximum slope allowed for a wheelchair ramp is $\frac{1}{12}$, which is an angle of about 4.8°. Properties of right triangles help builders construct ramps that meet this requirement.

By the AA Similarity Postulate, a right triangle with a given acute angle is similar to every other right triangle with that same acute angle measure. So $\triangle ABC \sim \triangle DEF \sim \triangle XYZ$, and $\frac{BC}{AC} = \frac{EF}{DF} = \frac{YZ}{XZ}$. These are *trigonometric ratios*. A **trigonometric ratio** is a ratio of two sides of a right triangle.

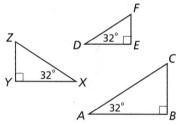

Trigonometric Ratios

DEFINITION	SYMBOLS	DIAGRAM
The **sine** of an angle is the ratio of the length of the leg opposite the angle to the length of the hypotenuse.	$\sin A = \dfrac{\text{opposite leg}}{\text{hypotenuse}} = \dfrac{a}{c}$ $\sin B = \dfrac{\text{opposite leg}}{\text{hypotenuse}} = \dfrac{b}{c}$	
The **cosine** of an angle is the ratio of the length of the leg adjacent to the angle to the length of the hypotenuse.	$\cos A = \dfrac{\text{adjacent leg}}{\text{hypotenuse}} = \dfrac{b}{c}$ $\cos B = \dfrac{\text{adjacent leg}}{\text{hypotenuse}} = \dfrac{a}{c}$	
The **tangent** of an angle is the ratio of the length of the leg opposite the angle to the length of the leg adjacent to the angle.	$\tan A = \dfrac{\text{opposite leg}}{\text{adjacent leg}} = \dfrac{a}{b}$ $\tan B = \dfrac{\text{opposite leg}}{\text{adjacent leg}} = \dfrac{b}{a}$	

Writing Math
In trigonometry, the letter of the vertex of the angle is often used to represent the measure of that angle. For example, the sine of $\angle A$ is written as $\sin A$.

COMMON CORE GPS
MCC9-12.G.SRT.6

EXAMPLE 1 Finding Trigonometric Ratios

Write each trigonometric ratio as a fraction and as a decimal rounded to the nearest hundredth.

A $\sin R$

$\sin R = \dfrac{12}{13} \approx 0.92$ *The sine of an $\angle$ is $\dfrac{\text{opp. leg}}{\text{hyp.}}$.*

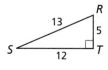

Online Video Tutor

Write each trigonometric ratio as a fraction and as a decimal rounded to the nearest hundredth.

 cos R

$\cos R = \dfrac{5}{13} \approx 0.38$ *The cosine of an $\angle$ is $\dfrac{adj.\ leg}{hyp.}$.*

 tan S

$\tan S = \dfrac{5}{12} \approx 0.42$ *The tangent of an $\angle$ is $\dfrac{opp.\ leg}{adj.\ leg}$.*

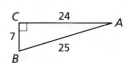

CHECK IT OUT! Write each trigonometric ratio as a fraction and as a decimal rounded to the nearest hundredth.

1a. $\cos A$ **1b.** $\tan B$ **1c.** $\sin B$

COMMON CORE GPS
EXAMPLE **2**
MCC9-12.G.SRT.6

Online Video Tutor

Finding Trigonometric Ratios in Special Right Triangles

Use a special right triangle to write sin 60° as a fraction.

Draw and label a 30°-60°-90° $\triangle$.

$\sin 60° = \dfrac{s\sqrt{3}}{2s} = \dfrac{\sqrt{3}}{2}$ *The sine of an $\angle$ is $\dfrac{opp.\ leg}{hyp.}$.*

 2. Use a special right triangle to write tan 45° as a fraction.

COMMON CORE GPS
EXAMPLE **3**
MCC9-12.G.SRT.6

Online Video Tutor

Calculating Trigonometric Ratios

Use your calculator to find each trigonometric ratio. Round to the nearest hundredth.

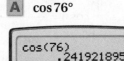

| **A** cos 76° | **B** sin 8° | **C** tan 82° |

cos(76)
.2419218956

sin(8)
.139173101

tan(82)
7.115369722

   $\cos 76° \approx 0.24$ $\sin 8° \approx 0.14$ $\tan 82° \approx 7.12$

Caution! ///////

Be sure your calculator is in degree mode, not radian mode.

CHECK IT OUT! Use your calculator to find each trigonometric ratio. Round to the nearest hundredth.

3a. $\tan 11°$ **3b.** $\sin 62°$ **3c.** $\cos 30°$

The hypotenuse is always the longest side of a right triangle. So the denominator of a sine or cosine ratio is always greater than the numerator. Therefore the sine and cosine of an acute angle are always positive numbers less than 1. Since the tangent of an acute angle is the ratio of the lengths of the legs, it can have any value greater than 0.

EXAMPLE 4 MCC9-12.G.SRT.8

Using Trigonometric Ratios to Find Lengths

Find each length. Round to the nearest hundredth.

A *AB*

$\overline{AB}$ is adjacent to the given angle, $\angle A$.
You are given BC, which is opposite $\angle A$.
Since the adjacent and opposite legs
are involved, use a tangent ratio.

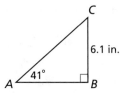

$\tan A = \dfrac{\text{opp. leg}}{\text{adj. leg}} = \dfrac{BC}{AB}$ *Write a trigonometric ratio.*

$\tan 41° = \dfrac{6.1}{AB}$ *Substitute the given values.*

$AB = \dfrac{6.1}{\tan 41°}$ *Multiply both sides by AB and divide by tan 41°.*

$AB \approx 7.02$ in.   *Simplify the expression.*

B *MP*

$\overline{MP}$ is opposite the given angle, $\angle N$.
You are given NP, which is the hypotenuse.
Since the opposite side and hypotenuse
are involved, use a sine ratio.

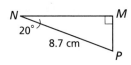

> **Caution!**
>
> Do not round until
> the final step of
> your answer. Use
> the values of the
> trigonometric ratios
> provided by your
> calculator.

$\sin N = \dfrac{\text{opp. leg}}{\text{hyp.}} = \dfrac{MP}{NP}$ *Write a trigonometric ratio.*

$\sin 20° = \dfrac{MP}{8.7}$ *Substitute the given values.*

$8.7(\sin 20°) = MP$ *Multiply both sides by 8.7.*

$MP \approx 2.98$ cm   *Simplify the expression.*

C *YZ*

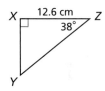

YZ is the hypotenuse. You are given XZ,
which is adjacent to the given angle, $\angle Z$.
Since the adjacent side and hypotenuse
are involved, use a cosine ratio.

$\cos Z = \dfrac{\text{adj. leg}}{\text{hyp.}} = \dfrac{XZ}{YZ}$ *Write a trigonometric ratio.*

$\cos 38° = \dfrac{12.6}{YZ}$ *Substitute the given values.*

$YZ = \dfrac{12.6}{\cos 38°}$ *Multiply both sides by YZ and divide by cos 38°.*

$YZ \approx 15.99$ cm   *Simplify the expression.*

CHECK IT OUT!

Find each length. Round to the nearest hundredth.

4a. *DF*

4b. *ST*

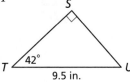

4c. *BC*

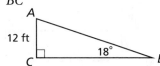

4d. *JL*

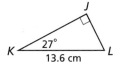

my.hrw.com

Online Video Tutor

EXAMPLE **5**
MCC9-12.G.SRT.8

Problem Solving Application

A contractor is building a wheelchair ramp for a doorway that is 1.2 ft above the ground. To meet ADA guidelines, the ramp will make an angle of 4.8° with the ground. To the nearest hundredth of a foot, what is the horizontal distance covered by the ramp?

1 Understand the Problem

Make a sketch. The **answer** is BC.

2 Make a Plan

$\overline{BC}$ is the leg adjacent to $\angle C$. You are given AB, which is the leg opposite $\angle C$. Since the opposite and adjacent legs are involved, write an equation using the tangent ratio.

3 Solve

$\tan C = \dfrac{AB}{BC}$ *Write a trigonometric ratio.*

$\tan 4.8° = \dfrac{1.2}{BC}$ *Substitute the given values.*

$BC = \dfrac{1.2}{\tan 4.8°}$ *Multiply both sides by BC and divide by tan 4.8°.*

$BC \approx 14.2904$ ft   *Simplify the expression.*

4 Look Back

The problem asks for BC rounded to the nearest hundredth, so round the length to 14.29. The ramp covers a horizontal distance of 14.29 ft.

 CHECK IT OUT!

5. Find AC, the length of the ramp in Example 5, to the nearest hundredth of a foot.

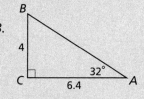
MCC.MP.4   MATHEMATICAL PRACTICES

THINK AND DISCUSS

1. Tell how you could use a sine ratio to find AB.

2. Tell how you could use a cosine ratio to find AB.

3. GET ORGANIZED Copy and complete the graphic organizer. In each cell, write the meaning of each abbreviation and draw a diagram for each.

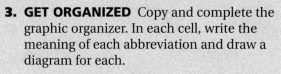

Abbreviation	Words	Diagram
$\sin = \dfrac{\text{opp. leg}}{\text{hyp.}}$		
$\cos = \dfrac{\text{adj. leg}}{\text{hyp.}}$		
$\tan = \dfrac{\text{opp. leg}}{\text{adj. leg}}$		

GUIDED PRACTICE

Vocabulary Apply the vocabulary from this lesson to answer each question.

1. In $\triangle JKL$, $\angle K$ is a right angle. Write the *sine* of $\angle J$ as a ratio of side lengths.

2. In $\triangle MNP$, $\angle M$ is a right angle. Write the *tangent* of $\angle N$ as a ratio of side lengths.

SEE EXAMPLE **1** Write each trigonometric ratio as a fraction and as a decimal rounded to the nearest hundredth.

3. $\sin C$ **4.** $\tan A$ **5.** $\cos A$

6. $\cos C$ **7.** $\tan C$ **8.** $\sin A$

SEE EXAMPLE **2** Use a special right triangle to write each trigonometric ratio as a fraction.

9. $\cos 60°$ **10.** $\tan 30°$ **11.** $\sin 45°$

SEE EXAMPLE **3** Use your calculator to find each trigonometric ratio. Round to the nearest hundredth.

12. $\tan 67°$ **13.** $\sin 23°$ **14.** $\sin 49°$

15. $\cos 88°$ **16.** $\cos 12°$ **17.** $\tan 9°$

SEE EXAMPLE **4** Find each length. Round to the nearest hundredth.

18. BC **19.** QR **20.** KL

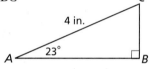
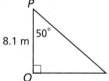
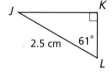

SEE EXAMPLE **5** **21. Architecture** A pediment has a pitch of 15°, as shown. If the width of the pediment, WZ, is 56 ft, what is XY to the nearest inch?

PRACTICE AND PROBLEM SOLVING

Write each trigonometric ratio as a fraction and as a decimal rounded to the nearest hundredth.

22. $\cos D$ **23.** $\tan D$ **24.** $\tan F$

25. $\cos F$ **26.** $\sin F$ **27.** $\sin D$

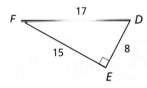

Use a special right triangle to write each trigonometric ratio as a fraction.

28. $\tan 60°$ **29.** $\sin 30°$ **30.** $\cos 45°$

Use your calculator to find each trigonometric ratio. Round to the nearest hundredth.

31. $\tan 51°$ **32.** $\sin 80°$ **33.** $\cos 77°$

34. $\tan 14°$ **35.** $\sin 55°$ **36.** $\cos 48°$

my.hrw.com

Online Extra Practice

Find each length. Round to the nearest hundredth.

37. *PQ*

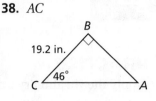

11 cm
19°

38. *AC*

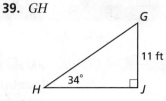

B
19.2 in.
46°
C   A

39. *GH*

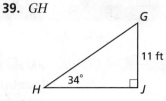

G
11 ft
34°
H   J

40. *XZ*

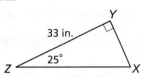

Y
33 in.
25°
Z   X

41. *KL*

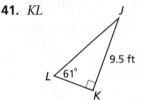

J
9.5 ft
61°
L
K

42. *EF*

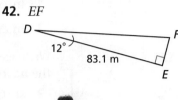

D   F
12°
83.1 m
E

H.O.T. 43. Sports A jump ramp for waterskiing makes an angle of 15° with the surface of the water. The ramp rises 1.58 m above the surface. What is the length of the ramp to the nearest hundredth of a meter?

1.58 m
15°

Use special right triangles to complete each statement.

44. An angle that measures ___?___ has a tangent of 1.

45. For a 45° angle, the ___?___ and ___?___ ratios are equal.

46. The sine of a ___?___ angle is 0.5.

47. The cosine of a 30° angle is equal to the sine of a ___?___ angle.

H.O.T. 48. Safety According to the Occupational Safety and Health Administration (OSHA), a ladder that is placed against a wall should make a 75.5° angle with the ground for optimal safety. To the nearest tenth of a foot, what is the maximum height that a 10-ft ladder can safely reach?

Find the indicated length in each rectangle. Round to the nearest tenth.

49. *BC*

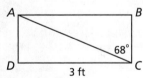

A   B
68°
D   3 ft   C

50. *SU*

R   S
49°
U   9.4 in.   T

H.O.T. 51. Critical Thinking For what angle measures is the tangent ratio less than 1? greater than 1? Explain.

Real-World Connections

52. A utility worker is installing a 25-foot pole $\overline{AB}$ at the foot of a hill. Two guy wires, $\overline{AC}$ and $\overline{AD}$, will help keep the pole vertical.

   a. To the nearest inch, how long should $\overline{AC}$ be?

   b. $\overline{AD}$ is perpendicular to the hill, which makes an angle of 28° with a horizontal line. To the nearest inch, how long should this guy wire be?

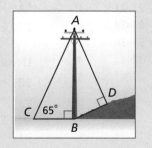

A
D
C 65°
B

(cr) Kevin Fleming/Corbis; (bl) Nicholas Eveleigh/Alamy

53. Find the sine of the smaller acute angle in a triangle with side lengths of 3, 4, and 5 inches.

54. Find the tangent of the greater acute angle in a triangle with side lengths of 7, 24, and 25 centimeters.

55. **History** The Great Pyramid of Cheops in Giza, Egypt, was completed around 2566 B.C.E. Its original height was 482 ft. Each face of the pyramid forms a 52° angle with the ground. To the nearest foot, how long is the base of the pyramid?

56. **Measurement** Follow these steps to calculate trigonometric ratios.

   a. Use a centimeter ruler to find AB, BC, and AC.

   b. Use your measurements from part **a** to find the sine, cosine, and tangent of $\angle A$.

   c. Use a protractor to find m$\angle A$.

   d. Use a calculator to find the sine, cosine, and tangent of $\angle A$.

   e. How do the values in part **d** compare to the ones you found in part **b**?

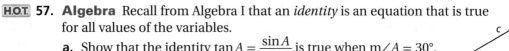

H.O.T. 57. **Algebra** Recall from Algebra I that an *identity* is an equation that is true for all values of the variables.

   a. Show that the identity $\tan A = \dfrac{\sin A}{\cos A}$ is true when m$\angle A = 30°$.

   b. Write $\tan A$, $\sin A$, and $\cos A$ in terms of a, b, and c.

   c. Use your results from part **b** to prove the identity $\tan A = \dfrac{\sin A}{\cos A}$.

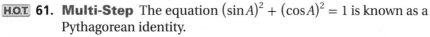

Verify that $(\sin A)^2 + (\cos A)^2 = 1$ **for each angle measure.**

58. m$\angle A = 45°$ **59.** m$\angle A = 30°$ **60.** m$\angle A = 60°$

H.O.T. 61. **Multi-Step** The equation $(\sin A)^2 + (\cos A)^2 = 1$ is known as a Pythagorean identity.

   a. Write $\sin A$ and $\cos A$ in terms of a, b, and c.

   b. Use your results from part **a** to prove the identity $(\sin A)^2 + (\cos A)^2 = 1$.

   c. **Write About It** Why do you think the identity is called a Pythagorean identity?

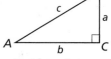

Find the perimeter and area of each triangle. Round to the nearest hundredth.

62.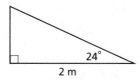
24°
2 m

63.
51°
7.2 cm

64.
58°
4 ft

65.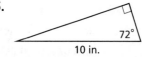
72°
10 in.

66. **Critical Thinking** Draw $\triangle ABC$ with $\angle C$ a right angle. Write $\sin A$ and $\cos B$ in terms of the side lengths of the triangle. What do you notice? How are $\angle A$ and $\angle B$ related? Make a conjecture based on your observations.

67. **Write About It** Explain how the tangent of an acute angle changes as the angle measure increases.

68. Which expression can be used to find AB?

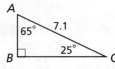

- Ⓐ $7.1(\sin 25°)$ Ⓒ $7.1(\sin 65°)$
- Ⓑ $7.1(\cos 25°)$ Ⓓ $7.1(\tan 65°)$

69. A steel cable supports an electrical tower as shown.
The cable makes a 65° angle with the ground.
The base of the cable is 17 ft from the tower.
What is the height of the tower to the nearest foot?

- Ⓕ 8 feet Ⓗ 36 feet
- Ⓖ 15 feet Ⓙ 40 feet

70. Which of the following has the same value as $\sin M$?

- Ⓐ $\sin N$ Ⓒ $\cos N$
- Ⓑ $\tan M$ Ⓓ $\cos M$

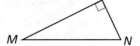

CHALLENGE AND EXTEND

Algebra Find the value of x. Then find AB, BC, and AC. Round each to the nearest unit.

71.

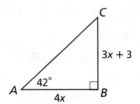

72.

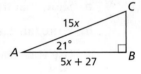

H.O.T. **73. Multi-Step** Prove the identity $(\tan A)^2 + 1 = \dfrac{1}{(\cos A)^2}$.

74. A regular pentagon with 1 in. sides is inscribed in a circle.
Find the radius of the circle rounded to the nearest hundredth.

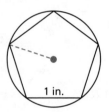

Each of the three trigonometric ratios has a reciprocal ratio,
as defined below. These ratios are *cosecant* (csc), *secant* (sec),
and *cotangent* (cot).

$$\csc A = \frac{1}{\sin A} \qquad \sec A = \frac{1}{\cos A} \qquad \cot A = \frac{1}{\tan A}$$

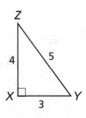

Find each trigonometric ratio to the nearest hundredth.

75. $\csc Y$ **76.** $\sec Z$ **77.** $\cot Y$

FOCUS ON MATHEMATICAL PRACTICES

H.O.T. **78. Analysis** Use the definitions of the sine and cosine ratios for acute angles.

a. For which acute angle A does $\sin A = \cos A$? Explain.

b. For which acute angles A is $\sin A > \cos A$? For which acute angles A is $\sin A < \cos A$? Explain.

H.O.T. **79. Error Analysis** For the question, "If $\angle A$ is an acute angle of a right triangle, which is greater, $\sin A$ or $\tan A$?" Danielle wrote the answer shown. Is she correct? If not, explain her error and correct her work.

> $\sin A = \dfrac{a}{c}$ and $\tan A = \dfrac{a}{b}$. Since the hypotenuse is the longest side
> of a right triangle, $c > b$, so $\dfrac{a}{c} > \dfrac{a}{b}$. Therefore $\sin A > \tan A$.

Trigonometric Ratios and Complementary Angles

 Essential Question: How is the sine ratio of one acute angle in a right triangle related to the cosine ratio of the other acute angle?

Objectives
Use the relationship between the sine and cosine of complementary angles.

The acute angles of a right triangle are complementary angles. If the measure of one of the two acute angles is given, the measure of the second acute angle can be found by subtracting the given measure from 90°.

COMMON CORE GPS MCC9-12.G.SRT.7 **EXAMPLE 1** Finding the Sine and Cosine of Acute Angles

Vocabulary
cofunction

Find the sine and cosine of the acute angles in the right triangle shown.

Start with the sine and cosine of $\angle A$.

$$\sin A = \frac{\text{opposite}}{\text{hypotenuse}} = \frac{6}{10} = \frac{3}{5}$$

$$\cos A = \frac{\text{adjacent}}{\text{hypotenuse}} = \frac{8}{10} = \frac{4}{5}$$

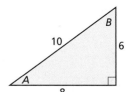

Then, find the sine and cosine of $\angle B$.

$$\sin B = \frac{\text{opposite}}{\text{hypotenuse}} = \frac{8}{10} = \frac{4}{5}$$

$$\cos B = \frac{\text{adjacent}}{\text{hypotenuse}} = \frac{6}{10} = \frac{3}{5}$$

 CHECK IT OUT! **1.** Find the sine and cosine of the acute angles of a right triangle with sides 10, 24, 26. (Use A for the angle opposite the side with length 10 and B for the angle opposite the side with length 24.)

In Example 1, notice that $\sin A = \cos B$ and $\cos A = \sin B$. In general, the sine of an acute angle is equal to the cosine of the complement of that angle.

The trigonometric function of the complement of an angle is called a **cofunction.** The sine and cosines are cofunctions of each other.

COMMON CORE GPS MCC9-12.G.SRT.7 **EXAMPLE 2** Writing Sine in Cosine Terms and Cosine in Sine Terms

A Write sin 42° in terms of the cosine.

$\sin 42° = \cos(90 - 42)°$
$\quad\quad = \cos 48°$

B Write cos 36° in terms of the sine.

$\cos 36° = \sin(90 - 36)°$
$\quad\quad = \sin 54°$

 CHECK IT OUT! **2a.** Write sin 28° in terms of the cosine.

2b. Write cos 51° in terms of the sine.

Find two angles that satisfy the equation.

$$\sin(2x - 4)° = \cos(3x + 9)°$$

If $\sin(2x - 4)° = \cos(3x + 9)°$, then $(2x - 4)°$ and $(3x + 9)°$ are the measures of complementary angles. The sum of the measures must be 90°.

$$(2x - 4) + (3x + 9) = 90$$
$$5x + 5 = 90$$
$$5x = 85$$
$$x = 17$$

Substitute the value of x into the original expression to find the angle measures.

$$2x - 4 = 2(17) - 4$$
$$= 30°$$

$$3x + 9 = 3(17) + 9$$
$$= 60°$$

The measurements of the two angles are 30° and 60°.

CHECK IT OUT! Find the two angles that satisfy the equation

3a. $\sin(3x + 2)° = \cos(x + 44)°$.

3b. $\sin(2x + 20)° = \cos(3x + 30)°$.

EXTENSION

Exercises

Find the cosine and sine of the acute angles in the triangles shown.

1.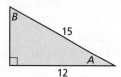

2.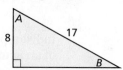

Write each trigonometric function in terms of its cofunction.

3. sin 64°

4. cos 84°

5. cos 38°

6. sin 24°

7. cos 72°

8. sin 45°

Find two angles that satisfy each equation.

9. $\sin(4x + 30)° = \cos(-2x + 54)°$

10. $\sin(-2x + 92)° = \cos(x + 8)°$

11. $\cos(5x + 49)° = \sin(3x + 57)°$

12. $\cos(-3x + 106)° = \sin(7x - 64)°$

13. $\sin(2x + 30)° = \cos(3x + 5)°$

14. $\sin(5x - 12)° = \cos(x + 54)°$

15. $\cos(3x - 10)° = \sin(3x - 20)°$

16. $\cos(7x - 68)° = \sin(-3x + 110)°$

Inverse Functions

In Algebra, you learned that a function is a relation in which each element of the domain is paired with exactly one element of the range. If you switch the domain and range of a one-to-one function, you create an *inverse function*.

The function $y = \sin^{-1} x$ is the inverse of the function $y = \sin x$.

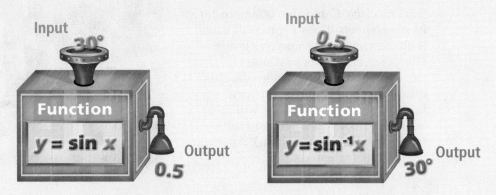

If you know the value of a trigonometric ratio, you can use the inverse trigonometric function to find the angle measure. You can do this either with a calculator or by looking at the graph of the function.

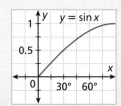
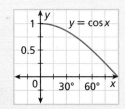
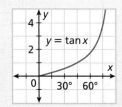

Example

Use the graphs above to find the value of x for $1 = \sin x$. Then write this expression using an inverse trigonometric function.

$1 = \sin x$ *Look at the graph of $y = \sin x$. Find where the graph intersects the line $y = 1$ and read the corresponding x-coordinate.*

$x = 90°$

$90° = \sin^{-1}(1)$ *Switch the x- and y-values.*

Try This

Use the graphs above to find the value of x for each of the following. Then write each expression using an inverse trigonometric function.

1. $0 = \sin x$ **2.** $\frac{1}{2} = \cos x$ **3.** $1 = \tan x$

4. $0 = \cos x$ **5.** $0 = \tan x$ **6.** $\frac{1}{2} = \sin x$

28-2 Solving Right Triangles

? Essential Question: How can you use inverse trigonometric functions to solve for the angles in a right triangle?

Objective
Use trigonometric ratios to find angle measures in right triangles and to solve real-world problems.

Why learn this?
You can convert the percent grade of a road to an angle measure by solving a right triangle.

San Francisco, California, is famous for its steep streets. The steepness of a road is often expressed as a *percent grade*. Filbert Street, the steepest street in San Francisco, has a 31.5% grade. This means the road rises 31.5 ft over a horizontal distance of 100 ft, which is equivalent to a 17.5° angle. You can use trigonometric ratios to change a percent grade to an angle measure.

my.hrw.com

Online Video Tutor

Identifying Angles from Trigonometric Ratios

Use the trigonometric ratio $\cos A = 0.6$ to determine which angle of the triangle is $\angle A$.

$\cos A = \dfrac{\text{adj. leg}}{\text{hyp.}}$ *Cosine is the ratio of the adjacent leg to the hypotenuse.*

$\cos \angle 1 = \dfrac{3.6}{6} = 0.6$ *The leg adjacent to $\angle 1$ is 3.6. The hypotenuse is 6.*

$\cos \angle 2 = \dfrac{4.8}{6} = 0.8$ *The leg adjacent to $\angle 2$ is 4.8. The hypotenuse is 6.*

Since $\cos A = \cos \angle 1$, $\angle 1$ is $\angle A$.

CHECK IT OUT! Use the given trigonometric ratio to determine which angle of the triangle is $\angle A$.

1a. $\sin A = \dfrac{8}{17}$ **1b.** $\tan A = 1.875$

You have learned that $\sin 30° = 0.5$. Conversely, if you know that the sine of an acute angle is 0.5, you can conclude that the angle measures 30°. This is written as $\sin^{-1}(0.5) = 30°$.

Reading Math

The expression $\sin^{-1}x$ is read "the inverse sine of x." It does *not* mean $\dfrac{1}{\sin x}$. You can think of $\sin^{-1}x$ as "the angle whose sine is x."

If you know the sine, cosine, or tangent of an acute angle measure, you can use the inverse trigonometric functions to find the measure of the angle.

Inverse Trigonometric Functions
If $\sin A = x$, then $\sin^{-1}x = m\angle A$.
If $\cos A = x$, then $\cos^{-1}x = m\angle A$.
If $\tan A = x$, then $\tan^{-1}x = m\angle A$.

Photo Edit Inc.

COMMON CORE GPS **EXAMPLE** MCC9-12.G.SRT.8 **2**

Calculating Angle Measures from Trigonometric Ratios

Use your calculator to find each angle measure to the nearest degree.

A $\cos^{-1}(0.5)$ **B** $\sin^{-1}(0.45)$ **C** $\tan^{-1}(3.2)$

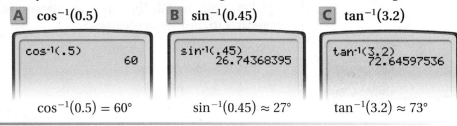

$\cos^{-1}(0.5) = 60°$ $\sin^{-1}(0.45) \approx 27°$ $\tan^{-1}(3.2) \approx 73°$

my.hrw.com

Online Video Tutor

 CHECK IT OUT! Use your calculator to find each angle measure to the nearest degree.

2a. $\tan^{-1}(0.75)$ **2b.** $\cos^{-1}(0.05)$ **2c.** $\sin^{-1}(0.67)$

Using given measures to find the unknown angle measures or side lengths of a triangle is known as *solving a triangle*. To solve a right triangle, you need to know two side lengths or one side length and an acute angle measure.

COMMON CORE GPS **EXAMPLE** MCC9-12.G.SRT.8 **3**

Solving Right Triangles

Find the unknown measures. Round lengths to the nearest hundredth and angle measures to the nearest degree.

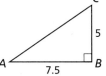

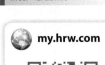

my.hrw.com

Online Video Tutor

Method 1:

By the Pythagorean Theorem,
$AC^2 = AB^2 + BC^2$.

$= (7.5)^2 + 5^2 = 81.25$

So $AC = \sqrt{81.25} \approx 9.01$.

$m\angle A = \tan^{-1}\left(\dfrac{5}{7.5}\right) \approx 34°$

Since the acute angles of a right triangle are complementary,
$m\angle C \approx 90° - 34° \approx 56°$.

Method 2:

$m\angle A = \tan^{-1}\left(\dfrac{5}{7.5}\right) \approx 34°$

Since the acute angles of a right triangle are complementary,
$m\angle C \approx 90° - 34° \approx 56°$.

$\sin A = \dfrac{5}{AC}$, so $AC = \dfrac{5}{\sin A}$.

$AC \approx \dfrac{5}{\sin\left[\tan^{-1}\left(\dfrac{5}{7.5}\right)\right]} \approx 9.01$

Helpful Hint

When using your calculator to find the value of an inverse trigonometric expression, you may need to press the [arc], [inv], or [2nd] key.

 CHECK IT OUT! **3.** Find the unknown measures. Round lengths to the nearest hundredth and angle measures to the nearest degree.

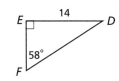

Student to Student   *Solving Right Triangles*

Kendell Waters
Marshall High School

Rounding can really make a difference! To find AC, I used the Pythagorean Theorem and got 15.62.

Then I did it a different way. I used $m\angle A = tan^{-1}\left(\dfrac{10}{12}\right)$ to find $m\angle A = 39.8056°$, which I rounded to 40°. $\sin 40° = \dfrac{10}{AC}$, so $AC = \dfrac{10}{\sin 40°} \approx 15.56$.

The difference in the two answers reminded me not to round values until the last step.

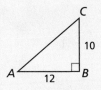

PhotoEdit

28-2 Solving Right Triangles   **853**

EXAMPLE 4
MCC9-12.G.SRT.8

Solving a Right Triangle in the Coordinate Plane

The coordinates of the vertices of $\triangle JKL$ are $J(-1, 2)$, $K(-1, -3)$, and $L(3, -3)$. Find the side lengths to the nearest hundredth and the angle measures to the nearest degree.

Step 1 Find the side lengths.

Plot points J, K, and L.

$JK = 5 \qquad KL = 4$

By the Distance Formula,

$JL = \sqrt{[3 - (-1)]^2 + (-3 - 2)^2}$.

$= \sqrt{4^2 + (-5)^2}$

$= \sqrt{16 + 25} = \sqrt{41} \approx 6.40$

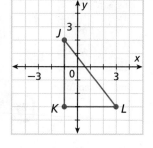

Step 2 Find the angle measures.

$m\angle K = 90°$ *$\overline{JK}$ and $\overline{KL}$ are $\perp$.*

$m\angle J = \tan^{-1}\left(\dfrac{4}{5}\right) \approx 39°$ *$\overline{KL}$ is opp. $\angle J$, and $\overline{JK}$ is adj. to $\angle J$.*

$m\angle L \approx 90° - 39° \approx 51°$ *The acute $\angle$ of a rt. $\triangle$ are comp.*

 4. The coordinates of the vertices of $\triangle RST$ are $R(-3, 5)$, $S(4, 5)$, and $T(4, -2)$. Find the side lengths to the nearest hundredth and the angle measures to the nearest degree.

EXAMPLE 5
MCC9-12.G.SRT.8

Travel Application

San Francisco's Lombard Street is known as one of "the crookedest streets in the world." The road's eight switchbacks were built in the 1920s to make the steep hill passable by cars. If the hill has a percent grade of 84%, what angle does the hill make with a horizontal line? Round to the nearest degree.

$84\% = \dfrac{84}{100}$ *Change the percent grade to a fraction.*

An 84% grade means the hill rises 84 ft for every 100 ft of horizontal distance.

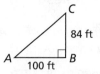

Draw a right triangle to represent the hill.

$\angle A$ is the angle the hill makes with a horizontal line.

$m\angle A = \tan^{-1}\left(\dfrac{84}{100}\right) \approx 40°$

 5. Baldwin St. in Dunedin, New Zealand, is the steepest street in the world. It has a grade of 38%. To the nearest degree, what angle does Baldwin St. make with a horizontal line?

Getty Images

THINK AND DISCUSS

1. Describe the steps you would use to solve △*RST*.

2. Given that cos *Z* = 0.35, write an equivalent statement using an inverse trigonometric function.

3. **GET ORGANIZED** Copy and complete the graphic organizer. In each box, write a trigonometric ratio for ∠*A*. Then write an equivalent statement using an inverse trigonometric function.

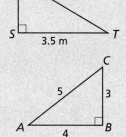

	Trigonometric Ratio	Inverse Trigonometric Function
Sine		
Cosine		
Tangent		

28-2 Exercises

my.hrw.com
Homework Help

GUIDED PRACTICE

SEE EXAMPLE 1

Use the given trigonometric ratio to determine which angle of the triangle is ∠*A*.

1. $\sin A = \dfrac{4}{5}$
2. $\tan A = 1\dfrac{1}{3}$
3. $\cos A = 0.6$
4. $\cos A = 0.8$
5. $\tan A = 0.75$
6. $\sin A = 0.6$

SEE EXAMPLE 2

Use your calculator to find each angle measure to the nearest degree.

7. $\tan^{-1}(2.1)$
8. $\cos^{-1}\left(\dfrac{1}{3}\right)$
9. $\cos^{-1}\left(\dfrac{5}{6}\right)$
10. $\sin^{-1}(0.5)$
11. $\sin^{-1}(0.61)$
12. $\tan^{-1}(0.09)$

SEE EXAMPLE 3

Multi-Step Find the unknown measures. Round lengths to the nearest hundredth and angle measures to the nearest degree.

13.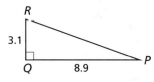

14. 15.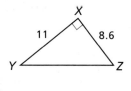

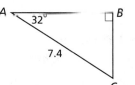

SEE EXAMPLE 4

Multi-Step For each triangle, find the side lengths to the nearest hundredth and the angle measures to the nearest degree.

16. $D(4, 1), E(4, -2), F(-2, -2)$
17. $R(3, 3), S(-2, 3), T(-2, -3)$
18. $X(4, -6), Y(-3, 1), Z(-3, -6)$
19. $A(-1, 1), B(1, 1), C(1, 5)$

SEE EXAMPLE 5 **20. Cycling** A hill in the Tour de France bike race has a grade of 8%. To the nearest degree, what is the angle that this hill makes with a horizontal line?

PRACTICE AND PROBLEM SOLVING

Independent Practice	
For Exercises	**See Example**
21–26	1
27–32	2
33–35	3
36–37	4
38	5

my.hrw.com

Online Extra Practice

Use the given trigonometric ratio to determine which angle of the triangle is ∠A.

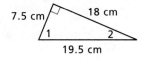

21. $\tan A = \dfrac{5}{12}$ **22.** $\tan A = 2.4$ **23.** $\sin A = \dfrac{12}{13}$

24. $\sin A = \dfrac{5}{13}$ **25.** $\cos A = \dfrac{12}{13}$ **26.** $\cos A = \dfrac{5}{13}$

Use your calculator to find each angle measure to the nearest degree.

27. $\sin^{-1}(0.31)$ **28.** $\tan^{-1}(1)$ **29.** $\cos^{-1}(0.8)$

30. $\cos^{-1}(0.72)$ **31.** $\tan^{-1}(1.55)$ **32.** $\sin^{-1}\left(\dfrac{9}{17}\right)$

Multi-Step Find the unknown measures. Round lengths to the nearest hundredth and angle measures to the nearest degree.

33. 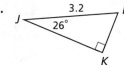   **34.** 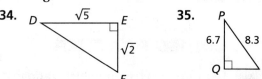   **35.**

Multi-Step For each triangle, find the side lengths to the nearest hundredth and the angle measures to the nearest degree.

36. $A(2, 0)$, $B(2, -5)$, $C(1, -5)$ **37.** $M(3, 2)$, $N(3, -2)$, $P(-1, -2)$

H.O.T. 38. Building For maximum accessibility, a wheelchair ramp should have a slope between $\dfrac{1}{16}$ and $\dfrac{1}{20}$. What is the range of angle measures that a ramp should make with a horizontal line? Round to the nearest degree.

Complete each statement. If necessary, round angle measures to the nearest degree. Round other values to the nearest hundredth.

39. $\tan \underline{\ \ ?\ \ } \approx 3.5$ **40.** $\sin \underline{\ \ ?\ \ } \approx \dfrac{2}{3}$ **41.** $\underline{\ \ ?\ \ }\ 42° \approx 0.74$

42. $\cos^{-1}\left(\underline{\ \ ?\ \ }\right) \approx 12°$ **43.** $\sin^{-1}\left(\underline{\ \ ?\ \ }\right) \approx 69°$ **44.** $\underline{\ \ ?\ \ }\ 60° = \dfrac{1}{2}$

H.O.T. 45. Critical Thinking Use trigonometric ratios to explain why the diagonal of a square forms a 45° angle with each of the sides.

46. Estimation You can use trigonometry to find angle measures when a protractor is not available.

a. Estimate the measure of ∠P.

b. Use a centimeter ruler to find RQ and PQ.

c. Use your measurements from part **b** and an inverse trigonometric function to find m∠P to the nearest degree.

d. How does your result in part **c** compare to your estimate in part **a**?

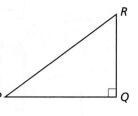

Getty Images Sport/ Bobby Julich

Real-World Connections

47. An electric company wants to install a vertical utility pole at the base of a hill that has an 8% grade.

    a. To the nearest degree, what angle does the hill make with a horizontal line?

    b. What is the measure of the angle between the pole and the hill? Round to the nearest degree.

    c. A utility worker installs a 31-foot guy wire from the top of the pole to the hill. Given that the guy wire is perpendicular to the hill, find the height of the pole to the nearest inch.

The side lengths of a right triangle are given below. Find the measures of the acute angles in the triangle. Round to the nearest degree.

48. 3, 4, 5   **49.** 5, 12, 13   **50.** 8, 15, 17

51. What if...? A right triangle has leg lengths of 28 and 45 inches. Suppose the length of the longer leg doubles. What happens to the measure of the acute angle opposite that leg?

52. Fitness As part of off-season training, the Houston Texans football team must sprint up a ramp with a 28% grade. To the nearest degree, what angle does this ramp make with a horizontal line?

53. The coordinates of the vertices of a triangle are $A(-1, 0)$, $B(6, 1)$, and $C(0, 3)$.

    a. Use the Distance Formula to find AB, BC, and AC.

    b. Use the Converse of the Pythagorean Theorem to show that $\triangle ABC$ is a right triangle. Identify the right angle.

    c. Find the measures of the acute angles of $\triangle ABC$. Round to the nearest degree.

Find the indicated measure in each rectangle. Round to the nearest degree.

54. $m\angle BDC$

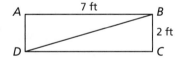

55. $m\angle STV$

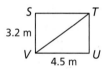

Find the indicated measure in each rhombus. Round to the nearest degree.

56. $m\angle DGF$

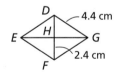

57. $m\angle LKN$

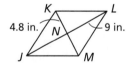

58. Critical Thinking Without using a calculator, compare the values of $\tan 60°$ and $\tan 70°$. Explain your reasoning.

The measure of an acute angle formed by a line with slope m and the x-axis can be found by using the expression $\tan^{-1}(m)$. Find the measure of the acute angle that each line makes with the x-axis. Round to the nearest degree.

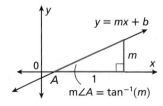

59. $y = 3x + 5$ **60.** $y = \frac{2}{3}x + 1$ **61.** $5y = 4x + 3$

H.O.T. 62. ///ERROR ANALYSIS/// A student was asked to find m∠C. Explain the error in the student's solution.

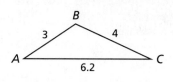

> Since tan $C = \frac{3}{4}$, m∠C = $\tan^{-1}\left(\frac{3}{4}\right)$, and $\tan^{-1}(0.75) \approx 37°$. So m∠C ≈ 37°.

H.O.T. 63. Write About It A student claims that you must know the three side lengths of a right triangle before you can use trigonometric ratios to find the measures of the acute angles. Do you agree? Why or why not?

64. $\overline{DC}$ is an altitude of right △ABC. Use trigonometric ratios to find the missing lengths in the figure. Then use these lengths to verify the three relationships in the Geometric Mean Corollaries.

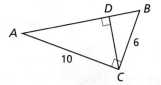

TEST PREP

65. Which expression can be used to find m∠A?

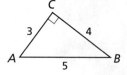

(A) $\tan^{-1}(0.75)$ (C) $\cos^{-1}(0.8)$

(B) $\sin^{-1}\left(\frac{3}{5}\right)$ (D) $\tan^{-1}\left(\frac{4}{3}\right)$

66. Which expression is NOT equivalent to cos 60°?

(F) $\frac{1}{2}$ (H) $\frac{\sin 60°}{\tan 60°}$

(G) $\sin 30°$ (J) $\cos^{-1}\left(\frac{1}{2}\right)$

67. To the nearest degree, what is the measure of the acute angle formed by Jefferson St. and Madison St.?

(A) 27°   (C) 59°

(B) 31°   (D) 63°

68. Gridded Response A highway exit ramp has a slope of $\frac{3}{20}$. To the nearest degree, find the angle that the ramp makes with a horizontal line.

CHALLENGE AND EXTEND

Find each angle measure. Round to the nearest degree.

69. m∠J

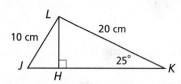

70. m∠A

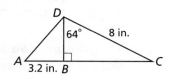

H.O.T. Simplify each expression.

71. $\cos^{-1}(\cos 34°)$ **72.** $\tan[\tan^{-1}(1.5)]$ **73.** $\sin(\sin^{-1} x)$

74. A ramp has a 6% grade. The ramp is 40 ft long. Find the vertical distance that the ramp rises. Round your answer to the nearest hundredth.

75. Critical Thinking Explain why the expression $\sin^{-1}(1.5)$ does not make sense.

76. If you are given the lengths of two sides of $\triangle ABC$ and the measure of the included angle, you can use the formula $\frac{1}{2}bc \sin A$ to find the area of the triangle. Derive this formula. (*Hint:* Draw an altitude from B to $\overline{AC}$. Use trigonometric ratios to find the length of this altitude.)

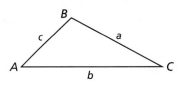

FOCUS ON MATHEMATICAL PRACTICES

H.O.T. 77. Problem Solving Find x to the nearest degree. What do you need to find out to solve for x?

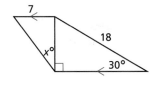

H.O.T. 78. Communication Is it possible to solve a right triangle if you know only its angle measures? Explain in terms of trigonometric ratios.

H.O.T. 79. Analysis Zach was puzzled by a problem because he had never seen one like it before: "Evaluate $\tan\left[\cos^{-1}\left(\frac{5}{13}\right)\right]$."

   a. Explain in words what the problem is asking Zach to find.

   b. A right triangle can be used to solve this problem without calculating any angle measures. What are its side lengths?

   c. Find the answer to the problem.

Using Technology

Use a spreadsheet to complete the following.

	A	B	C	D	E
1	a	b	c	m(angle A)	m(angle B)
2					

= SQRT(A2^2 + B2^2)   = DEGREES(ATAN(A2/B2))   = DEGREES(ATAN(B2/A2))

1. In cells A2 and B2, enter values for the leg lengths of a right triangle.

2. In cell C2, write a formula to calculate c, the length of the hypotenuse.

3. Write a formula to calculate the measure of $\angle A$ in cell D2. Be sure to use the Degrees function so that the answer is given in degrees. Format the value to include no decimal places.

4. Write a formula to calculate the measure of $\angle B$ in cell E2. Again, be sure to use the Degrees function and format the value to include no decimal places.

5. Use your spreadsheet to check your answers for Exercises 48–50.

28-3 Angles of Elevation and Depression

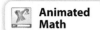

Essential Question: How can trigonometric ratios be used to estimate distances when you know an angle of elevation or depression?

Objective
Solve problems involving angles of elevation and angles of depression.

Vocabulary
angle of elevation
angle of depression

Who uses this?
Pilots and air traffic controllers use angles of depression to calculate distances.

An **angle of elevation** is the angle formed by a horizontal line and a line of sight to a point *above* the line. In the diagram, ∠1 is the angle of elevation from the tower *T* to the plane *P*.

An **angle of depression** is the angle formed by a horizontal line and a line of sight to a point *below* the line. ∠2 is the angle of depression from the plane to the tower.

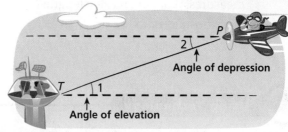

Since horizontal lines are parallel, ∠1 ≅ ∠2 by the Alternate Interior Angles Theorem. Therefore the angle of elevation from one point is congruent to the angle of depression from the other point.

COMMON CORE GPS
EXAMPLE 1 **Classifying Angles of Elevation and Depression**
Prep for MCC9-12.G.SRT.8

my.hrw.com

Online Video Tutor

Classify each angle as an angle of elevation or angle of depression.

A ∠3
∠3 is formed by a horizontal line and a line of sight to a point below the line. It is an angle of depression.

B ∠4
∠4 is formed by a horizontal line and a line of sight to a point above the line. It is an angle of elevation.

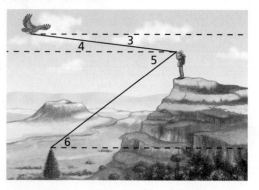

CHECK IT OUT! Use the diagram above to classify each angle as an angle of elevation or angle of depression.

1a. ∠5 **1b.** ∠6

Stone/Getty Images

EXAMPLE 2
MCC9-12.G.SRT.8

my.hrw.com

Online Video Tutor

Finding Distance by Using Angle of Elevation

An air traffic controller at an airport sights a plane at an angle of elevation of 41°. The pilot reports that the plane's altitude is 4000 ft. What is the horizontal distance between the plane and the airport? Round to the nearest foot.

Draw a sketch to represent the given information. Let *A* represent the airport and let *P* represent the plane. Let *x* be the horizontal distance between the plane and the airport.

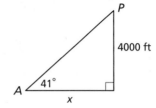

$$\tan 41° = \frac{4000}{x}$$ *You are given the side opposite ∠A, and x is the side adjacent to ∠A. So write a tangent ratio.*

$$x = \frac{4000}{\tan 41°}$$ *Multiply both sides by x and divide both sides by tan 41°.*

$$x \approx 4601 \text{ ft}$$ *Simplify the expression.*

2. What if...? Suppose the plane is at an altitude of 3500 ft and the angle of elevation from the airport to the plane is 29°. What is the horizontal distance between the plane and the airport? Round to the nearest foot.

EXAMPLE 3
MCC9-12.G.SRT.8

my.hrw.com

Online Video Tutor

Finding Distance by Using Angle of Depression

A forest ranger in a 90-foot observation tower sees a fire. The angle of depression to the fire is 7°. What is the horizontal distance between the tower and the fire? Round to the nearest foot.

Draw a sketch to represent the given information. Let *T* represent the top of the tower and let *F* represent the fire. Let *x* be the horizontal distance between the tower and the fire.

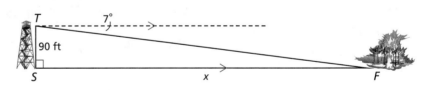

By the Alternate Interior Angles Theorem, m∠F = 7°.

$$\tan 7° = \frac{90}{x}$$ *Write a tangent ratio.*

$$x = \frac{90}{\tan 7°}$$ *Multiply both sides by x and divide both sides by tan 7°.*

$$x \approx 733 \text{ ft}$$ *Simplify the expression.*

3. What if...? Suppose the ranger sees another fire and the angle of depression to the fire is 3°. What is the horizontal distance to this fire? Round to the nearest foot.

Online Video Tutor

EXAMPLE **4** *Aviation Application*

A pilot flying at an altitude of 2.7 km sights two control towers directly in front of her. The angle of depression to the base of one tower is 37°. The angle of depression to the base of the other tower is 58°. What is the distance between the two towers? Round to the nearest tenth of a kilometer.

Step 1 Draw a sketch. Let *P* represent the plane and let *A* and *B* represent the two towers. Let *x* be the distance between the towers.

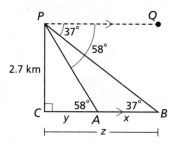

Helpful Hint

Always make a sketch to help you correctly place the given angle measure.

Step 2 Find *y*.

By the Alternate Interior Angles Theorem, $m\angle CAP = 58°$.

In $\triangle APC$, $\tan 58° = \dfrac{2.7}{y}$.

So $y = \dfrac{2.7}{\tan 58°} \approx 1.6871$ km.

Step 3 Find *z*.

By the Alternate Interior Angles Theorem, $m\angle CBP = 37°$.

In $\triangle BPC$, $\tan 37° = \dfrac{2.7}{z}$.

So $z = \dfrac{2.7}{\tan 37°} \approx 3.5830$ km.

Step 4 Find *x*.

$x = z - y$

$x \approx 3.5830 - 1.6871 \approx 1.9$ km

So the two towers are about 1.9 km apart.

4. A pilot flying at an altitude of 12,000 ft sights two airports directly in front of him. The angle of depression to one airport is 78°, and the angle of depression to the second airport is 19°. What is the distance between the two airports? Round to the nearest foot.

MCC.MP.2 | MATHEMATICAL PRACTICES

THINK AND DISCUSS

1. Explain what happens to the angle of elevation from your eye to the top of a skyscraper as you walk toward the skyscraper.

2. GET ORGANIZED Copy and complete the graphic organizer below. In each box, write a definition or make a sketch.

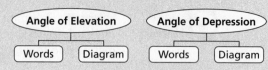

GUIDED PRACTICE

Vocabulary Apply the vocabulary from this lesson to answer each question.

1. An angle of ___?___ is measured from a horizontal line to a point above that line. (*elevation* or *depression*)

2. An angle of ___?___ is measured from a horizontal line to a point below that line. (*elevation* or *depression*)

SEE EXAMPLE 1 Classify each angle as an angle of elevation or angle of depression.

3. ∠1

4. ∠2

5. ∠3

6. ∠4

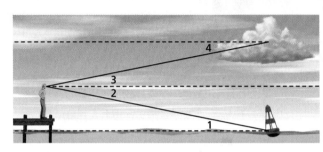

SEE EXAMPLE 2 7. **Measurement** When the angle of elevation to the sun is 37°, a flagpole casts a shadow that is 24.2 ft long. What is the height of the flagpole to the nearest foot?

SEE EXAMPLE 3 8. **Aviation** The pilot of a traffic helicopter sights an accident at an angle of depression of 18°. The helicopter's altitude is 1560 ft. What is the horizontal distance from the helicopter to the accident? Round to the nearest foot.

SEE EXAMPLE 4 9. **Surveying** From the top of a canyon, the angle of depression to the far side of the river is 58°, and the angle of depression to the near side of the river is 74°. The depth of the canyon is 191 m. What is the width of the river at the bottom of the canyon? Round to the nearest tenth of a meter.

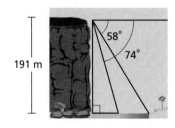

PRACTICE AND PROBLEM SOLVING

Classify each angle as an angle of elevation or angle of depression.

Independent Practice

For Exercises	See Example
10–13	1
14	2
15	3
16	4

10. ∠1

11. ∠2

12. ∠3

13. ∠4

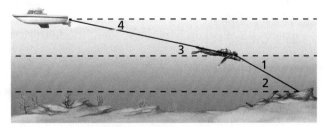

my.hrw.com

Online Extra Practice

14. **Geology** To measure the height of a rock formation, a surveyor places her transit 100 m from its base and focuses the transit on the top of the formation. The angle of elevation is 67°. The transit is 1.5 m above the ground. What is the height of the rock formation? Round to the nearest meter.

15. **Forestry** A forest ranger in a 120 ft observation tower sees a fire. The angle of depression to the fire is 3.5°. What is the horizontal distance between the tower and the fire? Round to the nearest foot.

16. **Space Shuttle** Marion is observing the launch of a space shuttle from the command center. When she first sees the shuttle, the angle of elevation to it is 16°. Later, the angle of elevation is 74°. If the command center is 1 mi from the launch pad, how far did the shuttle travel while Marion was watching? Round to the nearest tenth of a mile.

Tell whether each statement is true or false. If false, explain why.

17. The angle of elevation from your eye to the top of a tree increases as you walk toward the tree.

18. If you stand at street level, the angle of elevation to a building's tenth-story window is greater than the angle of elevation to one of its ninth-story windows.

19. As you watch a plane fly above you, the angle of elevation to the plane gets closer to 0° as the plane approaches the point directly overhead.

20. An angle of depression can never be more than 90°.

Use the diagram for Exercises 21 and 22.

21. Which angles are not angles of elevation or angles of depression?

22. The angle of depression from the helicopter to the car is 30°. Find m∠1, m∠2, m∠3, and m∠4.

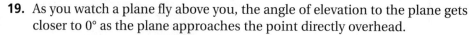

23. **Critical Thinking** Describe a situation in which the angle of depression to an object is decreasing.

24. An observer in a hot-air balloon sights a building that is 50 m from the balloon's launch point. The balloon has risen 165 m. What is the angle of depression from the balloon to the building? Round to the nearest degree.

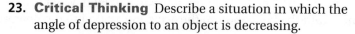

165 m

50 m

25. **Multi-Step** A surveyor finds that the angle of elevation to the top of a 1000 ft tower is 67°.

   a. To the nearest foot, how far is the surveyor from the base of the tower?

   b. How far back would the surveyor have to move so that the angle of elevation to the top of the tower is 55°? Round to the nearest foot.

H.O.T. 26. **Write About It** Two students are using shadows to calculate the height of a pole. One says that it will be easier if they wait until the angle of elevation to the sun is exactly 45°. Explain why the student made this suggestion.

27. The pilot of a rescue helicopter is flying over the ocean at an altitude of 1250 ft. The pilot sees a life raft at an angle of depression of 31°.

   a. What is the horizontal distance from the helicopter to the life raft, rounded to the nearest foot?

   b. The helicopter travels at 150 ft/s. To the nearest second, how long will it take until the helicopter is directly over the raft?

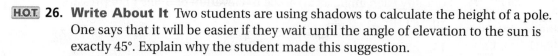

28. Mai is flying a plane at an altitude of 1600 ft. She sights a stadium at an angle of depression of 35°. What is Mai's approximate horizontal distance from the stadium?

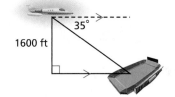

   Ⓐ 676 feet   Ⓒ 1450 feet

   Ⓑ 1120 feet   Ⓓ 2285 feet

29. Jeff finds that an office building casts a shadow that is 93 ft long when the angle of elevation to the sun is 60°. What is the height of the building?

   Ⓕ 54 feet   Ⓖ 81 feet   Ⓗ 107 feet   Ⓙ 161 feet

30. Short Response Jim is rafting down a river that runs through a canyon. He sees a trail marker ahead at the top of the canyon and estimates the angle of elevation from the raft to the marker as 45°. Draw a sketch to represent the situation. Explain what happens to the angle of elevation as Jim moves closer to the marker.

CHALLENGE AND EXTEND

H.O.T. 31. Susan and Jorge stand 38 m apart. From Susan's position, the angle of elevation to the top of Big Ben is 65°. From Jorge's position, the angle of elevation to the top of Big Ben is 49.5°. To the nearest meter, how tall is Big Ben?

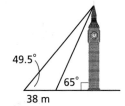

H.O.T. 32. A plane is flying at a constant altitude of 14,000 ft and a constant speed of 500 mi/h. The angle of depression from the plane to a lake is 6°. To the nearest minute, how much time will pass before the plane is directly over the lake?

H.O.T. 33. A skyscraper stands between two school buildings. The two schools are 10 mi apart. From school *A*, the angle of elevation to the top of the skyscraper is 5°. From school *B*, the angle of elevation is 2°. What is the height of the skyscraper to the nearest foot?

H.O.T. 34. Katie and Kim are attending a theater performance. Katie's seat is at floor level. She looks down at an angle of 18° to see the orchestra pit. Kim's seat is in the balcony directly above Katie. Kim looks down at an angle of 42° to see the pit. The horizontal distance from Katie's seat to the pit is 46 ft. What is the vertical distance between Katie's seat and Kim's seat? Round to the nearest inch.

FOCUS ON MATHEMATICAL PRACTICES

H.O.T. 35. Analysis If you are given the measure of the angle of depression from *Q* to *P*, what information can you find about the triangle?

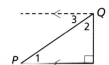

H.O.T. 36. Modeling A radio antenna is supported by guy wires, cables that run from the top of the antenna to the ground. How can you find the length of a guy wire if you can measure distance on the flat ground as well as angles from the ground?

H.O.T. 37. Problem Solving The angle of elevation from the top of a 55-ft tall building to the top of a nearby taller building is 43°. The angle of depression to the base of the taller building is 21°.

  a. Make a sketch illustrating this situation. Include all the given measurements. Label the unknown distances with variables.

  b. Describe in words how to calculate the height of the taller building.

  c. What is the height of the taller building to the nearest foot?

Ready to Go On?

my.hrw.com
Assessment and Intervention

28-1 Trigonometric Ratios

Use a special right triangle to write each trigonometric ratio as a fraction.

1. tan 45°

2. sin 30°

3. cos 30°

Use your calculator to find each trigonometric ratio. Round to the nearest hundredth.

4. sin 16°

5. cos 79°

6. tan 27°

Find each length. Round to the nearest hundredth.

7. *QR*

8. *AB*

9. *LM*

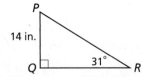
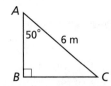
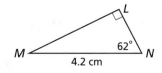

28-2 Solving Right Triangles

Find the unknown measures. Round lengths to the nearest hundredth and angle measures to the nearest degree.

10.
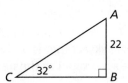

11.
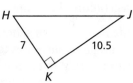

12.
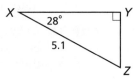

13. The wheelchair ramp at the entrance of the Mission Bay Library has a slope of $\frac{1}{18}$. What angle does the ramp make with the sidewalk? Round to the nearest degree.

28-3 Angles of Elevation and Depression

14. An observer in a blimp sights a football stadium at an angle of depression of 34°. The blimp's altitude is 1600 ft. What is the horizontal distance from the blimp to the stadium? Round to the nearest foot.

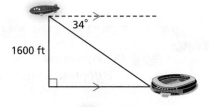

15. When the angle of elevation of the sun is 78°, a building casts a shadow that is 6 m long. What is the height of the building to the nearest tenth of a meter?

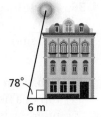

PARCC Assessment Readiness

Selected Response

1. Write cos 16° in terms of the sine.

   Ⓐ sin 164°

   Ⓑ sin 74°

   Ⓒ sin 84°

   Ⓓ sin 16°

2. Use the trigonometric ratio sin $A = 0.38$ to determine which angle of the triangle is $\angle A$.

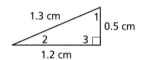

   Ⓕ $\angle 2$

   Ⓖ $\angle 1$

   Ⓗ $\angle 3$

   Ⓙ No solution

3. A pilot flying at an altitude of 1.8 km sights the runway directly in front of her. The angle of depression to the beginning of the runway is 31°. The angle of depression to the end of the runway is 23°. What is the length of the runway? Round to the nearest tenth of a kilometer.

   Ⓐ 1.2 km

   Ⓑ 0.9 km

   Ⓒ 1.3 km

   Ⓓ 1.0 km

4. Find the perimeter of the right triangle. Round to the nearest tenth of a centimeter.

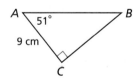

   Ⓕ 27.9 cm

   Ⓖ 30.7 cm

   Ⓗ 34.4 cm

   Ⓙ 36.0 cm

5. Nate built a skateboard ramp that covers a horizontal distance of 10 ft. The ramp rises a total of 3.5 ft. What angle does the ramp make with the ground? Round to the nearest degree.

   Ⓐ 19°

   Ⓑ 20°

   Ⓒ 28°

   Ⓓ 35°

6. The largest Egyptian pyramid is 146.5 m high. When Rowena stands far away from the pyramid, her line of sight to the top of the pyramid forms an angle of elevation of 20° with the ground. What is the horizontal distance between the center of the pyramid and Rowena? Round to the nearest meter.

   Ⓕ 402 m

   Ⓖ 427 m

   Ⓗ 156 m

   Ⓙ 65 m

7. The coordinates of the vertices of $\triangle RPQ$ are $R(2, -1)$, $P(2, 2)$, and $Q(-2, -1)$. Find $m\angle P$.

   Ⓐ $m\angle P = 53°$

   Ⓑ $m\angle P = 37°$

   Ⓒ $m\angle P = 93°$

   Ⓓ $m\angle P = 42°$

Mini-Tasks

8. Jessie is building a ramp for loading motorcycles onto a trailer. The trailer is 2.8 feet off of the ground. To avoid making it too difficult to push a motorcycle up the ramp, Jessie decides to make the angle between the ramp and the ground 15°. To the nearest hundredth of a foot, find the length of the ramp.

9. An observer at the top of a skyscraper sights a tour bus at an angle of depression of 61°. The skyscraper is 910 ft tall. What is the horizontal distance from the base of the skyscraper to the tour bus? Round to the nearest foot.

Selected Response

1. The length of one leg of a right triangle is 3 times the length of the other, and the length of the hypotenuse is 10. What is the length of the longest leg?

(A) 3

(B) $3\sqrt{10}$

(C) $\sqrt{10}$

(D) $12\sqrt{5}$

2. Which of the following is NOT equivalent to sin 60°?

(F) cos 30°

(G) $\dfrac{\sqrt{3}}{2}$

(H) $(\cos 60°)(\tan 60°)$

(J) $\dfrac{\tan 30°}{\sin 30°}$

3. $\triangle ABC$ is a right triangle. m∠A = 20°, m∠B = 90°, AC = 8, and AB = 3. Which expression can be used to find BC?

(A) $\dfrac{3}{\tan 70°}$

(B) $\dfrac{8}{\sin 20°}$

(C) $8 \tan 20°$

(D) $3 \cos 70°$

4. A slide at a park is 25 ft long, and the top of the slide is 10 ft above the ground. What is the approximate measure of the angle the slide makes with the ground?

(F) 21.8°

(G) 23.6°

(H) 66.4°

(J) 68.2°

5. Tell if the measures 6, 13, and 14 can be side lengths of a triangle. If so, classify the triangle as acute, right, or obtuse.

(A) Yes; acute triangle

(B) Yes; obtuse triangle

(C) Yes; right triangle

(D) No.

6. Find all the values of k so that $(-3, 4)$, $(-8, 5)$, and $(-5, k)$ are the vertices of a right triangle.

(F) $k = -6, 1, 9, 20$

(G) $k = -5, 2, 7, 19$

(H) $k = -5, 1, 9, 19$

(J) $k = -6, 2, 7, 20$

7. $\triangle ABC$ is a right triangle in which m∠A = 30° and m∠B = 60°. Which of the following are possible lengths for the sides of this triangle?

(A) $AB = \sqrt{3}$, $AC = \sqrt{2}$, and $BC = 1$

(B) $AB = 4$, $AC = 2$, and $BC = 2\sqrt{3}$

(C) $AB = 6\sqrt{3}$, $AC = 27$, and $BC = 3\sqrt{3}$

(D) $AB = 8$, $AC = 4\sqrt{3}$, and $BC = 4$

8. Find the values of x and y. Express your answers in simplest radical form.

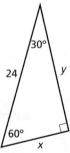

(F) $x = 12$, $y = 12\sqrt{3}$

(G) $x = 12\sqrt{3}$, $y = 12$

(H) $x = 12$, $y = 12\sqrt{2}$

(J) $x = 12\sqrt{2}$, $y = 12$

9. An architect designs the front view of a house with a gable roof that has a 45°-45°-90° triangle shape. The overhangs are 0.5 meter each from the exterior walls, and the width of the house is 16 meters. What should the side length *l* of the triangle be? Round your answer to the nearest meter.

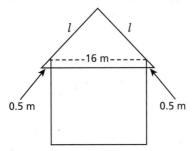

Ⓐ 12 m

Ⓑ 11 m

Ⓒ 24 m

Ⓓ 23 m

10. Write the trigonometric ratio for cos *X* as a fraction and as a decimal rounded to the nearest hundredth.

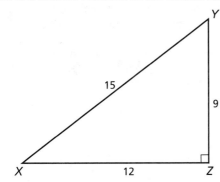

Ⓕ $\cos X = \dfrac{12}{9} \approx 1.33$

Ⓖ $\cos X = \dfrac{9}{15} = 0.60$

Ⓗ $\cos X = \dfrac{12}{15} = 0.80$

Ⓙ $\cos X = \dfrac{9}{12} = 0.75$

11. Use a special right triangle to write tan 60° as a fraction.

Ⓐ $\dfrac{\sqrt{3}}{1}$

Ⓑ $\dfrac{1}{\sqrt{3}}$

Ⓒ $\dfrac{\sqrt{2}}{1}$

Ⓓ $\dfrac{\sqrt{3}}{2}$

12. Use your calculator to find the trigonometric ratios sin 79°, cos 47°, and tan 77°. Round to the nearest hundredth.

Ⓕ sin 79° = −0.99,
cos 47° = −0.44,
tan 77° = −32.27

Ⓖ sin 79° = −0.44,
cos 47° = −0.99,
tan 77° = −32.27

Ⓗ sin 79° = 0.68,
cos 47° = 0.98,
tan 77° = 4.33

Ⓙ sin 79° = 0.98,
cos 47° = 0.68,
tan 77° = 4.33

13. Find sin ∠*A* to the nearest hundredth.

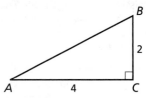

Ⓐ sin ∠*A* = 0.45

Ⓑ sin ∠*A* = 0.50

Ⓒ sin ∠*A* = 2.24

Ⓓ sin ∠*A* = 0.89

14. Some mountains in the Alps are very steep and have a grade of 42.7%. To the nearest degree, what angle do these mountains make with a horizontal line?

Ⓕ 23°

Ⓖ 67°

Ⓗ 47°

Ⓙ 32°

15. Classify each angle in the diagram as an angle of elevation or an angle of depression.

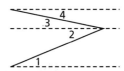

Ⓐ Angles of elevation: ∠1, ∠3
Angles of depression: ∠2, ∠4

Ⓑ Angles of elevation: ∠2, ∠4
Angles of depression: ∠1, ∠3

Ⓒ Angles of elevation: ∠1, ∠4
Angles of depression: ∠2, ∠3

Ⓓ Angles of elevation: ∠2, ∠3
Angles of depression: ∠1, ∠4

16. Find the missing side length. Tell if the side lengths form a Pythagorean triple. Explain.

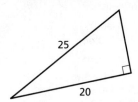

25

20

Ⓕ The missing side length is 15. The side lengths form a Pythagorean triple because they are nonzero whole numbers that satisfy the equation $a^2 + b^2 = c^2$.

Ⓖ The missing side length is 32.02. The side lengths do not form a Pythagorean triple because one of them is not a nonzero whole number.

Ⓗ The missing side length is 5. The side lengths form a Pythagorean triple because they are nonzero whole numbers that satisfy the equation $a^2 + b^2 = c^2$.

Ⓙ The missing side length is 32.02. The side lengths form a Pythagorean triple because they satisfy the equation $a^2 + b^2 = c^2$.

17. Find the value of x. Express your answer in simplest radical form.

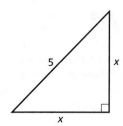

5

x

x

Ⓐ $x = \dfrac{5\sqrt{2}}{2}$

Ⓑ $x = 5\sqrt{2}$

Ⓒ $x = \dfrac{\sqrt{5}\sqrt{2}}{2}$

Ⓓ $x = \dfrac{5\sqrt{3}}{2}$

18. Find the value of x that satisfies the equation $\sin(4x + 14)° = \cos(-3x + 73)°$.

Ⓕ $x = \dfrac{3}{7}$

Ⓖ $x = 3$

Ⓗ $x = \dfrac{59}{7}$

Ⓙ $x = 93$

Mini-Tasks

19. Find the sine and cosine of the acute angles in the right triangle.

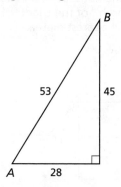

B

53   45

A 28

20. An eagle 300 feet in the air spots its prey on the ground. The angle of depression to its prey is 15°. What is the horizontal distance between the eagle and its prey? Round to the nearest foot.

21. Mike is standing between Lani and the Eiffel Tower. He and Lani are 21.2 meters apart. From Mike's position, the angle of elevation to the top of the Eiffel Tower is 40°. From Lani's position, the angle of elevation to the top of the Eiffel Tower is 38.5°. How many meters high is the Eiffel Tower? Round to the nearest meter.

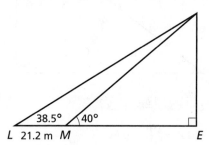

38.5°   40°

L 21.2 m M E

22. A building casts a shadow that is 85 ft long when the angle of elevation to the sun is 34°.

a. What is the height of the building? Round to the nearest inch and show your work.

b. What is the angle of elevation to the sun when the shadow is 42 ft 6 in. long? Round to the nearest tenth of a degree and show your work.

Performance Tasks

23. A 30°-60°-90° triangle is shown below. Draw another triangle similar to the given triangle, indicating the lengths of the sides. Show that the values of the sine, cosine, and tangent of the 30° and 60° angles of your triangle are the same as those for the given triangle.

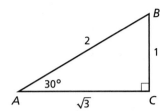

24. A new street is going to be constructed to connect Main Street, which runs in the east-west direction, and North Boulevard, which runs in the north-south direction, as shown in the diagram below. The construction cost has been estimated at $110 per linear foot, excluding the new intersections. The intersections are estimated to cost $1,450,000 each.

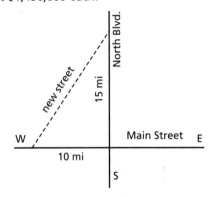

Part A: What type of triangle is bounded by the new street, North Boulevard, and Main Street? How do you know?

Part B: Let x represent the length of the new street. What is the name of the formula that can be used to find the value of x? Use that formula to write an equation that can be solved for x.

Part C: What is the length of the new street to the nearest thousandth of a mile? Convert that distance to the nearest foot. Show your work.

Part D: Estimate the cost of constructing the new street. Be sure to include the costs for intersections. Show your work and round the cost to the nearest thousand dollars.

Are You Ready?

my.hrw.com
Assessment and Intervention

✓ Vocabulary

Match each term on the left with a definition on the right.

1. equilateral
2. parallelogram
3. apothem
4. composite figure

A. the distance from the center of a regular polygon to a side of the polygon

B. a quadrilateral with four right angles

C. a quadrilateral with two pairs of parallel sides

D. having all sides congruent

E. a figure made up of simple shapes, such as triangles, rectangles, trapezoids, and circles

✓ Find Area in the Coordinate Plane

Find the area of each figure with the given vertices.

5. $\triangle ABC$ with $A(0, 3)$, $B(5, 3)$, and $C(2, -1)$
6. rectangle $KLMN$ with $K(-2, 3)$, $L(-2, 7)$, $M(6, 7)$, and $N(6, 3)$
7. $\odot P$ with center $P(2, 3)$ that passes through the point $Q(-6, 3)$

✓ Circumference and Area of Circles

Find the circumference and area of each circle. Give your answers in terms of π.

8.
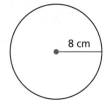
8 cm

9.
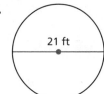
21 ft

10.
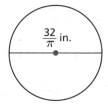
$\frac{32}{\pi}$ in.

✓ Distance and Midpoint Formulas

Find the length and midpoint of the segment with the given endpoints.

11. $A(-3, 2)$ and $B(5, 6)$
12. $C(-4, -4)$ and $D(2, -3)$

Career Readiness Transportation Engineer

Transportation engineers are civil engineers who specialize in highways, rail and bus systems, and airports. Some transportation engineers develop entire systems or supervise construction or repair of systems. They need to find areas of composite figures or volumes of composite solids to determine construction costs. A college degree in civil engineering is required. Most transportation engineers work for construction or engineering companies or government agencies.

Circles and Volume

Online Edition

my.hrw.com

Access the complete online textbook, interactive features, and additional resources.

Multilingual Glossary

Enhance your math vocabulary with this illustrated online glossary in 13 languages.

Homework Help

Get instant help with tutorial videos, practice problems, and step-by-step solutions.

Portable Devices

eTextbook

Access your full textbook on your tablet or e-reader.

HMH Fuse

Make your learning experience completely portable and interactive with this app for iPad®.

Chapter Resources

Scan with your smart phone to jump directly to the online edition.

 COMMON CORE GPS **Unit Contents**

Module 29   Area and Volume
MCC9-12.G.GMD.1, MCC9-12.G.GMD.2(+), MCC9-12.G.GMD.3, MCC9-12.G.SRT.9(+)

Module 30   Circles
MCC9-12.G.C.2, MCC9-12.G.C.3, MCC9-12.G.C.4, MCC9-12.G.C.5

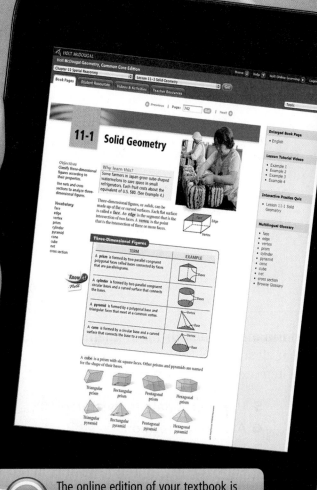

 The online edition of your textbook is enhanced with videos and interactive features for every lesson.

Area and Volume

MATHEMATICAL PRACTICES   The Common Core Georgia Performance Standards for Mathematical Practice describe varieties of expertise that all students should seek to develop. Opportunities to develop these practices are integrated throughout this program.

1 Make sense of problems and persevere in solving them.

2 Reason abstractly and quantitatively.

3 Construct viable arguments and critique the reasoning of others.

4 Model with mathematics.

5 Use appropriate tools strategically.

6 Attend to precision.

7 Look for and make use of structure.

8 Look for and express regularity in repeated reasoning.

Unpacking the Standards

my.hrw.com
Multilingual Glossary

Understanding the standards and the vocabulary terms in the standards will help you know exactly what you are expected to learn in this chapter.

 COMMON CORE GPS **MCC9-12.G.GMD.3**

Use volume formulas for cylinders, pyramids, cones, and spheres to solve problems.

Key Vocabulary

volume (volumen)
  The number of nonoverlapping unit cubes of a given size that will exactly fill the interior of a three-dimensional figure.

formula (formula)
  A literal equation that states a rule for a relationship among quantities.

cylinder (cilindro)
  A three-dimensional figure with two parallel congruent circular bases and a curved surface that connects the bases.

pyramid (pirámide)
  A polyhedron formed by a polygonal base and triangular lateral faces that meet at a common vertex.

cone (cono)
  A three-dimensional figure with a circular base and a curved surface that connects the base to a point called the vertex.

sphere (esfera)
  The set of points in space that are a fixed distance from a given point called the center of the sphere.

What It Means For You

Volume problems appear frequently in real-world contexts. Learning the relationships among volume formulas helps you understand, remember, and apply them.

EXAMPLE   **Volume of a cylinder**

A grain silo at a port has the dimensions shown. The volume is the base area B times the height h. Because the base is a circle, this gives:

$$V = Bh = \pi r^2 h$$
$$= \pi (15^2)(42)$$
$$\approx 30,000 \text{ ft}^3$$

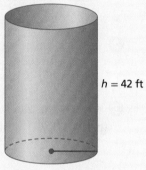

$h = 42$ ft

$r = 15$ ft

EXAMPLE   **Volume of a cone**

The silo above contains just enough grain so that the grain reaches to the outer edge of the floor, forming a cone. The volume is one third the base area times the height. This gives:

$$V = \frac{1}{3}Bh = \frac{1}{3}\pi r^2 h = \frac{1}{3}\pi(15^2)(8) \approx 1900 \text{ ft}^3$$

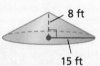

8 ft

15 ft

EXAMPLE   **Volume of a sphere**

A liquefied natural gas tank at the port is in the shape of a sphere with the radius shown. The volume is:

$$V = \frac{4}{3}\pi r^3 = \frac{4}{3}\pi(16^3) \approx 17,000 \text{ ft}^3$$

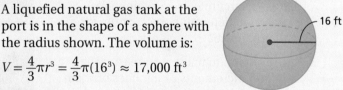

16 ft

EXAMPLE   **Volume of a pyramid**

A customs building at the port has a roof in the shape of a pyramid with the dimensions shown. As with a cone, the volume is one third the base area times the height. Because the base is a rectangle, this gives:

$$V = \frac{1}{3}Bh = \frac{1}{3}(72)(48)(24) \approx 28,000 \text{ ft}^3$$

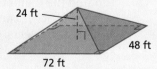

24 ft

48 ft

72 ft

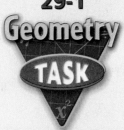

29-1

Geometry TASK

Develop π

The ratio of the circumference of a circle to its diameter is defined as π. All circles are similar, so this ratio is the same for all circles:

$$\pi = \frac{\text{circumference}}{\text{diameter}}.$$

Use with Developing Formulas for Circles and Regular Polygons

Use appropriate tools strategically.

MCC9-12.G.GMD.1 Give an informal argument for the formulas for the circumference of a circle, area of a circle …

Activity 1

① Use your compass to draw a large circle on a piece of cardboard and then cut it out.

② Use a measuring tape to measure the circle's diameter and circumference as accurately as possible.

③ Use the results from your circle to estimate π. Compare your answers with the results of the rest of the class.

Try This

1. Do you think it is possible to draw a circle whose ratio of circumference to diameter is not π? Why or why not?

2. How does knowing the relationship between circumference, diameter, and π help you determine the formula for circumference?

3. Use a ribbon to make a π measuring tape. Mark off increments of π inches or π cm on your ribbon as accurately as possible. How could you use this π measuring tape to find the diameter of a circular object? Use your π measuring tape to measure 5 circular objects. Give the circumference and diameter of each object.

Sam Dudgeon/HMH Photo

Archimedes used inscribed and circumscribed polygons to estimate the value of π. His "method of exhaustion" is considered to be an early version of calculus. In the figures below, the circumference of the circle is less than the perimeter of the larger polygon and greater than the perimeter of the smaller polygon. This fact is used to estimate π.

Activity 2

1 Construct a large square. Construct the perpendicular bisectors of two adjacent sides.

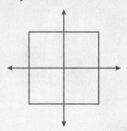

2 Use your compass to draw an inscribed circle as shown.

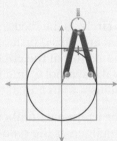

3 Connect the midpoints of the sides to form a square that is inscribed in the circle.

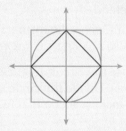

4 Let P_1 represent the perimeter of the smaller square, P_2 represent the perimeter of the larger square, and C represent the circumference of the circle. Measure the squares to find P_1 and P_2 and substitute the values into the inequality below.

$$P_1 < C < P_2$$

5 Divide each expression in the inequality by the diameter of the circle. Why does this give you an inequality in terms of π? Complete the inequality below.

$$\underline{\quad ? \quad} < \pi < \underline{\quad ? \quad}$$

Try This

4. Use the perimeters of the inscribed and circumscribed regular hexagons to write an inequality for π. Assume the diameter of each circle is 2 units.

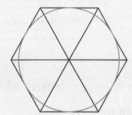
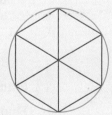

5. Compare the inequalities you found for π. What do you think would be true about your inequality if you used regular polygons with more sides? How could you use inscribed and circumscribed regular polygons to estimate π?

6. An alternate definition of π is the area of a circle with radius 1. How could you use this definition and the figures above to estimate the value of π?

29-1 Developing Formulas for Circles and Regular Polygons

Essential Question: How do you find the area of a regular polygon?

Objectives
Develop and apply the formulas for the area and circumference of a circle.

Develop and apply the formula for the area of a regular polygon.

Vocabulary
circle
center of a circle
center of a regular polygon
apothem
central angle of a regular polygon

Who uses this?

Drummers use drums of different sizes to produce different notes. The pitch is related to the area of the top of the drum. (See Example 2.)

A **circle** is the locus of points in a plane that are a fixed distance from a point called the **center of the circle**. A circle is named by the symbol $\odot$ and its center. $\odot A$ has radius $r = AB$ and diameter $d = CD$.

The irrational number π is defined as the ratio of the circumference C to the diameter d, or $\pi = \frac{C}{d}$. Solving for C gives the formula $C = \pi d$. Also $d = 2r$, so $C = 2\pi r$.

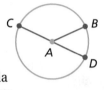

You can use the circumference of a circle to find its area. Divide the circle and rearrange the pieces to make a shape that resembles a parallelogram.

Animated Math

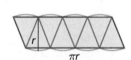

πr

The base of the parallelogram is about half the circumference, or πr, and the height is close to the radius r. So $A \cong \pi r \cdot r = \pi r^2$.

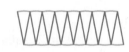

The more pieces you divide the circle into, the more accurate the estimate will be.

Know it!
Note

Circumference and Area   Circle
A circle with diameter d and radius r has circumference $C = \pi d$ or $C = 2\pi r$ and area $A = \pi r^2$.

COMMON CORE GPS MCC9-12.A.CED.1

EXAMPLE 1 **Finding Measurements of Circles**

Find each measurement.

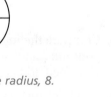

A the area of $\odot P$ in terms of π

$A = \pi r^2$ — *Area of a circle*

$A = \pi(8)^2$ — *Divide the diameter by 2 to find the radius, 8.*

$A = 64\pi \text{ cm}^2$ — *Simplify.*

Find each measurement.

B the radius of $\odot X$ in which $C = 24\pi$ in.

$C = 2\pi r$ *Circumference of a circle*

$24\pi = 2\pi r$ *Substitute 24π for C.*

$r = 12$ *in.*   *Divide both sides by 2π.*

C the circumference of $\odot S$ in which $A = 9x^2\,\pi$ cm^2

Step 1 Use the given area to solve for r.

$A = \pi r^2$ *Area of a circle*

$9x^2\pi = \pi r^2$ *Substitute $9x^2\pi$ for A.*

$9x^2 = r^2$ *Divide both sides by π.*

$3x = r$ *Take the square root of both sides.*

Step 2 Use the value of r to find the circumference.

$C = 2\pi r$

$C = 2\pi(3x)$ *Substitute 3x for r.*

$C = 6x\pi$ cm   *Simplify.*

CHECK IT OUT! **1.** Find the area of $\odot A$ in terms of π in which $C = (4x - 6)\pi$ m.

EXAMPLE **2**

Music Application

A drum kit contains three drums with diameters of 10 in., 12 in., and 14 in. Find the area of the top of each drum. Round to the nearest tenth.

10 in. diameter	12 in. diameter	14 in. diameter
$A = \pi(5^2)$ $r = \dfrac{10}{2} = 5$	$A = \pi(6^2)$ $r = \dfrac{12}{2} = 6$	$A = \pi(7)^2$ $r = \dfrac{14}{2} = 7$
$\cong 78.5$ in^2	$\cong 113.1$ in^2	$\cong 153.9$ in^2

CHECK IT OUT! **2.** Use the information above to find the circumference of each drum.

The **center of a regular polygon** is equidistant from the vertices. The **apothem** is the distance from the center to a side. A **central angle of a regular polygon** has its vertex at the center, and its sides pass through consecutive vertices. Each central angle measure of a regular n-gon is $\frac{360°}{n}$.

To find the area of a regular n-gon with side length s and apothem a, divide it into n congruent isosceles triangles.

area of each triangle: $\frac{1}{2}as$

total area of the polygon: $A = n\left(\frac{1}{2}as\right)$, or $A = \frac{1}{2}aP$ *The perimeter is $P = ns$.*

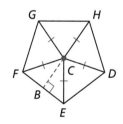

Regular pentagon *DEFGH* has center *C*, apothem *BC*, and central angle $\angle DCE$.

 Know it! Note

Area — **Regular Polygon**

The area of a regular polygon with apothem a and perimeter P is $A = \frac{1}{2}aP$.

my.hrw.com

Online Video Tutor

EXAMPLE 3

MCC9-12.G.SRT.8

Finding the Area of a Regular Polygon

Find the area of each regular polygon. Round to the nearest tenth.

A a regular hexagon with side length 6 m

The perimeter is $6(6) = 36$ m. The hexagon can be divided into 6 equilateral triangles with side length 6 m. By the 30°-60°-90° Triangle Theorem, the apothem is $3\sqrt{3}$ m.

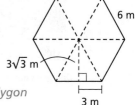

$A = \frac{1}{2}aP$ *Area of a regular polygon*

$A = \frac{1}{2}(3\sqrt{3})(36)$ *Substitute $3\sqrt{3}$ for a and 36 for P.*

$A = 54\sqrt{3} \cong 93.5$ m²   *Simplify.*

> **Remember!**
>
> The tangent of an angle in a right triangle is the ratio of the opposite leg length to the adjacent leg length.

B a regular pentagon with side length 8 in.

Step 1 Draw the pentagon. Draw an isosceles triangle with its vertex at the center of the pentagon. The central angle is $\frac{360°}{5} = 72°$. Draw a segment that bisects the central angle and the side of the polygon to form a right triangle.

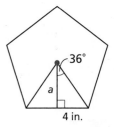

Step 2 Use the tangent ratio to find the apothem.

$\tan 36° = \frac{4}{a}$ *The tangent of an angle is $\frac{opp. \, leg}{adj. \, leg}$.*

$a = \frac{4}{\tan 36°}$ *Solve for a.*

Step 3 Use the apothem and the given side length to find the area.

$A = \frac{1}{2}aP$ *Area of a regular polygon*

$A = \frac{1}{2}\left(\frac{4}{\tan 36°}\right)(40)$ *The perimeter is $8(5) = 40$ in.*

$A \cong 110.1$ in²   *Simplify. Round to the nearest tenth.*

 3. Find the area of a regular octagon with a side length of 4 cm.

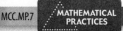

MCC.MP.7

THINK AND DISCUSS

1. Describe the relationship between the circumference of a circle and π.

2. Explain how you would find the central angle of a regular polygon with *n* sides.

3. **GET ORGANIZED** Copy and complete the graphic organizer.

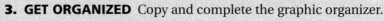

Regular Polygons (Side Length = 1)					
Polygon	Number of Sides	Perimeter	Central Angle	Apothem	Area
Triangle					
Square					
Hexagon					

GUIDED PRACTICE

1. **Vocabulary** Describe how to find the *apothem* of a square with side length *s*.

SEE EXAMPLE **1** **Find each measurement.**

2. the circumference of $\odot C$

3. the area of $\odot A$ in terms of π

4. the circumference of $\odot P$ in which $A = 36\pi$ in^2

SEE EXAMPLE **2** 5. **Food** A pizza parlor offers pizzas with diameters of 8 in., 10 in., and 12 in. Find the area of each size pizza. Round to the nearest tenth.

SEE EXAMPLE **3** **Find the area of each regular polygon. Round to the nearest tenth.**

6.

7.

8. an equilateral triangle with an apothem of 2 ft

9. a regular dodecagon with a side length of 5 m

PRACTICE AND PROBLEM SOLVING

Independent Practice

For Exercises	See Example
10–12	1
13	2
14–17	3

my.hrw.com

Online Extra Practice

Find each measurement. Give your answers in terms of π.

10. the area of $\odot M$

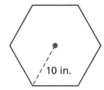

11. the circumference of $\odot Z$

12. the diameter of $\odot G$ in which $C = 10$ ft.

13. **Sports** A horse trainer uses circular pens that are 35 ft, 50 ft, and 66 ft in diameter. Find the area of each pen. Round to the nearest tenth.

Find the area of each regular polygon. Round to the nearest tenth, if necessary.

14.

15.

16. a regular nonagon with a perimeter of 144 in.

17. a regular pentagon with an apothem of 2 ft.

Find the central angle measure of each regular polygon. (*Hint:* To review polygon names.)

18. equilateral triangle   19. square   20. pentagon   21. hexagon

22. heptagon   23. octagon   24. nonagon   25. decagon

Find the area of each regular polygon. Round to the nearest tenth.

26.

14 in.

27.

5 cm

28.

6 in.

29.

3 m

30.
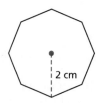
2 cm

31.

5 ft

Biology

Dendroclimatologists study tree rings for evidence of changes in weather patterns over time.

32. **Biology** You can estimate a tree's age in years by using the formula $a = \frac{r}{w}$, where r is the tree's radius without bark and w is the average thickness of the tree's rings. The circumference of a white oak tree is 100 in. The bark is 0.5 in. thick, and the average width of a ring is 0.2 in. Estimate the tree's age.

33. **///ERROR ANALYSIS///** A circle has a circumference of 2π in. Which calculation of the area is incorrect? Explain.

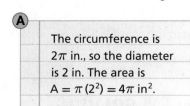
Ⓐ The circumference is 2π in., so the diameter is 2 in. The area is $A = \pi(2^2) = 4\pi$ in².

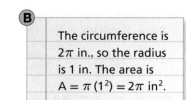
Ⓑ The circumference is 2π in., so the radius is 1 in. The area is $A = \pi(1^2) = 2\pi$ in².

Find the missing measurements for each circle. Give your answers in terms of π.

	Diameter d	Radius r	Area A	Circumference C
34.	6	▨	▨	▨
35.	▨	▨	100	▨
36.	▨	17	▨	▨
37.	▨	▨	▨	36 π

H.O.T. 38. **Multi-Step** Janet is designing a garden around a gazebo that is a regular hexagon with side length 6 ft. The garden will be a circle that extends 10 feet from the vertices of the hexagon. What is the area of the garden? Round to the nearest square foot.

Real-World Connections

39. A stop sign is a regular octagon. The signs are available in two sizes: 30 in. or 36 in.

   a. Find the area of a 30 in. sign. Round to the nearest tenth.

   b. Find the area of a 36 in. sign. Round to the nearest tenth.

   c. Find the percent increase in metal needed to make a 36 in. sign instead of a 30 in. sign.

30 in. or 36 in.

40. Measurement A *trundle wheel* is used to measure distances by rolling it on the ground and counting its number of turns. If the circumference of a trundle wheel is 1 meter, what is its diameter?

H.O.T. 41. Critical Thinking Which do you think would seat more people, a 4 ft by 6 ft rectangular table or a circular table with a diameter of 6 ft? How many people would you sit at each table? Explain your reasoning.

H.O.T. 42. Write About It The center of each circle in the figure lies on the number line. Describe the relationship between the circumference of the largest circle and the circumferences of the four smaller circles.

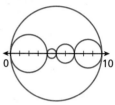

TEST PREP

43. Find the perimeter of the regular octagon to the nearest centimeter.

    (A) 5   (B) 40   (C) 20   (D) 68

6 cm

44. Which of the following ratios comparing a circle's circumference C to its diameter d gives the value of π?

    (F) $\dfrac{C}{d}$ (G) $\dfrac{4C}{d^2}$ (H) $\dfrac{d}{C}$ (J) $\dfrac{d}{2C}$

45. Alisa has a circular tabletop with a 2-foot diameter. She wants to paint a pattern on the table top that includes a 2-foot-by-1-foot rectangle and 4 squares with sides 0.5 foot long. Which information makes this scenario impossible?

    (A) There will be no room left on the tabletop after the rectangle has been painted.

    (B) A 2-foot-long rectangle will not fit on the circular tabletop.

    (C) Squares cannot be painted on the circle.

    (D) There will not be enough room on the table to fit all the 0.5-foot squares.

CHALLENGE AND EXTEND

H.O.T. 46. Two circles have the same center. The radius of the larger circle is 5 units longer than the radius of the smaller circle. Find the difference in the circumferences of the two circles.

5

47. Algebra Write the formula for the area of a circle in terms of its circumference.

48. Critical Thinking Show that the formula for the area of a regular n-gon approaches the formula for the area of a circle as n gets very large.

FOCUS ON MATHEMATICAL PRACTICES

H.O.T. 49. Reasoning A circle inscribed in a regular polygon touches each side of the polygon at its midpoint. What does the radius of the inscribed circle represent in the regular polygon?

H.O.T. 50. Communication The center of a circle is located at $(-5, 10)$. The point $(7, 15)$ is on the circle. Find the other point on the circle that lies on the same diameter as $(7, 15)$. Explain your solution process.

H.O.T. 51. Problem Solving The area of a regular hexagon is 500 square units. Find its perimeter to the nearest tenth of a unit. Show your work.

H.O.T. 52. Number Sense What is the radius of the circle whose numerical circumference is the same as its numerical area?

Connecting
Geometry to

Trigonometry

Triangle Area Formulas

You've used the formula $A = \frac{1}{2}bh$ to find the area of a triangle, and you've used trigonometric ratios to find missing lengths in right triangles. You can combine the two techniques to find the area of a triangle when you don't know the value of h.

 Reason abstractly and quantitatively.

MCC9-12.G.SRT.9(+) Derive the formula $A = 1/2\ ab\ \sin(C)$ for the area of a triangle by drawing an auxiliary line from a vertex perpendicular to the opposite side.

If you are given the lengths of two sides and the included angle, you can use this information to find the area of the triangle

$\dfrac{h}{a} = \sin C$ *Write the sine of C in terms of h and a.*

$h = a \sin C$ *Multiply both sides by a to isolate h.*

$A = \dfrac{1}{2} ba \sin C$ *Substitute the expression for h into the area formula.*

Example

Find the area of the triangle shown.

$A = \dfrac{1}{2} ba \sin B$

$A = \dfrac{1}{2} (7)(8)\sin 25°$ *Substitute the values for the side lengths and the measure of the included angle.*

$A \approx 11.8$ *Simplify.*

The area is approximately 11.8 in.^{2}.

Try This

Find the area of each triangle. Round to the nearest tenth.

1.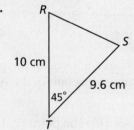

2.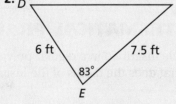

3.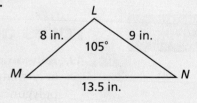

4. You can also find the area of a triangle if you only know the lengths of the sides. Heron's formula is $A = \sqrt{s(s-a)(s-b)(s-c)}$, where s is one-half of the perimeter of the triangle and a, b, and c are the side lengths of the triangle. Find s for the triangle in Exercise 3, and use Heron's formula to find the area. Round to the nearest tenth.

29-2 Volume of Prisms and Cylinders

? *Essential Question:* What are the volume formulas for prisms and cylinders?

Objectives
Learn and apply the formula for the volume of a prism.

Learn and apply the formula for the volume of a cylinder.

Vocabulary
volume

Who uses this?
Marine biologists must ensure that aquariums are large enough to accommodate the number of fish inside them. (See Example 2.)

The **volume** of a three-dimensional figure is the number of nonoverlapping unit cubes of a given size that will exactly fill the interior.

A cube built out of 27 unit cubes has a volume of 27 cubic units.

Cavalieri's principle says that if two three-dimensional figures have the same height and have the same cross-sectional area at every level, they have the same volume.

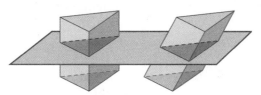

A right prism and an oblique prism with the same base and height have the same volume.

Know it!
note

Volume of a Prism		
The volume of a prism with base area B and height h is $V = Bh$. 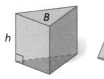	The volume of a right rectangular prism with length ℓ, width w, and height h is $V = \ell w h$. 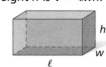	The volume of a cube with edge length s is $V = s^3$.

COMMON CORE GPS
MCC9-12.G.SRT.8

EXAMPLE 1 Finding Volumes of Prisms

Find the volume of each prism. Round to the nearest tenth, if necessary.

my.hrw.com

Online Video Tutor

A

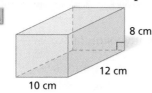

$V = \ell w h$ *Volume of a right rectangular prism*
$= (10)(12)(8) = 960 \text{ cm}^3$ *Substitute 10 for ℓ, 12 for w, and 8 for h.*

B a cube with edge length 10 cm

$V = s^3$ *Volume of a cube*
$= 10^3 = 1000 \text{ cm}^3$ *Substitute 10 for s.*

Find the volume of each prism. Round to the nearest tenth, if necessary.

 a right regular pentagonal prism with base edge length 5 m and height 7 m

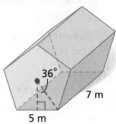

Step 1 Find the apothem *a* of the base. First draw a right triangle on one base as shown. The measure of the angle with its vertex at the center is $\dfrac{360°}{10} = 36°$.

$\tan 36° = \dfrac{2.5}{a}$ *The leg of the triangle is half the side length, or 2.5 m.*

$a = \dfrac{2.5}{\tan 36°}$ *Solve for a.*

Step 2 Use the value of *a* to find the base area.

$B = \dfrac{1}{2}aP = \dfrac{1}{2}\left(\dfrac{2.5}{\tan 36°}\right)(25) = \dfrac{31.25}{\tan 36°}$ $P = 5(5) = 25 \text{ m}$

Step 3 Use the base area to find the volume.

$V = Bh = \dfrac{31.25}{\tan 36°} \cdot 7 \approx 301.1 \text{ m}^3$

 1. Find the volume of a triangular prism with a height of 9 yd whose base is a right triangle with legs 7 yd and 5 yd long.

EXAMPLE 2
MCC9-12.G.MG.2

Marine Biology Application

my.hrw.com

Online Video Tutor

The aquarium at the right is a rectangular prism. Estimate the volume of the water in the aquarium in gallons. The density of water is about 8.33 pounds per gallon. Estimate the weight of the water in pounds.
(*Hint:* 1 gallon ≈ 0.134 ft^3)

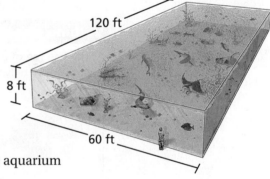

120 ft

8 ft

60 ft

Step 1 Find the volume of the aquarium in cubic feet.
$V = \ell wh = (120)(60)(8) = 57{,}600 \text{ ft}^3$

Step 2 Use the conversion factor $\dfrac{1 \text{ gallon}}{0.134 \text{ ft}^3}$ to estimate the volume in gallons.
$57{,}600 \text{ ft}^3 \cdot \dfrac{1 \text{ gallon}}{0.134 \text{ ft}^3} \approx 429{,}851 \text{ gallons}$ $\dfrac{1 \text{ gallon}}{0.134 \text{ ft}^3} = 1$

Step 3 Use the conversion factor $\dfrac{8.33 \text{ pounds}}{1 \text{ gallon}}$ to estimate the weight of the water.
$429{,}851 \text{ gallons} \cdot \dfrac{8.33 \text{ pounds}}{1 \text{ gallon}} \approx 3{,}580{,}659 \text{ pounds}$ $\dfrac{8.33 \text{ pounds}}{1 \text{ gallon}} = 1$

The aquarium holds about 429,851 gallons. The water in the aquarium weighs about 3,580,659 pounds.

 2. What if...? Estimate the volume in gallons and the weight of the water in the aquarium above if the height were doubled.

Cavalieri's principle also relates to cylinders. The two stacks have the same number of CDs, so they have the same volume.

 Know it! .Note

Volume of a Cylinder

The volume of a cylinder with base area B, radius r, and height h is $V = Bh$, or $V = \pi r^2 h$.

 COMMON CORE GPS | **EXAMPLE** 3 | MCC9-12.G.GMD.3

Finding Volumes of Cylinders

Find the volume of each cylinder. Give your answers both in terms of π and rounded to the nearest tenth.

 **my.hrw.com**

Online Video Tutor

A

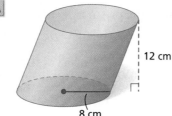

12 cm

8 cm

$$V = \pi r^2 h \qquad \text{\textit{Volume of a cylinder}}$$
$$= \pi(8)^2(12) \qquad \text{\textit{Substitute 8 for r and 12 for h.}}$$
$$= 768\pi \text{ cm}^3 \approx 2412.7 \text{ cm}^3$$

B **a cylinder with a base area of 36π in^2 and a height equal to twice the radius**

Step 1 Use the base area to find the radius.
$$\pi r^2 = 36\pi \qquad \text{\textit{Substitute 36}\pi \text{ for the base area.}}$$
$$r = 6 \qquad \text{\textit{Solve for r.}}$$

Step 2 Use the radius to find the height. The height is equal to twice the radius.
$$h = 2r$$
$$= 2(6) = 12 \text{ cm}$$

Step 3 Use the radius and height to find the volume.
$$V = \pi r^2 h \qquad \text{\textit{Volume of a cylinder}}$$
$$= \pi(6)^2(12) = 432\pi \text{ in}^3 \qquad \text{\textit{Substitute 6 for r and 12 for h.}}$$
$$\approx 1357.2 \text{ in}^3$$

 CHECK IT OUT!

3. Find the volume of a cylinder with a diameter of 16 in. and a height of 17 in. Give your answer both in terms of π and rounded to the nearest tenth.

© HMH

29-2 Volume of Prisms and Cylinders **887**

EXAMPLE 4
MCC9-12.G.GMD.3

Exploring Effects of Changing Dimensions

The radius and height of the cylinder are multiplied by $\frac{1}{2}$. Describe the effect on the volume.

6 m
12 m

original dimensions:	radius and height multiplied by $\frac{1}{2}$:
$V = \pi r^2 h$	$V = \pi r^2 h$
$\quad = \pi(6)^2(12)$	$\quad = \pi(3)^2(6)$
$\quad = 432\pi \text{ m}^3$	$\quad = 54\pi \text{ m}^3$

Notice that $54\pi = \frac{1}{8}(432\pi)$. If the radius and height are multiplied by $\frac{1}{2}$, the volume is multiplied by $\left(\frac{1}{2}\right)^3$, or $\frac{1}{8}$.

4. The length, width, and height of the prism are doubled. Describe the effect on the volume.

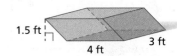
1.5 ft
4 ft
3 ft

EXAMPLE 5
MCC9-12.G.GMD.3

Finding Volumes of Composite Three-Dimensional Figures

Find the volume of the composite figure. Round to the nearest tenth.

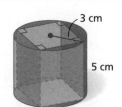
5 m
9 m
6 m
8 m

The base area of the prism is $B = \frac{1}{2}(6)(8) = 24 \text{ m}^2$.

The volume of the prism is $V = Bh = 24(9) = 216 \text{ m}^3$.

The cylinder's diameter equals the hypotenuse of the prism's base, 10 m. So the radius is 5 m.

The volume of the cylinder is $V = \pi r^2 h = \pi(5)^2(5) = 125\pi \text{ m}^3$.

The total volume of the figure is the sum of the volumes.
$V = 216 + 125\pi \approx 608.7 \text{ m}^3$

5. Find the volume of the composite figure. Round to the nearest tenth.

3 cm
5 cm

MCC.MP.8

MATHEMATICAL PRACTICES

THINK AND DISCUSS

1. Compare the formula for the volume of a prism with the formula for the volume of a cylinder.

2. Explain how Cavalieri's principle relates to the formula for the volume of an oblique prism.

Know it!
Note

3. GET ORGANIZED Copy and complete the graphic organizer. In each box, write the formula for the volume.

Shape	Volume
Prism	
Cube	
Cylinder	

GUIDED PRACTICE

1. **Vocabulary** In a right cylinder, the *altitude* is __?__ the axis. (*longer than, shorter than*, or *the same length as*)

SEE EXAMPLE 1 Find the volume of each prism.

2.

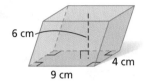

6 cm
4 cm
9 cm

3.

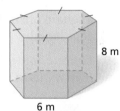

8 m

6 m

4. a cube with edge length 8 ft

SEE EXAMPLE 2 5. **Food** The world's largest ice cream cake, built in New York City on May 25, 2004, was approximately a 19 ft by 9 ft by 2 ft rectangular prism. Estimate the volume of the ice cream cake in gallons. If the density of the ice cream was 4.73 pounds per gallon, estimate the weight of the cake. (*Hint:* 1 gallon ≈ 0.134 cubic feet)

SEE EXAMPLE 3 Find the volume of each cylinder. Give your answers both in terms of π and rounded to the nearest tenth.

6.

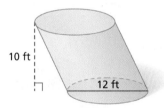

10 ft
12 ft

7.

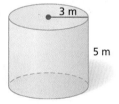

3 m
5 m

8. a cylinder with base area 25π cm^2 and height 3 cm more than the radius

SEE EXAMPLE 4 Describe the effect of each change on the volume of the given figure.

9. The dimensions are multiplied by $\frac{1}{4}$.

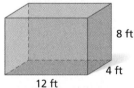

8 ft
4 ft
12 ft

10. The dimensions are tripled.

2 in.
7 in.

SEE EXAMPLE 5 Find the volume of each composite figure. Round to the nearest tenth.

11.

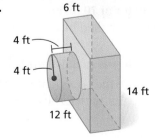

6 ft
4 ft
4 ft
14 ft
12 ft

12.

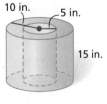

10 in.
5 in.
15 in.

AFP/TIMOTHY A. CLARY/Getty Images

PRACTICE AND PROBLEM SOLVING

Independent Practice

For Exercises	See Example
13–15	1
16	2
17–19	3
20–21	4
22–23	5

my.hrw.com

Online Extra Practice

Find the volume of each prism.

13.

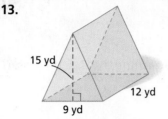

15 yd
12 yd
9 yd

14.

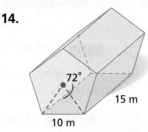

72°
15 m
10 m

15. a square prism with a base area of 49 ft² and a height 2 ft less than the base edge length

16. Landscaping Colin is buying dirt to fill a garden bed that is a 9 ft by 16 ft rectangle. If he wants to fill it to a depth of 4 in., how many cubic yards of dirt does he need? If dirt costs $25 per yd³, how much will the project cost? (*Hint:* 1 yd³ = 27 ft³)

Find the volume of each cylinder. Give your answers both in terms of π and rounded to the nearest tenth.

17.

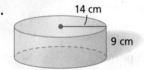

14 cm
9 cm

18.

6 in.
3 in.

19. a cylinder with base area 24π cm² and height 16 cm

H.O.T. **Describe the effect of each change on the volume of the given figure.**

20. The dimensions are multiplied by 5.

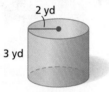

2 yd
3 yd

21. The dimensions are multiplied by $\frac{3}{5}$.

10 m
5 m

Find the volume of each composite figure.

22.

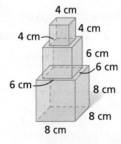

4 cm
4 cm
4 cm
6 cm
6 cm
6 cm
8 cm
8 cm
8 cm

23.

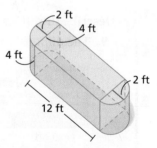

2 ft
4 ft
4 ft
2 ft
12 ft

24. One cup is equal to 14.4375 in³. If a 1 c cylindrical measuring cup has a radius of 2 in., what is its height? If the radius is 1.5 in., what is its height?

H.O.T. **25. Food** A cake is a cylinder with a diameter of 10 in. and a height of 3 in. For a party, a coin has been mixed into the batter and baked inside the cake. The person who gets the piece with the coin wins a prize.

　a. Find the volume of the cake. Round to the nearest tenth.

　b. Probability Keka gets a piece of cake that is a right rectangular prism with a 3 in. by 1 in. base. What is the probability that the coin is in her piece? Round to the nearest hundredth.

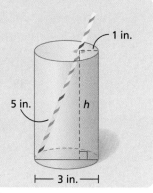

26. A cylindrical juice container with a 3 in. diameter has a hole for a straw that is 1 in. from the side. Up to 5 in. of a straw can be inserted.

    a. Find the height h of the container to the nearest tenth.

    b. Find the volume of the container to the nearest tenth.

    c. How many ounces of juice does the container hold? (*Hint:* 1 in^3 ≈ 0.55 oz)

27. Find the height of a rectangular prism with length 5 ft, width 9 ft, and volume 495 ft^3.

28. Find the area of the base of a rectangular prism with volume 360 in^3 and height 9 in.

29. Find the volume of a cylinder with surface area 210π m^2 and height 8 m.

30. Find the volume of a rectangular prism with vertices $(0, 0, 0)$, $(0, 3, 0)$, $(7, 0, 0)$, $(7, 3, 0)$, $(0, 0, 6)$, $(0, 3, 6)$, $(7, 0, 6)$, and $(7, 3, 6)$.

31. You can use *displacement* to find the volume of an irregular object, such as a stone. Suppose the tank shown is filled with water to a depth of 8 in. A stone is placed in the tank so that it is completely covered, causing the water level to rise by 2 in. Find the volume of the stone.

32. Food A 1 in. cube of cheese is one serving. How many servings are in a 4 in. by 4 in. by $\frac{1}{4}$ in. slice?

33. History In 1919, a cylindrical tank containing molasses burst and flooded the city of Boston, Massachusetts. The tank had a 90 ft diameter and a height of 52 ft. How many gallons of molasses were in the tank? (*Hint:* 1 gal ≈ 0.134 ft^3)

34. Meteorology If 3 in. of rain fall on the property shown, what is the volume in cubic feet? In gallons? The density of water is 8.33 pounds per gallon. What is the weight of the rain in pounds? (*Hint:* 1 gal ≈ 0.134 ft^3)

H.O.T. 35. Critical Thinking The dimensions of a prism with volume V and surface area S are multiplied by a scale factor of k to form a similar prism. Make a conjecture about the ratio of the surface area of the new prism to its volume. Test your conjecture using a cube with an edge length of 1 and a scale factor of 2.

H.O.T. 36. Write About It How can you change the edge length of a cube so that its volume is doubled?

TEST PREP

37. Abigail has a cylindrical candle mold with the dimensions shown. If Abigail has a rectangular block of wax measuring 15 cm by 12 cm by 18 cm, about how many candles can she make after melting the block of wax?

    Ⓐ 14   Ⓑ 31   Ⓒ 35   Ⓓ 76

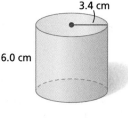

38. A 96-inch piece of wire was cut into equal segments that were then connected to form the edges of a cube. What is the volume of the cube?

(F) 512 in³   (G) 576 in³   (H) 729 in³   (J) 1728 in³

39. One juice container is a rectangular prism with a height of 9 in. and a 3 in. by 3 in. square base. Another juice container is a cylinder with a radius of 1.75 in. and a height of 9 in. Which best describes the relationship between the two containers?

(A) The prism has the greater volume.

(B) The cylinder has the greater volume.

(C) The volumes are equivalent.

(D) The volumes cannot be determined.

40. What is the volume of the three-dimensional object with the dimensions shown in the three views below?

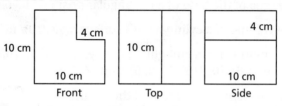

(F) 160 cm³   (G) 240 cm³   (H) 840 cm³   (J) 1000 cm³

CHALLENGE AND EXTEND

Algebra Find the volume of each three-dimensional figure in terms of x.

41.
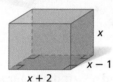

42.
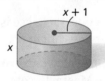

43.
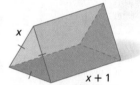

 44. The volume in cubic units of a cylinder is equal to its surface area in square units. Prove that the radius and height must both be greater than 2.

FOCUS ON MATHEMATICAL PRACTICES

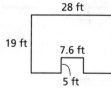

H.O.T. 45. Problem Solving The floor layout of a hotel suite is shown. The ceiling is 8.5 feet high. What is the volume of the suite?

H.O.T. 46. Number Sense The volume of a right square prism is 432 cubic centimeters. Every dimension is a whole number of centimeters. One of the dimensions is 6 centimeters. Find the other two dimensions.

H.O.T. 47. Estimation The volume of a cylinder, with diameter k inches, has the same volume as a right square prism with base of side length k inches.

a. For what values of k is the area of the cylinder's base greater than, or equal to, the area of the prism's base? Explain.

b. What can you conclude from part **a**?

c. Which figure is taller? Why?

d. Find the ratio of the taller figure to the shorter figure.

e. The height of the prism is 22 centimeters. What is the height of the cylinder to the nearest tenth of an inch?

892   *Module 29 Area and Volume*

29-3 Volume of Pyramids and Cones

? *Essential Question:* What are the volume formulas for pyramids and cones?

Objectives
Learn and apply the formula for the volume of a pyramid.

Learn and apply the formula for the volume of a cone.

Who uses this?
The builders of the Rainforest Pyramid in Galveston, Texas, needed to calculate the volume of the pyramid to plan the climate control system. (See Example 2.)

The volume of a pyramid is related to the volume of a prism with the same base and height. The relationship can be verified by dividing a cube into three congruent square pyramids, as shown.

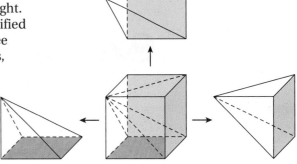

The square pyramids are congruent, so they have the same volume. The volume of each pyramid is one third the volume of the cube.

Volume of a Pyramid

The volume of a pyramid with base area B and height h is $V = \frac{1}{3}Bh$.

 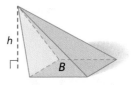

COMMON CORE GPS
MCC9-12.G.GMD.3

EXAMPLE 1 **Finding Volumes of Pyramids**

 my.hrw.com

Online Video Tutor

Find the volume of each pyramid.

A a rectangular pyramid with length 7 ft, width 9 ft, and height 12 ft

$$V = \frac{1}{3}Bh = \frac{1}{3}(7 \cdot 9)(12) = 252 \text{ ft}^3$$

B the square pyramid
The base is a square with a side length of 4 in., and the height is 6 in.

$$V = \frac{1}{3}Bh = \frac{1}{3}(4^2)(6) = 32 \text{ in}^3$$

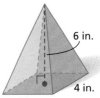

6 in.

4 in.

4 in.

Find the volume of the pyramid.

C the trapezoidal pyramid with base *ABCD*, where $\overline{AB} \parallel \overline{CD}$ and $\overline{AE} \perp$ plane *ABC*

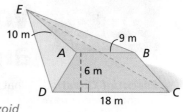

Step 1 Find the area of the base.

$B = \frac{1}{2}(b_1 + b_2)h$ *Area of a trapezoid*

$\quad = \frac{1}{2}(9 + 18)6$ *Substitute 9 for b_1, 18 for b_2, and 6 for h.*

$\quad = 81 \text{ m}^2$ *Simplify.*

Step 2 Use the base area and the height to find the volume. Because $\overline{AE} \perp$ plane *ABC*, $\overline{AE}$ is the altitude, so the height is equal to *AE*.

$V = \frac{1}{3}Bh$ *Volume of a pyramid*

$\quad = \frac{1}{3}(81)(10)$ *Substitute 81 for B and 10 for h.*

$\quad = 270 \text{ m}^3$

 1. Find the volume of a regular hexagonal pyramid with a base edge length of 2 cm and a height equal to the area of the base.

COMMON CORE GPS
EXAMPLE MCC9-12.G.MG.1 **2**

Online Video Tutor

Architecture Application

The Rainforest Pyramid in Galveston, Texas, is a square pyramid with a base area of about 1 acre and a height of 10 stories. Estimate the volume in cubic yards and in cubic feet. (*Hint:* 1 acre = 4840 yd², 1 story ≈ 10 ft)

The base is a square with an area of about 4840 yd². The base edge length is $\sqrt{4840} \approx 70$ yd. The height is about $10(10) = 100$ ft, or about 33 yd.

First find the volume in cubic yards.

$V = \frac{1}{3}Bh$ *Volume of a regular pyramid*

$\quad = \frac{1}{3}(70^2)(33) = 53{,}900 \text{ yd}^3$ *Substitute 70^2 for B and 33 for h.*

Then convert your answer to find the volume in cubic feet. The volume of one cubic yard is $(3 \text{ ft})(3 \text{ ft})(3 \text{ ft}) = 27 \text{ ft}^3$. Use the conversion factor $\frac{27 \text{ ft}^3}{1 \text{ yd}^3}$ to find the volume in cubic feet.

$53{,}900 \text{ yd}^3 \cdot \frac{27 \text{ ft}^3}{1 \text{ yd}^3} \approx 1{,}455{,}300 \text{ ft}^3$

Remember!

A *regular pyramid* has a base that is a regular polygon. Its lateral faces are congruent isosceles triangles. In a regular pyramid, the *slant height* is the distance from the vertex to the midpoint of an edge of the base.

 2. What if...? What would be the volume of the Rainforest Pyramid if the height were doubled?

© Lyndol Descant/LyndolDotCom

Know it! Note

The volume of a cone with base area B, radius r, and height h is $V = \frac{1}{3}Bh$, or $V = \frac{1}{3}\pi r^2 h$.

COMMON CORE GPS **EXAMPLE** **3**
MCC9-12.G.GMD.3

my.hrw.com

Online Video Tutor

Finding Volumes of Cones

Find the volume of each cone. Give your answers both in terms of π and rounded to the nearest tenth.

A a cone with radius 5 cm and height 12 cm

$V = \frac{1}{3}\pi r^2 h$ *Volume of a cone*

$= \frac{1}{3}\pi(5)^2(12)$ *Substitute 5 for r and 12 for h.*

$= 100\pi \text{ cm}^3 \approx 314.2 \text{ cm}^3$ *Simplify.*

B a cone with a base circumference of 21π cm and a height 3 cm less than twice the radius

Step 1 Use the circumference to find the radius.

$2\pi r = 21\pi$ *Substitute 21π for C.*

$r = 10.5$ cm   *Divide both sides by 2π.*

Step 2 Use the radius to find the height.

$2(10.5) - 3 = 18$ cm   *The height is 3 cm less than twice the radius.*

Step 3 Use the radius and height to find the volume.

$V = \frac{1}{3}\pi r^2 h$ *Volume of a cone*

$= \frac{1}{3}\pi(10.5)^2(18)$ *Substitute 10.5 for r and 18 for h.*

$= 661.5\pi \text{ cm}^3 \approx 2078.2 \text{ cm}^3$ *Simplify.*

C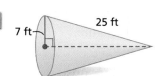
25 ft
7 ft

Step 1 Use the Pythagorean Theorem to find the height.

$7^2 + h^2 = 25^2$ *Pythagorean Theorem*

$h^2 = 576$ *Subtract 7^2 from both sides.*

$h = 24$ *Take the square root of both sides.*

Step 2 Use the radius and height to find the volume.

$V = \frac{1}{3}\pi r^2 h$ *Volume of a cone*

$= \frac{1}{3}\pi(7)^2(24)$ *Substitute 7 for r and 24 for h.*

$= 392\pi \text{ ft}^3 \approx 1231.5 \text{ ft}^3$ *Simplify.*

Remember!

A *right cone* has an axis perpendicular to the base. In a right cone, the *slant height* is the distance from the vertex of the cone to a point on the edge of the base. If ℓ is the *slant height* in a right cone with radius r and height h, then $r^2 + h^2 = \ell^2$ by the Pythagorean Theorem.

CHECK IT OUT! **3.** Find the volume of the cone.

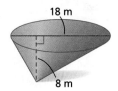
18 m
8 m

EXAMPLE 4
MCC9-12.G.GMD.3

my.hrw.com

Online Video Tutor

Exploring Effects of Changing Dimensions

The length, width, and height of the rectangular pyramid are multiplied by $\frac{1}{4}$. Describe the effect on the volume.

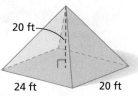

20 ft
24 ft   20 ft

original dimensions:	length, width, and height multiplied by $\frac{1}{4}$:
$V = \frac{1}{3}Bh$	$V = \frac{1}{3}Bh$
$= \frac{1}{3}(24 \cdot 20)(20)$	$= \frac{1}{3}(6 \cdot 5)(5)$
$= 3200 \text{ ft}^3$	$= 50 \text{ ft}^3$

Notice that $50 = \frac{1}{64}(3200)$. If the length, width, and height are multiplied by $\frac{1}{4}$, the volume is multiplied by $\left(\frac{1}{4}\right)^3$, or $\frac{1}{64}$.

 4. The radius and height of the cone are doubled. Describe the effect on the volume.

18 cm
9 cm

EXAMPLE 5
MCC9-12.G.GMD.3

my.hrw.com

Online Video Tutor

Finding Volumes of Composite Three-Dimensional Figures

Find the volume of the composite figure. Round to the nearest tenth.

The volume of the cylinder is
$V = \pi r^2 h = \pi(2)^2(2) = 8\pi \text{ in}^3$.

The volume of the cone is
$V = \frac{1}{3}\pi r^2 h = \frac{1}{3}\pi(2)^2(3) = 4\pi \text{ in}^3$.

The volume of the composite figure is the sum of the volumes.
$V = 8\pi + 4\pi = 12\pi \text{ in}^3 \approx 37.7 \text{ in}^3$

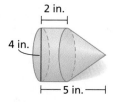

2 in.
4 in.
5 in.

 5. Find the volume of the composite figure.

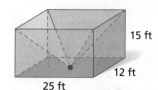

15 ft
12 ft
25 ft

MCC.MP.8   MATHEMATICAL PRACTICES

Know it!
Note

THINK AND DISCUSS

1. Explain how the volume of a pyramid is related to the volume of a prism with the same base and height.

2. GET ORGANIZED Copy and complete the graphic organizer.

Volumes of Three-Dimensional Figures		
Formula	$V = Bh$	$V = \frac{1}{3}Bh$
Shapes		
Examples		

GUIDED PRACTICE

1. **Vocabulary** The *altitude* of a pyramid is ___?___ to the base. (*perpendicular, parallel,* or *oblique*)

SEE EXAMPLE 1 **Find the volume of each pyramid. Round to the nearest tenth, if necessary.**

2.

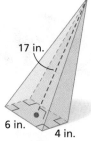

17 in.

6 in.   4 in.

3.

$4\sqrt{3}$ cm

4 cm

4. a hexagonal pyramid with a base area of 25 ft² and a height of 9 ft

SEE EXAMPLE 2 5. **Geology** A crystal is cut into the shape formed by two square pyramids joined at the base. Each pyramid has a base edge length of 5.7 mm and a height of 3 mm. What is the volume to the nearest cubic millimeter of the crystal?

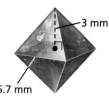

3 mm

5.7 mm

SEE EXAMPLE 3 **Find the volume of each cone. Give your answers both in terms of π and rounded to the nearest tenth.**

6.

14 cm

9 cm

7.

30 in.

24 in.

8. a cone with radius 12 m and height 20 m

SEE EXAMPLE 4 **Describe the effect of each change on the volume of the given figure.**

9. The dimensions are tripled.

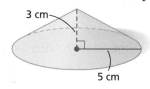

3 cm

5 cm

10. The dimensions are multiplied by $\frac{1}{2}$.

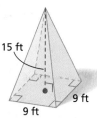

15 ft

9 ft

9 ft

SEE EXAMPLE 5 **Find the volume of each composite figure. Round to the nearest tenth, if necessary.**

11.

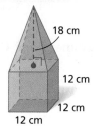

18 cm

12 cm

12 cm

12 cm

12.

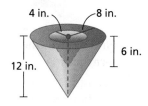

4 in.   8 in.

12 in.   6 in.

PRACTICE AND PROBLEM SOLVING

Independent Practice

For Exercises	See Example
13–15	1
16	2
17–19	3
20–21	4
22–23	5

my.hrw.com

Online Extra Practice

Find the volume of each pyramid. Round to the nearest tenth, if necessary.

13.
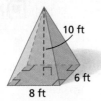
10 ft
6 ft
8 ft

14.
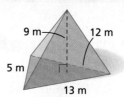
9 m
12 m
5 m
13 m

15. a regular square pyramid with base edge length 12 ft and slant height 10 ft

16. **Carpentry** A roof that encloses an attic is a square pyramid with a base edge length of 45 feet and a height of 5 yards. What is the volume of the attic in cubic feet? In cubic yards?

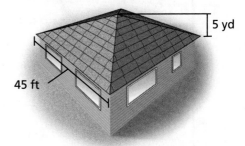
5 yd
45 ft

Find the volume of each cone. Give your answers both in terms of π and rounded to the nearest tenth.

17.

41 m
9 m

18.
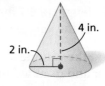
4 in.
2 in.

19. a cone with base area 36π ft^2 and a height equal to twice the radius

H.O.T. **Describe the effect of each change on the volume of the given figure.**

20. The dimensions are multiplied by $\frac{1}{3}$.
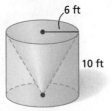
21 in.
15 in.

21. The dimensions are multiplied by 6.
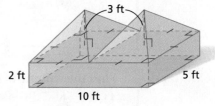
4 ft
7 ft   7 ft

Find the volume of each composite figure. Round to the nearest tenth, if necessary.

22.
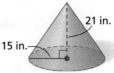
6 ft
10 ft

23.
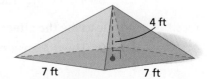
3 ft
2 ft
5 ft
10 ft

Find the volume of each right cone with the given dimensions. Give your answers in terms of π.

24. radius 3 in.
height 7 in.

25. diameter 5 m
height 2 m

26. radius 28 ft
slant height 53 ft

27. diameter 24 cm
slant height 13 cm

Find the volume of each regular pyramid with the given dimensions. Round to the nearest tenth, if necessary.

	Number of sides of base	Base edge length	Height	Volume
28.	3	10 ft	6 ft	
29.	4	15 m	18 m	
30.	5	9 in.	12 in.	
31.	6	8 cm	3 cm	

32. Find the height of a rectangular pyramid with length 3 m, width 8 m, and volume 112 m³.

33. Find the base circumference of a cone with height 5 cm and volume 125π cm³.

34. Find the volume of a cone with slant height 10 ft and height 8 ft.

35. Find the volume of a square pyramid with slant height 17 in. and surface area 800 in².

36. Find the surface area of a cone with height 20 yd and volume 1500π yd³. The surface area of a right cone with base radius r, height h, and slant height ℓ is $\pi r\ell + \pi r^2$.

37. Find the volume of a triangular pyramid with vertices $(0, 0, 0)$, $(5, 0, 0)$, $(0, 3, 0)$, and $(0, 0, 7)$.

38. **/// ERROR ANALYSIS ///** Which volume is incorrect? Explain the error.

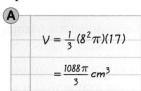

Ⓐ
$$V = \frac{1}{3}(8^2\pi)(17)$$
$$= \frac{1088\pi}{3} \text{ cm}^3$$

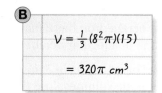

Ⓑ
$$V = \frac{1}{3}(8^2\pi)(15)$$
$$= 320\pi \text{ cm}^3$$

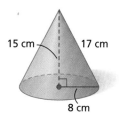

15 cm   17 cm   8 cm

H.O.T. 39. Critical Thinking Write a ratio comparing the volume of the prism to the volume of the composite figure. Explain your answer.

y x

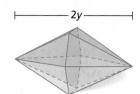

├──── $2y$ ────┤

H.O.T. 40. Write About It Explain how you would find the volume of a cone, given the radius and the surface area.

Real-World Connections

41. A juice stand sells smoothies in cone-shaped cups that are 8 in. tall. The regular size has a 4 in. diameter. The jumbo size has an 8 in. diameter.

  a. Find the volume of the regular size to the nearest tenth.

  b. Find the volume of the jumbo size to the nearest tenth.

  c. The regular size costs $1.25. What would be a reasonable price for the jumbo size? Explain your reasoning.

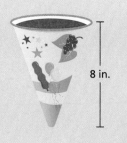

8 in.

42. Find the volume of the cone.

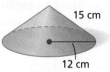

15 cm

12 cm

Ⓐ 432π cm³   Ⓒ 1296π cm³

Ⓑ 720π cm³   Ⓓ 2160π cm³

43. A square pyramid has a slant height of 25 m and a lateral area of 350 m². Which is closest to the volume?

Ⓕ 392 m³   Ⓖ 1176 m³   Ⓗ 404 m³   Ⓙ 1225 m³

44. A cone has a volume of 18π in³. Which are possible dimensions of the cone?

Ⓐ Diameter 1 in., height 18 in.   Ⓒ Diameter 3 in., height 6 in.

Ⓑ Diameter 6 in., height 6 in.   Ⓓ Diameter 6 in., height 3 in.

45. Gridded Response Find the height in centimeters of a square pyramid with a volume of 243 cm³ and a base edge length equal to the height.

CHALLENGE AND EXTEND

H.O.T. Each cone is inscribed in a regular pyramid with a base edge length of 2 ft and a height of 2 ft. Find the volume of each cone.

46.

47.

48.

49. A regular octahedron has 8 faces that are equilateral triangles. Find the volume of a regular octahedron with a side length of 10 cm.

50. A cylinder has a radius of 5 in. and a height of 3 in. Without calculating the volumes, find the height of a cone with the same base and the same volume as the cylinder. Explain your reasoning.

FOCUS ON MATHEMATICAL PRACTICES

H.O.T. 51. Communication How can Cavalieri's principle regarding the volume of prisms and cylinders be related to finding the area of triangles and parallelograms?

H.O.T. 52. Justify Two tents each have a volume of 1350 cubic feet. One is in the shape of a cone and the other is in the shape of a square pyramid. They are both 9 feet tall. Which is greater, the diagonal of the base of the pyramid or the diameter of the base of the cone? Justify your answer.

H.O.T. 53. Problem Solving The top portion of a cone is removed to make a new cone half as tall as the original.

a. If the radius of the original cone base is r, what is the radius of the new cone base? Explain.

b. Find the ratio of the volume of the new cone to that of the original cone. Justify your answer.

c. How can you use the ratio in part **b** to find the volume of the lower portion that was removed from the original cone?

d. A cone has a base with radius 10 cm and height 9 cm. The top portion is removed to make a new cone half as tall. Find the volume of the bottom half of the cone, to the nearest tenth of a cubic centimeter.

Cube Roots

If you know the area of a square, you can find the length of a side by taking the square root of the area. How can you find the length of a side of a cube if you know the volume?

$A = 16$ in^2

s s

$s^2 = A$

$s^2 = 16$

$s = \sqrt{16} = 4$

$V = 27$ in^3

s s

s

$s^3 = V$

$s^3 = 27$

$s = ?$

To find the side length, you need to find the *cube root* of 27. The cube root of 27 is 3 because $3^3 = 27$, so the side length of the cube above is 3 in. "The cube root of 27" can also be written as $\sqrt[3]{27}$.

Example

The volume of a cube is 64 m^3. Find the side length of the cube.

$s^3 = V$

$s^3 = 64$ *Substitute 64 for V.*

$s = \sqrt[3]{64} = 4$ *$4^3 = 64$, so the cube root of 64 is 4.*

The side length of the cube is 4 m.

Try This

Given the volume, find the side length of each cube.

1. $V = 8$ cm^3

2. $V = 125$ ft^3

3. $V = 216$ in.^{3}

4. $V = 1{,}000$ yd^3

5. $V = 1$ cm^3

6. $V = 0.064$ m^3

7. Carlos wants to buy an angelfish for a pet. The pet store recommends a fish tank that holds 2,197 in^3 of water. If the tank is in the shape of a cube, how long is each side?

For an integer $n > 1$, an *n*th root of x is a number a such that $a^n = x$. If n is also even and $x > 0$, x has both positive and negative *n*th roots, written as $\sqrt[n]{x}$ and $-\sqrt[n]{x}$. For example, the 4th roots of 16 are 2 and -2, because $2^4 = 16$ and $(-2)^4 = 16$. So, $\sqrt[4]{16} = 2$, and $-\sqrt[4]{16} = -2$. Simplify each expression.

8. $\sqrt[4]{81}$

9. $\sqrt[5]{32}$

10. $\sqrt[3]{729}$

11. $\sqrt[5]{243}$

12. $\sqrt[7]{1}$

13. $\sqrt[4]{0.0016}$

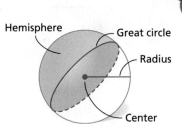

29-4 Spheres

Objectives
Learn and apply the formula for the volume of a sphere.

Learn and apply the formula for the surface area of a sphere.

Vocabulary
sphere
center of a sphere
radius of a sphere
hemisphere
great circle

Who uses this?

Biologists study the eyes of deep-sea predators such as the giant squid to learn about their behavior. (See Example 2.)

A **sphere** is the locus of points in space that are a fixed distance from a given point called the **center of a sphere** . A **radius of a sphere** connects the center of the sphere to any point on the sphere. A **hemisphere** is half of a sphere. A **great circle** divides a sphere into two hemispheres.

The figure shows a hemisphere and a cylinder with a cone removed from its interior. The cross sections have the same area at every level, so the volumes are equal by Cavalieri's Principle. You will prove that the cross sections have equal areas in Exercise 39.

$$V(\text{hemisphere}) = V(\text{cylinder}) - V(\text{cone})$$
$$= \pi r^2 h - \frac{1}{3}\pi r^2 h$$
$$= \frac{2}{3}\pi r^2 h$$
$$= \frac{2}{3}\pi r^2(r) \qquad \text{\textit{The height of the hemisphere is equal to the radius.}}$$
$$= \frac{2}{3}\pi r^3$$

 Animated Math

The volume of a sphere with radius r is twice the volume of the hemisphere, or $V = \frac{4}{3}\pi r^3$.

 Know it! Note

Volume of a Sphere

The volume of a sphere with radius r is $V = \frac{4}{3}\pi r^3$.

 COMMON CORE GPS MCC9-12.G.GMD.3

EXAMPLE 1 Finding Volumes of Spheres

Find each measurement. Give your answer in terms of π.

A the volume of the sphere

$$V = \frac{4}{3}\pi r^3$$

$$V = \frac{4}{3}\pi(9)^3 \qquad \text{\textit{Substitute 9 for r.}}$$

$$= 972\pi \text{ cm}^3 \qquad \text{\textit{Simplify.}}$$

9 cm

Online Video Tutor

Find each measurement. Give your answer in terms of π.

B the diameter of a sphere with volume 972π in^3

$972\pi = \frac{4}{3}\pi r^3$ *Substitute 972π for V.*

$729 = r^3$ *Divide both sides by $\frac{4}{3}\pi$.*

$r = 9$ *Take the cube root of both sides.*

$d = 18$ in.   *$d = 2r$*

C the volume of the hemisphere

$V = \frac{2}{3}\pi r^3$ *Volume of a hemisphere*

$= \frac{2}{3}\pi(4)^3 = \frac{128\pi}{3}$ m^3 *Substitute 4 for r.*

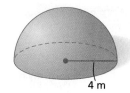

4 m

 1. Find the radius of a sphere with volume 2304π ft^3.

EXAMPLE 2
MCC9-12.G.MG.1

Online Video Tutor

Biology Application

Giant squid need large eyes to see their prey in low light. The eyeball of a giant squid is approximately a sphere with a diameter of 25 cm, which is bigger than a soccer ball. A human eyeball is approximately a sphere with a diameter of 2.5 cm. How many times as great is the volume of a giant squid eyeball as the volume of a human eyeball?

human eyeball:	giant squid eyeball:
$V = \frac{4}{3}\pi r^3$	$V = \frac{4}{3}\pi r^3$
$= \frac{4}{3}\pi(1.25)^3 \approx 8.18$ cm^3	$= \frac{4}{3}\pi(12.5)^3 \approx 8181.23$ cm^3

A giant squid eyeball is about 1000 times as great in volume as a human eyeball.

 2. A hummingbird eyeball has a diameter of approximately 0.6 cm. How many times as great is the volume of a human eyeball as the volume of a hummingbird eyeball?

In the figure, the vertex of the pyramid is at the center of the sphere. The height of the pyramid is approximately the radius r of the sphere. Suppose the entire sphere is filled with n pyramids that each have base area B and height r.

$V(\text{sphere}) \approx \frac{1}{3}Br + \frac{1}{3}Br + \ldots + \frac{1}{3}Br$ *The sphere's volume is close to the sum of the volumes of the pyramids.*

$\frac{4}{3}\pi r^3 \approx n\left(\frac{1}{3}Br\right)$

$4\pi r^2 \approx nB$ *Divide both sides by $\frac{1}{3}\pi r$.*

If the pyramids fill the sphere, the total area of the bases is approximately equal to the surface area of the sphere S, so $4\pi r^2 \approx S$. As the number of pyramids increases, the approximation gets closer to the actual surface area.

Surface Area of a Sphere

The surface area of a sphere with radius r is $S = 4\pi r^2$.

Online Video Tutor

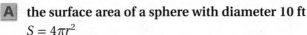

EXAMPLE **3** Finding Surface Area of Spheres

Find each measurement. Give your answers in terms of π.

A the surface area of a sphere with diameter 10 ft
$$S = 4\pi r^2$$
$$S = 4\pi(5)^2 = 200\pi \text{ ft}^2 \qquad \textit{Substitute 5 for r.}$$

B the volume of a sphere with surface area $144\pi \text{ m}^2$
$$S = 4\pi r^2$$
$$144\pi = 4\pi r^2 \qquad \textit{Substitute } 144\pi \textit{ for S.}$$
$$6 = r \qquad \textit{Solve for r.}$$
$$V = \frac{4}{3}\pi r^3$$
$$= \frac{4}{3}\pi(6)^3 = 288\pi \text{ m}^3 \qquad \textit{Substitute 6 for r.}$$

The volume of the sphere is $288\pi \text{ m}^3$.

C the surface area of a sphere with a great
circle that has an area of $4\pi \text{ in}^2$

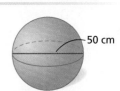

$$\pi r^2 = 4\pi \qquad \textit{Substitute } 4\pi \textit{ for A in the formula}$$
$$\qquad\qquad \textit{for the area of a circle.}$$
$$r = 2 \qquad \textit{Solve for r.}$$
$$S = 4\pi r^2$$
$$= 4\pi(2)^2 = 16\pi \text{ in}^2 \qquad \textit{Substitute 2 for r in the surface area formula.}$$

 3. Find the surface area of the sphere.

EXAMPLE **4** Exploring Effects of Changing Dimensions

The radius of the sphere is tripled. Describe the
effect on the volume.

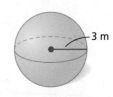

original dimensions:	radius tripled:
$V = \dfrac{4}{3}\pi r^3$	$V = \dfrac{4}{3}\pi r^3$
$= \dfrac{4}{3}\pi(3)^3$	$= \dfrac{4}{3}\pi(9)^3$
$= 36\pi \text{ m}^3$	$= 972\pi \text{ m}^3$

Online Video Tutor

Notice that $972\pi = 27(36\pi)$. If the radius is tripled, the volume is
multiplied by 27.

 4. The radius of the sphere above is divided by 3. Describe the
effect on the surface area.

EXAMPLE **5**

Finding Surface Areas and Volumes of Composite Figures

Find the surface area and volume of the composite figure. Give your answers in terms of π.

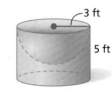
7 cm

25 cm

Step 1 Find the surface area of the composite figure.

The surface area of the composite figure is the sum of the surface area of the hemisphere and the lateral area of the cone.

$$S \text{ (hemisphere)} = \frac{1}{2}(4\pi r^2) = 2\pi(7)^2 = 98\pi \text{ cm}^2$$

$$L \text{ (cone)} = \pi r\ell = \pi(7)(25) = 175\pi \text{ cm}^2$$

The surface area of the composite figure is $98\pi + 175\pi = 273\pi \text{ cm}^2$.

Step 2 Find the volume of the composite figure.

First find the height of the cone.

$$h = \sqrt{25^2 - 7^2} \qquad \textit{Pythagorean Theorem}$$

$$= \sqrt{576} = 24 \text{ cm} \qquad \textit{Simplify.}$$

The volume of the composite figure is the sum of the volume of the hemisphere and the volume of the cone.

$$V \text{ (hemisphere)} = \frac{1}{2}\left(\frac{4}{3}\pi r^3\right) = \frac{2}{3}\pi(7)^3 = \frac{686\pi}{3} \text{ cm}^3$$

$$V \text{ (cone)} = \frac{1}{3}\pi r^2 h = \frac{1}{3}\pi(7)^2(24) = 392\pi \text{ cm}^3$$

The volume of the composite figure is $\dfrac{686\pi}{3} + 392\pi = \dfrac{1862\pi}{3} \text{ cm}^3$.

Remember!

The *lateral area* of a right cone is the area of its curved surface. The lateral area is given by the formula $\pi r\ell$, where r is the radius of the base and ℓ is the slant height of the cone.

 5. Find the surface area and volume of the composite figure.

3 ft

5 ft

MCC.MP.1 **MATHEMATICAL PRACTICES**

THINK AND DISCUSS

1. Explain how to find the surface area of a sphere when you know the area of a great circle.

2. Compare the volume of the sphere with the volume of the composite figure.

r

r
r
r

3. GET ORGANIZED Copy and complete the graphic organizer.

```
                If the radius of
                a sphere is r ...

   The area of a great    The volume of the    The surface area of
   circle is ...          sphere is ...        the sphere is ...
```

my.hrw.com
Homework Help

GUIDED PRACTICE

1. **Vocabulary** Describe the endpoints of a *radius of a sphere*.

SEE EXAMPLE **1** **Find each measurement. Give your answers in terms of π.**

2. the volume of the hemisphere

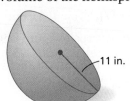

11 in.

3. the volume of the sphere

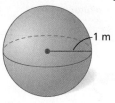

1 m

4. the radius of a sphere with volume 288π cm^3

SEE EXAMPLE **2** 5. **Food** Approximately how many times as great is the volume of the grapefruit as the volume of the lime?

10 cm

5 cm

SEE EXAMPLE **3** **Find each measurement. Give your answers in terms of π.**

6. the surface area of the sphere

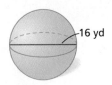

16 yd

7. the surface area of the sphere

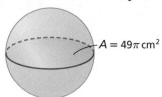

$A = 49\pi$ cm^2

8. the volume of a sphere with surface area 6724π ft^2

SEE EXAMPLE **4** **Describe the effect of each change on the given measurement of the figure.**

9. surface area

The dimensions are doubled.

15 in.

10. volume

The dimensions are multiplied by $\frac{1}{4}$.

16 cm

SEE EXAMPLE **5** **Find the surface area and volume of each composite figure.**

11.

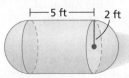

5 ft · 2 ft

12.

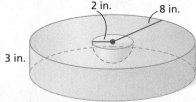

2 in.   8 in.

3 in.

PRACTICE AND PROBLEM SOLVING

Find each measurement. Give your answers in terms of π.

13. the volume of the sphere

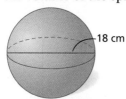

18 cm

14. the volume of the hemisphere

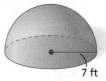

7 ft

15. the diameter of a sphere with volume 7776π in³

16. Jewelry The size of a cultured pearl is typically indicated by its diameter in mm. How many times as great is the volume of the 9 mm pearl as the volume of the 6 mm pearl?

6 mm

9 mm

Find each measurement. Give your answers in terms of π.

17. the surface area of the sphere

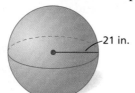

21 in.

18. the surface area of the sphere

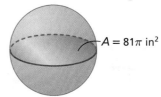

$A = 81\pi$ in²

19. the volume of a sphere with surface area 625π m²

H.O.T. **Describe the effect of each change on the given measurement of the figure.**

20. surface area
The dimensions are multiplied by $\frac{1}{5}$.

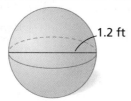

1.2 ft

21. volume
The dimensions are multiplied by 6.

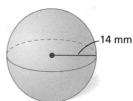

14 mm

Find the surface area and volume of each composite figure.

22.

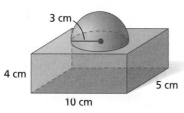

3 cm

4 cm

5 cm

10 cm

23.

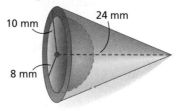

24 mm

10 mm

8 mm

24. Find the radius of a hemisphere with a volume of 144π cm³.

25. Find the circumference of a sphere with a surface area of 60π in².

26. Find the volume of a sphere with a circumference of 36π ft.

27. Find the surface area and volume of a sphere centered at $(0, 0, 0)$ that passes through the point $(2, 3, 6)$.

H.O.T. **28. Estimation** A bead is formed by drilling a cylindrical hole with a 2 mm diameter through a sphere with an 8 mm diameter. Estimate the surface area and volume of the bead.

Sports Find the unknown dimensions of the ball for each sport.

	Sport	Ball	Diameter	Circumference	Surface Area	Volume
29.	Golf		1.68 in.	▢	▢	▢
30.	Cricket		▢	9 in.	▢	▢
31.	Tennis		2.5 in.	▢	▢	▢
32.	Petanque		74 mm	▢	▢	▢

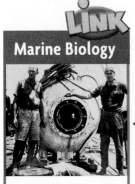

Marine Biology

In 1934, the bathysphere reached a record depth of 3028 feet. The pressure on the hull was about half a ton per square inch.

33. **Marine Biology** The *bathysphere* was an early version of a submarine, invented in the 1930s. The inside diameter of the bathysphere was 54 inches, and the steel used to make the sphere was 1.5 inches thick. It had three 8-inch diameter windows. Estimate the volume of steel used to make the bathysphere.

34. **Geography** Earth's radius is approximately 4000 mi. About two-thirds of Earth's surface is covered by water. Estimate the land area on Earth.

Astronomy Use the table for Exercises 35–38.

35. How many times as great is the volume of Jupiter as the volume of Earth?

36. The sum of the volumes of Venus and Mars is about equal to the volume of which planet?

37. Which is greater, the sum of the surface areas of Uranus and Neptune or the surface area of Saturn?

38. How many times as great is the surface area of Earth as the surface area of Mars?

Planet	Diameter (mi)
Mercury	3,032
Venus	7,521
Earth	7,926
Mars	4,222
Jupiter	88,846
Saturn	74,898
Uranus	31,763
Neptune	30,775

H.O.T. 39. **Critical Thinking** In the figure, the hemisphere and the cylinder both have radius and height r. Prove that the shaded cross sections have equal areas.

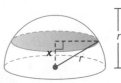
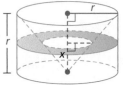

H.O.T. 40. **Write About It** Suppose a sphere and a cube have equal surface areas. Using r for the radius of the sphere and s for the side of a cube, write an equation to show the relationship between r and s.

Real-World Connections

41. A company sells orange juice in spherical containers that look like oranges. Each container has a surface area of approximately 50.3 in^2.

a. What is the volume of the container? Round to the nearest tenth.

b. The company decides to increase the radius of the container by 10%. What is the volume of the new container?

TEST PREP

42. A sphere with radius 8 cm is inscribed in a cube. Find the ratio of the volume of the cube to the volume of the sphere.

   Ⓐ $2:\frac{1}{3}\pi$ Ⓑ $2:3\pi$ Ⓒ $1:\frac{4}{3}\pi$ Ⓓ $1:\frac{2}{3}\pi$

43. What is the surface area of a sphere with volume $10\frac{2}{3}\pi$ in³?

   Ⓕ 8π in²   Ⓖ $10\frac{2}{3}\pi$ in²   Ⓗ 16π in²   Ⓙ 32π in²

44. Which expression represents the volume of the composite figure formed by a hemisphere with radius r and a cube with side length $2r$?

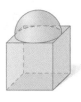

   Ⓐ $r^3\left(\frac{2}{3}\pi + 8\right)$ Ⓒ $2r^2(2\pi + 12)$

   Ⓑ $\frac{4}{3}\pi r^3 + 2r^3$ Ⓓ $\frac{4}{3}\pi r^3 + 8r^3$

CHALLENGE AND EXTEND

45. Food The top of a gumball machine is an 18 in. sphere. The machine holds a maximum of 3300 gumballs, which leaves about 43% of the space in the machine empty. Estimate the diameter of each gumball.

H.O.T. 46. The surface area of a sphere can be used to determine its volume.

   a. Solve the surface area formula of a sphere to get an expression for r in terms of S.

   b. Substitute your result from part **a** into the volume formula to find the volume V of a sphere in terms of its surface area S.

   c. Graph the relationship between volume and surface area with S on the horizontal axis and V on the vertical axis. What shape is the graph?

Use the diagram of a sphere inscribed in a cylinder for Exercises 47 and 48.

47. What is the relationship between the volume of the sphere and the volume of the cylinder?

48. What is the relationship between the surface area of the sphere and the lateral area of the cylinder?

FOCUS ON MATHEMATICAL PRACTICES

H.O.T. 49. Estimation The volume of a tennis ball is 157.5 cm³. What whole number of centimeters is the best approximation for its radius? Explain.

H.O.T. 50. Problem Solving A spherical scoop of frozen yogurt with a 6 cm diameter is placed in a cone with the same diameter. If left to melt, the yogurt exactly fills the cone, without overflowing. What is the height of the cone? Explain your reasoning.

H.O.T. 51. Justify The surface area of a sphere has the same numerical value as its volume. Find the diameter of this sphere. Justify your answer.

H.O.T. 52. Analysis A spherical piece of ice melts, and the water is poured into identical cylindrical buckets that have diameters and heights equal to the radius of the sphere. How many buckets are needed?

Ready to Go On?

my.hrw.com
Assessment and Intervention

✓ 29-1 Developing Formulas for Circles and Regular Polygons

Find each measurement.

1. the circumference of
⊙*R* in terms of π

R
18 in.

2. the area of ⊙*E*
in terms of π

E
6*x* ft

3. A store sells circular rugs in three different sizes. The rugs come in diameters of 8 ft, 12 ft, and 16 ft. Find the areas of the three different sizes of rugs. Use 3.14 for π and round answers to the nearest tenth.

Find the area of each regular polygon. Round to the nearest tenth.

4. a regular hexagon with apothem 6 ft

5. a regular pentagon with side length 12 m

✓ 29-2 Volume of Prisms and Cylinders

Find the volume of each figure. Round to the nearest tenth, if necessary.

6. a regular hexagonal prism with base area 23 in^2 and height 9 in.

7. a cylinder with radius 8 yd and height 14 yd

8. A brick patio measures 10 ft by 12 ft by 4 in. Find the volume of the bricks. If the density of brick is 130 pounds per cubic foot, what is the weight of the patio in pounds?

9. The dimensions of a cylinder with diameter 2 ft and height 1 ft are doubled. Describe the effect on the volume.

✓ 29-3 Volume of Pyramids and Cones

Find the volume of each figure. Round to the nearest tenth, if necessary.

10.

16 ft
24 ft

11.

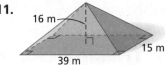

16 m
15 m
39 m

12.

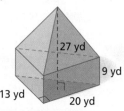

27 yd
9 yd
13 yd
20 yd

✓ 29-4 Spheres

Find the surface area and volume of each figure.

13. a sphere with diameter 20 in.

14. a hemisphere with radius 12 in.

15. A baseball has a diameter of approximately 3 in., and a softball has a diameter of approximately 5 in. About how many times as great is the volume of a softball as the volume of a baseball?

Selected Response

1. The radius and height of the cylinder are multiplied by 4. Describe the effect on the volume.

3 cm

6 cm

Ⓐ The volume is multiplied by 4.

Ⓑ The volume is multiplied by 8.

Ⓒ The volume is multiplied by 16.

Ⓓ The volume is multiplied by 64.

2. A human's eyeball is shaped like a sphere with a diameter of 2.5 cm. A dog's eyeball is shaped like a sphere with a diameter of 1.75 cm. About how many times greater is the volume of a human's eyeball than the volume of a dog's eyeball?

Ⓕ about 1.5 times greater

Ⓖ about 3 times greater

Ⓗ about 8 times greater

Ⓙ about 23 times greater

3. Find the volume of a cone with a base circumference of 19π cm and a height 6 cm less than twice the radius. Give your answer both in terms of π and rounded to the nearest tenth.

Ⓐ 752.1π cm^3 ≈ 2,362.7 cm^3

Ⓑ $1,173.3\pi$ cm^3 ≈ 3,685.9 cm^3

Ⓒ 391.1π cm^3 ≈ 1,228.6 cm^3

Ⓓ 17.2π cm^3 ≈ 54.1 cm^3

4. Two circles have the same center. The radius of the larger circle is 3 units longer than the radius of the smaller circle. Find the difference in the circumferences of the two circles. Round to the nearest hundredth.

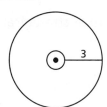

3

Ⓕ 6.00 units   Ⓗ 9.42 units

Ⓖ 18.84 units   Ⓙ 28.26 units

5. Find the surface area of a sphere with volume 288π m^3. Give your answer in terms of π.

Ⓐ 144 m^2 Ⓒ 144π m^2

Ⓑ 6π m^2 Ⓓ 864 m^2

6. Find the volume of the composite figure. Round to the nearest tenth.
(*Hint*: Volume of a cone is $V = \frac{1}{3}\pi r^2 h$.)

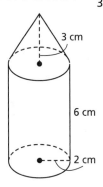

3 cm

6 cm

2 cm

Ⓕ 88.0 cm^3 Ⓗ 75.4 cm^3

Ⓖ 12.6 cm^3 Ⓙ 28.0 cm^3

7. The length, width, and height of the rectangular pyramid are multiplied by $\frac{1}{3}$. Describe the effect on the volume.

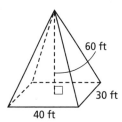

60 ft

30 ft

40 ft

Ⓐ The volume is multiplied by $\frac{1}{81}$.

Ⓑ The volume is multiplied by $\frac{1}{27}$.

Ⓒ The volume is multiplied by $\frac{1}{9}$.

Ⓓ The volume is multiplied by $\frac{1}{3}$.

Mini-Task

8. Find the height in centimeters of a square pyramid with a volume of 72 cm^3 and a base edge length equal to the height.

30 Circles

MATHEMATICAL
PRACTICES   The Common Core Georgia Performance Standards for Mathematical Practice
                   describe varieties of expertise that all students should seek to develop.
Opportunities to develop these practices are integrated throughout this program.

1 Make sense of problems and persevere in
solving them.

2 Reason abstractly and quantitatively.

3 Construct viable arguments and critique the
reasoning of others.

4 Model with mathematics.

5 Use appropriate tools strategically.

6 Attend to precision.

7 Look for and make use of structure.

8 Look for and express regularity in repeated
reasoning.

Unpacking the Standards

my.hrw.com
Multilingual Glossary

Understanding the standards and the vocabulary terms in the standards will help you know exactly what you are expected to learn in this chapter.

COMMON CORE GPS **MCC9-12.G.C.5**

Derive using similarity the fact that the length of the arc intercepted by an angle is proportional to the radius, and define the radian measure of the angle as the constant of proportionality; derive the formula for the area of a sector.

Key Vocabulary

similar (semejantes)
Two figures are similar if they have the same shape but not necessarily the same size.

intercepted arc (arco abarcado)
An arc that consists of endpoints that lie on the sides of an inscribed angle and all the points of the circle between the endpoints.

radian (radian)
A unit of angle measure based on arc length. In a circle of radius r, if a central angle has a measure of 1 radian, then the length of the intercepted arc is r units.
2π radians = 360°
1 radian ≈ 57°

sector of a circle (sector de un círculo)
A region inside a circle bounded by two radii of the circle and their intercepted arc.

What It Means For You

You can find the length of an arc with central angle m by multiplying the circumference by $\dfrac{m°}{360°}$ if m is in degrees or by $\dfrac{m\ \text{radians}}{2\pi\ \text{radians}}$ if m is in radians. You can also find the area of a sector by multiplying the area of the circle by $\dfrac{m°}{360°}$ or by $\dfrac{m\ \text{radians}}{2\pi\ \text{radians}}$.

EXAMPLE   **Finding Arc Length**

Find the length of $\overset{\frown}{CD}$.

$$\text{Arc length} = \text{Circumference} \times \frac{m°}{360°}$$

$$= 2\pi r \times \frac{m°}{360°}$$

$$= 2\pi(10)\left(\frac{90°}{360°}\right)$$

$$= 5\pi \approx 16 \text{ feet}$$

The radian measure of the central angle is

$$90°\left(\frac{2\pi\ \text{radians}}{360°}\right) = \frac{\pi}{2} \text{ radians, and } 2\pi r\left(\frac{\frac{\pi}{2}}{2\pi}\right) = 5\pi \approx 16 \text{ feet,}$$

which is the same as the answer above.

EXAMPLE   **Finding the Area of a Sector**

A farmer uses a rotating sprayer to irrigate a circular plot with radius 660 feet. What is the area that is irrigated as the sprayer moves through an angle of 60°?

$$\text{Area of sector} = \text{Area of plot} \times \frac{m°}{360°}$$

$$= \pi r^2 \times \frac{m°}{360°}$$

$$= \pi(660)^2 \times \left(\frac{60°}{360°}\right)$$

$$= 72,600\pi$$

$$\approx 228,000 \text{ square feet}$$

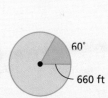

30-1 Lines That Intersect Circles

? Essential Question: What are various ways that lines and circles can intersect?

Objectives
Identify tangents, secants, and chords.

Use properties of tangents to solve problems.

Vocabulary
interior of a circle
exterior of a circle
chord
secant
tangent of a circle
point of tangency
congruent circles
concentric circles
tangent circles
common tangent

Why learn this?
You can use circle theorems to solve problems about Earth. (See Example 3.)

This photograph was taken 216 miles above Earth. From this altitude, it is easy to see the curvature of the horizon. Facts about circles can help us understand details about Earth.

Recall that a circle is the set of all points in a plane that are equidistant from a given point, called the center of the circle. A circle with center C is called circle C, or $\odot C$.

The **interior of a circle** is the set of all points inside the circle. The **exterior of a circle** is the set of all points outside the circle.

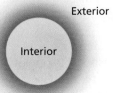

Lines and Segments That Intersect Circles

TERM	DIAGRAM
A **chord** is a segment whose endpoints lie on a circle.	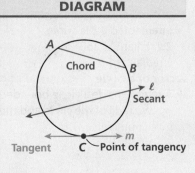
A **secant** is a line that intersects a circle at two points.	
A **tangent** is a line in the same plane as a circle that intersects it at exactly one point.	
The point where the tangent and a circle intersect is called the **point of tangency**.	

COMMON CORE GPS
Prep for MCC9-12.G.C.2

EXAMPLE 1 Identifying Lines and Segments That Intersect Circles

Identify each line or segment that intersects $\odot A$.

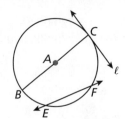

chords: $\overline{EF}$ and $\overline{BC}$

tangent: ℓ

radii: $\overline{AC}$ and $\overline{AB}$

secant: $\overleftrightarrow{EF}$

diameter: $\overline{BC}$

my.hrw.com

Online Video Tutor

PhotoDisc/Getty Images

1. Identify each line or segment that intersects ⊙*P*.

Remember that the terms *radius* and *diameter* may refer to line segments, or to the lengths of segments.

Pairs of Circles

TERM	DIAGRAM
Two circles are **congruent circles** if and only if they have congruent radii.	⊙*A* ≅ ⊙*B* if $\overline{AC}$ ≅ $\overline{BD}$. $\overline{AC}$ ≅ $\overline{BD}$ if ⊙*A* ≅ ⊙*B*.
Concentric circles are coplanar circles with the same center.	
Two coplanar circles that intersect at exactly one point are called **tangent circles**.	Internally tangent circles Externally tangent circles

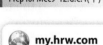

EXAMPLE 2
Prep for MCC9-12.G.C.4(+)

Identifying Tangents of Circles

my.hrw.com

Online Video Tutor

Find the length of each radius. Identify the point of tangency and write the equation of the tangent line at this point.

radius of ⊙*A*: 4   *Center is* $(-1, 0)$. *Pt. on* ⊙ *is* $(3, 0)$. *Dist. between the 2 pts. is 4.*

radius of ⊙*B*: 2   *Center is* $(1, 0)$. *Pt. on* ⊙ *is* $(3, 0)$. *Dist. between the 2 pts. is 2.*

point of tangency: $(3, 0)$ *Pt. where the* ⊙s *and tangent line intersect*

equation of tangent line: $x = 3$ *Vert. line through* $(3, 0)$

 2. Find the length of each radius. Identify the point of tangency and write the equation of the tangent line at this point.

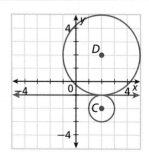

A **common tangent** is a line that is tangent to two circles.

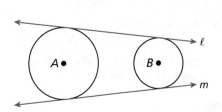 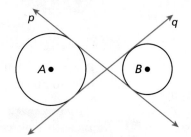

Lines ℓ and m are common external tangents to $\odot A$ and $\odot B$.

Lines p and q are common internal tangents to $\odot A$ and $\odot B$.

Construction Tangent to a Circle at a Point

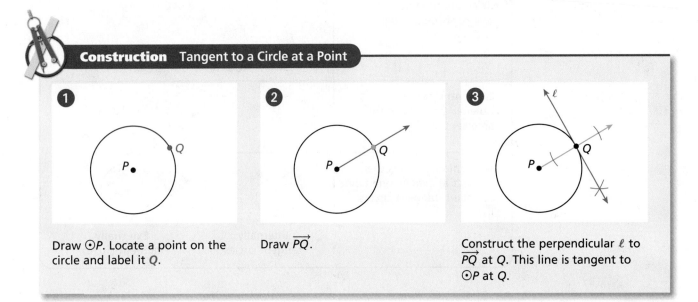

1 Draw $\odot P$. Locate a point on the circle and label it Q.

2 Draw $\overrightarrow{PQ}$.

3 Construct the perpendicular ℓ to $\overrightarrow{PQ}$ at Q. This line is tangent to $\odot P$ at Q.

Notice that in the construction, the tangent line is perpendicular to the radius at the point of tangency. This fact is the basis for the following theorems.

Know it! Note

Theorems

THEOREM	HYPOTHESIS	CONCLUSION
30-1-1 If a line is tangent to a circle, then it is perpendicular to the radius drawn to the point of tangency. (line tangent to $\odot$ → line ⊥ to radius)	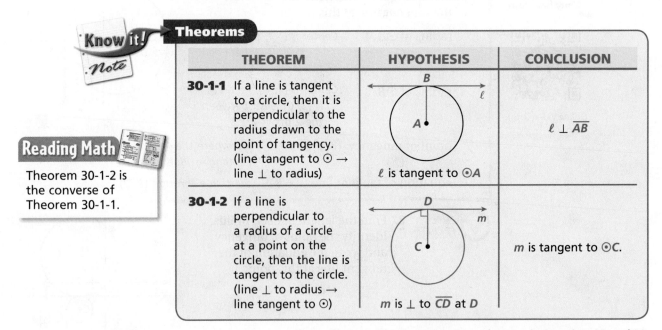 ℓ is tangent to $\odot A$	$\ell \perp \overline{AB}$
30-1-2 If a line is perpendicular to a radius of a circle at a point on the circle, then the line is tangent to the circle. (line ⊥ to radius → line tangent to $\odot$)	m is ⊥ to $\overline{CD}$ at D	m is tangent to $\odot C$.

You will prove Theorems 30-1-1 and 30-1-2 in Exercises 28 and 29.

EXAMPLE **3**
MCC9-12.G.SRT.8

my.hrw.com

Online Video Tutor

Make sense of problems and persevere in solving them.

Helpful Hint

5280 ft = 1 mi
Earth's radius ≈
4000 mi

Problem Solving Application

The summit of Mount Everest is approximately 29,000 ft above sea level. What is the distance from the summit to the horizon to the nearest mile?

1. Understand the Problem

The **answer** will be the length of an imaginary segment from the summit of Mount Everest to Earth's horizon.

2. Make a Plan

Draw a sketch. Let C be the center of Earth, E be the summit of Mount Everest, and H be a point on the horizon. You need to find the length of $\overline{EH}$, which is tangent to $\odot C$ at H. By Theorem 30-1-1, $\overline{EH} \perp \overline{CH}$. So $\triangle CHE$ is a right triangle.

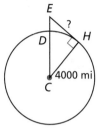

3. Solve

$ED = 29{,}000$ ft	*Given*
$= \dfrac{29{,}000}{5280} \approx 5.49$ mi	*Change ft to mi.*
$EC = CD + ED$	*Seg. Add. Post.*
$= 4000 + 5.49 = 4005.49$ mi	*Substitute 4000 for CD and 5.49 for ED.*
$EC^2 = EH^2 + CH^2$	*Pyth. Thm.*
$4005.49^2 = EH^2 + 4000^2$	*Substitute the given values.*
$43{,}950.14 \approx EH^2$	*Subtract 4000^2 from both sides.*
210 mi $\approx EH$	*Take the square root of both sides.*

4. Look Back

The problem asks for the distance to the nearest mile. Check if your answer is reasonable by using the Pythagorean Theorem. Is $210^2 + 4000^2 \approx 4005^2$? Yes, $16{,}044{,}100 \approx 16{,}040{,}025$.

3. Kilimanjaro, the tallest mountain in Africa, is 19,340 ft tall. What is the distance from the summit of Kilimanjaro to the horizon to the nearest mile?

Theorem 30-1-3

THEOREM	HYPOTHESIS	CONCLUSION
If two segments are tangent to a circle from the same external point, then the segments are congruent. (2 segs. tangent to $\odot$ from same ext. pt. → segs. ≅)	$\overline{AB}$ and $\overline{AC}$ are tangent to $\odot P$.	$\overline{AB} \cong \overline{AC}$

You will prove Theorem 30-1-3 in Exercise 30.

You can use Theorem 30-1-3 to find the length of segments drawn tangent to a circle from an exterior point.

EXAMPLE 4

Using Properties of Tangents

$\overline{DE}$ and $\overline{DF}$ are tangent to $\odot C$. Find DF.

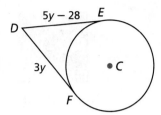

$DE = DF$	*2 segs. tangent to $\odot$ from same ext. pt. $\rightarrow$ segs. $\cong$.*
$5y - 28 = 3y$	*Substitute $5y - 28$ for DE and $3y$ for DF.*
$2y - 28 = 0$	*Subtract $3y$ from both sides.*
$2y = 28$	*Add 28 to both sides.*
$y = 14$	*Divide both sides by 2.*
$DF = 3(14)$	*Substitute 14 for y.*
$= 42$	*Simplify.*

CHECK IT OUT!

$\overline{RS}$ and $\overline{RT}$ are tangent to $\odot Q$. Find RS.

4a.

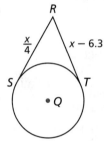

4b.

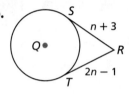

MCC.MP.6   MATHEMATICAL PRACTICES

THINK AND DISCUSS

1. Consider $\odot A$ and $\odot B$. How many different lines are common tangents to both circles? Copy the circles and sketch the common external and common internal tangent lines.

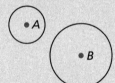

2. Is it possible for a line to be tangent to two concentric circles? Explain your answer.

3. Given $\odot P$, is the center P a part of the circle? Explain your answer.

4. In the figure, $\overline{RQ}$ is tangent to $\odot P$ at Q. Explain how you can find m$\angle PRQ$.

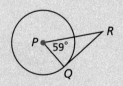

5. **GET ORGANIZED** Copy and complete the graphic organizer below. In each box, write a definition and draw a sketch.

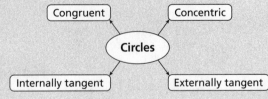

GUIDED PRACTICE

Vocabulary Apply the vocabulary from this lesson to answer each question.

1. A ___?___ is a line in the plane of a circle that intersects the circle at two points.
   (*secant* or *tangent*)

2. Coplanar circles that have the same center are called ___?___ .
   (*concentric* or *congruent*)

3. ⊙Q and ⊙R both have a radius of 3 cm. Therefore the circles are ___?___ .
   (*concentric* or *congruent*)

SEE EXAMPLE 1 Identify each line or segment that intersects each circle.

4.
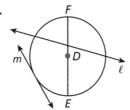

5.
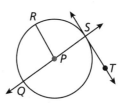

SEE EXAMPLE 2 **Multi-Step** Find the length of each radius. Identify the point of tangency and write the equation of the tangent line at this point.

6.
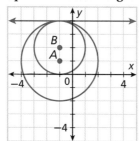

7.
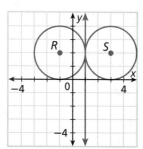

SEE EXAMPLE 3 8. **Space Exploration** The International Space Station orbits Earth at an altitude of 240 mi. What is the distance from the space station to Earth's horizon to the nearest mile?

SEE EXAMPLE 4 The segments in each figure are tangent to the circle. Find each length.

9. *JK*
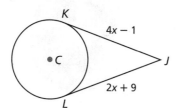

10. *ST*
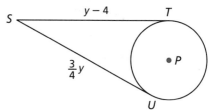

30-1 Lines That Intersect Circles **919**

© NASA

PRACTICE AND PROBLEM SOLVING

Independent Practice

For Exercises	See Example
11–12	1
13–14	2
15	3
16–17	4

Identify each line or segment that intersects each circle.

11.
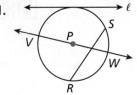

12.
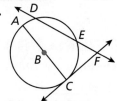

my.hrw.com

Online Extra Practice

Multi-Step Find the length of each radius. Identify the point of tangency and write the equation of the tangent line at this point.

13.
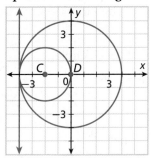

14.
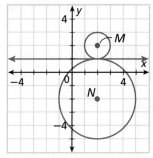

Astronomy

Olympus Mons, located on Mars, is the tallest known volcano in the solar system.

15. **Astronomy** Olympus Mons's peak rises 25 km above the surface of the planet Mars. The diameter of Mars is approximately 6794 km. What is the distance from the peak of Olympus Mons to the horizon to the nearest kilometer?

The segments in each figure are tangent to the circle. Find each length.

16. AB
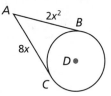

17. RT
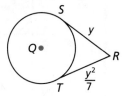

Tell whether each statement is sometimes, always, or never true.

18. Two circles with the same center are congruent.

19. A tangent to a circle intersects the circle at two points.

20. Tangent circles have the same center.

21. A tangent to a circle will form a right angle with a radius that is drawn to the point of tangency.

22. A chord of a circle is a diameter.

Graphic Design Use the following diagram for Exercises 23–25.

The peace symbol was designed in 1958 by Gerald Holtom, a professional artist and designer. Identify the following.

23. diameter

24. radii

25. chord

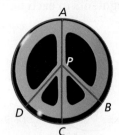

In each diagram, $\overline{PR}$ and $\overline{PS}$ are tangent to $\odot Q$. Find each angle measure.

26. m∠Q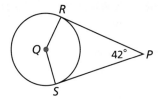

27. m∠P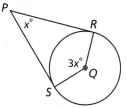

28. Complete this indirect proof of Theorem 30-1-1.
Given: ℓ is tangent to $\odot A$ at point B.
Prove: $\ell \perp \overline{AB}$

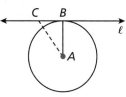

Proof: Assume that ℓ is not $\perp \overline{AB}$. Then it is possible to draw $\overline{AC}$ such that $\overline{AC} \perp \ell$. If this is true, then $\triangle ACB$ is a right triangle. $AC < AB$ because **a.** __?__ . Since ℓ is a tangent line, it can only intersect $\odot A$ at **b.** __?__ , and C must be in the exterior of $\odot A$. That means that $AC > AB$ since $\overline{AB}$ is a **c.** __?__ . This contradicts the fact that $AC < AB$. Thus the assumption is false, and **d.** __?__ .

H.O.T. 29. Prove Theorem 30-1-2.
Given: $m \perp \overline{CD}$
Prove: m is tangent to $\odot C$.

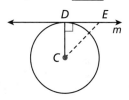

(*Hint:* Choose a point on m. Then use the Pythagorean Theorem to prove that if the point is not D, then it is not on the circle.)

H.O.T. 30. Prove Theorem 30-1-3.
Given: $\overline{AB}$ and $\overline{AC}$ are tangent to $\odot P$.
Prove: $\overline{AB} \cong \overline{AC}$

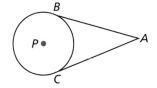

Plan: Draw auxiliary segments $\overline{PA}$, $\overline{PB}$, and $\overline{PC}$. Show that the triangles formed are congruent. Then use CPCTC.

Algebra Assume the segments that appear to be tangent are tangent. Find each length.

31. ST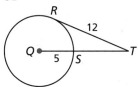

32. DE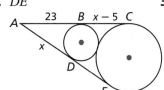

33. JL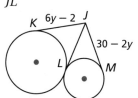

34. $\odot M$ has center $M(2, 2)$ and radius 3. $\odot N$ has center $N(-3, 2)$ and is tangent to $\odot M$. Find the coordinates of the possible points of tangency of the two circles.

35. The diagram shows the gears of a bicycle. $AD = 5$ in., and $BC = 3$ in. CD, the length of the chain between the gears, is 17 in.

a. What type of quadrilateral is $BCDE$? Why?

b. Find BE and AE.

c. What is AB to the nearest tenth of an inch?

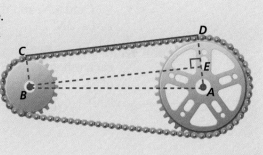

H.O.T. 36. Critical Thinking Given a circle with diameter $\overline{BC}$, is it possible to draw tangents to B and C from an external point X? If so, make a sketch. If not, explain why it is not possible.

37. Write About It $\overrightarrow{PR}$ and $\overrightarrow{PS}$ are tangent to $\odot Q$ at points R and S. Explain why $\angle RPS$ and $\angle SQR$ are supplementary.

TEST PREP

38. $\overline{AB}$ and $\overline{AC}$ are tangent to $\odot D$. Which of these is closest to AD?

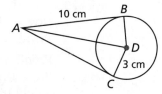

   Ⓐ 9.5 cm   Ⓒ 10.4 cm

   Ⓑ 10 cm   Ⓓ 13 cm

39. $\odot P$ has center $P(3, -2)$ and radius 2. Which of these lines is tangent to $\odot P$?

   Ⓕ $x = 0$ Ⓖ $y = -4$ Ⓗ $y = -2$ Ⓙ $x = 4$

40. $\odot A$ has radius 5. $\odot B$ has radius 6. What is the ratio of the area of $\odot A$ to that of $\odot B$?

   Ⓐ $\dfrac{125}{216}$ Ⓑ $\dfrac{25}{36}$ Ⓒ $\dfrac{5}{6}$ Ⓓ $\dfrac{36}{25}$

CHALLENGE AND EXTEND

H.O.T. 41. Given: $\odot G$ with $\overline{GH} \perp \overline{JK}$
Prove: $\overline{JH} \cong \overline{KH}$

H.O.T. 42. Multi-Step $\odot A$ has radius 5, $\odot B$ has radius 2, and $\overline{CD}$ is a common tangent. What is AB? (*Hint:* Draw a perpendicular segment from B to E, a point on $\overline{AC}$.)

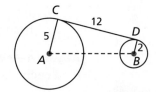

H.O.T. 43. Manufacturing A company builds metal stands for bicycle wheels. A new design calls for a V-shaped stand that will hold wheels with a 13 in. radius. The sides of the stand form a 70° angle. To the nearest tenth of an inch, what should be the length XY of a side so that it is tangent to the wheel?

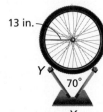

FOCUS ON MATHEMATICAL PRACTICES

H.O.T. 44. Proof $\overline{AB}$ and $\overline{CD}$ are common internal tangents to $\odot M$ and $\odot N$, and they intersect at point P. Prove that $\angle M \cong \angle N$.

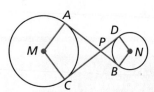

H.O.T. 45. Problem Solving Three circles, R, S, and T are tangent to each other. $RS = 13$, $RT = 14$, and $ST = 11$. Find the length of each radius. (*Hint:* Represent the radius of one circle with x. Represent each of the other radii in terms of x.)

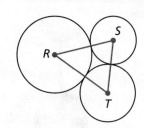

Circle Graphs

A circle graph compares data that are parts of a whole unit. When you make a circle graph, you find the measure of each *central angle*. A *central angle* is an angle whose vertex is the center of the circle.

Example

Make a circle graph to represent the following data.

Step 1 Add all the amounts. *110 + 40 + 300 + 150 = 600*

Step 2 Write each part as a fraction of the whole.

fiction: $\frac{110}{600}$; nonfiction: $\frac{40}{600}$; children's: $\frac{300}{600}$; audio books: $\frac{150}{600}$

Step 3 Multiply each fraction by 360° to calculate the central angle measure.

$\frac{110}{600}(360°) = 66°$; $\frac{40}{600}(360°) = 24°$; $\frac{300}{600}(360°) = 180°$; $\frac{150}{600}(360°) = 90°$

Step 4 Make a circle graph. Then color each section of the circle to match the data.

Books in the Bookmobile	
Fiction	110
Nonfiction	40
Children's	300
Audio books	150

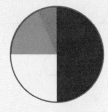

The section with a central angle of 66° is green, 24° is orange, 180° is purple, and 90° is yellow.

Try This

Choose the circle graph that best represents the data. Show each step.

A	B	C	D
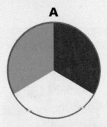		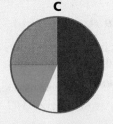	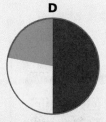

1.

Books in Linda's Library	
Novels	18
Reference	10
Textbooks	8

2.

Vacation Expenses ($)	
Travel	450
Meals	120
Lodging	900
Other	330

3.

Puppy Expenses ($)	
Food	190
Health	375
Training	120
Other	50

30-2 Arcs and Chords

 Essential Question: How are arcs of circles measured in relation to central angles?

Objectives
Apply properties of arcs.

Apply properties of chords.

Vocabulary
central angle
arc
minor arc
major arc
semicircle
adjacent arcs
congruent arcs

Who uses this?
Market analysts use circle graphs to compare sales of different products.

A **central angle** is an angle whose vertex is the center of a circle. An **arc** is an unbroken part of a circle consisting of two points called the endpoints and all the points on the circle between them.

Arcs and Their Measure

ARC	MEASURE	DIAGRAM
A **minor arc** is an arc whose points are on or in the interior of a central angle.	The measure of a minor arc is equal to the measure of its central angle. $\widehat{mAC} = m\angle ABC = x°$	
A **major arc** is an arc whose points are on or in the exterior of a central angle.	The measure of a major arc is equal to 360° minus the measure of its central angle. $\widehat{mADC} = 360° - m\angle ABC$ $= 360° - x°$	
If the endpoints of an arc lie on a diameter, the arc is a **semicircle**.	The measure of a semicircle is equal to 180°. $\widehat{mEFG} = 180°$	

Writing Math

Minor arcs may be named by two points. Major arcs and semicircles must be named by three points.

Data Application

The circle graph shows the types of music sold during one week at a music store. Find $\widehat{mBC}$.

$\widehat{mBC} = m\angle BMC$ *m of arc = m of central ∠.*

$m\angle BMC = 0.13(360°)$ *Central ∠ is 13% of the ⊙.*

$= 46.8°$

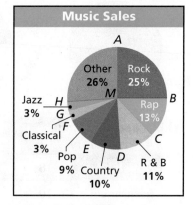

my.hrw.com

Online Video Tutor

 Use the graph to find each of the following.

1a. $m\angle FMC$ **1b.** $\widehat{mAHB}$ **1c.** $m\angle EMD$

©Brand X Pictures/PunchStock

Adjacent arcs are arcs of the same circle that intersect at exactly one point. $\overarc{RS}$ and $\overarc{ST}$ are adjacent arcs.

Postulate 30-2-1   Arc Addition Postulate

The measure of an arc formed by two adjacent arcs is the sum of the measures of the two arcs.

$$\text{m}\overarc{ABC} = \text{m}\overarc{AB} + \text{m}\overarc{BC}$$

EXAMPLE **2**
Prep for MCC9-12.G.C.2

Using the Arc Addition Postulate

Find $\text{m}\overarc{CDE}$

$\text{m}\overarc{CD} = 90°$	$m\angle CFD = 90°$
$m\angle DFE = 18°$	*Vert. $\angle$ Thm.*
$\text{m}\overarc{DE} = 18°$	$m\angle DFE = 18°$
$\text{m}\overarc{CE} = \text{m}\overarc{CD} + \text{m}\overarc{DE}$	*Arc Add. Post.*
$= 90° + 18° = 108°$	*Substitute and simplify.*

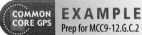

my.hrw.com

Online Video Tutor

CHECK IT OUT!

Find each measure.

2a. $\text{m}\overarc{JKL}$ **2b.** $\text{m}\overarc{LJN}$

Within a circle or congruent circles, **congruent arcs** are two arcs that have the same measure. In the figure, $\overarc{ST} \cong \overarc{UV}$.

Theorem 30-2-2

THEOREM	HYPOTHESIS	CONCLUSION
In a circle or congruent circles: **(1)** Congruent central angles have congruent chords.	$\angle EAD \cong \angle BAC$	$\overline{DE} \cong \overline{BC}$
(2) Congruent chords have congruent arcs.	$\overline{ED} \cong \overline{BC}$	$\overarc{DE} \cong \overarc{BC}$
(3) Congruent arcs have congruent central angles.	$\overarc{ED} \cong \overarc{BC}$	$\angle DAE \cong \angle BAC$

You will prove parts 2 and 3 of Theorem 30-2-2 in Exercises 40 and 41.

The converses of the parts of Theorem 30-2-2 are also true. For example, with part 1, congruent chords have congruent central angles.

PROOF   **Theorem 30-2-2 (Part 1)**

Given: $\angle BAC \cong \angle DAE$
Prove: $\overline{BC} \cong \overline{DE}$

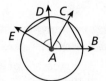

Proof:

Statements	Reasons
1. $\angle BAC \cong \angle DAE$	1. Given
2. $\overline{AB} \cong \overline{AD}$, $\overline{AC} \cong \overline{AE}$	2. All radii of a $\odot$ are $\cong$.
3. $\triangle BAC \cong \triangle DAE$	3. SAS *Steps 2, 1*
4. $\overline{BC} \cong \overline{DE}$	4. CPCTC

EXAMPLE 3
MCC9-12.A.CED.1

Applying Congruent Angles, Arcs, and Chords

Find each measure.

A $\overline{RS} \cong \overline{TU}$. Find m$\overparen{RS}$.

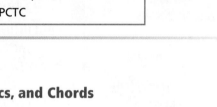

$\overparen{RS} \cong \overparen{TU}$	$\cong$ chords have $\cong$ arcs.
m$\overparen{RS}$ = m$\overparen{TU}$	Def. of $\cong$ arcs
$3x = 2x + 27$	Substitute the given measures.
$x = 27$	Subtract 2x from both sides.
m$\overparen{RS}$ = 3(27)	Substitute 27 for x.
$= 81°$	Simplify.

my.hrw.com

Online Video Tutor

B $\odot B \cong \odot E$, and $\overparen{AC} \cong \overparen{DF}$. Find m$\angle DEF$.

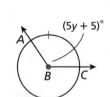
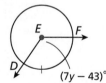

$\angle ABC \cong \angle DEF$	$\cong$ arcs have $\cong$ central $\angle$.
m$\angle ABC$ = m$\angle DEF$	Def. of $\cong$ $\angle$
$5y + 5 = 7y - 43$	Substitute the given measures.
$5 = 2y - 43$	Subtract 5y from both sides.
$48 = 2y$	Add 43 to both sides.
$24 = y$	Divide both sides by 2.
m$\angle DEF$ = 7(24) − 43	Substitute 24 for y.
$= 125°$	Simplify.

CHECK IT OUT!   Find each measure.

3a. $\overrightarrow{PT}$ bisects $\angle RPS$. Find RT.

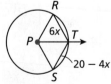

3b. $\odot A \cong \odot B$, and $\overline{CD} \cong \overline{EF}$.
Find m$\overparen{CD}$.

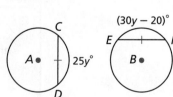

Know it! Note

Theorems

THEOREM	HYPOTHESIS	CONCLUSION
30-2-3 In a circle, if a radius (or diameter) is perpendicular to a chord, then it bisects the chord and its arc.	 $\overline{CD} \perp \overline{EF}$	$\overline{CD}$ bisects $\overline{EF}$ and $\overset{\frown}{EF}$.
30-2-4 In a circle, the perpendicular bisector of a chord is a radius (or diameter).	 $\overline{JK}$ is $\perp$ bisector of $\overline{GH}$.	$\overline{JK}$ is a diameter of $\odot A$.

You will prove Theorems 30-2-3 and 30-2-4 in Exercises 42 and 43.

COMMON CORE GPS MCC9-12.G.SRT.8

EXAMPLE 4 Using Radii and Chords

my.hrw.com

Online Video Tutor

Find BD.

Step 1 Draw radius $\overline{AD}$.

$AD = 5$ *Radii of a $\odot$ are $\cong$.*

Step 2 Use the Pythagorean Theorem.

$CD^2 + AC^2 = AD^2$

$CD^2 + 3^2 = 5^2$ *Substitute 3 for AC and 5 for AD.*

$CD^2 = 16$ *Subtract 3^2 from both sides.*

$CD = 4$ *Take the square root of both sides.*

Step 3 Find BD.

$BD = 2(4) = 8$ *$\overline{AE} \perp \overline{BD}$, so $\overline{AE}$ bisects $\overline{BD}$.*

CHECK IT OUT! **4.** Find QR to the nearest tenth.

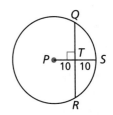

MCC.MP.2 **MATHEMATICAL PRACTICES**

THINK AND DISCUSS

1. What is true about the measure of an arc whose central angle is obtuse?

2. Under what conditions are two arcs the same measure but not congruent?

3. GET ORGANIZED Copy and complete the graphic organizer. In each box, write a definition and draw a sketch.

Know it! Note

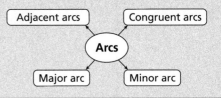

GUIDED PRACTICE

Vocabulary Apply the vocabulary from this lesson to answer each question.

1. An arc that joins the endpoints of a diameter is called a ___?___ . (*semicircle* or *major arc*)

2. How do you recognize a *central angle* of a circle?

3. In ⊙P m$\widehat{ABC}$ = 205°. Therefore $\widehat{ABC}$ is a ___?___ . (*major arc* or *minor arc*)

4. In a circle, an arc that is less than a semicircle is a ___?___ . (*major arc* or *minor arc*)

SEE EXAMPLE 1 **Consumer Application** Use the following information for Exercises 5–10.

The circle graph shows how a typical household spends money on energy. Find each of the following.

5. m∠*PAQ*   6. m∠*VAU*

7. m∠*SAQ*   8. m$\widehat{UT}$

9. m$\widehat{RQ}$ 10. m$\widehat{UPT}$

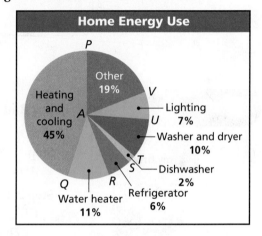

SEE EXAMPLE 2 Find each measure.

11. m$\widehat{DF}$

12. m$\widehat{DEB}$

13. m$\widehat{JL}$

14. m$\widehat{HLK}$

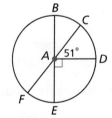

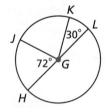

SEE EXAMPLE 3 15. ∠*QPR* ≅ ∠*RPS*. Find *QR*.

16. ⊙A ≅ ⊙B, and $\widehat{CD}$ ≅ $\widehat{EF}$. Find m∠*EBF*.

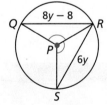

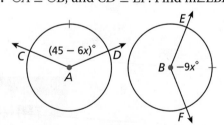

SEE EXAMPLE 4 **Multi-Step** Find each length to the nearest tenth.

17. *RS*

18. *EF*

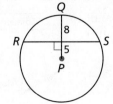

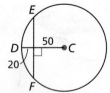

PRACTICE AND PROBLEM SOLVING

Independent Practice	
For Exercises	**See Example**
19–24	1
25–28	2
29–30	3
31–32	4

my.hrw.com

Online Extra Practice

Sports Use the following information for Exercises 19–24.

The key shows the number of medals won by U.S. athletes at the 2004 Olympics in Athens. Find each of the following to the nearest tenth.

Medals	
Gold	35
Silver	39
Bronze	29

19. m∠*ADB*

20. m∠*ADC*

21. m$\overset{\frown}{AB}$

22. m$\overset{\frown}{BC}$

23. m$\overset{\frown}{ACB}$

24. m$\overset{\frown}{CAB}$

Find each measure.

25. m$\overset{\frown}{MP}$

26. m$\overset{\frown}{QNL}$

27. m$\overset{\frown}{WT}$

28. m$\overset{\frown}{WTV}$

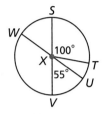

29. ⊙*A* ≅ ⊙*B*, and $\overset{\frown}{CD}$ ≅ $\overset{\frown}{EF}$. Find m∠*CAD*.

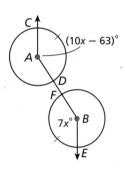

30. $\overline{JK}$ ≅ $\overline{LM}$. Find m$\overset{\frown}{JK}$.

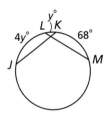

H.O.T. Multi-Step Find each length to the nearest tenth.

31. *CD*

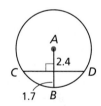

32. *RS*

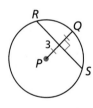

H.O.T. Determine whether each statement is true or false. If false, explain why.

33. The central angle of a minor arc is an acute angle.

34. Any two points on a circle determine a minor arc and a major arc.

35. In a circle, the perpendicular bisector of a chord must pass through the center of the circle.

H.O.T. 36. Data Collection Use a graphing calculator, a pH probe, and a data-collection device to collect information about the pH levels of ten different liquids. Then create a circle graph with the following sectors: strong basic $(9 < \text{pH} < 14)$, weak basic $(7 < \text{pH} < 9)$, neutral $(\text{pH} = 7)$, weak acidic $(5 < \text{pH} < 7)$, and strong acidic $(0 < \text{pH} < 5)$.

37. In ⊙*E*, the measures of ∠*AEB*, ∠*BEC*, and ∠*CED* are in the ratio 3:4:5. Find m$\overset{\frown}{AB}$, m$\overset{\frown}{BC}$, and m$\overset{\frown}{CD}$.

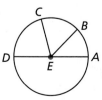

Algebra Find the indicated measure.

38. m$\widehat{JL}$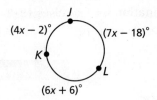

39. m∠*SPT*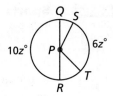

40. Prove ≅ chords have ≅ arcs.
Given: ⊙*A*, $\overline{BC}$ ≅ $\overline{DE}$
Prove: $\widehat{BC}$ ≅ $\widehat{DE}$

41. Prove ≅ arcs have ≅ central ∡.
Given: ⊙*A*, $\widehat{BC}$ ≅ $\widehat{DE}$
Prove: ∠*BAC* ≅ ∠*DAE*

42. Prove Theorem 30-2-3.
Given: ⊙*C*, $\overline{CD}$ ⊥ $\overline{EF}$
Prove: $\overline{CD}$ bisects $\overline{EF}$ and $\widehat{EF}$.
(*Hint:* Draw $\overline{CE}$ and $\overline{CF}$ and use the HL Theorem.)

43. Prove Theorem 30-2-4.
Given: ⊙*A*, $\overline{JK}$ ⊥ bisector of $\overline{GH}$
Prove: $\overline{JK}$ is a diameter
(*Hint:* Use the Converse of the ⊥ Bisector Theorem.)

44. Critical Thinking Roberto folds a circular piece of paper as shown. When he unfolds the paper, how many different-sized central angles will be formed?

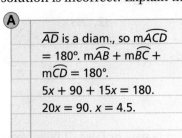 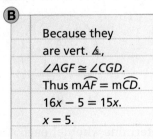 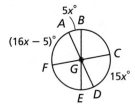

One fold   Two folds   Three folds

H.O.T. 45. ///ERROR ANALYSIS/// Below are two solutions to find the value of *x*. Which solution is incorrect? Explain the error.

A
$\overline{AD}$ is a diam., so m$\widehat{ACD}$ = 180°. m$\widehat{AB}$ + m$\widehat{BC}$ + m$\widehat{CD}$ = 180°.
5*x* + 90 + 15*x* = 180.
20*x* = 90. *x* = 4.5.

B
Because they are vert. ∡, ∠*AGF* ≅ ∠*CGD*. Thus m$\widehat{AF}$ = m$\widehat{CD}$.
16*x* − 5 = 15*x*.
x = 5.

46. Write About It According to a school survey, 40% of the students take a bus to school, 35% are driven to school, 15% ride a bike, and the remainder walk. Explain how to use central angles to create a circle graph from this data.

Real-World Connections

47. Chantal's bike has wheels with a 27 in. diameter.
  a. What are *AC* and *AD* if *DB* is 7 in.?
  b. What is *CD* to the nearest tenth of an inch?
  c. What is *CE*, the length of the top of the bike stand?

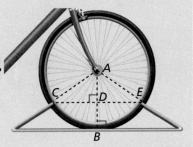

TEST PREP

48. Which of these arcs of ⊙Q has the greatest measure?

   (A) $\overset{\frown}{WT}$ (C) $\overset{\frown}{VR}$

   (B) $\overset{\frown}{UW}$ (D) $\overset{\frown}{TV}$

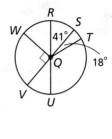

49. In ⊙A, CD = 10. Which of these is closest to the length of $\overline{AE}$?

   (F) 3.3 cm   (H) 5 cm

   (G) 4 cm   (J) 7.8 cm

50. Gridded Response ⊙P has center P(2, 1) and radius 3. What is the measure, in degrees, of the minor arc with endpoints A(−1, 1) and B(2, −2)?

CHALLENGE AND EXTEND

51. In the figure, $\overline{AB} \perp \overline{CD}$. Find m$\overset{\frown}{BD}$ to the nearest tenth of a degree.

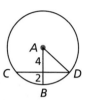

52. Two points on a circle determine two distinct arcs. How many arcs are determined by *n* points on a circle? (*Hint:* Make a table and look for a pattern.)

H.O.T. **53.** An angle measure other than degrees is *radian* measure. 360° converts to 2π radians, or 180° converts to π radians.

   a. Convert the following radian angle measures to degrees: $\frac{\pi}{2}, \frac{\pi}{3}, \frac{\pi}{4}$.

   b. Convert the following angle measures to radians: 135°, 270°.

FOCUS ON MATHEMATICAL PRACTICES

H.O.T. **54. Reasoning** In a circle, two chords are the same distance from the center of the circle. Are the chords necessarily congruent? Explain.

H.O.T. **55. Proof** In ⊙X, $\overset{\frown}{AP} \cong \overset{\frown}{QB}$ and $\overset{\frown}{AQ} \cong \overset{\frown}{PB}$. Prove $\overline{AP} \parallel \overline{QB}$.

Construction   Circle Through Three Noncollinear Points

1	**2**	**3**
	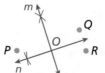	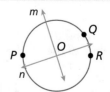
Draw three noncollinear points.	Construct *m* and *n*, the ⊥ bisectors of $\overline{PQ}$ and $\overline{QR}$. Label the intersection *O*.	Center the compass at *O*. Draw a circle through *P*.

1. Explain why ⊙O with radius $\overline{OP}$ also contains Q and R.

Sector Area and Arc Length

? Essential Question: How is proportional reasoning used to find areas of circle sectors and lengths of arcs?

Objectives
Find the area of sectors.

Find arc lengths.

Vocabulary
sector of a circle
segment of a circle
arc length

Who uses this?
Farmers use irrigation radii to calculate areas of sectors. (See Example 2.)

The area of a sector is a fraction of the circle containing the sector. To find the area of a sector whose central angle measures $m°$, multiply the area of the circle by $\frac{m°}{360°}$.

Sector of a Circle

 Animated Math

TERM	NAME	DIAGRAM	AREA
A **sector of a circle** is a region bounded by two radii of the circle and their intercepted arc.	sector *ACB*		$A = \pi r^2\left(\dfrac{m°}{360°}\right)$

EXAMPLE 1 Finding the Area of a Sector

 my.hrw.com

Online Video Tutor

Find the area of each sector. Give your answer in terms of π and rounded to the nearest hundredth.

A sector *MPN*

$$A = \pi r^2\left(\frac{m°}{360°}\right) \qquad \text{Use formula for area of a sector.}$$

$$= \pi(3)^2\left(\frac{80°}{360°}\right) \qquad \text{Substitute 3 for } r \text{ and 80 for } m.$$

$$= 2\pi \text{ in}^2 \approx 6.28 \text{ in}^2 \qquad \text{Simplify.}$$

B sector *EFG*

$$A = \pi r^2\left(\frac{m°}{360°}\right) \qquad \text{Use formula for area of a sector.}$$

$$= \pi(6)^2\left(\frac{120°}{360°}\right) \qquad \text{Substitute 6 for } r \text{ and 120 for } m.$$

$$= 12\pi \approx 37.70 \text{ cm}^2 \qquad \text{Simplify.}$$

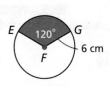

Helpful Hint

Write the degree symbol after m in the formula to help you remember to use degree measure not arc length.

✓ CHECK IT OUT! Find the area of each sector. Give your answer in terms of π and rounded to the nearest hundredth.

1a. sector *ACB*

1b. sector *JKL*

AP/Wide World Photos.

EXAMPLE **2** *Agriculture Application*

A circular plot with a 720 ft diameter is watered by a spray irrigation system. To the nearest square foot, what is the area that is watered as the sprinkler rotates through an angle of 50°?

$$A = \pi r^2 \left(\frac{m°}{360°}\right)$$

$$= \pi (360)^2 \left(\frac{50°}{360°}\right) \quad \textit{d = 720 ft, r = 360 ft.}$$

$$\approx 56{,}549 \text{ ft}^2 \quad \textit{Simplify.}$$

 2. To the nearest square foot, what is the area watered in Example 2 as the sprinkler rotates through a semicircle?

A **segment of a circle** is a region bounded by an arc and its chord. The shaded region in the figure is a segment.

 Area of a Segment

area of segment = area of sector − area of triangle

EXAMPLE **3** **Finding the Area of a Segment**

Find the area of segment *ACB* to the nearest hundredth.

Step 1 Find the area of sector *ACB*.

$$A = \pi r^2 \left(\frac{m°}{360°}\right) \quad \textit{Use formula for area of a sector.}$$

$$= \pi (12)^2 \left(\frac{60°}{360°}\right) \quad \textit{Substitute 12 for r and 60 for m.}$$

$$= 24\pi \text{ in}^2$$

Step 2 Find the area of △*ACB*.
Draw altitude $\overline{AD}$.

$$A = \frac{1}{2}bh = \frac{1}{2}(12)\left(6\sqrt{3}\right) \quad \textit{CD = 6 in., and h = 6}\sqrt{3} \textit{ in.}$$

$$= 36\sqrt{3} \text{ in}^2 \quad \textit{Simplify.}$$

Step 3 area of segment = area of sector *ACB* − area of △*ACB*

$$= 24\pi - 36\sqrt{3}$$

$$\approx 13.04 \text{ in}^2$$

Remember!

In a 30°-60°-90° triangle, the length of the leg opposite the 60° angle is $\sqrt{3}$ times the length of the shorter leg.

 3. Find the area of segment *RST* to the nearest hundredth.

In the same way that the area of a sector is a fraction of the area of the circle, the length of an arc is a fraction of the circumference of the circle.

 Arc Length

TERM	DIAGRAM	LENGTH
Arc length is the distance along an arc measured in linear units.		$L = 2\pi r\left(\dfrac{m°}{360°}\right)$

COMMON CORE GPS

EXAMPLE 4
MCC9-12.G.C.5

my.hrw.com

Online Video Tutor

Finding Arc Length

Find each arc length. Give your answer in terms of π and rounded to the nearest hundredth.

A $\overparen{CD}$

$$L = 2\pi r\left(\dfrac{m°}{360°}\right) \qquad \text{Use formula for arc length.}$$

$$= 2\pi(10)\left(\dfrac{90°}{360°}\right) \qquad \text{Substitute 10 for r and 90 for m.}$$

$$= 5\pi \text{ ft} \approx 15.71 \text{ ft} \qquad \text{Simplify.}$$

B an arc with measure 35° in a circle with radius 3 in.

$$L = 2\pi r\left(\dfrac{m°}{360°}\right) \qquad \text{Use formula for arc length.}$$

$$= 2\pi(3)\left(\dfrac{35°}{360°}\right) \qquad \text{Substitute 3 for r and 35 for m.}$$

$$= \dfrac{7}{12} \text{ in.} \approx 1.83 \text{ in.} \qquad \text{Simplify.}$$

 CHECK IT OUT! Find each arc length. Give your answer in terms of π and rounded to the nearest hundredth.

4a. $\overparen{GH}$

4b. an arc with measure 135° in a circle with radius 4 cm

MCC.MP.4 **MATHEMATICAL PRACTICES**

THINK AND DISCUSS

1. What is the difference between arc measure and arc length?

2. A slice of pizza is a sector of a circle. Explain what measurements you would need to make in order to calculate the area of the slice.

 3. GET ORGANIZED Copy and complete the graphic organizer.

	Formula	Diagram
Area of a Sector		
Area of a Segment		
Arc Length		

GUIDED PRACTICE

1. **Vocabulary** In a circle, the region bounded by a chord and an arc is called a ___?___ . (*sector* or *segment*)

SEE EXAMPLE 1

Find the area of each sector. Give your answer in terms of π and rounded to the nearest hundredth.

2. sector *PQR*

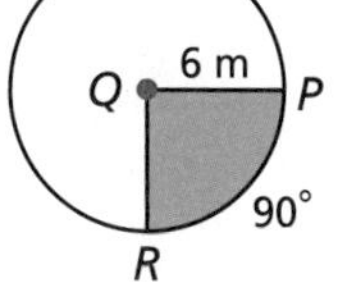

3. sector *JKL*
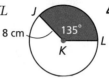

4. sector *ABC*

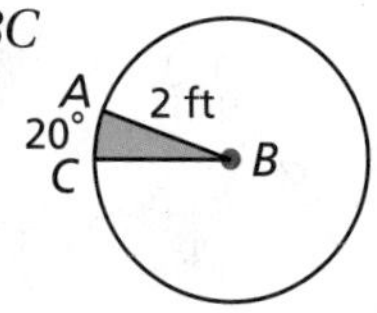

SEE EXAMPLE 2

5. **Navigation** The beam from a lighthouse is visible for a distance of 3 mi. To the nearest square mile, what is the area covered by the beam as it sweeps in an arc of 150°?

SEE EXAMPLE 3

Multi-Step Find the area of each segment to the nearest hundredth.

6.
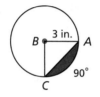

7.

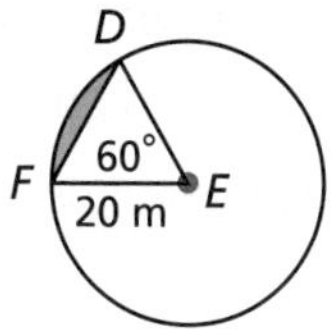

8.

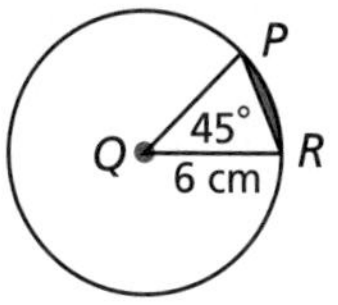

SEE EXAMPLE 4

Find each arc length. Give your answer in terms of π and rounded to the nearest hundredth.

9. $\widehat{EF}$

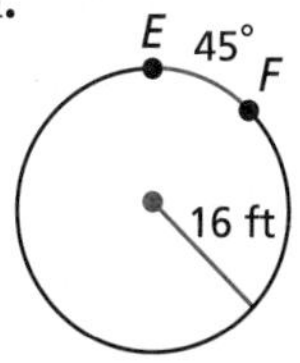

10. $\widehat{PQ}$

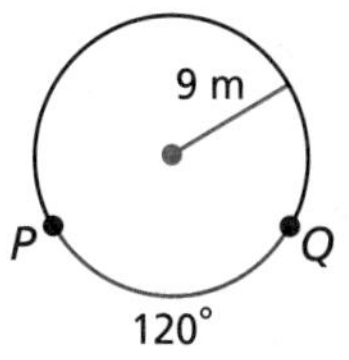

11. an arc with measure 20° in a circle with radius 6 in.

PRACTICE AND PROBLEM SOLVING

my.hrw.com

Online Extra Practice

Find the area of each sector. Give your answer in terms of π and rounded to the nearest hundredth.

12. sector *DEF*

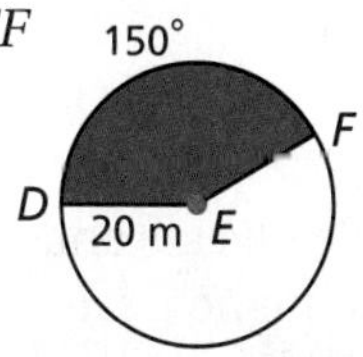

13. sector *GHJ*

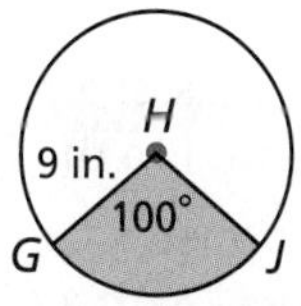

14. sector *RST*

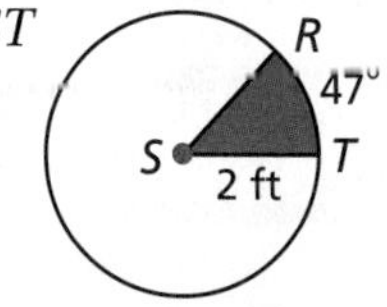

15. **Architecture** A *lunette* is a semicircular window that is sometimes placed above a doorway or above a rectangular window. To the nearest square inch, what is the area of the lunette?

├── 40 in. ──┤

H.O.T. **Multi-Step** Find the area of each segment to the nearest hundredth.

16.

17.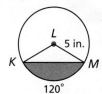

18.

Find each arc length. Give your answer in terms of π and rounded to the nearest hundredth.

19. $\overgroup{UV}$

20. $\overgroup{AB}$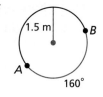

21. an arc with measure 9° in a circle with diameter 4 ft

22. **Math History** Greek mathematicians studied the *salinon*, a figure bounded by four semicircles. What is the perimeter of this salinon to the nearest tenth of an inch?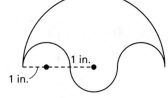

Tell whether each statement is sometimes, always, or never true.

23. The length of an arc of a circle is greater than the circumference of the circle.

24. Two arcs with the same measure have the same arc length.

25. In a circle, two arcs with the same length have the same measure.

Find the radius of each circle.

26. area of sector $ABC = 9\pi$

27. arc length of $\overgroup{EF} = 8\pi$

H.O.T. **28.** **Estimation** The fraction $\frac{22}{7}$ is an approximation for π.

   a. Use this value to estimate the arc length of $\overgroup{XY}$.

   b. Use the π key on your calculator to find the length of $\overgroup{XY}$ to 8 decimal places.

   c. Was your estimate in part **a** an overestimate or an underestimate?

29. The pedals of a penny-farthing bicycle are directly connected to the front wheel.

   a. Suppose a penny-farthing bicycle has a front wheel with a diameter of 5 ft. To the nearest tenth of a foot, how far does the bike move when you turn the pedals through an angle of 90°?

   b. Through what angle should you turn the pedals in order to move forward by a distance of 4.5 ft? Round to the nearest degree.

H.O.T. 30. Critical Thinking What is the length of the radius that makes the area of $\odot A = 24$ in^2 and the area of sector $BAC = 3$ in^2? Explain.

31. Write About It Given the length of an arc of a circle and the measure of the arc, explain how to find the radius of the circle.

TEST PREP

32. What is the area of sector AOB?

   Ⓐ 4π Ⓑ 16π Ⓒ 32π Ⓓ 64π

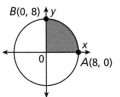

33. What is the length of $\overarc{AB}$?

   Ⓕ 2π Ⓖ 4π Ⓗ 8π Ⓙ 16π

34. Gridded Response To the nearest hundredth, what is the area of the sector determined by an arc with measure 35° in a circle with radius 12?

CHALLENGE AND EXTEND

H.O.T. 35. In the diagram, the larger of the two concentric circles has radius 5, and the smaller circle has radius 2. What is the area of the shaded region in terms of π?

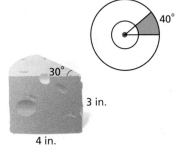

36. A wedge of cheese is a sector of a cylinder.

   a. To the nearest tenth, what is the volume of the wedge with the dimensions shown?

   b. What is the surface area of the wedge of cheese to the nearest tenth?

37. Probability The central angles of a target measure 45°. The inner circle has a radius of 1 ft, and the outer circle has a radius of 2 ft. Assuming that all arrows hit the target at random, find the following probabilities.

   a. hitting a red region

   b. hitting a blue region

   c. hitting a red or blue region

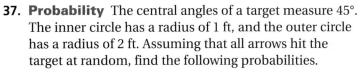

FOCUS ON MATHEMATICAL PRACTICES

H.O.T. 38. Number Sense Two congruent circles have a regular hexagon and a regular octagon inscribed in them, respectively. Which figure has segments with greater area? Explain.

H.O.T. 39. Problem Solving The circumference of a circle is 15.6 inches. The length of an arc in the circle is 5.2 inches.

   a. Find the measure of the central angle m.

   b. Explain how to find the length of the radius. Then find it to the nearest tenth of an inch.

   c. Find the length of the intercepted chord to the nearest tenth.

   d. Find the area of the sector to the nearest tenth.

   e. Find the area of the segment to the nearest tenth.

H.O.T. 40. Draw Conclusions Two sectors are in the same circle. The area of one is greater than the area of the other. What conclusions can you draw?

? ***Essential Question:*** How does the direct variation relationship between arc length and radius lead to the definition of radian measure?

Objective
Use proportions to convert angle measures from degrees to radians.

Vocabulary
radian

One unit of measurement for angles is degrees, which are based on a fraction of a circle. Another unit is called a *radian*, which is based on the relationship of the radius and arc length of a central angle in a circle.

Four concentric circles are shown, with radius 1, 2, 3, and 4. The measure of each arc is 60°.

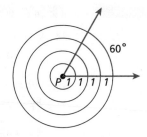

Radius	Arc Length
1	$2\pi(1)\left(\dfrac{60°}{360°}\right) = \dfrac{\pi}{3}$
2	$2\pi(2)\left(\dfrac{60°}{360°}\right) = \dfrac{2\pi}{3}$
3	$2\pi(3)\left(\dfrac{60°}{360°}\right) = \pi$
4	$2\pi(4)\left(\dfrac{60°}{360°}\right) = \dfrac{4\pi}{3}$

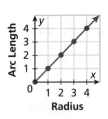

Remember!

Arc length is the distance along an arc measured in linear units. In a circle of radius r, the length of an arc with a central angle measure m is
$L = 2\pi r\left(\dfrac{m°}{360°}\right)$.

The relationship between the radius and arc length is linear, with a slope of $2\pi\left(\frac{60°}{360°}\right) = \frac{\pi}{3}$, or about 1.05. The slope represents the ratio of the arc length to the radius. This ratio is the *radian* measure of the angle, so 60° is the same as $\frac{\pi}{3}$ radians.

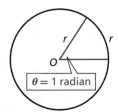

If a central angle θ in a circle of radius r intercepts an arc of length r, the measure of θ is defined as 1 **radian.** Since the circumference of a circle of radius r is $2\pi r$, an angle representing one complete rotation measures 2π radians, or 360°.

2π radians = 360°   and π radians = 180°

$1° = \left(\dfrac{\pi \text{ radians}}{180°}\right)$ and   1 radian $= \left(\dfrac{180°}{\pi \text{ radians}}\right)$

Use these facts to convert between radians and degrees.

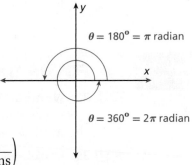

Converting Angle Measures

DEGREES TO RADIANS	RADIANS TO DEGREES
Multiply the number of degrees by	Multiply the number of radians by
$\left(\dfrac{\pi \text{ radians}}{180°}\right)$	$\left(\dfrac{180°}{\pi \text{ radians}}\right)$

 **EXAMPLE** MCC9-12.G.C.5 **1** **Converting Degrees to Radians**

Convert each measure from degrees to radians. *Multiply by $\left(\dfrac{\pi \text{ radians}}{180°}\right)$.*

A 30°

$$\overset{1}{\cancel{30°}}\left(\dfrac{\pi \text{ radians}}{\underset{6}{\cancel{180°}}}\right) = \dfrac{\pi}{6} \text{ radians}$$

B 75°

$$\overset{5}{\cancel{75°}}\left(\dfrac{\pi \text{ radians}}{\underset{12}{\cancel{180°}}}\right) = \dfrac{5\pi}{12} \text{ radians}$$

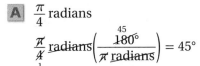 Convert each measure from degrees to radians.

1a. −36°   **1b.** 270°

 **EXAMPLE** MCC9-12.G.C.5 **2** **Converting Radians to Degrees**

Convert each measure from radians to degrees.

A $\dfrac{\pi}{4}$ radians

$$\underset{1}{\cancel{\dfrac{\pi}{4}}} \text{ radians}\left(\dfrac{\overset{45}{\cancel{180°}}}{\cancel{\pi} \text{ radians}}\right) = 45°$$

B $\dfrac{2\pi}{9}$ radians *Multiply by $\left(\dfrac{180°}{\pi \text{ radians}}\right)$.*

$$\underset{1}{\cancel{\dfrac{2\pi}{9}}} \text{ radians}\left(\dfrac{\overset{20}{\cancel{180°}}}{\cancel{\pi} \text{ radians}}\right) = 40°$$

Convert each measure from radians to degrees.

2a. $\dfrac{5\pi}{6}$ radians   **2b.** $-\dfrac{3\pi}{4}$ radians

EXTENSION

Exercises

my.hrw.com
Homework Help

1. Convert each measure from degrees to radians to complete the table.

0°	30°	45°	60°	90°	180°	270°	360°

Convert each measure from degrees to radians.

2. 215°   **3.** 25°   **4.** −180°   **5.** 35°

6. 120°   **7.** −315°   **8.** 400°   **9.** −60°

Convert each measure from radians to degrees.

10. $\dfrac{6\pi}{5}$ radians   **11.** $\dfrac{3\pi}{5}$ radians   **12.** $-\dfrac{\pi}{3}$ radians   **13.** $\dfrac{5\pi}{9}$ radians

14. $\dfrac{\pi}{6}$ radians   **15.** $\dfrac{2\pi}{3}$ radians   **16.** $\dfrac{5\pi}{8}$ radians   **17.** $\dfrac{7\pi}{2}$ radians

18. Electronics A DVD rotates through an angle of 20π radians in 1 second. At this speed, how many revolutions does the DVD make in 2 minutes?

19. Clocks Find the measure of the angle in radians formed by the minute hand on a clock at 7:35 and its position 15 minutes later.

20. Wheels A bicycle's wheel spins backwards, making 2 complete counterclockwise revolutions. What is the measure of the wheel's rotation angle in radians?

30-4 Inscribed Angles

Essential Question: How is the measure of an angle inscribed in a circle related to the measure of its associated central angle?

Objectives
Find the measure of an inscribed angle.

Use inscribed angles and their properties to solve problems.

Vocabulary
inscribed angle
intercepted arc
subtend

Why learn this?
You can use inscribed angles to find measures of angles in string art. (See Example 2.)

String art often begins with pins or nails that are placed around the circumference of a circle. A long piece of string is then wound from one nail to another. The resulting pattern may include hundreds of *inscribed angles*.

An **inscribed angle** is an angle whose vertex is on a circle and whose sides contain chords of the circle. An **intercepted arc** consists of endpoints that lie on the sides of an inscribed angle and all the points of the circle between them. A chord or arc **subtends** an angle if its endpoints lie on the sides of the angle.

$\angle DEF$ is an inscribed angle.

$\overset{\frown}{DF}$ is the intercepted arc.

$\overset{\frown}{DF}$ subtends $\angle DEF$.

| Theorem 30-4-1 | **Inscribed Angle Theorem** |

The measure of an inscribed angle is half the measure of its intercepted arc.

$m\angle ABC = \frac{1}{2}m\overset{\frown}{AC}$

Case 1   Case 2   Case 3

You will prove Cases 2 and 3 of Theorem 30-4-1 in Exercises 30 and 31.

PROOF ▮ **Inscribed Angle Theorem**

Given: $\angle ABC$ is inscribed in $\odot X$.
Prove: $m\angle ABC = \frac{1}{2}m\overset{\frown}{AC}$

Proof Case 1:

$\angle ABC$ is inscribed in $\odot X$ with X on $\overline{BC}$. Draw $\overline{XA}$. $m\overset{\frown}{AC} = m\angle AXC$. By the Exterior Angle Theorem $m\angle AXC = m\angle ABX + m\angle BAX$. Since $\overline{XA}$ and $\overline{XB}$ are radii of the circle, $\overline{XA} \cong \overline{XB}$. Then by definition $\triangle AXB$ is isosceles. Thus $m\angle ABX = m\angle BAX$.

By the Substitution Property, $m\overset{\frown}{AC} = 2m\angle ABX$ or $2m\angle ABC$. Thus $\frac{1}{2}m\overset{\frown}{AC} = m\angle ABC$.

940 *Module 30 Circles*

Victoria Smith/HMH

EXAMPLE 1

MCC9-12.G.C.2

Finding Measures of Arcs and Inscribed Angles

Find each measure.

A m∠RST

$$m\angle RST = \frac{1}{2}m\widehat{RT}$$ *Inscribed ∠ Thm.*

$$= \frac{1}{2}(120°) = 60°$$ *Substitute 120 for m$\widehat{RT}$.*

B m$\widehat{SU}$

$$m\angle SRU = \frac{1}{2}m\widehat{SU}$$ *Inscribed ∠ Thm.*

$$40° = \frac{1}{2}m\widehat{SU}$$ *Substitute 40 for m∠SRU.*

$$m\widehat{SU} = 80°$$ *Mult. both sides by 2.*

 CHECK IT OUT! Find each measure.

1a. m$\widehat{ADC}$

1b. m∠DAE

Corollary 30-4-2

COROLLARY	HYPOTHESIS	CONCLUSION
If inscribed angles of a circle intercept the same arc or are subtended by the same chord or arc, then the angles are congruent.	∠ACB, ∠ADB, and ∠AEB intercept $\widehat{AB}$.	∠ACB ≅ ∠ADB ≅ ∠AEB (and ∠CAE ≅ ∠CBE)

You will prove Corollary 30-4-2 in Exercise 32.

EXAMPLE 2

MCC9-12.G.C.2

Hobby Application

Find m∠DEC, if m$\widehat{AD}$ = 86°.

$$\angle BAC \cong \angle BDC$$ *∠BAC and ∠BDC intercept $\widehat{BC}$.*

$$m\angle BAC = m\angle BDC$$ *Def. of ≅*

$$m\angle BDC = 60°$$ *Substitute 60 for m∠BDC.*

$$m\angle ACD = \frac{1}{2}m\widehat{AD}$$ *Inscribed ∠ Thm.*

$$= \frac{1}{2}(86°)$$ *Substitute 86 for m$\widehat{AD}$.*

$$= 43°$$ *Simplify.*

$$m\angle DEC + 60 + 43 = 180$$ *△ Sum Theorem*

$$m\angle DEC = 77°$$ *Simplify.*

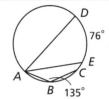

 **CHECK IT OUT!** **2.** Find m∠ABD and m$\widehat{BC}$ in the string art.

Theorem 30-4-3

An inscribed angle subtends a semicircle if and only if the angle is a right angle.

You will prove Theorem 30-4-3 in Exercise 43.

EXAMPLE 3

Finding Angle Measures in Inscribed Triangles

Find each value.

 my.hrw.com

Online Video Tutor

A *x*

∠*RQT* is a right angle   ∠*RQT* is inscribed in a
                         semicircle.

m∠*RQT* = 90°   *Def. of rt. ∠*

$4x + 6 = 90$ *Substitute $4x + 6$ for m∠RQT.*

$4x = 84$ *Subtract 6 from both sides.*

$x = 21$ *Divide both sides by 4.*

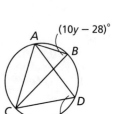

B m∠*ADC*

m∠*ABC* = m∠*ADC*   ∠*ABC* and ∠*ADC* both
                             intercept $\overset{\frown}{AC}$.

$10y - 28 = 7y - 1$ *Substitute the given values.*

$3y - 28 = -1$ *Subtract 7y from both sides.*

$3y = 27$ *Add 28 to both sides.*

$y = 9$ *Divide both sides by 3.*

m∠*ADC* = 7(9) −1 = 62°   *Substitute 9 for y.*

CHECK IT OUT! Find each value.

3a. *z*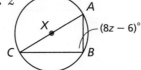

3b. m∠*EDF*

 Construction   Center of a Circle

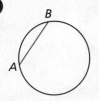

① Draw a circle and chord $\overline{AB}$.

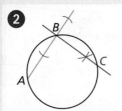

② Construct a line perpendicular to $\overline{AB}$ at *B*. Where the line and the circle intersect, label the point *C*.

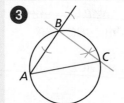

③ Draw chord $\overline{AC}$.

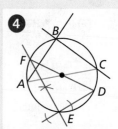

④ Repeat steps to draw chords $\overline{DE}$ and $\overline{DF}$. The intersection of $\overline{AC}$ and $\overline{DF}$ is the center of the circle.

Theorem 30-4-4

THEOREM	HYPOTHESIS	CONCLUSION
If a quadrilateral is inscribed in a circle, then its opposite angles are supplementary.	 *ABCD* is inscribed in ⊙*E*.	∠*A* and ∠*C* are supplementary. ∠*B* and ∠*D* are supplementary.

You will prove Theorem 30-4-4 in Exercise 44.

EXAMPLE 4
MCC9-12.G.C.3

Finding Angle Measures in Inscribed Quadrilaterals

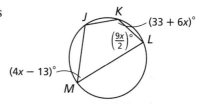

Find the angle measures of *PQRS*.

Step 1 Find the value of *y*.

$$m\angle P + m\angle R = 180°$$ *PQRS is inscribed in a ⊙.*

$$6y + 1 + 10y + 19 = 180$$ *Substitute the given values.*

$$16y + 20 = 180$$ *Simplify.*

$$16y = 160$$ *Subtract 20 from both sides.*

$$y = 10$$ *Divide both sides by 16.*

Step 2 Find the measure of each angle.

$$m\angle P = 6(10) + 1 = 61°$$ *Substitute 10 for y in each expression.*

$$m\angle R = 10(10) + 19 = 119°$$

$$m\angle Q = 10^2 + 48 = 148°$$

$$m\angle Q + m\angle S = 180°$$ *∠Q and ∠S are supp.*

$$148° + m\angle S = 180°$$ *Substitute 148 for m∠Q.*

$$m\angle S = 32°$$ *Subtract 148 from both sides.*

 4. Find the angle measures of *JKLM*.

MCC.MP.1

THINK AND DISCUSS

1. Can ▱*ABCD* be inscribed in a circle? Why or why not?

2. An inscribed angle intercepts an arc that is $\frac{1}{4}$ of the circle. Explain how to find the measure of the inscribed angle.

 3. GET ORGANIZED Copy and complete the graphic organizer. In each box write a definition, properties, an example, and a nonexample.

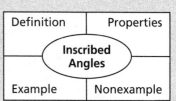

GUIDED PRACTICE

1. **Vocabulary** A, B, and C lie on $\odot P$. $\angle ABC$ is an example of an ___?___ angle. (*intercepted* or *inscribed*)

SEE EXAMPLE 1 Find each measure.

2. m$\angle DEF$

3. m$\widehat{EG}$

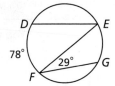

4. m$\widehat{JKL}$

5. m$\angle LKM$

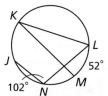

SEE EXAMPLE 2

6. **Crafts** A circular loom can be used for knitting. What is the m$\angle QTR$ in the knitting loom?

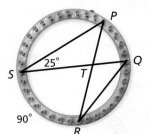

SEE EXAMPLE 3 Find each value.

7. x

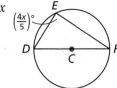

8. y

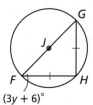

9. m$\angle XYZ$

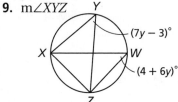

SEE EXAMPLE 4 **Multi-Step** Find the angle measures of each quadrilateral.

10. $PQRS$

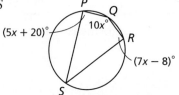

11. $ABCD$

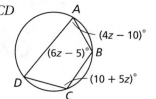

PRACTICE AND PROBLEM SOLVING

Independent Practice	
For Exercises	See Example
12–15	1
16	2
17–20	3
21–22	4

Find each measure.

12. m$\widehat{ML}$

13. m$\angle KMN$

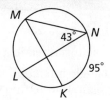

14. m$\widehat{EGH}$

15. m$\angle GFH$

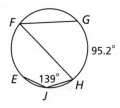

16. **Crafts** An artist created a stained glass window. If m$\angle BEC = 40°$ and m$\widehat{AB} = 44°$, what is m$\angle ADC$?

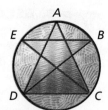

Algebra Find each value.

17. y

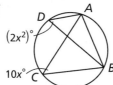

$(3y^2 - 18)°$

18. z

$30°$

$(6z - 4)°$

19. m$\widehat{AB}$

$(2x^2)°$

$10x°$

20. m$\angle MPN$

$(3x - 10)°$

$\left(\frac{11x}{3}\right)°$

H.O.T. **Multi-Step** Find the angle measures of each quadrilateral.

21. $BCDE$

$(z - 59)°$

$\left(\frac{z}{2}\right)°$

$\left(\frac{z}{4} + 30\right)°$

22. $TUVW$

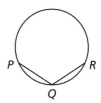

$(15y - 4)°$

$(6x - 14)°$

$(14 + 4x)°$

$(12y - 5)°$

Tell whether each statement is sometimes, always, or never true.

23. Two inscribed angles that intercept the same arc of a circle are congruent.

24. When a right triangle is inscribed in a circle, one of the legs of the triangle is a diameter of the circle.

25. A trapezoid can be inscribed in a circle.

H.O.T. **Multi-Step** Find each angle measure.

26. m$\angle ABC$ if
m$\angle ADC = 112°$

27. m$\angle PQR$ if
m$\widehat{PQR} = 130°$

28. Prove that the measure of a central angle subtended by a chord is twice the measure of the inscribed angle subtended by the chord.
Given: In $\odot H$ $\overline{JK}$ subtends $\angle JHK$ and $\angle JLK$.
Prove: m$\angle JHK = 2$m$\angle JLK$

Real-World Connections

29. A Native American sand painting could be used to indicate the direction of sunrise on the winter and summer solstices. You can make this design by placing six equally spaced points around the circumference of a circle and connecting them as shown.

   a. Find m$\angle BAC$.

   b. Find m$\angle CDE$.

   c. What type of triangle is $\triangle FBC$? Why?

H.O.T. **30.** **Given:** ∠ABC is inscribed in ⊙X with X in the interior of ∠ABC.
Prove: m∠ABC = $\frac{1}{2}$m$\overset{\frown}{AC}$
(*Hint:* Draw $\overrightarrow{BX}$ and use Case 1 of the Inscribed Angle Theorem.)

H.O.T. **31.** **Given:** ∠ABC is inscribed in ⊙X with X in the exterior of ∠ABC.
Prove: m∠ABC = $\frac{1}{2}$m$\overset{\frown}{AC}$

H.O.T. **32.** Prove Corollary 30-4-2.
Given: ∠ACB and ∠ADB intercept $\overset{\frown}{AB}$.
Prove: ∠ACB ≅ ∠ADB

33. **Multi-Step** In the diagram, m$\overset{\frown}{JKL}$ = 198°,
and m$\overset{\frown}{KLM}$ = 216°. Find the measures of the angles
of quadrilateral JKLM.

34. **Critical Thinking** A rectangle PQRS is inscribed
in a circle. What can you conclude about $\overline{PR}$? Explain.

35. **History** The diagram shows the Winchester Round
Table with inscribed △ABC. The table may
have been made at the request of King Edward III,
who created the Order of the Garter as a return to
the Round Table and an order of chivalry.

a. Explain why $\overline{BC}$ must be a diameter of
the circle.

b. Find m$\overset{\frown}{AC}$.

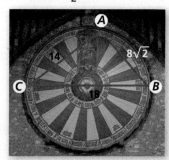

36. To inscribe an equilateral triangle in a circle, draw a
diameter $\overline{BC}$. Open the compass to the radius of the circle.
Place the point of the compass at C and make arcs
on the circle at D and E, as shown. Draw $\overline{BD}$, $\overline{BE}$, and
$\overline{DE}$. Explain why △BDE is an equilateral triangle.

37. **Write About It** A student claimed that if a parallelogram
contains a 30° angle, it cannot be inscribed in a circle.
Do you agree or disagree? Explain.

38. **Construction** Circumscribe a circle about a triangle. (*Hint:* Follow the steps
for the construction of a circle through three given noncollinear points.)

TEST PREP

39. What is m∠BAC?

  Ⓐ 38°   Ⓒ 66°

  Ⓑ 43°   Ⓓ 81°

40. Equilateral △XCZ is inscribed in a circle.
If $\overline{CY}$ bisects ∠C, what is m$\overset{\frown}{XY}$?

  Ⓕ 15°   Ⓖ 30°   Ⓗ 60°   Ⓙ 120°

41. Quadrilateral ABCD is inscribed in a circle. The ratio of
m∠A to m∠C is 4:5. What is m∠A?

  Ⓐ 20°   Ⓑ 40°   Ⓒ 80°   Ⓓ 100°

42. Which of these angles has the greatest measure?

  Ⓕ ∠STR   Ⓖ ∠QPR   Ⓗ ∠QSR   Ⓙ ∠PQS

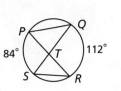

© Roy Rainford/Getty Images

CHALLENGE AND EXTEND

H.O.T. **43.** Prove that an inscribed angle subtends a semicircle if and only if the angle is a right angle. (*Hint:* There are two parts.)

H.O.T. **44.** Prove that if a quadrilateral is inscribed in a circle, then its opposite angles are supplementary. (*Hint:* There are two parts.)

45. Find m$\widehat{PQ}$ to the nearest degree.

46. Find m∠ABD.

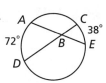

47. Construction To circumscribe an equilateral triangle about a circle, construct $\overline{AB}$ parallel to the horizontal diameter of the circle and tangent to the circle. Then use a 30°-60°-90° triangle to draw $\overline{AC}$ and $\overline{BC}$ so that they form 60° angles with $\overline{AB}$ and are tangent to the circle.

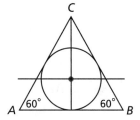

FOCUS ON MATHEMATICAL PRACTICES

MATHEMATICAL PRACTICES

H.O.T. **48. Reasoning** Solve for *x*. Explain your reasoning.

H.O.T. **49. Precision** A quadrilateral is inscribed in a circle. Its two diagonals are diameters of the circle. Classify the quadrilateral by its most precise name. Explain.

H.O.T. **50. Analysis** The inscribed angle has measure *x*°, *O* is the center of the circle, and $\overline{AP}$ and $\overline{BP}$ are tangent to the circle at *A* and *B*.

  a. What is m∠*O* in terms of *x*? Explain.

  b. What is m∠*P*? Explain.

  c. In ⊙*O*, *x* = 63. Find m∠*P*.

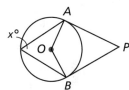

Construction Tangent to a Circle From an Exterior Point

❶	❷	❸	❹
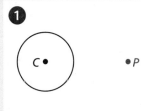		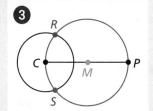	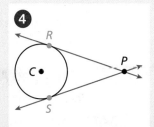

Draw ⊙C and locate *P* in the exterior of the circle.

Draw $\overline{CP}$. Construct *M*, the midpoint of $\overline{CP}$.

Center the compass at *M*. Draw a circle through *C* and *P*. It will intersect ⊙C at *R* and *S*.

R and *S* are the tangent points. Draw $\overleftrightarrow{PR}$ and $\overleftrightarrow{PS}$ tangent to ⊙C.

1. Can you draw $\overline{CR} \perp \overleftrightarrow{RP}$? Explain.

Ready to Go On?

my.hrw.com
Assessment and Intervention

✓ 30-1 Lines That Intersect Circles

Identify each line or segment that intersects each circle.

1.

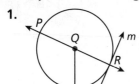

2.

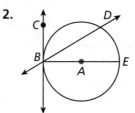

✓ 30-2 Arcs and Chords

Find each measure.

3. $\overset{\frown}{BC}$

4. $\overset{\frown}{BED}$

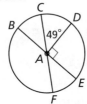

Find each length to the nearest tenth.

5. JK

6. NK

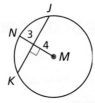

✓ 30-3 Sector Area and Arc Length

7. As part of an art project, Peter buys a circular piece of fabric and then cuts out the sector shown. What is the area of the sector to the nearest square centimeter?

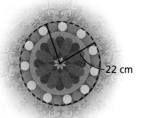

22 cm

Find each arc length. Give your answer in terms of π and rounded to the nearest hundredth.

8. $\overset{\frown}{AB}$

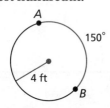

150°

4 ft

9. $\overset{\frown}{EF}$

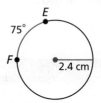

75°

2.4 cm

10. an arc with measure 44° in a circle with diameter 10 in.

11. a semicircle in a circle with diameter 92 m

✓ 30-4 Inscribed Angles

Find each measure.

12. $m\angle BAC$

13. $m\overset{\frown}{CD}$

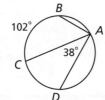

102°

38°

14. $m\angle FGH$

15. $m\overset{\frown}{JGF}$

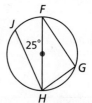

25°

PARCC Assessment Readiness

Selected Response

1. Find m$\widehat{CFB}$.

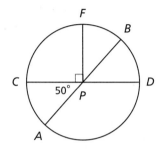

- (A) m$\widehat{CFB}$ = 130°
- (C) m$\widehat{CFB}$ = 230°
- (B) m$\widehat{CFB}$ = 140°
- (D) m$\widehat{CFB}$ = 90°

2. Find the area of sector *POM*.

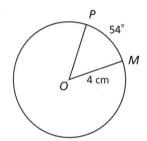

- (F) 0.6π cm²
- (H) 2.4π cm²
- (G) 1.2π cm²
- (J) 864π cm²

3. Carlos plays vinyl records on a turntable that rotates through an angle of $\frac{3}{2}\pi$ radians in 1 second. How many revolutions does the turntable make in one minute?

- (A) $33\frac{1}{3}$ revolutions per minute
- (B) 45 revolutions per minute
- (C) 78 revolutions per minute
- (D) $16\frac{2}{3}$ revolutions per minute

4. A satellite orbits 50 miles above Earth's atmosphere. An astronaut works on the satellite and sees the sun rise over Earth. To the nearest mile, what is the distance from the astronaut to the horizon? (*Hint:* Earth's radius is about 4,000 miles.)

- (F) 634 mi
- (H) 630 mi
- (G) 402,500 mi
- (J) 397,500 mi

5. Solve for *x*.

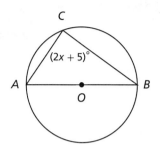

- (A) 42.5
- (C) 87.5
- (B) 47.5
- (D) 90

6. Identify the secant.

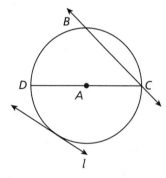

- (F) $\overleftrightarrow{BC}$
- (H) $\overline{DC}$
- (G) *l*
- (J) $\overline{DA}$

Mini-Task

7. $\overline{GK}$ is a diameter of the circle. Find m$\widehat{HK}$ to the nearest degree.

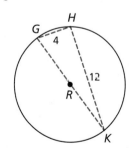

PARCC Assessment Readiness

Selected Response

1. The floor of a tent is a regular hexagon. If the side length of the tent floor is 5 feet, what is the area of the floor? Round to the nearest tenth.

- **(A)** 32.5 square feet
- **(B)** 65.0 square feet
- **(C)** 75.0 square feet
- **(D)** 129.9 square feet

2. Find the area of $\odot Q$ in terms of π.

- **(F)** 400π in.^{2}
- **(G)** 100 in.^{2}
- **(H)** 200π in.^{2}
- **(J)** 100π in.^{2}

3. Find the area of a regular hexagon with side length 4 m. Round to the nearest tenth.

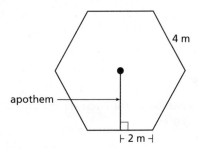

- **(A)** 83.1 m^2
- **(B)** 24 m^2
- **(C)** 41.6 m^2
- **(D)** 20.8 m^2

4. How many cubes with edge length 3 centimeters will fit in a box that is a rectangular prism with length 12 centimeters, width 15 centimeters, and height 24 centimeters?

- **(F)** 160
- **(G)** 480
- **(H)** 1440
- **(J)** 4320

5. Right $\triangle ABC$ with legs $AB = 9$ millimeters and $BC = 12$ millimeters is the base of a prism that has a volume of 513 cubic millimeters. What is the height of the prism?

- **(A)** 4.75 millimeters
- **(B)** 6 millimeters
- **(C)** 9.5 millimeters
- **(D)** 11 millimeters

6. The radius of a sphere is doubled. What happens to the ratio of the volume of the sphere to the surface area of the sphere?

- **(F)** It remains the same.
- **(G)** It is doubled.
- **(H)** It is increased by a factor of 4.
- **(J)** It is increased by a factor of 8.

7. To the nearest tenth of a cubic centimeter, what is the volume of a right regular octagonal prism with base edge length 4 centimeters and height 7 centimeters?

- **(A)** 180.3 cubic centimeters
- **(B)** 224.0 cubic centimeters
- **(C)** 270.4 cubic centimeters
- **(D)** 540.8 cubic centimeters

8. A square pyramid has a base area of 225 square meters and a volume of 2925 cubic meters. To the nearest meter, what is the height of the pyramid?

(F) 13 meters

(G) 26 meters

(H) 39 meters

(J) 52 meters

9. A cylinder has a height of 10 inches. The circumference of the base is 28.3 inches. To the nearest cubic inch, what is the volume of this cylinder?

(A) 141 cubic inches

(B) 283 cubic inches

(C) 637 cubic inches

(D) 2545 cubic inches

10. The volume of the smaller sphere is 288 cubic centimeters. Find the volume of the larger sphere.

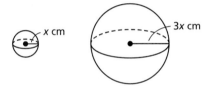

(F) 864 cubic centimeters

(G) 2,592 cubic centimeters

(H) 7,776 cubic centimeters

(J) 23,328 cubic centimeters

11. A cylinder has a volume of 24 cubic centimeters. The height of a cone with the same radius is two times the height of the cylinder. What is the volume of the cone?

(A) 8 cubic centimeters

(B) 12 cubic centimeters

(C) 16 cubic centimeters

(D) 48 cubic centimeters

12. The volume of a sphere is 288π cubic centimeters. What is its surface area, rounded to the nearest hundredth?

(F) 113.10 square centimeters

(G) 452.39 square centimeters

(H) 2842.45 square centimeters

(J) 8527.34 square centimeters

13. The circle graph shows the colors of automobiles sold at a car dealership. Find m$\overset{\frown}{CD}$.

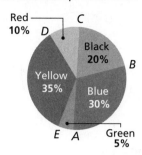

(A) m$\overset{\frown}{CD}$ = 36°

(B) m$\overset{\frown}{CD}$ = 10°

(C) m$\overset{\frown}{CD}$ = 170°

(D) m$\overset{\frown}{CD}$ = 20°

Use the diagram for Items 14–16.

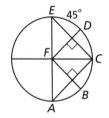

14. What is m$\overset{\frown}{BC}$?

(F) 36°

(G) 45°

(H) 54°

(J) 72°

15. If the length of $\overset{\frown}{ED}$ is 6π centimeters, what is the area of sector *EFD*?

(A) 20π square centimeters

(B) 72π square centimeters

(C) 120π square centimeters

(D) 240π square centimeters

16. Which of these line segments is NOT a chord of ⊙*F*?

(F) $\overline{EC}$

(G) $\overline{CA}$

(H) $\overline{AF}$

(J) $\overline{AE}$

17. A wheel from a motor has springs arranged as in the figure. Find m∠DOC.

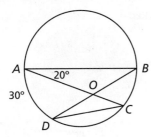

Ⓐ m∠DOC = 145°

Ⓑ m∠DOC = 150°

Ⓒ m∠DOC = 140°

Ⓓ m∠DOC = 130°

18. What is the arc length, rounded to the nearest hundredth, of a semicircle in a circle with radius 5 millimeters?

Ⓕ 3.14 millimeters

Ⓖ 6.28 millimeters

Ⓗ 15.71 millimeters

Ⓙ 31.42 millimeters

19. △ABC is inscribed in a circle with center P. Side $\overline{BC}$ passes through point P. Which of the following is true?

Ⓐ $\overline{BC}$ is a radius of the circle.

Ⓑ PA < PC

Ⓒ m$\overparen{BAC}$ = 90°

Ⓓ ∠BAC is a right angle.

20. A circle of radius r units has a central angle whose measure is 30°. What do you multiply r by to find the length of the arc intercepted by this central angle?

Ⓕ 2π

Ⓖ $\frac{\pi}{6}$

Ⓗ $\frac{\pi}{12}$

Ⓙ $\frac{1}{12}$

21. Circumscribed ∠ABC is tangent to ⊙P at points A and C. Which statement is not always true?

Ⓐ $\overline{BC} \perp \overline{PC}$

Ⓑ $\overline{BA} \perp \overline{PA}$

Ⓒ $\overline{BC} \cong \overline{PC}$

Ⓓ $\overline{BA} \cong \overline{BC}$

22. Which steps can you take to construct the tangent to ⊙M at point N on the circle?

Ⓕ Draw $\overrightarrow{MN}$. Then construct the line through N that is perpendicular to $\overrightarrow{MN}$.

Ⓖ Draw $\overrightarrow{MN}$. Then construct the line through M that is perpendicular to $\overrightarrow{MN}$.

Ⓗ Draw $\overrightarrow{MN}$. Then construct the perpendicular bisector of $\overline{MN}$.

Ⓙ Draw $\overleftrightarrow{MN}$ so that it intersects ⊙M at points P and N. Then construct the line through P that is perpendicular to $\overleftrightarrow{MN}$.

23. The illustration shows a fragment of a circular plate. AB = 8 in., and CD = 2 in. What is the diameter of the plate?

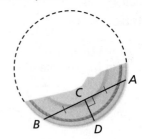

Ⓐ 4 in.

Ⓑ 5 in.

Ⓒ 8 in.

Ⓓ 10 in.

24. Which line of reasoning can be used to begin to derive the formula for the area of a circle with radius r and circumference C?

Ⓕ Divide the circle into eight congruent sectors and treat each sector as a triangle with base $\frac{1}{8}C$ and height $\frac{1}{2}r$.

Ⓖ Divide the circle into eight congruent sectors and arrange them to approximate a parallelogram with base C and height r.

Ⓗ Divide the circle into eight congruent sectors and arrange them to approximate a parallelogram with base $\frac{1}{8}C$ and height r.

Ⓙ Divide the circle into nine congruent sectors and arrange them to approximate a trapezoid with bases $\frac{5}{9}C$ and $\frac{4}{9}C$ and height r.

Mini-Tasks

25. Use the diagram to find the value of *x*. Show your work or explain in words how you determined your answer.

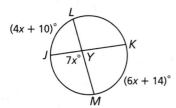

26. The figure shows the top view of a stack of cubes. The number on each cube represents the number of stacked cubes. The volume of each cube is 4 cubic inches. What is the volume of the three-dimensional figure formed by the cubes?

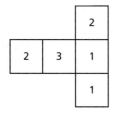

27. Find the volume of a cone with a base circumference of 15π m and a height 3 m less than twice the radius. Give your answer both in terms of π and rounded to the nearest tenth.

28. Find the area of segment *POM*. Round to the nearest tenth.

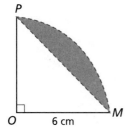

29. Find the volume of a sphere with diameter 24 ft. Give your answer in terms of π.

Performance Tasks

30. Zachary works for an outdoor supply company and is in charge of creating the specs for the tent shown below.

The tent will be in the shape of a regular hexagonal pyramid.

a. Zachary decides the distance from the center of the tent's base to any vertex of the base will be 8 feet and the distance from any vertex of the base to the top of the pyramid will be 10 feet. What is the height of the tent?

b. The base of the tent is a regular hexagon. What is the area of the base? Show your work, and round your answer to the nearest tenth of a square foot.

c. What is the volume of the tent? Show your work, and round your answer to the nearest cubic foot.

d. Zachary's boss says that if they keep the distance from the center to any vertex of the base 8 feet, and they keep the height of the tent the same, but they change the base of the tent to a regular polygon with 8 sides instead of 6 sides, the volume of the tent will increase by 33%. Is Zachary's boss correct? Explain why or why not.

31. The length of $\overline{TJ}$ is 10 inches and $m\overarc{JMB}$ is 225°.

Part A: Find the measure of ∠*JTB*. Find the circumference of circle *T*. Find the arc length of $\overarc{JB}$. Find the area of circle *T*. Find the area of sector *JTB*.

Part B: If the radius of circle *T* is doubled, will the area of sector *JTB* also double? Explain your reasoning by finding the area of sector *JTB* when the radius is doubled.

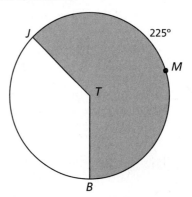

my.hrw.com
Online Assessment

Go online for updated, PARCC-aligned assessment readiness.

Student Handbook

Appendix of Additional Lessons

Appendix

Units in Algebra

? Essential Question: How can you use the units in problems to help you solve the problems?

Objective
Use units as a way to guide the solution of multi-step problems; choose and interpret the scale and the origin in graphs and data displays.

When solving real-world problems, it is important to pay attention to the units of measurement. If the numerical value is correct, but the units are missing or incorrect, then the solution is incorrect.

One of the most famous errors of this type caused the loss of the Mars Climate Orbiter in 1999. Miscalculations due to the use of customary units instead of metric units caused the spacecraft to be sent off course. It was a very expensive error: the spacecraft cost $125 million.

EXAMPLE 1 **Using Units to Guide Solutions**
Prep. for MCC9-12.N.Q.1

A container holds 5 liters of water. Convert this quantity to pints. There are about 2.1 pints in a liter.

Identify the given unit and the unit you need to find. Use that information to set up your conversion factor.

$$\boxed{\text{Unit Wanted}} = \boxed{\text{Given Unit}} \cdot \boxed{\text{Conversion Factor}}$$

Helpful Hint

Use ≈ because the word "about" shows the conversion is an approximation.

$$x \text{ pints} \approx \frac{5 \text{ liters}}{1} \cdot \frac{2.1 \text{ pints}}{1 \text{ liters}}$$ *The liters in the denominator cancel with the liters in the numerator.*

$$\approx 10.5 \text{ pints}$$

The container holds approximately 10.5 pints of water.

✓ CHECK IT OUT!
1. A box of fruit has a mass of 18 pounds. Convert this quantity to kilograms. There are about 2.2 pounds in a kilogram. Round your answer to the nearest hundredth.

EXAMPLE 2 **Using Units to Guide Solutions with Multiple Steps**
MCC9-12.N.Q.1

Monarch butterflies can fly at a rate of about 4 miles per hour. How many meters is that per minute? There are about 3.28 feet in 1 meter and 5280 feet in 1 mile.

Identify the given rate and the rate you need to find. Use that information to set up your conversion factors.

$$x \frac{\text{meters}}{\text{minute}} \approx 4 \frac{\text{miles}}{\text{hour}} \cdot \boxed{\text{conversion factor}} \cdot \boxed{\text{conversion factor}} \cdot \boxed{\text{conversion factor}}$$

Set up conversion factors so that both mile and hour units cancel.

$$x \frac{\text{meters}}{\text{minute}} \approx 4 \frac{\text{mi}}{\text{hr}} \cdot \left(\frac{1 \text{ hr}}{60 \text{ min}}\right) \cdot \left(\frac{5280 \text{ ft}}{1 \text{ mi}}\right) \cdot \left(\frac{1 \text{ m}}{3.28 \text{ ft}}\right)$$

$$\approx \frac{4 \cdot 5280 \text{ m}}{60 \cdot 3.28 \text{ min}}$$

$$\approx \frac{21,120 \text{ m}}{196.8 \text{ min}}$$

$$\approx 107.3 \frac{\text{m}}{\text{min}}$$

A monarch butterfly can fly at a rate of 107.3 meters per minute.

2. The mass of a newborn baby kitten is 95 grams. What is the kitten's mass in ounces? A kilogram is about 2.2 pounds.

EXAMPLE **3** **Using Units in Formulas**

MCC9-12.N.Q.1

A rectangular hallway rug is 18 inches by 8 feet. What is the area of the rug?

Draw and label a diagram.

18 in.

8 ft

The dimensions of the rug are given in two different units, inches and feet. To use the area formula, you need both dimensions to be in the same units.

You can change 18 inches to feet or 8 feet to inches.

Method 1: Using Feet

$$(18 \text{ inches}) \times \left(\frac{1 \text{ foot}}{12 \text{ inches}}\right) = 1.5 \text{ feet} \qquad \textit{Change inches to feet.}$$

$A = lw$ *Use the area formula.*

$A = (8 \text{ ft})(1.5 \text{ ft})$ *Substitute 8 ft for the length and 1.5 ft for the width.*

$A = 12 \text{ square feet}$ *The unit of measure is square feet.*

Method 2: Using Inches

$$(8 \text{ feet}) \times \left(\frac{12 \text{ inches}}{1 \text{ foot}}\right) = 96 \text{ inches} \qquad \textit{Change feet to inches.}$$

$A = lw$ *Use the area formula.*

$A = (96 \text{ in.})(18 \text{ in.})$ *Substitute 96 in. for the length and 18 in. for the width.*

$A = 1728 \text{ square inches}$ *The unit of measure is square inches.*

Check: Are the values the same?

$$(12 \text{ square feet}) \times \left(\frac{144 \text{ square inches}}{1 \text{ square foot}}\right) = 1728 \text{ square inches} \quad \textit{Change square feet to square inches.}$$

3. The dimensions of a rectangular painting are 15 inches by 3 feet. What is the perimeter of the painting?

When graphing a real-world situation or mathematical equation, it is important to choose a reasonable scale for each axis. If the scale has increments that are too small, the graph will take up too much space. If the scale has increments that are too large, then you can't get meaningful information from the graph.

EXAMPLE 4   Choosing an Appropriate Scale: Increments Greater than 1

Megan earns a base salary of $50 a day and a commission of 10% on her total daily sales. She often has sales of more than $300. She uses this equation to determine what her total earnings are in a day: $y = 0.1x + 50$.

a. Decide what scales should be used for the graph.

Since Megan often has sales of more than $300, the values on the x-axis can range from $0 to $600. Increments of $50 are reasonable.

To find the scale of the y-axis, substitute the largest x-value (600) into the equation to find the maximum y value: $y = 0.1(600) + 50 = 60 + 50 = 110$. The values on the y-axis can range from $0 to $120. Increments of $10 are reasonable.

b. Draw the graph.

Graph the equation $y = 0.1x + 50$. You can substitute values for x in the equation to find points that will help you draw the graph.

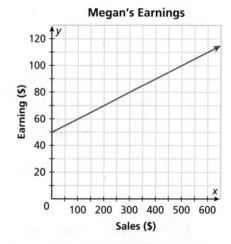

c. Use the graph to find the total earnings for Megan if her sales are $300.

To find Megan's total earnings when her sales are $300, find the y-coordinate of the point on the line that has an x-coordinate of 300. The point on the line with an x-coordinate of 300 is (300, 80). Megan's total earnings are $80.

d. What does the origin (0, 0) mean on this graph?

In this graph the origin (0, 0) would mean $0 salary and $0 sales. Note that the line does not go through the origin, because even when Megan has no sales, she still receives a base salary of $50.

 4. A water tank holds 2000 gallons. The tank has a leak and loses 100 gallons a day. Jeff is making a graph to show the volume of water in the tank. He uses the equation $y = 2000 - 100x$ where x is the number of days the water tank leaks.

   a. What scales should Jeff use for a graph?

   b. Draw the graph.

   c. Use the graph to find the volume of water in the tank if the tank leaks for 5 days.

   d. What does the origin (0, 0) mean on this graph?

EXAMPLE **5** **Choosing an Appropriate Scale: Increments Less than 1**
MCC9-12.N.Q.1

From 1901 to 2011 the ocean surface temperatures rose at an average rate of 0.013 F° every year. Jamil wrote the equation $y = 0.013x$ to describe the overall temperature change since 1901.

a. Decide what scales should be used for the graph.

Since the time period spans 110 years, increments of 10 years are reasonable for the *x*-axis. The rate of increase in the temperature is 0.013 per year, so the increments for the *y*-axis can be very small, such as 0.1 °F.

b. Draw the graph.

Graph the equation $y = 0.013x$ using the equation to help you plot the points.

Change in Surface Temperature

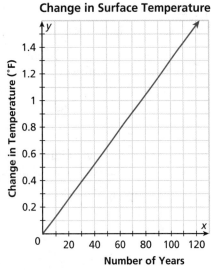

c. Use the graph to find the increase in ocean surface temperature in 1951.

1951 is 50 years after 1901. To find the amount of change after 50 years, find the *y*-coordinate of the point on the line that has an *x*-coordinate of 50. The point on the line with an *x*-coordinate of 50 is (50, 0.65). By 1951, the temperature had increased by 0.65 °F.

d. What does the point (0, 0) mean on this graph?

The origin (0, 0) on this graph represents no change in temperature in the year 1901.

 5. Jasmine wrote the equation $y = 0.17x$, where *x* represents the number of weeks, to describe the average weight gain of newborns in kilograms per week for the first 16 weeks of their lives.

    a. What scale should Jasmine use for a graph?

    b. Draw the graph.

    c. Use the graph to find the average total weight gain at 10 weeks.

    d. What does the origin (0, 0) mean on this graph?

1. Claire is making a soup that requires 3 liters of vegetable broth. There are about 2.1 pints in a liter. How many pints are in 3 liters?

2. To add a border to a curtain, Dion needs 4 meters of ribbon. There are about 3.28 feet in 1 meter. How many feet are in 4 meters?

3. Jermaine has collected 17 kilograms of aluminum cans to recycle. There are about 2.2 pounds in 1 kilogram. How many pounds are in 17 kilograms?

4. Brian has collected 6 ounces of sand. There are about 28.35 grams in an ounce. How many grams are in 6 ounces?

5. A rectangular patio is 4 yards by 10 feet. What is the perimeter of the patio?

6. A cylindrical water tank has a radius of 30 inches and a height of 10 feet. What is the volume of the water tank? Round your answer to the nearest hundredth. Round your answer to the nearest cubic foot or the nearest hundred thousand cubic inches.

7. Jared's rectangular garden is 30 feet by 6 yards. What is the area of the garden?

8. Irma buys 4 yards of fabric that is 45 inches wide. Is that enough fabric to cover an area that is 25 square feet? Justify your answer.

9. Delia's punch bowl holds 7 quarts.
   a. What conversion factor is needed to find the number of cups?
   b. How many cups does Delia's punch bowl hold?

10. Jason needs 10 quarts of paint. How many gallons is 10 quarts?

Use the table for Exercises 11–15.

11. Rita is traveling in England. She buys 11 liters of gasoline, paying in pounds, the English currency.
   a. How many gallons of gasoline did she buy?
   b. If the exchange rate for pounds to dollars is 1 pound = 1.5 dollars and 1 liter of gasoline costs 1.6 pounds, how much did Rita pay in dollars for the gasoline?
   c. What is the price per gallon in dollars for the gasoline that Rita bought? Round your answer to the nearest cent.

Metric and Customary Measurements	
Metric Unit	**Customary Equivalent**
1 liter	0.26 gal
1 kilometer	0.62 mi
1 meter	3.28 ft
1 kilogram	2.2 lb

12. A sign shows 18 kilometers to the next town. To the nearest tenth, how many miles away is the town?

13. Krista is driving at a speed of 50 kilometers per hour. How many minutes will it take her to drive 45 miles? Round to the nearest minute.

14. A loaf of bread has a mass of 0.75 kilograms. How many ounces does the bread weigh? Round your answer to the nearest ounce.

15. Zachary's destination is 95 kilometers away. It is 2:00 P.M. If he is traveling at a rate of 30 miles per hour will he arrive by 4:00 P.M.? Justify your answer.

16. A *board-foot* is a unit of volume used for lumber. It is equal to 1 inch × 1 foot × 1 foot. One inch is exactly 2.54 centimeters. Carson needs 7 board-feet of lumber to complete a project.

   a. How many cubic centimeters of lumber does Carson need? Round to the nearest hundred cubic centimeters.

   b. How many cubic feet of lumber does Carson need? Round to the nearest hundredth of a cubic foot.

17. Silver is usually bought and sold in troy ounces. A troy ounce is about 31.1 grams, whereas a customary ounce is about 28.35 grams.

   a. What was the price of a gram of silver in 2000, rounded to the nearest cent?

   b. To the nearest cent, by how much did the price of a gram of silver increase from 2010 to 2012?

Average Price of 1 Troy Ounce of Silver	
Year	Price
2000	$4.95
2010	$20.19
2012	$31.15

18. A league is an obsolete unit of length. It was the distance a person could walk in an hour, or about 3 miles. At sea, a league was defined as 3 nautical miles. Jules Verne wrote a book titled *20,000 Leagues Under the Sea*.

   a. Show how you could use equivalencies in the table to find out how long 20,000 leagues is in customary miles.

   b. To the nearest mile, how long is 20,000 leagues?

Equivalent Units of Measure	
Unit	Equivalent
1 league	3 nautical miles
1 nautical mile	1.85 kilometers
1 mile	1.61 kilometers

19. The Holderness coastline of England is eroding at an average rate of 1.5 meters per year.

   a. How many inches per month is the coastline eroding? Round your answer to the nearest inch.

   b. In some places along the Holderness coastline, the erosion is as much as 6 meters per year. How many more feet per year is that than the average erosion for the Holderness coastline?

20. Michael is growing pole bean plants for his science project. He bought the plants when they were 3 inches tall. The plants grew an average of 10 inches per week. The equation $y = 3 + 10x$ describes the average height of the bean plants during the 8 weeks of the experiment, with x the number of the week and y the height.

   a. What scales should Michael use for a graph?

   b. Draw the graph.

   c. Use the graph to find the height of the bean plants in the sixth week of the project.

   d. What does the origin (0, 0) represent on this graph?

21. In 2008 NASA's Phoenix spacecraft traveled toward Mars at a rate of 74,000 mph. It took 295 days for the spacecraft to reach Mars.

   a. At what rate did the spacecraft travel each day?

   b. Yoshi wants to create a graph to show the distance traveled by the Phoenix during the first 100 days of the flight. What equation could he use? What scale should he use for the graph?

   c. Draw the graph.

   d. Use the graph to find approximately how many miles the Phoenix had traveled by day 30.

   e. What does the origin (0, 0) represent on this graph?

Functions and Sequences

? **Essential Question:** How can you represent sequences as functions?

Objective
Recognize that sequences are functions whose domain is a subset of the set of integers.

Vocabulary
arithmetic sequence
common difference
geometric sequence
common ratio
recursive rule
explicit rule

You have studied two types of sequences, arithmetic sequences and geometric sequences. Recall that an **arithmetic sequence** is a sequence of numbers in which the difference between any two consecutive terms is the same number and is called the **common difference**. Recall that a **geometric sequence** is a sequence of numbers in which the ratio of any two consecutive terms is the same number and is called the **common ratio**.

Suppose that a sequence is represented as $a_1, a_2, a_3, a_4, \ldots$. The sequence can be defined by a **recursive rule**, a rule that shows what a_1 is and shows how to find a_n if you know what the preceding term, a_{n-1}, is for each $n > 1$.

Sequences can also be represented by functions. For example, the sequence $a_1, a_2, a_3, a_4, \ldots$ can be represented by the function $f(x)$ so that the following is true.

$$f(1) = a_1, f(2) = a_2, f(3) = a_3, f(4) = a_4, \text{ and so on.}$$

EXAMPLE MCC9-12.F.IF.3

1 **Interpreting a Recursive Rule**

An arithmetic sequence is defined by the recursive rule below:

$a_1 = 3$

$a_n = a_{n-1} + 2$ for $n > 1$

a. Find the first four terms of the sequence.

$a_1 = 3$

$a_2 = a_1 + 2 = 3 + 2 = 5$ *The number 2 is the common*
                              difference of the sequence.
$a_3 = a_2 + 2 = 5 + 2 = 7$

$a_4 = a_3 + 2 = 7 + 2 = 9$

The first four terms of the sequence are 3, 5, 7, and 9.

b. Represent the sequence as a function and identify the domain of the function.

$f(1) = 3$

$f(n) = f(n - 1) + 2$

The domain of the function is the set of positive integers.

 1. A geometric sequence is defined by the recursive rule below.

$a_1 = 4$

$a_n = a_{n-1} (0.5)$ for $n > 1$

a. Find the first five terms of the sequence.

b. Represent the sequence as a function and identify the domain of the function.

A sequence can also be defined by an **explicit rule**, a rule that allows you to find the nth term of the sequence without knowing what the preceding term is.

EXAMPLE 2

Interpreting an Explicit Rule

A geometric sequence is defined by the explicit rule below, where n may be any positive integer.

$$a_n = 2(3)^{n-1}$$

a. **Represent the sequence as a function and identify the domain of the function.**

$f(n) = 2(3)^{n-1}$; the domain of the function is the set of positive integers.

Note that 3 is the common ratio for the sequence.

b. **Find the first four terms of the sequence.**

$f(1) = 2(3)^{1-1} = 2(3)^0 = 2(1) = 2$

$f(2) = 2(3)^{2-1} = 2(3)^1 = 2(3) = 6$

$f(3) = 2(3)^{3-1} = 2(3)^2 = 2(9) = 18$

$f(4) = 2(3)^{4-1} = 2(3)^3 = 2(27) = 54$

c. **Find the 10th term of the sequence.**

$f(10) = 2(3)^{10-1} = 2(3)^9 = 2(19{,}683) = 39{,}366$

Notice that you do not need to know the 9th term of the sequence in order to find the 10th term of the sequence.

 CHECK IT OUT!

2. An arithmetic sequence is defined by the explicit rule below, where n may be any positive integer.

$$a_n = 9 + (n - 1)(-4)$$

a. Represent the sequence as a function and identify the domain of the function.

b. Find the first four terms of the sequence.

c. Find the 12th term of the sequence.

You can write a *recursive rule* for an arithmetic sequence by doing two things.

• Specify what the first term is. It would be denoted by a_1 or $f(1)$.

• Find the common difference d and write one of the following equivalent formulas.

$$a_n = a_{n-1} + d \text{ for } n > 1 \text{ or}$$

$$f(n) = f(n - 1) + d \text{ for } n > 1$$

You can write an *explicit rule* for an arithmetic sequence by writing one of the following equivalent formulas.

$$a_n = a_1 + (n - 1)d \text{ or}$$

$$f(n) = f(1) + (n - 1)d$$

3 **Writing Rules for an Arithmetic Sequence**

Annette is saving to buy a mountain bike. She received $75 from her aunt as a birthday present and after the first month, she has been saving an additional $25 per month toward her goal. The table shows her total savings so far.

Month	n	1	2	3	4	5
Total Savings ($)	$f(n)$	75	100	125	150	175

a. Write a recursive rule for the arithmetic sequence shown in the table.

The first term is 75. The common difference is 25.
Recursive rule:

$$f(1) = 75$$

$f(1)$ is the first term.

$$f(n) = f(n-1) + 25 \text{ for } n > 1$$

All other terms are the sum of the previous term and the common difference.

b. Write an explicit rule for the sequence.

n	$f(n)$
1	$75 = 75 + 25(0)$
2	$100 = 75 + 25(1)$
3	$125 = 75 + 25(2)$
n	$f(n) = 75 + 25(n-1)$

Write each term as the sum of the first term and a multiple of the common difference.

Explicit rule:

$$f(n) = 75 + 25(n-1) \text{ for } n \text{ a positive integer}$$

Write the explicit rule by generalizing the results.

 3. The table shows the number of members of the newly formed Metropolitan Chorus after n weeks.

Week	n	1	2	3	4	5
Members	$f(n)$	18	30	42	54	66

a. Write a recursive rule for the arithmetic sequence shown in the table.

b. Write an explicit rule for the sequence.

You can find a *recursive rule* for a geometric sequence by doing two things.

- Specify what the first term is. It would be denoted by a_1 or $f(1)$.

- Find the common ratio r and write one of the following equivalent formulas.

$$a_n = a_{n-1} r \text{ or}$$

$$f(n) = f(n-1) \cdot r$$

You can write an *explicit rule* for a geometric sequence by writing one of the following equivalent formulas.

$$a_n = a_1 r^{n-1} \text{ or}$$

$$f(n) = f(1) \cdot r^{n-1}$$

EXAMPLE 4 **Writing Rules for a Geometric Sequence**

MCC9-12.F.IF.3

Allan is conducting an experiment in biology lab about the growth rate of bacteria in a Petri dish. The table shows the number of bacteria in the dish n minutes after the start of the experiment.

Number of Minutes	n	1	2	3	4	5
Number of Bacteria	$f(n)$	10	20	40	80	160

a. Write a recursive rule for the geometric sequence shown in the table.

$\dfrac{20}{10} = 2 \quad \dfrac{40}{20} = 2 \quad \dfrac{80}{40} = 2 \quad \dfrac{160}{80} = 2$ *Find the common ratio. The common ratio, r, is 2.*

$f(1) = 10$ *Write the first term.*

$f(2) = f(1) \cdot 2$
$f(3) = f(2) \cdot 2$ *Each term in the sequence after the first term is equal to the previous term times 2.*
$f(4) = f(3) \cdot 2$

$f(n) = f(n - 1) \cdot 2$ *f(n − 1) represents the (n − 1)th term.*

Recursive rule:

$f(1) = 10$
$f(n) = f(n - 1) \cdot 2$ for $n > 1$ *Write the recursive rule by giving the first term and the rule for successive terms.*

b. Write an explicit rule for the sequence.

n	$f(n)$
1	$10(2)^0 = 10$
2	$10(2)^1 = 20$
3	$10(2)^2 = 40$
4	$10(2)^3 = 80$
5	$10(2)^4 = 160$

Write each term as the product of the first term and a power of the common ratio.

$f(n) = 10 \cdot 2^{n-1}$ *Write the explicit rule by generalizing the results.*

Explicit rule:

$f(n) = 10 \cdot 2^{n-1}$ for n a positive integer

c. Interpret the explicit rule in terms of the context of the problem.

In $f(n) = 10 \cdot 2^{n-1}$, 10 is number of bacteria after the first minute, 2 is the factor by which the number of bacteria increase each minute, and n is the number of minutes since the experiment began.

 4. The table shows the number of people called during each of the first 5 minutes of a phone tree.

Time (min)	n	1	2	3	4	5
Number contacted	$f(n)$	4	12	36	108	324

     a. Write a recursive rule for the geometric sequence shown in the table.

     b. Write an explicit rule for the sequence.

Write the first four terms of each sequence. Assume that the domain of each function is the set of positive integers.

1. $f(1) = 4$ and $f(n) = f(n-1) + 6$ for $n > 1$

2. $f(1) = -2$ and $f(n) = f(n-1) + (-3)$ for $n > 1$

3. $f(1) = 1$ and $f(n) = 3 \cdot f(n-1)$ for $n > 1$

4. $f(1) = 0.4$ and $f(n) = 2.5 \cdot f(n-1)$ for $n > 1$

5. $f(n) = 5 + (n-1)(-2)$

6. $f(n) = -7 + (n-1)(3)$

7. $f(n) = 3(2)^{n-1}$

8. $f(n) = 6(0.5)^{n-1}$

9. $f(n) = 2(-1)^{n-1}$

10. $f(n) = 4(-2)^{n-1}$

Write the 9th term of each sequence.

11. $f(n) = 181 + (n-1)(-17)$

12. $f(n) = 3.5 + (n-1)(1.5)$

13. $f(n) = -3(2)^{n-1}$

14. $f(n) = 0.5(-2)^{n-1}$

15. $f(n) = 4n + 19$

16. $f(n) = 21 - 3n$

17. $f(n) = (-3)(-1)^{n-1}$

18. $f(n) = 5(0.4)^{n-1}$

Write a recursive rule and an explicit rule for each sequence.

19.

n	1	2	3	4	5
$f(n)$	45	40	35	30	25

20.

n	1	2	3	4	5
$f(n)$	7	14	21	28	35

21.

n	1	2	3	4	5
$f(n)$	4	-12	36	-108	324

22.

n	1	2	3	4	5
$f(n)$	4374	1458	486	162	54

23. $9, 24, 39, 54, \ldots$

24. $19, 9, -1, -11, \ldots$

25. $15, 3, \dfrac{3}{5}, \dfrac{3}{25}, \ldots$

26. $3, 12, 48, 192, \ldots$

27. Write About It The first term of an arithmetic sequence is 7 and the common difference is 9. Explain how to find the sixth term of the sequence.

28. Problem Solving The numbers of points that a player must accumulate to reach the next level of a video game form a geometric sequence, where $f(n)$ is the number of points needed to complete Level n.

   a. A player needs 50 points to complete Level 1 and 8,000,000 points to complete Level 5. Write an explicit rule for the sequence.

   b. Interpret the explicit rule in terms of the context of the problem.

   c. How many points are needed to complete Level 7?

29. **Represent Real-World Problems** An economist predicts that the cost of food will increase by 3% per year for the next several years.

   a. Use the economist's prediction to write an explicit rule for a geometric sequence that gives the cost in dollars of a pound of cheese in year n that costs $4.50 in year 1.

   b. Interpret the explicit rule in terms of the context of the problem.

   c. What is the fourth term of the sequence rounded to the nearest cent, and what does it represent?

30. The Fibonacci sequence is a recursive sequence that has many applications in mathematics and science. The first two terms in the sequence are 0 and 1. Each succeeding number is found by adding the two numbers immediately before it. So the third term is $0 + 1 = 1$.

   a. Write the first 10 terms of the Fibonacci sequence.

   b. Write a recursive rule for the Fibonacci sequence.

31. One of the many interesting properties of the Fibonacci sequence appears when you divide terms of the sequence by the terms that immediately precede them. The curious result doesn't appear for the first few terms. In fact, the quotient is undefined for the first two terms in the sequence:

$$\frac{\text{second term}}{\text{first term}} = \frac{1}{0} \rightarrow \text{undefined}$$

   a. Find the following quotients to the nearest thousandth:
   $$\frac{\text{sixth term}}{\text{fifth term}}, \frac{\text{seventh term}}{\text{sixth term}}, \frac{\text{eighth term}}{\text{seventh term}}, \frac{\text{ninth term}}{\text{eighth term}}, \frac{\text{tenth term}}{\text{ninth term}}$$

   b. Describe the pattern in your results.

   c. Does the pattern continue for the next three quotients? Explain.

   d. Each shape in the figure is a square. Explain how the figure models the Fibonacci sequence.

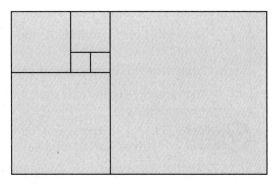

32. **Critical Thinking** Brittany drew the graph of a function that was an arithmetic sequence whose domain was the set of positive integers.

   a. Describe the graph.

   b. By looking at the graph, how could you tell that it is the graph of a function?

33. **Critical Thinking** A geometric sequence has a common ratio that is a negative number.

   a. Describe the signs of the terms of the sequence.

   b. Explain your reasoning.

34. **Represent Real-World Problems** Describe a real-world situation that could be represented by the explicit rule $f(n) = 10 + 4(n - 1)$.

Parts of Expressions

Essential Question: How can you interpret parts of an algebraic expression?

Objective
Interpret parts of expressions in terms of what the expression represents.

Vocabulary
term
coefficient
expression

A **term** is a number, or a variable, or a product or quotient of numbers and variables. The following are examples of terms.

number	$5, -8.3, \frac{2}{5}$
variable	x, y, a
product of number(s) and variable(s)	$3x, 5xy, -4x^3$
quotient of number(s) and variable(s)	$\frac{x}{9}, \frac{5}{c}, \frac{a}{b}$

When a term contains a number and one or more variables, the number part is called the **coefficient** of the term. For example, the coefficient of the term $5xy$ is 5.

Expressions are made up of terms. An **expression** may contain one term, or several terms that are combined using addition and/or subtraction. Here are some examples of expressions with several terms.

$$5x + 3y - 4, \; 6a^2 - 4a - 7, \; 4^x + 8x + 2$$

Expressions can be used to represent real-world situations.

EXAMPLE MCC9-12.A.SSE.1a

1 Interpreting a Simple Expression

Jason earns $30 each time he mows a lawn. The expression $30x$ represents the amount of money, in dollars, that he earned mowing lawns last month.

a. In this expression, what does the coefficient 30 represent?

The coefficient 30 represents the $30 Jason earned each time he mowed a lawn.

b. What does the variable x represent?

The variable x represents the number of lawns he mowed.

 1. Karly earns $15 a lesson for each private swimming lesson she gives. Karly's total pay for the day can be expressed as $15x$.

a. What does the coefficient 15 represent?

b. What does x represent?

EXAMPLE MCC9-12.A.SSE.1a

2 Interpreting an Expression with Multiple Terms

The cost of admission to the county fair is $8. Each ride ticket costs $1.25. The total cost of going to the fair and buying t ride tickets can be represented by the expression $8 + 1.25t$.

a. In this expression, what does the 8 represent?

The 8 represents the cost of admission to the fair.

b. What does the term $1.25t$ represent?

The term $1.25t$ represents the money spent on ride tickets.

c. What does the coefficient 1.25 represent?

The coefficient 1.25 represents the cost per ticket of the ride tickets.

2. The base cost of a house call by an electrician is $30. The electrician charges an additional $50 per hour for labor. The total cost of having the electrician work for h hours is $30 + 50h$.

   a. In this expression, what does the 30 represent?

   b. What does the term $50h$ represent?

   c. What does the coefficient 50 represent?

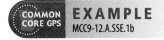

EXAMPLE 3   Interpreting Factors

An environmental biologist is studying ground squirrels. He estimates the current population as p. He uses the following expression to estimate the population in x years: $p(0.995)^x$

a. What are the factors in the expression?

   The factors are p and $(0.995)^x$.

b. Explain why $(0.995)^x$ does not depend on p.

   It does not depend on p because it does not change if p changes.

3. Oliver is writing a paper on population growth. He read that the population of the United States increases at about 1.5% per year. He uses this expression to estimate the population in the U.S in y years: $p(1 + 0.015)^y$

   a. What are the factors in the expression?

   b. Explain why $(1 + 0.015)^y$ does not depend on p.

EXAMPLE 4   Representing a Situation

Madison works h hours a week at a restaurant. She earns $12 an hour and each week she receives a $20 transportation voucher.

a. Write an expression to describe the amount of money she earns each week.

   $12h + 20$

b. What does each term in the expression represent?

   $12h$ represents her hourly pay and 20 represents the value of the voucher.

c. Is there a coefficient in the expression? If so, what does it represent?

   The coefficient 12 represents the amount Madison earns each hour.

4. Evan paid c dollars per dozen for 2 dozen eggs plus $5 for an insulated shopping bag.

   a. Write an expression to describe the amount of money Evan spent.

   b. What does each term in the expression represent?

   c. Is there a coefficient in the expression? If so, what does it represent?

1. Maria drives at a rate of 35 mi/h on her way to work. Maria uses the expression $35h$ to find the number miles she drives to work.

   a. What does the coefficient 35 represent in this context?

   b. What does h represent in this context?

2. **Home Improvement** Sean is planning a rectangular patio for his backyard. He wants the length to be 6 feet longer than the width. The expression for the perimeter of the patio with a width w is $2w + 2(w + 6)$.

   a. What does the term $2w$ represent?

   b. What does the term $2(w + 6)$ represent?

3. Hayley practices the violin for 45 minutes d days a week and 90 minutes one day a week. The expression for the amount of time she practices each week is $45d + 90$.

   a. What does the coefficient 45 represent in the expression?

   b. What does 90 represent in the expression?

4. Kyle ordered y cases of cans of pizza sauce. He received 24 cans of pizza sauce.

   a. Write an expression to describe the number of cans of pizza sauce in one case.

   b. What does 24 represent in the expression?

   c. If Kyle received 3 cases, how many cans were in each case?

5. The width of a rectangular prism with height 7 inches is increased by 2 inches. Ben wrote this expression for the volume of the prism:

   $$l \times (w + 2) \times 7$$

   a. What are the factors in the expression?

   b. Does the value of l depend on the value of $(w + 2)$? Explain.

6. Jason wrote this expression for the area of a trapezoid: $\frac{1}{2}(b_1 + b_2)h$.

   a. What are the factors in the expression?

   b. Does the value of $(b_1 + b_2)$ depend on h? Explain.

7. James has d dimes in his coin collection. The number of nickels he has is 5 more than 3 times the number of dimes in his collection.

   a. Write an expression to describe the number of nickels in James' collection.

   b. What does each term in the expression represent?

8. Jasmine is j years old. Her sister is three years younger than twice Jasmine's age.

   a. Write an expression to describe Jasmine's sister's age.

   b. What does each term in the expression represent?

9. A group of 15 coworkers bought several lottery tickets, and agreed to evenly split any winnings. They had only one winning ticket, worth x dollars.

   a. Write an expression that represents how much prize money each coworker should receive.

   b. What does 15 represent in the expression?

   c. If each coworker receives $180, how much was the winning ticket worth?

10. Tyrone buys z dozen donuts to take to work. On the way to work, he eats 4 of the donuts. He brings the rest to work.

    a. Write an expression that represents the number of donuts Tyrone brings to work.

b. What does each term in the expression represent?

c. If Tyrone buys 8 dozen donuts, how many donuts does he bring to work?

11. Kendall and Jenny each have a square piece of wrapping paper. Kendall's piece measures k centimeters on each side. Each side of Jenny's piece of paper measures twice that of Kendall's. Describe what each of the following expressions represents.

   a. k^2

   b. $(2k)^2$

   c. $k^2 + 4k^2$

12. **Business** Claire makes necklaces. She spends $39 on supplies and makes 13 necklaces using all of those supplies. She sells each necklace for n dollars.

   a. Write an expression that represents Claire's profit if she sells all 13 necklaces.

   b. What does each term in the expression represent?

   c. If Claire sells each necklace for $55, what is her total profit?

13. Franklin sells square frames made of wood. To find the area for the picture within the frame, he uses the expression $(s - 2w)^2$.

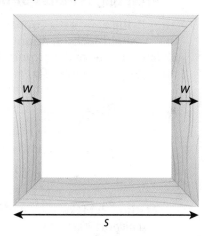

   a. What does $2w$ represent in the expression?

   b. Freida says the expression to find the area of the picture within the frame should be $2(s - 2w)$. Is she right? Justify your answer.

   c. If $s = 12$, what should w be so that the area within the frame is 81 square inches?

14. A company uses two different bakeries to make hamburger buns. The first bakery makes x dozen per batch and bakes A batches per day. The second bakery makes y dozen per batch and bakes B batches per day. What do the following expressions represent in this context?

   a. $A + B$

   b. $x + y$

   c. $|Ax - By|$

   d. $12(Ax - By)$

   e. In the expression $12(Ax - By)$, does the factor 12 depend on the factor $(Ax - By)$?

15. **Medicine** There are currently b bacteria present in a culture. When a new antibiotic is tested on the culture, the number of bacteria is reduced by $\frac{3}{4}$ every 4 hours. The following expression is used to find the number of bacteria left after a 24-hour day: $b\left(\frac{1}{4}\right)^6$.

   a. What does b represent in the expression?

   b. Why is the exponent 6 in the expression?

   c. If there are 1,000,000 bacteria in the culture, after 1 day would there be more or less than 1000 bacteria in the culture? Justify your answer.

Key Features of Graphs

? **Essential Question:** How can you interpret key features of graphs and sketch graphs given a description the relationship?

Objectives
Interpret key features of graphs and tables representing functions. Sketch graphs of relationships, showing key features.

Vocabulary
end behavior

You have seen that a function can represent a purely abstract relationship. The function $f(x) = 1.8x + 32$, for example, represents the relationship "$f(x)$ is the sum of 32 and the product of 1.8 and x."

The same function can also model a real-world relationship. The function $f(x) = 1.8x + 32$ gives the Fahrenheit temperature $f(x)$ that is equivalent to a given Celsius temperature x. By interpreting key features of the graph of a function—intercepts, slope, symmetries, and so on—you can learn more about the real-world situation represented by the graph.

EXAMPLE **1**

Interpreting Features of the Graph of a Linear Function

After flying across the country, a passenger jet is ready to begin its descent to Hartsfield-Jackson Atlanta International Airport. The plane is currently 32,000 feet above the airport. It will descend at a rate of 2000 feet per minute. The function $f(x) = 32,000 - 2000x$ gives the plane's height in feet above the airport after x minutes.

a. Graph $f(x) = 32,000 - 2000x$.

Method 1: Rewrite the function in $y = mx + b$ form and then use the slope and y-intercept to draw the graph.

$$f(x) = -2000x + 32{,}000 \qquad \text{slope} = -2000 \qquad y\text{-intercept} = 32{,}000$$

Method 2: Make a table of values showing the time, x, and height above the airport, $f(x)$, at several times. Notice that the time cannot be negative, so the domain must be $x \geq 0$.

x (minutes)	f(x) (feet)
0	32,000
2	28,000
4	24,000
6	20,000

Now draw the graph.

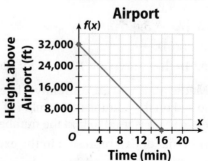

Atlanta International Airport

b. Interpret the key features of the graph.

- The *y*-intercept, 32,000, represents the plane's height above the airport in feet at the start of the descent, when the time *x* is 0.

- The *x*-intercept, 16, represents the number of minutes after the beginning of the descent when the plane touches down at the airport, when its height is 0.

- The slope is −2000, which indicates that as time increases, the height above the airport decreases at a rate of 2000 feet per minute.

- The maximum value for $f(x)$ is 32,000 feet, which is the plane's height above the airport at the beginning of its descent.

- The minimum value for $f(x)$ is 0, which is the plane's height above the ground at the end of its descent.

1. A pitcher with a maximum capacity of 4 cups contains 1 cup of apple juice concentrate. A faucet fills the pitcher at a rate of 0.25 cup per second. The amount of liquid in the pitcher in cups, $A(t)$, is given by the function $A(t) = 0.25t + 1$, where *t* is the time in seconds that the water runs from the faucet.

    a. Graph $A(t) = 0.25t + 1$ for $0 \le x \le 12$.

    b. Interpret the intercepts, slope, and maximum and minimum values of the graph.

EXAMPLE 2
MCC9-12.F.IF.4

Interpreting Features of the Graph of a Quadratic Function

A dolphin jumps out of the water. The function $f(x) = -16x^2 + 20x$ models the dolphin's height (in feet) above the water after *x* seconds.

a. Graph $f(x) = -16x^2 + 20x$.

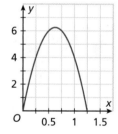

This is a quadratic function, so the graph is a parabola. The coefficient of x^2 is negative, so the parabola opens downward. The domain is $x \ge 0$.

You can plot points or use a graphing calculator to draw the graph. The graph shows that the *x*-intercepts are at 0 and 1.25. The vertex is (0.625, 6.25).

b. Interpret the key features of the graph.

- The *x*-intercepts of 0 and 1.25 mean that the dolphin is 0 feet above the water at $x = 0$ seconds and $x = 1.25$ seconds.

- The coordinates of the vertex of the parabola mean that the highest point of the dolphin's jump occurs at $x = 0.625$ seconds and $y = 6.25$ feet above the water.

- The graph of the parabola is symmetric about the line $x = 0.625$. This means that the path of the dolphin as it ascends to its highest point is a mirror image of its path as it descends to the water.

- The dolphin rises out of the water from $x = 0$ to $x = 0.625$, where the graph is increasing. It descends from $x = 0.625$ to $x = 1.25$, where the graph is decreasing.

2. A baseball coach hits a pop fly in practice. The quadratic function $y = -16x^2 + 80x$ models the height, y, of the baseball (in feet) above the point where it left the bat, after x seconds.

   a. Graph the function represented by the equation $y = -16x^2 + 80x$.

   b. Interpret the x-intercepts, vertex, and symmetry of the graph, and those intervals where the graph is increasing or decreasing.

The **end behavior** of the graph of a function is the behavior of the graph as it is followed in each direction farther and farther from 0.

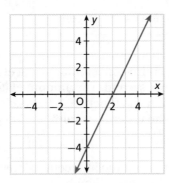

$$f(x) = 2x - 4$$

End behavior:
As x increases, the graph increases.
As x decreases, the graph decreases.

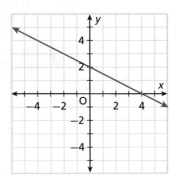

$$f(x) = -\frac{1}{2}x + 2$$

End behavior:
As x increases, the graph decreases.
As x decreases, the graph increases.

COMMON CORE GPS **EXAMPLE 3** MCC9-12.F.IF.4

Interpreting End Behavior of a Graph

Describe the end behavior of the parabola.

- The graph continues to increase as x increases.

- The graph continues to increase as x decreases.

Unlike the two graphs above, the end behavior of the graph of the parabola is the same as x increases and as it decreases.

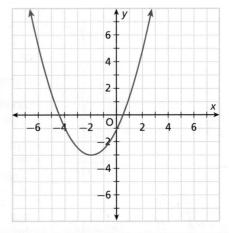

 **Helpful Hint**

When finding end behavior, think about whether the graph would be increasing, or decreasing, if you were to extend the graph beyond what is visible.

CHECK IT OUT!

3. Describe the end behavior of the parabola.

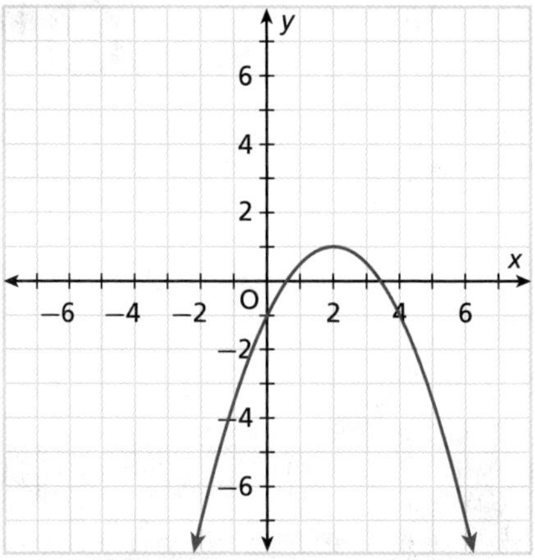

COMMON CORE GPS

EXAMPLE 4 MCC9-12.F.IF.4

Interpreting Features of the Graph of an Exponential Function

Compound interest is interest that is paid not only on an amount of money that has been invested (the principal), but also on interest that has already been earned. Seth invested \$5000 in a 30-year municipal bond issued by the city he lived in. The bond paid 4% interest compounded annually. The exponential function $f(t) = 5000(1.04)^t$ models the growth in the value of the bond in dollars, where t is the number of years after purchase.

a. Graph the function $f(t) = 5000(1.04)^t$.

Let y represent the value of the bond t years after Seth purchased it. Create a table of values, determine a scale, and graph the function.

t	y	(t, y)
0	5000	(0, 5000)
1	5200	(1, 5200)
2	5408	(2, 5408)
3	5624.32	(3, 5624.32)
4	5849.29	(4, 5849.29)
5	6083.26	(5, 6083.26)
10	7401.22	(10, 7401.22)
20	10,955.62	(20, 10,955.62)
30	16,216.99	(30, 16,216.99)

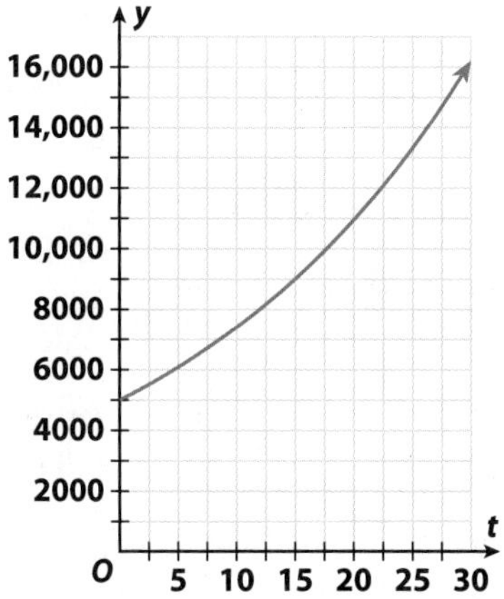

b. Interpret the key features of the graph.

- The y-intercept of 5000 represents the principal, which is Seth's initial investment of \$5000. There is no t-intercept, because the value of the investment is never \$0.
- As t increases, y increases at a rate that is, itself, also increasing. The end behavior represents the fact that the value of the investment continues to increase at an increasingly faster rate from Year 0 to Year 30.
- The minimum value of y is 5000, which represents \$5000, the least value shown on the graph. The maximum value of y is 16,216.99, which represents \$16,216.99, the value of the bond when it matures 30 years after Seth purchased it.

4. In a biology experiment, a culture began with 800 bacteria and is increasing at a rate of 12% per day. The exponential function $f(x) = 800(1.12)^x$ models the total number of bacteria, where x is the number of days since the experiment began.

   a. Graph the function $f(x) = 800(1.12)^x$.

   b. Interpret the intercepts, end behavior, and maximum and minimum values of the graph.

A-4 Exercises

1. A pump is set to dispense chlorine from a full 5-gallon container into a swimming pool to sanitize the water. The pump will dispense the chlorine at a rate of 0.5 gallon per minute and will shut off when the container is empty. The amount of chlorine in the container, $A(t)$, in gallons, is a function of the time t, in minutes, that the pump is running. The function that models this situation is $A(t) = -0.5t + 5$.

   a. Graph the function.

   b. Interpret the intercepts of the graph.

   c. Interpret the slope of the graph.

2. Physics Jean throws a ball up in the air. The ball returns to the height from which it was thrown 2.5 seconds later. The function $f(x) = 40t - 16x^2$ describes the ball's height $f(x)$, in feet, above the height at which it left her hand, after x seconds.

   a. Graph the function.

   b. Interpret the x-intercepts of the graph.

   c. Interpret the maximum value of $f(x)$.

   d. Describe the symmetry of the graph and explain what it means.

3. In 1995, the number of honor roll students at a high school was 300. Since then, it has been increasing at a rate of 8% per year. The function $y = 300(1.08)^t$, where t represents the number of years since 1995 and y represents the number of honor roll students, models this situation. The graph of this function is shown below.

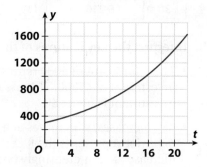

   a. Interpret the end behavior of this function.

   b. Interpret the y-intercept.

   c. Interpret the minimum and maximum values for y.

4. **Biology** Scientists studying changes in a particular insect population develop the function $y = 100(4)^x$ to model the changes. In the model, x represents the time in months since the start of the study and y represents the number of insects.

   a. Graph the function.

   b. Interpret the end behavior of the graph of this function.

   c. The biologists start a new study of the insects; now the model is $y = 200(4)^x$. What does this change tell you about the new study, compared to the original?

5. A company rents moving vans for a charge of $30 plus $0.50 per mile. The company allows its vans to be used only for local moves, limiting total mileage to 100 miles. The function $C(m) = 0.5m + 30$ gives the total rental cost, $C(m)$, in dollars, as a function of the distance driven m, in miles. The graph of this function is shown below.

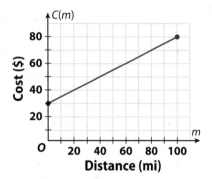

   a. Interpret the intercepts of the graph.

   b. Interpret the slope of the graph.

6. The population of Brownsville is presently 50,000. It has been decreasing by 7% every decade. If this pattern continues, the population of the town can be represented by the function $P(x) = 50{,}000(0.93)^t$, where t is the number of decades from the present.

   a. Graph the function.

   b. Interpret the y-intercept.

   c. Interpret the minimum and maximum values for y.

7. Ms. Lee sets out from home to drive to a city 500 miles away. The function $f(x) = -0.04x + 16$ represents the amount of gas she has in her car after driving x miles.

   a. Graph the function.

   b. Interpret the intercepts of the graph.

   c. Interpret the slope of the graph.

   d. Will Ms. Lee need to buy gas in order to get to her destination? Explain.

8. **Critical Thinking** A gym charges a joining fee of $50 and then a monthly membership fee of $25. The total cost C, in dollars, of being a member of the gym is given by the function $C(t) = 25t + 50$, where t is the time (in months) since joining the gym.

   a. The gym changes its fees. On a graph of the new function, the y-intercept is a lesser value than it was on the graph of the original function. Explain what this tells you about the new fees.

   b. After the change, the graph of the new function has a greater slope than the graph of the original function. Explain what this tells you about the new fees.

   c. In January, the gym offers a special for new members. The graph of this function has a y-intercept at the origin. Explain what this tells you about the fees during this special offer.

Approximating to Solve Problems

Objective
Identify the points of intersection of two functions by setting the functions equal to each other.

Given functions $f(x)$ and $g(x)$, you can find the values of x for which $f(x) = g(x)$ by graphing the functions and finding the x-coordinates of the points of intersection of the graphs.

COMMON CORE GPS MCC9-12.A.REI.11

EXAMPLE 1

Graphing to Solve Problems Involving Linear Functions

On January 1, Byron started losing weight and Roberto started gaining weight. The functions below represent their weights in pounds after x months.

- **Byron: $f(x) = 250 - 3x$**
- **Roberto: $g(x) = 132 + 9x$**

Approximate the number of months after which Byron weighs the same amount as Roberto. Round to the nearest tenth of a month.

Graph both functions using a graphing calculator. Use the intersect feature to find the point of intersection of the two graphs.

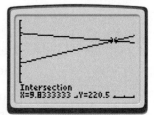

The x-value of the point of intersection, about 9.8, represents the number of months. The y-value of the point of intersection represents their weight at that time, which the problem does not ask for.

Byron and Roberto will weigh about the same amount about 9.8 months after January 1.

To check, substitute 9.8 into each function.

$f(x) = 250 - 3x$

$\quad = 250 - 3(9.8)$

$\quad = 250 - 29.4$

$\quad = 220.6$

$g(x) = 132 + 9x$

$\quad = 132 + 9(9.8)$

$\quad = 132 + 88.2$

$\quad = 220.2$

Since 220.6 and 220.2 are approximately equal, 9.8 months is a good approximation.

CHECK IT OUT!

1. Alfonso and Li open bank accounts at the same time. The amount of money, in dollars, in Alfonso's account after x weeks is represented by $f(x) = 400 - 7x$. The amount of money, in dollars, in Li's account after x weeks is represented by $g(x) = 95 + 20x$. After how many weeks will Alfonso and Li have the same amount in the bank? Round to the nearest tenth.

2 **Making Tables to Solve Problems**

Jason uses a taxi that charges $1.75 plus $0.20 per mile. Fran uses a taxi that charges $2.25 plus $0.13 per mile. Find the number of miles for which Jason and Fran would be charged the same amount.

The cost of a taxi ride in dollars for Jason can be represented by the function $Y_1(x) = 0.2x + 1.75$, where x is the number of miles driven.

The cost of a taxi ride in dollars for Fran can be represented by the function $Y_2(x) = 0.13x + 2.25$, where x is the number of miles driven.

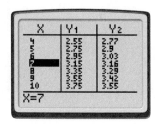

To find the number of miles, make a table of values for both functions using a graphing calculator. Then find an x-value that produces very similar y-values.

The y-values are closest when $x = 7$, so Jason and Fran would be charged about the same amount for a ride of about 7 miles.

 **2.** Rashid started draining his fish tank. The function $f(x) = 240 - 8x$ describes the number of gallons in the tank after x minutes. At the same time, Delores started filling her fish tank. The function $g(x) = 15.8x$ describes the number of gallons in her tank after x minutes. Find the approximate number of minutes it takes for both tanks to contain the same amount of water.

3 **Graphing to Solve Problems Involving Exponential Functions**

Norton has 127,765 residents. The population is increasing at a rate of 9% per year. The town council wants to renovate the courthouse before the population reaches 200,000. How long does the town council have to renovate the courthouse? Round to the nearest tenth of a year.

Step 1 Write a function $f(x)$ to represent the population of the town after x years, and a function $g(x)$ to represent the population of the town when the courthouse must be renovated.

$f(x) = 127,765(1 + 0.09)^x$ *f(x) is an exponential function.*

$g(x) = 200,000$ *g(x) is a constant function.*

Step 2 Graph the functions on a graphing calculator. Let $Y_1 = f(x)$ and $Y_2 = g(x)$. Use a viewing window from −2 to 12 for x, at a scale of 1, and a viewing window from −50,000 to 300,000 for y, at a scale of 25,000.

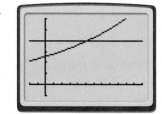

Step 3 Use the intersect feature on the CALC menu to find the value of x for which the graphs intersect.

The town council has about 5.2 years to renovate the courthouse.

 3. Eton has a population of 385,184. The population is decreasing at a rate of 11% per year. How long will it take for the population to reach 250,000? Round to the nearest tenth of a year.

EXAMPLE 4 Using Successive Approximations

MCC9-12.A.REI.11

For the functions $f(x) = 2^x$ and $g(x) = -85x + 725$, use successive approximations to find the integer that is closest to the value of x for which $f(x) = g(x)$.

Choose a value for x, and evaluate both $f(x)$ and $g(x)$ with it. Since the range for $f(x)$ is the set of all positive numbers, choose an x value that makes $g(x)$ a positive number. Evaluate both functions when $x = 8$.

$f(8) = 2^8 = 256$
$g(8) = -85(8) + 725 = 45$
$f(8) > g(8)$

Since, $f(8) > g(8)$, choose a smaller value for x. Evaluate both functions when $x = 4$.

$f(4) = 2^4 = 16$
$g(4) = -85(4) + 725 = 385$
$f(4) < g(4)$

Since, $f(4) < g(4)$, choose a value for x that is greater than 4 but less than 8. Evaluate both functions when $x = 7$.

$f(7) = 2^7 = 128$
$g(7) = -85(7) + 725 = 130$
$f(7) \approx g(7)$

Since $f(7) \approx g(7)$, 7 is an approximate solution for $f(x) = g(x)$.

 CHECK IT OUT! **4.** For the functions $f(x) = -3^x$ and $g(x) = 145x - 975$, use successive approximations to find the integer that is closest to the value of x for which $f(x) = g(x)$.

A-5 Exercises

For each pair of functions, use successive approximations to find the integer that is closest to the value of x for which $f(x) = g(x)$.

1. $f(x) = 5^x$ and $g(x) = 1000 - 94x$

2. $f(x) = -2^x$ and $g(x) = 75x - 85$

3. $f(x) = -40x + 960$ and $g(x) = 3^x$

4. $f(x) = 2^x$ and $g(x) = -14x + 650$

5. $f(x) = 3^x$ and $g(x) = -85x + 2800$

6. $f(x) = -28x + 150$ and $g(x) = 4^x$

For Exercises 7–13, use a graphing calculator to approximate the answer.

7. On the same day, Nate and Craig each bought a new car. The function $f(x) = 15,000 - 300x$ represents the value of Nate's car x months after the purchase, and the function $g(x) = 8500 - 125x$ represents the value of Craig's car x months after its purchase. After how many months will the value of both cars be the same? Round to the nearest hundredth.

8. Rita and Leticia are on the same social network. They challenge each other to collect the most fans. The function $f(x) = 585 + 22x$ represents the number of Rita's fans x days after the start of the challenge, and $g(x) = 1215 + 8x$ represents the number of Leticia's fans x days after the start of the challenge. After how many days will each have the same number of fans?

9. Al's Bike Shop and Braker Bike Shop charge different amounts to repair bikes. The amount Al's Bike Shop charges is found by using $f(x) = 100 + 25x$, where x is the number of hours needed to repair the bike. The amount Braker Bike Shop charges is found by using $g(x) = 150 + 18x$, where x is also the number of repair hours. If both shops charge the same for a rear-wheel rebuild, how many hours are needed to fix the bike? Round to the nearest hundredth.

10. Kendall and Baxter both collect books. On the same day, Kendall starts decreasing the size of her collection and Baxter starts increasing the size of his. The function $f(x) = 301 - 20x$ describes the size of Kendall's collection after x weeks, and $g(x) = 86 + 7x$ describes the size of Baxter's collection after x weeks. Use tables to find the approximate number of weeks it will take for the collections to be the same size.

11. Two athletes are practicing hang-gliding. One jumps from a height of 800 feet; $f(x) = 800 - 2x$ describes his height after x seconds. The other jumps from a height of 1350 feet, and $g(x) = 1350 - 34.5x$ describes her height after x seconds. Use tables of values to find the approximate number of seconds it takes for both athletes to reach the same elevation.

12. Joyce bought a sculpture and a painting on the same day. The function $f(x) = 1000 + 600x$ represents the value of the sculpture x months after Joyce bought it, and the function $g(x) = 4500 + 150x$ represents the value of the painting x months after Joyce bought it. Approximate the number of months until the value of the sculpture and the value of the painting will be the same. Round to the nearest tenth of a month.

13. A biologist is testing two different fertilizers to see which one works best on flowers. Each fertilizer is tested in a different field. The initial number of flowers in each field is shown in the table, as well as the monthly change to the flower population in each field.

	Fertilizer A, in Field A	Fertilizer B, in Field B
Flowers in field at start of experiment	1	100
Monthly change	Each month, the number of flowers triples.	Each month, the number of flowers increases by 800.

a. Define a function $a(x)$ that can be used to find the number of flowers in Field A after x months.
b. Define a function $b(x)$ that can be used to find the number of flowers in Field B after x months.
c. Use successive approximations to find the integer that is closest to the value of x for which a(x) = b(x).
d. After how many months will the number of flowers in the two fields be about equal?

14. Dorie and Shane start wrapping presents at the same time. Dorie starts with 190 yards of ribbon and uses 1.5 yards of ribbon per minute. Shane starts with 270 yards of ribbon and uses 4.5 yards of ribbon per minute.

a. Write a function $f(x)$ that describes the amount of ribbon, in yards, that Dorie has after wrapping for x minutes.
b. Write a function $g(x)$ that describes the amount of ribbon, in yards, that Shane has after wrapping for x minutes.
c. Use tables to find the approximate number of minutes it takes for Dorie and Shane to have the same amount of ribbon.

15. A gardener has a tree that is 70 inches tall and grows at a rate of 7% per year. The gardener wants to sell the tree when it is 95 inches tall.

a. Write a function $f(x)$ that describes the height of the tree after x years.
b. Write a function $g(x)$ that describes the height of the tree in inches when the gardener sells it.
c. Use a graphing calculator to determine the number of years it will take for the tree to reach 95 inches. Round to the nearest tenth.

Compare Linear and Exponential Functions

Essential Question: How can you decide whether to use a linear or exponential function to model a situation?

Objective
Compare linear and exponential models. Interpret the parameters of a linear or exponential function in terms of a context.

Vocabulary
parameter

A freight train leaves a depot at noon. When it is 5 miles from the depot, it passes the Forest Park station and begins to travel at a constant speed of 40 miles per hour. The linear function $f(x) = 40x + 5$ gives the train's distance $f(x)$ from the depot x hours after it passes Forest Park. The table records the times and distances.

x	0	1	2	3	4	5	6	7	8	9	10	11	12
$f(x)$	5	45	85	125	165	205	245	285	325	365	405	445	485

The table shows these results:

During every 1-hour period, the train traveled 40 miles:
Examples: $f(3) - f(2) = 125 - 85 = 40$ $f(9) - f(8) = 365 - 325 = 40$

During every 2-hour period, the train traveled 80 miles:
Examples: $f(6) - f(4) = 245 - 165 = 80$ $f(12) - f(10) = 485 - 405 = 80$

The table illustrates a general rule about linear functions: **Linear functions change by equal differences over equal intervals.** The rule explains why no matter which 3-hour interval you choose in the table above, you find that the train traveled 120 miles.

Now look at a table for the exponential function $g(x) = 5(2)^x$.

x	1	2	3	4	5	6	7	8
$g(x)$	10	20	40	80	160	320	640	1280

The table shows these results:

When x changes by 1, $g(x)$ changes by a *factor* of 2:
Examples: $\dfrac{g(2)}{g(1)} = \dfrac{20}{10} = 2$ $\dfrac{g(5)}{g(4)} = \dfrac{160}{80} = 2$ $\dfrac{g(7)}{g(6)} = \dfrac{640}{320} = 2$

When x changes by 2, $g(x)$ changes by a *factor* of 4:
Examples: $\dfrac{g(3)}{g(1)} = \dfrac{40}{10} = 4$ $\dfrac{g(5)}{g(3)} = \dfrac{160}{40} = 4$ $\dfrac{g(8)}{g(6)} = \dfrac{1280}{320} = 4$

The table illustrates a general rule about exponential functions: **Exponential functions change by equal factors over equal intervals.**

You will look more closely at these results in the following two examples.

EXAMPLE 1   **Understanding How Linear Functions Grow**

MCC9-12.F.LE.1a

Prove that the linear function $f(x) = 0.5x + 3$ changes by equal differences over equal intervals.

First, choose two equal intervals on the x-axis. Let x_1 and x_2 be the endpoints of one interval and x_3 and x_4 be the endpoints of the other interval. (The interval from x_1 to x_2 on the x-axis is the line segment on the x-axis with endpoints x_1 and x_2.) Since the intervals are equal, $x_2 - x_1 = x_4 - x_3$.

To find the change in $f(x)$ over the interval from x_1 to x_2, substitute x_1 and x_2 in $f(x) = 0.5x + 3$ and then subtract.

$f(x) = 0.5x + 3$ *Write the equation of the function.*

$f(x_1) = 0.5x_1 + 3$ *Substitute x_1 for x.*

$$f(x_2) = 0.5x_2 + 3 \qquad \text{\textit{Substitute } } x_2 \text{ for } x.$$

$$f(x_2) - f(x_1) = (0.5x_2 + 3) - (0.5x_1 + 3) \qquad \text{\textit{Subtract to find the difference.}}$$

This gives the change in $f(x)$ over the interval from x_1 to x_2.
Now simplify the right side of the equation.

$$f(x_2) - f(x_1) = (0.5x_2 + 3) - (0.5x_1 + 3)$$

$$= 0.5x_2 + 3 - 0.5x_1 - 3 \qquad \text{\textit{Use the Distributive Property.}}$$

$$= 0.5x_2 + 3 + (-0.5x_1) + (-3) \quad \text{\textit{Definition of Subtraction}}$$

$$= 0.5x_2 + (-0.5x_1) + 3 + (-3) \quad \text{\textit{Commutative Property of Addition}}$$

$$= 0.5x_2 + (-0.5x_1) + 0 \qquad \text{\textit{Additive Inverse Property}}$$

$$= 0.5x_2 + (-0.5x_1) \qquad \text{\textit{Additive Identity Property}}$$

$$= 0.5x_2 - 0.5x_1 \qquad \text{\textit{Definition of Subtraction}}$$

$$= 0.5(x_2 - x_1) \qquad \text{\textit{Distributive Property}}$$

So, the change in $f(x)$ over the interval from x_1 to x_2 is $0.5(x_2 - x_1)$.

To find the change in $f(x)$ over the interval x_3 to x_4, follow the same steps used above. The results are similar: $f(x_4) - f(x_3)$, the change in $f(x)$ over the interval from x_3 to x_4, is $0.5(x_4 - x_3)$.

To finish the proof, return to the fact that $x_2 - x_1 = x_4 - x_3$.

$$x_2 - x_1 = x_4 - x_3 \qquad \text{\textit{The intervals are equal.}}$$

$$0.5(x_2 - x_1) = 0.5(x_4 - x_3) \qquad \text{\textit{Multiplication Property of Equality}}$$

$$f(x_2) - f(x_1) = f(x_4) - f(x_3) \qquad \text{\textit{Substitution.}}$$

So, $f(x_2) - f(x_1) = f(x_4) - f(x_3)$.
This proves that the linear function
$f(x) = 0.5x + 3$ changes by equal
differences over equal intervals.

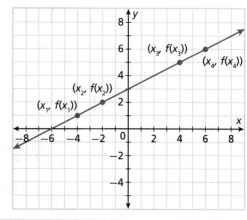

You can see that these results
make sense by looking at a graph
of $f(x) = 0.5x + 3$. Equal intervals
of 2 units horizontally ($x = -4$ to
$x = -2$ and $x = 4$ to $x = 6$) result in
equal differences of 1 vertically
($y = 1$ to $y = 2$ and $y = 5$ to $y = 6$).

1. Complete the above proof by showing that
$f(x_4) - f(x_3) = 0.5(x_4 - x_3)$.

COMMON CORE GPS MCC9-12.F.LE.1a

EXAMPLE 2

Understanding How Exponential Functions Grow

Prove that the exponential function $g(x) = 2(1.5)^x$ changes by equal factors over equal intervals.

This proof depends on the Quotient of Powers Property: For all real numbers b, x, and y, if $b \neq 0$, $\dfrac{b^x}{b^y} = b^{x-y}$.

Again, choose two equal intervals such that $x_2 - x_1 = x_4 - x_3$. To find the change in $g(x)$ over the interval from x_1 to x_2, substitute x_2 and x_1 in the equation $g(x) = 2(1.5)^x$ and then divide.

$g(x) = 2(1.5)^x$ *Write the equation of the function.*

$g(x_1) = 2(1.5)^{x_1}$ *Substitute x_1 for x.*

$g(x_2) = 2(1.5)^{x_2}$ *Substitute x_2 for x.*

$\dfrac{g(x_2)}{g(x_1)} = \dfrac{2(1.5)^{x_2}}{2(1.5)^{x_1}}$ *Divide to find the quotient.*

$\dfrac{g(x_2)}{g(x_1)} = \dfrac{(1.5)^{x_2}}{(1.5)^{x_1}}$ *Divide numerator and denominator by 2.*

$\dfrac{g(x_2)}{g(x_1)} = (1.5)^{x_2 - x_1}$ *Quotient of Powers Property*

So, the change in $g(x)$ over the interval from x_1 to x_2 is $(1.5)^{x_2 - x_1}$. To find the change in $g(x)$ over the interval x_3 to x_4, follow the same steps used above. The results are similar: $\frac{g(x_4)}{g(x_3)}$, the change in $g(x)$ over the interval x_3 to x_4, is $(1.5)^{x_4 - x_3}$.

To finish the proof, return to the fact that $x_2 - x_1 = x_4 - x_3$.

$x_2 - x_1 = x_4 - x_3$ *The intervals are equal.*

$(1.5)^{x_2 - x_1} = (1.5)^{x_4 - x_3}$ *Equal bases raised to equal powers are equal.*

$\dfrac{g(x_2)}{g(x_1)} = \dfrac{g(x_4)}{g(x_3)}$ *Substitution.*

So, $\frac{g(x_2)}{g(x_1)} = \frac{g(x_4)}{g(x_3)}$. This proves that the exponential function $g(x) = 2(1.5)^x$ changes by equal factors over equal intervals.

 2. Complete the above proof by showing that $\frac{g(x_4)}{g(x_3)} = (1.5)^{x_4 - x_3}$.

 **EXAMPLE** **3**   MCC9-12.F.LE.1b, F.LE.1c

Recognizing Constant Change and Constant Percent Change

A   A tank that contained 300 gallons of water loses water each day due to evaporation. The table shows the amounts in the tank for Days 1–6.

Day	0	1	2	3	4	5	6
Amount (gal)	300	288	276	264	252	240	228

Describe the rate at which the tank is losing water. Then write an equation relating x, the number of days since evaporation began, and $f(x)$, the amount of water in the tank.

To measure a rate of increase or decrease, identify a *unit interval*, a constant interval across which you can calculate the rate. Here, the volume of water in the tank decreases at a rate of 12 gallons per day, so the unit interval is 1 day.

A function like this one that increases or decreases at a constant rate per unit interval is a linear function. To find the equation of this function, think: The tank begins with 300 gallons. After x days, the total amount of water that has evaporated is $12x$. So, $f(x) = 300 - 12x$.

B   The table shows the height of a ball after each of 5 bounces.

Bounce	0	1	2	3	4	5
Height (in.)	240	120	60	30	15	7.5

Describe the rate at which the bounces are decreasing in height. Then write an equation relating x, the number of bounces, and $g(x)$, the height of the ball after each bounce.

A function like this one that increases or decreases at a constant percent rate per unit interval is an exponential function. To find the equation of this function, think: The first bounce measured 240 inches. On each succeeding bounce, the height measured 50% or 0.5 times the previous height. So, $g(x) = 240(0.5)^x$.

 3a. The table shows the prices of 1 to 6 concert tickets, including a single $5 service fee.

Number of Tickets	1	2	3	4	5	6
Total Price ($)	17	29	41	53	65	77

Describe the rate at which prices increase per ticket purchased. Then write an equation relating x, the number of tickets purchased, and $f(x)$, the total price.

b. The table shows the prices of Gizmo Computers over a 4-year period.

Year	0	1	2	3	4
Price ($)	800	1000	1250	1562.50	1953.13

Describe the annual rate at which prices increased. Then write an equation relating x, the number of years, and $f(x)$, the total price.

 **EXAMPLE 4** **Comparing Linear and Exponential Functions**

MCC9-12.F.LE.3

Compare two salary plans. Will Job B ever have a higher monthly salary than Job A? If so, in which month will this occur?

• **Job A: $1000 for month 0 with $100 raise every month thereafter**

• **Job B: $1000 for month 0 with a 1% raise every month thereafter**

Notice that the salary for Job A increases at a constant rate per unit interval of 1 month, indicating a linear function. Job B increases at a constant percent rate per month, indicating an exponential function.

Write equations to represent $Y(t)$, the monthly salaries after t months.

$Y_A(t) = 1000 + 100t$ $Y_A(t)$ is linear.
$Y_B(t) = 1000(1.01)^t$ $Y_B(t)$ is exponential.

Graph the function using a table of values or a graphing calculator.

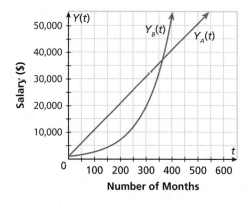

Whichever method you use to draw the graph, you will see that in the beginning, Job B pays a lower salary than Job A. Eventually, however, the Job B salary will exceed that of Job A. Using a graphing calculator, you will find that Job B passes Job A for the first time in the 364th month.

 4. Canton has 2500 residents and Easton has 2000 residents. Canton's population decreases by 80 people per year. Easton's population decreases by 3% per year. Will Easton ever have a population greater than Canton's? If so, when?

 **EXAMPLE** MCC9-12.F.LE.5 **5** **Interpreting the Parameters of a Function**

Interpret the parameters of the two jobs in Example 4.

Job A: $Y(t) = 1000 + 100t$

- The parameter 100 represents the monthly increase in salary for Job A. It is the slope of the graph.
- The parameter 1000 represents the beginning salary. On the graph, 1000 is the y-intercept.

Job B: $Y_B(t) = 1000(1.01)^t$

- The parameter 1000 represents the beginning salary. On the graph, 1000 is the y-intercept.
- The parameter 1.01 represents the 1% monthly increase in salary. The parameter shows the rate of growth for the graph.

Reading Math

Parameters are numbers that appear in the definition of a function.

 5. Interpret the parameters of the two functions in Example 3, $f(x) = 300 - 12x$ and $g(x) = 240(0.5)^x$.

A-6 Exercises

1. Without graphing, tell whether each quantity is changing at a constant rate per unit of time, a constant percent rate per unit of time, or neither. Justify your reasoning.

   a. Amy received a $15,000 interest-free loan from her parents and agreed to make monthly payments of $150.

   b. Carla's salary is $50,000 a year plus a 1% commission on sales.

   c. Enrollment at school is 976 students initially, increasing 2.5% each year thereafter.

2. **a.** Which table below represents a linear function and which represents an exponential function?

Table 1

x	0	1	2	3	4
f(x)	3200	800	200	50	12.5

Table 2

x	0	1	2	3	4
f(x)	3200	2600	2000	1400	800

   b. Explain how you decided which table represents each function.

   c. For each table, write an equation relating x and $f(x)$.

3. **Critical Thinking** Beyond a certain point, will an exponential growth function always exceed a linear growth function? Explain.

4. **Draw Conclusions** Maria would like to put $500 in savings for a 5-year period. Should she choose a simple interest account that pays an interest rate of 10% of the principal (initial amount) each year, or a compounded interest account paying 3% of the total account value each month?

5. **Interpret the Answer** Dale and Manor each have 40,000 residents. Dale's population decreases by 900 people per year and Manor's population decreases by 2% per year. Will Dale's population ever be greater than Manor's? If so, when? Explain.

6. State whether the situation describes a linear function or an exponential function.

   a. In Willowbrook, the rate of computer hackings has been falling at a rate of 27% per year.

   b. At sea level, sound travels at a speed of 390 meters per second.

   c. Carmine is saving $25 per month for the purchase of a new bicycle.

   d. Since 2008, the price of a ticket to the planetarium has been increasing at a rate of 14.2% per year.

7. a. By how much does the linear function $f(x) = 3x - 7$ change over equal intervals of 5 units?

   b. By what factor does the exponential function $g(x) = 10,000(0.9)^x$ change over equal intervals of 5 units?

8. At time $t = 0$ months, there were 40 trout in a lake. Each month after that, the trout population increased by 8.

   a. Write a function relating t, the number of months, and $f(t)$, the number of trout in the lake.

   b. Interpret the parameters in the function.

   c. Explain the relationship of the parameters to the graph of the equation.

9. At time $t = 0$ months, there were 40 trout in a lake. Each month after that, the trout population increased by 10%.

   a. Write a function relating t, the number of months, and $f(t)$, the number of trout in the lake.

   b. Interpret the parameters in the function.

   c. Explain the relationship of the parameters to the graph of the equation.

10. Prove that the linear function $f(x) = 3x - 5$ changes by equal differences over equal intervals.

11. Prove that a linear function of the form $f(x) = mx + b$, where m and b are real numbers, changes by equal differences over equal intervals.

12. Prove that the exponential function $g(x) = 3(4)^x$ changes by equal factors over equal intervals.

13. Prove that an exponential function of the form $g(x) = a(b)^x$, where a and b are real numbers, changes by equal factors over equal intervals.

Combine Functions

 Essential Question: How can you combine functions using arithmetic operations?

Objective
Combine standard function types using arithmetic operations.

Vocabulary
arithmetic operations

You know how to add, subtract, multiply, and divide algebraic expressions by combining like terms. You can also peform these **arithmetic operations** on functions, as shown in the table.

Notation for Function Operations	
Operations	**Notation**
Addition	$(f + g)(x) = f(x) + g(x)$
Subtraction	$(f - g)(x) = f(x) - g(x)$
Multiplication	$(f \cdot g)(x) = f(x) \cdot g(x)$
Division	$\left(\dfrac{f}{g}\right)(x) = \dfrac{f(x)}{g(x)}$, where $g(x) \neq 0$

 EXAMPLE MCC9-12.F.BF.1b

1 **Adding and Subtracting Functions**

Given $f(x) = x + 4$ and $g(x) = 5x$, find each function.

A $(f + g)(x)$

$(f + g)(x) = f(x) + g(x)$

$\quad = (x + 4) + (5x)$ *Substitute function rules.*

$\quad = 6x + 4$ *Combine like terms.*

B $(f - g)(x)$

$(f - g)(x) = f(x) - g(x)$

$\quad = (x + 4) - (5x)$ *Substitute function rules.*

$\quad = -4x + 4$ *Combine like terms.*

C $(g - f)(x)$

$(g - f)(x) = g(x) - f(x)$

$\quad = (5x) - (x + 4)$ *Substitute function rules.*

$\quad = 4x - 4$ *Combine like terms.*

Helpful Hint

Remember to read $f(x)$ as 'f of x.' So, $(f + g)(x)$ is read as 'f plus g of x.'

 CHECK IT OUT!

1. Given $f(x) = 3 - 2x$ and $g(x) = -x$, find each function.

   a. $(f + g)(x)$ **b.** $(f - g)(x)$

   c. $(g - f)(x)$

Notice in Example 1 that $(f - g)(x) \neq (g - f)(x)$. When you subtract functions, order makes a difference, just as it does when you subtract numbers or expressions.

Notice also in Example 1 that the domains of $f(x)$, $g(x)$, and the new functions $(f + g)(x)$, $(f - g)(x)$, and $(g - f)(x)$ are all real numbers. In general, the domain of a function created by adding or subtracting functions will consist of the x-values that are in the domains of the combined functions.

EXAMPLE **2** | **Representing a Consumer Application with a Sum of Functions**

An attorney charges new clients $200 for an initial meeting of up to one hour, and $125 for each additional hour. Represent the total cost of an initial meeting that lasts h hours, using a combination of two functions.

Translate the description into two functions in terms of h hours.

variable cost function   **fixed cost function**

$$v(h) = 125(h - 1) \qquad\qquad f(h) = 200$$

Write the total cost function $c(h)$ in dollars.

$$c(h) = v(h) + f(h)$$
$$= 125(h - 1) + 200 \qquad \text{\textit{c(h) is a vertical translation of v(h) by 200, or f(h).}}$$
$$= 125h + 75$$

 **2.** Carpet cleaning costs $3.50 per square foot. New customers get a $25-off coupon. Represent the total cost for new customers using a combination of two functions.

EXAMPLE **3** | **Representing a Business Application with a Difference of Functions**

A business purchases a new computer for $2400. The business can depreciate the computer using the exponential model $e(t) = 2400(0.8)^t$, or the linear model $l(t) = -480t + 2400$, where t is the time in years. Find the difference function $d(t) = e(t) - l(t)$ and describe what it represents.

$$d(t) = e(t) - l(t)$$
$$= 2400(0.8)^t - (-480t + 2400) \qquad \text{\textit{Substitute function rules.}}$$
$$= 2400(0.8)^t + 480t - 2400$$

Make a table and graph each function to visualize what they represent.

Year t	$e(t)$	$l(t)$	$d(t)$
0	2400	2400	0
1	1920	1920	0
2	1536	1440	96
3	1229	960	269
4	983	480	503
5	786	0	786
6	629	−480	1109

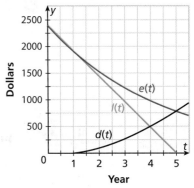

The difference function $d(t)$ shows how much more money can be deducted using the linear depreciation model $l(t)$ instead of the exponential model $e(t)$. Notice that $d(t)$ is an increasing function.

 3. The temperature of the coffee in a cup is initially 160°F and it starts cooling down to the temperature of the room, which is 70°F. If t is the number of minutes since the coffee was 160°F, the function $c(t) = (160 - 70)(1 - 0.09)^t$ represents how much warmer the coffee is than the room temperature, in degrees Fahrenheit, at time t. The function $R(t) = 70$ represents the room temperature. Find the function $T(t) = (c + R)(t)$ and explain what it represents.

In general, when multiplying or dividing two functions, the domain of the new function will consist of the *x*-values that are in the domains of the two original functions, except for *x*-values that make a denominator 0.

EXAMPLE 4

Multiplying and Dividing Functions

Given $f(x) = x - 1$ and $g(x) = 3x + 2$, find each function.

A $(f \cdot g)(x)$

$$(f \cdot g)(x) = f(x) \cdot g(x)$$

$$= (x - 1)(3x + 2) \qquad \text{Substitute function rules.}$$

$$= x(3x + 2) - 1(3x + 2) \qquad \text{Apply the Distributive Property.}$$

$$= 3x^2 + 2x - 3x - 2 \qquad \text{Multiply.}$$

$$= 3x^2 - x - 2 \qquad \text{Combine like terms.}$$

B $\left(\dfrac{g}{f}\right)(x)$

$$\left(\dfrac{g}{f}\right)(x) = \dfrac{g(x)}{f(x)}$$

$$= \dfrac{3x + 2}{x - 1}$$

No simplification can be performed.

Because division by zero is undefined, $f(x) \neq 0$. This means $x \neq 1$.

So the domain of $\left(\dfrac{g}{f}\right)(x)$ is all real numbers *except* 1.

C $\left(\dfrac{f}{g}\right)(x)$

$$\left(\dfrac{f}{g}\right)(x) = \dfrac{f(x)}{g(x)}$$

$$= \dfrac{x - 1}{3x + 2}$$

Because division by zero is undefined, $g(x) \neq 0$. Since $3x + 2 \neq 0$, $3x \neq -2$, so $x \neq -\frac{2}{3}$. So the domain of $\left(\dfrac{f}{g}\right)(x)$ is all real numbers *except* $-\frac{2}{3}$.

CHECK IT OUT!

4. Given $f(x) = 1 - 4x$ and $g(x) = -2x$, find each function.

 a. $(f \cdot g)(x)$ **b.** $\left(\dfrac{f}{g}\right)(x)$ **c.** $\left(\dfrac{g}{f}\right)(x)$

Notice in Example 4 that $\left(\dfrac{f}{g}\right)(x) \neq \left(\dfrac{g}{f}\right)(x)$. When you divide functions, order makes a difference, just as it does when you divide numbers or expressions.

EXAMPLE 5

Representing a Business Application with a Product of Functions

A business imports scooters from Italy. Each scooter costs 850 euro, plus a flat fee of 75 euro for each order. The current exchange rate is 1.3 dollars for each euro. Write a function for the cost of *n* scooters in dollars.

Write the cost function $c(n)$ in euros for *n* scooters. $c(n) = 850n + 75$

Convert euros to dollars. Use the conversion factor $1.3 \frac{\text{dollars}}{\text{euro}}$.

$$d(n) = 1.3 \cdot c(n)$$

$$= 1.3(850n + 75)$$

$$= 1105n + 97.5$$

The cost of *n* scooters in dollars is $d(n) = 1105n + 97.5$.

CHECK IT OUT!

5. Fuel oil costs $4.25 per gallon plus a $50 delivery charge, plus an 8% tax on the cost of the fuel and the delivery charge. Write a function for the total cost of *x* gallons of fuel oil in dollars.

Given $f(x) = 12x - 3$ and $g(x) = 1 - x$, find each function.

1. $(f + g)(x)$
2. $(f - g)(x)$
3. $(g - f)(x)$

4. $(fg)(x)$
5. $\left(\dfrac{f}{g}\right)(x)$
6. $\left(\dfrac{g}{f}\right)(x)$

7. To get to work, Sade uses Fast Taxi Company, which charges $5 plus $1.35 per mile. Going home, Sade uses a different taxi company that charges $2 plus $1.85 per mile. Write a function for each cab ride, and the total cost function for the distance x between her home and workplace.

8. A police department issues speeding tickets for $50 plus an additional dollar for each mile per hour over the speed limit. Half of the money from speeding tickets goes toward buying new equipment for the department.
   a. Write a function rule $A(x)$ for the amount of a speeding ticket for driving x miles per hour over the speed limit.
   b. Write a function rule $E(x)$ for the amount of money generated for new equipment by a speeding ticket for driving x miles per hour over the speed limit.

9. **Depreciation** A new computer costs $2000, and its value depreciates linearly by $500 each year. A new printer costs $800, and its value depreciates linearly by $200 each year.
   a. Write a function rule for the combined value of the computer and printer in terms of t years since the equipment was purchased.
   b. When will the computer and printer have a combined value of $700?

10. A school is raising money for a new scoreboard. They have collected $400 in donations. They have also sold t dinner tickets for $25 per ticket. Every ticket purchaser has also bought a $20 raffle ticket. The winner of the raffle will get $500.
    a. Write a function rule $R(t)$ for the profit the school makes on the raffle.
    b. Write a function rule $D(t)$ for the income made from the donations and dinner.
    c. Write a function rule $T(t)$ for the total amount of money raised by the school.
    d. How many tickets must be sold to raise $3500?

11. **Modeling** The population of a city can be approximated by $p(t) = 175{,}000(1.05)^t$, where t is the number of years since 2010. Its number of doctors can be approximated by $d(t) = 70t + 1240$, where t is the number of years since 2010.
    a. Define a function that represents the number of doctors per person in the city t years after 2010.
    b. Is the number of doctors per person increasing or decreasing each year? Explain.

12. Malori is building a rectangular area for her dog. One side of the pen will be the house, so her fencing needs to complete the other three sides. Malori buys 20 yards of fence.

    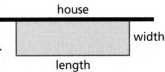

    a. Let x represent the width of the rectangle in yards. Let $w(x) = x$. Write the length function $l(x)$ in terms of $w(x)$.
    b. What is the domain for $l(x)$?
    c. Write the area function $A(x)$ for the area enclosed by the pen.
    d. What is the domain of $A(x)$? Do the numbers in the domain and range of $A(x)$ go with the same units?

13. Is the sum of two linear functions always a linear function? Explain.

Geometric Terms

? Essential Question: How can you give precise definitions of important geometric terms?

Objective
Know precise definitions of angle, circle, perpendicular line, parallel line, and line segment, based on the undefined notions of point, line, and distance along a line.

Vocabulary
point
line
plane
line segment
endpoint
ray
collinear
coplanar
coordinate
distance
length
directed line segment
angle
vertex
measure of an angle
acute angle
right angle
obtuse angle
straight angle
parallel lines
perpendicular lines

Suppose you define a rose as a plant with prickly stems and bright flowers. To define the word completely, you would also need to define "plant," "prickly," "flower," and all the other words in the definition, plus the words in those definitions, and so on. Eventually you would come to some very basic words and leave them undefined.

In geometry, the terms *point*, *line*, and *plane* are left undefined. Athough formal definitions of those terms are not given, informal descriptions of their meanings can be given.

- A **point** is a specific location. It has no length, width, or thickness, but it can be represented with a dot. A capital letter is usually used to name a point, like point *G* at the right.

  G •

- A **line** is a straight set of points with no thickness. It extends without end in both directions. It can be represented by a straight line with arrows at the ends and named by a single lowercase letter or by two points on the line. The line *ST* at right can also be called line *w*. It can be represented by $\overleftrightarrow{ST}$ and by $\overleftrightarrow{TS}$.

- A **plane** is a flat surface with no thickness. It extends without end in all directions. A plane is named by a capital letter or by three points not in line with one another. It can be represented by a parallelogram with edges (but remember that it has no boundaries!). The plane at the right can be named plane *R* or plane *JKL*.

With those three terms, it is possible to begin building the structure of geometry by defining *line segment*, *endpoint*, and *ray*.

A **line segment** is part of a line consisting of two points and all the points between them.

Each of the two points is an **endpoint**. A line segment is named by its endpoints. The line segment *MN* above can be represented by $\overline{MN}$ and by $\overline{NM}$.

A **ray** is also part of a line. It has one endpoint and extends without end in one direction.

When naming a ray, use the endpoint as the first letter. The ray *PQ* above is represented by $\overrightarrow{PQ}$.

Two useful terms describe groups of points. **Collinear** points lie on the same line. **Coplanar** points lie in the same plane.

EXAMPLE **1** MCC9-12.G.CO.1

Naming Points, Lines, Rays, and Planes

Use the figure shown.

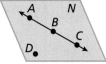

A Name three different line segments.
$\overline{AB}$, $\overline{AC}$, and $\overline{BC}$

B Name the line six ways.
$\overleftrightarrow{AC}$, $\overleftrightarrow{CA}$, $\overleftrightarrow{AB}$, $\overleftrightarrow{BA}$, $\overleftrightarrow{BC}$, and $\overleftrightarrow{CB}$

C Name four different rays.
$\overrightarrow{BC}$, $\overrightarrow{BA}$, $\overrightarrow{AB}$ (which is also named $\overrightarrow{AC}$), and $\overrightarrow{CB}$ (which is also named $\overrightarrow{CA}$). Note that $\overrightarrow{BC}$ is not the same ray as $\overrightarrow{CB}$. $\overrightarrow{BC}$ has B as its endpoint. $\overrightarrow{CB}$ has C as its endpoint.

D Name the plane four ways.
N, DAB, DAC, and DBC
Note that ABC does not name the plane because the points are collinear.

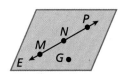

CHECK IT OUT! Use the figure shown.

1a. Name three different line segments.

b. Name the line four ways.

c. Name four different rays.

d. Name the plane four ways.

Because lines, rays, and planes extend without end, it is not possible to describe their sizes. A line segment, however, has two endpoints, so its size can be measured. To understand how, suppose you want to know the length of line segment $\overline{AB}$. Place the segment beside a number line.

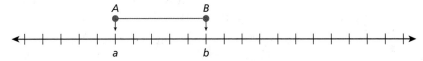

Each point on the line segment can be matched one-to-one with a real number on the number line. The real number that corresponds to a given point on the line segment is called the **coordinate** of the point. In the figure, a is the coordinate of endpoint A and b is the coordinate of endpoint B.

The **distance** between two points A and B is defined to be the absolute value of the difference between the coordinates of A and B. The distance between A and B is also called the **length** of $\overline{AB}$ and is denoted AB.

$$AB = |a - b|, \text{ which is equal to } |b - a|$$

Be sure to distinguish between a line segment, which is a set of points that is part of a line, and the *length* of the segment, which is the absolute value of the difference between the coordinates of the endpoints.

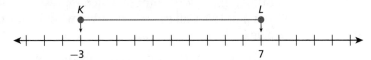

$\overline{KL}$, the line segment: K————L

KL, the length of $\overline{KL}$: $|-3 - 7| = |-10| = 10$

2 **Finding the Length of a Line Segment**

Find each length.

A *HP*

$HP = |-4 - (-1)|$
$\quad = |-4 + 1|$
$\quad = |-3|$
$\quad = 3$

B *TH*

$TH = |3 - (-4)|$
$\quad = |3 + 4|$
$\quad = |7|$
$\quad = 7$

C *BC*, if *AC* = 29 and *AB* = 15

$BC = AC - AB$
$\quad = 29 - 15$
$\quad = 14$

CHECK IT OUT!

Find each length.

2a. *NY*

b. *YS*

c. *FG*, if *FH* = 41 and *GH* = 19

A **circle** is a set of points in a plane, all of which are the same distance from a given point called the center of the circle.

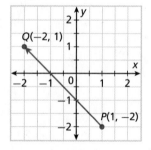

A **directed line segment** is a line segment that points in one direction or the other. A directed line segment has an initial point and a terminal point.

The directed line segment at the right has $P(1, -2)$ as its initial point and $Q(-2, 1)$ as its terminal point.

An **angle** is a figure formed by two rays with a common endpoint called the **vertex** (plural: vertices). An angle can be named by a point on each ray and the vertex, or by giving its vertex a number, or, if there is no danger of confusion with another angle, by its vertex alone.

When naming an angle by a point on each ray and the vertex, write the vertex letter in the middle. The angle at right is can be represented by $\angle ABC$, $\angle CBA$, $\angle B$, and $\angle 3$.

To measure an angle, place the vertex at the center of a semicircle as shown. Think of the semicircle as a curved number line, every point of which represents a real number from 0 to 180. Call the real number where a ray of the angle intersects the semicircle the coordinate of the ray.

The **measure** of the angle is the absolute value of the difference of the coordinates of the two rays.

$$m\angle POQ = |p - q|, \text{ which is equal to } |q - p|$$

The units of the measure of an angle are *degrees* (°). Angles can be measured using a protractor, which is shaped like the semicircle in the diagram at the right.

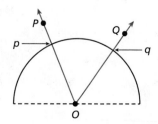

Angles are classified by their measures.

Acute Angle	Right Angle	Obtuse Angle	Straight Angle
Measures greater than 0° and less than 90°	Measures 90°	Measures greater than 90° and less than 180°	Formed by two opposite rays and measures 180°

Two lines are **perpendicular lines** if they intersect at a right angle. Two lines are **parallel lines** if they are coplanar and do not intersect no matter how far they are extended.

EXAMPLE 3

Naming and Finding the Measure of an Angle

A Give all possible names for the angles in the figure.
∠FEM, ∠MEF, ∠MEK, ∠KEM, ∠FEK, ∠KEF, ∠5, ∠6

B The rays of ∠GRS intersect the edge of a protractor at 47° and 111°. Find the measure of the angle and classify the angle.
m∠GRS = |47 − 111| = |−64| = 64°
64° is greater than 0° and less than 90°, so ∠GRS is acute.

CHECK IT OUT!

3a. Give all possible names for the angles in the figure.

b. The rays of ∠BDU intersect the edge of a protractor at 49° and 175°. Find the measure of the angle and classify it.

A-8

Exercises

1. Name each of the following.
   a. the intersection of two lines
   b. the intersection of two planes
   c. the intersection of a plane and a line not on the plane
   d. the intersection of two rays
   e. the intersection of $\overrightarrow{AB}$ and $\overrightarrow{BA}$

2. Name the geometrical figure or figures that can be named with each of the following.
   a. one point
   b. two points
   c. three points

3. Points *B*, *H*, and *K* are coplanar and non-collinear. List all of the possible names for the plane the points lie on.

4. Draw and label each of the following.
   a. a ray with endpoint *Y* that contains *C*
   b. opposite rays with common endpoint *W*
   c. a line containing *D* and *J*
   d. a line that intersects a plane but does not lie in the plane
   e. two intersecting planes
   f. plane *M* containing $\overleftrightarrow{GT}$ and $\overleftrightarrow{AF}$, which intersect at *V*

5a. Name a plane containing non-collinear points *Z*, *M*, and *P*.

   b. Points *K*, *O*, and *N* are collinear. *KN* = 12.7 cm and *NO* = 8.9 cm. Find the length of $\overline{OK}$.

   c. Explain the difference between $\overrightarrow{RS}$ and $\overrightarrow{SR}$.

   d. A plane can be named by any three non-collinear points on the plane. Explain why the three points must be non-collinear.

   e. Parallel lines are coplanar lines that do not intersect no matter how far they are extended. Why does the definition state that the lines must be coplanar?

   f. The instructions for a math problem say: "Draw a line 5 inches long." Explain the error in the instructions.

6. Answer *always*, *never*, or *sometimes*.

   a. A line segment has length but no thickness.

   b. Coplanar points are also collinear.

   c. If points *A*, *B*, and *C* are collinear, then *AC* = *AB* + *BC*.

   d. Another name for ∠*GWJ* is ∠*JGW*.

   e. Point *A* has coordinate −5. Point *B* has coordinate 3. *AB* = −8.

   f. Perpendicular lines lie in the same plane.

7. Draw Conclusions Three lines are coplanar. In how many points may they intersect? Draw sketches to support your answer.

8. Manufacturing Many stools are made with three legs instead of four. Explain why a three-legged stool might be preferable to one with four legs.

9. Problem Solving ∠*A* is an obtuse angle. The measure of ∠*B* is half the measure of ∠*A*.

   a. Classify ∠*B*.

   b. Explain how you found the classification.

10a. Complete the table.

Figure			
Number of Points	2	3	4
Maximum Number of Segments Joining the Points	1	3	

   b. What is the maximum number of segments that can be drawn joining 5 points?

   c. What is the maximum number of segments that can be drawn joining 6 points?

   d. Describe the pattern you see in the maximum number of segments that can be drawn joining a given number of points?

   e. Use the pattern to find the maximum number of segments that can be drawn joining 10 points.

11. Reasoning Give a real-world example that models each of the following.

   a. two intersecting lines

   b. two intersecting planes

   c. a line and a plane intersecting

   d. a point on a plane

Perimeter and Area in the Coordinate Plane

Objective

Use coordinates to compute perimeters of polygons and areas of triangles, e.g., using the distance formula.

You can use the distance formula to find the perimeter of a polygon and the area of triangles and rectangles using the coordinates of the vertices on the coordinate plane.

EXAMPLE **1** **Finding the Area of a Rectangle**

MCC9-12.G.GPE.7

Find the area of rectangle *GHJK*.

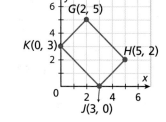

Use $A = bh$ for the area of a rectangle.

Find the length of the base and the height.

Find the length of the base, $\overline{KJ}$.

$d = \sqrt{(x_2 - x_1)^2 + (y_2 - y_1)^2}$ *Distance Formula*

$d = \sqrt{(3 - 0)^2 + (0 - 3)^2}$ *Substitute, using K(0, 3) and J(3, 0).*

$d = \sqrt{(3)^2 + (-3)^2}$ *Subtract.*

$d = \sqrt{9 + 9}$ *Simplify powers.*

$d = \sqrt{18}$ *Add.*

$d \approx 4.24$

Find the length of the height, $\overline{KG}$.

$d = \sqrt{(x_2 - x_1)^2 + (y_2 - y_1)^2}$ *Distance Formula*

$d = \sqrt{(2 - 0)^2 + (5 - 3)^2}$ *Substitute, using K(0, 3) and G(2, 5).*

$d = \sqrt{(2)^2 + (2)^2}$ *Subtract.*

$d = \sqrt{4 + 4}$ *Simplify powers.*

$d = \sqrt{8}$ *Add.*

$d \approx 2.83$ *Find the square root to the nearest hundredth.*

Find the area.

$A = bh$ *Formula for the area of a rectangle*

$A \approx (4.24)(2.83)$ *Substitute.*

$A \approx 11.9992$ *Multiply.*

$A \approx 12.00$ *Round to the nearest hundredth.*

The area of the rectangle *GHJK* is about 12 square units.

 CHECK IT OUT!

1. Find the area of a rectangle with vertices at $D(0, 3)$, $E(1, 4)$, $F(4, -1)$, and $G(3, -2)$. Round to the nearest tenth.

EXAMPLE **2**
MCC9-12.G.GPE.7

Finding the Perimeter of a Polygon

Find the perimeter of polygon ABCDE.

Find the length of each side of the polygon:

$\overline{AB}, \overline{BC}, \overline{CD}, \overline{DE}$ and $\overline{EA}$.

Find the length of $\overline{AB}$.

$A(-3, 2)$ and $B(1, 2)$ have the same y-coordinate, 2.

Distance is the absolute value of the difference between the x-coordinates.

$$d = |1-(-3)|$$

$$d = |4|$$

$$d = 4$$

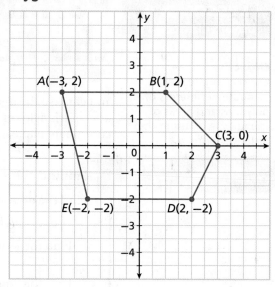

Find the length of $\overline{BC}$.

$d = \sqrt{(x_2 - x_1)^2 + (y_2 - y_1)^2}$	*Distance Formula*
$d = \sqrt{(3 - 1)^2 + (0 - 2)^2}$	*Substitute, using B(1, 2) and C(3, 0).*
$d = \sqrt{(2)^2 + (-2)^2}$	*Subtract.*
$d = \sqrt{4 + 4}$	*Simplify powers.*
$d = \sqrt{8}$	*Add.*
$d \approx 2.83$	*Find the square root to the nearest hundredth.*

Find the length of $\overline{CD}$.

$d = \sqrt{(x_2 - x_1)^2 + (y_2 - y_1)^2}$	*Distance Formula*
$d = \sqrt{(2 - 3)^2 + (-2 - 0)^2}$	*Substitute, using C(3, 0) and C(2, −2).*
$d = \sqrt{(-1)^2 + (-2)^2}$	*Subtract.*
$d = \sqrt{1 + 4}$	*Simplify powers.*
$d = \sqrt{5}$	*Add.*
$d \approx 2.24$	*Find the square root to the nearest hundredth.*

Find the length of $\overline{DE}$.

$D(2, -2)$ and $E(-2, -2)$ have the same y-coordinate, −2.

$d = |-2 - 2|$	*Distance is the absolute value of the difference*
$d = |-4|$	*between the x-coordinates.*
$d = 4$	

Find the length of $\overline{EA}$.

$d = \sqrt{(x_2 - x_1)^2 + (y_2 - y_1)^2}$	*Distance Formula*
$d = \sqrt{(-3 - (-2))^2 + (2 - (-2))^2}$	*Substitute, using E(−2, −2) and A(−3, 2).*
$d = \sqrt{(-1)^2 + (4)^2}$	*Subtract.*
$d = \sqrt{1 + 16}$	*Simplify powers.*
$d = \sqrt{17}$	*Add.*
$d \approx 4.12$	*Find the square root to the nearest hundredth.*

Find the sum of the lengths of the sides to find the perimeter of the polygon.

$$P \approx 4 + 2.83 + 2.24 + 4 + 4.12 = 17.19$$

The perimeter of polygon *ABCDE* is about 17.19 units.

 2. Find the perimeter of a triangle with vertices at $Q(-2, 1)$, $R(1, -2)$, and $S(5, 2)$. Round the answer to the nearest hundredth.

 **EXAMPLE 3** **Finding the Area of a Triangle**

Find the area of the triangle *XYZ*.

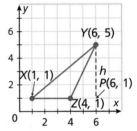

Use $A = \frac{1}{2}bh$ for the area of a triangle.

Find the base and the height.

Find the length of the base, $\overline{XY}$.

$X(1, 1)$ and $Z(4, 1)$ have the same *y*-coordinate, 1.

$b = |4 - 1|$	*Distance is the absolute value of the difference between the x-coordinates.*
$b = |3|$	
$b = 3$	

Find the length of the height, $\overline{YP}$.

$Y(6, 5)$ and $P(6, 1)$ have the same *x*-coordinate, 6.

$h = |1 - 5|$	*Distance is the absolute value of the difference between the y-coordinates.*
$h = |-4|$	
$h = 4$	

Find the area.

$A = \frac{1}{2}bh$	*Formula for the area of a triangle*
$A = \frac{1}{2}(3)(4)$	*Substitute.*
$A = \frac{1}{2}(12) = 6$	*Multiply and simplify.*

The area of the triangle *XYZ* is 6 square units.

 3. Find the area of a triangle with vertices at $A(0, 0)$, $B(3, 5)$, and $S(7, 0)$.

EXAMPLE **4** **Solving a Problem Involving Distance**

The cross-country team begins a route at the entrance to a park at $S(0, 0)$. The route goes to the rose garden at $R(2, 1)$, turns left and heads through the wilderness area to $W(2, 3)$, then leads back to the park entrance.

a. Draw the team's route on the coordinate plane.

Plot the points on a coordinate grid.

b. If one grid unit represents 1 mile, what is the total distance of the cross-country team's route? Round to the nearest tenth.

To find the length of the route, find the perimeter of the triangle.

Find the length of $\overline{SR}$.

$d = \sqrt{(x_2 - x_1)^2 + (y_2 - y_1)^2}$	*Distance Formula*
$d = \sqrt{(2 - 0)^2 + (1 - 0)^2}$	*Substitute, using S(0, 0) and R(2, 1).*
$d = \sqrt{(2)^2 + (1)^2}$	*Subtract.*
$d = \sqrt{4 + 1}$	*Simplify powers.*
$d = \sqrt{5}$	*Add.*
$d \approx 2.24$	*Find the square root to the nearest hundredth.*

Find the length of $\overline{RW}$.

$R(2, 1)$ and $P(2, 3)$ have the same x-coordinate, 2.

$$d = |3 - 1| = |2| = 2$$

Find the length of $\overline{WS}$.

$d = \sqrt{(x_2 - x_1)^2 + (y_2 - y_1)^2}$	*Distance Formula*
$d = \sqrt{(0 - 2)^2 + (0 - 3)^2}$	*Substitute, using W(2, 3) and S(0, 0).*
$d = \sqrt{(-2)^2 + (-3)^2}$	*Subtract.*
$d = \sqrt{4 + 9}$	*Simplify powers.*
$d = \sqrt{13}$	*Add.*
$d \approx 3.61$	*Find the square root to the nearest hundredth.*

Find the sum of the lengths of the sides.

$$P \approx 2.24 + 2 + 3.61 = 7.85 \approx 7.9$$

The distance of the cross-country route is about 7.9 miles.

4. Sean visits three towns that lie on a coordinate grid at $(-3, 4)$, $(6, 4)$, and $(0, 0)$, ending at the town where he started. If each square on the coordinate grid represents a mile, how far did he travel? Round to the nearest tenth.

1. A search-and-rescue team is searching for a lost hiker. The search area is defined by the coordinates shown at right. Each square on the grid is 1 square mile.

   a. What is the perimeter of the area being searched? Round your answer to the nearest tenth of a mile.

   b. How many square miles are being searched? Round your answer to the nearest tenth of a square mile.

   c. Explain how to partition the area to find the number of square miles being searched.

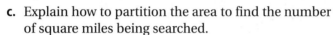

2. Erin says a triangle with vertices at $P(2, 2)$, $Q(4, 5)$, and $R(6, 0)$ is a right triangle. Is she right? Justify your answer.

3. A right triangle has vertices at $(1, 1)$, $(4, -3)$, and $(7, -1)$. Find the perimeter and area of the triangle. Round your answers to the nearest tenth.

4. Three vertices of a square $STQR$ are $S(-1, 1)$, $T(3, 3)$, and $Q(1, 7)$.

   a. What is the fourth vertex R?

   b. What is the length of a diagonal rounded to the nearest tenth?

   c. What is the area of the square?

5. The sides of a quadrilateral lie on the following lines: $x + y = 8$, $x - y = 8$, $x + y = -8$, and $x - y = -8$.

   a. Draw the quadrilateral. What are the vertices of the quadrilateral?

   b. What is the perimeter and area of the quadrilateral?

   c. What type of quadrilateral is defined by the lines? Justify your answer.

The coordinate grid shows the plans for a park. The scale on the grid is 1:2 yards. All the vertices of the diagram lie on integer coordinates. Round your answers to the nearest tenth.

6. A fence is planned for the perimeter of the park. What is the length of the fence?

7. What is the area of the Plaza?

8. Safety matting for playgrounds costs $15 per square foot. What is the cost of the safety matting for the Play Equipment Area?

9. What percent of the park is the Native Plants Garden?

10. Mr. Ryan says that the Picnic Area is 40.5 square yards. Is he correct? Explain.

11. The proposed budget for constructing the park is $325,000. What is the budget per square foot for the project?

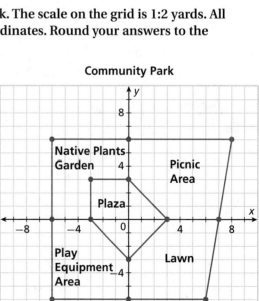

Partitions of Directed Line Segments

Essential Question: How can you find the point on a directed line segment that partitions the segment in a given ratio?

Objective
Find the point on a directed line segment between two given points that partitions the segment in a given ratio.

In this lesson, you will learn to find points that divide directed line segments into two parts, whose lengths are given ratios. One way to develop a method for solving problems like this is to consider a problem involving a directed line segment that is horizontal.

The diagram shows a portion of the timeline for the launch of a rocket carrying a satellite.

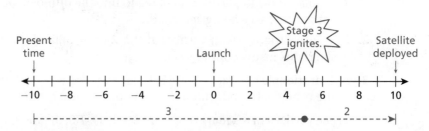

The diagram shows that sometime between now (T − 10 minutes) and the time the satellite is deployed (T + 10 minutes), Stage 3 will ignite. The exact time will divide the total time into two segments whose lengths are in the ratio 3 to 2. When will ignition occur?

To solve the problem, you might follow these steps:

- Find the total time until deployment: $10 - (-10) = 20$ minutes
- Find the ratio $\dfrac{\text{time to Stage 3 ignition}}{\text{total time}} : \dfrac{3}{3+2} = \dfrac{3}{5}$
- Solve a proportion to find x, the time of Stage 3 ignition: $\dfrac{3}{5} = \dfrac{x}{20} \rightarrow x = 12$
- Find the time since launch: $-10 + 12 = 2$

So, Stage 3 ignition will be at T + 2 minutes, or 2 minutes after launch.

You can apply similar reasoning to solve a problem involving a sloping line segment on the coordinate plane.

EXAMPLE 1 Using a Ratio to Find an Indicated Point

Find the coordinates of the point P that lies on the directed line segment from $A(-3, -2)$ to $B(5, 2)$, and partitions the segment in the ratio 3 to 5.

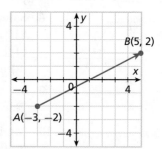

It's important to note that P lies on a directed line segment that *starts* at A and *ends* at B. The point that lies on the segment that starts at B, ends at A, and partitions the segment in the ratio 3 to 5 in *that* direction, is a different point than P.

The given ratio, 3 to 5, compares P's distance from A with P's distance from B. Start by converting that ratio to one that compares P's distance from A with the entire distance from A to B.

$$\frac{AP}{PB} = \frac{3}{5}$$ *Write the given ratio.*

$$\frac{AP}{AP + PB} = \frac{3}{3 + 5}$$ *Convert to a ratio comparing AP with AB.*

$$\frac{AP}{AB} = \frac{3}{8}$$

So, P is three-eighths of the distance from A to B. Use that fact together with the rise and run from A to B to find the coordinates of P.

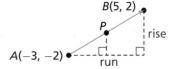

Find the x-coordinate.

$5 - (-3) = 5 + 3 = 8$ *Subtract x-coordinates to find the run from A to B.*

$\frac{3}{8} \cdot 8 = 3$ *The run from A to P is $\frac{3}{8}$ of the run from A to B.*

$-3 + 3 = 0$ *Add the run from A to P to the x-coordinate of A.*

Find the y-coordinate.

$2 - (-2) = 2 + 2 = 4$ *Subtract y-coordinates to find the rise from A to B.*

$\frac{3}{8} \cdot 4 = \frac{12}{8} = 1.5$ *The rise from A to P is $\frac{3}{8}$ of the rise from A to B.*

$-2 + 1.5 = -0.5$ *Add the rise from A to P to the y-coordinate of A.*

So, the coordinates of P are $(0, -0.5)$.

 1. Find the coordinates of the point P that lies on the directed line segment from $A(2, 3)$ and $B(7, 13)$, and partitions the segment in the ratio 3 to 2.

Sometimes the partitioning of a segment is given as a fraction rather than a ratio.

 **EXAMPLE 2**
MCC9-12.G.GPE.6

Using a Fraction to Find an Indicated Point

The map shows New York City from West 24th to West 33rd Streets between 5th and 6th Avenues. The slanted line is Broadway. The map is marked in units of 75 meters. Soupy's Subs is on Broadway at S, $\frac{7}{25}$ of the way from $G(300, 0)$ to $H(0, 675)$. Find the shop's coordinates.

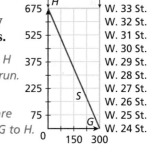

run: $0 - 300 = -300$ *Subtract coordinates of G and H*
rise: $675 - 0 = 675$ *to find Broadway's rise and run.*

run: $\frac{7}{25} \cdot (-300) = -84$ *The rise and run from G to S are*
                  $\frac{7}{25}$ of the rise and run from G to H.
rise: $\frac{7}{25} \cdot (675) = 189$

x-coordinate of shop: $300 + (-84) = 216$ *Add the rise and run from G to S to*
                                   the coordinates of G.
y-coordinate of shop: $0 + 189 = 189$

So, the coordinates of Soupy's Subs are $S(216, 189)$.

 2. The map shows the freeway between Xenon and Yardley. The map is marked in units of 1 mile. The only exit from the freeway is $\frac{2}{5}$ of the way from Xenon to Yardley. Find the coordinates of the exit.

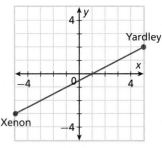

1. Point P lies on the directed line segment $\overline{AB}$, and partitions the segment in the ratio 5 to 11. Write a fraction to complete this sentence: P is located _____ of the way from A to B.

2. Point E is four-ninths of the way from C to D on the directed line segment $\overline{CD}$. Write a ratio to complete this sentence: E partitions $\overline{CD}$ in the ratio _____ to _____.

3. Point K lies on the directed line segment $\overline{JL}$ and partitions the segment in the ratio 7 to 12. Write a ratio to compete this sentence: K partitions the directed line segment $\overline{LJ}$ in the ratio _____ to _____.

4. Point Q is three-eighths of the way from P to R on the directed line segment $\overline{PR}$. Write a fraction to complete this sentence: P is located _____ of the way from R to P on directed line segment $\overline{RP}$.

5. On a number line, A is at -16 and B is at 9. Find the coordinate of the point that is four-fifths of the distance from A to B.

6. On a number line, X is at -23 and Y is at 13. Find the coordinate of the point that is two-thirds of the distance from Y to X.

7. The time is T $-$ 14 at a rocket launch site. (Times are measured in minutes.) At T $+$ 16 the rocket will rendezvous with an orbiting space station. Stage 4 of the rocket will ignite at a time that divides the total time in the ratio 7 to 3. How many minutes after launch will Stage 4 ignite?

8. The ground level of the Segment Building is Level 0. Above-ground levels are numbered 1 to 85. Below-ground parking levels are numbered -1 to -6. Each morning, Bettina parks her car at the lowest level and takes the elevator to her office, a distance that is $\frac{5}{7}$ of the total distance from the lowest level to the highest. The distance between levels is constant throughout the building. On which level is Bettina's office?

9. Given the points $A(-2, 0)$ and $B(3, 5)$, find the coordinates of the point P on the directed line segment $\overline{AB}$ that partitions $\overline{AB}$ in the ratio 2 to 3.

10. Given the points $A(-2, 0)$ and $B(3, 5)$, find the coordinates of the point P on the directed line segment $\overline{BA}$ that partitions $\overline{BA}$ in the ratio 2 to 3.

11. Given the points $J(-8, 5)$ and $K(7, -5)$, find the coordinates of the point P on the directed line segment $\overline{JK}$ that partitions $\overline{JK}$ in the ratio 4 to 1.

12. Given the points $J(-8, 5)$ and $K(7, -5)$, find the coordinates of the point P on the directed line segment $\overline{KJ}$ that partitions $\overline{KJ}$ in the ratio 4 to 1.

13. Given the points $C(-9, 1)$ and $D(-3, -2)$, find the coordinates of the point N on the directed line segment $\overline{CD}$ that partitions $\overline{CD}$ in the ratio $\frac{1}{3}$.

14. Given the points $C(-9, 1)$ and $D(-3, -2)$, find the coordinates of the point N on the directed line segment $\overline{DC}$ that partitions $\overline{DC}$ in the ratio $\frac{1}{3}$.

15. Find the point on the directed line segment $\overline{AB}$ that is three-fifths of the distance from $A(3, -1)$ to $B(-2, 9)$.

16. Find the point on the directed line segment $\overline{MN}$ that is five-sixths of the distance from $M(-7, 2)$ to $N(-1, -4)$.

17. Find the point on the directed line segment $\overline{YZ}$ that is seven-eighths of the distance from $Y(-7, 1)$ to $Z(1, -7)$.

Mastering *the* Standards
for Mathematical Practice

The topics described in the Standards for Mathematical Content will vary from year to year. However, the *way* in which you learn, study, and think about mathematics will not. The Standards for Mathematical Practice describe skills that you will use in all of your math courses.

Mathematical Practices

1. Make sense of problems and persevere in solving them.
2. Reason abstractly and quantitatively.
3. Construct viable arguments and critique the reasoning of others.
4. Model with mathematics.
5. Use appropriate tools strategically.
6. Attend to precision.
7. Look for and make use of structure.
8. Look for and express regularity in repeated reasoning.

④ Model with mathematics.

Mathematically proficient students can apply... mathematics... to... problems... in everyday life, society, and the workplace...

In your book

Real-World Connections and **Focus on Mathematical Practices** exercises apply mathematics to other disciplines and in real-world scenarios.

Real-World Connections

61.
a. A band wants to create a CD of their last concert. They received a donation of $500 to cover the cost. The total cost is $350 plus $3 per CD. Complete the table to find a relationship between the number of CDs and the total cost.

b. Write an equation for the cost c of the CDs based on the number of CDs n.

c. Write an inequality that can be used to determine how many CDs can be made with the $500 donation. Solve the inequality and determine how many CDs the band can have made from the $500 donation.

Number	Process	Cost
1	350 + 3	353
2		
3		
10		
n		

124 Chapter 2 Inequalities

FOCUS ON MATHEMATICAL PRACTICES

HOT 70. Modeling In order for Ramon to remain in his current weight class for a wrestling match on Saturday morning, he must weigh in at 152 pounds or more, but less than 160 pounds. Write a pair of inequalities that expresses the set of acceptable weights for Ramon. Define your variable.

HOT 71. Problem Solving Cary is making brownies using a recipe that calls for "at least 5 cups of flour but no more than 6 cups of flour." The only measuring cup he could find holds one quarter of a cup. Write a pair of inequalities to express how many *quarter cups* of flour Cary can use.

HOT 72. Analysis Imani and Trey are planning the seating at their wedding reception. They have 168 guests and each table can hold up to 16 guests, so they calculate that they need at least 10.5 tables to seat all of their guests. Graph their solution. In this context, how is the graph inaccurate? Make another graph that takes the context into account.

2-1 Graphing and Writing Inequalities **105**

PhotoDisc/Getty Images

1-1

Check It Out! **1a.** 4 decreased by n; n less than 4 **1b.** the quotient of t and 5; t divided by 5 **1c.** the sum of 9 and q; q added to 9 **1d.** the product of 3 and h; 3 times h
2a. $65t$ **2b.** $m + 5$ **2c.** $32d$ **3a.** 6
3b. 7 **3c.** 3 **4. a.** $63s$, **b.** 756 bottles; 1575 bottles; 3150 bottles

Exercises **1.** variable **3.** the quotient of f and 3; f divided by 3 **5.** 9 decreased by y; y less than 9 **7.** the sum of t and 12; t increased by 12 **9.** x decreased by 3; the difference of x and 3
11. $w + 4$ **13.** 12 **15.** 6 **17.** the product of 5 and p; 5 groups of p **19.** the sum of 3 and x; 3 increased by x **21.** negative 3 times s; the product of negative 3 and s **23.** 14 decreased by t; the difference of 14 and t **25.** $t + 20$
27. 1 **29.** 2 **31a.** $h - 40$, **b.** 0; 4; 8; 12 **33.** $2x$ **35.** $y + 10$ **37.** $9w$; 9 in^2; 72 in^2; 81 in^2; 99 in^2 **39.** 13; 14; 15; 16 **41.** 6; 10; 13; 15 **43a.** $47.84 + m$;
b. $58.53 - s$ **45.** $x + 7$; 19; 21
47. $x + 3$; 15; 17 **49.** F **51.** 36
53. 1.

1-2

Check It Out! **1a.** 8.8 **1b.** 0 **1c.** 25
2a. $\frac{1}{2}$ **2b.** -10 **2c.** 8 **3a.** 9.3 **3b.** 2
3c. 44 **4.** 35 years old

Exercises **3.** 21 **5.** 16.3 **7.** $\frac{1}{2}$ **9.** 0
11. 2.3 **13.** 1.2 **15.** 32 **17.** 3.7 **19.** $\frac{17}{6}$
21. 9 **23.** 17 **25.** $\frac{4}{7}$ **27.** 10.5 **29.** 9
31. 0 **33.** -17 **35.** -3100 **37.** -0.5
39. 0.05 **41.** 15 **43.** 1545 **45.** 30
47. $\frac{1}{3}$ **49.** $a + 500 = 4732$; $4232
51. $x - 10 = 12$; $x = 22$ **53.** $x + 8 = 16$; $x = 8$ **55.** $5 + x = 6$; $x = 1$
57. $x - 4 = 9$; $x = 13$ **59.** $m + 560 = 1680$; $1120 **61.** $63 + x = 90$;
$x = 27$ **63.** $x + 15 = 90$; $x = 75$
65. $h - 47 = 28$; 75 **69.** J **71.** $-\frac{12}{5}$
73. $-\frac{13}{12}$ **75.** 10 **77.** 90

1-3

Check It Out! **1a.** 50 **1b.** -39
1c. 56 **2a.** 4 **2b.** -20 **2c.** 5 **3a.** $-\frac{5}{4}$
3b. 1 **3c.** 612 **4.** 15,000 ft

Exercises **1.** 32 **3.** 14 **5.** 19 **7.** 7
9. 5 **11.** 2.5 **13.** 14 **15.** -9 **17.** $\frac{1}{8}$
19. $16c = 192$; $12 **21.** 24 **23.** -36
25. -150 **27.** 55 **29.** -3 **31.** 1
33. 13 **35.** 0.3 **37.** 2 **39.** -16 **41.** -3.5
43. -2 **45.** $\frac{7}{10}s = 392$; $560
49. $4s = 84$; 21 in. **51.** $4s = 16.4$;
4.1 cm **53.** $-3x = 12$; $x = -4$
55. $\frac{x}{3} = -8$; $x = -24$ **57.** $6.25h = 50$;
8 h **59.** $0.05m = 13.80$; 276 min
61. -2 **63.** 0; $8y = 0$; 0 **65a.** number of data values **c.** 185,300 acres
67. 7 **69.** 605 **71.** $\frac{3}{16}$ **73.** 5.7
75. $\frac{2}{3}g = 2$; 3 g **77.** D **79.** B
81a. $6c = 4.80$ **b.** $c = $0.80 **83.** 2
85. 9 **87.** 2 **89.** -20 **91.** -132
93. Multiply both sides by a.

2-1

Check It Out! **1.** 12 **2.** $7.50/h
3. 20.5 ft/s **4a.** -20 **4b.** 5.75
5. 6 in.

Exercises **1.** The ratios are equivalent. **3.** 682 trillion
5. 18,749 lb/cow **7.** 0.075 page/min
9. 18 mi/gal **11.** $\frac{3}{5}$ **13.** 39 **15.** 6.5
17. 23 **19.** $\frac{3}{5} = \frac{h}{4.9}$; 2.94 m **21.** 72
23. $403.90/oz **25.** 2498.4 km/h
27. 10 **29.** -1 **31.** 13 **33.** 1.2 **35.** $\frac{1}{9}$
37. 45 **39.** $84 **43.** 1.625 **45.** 3
47. $-\frac{2}{7}$ **49.** $\frac{11}{3}$ **51.** 3 **53.** 24
55. -120 **59.** A **61.** D **63.** 40°; 50°
65. 0.0006722 people/m^2

2-2

Check It Out! **1.** 2.8 in.
2a. $\frac{150}{x} = \frac{45}{195}$; 650 cm **2b.** $\frac{5.5}{x} = \frac{3.5}{28}$;
44 ft **3.** The ratio of the perimeters is equal to the ratio of the corresponding sides.

Exercises **3.** 10 ft **7.** 7 in. **11.** 480 ft^2
13. 4 **15.** 2.8 ft **17.** 4 cm
21. $\frac{1.5}{x} = \frac{4.5}{36}$; 12 m **23.** k^2 **25.** G
27. $w = 4$; $x = 7.5$; $y = 8$
29. 16.6 cm

2-3

Check It Out! **1a.** 17 oz **1b.** 7.85 m
1c. 6000 g **2a.** C **2b.** C **3.** no; C
4a. 3.89 cm–4.31 cm
4b. 463.12 m–486.88 m
4c. 84.57 mg–85.43 mg

Exercises **1.** precise **3.** 4.3 mL
5. 2.37 mg **7.** 47.3 ft **9a.** 1 **9b.** 1
11. no; ball 4 **13.** 49 lb–51 lb
15. 24 cm–26 cm
17. 240 mm–260 mm
19. 4337 mg **21.** 11,000 lb
23. 6.83 cm **25.** 0.0127 m
27a. Chandra **27b.** Lucy
29. 44.1 lb–45.9 lb
31. 36.44°C–37.56°C
33. 28.8 ft–31.2 ft
35. 0.19 cm–0.21 cm
37. 5456 mi **39.** 120 ft
41. 6 kg **43.** 16,453.2 mL
45. 0.265 cm **47.** 165 ft
49. neither **51.** 475.0 mL
53. 50 kg $\pm$ 4% **55.** 750 kg $\pm$ 2%
57. 425 lb $\pm$ 2% **59.** 175 km $\pm$ 3%
61. ball 4 **65.** J **67.** 0.04%
69. 384,326 km–384,480 km

Selected Answers ▪ Unit 2

3-1

Check It Out! **1a.** 1 **1b.** 6 **1c.** 0
2a. $\frac{55}{4}$ **2b.** $\frac{1}{2}$ **2c.** 15 **3a.** $-\frac{5}{6}$ **3b.** 5
3c. 8 **4.** $60 **5.** -42

Exercises **1.** 2 **3.** -18 **5.** 2 **7.** 66
9. $\frac{5}{4}$ **11.** -12 **13.** 16 **15.** -3.2 **17.** 4
19. 15 passes **21.** 4 **23.** -4 **25.** 4
27. 5 **29.** -9 **31.** $\frac{1}{4}$ **33.** 1 **35.** 3
37. $\frac{28}{5}$ **39.** 3 **41.** 8 **43.** 7 **45.** $-\frac{1}{2}$
47. $x = 40$ **49.** $x = 35$
51. $8 - 3n = 2$; $n = 2$
53a. $1963 - 5s = 1863$; $s = 20$ **53b.** 3
55. 8 **57.** 4.5 **59.** -10 **61.** 10
63. $5k - 70 = 60$; 26 in. **65.** Stan: 36;
Mark: 37; Wayne: 38 **67a.** 45,000;
112,500; 225,000; 337,500; 225n
67b. $c = 225n$ **71.** H **73.** 27 **75.** $6\frac{1}{5}$
77. 14.5 **79.** -6

3-2

Check It Out! **1a.** -2 **1b.** 2
2a. 4 **2b.** -2 **3a.** no solution
3b. all real numbers **4.** 10 years old

Exercises **3.** 1 **5.** 40 **7.** $-\frac{2}{3}$
9. 3 **11.** no solution **13.** all real
numbers **15.** 6 **17.** 6 **19.** 2.85
21. 10 **23.** 6 **25.** 14 **27.** $\frac{3}{4}$
29. -4 **31.** no solution **33a.** 15 weeks
33b. 180 lb **35.** $x - 30 = 14 - 3x$;
$x = 11$ **37.** -4 **39.** 7 **41.** -3 **43.** 2
45. 1 **47.** $-\frac{7}{5}$ **49.** 4 **51.** no solution
53. 9 **59.** F **61.** H **63.** 2 **65.** no
solution **67.** -20 **69.** 6, 7, 8 **71.** $1.68

3-3

Check It Out! **1.** about 1.46 h
2. $i = f + gt$ **3a.** $t = \frac{5-b}{2}$ **3b.** $V = \frac{m}{D}$

Exercises **3.** $w = \frac{V}{\ell h}$ **5.** $m = 4n + 8$
7. $a = \frac{10}{b+c}$ **9.** $I = A - P$
11. $x = \frac{k+5}{y}$ **13.** $\frac{x-2}{z} = y$
15. $x = 5(a + g)$ **17.** $x = \frac{y-b}{m}$
19. $T = \frac{PV}{nR}$ **21.** $T = M + R$
23. $b = \frac{c-2a}{2}$ **25.** $r = 7 - ax$
27. $x = \frac{5-4y}{3}$ **31.** $a = \frac{t-g}{-0.0035}$
35. C **37.** D **39.** $a = \frac{5}{2}\left(c + \frac{3}{4}b\right)$
41. $d = 500\left(t - \frac{1}{2}\right)$ **43.** $s = \frac{v^2 - u^2}{2a}$
45. 120 s

4-1

Check It Out! **1.** all real numbers
greater than 4

2a.
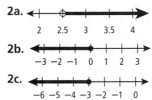

2b.

2c.

3. $x < 2.5$ **4.** $d =$ amount employee
can earn per hour; $d \geq 8.25$

Exercises **1.** A solution of an
inequality makes the inequality
true when substituted for the
variable. **3.** all real numbers greater
than -3 **5.** all real numbers greater
than or equal to 3 **11.** $b > -8\frac{1}{2}$
13. $d < -7$ **15.** $f \leq 14$ **17.** $r < 140$
where r is positive **19.** all real
numbers less than 2 **21.** all real
numbers less than or equal to 12
27. $v < -11$ **29.** $x > -3.3$ **31.** $z \geq$
9 **33.** $y =$ years of experience;
$y \geq 5$ **35.** h is less than -5. **37.** r is
greater than or equal to -2.
39. $p \leq 17$ **41.** $f > 0$ **43.** $p =$ profits;
$p < 10,000$ **45.** $e =$ elevation;
$e \leq 5000$ **51.** D **53.** C **59.** D **61.** C
65. $<$

4-2

Check It Out! **1a.** $s \leq 9$

1b. $t < 5\frac{1}{2}$

1c. $q < 11$

2. $11 + m \leq 15$; $m \leq 4$ where m is
nonnegative; Sarah can consume
4 mg or less without exceeding the
RDA. **3.** $250 + p > 282$; $p > 32$; Josh
needs to bench press more than
32 additional pounds to break the
school record.

Exercises **1.** $p > 6$ **3.** $x \leq -15$
5. $102 + t \leq 104$; $t \leq 2$ where t is

nonnegative **7.** $a \geq 5$ **9.** $x < 15$
11. $1400 + 243 + w \leq 2000$;
$w \leq 357$ where w is nonnegative
13. $x - 10 > 32$; $x > 42$
15. $r - 13 \leq 15$; $r \leq 28$ **17.** $q > 51$
19. $p \leq 0.8$ **21.** $c > -202$ **23.** $x \geq 0$
25. $21 + d \leq 30$; $d \leq 9$ where d is
nonnegative **27.** $x < 3$; B
29. $x \leq 3$; D **31.** $p \leq 40,421$ where p
is nonnegative **35.** **a.** $411 + 411 =$
882 miles **b.** $822 + m \leq 1000$
c. $m \leq 178$, but m cannot be negative.
37. F **39.** J **41.** $r \leq 5\frac{1}{10}$
43. sometimes **45.** always

4-3

Check It Out! **1a.** $k > 6$

1b. $q \leq -10$

1c. $g > 36$

2a. $x \geq -10$

2b. $h > -17$

3. 0, 1, 2, 3, 4, 5, 6, 7, 8, 9, 10, 11, or
12 servings

Exercises **1.** $b > 9$ **3.** $d > 18$
5. $m \leq 1.1$ **7.** $s > -2$ **9.** $x > 5$
11. $n > -0.4$ **13.** $d > -3$ **15.** $t > -72$
17. 0, 1, 2, 3, 4, 5, or 6 nights **19.** $j \leq$
12 **21.** $d < 7$ **23.** $h \leq \frac{8}{7}$ **25.** $c \leq$
-12 **27.** $b \geq \frac{1}{10}$ **29.** $b \leq -16$
31. $r < -\frac{3}{2}$ **33.** $y < 2$ **35.** $t > 4$
37. $z < -11$ **39.** $k \leq -7$ **41.** $p \geq$
-12 **43.** $x > -3$ **45.** $x < 20$
47. $p \leq -6$ **49.** $b < 2$ **51.** $7x \geq 21$;
$x \geq 3$ **53.** $-\frac{4}{5}b \leq -16$; $b \geq 20$ **57.** C
59. A **67.** B **71.** $g \leq -\frac{14}{5}$ **73.** $m > \frac{4}{15}$
75. $x = 5$

5-1

Check It Out! **1a.** $x \leq -6$

1b. $x < -11$

Selected Answers ■ Unit 2

1c. $n \le -10$

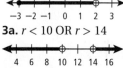

2a. $m > 10$

2b. $x > -4$

2c. $x > 2\frac{1}{3}$

3. $\frac{95+x}{2} \ge 90$; $95 + x \ge 180$; $x \ge 85$; Jim's score must be at least 85.

Exercises 1. $m > 6$ **3.** $x \le -2$
5. $x > -16$ **7.** $x \ge -9$ **9.** $x > -\frac{1}{2}$
11. $x \le 19$ **13.** $x > 1$ **15.** sales of more than $9000 **17.** $x \le 1$
19. $w < -2$ **21.** $x < -6$ **23.** $f < -4.5$ **25.** $w > 0$ **27.** $v > \frac{2}{3}$ **29.** $x > -5$ **31.** $x < -2$ **33.** $a \ge 11$ **35.** $x > 3$
37. starting at 29 min **39.** $x \le 2$
41. $x < 4$ **43.** $x < -6$ **45.** $r < 8$
47. $x < 7$ **49.** $p \ge 18$ **51.** $\frac{1}{2}x + 9 < 33$; $x < 48$ **53.** $4(x + 12) \le 16$; $x \le -8$
55. B **57.** A **59.** 24 months or more
61a.

Number	Process	Cost
1	350 + 3	353
2	350 + 3(2)	356
3	350 + 3(3)	359
10	350 + 3(10)	380
n	350 + 3n	350 + 3n

b. $c = 350 + 3n$ **c.** $350 + 3n \le 500$; $n \le 50$; 50 CDs or fewer **65.** G **67.** 59
69. $x > 5$ **71.** $x > 0$ **73.** $x \ge 0$
75. $-3x > 0$

5-2

Check It Out! 1a. $x \le -2$

1b. $t < -1$

2. more than 160 flyers
3a. $r \le 2$

3b. $x < 3$

4a. no solutions **4b.** all real numbers

Exercises 1. $x < 3$ **3.** $x < 2$
5. $c < -2$ **7.** at least 34 pizzas
9. $p < -17$ **11.** $x > 3$ **13.** $t < 6.8$
15. no solutions **17.** all real numbers **19.** no solutions
21. $y > -2$ **23.** $b \ge -7$ **25.** $m > 5$
27. $x \ge 2$ **29.** $w \ge 6$ **31.** $r \ge -4$
33. no solutions **35.** all real numbers
37. all real numbers **39.** $t < -7$
41. $x > 3$ **43.** $x < 2$ **45.** $x > -2$
47. $x \le -6$ **49.** 27 s
51a. $400 + 4.50n$ **b.** $12n$ **c.** $400 + 4.50n < 12n$; $n > 53\frac{1}{3}$; 54 CDs or more **53.** $5x - 10 < 6x - 8$; $x > -2$
55. $\frac{3}{4}x \ge x - 5$; $x \le 20$
59. x can never be greater than itself plus 1. **61.** D **63.** A
67. $x < -3$ **69.** $w \ge -1\frac{6}{7}$

5-3

Check It Out! 1. $1.0 < c < 3.0$

2a. $1 < x < 5$

2b. $-3 \le n < 2$

3a. $r < 10$ OR $r > 14$

3b. $x \ge 3$ OR $x < -1$

4a. $-9 < y < -2$

4b. $x \le -13$ OR $x \ge 2$

Exercises **1.** intersection
3. $-5 < x < 5$ **5.** $0 < x < 3$
7. $x < -8$ OR $x > 4$ **9.** $n < 1$ OR $n > 4$
11. $-5 \le a \le -3$ **13.** $c < 1$ OR $c \ge 9$
15. $16 \le k \le 50$ **17.** $3 \le n \le 6$
19. $2 < x < 6$ **21.** $x < 0$ OR $x > 3$
23. $x < -3$ OR $x > 2$
25. $q < 0$ OR $q \ge 2$ **27.** $-2 < s < 1$
29a. $225 + 80n$ gives the cost of the studio and technicians; the band will spend between $200 and $550.

---

b. $-0.3125 \le n \le 4.0625$; n cannot be a negative number **c.** $155
31. $1 \le x \le 2$ **33.** $-10 \le x \le 10$
35. $t < 0$ OR $t > 100$ **37.** $-2 < x < 5$
39. $a < 0$ OR $a > 1$ **41.** $n < 2$ OR $n > 5$
43. $7 \le m \le 60$ **47.** D **49.** B
51. $0.5 < c < 3$ **53.** $s \le 6$ OR $s \ge 9$
55. $-1 \le x \le 3$mm

6-1

Check It Out! 1a. yes **1b.** no
2a. $(-2, 3)$ **2b.** $(3, -2)$ **3.** 5 movies; $25

Exercises 1. an ordered pair that satisfies both equations **3.** yes
5. $(2, 1)$ **7.** $(-4, 7)$ **9.** no **11.** yes
13. $(3, 3)$ **15.** $(3, -1)$

17a. $\begin{cases} y = 2x \\ y = 16 + 0.50x \end{cases}$

b.

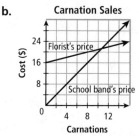

It represents how many carnations need to be sold to break even.
c. No, because the solution is not a whole number of carnations; 11 carnations. **19.** $(-2.4, -9.3)$
21. $(0.3, -0.3)$ **23.** 45 white; 120 pink **25.** 8 yr **29.** C **31.** month 11; 400

6-2

Check It Out! 1a. $(-2, 1)$
1b. $(0, 2)$ **1c.** $(3, -10)$ **2.** $(-1, 6)$
3. 10 months; $860; the first option; the first option is cheaper for the first 9 months; the second option is cheaper after 10 months.

Exercises 1. $(9, 35)$ **3.** $(3, 8)$
5. $(-3, -9)$ **7a.** 3 months; $136
b. Green Lawn **9.** $(-4, 2)$
11. $(-1, 2)$ **13.** $(1, 5)$
15. $(3, -2)$ **17.** 6 months; $360; the second option **19.** $(2, -2)$
21. $(8, 6)$ **23.** $(-9, -14.8)$
25. 12 nickels; 8 dimes

27. $\begin{cases} x + y = 1000 \\ 0.05x + 0.06y = 58 \end{cases}$; $200 at 5%; $800 at 6%

29. $x = 60°$; $y = 30°$

35. Possible estimate: $(1.75, -2.5)$; $(1.8, -2.4)$ **37.** F **39.** $r = 5$; $s = -2$; $t = 4$ **41.** $a = 9$; $b = 5$; $c = 0$

6-3

Check It Out! 1. $(-2, 4)$ **2.** $(4, 1)$ **3a.** $(2, 0)$ **3b.** $(3, 4)$ **4.** 9 lilies; 4 tulips

Exercises 1. $(-4, 1)$ **3.** $(-2, -4)$ **5.** $(-6, 30)$ **7.** $(3, 2)$ **9.** $(4, -3)$ **11.** $(-1, -2)$ **13.** $(1, 5)$ **15.** $\left(6, -\frac{1}{2}\right)$ **17.** $(-1, 2)$ **19.** $(-1, 2)$

21. $\begin{cases} \ell - w = 2 \\ 2\ell + 2w = 40 \end{cases}$; length: 11 units; width: 9 units

25. $(3, 3)$ **27.** $\left(\frac{46}{7}, \frac{8}{7}\right)$ **29.** $\left(\frac{15}{7}, \frac{9}{7}\right)$

31a. $\begin{cases} 3A + 2B = 16 \\ 2A + 3B = 14 \end{cases}$ **b.** $A = 4$; $B = 2$
c. Buying the first package will save $8; buying the second package will save $7. **33.** A **35a.** s = number of student tickets; n = number of nonstudent tickets;
$\begin{cases} s + n = 358 \\ 1.50s + 3.25n = 752.25 \end{cases}$
b. $s = 235$; $n = 123$; 235 student tickets, 123 nonstudent tickets

7-1

Check It Out! 1. Possible answer: Substitute $-2x + 5$ for y in the second equation: $2x + (-2x + 5) = 1$; $5 = 1$ ✗ **2.** Possible answer: Substitute $x - 3$ for y in the second equation: $x - (x - 3) - 3 = 0$; $3 - 3 = 0$; $0 = 0$ ✔
3a. consistent, dependent; infinitely many solutions
3b. consistent, independent; one solution **3c.** inconsistent; no solution **4.** Yes; the graphs of the two equations have different slopes so they intersect.

Exercises 1. consistent **3.** Possible answer: Substitute $-3x + 2$ for y in the first equation: $3x + (-3x + 2) = 6$; $2 = 6$ ✗ **5.** Possible answer: Substitute $-x + 3$ for y in the

second equation: $x + (-x + 3) - 3 = 0$; $0 = 0$ ✔ **7.** Possible answer: Add the two equations:
$-7x + y = -2$
$+7x - y = \underline{\quad 2}$
$0 + 0 = 0$
$\quad 0 = 0$ ✔

9. inconsistent; no solutions
11. yes **13.** Possible answer: Substitute $-x - 1$ for y in the first equation: $x + (-x - 1) = 3$; $-1 = 3$ ✗ **15.** Possible answer: Compare slopes and intercepts. $-6 + y = 2x \rightarrow y = 2x - 6$; $y = 2x - 36$; the lines have the same slope and different y-intercepts. Therefore the lines are parallel. **17.** Possible answer: Substitute $x - 2$ for y in the second equation: $x - (x - 2) - 2 = 0$; $2 - 2 = 0$; $0 = 0$ ✔
19. Possible answer: Compare slopes and intercepts. $-9x - 3y = -18 \rightarrow y = -3x + 6$; $3x + y = 6 \rightarrow y = -3x + 6$; the lines have the same slope and the same y-intercepts. Therefore the graphs are one line. **21.** consistent, independent; one solution **23.** Yes; the graphs of the two equations have different slopes, so they intersect. **27.** They will always have the same number; both started with 2 and add 4 every year. **29.** The graph will be 2 parallel lines. **31.** A **33.** D
35. $p = q$; $p \neq q$

7-2

Check It Out! 1a. no **1b.** yes
2a.

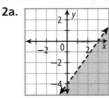

2b.

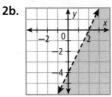

2c.

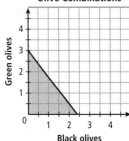

3a. $2.5b + 2g \leq 6$

3b.

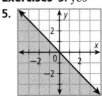

Olive Combinations

3c. Possible answer: (1 lb black, 1 lb green), (0.5 lb black, 2 lb green)
4a. $y < -x$ **4b.** $y \geq -2x - 3$

Exercises 3. yes
5.

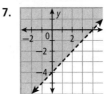

7.

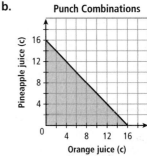

9a. $r + p \leq 16$
b.

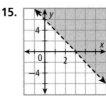

Punch Combinations

c. Possible answer: (2 c orange, 2 c pineapple), (4 c orange, 10 c pineapple) **11.** $y \geq x + 5$ **13.** yes

15.

19a. $3x + 2y \leq 30$

b.

Food Combinations

Hot dogs (lb) vs *Hamburger meat (lb)*

c. Possible answer: (3 lb hamburger, 2 lb hot dogs), (5 lb hamburger, 6 lb hot dogs) **21.** $y \leq -\frac{1}{5}x + 3$

23.

25.

29.

31.

33.

35.

37. $7a + 4s \geq 280$ **41.** A **43.** B **45.** C

47.

49. $y \geq \frac{1}{2}x + 3$

7-3

Check It Out! **1a.** yes **1b.** no

2a.

Possible answer: solutions: $(3, 3)$, $(4, 4)$; not solutions: $(-3, 1)$, $(-1, -4)$

2b.

Possible answer: solutions: $(0, 0)$, $(3, -2)$; not solutions: $(4, 4)$, $(1, -6)$

3a.

no solutions

3b.

all points between and on the parallel lines

3c.

same as solutions of $y > -2x + 3$

4.

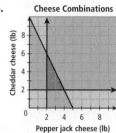

Cheese Combinations

Cheddar cheese (lb) vs *Pepper jack cheese (lb)*

Possible answer: (3 lb pepper jack, 2 lb cheddar), (2.5 lb pepper jack, 4 lb cheddar)

Exercises **1.** all **3.** yes

5.

Possible answer: solutions: $(3, 3)$, $(4, 3)$; not solutions: $(0, 0)$, $(2, 1)$

7.

Possible answer: solutions: $(0, 4)$, $(1, 4)$; not solutions: $(2, -1)$, $(3, 1)$

9.

no solutions

11.

all points between the parallel lines and on the solid line

13.

same solutions as $y > 2x - 1$

15.

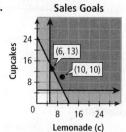

Sales Goals

Cupcakes vs *Lemonade (c)*

(6, 13) (10, 10)

Possible answer: (6 lemonade, 13 cupcakes), (10 lemonade, 10 cupcakes) **17.** yes

19.

Possible answer: solutions: $(-2, 0)$, $(-3, 1)$; not solutions: $(0, 0)$, $(1, 4)$

21.

Possible answer: solutions: $(-1, 3)$, $(0, 5)$; not solutions: $(0, 0)$, $(1, 4)$

23.

no solutions

25.

All points are solutions.

27.

same solutions as $y > 2$

29.

Possible answer:
$\big(0$ h at pharmacy, 9 h babysitting$\big)$,
$\big(8.5$ h at pharmacy, 10 h babysitting$\big)$

31.

33.

35. $\begin{cases} y > x + 1 \\ y < x + 3 \end{cases}$

37. $\begin{cases} y < 2 \\ x \geq -2 \end{cases}$

39. Student B **45.** G

47. about 12 square units

49.

8-1

Check It Out! 1. C
2a. discrete;

Keyboarding

2b. continuous;

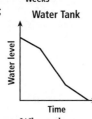
Water Tank

3. Possible answer: When the number of students reaches a certain point, the number of pizzas bought increases.

Exercises 1. continuous **3.** B
5. C **11.** A **13.** continuous **19.** The point of intersection represents the time of day when you will be the same distance from the base of the mountain on both the hike up and the hike down. **23.** C

8-2

Check It Out! 1.

x	y
1	3
2	4
3	5

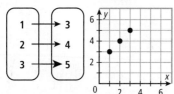

2a. D: $\{6, 5, 2, 1\}$; R: $\{-4, -1, 0\}$
2b. D: $\{1, 4, 8\}$; R: $\{1, 4\}$
3a. D: $\{-6, -4, 1, 8\}$; R: $\{1, 2, 9\}$; yes; each domain value is paired with exactly one range value.
3b. D: $\{2, 3, 4\}$; R: $\{-5, -4, -3\}$; no; the domain value 2 is paired with both -5 and -4.

Exercises

3.

x	y
1	1
1	2

5.

x	y
-7	7
-3	3
-1	1
5	-5

7. D: $\{-5, 0, 2, 5\}$; R: $\{-20, -8, 0, 7\}$ **9.** D: $\{2, 3, 5, 6, 8\}$; R: $\{4, 9, 25, 36, 81\}$ **11.** D: $\{1\}$; R: $\{-2, 0, 3, 8\}$; no **13.** D: $\{-2, -1, 0, 1, 2\}$; R: $\{1\}$; yes

15.

x	y
-2	-4
-1	-1
0	0
1	-1
2	-4

17. D: $\{3\}$; R: $1 \le y \le 5$
19. D: $-2 \le x \le 2$; R: $0 \le y \le 2$; yes **21.** yes **23.** yes **25.** yes
27. no **29a.** D: $0 \le t \le 5$; R: $0 \le v \le 750$ **b.** yes **c.** $(2, 300)$; $(3.5, 525)$
33. G **35a.** $\{(-3, 5), (-1, 7), (0, 9), (1, 11), (3, 13)\}$ **b.** D: $\{-3, -1, 0, 1, 3\}$; R: $\{5, 7, 9, 11, 13\}$ **c.** yes
37. all real numbers

8-3

Check It Out! 1. $y = 3x$
2a. independent: time; dependent: cost **2b.** independent: pounds; dependent: cost **3a.** independent: pounds; dependent: cost; $f(x) = 1.69x$ **3b.** independent: people; dependent: cost; $f(x) = 6 + 29.99x$
4a. 1; -7 **4b.** -5; 101 **5.** $f(x) = 500x$; D: $\{0, 1, 2, 3\}$; R: $\{0, 500, 1000, 1500\}$

Exercises 1. dependent
3. $y = x - 2$ **5.** independent: size of bottle; dependent: cost of water
7. independent: hours; dependent: cost; $f(h) = 75h$ **9.** 2; 9 **11.** -1; -15
13. $y = -2x$ **15.** independent: size of lawn; dependent: cost
17. independent: days late; dependent: total cost; $f(x) = 3.99 + 0.99x$ **19.** independent: gallons of gas; dependent: miles; $f(x) = 28x$

21. 7; 10 **23.** $f(n) = 2n + 5$; D: $\{1, 2, 3, 4\}$; R: $\{\$7, \$9, \$11, \$13\}$
25.

z	1	2	3	4
g(z)	-3	-1	1	3

27. $f(-6.89) \approx -16$; $f(1.01) \approx 8$; $f(4.67) \approx 20$ **33.** D **35.** 3.5
37. 44.1 m

9-1

Check It Out! 1a.

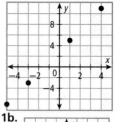

1b.

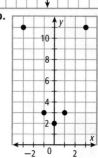

2a.

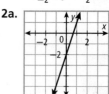

2b.

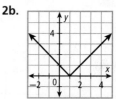

3. $x = 3$ **4.** Possible answer: about 32.5 mi

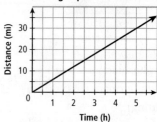
Average Speed of Lava Flow

Exercises

1.
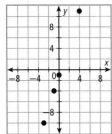

3.
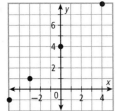

5.

7.
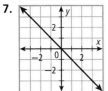

9.
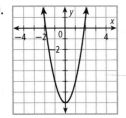

11. $y = -1$

13.
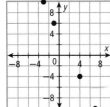

15.
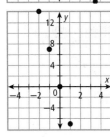

17.
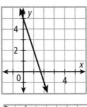

19.

21.
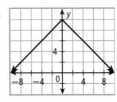

23.
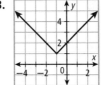

25. $y = 5$

29.
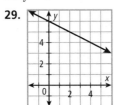

31.

33.

35.

37. $x = 1$ **39.** $y = -8$ **41.** yes; yes **43.** no; yes **45.** no; yes; yes

47. yes; no; yes **55a.** $v = 10,000 - 1500h$ **b.** 8500 gal

c.

Time (h)	Volume (gal)
0	10,000
1	8,500
2	7,000
3	5,500
4	4,000

59. J **61.** J **63.** $y = 4x + 64$

9-2

Check It Out!

1a. $(3, 3)$ **b.** $(-2, 1)$

2a.

$x + 3$	x	y
1	-2	4
2	-1	0
3	x	2
5	x	2

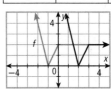

b.

x	y	$-y$
-2	4	-4
-1	0	x
x	2	-2
x	2	-2

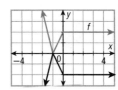

3.

x	y	$2y$
-1	3	6
0	0	0
2	2	4
4	2	4

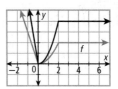

4. vertical compression by a factor of $\frac{3}{4}$

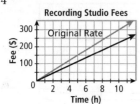
Recording Studio Fees

Exercises 1. compression
3. $(4, -1)$

5.
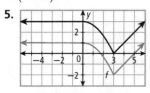

7.
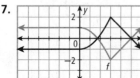

9.
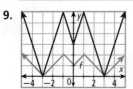

11. vertical compression by a factor of $\frac{1}{2}$ **13.** horizontal shift right 5 units **15.** $(3, 5)$

17.
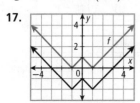

21.
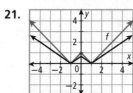

25. vertical shift down 5 units
27. horizontal stretch by a factor of 2 **29.** 10 square units; the same as the original **31.** 7 square units; smaller than the original
33. 10 square units; the same as the original **35.** 30 square units; larger than the original
37a. vertical translation
b. horizontal compression

c. the increase in the per-hour labor rate

39.
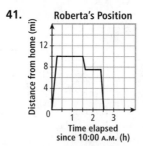
Roberta's Position

41.
Roberta's Position
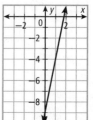

43. The library is half as far from Roberta's house. **47.** H
49. H **53a.** $c(n) = 0.37n$
b. vertical stretch **c.** 15 in 1999 and 13 in 2002 **d.** The number of letters that can be mailed for $5.00 must be rounded down to the nearest whole number.

9-3

Check It Out! 1a. yes; $\frac{1}{2}, \frac{5}{4}, \frac{7}{4}, \frac{9}{4}$
1b. no **2a.** -343 **2b.** 19.6 **3.** 750 lb

Exercises 1. common difference
3. yes; -0.7; $-0.7, -1.4, -2.1$
5. no **7.** -53 **9.** no **11.** yes; -9; $-58, -67, -76$ **13.** 5.9 **15.** 9500 mi **17.** $\frac{1}{4}$ **19.** -2.2 **21.** 0.07
23. $-\frac{3}{8}, -\frac{1}{2}, -\frac{5}{8}, -\frac{3}{4}$ **25.** $-0.2, -0.7, -1.2, -1.7$ **27.** $-0.3, -0.1, 0.1, 0.3$ **29.** 22 **31.** 122 **33b.** $9, $11, $13, $15; $a_n = 2n + 7$ **c.** $37
d. no **35.** -104.5 **37.** $\frac{20}{3}$ **39a.** $a_n = 6 + 3(n - 1)$ **b.** 48 **c.** $7800 **d.** $a_n = 7 + 3(n - 1)$; $8200

41a.

Time Interval	Mile Marker
1	520
2	509
3	498
4	487
5	476
6	465

b. $a_n = 520 + (n - 1)(-11)$
c. number of miles per interval
d. 421 **43.** F **45.** 173 and 182; 20th and 21st terms **47a.** session 16; yes
b. Thursday

10-1

Check It Out! 1a. Yes; each domain value is paired with exactly one range value; yes **1b.** Yes; each domain value is paired with exactly one range value; yes **1c.** No; each domain value is not paired with exactly one range value.
2. Yes; a constant change of $+2$ in x corresponds to a constant change of -1 in y.
3a. yes

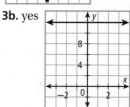

3b. yes

3c. no
4.
Rental Payment

D: {0, 1, 2, 3, …}
R: {$10, $13, $16, $19, …}

Exercises 1. No; it is not in the form $Ax + By = C$. **3.** yes; yes
5. yes **7.** yes **9.** yes **11.** no **15.** yes; no **17.** yes; no **19.** yes **23.** no
27. yes; yes **29.** yes; yes
31. yes; $-4x + y = 2$; $A = -4$; $B = 1$; $C = 2$ **33.** no **35.** yes; $x = 7$; $A = 1$; $B = 0$; $C = 7$ **37.** yes; $3x - y = 1$; $A = 3$; $B = -1$; $C = 1$ **39.** yes; $5x - 2y = -3$; $A = 5$, $B = -2$, $C = -3$ **41.** no **55.** no **57.** C
63. not linear

10-2

Check It Out! 1a. x-intercept: -2; y-intercept: 3 **1b.** x-intercept: -10; y-intercept: 6 **1c.** x-intercept: 4; y-intercept: 8

2a. School Store Purchases

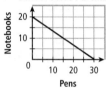

x-intercept: 30; y-intercept: 20
2b. x-intercept: number of pens that can be purchased if no notebooks are purchased; y-intercept: number of notebooks that can be purchased if no pens are purchased

3a.

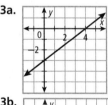

3b.

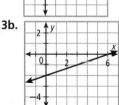

Exercises 1. y-intercept
3. x-intercept: 2; y-intercept: -4
5. x-intercept: 2; y-intercept: -1
7. x-intercept: 2; y-intercept: 8
13. x-intercept: -1; y-intercept: 3
15. x-intercept: -4; y-intercept: 2
17. x-intercept: -4; y-intercept: 2
19. x-intercept: 2; y-intercept: 8

21. x-intercept: $\frac{1}{8}$; y-intercept: -1
35. A **37.** B **41.** F **47.** x-intercept: 950; y-intercept: -55

10-3

Check It Out! 1. day 1 to day 6: -53; day 6 to day 16: -7.5; day 16 to day 22: 0; day 22 to day 30: -4.375; from day 1 to day 6

2. Bank Balance

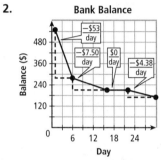

3. $-\frac{2}{5}$ **4a.** undefined **4b.** 0
5a. undefined **5b.** positive

Exercises 1. constant **5.** $-\frac{3}{4}$
7. undefined **9.** undefined
11. positive **15.** 1 **17.** 0
19. positive **23.** $\frac{17}{18}$ **29.** C **31.** G

10-4

Check It Out! 1a. $m = 0$ **1b.** $m = 3$
1c. $m = 2$ **2a.** $m = \frac{1}{2}$ **2b.** $m = -3$
2c. $m = 2$ **2d.** $m = -\frac{3}{2}$ **3.** $m = \frac{1}{2}$; the height of the plant is increasing at a rate of 1 cm every 2 days.
4. $m = -\frac{2}{3}$

Exercises 1. 1 **3.** $-\frac{1}{2}$ **5.** 10 **7.** $\frac{1}{540}$
9. $-\frac{5}{9}$ **11.** -4 **13.** undefined
15. $-\frac{3}{4}$ **17.** $-\frac{9}{5000}$ **19.** $-\frac{13}{5}$
23a. Car 1; 20 mi/h **b.** The speed and the slope are both equal to the distance divided by time. **c.** 20 mi/h
25a. $y = 220 - x$ **27.** G **29.** $-\frac{b}{u}$
31. $\frac{3}{2} - y$ **33.** $x = \frac{1}{2}$ **35.** $x = -3$
37. $x = 0$

11-1

Check It Out! 1a. no **1b.** yes; $-\frac{3}{4}$
1c. yes; -3 **2a.** No; possible answer: the value of $\frac{y}{x}$ is not the same for each ordered pair. **2b.** Yes; possible answer: the value of $\frac{y}{x}$ is the same for each ordered pair.
2c. No; possible answer: the value

of $\frac{y}{x}$ is not the same for each ordered pair. **3.** 90

4. $y = 4x$ Perimeter of a Square

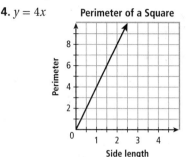

Exercises 1. direct variation
3. yes; -4 **5.** no **7.** 18 **9.** $y = 7x$
11. yes; $\frac{1}{4}$ **13.** yes **15.** -16
17. $y = 2.50x$ **19.** no **21.** $y = -3x$

The value of k is -3, and the graph shows that the slope of the line is -3.
25. $y = 2x$

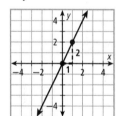

The value of k is 2, and the graph shows that the slope of the line is 2.
29. $y = -\frac{2}{9}x$

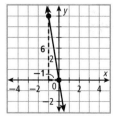

The value of k is $-\frac{2}{9}$, and the graph shows that the slope of the line is $-\frac{2}{9}$.
33. $y = -6x$

The value of k is -6, and the graph shows that the slope of the line is -6. **41.** C **43.** B

11-2

Check It Out!

1a.

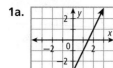

1b.

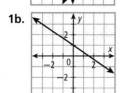

2a. $y = -12x - \frac{1}{2}$ **2b.** $y = x$
2c. $y = 8x - 25$
3a. $y = \frac{2}{3}x$

3b. $y = -3x + 5$

3c. $y = -4$

4a. $y = 18x + 200$ **4b.** slope: 18; cost per person; y-intercept: 200; fee **4c.** $3800

Exercises

1.

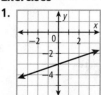

5. $y = x - 2$ **7.** $y = -3$

9. $y = -2x - 1$ **11.** $y = 3x - 1$
13a. $y = 18x + 10$ **b.** slope: 18; Helen's speed; y-intercept: 10; distance she has already biked
c. 46 mi

15.

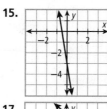

17.

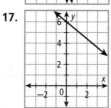

19. $y = 5x - 9$ **21.** $y = -\frac{1}{2}x + 7$
23. $y = \frac{1}{2}x + 4$ **25.** $y = -2x + 8$
29. possible **31.** impossible
33. C **37.** B **39.** B **41.** $y = \frac{1}{3}x - 3$
43. -6

11-3

Check It Out!
1a. $y - 1 = 2\left(x - \frac{1}{2}\right)$
1b. $y + 4 = 0(x - 3)$

2a.

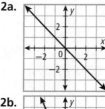

2b.

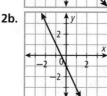

3a. $y = \frac{1}{3}x + 2$ **3b.** $y = 6x - 8$
4. x-intercept: -3; y-intercept: 9
5. $y = 2.25x + 6$; $53.25

Exercises 1. $y + 6 = \frac{1}{5}(x - 2)$
3. $y + 7 = 0(x - 3)$ **7.** $y = -\frac{1}{3}x + 7$
9. $y = -x$ **11.** $y = -\frac{1}{2}x + 4$
13. x-intercept: 3; y-intercept: -3
15. x-intercept: -1; y-intercept: 3
17. $y - 5 = \frac{2}{9}(x + 1)$ **19.** $y - 8 =$
$8(x - 1)$ **23.** $y = -\frac{2}{7}x + 1$ **25.** $y =$
$-6x + 57$ **27.** $y = -\frac{11}{2}x + 18$
29. $y = 2x - 6$ **31.** x-intercept: 1;
y-intercept: -2 **33.** x-intercept: -6;

y-intercept: 9 **35.** $y = -\frac{1}{500}x + 212$;
200 °F **41.** never **43a.** $y - 11 = 2.5$
$(x - 2)$ **b.** 6 in. **c.** $16\frac{5}{8}$ in.
47. $y = -8$; $x = 4$ **49.** A **53a.** (0, 12)
and (6, 8) **b.** $y = -\frac{2}{3}x + 12$
c. 18 min **55.** H **57.** $y = -3x + \frac{11}{4}$

11-4

Check It Out!
1a. $g(x) = 3(x - 2) + 1$
b. $g(x) = -(x + 2)$
2. $g(x) = \frac{1}{4}(3x + 2)$

3. $g(x) = \frac{1}{2}(x + 8)$
4a. $S(n) = 25n - 75$
b.

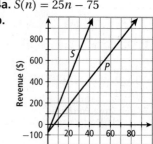

4c. horizontal compression by a factor of $\frac{1}{2}$

Exercises 1. $g(x) = -\frac{3}{2}x + 2$

3. $g(x) = x - 6$

5. $g(x) = \frac{2}{3}x - 6$
7a. $D(n) = 0.60n + 5.00$
b.

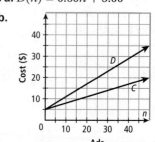

c. horizontal compression by a factor of $\frac{1}{2}$

9. $g(x) = \frac{1}{2}x - 4$
11. $g(x) = 1.2(-0.5x + 0.5)$
13. $g(x) = \frac{1}{2.75}(x + 1)$

15a. $g(x) = 0.15x + 0.35$

b.

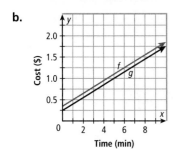

c. vertical shift up 0.1 unit
17. $g(x) = 2x$
19. $T(n) = 0.10\left(\dfrac{n}{15}\right) = \dfrac{n}{150}$; vertical stretch by a factor of 1.6
21a. $g(x) = -x - 2$
b. $h(x) = -x + 2$
23a. 22.125; 20; 23; 59 **b.** Mean, median, and mode are increased by 7. Range stays the same.
c. All are multiplied by 4.
d. Mean, median, and mode are multiplied by 2, and 5 is added. Range is multiplied by 2. **25.** H

27. F

12-1

Check It Out! 1a. 80, −160, 320
1b. 216, 162, 121.5 **2.** 7.8125
3. $1342.18

Exercises 3. 25, 12.5, 6.25
5. 1,000,000,000 **7.** 4 **9.** 162, 243, 364.5 **11.** 2058; 14,406; 100,842
13. $\dfrac{5}{32}, \dfrac{5}{128}, \dfrac{5}{512}$ **15.** 0.0000000001, or 1×10^{-10} **17.** 80; 160 **19.** $\dfrac{1}{3}$ **21.** $\dfrac{1}{7}; \dfrac{1}{49}$
23. 6; −48 **25.** 4913 **27.** yes; $\dfrac{1}{3}$ **29.** no
31. no **33a.** 1.28 cm **b.** 40.96 cm
35. −2, −8, −32, −128
37. 2, 4, 8, 16 **39.** 12, 3, $\dfrac{3}{4}, \dfrac{3}{16}$
43a. $3993; $4392.30 **b.** 1.1
c. $2727.27 **45.** J **47.** x^4, x^5, x^6
49. 1, y, y^2 **51.** −400 **53.** the 7th term

12-2

Check It Out! 1. 3.375 in. **2a.** no
2b. yes

3a.

3b.

4a.

4b.

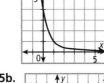

5a.

5b.

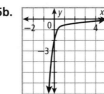

6. after about 13 yr

Exercises 1. no **3.** no **17.** about 2023 **19.** 289 ft **21.** yes **23.** no
35. $y = 4.8(2)^x$ **41.** −0.125
43a. $2000 **b.** 8% **c.** $2938.66
45. C **45.** C **47.** D **49.** 3 **51.** The value of a is the y-intercept.

12-3

Check It Out! 1. $y = 1200(1.08)^t$; $1904.25 **2a.** $A = 1200(1.00875)^{4t}$; $1379.49 **2b.** $A = 4000(1.0025)^{12t}$; $5083.47 **3.** $y = 48,000(0.97)^t$; 38,783
4a. 1.5625 mg **4b.** 0.78125 g

Exercises 1. exponential growth
3. $y = 300(1.08)^t$; 441 **5.** $A = 4200(1.007)^{4t}$; $4965.43 **7.** $y = 10(0.84)^t$; 4.98 mg **9.** 5.5 g **11.** $y = 1600(1.03)^t$; 2150 **13.** $A = 30(1.078)^t$; 47 members **15.** $A = 7000(1.0075)^{4t}$; $9438.44 **17.** $A = 12,000(1.026)^t$; $17,635.66 **19.** $y = 58(0.9)^t$; $24.97

21. growth; 61% **23.** decay; $33\frac{1}{3}$%
25. growth; 10% **27.** growth; 25%
29. $y = 58,000,000(1.001)^t$;
58,174,174 **31.** $y = 8200(0.98)^t$;
$7118.63 **33.** $y = 970(1.012)^t$; 1030
35. B **37.** 18 yr **39.** A; B **45.** D **47.** D
49. about 20 yr **51.** 100 min, or 1 h 40 min **53.** $225,344

13-1

Check It Out!

1a.

exponential

1b.

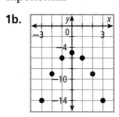

quadratic
2. quadratic **3.** The oven temperature decreases by 50 °F every 10 min; $y = -5x + 375$; 75 °F

Exercises 1. exponential
3. linear **5.** exponential **7.** Grapes cost $1.79/lb; $y = 1.79x$; $10.74
11. linear **13.** exponential
15. $\ell = 6k$; linear **17.** linear
19. $y = 0.2(4)^x$ **21.** linear **27.** C
29. C

13-2

Check It Out! 1. Slope: Dave is saving at a higher rate ($12/wk) than Arturo ($8/wk); y-int.: Dave started with more money ($30) than Arturo ($24). **2.** A increased about $1.67/yr; B increased about $1.13/yr. **3.** A: $y = 100x + 850$; B: $y = 850(1.08)^x$; school A's enrollment will exceed school B's enrollment at first, but school B will have more students by the end of the 11th year. After that, school B's enrollment exceeds school A's enrollment by ever-increasing amounts each year.

Exercises **1.** Slope: Kara is withdrawing at a higher rate ($75/wk) than Fay ($50/wk); y-int.: Kara started with more money ($500) than Fay ($425). **3.** Plan A will result in more bicycles at first, but plan B surpasses plan A by the end of the 8th year. After that, B exceeds A by ever-increasing amounts each year. **5. A:** 6.3 people per square mile; **B:** about 5.25 people per square mile **7a.** about 120 **b.** $5

13-2 Extension

Check It Out!

1.

x	−2	−1	0	1	2
$j(x)$	$\frac{1}{16}$	$\frac{1}{8}$	$\frac{1}{4}$	$\frac{1}{2}$	1

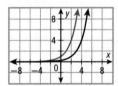

$y = 0$; $j(x) = 2^x$ translation 2 units right

2a.

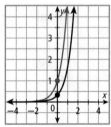

$\frac{1}{3}$; $y = 0$; $f(x) = 5^x$ vertical compression by a factor of 3

b.

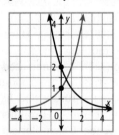

2; $y = 0$; $j(x) = 2^x$ reflection across y-axis and vertical stretch by a factor of 2

Exercises

1.

x	−2	−1	0	1	2
$g(x)$	2.1	2.3	3	5	11

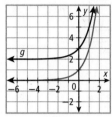

$y = 2$; translation 2 units up; R: $\{y \mid y > 2\}$

3.

x	−3	−2	−1	0	1
$j(x)$	0.11	0.33	1	3	9

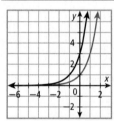

$y = 0$; translation 1 unit left

5. $\frac{1}{3}$; $y = 0$; vertical compression by a factor of $\frac{1}{3}$

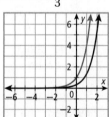

7. −2; $y = 0$; vertical stretch by a factor of 2 and reflection across the x-axis; R: $\{y \mid y < 0\}$

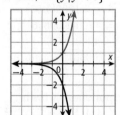

9. 1; $y = 0$; horizontal compression by a factor of $\frac{1}{2}$

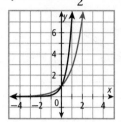

11.

x	−2	−1	0	1	2
$h(x)$	1	5	25	125	625

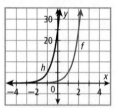

$y = 0$; translation 2 units left

13. 4; $y = 0$; vertical stretch by a factor of 4 **15.** −0.25; $y = 0$; vertical compression by a factor of 0.25 and reflection across the x-axis; R: $\{y \mid y < 0\}$ **17.** 4; $y = 0$; vertical stretch by a factor of 4 and reflection across the y-axis

14-1

Check It Out! 1a. bread
1b. cheese and mayonnaise
2. 2001, 2002, and 2005; about
13,000 **3.** about 18 °F **4.** Prices
increased from January through
July or August, and then prices
decreased through November.
5. 31.25%
6.

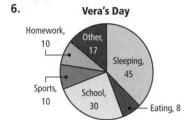

Vera's Day

Homework, 10; Other, 17; Sleeping, 45; Sports, 10; School, 30; Eating, 8

A circle graph shows parts of a
whole.

Exercises 1. one part of a whole
3. 82 animals **5.** $15 **7.** Prices at
stadium A are greater than prices at
stadium B. **9.** between weeks 4 and
5 **11.** 18% **13.** purple **15.** blue and
green **17.** 225,000 **19.** Friday
21. 3.5 times **23.** games 3, 4, and 5
25. Stock Y changed the most
between April and July of 2004.
27. $8\frac{1}{3}$% **31.** double line **33.** circle
35a. Greece; about 40% **b.** United
States; about 15% **37.** D **41.** 19
girls

14-2

Check It Out!

1.

Temperature (°C)

Stem	Leaves
0	7
1	9
2	2 3 6 7 9
3	0 1 1 2 4 5 6 6

Key: 1|9 means 19

2.

Interval	Frequency
4–6	5
7–9	4
10–12	4
13–15	2

3.

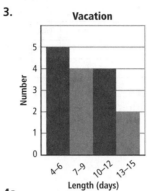

Vacation

Number vs. Length (days)

4a.

Interval	Frequency	Cumulative Frequency
28–31	2	2
32–35	7	9
36–39	5	14
40–43	3	17

4b. 9

Exercises 1. stem-and-leaf plot
3.

Austin	Stem	New York
9 9 9	1	
4 3 2 1	2	
6 5 3 2 0	3	1 3 3 3 6 6 7 9
	4	1 1 2 2

5.

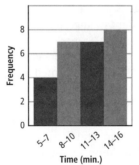

Breathing Intervals

Frequency vs. Time (min.)

7.

Summer	Stem	Winter
	0	4 9 9
	1	1 2 3 4 9 9
9 7 / 6 5 5 3 3 2 2	2	1 7
	3	0 3 5
	4	
9 7 4 3	5	

Key: |2|1 means 21
7|2| means 27

9.

Interval	Frequency
2.0–2.4	2
2.5–2.9	7
3.0–3.4	5
3.5–3.9	3

11a.

Interval	Frequency	Cumulative Frequency
36–38	4	4
39–41	6	10
42–44	5	15
45–47	1	16

b. 10

15a.

Interval	Frequency
160–169.9	2
170–179.9	4
180–189.9	3
190–199.9	1
200–209.9	2
210–219.9	1

19. G **21.** 8; 8; 41; 66

14-3

Check It Out!

1.

	Fiction	Nonfiction	Total
Hardcover	0.133	0.248	0.381
Paperback	0.448	0.171	0.619
Total	0.581	0.419	1

2a.

		Ballet		
		Yes	No	Total
Tap	**Yes**	0.19	0.26	0.45
	No	0.43	0.12	0.55
	Total	0.62	0.38	1

b. 0.69 or 69%

3. Al's Driving has the best pass
rate, about 64%, versus 61% for
Drive Time and 50% for Crash
Course.

Exercises 1. marginal

3.

	Under-classmates	Upper-classmates	Total
Morning	0.16	0.28	0.44
Afternoon	0.36	0.2	0.56
Total	0.52	0.48	1

5a.

Play Sport

Play instrument		Yes	No	Total
	Yes	0.23	0.19	0.42
	No	0.25	0.33	0.58
	Total	0.48	0.52	1

b. 0.55

c. 0.48

7.

	Students	Adults	Total
T-Shirts	0.267	0.383	0.65
Sweatshirts	0.117	0.233	0.35
Total	0.384	0.616	1

9a.

	Satisfied	Dissatisfied	Total
Team 1	0.17	0.07	0.24
Team 2	0.29	0.1	0.39
Team 3	0.29	0.08	0.37
Total	0.75	0.25	1

b. Team 1: 0.71; Team 2: 0.74; Team 3: 0.78

c. Team 3 has the highest rate of customer satisfaction.

11. Maria made an error; Possible answer: You can tell because the four relative frequencies have a sum of 1.1, rather than 1.

13a.

Work less than 5 miles from home?

Use new system?		Yes	No	Total
	Yes	0.2	0.27	0.47
	No	0.37	0.17	0.54
	Total	0.57	0.44	1

b. 0.35

c. 0.57

15. C

17.

	Yes	No	Total
Children	0.125	0.1	0.225
Teenagers	0.725	0.05	0.775
Total	0.85	0.15	1

19. 10 children

21. 0

14-4

Check It Out! 1. mean: 14 lb; median: 14 lb; modes: 12 lb and 16 lb; range: 4 lb **2.** 3; the outlier decreases the mean by 3.7 and increases the range by 18. It has no effect on the median and mode. **3a.** mode: 7 **3b.** Median: 81; the median is greater than either the mean or the mode.

4.

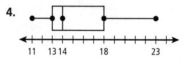

5a. The data set for 2000; the distance between the points for the least and greatest values is less for 2000 than for 2007. **5b.** about $40 million

Exercises 3. mean: 31.5; median: 33.5; mode: 44; range: 32 **5.** mean: 78.25; median: 78; mode: 78; range: 15 **7.** 13; the outlier decreases the mean by 11.15 and the median by 4. It increases the range by 51 and has no effect on the mode. **9.** Median: 83; the median is greater than the mean, and there is no mode. **13.** Simon; about 3000 points **15.** mean: 2.5; median: 2.5; modes: 2 and 3; range: 3 **17.** mean: 60; median: 60; mode: 60; range: 5 **19.** 23; the outlier increases the mean by 3, the median by 2.5, and the range by 15. It has no effect on the mode. **21.** Mean: 153; the mean is greater than the median, and there is no mode. **25.** Sneaks R Us; the middle half of the data doesn't vary as much at Sneaks R Us as at Jump N Run. **27.** mean: 5.5; median: 5.5; mode: none; range: 9 **29.** mean: 3.5; median: 3.4; mode: none; range: 5.3

31. mean: 24.4; median: 25; modes: 23 and 25; range: 3 **33.** mean: $15\frac{1}{6}$; median: $12\frac{1}{2}$; mode: none; range: 35 **37.** sometimes **39.** always **41.** Median; the mean is affected by the outlier of 1218, and there is no mode. **43.** Median or mode; the store wants their prices to seem low, and the median and mode are both $2.80 less than the mean. **49.** Mean: $32,000; median: $25,000; median; the outlier of $78,000 increases the mean significantly. **51.** 96 **53.** increase the mean; decrease the mean **55.** G **57.** The mean decreases by 6.6 lb.

15-1

Check It Out!

1. Football Team Score

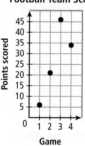

2. positive **3a.** No correlation; the temperature in Houston has nothing to do with the number of cars sold in Boston. **3b.** Positive; as the number of family members increases, more food is needed, so the grocery bill increases too. **3c.** Negative; as the number of times you sharpen your pencil increases, the length of the pencil decreases. **4.** Graph A; it cannot be graph B because graph B shows negative minutes; it cannot be graph C because graph C shows the temperature of the pie increasing, a positive correlation. **5.** about 75 rolls

Exercises 3. no **5.** positive **7.** negative **9.** positive **11.** A **15.** positive **17.** positive **19.** A **23.** positive **25.** B

27a.

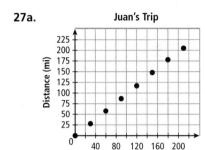

Juan's Trip

b. positive **29.** C

15-2

Check It Out! 1. $y = -\frac{1}{2}x + 6$:
16; $y = -x + 8$: 30; $y = -\frac{1}{2}x + 6$ is
better. **2a.** $y < 0.04x + 6.38$
2b. slope: cost is \$0.04/yd; y-int.:
\$6.38 is added to the cost of every
ball of yarn. **2c.** \$46.38
3. $y < -2.74x + 84.32$; very well
($r < -0.88$) **4.** strong positive
correlation; likely cause-and-effect
(more education often contributes
to higher earnings)

Exercises 1. residual **3.** $y = x +$
1: 19; $y = x - 1$: 23; $y = x + 1$ is
better. **5.** $y < -0.53x + 8.8$; very
well ($y < -0.91$) **7.** $y = -x + 8$: 7;
$y = -\frac{1}{2}x + 6$: 9; $y = -x + 8$ is
better. **9.** $y < 0.2x + 2$; very well
($r < 0.94$) **13a.** $y < 0.48x + 12.03$
13b. A player will score 0.48 run for
every hit. **13c.** A player with no hits
will score 12.03 runs. **13d.** There
is a strong correlation between the
number of hits and the number
of runs, since the correlation
cofficient is $r < 0.84$. **13e.** <60 runs
15a. $y < 115.36x + 1065$; $r < 0.96$
15b. Slope: each year there will
be 115.36 more visitors than the
previous year; y-intercept: there
were 1065 visitors in year 0.
15c. yes; $r < 0.96$, which is very
close to 1. **15d.** No; the passage of
time likely does not cause changes
in the number of visitors. **17.** B
19a. 1000

15-2 Extension

Check It Out!
1a. yes; 1.5 **b.** no
2. $B(t) \approx 199(1.25)^t$; ≈ 10.3 min

Exercises
1. no **3.** no
5. $T(t) \approx 131(0.92)^t$; ≈ 13.6 min
7. no **9.** yes; $\frac{1}{2}$
11. $T(t) \approx 4.45(1.165)^t$; ≈ 2011
13. yes; $f(x) = 2(0.5)^x$
15. $r(d) \approx 10.99(0.9995)^d$; 1.40 per
100 cows

16-1

Check It Out! 1a. translation; $MNOP \rightarrow M'N'O'P'$ **1b.** rotation; $\triangle XYZ \rightarrow \triangle X'Y'Z'$ **2.** rotation; 90° **3.** $J'(-1, -5)$; $K'(1, 5)$; $L'(1, 0)$; $M'(-1, 0)$ **4.** $(x, y) \rightarrow (x - 4, y - 4)$

Exercises 1. Preimage is $\triangle XYZ$; image is $\triangle X'Y'Z'$ **3.** reflection; $\triangle ABC \rightarrow \triangle A'B'C'$ **5.** reflection across the y-axis **7.** $(x, y) \rightarrow (x + 4, y + 4)$ **9.** reflection; $WXYZ \rightarrow W'X'Y'Z'$ **11.** $A'(-1, -1)$, $B'(4, -1)$, $C'(4, -4)$, $D'(-1, -4)$ **13.** reflection **15.** reflection

17.
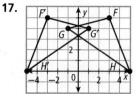

19. B **21.** D **23.** $R'(-1, -12)$; $S'(-3, -9)$; $T'(-7, -7)$

25.
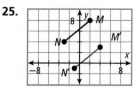

29. A **31.** A **33a.** $R''(1, 0)$; $S''(0, 3)$; $T''(4, 3)$ **b.** $(x, y) \rightarrow (x + 3, y + 2)$

35.
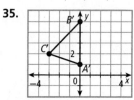

37. $(-x, y)$

16-2

Check It Out! 1a. no **1b.** yes

2.

3. $\overline{AX}$ and $\overline{BX}$ would be $\cong$.

4.
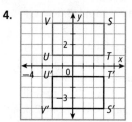

Exercises 1. They are $\cong$. **3.** no **5.** no

7.
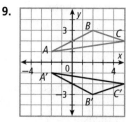

9.
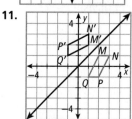

11.
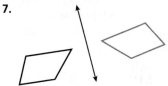

13. no **15.** yes

17.
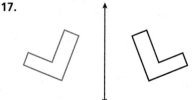

19.
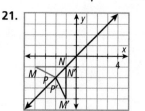

21.

23.

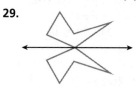

27.

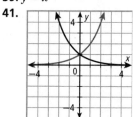

R-(+)-limonene $\quad$ S-(−)-limonene

29.

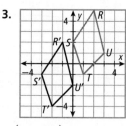

31. $(5, 2) \rightarrow (5, -2)$ **33.** $(0, 12) \rightarrow (0, -12)$ **35.** $(0, -5) \rightarrow (-5, 0)$ **37a.** no **b.** $(7, 4)$ **c.** $(6, 3.5)$ **39.** $y = x$

41.

43. A **45.** C **47.** $(5, 2)$

16-3

Check It Out! 1a. Yes **1b.** no

2.

$\vec{w}$

3.

4. $(16, -24)$

SA18

Selected Answers ▪ Unit 5

Exercises 1. no **3.** yes

7.
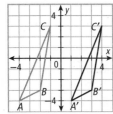

9.
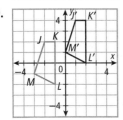

11. yes **13.** no

17.
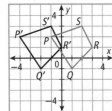

19.
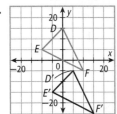

21.
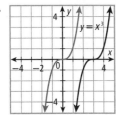

23a. $\frac{1}{4}$ **b.** $\frac{1}{2}$. **c.** 0 **27.** No; there are no fixed pts. because, by def. of a translation, every pt. must move by the same distance.
29. $\langle 4, 0 \rangle$, $(-3, 2) \rightarrow (1, 2)$
31. $\langle -3, -2 \rangle$, $(3, -1) \rightarrow (0, -3)$
33. $\langle -3, 1 \rangle$, $(3, -1) \rightarrow (0, 0)$
37. G **39.** $(0, 0)$ and $(2, 4)$

16-4

Check It Out! 1a. no **1b.** yes

2.
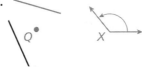

3a.
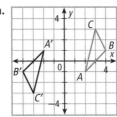

3b. $(-59, 34)$

Exercises 1. yes **3.** no

5.
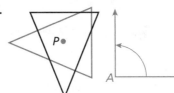

7.
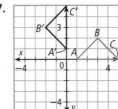

9.
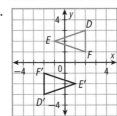

11. no **13.** yes
15.

17.
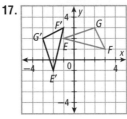

19.
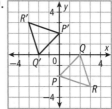

21. $(-10, 50)$
25a. 180°
b. $(-3, 2)$
27. M
29. $\overrightarrow{NP}$
35a. Possible answer: about 45°
b. Draw $\overrightarrow{AP}$ and $\overrightarrow{AQ}$ and use the protractor to measure $\angle AQA$.
c. 50°
37. $A'(3, 2)$, $B'(0, 3)$, $C'(3, 0)$, $D'(0, -3)$, $E'(3, -2)$
41. H
43. 160°; clockwise; gear B has 8 teeth, so one complete rotation of gear B in the counterclockwise direction will move gear A by 8 teeth in the clockwise direction. Gear A has 18 teeth, so 8 teeth is $\frac{4}{9}$ of a complete rotation, or $\frac{4}{9}(360°) = 160°$.

17-1

Check It Out!

1.
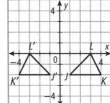

2. a translation in direction $\perp$ to n and p, by distance of 6 in.

3.
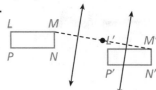

Exercises 1. Draw a figure and translate it along a vector. Then reflect the image across a line.

3.

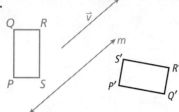

5. a rotation of 100° about the pt. of intersection of the lines

7.

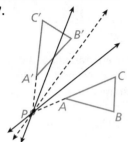

9.

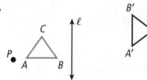

11a. The move is a horiz. or vert. translation by 2 spaces followed by a vert. or horiz. translation by 1 space.

11b.

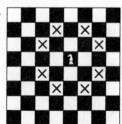

11c.

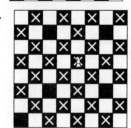

13.

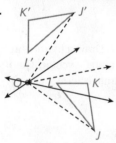

17. never **19.** always **23.** A

---

25. C

17-2

Check It Out!
1a. yes; 2 lines of symmetry

1b. yes; 1 line of symmetry

1c. yes; 1 line of symmetry

2a. yes; 120°; order: 3 **2b.** yes; 180°; order: 2° **2c.** no
3a. line symmetry and rotational symmetry; 72°; order: 5

3b. line symmetry and rotational symmetry; 51.4°; order: 7
4a. both **4b.** neither

Exercises 1. The line of symmetry is the ⊥ bisector of the base.
3. yes; 2 lines of symmetry
5. no **7.** no
9. 72°; order: 5
11. both
13. yes; 1 line of symmetry
15. no **17.** yes; 72°; order: 5
19. 90; order: 4 **21.** neither
23. isosc. **25.** scalene **27.** 0

---

29. line symmetry

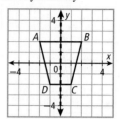

31. line symmetry

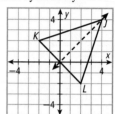

33. rotational symmetry of order 4
35. line symmetry; $x = 2$ **37a.** no
b. yes; 180°; 2. **c.** Yes; if color is not taken into account the ∠ of rotational symmetry is 90.
39. parallelogram **41.** square
43. 15° **45.** It has rotational symmetry of order 3, with an ∠ of rotational symmetry of 120°.
47.

49.

51. A **53.** C **55.** 72 **57.** 13
59. 13

17-3

Check It Out! 1a. translation symmetry **1b.** translation symmetry and glide reflection symmetry

2.

3a. regular **3b.** neither.
3c. semiregular
4a. yes

4b. no

Exercises 3. translation symmetry and glide reflection symmetry
5. translation symmetry and glide reflection symmetry **9.** regular
11. semiregular
13. yes; possible answer

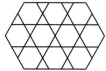

15. translation symmetry
17. translation symmetry
19.
21. neither **23.** neither **25.** no
27. translation symmetry and glide reflection symmetry
29. translation, glide reflection, rotation **31.** always **33.** always
35. never **41.** The tessellation has translation symmetry, reflection symmetry, and order 3 rotation symmetry.

43. $CH_2 - CH$
$|$
CH_3

47. H **51.** yes

18-1

Check It Out! **1a.** $y = 2x + 2$ and $y = 2x + 1$ **1b.** $y = 3x$ and $y - 1 = 3(x + 2)$

2. slope of $\overline{AB} = 0$; slope of $\overline{BC} = \frac{5}{3}$; slope of $\overline{CD} = 0$; slope of $\overline{AD} = \frac{5}{3}$; $\overline{AB}$ is parallel to $\overline{CD}$ because they have the same slope. $\overline{AD}$ is parallel to $\overline{BC}$ because they have the same slope. Since opposite sides are parallel, $ABCD$ is a parallelogram. **3.** $y = -4$ and $x = 3$; $y - 6 = 5(x + 4)$ and $y = -\frac{1}{5}x + 2$
4. slope of $\overline{PQ} = 2$; slope of $\overline{QR} = -1$; slope of $\overline{PR} = -\frac{1}{2}$; $\overline{PQ}$ is perpendicular to $\overline{PR}$ because the product of their slopes is -1. Since PQR contains a right angle, PQR is a right triangle. **5a.** $y = \frac{4}{5}x + 3$
5b. $y = -\frac{1}{5}x + 2$

Exercises **1.** parallel **3.** $y = \frac{3}{4}x - 1$ and $y - 3 = \frac{3}{4}(x - 5)$ **5.** $y = \frac{2}{3}x - 4$ and $y = -\frac{3}{2}x + 2$; $y = -1$ and $x = 3$
9. $x = 7$ and $x = -9$; $y = -\frac{5}{6}x + 8$ and $y = -\frac{5}{6}x - 4$ **11.** $y = -3x + 2$ and $3x + y = 27$; $y = \frac{1}{2}x - 1$ and $-x + 2y = 17$ **13.** $y = 6x$ and $y = -\frac{1}{6}x$; $y = \frac{1}{6}x$ and $y = -6x$ **15.** $x - 6y = 15$ and $y = -6x - 8$; $y = 3x - 2$ and $3y = -x - 11$ **17.** $y = -\frac{6}{7}x$ **19.** neither
21. parallel **23.** $y = \frac{1}{2}x - 5$
25. $y = 2x + 5$ **27.** $y = 3x + 13$
29. $y = -x + 5$ **31.** $y = 4x - 23$
33. $y = -\frac{3}{4}x$ **35.** $y = -x + 1$
37. $y = \frac{2}{5}x - \frac{31}{5}$ **39.** $y = -\frac{1}{5}x - \frac{11}{5}$
41. $y = -\frac{1}{2}x - \frac{1}{2}$ **43.** $y = \frac{1}{2}x + 6$
45. $y = x - 3$ **47.** $y = -4$ **51a.** $y = 50x$ **b.** $y = 50x + 30$ **53.** H **57.** $-\frac{1}{5}$

18-2

Check It Out! **1.** $\left(\frac{3}{2}, 0\right)$ **2.** $(4, 3)$
3. 6.71 **4.** 17.7 mi
Exercises **3.** $\left(1\frac{1}{2}, -4\right)$ **5.** $(3, 3)$
7. 5.39 **9.** 10.82 **11.** $(-2, -3)$
13. $(17, -23)$ **15.** $(2, -8)$ **17.** 8.94
19. 9.22 **21.** 6.1 mi **25.** 13.42
27. 14.32 **29a.** 7.2 **b.** $(0, -2)$ **c.** 23
31. $\overline{CD}, \overline{EF}, \overline{AB}$ **35.** B **37.** D
39. 12.5 square units **41.** ± 8
43. 26

Selected Answers ▪ Unit 7

19-1

Check It Out! 1a. $3\frac{1}{2}$ **1b.** $4\frac{1}{2}$
3a. $1\frac{2}{3}$ **3b.** 24 **4.** 591.25 m
5. $RS = 4$; $ST = 4$; $RT = 8$

Exercises 1. $\overline{XM}$ and $\overline{MY}$ **3.** 3.5
7. 29 **9.** $x = 4$; $KL = 7$; $JL = 14$
11. $5\frac{11}{12}$ **15.** 5 **17.** $DE = EF = 14$; DF
$= 28$ **19a.** C is the mdpt. of $\overline{AE}$.
b. 16 **21.** 7.1 **23.** 4 **25.** S
27. Statement A **29.** 6.5; -1.5
31. 3.375 **33.** 9 **37.** J **39.** H

41.

43. 14.02 m

19-2

Check It Out! 1. $\angle RTQ$, $\angle T$,
$\angle STR$, $\angle 1$, $\angle 2$ **2a.** 40°; acute
2b. 125°; obtuse **2c.** 105°; obtuse
3. 62° **4a.** 34° **4b.** 46°

Exercises 1. $\angle A$, $\angle R$, $\angle O$
3. $\angle AOB$, $\angle BOA$, or $\angle 1$; $\angle BOC$,
$\angle COB$, or $\angle 2$; $\angle AOC$ or $\angle COA$
5. 105°; obtuse **7.** 70° **9.** 28°
11. $\angle 1$ or $\angle JMK$; $\angle 2$ or $\angle LMK$;
$\angle M$ or $\angle JML$ **13.** 93°; obtuse
15. 66.6° **17.** 20° **19.** acute
21. acute **27.** 67.5°; 22.5° **29.** $16\frac{1}{3}$
31. 9 **33a.** 9 **b.** 12 **c.** $0 < x < 15.6$
35. $m\angle COD = 72°$; $m\angle BOC = 90°$
37. No; an obtuse $\angle$ measures
greater than 90°, so it cannot be $\cong$
to an acute $\angle$ (less than 90°).
41. D **43.** C **45.** The $\triangle$ are acute.
An obtuse $\angle$ measures between 90°
and 180°. Since $\frac{1}{2}$ of 180 is 90, the
resulting $\triangle$ must measure less than
90°. **47.** 36° or 4° **49.** 8100

19-3

Check It Out! 1. 0.0004 **2.** odd
3. Female whales are longer than
male whales. **4a.** Possible answer: x
$= \frac{1}{2}$ **4b.** Possible answer:

4c. Jupiter or Saturn

Exercises 3. $\frac{4}{6}$ **5.** even
7. The number of bacteria doubles
every 20 minutes. **9.** The 3 pts. are
collinear. **11.** 5 P.M.

13.

15. $n - 1$ **17.** Possible answer:
$y = -1$ **19.** $m\angle 1 = m\angle 2 = 90°$
21. Possible answer: each term is
the previous term multiplied
by $\frac{1}{2}$; $\frac{1}{16}$; $\frac{1}{32}$. **23.** $2n + 1$ **25.** F
27. T **29.** $\frac{1}{11} = 0.\overline{09}$, $\frac{2}{11} = 0.\overline{18}$, $\frac{3}{11}$
$= 0.\overline{27}$,...; the fraction pattern is
multiples of $\frac{1}{11}$, and the decimal
pattern is repeating multiples of
0.09. **31.** 34, 55, 89; each term is
the sum of the 2 previous terms.
33. odd **37.** C **39.** D **41.** 12 years
43. $m\angle CAB = m\angle CBA$; $AC = CB$

19-4

Check It Out! 1. Hypothesis:
A number is divisible by 6.
Conclusion: A number is divisible
by 3. **2.** If 2 $\triangle$ are comp., then they
are acute. **3.** F; possible answer: 7
4. Converse: If an animal has
4 paws, then it is a cat; F. Inverse: If
an animal is not a cat, then it does
not have 4 paws; F. Contrapositive:
If an animal does not have 4 paws,
then it is not a cat; T.

Exercises 1. converse
3. Hypothesis: A person is at least
16 years old. Conclusion: A person
can drive a car. **5.** Hypothesis:
$a - b < a$. Conclusion: b is a
positive number. **7.** If $0 < a < b$,
then $\left(\frac{a}{b}\right)^2 < \frac{a}{b}$. **9.** T **11.** F
13. Hypothesis: An animal is a
tabby. Conclusion: An animal is a
cat. **15.** Hypothesis: 8 ounces of
cereal cost $2.99. Conclusion:
16 ounces of cereal cost $5.98.
17. If the batter makes 3 strikes,
then the batter is out. **19.** T **21.** T
25. T **27.** F **29.** F **35.** If a person
is a Texan, then the person is an
American. **37a.** H: Only you can
find it. C: Everything's got a moral.
b. If only you can find it, then
everything's got a moral. **43.** If a
mineral has a hardness less than 5,
then it is not apatite; T. **45.** If a
mineral is not apatite, then it is
calcite; F. **47.** If a mineral is calcite,
then it has a hardness less than 5; T.

---

51. H **53.** J **55.** Some students are
adults. Some adults are students.
57. 3

19-5

Check It Out! 1. deductive
reasoning **2.** valid **3.** valid
4. Polygon P is not a quad.

Exercises 3. deductive
reasoning **5.** valid **7.** invalid
9. deductive reasoning
11. invalid **13.** Dakota gets better
grades in Social Studies.
15. valid **17.** valid **19.** yes; no;
because the first conditional is false
23. D **25.** 196 **27a.** If you live in
San Diego, then you live in the
United States. **b.** If you do not live
in California, then you do not live
in San Diego. If you do not live in
the United States, then you do not
live in California. **c.** If you do not
live in the United States, then you
do not live in San Diego. **d.** They
are contrapositives of each other.

20-1

Check It Out! 1a. Conditional: If
an $\angle$ is acute, then its measure is
greater than 0° and less than 90°.
Converse: If an $\angle$'s measure is
greater than 0° and less than 90°,
then the $\angle$ is acute.
1b. Conditional: If Cho is a
member, then he has paid the
$5 dues. Converse: If Cho has paid
the $5 dues, then he is a member.
2a. Converse: If it is Independence
Day, then the date is July 4th.
Biconditional: It is July 4th if and
only if it is Independence Day.
2b. Converse: If pts. are collinear,
then they lie on the same line.
Biconditional: Pts. lie on the
same line if and only if they are
collinear. **3a.** T **3b.** F; $y = 5$
4a. A figure is a quad. if and only
if it is a 4-sided polygon. **4b.** An
$\angle$ is a straight $\angle$ if and only if its
measure is 180°.

Exercises 3. Conditional: If
your medicine will be ready by

---

5 P.M. , then you dropped your prescription off by 8 A.M. Converse: If you drop your prescription off by 8 A.M. , then your medicine will be ready by 5 P.M. **5.** Converse: If 2 segs. are ≅, then they have the same length. Biconditional: 2 segs. have the same length if and only if they are ≅. **7.** F **9.** An animal is a hummingbird if and only if it is a tiny, brightly colored bird with narrow wings, a slender bill, and a long tongue. **11.** Conditional: If a ▭ is a rect., then it has 4 rt. ∡. Converse: If a ▭ has 4 rt. ∡, then it is a rect. **13.** Converse: If it is the weekend, then today is Saturday or Sunday. Biconditional: Today is Saturday or Sunday if and only if it is the weekend. **15.** Converse: If a △ is a rt. △, then it contains a rt. ∠. Biconditional: A △ contains a rt. ∠ if and only if it is a rt. △. **17.** T **19.** A player is a catcher if and only if the player is positioned behind home plate and catches throws from the pitcher. **21.** yes **23.** no **25.** A square is a quad. with 4 ≅ sides and 4 rt. ∡. **31.** no **33.** 5 **37a.** If I say it, then I mean it. If I mean it, then I say it. **39.** G **43a.** If an ∠ does not measure 105°, then the ∠ is not obtuse. **b.** If an ∠ is not obtuse, then it does not measure 105°. **c.** It is the contrapositive of the original. **d.** F; the inverse is false, and its converse is true.

20-2

Check It Out! 1. $\frac{1}{2}t = -7$ (Given); $2\left(\frac{1}{2}t\right) = 2(-7)$ (Mult. Prop. of =); $t = -14$ (Simplify.) **2.** $C = \frac{5}{9}(F - 32)$ (Given); $C = \frac{5}{9}(86 - 32)$ (Subst.); $C = \frac{5}{9}(54)$ (Simplify.); $C = 30$ (Simplify.) **3.** ∠ Add. Post.; Subst.; Simplify.; Subtr. Prop. of =; Mult. Prop. of = **4a.** Sym. Prop. of = **4b.** Reflex. Prop. of = **4c.** Trans. Prop. of = **4d.** Sym. Prop. of ≅

Exercises 3. $t - 3.2 = -8.3$ (Given); $t = -5.1$ (Add. Prop. of =) **5.** $\frac{x+3}{-2} = 8$ (Given); $x + 3 = -16$ (Mult. Prop.

of =); $x = -19$ (Subtr. Prop. of =) **7.** $0 = 2(r - 3) + 4$ (Given); $0 = 2r - 6 + 4$ (Distrib. Prop.); $0 = 2r - 2$ (Simplify.); $2 = 2r$ (Add. Prop. of =); $1 = r$ (Div. Prop. of =) **9.** $C = \$5.75 + \$0.89m$ (Given); $\$11.98 = \$5.75 + \$0.89m$ (Subst.); $\$6.23 = \$0.89m$ (Subtr. Prop. of =); $m = 7$ (Div. Prop. of =) **11.** Seg. Add. Post.; Subst.; Subtr. Prop. of =; Add. Prop. of =; Div. Prop. of = **13.** Trans. Prop. of = **15.** Trans. Prop. of ≅ **17.** $1.6 = 3.2n$ (Given); $0.5 = n$ (Div. Prop. of =) **19.** $-(h + 3) = 72$ (Given); $-h - 3 = 72$ (Distrib. Prop.); $-h = 75$ (Add. Prop. of =); $h = -75$ (Mult. Prop. of =) **21.** $\frac{1}{2}(p - 16) = 13$ (Given); $\frac{1}{2}p - 8 = 13$ (Distrib. Prop.); $\frac{1}{2}p = 21$ (Add. Prop. of =); $p = 42$ (Mult. Prop. of =) **23.** ∠ Add. Post.; Subst.; Simplify.; Subtr. Prop. of =; Add. Prop. of =; Div. Prop. of = **25.** Sym. Prop. of ≅ **27.** Trans. Prop. of = **29.** $x = 16$; $2(3.1x - 0.87) = 94.36$ (Given); $6.2x - 1.74 = 94.36$ (Distrib. Prop.); $6.2x = 96.1$ (Add. Prop. of =); $x = 15.5$ (Div. Prop. of =); possible answer: the exact solution rounds to the estimate. **31.** $\angle A \cong \angle T$ **33.** $\frac{x+1}{2} = 3$ (Mdpt. Formula;) $x + 1 = 6$ (Mult. Prop. of =); $x = 5$ (Subtr. Prop. of =); $\frac{1+y}{2} = 5$ (Mdpt. Formula); $1 + y = 10$ (Mult. Prop. of =); $y = 9$ (Subtr. Prop. of =) **35a.** $1733.65 = 92.50 + 79.96 + 983 + 10,820x$ (Given); $1733.65 = 1155.46 + 10,820x$ (Simplify.); $578.19 = 10,820x$ (Subtr. Prop. of =); $0.05 \approx x$ (Div. Prop. of =) **b.** \$1.71 **37a.** $x + 15 \leq 63$ (Given); $x \leq 48$ (Subtr. Prop. of Inequal.) **b.** $-2x > 36$ (Given); $x < -18$ (Div. Prop. of Inequal.) **39.** B **41.** D **43.** $PR = PA + RA$ (Seg. Add. Post.); $PA = QB, QB = RA$ (Given); $PA = RA$ (Trans. Prop. of =); $PR = PA + PA$ (Subst.); $PA = 18$(Given); $PR = 18 + 18$ (Subst.); $PR = 36$ in. (Simplify.) **45.** $7 - 3x > 19$ (Given); $-3x > 12$ (Subtr. Prop. of Inequal.); $x < -4$ (Div. Prop. of Inequal.)

20-3

Check It Out!
1. 1. Given
2. Def. of mdpt.
3. Given
4. Trans. Prop. of ≅

2a. ∠1 and ∠2 are supp., and ∠2 and ∠3 are supp. **2b.** m∠1 + m∠2 = m∠2 + m∠3 **2c.** Subtr. Prop. of = **2d.** ∠1 ≅ ∠3

3. 1. ∠1 and ∠2 are comp. ∠2 and ∠3 are comp. (Given)
2. m∠1 + m∠2 = 90°, m∠2 + m∠3 = 90° (Def. of comp. ∡)
3. m∠1 + m∠2 = m∠2 + m∠3 (Subst.)
4. m∠2 = m∠2 (Reflex. Prop. of =)
5. m∠1 = m∠3 (Subtr. Prop. of =)
6. ∠1 ≅ ∠3 (Def. of ≅ ∡)

Exercises 1. statements; reasons

3. 1. Given
2. Subst.
3. Simplify.
4. Add. Prop. of =
5. Simplify.
6. Def. of supp. ∡

5. 1. X is the mdpt. of $\overline{AY}$. Y is the mdpt. of $\overline{XB}$. (Given)
2. $\overline{AX} \cong \overline{XY}, \overline{XY} \cong \overline{YB}$ (Def. of mdpt.)
3. $\overline{AX} \cong \overline{YB}$ (Trans. Prop. of ≅)
7a. m∠1 + m∠2 = 180°, m∠3 + m∠4 = 180° **b.** Subst. **c.** m∠1 = m∠4 **d.** Def. of ≅ ∡

9. 1. $\overline{BE} \cong \overline{CE}, \overline{DE} \cong \overline{AE}$ (Given)
2. $BE = CE, DE = AE$ (Def. of ≅ segs.)
3. $AE + BE = AB, CE + DE = CD$ (Seg. Add. Post.)
4. $DE + CE = AB$ (Subst.)
5. $AB = CD$ (Subst.)
6. $\overline{AB} \cong \overline{CD}$ (Def. of ≅ segs.)
11. 132° **13.** 59° **17.** S **19.** N
21. $x = 16$ **25.** C **27.** D **29.** $a = 17$; 37.5°, 52.5°, and 37.5°

20-4

Check It Out!
1. 1. $RS = UV, ST = TU$ (Given)
2. $RS + ST = TU + UV$ (Add. Prop. of =)

3. $RS + ST = RT$, $TU + UV = TV$ (Seg. Add. Post.)
4. $RT = TV$ (Subst.)
5. $\overline{RT} \cong \overline{TV}$ (Def. of $\cong$ segs.)

2.

3. 1. $\angle WXY$ is a rt. $\angle$. (Given)
2. $m\angle WXY = 90°$ (Def. of rt. $\angle$)
3. $m\angle 2 + m\angle 3 = m\angle WXY$ ($\angle$ Add. Post.)
4. $m\angle 2 + m\angle 3 = 90°$ (Subst.)
5. $\angle 1 \cong \angle 3$ (Given)
6. $m\angle 1 = m\angle 3$ (Def. of $\cong$ $\angle$)
7. $m\angle 2 + m\angle 1 = 90°$ (Subst.)
8. $\angle 1$ and $\angle 2$ are comp. (Def. of comp. $\angle$)

4. It is given that $\angle 1 \cong \angle 4$. By the Vert. $\angle$ Thm., $\angle 1 \cong \angle 2$ and $\angle 3 \cong \angle 4$. By the Trans. Prop. of $\cong$, $\angle 2 \cong \angle 4$. Similarly, $\angle 2 \cong \angle 3$.

Exercises 1. flowchart
3. 1. $\angle 1 \cong \angle 2$ (Given)
2. $\angle 1$ and $\angle 2$ are supp. (Lin. Pair Thm.)
3. $\angle 1$ and $\angle 2$ are rt. $\angle$. ($\cong$ $\angle$ supp. $\rightarrow$ rt. $\angle$)
5. 1. $\angle 2 \cong \angle 4$ (Given)
2. $\angle 1 \cong \angle 2$, $\angle 3 \cong \angle 4$ (Vert. $\angle$ Thm.)
3. $\angle 1 \cong \angle 4$ (Trans. Prop. of $\cong$)
4. $\angle 1 \cong \angle 3$ (Trans. Prop. of $\cong$)
7. 1. B is the mdpt. of $\overline{AC}$. (Given)
2. $\overline{AB} \cong \overline{BC}$ (Def. of mdpt.)
3. $AB = BC$ (Def. of $\cong$ segs.)
4. $AD + DB = AB$, $BE + EC = BC$ (Seg. Add. Post.)
5. $AD + DB = BE + EC$ (Subst.)
6. $AD = EC$ (Given)
7. $DB = BE$ (Subtr. Prop. of $=$)
9. 1. $\angle 1 \cong \angle 4$ (Given)
2. $\angle 1 \cong \angle 2$ (Vert. $\angle$ Thm.)
3. $\angle 4 \cong \angle 2$ (Trans. Prop. of $\cong$)
4. $m\angle 4 = m\angle 2$ (Def. of $\cong$ $\angle$)
5. $\angle 3$ and $\angle 4$ are supp. (Lin. Pair Thm.)

6. $m\angle 3 + m\angle 4 = 180°$ (Def. of supp. $\angle$)
7. $m\angle 3 + m\angle 2 = 180°$ (Subst.)
8. $\angle 2$ and $\angle 3$ are supp. (Def. of supp. $\angle$)
11. 13 cm; conv. of the Common Segs. Thm. **13.** 37°, Vert. $\angle$ Thm.
15. $y = 11$ **17.** A **21.** C **23.** D
25. 1. $\angle AOC \cong \angle BOD$ (Given)
2. $m\angle AOC = m\angle BOD$ (Def. of $\cong$ $\angle$)
3. $m\angle AOB + m\angle BOC = m\angle AOC$, $m\angle BOC + m\angle COD = m\angle BOD$ ($\angle$ Add. Post.)
4. $m\angle AOB + m\angle BOC = m\angle BOC + m\angle COD$ (Subst.)
5. $m\angle BOC = m\angle BOC$ (Reflex. Prop. of $=$)
6. $m\angle AOB = m\angle COD$ (Subtr. Prop. of $=$)
7. $\angle AOB \cong \angle COD$ (Def. of $\cong$ $\angle$)
27. $x = 31$ and $y = 11.5$; 86°, 94°, 86°, and 94°

21-1

Check It Out! 1. $m\angle QRS = 62°$
2. $m\angle ABD = 60°$ **3.** 55° and 60°

Exercises 1. $m\angle JKL = 127°$ **3.** $m\angle 1 = 90°$ **5.** $x = 8$; $y = 9$ **7.** $m\angle VYX = 100°$ **9.** $m\angle EFG = 102°$ **11.** $m\angle STU = 90°$ **13.** 120°; Corr. $\angle$ Post.
15. 60°; Same-Side Int. $\angle$ Thm.
17. 60°; Lin. Pair Thm. **19.** 120°; Vert. $\angle$ Thm. **21.** $x = 4$; Same-Side Int. $\angle$ Thm.; $m\angle 3 = 103°$; $m\angle 4 = 77°$
23. $x = 3$; Corr. $\angle$ Post.; $m\angle 1 = m\angle 4 = 42°$ **25a.** $\angle 1 \cong \angle 3$ **b.** Corr. $\angle$ Post. **c.** $\angle 1 \cong \angle 2$ **d.** Trans. Prop. of $\cong$ **29a.** same-side int. $\angle$ **b.** By the Same-Side Int. $\angle$ Thm., $m\angle QRT + m\angle STR = 180°$. $m\angle QRT = 25° + 90° = 115°$, so $m\angle STR = 65°$.
31. A **35.** J **37.** $m\angle 1 = 75°$
39. $x = 4$; $y = 12$

21-2

Check It Out! 1a. $\angle 1 \cong \angle 3$, so $\ell \parallel m$ by the Conv. of Corr. $\angle$ Post.
1b. $m\angle 7 = 77°$ and $m\angle 5 = 77°$, so $\angle 7 \cong \angle 5$. $\ell \parallel m$ by the Conv. of Corr. $\angle$ Post. **2a.** $\angle 4 \cong \angle 8$, so $r \parallel s$ by the Conv. of Alt. Int. $\angle$ Thm.

2b. $m\angle 3 = 100°$ and $m\angle 7 = 100°$, so $\angle 3 \cong \angle 7$. $r \parallel s$ by the Conv. of Alt. Int. $\angle$ Thm.
3. 1. $\angle 1 \cong \angle 4$ (Given)
2. $m\angle 1 = m\angle 4$ (Def. $\cong$ $\angle$)
3. $\angle 3$ and $\angle 4$ are supp. (Given)
4. $m\angle 3 + m\angle 4 = 180°$ (Def. supp. $\angle$)
5. $m\angle 3 + m\angle 1 = 180°$ (Subst.)
6. $m\angle 2 = m\angle 3$ (Vert. $\angle$ Thm.)
7. $m\angle 2 + m\angle 1 = 180°$ (Subst.)
8. $\ell \parallel m$ (Conv. of Same-Side Int. $\angle$ Thm.)
4. $4y - 2 = 4(8) - 2 = 30°$; $3y + 6 = 3(8) + 6 = 30°$; The $\angle$ are $\cong$, so the oars are $\parallel$ by the Conv. of Corr. $\angle$ Post.

Exercises 1. $\angle 4 \cong \angle 5$, so $p \parallel q$ by the Conv. of Corr. $\angle$ Post. **3.** $m\angle 4 = 47°$, and $m\angle 5 = 47°$, so $\angle 4 \cong \angle 5$. $p \parallel q$ by the Conv. of Corr. $\angle$ Post.
5. $\angle 3$ and $\angle 4$ are supp., so $r \parallel s$ by the Conv. of Same-Side Int. $\angle$ Thm. **7.** $m\angle 4 = 61°$, and $m\angle 8 = 61°$, so $\angle 4 \cong \angle 8$. $r \parallel s$ by the Conv. of Alt. Int. $\angle$ Thm. **9.** $m\angle 2 = 132°$, and $m\angle 6 = 132°$, so $\angle 2 \cong \angle 6$. $r \parallel s$ by the Conv. of Alt. Ext. $\angle$ Thm. **11.** $m\angle 1 = 60°$, and $m\angle 2 = 60°$, so $\angle 1 \cong \angle 2$. By the Conv. of Alt. Int. $\angle$ Thm., the landings are $\parallel$.
13. $m\angle 4 = 54°$, and $m\angle 8 = 54°$, so $\angle 4 \cong \angle 8$. $\ell \parallel m$ by the Conv. of Corr. $\angle$ Post. **15.** $m\angle 1 = 55°$, and $m\angle 5 = 55°$, so $\angle 1 \cong \angle 5$. $\ell \parallel m$ by the Conv. of Corr. $\angle$ Post. **17.** $\angle 2 \cong \angle 7$, so $n \parallel p$ by the Conv. of Alt. Ext. $\angle$ Thm. **19.** $m\angle 1 = 105°$, and $m\angle 8 = 105°$, so $\angle 1 \cong \angle 8$. $n \parallel p$ by the Conv. of Alt. Ext. $\angle$ Thm. **21.** $m\angle 3 = 75°$, and $m\angle 5 = 105°$. $75° + 105° = 180°$, so $\angle 3$ and $\angle 5$ are supp. $n \parallel p$ by the Conv. of Same-Side Int. $\angle$ Thm. **23.** If $x = 6$, then $m\angle 1 = 20°$ and $m\angle 2 = 20°$. So $\overline{DJ} \parallel \overline{EK}$ by the Conv. of Corr. $\angle$ Post. **25.** Conv. of Alt. Ext. $\angle$ Thm. **27.** Conv. of Corr. $\angle$ Post. **29.** Conv. of Same-Side Int. $\angle$ Thm. **31.** $m \parallel n$; Conv. of Same-Side Int. $\angle$ Thm. **33.** $m \parallel n$; Conv. of Alt. Ext. $\angle$ Thm. **35.** $\ell \parallel n$; Conv. of Same-Side Int. $\angle$ Thm.

37a. ∠*URT* ; m∠*URT* = m∠*URS* + m∠*SRT* by the ∠ Add. Post. It is given that m∠*SRT* = 25° and m∠*URS* = 90°, so m∠*URT* = 25° + 90° = 115°. **b.** It is given that m∠*SUR* = 65°. From part **a,** m∠*URT* = 115°. 65° + 115° = 180°, so $\overleftrightarrow{SU} \parallel \overleftrightarrow{RT}$ by the Conv. of Same-Side Int. ⦟ Thm. **39.** It is given that ∠1 and ∠2 are supp., so m∠1 + m∠2 = 180°. By the Lin. Pair Thm., m∠2 + m∠3 = 180°. By the Trans. Prop. of =, m∠1 + m∠2 = m∠2 + m∠3. By the Subtr. Prop. of =, m∠1 = m∠3. By the Conv. of Corr. ⦟ Post., ℓ ∥ *m*. **41.** The Reflex. Prop. is not true for ∥ lines, because a line is not ∥ to itself. The Sym. Prop. is true, because if ℓ ∥ *m*, then ℓ and *m* are coplanar and do not intersect. So *m* ∥ ℓ . The Trans. Prop. is not true for ∥ lines, because if ℓ ∥ *m* and *m* ∥ *n*, then ℓ and *n* could be the same line. So they would not be ∥. **43.** C **45.** 15 **47.** No lines can be proven ∥. **49.** *q* ∥ *r* by the Conv. of Alt. Int. ⦟ Thm. **51.** *s* ∥ *t* by the Conv. of Alt. Ext. ⦟ Thm. **53.** No lines can be proven ∥. **55.** By the Vert. ⦟ Thm., ∠6 ≅ ∠3, so m∠6 = m∠3. It is given that m∠2 + m∠3 = 180°. By subst., m∠2 + m∠6 = 180°. By the Conv. of Same-Side Int. ⦟ Thm., ℓ ∥ *m*.

21-3

Check It Out! 1a. $\overline{AB}$ **1b.** *x* < 17
2. 1. ∠*EHF* ≅ ∠*HFG* (Given)
  2. $\overleftrightarrow{EH} \parallel \overleftrightarrow{FG}$ (Conv. of Alt. Int. ⦟ Thm.)
  3. $\overleftrightarrow{FG} \perp \overleftrightarrow{GH}$ (Given)
  4. $\overleftrightarrow{EH} \perp \overleftrightarrow{GH}$ (⊥ Transv. Thm.)

3. The shoreline and the path of the swimmer should both be ⊥ to the current, so they should be ∥ to each other.

Exercises 1. $\overline{AB}$ and $\overleftrightarrow{CD}$ are ⊥. $\overline{AC}$ and $\overline{BC}$ are ≅. **3.** *x* > −5
5. The service lines are coplanar lines that are ⊥ to the same line (the center line), so they must be ∥ to each other. **7.** *x* < 11 **9.** Both

the frets are lines that are ⊥ to the same line (the string), so the frets must be ∥ to each other. **11.** $x > \frac{8}{3}$
13. *x* = 6, *y* = 15 **15.** *x* = 60, *y* = 60
17. no **19.** no **21.** yes **23a.** It is given that $\overline{QR} \perp \overline{PQ}$ and $\overline{PQ} \parallel \overline{RS}$, so $\overline{QR} \perp \overline{RS}$ by the ⊥ Transv. Thm. It is given that $\overline{PS} \parallel \overline{QR}$. Since $\overline{QR}$ ⊥ $\overline{RS}$, $\overline{PS} \perp \overline{RS}$ by the ⊥ Transv. Thm. **b.** It is given that $\overline{PS} \parallel \overline{QR}$ and $\overline{QR} \perp \overline{PQ}$. So $\overline{PQ} \perp \overline{PS}$ by the ⊥ Transv. Thm.
25. Possible answer: 1.6 cm
31. C **33.** D **35a.** *n* ⊥ *p* **b.** *AB*; *AB*; the shortest distance from a point to a line is measured along a perpendicular segment. **c.** The distance between two parallel lines is the length of a segment that is perpendicular to both lines and has one endpoint on each line.

22-1

Check It Out! 1. *D*′(3, 9), *E*′(3, –6), *F*′(9, 0); dilation with scale factor 3 **2.** The triangles are congruent because △*ABC* can be mapped to △*PQR* by a rotation: (*x*, *y*) ⟶ (−*y*, *x*). **3.** The polygons are congruent because △*ABC* can be mapped to △*A*′*B*′*C*′ by a translation: (*x*, *y*) ⟶ (*x* + 5, *y* + 2); and then △*A*′*B*′*C*′ can be mapped to △*PQR* by a reflection (*x*, *y*) ⟶ (*x*, −*y*).

Exercises 1. are not **3.** *A*′(2, −1), *B*′(5, −4), *C*′(5, −1); This is a reflection across the x-axis.
5. *L*′(2, −1), *M*′(5, −4), *N*′(5, −1), *O*′(5, −1); This is a 90° rotation clockwise with a center of rotation (0, 0). **7.** The rectangles are not congruent because rectangle *ABCD* can be mapped to rectangle *WXYZ* by a dilation with scale factor *k* ≠ 1. (*x*, *y*) ⟶ (0.5*x*, 0.5*y*). **9.** The triangles are congruent because △*MNO* can be mapped to △*M*′*N*′*O*′ by a reflection: (*x*, *y*) ⟶ (−*x*, *y*). And then △*M*′*N*′*O*′ can be mapped to △*JKL* by a translation: (*x*, *y*) ⟶ (*x*, *y* + 2). **11.** Repeated horizontal reflections and horizontal

translations create the wallpaper pattern. The large flower at the top is translated right and left while the stem, leaves, smaller flowers, and background design are reflected to the left and right to create an image that is congruent to the pre-image. **13.** *G*′(9, −5), *H*′(12, −1), *I*′(12, −5); This is a translation 5 units right and 4 units down. **15.** *L*′(−1.5, 6), *M*′(−6, 6), *N*′(−6, 4.5); This is a dilation with scale factor 1.5 and center (0, 0). **17.** *N*′(0, −1), *O*′(−1, 5), *P*′(1, 5); This is a translation 1 unit left and 1 unit up. **19.** Yes, the rectangles are congruent because rectangle *JKLM* can be mapped to rectangle *ABCD* by a rotation: (*x*, *y*) ⟶ (*y*, –*x*). **21.** Yes, the triangles are congruent because △*EFG* can be mapped to △*UVW* by a translation: (*x*, *y*) ⟶ (*x*, *y* + 3). **23.** The triangles are congruent because △*ABC* can be mapped to △*A*′*B*′*C*′ by a rotation: (*x*, *y*) ⟶ (*y*, –*x*), and then △*A*′*B*′*C*′ can be mapped to △*DEF* by a translation: (*x*, *y*) ⟶ (*x* − 2, *y*). **25a.** The pattern was created with a 90° counterclockwise rotation and translation to the right and down. Then another 90° rotation clockwise and a translation right and down. This then repeats to fill the rectangular quilt area. **b.** The thin rectangles are congruent, as are the quilt block squares. **c.** The quilt would look more like a checkerboard pattern. **27.** *X*′(4, 6), *Y*′(4, −4), *Z*′(−2, 0); This is a rotation 90° clockwise about (0, 0) **29.** *A*′(2, −5), *B*′(4, −4), *C*′(−1, 2); This is a reflection across the x-axis and a translation 3 units to the right. **31.** Starting in the upper left, Frank reflected his shape horizontally. Then he rotated it 90° counterclockwise and translated it to the right and up. The he reflected it vertically. This whole row he then rotated 180° and translated down. **33.** Dave is correct because the triangle was reflected, not rotated. **35.** The dilation of the figure with a scale factor of 2 will be 4 times as large as the figure with a scale factor of 0.5. A scale factor of 2 increases the figure to twice its original size. A scale factor of 0.5 decreases the figure to half its original size. **37.** D

22-2

Check It Out! 1. 32° **2a.** 26.3° **2b.** $(90 - x)°$ **2c.** $41\frac{3}{5}°$ **3.** 141° **4.** 32°; 32°

Exercises 3. auxiliary lines **5.** 36°; 80°; 64° **7.** $(90 - y)°$ **9.** 28° **11.** 52°; 63° **13.** 89°; 89° **15.** 84° **17.** $(90 - 2x)°$ **19.** 162° **21.** 48°; 48° **23.** 15°; 60°; 105° **29.** 36° **31.** 48° **33.** 120°; 360° **35.** 18° **37.** The ext. ∡ at the same vertex of a △ are vert. ∡. Since vert. ∡ are ≅, the 2 ext. ∡ have the same measure. **41.** C **43.** D **45.** $y = 7$ or $y = -7$ **47.** Since an ext. ∠ is = to a sum of 2 remote int. ∡, it must be greater than either ∠. Therefore it cannot be ≅ to a remote int. ∠. **49.** 38°

22-3

Check It Out! 1. $\angle L \cong \angle E$, $\angle M \cong \angle F$, $\angle N \cong \angle G$, $\angle P \cong \angle H$, $\overline{LM} \cong \overline{EF}$, $\overline{MN} \cong \overline{FG}$, $\overline{NP} \cong \overline{GH}$, $\overline{LP} \cong \overline{EH}$ **2a.** 4 **2b.** 37°
3. 1. $\angle A \cong \angle D$ (Given)
2. $\angle BCA \cong \angle ECD$ (Vert. ∡ are ≅.)
3. $\angle ABC \cong \angle DEC$ (Third ∡ Thm.)
4. $\overline{AB} \cong \overline{DE}$ (Given)
5. $\overline{AD}$ bisects $\overline{BE}$, and $\overline{BE}$ bisects $\overline{AD}$. (Given)
6. $\overline{BC} \cong \overline{EC}$, $\overline{AC} \cong \overline{DC}$ (Def. of bisector)
7. $\triangle ABC \cong \triangle DEC$ (Def. of ≅ △)
4. 1. $\overline{JK} \parallel \overline{ML}$ (Given)
2. $\angle KJN \cong \angle MLN$, $\angle JKN \cong \angle LMN$ (Alt. Int. ∡ Thm.)
3. $\angle JNK \cong \angle LNM$ (Vert. ∡ Thm.)
4. $\overline{JK} \cong \overline{ML}$ (Given)
5. $\overline{MK}$ bisects $\overline{JL}$, and $\overline{JL}$ bisects $\overline{MK}$. (Given)
6. $\overline{JN} \cong \overline{LN}$, $\overline{MN} \cong \overline{KN}$ (Def. of bisector)
7. $\triangle JKN \cong \triangle MLN$ (Def. of ≅ △)

Exercises 1. You find the ∡ and sides that are in the same, or matching, places in the 2 △. **3.** $\overline{LM}$ **5.** $\angle M$ **7.** $\angle R$ **9.** $KL = 9$ **11a.** Given **b.** Alt. Int. ∡ Thm. **c.** Given **d.** Given **e.** $\overline{AE} \cong \overline{CE}$, $\overline{DE} \cong \overline{BE}$; **f.** Vert. ∡ Thm. **g.** Def. of ≅ ∡ **13.** $\overline{LM}$ **15.** $\angle N$ **17.** m∠C = 31° **19a.** Given **b.** Given **c.** $\angle NMP \cong \angle RMP$ **d.** $\angle NPM \cong \angle RPM$ **e.** Given **f.** $\overline{PN} \cong \overline{PR}$ **g.** Given **h.** Reflex. Prop. of ≅ **21.** $\triangle GSR \cong \triangle KPH$; $\triangle SRG \cong \triangle PHK$; $\triangle RGS \cong \triangle HKP$ **23.** $x = 30$; $AB = 50$ **25.** $x = 2$; $BC = 17$ **29.** solution A **31.** B **33.** D **35.** $x = 5.5$; yes; $UV = WV = 41.5$, and $UT = WT = 33$. $TV = TV$ by the Reflex. Prop. of =. It is given that $\angle VWT \cong \angle VUT$ and $\angle WTV \cong \angle UTV$. $\angle WVT \cong \angle UVT$ by the Third ∡ Thm. Thus $\triangle TUV \cong \triangle TWV$ by the def. of ≅ △.

23-1

Check It Out! 1. It is given that $\overline{AB} \cong \overline{CD}$ and $\overline{BC} \cong \overline{DA}$. By the Reflex. Prop. of ≅, $\overline{AC} \cong \overline{CA}$. So $\triangle ABC \cong \triangle CDA$ by SSS. **2.** It is given that $\overline{BA} \cong \overline{BD}$ and $\angle ABC \cong \angle DBC$. By the Reflex. Prop. of ≅, $\overline{BC} \cong \overline{BC}$. So $\triangle ABC \cong \triangle DBC$ by SAS. **3.** $DA = DC = 13$, so $\overline{DA} \cong \overline{DC}$ by def. of ≅. m∠ADB = m∠CDB = 32°, so $\angle ADB \cong \angle CDB$ by def. of ≅. $\overline{DB} \cong \overline{DB}$ by the Reflex. Prop. of ≅. Therefore $\triangle ADB \cong \triangle CDB$ by SAS.
4. 1. $\overline{QR} \cong \overline{QS}$ (Given)
2. $\overrightarrow{QP}$ bisects $\angle RQS$. (Given)
3. $\angle RQP \cong \angle SQP$ (Def. of bisector)
4. $\overline{QP} \cong \overline{QP}$ (Reflex. Prop. of ≅)
5. $\triangle RQP \cong \triangle SQP$ (SAS Steps 1, 3, 4)

Exercises 1. $\angle T$ **3.** It is given that $\overline{MN} \cong \overline{MQ}$ and $\overline{NP} \cong \overline{QP}$. $\overline{MP} \cong \overline{MP}$ by the Reflex. Prop. of ≅. Thus $\triangle MNP \cong \triangle MQP$ by SSS. **5.** When $x = 4$, $HI = GH = 3$, and $IJ = GJ = 5$. $\overline{HJ} \cong \overline{HJ}$ by the Reflex. Prop. of ≅. Therefore $\triangle GHJ \cong \triangle IHJ$ by SSS. **7a.** Given **b.** $\angle JKL \cong \angle MLK$ **c.** Reflex. Prop. of ≅

d. SAS Steps 1, 2, 3 **9.** It is given that $\overline{KJ} \cong \overline{LJ}$ and $\overline{GK} \cong \overline{GL}$. $\overline{GJ} \cong \overline{GJ}$ by the Reflex. Prop. of ≅. So $\triangle GJK \cong \triangle GJL$ by SSS. **11.** When $y = 3$, $NQ = NM = 3$, and $QP = MP = 4$. So by the def. of ≅, $\overline{NQ} \cong \overline{NM}$ and $\overline{QP} \cong \overline{MP}$. m∠M = m∠Q = 90°, so $\angle M \cong \angle Q$ by the def. of ≅. Thus $\triangle MNP \cong \triangle QNP$ by SAS. **13a.** Given **b.** $\overline{DB} \cong \overline{CB}$ **c.** $\overline{AB} \perp \overline{DC}$ **d.** Def. of ⊥ **e.** Rt. ∠ ≅ Thm. **f.** $\overline{AB} \cong \overline{AB}$ **g.** SAS Steps 2, 5, 6 **15.** SAS **17.** neither **19.** $QS = TV = \sqrt{5}$. $SR = VU = 4$. $QR = TU = \sqrt{13}$. The △ are ≅ by SSS. **21a.** Given **b.** Def. of ≅ **c.** m∠WVY = m∠ZYV **d.** Def. of ≅ **e.** Given **f.** $\overline{VY} \cong \overline{YV}$ **g.** SAS Steps 6, 5, 7 **25.** Measure the lengths of the logs. If the lengths of the logs in 1 wing deflector match the lengths of the logs in the other wing deflector, the △ will be ≅ by SAS or SSS. **27.** Yes; if each side is ≅ to the corr. side of the second △, they can be in any order. **29.** G **31.** J **35.** $x = 27$; $FK = FH = 171$, so $\overline{FK} \cong \overline{FH}$ by the def of ≅. $\angle KFJ \cong \angle HFJ$ by the def. of ∠ bisector. $\overline{FJ} = \overline{FJ}$ by the Reflex. Prop. of ≅. So $\triangle FJK \cong \triangle FJH$ by SAS.

23-2

Check It Out! 1. Yes; the △ is uniquely determined by AAS. **2.** By the Alt. Int. ∡ Thm., $\angle KLN \cong \angle MNL$. $\overline{LN} \cong \overline{LN}$ by the Reflex. Prop. of ≅. No other congruence relationships can be determined, so ASA cannot be applied. **3. Given:** $\overline{JL}$ bisects $\angle KLM$, and $\angle K \cong \angle M$. **Prove:** $\triangle JKL \cong \triangle JML$

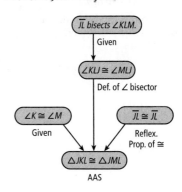

4. Yes; it is given that $\overline{AC} \cong \overline{DB}$. $\overline{CB} \cong \overline{CB}$ by the Reflex. Prop. of $\cong$. Since $\angle ABC$ and $\angle DCB$ are rt. $\angle$, $\triangle ABC$ and $\triangle DCB$ are rt. $\triangle$, $\triangle ABC \cong \triangle DCB$ by HL.

Exercises 1. The included side $\overline{BC}$ is enclosed between $\angle ABC$ and $\angle ACB$. **3.** Yes, the $\triangle$ is determined by AAS. **5.** No; you need to know that a pair of corr. sides are $\cong$. **7.** Yes; it is given that $\angle D$ and $\angle B$ are rt. $\angle$ and $\overline{AD} \cong \overline{BC}$. $\triangle ABC$ and $\triangle CDA$ are rt. $\triangle$ by def. $\overline{AC} \cong \overline{CA}$ by the Reflex. Prop. of $\cong$. So $\triangle ABC \cong \triangle CDA$ by HL.

9.

11. No; you need to know that $\angle MKJ \cong \angle MKL$. **13a.** $\angle A \cong \angle D$ **b.** Given **c.** $\angle C \cong \angle F$ **d.** AAS **15.** Yes; E is a mdpt. So by def., $\overline{BE} \cong \overline{CE}$, and $\overline{AE} \cong \overline{DE}$. $\angle A$ and $\angle D$ are $\cong$ by the Rt. $\angle$ Thm. By def. $\triangle ABE$ and $\triangle DCE$ are rt. $\triangle$. So $\triangle ABE \cong \triangle DCE$ by HL. **17.** $\triangle FEG \cong \triangle QSR$; rotation **19a.** No; there is not enough information given to use any of the congruence theorems. **b.** HL **21.** It is given that $\triangle ABC$ and $\triangle DEF$ are rt.$\triangle$. $\overline{AC} \cong \overline{DF}$, $\overline{BC} \cong \overline{EF}$, and $\angle C$ and $\angle F$ are rt. $\angle$. $\angle C \cong \angle F$ by the Rt. $\angle \cong$ Thm. Thus $\triangle ABC \cong \triangle DEF$ by SAS. **27.** J **29.** G **31.** Yes; the sum of the $\angle$ measures in each $\triangle$ must be 180°, which makes it possible to solve for x and y. The value of x is 15, and the value of y is 12. Each $\triangle$ has $\angle$ measuring 82°, 68°, and 30°. $\overline{VU} \cong \overline{VU}$ by the Reflex. Prop. of $\cong$. So $\triangle VSU \cong \triangle VTU$ by ASA or AAS.

23-3

Check It Out! 1. 41 ft

2.

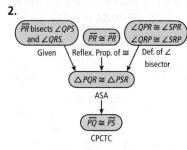

3. 1. J is the mdpt. of $\overline{KM}$ and $\overline{NL}$. (Given)
2. $\overline{KJ} \cong \overline{MJ}$, $\overline{NJ} \cong \overline{LJ}$ (Def. of mdpt.)
3. $\angle KJL \cong \angle MJN$ (Vert. $\angle$ Thm.)
4. $\triangle KJL \cong \triangle MJN$ (SAS *Steps 2, 3*)
5. $\angle LKJ \cong \angle NMJ$ (CPCTC)
6. $\overline{KL} \parallel \overline{MN}$ (Conv. of Alt. Int. $\angle$ Thm.)
4. $RJ = JL = \sqrt{5}$, $RS = JK = \sqrt{10}$, and $ST = KL = \sqrt{17}$. So $\triangle JKL \cong \triangle RST$ by SSS. $\angle JKL \cong \angle RST$ by CPCTC.

Exercises 1. corr. $\angle$ and corr. sides. **3a.** Def. of $\perp$ **b.** Rt. $\angle \cong$ Thm. **c.** Reflex. Prop. of $\cong$ **d.** Def. of mdpt. **e.** $\triangle RXS \cong \triangle RXT$ **f.** CPCTC **5.** $EF = JK = 2$ and $EG = FG = JL = KL = \sqrt{10}$. So $\triangle EFG \cong \triangle JKL$ by SSS. $\angle EFG \cong \angle JKL$ by CPCTC. **7.** 420 ft **9. 1.** $\overline{WX} \cong \overline{XY} \cong \overline{YZ} \cong \overline{ZW}$ (Given)
2. $\overline{ZX} \cong \overline{ZX}$ (Reflex. Prop. of $\cong$)
3. $\triangle WXZ \cong \triangle YZX$ (SSS)
4. $\angle W \cong \angle Y$ (CPCTC)
11. 1. $\overline{LM}$ bisects $\angle JLK$. (Given)
2. $\angle JLM \cong \angle KLM$ (Def. of $\angle$ bisector)
3. $\overline{JL} \cong \overline{KL}$ (Given)
4. $\overline{LM} \cong \overline{LM}$ (Reflex. Prop. of $\cong$)
5. $\triangle JLM \cong \triangle KLM$ (SAS *Steps 3, 2, 4*)
6. $\overline{JM} \cong \overline{KM}$ (CPCTC)
7. M is the mdpt. of $\overline{JK}$. (Def. of mdpt.)
13. $AB = DE = \sqrt{13}$, $BC = EF = 5$, and $AC = DF = \sqrt{18} = 3\sqrt{2}$. So $\triangle ABC \cong \triangle DEF$ by SSS. $\angle BAC \cong \angle EDF$ by CPCTC.
15. 1. E is the mdpt. of $\overline{AC}$ and $\overline{BD}$. (Given)
2. $\overline{AE} \cong \overline{CE}$; $\overline{BE} \cong \overline{DE}$ (Def. of mdpt.)

3. $\angle AEB \cong \angle CED$ (Vert. $\angle$ Thm.)
4. $\triangle AEB \cong \triangle CED$ (SAS *Steps 2, 3*)
5. $\angle A \cong \angle C$ (CPCTC)
6. $\overline{AB} \parallel \overline{CD}$ (Conv. of Alt. Int. $\angle$ Thm.)
17. 14 **25.** G **27.** G **29.** Any diag. on any face of the cube is the hyp. of a rt. $\triangle$ whose legs are edges of the cube. Any 2 of these $\triangle$ are $\cong$ by SAS. Therefore any 2 diags. are $\cong$ by CPCTC.

23-4

Check It Out! 1. 4.2×10^{13}; since it is 6 months between September and March, the $\angle$ measures will be the same between Earth and the star. By the Conv. of the Isosc. $\triangle$ Thm., the $\triangle$ created are isosc. and the dist. is the same. **2a.** 66° **2b.** 48° **3.** 10 **4.** By the Mdpt. Formula, the coords. of X are $(-a, b)$, the coords. of Y are (a, b), and the coords. of Z are $(0, 0)$. By the Dist. Formula, $XZ = YZ = \sqrt{a^2 + b^2}$. So $\overline{XZ} \cong \overline{YZ}$ and $\triangle XYZ$ is isosc.

Exercises 1. legs: $\overline{KJ}$ and $\overline{KL}$; base: $\overline{JL}$; base $\angle$: $\angle J$ and $\angle L$ **3.** 118° **5.** 27° **7.** $y = 5$ **9.** 20 **11.** It is given that $\triangle ABC$ is rt. isosc., $\overline{AB} \cong \overline{BC}$, and X is the mdpt. of $\overline{AC}$. By the Mdpt. Formula, the coords. of X are (a, a). By the Dist. Formula, $AX = BX = a\sqrt{2}$. So $\triangle AXB$ is isosc. by def. of an isosc. $\triangle$. **13.** 69° **15.** 130° or 172° **17.** $z = 92$ **19.** 26 **21.** It is given that $\triangle ABC$ is isosc., $\overline{AB} \cong \overline{AC}$, P is the mdpt. of $\overline{AB}$, and Q is the mdpt. of $\overline{AC}$. By the Mdpt. Formula, the coords. of P are (a, b) and the coords. of Q are $(3a, b)$. By the Dist. Formula, $PC = QB = \sqrt{9a^2 + b^2}$, so $\overline{PC} \cong \overline{QB}$ by the def of $\cong$ segs. **23.** S **25.** N **27a.** 38° **b.** $m\angle PQR = m\angle PRQ = 53°$ **29.** $m\angle 1 = 127°$; $m\angle 2 = 26.5°$; $m\angle 3 = 53°$ **33.** 20 **39. 1.** $\triangle ABC \cong \triangle CBA$ (Given)
2. $\overline{AB} \cong \overline{CB}$ (CPCTC)
3. $\triangle ABC$ is isosceles (Def. ofIsosc)

43. H **47.** $(2a, 0)$, $(0, 2b)$, or any pt. on the ⊥ bisector of $\overline{AB}$

24-1

Check It Out! 1a. 14.6 **1b.** 10.4
2a. 3.05 **2b.** 126° **3.** $\overrightarrow{QS}$ bisects $\angle PQR$. **4.** $y + 1 = -\frac{2}{3}(x - 3)$

Exercises 1. perpendicular bisector
3. 25.9 **5.** 21.9 **7.** 38° **9.** $y - 1 = x + 2$ **11.** $y - 2 = \frac{4}{3}(x + 3)$
13. 26.5 **15.** 1.3 **17.** 54° **19.** $y + 3 = -\frac{1}{2}(x + 2)$ **21.** $y + 3 = \frac{5}{2}(x - 2)$
23. 38 **25.** 38 **27.** 24 **29.** Possible answer: $C(3, 2)$
31. 1. $\overrightarrow{PS}$ bisects $\angle QPR$. $\overline{SQ} \perp \overrightarrow{PQ}$, $\overline{SR} \perp \overrightarrow{PR}$ (Given)
　2. $\angle QPS \cong \angle RPS$ (Def. of ∠ bisector)
　3. $\angle SQP$ and $\angle SRP$ are rt. ∠s. (Def. of ⊥)
　4. $\angle SQP \cong \angle SRP$ (Rt. ∠ ≅ Thm.)
　5. $\overline{PS} \cong \overline{PS}$ (Reflex. Prop. of ≅)
　6. $\triangle PQS \cong \triangle PRS$ (AAS)
　7. $\overline{SQ} \cong \overline{SR}$ (CPCTC)
　8. $SQ = SR$ (Def. of ≅ segs.)
33a. $y = -\frac{3}{4}x + 2$ **b.** 2 **c.** 6.4 mi
35. D **39.** the lines $y = x$ and $y = -x$

24-2

Check It Out! 1a. 14.5 **1b.** 18.6
1c. 19.9 **2.** $(4, -4.5)$ **3a.** 19.2
3b. 52°

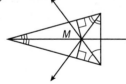

4. By the Incenter Thm., the incenter of a △ is equidistant from the sides of the △. Draw the △ formed by the streets and draw the ∠ bisectors to find the incenter, point M. The city should place the monument at point M.

Exercises 1. They do not intersect at a single point. **3.** 5.64 **5.** 3.95
7. $(2, 6)$ **9.** 42.1 **11.** The largest possible ⊙ in the int. of the △ is its inscribed ⊙, and the center of the inscribed ⊙ is the incenter. Draw the △ and its ∠ bisectors. Center the ⊙ at E, the pt. of concurrency of the ∠ bisectors. **13.** 63.9

15. 63.9 **17.** $(-1.5, 9.5)$ **19.** 55°
23. perpendicular bisector **25.** angle bisector **27.** neither **29.** S **31.** N
33. $(4, 3)$ **35a.** ∠ Bisector Thm.
b. the bisector of $\angle B$ **c.** $PX = PZ$
37a. $\left(4, -\frac{7}{6}\right)$ **b.** outside **c.** 4.2 mi
41. F

24-3

Check It Out! 1a. 21 **1b.** 5.4
2. 3; 4; possible answer: the x-coordinate of the centroid is the average of the x-coordinates of the vertices of the △, and the y-coordinate of the centroid is the average of the y-coordinates of the vertices of the △. **3.** Possible answer: An equation of the altitude to $\overline{JK}$ is $y = -\frac{1}{2}x + 3$. It is true that $4 = -\frac{1}{2}(-2) + 3$, so $(-2, 4)$ is a solution of this equation. Therefore this altitude passes through the orthocenter.

Exercises 1. centroid **3.** 136 **5.** 156
7. $(4, 2)$ **9.** $(2, -3)$ **11.** $(-1, 2)$
13. 7.2 **15.** 5.8 **17.** $(0, -2)$
19. $(-2, 9)$ **21.** 12 **23.** 5 **25.** 36 units
27. $(10, -2)$ **29.** 54 **31.** 48
33. Possible answer: ⊥ bisector of the base; bisector of the vertex ∠; median to the base; altitude to the base **35.** A **37.** A **41.** D **43.** D
45a. slope of $\overline{RS} = \frac{c}{b}$; slope of $\overline{ST} = \frac{c}{b-a}$; slope of $\overline{RT} = 0$
b. Since $\ell \perp \overline{RS}$, slope of $\ell = -\frac{b}{c}$. Since $m \perp \overline{ST}$, slope of $m = -\frac{b-a}{c} = \frac{a-b}{c}$. Since $n \perp \overline{RT}$, n is a vertical line, and its slope is undefined.
c. An equation of ℓ is $y - 0 = -\frac{b}{c}(x - a)$, or $y = -\frac{b}{c}x + \frac{ab}{c}$. An equation of m is $y - 0 = \frac{a-b}{c}(x - 0)$, or $y = \frac{a-b}{c}x$. An equation of n is $x = b$.
d. $\left(b, \frac{ab - b^2}{c}\right)$ **e.** Since the equation of line n is $x = b$ and the x-coordinate of P is b, P lies on n.
f. Lines ℓ, m, and n are concurrent at P.

24-4

Check It Out! 1. $M(1, 1)$; $N(3, 4)$; slope of $\overline{MN} = \frac{3}{2}$; slope of $\overline{RS} = \frac{3}{2}$; since the slopes are the same,

$\overline{MN} \parallel \overline{RS}$. $MN = \sqrt{13}$; $RS = \sqrt{52} = 2\sqrt{13}$; the length of $\overline{MN}$ is half the length of $\overline{RS}$. **2a.** 72 **2b.** 48.5
2c. 102° **3.** 775 m

Exercises 1. midpoints **3.** 5.1
5. 5.6 **7.** 29° **9.** less than 5 yd
11. 38 **13.** 19 **15.** 55° **17.** yes
19. 17 **21.** $n = 36$ **23.** $n = 8$
25. $n = 4$ **27.** B **29.** Possible answer: about 18 parking spaces
31. 11 **33.** 57° **35.** 123°
37a. 2.25 mi **b.** 28.5 mi **39.** D
41. D **43.** equilateral and equiangular **45.** 7 **47a.** 32; 16; 8; 4
b. $\frac{1}{4}$ **c.** $64\left(\frac{1}{2}\right)^n = 2^{6-n}$

25-1

Check It Out! 1a. 28 in. **1b.** 74°
1c. 13 in. **2a.** 12 **2b.** 18 **3.** $(7,6)$
4. 1. $GHJN$ and $JKLM$ are ▱. (Given)
　2. $\angle N$ and $\angle HJN$ are supp. $\angle K$ and $\angle MJK$ are supp. (▱ →cons. ∠ supp.)
　3. $\angle HJN \cong \angle MJK$ (Vert. ∠ Thm.)
　4. $\angle N \cong \angle K$ (≅ Supps. Thm.)

Exercises 3. 36 **5.** 18 **7.** 70°
9. 24.5 **11.** 51° **13.** $(-6, -1)$
15. 82.9 **17.** 82.9 **19.** 130° **21.** 10
23. 28 **25.** $(-1, 3)$ **27.** $PQ = QR = RS = SP = 21$ **29.** $PQ = RS = 17.5$; $QR = SP = 24.5$ **31a.** $\angle 3 \cong \angle 1$ (Corr. ∠ Post.); $\angle 6 \cong \angle 1$ (▱ → opp. ∠ ≅); $\angle 8 \cong \angle 1$ (▱ → opp. ∠ ≅) **b.** $\angle 2$ is supp. to $\angle 1$ (▱ → cons. ∠ supp.); $\angle 4$ is supp. to $\angle 1$ (▱ → cons. ∠ supp.); $\angle 5$ is supp. to $\angle 1$ (▱ → cons. ∠ supp.); $\angle 7$ is supp. to $\angle 1$ (Subst.) **33.** $\angle KMP$ (▱ → opp. ∠ ≅) **35.** $\overline{KM}$ (▱ → opp. sides ≅) **37.** $\overline{RP}$ (Def. of ▱) **39.** $\angle RTP$ (Vert. ∠ Thm.) **41.** $x = 119$; $y = 61$; $z = 119$ **43.** $x = 24$; $y = 50$; $z = 50$
47. $x = 5$; $y = 8$ **49a.** no **b.** no
51. A **53.** 26.4 **55.** $(2, 4)$, $(4, -6)$, $(-6, -2)$

25-2

Check It Out! 1. $PQ = RS = 16.8$, so $\overline{PQ} \cong \overline{RS}$. $m\angle Q = 74°$, and $m\angle R = 106°$, so $\angle Q$ and $\angle R$ are supp., which means that $\overline{PQ} \parallel \overline{RS}$. So 1 pair of opp. sides of $PQRS$ are ∥ and ≅. By Thm. 7-2-1, $PQRS$ is a ▱.

2a. Yes; possible answer: the diag. of the quad. forms 2 △. 2 ∠ of 1 △ are ≅ to 2 ∠ of the other, so the third pair of ∠ are ≅ by the Third ∠ Thm. So both pairs of opp. ∠ of the quad. are ≅. By Thm. 7-2-3, the quad. is a ▱. **2b.** No; 2 pairs of cons. sides are ≅. None of the sets of conditions for a ▱ are met. **3.** Possible answer: slope of $\overline{KL}$ = slope of $\overline{MN} = -\frac{7}{2}$; slope of $\overline{LM}$ = slope of $\overline{NK} = -\frac{1}{4}$; both pairs of opp. sides have the same slope, so $\overline{KL} \parallel \overline{MN}$ and $\overline{LM} \parallel \overline{NK}$; by def., KLMN is a ▱. **4.** Possible answer: Since ABRS is a ▱, it is always true that $\overline{AB} \parallel \overline{RS}$. Since $\overline{AB}$ stays vert., $\overline{RS}$ also remains vert. no matter how the frame is adjusted. Therefore the viewing ∠ never changes.

Exercises 1. FJ = HJ = 10, so $\overline{FJ} \cong \overline{HJ}$. Thus $\overline{EG}$ bisects $\overline{FH}$. EJ = GJ = 18, so $\overline{EJ} \cong \overline{GJ}$. Thus $\overline{FH}$ bisects $\overline{EG}$. So the diags. of EFGH bisect each other. By Thm. 7-2-5, EFGH is a ▱. **3.** yes **5.** yes **7.** Possible answer: slope of $\overline{ST}$ = slope of $\overline{UR} = 0$; $\overline{ST}$ and $\overline{UR}$ have the same slope, so $\overline{ST} \parallel \overline{UR}$; ST = UR = 6; 1 pair of opp. sides are ∥ and ≅; by Thm. 6-3-1, RSTU is a ▱. **9.** BC = GH = 16.6, so $\overline{BC} \cong \overline{GH}$. CG = HB = 28, so $\overline{CG} \cong \overline{HB}$. Since both pairs of opp. sides of BCGH are ≅, BCGH is a ▱ by Thm. 7-2-2. **11.** yes **13.** no **15.** Possible answer: slope of $\overline{PQ}$ = slope of $\overline{RS} = \frac{5}{3}$; $\overline{PQ}$ and $\overline{RS}$ have the same slope, so $\overline{PQ} \parallel \overline{RS}$; PQ = RS = √34; 1 pair of opp. sides are ∥ and ≅; by Thm. 7-2-1, PQRS is a ▱. **17.** no **19.** yes **21.** a = 16.5; b = 23.2 **23.** a = 8.4; b = 20 **27a.** ∠Q **b.** ∠S. **c.** $\overline{SP}$. **d.** $\overline{RS}$ **e.** ▱ **35.** B **37.** no **39.** (3, 1); (−6, −3.5)

25-3

Check It Out! 1a. 48 in. **1b.** 61.6 in. **2a.** 42.5 **2b.** 17° **3.** SV = TW = √122, so $\overline{SV} \cong \overline{TW}$. Slope of $\overline{SV} = \frac{1}{11}$, and slope of $\overline{TW} = -11$, so $\overline{SV} \perp \overline{TW}$. The coordinates of the

mdpt. of $\overline{SV}$ and $\overline{TW}$ are $\left(\frac{1}{2}, -\frac{7}{2}\right)$, so $\overline{SV}$ and $\overline{TW}$ bisect each other. So the diags. of STVW are ≅ ⊥ bisectors of each other.
4. Possible answer:
   1. PQTS is a rhombus. (Given)
   2. $\overline{PT}$ bisects ∠QPS. (Rhombus → each diag. bisects opp. ∠)
   3. ∠QPR ≅ ∠SPR (Def. of ∠ bisector)
   4. $\overline{PQ} \cong \overline{PS}$ (Def. of rhombus)
   5. $\overline{PR} \cong \overline{PR}$ (Reflex. Prop. of ≅)
   6. △QPR ≅ △SPR (SAS)
   7. $\overline{RQ} \cong \overline{RS}$ (CPCTC)

Exercises 1. rhombus; rectangle; square **3.** 160 ft **5.** 380 ft **7.** 122° **9.** Possible answer:
   1. RECT is a rect. $\overline{RX} \cong \overline{TY}$ (Given)
   2. $\overline{XY} \cong \overline{XY}$ (Reflex. Prop. of ≅)
   3. RX = TY, XY = XY (Def. of ≅ segs.)
   4. RX + XY = TY + XY (Add. Prop. of =)
   5. RX + XY = RY, TY + XY = TX (Seg. Add. Post.)
   6. RY = TX (Subst.)
   7. $\overline{RY} \cong \overline{TX}$ (Def. of ≅ segs.)
   8. ∠R and ∠T are rt. ∠. (Def. of rect.)
   9. ∠R ≅ ∠T (Rt. ∠ ≅ Thm.)
   10. RECT is a ▱. (Rect. → ▱)
   11. $\overline{RE} \cong \overline{TC}$ (▱ → opp. sides ≅)
   12. △REY ≅ △TCX (SAS)
11. 25 **13.** $14\frac{1}{2}$ **15.** m∠VWX = 132°; m∠WYX = 66°
17. Possible answer:
   1. RHMB is a rhombus. $\overline{HB}$ is a diag. of RHMB. (Given)
   2. $\overline{MH} \cong \overline{RH}$ (Def. of rhombus)
   3. $\overline{HB}$ bisects ∠RHM. (Rhombus → each diag. bisects opp. ∠)
   4. ∠MHX ≅ ∠RHX (Def. of ∠ bisector)
   5. $\overline{HX} \cong \overline{HX}$ (Reflex. Prop. of ≅)
   6. △MHX ≅ △RHX (SAS)
   7. ∠HMX ≅ ∠HRX (CPCTC)
19. m∠1 = 54°; m∠2 = 36°; m∠3 = 54°; m∠4 = 108°; m∠5 = 72°
21. m∠1 = 126°; m∠2 = 27°; m∠3 = 27°; m∠4 = 126°; m∠5 = 27°
23. m∠1 = 64°; m∠2 = 64°; m∠3 =

26°; m∠4 = 90°; m∠5 = 64° **25.** S **27.** S **29.** A **31.** S **35a.** Rect. → ▱ **b.** $\overline{HG}$ **c.** Reflex. Prop. of ≅ **d.** Def. of rect. **e.** ∠GHE **f.** SAS **g.** CPCTC **41.** 28√2 in. ≈ 39.60 in.; 98 in² **45.** D **47.** H **51.** 45

25-4

Check It Out! 1. Both pairs of opp. sides of WXYZ are ≅, so WXYZ is a ▱. The contractor can use the carpenter's square to see if 1 ∠ of WXYZ is a rt. ∠. If 1 ∠ is a rt. ∠, then by Thm. 7-4-1 the frame is a rect. **2.** Not valid; by Thm. 7-4-1, if 1 ∠ of a ▱ is a rt. ∠, then the ▱ is a rect. To apply this thm., you need to know that ABCD is a ▱. **3a.** rect., rhombus, square **3b.** rhombus

Exercises 3. valid **5.** rhombus **7.** valid **9.** square, rect., rhombus **11.** ▱, rect. **13.** ▱, rect., rhombus, square **15.** ▱, rect., rhombus, square **17.** B **19.** $\overline{PR} \cong \overline{QS}$ **21.** (2, 6) **23.** (−2, −2) **25.** x = 3 **27.** rhombus **29a.** slope of $\overline{AB}$ = slope of $\overline{CD} = -\frac{1}{3}$; slope of $\overline{AD}$ = slope of $\overline{CB} = -3$ **b.** Slope of $\overline{AC}$ = −1; slope of $\overline{BD}$ = 1; the slopes are negative reciprocals of each other, so $\overline{AC} \perp \overline{BD}$. **c.** ABCD is a rhombus, since it is a ▱ and its diags. are ⊥ (Thm. 7-4-4.) **33b.** ▱ **c.** square **39.** A **41a.** 15x = 13x + 12; x = 6 **b.** yes **c.** no **d.** yes **43b.** no **c.** no

26-1

Check It Out! 1. ∠A ≅ ∠J; ∠B ≅ ∠G; ∠C ≅ ∠H; $\frac{AB}{JG} = \frac{BC}{GH} = \frac{AC}{JH} = 2$ **2.** yes; $\frac{5}{2}$; △LMJ ~ △PNS **3.** 5 in.

Exercises 3. ∠A ≅ ∠H; ∠B ≅ ∠J; ∠C ≅ ∠K; ∠D ≅ ∠L; $\frac{AB}{HJ} = \frac{BC}{JK} = \frac{CD}{KL} = \frac{DA}{LH} = \frac{2}{3}$ **5.** yes; $\frac{2}{3}$; △RMP ~ △XWU **7.** ∠J ≅ ∠S; ∠K ≅ ∠T; ∠L ≅ ∠U; ∠M ≅ ∠V; $\frac{JK}{ST} = \frac{KL}{TU} = \frac{LM}{UV} = \frac{MJ}{VS}$ = $\frac{5}{6}$ **9.** yes; $\frac{7}{8}$; △RSQ ~ △UZX **11.** 14 ft **13.** S **15.** N **17.** S **19.** 5 **23.** ∠O; ∠Q **27.** C **29.** The ratios of the sides are not the same; $\frac{12}{3.5} = \frac{24}{7}$; $\frac{10}{2.5} = 4$; $\frac{6}{1.5} = 4$. **33a.** rect. ABCD ~ rect. BCFE. **b.** $\frac{\ell}{1} = \frac{1}{\ell - 1}$ **c.** $\ell = \frac{1 + \sqrt{5}}{2}$ **d.** $\ell ≈ 1.6$

26-2

Check It Out! 1. $D'(-2, 0)$, $E'(-2, -1)$, $F'(-1, -2)$; dilation with center $(0, 0)$ and scale factor $\frac{1}{4}$ **2.** The triangles are similar because $\triangle ABC$ can be mapped to $\triangle A'B'C'$ by a rotation: $(x, y) \longrightarrow (-y, x)$, and then $\triangle A'B'C'$ can be mapped to $\triangle PQR$ by a dilation: $(x, y) \longrightarrow (3x, 3y)$. **3.** Circle A can be mapped to circle A' by a translation: $(x, y) \longrightarrow (x - 3, y - 2)$. Then circle A' can be mapped to circle B by a dilation with center $(-1, -1)$ and scale factor $\frac{1}{2}$. So, circles A and B are similar. **4.** Apply the dilation with center $(0, 0)$ and scale factor 4: $(x, y) \longrightarrow (4x, 4y)$.

Exercises 1. similarity **3.** dilation about $(0, 0)$ with a scale factor of 4; $A'(-4, -4)$, $B'(8, 4)$, $C'(-8, 4)$ **5.** dilation about $(0, 0)$ with a scale factor of 2.5; $A'(5, 7.5)$, $B'(12.5, -5)$, $C'(-10, -5)$ **7.** Similar; to map $LMNO$ to $PQRS$, first dilate by a scale factor of 2: $(x, y) \longrightarrow (2x, 2y)$. Then translate 13 units up: $(x, y) \longrightarrow (x, y + 13)$. **9.** Similar; to map ABC to XYZ, first reflect: $(x, y) \longrightarrow (x, -y)$. Then dilate by a scale factor of $\frac{4}{3}$: $(x, y) \longrightarrow (\frac{4}{3}x, \frac{4}{3}y)$. The transformations could also be done in the other order. **11.** To map A to B, first translate 10 units to the left and 3 units down: $(x, y) \longrightarrow (x - 10, y - 3)$. Then dilate by a scale factor of $\frac{3}{5}$: $(x, y) \longrightarrow (\frac{3}{5}x, \frac{3}{5}y)$. **13.** Apply a dilation with center $(0, 0)$ and scale factor 4 to the small triangle on the grid: $(x, y) \longrightarrow (4x, 4y)$. The image represents the shape of the large triangle. **15.** dilation about $(0, 0)$ with a scale factor of 0.5; $A'(6, 3)$, $B'(0, -3)$, $C'(3, 9)$ **17.** Similar; to map ABC to XYZ, first translate 4 units to the left and 6 units up: $(x, y) \longrightarrow (x - 4, y + 6)$. Then dilate by a scale factor of $\frac{2}{3}$: $(x, y) \longrightarrow (\frac{2}{3}x, \frac{2}{3}y)$. **19.** Similar; to map $GHJK$ to $LMNO$, dilate by a scale factor of 0.5: $(x, y) \longrightarrow (0.5x, 0.5y)$; to map $LMNO$ to $GHJK$, dilate by a scale factor of 2: $(x, y) \longrightarrow (2x, 2y)$. **21.** Reggie made an

error. The scale factor from ABC to $A'B'C'$ is $\frac{2}{3}$, not $\frac{3}{2}$. **23.** Place the drawing of the smaller building on a coordinate plane in a convenient position in the first quadrant. Apply the dilation with center $(0, 0)$ and scale factor 5: $(x, y) \longrightarrow (5x, 5y)$. The image represents the larger building. **25.** A

26-3

Check It Out! 1. By the $\triangle$ Sum Thm., $m\angle C = 47°$, so $\angle C \cong \angle F$. $\angle B \cong \angle E$ by the Rt. $\angle \cong$ Thm. Therefore $\triangle ABC \sim \triangle DEF$ by AA $\sim$. **2.** $\angle TXU \cong \angle VXW$ by the Vert. $\angle$ Thm. $\frac{TX}{VX} = \frac{12}{16} = \frac{3}{4}$, and $\frac{XU}{XW} = \frac{15}{20} = \frac{3}{4}$. Therefore $\triangle TXU \sim \triangle VXW$ by SAS $\sim$. **3.** It is given that $\angle RSV \cong \angle T$. By the Reflex. Prop. of $\cong$, $\angle R \cong \angle R$. Therefore $\triangle RSV \sim \triangle RTU$ by AA $\sim$. $RT = 15$.
4.1. M is the mdpt. of $\overline{JK}$, N is the mdpt. of $\overline{KL}$, and P is the mdpt. of $\overline{JL}$. (Given)
   2. $MP = \frac{1}{2}KL$, $MN = \frac{1}{2}JL$, $NP = \frac{1}{2}KJ$ ($\triangle$Midsegs. Thm.)
   3. $\frac{MP}{KL} = \frac{MN}{JL} = \frac{NP}{KJ} = \frac{1}{2}$ (Div. Prop. of =)
   4. $\triangle JKL \sim \triangle NPM$ (SSS $\sim$ Step 3)
   5. 5

Exercises 1. By the $\triangle$ Sum Thm., $m\angle A = 47°$. So by the def. of $\cong$, $\angle A \cong \angle F$, and $\angle C \cong \angle H$. Therefore $\triangle ABC \sim \triangle FGH$ by AA $\sim$. **3.** $\frac{DF}{JL} = \frac{DE}{JK} = \frac{EF}{KL} = \frac{1}{2}$, so $\triangle DEF \sim \triangle JKL$ by SSS $\sim$. **5.** It is given that $\angle AED \cong \angle ACB$. $\angle A \cong \angle A$ by the Reflex. Prop. of $\cong$. Therefore $\triangle AED \sim \triangle ACB$ by AA $\sim$. $AB = 10$
7.1. $\overline{MN} \parallel \overline{KL}$ (Given)
   2. $\angle JMN \cong \angle JKL$, $\angle JNM \cong \angle JLK$ (Corr. $\angle$ Post.)
   3. $\triangle JMN \sim \triangle JKL$ (AA $\sim$ Step 2)
9. SAS or SSS $\sim$ Thm. **11.** It is given that $\angle GLH \cong \angle K$. $\angle G \cong \angle G$ by the Reflex. Prop. of $\cong$. Therefore $\triangle HLG \sim \triangle JKG$ by AA $\sim$. **13.** $\angle K \cong \angle K$ by the Reflex. Prop. of $\cong$. $\frac{KL}{KN} = \frac{KM}{KL} = \frac{3}{2}$. Therefore $\triangle KLM \sim \triangle KNL$ by SAS $\sim$. **15.** It is given that $\angle ABD \cong \angle C$. $\angle A \cong \angle A$ by the Reflex. Prop. of $\cong$.

Therefore $\triangle ABD \sim \triangle ACB$ by AA $\sim$. $AB = 8$

17.1. $CD = 3AC$, $CE = 3BC$ (Given)
   2. $\frac{CD}{AC} = 3$, $\frac{CE}{BC} = 3$ (Div. Prop. of =)
   3. $\angle ACB \cong \angle DCE$ (Vert. $\angle$ Thm.)
   4. $\triangle ABC \sim \triangle DEC$ (SAS $\sim$ Steps 2, 3)
19. 1.5 ft **21.** yes; SSS $\sim$ **23.** $x = 3$ **25a.** Pyramids A and C are $\sim$ because the ratios of their corr. side lengths are =. **b.** $\frac{5}{4}$ **27.** 2 ft; 4 ft **31a.** The $\triangle$ are $\sim$ by AA $\sim$ if you assume that the camera is $\parallel$ to the hurricane (that is, $\overline{YX} \parallel \overline{AB}$). **b.** $\triangle YWZ \sim \triangle BCZ$, and $\triangle XWZ \sim \triangle ACZ$, also by AA $\sim$. **c.** 105 mi **35.** J **37.** 30

26-4

Check It Out! 1. 7.5 **2.** $AD = 16$, and $BE = 12$, so $\frac{DC}{AD} = \frac{20}{16} = \frac{5}{4}$, and $\frac{EC}{BE} = \frac{15}{12} = \frac{5}{4}$. Since $\frac{DC}{AD} = \frac{EC}{BE}$, $\overline{DE} \parallel \overline{AB}$ by the Conv. of the $\triangle$ Proportionality Thm. **3.** $LM \approx 1.5$ cm; $MN \approx 2.4$ cm **4.** $AC = 16$; $DC = 9$

Exercises 1. 30 **3.** $\frac{EC}{AC} = 1$, and $\frac{ED}{DB} = 1$. Since $\frac{EC}{AC} = \frac{ED}{DB}$, $\overline{AB} \parallel \overline{CD}$ by the Conv. of the $\triangle$ Proportionality Thm. **5.** 286 ft **7.** $CD = 4$; $AD = 6$ **9.** 20 **11.** $\frac{PM}{MQ} = \frac{6.3}{2.7} = 2\frac{1}{3}$, and $\frac{PN}{NR} = \frac{7}{3} = 2\frac{1}{3}$. Since $\frac{PM}{MQ} = \frac{PN}{NR}$, $\overline{MN} \parallel \overline{QR}$ by the Conv. of the $\triangle$ Proportionality Thm. **13.** $BC = 6$; $CD = 5$ **15.** CE **17.** BD **19.** DF **21.** 15 in. or $26\frac{2}{3}$ in.
23.1. $\frac{AE}{EB} = \frac{AF}{FC}$ (Given)
   2. $\angle A \cong \angle A$ (Reflex. Prop. of $\square$)
   3. $\triangle AEF \sim \triangle ABC$ (SAS $\sim$ Steps 1, 2)
   4. $\angle AEF \cong \angle ABC$ (Def. of $\sim \triangle$)
   5. $\overleftrightarrow{EF} \parallel \overline{BC}$ (Conv. of Corr. $\angle$ Post.)
25a. $PR = 6$; $RT = 8$; $QS = 3$; $SU = 4$ **b.** $\frac{PR}{RT} = \frac{QS}{SU}$, or $\frac{6}{8} = \frac{3}{4}$ **27.** 15 **33.** J

26-5

Check It Out! 1. The photo should have vertices $A'(0, 0)$, $B'(0, 2)$, $C'(1.5, 2)$, and $D'(1.5, 0)$. **2.** $N(0, -20)$; $\frac{2}{3}$ **3.** $RS = \sqrt{2}$, $RU =$

$3\sqrt{2}$, $RT = \sqrt{5}$, and $RV = 3\sqrt{5}$, so $\frac{RS}{RU} = \frac{RT}{RV} = \frac{1}{3}$. $\angle R \cong \angle R$ by the Reflex. Prop. of $\cong$. So $\triangle RST \sim \triangle RUV$ by SAS $\sim$. **4.** Check students' work. The image of $\triangle MNP$ has vertices $M'(-6, 3)$, $N'(6, 6)$, and $P'(-3, -3)$. $MP = \sqrt{5}$, $MN = \sqrt{17}$, and $PN = 3\sqrt{2}$. $M'P' = 3\sqrt{5}$, $M'N' = 3\sqrt{17}$, and $P'N' = 9\sqrt{2}$. $\frac{M'P'}{MP} = \frac{M'N'}{MN} = \frac{P'N'}{PN} = 3$. So $\triangle M'N'P' \sim \triangle MNP$ by SSS $\sim$.

Exercises 1. dilation

5. $S(0, -8)$; $\frac{5}{2}$ **7.** $JK = 2\sqrt{5}$, $JM = 3\sqrt{5}$, $JL = 2\sqrt{5}$, and $JN = 3\sqrt{5}$,

so $\frac{JK}{JM} = \frac{JL}{JN} = \frac{2}{3}$. $\angle J \cong \angle J$ by the Reflex. Prop. of $\cong$. So $\triangle JKL \sim \triangle JMN$ by SAS $\sim$. **9.** The image of $\triangle RST$ has vertices $R'(-3, 3)$, $S'(3, 6)$, and $T'(0, -3)$. $RS = 2\sqrt{5}$, $RT = 2\sqrt{5}$, and $ST = 2\sqrt{10}$. $R'S' = 3\sqrt{5}$, $R'T' = 3\sqrt{5}$, and $S'T' = 3\sqrt{10}$. $\frac{R'S'}{RS} = \frac{R'T'}{RT} = \frac{S'T'}{ST} = \frac{3}{2}$. So $\triangle RST \sim \triangle R'S'T'$ by SSS $\sim$. **11.** $X(-24, 0)$; $\frac{8}{3}$ **13.** $DE = 2\sqrt{5}$, $DG = 3\sqrt{5}$, $DF = 4\sqrt{2}$, and $DH = 6\sqrt{2}$, so $\frac{DE}{DG} = \frac{DF}{DH} = \frac{2}{3}$. $\angle D \cong \angle D$ by the Reflex. Prop. of $\cong$. So $\triangle DEF \sim \triangle DGH$ by SAS $\sim$. **15.** The image of $\triangle JKL$ has vertices

$J'(-6, 0)$, $K'(-3, -3)$, and $L'(-9, -6)$. $JK = \sqrt{2}$, $JL = \sqrt{5}$, and $LK = \sqrt{5}$. $J'K' = 3\sqrt{2}$, $J'L' = 3\sqrt{5}$, and $L'K' = 3\sqrt{5}$. $\frac{J'K'}{JK} = \frac{J'L'}{JL} = \frac{L'K'}{LK} = 3$. So $\triangle JKL \sim \triangle J'K'L'$ by SSS $\sim$. **17.** It is not a dilation; because it changes the shape of the figure. **21.** A **23.** A **25.** 12

27-1

Check It Out! **1a.** $x = 4\sqrt{5}$
1b. $x = 16$ **2.** 29 ft 1 in. **3a.** $2\sqrt{41}$;
no; $2\sqrt{41}$ is not a whole number.
3b. 10; yes; the 3 side lengths are
nonzero whole numbers that
satisfy the equation $a^2 + b^2 = c^2$.
3c. 2.6; no; 2.4 and 2.6 are not
whole numbers. **3d.** 34; yes; the
3 side lengths are nonzero whole
numbers that satisfy the equation
$a^2 + b^2 = c^2$. **4a.** yes; obtuse **4b.** no
4c. yes, acute

Exercises **1.** no **3.** $x = 6\sqrt{2}$
5. width: 14.8 in.; height: 11.9 in.
7. 16; yes **9.** triangle; acute
11. triangle; right **13.** triangle;
acute **15.** $x = 10$ **17.** $x = 24$ **19.** 6;
no **21.** $3\sqrt{5}$; no **23.** not a triangle
25. triangle; right **27.** triangle;
acute **29.** B **31.** $x = 8 + \sqrt{13}$
33. $x = 4\sqrt{6}$ **35.** $x = 6\sqrt{13}$
39. perimeter: $16 + 4\sqrt{7}$ units; area:
$12\sqrt{7}$ square units
41. perimeter: $14 + 2\sqrt{13}$ units;
area: 18 square units
43. perimeter: 22 units; area:
26 square units **47a.** King City
b. m∠SRM > 90° **49.** B
51a. $PA = \sqrt{2}$; $PB = \sqrt{3}$; $PC = 2$;
$PD = \sqrt{5}$; $PE = \sqrt{6}$; $PF = \sqrt{7}$
55a. no **b.** yes. **c.** no **d.** no

27-2

Check It Out! **1a.** $x = 20$ **1b.** $x = 8\sqrt{2}$ **2.** 43 cm **3a.** $x = 9\sqrt{3}$; $y = 27$
3b. $x = 5\sqrt{3}$; $y = 10$ **3c.** $x = 12$;
$y = 12\sqrt{3}$ **3d.** $x = 6\sqrt{3}$; $y = 3\sqrt{3}$
4. 34.6 cm

Exercises **1.** $x = 14\sqrt{2}$ **3.** $x = 9$
5. $x = 3$; $y = 3\sqrt{3}$ **7.** $x = 21$;
$y = 14\sqrt{3}$ **9.** $x = \frac{15\sqrt{2}}{2}$ **11.** $x = 18$

13. $x = 48$; $y = 24\sqrt{3}$ **15.** $x = \frac{2\sqrt{3}}{3}$;
$y = \frac{4\sqrt{3}}{3}$ **17.** perimeter:
$\left(12 + 12\sqrt{2}\right)$ in.; area: 36 in²
19. perimeter: $36\sqrt{2}$ m; area:
162 m² **21.** perimeter: $60\sqrt{3}$ yd;
area: $300\sqrt{3}$ yd² **23.** no **25.** $(10, 3)$
27. $\left(5, 10 - 12\sqrt{3}\right)$ **29a.** 640 mi
b. 453 mi **c.** 234 mi **31.** F
33. 443.4 **35.** $x = \frac{32}{9}$

28-1

Check It Out! **1a.** $\frac{24}{25} = 0.96$ **1b.** $\frac{24}{7}$
≈ 3.43 **1c.** $\frac{24}{25} = 0.96$ **2.** $\frac{s}{s} = 1$
3a. 0.19 **3b.** 0.88 **3c.** 0.87
4a. 21.87 m **4b.** 7.06 in. **4c.** 36.93 ft
4d. 6.17 cm **5.** 14.34 ft

Exercises **1.** $\frac{LK}{JL}$ **3.** $\frac{4}{5} = 0.80$ **5.** $\frac{4}{5} =$
0.80 **7.** $\frac{4}{3} \approx 1.33$ **9.** $\frac{1}{2}$ **11.** $\frac{\sqrt{2}}{2}$ **13.** 0.39
15. 0.03 **17.** 0.16 **19.** 9.65 m
21. 7 ft 6 in. **23.** $\frac{15}{8} \approx 1.88$ **25.** $\frac{15}{17} \approx$
0.88 **27.** $\frac{15}{17} \approx 0.88$ **29.** $\frac{1}{2}$ **31.** 1.23
33. 0.22 **35.** 0.82 **37.** 3.58 cm
39. 19.67 ft **41.** 5.27 ft **43.** 6.10 m
45. sine; cosine **47.** 60° **49.** 1.2 ft
53. 0.6 **55.** 753 ft **59.** $\left(\frac{1}{2}\right)^2 + \left(\frac{\sqrt{3}}{2}\right)^2 =$
$\frac{1}{4} + \frac{3}{4} = 1$ **61a.** $\sin A = \frac{a}{c}$; $\cos A = \frac{b}{c}$
b. $(\sin A)^2 + (\cos A)^2 = \left(\frac{a}{c}\right)^2 + \left(\frac{b}{c}\right)^2$
$= \frac{a^2}{c^2} + \frac{b^2}{c^2} = \frac{a^2 + b^2}{c^2} = \frac{c^2}{c^2} = 1$
63. 18.64 cm; 16.00 cm²
65. 22.60 in.; 14.69 in² **69.** H
71. $x \approx 5$; $AB \approx 20$; $BC \approx 18$;
$AC \approx 27$ **75.** 1.25 **77.** 0.75

28-2

Check It Out! **1a.** ∠2 **1b.** ∠1
2a. 37° **2b.** 87° **2c.** 42° **3.** $DF \approx$
16.51; $EF \approx 8.75$; m∠D = 32°
4. $RS = ST = 7$; $RT \approx 9.90$; m∠S =
90°; m∠R = m∠T = 45° **5.** 21°

Exercises **1.** ∠1 **3.** ∠1 **5.** ∠2 **7.** 65°
9. 34° **11.** 38° **13.** $RP \approx 9.42$; m∠P

$\approx 19°$; m∠R ≈ 71° **15.** $YZ \approx 13.96$;
m∠Y ≈ 38°; m∠Z ≈ 52° **17.** $RS = 5$;
$ST = 6$; $RT \approx 7.81$; m∠S = 90°; m∠R
≈ 50°; m∠T ≈ 40° **19.** $AB = 2$; BC
$= 4$; $AC \approx 4.47$; m∠B = 90°; m∠A ≈
63°; m∠C ≈ 27° **21.** ∠2 **23.** ∠1
25. ∠2 **27.** 18° **29.** 37° **31.** 57°
33. $JK \approx 2.88$; $LK \approx 1.40$; m∠L = 64°
35. $QR \approx 4.90$; m∠P ≈ 36°; m∠R ≈
54° **37.** $MN = NP = 4$; $MP \approx 5.66$;
m∠N = 90°; m∠M = m∠P = 45°
39. 74° **41.** cos **43.** 0.93 **47a.** 5°
b. 85° **c.** 31 ft 1 in. **49.** 23°; 67°
51. The acute ∠ measure changes
from about 58° to about 73°, an
increase by a factor of 1.26.
53a. $AB = 5\sqrt{2}$; $BC = 2\sqrt{10}$; AC
$= \sqrt{10}$ **b.** $AC^2 + BC^2 = AB^2$, so
△ABC is a rt. △, and ∠C is the rt. ∠.
c. m∠A = 63°; m∠B = 27° **55.** 35°
57. 62° **59.** 72° **61.** 39° **65.** D **67.** A
69. 58° **71.** 34° **73.** x

28-3

Check It Out! **1a.** angle of
depression **1b.** angle of elevation
2. 6314 ft **3.** 1717 ft **4.** 32,300 ft

Exercises **1.** elevation **3.** angle of
elevation **5.** angle of elevation
7. 18 ft **9.** 64.6 m **11.** angle of
elevation **13.** angle of depression
15. 1962 ft **17.** T **19.** F **21.** ∠1 and
∠3 **25a.** 424 ft **b.** 276 ft
27a. 2080 ft **b.** 14 s **29.** J **31.** 98 m
33. 1318 ft

Selected Answers ▪ Unit 9

29-1

Check It Out! 1. $A = \left(4x^2 - 12x + 9\right)\pi$ m^2
2. $C \approx 31.4$ in.; $C \approx 37.7$ in.; $C \approx 44.0$ in. **3.** $A \approx 77.3$ cm^2

Exercises 1. Draw a segment perpendicular to a side with one endpoint at the center. The apothem is $\frac{1}{2}s$. **3.** $A = 9x^2\pi$ in^2 **5.** $A \approx 50.3$ in^2; $A \approx 78.5$ in^2; $A \approx 113.1$ in^2 **7.** $A \approx 32.7$ cm^2 **9.** $A \approx 279.9$ m^2 **11.** $C = 5\pi$ m **13.** $A \approx 962.1$ ft^2; $A \approx 1963.5$ ft^2; $A \approx 3421.2$ ft^2 **15.** $A \approx 13.3$ ft^2 **17.** $A \approx 14.5$ ft^2 **19.** 90° **21.** 60° **23.** 45° **25.** 36° **27.** $A \approx 84.3$ cm^2 **29.** $A \approx 46.8$ m^2 **31.** $A \approx 90.8$ ft^2 **35.** $20\frac{\sqrt{\pi}}{\pi}$; $10\frac{\sqrt{\pi}}{\pi}$; $20\sqrt{\pi}$ **37.** 36; 18; 324π **39a.** $A \approx 745.6$ in^2 **b.** $A \approx 1073.6$ in^2 **c.** 44% **43.** B **45.** B **47.** $A = \frac{C^2}{4\pi}$

29-2

Check It Out! 1. $V = 157.5$ yd^3 **2.** 859,702 gal; 7,161,318 lb **3.** $V = 1088\pi$ in$^3 \approx 3418.1$ in^3 **4.** The volume is multiplied by 8. **5.** $V \approx 51.4$ cm^3

Exercises 1. the same length as **3.** $V \approx 748.2$ m^3 **5.** 2552 gal; 12,071 lb **7.** $V = 45\pi$ m$^3 \approx 141.4$ m^3 **9.** The volume is multiplied by $\frac{1}{64}$. **11.** $V \approx 1209.1$ ft^3 **13.** $V = 810$ yd^3 **15.** $V = 245$ ft^3 **17.** $V = 1764\pi$ cm$^3 \approx 5541.8$ cm^3 **19.** $V = 384\pi$ cm$^3 \approx 1206.4$ cm^3 **21.** The volume is multiplied by $\frac{27}{125}$. **23.** $V \approx 242.3$ ft^3 **25a.** 235.6 in^2 **25b.** 0.04 **27.** $h = 11$ ft **29.** $V = 392\pi$ m^3 **31.** 576 in^3, or $\frac{1}{3}$ ft^3 **33.** 2,468,729 gal **37.** A **39.** B **41.** $V = x^3 + x^2 - 2x$ **43.** $V = \frac{x^3\sqrt{3} + x^2\sqrt{3}}{4}$

29-3

Check It Out! 1. $V = 36$ cm^3 **2.** 107,800 yd^3 or 2,910,600 ft^3 **3.** $V = 216\pi$ m$^3 \approx 678.6$ m^3 **4.** The volume is multiplied by 8. **5.** $V = 3000$ ft^3

Exercises 1. perpendicular **3.** $V = 96$ cm^3 **5.** $V \approx 65$ mm^3 **7.** $V =$ 1440π in$^3 \approx 4523.9$ in^3 **9.** The volume is multiplied by 27. **11.** $V = 2592$ cm^3 **13.** $V = 160$ ft^3 **15.** $V = 384$ ft^3 **17.** $V = 1107\pi$ m$^3 \approx 3477.7$ m^3 **19.** $V = 144\pi$ ft$^3 \approx 452.4$ ft^3 **21.** The volume is multiplied by 216. **23.** $V = 150$ ft^3 **25.** $V = \frac{25\pi}{6}$ m^3 **27.** $V = 240\pi$ cm^3 **29.** 1350 m^3 **31.** 166.3 cm^3 **33.** $C = 10\pi\sqrt{3}$ cm **35.** $V = 1280$ in^3 **37.** $V = 17.5$ units^3 **39.** 3:2 **41a.** 33.5 in^3 **b.** 134.0 in^3 **c.** \$5; the large size holds 4 times as much. **43.** H **45.** 9 **47.** $V = \frac{2\pi}{3}$ ft^3 **49.** $V = \frac{1000\sqrt{2}}{3}$ cm^3

29-4

Check It Out! 1. $r = 12$ ft **2.** about 72.3 times as great **3.** $S = 2500\pi$ cm^2 **4.** The surface area is divided by 9. **5.** $S = 57\pi$ ft^2; $V = 27\pi$ ft^3

Exercises 1. One endpoint is the center of the sphere, and the other is a point on the sphere. **3.** $V = \frac{4\pi}{3}$ m^3 **5.** about 8 times as great **7.** $S = 196\pi$ cm^2 **9.** The surface area is multiplied by 4. **11.** $S = 36\pi$ ft^2; $V = \frac{92\pi}{3}$ ft^3 **13.** $V = 972\pi$ cm^3 **15.** $d = 36$ in. **17.** $S = 1764\pi$ in^2 **19.** $V = \frac{15,625\pi}{6}$ m^3 **21.** The volume is multiplied by 216. **23.** $S \approx 1332.0$ mm^2; $V \approx 1440.9$ mm^3 **25.** $C = 2\pi\sqrt{15}$ in. **27.** $S = 196\pi$ units^2; $V = \frac{1372\pi}{3}$ units^3 **29.** 5.28 in.; 8.87 in^2; 2.48 in^3 **31.** 7.85 in.; 19.63 in^2; 8.18 in^3 **33.** Possible answer: 14,293 in^3 **35.** about 1408 times as great **37.** The surface area of Saturn is greater. **39.** The cross section of the hemisphere is a circle with radius $\sqrt{r^2 - x^2}$, so its area is $A = \pi\left(r^2 - x^2\right)$. The cross section of the cylinder with the cone removed has an outer radius of r and an inner radius of x, so the area is $A = \pi r^2 - \pi x^2 = \pi\left(r^2 - x^2\right)$. **41a.** 33.5 in^3 **b.** 44.6 in^3 **43.** H **45.** 1 in. **47.** The volume of the cylinder is 1.5 times the volume of the sphere.

30-1

Check It Out! 1. chords: $\overline{QR}$, $\overline{ST}$; secant: $\overleftrightarrow{ST}$; tangent: $\overleftrightarrow{UV}$; diam.: $\overline{ST}$; radii: $\overline{PQ}$, $\overline{PT}$, $\overline{PS}$ **2.** radius of $\odot C$: 1; radius of $\odot D$: 3; pt. of tangency: $(2, -1)$; eqn. of tangent line: $y = -1$ **3.** 171 mi **4a.** 2.1 **4b.** 7

Exercises 1. secant **3.** congruent **5.** chord: $\overline{QS}$; secant: $\overleftrightarrow{QS}$; tangent: $\overleftrightarrow{ST}$; diam.: $\overline{QS}$; radii: $\overline{PR}$, $\overline{PQ}$, $\overline{PS}$ **7.** radius of $\odot R$: 2; radius of $\odot S$: 2; pt. of tangency: $(1, 2)$; eqn. of tangent line: $x = 1$ **9.** 19 **11.** chords: $\overline{RS}$, $\overline{VW}$; secant: $\overleftrightarrow{VW}$; tangent: ℓ; diam.: $\overline{VW}$; radii: $\overline{PV}$, $\overline{PW}$ **13.** radius of $\odot C$: 2; radius of $\odot D$: 4; pt. of tangency: $(-4, 0)$; eqn. of tangent line: $x = -4$ **15.** 413 km **17.** 7 **19.** N **21.** A **23.** $\overline{AC}$ **25.** $\overline{AC}$ **27.** 45° **31.** 8 **33.** 22 **35a.** rect.; $\angle BCD$ and $\angle EDC$ are rt. $\angle$ because a line tangent to a $\odot$ is $\perp$ to a radius. It is given that $\angle DEB$ is a rt. $\angle$. $\angle CBE$ must also be a rt. $\angle$ because the sum of the $\angle$ of a quad. is 360°. Thus $BCDE$ has 4 rt. $\angle$ and is a rect. **b.** 17 in.; 2 in. **c.** 17.1 in. **39.** G **43.** 18.6 in.

30-2

Check It Out! 1a. 108° **1b.** 270° **1c.** 36° **2a.** 140° **2b.** 295° **3a.** 12 **3b.** 100° **4.** 34.6

Exercises 1. semicircle **3.** major arc **5.** 162° **7.** 61.2° **9.** 39.6° **11.** 129° **13.** 108° **15.** 24 **17.** 24.0 **19.** 122.3° **21.** 122.3° **23.** 237.7° **25.** 152° **27.** 155° **29.** 147° **31.** 6.6 **33.** F **35.** T **37.** 45°; 60°; 75° **39.** 108° **41. 1.** $\overset{\frown}{BC} \cong \overset{\frown}{DE}$ (Given)
  2. $m\overset{\frown}{BC} = m\overset{\frown}{DE}$ (Def. of $\cong$ arcs)
  3. $m\angle BAC = m\angle DAE$ (Def. of arc measures)
  4. $\angle BAC \cong \angle DAE$ (Def. of $\cong \angle$)
43. 1. $\overleftrightarrow{JK}$ is the $\perp$ bisector of $\overline{GH}$. (Given)
  2. A is equidistant from G and H. (Def. of center of $\odot$)

3. *A* lies on the ⊥ bisector of $\overline{GH}$. (⊥ Bisector Thm.)
4. $\overline{JK}$ is a diam. of ⊙*A*. (Def. of diam.)
45. Solution A **47a.** 13.5 in.; 6.5 in.
b. 11.8 in. **c.** 23.7 in. **49.** F
51. 48.2° **53a.** 90°; 60°; 45° **b.** $\frac{3}{4}\pi$; $\frac{3}{2}\pi$

30-3

Check It Out! 1a. $\frac{\pi}{4}$ m²; 0.79 m²
1b. 25.6π in²; 80.42 in² **2.** 203,575 ft²
3. 4.57 m² **4a.** $\frac{4}{3}\pi$ m; 4.19 m
4b. 3π cm; 9.42 cm

Exercises 1. seg. **3.** 24π cm²;
75.40 cm² **5.** 12 mi² **7.** 36.23 m²

9. 4π ft; 12.57 ft **11.** $\frac{2}{3}\pi$ in; 2.09 in.
13. $\frac{45}{2}\pi$ in²; 70.69 in² **15.** 628 in²
17. 15.35 in² **19.** $\frac{25}{18}\pi$ mm; 4.36 mm
21. $\frac{1}{10}\pi$ ft; 0.31 ft **23.** N **25.** A **27.** 12
29a. 3.9 ft **b.** 103° **33.** G **35.** $\frac{7}{3}\pi$
37a. $\frac{1}{8}$ **b.** $\frac{3}{8}$ **c.** $\frac{1}{2}$

30-4

Check It Out! 1a. 270° **1b.** 38°
2. 43°; 120° **3a.** 12 **3b.** 39° **4.** 51°;
129°; 72°; 108°

Exercises 1. inscribed **3.** 58°
5. 26° **7.** 112.5 **9.** 46° **11.** 70°; 110°;
115°; 65° **13.** 47.5° **15.** 47.6° **17.** ±6
19. 100° **21.** 100°; 39°; 80°; 141°
23. A **25.** S **27.** 115° **29a.** 30°

b. 120° **c.** Rt.; ∠*FBC* is inscribed in a semicircle, so it must be a rt. ∠; therefore △*FBC* is a rt. △.
33. 72°; 99°; 108°; 81° **35a.** $AB^2 + AC^2 = BC^2$, so by the Conv. of the Pyth. Thm., △*ABC* is a rt. △ with rt. ∠*A*. Since ∠*A* is an inscribed rt. ∠, it intercepts a semicircle. This means that $\overline{BC}$ is a diam. **b.** 102° **39.** D
41. C **45.** 134°

Mastering the Standards

for Mathematical Practice

The topics described in the Standards for Mathematical Content will vary from year to year. However, the *way* in which you learn, study, and think about mathematics will not. The Standards for Mathematical Practice describe skills that you will use in all of your math courses.

Mathematical Practices

1. Make sense of problems and persevere in solving them.
2. Reason abstractly and quantitatively.
3. Construct viable arguments and critique the reasoning of others.
4. Model with mathematics.
5. Use appropriate tools strategically.
6. Attend to precision.
7. Look for and make use of structure.
8. Look for and express regularity in repeated reasoning.

---

⑤ Use appropriate tools strategically.

Mathematically proficient students consider the available tools when solving a... problem... [and] are... able to use technological tools to explore and deepen their understanding...

In your book

Algebra Tasks and **Technology Tasks** use concrete and technological tools to explore mathematical concepts.

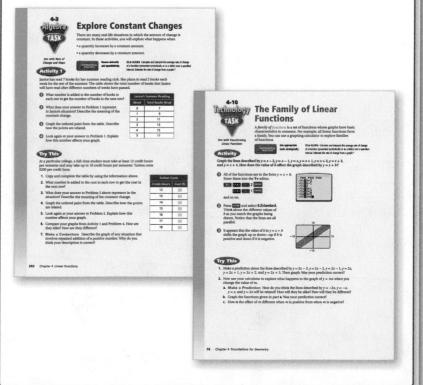

Glossary/Glosario

ENGLISH	SPANISH	EXAMPLES
absolute value The absolute value of x is the distance from zero to x on a number line, denoted $\lvert x \rvert$. $$\lvert x \rvert = \begin{cases} x & \text{if } x \geq 0 \\ -x & \text{if } x < 0 \end{cases}$$	**valor absoluto** El valor absoluto de x es la distancia de cero a x en una recta numérica, y se expresa $\lvert x \rvert$. $$\lvert x \rvert = \begin{cases} x & \text{si } x \geq 0 \\ -x & \text{si } x < 0 \end{cases}$$	$\lvert 3 \rvert = 3$ $\lvert -3 \rvert = 3$
absolute-value equation An equation that contains absolute-value expressions.	**ecuación de valor absoluto** Ecuación que contiene expresiones de valor absoluto.	$\lvert x + 4 \rvert = 7$
absolute-value function A function whose rule contains absolute-value expressions.	**función de valor absoluto** Función cuya regla contiene expresiones de valor absoluto.	$y = \lvert x + 4 \rvert$
absolute-value inequality An inequality that contains absolute-value expressions.	**desigualdad de valor absoluto** Desigualdad que contiene expresiones de valor absoluto.	$\lvert x + 4 \rvert > 7$
accuracy The closeness of a given measurement or value to the actual measurement or value.	**exactitud** Cercanía de una medida o un valor a la medida o el valor real.	
acute angle An angle that measures greater than 0° and less than 90°.	**ángulo agudo** Ángulo que mide más de 0° y menos de 90°.	
acute triangle A triangle with three acute angles.	**triángulo acutángulo** Triángulo con tres ángulos agudos.	
Addition Property of Equality For real numbers a, b, and c, if $a = b$, then $a + c = b + c$.	**Propiedad de igualdad de la suma** Dados los números reales a, b y c, si $a = b$, entonces $a + c = b + c$.	$\begin{aligned} x - 6 &= 8 \\ +6 \ \ &\ \ +6 \\ \hline x \ \ \ &= 14 \end{aligned}$
Addition Property of Inequality For real numbers a, b, and c, if $a < b$, then $a + c < b + c$. Also holds true for $>$, $\leq$, $\geq$, and $\neq$.	**Propiedad de desigualdad de la suma** Dados los números reales a, b y c, si $a < b$, entonces $a + c < b + c$. Es válido también para $>$, $\leq$, $\geq$ y $\neq$.	$\begin{aligned} x - 6 &< 8 \\ +6 \ \ &\ \ +6 \\ \hline x \ \ \ &< 14 \end{aligned}$
additive inverse The opposite of a number. Two numbers are additive inverses if their sum is zero.	**inverso aditivo** El opuesto de un número. Dos números son inversos aditivos si su suma es cero.	The additive inverse of 5 is −5. The additive inverse of −5 is 5.
adjacent arcs Two arcs of the same circle that intersect at exactly one point.	**arcos adyacentes** Dos arcos del mismo círculo que se cruzan en un punto exacto.	$\overset{\frown}{RS}$ and $\overset{\frown}{ST}$ are adjacent arcs.

altitude of a triangle
A perpendicular segment from a vertex to the line containing the opposite side.

altura de un triángulo Segmento perpendicular que se extiende desde un vértice hasta la línea que forma el lado opuesto.

AND A logical operator representing the intersection of two sets.

Y Operador lógico que representa la intersección de dos conjuntos.

$A = \{2, 3, 4, 5\}$ $B = \{1, 3, 5, 7\}$
The set of values that are in A AND B is $A \cap B = \{3, 5\}$.

---

angle A figure formed by two rays with a common endpoint.

ángulo Figura formada por dos rayos con un extremo común.

---

angle bisector A ray that divides an angle into two congruent angles.

bisectriz de un ángulo Rayo que divide un ángulo en dos ángulos congruentes.

$\overrightarrow{JK}$ is an angle bisector of $\angle LJM$.

---

angle of depression The angle formed by a horizontal line and a line of sight to a point below.

ángulo de depresión Ángulo formado por una línea horizontal y una línea visual a un punto inferior.

---

angle of elevation The angle formed by a horizontal line and a line of sight to a point above.

ángulo de elevación Ángulo formado por una línea horizontal y una línea visual a un punto superior.

---

apothem The perpendicular distance from the center of a regular polygon to a side of the polygon.

apotema Distancia perpendicular desde el centro de un polígono regular hasta un lado del polígono.

---

arc An unbroken part of a circle consisting of two points on the circle, called the endpoints, and all the points on the circle between them.

arco Parte continua de una circunferencia formada por dos puntos de la circunferencia denominados extremos y todos los puntos de la circunferencia comprendidos entre éstos.

---

arc length The distance along an arc measured in linear units.

longitud de arco Distancia a lo largo de un arco medida en unidades lineales.

$m\overset{\frown}{CD} = 5\pi$ ft

---

area The number of nonoverlapping unit squares of a given size that will exactly cover the interior of a plane figure.

área Cantidad de cuadrados unitarios de un determinado tamaño no superpuestos que cubren exactamente el interior de una figura plana.

The area is 10 square units.

---

arithmetic sequence A sequence whose successive terms differ by the same nonzero number d, called the *common difference*.

sucesión aritmética Sucesión cuyos términos sucesivos difieren en el mismo número distinto de cero d, denominado *diferencia común*.

4, 7, 10, 13, 16, …
$+ 3 + 3 + 3 + 3$
$d = 3$

ENGLISH	SPANISH	EXAMPLES

Associative Property of Addition
For all numbers a, b, and c,
$(a + b) + c = a + (b + c)$.

Propiedad asociativa de la suma
Dados tres números cualesquiera
a, b y c, $(a + b) + c = a + (b + c)$.

$$(5 + 3) + 7 = 5 + (3 + 7)$$

Associative Property of Multiplication For all numbers a, b, and c, $(a \cdot b) \cdot c = a \cdot (b \cdot c)$.

Propiedad asociativa de la multiplicación Dados tres números cualesquiera a, b y c, $(a \cdot b) \cdot c = a \cdot (b \cdot c)$.

$$(5 \cdot 3) \cdot 7 = 5 \cdot (3 \cdot 7)$$

---

asymptote A line that a graph gets closer to as the value of a variable becomes extremely large or small.

asíntota Línea recta a la cual se aproxima una gráfica a medida que el valor de una variable se hace sumamente grande o pequeño.

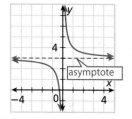

---

auxiliary line A line drawn in a figure to aid in a proof.

línea auxiliar Línea dibujada en una figura como ayuda en una demostración.

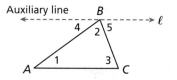

---

average *See* mean.

promedio *Ver* media.

---

axis of a coordinate plane One of two perpendicular number lines, called the x-axis and the y-axis, used to define the location of a point in a coordinate plane.

eje de un plano cartesiano Una de las dos rectas numéricas perpendiculares, denominadas eje x y eje y, utilizadas para definir la ubicación de un punto en un plano cartesiano.

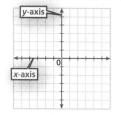

---

axis of symmetry A line that divides a plane figure or a graph into two congruent reflected halves.

eje de simetría Línea que divide una figura plana o una gráfica en dos mitades reflejadas congruentes.

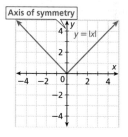

B

---

back-to-back stem-and-leaf plot (A graph used to organize and compare two sets of data so that the frequencies can be compared. *See also* stem-and-leaf plot.

diagrama doble de tallo y hojas Gráfica utilizada para organizar y comparar dos conjuntos de datos para poder comparar las frecuencias. *Ver también* diagrama de tallo y hojas.

Data set A: 9, 12, 14, 16, 23, 27
Data set B: 6, 8, 10, 13, 15, 16, 21

Set A		Set B
9	0	6 8
6 4 2	1	0 3 5 6
7 3	2	1

Key: |2| 1 means 21
7 |2| means 27

ENGLISH	SPANISH	EXAMPLES
bar graph A graph that uses vertical or horizontal bars to display data.	**gráfica de barras** Gráfica con barras horizontales o verticales para mostrar datos.	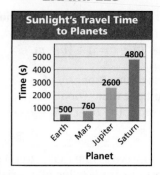
base of a power The number in a power that is used as a factor.	**base de una potencia** Número de una potencia que se utiliza como factor.	$3^4 = 3 \cdot 3 \cdot 3 \cdot 3 = 81$ 3 is the base.
base of an exponential function The value of b in a function of the form $f(x) = ab^x$, where a and b are real numbers with $a \neq 0$, $b > 0$, and $b \neq 1$.	**base de una función exponencial** Valor de b en una función del tipo $f(x) = ab^x$, donde a y b son números reales con $a \neq 0$, $b > 0$ y $b \neq 1$.	In the function $f(x) = 5(2)^x$, the base is 2.
base of an isosceles triangle The side opposite the vertex angle.	**base de un triángulo isósceles** Lado opuesto al ángulo del vértice.	
between Given three points A, B, and C, B is between A and C if and only if all three of the points lie on the same line, and $AB + BC = AC$.	**entre** Dados tres puntos A, B y C, B está entre A y C si y sólo si los tres puntos se encuentran en la misma línea y $AB + BC = AC$.	
biased sample A sample that does not fairly represent the population.	**muestra no representativa** Muestra que no representa adecuadamente una población.	To find out about the exercise habits of average Americans, a fitness magazine surveyed its readers about how often they exercise. The population is all Americans and the sample is readers of the fitness magazine. This sample will likely be biased because readers of fitness magazines may exercise more often than other people do.
biconditional statement A statement that can be written in the form "p if and only if q."	**enunciado bicondicional** Enunciado que puede expresarse en la forma "p si y sólo si q".	A figure is a triangle if and only if it is a three-sided polygon.
binomial A polynomial with two terms.	**binomio** Polinomio con dos términos.	$x + y$ $2a^2 + 3$ $4m^3n^2 + 6mn^4$
bisect To divide into two congruent parts.	**trazar una bisectriz** Dividir en dos partes congruentes.	 $\overrightarrow{JK}$ bisects $\angle LJM$.

ENGLISH	SPANISH	EXAMPLES

boundary line A line that divides a coordinate plane into two half-planes.

línea de límite Línea que divide un plano cartesiano en dos semiplanos.

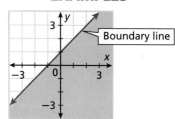

---

box-and-whisker plot A method of showing how data are distributed by using the median, quartiles, and minimum and maximum values; also called a *box plot*.

gráfica de mediana y rango Método para mostrar la distribución de datos utilizando la mediana, los cuartiles y los valores mínimo y máximo; también llamado *gráfica de caja*.

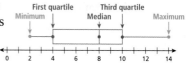

Cartesian coordinate system *See* coordinate plane.

sistema de coordenadas cartesianas *Ver* plano cartesiano.

---

center of a circle The point inside a circle that is the same distance from every point on the circle.

centro de un círculo Punto dentro de un círculo que se encuentra a la misma distancia de todos los puntos del círculo.

---

center of a regular polygon The point that is equidistant from all vertices of the regular polygon.

centro de un polígono regular Punto equidistante de todos los vértices del polígono regular.

---

center of a sphere The point inside a sphere that is the same distance from every point on the sphere.

centro de una esfera Punto dentro de una esfera que está a la misma distancia de cualquier punto de la esfera.

---

central angle of a circle An angle whose vertex is the center of a circle.

ángulo central de un círculo Ángulo cuyo vértice es el centro de un círculo.

---

central angle of a regular polygon An angle whose vertex is the center of the regular polygon and whose sides pass through consecutive vertices.

ángulo central de un polígono regular Ángulo cuyo vértice es el centro del polígono regular y cuyos lados pasan por vértices consecutivos.

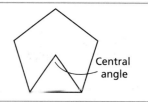

---

centroid of a triangle The point of concurrency of the three medians of a triangle. Also known as the *center of gravity*.

centroide de un triángulo Punto donde se encuentran las tres medianas de un triángulo. También conocido como *centro de gravedad*.

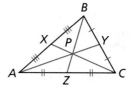

The centroid is *P*.

---

chord A segment whose endpoints lie on a circle.

cuerda Segmento cuyos extremos se encuentran en un círculo.

ENGLISH	SPANISH	EXAMPLES
circle The set of points in a plane that are a fixed distance from a given point called the center of the circle.	**círculo** Conjunto de puntos en un plano que se encuentran a una distancia fija de un punto determinado denominado centro del círculo.	
circle graph A way to display data by using a circle divided into non-overlapping sectors.	**gráfica circular** Forma de mostrar datos mediante un círculo dividido en sectores no superpuestos.	Residents of Mesa, AZ
circumcenter of a triangle The point of concurrency of the three perpendicular bisectors of a triangle.	**circuncentro de un triángulo** Punto donde se cortan las tres mediatrices de un triángulo.	The circumcenter is *P*.
circumference The distance around a circle.	**circunferencia** Distancia alrededor de un círculo.	Circumference
circumscribed polygon Each side of the polygon is tangent to the circle.	**polígono circunscrito** Todos los lados del polígono son tangentes al círculo.	
closure A set of numbers is said to be closed, or to have closure, under a given operation if the result of the operation on any two numbers in the set is also in the set.	**cerradura** Se dice que un conjunto de números es cerrado, o tiene cerradura, respecto de una operación determinada, si el resultado de la operación entre dos números cualesquiera del conjunto también está en el conjunto.	The natural numbers are closed under addition because the sum of two natural numbers is always a natural number.
coefficient A number that is multiplied by a variable.	**coeficiente** Número que se multiplica por una variable.	In the expression $2x + 3y$, 2 is the coefficient of x and 3 is the coefficient of y.
cofunction The trigonometric function of the complement of an angle.	**cofuncion** La funciona trigonométrica del complemento de un ángulo.	
common difference In an arithmetic sequence, the nonzero constant difference of any term and the previous term.	**diferencia común** En una sucesión aritmética, diferencia constante distinta de cero entre cualquier término y el término anterior.	In the arithmetic sequence 3, 5, 7, 9, 11, ..., the common difference is 2.
common factor A factor that is common to all terms of an expression or to two or more expressions.	**factor común** Factor que es común a todos los términos de una expresión o a dos o más expresiones.	Expression: $4x^2 + 16x^3 - 8x$ Common factor: $4x$ Expressions: 12 and 18 Common factors: 2, 3, and 6

Glossary/Glosario

ENGLISH	SPANISH	EXAMPLES
common ratio In a geometric sequence, the constant ratio of any term and the previous term.	**razón común** En una sucesión geométrica, la razón constante entre cualquier término y el término anterior.	In the geometric sequence 32, 16, 8, 4, 2, . . ., the common ratio is $\frac{1}{2}$.
common tangent A line that is tangent to two circles.	**tangente común** Línea que es tangente a dos círculos.	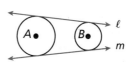 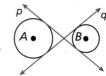
Commutative Property of Addition For any two numbers a and b, $a + b = b + a$.	**Propiedad conmutativa de la suma** Dados dos números cualesquiera a y b, $a + b = b + a$.	$3 + 4 = 4 + 3 = 7$
Commutative Property of Multiplication For any two numbers a and b, $a \cdot b = b \cdot a$.	**Propiedad conmutativa de la multiplicación** Dados dos números cualesquiera a y b, $a \cdot b = b \cdot a$.	$3 \cdot 4 = 4 \cdot 3 = 12$
complement of an event The set of all outcomes that are not the event.	**complemento de un suceso** Todos los resultados que no están en el suceso.	In the experiment of rolling a number cube, the complement of rolling a 3 is rolling a 1, 2, 4, 5, or 6.
complementary angles Two angles whose measures have a sum of 90°.	**ángulos complementarios** Dos ángulos cuyas medidas suman 90°.	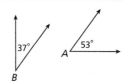
completing the square A process used to form a perfect-square trinomial. To complete the square of $x^2 + bx$, add $\left(\frac{b}{2}\right)^2$.	**completar el cuadrado** Proceso utilizado para formar un trinomio cuadrado perfecto. Para completar el cuadrado de $x^2 + bx$, hay que sumar $\left(\frac{b}{2}\right)^2$.	$x^2 + 6x +$ ▮ Add $\left(\frac{6}{2}\right)^2 = 9$. $x^2 + 6x + 9$
complex fraction A fraction that contains one or more fractions in the numerator, the denominator, or both.	**fracción compleja** Fracción que contiene una o más fracciones en el numerador, en el denominador, o en ambos.	$\dfrac{\frac{1}{2}}{1 + \frac{2}{3}}$
composite figure A plane figure made up of triangles, rectangles, trapezoids, circles, and other simple shapes, or a three-dimensional figure made up of prisms, cones, pyramids, cylinders, and other simple three-dimensional figures.	**figura compuesta** Figura plana compuesta por triángulos, rectángulos, trapecios, círculos y otras figuras simples, o figura tridimensional compuesta por prismas, conos, pirámides, cilindros y otras figuras tridimensionales simples.	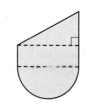
composition of transformations One transformation followed by another transformation.	**composición de transformaciones** Una transformación seguida de otra transformación.	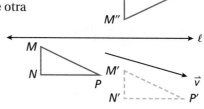

ENGLISH	SPANISH	EXAMPLES
compound event An event made up of two or more simple events.	**suceso compuesto** Suceso formado por dos o más sucesos simples.	In the experiment of tossing a coin and rolling a number cube, the event of the coin landing heads and the number cube landing on 3.
compound inequality Two inequalities that are combined into one statement by the word *and* or *or*.	**desigualdad compuesta** Dos desigualdades unidas en un enunciado por la palabra *y* u *o*.	$x \geq 2$ AND $x < 7$ (also written $2 \leq x < 7$) 0 2 4 6 8 $x < 2$ OR $x > 6$ 0 2 4 6 8
compound interest Interest earned or paid on both the principal and previously earned interest. The formula for compound interest is $A = P\left(1 + \frac{r}{n}\right)^{nt}$, where A is the final amount, P is the principal, r is the interest rate expressed as a decimal, n is the number of times interest is compounded, and t is the time.	**interés compuesto** Intereses ganados o pagados sobre el capital y los intereses ya devengados. La fórmula de interés compuesto es $A = P\left(1 + \frac{r}{n}\right)^{nt}$, donde A es la cantidad final, P es el capital, r es la tasa de interés expresada como un decimal, n es la cantidad de veces que se capitaliza el interés y t es el tiempo.	If \$100 is put into an account with an interest rate of 5% compounded monthly, then after 2 years, the account will have $100\left(1 + \frac{0.05}{12}\right)^{12 \cdot 2} = \$110.49$.
compound statement Two statements that are connected by the word *and* or *or*.	**enunciado compuesto** Dos enunciados unidos por la palabra *y* u *o*.	The sky is blue and the grass is green. I will drive to school or I will take the bus.
compression A transformation that pushes the points of a graph horizontally toward the *y*-axis or vertically toward the *x*-axis.	**compresión** Transformación que desplaza los puntos de una gráfica horizontalmente hacia el eje *y* o verticalmente hacia el eje *x*.	
conclusion The part of a conditional statement following the word *then*.	**conclusión** Parte de un enunciado condicional que sigue a la palabra *entonces*.	If $x + 1 = 5$, then $\underline{x = 4}$. Conclusion
concurrent Three or more lines that intersect at one point.	**concurrente** Tres o más líneas que se cortan en un punto.	
conditional relative frequency The ratio of a joint relative frequency to a related marginal relative frequency in a two-way table.	**frecuencia relativa condicional** Razón de una frecuencia relativa conjunta a una frecuencia relativa marginal en una tabla de doble entrada.	
conditional statement A statement that can be written in the form "if *p*, then *q*," where *p* is the hypothesis and *q* is the conclusion.	**enunciado condicional** Enunciado que se puede expresar como "si *p*, entonces *q*", donde *p* es la hipótesis y *q* es la conclusión.	If $x + 1 = 5$, then $\underline{x = 4}$. Hypothesis Conclusion

ENGLISH	SPANISH	EXAMPLES
cone A three-dimensional figure with a circular base and a curved surface that connects the base to a point called the vertex.	**cono** Figura tridimensional con una base circular y una superficie lateral curva que conecta la base con un punto denominado vértice.	
congruent Having the same size and shape, denoted by ≅.	**congruente** Que tiene el mismo tamaño y la misma forma, expresado por ≅.	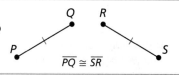 $\overline{PQ} \cong \overline{SR}$
congruent angles Angles that have the same measure.	**ángulos congruentes** Ángulos que tienen la misma medida.	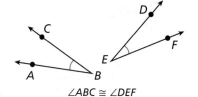 $\angle ABC \cong \angle DEF$
congruent arcs Two arcs that are in the same or congruent circles and have the same measure.	**arcos congruentes** Dos arcos que se encuentran en el mismo círculo o en círculos congruentes y que tienen la misma medida.	
congruent circles Two circles that have congruent radii.	**círculos congruentes** Dos círculos que tienen radios congruentes.	
congruent polygons Two polygons whose corresponding sides and angles are congruent.	**polígonos congruentes** Dos polígonos cuyos lados y ángulos correspondientes son congruentes.	
congruent segments Two segments that have the same length.	**segmentos congruentes** Dos segmentos que tienen la misma longitud.	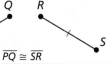 $\overline{PQ} \cong \overline{SR}$
conjecture A statement that is believed to be true.	**conjetura** Enunciado que se supone verdadero.	A sequence begins with the terms 2, 4, 6, 8, 10. A reasonable conjecture is that the next term in the sequence is 12.
consistent system A system of equations or inequalities that has at least one solution.	**sistema consistente** Sistema de ecuaciones o desigualdades que tiene por lo menos una solución.	$\begin{cases} x + y = 6 \\ x - y = 4 \end{cases}$ solution: $(5, 1)$
constant A value that does not change.	**constante** Valor que no cambia.	$3, 0, \pi$
constant of variation The constant k in direct and inverse variation equations.	**constante de variación** La constante k en ecuaciones de variación directa e inversa.	$y = 5x$ constant of variation
construction A method of creating a figure that is considered to be mathematically precise. Figures may be constructed by using a compass and straightedge, geometry software, or paper folding.	**construcción** Método para crear una figura que es considerado matemáticamente preciso. Se pueden construir figuras utilizando un compás y una regla, un programa de computación de geometría o plegando papeles.	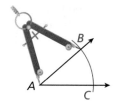

ENGLISH	SPANISH	EXAMPLES
continuous graph A graph made up of connected lines or curves.	**gráfica continua** Gráfica compuesta por líneas rectas o curvas conectadas.	**Angelique's Heart Rate**
contrapositive The statement formed by both exchanging and negating the hypothesis and conclusion of a conditional statement.	**contrarrecíproco** Enunciado que se forma al intercambiar y negar la hipótesis y la conclusión de un enunciado condicional.	Statement: If $n + 1 = 3$, then $n = 2$ Contrapositive: If $n \neq 2$, then $n + 1 \neq 3$
convenience sample A sample based on members of the population that are readily available.	**muestra de conveniencia** Una muestra basada en miembros de la población que están fácilmente disponibles.	A reporter surveys people he personally knows.
converse The statement formed by exchanging the hypothesis and conclusion of a conditional statement.	**recíproco** Enunciado que se forma intercambiando la hipótesis y la conclusión de un enunciado condicional.	Statement: If $n + 1 = 3$, then $n = 2$ Converse: If $n = 2$, then $n + 1 = 3$
conversion factor The ratio of two equal quantities, each measured in different units.	**factor de conversión** Razón entre dos cantidades iguales, cada una medida en unidades diferentes.	$$\frac{12 \text{ inches}}{1 \text{ foot}}$$
coordinate A number used to identify the location of a point. On a number line, one coordinate is used. On a coordinate plane, two coordinates are used, called the x-coordinate and the y-coordinate. In space, three coordinates are used, called the x-coordinate, the y-coordinate, and the z-coordinate.	**coordenada** Número utilizado para identificar la ubicación de un punto. En una recta numérica se utiliza una coordenada. En un plano cartesiano se utilizan dos coordenadas, denominadas coordenada x y coordenada y. En el espacio se utilizan tres coordenadas, denominadas coordenada x, coordenada y y coordenada z.	◄─┼─┼─┼─●─┼─┼─► −1 0 1 2 3 4 5 The coordinate of point A is 3. The coordinates of point B are (1, 4).
coordinate plane A plane that is divided into four regions by a horizontal line called the x-axis and a vertical line called the y-axis.	**plano cartesiano** Plano dividido en cuatro regiones por una línea horizontal denominada eje x y una línea vertical denominada eje y.	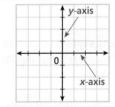
corollary A theorem whose proof follows directly from another theorem.	**corolario** Teorema cuya demostración proviene directamente de otro teorema.	
correlation A measure of the strength and direction of the relationship between two variables or data sets.	**correlación** Medida de la fuerza y dirección de la relación entre dos variables o conjuntos de datos.	**Positive correlation** **No correlation** **Negative correlation** 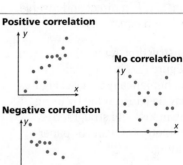

ENGLISH	SPANISH	EXAMPLES
correlation coefficient A number r, where $-1 \leq r \leq 1$, that describes how closely the points in a scatter plot cluster around the least-squares line.	**coeficiente de correlación** Número r, donde $-1 \leq r \leq 1$, que describe a qué distancia de la recta de mínimos cuadrados se agrupan los puntos de un diagrama de dispersión.	An r-value close to 1 describes a strong positive correlation. An r-value close to 0 describes a weak correlation or no correlation. An r-value close to -1 describes a strong negative correlation.
corresponding angles of lines intersected by a transversal For two lines intersected by a transversal, a pair of angles that lie on the same side of the transversal and on the same sides of the other two lines.	**ángulos correspondientes de líneas cortadas por una transversal** Dadas dos líneas cortadas por una transversal, el par de ángulos ubicados en el mismo lado de la transversal y en los mismos lados de las otras dos líneas.	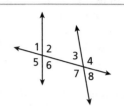 $\angle 1$ and $\angle 3$ are corresponding.
corresponding angles of polygons Angles in the same position in two different polygons that have the same number of angles.	**ángulos correspondientes de los polígonos** Ángulos que tienen la misma posición en dos polígonos diferentes que tienen el mismo número de ángulos.	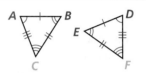 $\angle A$ and $\angle D$ are corresponding angles.
corresponding sides of polygons Sides in the same position in two different polygons that have the same number of sides.	**lados correspondientes de los polígonos** Lados que tienen la misma posición en dos polígonos diferentes que tienen el mismo número de lados.	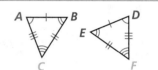 $\overline{AB}$ and $\overline{DE}$ are corresponding sides.
cosine In a right triangle, the cosine of angle A is the ratio of the length of the leg adjacent to angle A to the length of the hypotenuse. It is the reciprocal of the secant function.	**coseno** En un triángulo rectángulo, el coseno del ángulo A es la razón entre la longitud del cateto adyacente al ángulo A y la longitud de la hipotenusa. Es la inversa de la función secante.	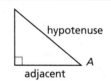 $\cos A = \dfrac{\text{adjacent}}{\text{hypotenuse}} = \dfrac{1}{\sec A}$
counterexample An example that proves that a conjecture or statement is false.	**contraejemplo** Ejemplo que demuestra que una conjetura o enunciado es falso.	
CPCTC An abbreviation for "Corresponding Parts of Congruent Triangles are Congruent," which can be used as a justification in a proof after two triangles are proven congruent.	**PCTCC** Abreviatura que significa "Las partes correspondientes de los triángulos congruentes son congruentes", que se puede utilizar para justificar una demostración después de demostrar que dos triángulos son congruentes (CPCTC, por sus siglas en inglés).	
Cross Product Property For any real numbers a, b, c, and d, where $b \neq 0$ and $d \neq 0$, if $\frac{a}{b} = \frac{c}{d}$, then $ad = bc$.	**Propiedad de productos cruzados** Dados los números reales a, b, c y d, donde $b \neq 0$ y $d \neq 0$, si $\frac{a}{b} = \frac{c}{d}$, entonces $ad = bc$.	If $\frac{4}{6} = \frac{10}{x}$, then $4x = 60$, so $x = 15$.

ENGLISH	SPANISH	EXAMPLES

cross products In the statement $\frac{a}{b} = \frac{c}{d}$, bc and ad are the cross products.

productos cruzados En el enunciado $\frac{a}{b} = \frac{c}{d}$, bc y ad son productos cruzados.

$$\frac{1}{2} = \frac{3}{6}$$
Cross products: $2 \cdot 3 = 6$ and $1 \cdot 6 = 6$

---

cube A prism with six square faces.

cubo Prisma con seis caras cuadradas.

---

cube in numeration The third power of a number.

cubo en numeración Tercera potencia de un número.

8 is the cube of 2.

---

cube root A number, written as $\sqrt[3]{x}$, whose cube is x.

raíz cúbica Número, expresado como $\sqrt[3]{x}$, cuyo cubo es x.

$\sqrt[3]{64} = 4$, because $4^3 = 64$; 4 is the cube root of 64.

---

cubic equation An equation that can be written in the form $ax^3 + bx^2 + cx + d = 0$, where a, b, c, and d are real numbers and $a \neq 0$.

ecuación cúbica Ecuación que se puede expresar como $ax^3 + bx^2 + cx + d = 0$, donde a, b, c, y d son números reales y $a \neq 0$.

$4x^3 + x^2 - 3x - 1 = 0$

---

cubic function A function that can be written in the form $f(x) = ax^3 + bx^2 + cx + d$, where a, b, c, and d are real numbers and $a \neq 0$.

función cúbica Función que se puede expresar como $f(x) = ax^3 + bx^2 + cx + d$, donde a, b, c, y d son números reales y $a \neq 0$.

$f(x) = x^3 + 2x^2 - 6x + 8$

---

cubic polynomial A polynomial of degree 3.

polinomio cúbico Polinomio de grado 3.

$x^3 + 4x^2 - 6x + 2$

---

cumulative frequency The frequency of all data values that are less than or equal to a given value.

frecuencia acumulativa Frecuencia de todos los valores de los datos que son menores que o iguales a un valor dado.

For the data set 2, 2, 3, 5, 5, 6, 7, 7, 8, 8, 8, 9, the cumulative frequency table is shown below.

Data	Frequency	Cumulative Frequency
2	2	2
3	1	3
5	2	5
6	1	6
7	2	8
8	3	11
9	1	12

---

cylinder A three-dimensional figure with two parallel congruent circular bases and a curved surface that connects the bases.

cilindro Figura tridimensional con dos bases circulares congruentes paralelas y una superficie lateral curva que conecta las bases.

---

data Information gathered from a survey or experiment.

datos Información reunida en una encuesta o experimento.

---

deductive reasoning The process of using logic to draw conclusions.

razonamiento deductivo Proceso en el que se utiliza la lógica para sacar conclusiones.

ENGLISH	SPANISH	EXAMPLES
definition A statement that describes a mathematical object and can be written as a true biconditional statement.	**definición** Enunciado que describe un objeto matemático y se puede expresar como un enunciado bicondicional verdadero.	
degree measure of an angle A unit of angle measure; one degree is $\frac{1}{360}$ of a circle.	**medida en grados de un ángulo** Unidad de medida de los ángulos; un grado es $\frac{1}{360}$ de un círculo.	
degree of a monomial The sum of the exponents of the variables in the monomial.	**grado de un monomio** Suma de los exponentes de las variables del monomio.	$4x^2y^5z^3$ Degree: $2 + 5 + 3 = 10$ $5 = 5x^0$ Degree: 0
degree of a polynomial The degree of the term of the polynomial with the greatest degree.	**grado de un polinomio** Grado del término del polinomio con el grado máximo.	$3x^2y^2 + 4xy^5 - 12x^3y^2$ Degree 4 Degree 6 Degree 5 Degree 6
dependent events Events for which the occurrence or nonoccurrence of one event affects the probability of the other event.	**sucesos dependientes** Dos sucesos son dependientes si el hecho de que uno de ellos ocurra o no afecta la probabilidad del otro suceso.	From a bag containing 3 red marbles and 2 blue marbles, draw a red marble, and then draw a blue marble without replacing the first marble.
dependent system A system of equations that has infinitely many solutions.	**sistema dependiente** Sistema de ecuaciones que tiene infinitamente muchas soluciones.	$\begin{cases} x + y = 2 \\ 2x + 2y = 4 \end{cases}$
dependent variable The output of a function; a variable whose value depends on the value of the input, or independent variable.	**variable dependiente** Salida de una función; variable cuyo valor depende del valor de la entrada, o variable independiente.	For $y = 2x + 1$, y is the dependent variable. input: x output: y
diameter A segment that has endpoints on the circle and that passes through the center of the circle; also the length of that segment.	**diámetro** Segmento que atraviesa el centro de un círculo y cuyos extremos están sobre la circunferencia; longitud de dicho segmento.	
difference of two cubes A polynomial of the form $a^3 - b^3$, which may be written as the product $(a - b)(a^2 + ab + b^2)$.	**diferencia de dos cubos** Polinomio del tipo $a^3 - b^3$, que se puede expresar como el producto $(a - b)(a^2 + ab + b^2)$.	$x^3 - 8 = (x - 2)(x^2 + 2x + 4)$
difference of two squares A polynomial of the form $a^2 - b^2$, which may be written as the product $(a + b)(a - b)$.	**diferencia de dos cuadrados** Polinomio del tipo $a^2 - b^2$, que se puede expresar como el producto $(a + b)(a - b)$.	$x^2 - 4 = (x + 2)(x - 2)$
dilation A transformation in which the lines connecting every point P with its preimage P' all intersect at a point C known as the center of dilation, and $\frac{CP'}{CP}$ is the same for every point P; a transformation that changes the size of a figure but not its shape.	**dilatación** Transformación en la cual las líneas que conectan cada punto P con su imagen original P' se cruzan en un punto C conocido como centro de dilatación, y $\frac{CP'}{CP}$ es igual para cada punto P; transformación que cambia el tamaño de una figura pero no su forma.	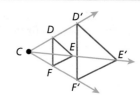

dimensional analysis A process that uses rates to convert measurements from one unit to another.

análisis dimensional Un proceso que utiliza tasas para convertir medidas de unidad a otra.

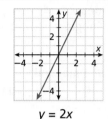

$$12 \text{ pt} \cdot \frac{1 \text{ qt}}{2 \text{ pt}} = 6 \text{ qt}$$

---

direct variation A linear relationship between two variables, x and y, that can be written in the form $y = kx$, where k is a nonzero constant.

variación directa Relación lineal entre dos variables, x e y, que puede expresarse en la forma $y = kx$, donde k es una constante distinta de cero.

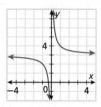

$y = 2x$

---

discontinuous function A function whose graph has one or more jumps, breaks, or holes.

función discontinua Función cuya gráfica tiene uno o más saltos, interrupciones u hoyos.

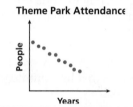

---

discrete graph A graph made up of unconnected points.

gráfica discreta Gráfica compuesta de puntos no conectados.

Theme Park Attendance

---

distance between two points The absolute value of the difference of the coordinates of the points.

distancia entre dos puntos Valor absoluto de la diferencia entre las coordenadas de los puntos.

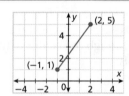

$$AB = |a - b| = |b - a|$$

Distance Formula In a coordinate plane, the distance from (x_1, y_1) to (x_2, y_2) is

$$d = \sqrt{(x_2 - x_1)^2 + (y_2 - y_1)^2}.$$

Fórmula de distancia En un plano cartesiano, la distancia desde (x_1, y_1) hasta (x_2, y_2) es

$$d = \sqrt{(x_2 - x_1)^2 + (y_2 - y_1)^2}.$$

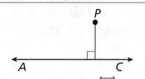

The distance from $(2, 5)$ to $(-1, 1)$ is
$$d = \sqrt{(-1 - 2)^2 + (1 - 5)^2}$$
$$= \sqrt{(-3)^2 + (-4)^2} = \sqrt{25} = 5.$$

---

distance from a point to a line The length of the perpendicular segment from the point to the line.

distancia desde un punto hasta una línea Longitud del segmento perpendicular desde el punto hasta la línea.

The distance from P to $\overleftrightarrow{AC}$ is 5 units.

Distributive Property For all real numbers a, b, and c, $a(b + c) = ab + ac$, and $(b + c)a = ba + ca$.

Propiedad distributiva Dados los números reales a, b y c, $a(b + c) = ab + ac$, y $(b + c)a = ba + ca$.

$$3(4 + 5) = 3 \cdot 4 + 3 \cdot 5$$
$$(4 + 5)3 = 4 \cdot 3 + 5 \cdot 3$$

Division Property of Equality For real numbers a, b, and c, where $c \neq 0$, if $a = b$, then $\frac{a}{c} = \frac{b}{c}$.

Propiedad de igualdad de la división Dados los números reales a, b y c, donde $c \neq 0$, si $a = b$, entonces $\frac{a}{c} = \frac{b}{c}$.

$$4x = 12$$
$$\frac{4x}{4} = \frac{12}{4}$$
$$x = 3$$

Glossary/Glosario

ENGLISH	SPANISH	EXAMPLES
Division Property of Inequality If both sides of an inequality are divided by the same positive quantity, the new inequality will have the same solution set. If both sides of an inequality are divided by the same negative quantity, the new inequality will have the same solution set if the inequality symbol is reversed.	**Propiedad de desigualdad de la división** Cuando ambos lados de una desigualdad se dividen entre el mismo número positivo, la nueva desigualdad tiene el mismo conjunto solución. Cuando ambos lados de una desigualdad se dividen entra el mismo número negativo, la nueva desigualdad tiene el mismo conjunto solución si se invierte el símbolo de desigualdad.	$4x \geq 12$ $$\frac{4x}{4} \geq \frac{12}{4}$$ $x \geq 3$ $-4x \geq 12$ $$\frac{-4x}{-4} \leq \frac{12}{-4}$$ $x \leq -3$
domain The set of all first coordinates (or x-values) of a relation or function.	**dominio** Conjunto de todos los valores de la primera coordenada (o valores de x) de una función o relación.	The domain of the function $\{(-5, 3), (-3, -2), (-1, -1), (1, 0)\}$ is $\{-5, -3, -1, 1\}$.

element Each member in a set or matrix. *See also* entry.	**elemento** Cada miembro en un conjunto o matriz. *Ver también* entrada.	
elimination method A method used to solve systems of equations in which one variable is eliminated by adding or subtracting two equations of the system.	**eliminación** Método utilizado para resolver sistemas de ecuaciones por el cual se elimina una variable sumando o restando dos ecuaciones del sistema.	
empty set A set with no elements.	**conjunto vacío** Conjunto sin elementos.	The solution set of $|x| < 0$ is the empty set, $\{\ \}$, or $\varnothing$.
entry Each value in a matrix; also called an element.	**entrada** Cada valor de una matriz, también denominado elemento.	3 is the entry in the first row and second column of $A = \begin{bmatrix} 2 & 3 \\ 0 & 1 \end{bmatrix}$, denoted a_{12}.
equally likely outcomes Outcomes are equally likely if they have the same probability of occurring. If an experiment has n equally likely outcomes, then the probability of each outcome is $\frac{1}{n}$.	**resultados igualmente probables** Los resultados son igualmente probables si tienen la misma probabilidad de ocurrir. Si un experimento tiene n resultados igualmente probables, entonces la probabilidad de cada resultado es $\frac{1}{n}$.	If a fair coin is tossed, then $P(\text{heads}) = P(\text{tails}) = \frac{1}{2}$. So the outcome "heads" and the outcome "tails" are equally likely.
equation A mathematical statement that two expressions are equivalent.	**ecuación** Enunciado matemático que indica que dos expresiones son equivalentes.	$x + 4 = 7$ $2 + 3 = 6 - 1$ $(x - 1)^2 + (y + 2)^2 = 4$
equidistant The same distance from two or more objects.	**equidistante** Igual distancia de dos o más objetos.	X is equidistant from A and B.

ENGLISH	SPANISH	EXAMPLES
equilateral polygon A polygon in which all sides are congruent.	**polígono equilátero** Polígono cuyos lados son todos congruentes.	
equilateral triangle A triangle with three congruent sides.	**triángulo equilátero** Triángulo con tres lados congruentes.	
equivalent ratios Ratios that name the same comparison.	**razones equivalentes** Razones que expresan la misma comparación.	$\frac{1}{2}$ and $\frac{2}{4}$ are equivalent ratios.
evaluate To find the value of an algebraic expression by substituting a number for each variable and simplifying by using the order of operations.	**evaluar** Calcular el valor de una expresión algebraica sustituyendo cada variable por un número y simplificando mediante el orden de las operaciones.	Evaluate $2x + 7$ for $x = 3$. $2x + 7$ $2(3) + 7$ $6 + 7$ 13
event An outcome or set of outcomes of an experiment.	**suceso** Resultado o conjunto de resultados en un experimento.	In the experiment of rolling a number cube, the event "an odd number" consists of the outcomes 1, 3, and 5.
excluded values Values of x for which a function or expression is not defined.	**valores excluidos** Valores de x para los cuales no está definida una función o expresión.	The excluded values of $\frac{(x + 2)}{(x - 1)(x + 4)}$ are $x = 1$ and $x = -4$, which would make the denominator equal to 0.
experiment An operation, process, or activity in which outcomes can be used to estimate probability.	**experimento** Una operación, proceso o actividad en la que se usan los resultados para estimar una probabilidad.	Tossing a coin 10 times and noting the number of heads
experimental probability The ratio of the number of times an event occurs to the number of trials, or times, that an activity is performed.	**probabilidad experimental** Razón entre la cantidad de veces que ocurre un suceso y la cantidad de pruebas, o veces, que se realiza una actividad.	Kendra attempted 27 free throws and made 16 of them. The experimental probability that she will make her next free throw is $P(\text{free throw}) = $ $\frac{\text{number made}}{\text{number attempted}} = \frac{16}{27} \approx 0.59$.
exponent The number that indicates how many times the base in a power is used as a factor.	**exponente** Número que indica la cantidad de veces que la base de una potencia se utiliza como factor.	$3^4 = 3 \cdot 3 \cdot 3 \cdot 3 = 81$ 4 is the exponent.
exponential decay An exponential function of the form $f(x) = ab^x$ in which $0 < b < 1$. If r is the rate of decay, then the function can be written $y = a(1 - r)^t$, where a is the initial amount and t is the time.	**decremento exponencial** Función exponencial del tipo $f(x) = ab^x$ en la cual $0 < b < 1$. Si r es la tasa decremental, entonces la función se puede expresar como $y = a(1 - r)^t$, donde a es la cantidad inicial y t es el tiempo.	$f(x) = 3\left(\frac{1}{2}\right)^x$

ENGLISH	SPANISH	EXAMPLES
exponential expression An algebraic expression in which the variable is in an exponent with a fixed number as the base.	**expresión exponencial** Expresión algebraica en la que la variable está en un exponente y que tiene un número fijo como base.	2^{x+1}
exponential function A function of the form $f(x) = ab^x$, where a and b are real numbers with $a \neq 0$, $b > 0$, and $b \neq 1$.	**función exponencial** Función del tipo $f(x) = ab^x$, donde a y b son números reales con $a \neq 0$, $b > 0$ y $b \neq 1$.	$f(x) = 3 \cdot 4^x$
exponential growth An exponential function of the form $f(x) = ab^x$ in which $b > 1$. If r is the rate of growth, then the function can be written $y = a(1 + r)^t$, where a is the initial amount and t is the time.	**crecimiento exponencial** Función exponencial del tipo $f(x) = ab^x$ en la que $b > 1$. Si r es la tasa de crecimiento, entonces la función se puede expresar como $y = a(1 + r)^t$, donde a es la cantidad inicial y t es el tiempo.	$f(x) = 2^x$
exponential regression A statistical method used to fit an exponential model to a given data set.	**regresión exponencial** Método estadístico utilizado para ajustar un modelo exponencial a un conjunto de datos determinado.	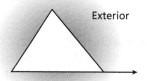
expression A mathematical phrase that contains operations, numbers, and/or variables.	**expresión** Frase matemática que contiene operaciones, números y/o variables.	$6x + 1$
exterior of a circle The set of all points outside a circle.	**exterior de un círculo** Conjunto de todos los puntos que se encuentran fuera de un círculo.	Exterior
exterior of a polygon The set of all points outside a polygon.	**exterior de un polígono** Conjunto de todos los puntos que se encuentran fuera de un polígono.	Exterior
exterior of an angle The set of all points outside an angle.	**exterior de un ángulo** Conjunto de todos los puntos que se encuentran fuera de un ángulo.	Exterior
extraneous solution A solution of a derived equation that is not a solution of the original equation.	**solución extraña** Solución de una ecuación derivada que no es una solución de la ecuación original.	To solve $\sqrt{x} = -2$, square both sides; $x = 4$. **Check** $\sqrt{4} = -2$ is false; so 4 is an extraneous solution.

ENGLISH	SPANISH	EXAMPLES

factor A number or expression that is multiplied by another number or expression to get a product. *See also* factoring.

factor Número o expresión que se multiplica por otro número o expresión para obtener un producto. *Ver también* factoreo.

$12 = 3 \cdot 4$
3 and 4 are factors of 12.
$x^2 - 1 = (x - 1)(x + 1)$
$(x - 1)$ and $(x + 1)$ are factors of $x^2 - 1$.

---

factorial If n is a positive integer, then n factorial, written $n!$, is $n \cdot (n - 1) \cdot (n - 2) \cdot \ldots \cdot 2 \cdot 1$. The factorial of 0 is defined to be 1.

factorial Si n es un entero positivo, entonces el factorial de n, expresado como $n!$, es $n \cdot (n - 1) \cdot (n - 2) \cdot \ldots \cdot 2 \cdot 1$. Por definición, el factorial de 0 será 1.

$7! = 7 \cdot 6 \cdot 5 \cdot 4 \cdot 3 \cdot 2 \cdot 1$
$= 5040$

---

factoring The process of writing a number or algebraic expression as a product.

factorización Proceso por el que se expresa un número o expresión algebraica como un producto.

$x^2 - 4x - 21 = (x - 7)(x + 3)$

---

fair When all outcomes of an experiment are equally likely.

justo Cuando todos los resultados de un experimento son igualmente probables.

When tossing a fair coin, heads and tails are equally likely. Each has a probability of $\frac{1}{2}$.

---

family of functions A set of functions whose graphs have basic characteristics in common. Functions in the same family are transformations of their parent function.

familia de funciones Conjunto de funciones cuyas gráficas tienen características básicas en común. Las funciones de la misma familia son transformaciones de su función madre.

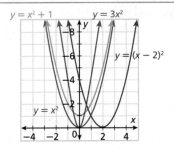

---

first differences The differences between y-values of a function for evenly spaced x-values.

primeras diferencias Diferencias entre los valores de y de una función para valores de x espaciados uniformemente.

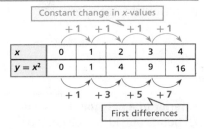

---

first quartile The median of the lower half of a data set, denoted Q_1. Also called *lower quartile*.

primer cuartil Mediana de la mitad inferior de un conjunto de datos, expresada como Q_1. También se llama *cuartil inferior*.

Lower half   Upper half
18, (23), 28,   29, 36, 42
First quartile

---

flowchart proof A style of proof that uses boxes and arrows to show the structure of the proof.

demostración con diagrama de flujo Tipo de demostración que se vale de cuadros y flechas para mostrar la estructura de la prueba.

$\angle 1 \cong \angle 2$
Given
$\angle 1$ and $\angle 2$ are supplementary. → $\angle 1$ and $\angle 2$ are right angles.
Lin. Pair Thm. $\cong \angle$ supp. → rt. $\angle$

Glossary/Glosario

ENGLISH	SPANISH	EXAMPLES

FOIL A mnemonic (memory) device for a method of multiplying two binomials:

Multiply the **First** terms.
Multiply the **Outer** terms.
Multiply the **Inner** terms.
Multiply the **Last** terms.

FOIL Regla mnemotécnica para recordar el método de multiplicación de dos binomios:

Multiplicar los términos **Primeros** (*First*).
Multiplicar los términos **Externos** (*Outer*).
Multiplicar los términos **Internos** (*Inner*).
Multiplicar los términos **Últimos** (*Last*).

$$(x + 2)(x - 3) = x^2 - 3x + 2x - 6$$
$$= x^2 - x - 6$$

---

formula A literal equation that states a rule for a relationship among quantities.

fórmula Ecuación literal que establece una regla para una relación entre cantidades.

$$A = \pi r^2$$

---

fractional exponent *See* rational exponent.

exponente fraccionario *Ver* exponente racional.

---

frequency The number of times the value appears in the data set.

frecuencia Cantidad de veces que aparece el valor en un conjunto de datos.

In the data set 5, 6, 6, 7, 8, 9, the data value 6 has a frequency of 2.

---

frequency table A table that lists the number of times, or frequency, that each data value occurs.

tabla de frecuencia Tabla que enumera la cantidad de veces que ocurre cada valor de datos, o la frecuencia.

Data set: 1, 1, 2, 2, 3, 4, 5, 5, 5, 6, 6, 6, 6
Frequency table:

Data	Frequency
1	2
2	2
3	1
4	1
5	3
6	4

---

function A relation in which every domain value is paired with exactly one range value.

función Relación en la que a cada valor de dominio corresponde exactamente un valor de rango.

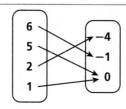

---

function notation If x is the independent variable and y is the dependent variable, then the function notation for y is $f(x)$, read "f of x," where f names the function.

notación de función Si x es la variable independiente e y es la variable dependiente, entonces la notación de función para y es $f(x)$, que se lee "f de x," donde f nombra la función.

equation: $y = 2x$
function notation: $f(x) = 2x$

---

function rule An algebraic expression that defines a function.

regla de función Expresión algebraica que define una función.

$$f(x) = \underset{\uparrow \text{ function rule}}{2x^2 + 3x - 7}$$

Fundamental Counting Principle If one event has m possible outcomes and a second event has n possible outcomes after the first event has occurred, then there are mn total possible outcomes for the two events.

Principio fundamental de conteo Si un suceso tiene m resultados posibles y otro suceso tiene n resultados posibles después de ocurrido el primer suceso, entonces hay mn resultados posibles en total para los dos sucesos.

If there are 4 colors of shirts, 3 colors of pants, and 2 colors of shoes, then there are $4 \cdot 3 \cdot 2 = 24$ possible outfits.

G

geometric sequence A sequence in which the ratio of successive terms is a constant r, called the common ratio, where $r \neq 0$ and $r \neq 1$.

sucesión geométrica Sucesión en la que la razón de los términos sucesivos es una constante r, denominada razón común, donde $r \neq 0$ y $r \neq 1$.

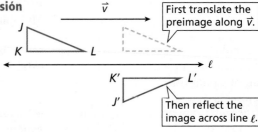

glide reflection A composition of a translation and a reflection across a line parallel to the translation vector.

deslizamiento con inversión Composición de una traslación y una reflexión sobre una línea paralela al vector de traslación.

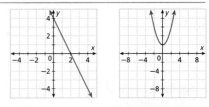

graph of a function The set of points in a coordinate plane with coordinates (x, y), where x is in the domain of the function f and $y = f(x)$.

gráfica de una función Conjunto de los puntos de un plano cartesiano con coordenadas (x, y), donde x está en el dominio de la función f e $y = f(x)$.

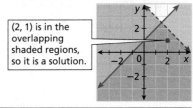

graph of a system of linear inequalities The region in a coordinate plane consisting of points whose coordinates are solutions to all of the inequalities in the system.

gráfica de un sistema de desigualdades lineales Región de un plano cartesiano que consta de puntos cuyas coordenadas son soluciones de todas las desigualdades del sistema.

graph of an inequality in one variable The set of points on a number line that are solutions of the inequality.

gráfica de una desigualdad en una variable Conjunto de los puntos de una recta numérica que representan soluciones de la desigualdad.

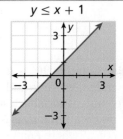

graph of an inequality in two variables The set of points in a coordinate plane whose coordinates (x, y) are solutions of the inequality.

gráfica de una desigualdad en dos variables Conjunto de los puntos de un plano cartesiano cuyas coordenadas (x, y) son soluciones de la desigualdad.

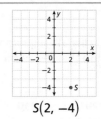

graph of an ordered pair For the ordered pair (x, y), the point in a coordinate plane that is a horizontal distance of x units from the origin and a vertical distance of y units from the origin.

gráfica de un par ordenado Dado el par ordenado (x, y), punto en un plano cartesiano que está a una distancia horizontal de x unidades desde el origen y a una distancia vertical de y unidades desde el origen.

Glossary/Glosario

ENGLISH	SPANISH	EXAMPLES

great circle A circle on a sphere that divides the sphere into two hemispheres.

círculo máximo En una esfera, círculo que divide la esfera en dos hemisferios.

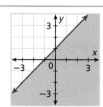
Great circle

---

greatest common factor (monomials) (GCF) The product of the greatest integer and the greatest power of each variable that divide evenly into each monomial.

máximo común divisor (monomios) (MCD) Producto del entero mayor y la potencia mayor de cada variable que divide exactamente cada monomio.

The GCF of $4x^3y$ and $6x^2y$ is $2x^2y$.

---

greatest common factor (numbers) (GCF) The largest common factor of two or more given numbers.

máximo común divisor (números) (MCD) El mayor de los factores comunes compartidos por dos o más números dados.

The GCF of 27 and 45 is 9.

---

grouping symbols Symbols such as parentheses ( ), brackets [ ], and braces { } that separate part of an expression. A fraction bar, absolute-value symbols, and radical symbols may also be used as grouping symbols.

símbolos de agrupación Símbolos tales como paréntesis ( ), corchetes [ ] y llaves { } que separan parte de una expresión. La barra de fracciones, los símbolos de valor absoluto y los símbolos de radical también se pueden utilizar como símbolos de agrupación.

$6 + \{3 - [(4 - 3) + 2] + 1\} - 5$
$6 + \{3 - [1 + 2] + 1\} - 5$
$6 + \{3 - 3 + 1\} - 5$
$6 + 1 - 5$
2

---

half-life The half-life of a substance is the time it takes for one-half of the substance to decay into another substance.

vida media La vida media de una sustancia es el tiempo que tarda la mitad de la sustancia en desintegrarse y transformarse en otra sustancia.

Carbon-14 has a half-life of 5730 years, so 5 g of an initial amount of 10 g will remain after 5730 years.

---

half-plane The part of the coordinate plane on one side of a line, which may include the line.

semiplano La parte del plano cartesiano de un lado de una línea, que puede incluir la línea.

---

hemisphere Half of a sphere.

hemisferio Mitad de una esfera.

Heron's Formula A triangle with side lengths a, b, and c has area $A = \sqrt{s(s - a)(s - b)(s - c)}$, where s is one-half the perimeter, or $s = \frac{1}{2}(a + b + c)$.

fórmula de Herón Un triángulo con longitudes de lado a, b y c tiene un área $A = \sqrt{s(s - a)(s - b)(s - c)}$, donde s es la mitad del perímetro ó $s = \frac{1}{2}(a + b + c)$.

ENGLISH	SPANISH	EXAMPLES
histogram A bar graph used to display data grouped in intervals.	**histograma** Gráfica de barras utilizada para mostrar datos agrupados en intervalos de clases.	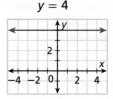
horizontal line A line described by the equation $y = b$, where b is the y-intercept.	**línea horizontal** Línea descrita por la ecuación $y = b$, donde b es la intersección con el eje y.	
hypotenuse The side opposite the right angle in a right triangle.	**hipotenusa** Lado opuesto al ángulo recto de un triángulo rectángulo.	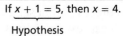
hypothesis The part of a conditional statement following the word *if*.	**hipótesis** La parte de un enunciado condicional que sigue a la palabra *si*.	If $x + 1 = 5$, then $x = 4$. Hypothesis

ENGLISH	SPANISH	EXAMPLES
identity An equation that is true for all values of the variables.	**identidad** Ecuación verdadera para todos los valores de las variables.	$3 = 3$ $2(x - 1) = 2x - 2$
incenter of a triangle The point of concurrency of the three angle bisectors of a triangle.	**incentro de un triángulo** Punto donde se encuentran las tres bisectrices de los ángulos de un triángulo.	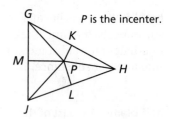 P is the incenter.
included angle The angle formed by two adjacent sides of a polygon.	**ángulo incluido** Ángulo formado por dos lados adyacentes de un polígono.	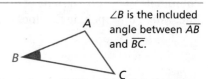 $\angle B$ is the included angle between $\overline{AB}$ and $\overline{BC}$.
included side The common side of two consecutive angles of a polygon.	**lado incluido** Lado común de dos ángulos consecutivos de un polígono.	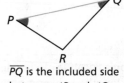 $\overline{PQ}$ is the included side between $\angle P$ and $\angle Q$.
inclusive events Events that have one or more outcomes in common	**sucesos inclusivos** Sucesos que tienen uno o más resultados en común.	In the experiment of rolling a number cube, rolling an even number and rolling a number less than 3 are inclusive events because both contain the outcome 2.

ENGLISH	SPANISH	EXAMPLES
inconsistent system A system of equations or inequalities that has no solution.	**sistema inconsistente** Sistema de ecuaciones o desigualdades que no tiene solución.	$\begin{cases} x + y = 0 \\ x + y = 1 \end{cases}$
independent events Events for which the occurrence or nonoccurrence of one event does not affect the probability of the other event.	**sucesos independientes** Dos sucesos son independientes si el hecho de que se produzca o no uno de ellos no afecta la probabilidad del otro suceso.	From a bag containing 3 red marbles and 2 blue marbles, draw a red marble, replace it, and then draw a blue marble.
independent system A system of equations that has exactly one solution.	**sistema independiente** Sistema de ecuaciones que tiene sólo una solución.	$\begin{cases} x + y = 7 \\ x - y = 1 \end{cases}$ Solution: (4, 3)
independent variable The input of a function; a variable whose value determines the value of the output, or dependent variable.	**variable independiente** Entrada de una función; variable cuyo valor determina el valor de la salida, o variable dependiente.	For $y = 2x + 1$, x is the independent variable.
index In the radical $\sqrt[n]{x}$, which represents the nth root of x, n is the index. In the radical $\sqrt{x}$, the index is understood to be 2.	**índice** En el radical $\sqrt[n]{x}$, que representa la enésima raíz de x, n es el índice. En el radical $\sqrt{x}$, se da por sentado que el índice es 2.	The radical $\sqrt[3]{8}$ has an index of 3.
indirect measurement A method of measurement that uses formulas, similar figures, and/or proportions.	**medición indirecta** Método de medición en el que se usan fórmulas, figuras semejantes y/o proporciones.	
inductive reasoning The process of reasoning that a rule or statement is true because specific cases are true.	**razonamiento inductivo** Proceso de razonamiento por el que se determina que una regla o enunciado son verdaderos porque ciertos casos específicos son verdaderos.	
inequality A statement that compares two expressions by using one of the following signs: $<$, $>$, $\leq$, $\geq$, or $\neq$.	**desigualdad** Enunciado que compara dos expresiones utilizando uno de los siguientes signos: $<$, $>$, $\leq$, $\geq$, o $\neq$.	$x \geq 2$ ←+−+−+−+−+−+−+−+→ −4 −3 −2 −1 0 1 2 3 4 5 6
input A value that is substituted for the independent variable in a relation or function.	**entrada** Valor que sustituye a la variable independiente en una relación o función.	For the function $f(x) = x + 5$, the input 3 produces an output of 8.
input-output table A table that displays input values of a function or expression together with the corresponding outputs.	**tabla de entrada y salida** Tabla que muestra los valores de entrada de una función o expresión junto con las correspondientes salidas.	Input | x | 1 | 2 | 3 | 4 | Output | y | 4 | 7 | 10 | 13 |
inscribed circle A circle in which each side of the polygon is tangent to the circle.	**círculo inscrito** Círculo en el que cada lado del polígono es tangente al círculo.	
integer A member of the set of whole numbers and their opposites.	**entero** Miembro del conjunto de números cabales y sus opuestos.	..., −3, −2, −1, 0, 1, 2, 3, ...

ENGLISH	SPANISH	EXAMPLES
intercept *See x*-intercept and *y*-intercept.	**intersección** *Ver* intersección con el eje *x* e intersección con el eje *y*.	
intercepted arc An arc that consists of endpoints that lie on the sides of an inscribed angle and all the points of the circle between the endpoints.	**arco abarcado** Arco cuyos extremos se encuentran en los lados de un ángulo inscrito y consta de todos los puntos del círculo ubicados entre dichos extremos.	$\overset{\frown}{DF}$ is the intercepted arc.
interior angle An angle formed by two sides of a polygon with a common vertex.	**ángulo interno** Ángulo formado por dos lados de un polígono con un vértice común.	∠1 is an interior angle.
interior of a circle The set of all points inside a circle.	**interior de un círculo** Conjunto de todos los puntos que se encuentran dentro de un círculo.	Interior
interior of an angle The set of all points between the sides of an angle.	**interior de un ángulo** Conjunto de todos los puntos entre los lados de un ángulo.	Interior
interquartile range (IQR) The difference of the third (upper) and first (lower) quartiles in a data set, representing the middle half of the data.	**rango entre cuartiles** Diferencia entre el tercer cuartil (superior) y el primer cuartil (inferior) de un conjunto de datos, que representa la mitad central de los datos.	Lower half Upper half 18, 23, 28, 29, 36, 42 First quartile Third quartile Interquartile range: $36 - 23 = 13$
intersection The intersection of two sets is the set of all elements that are common to both sets, denoted by ∩.	**intersección de conjuntos** La intersección de dos conjuntos es el conjunto de todos los elementos que son comunes a ambos conjuntos, expresado por ∩.	$A = \{1, 2, 3, 4\}$ $B = \{1, 3, 5, 7, 9\}$ $A \cap B = \{1, 3\}$
inverse The statement formed by negating the hypothesis and conclusion of a conditional statement.	**inverso** Enunciado formado al negar la hipótesis y la conclusión de un enunciado condicional.	Statement: If $n + 1 = 3$, then $n = 2$ Inverse: If $n + 1 \neq 3$, then $n \neq 2$
inverse function The function that results from exchanging the input and output values of a one-to-one function. The inverse of $f(x)$ is denoted $f^{-1}(x)$.	**función inversa** Función que resulta de intercambiar los valores de entrada y salida de una función uno a uno. La función inversa de $f(x)$ se expresa $f^{-1}(x)$.	$f(x)=x^1$ $y = x$ $f^{-1}(x)=\sqrt[3]{x}$

Glossary/Glosario

ENGLISH	SPANISH	EXAMPLES
inverse operations Operations that undo each other.	**operaciones inversas** Operaciones que se anulan entre sí.	Addition and subtraction of the same quantity are inverse operations: $5 + 3 = 8$, $8 - 3 = 5$ Multiplication and division by the same quantity are inverse operations: $2 \cdot 3 = 6$, $6 \div 3 = 2$
inverse variation A relationship between two variables, x and y, that can be written in the form $y = \frac{k}{x}$, where k is a nonzero constant and $x \neq 0$.	**variación inversa** Relación entre dos variables, x e y, que puede expresarse en la forma $y = \frac{k}{x}$, donde k es una constante distinta de cero y $x \neq 0$.	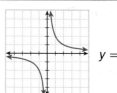 $y = \frac{8}{x}$
irrational number A real number that cannot be expressed as the ratio of two integers.	**número irracional** Número real que no se puede expresar como una razón de enteros.	$\sqrt{2}$, π, e
isolate the variable To isolate a variable in an equation, use inverse operations on both sides until the variable appears by itself on one side of the equation and does not appear on the other side.	**despejar la variable** Para despejar la variable de una ecuación, utiliza operaciones inversas en ambos lados hasta que la variable aparezca sola en uno de los lados de la ecuación y no aparezca en el otro lado.	$10 = 6 - 2x$ $\underline{-6 \quad -6}$ $4 = \qquad -2x$ $\frac{4}{-2} = \frac{-2x}{-2}$ $-2 = x$
isometry A transformation that does not change the size or shape of a figure.	**isometría** Transformación que no cambia el tamaño ni la forma de una figura.	Reflections, translations, and rotations are all examples of isometries.
isosceles triangle A triangle with at least two congruent sides.	**triángulo isósceles** Triángulo que tiene al menos dos lados congruentes.	

J

joint relative frequency The ratio of the frequency in a particular category divided by the total number of data values.	**frecuencia relativa conjunta** La razón de la frecuencia en una determinada categoría dividida entre el número total de valores.	

L

leading coefficient The coefficient of the first term of a polynomial in standard form.	**coeficiente principal** Coeficiente del primer término de un polinomio en forma estándar.	$3x^2 + 7x - 2$ Leading coefficient: 3
least common denominator (LCD) The least common multiple of the denominators of two or more given fractions or rational expressions.	**mínimo común denominador (MCD)** Mínimo común múltiplo de los denominadores de dos o más fracciones dadas o expresionnes racionales.	The LCD of $\frac{3}{4}$ and $\frac{5}{6}$ is 12.

ENGLISH	SPANISH	EXAMPLES
least common multiple (monomials) (LCM) The product of the smallest positive number and the lowest power of each variable that divide evenly into each monomial.	**mínimo común múltiplo (monomios) (MCM)** El producto del número positivo más pequeño y la menor potencia de cada variable que divide exactamente cada monomio.	The LCM of $6x^2$ and $4x$ is $12x^2$.
least common multiple (numbers) (LCM) The smallest whole number, other than zero, that is a multiple of two or more given numbers.	**mínimo común múltiplo (números) (MCM)** El menor de los números cabales, distinto de cero, que es múltiplo de dos o más números dados.	The LCM of 10 and 18 is 90.
least-squares line The line of fit for which the sum of the squares of the residuals is as small as possible.	**línea de mínimos cuadrados** La línea de ajuste en que la suma de cuadrados de los residuos es la menor.	
leg of a right triangle One of the two sides of the right triangle that form the right angle.	**cateto de un triángulo rectángulo** Uno de los dos lados de un triángulo rectángulo que forman el ángulo recto.	
leg of an isosceles triangle One of the two congruent sides of the isosceles triangle.	**cateto de un triángulo isósceles** Uno de los dos lados congruentes del triángulo isósceles.	
length The distance between the two endpoints of a segment.	**longitud** Distancia entre los dos extremos de un segmento.	$AB = \lvert a - b \rvert = \lvert b - a \rvert$
line An undefined term in geometry, a line is a straight path that has no thickness and extends forever.	**línea** Término indefinido en geometría; una línea es un trazo recto que no tiene grosor y se extiende infinitamente.	
line of best fit The line that comes closest to all of the points in a data set.	**línea de mejor ajuste** Línea que más se acerca a todos los puntos de un conjunto de datos.	
line symmetry A figure that can be reflected across a line so that the image coincides with the preimage.	**simetría axial** Figura que puede reflejarse sobre una línea de forma tal que la imagen coincida con la imagen original.	
linear equation in one variable An equation that can be written in the form $ax = b$ where a and b are constants and $a \neq 0$.	**ecuación lineal en una variable** Ecuación que puede expresarse en la forma $ax = b$ donde a y b son constantes y $a \neq 0$.	$x + 1 = 7$
linear equation in two variables An equation that can be written in the form $Ax + By = C$ where A, B, and C are constants and A and B are not both 0.	**ecuación lineal en dos variables** Ecuación que puede expresarse en la forma $Ax + By = C$ donde A, B y C son constantes y A y B no son ambas 0.	$2x + 3y = 6$

ENGLISH	SPANISH	EXAMPLES

linear function A function that can be written in the form $y = mx + b$, where x is the independent variable and m and b are real numbers. Its graph is a line.

función lineal Función que puede expresarse en la forma $y = mx + b$, donde x es la variable independiente y m y b son números reales. Su gráfica es una línea.

$y = x - 1$

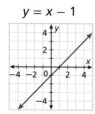

linear inequality in one variable An inequality that can be written in one of the following forms: $ax < b$, $ax > b$, $ax \leq b$, $ax \geq b$, or $ax \neq b$, where a and b are constants and $a \neq 0$.

desigualdad lineal en una variable Desigualdad que puede expresarse de una de las siguientes formas: $ax < b$, $ax > b$, $ax \leq b$, $ax \geq b$ o $ax \neq b$, donde a y b son constantes y $a \neq 0$.

$3x - 5 \leq 2(x + 4)$

linear inequality in two variables An inequality that can be written in one of the following forms: $Ax + By < C$, $Ax + By > C$, $Ax + By \leq C$, $Ax + By \geq C$, or $Ax + By \neq C$, where A, B, and C are constants and A and B are not both 0.

desigualdad lineal en dos variables Desigualdad que puede expresarse de una de las siguientes formas: $Ax + By < C$, $Ax + By > C$, $Ax + By \leq C$, $Ax + By \geq C$ o $Ax + By \neq C$, donde A, B y C son constantes y A y B no son ambas 0.

$2x + 3y > 6$

linear regression A statistical method used to fit a linear model to a given data set.

regresión lineal Método estadístico utilizado para ajustar un modelo lineal a un conjunto de datos determinado.

literal equation An equation that contains two or more variables.

ecuación literal Ecuación que contiene dos o más variables.

$d = rt$

$A = \frac{1}{2}h(b_1 + b_2)$

locus A set of points that satisfies a given condition.

lugar geométrico Conjunto de puntos que cumple con una condición determinada.

logically equivalent statements Statements that have the same truth value.

enunciados lógicamente equivalentes Enunciados que tienen el mismo valor de verdad.

lower quartile *See* first quartile.

cuartil inferior *Ver* primer cuartil.

major arc An arc of a circle whose points are on or in the exterior of a central angle.

arco mayor Arco de un círculo cuyos puntos están sobre un ángulo central o en su exterior.

$\overset{\frown}{ADC}$ is a major arc of the circle.

mapping diagram A diagram that shows the relationship of elements in the domain to elements in the range of a relation or function.

diagrama de correspondencia Diagrama que muestra la relación entre los elementos del dominio y los elementos del rango de una función.

Mapping Diagram

Domain   Range

2 → A
→ B
→ C

ENGLISH	SPANISH	EXAMPLES
marginal relative frequency The sum of the joint relative frequencies in a row or column of a two-way table.	**frecuencia relativa marginal** La suma de las frecuencias relativas conjuntas en una fila o columna de una tabla de doble entrada.	
maximum of a function The *y*-value of the highest point on the graph of the function.	**máximo de una función** Valor de *y* del punto más alto en la gráfica de la función.	The maximum of the function is 2.
mean The sum of all the values in a data set divided by the number of data values. Also called the *average*.	**media** Suma de todos los valores de un conjunto de datos dividida entre el número de valores de datos. También llamada *promedio*.	Data set: 4, 6, 7, 8, 10 Mean: $\dfrac{4 + 6 + 7 + 8 + 10}{5}$ $= \dfrac{35}{5} = 7$
measure of a major arc The difference of 360° and the measure of the associated minor arc.	**medida de un arco mayor** Diferencia entre 360° y la medida del arco menor asociado.	$m\widehat{ADC} = 360° - x°$
measure of a minor arc The measure of its central angle.	**medida de un arco menor** Medida de su ángulo central.	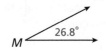 $m\widehat{AC} = x°$
measure of an angle Angles are measured in degrees. A degree is $\frac{1}{360}$ of a complete circle.	**medida de un ángulo** Los ángulos se miden en grados. Un grado es $\frac{1}{360}$ de un círculo completo.	M $\overset{26.8°}{\diagup}$
measure of central tendency A measure that describes the center of a data set.	**medida de tendencia dominante** Medida que describe el centro de un conjunto de datos.	mean, median, or mode
median For an ordered data set with an odd number of values, the median is the middle value. For an ordered data set with an even number of values, the median is the average of the two middle values.	**mediana** Dado un conjunto de datos ordenado con un número impar de valores, la mediana es el valor medio. Dado un conjunto de datos con un número par de valores, la mediana es el promedio de los dos valores medios.	8, 9, (9,) 12, 15 Median: 9 4, 6, (7, 10) 10, 12 Median: $\dfrac{7 + 10}{2} = 8.5$
median of a triangle A segment whose endpoints are a vertex of the triangle and the midpoint of the opposite side.	**mediana de un triángulo** Segmento cuyos extremos son un vértice del triángulo y el punto medio del lado opuesto.	Median diagram with triangle A, B, C, D
midpoint The point that divides a segment into two congruent segments.	**punto medio** Punto que divide un segmento en dos segmentos congruentes.	A —•— B —•— C Point B is the midpoint of AC.

ENGLISH	SPANISH	EXAMPLES

midsegment of a triangle
A segment that joins
the midpoints of two sides of
the triangle.

segmento medio de un triángulo
Segmento que une los puntos
medios de dos lados del triángulo.

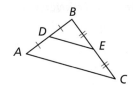

---

midsegment triangle The triangle
formed by the three midsegments
of a triangle.

triángulo de segmentos medios
Triángulo formado por los tres
segmentos medios de un triángulo.

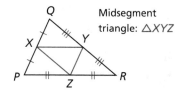

Midsegment
triangle: $\triangle XYZ$

---

minimum of a function The
y-value of the lowest point on the
graph of the function.

mínimo de una función Valor de
y del punto más bajo en la gráfica
de la función.

$(0, -2)$

The minimum of the function
is -2.

---

minor arc An arc of a circle whose
points are on or in the interior of
a central angle.

arco menor Arco de un círculo cuyos
puntos están sobre un ángulo central
o en su interior.

$\overset{\frown}{AC}$ is a minor arc of the circle.

---

mode The value or values that
occur most frequently in a data
set; if all values occur with the
same frequency, the data set is
said to have no mode.

moda El valor o los valores que se
presentan con mayor frecuencia
en un conjunto de datos. Si todos
los valores se presentan con la
misma frecuencia, se dice que el
conjunto de datos no tiene moda.

Data set: 3, 6, 8, 8, 10 Mode: 8
Data set: 2, 5, 5, 7, 7 Modes: 5
and 7
Data set: 2, 3, 6, 9, 11 No mode

---

monomial A number or a product
of numbers and variables with
whole-number exponents, or a
polynomial with one term.

monomio Número o producto de
números y variables con exponentes
de números cabales, o polinomio
con un término.

$3x^2y^4$

**Multiplication Property of
Equality** If *a*, *b*, and *c* are real
numbers and $a = b$, then $ac = bc$.

**Propiedad de igualdad de la
multiplicación** Si *a*, *b* y *c* son
números reales y $a = b$,
entonces $ac = bc$.

$\frac{1}{3}x = 7$

$(3)\left(\frac{1}{3}x\right) = (3)(7)$

$x = 21$

**Multiplication Property of
Inequality** If both sides of an
inequality are multiplied by the
same positive quantity, the new
inequality will have the same
solution set.
If both sides of an inequality
are multiplied by the same
negative quantity, the new
inequality will have the same
solution set if the inequality
symbol is reversed.

**Propiedad de desigualdad de la
multiplicación** Si ambos lados de
una desigualdad se multiplican
por el mismo número positivo,
la nueva desigualdad tendrá el
mismo conjunto solución.
Si ambos lados de una desigualdad
se multiplican por el mismo número
negativo, la nueva desigualdad
tendrá el mismo conjunto solución si
se invierte el símbolo de desigualdad.

$\frac{1}{3}x > 7$

$(3)\left(\frac{1}{3}x\right) > (3)(7)$

$x > 21$

$-x \leq 2$

$(-1)(-x) \geq (-1)(2)$

$x \geq -2$

ENGLISH	SPANISH	EXAMPLES
multiplicative inverse The reciprocal of the number.	**inverso multiplicativo** Recíproco de un número.	The multiplicative inverse of 5 is $\frac{1}{5}$.
mutually exclusive events Two events are mutually exclusive if they cannot both occur in the same trial of an experiment.	**sucesos mutuamente excluyentes** Dos sucesos son mutuamente excluyentes si ambos no pueden ocurrir en la misma prueba de un experimento.	In the experiment of rolling a number cube, rolling a 3 and rolling an even number are mutually exclusive events.

N

ENGLISH	SPANISH	EXAMPLES
natural number A counting number.	**número natural** Número que se utiliza para contar.	1, 2, 3, 4, 5, 6, …
negation The negation of statement p is "not p," written as $\sim p$.	**negación** La negación de un enunciado p es "no p", que se escribe p.	
negative correlation Two data sets have a negative correlation if one set of data values increases as the other set decreases.	**correlación negativa** Dos conjuntos de datos tienen una correlación negativa si un conjunto de valores de datos aumenta a medida que el otro conjunto disminuye.	
negative exponent For any nonzero real number x and any integer n, $x^{-n} = \frac{1}{x^n}$.	**exponente negativo** Para cualquier número real distinto de cero x y cualquier entero n, $x^{-n} = \frac{1}{x^n}$.	$x^{-2} = \frac{1}{x^2}$; $3^{-2} = \frac{1}{3^2}$
negative number A number that is less than zero. Negative numbers lie to the left of zero on a number line.	**número negativo** Número menor que cero. Los números negativos se ubican a la izquierda del cero en una recta numérica.	-2 is a negative number.
net A diagram of the faces of a three-dimensional figure arranged in such a way that the diagram can be folded to form the three-dimensional figure.	**plantilla** Diagrama de las caras de una figura tridimensional que se puede plegar para formar la figura tridimensional.	
no correlation Two data sets have no correlation if there is no relationship between the sets of values.	**sin correlación** Dos conjuntos de datos no tienen correlación si no existe una relación entre los conjuntos de valores.	
nonlinear system of equations A system in which at least one of the equations is not linear.	**sistema no lineal de ecuaciones** Sistema en el cual por lo menos una de las ecuaciones no es lineal.	A system that contains one quadratic equation and one linear equation is a nonlinear system.
nth root The nth root of a number a, written as $\sqrt[n]{a}$ or $a^{\frac{1}{n}}$, is a number that is equal to a when it is raised to the nth power.	**enésima raíz** La enésima raíz de un número a, que se escribe $\sqrt[n]{a}$ o $a^{\frac{1}{n}}$, es un número igual a a cuando se eleva a la enésima potencia.	$\sqrt[5]{32} = 2$, because $2^5 = 32$.

Glossary/Glosario

ENGLISH	SPANISH	EXAMPLES
number line A line used to represent the real numbers.	**recta numérica** Línea utilizada para representar los números reales.	

ENGLISH	SPANISH	EXAMPLES
obtuse angle An angle that measures greater than 90° and less than 180°.	**ángulo obtuso** Ángulo que mide más de 90° y menos de 180°.	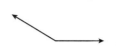
obtuse triangle A triangle with one obtuse angle.	**triángulo obtusángulo** Triángulo con un ángulo obtuso.	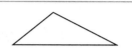
odds A comparison of favorable and unfavorable outcomes. The odds in favor of an event are the ratio of the number of favorable outcomes to the number of unfavorable outcomes. The odds against an event are the ratio of the number of unfavorable outcomes to the number of favorable outcomes.	**probabilidades a favor y en contra** Comparación de los resultados favorables y desfavorables. Las probabilidades a favor de un suceso son la razón entre la cantidad de resultados favorables y la cantidad de resultados desfavorables. Las probabilidades en contra de un suceso son la razón entre la cantidad de resultados desfavorables y la cantidad de resultados favorables.	The odds in favor of rolling a 3 on a number cube are $1:5$. The odds against rolling a 3 on a number cube are $5:1$.
opposite The opposite of a number a, denoted $-a$, is the number that is the same distance from zero as a, on the opposite side of the number line. The sum of opposites is 0.	**opuesto** El opuesto de un número a, expresado $-a$, es el número que se encuentra a la misma distancia de cero que a, del lado opuesto de la recta numérica. La suma de los opuestos es 0.	 5 and -5 are opposites.
opposite reciprocal The opposite of the reciprocal of a number. The opposite reciprocal of any nonzero number a is $-\frac{1}{a}$.	**recíproco opuesto** Opuesto del recíproco de un número. El recíproco opuesto de a es $-\frac{1}{a}$.	The opposite reciprocal of $\frac{2}{3}$ is $-\frac{3}{2}$.
OR A logical operator representing the union of two sets.	**O** Operador lógico que representa la unión de dos conjuntos.	$A = \{2, 3, 4, 5\}$ $B = \{1, 3, 5, 7\}$ The set of values that are in A OR B is $A \cup B = \{1, 2, 3, 4, 5, 7\}$.
order of operations A process for evaluating expressions: First, perform operations in parentheses or other grouping symbols. Second, simplify powers and roots. Third, perform all multiplication and division from left to right. Fourth, perform all addition and subtraction from left to right.	**orden de las operaciones** Regla para evaluar las expresiones: Primero, realizar las operaciones entre paréntesis u otros símbolos de agrupación. Segundo, simplificar las potencias y las raíces. Tercero, realizar todas las multiplicaciones y divisiones de izquierda a derecha. Cuarto, realizar todas las sumas y restas de izquierda a derecha.	$2 + 3^2 - (7 + 5) \div 4 \cdot 3$ $2 + 3^2 - 12 \div 4 \cdot 3$ Add inside parentheses. $2 + 9 - 12 \div 4 \cdot 3$ Simplify the power. $2 + 9 - 3 \cdot 3$ Divide. $2 + 9 - 9$ Multiply. $11 - 9$ Add. 2 Subtract.

ENGLISH	SPANISH	EXAMPLES
ordered pair A pair of numbers (x, y) that can be used to locate a point on a coordinate plane. The first number x indicates the distance to the left or right of the origin, and the second number y indicates the distance above or below the origin.	**par ordenado** Par de números (x, y) que se pueden utilizar para ubicar un punto en un plano cartesiano. El primer número, x, indica la distancia a la izquierda o derecha del origen y el segundo número, y, indica la distancia hacia arriba o hacia abajo del origen.	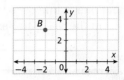 The ordered pair $(-2, 3)$ can be used to locate B.
origin The intersection of the x- and y-axes in a coordinate plane. The coordinates of the origin are $(0, 0)$.	**origen** Intersección de los ejes x e y en un plano cartesiano. Las coordenadas de origen son $(0, 0)$.	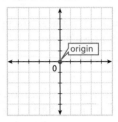
orthocenter of a triangle The point of concurrency of the three altitudes of a triangle.	**ortocentro de un triángulo** Punto de intersección de las tres alturas de un triángulo.	P is the orthocenter. 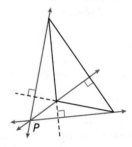
outcome A possible result of a probability experiment.	**resultado** Resultado posible de un experimento de probabilidad.	In the experiment of rolling a number cube, the possible outcomes are 1, 2, 3, 4, 5, and 6.
outlier A data value that is far removed from the rest of the data.	**valor extremo** Valor de datos que está muy alejado del resto de los datos.	
output The result of substituting a value for a variable in a function.	**salida** Resultado de la sustitución de una variable por un valor en una función.	For the function $f(x) = x^2 + 1$, the input 3 produces an output of 10.

parabola The shape of the graph of a quadratic function.	**parábola** Forma de la gráfica de una función cuadrática.	
paragraph proof A style of proof in which the statements and reasons are presented in paragraph form.	**demostración con párrafos** Tipo de demostración en la cual los enunciados y las razones se presentan en forma de párrafo.	
parallel lines Lines in the same plane that do not intersect.	**líneas paralelas** Líneas en el mismo plano que no se cruzan.	

Glossary/Glosario

ENGLISH	SPANISH	EXAMPLES
parallelogram A quadrilateral with two pairs of parallel sides.	**paralelogramo** Cuadrilátero con dos pares de lados paralelos.	
parent function The simplest function with the defining characteristics of the family. Functions in the same family are transformations of their parent function.	**función madre** La función más básica que tiene las características distintivas de una familia. Las funciones de la misma familia son transformaciones de su función madre.	$f(x) = x^2$ is the parent function for $g(x) = x^2 + 4$ and $h(x) = (5x + 2)^2 - 3$.
Pascal's triangle A triangular arrangement of numbers in which every rowstarts and ends with 1 and each other number is the sum of the two numbers above it.	**triángulo de Pascal** Arreglo triangular de números en el cual cada fila comienza y termina con 1 y los demás números son la suma de los dos valores que están arriba de cada uno.	1 1 1 1 2 1 1 3 3 1 1 4 6 4 1
percent A ratio that compares a number to 100.	**porcentaje** Razón que compara un número con 100.	$\dfrac{17}{100} = 17\%$
percent change An increase or decrease given as a percent of the original amount. *See also* percent decrease, percent increase.	**porcentaje de cambio** Incremento o disminución dada como un porcentaje de la cantidad original. *Ver también* porcentaje de disminución, porcentaje de incremento.	
percent decrease A decrease given as a percent of the original amount.	**porcentaje de disminución** Disminución dada como un porcentaje de la cantidad original.	If an item that costs $8.00 is marked down to $6.00, the amount of the decrease is $2.00, so the percent decrease is $\frac{2.00}{8.00} = 0.25 = 25\%$.
percent increase An increase given as a percent of the original amount.	**porcentaje de incremento** Incremento dado como un porcentaje de la cantidad original.	If an item's wholesale cost of $8.00 is marked up to $12.00, the amount of the increase is $4.00, so the percent increase is $\frac{4.00}{8.00} = 0.5 = 50\%$.
perfect square A number whose positive square root is a whole number.	**cuadrado perfecto** Número cuya raíz cuadrada positiva es un número cabal.	36 is a perfect square because $\sqrt{36} = 6$.
perfect-square trinomial A trinomial whose factored form is the square of a binomial. A perfect-square trinomial has the form $a^2 - 2ab + b^2 = (a - b)^2$ or $a^2 + 2ab + b^2 = (a + b)^2$.	**trinomio cuadrado perfecto** Trinomio cuya forma factorizada es el cuadrado de un binomio. Un trinomio cuadrado perfecto tiene la forma $a^2 - 2ab + b^2 = (a - b)^2$ o $a^2 + 2ab + b^2 = (a + b)^2$.	$x^2 + 6x + 9$ is a perfect-square trinomial, because $x^2 + 6x + 9 = (x + 3)^2$.
perimeter The sum of the side lengths of a closed plane figure.	**perímetro** Suma de las longitudes de los lados de una figura plana cerrada.	 Perimeter $= 18 + 6 + 18 + 6 = 48$ ft

ENGLISH	SPANISH	EXAMPLES
permutation An arrangement of a group of objects in which order is important.	**permutación** Arreglo de un grupo de objetos en el cual el orden es importante.	For objects *A*, *B*, *C*, and *D*, there are 12 different permutations of 2 objects. *AB, AC, AD, BC, BD, CD* *BA, CA, DA, CB, DB, DC*
perpendicular Intersecting to form 90° angles.	**perpendicular** Que se cruza para formar ángulos de 90°.	
perpendicular bisector of a segment A line perpendicular to a segment at the segment's midpoint.	**mediatriz de un segmento** Línea perpendicular a un segmento en el punto medio del segmento.	ℓ is the perpendicular bisector of $\overline{AB}$.
perpendicular lines Lines that intersect at 90° angles.	**líneas perpendiculares** Líneas que se cruzan en ángulos de 90°.	
plane A flat surface that has no thickness and extends forever.	**plano** Una superficie plana que no tiene grosor y se extiende infinitamente.	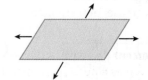
point A location that has no size.	**punto** Ubicación exacta que no tiene ningún tamaño.	point *P*
point of concurrency A point where three or more lines coincide.	**punto de concurrencia** Punto donde se cruzan tres o más líneas.	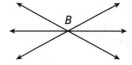
point of tangency The point of intersection of a circle or sphere with a tangent line or plane.	**punto de tangencia** Punto de intersección de un círculo o esfera con una línea o plano tangente.	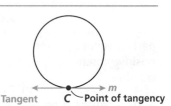
point-slope form The point-slope form of a linear equation is $y - y_1 = m(x - x_1)$, where *m* is the slope and (x_1, y_1) is a point on the line.	**forma de punto y pendiente** La forma de punto y pendiente de una ecuación lineal es $y - y_1 = m(x - x_1)$, donde *m* es la pendiente y (x_1, y_1) es un punto en la línea.	$y - 3 = 2(x - 3)$
polygon A closed plane figure formed by three or more segments such that each segment intersects exactly two other segments only at their endpoints and no two segments with a common endpoint are collinear.	**polígono** Figura plana cerrada formada por tres o más segmentos tal que cada segmento se cruza únicamente con otros dos segmentos sólo en sus extremos y ningún segmento con un extremo común a otro es colineal con éste.	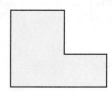

ENGLISH	SPANISH	EXAMPLES
polynomial A monomial or a sum or difference of monomials.	**polinomio** Monomio o suma o diferencia de monomios.	$2x^2 + 3xy - 7y^2$
polynomial long division A method of dividing one polynomial by another.	**división larga polinomial** Método por el que se divide un polinomio entre otro.	$$\begin{array}{r} x + 1 \\ x + 2 \overline{)\, x^2 + 3x + 5} \\ -(x^2 + 2x) \\ \hline x + 5 \\ -(x + 2) \\ \hline 3 \end{array}$$ $$\frac{x^2 + 3x + 5}{x + 2} = x + 1 + \frac{3}{x + 2}$$
population The entire group of objects or individuals considered for a survey.	**población** Grupo completo de objetos o individuos que se desea estudiar.	In a survey about the study habits of high school students, the population is all high school students.
positive correlation Two data sets have a positive correlation if both sets of data values increase.	**correlación positiva** Dos conjuntos de datos tienen correlación positiva si los valores de ambos conjuntos de datos aumentan.	
positive number A number greater than zero.	**número positivo** Número mayor que cero.	2 is a positive number.
Power of a Power Property If a is any nonzero real number and m and n are integers, then $(a^m)^n = a^{mn}$.	**Propiedad de la potencia de una potencia** Dado un número real a distinto de cero y los números enteros m y n, entonces $(a^m)^n = a^{mn}$.	$(6^7)^4 = 6^{7 \cdot 4}$ $= 6^{28}$
Power of a Product Property If a and b are any nonzero real numbers and n is any integer, then $(ab)^n = a^n b^n$.	**Propiedad de la potencia de un producto** Dados los números reales a y b distintos de cero y un número entero n, entonces $(ab)^n = a^n b^n$.	$(2 \cdot 4)^3 = 2^3 \cdot 4^3$ $= 8 \cdot 64$ $= 512$
Power of a Quotient Property If a and b are any nonzero real numbers and n is an integer, then $\left(\frac{a}{b}\right)^n = \frac{a^n}{b^n}$.	**Propiedad de la potencia de un cociente** Dados los números reales a y b distintos de cero y un número entero n, entonces $\left(\frac{a}{b}\right)^n = \frac{a^n}{b^n}$.	$\left(\frac{3}{5}\right)^4 = \frac{3}{5} \cdot \frac{3}{5} \cdot \frac{3}{5} \cdot \frac{3}{5}$ $= \frac{3 \cdot 3 \cdot 3 \cdot 3}{5 \cdot 5 \cdot 5 \cdot 5}$ $= \frac{3^4}{5^4}$
precision The level of detail of a measurement, determined by the unit of measure.	**precisión** Detalle de una medición, determinado por la unidad de medida.	A ruler marked in millimeters has a greater level of precision than a ruler marked in centimeters.
prediction An estimate or guess about something that has not yet happened.	**predicción** Estimación o suposición sobre algo que todavía no ha sucedido.	
prime factorization A representation of a number or a polynomial as a product of primes.	**factorización prima** Representación de un número o de un polinomio como producto de números primos.	The prime factorization of 60 is $2 \cdot 2 \cdot 3 \cdot 5$.

ENGLISH	SPANISH	EXAMPLES
prime number A whole number greater than 1 that has exactly two positive factors, itself and 1.	**número primo** Número cabal mayor que 1 que es divisible únicamente entre sí mismo y entre 1.	5 is prime because its only positive factors are 5 and 1.
principal An amount of money borrowed or invested.	**capital** Cantidad de dinero que se pide prestado o se invierte.	
prism A polyhedron formed by two parallel congruent polygonal bases connected by faces that are parallelograms.	**prisma** Poliedro formado por dos bases poligonales congruentes y paralelas conectadas por caras laterales que son paralelogramos.	
probability A number from 0 to 1 (or 0% to 100%) that is the measure of how likely an event is to occur.	**probabilidad** Número entre 0 y 1 (o entre 0% y 100%) que describe cuán probable es que ocurra un suceso.	A bag contains 3 red marbles and 4 blue marbles. The probability of randomly choosing a red marble is $\frac{3}{7}$.
Product of Powers Property If a is any nonzero real number and m and n are integers, then $a^m \cdot a^n = a^{m+n}$.	**Propiedad del producto de potencias** Dado un número real a distinto de cero y los números enteros m y n, entonces $a^m \cdot a^n = a^{m+n}$.	$6^7 \cdot 6^4 = 6^{7+4}$ $= 6^{11}$
Product Property of Square Roots For $a \geq 0$ and $b \geq 0$, $\sqrt{ab} = \sqrt{a} \cdot \sqrt{b}$.	**Propiedad del producto de raíces cuadradas** Dados $a \geq 0$ y $b \geq 0$, $\sqrt{ab} = \sqrt{a} \cdot \sqrt{b}$.	$\sqrt{9 \cdot 25} = \sqrt{9} \cdot \sqrt{25}$ $= 3 \cdot 5 = 15$
proof An argument that uses logic to show that a conclusion is true.	**demostración** Argumento que se vale de la lógica para probar que una conclusión es verdadera.	
proportion A statement that two ratios are equal; $\frac{a}{b} = \frac{c}{d}$.	**proporción** Ecuación que establece que dos razones son iguales; $\frac{a}{b} = \frac{c}{d}$.	$\frac{2}{3} = \frac{4}{6}$
pyramid A polyhedron formed by a polygonal base and triangular lateral faces that meet at a common vertex.	**pirámide** Poliedro formado por una base poligonal y caras laterales triangulares que se encuentran en un vértice común.	
Pythagorean Theorem If a right triangle has legs of lengths a and b and a hypotenuse of length c, then $a^2 + b^2 = c^2$.	**Teorema de Pitágoras** Dado un triángulo rectángulo con catetos de longitudes a y b y una hipotenusa de longitud c, entonces $a^2 + b^2 = c^2$.	 $5^2 + 12^2 = 13^2$ $25 + 144 = 169$
Pythagorean triple A set of three positive integers a, b, and c such that $a^2 + b^2 = c^2$.	**Tripleta de Pitágoras** Conjunto de tres enteros positivos a, b y c tal que $a^2 + b^2 = c^2$.	The numbers 3, 4, and 5 form a Pythagorean triple because $3^2 + 4^2 = 5^2$.

Q

quadrant One of the four regions into which the x- and y-axes divide the coordinate plane.

cuadrante Una de las cuatro regiones en las que los ejes x e y dividen el plano cartesiano.

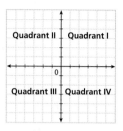

quadratic equation An equation that can be written in the form $ax^2 + bx + c = 0$, where a, b, and c are real numbers and $a \neq 0$.

ecuación cuadrática Ecuación que se puede expresar como $ax^2 + bx + c = 0$, donde a, b y c son números reales y $a \neq 0$.

$$x^2 + 3x - 4 = 0$$
$$x^2 - 9 = 0$$

Quadratic Formula

The formula $x = \frac{-b \pm \sqrt{b^2 - 4ac}}{2a}$, which gives solutions, or roots, of equations in the form $ax^2 + bx + c = 0$, where $a \neq 0$.

fórmula cuadrática La fórmula $x = \frac{-b \pm \sqrt{b^2 - 4ac}}{2a}$, que da soluciones, o raíces, para las ecuaciones del tipo $ax^2 + bx + c = 0$, donde $a \neq 0$.

The solutions of $2x^2 - 5x - 3 = 0$ are given by
$$x = \frac{-(-5) \pm \sqrt{(-5)^2 - 4(2)(-3)}}{2(2)}$$
$$= \frac{5 \pm \sqrt{25 + 24}}{4} = \frac{5 \pm 7}{4}$$
$$x = 3 \text{ or } x = -\frac{1}{2}$$

quadratic function A function that can be written in the form $f(x) = a\,x^2 + bx + c$, where a, b, and c are real numbers and $a \neq 0$.

función cuadrática Función que se puede expresar como $f(x) = ax^2 + bx + c$, donde a, b y c son números reales y $a \neq 0$.

$$f(x) = x^2 - 6x + 8$$

quadratic polynomial A polynomial of degree 2.

polinomio cuadrático Polinomio de grado 2.

$$x^2 - 6x + 8$$

quadrilateral A four-sided polygon.

cuadrilátero Polígono de cuatro lados.

quartile The median of the upper or lower half of a data set. *See also* first quartile, third quartile.

cuartil La mediana de la mitad superior o inferior de un conjunto de datos. *Ver también* primer cuartil, tercer cuartil.

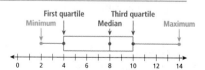

Quotient of Powers Property If a is a nonzero real number and m and n are integers, then $\frac{a^m}{a^n} = a^{m-n}$.

Propiedad del cociente de potencias Dado un número real a distinto de cero y los números enteros m y n, entonces $\frac{a^m}{a^n} = a^{m-n}$.

$$\frac{6^7}{6^4} = 6^{7-4} = 6^3$$

Quotient Property of Square Roots For $a \geq 0$ and $b > 0$, $\sqrt{\frac{a}{b}} = \frac{\sqrt{a}}{\sqrt{b}}$.

Propiedad del cociente de raíces cuadradas Dados $a \geq 0$ y $b > 0$, $\sqrt{\frac{a}{b}} = \frac{\sqrt{a}}{\sqrt{b}}$.

$$\sqrt{\frac{9}{25}} = \frac{\sqrt{9}}{\sqrt{25}} = \frac{3}{5}$$

Glossary/Glosario

R

radian A unit of angle measure based on arc length. In a circle of radius r, if a central angle has a measure of 1 radian, then the length of the intercepted arc is r units.

2π radians = 360°

1 radian ≈ 57°

radián Unidad de medida de un ángulo basada en la longitud del arco. En un círculo de radio r, si un ángulo central mide 1 radián, entonces la longitud del arco abarcado es r unidades.

2π radians = 360°

1 radian ≈ 57°

$\theta = 1$ radian

---

radical equation An equation that contains a variable within a radical.

ecuación radical Ecuación que contiene una variable dentro de un radical.

$\sqrt{x + 3} + 4 = 7$

---

radical expression An expression that contains a radical sign.

expresión radical Expresión que contiene un signo de radical.

$\sqrt{x + 3} + 4$

---

radical symbol The symbol $\sqrt{\ }$ used to denote a root. The symbol is used alone to indicate a square root or with an index, $\sqrt[n]{\ }$, to indicate the *n*th root.

símbolo de radical Símbolo $\sqrt{\ }$ que se utiliza para expresar una raíz. Puede utilizarse solo para indicar una raíz cuadrada, o con un índice, $\sqrt[n]{\ }$, para indicar la enésima raíz.

$\sqrt{36} = 6$

$\sqrt[3]{27} = 3$

---

radicand The expression under a radical sign.

radicando Número o expresión debajo del signo de radical.

Expression: $\sqrt{x + 3}$

Radicand: $x + 3$

---

radius A segment whose endpoints are the center of a circle and a point on the circle; the distance from the center of a circle to any point on the circle.

radio Segmento cuyos extremos son el centro de un círculo y un punto de la circunferencia; distancia desde el centro de un círculo hasta cualquier punto de la circunferencia.

Radius

---

radius of a sphere A segment whose endpoints are the center of a sphere and any point on the sphere; the distance from the center of a sphere to any point on the sphere.

radio de una esfera Segmento cuyos extremos son el centro de una esfera y cualquier punto sobre la esfera; distancia desde el centro de una esfera hasta cualquier punto sobre la esfera.

r

---

random sample A sample selected from a population so that each member of the population has an equal chance of being selected.

muestra aleatoria Muestra seleccionada de una población tal que cada miembro de ésta tenga igual probabilidad de ser seleccionada.

Mr. Hansen chose a random sample of the class by writing each student's name on a slip of paper, mixing up the slips, and drawing five slips without looking.

---

range of a data set The difference of the greatest and least values in the data set.

rango de un conjunto de datos La diferencia del mayor y menor valor en un conjunto de datos.

The data set {3, 3, 5, 7, 8, 10, 11, 11, 12} has a range of 12 − 3 = 9.

---

range of a function or relation The set of all second coordinates (or *y*-values) of a function or relation.

rango de una función o relación Conjunto de todos los valores de la segunda coordenada (o valores de *y*) de una función o relación.

The range of the function {(−5, 3), (−3, −2), (−1, −1), (1, 0)} is {−2, −1, 0, 3}.

Glossary/Glosario

ENGLISH	SPANISH	EXAMPLES
rate A ratio that compares two quantities measured in different units.	**tasa** Razón que compara dos cantidades medidas en diferentes unidades.	$\dfrac{55 \text{ miles}}{1 \text{ hour}} = 55 \text{ mi/h}$
rate of change A ratio that compares the amount of change in a dependent variable to the amount of change in an independent variable.	**tasa de cambio** Razón que compara la cantidad de cambio de la variable dependiente con la cantidad de cambio de la variable independiente.	The cost of mailing a letter increased from 22 cents in 1985 to 25 cents in 1988. During this period, the rate of change was $\dfrac{\text{change in cost}}{\text{change in year}} = \dfrac{25 - 22}{1988 - 1985} = \dfrac{3}{3}$ $= 1$ cent per year.
ratio A comparison of two quantities by division.	**razón** Comparación de dos cantidades mediante una división.	$\dfrac{1}{2}$ or $1:2$
rational equation An equation that contains one or more rational expressions.	**ecuación racional** Ecuación que contiene una o más expresiones racionales.	$\dfrac{x + 2}{x^2 + 3x - 1} = 6$
rational exponent An exponent that can be expressed as $\frac{m}{n}$ such that if m and n are integers, then $b^{\frac{m}{n}} = \sqrt[n]{b^m} = \left(\sqrt[n]{b}\right)^m$.	**exponente racional** Exponente que se puede expresar como $\frac{m}{n}$ tal que si m y n son números enteros, entonces $b^{\frac{m}{n}} = \sqrt[n]{b^m} = \left(\sqrt[n]{b}\right)^m$.	$64^{\frac{1}{6}} = \sqrt[6]{64}$
rational expression An algebraic expression whose numerator and denominator are polynomials and whose denominator has a degree ≥ 1.	**expresión racional** Expresión algebraica cuyo numerador y denominador son polinomios y cuyo denominador tiene un grado ≥ 1.	$\dfrac{x + 2}{x^2 + 3x - 1}$
rational function A function whose rule can be written as a rational expression.	**función racional** Función cuya regla se puede expresar como una expresión racional.	$f(x) = \dfrac{x + 2}{x^2 + 3x - 1}$
rational number A number that can be written in the form $\frac{a}{b}$, where a and b are integers and $b \neq 0$.	**número racional** Número que se puede expresar como $\frac{a}{b}$, donde a y b son números enteros y $b \neq 0$.	$3, 1.75, 0.\overline{3}, -\dfrac{2}{3}, 0$
rationalizing the denominator A method of rewriting a fraction by multiplying by another fraction that is equivalent to 1 in order to remove radical terms from the denominator.	**racionalizar el denominador** Método que consiste en escribir nuevamente una fracción multiplicándola por otra fracción equivalente a 1 a fin de eliminar los términos radicales del denominador.	$\dfrac{1}{\sqrt{2}} \cdot \dfrac{\sqrt{2}}{\sqrt{2}} = \dfrac{\sqrt{2}}{2}$
ray A part of a line that starts at an endpoint and extends forever in one direction.	**rayo** Parte de una recta que comienza en un extremo y se extiende infinitamente en una dirección.	$D \; \bullet\!\longrightarrow$
real number A rational or irrational number. Every point on the number line represents a real number.	**número real** Número racional o irracional. Cada punto de la recta numérica representa un número real.	

ENGLISH	SPANISH	EXAMPLES

reciprocal For a real number $a \neq 0$, the reciprocal of a is $\frac{1}{a}$. The product of reciprocals is 1.

recíproco Dado el número real $a \neq 0$, el recíproco de a es $\frac{1}{a}$. El producto de los recíprocos es 1.

Number	Reciprocal
2	$\frac{1}{2}$
1	1
−1	−1
0	No reciprocal

rectangle A quadrilateral with four right angles.

rectángulo Cuadrilátero con cuatro ángulos rectos.

rectangular prism A prism whose bases are rectangles.

prisma rectangular Prisma cuyas bases son rectángulos.

rectangular pyramid A pyramid whose base is a rectangle.

pirámide rectangular Pirámide cuya base es un rectángulo.

reflection A transformation that reflects, or "flips," a graph or figure across a line, called the line of reflection.

reflexión Transformación en la que una gráfica o figura se refleja o se invierte sobre una línea, denominada la línea de reflexión.

regular polygon A polygon that is both equilateral and equiangular.

polígono regular Polígono equilátero de ángulos iguales.

relation A set of ordered pairs.

relación Conjunto de pares ordenados.

$$\{(0, 5), (0, 4), (2, 3), (4, 0)\}$$

remote interior angle An interior angle of a polygon that is not adjacent to the exterior angle.

ángulo interno remoto Ángulo interno de un polígono que no es adyacente al ángulo externo.

The remote interior angles of $\angle 4$ are $\angle 1$ and $\angle 2$

repeating decimal A rational number in decimal form that has a nonzero block of one or more digits that repeat continuously.

decimal periódico Número racional en forma decimal que tiene un bloque de uno o más dígitos que se repite continuamente.

$1.\overline{3}, 0.\overline{6}, 2.\overline{14}, 6.77\overline{3}$

replacement set A set of numbers that can be substituted for a variable.

conjunto de reemplazo Conjunto de números que pueden sustituir una variable.

residual The signed vertical distance between a data point and a line of fit.

residuo La diferencia vertical entre un dato y una línea de ajuste.

rhombus A quadrilateral with four congruent sides.

rombo Cuadrilátero con cuatro lados congruentes.

ENGLISH	SPANISH	EXAMPLES
right angle An angle that measures 90°.	**ángulo recto** Ángulo que mide 90°.	
right triangle A triangle with one right angle.	**triángulo rectángulo** Triángulo con un ángulo recto.	
rigid transformation A transformation that does not change the size or shape of a figure.	**transformación rígida** Transformación que no cambia el tamaño o la forma de una figura.	
rise The difference in the y-values of two points on a line.	**distancia vertical** Diferencia entre los valores de y de dos puntos de una línea.	For the points $(3, -1)$ and $(6, 5)$, the rise is $5 - (-1) = 6$.
rotation A transformation that rotates or turns a figure about a point called the center of rotation.	**rotación** Transformación que rota o gira una figura sobre un punto llamado centro de rotación.	
rotational symmetry A figure that can be rotated about a point by an angle less than 360° so that the image coincides with the preimage has rotational symmetry.	**simetría de rotación** Una figura que puede rotarse alrededor de un punto en un ángulo menor de 360° de forma tal que la imagen coincide con la imagen original tiene simetría de rotación.	Order of rotational symmetry: 4
run The difference in the x-values of two points on a line.	**distancia horizontal** Diferencia entre los valores de x de dos puntos de una línea.	For the points $(3, -1)$ and $(6, 5)$, the run is $6 - 3 = 3$.

S

sample A part of the population.	**muestra** Una parte de la población.	In a survey about the study habits of high school students, a sample is a survey of 100 high school students.
sample space The set of all possible outcomes of a probability experiment.	**espacio muestral** Conjunto de todos los resultados posibles de un experimento de probabilidad.	In the experiment of rolling a number cube, the sample space is $\{1, 2, 3, 4, 5, 6\}$.
scale The ratio between two corresponding measurements.	**escala** Razón entre dos medidas correspondientes.	1 cm : 5 mi
scale drawing A drawing that uses a scale to represent an object as smaller or larger than the actual object.	**dibujo a escala** Dibujo que utiliza una escala para representar un objeto como más pequeño o más grande que el objeto original.	A blueprint is an example of a scale drawing.

ENGLISH	SPANISH	EXAMPLES
scale factor The multiplier used on each dimension to change one figure into a similar figure.	**factor de escala** El multiplicador utilizado en cada dimensión para transformar una figura en una figura semejante.	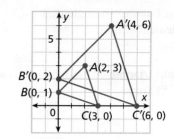 Scale factor: 2
scale model A three-dimensional model that uses a scale to represent an object as smaller or larger than the actual object.	**modelo a escala** Modelo tridimensional que utiliza una escala para representar un objeto como más pequeño o más grande que el objeto real.	
scalene triangle A triangle with no congruent sides.	**triángulo escaleno** Triángulo sin lados congruentes.	
scatter plot A graph with points plotted to show a possible relationship between two sets of data.	**diagrama de dispersión** Gráfica con puntos que se usa para demostrar una relación posible entre dos conjuntos de datos.	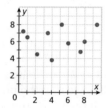
secant of a circle A line that intersects a circle at two points.	**secante de un círculo** Línea que corta un círculo en dos puntos.	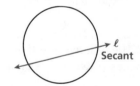
second differences Differences between first differences of a function.	**segundas diferencias** Diferencias entre las primeras diferencias de una función.	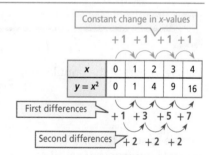
sector of a circle A region inside a circle bounded by two radii of the circle and their intercepted arc.	**sector de un círculo** Región dentro de un círculo delimitado por dos radios del círculo y por su arco abarcado.	
segment bisector A line, ray, or segment that divides a segment into two congruent segments.	**bisectriz de un segmento** Línea, rayo o segmento que divide un segmento en dos segmentos congruentes.	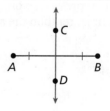

segment of a circle A region inside a circle bounded by a chord and an arc.	**segmento de un círculo** Región dentro de un círculo delimitada por una cuerda y un arco.	
sequence A list of numbers that often form a pattern.	**sucesión** Lista de números que generalmente forman un patrón.	1, 2, 4, 8, 16, …
set A collection of items called elements.	**conjunto** Grupo de componentes denominados elementos.	{1, 2, 3}
set-builder notation A notation for a set that uses a rule to describe the properties of the elements of the set.	**notación de conjuntos** Notación para un conjunto que se vale de una regla para describir las propiedades de los elementos del conjunto.	$\{x \mid x > 3\}$ is read "The set of all x such that x is greater than 3."
similar Two figures are similar if they have the same shape but not necessarily the same size.	**semejantes** Dos figuras con la misma forma pero no necesariamente del mismo tamaño.	
similar polygons Two polygons whose corresponding angles are congruent and whose corresponding side lengths are proportional.	**polígonos semejantes** Dos polígonos cuyos ángulos correspondientes son congruentes y cuyos lados correspondientes tienen longitudes proporcionales.	
similarity ratio The ratio of two corresponding linear measurements in a pair of similar figures.	**razón de semejanza** Razón de dos medidas lineales correspondientes en un par de figuras semejantes.	Similarity ratio: $\dfrac{3.5}{2.1} = \dfrac{5}{3}$
similarity statement A statement that indicates that two polygons are similar by listing the vertices in the order of correspondence.	**enunciado de semejanza** Enunciado que indica que dos polígonos son semejantes enumerando los vértices en orden de correspondencia.	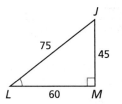 quadrilateral *ABCD* ~ quadrilateral *EFGH*
similarity transformation A transformation that produces similar figures.	**transformación de semejanza** Una transformación que resulta en figuras semejantes.	Dilations are similarity transformations.
simple event An event consisting of only one outcome.	**suceso simple** Suceso que tiene sólo un resultado.	In the experiment of rolling a number cube, the event consisting of the outcome 3 is a simple event.
simple interest A fixed percent of the principal. For principal *P*, interest rate *r*, and time *t* in years, the simple interest is $I = Prt$.	**interés simple** Porcentaje fijo del capital. Dado el capital *P*, la tasa de interés *r* y el tiempo *t* expresado en años, el interés simple es $I = Prt$.	If $100 is put into an account with a simple interest rate of 5%, then after 2 years, the account will have earned $I = 100 \cdot 0.05 \cdot 2 = \$10$ in interest.

ENGLISH	SPANISH	EXAMPLES

simplest form of a rational expression A rational expression is in simplest form if the numerator and denominator have no common factors.

forma simplificada de una expresión racional Una expresión racional está en forma simplificada cuando el numerador y el denominador no tienen factores comunes.

$$\frac{x^2 - 1}{x^2 + x - 2} = \frac{(x - 1)(x + 1)}{(x - 1)(x + 2)}$$
$$= \frac{x + 1}{x + 2}$$

↑ Simplest form

---

simplest form of a square root expression A square root expression is in simplest form if it meets the following criteria:
1. No perfect squares are in the radicand.
2. No fractions are in the radicand.
3. No square roots appear in the denominator of a fraction.

See also rationalizing the denominator.

forma simplificada de una expresión de raíz cuadrada Una expresión de raíz cuadrada está en forma simplificada si reúne los siguientes requisitos:
1. No hay cuadrados perfectos en el radicando.
2. No hay fracciones en el radicando.
3. No aparecen raíces cuadradas en el denominador de una fracción.

Ver también racionalizar el denominador.

Not Simplest Form	Simplest Form
$\sqrt{180}$	$6\sqrt{5}$
$\sqrt{216a^2b^2}$	$6ab\sqrt{6}$
$\dfrac{\sqrt{7}}{\sqrt{2}}$	$\dfrac{\sqrt{14}}{2}$

---

simplest form of an exponential expression An exponential expression is in simplest form if it meets the following criteria:
1. There are no negative exponents.
2. The same base does not appear more than once in a product or quotient.
3. No powers, products, or quotients are raised to powers.
4. Numerical coefficients in a quotient do not have any common factor other than 1.

forma simplificada de una expresión exponencial Una expresión exponencial está en forma simplificada si reúne los siguientes requisitos:
1. No hay exponentes negativos.
2. La misma base no aparece más de una vez en un producto o cociente.
3. No se elevan a potencias productos, cocientes ni potencias.
4. Los coeficientes numéricos en un cociente no tienen ningún factor común que no sea 1.

Not Simplest Form	Simplest Form
$7^8 \cdot 7^4$	7^{12}
$(x^2)^{-4} \cdot x^5$	$\dfrac{1}{x^3}$
$\dfrac{a^5b^9}{(ab)^4}$	ab^5

---

simplify To perform all indicated operations.

simplificar Realizar todas las operaciones indicadas.

$$13 - 20 + 8$$
$$-7 + 8$$
$$1$$

---

simulation A model of an experiment, often one that would be too difficult or time-consuming to actually perform.

simulación Modelo de un experimento; generalmente se recurre a la simulación cuando realizar dicho experimento sería demasiado difícil o llevaría mucho tiempo.

---

sine In a right triangle, the ratio of the length of the leg opposite ∠A to the length of the hypotenuse.

seno En un triángulo rectángulo, razón entre la longitud del cateto opuesto a ∠A y la longitud de la hipotenusa.

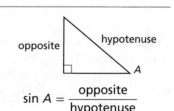

$$\sin A = \frac{\text{opposite}}{\text{hypotenuse}}$$

ENGLISH	SPANISH	EXAMPLES

slope A measure of the steepness of a line. If (x_1, y_1) and (x_2, y_2) are any two points on the line, the slope of the line, known as m, is represented by the equation $m = \frac{y_2 - y_1}{x_2 - x_1}$.

pendiente Medida de la inclinación de una línea. Dados dos puntos (x_1, y_1) y (x_2, y_2) en una línea, la pendiente de la línea, denominada m, se representa con la ecuación $m = \frac{y_2 - y_1}{x_2 - x_1}$.

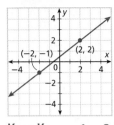

$$m = \frac{y_2 - y_1}{x_2 - x_1} = \frac{-1 - 2}{-2 - 2} = \frac{3}{4}$$

---

slope-intercept form The slope-intercept form of a linear equation is $y = mx + b$, where m is the slope and b is the y-intercept.

forma de pendiente-intersección La forma de pendiente-intersección de una ecuación lineal es $y = mx + b$, donde m es la pendiente y b es la intersección con el eje y.

$y = -2x + 4$
The slope is -2.
The y-intercept is 4.

---

solution of a linear equation in two variables An ordered pair or ordered pairs that make the equation true.

solución de una ecuación lineal en dos variables Un par ordenado o pares ordenados que hacen que la ecuación sea verdadera.

$(4, 2)$ is a solution of $x + y = 6$.

---

solution of a linear inequality in two variables An ordered pair or ordered pairs that make the inequality true.

solución de una desigualdad lineal en dos variables Un par ordenado o pares ordenados que hacen que la desigualdad sea verdadera.

$(3, 1)$ is a solution of $x + y < 6$.

---

solution of a system of linear equations Any ordered pair that satisfies all the equations in a system.

solución de un sistema de ecuaciones lineales Cualquier par ordenado que resuelva todas las ecuaciones de un sistema.

$\begin{cases} x + y = -1 \\ -x + y = -3 \end{cases}$
Solution: $(1, -2)$

---

solution of a system of linear inequalities Any ordered pair that satisfies all the inequalities in a system.

solución de un sistema de desigualdades lineales Cualquier par ordenado que resuelva todas las desigualdades de un sistema.

$\begin{cases} y \le x + 1 \\ y < -x + 4 \end{cases}$

(2, 1) is in the overlapping shaded regions, so it is a solution.
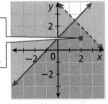

---

solution of an equation in one variable A value or values that make the equation true.

solución de una ecuación en una variable Valor o valores que hacen que la ecuación sea verdadera.

Equation: $x + 2 = 6$
Solution: $x = 4$

---

solution of an inequality in one variable A value or values that make the inequality true.

solución de una desigualdad en una variable Valor o valores que hacen que la desigualdad sea verdadera.

Inequality: $x + 2 < 6$
Solution: $x < 4$

---

solution set The set of values that make a statement true.

conjunto solución Conjunto de valores que hacen verdadero un enunciado.

Inequality: $x + 3 \ge 5$
Solution set: $\{x | x \ge 2\}$

-4 -3 -2 -1 0 1 2 3 4 5 6

Glossary/Glosario

Glossary/Glosario

sphere The set of points in space that are a fixed distance from a given point called the center of the sphere.

esfera Conjunto de puntos en el espacio que se encuentran a una distancia fija de un punto determinado denominado centro de la esfera.

square A quadrilateral with four congruent sides and four right angles.

cuadrado Cuadrilátero con cuatro lados congruentes y cuatro ángulos rectos.

square in numeration The second power of a number.

cuadrado en numeración La segunda potencia de un número.

16 is the square of 4.

standard form of a linear equation $Ax + By = C$, where A, B, and C are real numbers and A and B are not both 0.

forma estándar de una ecuación lineal $Ax + By = C$, donde A, B y C son números reales y A y B no son ambos cero.

$2x + 3y = 6$

standard form of a polynomial A polynomial in one variable is written in standard form when the terms are in order from greatest degree to least degree.

forma estándar de un polinomio Un polinomio de una variable se expresa en forma estándar cuando los términos se ordenan de mayor a menor grado.

$4x^5 - 2x^4 + x^2 - x + 1$

standard form of a quadratic equation $ax^2 + bx + c = 0$, where a, b, and c are real numbers and $a \neq 0$.

forma estándar de una ecuación cuadrática $ax^2 + bx + c = 0$, donde a, b y c son números reales y $a \neq 0$.

$2x^2 + 3x - 1 = 0$

stem-and-leaf plot A graph used to organize and display data by dividing each data value into two parts, a stem and a leaf.

diagrama de tallo y hojas Gráfica utilizada para organizar y mostrar datos dividiendo cada valor de datos en dos partes, un tallo y una hoja.

Stem	Leaves
3	2 3 4 4 7 9
4	0 1 5 7 7 7 8
5	1 2 2 3

Key: 3|2 means 3.2

straight angle A 180° angle.

ángulo llano Ángulo que mide 180°.

stratified random sample A sample in which a population is divided into distinct groups and members are selected at random from each group.

muestra aleatoria estratificada Muestra en la que la población está dividida en grupos diferenciados y los miembros de cada grupo se seleccionan al azar.

Ms. Carter chose a stratified random sample of her school's student population by randomly selecting 30 students from each grade level.

stretch A transformation that pulls the points of a graph horizontally away from the y-axis or vertically away from the x-axis.

estiramiento Transformación que desplaza los puntos de una gráfica en forma horizontal alejándolos del eje y o en forma vertical alejándolos del eje x.

subset A set that is contained entirely within another set. Set B is a subset of set A if every element of B is contained in A, denoted $B \subset A$.

subconjunto Conjunto que se encuentra dentro de otro conjunto. El conjunto B es un subconjunto del conjunto A si todos los elementos de B son elementos de A; se expresa $B \subset A$.

The set of integers is a subset of the set of rational numbers.

ENGLISH	SPANISH	EXAMPLES

substitution method A method used to solve systems of equations by solving an equation for one variable and substituting the resulting expression into the other equation(s).

sustitución Método utilizado para resolver sistemas de ecuaciones resolviendo una ecuación para una variable y sustituyendo la expresión resultante en las demás ecuaciones.

---

subtend A segment or arc subtends an angle if the endpoints of the segment or arc lie on the sides of the angle.

subtender Un segmento o arco subtiende un ángulo si los extremos del segmento o arco se encuentran sobre los lados del ángulo.

If D and F are the endpoints of an arc or chord, and E is a point not on $\overline{DF}$, then $\overset{\frown}{DF}$ or $\overline{DF}$ is said to subtend $\angle DEF$.

Subtraction Property of Equality If a, b, and c are real numbers and $a = b$, then $a - c = b - c$.

Propiedad de igualdad de la resta Si a, b y c son números reales y $a = b$, entonces $a - c = b - c$.

$$\begin{array}{r} x + 6 = 8 \\ \underline{-6 \quad -6} \\ x \quad = 2 \end{array}$$

Subtraction Property of Inequality For real numbers a, b, and c, if $a < b$, then $a - c < b - c$. Also holds true for $>$, $\leq$, $\geq$, and $\neq$.

Propiedad de desigualdad de la resta Dados los números reales a, b y c, si $a < b$, entonces $a - c < b - c$. Es válido también para $>$, $\leq$, $\geq$ y $\neq$.

$$\begin{array}{r} x + 6 < 8 \\ \underline{-6 \quad -6} \\ x \quad < 2 \end{array}$$

---

supplementary angles Two angles whose measures have a sum of 180°.

ángulos suplementarios Dos ángulos cuyas medidas suman 180°.

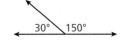

---

surface area The total area of all faces and curved surfaces of a three-dimensional figure.

área total Área total de todas las caras y superficies curvas de una figura tridimensional.

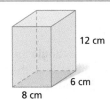

Surface area
$= 2(8)(12) + 2(8)(6) + 2(12)(6)$
$= 432 \text{ cm}^2$

---

symmetry In the transformation of a figure such that the image coincides with the preimage, the image and preimage have symmetry.

simetría En la transformación de una figura tal que la imagen coincide con la imagen original, la imagen y la imagen original tienen simetría.

---

system of linear equations A system of equations in which all of the equations are linear.

sistema de ecuaciones lineales Sistema de ecuaciones en el que todas las ecuaciones son lineales.

$$\begin{cases} 2x + 3y = -1 \\ x - 3y = 4 \end{cases}$$

---

system of linear inequalities A system of inequalities in which all of the inequalities are linear.

sistema de desigualdades lineales Sistema de desigualdades en el que todas las desigualdades son lineales.

$$\begin{cases} 2x + 3y > -1 \\ x - 3y \leq 4 \end{cases}$$

ENGLISH	SPANISH	EXAMPLES
systematic random sample A sample based on selecting one member of the population at random and then selecting other members by using a pattern.	**muestra sistemática** Muestra en la que se elige a un miembro de la población al azar y luego se elige a otros miembros mediante un patrón.	Mr. Martin chose a systematic random sample of customers visiting a store by selecting one customer at random and then selecting every tenth customer after that.

tangent In a right triangle, the ratio of the length of the leg opposite ∠A to the length of the leg adjacent to ∠A.	**tangente** En un triángulo rectángulo, razón entre la longitud del cateto opuesto a ∠A y la longitud del cateto adyacente a ∠A.	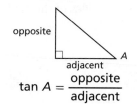 $$\tan A = \frac{\text{opposite}}{\text{adjacent}}$$
tangent circles Two coplanar circles that intersect at exactly one point. If one circle is contained inside the other, they are *internally tangent*. If not, they are *externally tangent*.	**círculos tangentes** Dos círculos coplanares que se cruzan únicamente en un punto. Si un círculo contiene a otro, son *tangentes internamente*. De lo contrario, son *tangentes externamente*.	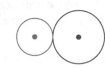
tangent of a circle A line that is in the same plane as a circle and intersects the circle at exactly one point.	**tangente de un círculo** Línea que se encuentra en el mismo plano que un círculo y lo cruza únicamente en un punto.	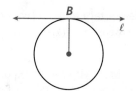
tangent of an angle In a right triangle, the ratio of the length of the leg opposite ∠A to the length of the leg adjacent to ∠A.	**tangente de un ángulo** En un triángulo rectángulo, razón entre la longitud del cateto opuesto a ∠A y la longitud del cateto adyacente a ∠A.	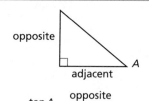 $$\tan A = \frac{\text{opposite}}{\text{adjacent}}$$
term of a sequence An element or number in the sequence.	**término de una sucesión** Elemento o número de una sucesión.	5 is the third term in the sequence 1, 3, 5, 7, …
term of an expression The parts of the expression that are added or subtracted.	**término de una expresión** Parte de una expresión que debe sumarse o restarse.	$3x^2 + 6x - 8$ Term Term Term
terminating decimal A decimal that ends, or terminates.	**decimal finito** Decimal con un número determinados de posiciones decimales.	1.5, 2.75, 4.0
tessellation A repeating pattern of plane figures that completely covers a plane with no gaps or overlaps.	**teselado** Patrón que se repite formado por figuras planas que cubren completamente un plano sin dejar espacios libres y sin superponerse.	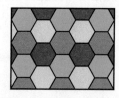

ENGLISH	SPANISH	EXAMPLES
theorem A statement that has been proven.	**teorema** Enunciado que ha sido demostrado.	
theoretical probability The ratio of the number of equally likely outcomes in an event to the total number of possible outcomes.	**probabilidad teórica** Razón entre el número de resultados igualmente probables de un suceso y el número total de resultados posibles.	In the experiment of rolling a number cube, the theoretical probability of rolling an odd number is $\frac{3}{6} = \frac{1}{2}$.
third quartile The median of the upper half of a data set. Also called *upper quartile*.	**tercer cuartil** La mediana de la mitad superior de un conjunto de datos. También se llama *cuartil superior*.	Lower half Upper half 18, 23, 28, 29, ⃝36 42 Third quartile
tolerance The amount by which a measurement is permitted to vary from a specified value.	**tolerancia** La cantidad por que una medida se permite variar de un valor especificado.	
transformation A change in the position, size, or shape of a figure or graph.	**transformación** Cambio en la posición, tamaño o forma de una figura o gráfica.	 $\triangle ABC \rightarrow \triangle A'B'C'$
translation A transformation that shifts or slides every point of a figure or graph the same distance in the same direction.	**traslación** Transformación en la que todos los puntos de una figura o gráfica se mueven la misma distancia en la misma dirección.	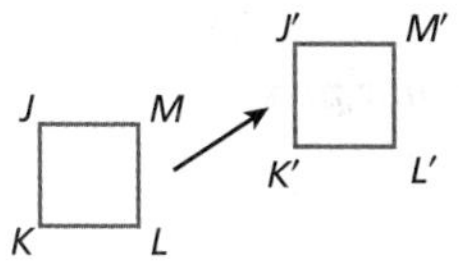
translation symmetry A figure has translation symmetry if it can be translated along a vector so that the image coincides with the preimage.	**simetría de traslación** Una figura tiene simetría de traslación si se puede trasladar a lo largo de un vector de forma tal que la imagen coincida con la imagen original.	
trapezoid A quadrilateral with exactly one pair of parallel sides.	**trapecio** Cuadrilátero con sólo un par de lados paralelos.	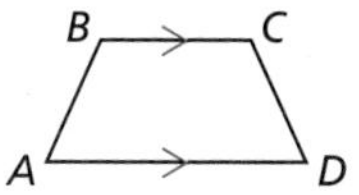
tree diagram A branching diagram that shows all possible combinations or outcomes of an experiment.	**diagrama de árbol** Diagrama con ramificaciones que muestra todas las combinaciones o resultados posibles de un experimento.	 The tree diagram shows the possible outcomes when tossing a coin and rolling a number cube.

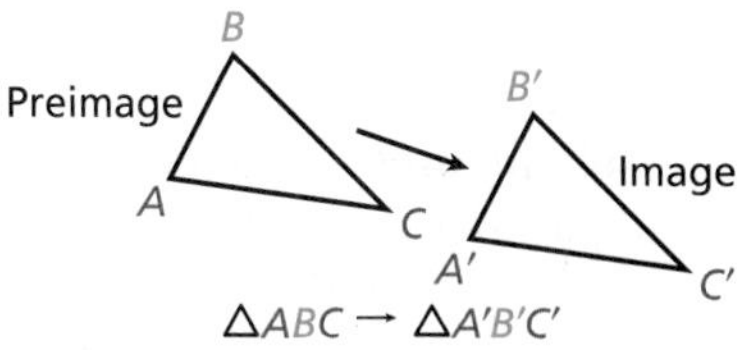

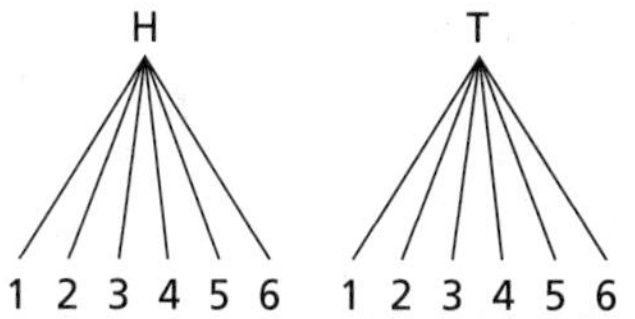

ENGLISH	SPANISH	EXAMPLES
trend line A line on a scatter plot that helps show the correlation between data sets more clearly.	**línea de tendencia** Línea en un diagrama de dispersión que sirve para mostrar la correlación entre conjuntos de datos más claramente.	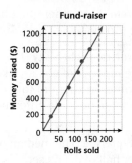
trial Each repetition or observation of an experiment.	**prueba** Una sola repetición u observación de un experimento.	In the experiment of rolling a number cube, each roll is one trial.
triangle A three-sided polygon.	**triángulo** Polígono de tres lados.	
triangle rigidity A property of triangles that states that if the side lengths of a triangle are fixed, the triangle can have only one shape.	**rigidez del triángulo** Propiedad de los triángulos que establece que, si las longitudes de los lados de un triángulo son fijas, el triángulo puede tener sólo una forma.	
triangular prism A prism whose bases are triangles.	**prisma triangular** Prisma cuyas bases son triángulos.	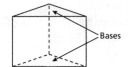
triangular pyramid A pyramid whose base is a triangle.	**pirámide triangular** Pirámide cuya base es un triángulo.	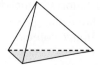
trigonometric ratio Ratio of the lengths of two sides of a right triangle.	**razón trigonométrica** Razón entre dos lados de un triángulo rectángulo.	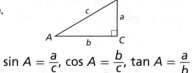$\sin A = \dfrac{a}{c}$, $\cos A = \dfrac{b}{c}$, $\tan A = \dfrac{a}{b}$
trinomial A polynomial with three terms.	**trinomio** Polinomio con tres términos.	$4x^2 + 3xy - 5y^2$
truth value A statement can have a truth value of true (T) or false (F).	**valor de verdad** Un enunciado puede tener un valor de verdad verdadero (V) o falso (F).	
two-column proof A style of proof in which the statements are written in the left-hand column and the reasons are written in the right-hand column.	**demostración a dos columnas** Estilo de demostración en la que los enunciados se escriben en la columna de la izquierda y las razones en la columna de la derecha.	

union The union of two sets is the set of all elements that are in either set, denoted by ∪.

unión La unión de dos conjuntos es el conjunto de todos los elementos que se encuentran en ambos conjuntos, expresado por ∪.

$A = \{1, 2, 3, 4\}$
$B = \{1, 3, 5, 7, 9\}$
$A \cup B = \{1, 2, 3, 4, 5, 7, 9\}$

unit rate A rate in which the second quantity in the comparison is one unit.

tasa unitaria Tasa en la que la segunda cantidad de la comparación es una unidad.

$\dfrac{30 \text{ mi}}{1 \text{ h}} = 30 \text{ mi/h}$

unlike radicals Radicals with a different quantity under the radical.

radicales distintos Radicales con cantidades diferentes debajo del signo de radical.

$2\sqrt{2}$ and $2\sqrt{3}$

unlike terms Terms with different variables or the same variables raised to different powers.

términos distintos Términos con variables diferentes o las mismas variables elevadas a potencias diferentes.

$4xy^2$ and $6x^2y$

upper quartile *See* third quartile.

cuartil superior *Ver* tercer cuartil.

value of a function The result of replacing the independent variable with a number and simplifying.

valor de una función Resultado de reemplazar la variable independiente por un número y luego simplificar.

The value of the function $f(x) = x + 1$ for $x = 3$ is 4.

value of a variable A number used to replace a variable to make an equation true.

valor de una variable Número utilizado para reemplazar una variable y hacer que una ecuación sea verdadera.

In the equation $x + 1 = 4$, the value of x is 3.

value of an expression The result of replacing the variables in an expression with numbers and simplifying.

valor de una expresión Resultado de reemplazar las variables de una expresión por un número y luego simplificar.

The value of the expression $x + 1$ for $x = 3$ is 4.

variable A symbol used to represent a quantity that can change.

variable Símbolo utilizado para representar una cantidad que puede cambiar.

In the expression $2x + 3$, x is the variable.

Venn diagram A diagram used to show relationships between sets.

diagrama de Venn Diagrama utilizado para mostrar la relación entre conjuntos.

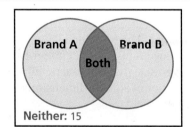

vertex angle of an isosceles triangle The angle formed by the legs of an isosceles triangle.

ángulo del vértice de un triángulo isósceles Ángulo formado por los catetos de un triángulo isósceles.

vertex angle

E   *F*

ENGLISH	SPANISH	EXAMPLES
vertex of a parabola The highest or lowest point on the parabola.	**vértice de una parábola** Punto más alto o más bajo de una parábola.	 The vertex is $(0, -2)$.
vertex of an absolute-value graph The point on the axis of symmetry of the graph.	**vértice de una gráfica de valor absoluto** Punto en el eje de simetría de la gráfica.	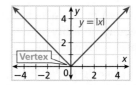
vertex of an angle The common endpoint of the sides of the angle.	**vértice de un ángulo** Extremo común de los lados del ángulo.	 A is the vertex of $\angle CAB$.
vertical angles The nonadjacent angles formed by two intersecting lines.	**ángulos opuestos por el vértice** Ángulos no adyacentes formados por dos líneas que se cruzan.	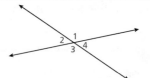 $\angle 1$ and $\angle 3$ are vertical angles. $\angle 2$ and $\angle 4$ are vertical angles.
vertical line A line whose equation is $x = a$, where a is the x-intercept.	**línea vertical** Línea cuya ecuación es $x = a$, donde a es la intersección con el eje x.	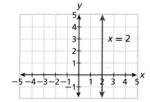
vertical-line test A test used to determine whether a relation is a function. If any vertical line crosses the graph of a relation more than once, the relation is not a function.	**prueba de la línea vertical** Prueba utilizada para determinar si una relación es una función. Si una línea vertical corta la gráfica de una relación más de una vez, la relación no es una función.	 Function Not a function
volume The number of nonoverlapping unit cubes of a given size that will exactly fill the interior of a three-dimensional figure.	**volumen** Cantidad de cubos unitarios no superpuestos de un determinado tamaño que llenan exactamente el interior de una figura tridimensional.	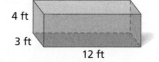 Volume $= (3)(4)(12) = 144$ ft^3
voluntary response sample A sample in which members choose to be in the sample.	**muestra de respuesta voluntaria** Una muestra en la que los miembros eligen participar.	A store provides survey cards for customers who wish to fill them out.

ENGLISH	SPANISH	EXAMPLES

whole number A member of the set of natural numbers and zero. | **número cabal** Miembro del conjunto de los números naturales y cero. | 0, 1, 2, 3, 4, 5, …

x-axis The horizontal axis in a coordinate plane. | **eje x** Eje horizontal en un plano cartesiano. |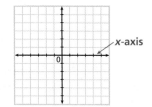

x-coordinate The first number in an ordered pair, which indicates the horizontal distance of a point from the origin on the coordinate plane. | **coordenada x** Primer número de un par ordenado, que indica la distancia horizontal de un punto desde el origen en un plano cartesiano. |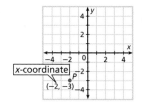

x-intercept The x-coordinate(s) of the point(s) where a graph intersects the x-axis. | **intersección con el eje x** Coordenada(s) x de uno o más puntos donde una gráfica corta el eje x. |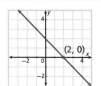

The x-intercept is 2.

y-axis The vertical axis in a coordinate plane. | **eje y** Eje vertical en un plano cartesiano. |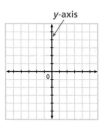

y-coordinate The second number in an ordered pair, which indicates the vertical distance of a point from the origin on the coordinate plane. | **coordenada y** Segundo número de un par ordenado, que indica la distancia vertical de un punto desde el origen en un plano cartesiano. |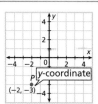

y-intercept The y-coordinate(s) of the point(s) where a graph intersects the y-axis. | **intersección con el eje y** Coordenada(s) y de uno o más puntos donde una gráfica corta el eje y. |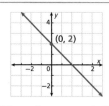

The y-intercept is 2.

Z

zero exponent For any nonzero real number x, $x^0 = 1$.	**exponente cero** Dado un número real distinto de cero x, $x^0 = 1$.	$5^0 = 1$
zero of a function For the function f, any number x such that $f(x) = 0$.	**cero de una función** Dada la función f, todo número x tal que $f(x) = 0$.	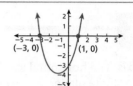 (−3, 0) (1, 0) The zeros are −3 and 1.
Zero Product Property For real numbers p and q, if $pq = 0$, then $p = 0$ or $q = 0$.	**Propiedad del producto cero** Dados los números reales p y q, si $pq = 0$, entonces $p = 0$ o $q = 0$.	If $(x - 1)(x + 2) = 0$, then $x - 1 = 0$ or $x + 2 = 0$, so $x = 1$ or $x = -2$.

Glossary/Glosario

Index

A

Index

Index

B

C

Index

Index

Index

Index

Index

Index

Index

Index

Physical Science, 246, 311, 350
Physics, 318, 432, 489, 543
piano strings, 603
Pimlico Race Course, 192
plane symmetry, 486
Plimpton tablet, 710
plumb bob, 616
point(s)
  and a line distance between a, 620
  constructing a tangent to a circle at a, 916
  equidistant, 914
  exterior constructing a tangent to a circle from an, 947
  of concurrency, 707
  of tangency, 914
  three noncollinear constructing a circle through, 931
point-slope form of linear equations, 287, 288, 289, 290, 291
Politics, 644
Polygon(s)
  congruent, 649
  quadrilaterals and, 733, 734, 735, 736, 737, 738, 739, 740, 741, 742, 743, 744, 745, 746, 747, 748, 749, 750, 751, 752, 753, 754, 755, 758, 759, 760, 761, 762, 763, 764, 765
Pompeii, 753
Population, 38
positive correlation, 413
positive slope, 256
precision of measurements, 45, 46, 47, 48
preimage, 444
primes, 444
probability, 463, 557, 648, 655
  conditional relative frequency to find, 387
Problem-Solving Applications, 64, 93, 94, 135, 217, 290, 343, 344, 453, 670, 671, 715, 716, 917
proof(s), 626, 646, 712, 733, 739, 746, 747, 751, 752, 753, 754, 755, 765, 921, 926, 930, 946, 947
  flowchart, 590, 591, 594, 595, 616
  of angle-angle-side (AAS) congruence, 672
  of the Circumcenter Theorem, 708
  of the Common Segments Theorem, 590
  of the Converse of the Alternate Interior Angles Theorem, 616
  of the Converse of the Common Segments Theorem, 590
  of the Distance Formula, 826
  of the Inscribed Angle Theorem, 940, 946

  of the Isosceles Triangle Theorem, 687
  of the Pythagorean Theorem, 820
  of the Triangle Midsegment Theorem, 726
  of the Triangle Sum Theorem, 641
  paragraph, 592, 593, 594, 595, 596, 607, 616, 617, 621, 738, 746, 764, 826, 834
  of the Converse of the Same-Side Interior Angles Theorem, 616
  of the Perpendicular Transversal Theorem, 621
  of the Same-Side Interior Angles Theorem, 607
  of the Vertical Angles Theorem, 592
  two-column, 590, 591, 592, 593, 594, 595, 596, 597, 607, 612, 621, 623, 718, 736, 737, 738, 745, 753, 763, 764, 788
  of the Alternate Exterior Angles Theorem, 607
Properties, 229
  of equality, 15, 22
  of inequality, 92, 98, 99
  of parallelograms, 733, 734
  of rectangles, 748
  of rhombuses, 749
  of squares, 750
proportions
  applications of, 39, 40, 41
  cross products in, 33
  definition of, 32
  rates, ratios and, 32, 33, 34, 35
proportions solving, 713
protractor, 538
  using, 539
Protractor Postulate, 538
proving theorems about lines and angles, 600
proving theorems about parallelograms, 730
proving triangles congruent, 658
Pythagorean Inequalities Theorem, 823
Pythagorean Theorem, 820, 821, 822, 823, 824, 917
  Converse of the, 822
  proof of the, 820
  solving quadratic equations using, 928, 929
Pythagorean triple, 821

Q

Qin Jiushao, 152
Quadratic Formula
  using, 693
quadratic models, 341, 342, 343, 344

quadrilaterals
  opposite angles, 733
  opposite sides, 733
  polygons and, 733, 734, 735, 736, 737, 738, 739, 740, 741, 742, 743, 744, 745, 746, 747, 748, 749, 750, 751, 752, 753, 754, 755, 758, 759, 760, 761, 762, 763, 764, 765
  special, 733

R

Racing, 734
radian, 931
radius, 915
range, 18, 194, 195, 196, 197, 198, 199, 200, 206, 207, 208, 209, 218
range of a data set, 394, 395
rate of change
  constant and variable, 348, 349
  decrease, 321
  definition of, 254, 348
  identifying linear and nonlinear functions from, 349, 350
  increase, 321
  slope and, 254, 255, 256, 257
rates, 32, 33, 34, 35
ratio(s), 922
  equivalent, 32
  rates and proportions, 32, 33, 34, 35
Reading Math, 32, 34, 39, 88, 160, 205, 230, 264, 324, 353, 372, 396, 687, 916
Reading Strategies
  Read and Interpret Graphics, 381
Real Estate, 43
Real-World Connections
  Real-World Connections are found in every chapter.
reasonable answer, 15, 16, 17, 18, 24, 25, 33, 35, 36, 38, 40, 42, 65, 74, 88, 94, 100, 135, 136, 166, 173, 189, 217, 314, 323, 325
reasonable domain, 206, 207, 208, 209, 217, 243, 248
reasonableness, 15, 16, 17, 18, 24, 25, 65, 74, 35, 36, 38, 40, 42, 208, 209, 217, 415, 917
reasonable range, 206, 207, 208, 209, 217, 243, 248
reasoning, 303, 393, 521
Recreation, 23, 118, 144, 175, 192, 198, 226, 234, 261, 456, 480, 519, 533, 564, 792
rectangle
  proof of, 748
  properties of, 748
rectangles, area of, 19
recursive patterns, 332

Index

S

Index

T

Index

Index